S0-BBR-992

Econometric Analysis of Cross Section and Panel Data

Econometric Analysis of Cross Section and Panel Data

Jeffrey M. Wooldridge

The MIT Press
Cambridge, Massachusetts
London, England

This book was set in Times Roman by Asco Typesetters, Hong Kong, and was printed and bound in the United States of America.

Library of Congress Cataloging-in-Publication Data

Wooldridge, Jeffrey M., 1960–
Econometric analysis of cross section and panel data / Jeffrey M. Wooldridge.
p. cm.
Includes bibliographical references and index.
ISBN-13 978-0-262-23219-7 (cloth)
ISBN 0-262-23219-7 (cloth)
1. Econometrics—Asymptotic theory. I. Title.

HB139.W663 2001
330′.01′5195—dc21 2001044263

20 19 18 17 16 15 14

Contents

Preface

This book is intended primarily for use in a second-semester course in graduate econometrics, after a first course at the level of Goldberger (1991) or Greene (1997). Parts of the book can be used for special-topics courses, and it should serve as a general reference.

My focus on cross section and panel data methods—in particular, what is often dubbed *microeconometrics*—is novel, and it recognizes that, after coverage of the basic linear model in a first-semester course, an increasingly popular approach is to treat advanced cross section and panel data methods in one semester and time series methods in a separate semester. This division reflects the current state of econometric practice.

Modern empirical research that can be fitted into the classical linear model paradigm is becoming increasingly rare. For instance, it is now widely recognized that a student doing research in applied time series analysis cannot get very far by ignoring recent advances in estimation and testing in models with trending and strongly dependent processes. This theory takes a very different direction from the classical linear model than does cross section or panel data analysis. Hamilton's (1994) time series text demonstrates this difference unequivocally.

Books intended to cover an econometric sequence of a year or more, beginning with the classical linear model, tend to treat advanced topics in cross section and panel data analysis as direct applications or minor extensions of the classical linear model (if they are treated at all). Such treatment needlessly limits the scope of applications and can result in poor econometric practice. The focus in such books on the algebra and geometry of econometrics is appropriate for a first-semester course, but it results in oversimplification or sloppiness in stating assumptions. Approaches to estimation that are acceptable under the fixed regressor paradigm so prominent in the classical linear model can lead one badly astray under practically important departures from the fixed regressor assumption.

Books on "advanced" econometrics tend to be high-level treatments that focus on general approaches to estimation, thereby attempting to cover all data configurations—including cross section, panel data, and time series—in one framework, without giving special attention to any. A hallmark of such books is that detailed regularity conditions are treated on par with the practically more important assumptions that have economic content. This is a burden for students learning about cross section and panel data methods, especially those who are empirically oriented: definitions and limit theorems about dependent processes need to be included among the regularity conditions in order to cover time series applications.

In this book I have attempted to find a middle ground between more traditional approaches and the more recent, very unified approaches. I present each model and method with a careful discussion of assumptions of the underlying population model. These assumptions, couched in terms of correlations, conditional expectations, conditional variances and covariances, or conditional distributions, usually can be given behavioral content. Except for the three more technical chapters in Part III, regularity conditions—for example, the existence of moments needed to ensure that the central limit theorem holds—are not discussed explicitly, as these have little bearing on applied work. This approach makes the assumptions relatively easy to understand, while at the same time emphasizing that assumptions concerning the underlying population and the method of sampling need to be carefully considered in applying any econometric method.

A unifying theme in this book is the analogy approach to estimation, as exposited by Goldberger (1991) and Manski (1988). [For nonlinear estimation methods with cross section data, Manski (1988) covers several of the topics included here in a more compact format.] Loosely, the analogy principle states that an estimator is chosen to solve the sample counterpart of a problem solved by the population parameter. The analogy approach is complemented nicely by asymptotic analysis, and that is the focus here.

By focusing on asymptotic properties I do not mean to imply that small-sample properties of estimators and test statistics are unimportant. However, one typically first applies the analogy principle to devise a sensible estimator and then derives its asymptotic properties. This approach serves as a relatively simple guide to doing inference, and it works well in large samples (and often in samples that are not so large). Small-sample adjustments may improve performance, but such considerations almost always come after a large-sample analysis and are often done on a case-by-case basis.

The book contains proofs or outlines the proofs of many assertions, focusing on the role played by the assumptions with economic content while downplaying or ignoring regularity conditions. The book is primarily written to give applied researchers a very firm understanding of why certain methods work and to give students the background for developing new methods. But many of the arguments used throughout the book are representative of those made in modern econometric research (sometimes without the technical details). Students interested in doing research in cross section or panel data methodology will find much here that is not available in other graduate texts.

I have also included several empirical examples with included data sets. Most of the data sets come from published work or are intended to mimic data sets used in modern empirical analysis. To save space I illustrate only the most commonly used methods on the most common data structures. Not surprisingly, these overlap considerably with methods that are packaged in econometric software programs. Other examples are of models where, given access to the appropriate data set, one could undertake an empirical analysis.

The numerous end-of-chapter problems are an important component of the book. Some problems contain important points that are not fully described in the text; others cover new ideas that can be analyzed using the tools presented in the current and previous chapters. Several of the problems require using the data sets that are included with the book.

As with any book, the topics here are selective and reflect what I believe to be the methods needed most often by applied researchers. I also give coverage to topics that have recently become important but are not adequately treated in other texts. Part I of the book reviews some tools that are elusive in mainstream econometrics books—in particular, the notion of conditional expectations, linear projections, and various convergence results. Part II begins by applying these tools to the analysis of single-equation linear models using cross section data. In principle, much of this material should be review for students having taken a first-semester course. But starting with single-equation linear models provides a bridge from the classical analysis of linear models to a more modern treatment, and it is the simplest vehicle to illustrate the application of the tools in Part I. In addition, several methods that are used often in applications—but rarely covered adequately in texts—can be covered in a single framework.

I approach estimation of linear systems of equations with endogenous variables from a different perspective than traditional treatments. Rather than begin with simultaneous equations models, we study estimation of a general linear system by instrumental variables. This approach allows us to later apply these results to models with the same statistical structure as simultaneous equations models, including panel data models. Importantly, we can study the generalized method of moments estimator from the beginning and easily relate it to the more traditional three-stage least squares estimator.

The analysis of general estimation methods for nonlinear models in Part III begins with a general treatment of asymptotic theory of estimators obtained from nonlinear optimization problems. Maximum likelihood, partial maximum likelihood, and generalized method of moments estimation are shown to be generally applicable estimation approaches. The method of nonlinear least squares is also covered as a method for estimating models of conditional means.

Part IV covers several nonlinear models used by modern applied researchers. Chapters 15 and 16 treat limited dependent variable models, with attention given to handling certain endogeneity problems in such models. Panel data methods for binary response and censored variables, including some new estimation approaches, are also covered in these chapters.

Chapter 17 contains a treatment of sample selection problems for both cross section and panel data, including some recent advances. The focus is on the case where the population model is linear, but some results are given for nonlinear models as well. Attrition in panel data models is also covered, as are methods for dealing with stratified samples. Recent approaches to estimating average treatment effects are treated in Chapter 18.

Poisson and related regression models, both for cross section and panel data, are treated in Chapter 19. These rely heavily on the method of quasi-maximum likelihood estimation. A brief but modern treatment of duration models is provided in Chapter 20.

I have given short shrift to some important, albeit more advanced, topics. The setting here is, at least in modern parlance, essentially *parametric*. I have not included detailed treatment of recent advances in semiparametric or nonparametric analysis. In many cases these topics are not conceptually difficult. In fact, many semiparametric methods focus primarily on estimating a finite dimensional parameter in the presence of an infinite dimensional nuisance parameter—a feature shared by traditional parametric methods, such as nonlinear least squares and partial maximum likelihood. It is estimating infinite dimensional parameters that is conceptually and technically challenging.

At the appropriate point, in lieu of treating semiparametric and nonparametric methods, I mention when such extensions are possible, and I provide references. A benefit of a modern approach to parametric models is that it provides a seamless transition to semiparametric and nonparametric methods. General surveys of semiparametric and nonparametric methods are available in Volume 4 of the *Handbook of Econometrics*—see Powell (1994) and Härdle and Linton (1994)—as well as in Volume 11 of the *Handbook of Statistics*—see Horowitz (1993) and Ullah and Vinod (1993).

I only briefly treat simulation-based methods of estimation and inference. Computer simulations can be used to estimate complicated nonlinear models when traditional optimization methods are ineffective. The bootstrap method of inference and confidence interval construction can improve on asymptotic analysis. Volume 4 of the *Handbook of Econometrics* and Volume 11 of the *Handbook of Statistics* contain nice surveys of these topics (Hajivassilou and Ruud, 1994; Hall, 1994; Hajivassilou, 1993; and Keane, 1993).

On an organizational note, I refer to sections throughout the book first by chapter number followed by section number and, sometimes, subsection number. Therefore, Section 6.3 refers to Section 3 in Chapter 6, and Section 13.8.3 refers to Subsection 3 of Section 8 in Chapter 13. By always including the chapter number, I hope to minimize confusion.

Possible Course Outlines

If all chapters in the book are covered in detail, there is enough material for two semesters. For a one-semester course, I use a lecture or two to review the most important concepts in Chapters 2 and 3, focusing on conditional expectations and basic limit theory. Much of the material in Part I can be referred to at the appropriate time. Then I cover the basics of ordinary least squares and two-stage least squares in Chapters 4, 5, and 6. Chapter 7 begins the topics that most students who have taken one semester of econometrics have not previously seen. I spend a fair amount of time on Chapters 10 and 11, which cover linear unobserved effects panel data models.

Part III is technically more difficult than the rest of the book. Nevertheless, it is fairly easy to provide an overview of the analogy approach to nonlinear estimation, along with computing asymptotic variances and test statistics, especially for maximum likelihood and partial maximum likelihood methods.

In Part IV, I focus on binary response and censored regression models. If time permits, I cover the rudiments of quasi-maximum likelihood in Chapter 19, especially for count data, and give an overview of some important issues in modern duration analysis (Chapter 20).

For topics courses that focus entirely on nonlinear econometric methods for cross section and panel data, Part III is a natural starting point. A full-semester course would carefully cover the material in Parts III and IV, probably supplementing the parametric approach used here with popular semiparametric methods, some of which are referred to in Part IV. Parts III and IV can also be used for a half-semester course on nonlinear econometrics, where Part III is not covered in detail if the course has an applied orientation.

A course in applied econometrics can select topics from all parts of the book, emphasizing assumptions but downplaying derivations. The several empirical examples and data sets can be used to teach students how to use advanced econometric methods. The data sets can be accessed by visiting the website for the book at MIT Press: http://mitpress.mit.edu/Wooldridge-EconAnalysis.

Acknowledgments

My interest in panel data econometrics began in earnest when I was an assistant professor at MIT, after I attended a seminar by a graduate student, Leslie Papke, who would later become my wife. Her empirical research using nonlinear panel data methods piqued my interest and eventually led to my research on estimating nonlinear panel data models without distributional assumptions. I dedicate this text to Leslie.

My former colleagues at MIT, particularly Jerry Hausman, Daniel McFadden, Whitney Newey, Danny Quah, and Thomas Stoker, played significant roles in encouraging my interest in cross section and panel data econometrics. I also have learned much about the modern approach to panel data econometrics from Gary Chamberlain of Harvard University.

I cannot discount the excellent training I received from Robert Engle, Clive Granger, and especially Halbert White at the University of California at San Diego. I hope they are not too disappointed that this book excludes time series econometrics.

I did not teach a course in cross section and panel data methods until I started teaching at Michigan State. Fortunately, my colleague Peter Schmidt encouraged me to teach the course at which this book is aimed. Peter also suggested that a text on panel data methods that uses "vertical bars" would be a worthwhile contribution.

Several classes of students at Michigan State were subjected to this book in manuscript form at various stages of development. I would like to thank these students for their perseverance, helpful comments, and numerous corrections. I want to specifically mention Scott Baier, Linda Bailey, Ali Berker, Yi-Yi Chen, William Horrace, Robin Poston, Kyosti Pietola, Hailong Qian, Wendy Stock, and Andrew Toole. Naturally, they are not responsible for any remaining errors.

I was fortunate to have several capable, conscientious reviewers for the manuscript. Jason Abrevaya (University of Chicago), Joshua Angrist (MIT), David Drukker (Stata Corporation), Brian McCall (University of Minnesota), James Ziliak (University of Oregon), and three anonymous reviewers provided excellent suggestions, many of which improved the book's organization and coverage.

The people at MIT Press have been remarkably patient, and I have very much enjoyed working with them. I owe a special debt to Terry Vaughn (now at Princeton University Press) for initiating this project and then giving me the time to produce a manuscript with which I felt comfortable. I am grateful to Jane McDonald and Elizabeth Murry for reenergizing the project and for allowing me significant leeway in crafting the final manuscript. Finally, Peggy Gordon and her crew at P. M. Gordon Associates, Inc., did an expert job in editing the manuscript and in producing the final text.

I INTRODUCTION AND BACKGROUND

In this part we introduce the basic approach to econometrics taken throughout the book and cover some background material that is important to master before reading the remainder of the text. Students who have a solid understanding of the algebra of conditional expectations, conditional variances, and linear projections could skip Chapter 2, referring to it only as needed. Chapter 3 contains a summary of the asymptotic analysis needed to read Part II and beyond. In Part III we introduce additional asymptotic tools that are needed to study nonlinear estimation.

1 Introduction

1.1 Causal Relationships and Ceteris Paribus Analysis

The goal of most empirical studies in economics and other social sciences is to determine whether a change in one variable, say w, causes a change in another variable, say y. For example, does having another year of education cause an increase in monthly salary? Does reducing class size cause an improvement in student performance? Does lowering the business property tax rate cause an increase in city economic activity? Because economic variables are properly interpreted as random variables, we should use ideas from probability to formalize the sense in which a change in w causes a change in y.

The notion of **ceteris paribus**—that is, holding all other (relevant) factors fixed—is at the crux of establishing a **causal relationship**. Simply finding that two variables are correlated is rarely enough to conclude that a change in one variable causes a change in another. This result is due to the nature of economic data: rarely can we run a controlled experiment that allows a simple correlation analysis to uncover causality. Instead, we can use econometric methods to effectively hold other factors fixed.

If we focus on the average, or expected, response, a ceteris paribus analysis entails estimating $\mathrm{E}(y \mid w, \mathbf{c})$, the expected value of y conditional on w and $\mathbf{c}$. The vector $\mathbf{c}$—whose dimension is not important for this discussion—denotes a set of **control variables** that we would like to explicitly hold fixed when studying the effect of w on the expected value of y. The reason we control for these variables is that we think w is correlated with other factors that also influence y. If w is continuous, interest centers on $\partial \mathrm{E}(y \mid w, \mathbf{c})/\partial w$, which is usually called the **partial effect** of w on $\mathrm{E}(y \mid w, \mathbf{c})$. If w is discrete, we are interested in $\mathrm{E}(y \mid w, \mathbf{c})$ evaluated at different values of w, with the elements of $\mathbf{c}$ fixed at the same specified values.

Deciding on the list of proper controls is not always straightforward, and using different controls can lead to different conclusions about a causal relationship between y and w. This is where establishing causality gets tricky: it is up to us to decide which factors need to be held fixed. If we settle on a list of controls, and if all elements of $\mathbf{c}$ can be observed, then estimating the partial effect of w on $\mathrm{E}(y \mid w, \mathbf{c})$ is relatively straightforward. Unfortunately, in economics and other social sciences, many elements of $\mathbf{c}$ are not observed. For example, in estimating the causal effect of education on wage, we might focus on $\mathrm{E}(wage \mid educ, exper, abil)$ where *educ* is years of schooling, *exper* is years of workforce experience, and *abil* is innate ability. In this case, $\mathbf{c} = (exper, abil)$, where *exper* is observed but *abil* is not. (It is widely agreed among labor economists that experience and ability are two factors we should hold fixed to obtain the causal effect of education on wages. Other factors, such as years with the current employer, might belong as well. We can all agree that something such as the last digit of one's social security number need not be included as a control, as it has nothing to do with wage or education.)

As a second example, consider establishing a causal relationship between student attendance and performance on a final exam in a principles of economics class. We might be interested in $\mathrm{E}(score \mid attend, SAT, priGPA)$, where *score* is the final exam score, *attend* is the attendance rate, *SAT* is score on the scholastic aptitude test, and *priGPA* is grade point average at the beginning of the term. We can reasonably collect data on all of these variables for a large group of students. Is this setup enough to decide whether attendance has a causal effect on performance? Maybe not. While *SAT* and *priGPA* are general measures reflecting student ability and study habits, they do not necessarily measure one's interest in or aptitude for econonomics. Such attributes, which are difficult to quantify, may nevertheless belong in the list of controls if we are going to be able to infer that attendance rate has a causal effect on performance.

In addition to not being able to obtain data on all desired controls, other problems can interfere with estimating causal relationships. For example, even if we have good measures of the elements of $\mathbf{c}$, we might not have very good measures of y or w. A more subtle problem—which we study in detail in Chapter 9—is that we may only observe equilibrium values of y and w when these variables are simultaneously determined. An example is determining the causal effect of conviction rates (w) on city crime rates (y).

A first course in econometrics teaches students how to apply multiple regression analysis to estimate ceteris paribus effects of explanatory variables on a response variable. In the rest of this book, we will study how to estimate such effects in a variety of situations. Unlike most introductory treatments, we rely heavily on conditional expectations. In Chapter 2 we provide a detailed summary of properties of conditional expectations.

1.2 The Stochastic Setting and Asymptotic Analysis

1.2.1 Data Structures

In order to give proper treatment to modern cross section and panel data methods, we must choose a stochastic setting that is appropriate for the kinds of cross section and panel data sets collected for most econometric applications. Naturally, all else equal, it is best if the setting is as simple as possible. It should allow us to focus on interpreting assumptions with economic content while not having to worry too much about technical regularity conditions. (Regularity conditions are assumptions involving things such as the number of absolute moments of a random variable that must be finite.)

For much of this book we adopt a **random sampling** assumption. More precisely, we assume that (1) a **population model** has been specified and (2) an **independent, identically distributed** (**i.i.d.**) sample can be drawn from the population. Specifying a population model—which may be a model of $\mathrm{E}(y \mid w, \mathbf{c})$, as in Section 1.1—requires us first to clearly define the population of interest. Defining the relevant population may seem to be an obvious requirement. Nevertheless, as we will see in later chapters, it can be subtle in some cases.

An important virtue of the random sampling assumption is that it allows us to separate the sampling assumption from the assumptions made on the population model. In addition to putting the proper emphasis on assumptions that impinge on economic behavior, stating all assumptions in terms of the population is actually much easier than the traditional approach of stating assumptions in terms of full data matrices.

Because we will rely heavily on random sampling, it is important to know what it allows and what it rules out. Random sampling is often reasonable for **cross section data**, where, at a given point in time, units are selected at random from the population. In this setup, any explanatory variables are treated as random outcomes along with data on response variables. Fixed regressors cannot be identically distributed across observations, and so the random sampling assumption technically excludes the classical linear model. This result is actually desirable for our purposes. In Section 1.4 we provide a brief discussion of why it is important to treat explanatory variables as random for modern econometric analysis.

We should not confuse the random sampling assumption with so-called **experimental data**. Experimental data fall under the fixed explanatory variables paradigm. With experimental data, researchers set values of the explanatory variables and then observe values of the response variable. Unfortunately, true experiments are quite rare in economics, and in any case nothing practically important is lost by treating explanatory variables that are set ahead of time as being random. It is safe to say that no one ever went astray by assuming random sampling in place of independent sampling with fixed explanatory variables.

Random sampling does exclude cases of some interest for cross section analysis. For example, the identical distribution assumption is unlikely to hold for a **pooled cross section**, where random samples are obtained from the population at different points in time. This case is covered by **independent, not identically distributed** (**i.n.i.d.**) observations. Allowing for non-identically distributed observations under independent sampling is not difficult, and its practical effects are easy to deal with. We will mention this case at several points in the book after the analyis is done under random sampling. We do not cover the i.n.i.d. case explicitly in derivations because little is to be gained from the additional complication.

A situation that does require special consideration occurs when cross section observations are not independent of one another. An example is **spatial correlation** models. This situation arises when dealing with large geographical units that cannot be assumed to be independent draws from a large population, such as the 50 states in the United States. It is reasonable to expect that the unemployment rate in one state is correlated with the unemployment rate in neighboring states. While standard estimation methods—such as ordinary least squares and two-stage least squares—can usually be applied in these cases, the asymptotic theory needs to be altered. Key statistics often (although not always) need to be modified. We will briefly discuss some of the issues that arise in this case for single-equation linear models, but otherwise this subject is beyond the scope of this book. For better or worse, spatial correlation is often ignored in applied work because correcting the problem can be difficult.

Cluster sampling also induces correlation in a cross section data set, but in most cases it is relatively easy to deal with econometrically. For example, retirement saving of employees within a firm may be correlated because of common (often unobserved) characteristics of workers within a firm or because of features of the firm itself (such as type of retirement plan). Each firm represents a group or cluster, and we may sample several workers from a large number of firms. As we will see later, provided the number of clusters is large relative to the cluster sizes, standard methods can correct for the presence of within-cluster correlation.

Another important issue is that cross section samples often are, either intentionally or unintentionally, chosen so that they are not random samples from the population of interest. In Chapter 17 we discuss such problems at length, including **sample selection** and **stratified sampling**. As we will see, even in cases of nonrandom samples, the assumptions on the population model play a central role.

For **panel data** (or **longitudinal data**), which consist of repeated observations on the same cross section of, say, individuals, households, firms, or cities, over time, the random sampling assumption initially appears much too restrictive. After all, any reasonable stochastic setting should allow for correlation in individual or firm behavior over time. But the random sampling assumption, properly stated, does allow for temporal correlation. What we will do is assume random sampling in the *cross* *section* dimension. The dependence in the time series dimension can be entirely unrestricted. As we will see, this approach is justified in panel data applications with many cross section observations spanning a relatively short time period. We will also be able to cover panel data sample selection and stratification issues within this paradigm.

A panel data setup that we will not adequately cover—although the estimation methods we cover can be usually used—is seen when the cross section dimension and time series dimensions are roughly of the same magnitude, such as when the sample consists of countries over the post–World War II period. In this case it makes little sense to fix the time series dimension and let the cross section dimension grow. The research on asymptotic analysis with these kinds of panel data sets is still in its early stages, and it requires special limit theory. See, for example, Quah (1994), Pesaran and Smith (1995), Kao (1999), and Phillips and Moon (1999).

1.2.2 Asymptotic Analysis

Throughout this book we focus on asymptotic properties, as opposed to finite sample properties, of estimators. The primary reason for this emphasis is that finite sample properties are intractable for most of the estimators we study in this book. In fact, most of the estimators we cover will not have desirable finite sample properties such as unbiasedness. Asymptotic analysis allows for a unified treatment of estimation procedures, and it (along with the random sampling assumption) allows us to state all assumptions in terms of the underlying population. Naturally, asymptotic analysis is not without its drawbacks. Occasionally, we will mention when asymptotics can lead one astray. In those cases where finite sample properties can be derived, you are sometimes asked to derive such properties in the problems.

In cross section analysis the asymptotics is as the number of observations, denoted N throughout this book, tends to infinity. Usually what is meant by this statement is obvious. For panel data analysis, the asymptotics is as the cross section dimension gets large while the time series dimension is fixed.

1.3 Some Examples

In this section we provide two examples to emphasize some of the concepts from the previous sections. We begin with a standard example from labor economics.

Example 1.1 (Wage Offer Function): Suppose that the natural log of the *wage offer*, $wage^o$, is determined as

$$\log(wage^o) = \beta_0 + \beta_1 educ + \beta_2 exper + \beta_3 married + u \tag{1.1}$$

where *educ* is years of schooling, *exper* is years of labor market experience, and *married* is a binary variable indicating marital status. The variable u, called the **error term** or **disturbance**, contains unobserved factors that affect the wage offer. Interest lies in the unknown parameters, the β_j.

We should have a concrete population in mind when specifying equation (1.1). For example, equation (1.1) could be for the population of all *working* women. In this case, it will not be difficult to obtain a random sample from the population.

All assumptions can be stated in terms of the population model. The crucial assumptions involve the relationship between u and the observable explanatory variables, *educ*, *exper*, and *married*. For example, is the expected value of u given the explanatory variables *educ*, *exper*, and *married* equal to zero? Is the variance of u conditional on the explanatory variables constant? There are reasons to think the answer to both of these questions is no, something we discuss at some length in Chapters 4 and 5. The point of raising them here is to emphasize that all such questions are most easily couched in terms of the population model.

What happens if the relevant population is *all* women over age 18? A problem arises because a random sample from this population will include women for whom the wage offer cannot be observed because they are not working. Nevertheless, we can think of a random sample being obtained, but then $wage^o$ is unobserved for women not working.

For deriving the properties of estimators, it is often useful to write the population model for a generic draw from the population. Equation (1.1) becomes

$$\log(wage_i^o) = \beta_0 + \beta_1 educ_i + \beta_2 exper_i + \beta_3 married_i + u_i, \tag{1.2}$$

where i indexes person. Stating assumptions in terms of u_i and $\mathbf{x}_i \equiv (educ_i, exper_i, married_i)$ is the same as stating assumptions in terms of u and $\mathbf{x}$. Throughout this book, the i subscript is reserved for indexing cross section units, such as individual, firm, city, and so on. Letters such as j, g, and h will be used to index variables, parameters, and equations.

Before ending this example, we note that using matrix notation to write equation (1.2) for all N observations adds nothing to our understanding of the model or sampling scheme; in fact, it just gets in the way because it gives the mistaken impression that the matrices tell us something about the assumptions in the underlying population. It is much better to focus on the population model (1.1).

The next example is illustrative of panel data applications.

Example 1.2 (Effect of Spillovers on Firm Output): Suppose that the population is all manufacturing firms in a country operating during a given three-year period. A production function describing output in the population of firms is

$$\log(output_t) = \delta_t + \beta_1 \log(labor_t) + \beta_2 \log(capital_t) + \beta_3 spillover_t + quality + u_t, \qquad t = 1, 2, 3 \tag{1.3}$$

Here, $spillover_t$ is a measure of foreign firm concentration in the region containing the firm. The term *quality* contains unobserved factors—such as unobserved managerial or worker quality—which affect productivity and are constant over time. The error u_t represents unobserved shocks in each time period. The presence of the parameters δ_t, which represent different intercepts in each year, allows for aggregate productivity to change over time. The coefficients on $labor_t$, $capital_t$, and $spillover_t$ are assumed constant across years.

As we will see when we study panel data methods, there are several issues in deciding how best to estimate the β_j. An important one is whether the unobserved productivity factors (*quality*) are correlated with the observable inputs. Also, can we assume that $spillover_t$ at, say, $t = 3$ is uncorrelated with the error terms in all time periods?

For panel data it is especially useful to add an i subscript indicating a generic cross section observation—in this case, a randomly sampled firm:

$$\log(output_{it}) = \delta_t + \beta_1 \log(labor_{it}) + \beta_2 \log(capital_{it}) + \beta_3 spillover_{it} + quality_i + u_{it}, \qquad t = 1, 2, 3 \tag{1.4}$$

Equation (1.4) makes it clear that $quality_i$ is a firm-specific term that is constant over time and also has the same effect in each time period, while u_{it} changes across time and firm. Nevertheless, the key issues that we must address for estimation can be discussed for a generic i, since the draws are assumed to be randomly made from the population of all manufacturing firms.

Equation (1.4) is an example of another convention we use throughout the book: the subscript t is reserved to index time, just as i is reserved for indexing the cross section.

1.4 Why Not Fixed Explanatory Variables?

We have seen two examples where, generally speaking, the error in an equation can be correlated with one or more of the explanatory variables. This possibility is so prevalent in social science applications that it makes little sense to adopt an assumption—namely, the assumption of fixed explanatory variables—that rules out such correlation a priori.

In a first course in econometrics, the method of ordinary least squares (OLS) and its extensions are usually learned under the fixed regressor assumption. This is appropriate for understanding the mechanics of least squares and for gaining experience with statistical derivations. Unfortunately, reliance on fixed regressors or, more generally, fixed "exogenous" variables, can have unintended consequences, especially in more advanced settings. For example, in Chapters 7, 10, and 11 we will see that assuming fixed regressors or fixed instrumental variables in panel data models imposes often unrealistic restrictions on dynamic economic behavior. This is not just a technical point: estimation methods that are consistent under the fixed regressor assumption, such as generalized least squares, are no longer consistent when the fixed regressor assumption is relaxed in interesting ways.

To illustrate the shortcomings of the fixed regressor assumption in a familiar context, consider a linear model for cross section data, written for each observation i as

$$y_i = \beta_0 + \mathbf{x}_i\boldsymbol{\beta} + u_i, \qquad i = 1, 2, \ldots, N$$

where $\mathbf{x}_i$ is a $1 \times K$ vector and $\boldsymbol{\beta}$ is a $K \times 1$ vector. It is common to see the "ideal" assumptions for this model stated as "The errors $\{u_i\colon i = 1, 2, \ldots, N\}$ are i.i.d. with $\mathrm{E}(u_i) = 0$ and $\mathrm{Var}(u_i) = \sigma^2$." (Sometimes the u_i are also assumed to be normally distributed.) The problem with this statement is that it omits the most important consideration: What is assumed about the relationship between u_i and $\mathbf{x}_i$? If the $\mathbf{x}_i$ are taken as nonrandom—which, evidently, is very often the implicit assumption—then u_i and $\mathbf{x}_i$ are independent of one another. In nonexperimental environments this assumption rules out too many situations of interest. Some important questions, such as efficiency comparisons across models with different explanatory variables, cannot even be asked in the context of fixed regressors. (See Problems 4.5 and 4.15 of Chapter 4 for specific examples.)

In a random sampling context, the u_i are *always* independent and identically distributed, regardless of how they are related to the $\mathbf{x}_i$. Assuming that the population mean of the error is zero is without loss of generality when an intercept is included in the model. Thus, the statement "The errors $\{u_i\colon i = 1, 2, \ldots, N\}$ are i.i.d. with $\mathrm{E}(u_i) = 0$ and $\mathrm{Var}(u_i) = \sigma^2$" is vacuous in a random sampling context. Viewing the $\mathbf{x}_i$ as random draws along with y_i forces us to think about the relationship between the error and the explanatory variables in the *population*. For example, in the population model $y = \beta_0 + \mathbf{x}\boldsymbol{\beta} + u$, is the expected value of u given $\mathbf{x}$ equal to zero? Is u correlated with one or more elements of $\mathbf{x}$? Is the variance of u given $\mathbf{x}$ constant, or does it depend on $\mathbf{x}$? These are the assumptions that are relevant for estimating $\boldsymbol{\beta}$ and for determining how to perform statistical inference.

Because our focus is on asymptotic analysis, we have the luxury of allowing for random explanatory variables throughout the book, whether the setting is linear models, nonlinear models, single-equation analysis, or system analysis. An incidental but nontrivial benefit is that, compared with frameworks that assume fixed explanatory variables, the unifying theme of random sampling actually simplifies the asymptotic analysis. We will never state assumptions in terms of full data matrices, because such assumptions can be imprecise and can impose unintended restrictions on the population model.

2 Conditional Expectations and Related Concepts in Econometrics

2.1 The Role of Conditional Expectations in Econometrics

As we suggested in Section 1.1, the conditional expectation plays a crucial role in modern econometric analysis. Although it is not always explicitly stated, the goal of most applied econometric studies is to estimate or test hypotheses about the expectation of one variable—called the **explained variable**, the **dependent variable**, the **regressand**, or the **response variable**, and usually denoted y—conditional on a set of **explanatory variables**, **independent variables**, **regressors**, **control variables**, or **covariates**, usually denoted $\mathbf{x} = (x_1, x_2, \ldots, x_K)$.

A substantial portion of research in econometric methodology can be interpreted as finding ways to estimate conditional expectations in the numerous settings that arise in economic applications. As we briefly discussed in Section 1.1, most of the time we are interested in conditional expectations that allow us to infer causality from one or more explanatory variables to the response variable. In the setup from Section 1.1, we are interested in the effect of a variable w on the expected value of y, holding fixed a vector of controls, $\mathbf{c}$. The conditional expectation of interest is $\mathrm{E}(y \mid w, \mathbf{c})$, which we will call a **structural conditional expectation**. If we can collect data on y, w, and $\mathbf{c}$ in a random sample from the underlying population of interest, then it is fairly straightforward to estimate $\mathrm{E}(y \mid w, \mathbf{c})$—especially if we are willing to make an assumption about its functional form—in which case the effect of w on $\mathrm{E}(y \mid w, \mathbf{c})$, holding $\mathbf{c}$ fixed, is easily estimated.

Unfortunately, complications often arise in the collection and analysis of economic data because of the nonexperimental nature of economics. Observations on economic variables can contain measurement error, or they are sometimes properly viewed as the outcome of a simultaneous process. Sometimes we cannot obtain a random sample from the population, which may not allow us to estimate $\mathrm{E}(y \mid w, \mathbf{c})$. Perhaps the most prevalent problem is that some variables we would like to control for (elements of $\mathbf{c}$) cannot be observed. In each of these cases there is a conditional expectation (CE) of interest, but it generally involves variables for which the econometrician cannot collect data or requires an experiment that cannot be carried out.

Under additional assumptions—generally called **identification assumptions**—we can sometimes recover the structural conditional expectation originally of interest, even if we cannot observe all of the desired controls, or if we only observe equilibrium outcomes of variables. As we will see throughout this text, the details differ depending on the context, but the notion of conditional expectation is fundamental.

In addition to providing a unified setting for interpreting economic models, the CE operator is useful as a tool for manipulating structural equations into estimable equations. In the next section we give an overview of the important features of the conditional expectations operator. The appendix to this chapter contains a more extensive list of properties.

2.2 Features of Conditional Expectations

2.2.1 Definition and Examples

Let y be a random variable, which we refer to in this section as the *explained variable*, and let $\mathbf{x} \equiv (x_1, x_2, \ldots, x_K)$ be a $1 \times K$ random vector of *explanatory variables*. If $\mathrm{E}(|y|) < \infty$, then there is a function, say μ: $\mathbb{R}^K \to \mathbb{R}$, such that

$$\mathrm{E}(y \mid x_1, x_2, \ldots, x_K) = \mu(x_1, x_2, \ldots, x_K) \tag{2.1}$$

or $\mathrm{E}(y \mid \mathbf{x}) = \mu(\mathbf{x})$. The function $\mu(\mathbf{x})$ determines how the *average* value of y changes as elements of $\mathbf{x}$ change. For example, if y is wage and $\mathbf{x}$ contains various individual characteristics, such as education, experience, and IQ, then $\mathrm{E}(wage \mid educ, exper, IQ)$ is the average value of *wage* for the given values of *educ*, *exper*, and *IQ*. Technically, we should distinguish $\mathrm{E}(y \mid \mathbf{x})$—which is a random variable because $\mathbf{x}$ is a random vector defined in the population—from the conditional expectation when $\mathbf{x}$ takes on a particular value, such as $\mathbf{x}_0$: $\mathrm{E}(y \mid \mathbf{x} = \mathbf{x}_0)$. Making this distinction soon becomes cumbersome and, in most cases, is not overly important; for the most part we avoid it. When discussing probabilistic features of $\mathrm{E}(y \mid \mathbf{x})$, $\mathbf{x}$ is necessarily viewed as a random variable.

Because $\mathrm{E}(y \mid \mathbf{x})$ is an expectation, it can be obtained from the conditional density of y given $\mathbf{x}$ by integration, summation, or a combination of the two (depending on the nature of y). It follows that the conditional expectation operator has the same linearity properties as the unconditional expectation operator, and several additional properties that are consequences of the randomness of $\mu(\mathbf{x})$. Some of the statements we make are proven in the appendix, but general proofs of other assertions require measure-theoretic probabability. You are referred to Billingsley (1979) for a detailed treatment.

Most often in econometrics a model for a conditional expectation is specified to depend on a finite set of parameters, which gives a **parametric model** of $\mathrm{E}(y \mid \mathbf{x})$. This considerably narrows the list of possible candidates for $\mu(\mathbf{x})$.

Example 2.1: For $K = 2$ explanatory variables, consider the following examples of conditional expectations:

$$\mathrm{E}(y \mid x_1, x_2) = \beta_0 + \beta_1 x_1 + \beta_2 x_2 \tag{2.2}$$

$$E(y \mid x_1, x_2) = \beta_0 + \beta_1 x_1 + \beta_2 x_2 + \beta_3 x_2^2 \tag{2.3}$$

$$E(y \mid x_1, x_2) = \beta_0 + \beta_1 x_1 + \beta_2 x_2 + \beta_3 x_1 x_2 \tag{2.4}$$

$$E(y \mid x_1, x_2) = \exp[\beta_0 + \beta_1 \log(x_1) + \beta_2 x_2], \qquad y \geq 0, \; x_1 > 0 \tag{2.5}$$

The model in equation (2.2) is linear in the explanatory variables x_1 and x_2. Equation (2.3) is an example of a conditional expectation nonlinear in x_2, although it is linear in x_1. As we will review shortly, from a statistical perspective, equations (2.2) and (2.3) can be treated in the same framework because they are linear in the *parameters* β_j. The fact that equation (2.3) is nonlinear in $\mathbf{x}$ has important implications for interpreting the β_j, but not for estimating them. Equation (2.4) falls into this same class: it is nonlinear in $\mathbf{x} = (x_1, x_2)$ but linear in the β_j.

Equation (2.5) differs fundamentally from the first three examples in that it is a nonlinear function of the parameters β_j, as well as of the x_j. Nonlinearity in the parameters has implications for estimating the β_j; we will see how to estimate such models when we cover nonlinear methods in Part III. For now, you should note that equation (2.5) is reasonable only if $y \geq 0$.

2.2.2 Partial Effects, Elasticities, and Semielasticities

If y and $\mathbf{x}$ are related in a deterministic fashion, say $y = f(\mathbf{x})$, then we are often interested in how y changes when elements of $\mathbf{x}$ change. In a stochastic setting we cannot assume that $y = f(\mathbf{x})$ for some known function and observable vector $\mathbf{x}$ because there are always unobserved factors affecting y. Nevertheless, we can define the partial effects of the x_j on the conditional expectation $E(y \mid \mathbf{x})$. Assuming that $\mu(\cdot)$ is appropriately differentiable and x_j is a continuous variable, the partial derivative $\partial\mu(\mathbf{x})/\partial x_j$ allows us to approximate the marginal change in $E(y \mid \mathbf{x})$ when x_j is increased by a small amount, holding $x_1, \ldots, x_{j-1}, x_{j+1}, \ldots x_K$ constant:

$$\Delta E(y \mid \mathbf{x}) \approx \frac{\partial\mu(\mathbf{x})}{\partial x_j} \cdot \Delta x_j, \quad \text{holding } x_1, \ldots, x_{j-1}, x_{j+1}, \ldots x_K \text{ fixed} \tag{2.6}$$

The partial derivative of $E(y \mid \mathbf{x})$ with respect to x_j is usually called the **partial effect** of x_j on $E(y \mid \mathbf{x})$ (or, to be somewhat imprecise, the partial effect of x_j on y). Interpreting the magnitudes of coefficients in parametric models usually comes from the approximation in equation (2.6).

If x_j is a discrete variable (such as a binary variable), partial effects are computed by comparing $E(y \mid \mathbf{x})$ at different settings of x_j (for example, zero and one when x_j is binary), holding other variables fixed.

Example 2.1 (continued): In equation (2.2) we have

$$\frac{\partial \mathrm{E}(y \mid \mathbf{x})}{\partial x_1} = \beta_1, \qquad \frac{\partial \mathrm{E}(y \mid \mathbf{x})}{\partial x_2} = \beta_2$$

As expected, the partial effects in this model are constant. In equation (2.3),

$$\frac{\partial \mathrm{E}(y \mid \mathbf{x})}{\partial x_1} = \beta_1, \qquad \frac{\partial \mathrm{E}(y \mid \mathbf{x})}{\partial x_2} = \beta_2 + 2\beta_3 x_2$$

so that the partial effect of x_1 is constant but the partial effect of x_2 depends on the level of x_2. In equation (2.4),

$$\frac{\partial \mathrm{E}(y \mid \mathbf{x})}{\partial x_1} = \beta_1 + \beta_3 x_2, \qquad \frac{\partial \mathrm{E}(y \mid \mathbf{x})}{\partial x_2} = \beta_2 + \beta_3 x_1$$

so that the partial effect of x_1 depends on x_2, and vice versa. In equation (2.5),

$$\frac{\partial \mathrm{E}(y \mid \mathbf{x})}{\partial x_1} = \exp(\cdot)(\beta_1/x_1), \qquad \frac{\partial \mathrm{E}(y \mid \mathbf{x})}{\partial x_2} = \exp(\cdot)\beta_2 \tag{2.7}$$

where $\exp(\cdot)$ denotes the function $\mathrm{E}(y \mid \mathbf{x})$ in equation (2.5). In this case, the partial effects of x_1 and x_2 both depend on $\mathbf{x} = (x_1, x_2)$.

Sometimes we are interested in a particular function of a partial effect, such as an elasticity. In the determinstic case $y = f(\mathbf{x})$, we define the elasticity of y with respect to x_j as

$$\frac{\partial y}{\partial x_j} \cdot \frac{x_j}{y} = \frac{\partial f(\mathbf{x})}{\partial x_j} \cdot \frac{x_j}{f(\mathbf{x})} \tag{2.8}$$

again assuming that x_j is continuous. The right-hand side of equation (2.8) shows that the elasticity is a function of $\mathbf{x}$. When y and $\mathbf{x}$ are random, it makes sense to use the right-hand side of equation (2.8), but where $f(\mathbf{x})$ is the conditional mean, $\mu(\mathbf{x})$. Therefore, the (partial) **elasticity** of $\mathrm{E}(y \mid \mathbf{x})$ with respect to x_j, holding $x_1, \ldots, x_{j-1}, x_{j+1}, \ldots, x_K$ constant, is

$$\frac{\partial \mathrm{E}(y \mid \mathbf{x})}{\partial x_j} \cdot \frac{x_j}{\mathrm{E}(y \mid \mathbf{x})} = \frac{\partial \mu(\mathbf{x})}{\partial x_j} \cdot \frac{x_j}{\mu(\mathbf{x})}. \tag{2.9}$$

If $\mathrm{E}(y \mid \mathbf{x}) > 0$ and $x_j > 0$ (as is often the case), equation (2.9) is the same as

$$\frac{\partial \log[\mathrm{E}(y \mid \mathbf{x})]}{\partial \log(x_j)} \tag{2.10}$$

This latter expression gives the elasticity its interpretation as the approximate percentage change in $\mathrm{E}(y \mid \mathbf{x})$ when x_j increases by 1 percent.

Example 2.1 (continued): In equations (2.2) to (2.5), most elasticities are not constant. For example, in equation (2.2), the elasticity of $\mathrm{E}(y \mid \mathbf{x})$ with respect to x_1 is $(\beta_1 x_1)/(\beta_0 + \beta_1 x_1 + \beta_2 x_2)$, which clearly depends on x_1 and x_2. However, in equation (2.5) the elasticity with respect to x_1 is constant and equal to β_1.

How does equation (2.10) compare with the definition of elasticity from a model linear in the natural logarithms? If $y > 0$ and $x_j > 0$, we could define the elasticity as

$$\frac{\partial \mathrm{E}[\log(y) \mid \mathbf{x}]}{\partial \log(x_j)} \tag{2.11}$$

This is the natural definition in a model such as $\log(y) = g(\mathbf{x}) + u$, where $g(\mathbf{x})$ is some function of $\mathbf{x}$ and u is an unobserved disturbance with zero mean conditional on $\mathbf{x}$. How do equations (2.10) and (2.11) compare? Generally, they are different (since the expected value of the log and the log of the expected value can be very different). *If* u is *independent* of $\mathbf{x}$, then equations (2.10) and (2.11) are the same, because then

$$\mathrm{E}(y \mid \mathbf{x}) = \delta \cdot \exp[g(\mathbf{x})]$$

where $\delta \equiv \mathrm{E}[\exp(u)]$. (If u and $\mathbf{x}$ are independent, so are $\exp(u)$ and $\exp[g(\mathbf{x})]$.) As a specific example, if

$$\log(y) = \beta_0 + \beta_1 \log(x_1) + \beta_2 x_2 + u \tag{2.12}$$

where u has zero mean and is independent of (x_1, x_2), then the elasticity of y with respect to x_1 is β_1 using *either* definition of elasticity. If $\mathrm{E}(u \mid \mathbf{x}) = 0$ but u and $\mathbf{x}$ are not independent, the definitions are generally different.

For the most part, little is lost by treating equations (2.10) and (2.11) as the same when $y > 0$. We will view models such as equation (2.12) as constant elasticity models of y with respect to x_1 whenever $\log(y)$ and $\log(x_j)$ are well defined. Definition (2.10) is more general because sometimes it applies even when $\log(y)$ is not defined. (We will need the general definition of an elasticity in Chapters 16 and 19.)

The percentage change in $\mathrm{E}(y \mid \mathbf{x})$ when x_j is increased by one *unit* is approximated as

$$100 \cdot \frac{\partial \mathrm{E}(y \mid \mathbf{x})}{\partial x_j} \cdot \frac{1}{\mathrm{E}(y \mid \mathbf{x})} \tag{2.13}$$

which equals

$$100 \cdot \frac{\partial \log[\mathrm{E}(y \mid \mathbf{x})]}{\partial x_j} \tag{2.14}$$

if $\mathrm{E}(y \mid \mathbf{x}) > 0$. This is sometimes called the **semielasticity** of $\mathrm{E}(y \mid \mathbf{x})$ with respect to x_j.

Example 2.1 (continued): In equation (2.5) the semielasticity with respect to x_2 is constant and equal to $100 \cdot \beta_2$. No other semielasticities are constant in these equations.

2.2.3 The Error Form of Models of Conditional Expectations

When y is a random variable we would like to explain in terms of observable variables $\mathbf{x}$, it is useful to decompose y as

$$y = \mathrm{E}(y \mid \mathbf{x}) + u \tag{2.15}$$

$$\mathrm{E}(u \mid \mathbf{x}) = 0 \tag{2.16}$$

In other words, equations (2.15) and (2.16) are *definitional*: we can always write y as its conditional expectation, $\mathrm{E}(y \mid \mathbf{x})$, plus an **error term** or **disturbance term** that has *conditional* mean zero.

The fact that $\mathrm{E}(u \mid \mathbf{x}) = 0$ has the following important implications: (1) $\mathrm{E}(u) = 0$; (2) u is uncorrelated with *any* function of $x_1, x_2, \ldots, x_K$, and, in particular, u is uncorrelated with each of $x_1, x_2, \ldots, x_K$. That u has zero unconditional expectation follows as a special case of the **law of iterated expectations** (**LIE**), which we cover more generally in the next subsection. Intuitively, it is quite reasonable that $\mathrm{E}(u \mid \mathbf{x}) = 0$ implies $\mathrm{E}(u) = 0$. The second implication is less obvious but very important. The fact that u is uncorrelated with any function of $\mathbf{x}$ is much stronger than merely saying that u is uncorrelated with $x_1, \ldots, x_K$.

As an example, if equation (2.2) holds, then we can write

$$y = \beta_0 + \beta_1 x_1 + \beta_2 x_2 + u, \qquad \mathrm{E}(u \mid x_1, x_2) = 0 \tag{2.17}$$

and so

$$\mathrm{E}(u) = 0, \qquad \mathrm{Cov}(x_1, u) = 0, \qquad \mathrm{Cov}(x_2, u) = 0 \tag{2.18}$$

But we can say much more: under equation (2.17), u is also uncorrelated with any other function we might think of, such as $x_1^2, x_2^2, x_1 x_2, \exp(x_1)$, and $\log(x_2^2 + 1)$. This fact ensures that we have fully accounted for the effects of x_1 and x_2 on the expected value of y; another way of stating this point is that we have the functional form of $\mathrm{E}(y \mid \mathbf{x})$ properly specified.

If we only assume equation (2.18), then u can be correlated with nonlinear functions of x_1 and x_2, such as quadratics, interactions, and so on. If we hope to estimate the partial effect of each x_j on $\mathrm{E}(y \mid \mathbf{x})$ over a broad range of values for $\mathbf{x}$, we want $\mathrm{E}(u \mid \mathbf{x}) = 0$. [In Section 2.3 we discuss the weaker assumption (2.18) and its uses.]

Example 2.2: Suppose that housing prices are determined by the simple model

$$hprice = \beta_0 + \beta_1 sqrft + \beta_2 distance + u,$$

where *sqrft* is the square footage of the house and *distance* is distance of the house from a city incinerator. For β_2 to represent $\partial \mathrm{E}(hprice \mid sqrft, distance)/\partial\, distance$, we must assume that $\mathrm{E}(u \mid sqrft, distance) = 0$.

2.2.4 Some Properties of Conditional Expectations

One of the most useful tools for manipulating conditional expectations is the law of iterated expectations, which we mentioned previously. Here we cover the most general statement needed in this book. Suppose that $\mathbf{w}$ is a random vector and y is a random variable. Let $\mathbf{x}$ be a random vector that is some function of $\mathbf{w}$, say $\mathbf{x} = \mathbf{f}(\mathbf{w})$. (The vector $\mathbf{x}$ could simply be a subset of $\mathbf{w}$.) This statement implies that if we know the outcome of $\mathbf{w}$, then we know the outcome of $\mathbf{x}$. The most general statement of the LIE that we will need is

$$\mathrm{E}(y \mid \mathbf{x}) = \mathrm{E}[\mathrm{E}(y \mid \mathbf{w}) \mid \mathbf{x}] \tag{2.19}$$

In other words, if we write $\mu_1(\mathbf{w}) \equiv \mathrm{E}(y \mid \mathbf{w})$ and $\mu_2(\mathbf{x}) \equiv \mathrm{E}(y \mid \mathbf{x})$, we can obtain $\mu_2(\mathbf{x})$ by computing the expected value of $\mu_2(\mathbf{w})$ given $\mathbf{x}$: $\mu_1(\mathbf{x}) = \mathrm{E}[\mu_1(\mathbf{w}) \mid \mathbf{x}]$.

There is another result that looks similar to equation (2.19) but is much simpler to verify. Namely,

$$\mathrm{E}(y \mid \mathbf{x}) = \mathrm{E}[\mathrm{E}(y \mid \mathbf{x}) \mid \mathbf{w}] \tag{2.20}$$

Note how the positions of $\mathbf{x}$ and $\mathbf{w}$ have been switched on the right-hand side of equation (2.20) compared with equation (2.19). The result in equation (2.20) follows easily from the conditional aspect of the expection: since $\mathbf{x}$ is a function of $\mathbf{w}$, knowing $\mathbf{w}$ implies knowing $\mathbf{x}$; given that $\mu_2(\mathbf{x}) = \mathrm{E}(y \mid \mathbf{x})$ is a function of $\mathbf{x}$, the expected value of $\mu_2(\mathbf{x})$ given $\mathbf{w}$ is just $\mu_2(\mathbf{x})$.

Some find a phrase useful for remembering both equations (2.19) and (2.20): "The smaller information set always dominates." Here, $\mathbf{x}$ represents less information than $\mathbf{w}$, since knowing $\mathbf{w}$ implies knowing $\mathbf{x}$, but not vice versa. We will use equations (2.19) and (2.20) almost routinely throughout the book.

For many purposes we need the following special case of the general LIE (2.19). If $\mathbf{x}$ and $\mathbf{z}$ are any random vectors, then

$$\mathrm{E}(y \mid \mathbf{x}) = \mathrm{E}[\mathrm{E}(y \mid \mathbf{x}, \mathbf{z}) \mid \mathbf{x}] \tag{2.21}$$

or, defining $\mu_1(\mathbf{x}, \mathbf{z}) \equiv \mathrm{E}(y \mid \mathbf{x}, \mathbf{z})$ and $\mu_2(\mathbf{x}) \equiv \mathrm{E}(y \mid \mathbf{x})$,

$$\mu_2(\mathbf{x}) = \mathrm{E}[\mu_1(\mathbf{x}, \mathbf{z}) \mid \mathbf{x}] \tag{2.22}$$

For many econometric applications, it is useful to think of $\mu_1(\mathbf{x}, \mathbf{z}) = \mathrm{E}(y \mid \mathbf{x}, \mathbf{z})$ as a structural conditional expectation, but where $\mathbf{z}$ is unobserved. If interest lies in $\mathrm{E}(y \mid \mathbf{x}, \mathbf{z})$, then we want the effects of the x_j holding the other elements of $\mathbf{x}$ *and* $\mathbf{z}$ fixed. If $\mathbf{z}$ is not observed, we cannot estimate $\mathrm{E}(y \mid \mathbf{x}, \mathbf{z})$ directly. Nevertheless, since y and $\mathbf{x}$ are observed, we can generally estimate $\mathrm{E}(y \mid \mathbf{x})$. The question, then, is whether we can relate $\mathrm{E}(y \mid \mathbf{x})$ to the original expectation of interest. (This is a version of the *identification problem* in econometrics.) The LIE provides a convenient way for relating the two expectations.

Obtaining $\mathrm{E}[\mu_1(\mathbf{x}, \mathbf{z}) \mid \mathbf{x}]$ generally requires integrating (or summing) $\mu_1(\mathbf{x}, \mathbf{z})$ against the conditional density of $\mathbf{z}$ given $\mathbf{x}$, but in many cases the form of $\mathrm{E}(y \mid \mathbf{x}, \mathbf{z})$ is simple enough not to require explicit integration. For example, suppose we begin with the model

$$\mathrm{E}(y \mid x_1, x_2, z) = \beta_0 + \beta_1 x_1 + \beta_2 x_2 + \beta_3 z \tag{2.23}$$

but where z is unobserved. By the LIE, and the linearity of the CE operator,

$$\begin{aligned} \mathrm{E}(y \mid x_1, x_2) &= \mathrm{E}(\beta_0 + \beta_1 x_1 + \beta_2 x_2 + \beta_3 z \mid x_1, x_2) \\ &= \beta_0 + \beta_1 x_1 + \beta_2 x_2 + \beta_3 \mathrm{E}(z \mid x_1, x_2) \end{aligned} \tag{2.24}$$

Now, if we make an assumption about $\mathrm{E}(z \mid x_1, x_2)$, for example, that it is linear in x_1 and x_2,

$$\mathrm{E}(z \mid x_1, x_2) = \delta_0 + \delta_1 x_1 + \delta_2 x_2 \tag{2.25}$$

then we can plug this into equation (2.24) and rearrange:

$$= \beta_0 + \beta_1 x_1 + \beta_2 x_2 + \beta_3(\delta_0 + \delta_1 x_1 + \delta_2 x_2)$$

$$= (\beta_0 + \beta_3 \delta_0) + (\beta_1 + \beta_3 \delta_1) x_1 + (\beta_2 + \beta_3 \delta_2) x_2$$

This last expression is $\mathrm{E}(y \mid x_1, x_2)$; given our assumptions it is necessarily linear in (x_1, x_2).

Now suppose equation (2.23) contains an interaction in x_1 and z:

$$\mathrm{E}(y \mid x_1, x_2, z) = \beta_0 + \beta_1 x_1 + \beta_2 x_2 + \beta_3 z + \beta_4 x_1 z \tag{2.26}$$

Then, again by the LIE,

$$\mathrm{E}(y \mid x_1, x_2) = \beta_0 + \beta_1 x_1 + \beta_2 x_2 + \beta_3 \mathrm{E}(z \mid x_1, x_2) + \beta_4 x_1 \mathrm{E}(z \mid x_1, x_2)$$

If $\mathrm{E}(z \mid x_1, x_2)$ is again given in equation (2.25), you can show that $\mathrm{E}(y \mid x_1, x_2)$ has terms linear in x_1 and x_2 and, in addition, contains x_1^2 and $x_1 x_2$. The usefulness of such derivations will become apparent in later chapters.

The general form of the LIE has other useful implications. Suppose that for some (vector) function $\mathbf{f}(\mathbf{x})$ and a real-valued function $g(\cdot)$, $\mathrm{E}(y \mid \mathbf{x}) = g[\mathbf{f}(\mathbf{x})]$. Then

$$\mathrm{E}[y \mid \mathbf{f}(\mathbf{x})] = \mathrm{E}(y \mid \mathbf{x}) = g[\mathbf{f}(\mathbf{x})] \tag{2.27}$$

There is another way to state this relationship: If we define $\mathbf{z} \equiv \mathbf{f}(\mathbf{x})$, then $\mathrm{E}(y \mid \mathbf{z}) = g(\mathbf{z})$. The vector $\mathbf{z}$ can have smaller or greater dimension than $\mathbf{x}$. This fact is illustrated with the following example.

Example 2.3: If a wage equation is

$$\mathrm{E}(wage \mid educ, exper) = \beta_0 + \beta_1 educ + \beta_2 exper + \beta_3 exper^2 + \beta_4 educ{\cdot}exper$$

then

$$\mathrm{E}(wage \mid educ, exper, exper^2, educ{\cdot}exper)$$
$$= \beta_0 + \beta_1 educ + \beta_2 exper + \beta_3 exper^2 + \beta_4 educ{\cdot}exper.$$

In other words, once *educ* and *exper* have been conditioned on, it is redundant to condition on $exper^2$ and $educ{\cdot}exper$.

The conclusion in this example is much more general, and it is helpful for analyzing models of conditional expectations that are linear in parameters. Assume that, for some functions $g_1(\mathbf{x}), g_2(\mathbf{x}), \ldots, g_M(\mathbf{x})$,

$$\mathrm{E}(y \mid \mathbf{x}) = \beta_0 + \beta_1 g_1(\mathbf{x}) + \beta_2 g_2(\mathbf{x}) + \cdots + \beta_M g_M(\mathbf{x}) \tag{2.28}$$

This model allows substantial flexibility, as the explanatory variables can appear in all kinds of nonlinear ways; the key restriction is that the model is linear in the β_j. If we define $z_1 \equiv g_1(\mathbf{x}), \ldots, z_M \equiv g_M(\mathbf{x})$, then equation (2.27) implies that

$$\mathrm{E}(y \mid z_1, z_2, \ldots, z_M) = \beta_0 + \beta_1 z_1 + \beta_2 z_2 + \cdots + \beta_M z_M \tag{2.29}$$

This equation shows that any conditional expectation linear in parameters can be written as a conditional expectation linear in parameters and linear in *some* conditioning variables. If we write equation (2.29) in error form as $y = \beta_0 + \beta_1 z_1 + \beta_2 z_2 + \cdots + \beta_M z_M + u$, then, because $\mathrm{E}(u \mid \mathbf{x}) = 0$ and the z_j are functions of $\mathbf{x}$, it follows that u is uncorrelated with $z_1, \ldots, z_M$ (and any functions of them). As we will see in Chapter 4, this result allows us to cover models of the form (2.28) in the same framework as models linear in the original explanatory variables.

We also need to know how the notion of statistical independence relates to conditional expectations. If u is a random variable independent of the random vector $\mathbf{x}$, then $\mathrm{E}(u \mid \mathbf{x}) = \mathrm{E}(u)$, so that if $\mathrm{E}(u) = 0$ and u and $\mathbf{x}$ are independent, then $\mathrm{E}(u \mid \mathbf{x}) = 0$. The converse of this is not true: $\mathrm{E}(u \mid \mathbf{x}) = \mathrm{E}(u)$ does not imply statistical independence between u and $\mathbf{x}$ (just as zero correlation between u and $\mathbf{x}$ does not imply independence).

2.2.5 Average Partial Effects

When we explicitly allow the expectation of the response variable, y, to depend on unobservables—usually called **unobserved heterogeneity**—we must be careful in specifying the partial effects of interest. Suppose that we have in mind the (structural) conditional mean $\mathrm{E}(y \mid \mathbf{x}, q) = \mu_1(\mathbf{x}, q)$, where $\mathbf{x}$ is a vector of observable explanatory variables and q is an unobserved random variable—the unobserved heterogeneity. (We take q to be a scalar for simplicity; the discussion for a vector is essentially the same.) For continuous x_j, the partial effect of immediate interest is

$$\theta_j(\mathbf{x}, q) \equiv \partial \mathrm{E}(y \mid \mathbf{x}, q)/\partial x_j = \partial \mu_1(\mathbf{x}, q)/\partial x_j \tag{2.30}$$

(For discrete x_j, we would simply look at differences in the regression function for x_j at two different values, when the other elements of $\mathbf{x}$ and q are held fixed.) Because $\theta_j(\mathbf{x}, q)$ generally depends on q, we cannot hope to estimate the partial effects across many different values of q. In fact, even if we could estimate $\theta_j(\mathbf{x}, q)$ for all $\mathbf{x}$ and q, we would generally have little guidance about inserting values of q into the mean function. In many cases we can make a normalization such as $\mathrm{E}(q) = 0$, and estimate $\theta_j(\mathbf{x}, 0)$, but $q = 0$ typically corresponds to a very small segment of the population. (Technically, $q = 0$ corresponds to no one in the population when q is continuously distributed.) Usually of more interest is the partial effect averaged across the population distribution of q; this is called the **average partial effect** (**APE**).

For emphasis, let $\mathbf{x}^o$ denote a fixed value of the covariates. The average partial effect evaluated at $\mathbf{x}^o$ is

$$\delta_j(\mathbf{x}^o) \equiv \mathrm{E}_q[\theta_j(\mathbf{x}^o, q)] \tag{2.31}$$

where $\mathrm{E}_q[\cdot]$ denotes the expectation with respect to q. In other words, we simply average the partial effect $\theta_j(\mathbf{x}^o, q)$ across the population distribution of q. Definition (2.31) holds for any population relationship between q and $\mathbf{x}$; in particular, they need not be independent. But remember, in definition (2.31), $\mathbf{x}^o$ is a nonrandom vector of numbers.

For concreteness, assume that q has a continuous distribution with density function $g(\cdot)$, so that

$$\delta_j(\mathbf{x}^o) = \int_{\mathbb{R}} \theta_j(\mathbf{x}^o, \varphi) g(\varphi)\, d\varphi \tag{2.32}$$

where φ is simply the dummy argument in the integration. The question we answer here is, Is it possible to estimate $\delta_j(\mathbf{x}^o)$ from conditional expectations that depend only on *observable* conditioning variables? Generally, the answer must be no, as q and $\mathbf{x}$ can be arbitrarily related. Nevertheless, if we appropriately restrict the relationship between q and $\mathbf{x}$, we can obtain a very useful equivalance.

One common assumption in nonlinear models with unobserved heterogeneity is that q and $\mathbf{x}$ are independent. We will make the weaker assumption that q and $\mathbf{x}$ are independent *conditional* on a vector of observables, $\mathbf{w}$:

$$\mathrm{D}(q \mid \mathbf{x}, \mathbf{w}) = \mathrm{D}(q \mid \mathbf{w}) \tag{2.33}$$

where $\mathrm{D}(\cdot \mid \cdot)$ denotes conditional distribution. (If we take $\mathbf{w}$ to be empty, we get the special case of independence between q and $\mathbf{x}$.) In many cases, we can interpret equation (2.33) as implying that $\mathbf{w}$ is a vector of good **proxy variables** for q, but equation (2.33) turns out to be fairly widely applicable. We also assume that $\mathbf{w}$ is *redundant* or *ignorable* in the structural expectation

$$\mathrm{E}(y \mid \mathbf{x}, q, \mathbf{w}) = \mathrm{E}(y \mid \mathbf{x}, q) \tag{2.34}$$

As we will see in subsequent chapters, many econometric methods hinge on being able to exclude certain variables from the equation of interest, and equation (2.34) makes this assumption precise. Of course, if $\mathbf{w}$ is empty, then equation (2.34) is trivially true.

Under equations (2.33) and (2.34), we can show the following important result, provided that we can interchange a certain integral and partial derivative:

$$\delta_j(\mathbf{x}^o) = \mathrm{E}_w[\partial \mathrm{E}(y \mid \mathbf{x}^o, \mathbf{w})/\partial x_j] \tag{2.35}$$

where $\mathrm{E}_w[\cdot]$ denotes the expectation with respect to the distribution of $\mathbf{w}$. Before we verify equation (2.35) for the special case of continuous, scalar q, we must understand its usefulness. The point is that the unobserved heterogeneity, q, has disappeared entirely, and the conditional expectation $\mathrm{E}(y \mid \mathbf{x}, \mathbf{w})$ can be estimated quite generally because we assume that a random sample can be obtained on $(y, \mathbf{x}, \mathbf{w})$. [Alternatively, when we write down parametric econometric models, we will be able to derive $\mathrm{E}(y \mid \mathbf{x}, \mathbf{w})$.] Then, estimating the average partial effect at any chosen $\mathbf{x}^o$ amounts to averaging $\partial \hat{\mu}_2(\mathbf{x}^o, \mathbf{w}_i)/\partial x_j$ across the random sample, where $\mu_2(\mathbf{x}, \mathbf{w}) \equiv \mathrm{E}(y \mid \mathbf{x}, \mathbf{w})$.

Proving equation (2.35) is fairly simple. First, we have

$$\mu_2(\mathbf{x}, \mathbf{w}) = \mathrm{E}[\mathrm{E}(y \mid \mathbf{x}, q, \mathbf{w}) \mid \mathbf{x}, \mathbf{w}] = \mathrm{E}[\mu_1(\mathbf{x}, q) \mid \mathbf{x}, \mathbf{w}] = \int_{\mathbb{R}} \mu_1(\mathbf{x}, q) g(q \mid \mathbf{w})\, dq$$

where the first equality follows from the law of iterated expectations, the second equality follows from equation (2.34), and the third equality follows from equation (2.33). If we now take the partial derivative with respect to x_j of the equality

$$\mu_2(\mathbf{x}, \mathbf{w}) = \int_{\mathbb{R}} \mu_1(\mathbf{x}, q) g(q \mid \mathbf{w})\, dq \tag{2.36}$$

and interchange the partial derivative and the integral, we have, for any $(\mathbf{x}, \mathbf{w})$,

$$\partial \mu_2(\mathbf{x}, \mathbf{w})/\partial x_j = \int_{\mathbb{R}} \theta_j(\mathbf{x}, q) g(q \mid \mathbf{w})\, dq \tag{2.37}$$

For fixed $\mathbf{x}^o$, the right-hand side of equation (2.37) is simply $\mathrm{E}[\theta_j(\mathbf{x}^o, q) \mid \mathbf{w}]$, and so another application of iterated expectations gives, for any $\mathbf{x}^o$,

$$\mathrm{E}_w[\partial \mu_2(\mathbf{x}^o, \mathbf{w})/\partial x_j] = \mathrm{E}\{\mathrm{E}[\theta_j(\mathbf{x}^o, q) \mid \mathbf{w}]\} = \delta_j(\mathbf{x}^o)$$

which is what we wanted to show.

As mentioned previously, equation (2.35) has many applications in models where unobserved heterogeneity enters a conditional mean function in a nonadditive fashion. We will use this result (in simplified form) in Chapter 4, and also extensively in Part III. The special case where q is independent of $\mathbf{x}$—and so we do not need the proxy variables $\mathbf{w}$—is very simple: the APE of x_j on $\mathrm{E}(y \mid \mathbf{x}, q)$ is simply the partial effect of x_j on $\mu_2(\mathbf{x}) = \mathrm{E}(y \mid \mathbf{x})$. In other words, if we focus on average partial effects, there is no need to introduce heterogeneity. If we do specify a model with heterogeneity independent of $\mathbf{x}$, then we simply find $\mathrm{E}(y \mid \mathbf{x})$ by integrating $\mathrm{E}(y \mid \mathbf{x}, q)$ over the distribution of q.

2.3 Linear Projections

In the previous section we saw some examples of how to manipulate conditional expectations. While structural equations are usually stated in terms of CEs, making linearity assumptions about CEs involving unobservables or auxiliary variables is undesirable, especially if such assumptions can be easily relaxed.

By using the notion of a linear projection we can often relax linearity assumptions in auxiliary conditional expectations. Typically this is done by first writing down a structural model in terms of a CE and then using the linear projection to obtain an estimable equation. As we will see in Chapters 4 and 5, this approach has many applications.

Generally, let $y, x_1, \dots, x_K$ be random variables representing some population such that $\mathrm{E}(y^2) < \infty$, $\mathrm{E}(x_j^2) < \infty$, $j = 1, 2, \dots, K$. These assumptions place no practical restrictions on the joint distribution of $(y, x_1, x_2, \dots, x_K)$: the vector can contain discrete and continuous variables, as well as variables that have both characteristics. In many cases y and the x_j are nonlinear functions of some underlying variables that are initially of interest.

Define $\mathbf{x} \equiv (x_1, \dots, x_K)$ as a $1 \times K$ vector, and make the assumption that the $K \times K$ variance matrix of $\mathbf{x}$ is nonsingular (positive definite). Then the **linear projection** of y on $1, x_1, x_2, \dots, x_K$ always exists and is unique:

$$\mathrm{L}(y \mid 1, x_1, \dots x_K) = \mathrm{L}(y \mid 1, \mathbf{x}) = \beta_0 + \beta_1 x_1 + \cdots + \beta_K x_K = \beta_0 + \mathbf{x}\boldsymbol{\beta} \tag{2.38}$$

where, by definition,

$$\boldsymbol{\beta} \equiv [\mathrm{Var}(\mathbf{x})]^{-1} \,\mathrm{Cov}(\mathbf{x}, y) \tag{2.39}$$

$$\beta_0 \equiv \mathrm{E}(y) - \mathrm{E}(\mathbf{x})\boldsymbol{\beta} = \mathrm{E}(y) - \beta_1 \mathrm{E}(x_1) - \cdots - \beta_K \mathrm{E}(x_K) \tag{2.40}$$

The matrix $\mathrm{Var}(\mathbf{x})$ is the $K \times K$ symmetric matrix with (j,k)th element given by $\mathrm{Cov}(x_j, x_k)$, while $\mathrm{Cov}(\mathbf{x}, y)$ is the $K \times 1$ vector with jth element $\mathrm{Cov}(x_j, y)$. When $K = 1$ we have the familiar results $\beta_1 \equiv \mathrm{Cov}(x_1, y)/\mathrm{Var}(x_1)$ and $\beta_0 \equiv \mathrm{E}(y) - \beta_1 \mathrm{E}(x_1)$. As its name suggests, $\mathrm{L}(y \mid 1, x_1, x_2, \dots, x_K)$ is always a linear function of the x_j.

Other authors use a different notation for linear projections, the most common being $\mathrm{E}^*(\cdot \mid \cdot)$ and $\mathrm{P}(\cdot \mid \cdot)$. [For example, Chamberlain (1984) and Goldberger (1991) use $\mathrm{E}^*(\cdot \mid \cdot)$.] Some authors omit the 1 in the definition of a linear projection because it is assumed that an intercept is always included. Although this is usually the case, we put unity in explicitly to distinguish equation (2.38) from the case that a zero intercept is intended. The linear projection of y on $x_1, x_2, \dots, x_K$ is defined as

$$\mathrm{L}(y \mid \mathbf{x}) = \mathrm{L}(y \mid x_1, x_2, \dots, x_K) = \gamma_1 x_1 + \gamma_2 x_2 + \cdots + \gamma_K x_K = \mathbf{x}\boldsymbol{\gamma}$$

where $\boldsymbol{\gamma} \equiv (\mathrm{E}(\mathbf{x}'\mathbf{x}))^{-1}\mathrm{E}(\mathbf{x}'y)$. Note that $\boldsymbol{\gamma} \neq \boldsymbol{\beta}$ unless $\mathrm{E}(\mathbf{x}) = \mathbf{0}$. Later, we will include unity as an element of $\mathbf{x}$, in which case the linear projection including an intercept can be written as $\mathrm{L}(y \mid \mathbf{x})$.

The linear projection is just another way of writing down a population linear model where the disturbance has certain properties. Given the linear projection in equation (2.38) we can *always* write

$$y = \beta_0 + \beta_1 x_1 + \cdots + \beta_K x_K + u \tag{2.41}$$

where the error term u has the following properties (by definition of a linear projection): $\mathrm{E}(u^2) < \infty$ and

$$\mathrm{E}(u) = 0, \qquad \mathrm{Cov}(x_j, u) = 0, \qquad j = 1, 2, \ldots, K \tag{2.42}$$

In other words, u has zero mean and is uncorrelated with every x_j. Conversely, given equations (2.41) and (2.42), the parameters β_j in equation (2.41) must be the parameters in the linear projection of y on $1, x_1, \ldots, x_K$ given by definitions (2.39) and (2.40). Sometimes we will write a linear projection in error form, as in equations (2.41) and (2.42), but other times the notation (2.38) is more convenient.

It is important to emphasize that when equation (2.41) represents the linear projection, all we can say about u is contained in equation (2.42). In particular, it is not generally true that u is independent of $\mathbf{x}$ or that $\mathrm{E}(u \mid \mathbf{x}) = 0$. Here is another way of saying the same thing: equations (2.41) and (2.42) are *definitional*. Equation (2.41) under $\mathrm{E}(u \mid \mathbf{x}) = 0$ is an *assumption* that the conditional expectation is linear.

The linear projection is sometimes called the **minimum mean square linear predictor** or the **least squares linear predictor** because β_0 and $\boldsymbol{\beta}$ can be shown to solve the following problem:

$$\min_{b_0, \mathbf{b} \in \mathbb{R}^K} \mathrm{E}[(y - b_0 - \mathbf{x}\mathbf{b})^2] \tag{2.43}$$

(see Property LP.6 in the appendix). Because the CE is the minimum mean square predictor—that is, it gives the smallest mean square error out of all (allowable) functions (see Property CE.8)—it follows immediately that *if* $\mathrm{E}(y \mid \mathbf{x})$ is linear in $\mathbf{x}$ then the linear projection coincides with the conditional expectation.

As with the conditional expectation operator, the linear projection operator satisfies some important iteration properties. For vectors $\mathbf{x}$ and $\mathbf{z}$,

$$\mathrm{L}(y \mid 1, \mathbf{x}) = \mathrm{L}[\mathrm{L}(y \mid 1, \mathbf{x}, \mathbf{z}) \mid 1, \mathbf{x}] \tag{2.44}$$

This simple fact can be used to derive omitted variables bias in a general setting as well as proving properties of estimation methods such as two-stage least squares and certain panel data methods.

Another iteration property that is useful involves taking the linear projection of a conditional expectation:

$$\mathrm{L}(y \mid 1, \mathbf{x}) = \mathrm{L}[\mathrm{E}(y \mid \mathbf{x}, \mathbf{z}) \mid 1, \mathbf{x}] \tag{2.45}$$

Often we specify a structural model in terms of a conditional expectation $\mathrm{E}(y \mid \mathbf{x}, \mathbf{z})$ (which is frequently linear), but, for a variety of reasons, the estimating equations are based on the linear projection $\mathrm{L}(y \mid 1, \mathbf{x})$. If $\mathrm{E}(y \mid \mathbf{x}, \mathbf{z})$ is linear in $\mathbf{x}$ and $\mathbf{z}$, then equations (2.45) and (2.44) say the same thing.

For example, assume that

$$\mathrm{E}(y \mid x_1, x_2) = \beta_0 + \beta_1 x_1 + \beta_2 x_2 + \beta_3 x_1 x_2$$

and define $z_1 \equiv x_1 x_2$. Then, from Property CE.3,

$$\mathrm{E}(y \mid x_1, x_2, z_1) = \beta_0 + \beta_1 x_1 + \beta_2 x_2 + \beta_3 z_1 \tag{2.46}$$

The right-hand side of equation (2.46) is also the linear projection of y on $1, x_1, x_2$, and z_1; it is not generally the linear projection of y on $1, x_1, x_2$.

Our primary use of linear projections will be to obtain estimable equations involving the parameters of an underlying conditional expectation of interest. Problems 2.2 and 2.3 show how the linear projection can have an interesting interpretation in terms of the structural parameters.

Problems

2.1. Given random variables y, x_1, and x_2, consider the model

$$\mathrm{E}(y \mid x_1, x_2) = \beta_0 + \beta_1 x_1 + \beta_2 x_2 + \beta_3 x_2^2 + \beta_4 x_1 x_2$$

a. Find the partial effects of x_1 and x_2 on $\mathrm{E}(y \mid x_1, x_2)$.

b. Writing the equation as

$$y = \beta_0 + \beta_1 x_1 + \beta_2 x_2 + \beta_3 x_2^2 + \beta_4 x_1 x_2 + u$$

what can be said about $\mathrm{E}(u \mid x_1, x_2)$? What about $\mathrm{E}(u \mid x_1, x_2, x_2^2, x_1 x_2)$?

c. In the equation of part b, what can be said about $\mathrm{Var}(u \mid x_1, x_2)$?

2.2. Let y and x be scalars such that

$$\mathrm{E}(y \mid x) = \delta_0 + \delta_1 (x - \mu) + \delta_2 (x - \mu)^2$$

where $\mu = \mathrm{E}(x)$.

a. Find $\partial \mathrm{E}(y \mid x)/\partial x$, and comment on how it depends on x.

b. Show that δ_1 is equal to $\partial \mathrm{E}(y \mid x)/\partial x$ averaged across the distribution of x.

c. Suppose that x has a symmetric distribution, so that $\mathrm{E}[(x-\mu)^3] = 0$. Show that $\mathrm{L}(y \mid 1, x) = \alpha_0 + \delta_1 x$ for some α_0. Therefore, the coefficient on x in the linear projection of y on $(1, x)$ measures something useful in the nonlinear model for $\mathrm{E}(y \mid x)$: it is the partial effect $\partial \mathrm{E}(y \mid x)/\partial x$ averaged across the distribution of x.

2.3. Suppose that

$$\mathrm{E}(y \mid x_1, x_2) = \beta_0 + \beta_1 x_1 + \beta_2 x_2 + \beta_3 x_1 x_2 \tag{2.47}$$

a. Write this expectation in error form (call the error u), and describe the properties of u.

b. Suppose that x_1 and x_2 have zero means. Show that β_1 is the expected value of $\partial \mathrm{E}(y \mid x_1, x_2)/\partial x_1$ (where the expectation is across the population distribution of x_2). Provide a similar interpretation for β_2.

c. Now add the assumption that x_1 and x_2 are independent of one another. Show that the linear projection of y on $(1, x_1, x_2)$ is

$$\mathrm{L}(y \mid 1, x_1, x_2) = \beta_0 + \beta_1 x_1 + \beta_2 x_2 \tag{2.48}$$

(Hint: Show that, under the assumptions on x_1 and x_2, $x_1 x_2$ has zero mean and is uncorrelated with x_1 and x_2.)

d. Why is equation (2.47) generally more useful than equation (2.48)?

2.4. For random scalars u and v and a random vector $\mathbf{x}$, suppose that $\mathrm{E}(u \mid \mathbf{x}, v)$ is a linear function of $(\mathbf{x}, v)$ and that u and v each have zero mean and are uncorrelated with the elements of $\mathbf{x}$. Show that $\mathrm{E}(u \mid \mathbf{x}, v) = \mathrm{E}(u \mid v) = \rho_1 v$ for some ρ_1.

2.5. Consider the two representations

$$y = \mu_1(\mathbf{x}, \mathbf{z}) + u_1, \qquad \mathrm{E}(u_1 \mid \mathbf{x}, \mathbf{z}) = 0$$

$$y = \mu_2(\mathbf{x}) + u_2, \qquad \mathrm{E}(u_2 \mid \mathbf{x}) = 0$$

Assuming that $\mathrm{Var}(y \mid \mathbf{x}, \mathbf{z})$ and $\mathrm{Var}(y \mid \mathbf{x})$ are both constant, what can you say about the relationship between $\mathrm{Var}(u_1)$ and $\mathrm{Var}(u_2)$? (Hint: Use Property CV.4 in the appendix.)

2.6. Let $\mathbf{x}$ be a $1 \times K$ random vector, and let q be a random scalar. Suppose that q can be expressed as $q = q^* + e$, where $\mathrm{E}(e) = 0$ and $\mathrm{E}(\mathbf{x}'e) = \mathbf{0}$. Write the linear projection of q^* onto $(1, \mathbf{x})$ as $q^* = \delta_0 + \delta_1 x_1 + \cdots + \delta_K x_K + r^*$, where $\mathrm{E}(r^*) = 0$ and $\mathrm{E}(\mathbf{x}'r^*) = \mathbf{0}$.

a. Show that

$\mathrm{L}(q \mid 1, \mathbf{x}) = \delta_0 + \delta_1 x_1 + \cdots + \delta_K x_K$

b. Find the projection error $r \equiv q - \mathrm{L}(q \mid 1, \mathbf{x})$ in terms of r^* and e.

2.7. Consider the conditional expectation

$\mathrm{E}(y \mid \mathbf{x}, \mathbf{z}) = g(\mathbf{x}) + \mathbf{z}\boldsymbol{\beta}$

where $g(\cdot)$ is a general function of $\mathbf{x}$ and $\boldsymbol{\beta}$ is a $1 \times M$ vector. Show that

$\mathrm{E}(\tilde{y} \mid \tilde{\mathbf{z}}) = \tilde{\mathbf{z}}\boldsymbol{\beta}$

where $\tilde{y} \equiv y - \mathrm{E}(y \mid \mathbf{x})$ and $\tilde{\mathbf{z}} \equiv \mathbf{z} - \mathrm{E}(\mathbf{z} \mid \mathbf{x})$.

Appendix 2A

2.A.1 Properties of Conditional Expectations

PROPERTY CE.1: Let $a_1(\mathbf{x}), \ldots, a_G(\mathbf{x})$ and $b(\mathbf{x})$ be scalar functions of $\mathbf{x}$, and let $y_1, \ldots, y_G$ be random scalars. Then

$$\mathrm{E}\left(\sum_{j=1}^{G} a_j(\mathbf{x}) y_j + b(\mathbf{x}) \mid \mathbf{x}\right) = \sum_{j=1}^{G} a_j(\mathbf{x}) \mathrm{E}(y_j \mid \mathbf{x}) + b(\mathbf{x})$$

provided that $\mathrm{E}(|y_j|) < \infty$, $\mathrm{E}[|a_j(\mathbf{x}) y_j|] < \infty$, and $\mathrm{E}[|b(\mathbf{x})|] < \infty$. This is the sense in which the conditional expectation is a linear operator.

PROPERTY CE.2: $\mathrm{E}(y) = \mathrm{E}[\mathrm{E}(y \mid \mathbf{x})] \equiv \mathrm{E}[\mu(\mathbf{x})]$.

Property CE.2 is the simplest version of the law of iterated expectations. As an illustration, suppose that $\mathbf{x}$ is a discrete random vector taking on values $\mathbf{c}_1, \mathbf{c}_2, \ldots, \mathbf{c}_M$ with probabilities $p_1, p_2, \ldots, p_M$. Then the LIE says

$$\mathrm{E}(y) = p_1 \mathrm{E}(y \mid \mathbf{x} = \mathbf{c}_1) + p_2 \mathrm{E}(y \mid \mathbf{x} = \mathbf{c}_2) + \cdots + p_M \mathrm{E}(y \mid \mathbf{x} = \mathbf{c}_M) \tag{2.49}$$

In other words, $\mathrm{E}(y)$ is simply a weighted average of the $\mathrm{E}(y \mid \mathbf{x} = \mathbf{c}_j)$, where the weight p_j is the probability that $\mathbf{x}$ takes on the value $\mathbf{c}_j$.

PROPERTY CE.3: (1) $\mathrm{E}(y \mid \mathbf{x}) = \mathrm{E}[\mathrm{E}(y \mid \mathbf{w}) \mid \mathbf{x}]$, where $\mathbf{x}$ and $\mathbf{w}$ are vectors with $\mathbf{x} = \mathbf{f}(\mathbf{w})$ for some nonstochastic function $\mathbf{f}(\cdot)$. (This is the general version of the law of iterated expectations.)

(2) As a special case of part 1, $\mathrm{E}(y \mid \mathbf{x}) = \mathrm{E}[\mathrm{E}(y \mid \mathbf{x}, \mathbf{z}) \mid \mathbf{x}]$ for vectors $\mathbf{x}$ and $\mathbf{z}$.

PROPERTY CE.4: If $\mathbf{f}(\mathbf{x}) \in \mathbb{R}^J$ is a function of $\mathbf{x}$ such that $\mathrm{E}(y \mid \mathbf{x}) = g[\mathbf{f}(\mathbf{x})]$ for some scalar function $g(\cdot)$, then $\mathrm{E}[y \mid \mathbf{f}(\mathbf{x})] = \mathrm{E}(y \mid \mathbf{x})$.

PROPERTY CE.5: If the vector $(\mathbf{u}, \mathbf{v})$ is independent of the vector $\mathbf{x}$, then $\mathrm{E}(\mathbf{u} \mid \mathbf{x}, \mathbf{v}) = \mathrm{E}(\mathbf{u} \mid \mathbf{v})$.

PROPERTY CE.6: If $u \equiv y - \mathrm{E}(y \mid \mathbf{x})$, then $\mathrm{E}[\mathbf{g}(\mathbf{x})u] = \mathbf{0}$ for any function $\mathbf{g}(\mathbf{x})$, provided that $\mathrm{E}[|g_j(\mathbf{x})u|] < \infty$, $j = 1, \ldots, J$, and $\mathrm{E}(|u|) < \infty$. In particular, $\mathrm{E}(u) = 0$ and $\mathrm{Cov}(x_j, u) = 0$, $j = 1, \ldots, K$.

Proof: First, note that

$$\mathrm{E}(u \mid \mathbf{x}) = \mathrm{E}[(y - \mathrm{E}(y \mid \mathbf{x})) \mid \mathbf{x}] = \mathrm{E}[(y - \mu(\mathbf{x})) \mid \mathbf{x}] = \mathrm{E}(y \mid \mathbf{x}) - \mu(\mathbf{x}) = 0$$

Next, by property CE.2, $\mathrm{E}[\mathbf{g}(\mathbf{x})u] = \mathrm{E}(\mathrm{E}[\mathbf{g}(\mathbf{x})u \mid \mathbf{x}]) = \mathrm{E}[\mathbf{g}(\mathbf{x})\mathrm{E}(u \mid \mathbf{x})]$ (by property CE.1) $= \mathbf{0}$ because $\mathrm{E}(u \mid \mathbf{x}) = 0$.

PROPERTY CE.7 (Conditional Jensen's Inequality): If $c\colon \mathbb{R} \to \mathbb{R}$ is a convex function defined on $\mathbb{R}$ and $\mathrm{E}[|y|] < \infty$, then

$$c[\mathrm{E}(y \mid \mathbf{x})] \le \mathrm{E}[c(y) \mid \mathbf{x}]$$

Technically, we should add the statement "almost surely-$\mathrm{P}_{\mathbf{x}}$," which means that the inequality holds for all $\mathbf{x}$ in a set that has probability equal to one. As a special case, $[\mathrm{E}(y)]^2 \le \mathrm{E}(y^2)$. Also, if $y > 0$, then $-\log[\mathrm{E}(y)] \le \mathrm{E}[-\log(y)]$, or $\mathrm{E}[\log(y)] \le \log[\mathrm{E}(y)]$.

PROPERTY CE.8: If $\mathrm{E}(y^2) < \infty$ and $\mu(\mathbf{x}) \equiv \mathrm{E}(y \mid \mathbf{x})$, then μ is a solution to

$$\min_{m \in \mathscr{M}} \mathrm{E}[(y - m(\mathbf{x}))^2]$$

where $\mathscr{M}$ is the set of functions $m\colon \mathbb{R}^K \to \mathbb{R}$ such that $\mathrm{E}[m(\mathbf{x})^2] < \infty$. In other words, $\mu(\mathbf{x})$ is the best mean square predictor of y based on information contained in $\mathbf{x}$.

Proof: By the conditional Jensen's inequality, if follows that $\mathrm{E}(y^2) < \infty$ implies $\mathrm{E}[\mu(\mathbf{x})^2] < \infty$, so that $\mu \in \mathscr{M}$. Next, for any $m \in \mathscr{M}$, write

$$\begin{aligned}\mathrm{E}[(y - m(\mathbf{x}))^2] &= \mathrm{E}[\{(y - \mu(\mathbf{x})) + (\mu(\mathbf{x}) - m(\mathbf{x}))\}^2] \\ &= \mathrm{E}[(y - \mu(\mathbf{x}))^2] + \mathrm{E}[(\mu(\mathbf{x}) - m(\mathbf{x}))^2] + 2\mathrm{E}[(\mu(\mathbf{x}) - m(\mathbf{x}))u]\end{aligned}$$

where $u \equiv y - \mu(\mathbf{x})$. Thus, by CE.6,

$$\mathrm{E}[(y - m(\mathbf{x}))^2] = \mathrm{E}(u^2) + \mathrm{E}[(\mu(\mathbf{x}) - m(\mathbf{x}))^2].$$

The right-hand side is clearly minimized at $m \equiv \mu$.

2.A.2 Properties of Conditional Variances

The **conditional variance** of y given $\mathbf{x}$ is defined as

$$\mathrm{Var}(y \mid \mathbf{x}) \equiv \sigma^2(\mathbf{x}) \equiv \mathrm{E}[\{y - \mathrm{E}(y \mid \mathbf{x})\}^2 \mid \mathbf{x}] = \mathrm{E}(y^2 \mid \mathbf{x}) - [\mathrm{E}(y \mid \mathbf{x})]^2$$

The last representation is often useful for computing $\mathrm{Var}(y \mid \mathbf{x})$. As with the conditional expectation, $\sigma^2(\mathbf{x})$ is a random variable when $\mathbf{x}$ is viewed as a random vector.

PROPERTY CV.1: $\mathrm{Var}[a(\mathbf{x})y + b(\mathbf{x}) \mid \mathbf{x}] = [a(\mathbf{x})]^2 \, \mathrm{Var}(y \mid \mathbf{x})$.

PROPERTY CV.2: $\mathrm{Var}(y) = \mathrm{E}[\mathrm{Var}(y \mid \mathbf{x})] + \mathrm{Var}[\mathrm{E}(y \mid \mathbf{x})] = \mathrm{E}[\sigma^2(\mathbf{x})] + \mathrm{Var}[\mu(\mathbf{x})]$.

Proof:

$$\begin{aligned}\mathrm{Var}(y) &\equiv \mathrm{E}[(y - \mathrm{E}(y))^2] = \mathrm{E}[(y - \mathrm{E}(y \mid \mathbf{x}) + \mathrm{E}(y \mid \mathbf{x}) + \mathrm{E}(y))^2] \\ &= \mathrm{E}[(y - \mathrm{E}(y \mid \mathbf{x}))^2] + \mathrm{E}[(\mathrm{E}(y \mid \mathbf{x}) - \mathrm{E}(y))^2] \\ &\quad + 2\mathrm{E}[(y - \mathrm{E}(y \mid \mathbf{x}))(\mathrm{E}(y \mid \mathbf{x}) - \mathrm{E}(y))]\end{aligned}$$

By CE.6, $\mathrm{E}[(y - \mathrm{E}(y \mid \mathbf{x}))(\mathrm{E}(y \mid \mathbf{x}) - \mathrm{E}(y))] = 0$; so

$$\begin{aligned}\mathrm{Var}(y) &= \mathrm{E}[(y - \mathrm{E}(y \mid \mathbf{x}))^2] + \mathrm{E}[(\mathrm{E}(y \mid \mathbf{x}) - \mathrm{E}(y))^2] \\ &= \mathrm{E}\{\mathrm{E}[(y - \mathrm{E}(y \mid \mathbf{x}))^2 \mid \mathbf{x}]\} + \mathrm{E}[(\mathrm{E}(y \mid \mathbf{x}) - \mathrm{E}[\mathrm{E}(y \mid \mathbf{x})])^2\end{aligned}$$

by the law of iterated expectations

$$\equiv \mathrm{E}[\mathrm{Var}(y \mid \mathbf{x})] + \mathrm{Var}[\mathrm{E}(y \mid \mathbf{x})]$$

An extension of Property CV.2 is often useful, and its proof is similar:

PROPERTY CV.3: $\mathrm{Var}(y \mid \mathbf{x}) = \mathrm{E}[\mathrm{Var}(y \mid \mathbf{x}, \mathbf{z}) \mid \mathbf{x}] + \mathrm{Var}[\mathrm{E}(y \mid \mathbf{x}, \mathbf{z}) \mid \mathbf{x}]$.

Consequently, by the law of iterated expectations CE.2,

PROPERTY CV.4: $\mathrm{E}[\mathrm{Var}(y \mid \mathbf{x})] \geq \mathrm{E}[\mathrm{Var}(y \mid \mathbf{x}, \mathbf{z})]$.

For any function $m(\cdot)$ define the mean squared error as $\mathrm{MSE}(y; m) \equiv \mathrm{E}[(y - m(\mathbf{x}))^2]$. Then CV.4 can be loosely stated as $\mathrm{MSE}[y; \mathrm{E}(y \mid \mathbf{x})] \geq \mathrm{MSE}[y; \mathrm{E}(y \mid \mathbf{x}, \mathbf{z})]$. In other words, in the population one never does worse for predicting y when additional variables are conditioned on. In particular, if $\mathrm{Var}(y \mid \mathbf{x})$ and $\mathrm{Var}(y \mid \mathbf{x}, \mathbf{z})$ are both constant, then $\mathrm{Var}(y \mid \mathbf{x}) \geq \mathrm{Var}(y \mid \mathbf{x}, \mathbf{z})$.

2.A.3 Properties of Linear Projections

In what follows, y is a scalar, $\mathbf{x}$ is a $1 \times K$ vector, and $\mathbf{z}$ is a $1 \times J$ vector. We allow the first element of $\mathbf{x}$ to be unity, although the following properties hold in either case. All of the variables are assumed to have finite second moments, and the appropriate variance matrices are assumed to be nonsingular.

PROPERTY LP.1: If $\mathrm{E}(y \mid \mathbf{x}) = \mathbf{x}\boldsymbol{\beta}$, then $\mathrm{L}(y \mid \mathbf{x}) = \mathbf{x}\boldsymbol{\beta}$. More generally, if

$$\mathrm{E}(y \mid \mathbf{x}) = \beta_1 g_1(\mathbf{x}) + \beta_2 g_2(\mathbf{x}) + \cdots + \beta_M g_M(\mathbf{x})$$

then

$$\mathrm{L}(y \mid w_1, \ldots, w_M) = \beta_1 w_1 + \beta_2 w_2 + \cdots + \beta_M w_M$$

where $w_j \equiv g_j(\mathbf{x})$, $j = 1, 2, \ldots, M$. This property tells us that, if $\mathrm{E}(y \mid \mathbf{x})$ is known to be linear in some functions $g_j(\mathbf{x})$, then this linear function also represents a linear projection.

PROPERTY LP.2: Define $u \equiv y - \mathrm{L}(y \mid \mathbf{x}) = y - \mathbf{x}\boldsymbol{\beta}$. Then $\mathrm{E}(\mathbf{x}'u) = \mathbf{0}$.

PROPERTY LP.3: Suppose y_j, $j = 1, 2, \ldots, G$ are each random scalars, and $a_1, \ldots, a_G$ are constants. Then

$$\mathrm{L}\left(\sum_{j=1}^{G} a_j y_j \mid \mathbf{x}\right) = \sum_{j=1}^{G} a_j \mathrm{L}(y_j \mid \mathbf{x})$$

Thus, the linear projection is a linear operator.

PROPERTY LP.4 (Law of Iterated Projections): $\mathrm{L}(y \mid \mathbf{x}) = \mathrm{L}[\mathrm{L}(y \mid \mathbf{x}, \mathbf{z}) \mid \mathbf{x}]$. More precisely, let

$$\mathrm{L}(y \mid \mathbf{x}, \mathbf{z}) \equiv \mathbf{x}\boldsymbol{\beta} + \mathbf{z}\boldsymbol{\gamma} \qquad \text{and} \qquad \mathrm{L}(y \mid \mathbf{x}) = \mathbf{x}\boldsymbol{\delta}$$

For each element of $\mathbf{z}$, write $\mathrm{L}(z_j \mid \mathbf{x}) = \mathbf{x}\boldsymbol{\pi}_j$, $j = 1, \ldots, J$, where $\boldsymbol{\pi}_j$ is $K \times 1$. Then $\mathrm{L}(\mathbf{z} \mid \mathbf{x}) = \mathbf{x}\boldsymbol{\Pi}$ where $\boldsymbol{\Pi}$ is the $K \times J$ matrix $\boldsymbol{\Pi} \equiv (\boldsymbol{\pi}_1, \boldsymbol{\pi}_2, \ldots, \boldsymbol{\pi}_J)$. Property LP.4 implies that

$$\begin{aligned} \mathrm{L}(y \mid \mathbf{x}) &= \mathrm{L}(\mathbf{x}\boldsymbol{\beta} + \mathbf{z}\boldsymbol{\gamma} \mid \mathbf{x}) = \mathrm{L}(\mathbf{x} \mid \mathbf{x})\boldsymbol{\beta} + \mathrm{L}(\mathbf{z} \mid \mathbf{x})\boldsymbol{\gamma} \qquad \text{(by LP.3)} \\ &= \mathbf{x}\boldsymbol{\beta} + (\mathbf{x}\boldsymbol{\Pi})\boldsymbol{\gamma} = \mathbf{x}(\boldsymbol{\beta} + \boldsymbol{\Pi}\boldsymbol{\gamma}) \end{aligned} \tag{2.50}$$

Thus, we have shown that $\boldsymbol{\delta} = \boldsymbol{\beta} + \boldsymbol{\Pi}\boldsymbol{\gamma}$. This is, in fact, the population analogue of the omitted variables bias formula from standard regression theory, something we will use in Chapter 4.

Another iteration property involves the linear projection and the conditional expectation:

PROPERTY LP.5: $\mathrm{L}(y \mid \mathbf{x}) = \mathrm{L}[\mathrm{E}(y \mid \mathbf{x}, \mathbf{z}) \mid \mathbf{x}]$.

Proof: Write $y = \mu(\mathbf{x}, \mathbf{z}) + u$, where $\mu(\mathbf{x}, \mathbf{z}) = \mathrm{E}(y \mid \mathbf{x}, \mathbf{z})$. But $\mathrm{E}(u \mid \mathbf{x}, \mathbf{z}) = 0$; so $\mathrm{E}(\mathbf{x}'u) = \mathbf{0}$, which implies by LP.3 that $\mathrm{L}(y \mid \mathbf{x}) = \mathrm{L}[\mu(\mathbf{x}, \mathbf{z}) \mid \mathbf{x}] + \mathrm{L}(u \mid \mathbf{x}) = \mathrm{L}[\mu(\mathbf{x}, \mathbf{z}) \mid \mathbf{x}] = \mathrm{L}[\mathrm{E}(y \mid \mathbf{x}, \mathbf{z}) \mid \mathbf{x}]$.

A useful special case of Property LP.5 occurs when $\mathbf{z}$ is empty. Then $\mathrm{L}(y \mid \mathbf{x}) = \mathrm{L}[\mathrm{E}(y \mid \mathbf{x}) \mid \mathbf{x}]$.

PROPERTY LP.6: $\boldsymbol{\beta}$ is a solution to

$$\min_{\mathbf{b} \in \mathbb{R}^K} \mathrm{E}[(y - \mathbf{x}\mathbf{b})^2] \tag{2.51}$$

If $\mathrm{E}(\mathbf{x}'\mathbf{x})$ is positive definite, then $\boldsymbol{\beta}$ is the *unique* solution to this problem.

Proof: For any $\mathbf{b}$, write $y - \mathbf{x}\mathbf{b} = (y - \mathbf{x}\boldsymbol{\beta}) + (\mathbf{x}\boldsymbol{\beta} - \mathbf{x}\mathbf{b})$. Then

$$\begin{aligned}(y - \mathbf{x}\mathbf{b})^2 &= (y - \mathbf{x}\boldsymbol{\beta})^2 + (\mathbf{x}\boldsymbol{\beta} - \mathbf{x}\mathbf{b})^2 + 2(\mathbf{x}\boldsymbol{\beta} - \mathbf{x}\mathbf{b})(y - \mathbf{x}\boldsymbol{\beta}) \\ &= (y - \mathbf{x}\boldsymbol{\beta})^2 + (\boldsymbol{\beta} - \mathbf{b})'\mathbf{x}'\mathbf{x}(\boldsymbol{\beta} - \mathbf{b}) + 2(\boldsymbol{\beta} - \mathbf{b})'\mathbf{x}'(y - \mathbf{x}\boldsymbol{\beta})\end{aligned}$$

Therefore,

$$\begin{aligned}\mathrm{E}[(y - \mathbf{x}\mathbf{b})^2] &= \mathrm{E}[(y - \mathbf{x}\boldsymbol{\beta})^2] + (\boldsymbol{\beta} - \mathbf{b})'\mathrm{E}(\mathbf{x}'\mathbf{x})(\boldsymbol{\beta} - \mathbf{b}) \\ &\quad + 2(\boldsymbol{\beta} - \mathbf{b})'\mathrm{E}[\mathbf{x}'(y - \mathbf{x}\boldsymbol{\beta})] \\ &= \mathrm{E}[(y - \mathbf{x}\boldsymbol{\beta})^2] + (\boldsymbol{\beta} - \mathbf{b})'\mathrm{E}(\mathbf{x}'\mathbf{x})(\boldsymbol{\beta} - \mathbf{b})\end{aligned} \tag{2.52}$$

because $\mathrm{E}[\mathbf{x}'(y - \mathbf{x}\boldsymbol{\beta})] = \mathbf{0}$ by LP.2. When $\mathbf{b} = \boldsymbol{\beta}$, the right-hand side of equation (2.52) is minimized. Further, if $\mathrm{E}(\mathbf{x}'\mathbf{x})$ is positive definite, $(\boldsymbol{\beta} - \mathbf{b})'\mathrm{E}(\mathbf{x}'\mathbf{x})(\boldsymbol{\beta} - \mathbf{b}) > 0$ if $\mathbf{b} \neq \boldsymbol{\beta}$; so in this case $\boldsymbol{\beta}$ is the unique minimizer.

Property LP.6 states that the linear projection is the minimum mean square *linear* predictor. It is not necessarily the minimum mean square predictor: if $\mathrm{E}(y \mid \mathbf{x}) = \mu(\mathbf{x})$ is not linear in $\mathbf{x}$, then

$$\mathrm{E}[(y - \mu(\mathbf{x}))^2] < \mathrm{E}[(y - \mathbf{x}\boldsymbol{\beta})^2] \tag{2.53}$$

PROPERTY LP.7: This is a partitioned projection formula, which is useful in a variety of circumstances. Write

$$\mathrm{L}(y \mid \mathbf{x}, \mathbf{z}) = \mathbf{x}\boldsymbol{\beta} + \mathbf{z}\boldsymbol{\gamma} \tag{2.54}$$

Define the $1 \times K$ vector of population residuals from the projection of $\mathbf{x}$ on $\mathbf{z}$ as $\mathbf{r} \equiv \mathbf{x} - \mathrm{L}(\mathbf{x} \mid \mathbf{z})$. Further, define the population residual from the projection of y on $\mathbf{z}$ as $v \equiv y - \mathrm{L}(y \mid \mathbf{z})$. Then the following are true:

$$\mathrm{L}(v \mid \mathbf{r}) = \mathbf{r}\boldsymbol{\beta} \tag{2.55}$$

and

$$\mathrm{L}(y \mid \mathbf{r}) = \mathbf{r}\boldsymbol{\beta} \tag{2.56}$$

The point is that the $\boldsymbol{\beta}$ in equations (2.55) and (2.56) is the *same* as that appearing in equation (2.54). Another way of stating this result is

$$\boldsymbol{\beta} = [\mathrm{E}(\mathbf{r}'\mathbf{r})]^{-1}\mathrm{E}(\mathbf{r}'v) = [\mathrm{E}(\mathbf{r}'\mathbf{r})]^{-1}\mathrm{E}(\mathbf{r}'y). \tag{2.57}$$

Proof: From equation (2.54) write

$$y = \mathbf{x}\boldsymbol{\beta} + \mathbf{z}\boldsymbol{\gamma} + u, \qquad \mathrm{E}(\mathbf{x}'u) = \mathbf{0}, \qquad \mathrm{E}(\mathbf{z}'u) = \mathbf{0} \tag{2.58}$$

Taking the linear projection gives

$$\mathrm{L}(y \mid \mathbf{z}) = \mathrm{L}(\mathbf{x} \mid \mathbf{z})\boldsymbol{\beta} + \mathbf{z}\boldsymbol{\gamma} \tag{2.59}$$

Subtracting equation (2.59) from (2.58) gives $y - \mathrm{L}(y \mid \mathbf{z}) = [\mathbf{x} - \mathrm{L}(\mathbf{x} \mid \mathbf{z})]\boldsymbol{\beta} + u$, or

$$v = \mathbf{r}\boldsymbol{\beta} + u \tag{2.60}$$

Since $\mathbf{r}$ is a linear combination of $(\mathbf{x}, \mathbf{z})$, $\mathrm{E}(\mathbf{r}'u) = \mathbf{0}$. Multiplying equation (2.60) through by $\mathbf{r}'$ and taking expectations, it follows that

$$\boldsymbol{\beta} = [\mathrm{E}(\mathbf{r}'\mathbf{r})]^{-1}\mathrm{E}(\mathbf{r}'v)$$

[We assume that $\mathrm{E}(\mathbf{r}'\mathbf{r})$ is nonsingular.] Finally, $\mathrm{E}(\mathbf{r}'v) = \mathrm{E}[\mathbf{r}'(y - \mathrm{L}(y \mid \mathbf{z}))] = \mathrm{E}(\mathbf{r}'y)$, since $\mathrm{L}(y \mid \mathbf{z})$ is linear in $\mathbf{z}$ and $\mathbf{r}$ is orthogonal to any linear function of $\mathbf{z}$.

3 Basic Asymptotic Theory

This chapter summarizes some definitions and limit theorems that are important for studying large-sample theory. Most claims are stated without proof, as several require tedious epsilon-delta arguments. We do prove some results that build on fundamental definitions and theorems. A good, general reference for background in asymptotic analysis is White (1984). In Chapter 12 we introduce further asymptotic methods that are required for studying nonlinear models.

3.1 Convergence of Deterministic Sequences

Asymptotic analysis is concerned with the various kinds of convergence of sequences of estimators as the sample size grows. We begin with some definitions regarding nonstochastic sequences of numbers. When we apply these results in econometrics, N is the sample size, and it runs through all positive integers. You are assumed to have some familiarity with the notion of a limit of a sequence.

DEFINITION 3.1: (1) A sequence of nonrandom numbers $\{a_N: N = 1, 2, \dots\}$ *converges to a* (has limit a) if for all $\varepsilon > 0$, there exists N_ε such that if $N > N_\varepsilon$ then $|a_N - a| < \varepsilon$. We write $a_N \to a$ as $N \to \infty$.

(2) A sequence $\{a_N: N = 1, 2, \dots\}$ is *bounded* if and only if there is some $b < \infty$ such that $|a_N| \le b$ for all $N = 1, 2, \dots$. Otherwise, we say that $\{a_N\}$ is *unbounded*.

These definitions apply to vectors and matrices element by element.

Example 3.1: (1) If $a_N = 2 + 1/N$, then $a_N \to 2$. (2) If $a_N = (-1)^N$, then a_N does not have a limit, but it is bounded. (3) If $a_N = N^{1/4}$, a_N is not bounded. Because a_N increases without bound, we write $a_N \to \infty$.

DEFINITION 3.2: (1) A sequence $\{a_N\}$ is $\mathrm{O}(N^\lambda)$ (*at most of order* N^λ) if $N^{-\lambda}a_N$ is bounded. When $\lambda = 0$, $\{a_N\}$ is bounded, and we also write $a_N = \mathrm{O}(1)$ (*big oh one*). (2) $\{a_N\}$ is $\mathrm{o}(N^\lambda)$ if $N^{-\lambda}a_N \to 0$. When $\lambda = 0$, a_N converges to zero, and we also write $a_N = \mathrm{o}(1)$ (*little oh one*).

From the definitions, it is clear that if $a_N = \mathrm{o}(N^\lambda)$, then $a_N = \mathrm{O}(N^\lambda)$; in particular, if $a_N = \mathrm{o}(1)$, then $a_N = \mathrm{O}(1)$. If each element of a sequence of vectors or matrices is $\mathrm{O}(N^\lambda)$, we say the sequence of vectors or matrices is $\mathrm{O}(N^\lambda)$, and similarly for $\mathrm{o}(N^\lambda)$.

Example 3.2: (1) If $a_N = \log(N)$, then $a_N = \mathrm{o}(N^\lambda)$ for any $\lambda > 0$. (2) If $a_N = 10 + \sqrt{N}$, then $a_N = \mathrm{O}(N^{1/2})$ and $a_N = \mathrm{o}(N^{(1/2+\gamma)})$ for any $\gamma > 0$.

3.2 Convergence in Probability and Bounded in Probability

DEFINITION 3.3: (1) A sequence of random variables $\{x_N: N = 1, 2, \ldots\}$ **converges in probability** to the constant a if for all $\varepsilon > 0$,

$$P[|x_N - a| > \varepsilon] \to 0 \qquad \text{as } N \to \infty$$

We write $x_N \xrightarrow{p} a$ and say that a is the **probability limit (plim)** of x_N: plim $x_N = a$.

(2) In the special case where $a = 0$, we also say that $\{x_N\}$ is $o_p(1)$ (*little oh p one*). We also write $x_N = o_p(1)$ or $x_N \xrightarrow{p} 0$.

(3) A sequence of random variables $\{x_N\}$ is **bounded in probability** if and only if for every $\varepsilon > 0$, there exists a $b_\varepsilon < \infty$ and an integer N_ε such that

$$P[|x_N| \geq b_\varepsilon] < \varepsilon \qquad \text{for all } N \geq N_\varepsilon$$

We write $x_N = O_p(1)$ ($\{x_N\}$ is *big oh p one*).

If c_N is a nonrandom sequence, then $c_N = O_p(1)$ if and only if $c_N = O(1)$; $c_N = o_p(1)$ if and only if $c_N = o(1)$. A simple, and very useful, fact is that if a sequence converges in probability to any real number, then it is bounded in probability.

LEMMA 3.1: If $x_N \xrightarrow{p} a$, then $x_N = O_p(1)$. This lemma also holds for vectors and matrices.

The proof of Lemma 3.1 is not difficult; see Problem 3.1.

DEFINITION 3.4: (1) A random sequence $\{x_N: N = 1, 2, \ldots\}$ is $o_p(a_N)$, where $\{a_N\}$ is a nonrandom, positive sequence, if $x_N/a_N = o_p(1)$. We write $x_N = o_p(a_N)$.

(2) A random sequence $\{x_N: N = 1, 2, \ldots\}$ is $O_p(a_N)$, where $\{a_N\}$ is a nonrandom, positive sequence, if $x_N/a_N = O_p(1)$. We write $x_N = O_p(a_N)$.

We could have started by defining a sequence $\{x_N\}$ to be $o_p(N^\delta)$ for $\delta \in \mathbb{R}$ if $N^{-\delta} x_N \xrightarrow{p} 0$, in which case we obtain the definition of $o_p(1)$ when $\delta = 0$. This is where the one in $o_p(1)$ comes from. A similar remark holds for $O_p(1)$.

Example 3.3: If z is a random variable, then $x_N \equiv \sqrt{N} z$ is $O_p(N^{1/2})$ and $x_N = o_p(N^\delta)$ for any $\delta > \frac{1}{2}$.

LEMMA 3.2: If $w_N = o_p(1)$, $x_N = o_p(1)$, $y_N = O_p(1)$, and $z_N = O_p(1)$, then (1) $w_N + x_N = o_p(1)$; (2) $y_N + z_N = O_p(1)$; (3) $y_N z_N = O_p(1)$; and (4) $x_N z_N = o_p(1)$.

In derivations, we will write relationships 1 to 4 as $o_p(1) + o_p(1) = o_p(1)$, $O_p(1) + O_p(1) = O_p(1)$, $O_p(1) \cdot O_p(1) = O_p(1)$, and $o_p(1) \cdot O_p(1) = o_p(1)$, respectively. Because a $o_p(1)$ sequence is $O_p(1)$, Lemma 3.2 also implies that $o_p(1) + O_p(1) = O_p(1)$ and $o_p(1) \cdot o_p(1) = o_p(1)$.

All of the previous definitions apply element by element to sequences of random vectors or matrices. For example, if $\{\mathbf{x}_N\}$ is a sequence of random $K \times 1$ random vectors, $\mathbf{x}_N \xrightarrow{p} \mathbf{a}$, where $\mathbf{a}$ is a $K \times 1$ nonrandom vector, if and only if $x_{Nj} \xrightarrow{p} a_j$, $j = 1, \ldots, K$. This is equivalent to $\|\mathbf{x}_N - \mathbf{a}\| \xrightarrow{p} 0$, where $\|\mathbf{b}\| \equiv (\mathbf{b}'\mathbf{b})^{1/2}$ denotes the Euclidean length of the $K \times 1$ vector $\mathbf{b}$. Also, $\mathbf{Z}_N \xrightarrow{p} \mathbf{B}$, where $\mathbf{Z}_N$ and $\mathbf{B}$ are $M \times K$, is equivalent to $\|\mathbf{Z}_N - \mathbf{B}\| \xrightarrow{p} 0$, where $\|\mathbf{A}\| \equiv [\mathrm{tr}(\mathbf{A}'\mathbf{A})]^{1/2}$ and $\mathrm{tr}(\mathbf{C})$ denotes the trace of the square matrix $\mathbf{C}$.

A result that we often use for studying the large-sample properties of estimators for linear models is the following. It is easily proven by repeated application of Lemma 3.2 (see Problem 3.2).

LEMMA 3.3: Let $\{\mathbf{Z}_N: N = 1, 2, \ldots\}$ be a sequence of $J \times K$ matrices such that $\mathbf{Z}_N = o_p(1)$, and let $\{\mathbf{x}_N\}$ be a sequence of $J \times 1$ random vectors such that $\mathbf{x}_N = O_p(1)$. Then $\mathbf{Z}_N'\mathbf{x}_N = o_p(1)$.

The next lemma is known as **Slutsky's theorem**.

LEMMA 3.4: Let $\mathbf{g}: \mathbb{R}^K \to \mathbb{R}^J$ be a function continuous at some point $\mathbf{c} \in \mathbb{R}^K$. Let $\{\mathbf{x}_N: N = 1, 2, \ldots\}$ be sequence of $K \times 1$ random vectors such that $\mathbf{x}_N \xrightarrow{p} \mathbf{c}$. Then $\mathbf{g}(\mathbf{x}_N) \xrightarrow{p} \mathbf{g}(\mathbf{c})$ as $N \to \infty$. In other words,

$$\operatorname{plim} \mathbf{g}(\mathbf{x}_N) = \mathbf{g}(\operatorname{plim} \mathbf{x}_N) \tag{3.1}$$

if $\mathbf{g}(\cdot)$ is continuous at $\operatorname{plim} \mathbf{x}_N$.

Slutsky's theorem is perhaps the most useful feature of the plim operator: it shows that the plim passes through nonlinear functions, provided they are continuous. The expectations operator does not have this feature, and this lack makes finite sample analysis difficult for many estimators. Lemma 3.4 shows that plims behave just like regular limits when applying a continuous function to the sequence.

DEFINITION 3.5: Let $(\Omega, \mathscr{F}, \mathrm{P})$ be a probability space. A sequence of events $\{\Omega_N: N = 1, 2, \ldots\} \subset \mathscr{F}$ is said to occur **with probability approaching one (w.p.a.1)** if and only if $\mathrm{P}(\Omega_N) \to 1$ as $N \to \infty$.

Definition 3.5 allows that Ω_N^c, the complement of Ω_N, can occur for each N, but its chance of occuring goes to zero as $N \to \infty$.

COROLLARY 3.1: Let $\{\mathbf{Z}_N: N = 1, 2, \ldots\}$ be a sequence of random $K \times K$ matrices, and let $\mathbf{A}$ be a nonrandom, invertible $K \times K$ matrix. If $\mathbf{Z}_N \xrightarrow{p} \mathbf{A}$ then

(1) $\mathbf{Z}_N^{-1}$ exists w.p.a.1;
(2) $\mathbf{Z}_N^{-1} \xrightarrow{p} \mathbf{A}^{-1}$ or plim $\mathbf{Z}_N^{-1} = \mathbf{A}^{-1}$ (in an appropriate sense).

Proof: Because the determinant is a continuous function on the space of all square matrices, $\det(\mathbf{Z}_N) \xrightarrow{p} \det(\mathbf{A})$. Because $\mathbf{A}$ is nonsingular, $\det(\mathbf{A}) \neq 0$. Therefore, it follows that $\mathrm{P}[\det(\mathbf{Z}_N) \neq 0] \to 1$ as $N \to \infty$. This completes the proof of part 1.

Part 2 requires a convention about how to define $\mathbf{Z}_N^{-1}$ when $\mathbf{Z}_N$ is nonsingular. Let Ω_N be the set of ω (outcomes) such that $\mathbf{Z}_N(\omega)$ is nonsingular for $\omega \in \Omega_N$; we just showed that $\mathrm{P}(\Omega_N) \to 1$ as $N \to \infty$. Define a new sequence of matrices by

$$\tilde{\mathbf{Z}}_N(\omega) \equiv \mathbf{Z}_N(\omega) \text{ when } \omega \in \Omega_N, \qquad \tilde{\mathbf{Z}}_N(\omega) \equiv \mathbf{I}_K \text{ when } \omega \notin \Omega_N$$

Then $\mathrm{P}(\tilde{\mathbf{Z}}_N = \mathbf{Z}_N) = \mathrm{P}(\Omega_N) \to 1$ as $N \to \infty$. Then, because $\mathbf{Z}_N \xrightarrow{p} \mathbf{A}$, $\tilde{\mathbf{Z}}_N \xrightarrow{p} \mathbf{A}$. The inverse operator is continuous on the space of invertible matrices, so $\tilde{\mathbf{Z}}_N^{-1} \xrightarrow{p} \mathbf{A}^{-1}$. This is what we mean by $\mathbf{Z}_N^{-1} \xrightarrow{p} \mathbf{A}^{-1}$; the fact that $\mathbf{Z}_N$ can be singular with vanishing probability does not affect asymptotic analysis.

3.3 Convergence in Distribution

DEFINITION 3.6: A sequence of random variables $\{x_N : N = 1, 2, \ldots\}$ **converges in distribution** to the continuous random variable x if and only if

$$F_N(\xi) \to F(\xi) \qquad \text{as } N \to \infty \text{ for all } \xi \in \mathbb{R}$$

where F_N is the cumulative distribution function (c.d.f.) of x_N and F is the (continuous) c.d.f. of x. We write $x_N \xrightarrow{d} x$.

When $x \sim \mathrm{Normal}(\mu, \sigma^2)$ we write $x_N \xrightarrow{d} \mathrm{Normal}(\mu, \sigma^2)$ or $x_N \overset{a}{\sim} \mathrm{Normal}(\mu, \sigma^2)$ (x_N is **asymptotically normal**).

In Definition 3.6, x_N is not required to be continuous for any N. A good example of where x_N is discrete for all N but has an asymptotically normal distribution is the Demoivre-Laplace theorem (a special case of the central limit theorem given in Section 3.4), which says that $x_N \equiv (s_N - Np)/[Np(1-p)]^{1/2}$ has a limiting standard normal distribution, where s_N has the binomial (N, p) distribution.

DEFINITION 3.7: A sequence of $K \times 1$ random vectors $\{\mathbf{x}_N : N = 1, 2, \ldots\}$ converges in distribution to the continuous random vector $\mathbf{x}$ if and only if for any $K \times 1$ nonrandom vector $\mathbf{c}$ such that $\mathbf{c}'\mathbf{c} = 1$, $\mathbf{c}'\mathbf{x}_N \xrightarrow{d} \mathbf{c}'\mathbf{x}$, and we write $\mathbf{x}_N \xrightarrow{d} \mathbf{x}$.

When $\mathbf{x} \sim \mathrm{Normal}(\mathbf{m}, \mathbf{V})$ the requirement in Definition 3.7 is that $\mathbf{c}'\mathbf{x}_N \xrightarrow{d} \mathrm{Normal}(\mathbf{c}'\mathbf{m}, \mathbf{c}'\mathbf{V}\mathbf{c})$ for every $\mathbf{c} \in \mathbb{R}^K$ such that $\mathbf{c}'\mathbf{c} = 1$; in this case we write $\mathbf{x}_N \xrightarrow{d} \mathrm{Normal}(\mathbf{m}, \mathbf{V})$ or $\mathbf{x}_N \overset{a}{\sim} \mathrm{Normal}(\mathbf{m}, \mathbf{V})$. For the derivations in this book, $\mathbf{m} = \mathbf{0}$.

LEMMA 3.5: If $\mathbf{x}_N \xrightarrow{d} \mathbf{x}$, where $\mathbf{x}$ is any $K \times 1$ random vector, then $\mathbf{x}_N = \mathrm{O}_p(1)$.

As we will see throughout this book, Lemma 3.5 turns out to be very useful for establishing that a sequence is bounded in probability. Often it is easiest to first verify that a sequence converges in distribution.

LEMMA 3.6: Let $\{\mathbf{x}_N\}$ be a sequence of $K \times 1$ random vectors such that $\mathbf{x}_N \xrightarrow{d} \mathbf{x}$. If $\mathbf{g}\colon \mathbb{R}^K \to \mathbb{R}^J$ is a continuous function, then $\mathbf{g}(\mathbf{x}_N) \xrightarrow{d} \mathbf{g}(\mathbf{x})$.

The usefulness of Lemma 3.6, which is called the **continuous mapping theorem**, cannot be overstated. It tells us that once we know the limiting distribution of $\mathbf{x}_N$, we can find the limiting distribution of many interesting functions of $\mathbf{x}_N$. This is especially useful for determining the asymptotic distribution of test statistics once the limiting distribution of an estimator is known; see Section 3.5.

The continuity of $\mathbf{g}$ is not necessary in Lemma 3.6, but some restrictions are needed. We will only need the form stated in Lemma 3.6.

COROLLARY 3.2: If $\{\mathbf{z}_N\}$ is a sequence of $K \times 1$ random vectors such that $\mathbf{z}_N \xrightarrow{d}$ Normal$(\mathbf{0}, \mathbf{V})$ then

(1) For any $K \times M$ nonrandom matrix $\mathbf{A}$, $\mathbf{A}'\mathbf{z}_N \xrightarrow{d}$ Normal$(\mathbf{0}, \mathbf{A}'\mathbf{V}\mathbf{A})$.

(2) $\mathbf{z}_N'\mathbf{V}^{-1}\mathbf{z}_N \xrightarrow{d} \chi_K^2$ (or $\mathbf{z}_N'\mathbf{V}^{-1}\mathbf{z}_N \overset{a}{\sim} \chi_K^2$).

LEMMA 3.7: Let $\{\mathbf{x}_N\}$ and $\{\mathbf{z}_N\}$ be sequences of $K \times 1$ random vectors. If $\mathbf{z}_N \xrightarrow{d} \mathbf{z}$ and $\mathbf{x}_N - \mathbf{z}_N \xrightarrow{p} \mathbf{0}$, then $\mathbf{x}_N \xrightarrow{d} \mathbf{z}$.

Lemma 3.7 is called the **asymptotic equivalence lemma**. In Section 3.5.1 we discuss generally how Lemma 3.7 is used in econometrics. We use the asymptotic equivalence lemma so frequently in asymptotic analysis that after a while we will not even mention that we are using it.

3.4 Limit Theorems for Random Samples

In this section we state two classic limit theorems for independent, identically distributed (i.i.d.) sequences of random vectors. These apply when sampling is done randomly from a population.

THEOREM 3.1: Let $\{\mathbf{w}_i\colon i = 1, 2, \ldots\}$ be a sequence of independent, identically distributed $G \times 1$ random vectors such that $E(|w_{ig}|) < \infty$, $g = 1, \ldots, G$. Then the sequence satisfies the **weak law of large numbers (WLLN)**: $N^{-1}\sum_{i=1}^N \mathbf{w}_i \xrightarrow{p} \boldsymbol{\mu}_w$, where $\boldsymbol{\mu}_w \equiv \mathrm{E}(\mathbf{w}_i)$.

THEOREM 3.2 (Lindeberg-Levy): Let $\{\mathbf{w}_i: i = 1, 2, \ldots\}$ be a sequence of independent, identically distributed $G \times 1$ random vectors such that $E(w_{ig}^2) < \infty$, $g = 1, \ldots, G$, and $E(\mathbf{w}_i) = \mathbf{0}$. Then $\{\mathbf{w}_i: i = 1, 2, \ldots\}$ satisfies the **central limit theorem (CLT)**; that is,

$$N^{-1/2} \sum_{i=1}^{N} \mathbf{w}_i \xrightarrow{d} \text{Normal}(\mathbf{0}, \mathbf{B})$$

where $\mathbf{B} = \text{Var}(\mathbf{w}_i) = \text{E}(\mathbf{w}_i \mathbf{w}_i')$ is necessarily positive semidefinite. For our purposes, $\mathbf{B}$ is almost always positive definite.

3.5 Limiting Behavior of Estimators and Test Statistics

In this section, we apply the previous concepts to sequences of estimators. Because estimators depend on the random outcomes of data, they are properly viewed as random vectors.

3.5.1 Asymptotic Properties of Estimators

DEFINITION 3.8: Let $\{\hat{\boldsymbol{\theta}}_N: N = 1, 2, \ldots\}$ be a sequence of estimators of the $P \times 1$ vector $\boldsymbol{\theta} \in \boldsymbol{\Theta}$, where N indexes the sample size. If

$$\hat{\boldsymbol{\theta}}_N \xrightarrow{p} \boldsymbol{\theta} \tag{3.2}$$

for any value of $\boldsymbol{\theta}$, then we say $\hat{\boldsymbol{\theta}}_N$ is a **consistent estimator** of $\boldsymbol{\theta}$.

Because there are other notions of convergence, in the theoretical literature condition (3.2) is often referred to as *weak consistency*. This is the only kind of consistency we will be concerned with, so we simply call condition (3.2) *consistency*. (See White, 1984, Chapter 2, for other kinds of convergence.) Since we do not know $\boldsymbol{\theta}$, the consistency definition requires condition (3.2) for any possible value of $\boldsymbol{\theta}$.

DEFINITION 3.9: Let $\{\hat{\boldsymbol{\theta}}_N: N = 1, 2, \ldots\}$ be a sequence of estimators of the $P \times 1$ vector $\boldsymbol{\theta} \in \boldsymbol{\Theta}$. Suppose that

$$\sqrt{N}(\hat{\boldsymbol{\theta}}_N - \boldsymbol{\theta}) \xrightarrow{d} \text{Normal}(\mathbf{0}, \mathbf{V}) \tag{3.3}$$

where $\mathbf{V}$ is a $P \times P$ positive semidefinite matrix. Then we say that $\hat{\boldsymbol{\theta}}_N$ is $\sqrt{\mathbf{N}}$**-asymptotically normally distributed** and $\mathbf{V}$ is the **asymptotic variance** of $\sqrt{N}(\hat{\boldsymbol{\theta}}_N - \boldsymbol{\theta})$, denoted Avar $\sqrt{N}(\hat{\boldsymbol{\theta}}_N - \boldsymbol{\theta}) = \mathbf{V}$.

Even though $\mathbf{V}/N = \text{Var}(\hat{\boldsymbol{\theta}}_N)$ holds only in special cases, and $\hat{\boldsymbol{\theta}}_N$ rarely has an exact normal distribution, we treat $\hat{\boldsymbol{\theta}}_N$ *as if*

$$\hat{\boldsymbol{\theta}}_N \sim \text{Normal}(\boldsymbol{\theta}, \mathbf{V}/N) \tag{3.4}$$

whenever statement (3.3) holds. For this reason, $\mathbf{V}/N$ is called the **asymptotic variance** of $\hat{\boldsymbol{\theta}}_N$, and we write

$$\text{Avar}(\hat{\boldsymbol{\theta}}_N) = \mathbf{V}/N \tag{3.5}$$

However, the only sense in which $\hat{\boldsymbol{\theta}}_N$ is approximately normally distributed with mean $\boldsymbol{\theta}$ and variance $\mathbf{V}/N$ is contained in statement (3.3), and this is what is needed to perform inference about $\boldsymbol{\theta}$. Statement (3.4) is a heuristic statement that leads to the appropriate inference.

When we discuss consistent estimation of asymptotic variances—a topic that will arise often—we should technically focus on estimation of $\mathbf{V} \equiv \text{Avar}\,\sqrt{N}(\hat{\boldsymbol{\theta}}_N - \boldsymbol{\theta})$. In most cases, we will be able to find at least one, and usually more than one, consistent estimator $\hat{\mathbf{V}}_N$ of $\mathbf{V}$. Then the corresponding estimator of $\text{Avar}(\hat{\boldsymbol{\theta}}_N)$ is $\hat{\mathbf{V}}_N/N$, and we write

$$\widehat{\text{Avar}}(\hat{\boldsymbol{\theta}}_N) = \hat{\mathbf{V}}_N/N \tag{3.6}$$

The division by N in equation (3.6) is practically very important. What we call the asymptotic variance of $\hat{\boldsymbol{\theta}}_N$ is estimated as in equation (3.6). Unfortunately, there has not been a consistent usage of the term "asymptotic variance" in econometrics.

Taken literally, a statement such as "$\hat{\mathbf{V}}_N/N$ is consistent for $\text{Avar}(\hat{\boldsymbol{\theta}}_N)$" is not very meaningful because $\mathbf{V}/N$ converges to $\mathbf{0}$ as $N \to \infty$; typically, $\hat{\mathbf{V}}_N/N \xrightarrow{p} \mathbf{0}$ whether or not $\hat{\mathbf{V}}_N$ is not consistent for $\mathbf{V}$. Nevertheless, it is useful to have an admittedly imprecise shorthand. In what follows, if we say that "$\hat{\mathbf{V}}_N/N$ consistently estimates $\text{Avar}(\hat{\boldsymbol{\theta}}_N)$," we mean that $\hat{\mathbf{V}}_N$ consistently estimates $\text{Avar}\,\sqrt{N}(\hat{\boldsymbol{\theta}}_N - \boldsymbol{\theta})$.

Definition 3.10: If $\sqrt{N}(\hat{\boldsymbol{\theta}}_N - \boldsymbol{\theta}) \overset{a}{\sim} \text{Normal}(0, \mathbf{V})$ where $\mathbf{V}$ is positive definite with jth diagonal v_{jj}, and $\hat{\mathbf{V}}_N \xrightarrow{p} \mathbf{V}$, then the **asymptotic standard error** of $\hat{\theta}_{Nj}$, denoted $\text{se}(\hat{\theta}_{Nj})$, is $(\hat{v}_{Njj}/N)^{1/2}$.

In other words, the asymptotic standard error of an estimator, which is almost always reported in applied work, is the square root of the appropriate diagonal element of $\hat{\mathbf{V}}_N/N$. The asymptotic standard errors can be loosely thought of as estimating the standard deviations of the elements of $\hat{\boldsymbol{\theta}}_N$, and they are the appropriate quantities to use when forming (asymptotic) t statistics and confidence intervals. Obtaining valid asymptotic standard errors (after verifying that the estimator is asymptotically normally distributed) is often the biggest challenge when using a new estimator.

If statement (3.3) holds, it follows by Lemma 3.5 that $\sqrt{N}(\hat{\boldsymbol{\theta}}_N - \boldsymbol{\theta}) = \text{O}_p(1)$, or $\hat{\boldsymbol{\theta}}_N - \boldsymbol{\theta} = \text{O}_p(N^{-1/2})$, and we say that $\hat{\boldsymbol{\theta}}_N$ is a $\sqrt{\mathbf{N}}$**-consistent estimator** of $\boldsymbol{\theta}$. $\sqrt{N}$-

consistency certainly implies that plim $\hat{\boldsymbol{\theta}}_N = \boldsymbol{\theta}$, but it is much stronger because it tells us that the rate of convergence is almost the square root of the sample size N: $\hat{\boldsymbol{\theta}}_N - \boldsymbol{\theta} = \mathrm{o}_p(N^{-c})$ for any $0 \leq c < \frac{1}{2}$. In this book, almost every consistent estimator we will study—and every one we consider in any detail—is $\sqrt{N}$-asymptotically normal, and therefore $\sqrt{N}$-consistent, under reasonable assumptions.

If one $\sqrt{N}$-asymptotically normal estimator has an asymptotic variance that is smaller than another's asymptotic variance (in the matrix sense), it makes it easy to choose between the estimators based on asymptotic considerations.

DEFINITION 3.11: Let $\hat{\boldsymbol{\theta}}_N$ and $\tilde{\boldsymbol{\theta}}_N$ be estimators of $\boldsymbol{\theta}$ each satisfying statement (3.3), with asymptotic variances $\mathbf{V} = \text{Avar}\, \sqrt{N}(\hat{\boldsymbol{\theta}}_N - \boldsymbol{\theta})$ and $\mathbf{D} = \text{Avar}\, \sqrt{N}(\tilde{\boldsymbol{\theta}}_N - \boldsymbol{\theta})$ (these generally depend on the value of $\boldsymbol{\theta}$, but we suppress that consideration here). (1) $\hat{\boldsymbol{\theta}}_N$ is **asymptotically efficient relative to** $\tilde{\boldsymbol{\theta}}_N$ if $\mathbf{D} - \mathbf{V}$ is positive semidefinite for all $\boldsymbol{\theta}$; (2) $\hat{\boldsymbol{\theta}}_N$ and $\tilde{\boldsymbol{\theta}}_N$ are $\sqrt{\mathbf{N}}$**-equivalent** if $\sqrt{N}(\hat{\boldsymbol{\theta}}_N - \tilde{\boldsymbol{\theta}}_N) = \mathrm{o}_p(1)$.

When two estimators are $\sqrt{N}$-equivalent, they have the same limiting distribution (multivariate normal in this case, with the same asymptotic variance). This conclusion follows immediately from the asymptotic equivalence lemma (Lemma 3.7). Sometimes, to find the limiting distribution of, say, $\sqrt{N}(\hat{\boldsymbol{\theta}}_N - \boldsymbol{\theta})$, it is easiest to first find the limiting distribution of $\sqrt{N}(\tilde{\boldsymbol{\theta}}_N - \boldsymbol{\theta})$, and then to show that $\hat{\boldsymbol{\theta}}_N$ and $\tilde{\boldsymbol{\theta}}_N$ are $\sqrt{N}$-equivalent. A good example of this approach is in Chapter 7, where we find the limiting distribution of the feasible generalized least squares estimator, after we have found the limiting distribution of the GLS estimator.

DEFINITION 3.12: Partition $\hat{\boldsymbol{\theta}}_N$ satisfying statement (3.3) into vectors $\hat{\boldsymbol{\theta}}_{N1}$ and $\hat{\boldsymbol{\theta}}_{N2}$. Then $\hat{\boldsymbol{\theta}}_{N1}$ and $\hat{\boldsymbol{\theta}}_{N2}$ are **asymptotically independent** if

$$\mathbf{V} = \begin{pmatrix} \mathbf{V}_1 & \mathbf{0} \\ \mathbf{0} & \mathbf{V}_2 \end{pmatrix}$$

where $\mathbf{V}_1$ is the asymptotic variance of $\sqrt{N}(\hat{\boldsymbol{\theta}}_{N1} - \boldsymbol{\theta}_1)$ and similarly for $\mathbf{V}_2$. In other words, the asymptotic variance of $\sqrt{N}(\hat{\boldsymbol{\theta}}_N - \boldsymbol{\theta})$ is block diagonal.

Throughout this section we have been careful to index estimators by the sample size, N. This is useful to fix ideas on the nature of asymptotic analysis, but it is cumbersome when applying asymptotics to particular estimation methods. After this chapter, an estimator of $\boldsymbol{\theta}$ will be denoted $\hat{\boldsymbol{\theta}}$, which is understood to depend on the sample size N. When we write, for example, $\hat{\boldsymbol{\theta}} \xrightarrow{p} \boldsymbol{\theta}$, we mean convergence in probability as the sample size N goes to infinity.

3.5.2 Asymptotic Properties of Test Statistics

We begin with some important definitions in the large-sample analysis of test statistics.

DEFINITION 3.13: (1) The **asymptotic size** of a testing procedure is defined as the limiting probability of rejecting H_0 when it is true. Mathematically, we can write this as $\lim_{N\to\infty} P_N(\text{reject } H_0 \mid H_0)$, where the N subscript indexes the sample size.

(2) A test is said to be **consistent** against the alternative H_1 if the null hypothesis is rejected with probability approaching one when H_1 is true: $\lim_{N\to\infty} P_N(\text{reject } H_0 \mid H_1) = 1$.

In practice, the asymptotic size of a test is obtained by finding the limiting distribution of a test statistic—in our case, normal or chi-square, or simple modifications of these that can be used as t distributed or F distributed—and then choosing a critical value based on this distribution. Thus, testing using asymptotic methods is practically the same as testing using the classical linear model.

A test is consistent against alternative H_1 if the probability of rejecting H_1 tends to unity as the sample size grows without bound. Just as consistency of an estimator is a minimal requirement, so is consistency of a test statistic. Consistency rarely allows us to choose among tests: most tests are consistent against alternatives that they are supposed to have power against. For consistent tests with the same asymptotic size, we can use the notion of *local power analysis* to choose among tests. We will cover this briefly in Chapter 12 on nonlinear estimation, where we introduce the notion of *local alternatives*—that is, alternatives to H_0 that converge to H_0 at rate $1/\sqrt{N}$. Generally, test statistics will have desirable asymptotic properties when they are based on estimators with good asymptotic properties (such as efficiency).

We now derive the limiting distribution of a test statistic that is used very often in econometrics.

LEMMA 3.8: Suppose that statement (3.3) holds, where $\mathbf{V}$ is positive definite. Then for any nonstochastic matrix $Q \times P$ matrix $\mathbf{R}$, $Q \leq P$, with $\text{rank}(\mathbf{R}) = Q$,

$$\sqrt{N}\mathbf{R}(\hat{\boldsymbol{\theta}}_N - \boldsymbol{\theta}) \overset{a}{\sim} \text{Normal}(\mathbf{0}, \mathbf{RVR}')$$

and

$$[\sqrt{N}\mathbf{R}(\hat{\boldsymbol{\theta}}_N - \boldsymbol{\theta})]'[\mathbf{RVR}']^{-1}[\sqrt{N}\mathbf{R}(\hat{\boldsymbol{\theta}}_N - \boldsymbol{\theta})] \overset{a}{\sim} \chi_Q^2$$

In addition, if $\text{plim}\ \hat{\mathbf{V}}_N = \mathbf{V}$ then

$$\begin{aligned}&[\sqrt{N}\mathbf{R}(\hat{\boldsymbol{\theta}}_N - \boldsymbol{\theta})]'[\mathbf{R}\hat{\mathbf{V}}_N\mathbf{R}']^{-1}[\sqrt{N}\mathbf{R}(\hat{\boldsymbol{\theta}}_N - \boldsymbol{\theta})]\\ &\quad = (\hat{\boldsymbol{\theta}}_N - \boldsymbol{\theta})'\mathbf{R}'[\mathbf{R}(\hat{\mathbf{V}}_N/N)\mathbf{R}']^{-1}\mathbf{R}(\hat{\boldsymbol{\theta}}_N - \boldsymbol{\theta}) \overset{a}{\sim} \chi_Q^2\end{aligned}$$

For testing the null hypothesis H_0: $\mathbf{R}\boldsymbol{\theta} = \mathbf{r}$, where $\mathbf{r}$ is a $Q \times 1$ nonrandom vector, define the **Wald statistic** for testing H_0 against H_1: $\mathbf{R}\boldsymbol{\theta} \neq \mathbf{r}$ as

$$W_N \equiv (\mathbf{R}\hat{\boldsymbol{\theta}}_N - \mathbf{r})'[\mathbf{R}(\hat{\mathbf{V}}_N/N)\mathbf{R}']^{-1}(\mathbf{R}\hat{\boldsymbol{\theta}}_N - \mathbf{r}) \tag{3.7}$$

Under H_0, $W_N \overset{a}{\sim} \chi^2_Q$. If we abuse the asymptotics and treat $\hat{\boldsymbol{\theta}}_N$ as being distributed as $\mathrm{Normal}(\boldsymbol{\theta}, \hat{\mathbf{V}}_N/N)$, we get equation (3.7) exactly.

LEMMA 3.9: Suppose that statement (3.3) holds, where $\mathbf{V}$ is positive definite. Let $\mathbf{c}$: $\boldsymbol{\Theta} \to \mathbb{R}^Q$ be a continuously differentiable function on the parameter space $\boldsymbol{\Theta} \subset \mathbb{R}^P$, where $Q \leq P$, and assume that $\boldsymbol{\theta}$ is in the interior of the parameter space. Define $\mathbf{C}(\boldsymbol{\theta}) \equiv \nabla_\theta \mathbf{c}(\boldsymbol{\theta})$ as the $Q \times P$ Jacobian of $\mathbf{c}$. Then

$$\sqrt{N}[\mathbf{c}(\hat{\boldsymbol{\theta}}_N) - \mathbf{c}(\boldsymbol{\theta})] \overset{a}{\sim} \mathrm{Normal}[\mathbf{0}, \mathbf{C}(\boldsymbol{\theta})\mathbf{V}\mathbf{C}(\boldsymbol{\theta})'] \tag{3.8}$$

and

$$\{\sqrt{N}[\mathbf{c}(\hat{\boldsymbol{\theta}}_N) - \mathbf{c}(\boldsymbol{\theta})]\}'[\mathbf{C}(\boldsymbol{\theta})\mathbf{V}\mathbf{C}(\boldsymbol{\theta})']^{-1}\{\sqrt{N}[\mathbf{c}(\hat{\boldsymbol{\theta}}_N) - \mathbf{c}(\boldsymbol{\theta})]\} \overset{a}{\sim} \chi^2_Q$$

Define $\hat{\mathbf{C}}_N \equiv \mathbf{C}(\hat{\boldsymbol{\theta}}_N)$. Then $\mathrm{plim}\ \hat{\mathbf{C}}_N = \mathbf{C}(\boldsymbol{\theta})$. If $\mathrm{plim}\ \hat{\mathbf{V}}_N = \mathbf{V}$, then

$$\{\sqrt{N}[\mathbf{c}(\hat{\boldsymbol{\theta}}_N) - \mathbf{c}(\boldsymbol{\theta})]\}'[\hat{\mathbf{C}}_N\hat{\mathbf{V}}_N\hat{\mathbf{C}}_N']^{-1}\{\sqrt{N}[\mathbf{c}(\hat{\boldsymbol{\theta}}_N) - \mathbf{c}(\boldsymbol{\theta})]\} \overset{a}{\sim} \chi^2_Q \tag{3.9}$$

Equation (3.8) is very useful for obtaining asymptotic standard errors for nonlinear functions of $\hat{\boldsymbol{\theta}}_N$. The appropriate estimator of $\mathrm{Avar}[\mathbf{c}(\hat{\boldsymbol{\theta}}_N)]$ is $\hat{\mathbf{C}}_N(\hat{\mathbf{V}}_N/N)\hat{\mathbf{C}}_N' = \hat{\mathbf{C}}_N[\mathrm{Avar}(\hat{\boldsymbol{\theta}}_N)]\hat{\mathbf{C}}_N'$. Thus, once $\mathrm{Avar}(\hat{\boldsymbol{\theta}}_N)$ and the estimated Jacobian of $\mathbf{c}$ are obtained, we can easily obtain

$$\mathrm{Avar}[\mathbf{c}(\hat{\boldsymbol{\theta}}_N)] = \hat{\mathbf{C}}_N[\mathrm{Avar}(\hat{\boldsymbol{\theta}}_N)]\hat{\mathbf{C}}_N' \tag{3.10}$$

The asymptotic standard errors are obtained as the square roots of the diagonal elements of equation (3.10). In the scalar case $\hat{\gamma}_N = c(\hat{\boldsymbol{\theta}}_N)$, the asymptotic standard error of $\hat{\gamma}_N$ is $[\nabla_\theta c(\hat{\boldsymbol{\theta}}_N)[\mathrm{Avar}(\hat{\boldsymbol{\theta}}_N)]\nabla_\theta c(\hat{\boldsymbol{\theta}}_N)']^{1/2}$.

Equation (3.9) is useful for testing nonlinear hypotheses of the form H_0: $\mathbf{c}(\boldsymbol{\theta}) = \mathbf{0}$ against H_1: $\mathbf{c}(\boldsymbol{\theta}) \neq \mathbf{0}$. The Wald statistic is

$$W_N = \sqrt{N}\mathbf{c}(\hat{\boldsymbol{\theta}}_N)'[\hat{\mathbf{C}}_N\hat{\mathbf{V}}_N\hat{\mathbf{C}}_N']^{-1}\sqrt{N}\mathbf{c}(\hat{\boldsymbol{\theta}}_N) = \mathbf{c}(\hat{\boldsymbol{\theta}}_N)'[\hat{\mathbf{C}}_N(\hat{\mathbf{V}}_N/N)\hat{\mathbf{C}}_N']^{-1}\mathbf{c}(\hat{\boldsymbol{\theta}}_N) \tag{3.11}$$

Under H_0, $W_N \overset{a}{\sim} \chi^2_Q$.

The method of establishing equation (3.8), given that statement (3.3) holds, is often called the **delta method**, and it is used very often in econometrics. It gets its name from its use of calculus. The argument is as follows. Because $\boldsymbol{\theta}$ is in the interior of $\boldsymbol{\Theta}$, and because $\mathrm{plim}\ \hat{\boldsymbol{\theta}}_N = \boldsymbol{\theta}$, $\hat{\boldsymbol{\theta}}_N$ is in an open, convex subset of $\boldsymbol{\Theta}$ containing $\boldsymbol{\theta}$ with probability approaching one, therefore w.p.a.1 we can use a mean value expansion $\mathbf{c}(\hat{\boldsymbol{\theta}}_N) = \mathbf{c}(\boldsymbol{\theta}) + \ddot{\mathbf{C}}_N \cdot (\hat{\boldsymbol{\theta}}_N - \boldsymbol{\theta})$, where $\ddot{\mathbf{C}}_N$ denotes the matrix $\mathbf{C}(\boldsymbol{\theta})$ with rows evaluated at mean values between $\hat{\boldsymbol{\theta}}_N$ and $\boldsymbol{\theta}$. Because these mean values are trapped between $\hat{\boldsymbol{\theta}}_N$ and $\boldsymbol{\theta}$, they converge in probability to $\boldsymbol{\theta}$. Therefore, by Slutsky's theorem, $\ddot{\mathbf{C}}_N \xrightarrow{p} \mathbf{C}(\boldsymbol{\theta})$, and we can write

$$\begin{aligned}\sqrt{N}[\mathbf{c}(\hat{\boldsymbol{\theta}}_N) - \mathbf{c}(\boldsymbol{\theta})] &= \ddot{\mathbf{C}}_N \cdot \sqrt{N}(\hat{\boldsymbol{\theta}}_N - \boldsymbol{\theta}) \\ &= \mathbf{C}(\boldsymbol{\theta})\sqrt{N}(\hat{\boldsymbol{\theta}}_N - \boldsymbol{\theta}) + [\ddot{\mathbf{C}}_N - \mathbf{C}(\boldsymbol{\theta})]\sqrt{N}(\hat{\boldsymbol{\theta}}_N - \boldsymbol{\theta}) \\ &= \mathbf{C}(\boldsymbol{\theta})\sqrt{N}(\hat{\boldsymbol{\theta}}_N - \boldsymbol{\theta}) + \mathrm{o}_p(1) \cdot \mathrm{O}_p(1) = \mathbf{C}(\boldsymbol{\theta})\sqrt{N}(\hat{\boldsymbol{\theta}}_N - \boldsymbol{\theta}) + \mathrm{o}_p(1)\end{aligned}$$

We can now apply the asymptotic equivalence lemma and Lemma 3.8 [with $\mathbf{R} \equiv \mathbf{C}(\boldsymbol{\theta})$] to get equation (3.8).

Problems

3.1. Prove Lemma 3.1.

3.2. Using Lemma 3.2, prove Lemma 3.3.

3.3. Explain why, under the assumptions of Lemma 3.4, $\mathbf{g}(\mathbf{x}_N) = \mathrm{O}_p(1)$.

3.4. Prove Corollary 3.2.

3.5. Let $\{y_i: i = 1, 2, \ldots\}$ be an independent, identically distributed sequence with $\mathrm{E}(y_i^2) < \infty$. Let $\mu = \mathrm{E}(y_i)$ and $\sigma^2 = \mathrm{Var}(y_i)$.

a. Let $\bar{y}_N$ denote the sample average based on a sample size of N. Find $\mathrm{Var}[\sqrt{N}(\bar{y}_N - \mu)]$.

b. What is the asymptotic variance of $\sqrt{N}(\bar{y}_N - \mu)$?

c. What is the asymptotic variance of $\bar{y}_N$? Compare this with $\mathrm{Var}(\bar{y}_N)$.

d. What is the asymptotic standard deviation of $\bar{y}_N$?

e. How would you obtain the asymptotic standard error of $\bar{y}_N$?

3.6. Give a careful (albeit short) proof of the following statement: If $\sqrt{N}(\hat{\boldsymbol{\theta}}_N - \boldsymbol{\theta}) = \mathrm{O}_p(1)$, then $\hat{\boldsymbol{\theta}}_N - \boldsymbol{\theta} = \mathrm{o}_p(N^{-c})$ for any $0 \le c < \frac{1}{2}$.

3.7. Let $\hat{\theta}$ be a $\sqrt{N}$-asymptotically normal estimator for the scalar $\theta > 0$. Let $\hat{\gamma} = \log(\hat{\theta})$ be an estimator of $\gamma = \log(\theta)$.

a. Why is $\hat{\gamma}$ a consistent estimator of γ?

b. Find the asymptotic variance of $\sqrt{N}(\hat{\gamma} - \gamma)$ in terms of the asymptotic variance of $\sqrt{N}(\hat{\theta} - \theta)$.

c. Suppose that, for a sample of data, $\hat{\theta} = 4$ and $\text{se}(\hat{\theta}) = 2$. What is $\hat{\gamma}$ and its (asymptotic) standard error?

d. Consider the null hypothesis H_0: $\theta = 1$. What is the asymptotic t statistic for testing H_0, given the numbers from part c?

e. Now state H_0 from part d equivalently in terms of γ, and use $\hat{\gamma}$ and $\text{se}(\hat{\gamma})$ to test H_0. What do you conclude?

3.8. Let $\hat{\boldsymbol{\theta}} = (\hat{\theta}_1, \hat{\theta}_2)'$ be a $\sqrt{N}$-asymptotically normal estimator for $\boldsymbol{\theta} = (\theta_1, \theta_2)'$, with $\theta_2 \neq 0$. Let $\hat{\gamma} = \hat{\theta}_1/\hat{\theta}_2$ be an estimator of $\gamma = \theta_1/\theta_2$.

a. Show that plim $\hat{\gamma} = \gamma$.

b. Find $\text{Avar}(\hat{\gamma})$ in terms of $\boldsymbol{\theta}$ and $\text{Avar}(\hat{\boldsymbol{\theta}})$ using the delta method.

c. If, for a sample of data, $\hat{\boldsymbol{\theta}} = (-1.5, .5)'$ and $\text{Avar}(\hat{\boldsymbol{\theta}})$ is estimated as $\begin{pmatrix} 1 & -.4 \\ -.4 & 2 \end{pmatrix}$, find the asymptotic standard error of $\hat{\gamma}$.

3.9. Let $\hat{\boldsymbol{\theta}}$ and $\tilde{\boldsymbol{\theta}}$ be two consistent, $\sqrt{N}$-asymptotically normal estimators of the $P \times 1$ parameter vector $\boldsymbol{\theta}$, with Avar $\sqrt{N}(\hat{\boldsymbol{\theta}} - \boldsymbol{\theta}) = \mathbf{V}_1$ and Avar $\sqrt{N}(\tilde{\boldsymbol{\theta}} - \boldsymbol{\theta}) = \mathbf{V}_2$. Define a $Q \times 1$ parameter vector by $\gamma = \mathbf{g}(\boldsymbol{\theta})$, where $\mathbf{g}(\cdot)$ is a continuously differentiable function. Show that, if $\hat{\boldsymbol{\theta}}$ is asymptotically more efficient than $\tilde{\boldsymbol{\theta}}$, then $\hat{\gamma} \equiv \mathbf{g}(\hat{\boldsymbol{\theta}})$ is asymptotically efficient relative to $\tilde{\gamma} \equiv \mathbf{g}(\tilde{\boldsymbol{\theta}})$.

II LINEAR MODELS

In this part we begin our econometric analysis of linear models for cross section and panel data. In Chapter 4 we review the single-equation linear model and discuss ordinary least squares estimation. Although this material is, in principle, review, the approach is likely to be different from an introductory linear models course. In addition, we cover several topics that are not traditionally covered in texts but that have proven useful in empirical work. Chapter 5 discusses instrumental variables estimation of the linear model, and Chapter 6 covers some remaining topics to round out our treatment of the single-equation model.

Chapter 7 begins our analysis of systems of equations. The general setup is that the number of population equations is small relative to the (cross section) sample size. This allows us to cover seemingly unrelated regression models for cross section data as well as begin our analysis of panel data. Chapter 8 builds on the framework from Chapter 7 but considers the case where some explanatory variables may be uncorrelated with the error terms. Generalized method of moments estimation is the unifying theme. Chapter 9 applies the methods of Chapter 8 to the estimation of simultaneous equations models, with an emphasis on the conceptual issues that arise in applying such models.

Chapter 10 explicitly introduces unobserved-effects linear panel data models. Under the assumption that the explanatory variables are strictly exogenous conditional on the unobserved effect, we study several estimation methods, including fixed effects, first differencing, and random effects. The last method assumes, at a minimum, that the unobserved effect is uncorrelated with the explanatory variables in all time periods. Chapter 11 considers extensions of the basic panel data model, including failure of the strict exogeneity assumption.

4 The Single-Equation Linear Model and OLS Estimation

4.1 Overview of the Single-Equation Linear Model

This and the next couple of chapters cover what is still the workhorse in empirical economics: the single-equation linear model. Though you are assumed to be comfortable with ordinary least squares (OLS) estimation, we begin with OLS for a couple of reasons. First, it provides a bridge between more traditional approaches to econometrics—which treats explanatory variables as fixed—and the current approach, which is based on random sampling with stochastic explanatory variables. Second, we cover some topics that receive at best cursory treatment in first-semester texts. These topics, such as proxy variable solutions to the omitted variable problem, arise often in applied work.

The population model we study is linear in its parameters,

$$y = \beta_0 + \beta_1 x_1 + \beta_2 x_2 + \cdots + \beta_K x_K + u \tag{4.1}$$

where $y, x_1, x_2, x_3, \ldots, x_K$ are observable random scalars (that is, we can observe them in a random sample of the population), u is the unobservable random disturbance or error, and $\beta_0, \beta_1, \beta_2, \ldots, \beta_K$ are the parameters (constants) we would like to estimate.

The error form of the model in equation (4.1) is useful for presenting a unified treatment of the statistical properties of various econometric procedures. Nevertheless, the steps one uses for getting to equation (4.1) are just as important. Goldberger (1972) defines a **structural model** as one representing a causal relationship, as opposed to a relationship that simply captures statistical associations. A structural equation can be obtained from an economic model, or it can be obtained through informal reasoning. Sometimes the structural model is directly estimable. Other times we must combine auxiliary assumptions about other variables with algebraic manipulations to arrive at an **estimable model**. In addition, we will often have reasons to estimate nonstructural equations, sometimes as a precursor to estimating a structural equation.

The error term u can consist of a variety of things, including omitted variables and measurement error (we will see some examples shortly). The parameters β_j hopefully correspond to the parameters of interest, that is, the parameters in an underlying structural model. Whether this is the case depends on the application and the assumptions made.

As we will see in Section 4.2, the key condition needed for OLS to consistently estimate the β_j (assuming we have available a random sample from the population) is that the error (in the population) has mean zero and is uncorrelated with each of the regressors:

$$\mathrm{E}(u) = 0, \qquad \mathrm{Cov}(x_j, u) = 0, \qquad j = 1, 2, \ldots, K \tag{4.2}$$

The zero-mean assumption is for free when an intercept is included, and we will restrict attention to that case in what follows. It is the zero covariance of u with each x_j that is important. From Chapter 2 we know that equation (4.1) and assumption (4.2) are equivalent to defining the linear projection of y onto $(1, x_1, x_2, \ldots, x_K)$ as $\beta_0 + \beta_1 x_1 + \beta_2 x_2 + \cdots + \beta_K x_K$.

Sufficient for assumption (4.2) is the zero conditional mean assumption

$$\mathrm{E}(u \mid x_1, x_2, \ldots, x_K) = \mathrm{E}(u \mid \mathbf{x}) = 0 \tag{4.3}$$

Under equation (4.1) and assumption (4.3) we have the population regression function

$$\mathrm{E}(y \mid x_1, x_2, \ldots, x_K) = \beta_0 + \beta_1 x_1 + \beta_2 x_2 + \cdots + \beta_K x_K \tag{4.4}$$

As we saw in Chapter 2, equation (4.4) includes the case where the x_j are nonlinear functions of underlying explanatory variables, such as

$$\begin{aligned} \mathrm{E}(savings \mid income, size, age, college) = \beta_0 + \beta_1 \log(income) + \beta_2 size + \beta_3 age \\ + \beta_4 college + \beta_5 college{\cdot}age \end{aligned}$$

We will study the asymptotic properties of OLS primarily under assumption (4.2), since it is weaker than assumption (4.3). As we discussed in Chapter 2, assumption (4.3) is natural when a structural model is directly estimable because it ensures that no additional functions of the explanatory variables help to explain y.

An explanatory variable x_j is said to be **endogenous** in equation (4.1) if it is correlated with u. You should not rely too much on the meaning of "endogenous" from other branches of economics. In traditional usage, a variable is endogenous if it is determined within the context of a model. The usage in econometrics, while related to traditional definitions, is used broadly to describe any situation where an explanatory variable is correlated with the disturbance. If x_j is uncorrelated with u, then x_j is said to be **exogenous** in equation (4.1). If assumption (4.3) holds, then each explanatory variable is necessarily exogenous.

In applied econometrics, endogeneity usually arises in one of three ways:

Omitted Variables Omitted variables appear when we would like to control for one or more additional variables but, usually because of data unavailability, we cannot include them in a regression model. Specifically, suppose that $\mathrm{E}(y \mid \mathbf{x}, q)$ is the conditional expectation of interest, which can be written as a function linear in parameters and additive in q. If q is unobserved, we can always estimate $\mathrm{E}(y \mid \mathbf{x})$, but this need have no particular relationship to $\mathrm{E}(y \mid \mathbf{x}, q)$ when q and $\mathbf{x}$ are allowed to be correlated. One way to represent this situation is to write equation (4.1) where q is part of the error term u. If q and x_j are correlated, then x_j is endogenous. The correlation of explanatory variables with unobservables is often due to *self-selection*: if agents choose the value of x_j, this might depend on factors (q) that are unobservable to the analyst. A good example is omitted ability in a wage equation, where an individual's years of schooling are likely to be correlated with unobserved ability. We discuss the omitted variables problem in detail in Section 4.3.

Measurement Error In this case we would like to measure the (partial) effect of a variable, say x_K^*, but we can observe only an imperfect measure of it, say x_K. When we plug x_K in for x_K^*—thereby arriving at the estimable equation (4.1)—we necessarily put a measurement error into u. Depending on assumptions about how x_K^* and x_K are related, u and x_K may or may not be correlated. For example, x_K^* might denote a marginal tax rate, but we can only obtain data on the average tax rate. We will study the measurement error problem in Section 4.4.

Simultaneity Simultaneity arises when at least one of the explanatory variables is determined simultaneously along with y. If, say, x_K is determined partly as a function of y, then x_K and u are generally correlated. For example, if y is city murder rate and x_K is size of the police force, size of the police force is partly determined by the murder rate. Conceptually, this is a more difficult situation to analyze, because we must be able to think of a situation where we *could* vary x_K exogenously, even though in the data that we collect y and x_K are generated simultaneously. Chapter 9 treats simultaneous equations models in detail.

The distinctions among the three possible forms of endogeneity are not always sharp. In fact, an equation can have more than one source of endogeneity. For example, in looking at the effect of alcohol consumption on worker productivity (as typically measured by wages), we would worry that alcohol usage is correlated with unobserved factors, possibly related to family background, that also affect wage; this is an omitted variables problem. In addition, alcohol demand would generally depend on income, which is largely determined by wage; this is a simultaneity problem. And measurement error in alcohol usage is always a possibility. For an illuminating discussion of the three kinds of endogeneity as they arise in a particular field, see Deaton's (1995) survey chapter on econometric issues in development economics.

4.2 Asymptotic Properties of OLS

We now briefly review the asymptotic properties of OLS for random samples from a population, focusing on inference. It is convenient to write the population equation of interest in vector form as

$$y = \mathbf{x}\boldsymbol{\beta} + u \tag{4.5}$$

where $\mathbf{x}$ is a $1 \times K$ vector of regressors and $\boldsymbol{\beta} \equiv (\beta_1, \beta_2, \ldots, \beta_K)'$ is a $K \times 1$ vector. Since most equations contain an intercept, we will just assume that $x_1 \equiv 1$, as this assumption makes interpreting the conditions easier.

We assume that we can obtain a random sample of size N from the population in order to estimate $\boldsymbol{\beta}$; thus, $\{(\mathbf{x}_i, y_i): i = 1, 2, \ldots, N\}$ are treated as independent, identically distributed random variables, where $\mathbf{x}_i$ is $1 \times K$ and y_i is a scalar. For each observation i we have

$$y_i = \mathbf{x}_i\boldsymbol{\beta} + u_i \tag{4.6}$$

which is convenient for deriving statistical properties of estimators. As for stating and interpreting assumptions, it is easiest to focus on the population model (4.5).

4.2.1 Consistency

As discussed in Section 4.1, the key assumption for OLS to consistently estimate $\boldsymbol{\beta}$ is the **population orthogonality condition**:

ASSUMPTION OLS.1: $\mathrm{E}(\mathbf{x}'u) = \mathbf{0}$.

Because $\mathbf{x}$ contains a constant, Assumption OLS.1 is equivalent to saying that u has mean zero and is uncorrelated with each regressor, which is how we will refer to Assumption OLS.1. Sufficient for Assumption OLS.1 is the zero conditional mean assumption (4.3).

The other assumption needed for consistency of OLS is that the expected outer product matrix of $\mathbf{x}$ has full rank, so that there are no exact linear relationships among the regressors in the population. This is stated succinctly as follows:

ASSUMPTION OLS.2: rank $\mathrm{E}(\mathbf{x}'\mathbf{x}) = K$.

As with Assumption OLS.1, Assumption OLS.2 is an assumption about the population. Since $\mathrm{E}(\mathbf{x}'\mathbf{x})$ is a symmetric $K \times K$ matrix, Assumption OLS.2 is equivalent to assuming that $\mathrm{E}(\mathbf{x}'\mathbf{x})$ is positive definite. Since $x_1 = 1$, Assumption OLS.2 is also equivalent to saying that the (population) variance matrix of the $K - 1$ nonconstant elements in $\mathbf{x}$ is nonsingular. This is a standard assumption, which fails if and only if at least one of the regressors can be written as a linear function of the other regressors (in the population). Usually Assumption OLS.2 holds, but it can fail if the population model is improperly specified [for example, if we include too many dummy variables in $\mathbf{x}$ or mistakenly use something like $\log(age)$ and $\log(age^2)$ in the same equation].

Under Assumptions OLS.1 and OLS.2, the parameter vector $\boldsymbol{\beta}$ is **identified**. In the context of models that are linear in the parameters under random sampling, identification of $\boldsymbol{\beta}$ simply means that $\boldsymbol{\beta}$ can be written in terms of population moments in observable variables. (Later, when we consider nonlinear models, the notion of identification will have to be more general. Also, special issues arise if we cannot obtain a random sample from the population, something we treat in Chapter 17.) To see that $\boldsymbol{\beta}$ is identified under Assumptions OLS.1 and OLS.2, premultiply equation (4.5) by $\mathbf{x}'$, take expectations, and solve to get

$$\boldsymbol{\beta} = [\mathrm{E}(\mathbf{x}'\mathbf{x})]^{-1}\mathrm{E}(\mathbf{x}'y)$$

Because $(\mathbf{x}, y)$ is observed, $\boldsymbol{\beta}$ is identified. The **analogy principle** for choosing an estimator says to turn the population problem into its sample counterpart (see Goldberger, 1968; Manski, 1988). In the current application this step leads to the **method of moments**: replace the population moments $\mathrm{E}(\mathbf{x}'\mathbf{x})$ and $\mathrm{E}(\mathbf{x}'y)$ with the corresponding sample averages. Doing so leads to the OLS estimator:

$$\hat{\boldsymbol{\beta}} = \left(N^{-1}\sum_{i=1}^{N}\mathbf{x}_i'\mathbf{x}_i\right)^{-1}\left(N^{-1}\sum_{i=1}^{N}\mathbf{x}_i'y_i\right) = \boldsymbol{\beta} + \left(N^{-1}\sum_{i=1}^{N}\mathbf{x}_i'\mathbf{x}_i\right)^{-1}\left(N^{-1}\sum_{i=1}^{N}\mathbf{x}_i'u_i\right)$$

which can be written in full matrix form as $(\mathbf{X}'\mathbf{X})^{-1}\mathbf{X}'\mathbf{Y}$, where $\mathbf{X}$ is the $N \times K$ data matrix of regressors with ith row $\mathbf{x}_i$ and $\mathbf{Y}$ is the $N \times 1$ data vector with ith element y_i. Under Assumption OLS.2, $\mathbf{X}'\mathbf{X}$ is nonsingular with probability approaching one and $\text{plim}[(N^{-1}\sum_{i=1}^{N}\mathbf{x}_i'\mathbf{x}_i)^{-1}] = \mathbf{A}^{-1}$, where $\mathbf{A} \equiv \mathrm{E}(\mathbf{x}'\mathbf{x})$ (see Corollary 3.1). Further, under Assumption OLS.1, $\text{plim}(N^{-1}\sum_{i=1}^{N}\mathbf{x}_i'u_i) = \mathrm{E}(\mathbf{x}'u) = \mathbf{0}$. Therefore, by Slutsky's theorem (Lemma 3.4), $\text{plim}\,\hat{\boldsymbol{\beta}} = \boldsymbol{\beta} + \mathbf{A}^{-1}\cdot\mathbf{0} = \boldsymbol{\beta}$. We summarize with a theorem:

THEOREM 4.1 (Consistency of OLS): Under Assumptions OLS.1 and OLS.2, the OLS estimator $\hat{\boldsymbol{\beta}}$ obtained from a random sample following the population model (4.5) is consistent for $\boldsymbol{\beta}$.

The simplicity of the proof of Theorem 4.1 should not undermine its usefulness. Whenever an equation can be put into the form (4.5) and Assumptions OLS.1 and OLS.2 hold, OLS using a random sample consistently estimates $\boldsymbol{\beta}$. It does not matter where this equation comes from, or what the β_j actually represent. As we will see in Sections 4.3 and 4.4, often an estimable equation is obtained only after manipulating an underlying structural equation. An important point to remember is that, once the linear (in parameters) equation has been specified with an additive error and Assumptions OLS.1 and OLS.2 are verified, there is no need to reprove Theorem 4.1.

Under the assumptions of Theorem 4.1, $\mathbf{x}\boldsymbol{\beta}$ is the linear projection of y on $\mathbf{x}$. Thus, Theorem 4.1 shows that OLS consistently estimates the parameters in a linear projection, subject to the rank condition in Assumption OLS.2. This is very general, as it places no restrictions on the nature of y—for example, y could be a binary variable or some other variable with discrete characteristics. Since a conditional expectation that is linear in parameters is also the linear projection, Theorem 4.1 also shows that OLS consistently estimates conditional expectations that are linear in parameters. We will use this fact often in later sections.

There are a few final points worth emphasizing. First, if either Assumption OLS.1 or OLS.2 fails, then $\boldsymbol{\beta}$ is not identified (unless we make other assumptions, as in Chapter 5). Usually it is correlation between u and one or more elements of $\mathbf{x}$ that causes lack of identification. Second, the OLS estimator is *not* necessarily unbiased even under Assumptions OLS.1 and OLS.2. However, if we impose the zero conditional mean assumption (4.3), then it can be shown that $\mathrm{E}(\hat{\boldsymbol{\beta}} \mid \mathbf{X}) = \boldsymbol{\beta}$ if $\mathbf{X}'\mathbf{X}$ is nonsingular; see Problem 4.2. By iterated expectations, $\hat{\boldsymbol{\beta}}$ is then also unconditionally unbiased, provided the expected value $\mathrm{E}(\hat{\boldsymbol{\beta}})$ exists.

Finally, we have not made the much more restrictive assumption that u and $\mathbf{x}$ are *independent*. If $\mathrm{E}(u) = 0$ and u is independent of $\mathbf{x}$, then assumption (4.3) holds, but not vice versa. For example, $\mathrm{Var}(u \mid \mathbf{x})$ is entirely unrestricted under assumption (4.3), but $\mathrm{Var}(u \mid \mathbf{x})$ is necessarily constant if u and $\mathbf{x}$ are independent.

4.2.2 Asymptotic Inference Using OLS

The asymptotic distribution of the OLS estimator is derived by writing

$$\sqrt{N}(\hat{\boldsymbol{\beta}} - \boldsymbol{\beta}) = \left(N^{-1}\sum_{i=1}^{N}\mathbf{x}_i'\mathbf{x}_i\right)^{-1}\left(N^{-1/2}\sum_{i=1}^{N}\mathbf{x}_i'u_i\right)$$

As we saw in Theorem 4.1, $(N^{-1}\sum_{i=1}^{N}\mathbf{x}_i'\mathbf{x}_i)^{-1} - \mathbf{A}^{-1} = \mathrm{o}_p(1)$. Also, $\{(\mathbf{x}_i'u_i): i = 1, 2, \ldots\}$ is an i.i.d. sequence with zero mean, and we assume that each element has finite variance. Then the central limit theorem (Theorem 3.2) implies that $N^{-1/2}\sum_{i=1}^{N}\mathbf{x}_i'u_i \xrightarrow{d} \mathrm{Normal}(\mathbf{0}, \mathbf{B})$, where $\mathbf{B}$ is the $K \times K$ matrix

$$\mathbf{B} \equiv \mathrm{E}(u^2\mathbf{x}'\mathbf{x}) \tag{4.7}$$

This implies $N^{-1/2}\sum_{i=1}^{N}\mathbf{x}_i'u_i = \mathrm{O}_p(1)$, and so we can write

$$\sqrt{N}(\hat{\boldsymbol{\beta}} - \boldsymbol{\beta}) = \mathbf{A}^{-1}\left(N^{-1/2}\sum_{i=1}^{N}\mathbf{x}_i'u_i\right) + \mathrm{o}_p(1) \tag{4.8}$$

since $\mathrm{o}_p(1)\cdot\mathrm{O}_p(1) = \mathrm{o}_p(1)$. We can use equation (4.8) to immediately obtain the asymptotic distribution of $\sqrt{N}(\hat{\boldsymbol{\beta}} - \boldsymbol{\beta})$. A **homoskedasticity** assumption simplifies the form of OLS asymptotic variance:

ASSUMPTION OLS.3: $\mathrm{E}(u^2\mathbf{x}'\mathbf{x}) = \sigma^2\mathrm{E}(\mathbf{x}'\mathbf{x})$, where $\sigma^2 \equiv \mathrm{E}(u^2)$.

Because $\mathrm{E}(u) = 0$, σ^2 is also equal to $\mathrm{Var}(u)$. Assumption OLS.3 is the weakest form of the homoskedasticity assumption. If we write out the $K \times K$ matrices in Assumption OLS.3 element by element, we see that Assumption OLS.3 is equivalent to assuming that the squared error, u^2, is uncorrelated with each x_j, x_j^2, and all cross products of the form $x_j x_k$. By the law of iterated expectations, sufficient for Assumption OLS.3 is $\mathrm{E}(u^2 \mid \mathbf{x}) = \sigma^2$, which is the same as $\mathrm{Var}(u \mid \mathbf{x}) = \sigma^2$ when $\mathrm{E}(u \mid \mathbf{x}) = 0$. The constant conditional variance assumption for u given $\mathbf{x}$ is the easiest to interpret, but it is stronger than needed.

THEOREM 4.2 (Asymptotic Normality of OLS): Under Assumptions OLS.1–OLS.3,

$$\sqrt{N}(\hat{\boldsymbol{\beta}} - \boldsymbol{\beta}) \overset{a}{\sim} \mathrm{Normal}(0, \sigma^2 \mathbf{A}^{-1}) \tag{4.9}$$

Proof: From equation (4.8) and definition of $\mathbf{B}$, it follows from Lemma 3.7 and Corollary 3.2 that

$$\sqrt{N}(\hat{\boldsymbol{\beta}} - \boldsymbol{\beta}) \overset{a}{\sim} \mathrm{Normal}(0, \mathbf{A}^{-1}\mathbf{B}\mathbf{A}^{-1})$$

Under Assumption OLS.3, $\mathbf{B} = \sigma^2 \mathbf{A}$, which proves the result.

Practically speaking, equation (4.9) allows us to treat $\hat{\boldsymbol{\beta}}$ as approximately normal with mean $\boldsymbol{\beta}$ and variance $\sigma^2[\mathrm{E}(\mathbf{x}'\mathbf{x})]^{-1}/N$. The usual estimator of σ^2, $\hat{\sigma}^2 \equiv \mathrm{SSR}/(N - K)$, where $\mathrm{SSR} = \sum_{i=1}^{N} \hat{u}_i^2$ is the OLS sum of squared residuals, is easily shown to be consistent. (Using N or $N - K$ in the denominator does not affect consistency.) When we also replace $\mathrm{E}(\mathbf{x}'\mathbf{x})$ with the sample average $N^{-1}\sum_{i=1}^{N} \mathbf{x}_i'\mathbf{x}_i = (\mathbf{X}'\mathbf{X}/N)$, we get

$$\widehat{\mathrm{Avar}}(\hat{\boldsymbol{\beta}}) = \hat{\sigma}^2 (\mathbf{X}'\mathbf{X})^{-1} \tag{4.10}$$

The right-hand side of equation (4.10) should be familiar: it is the usual OLS variance matrix estimator under the classical linear model assumptions. The bottom line of Theorem 4.2 is that, under Assumptions OLS.1–OLS.3, the usual OLS standard errors, t statistics, and F statistics are asymptotically valid. Showing that the F statistic is approximately valid is done by deriving the Wald test for linear restrictions of the form $\mathbf{R}\boldsymbol{\beta} = \mathbf{r}$ (see Chapter 3). Then the F statistic is simply a degrees-of-freedom-adjusted Wald statistic, which is where the F distribution (as opposed to the chi-square distribution) arises.

4.2.3 Heteroskedasticity-Robust Inference

If Assumption OLS.1 fails, we are in potentially serious trouble, as OLS is not even consistent. In the next chapter we discuss the important method of instrumental variables that can be used to obtain consistent estimators of $\boldsymbol{\beta}$ when Assumption

OLS.1 fails. Assumption OLS.2 is also needed for consistency, but there is rarely any reason to examine its failure.

Failure of Assumption OLS.3 has less serious consequences than failure of Assumption OLS.1. As we have already seen, Assumption OLS.3 has nothing to do with consistency of $\hat{\boldsymbol{\beta}}$. Further, the proof of asymptotic normality based on equation (4.8) is still valid without Assumption OLS.3, but the final asymptotic variance is different. We have assumed OLS.3 for deriving the limiting distribution because it implies the asymptotic validity of the usual OLS standard errors and test statistics. All regression packages assume OLS.3 as the default in reporting statistics.

Often there are reasons to believe that Assumption OLS.3 might fail, in which case equation (4.10) is no longer a valid estimate of even the asymptotic variance matrix. If we make the zero conditional mean assumption (4.3), one solution to violation of Assumption OLS.3 is to specify a model for $\text{Var}(y \mid \mathbf{x})$, estimate this model, and apply **weighted least squares** (WLS): for observation i, y_i and every element of $\mathbf{x}_i$ (including unity) are divided by an estimate of the conditional standard deviation $[\text{Var}(y_i \mid \mathbf{x}_i)]^{1/2}$, and OLS is applied to the weighted data (see Wooldridge, 2000a, Chapter 8, for details). This procedure leads to a different estimator of $\boldsymbol{\beta}$. We discuss WLS in the more general context of nonlinear regression in Chapter 12. Lately, it has become more popular to estimate $\boldsymbol{\beta}$ by OLS even when heteroskedasticity is suspected but to adjust the standard errors and test statistics so that they are valid in the presence of arbitrary heteroskedasticity. Since these standard errors are valid whether or not Assumption OLS.3 holds, this method is much easier than a weighted least squares procedure. What we sacrifice is potential efficiency gains from weighted least squares (WLS) (see Chapter 14). But, efficiency gains from WLS are guaranteed only if the model for $\text{Var}(y \mid \mathbf{x})$ is correct. Further, WLS is generally inconsistent if $\text{E}(u \mid \mathbf{x}) \neq 0$ but Assumption OLS.1 holds, so WLS is inappropriate for estimating linear projections. Especially with large sample sizes, the presence of heteroskedasticity need not affect one's ability to perform accurate inference using OLS. But we need to compute standard errors and test statistics appropriately.

The adjustment needed to the asymptotic variance follows from the proof of Theorem 4.2: without OLS.3, the asymptotic variance of $\hat{\boldsymbol{\beta}}$ is $\text{Avar}(\hat{\boldsymbol{\beta}}) = \mathbf{A}^{-1}\mathbf{B}\mathbf{A}^{-1}/N$, where the $K \times K$ matrices $\mathbf{A}$ and $\mathbf{B}$ were defined earlier. We already know how to consistently estimate $\mathbf{A}$. Estimation of $\mathbf{B}$ is also straightforward. First, by the law of large numbers, $N^{-1}\sum_{i=1}^{N} u_i^2 \mathbf{x}_i'\mathbf{x}_i \xrightarrow{p} \text{E}(u^2\mathbf{x}'\mathbf{x}) = \mathbf{B}$. Now, since the u_i are not observed, we replace u_i with the OLS residual $\hat{u}_i = y_i - \mathbf{x}_i\hat{\boldsymbol{\beta}}$. This leads to the consistent estimator $\hat{\mathbf{B}} \equiv N^{-1}\sum_{i=1}^{N} \hat{u}_i^2 \mathbf{x}_i'\mathbf{x}_i$. See White (1984) and Problem 4.4.

The heteroskedasticity-robust variance matrix estimator of $\hat{\boldsymbol{\beta}}$ is $\hat{\mathbf{A}}^{-1}\hat{\mathbf{B}}\hat{\mathbf{A}}^{-1}/N$ or, after cancellations,

$$\text{Av}\hat{\text{a}}\text{r}(\hat{\boldsymbol{\beta}}) = (\mathbf{X}'\mathbf{X})^{-1}\left(\sum_{i=1}^{N} \hat{u}_i^2 \mathbf{x}_i'\mathbf{x}_i\right)(\mathbf{X}'\mathbf{X})^{-1} \tag{4.11}$$

This matrix was introduced in econometrics by White (1980b), although some attribute it to either Eicker (1967) or Huber (1967), statisticians who discovered robust variance matrices. The square roots of the diagonal elements of equation (4.11) are often called the **White standard errors** or **Huber standard errors**, or some hyphenated combination of the names Eicker, Huber, and White. It is probably best to just call them **heteroskedasticity-robust standard errors**, since this term describes their purpose. Remember, these standard errors are asymptotically valid in the presence of any kind of heteroskedasticity, including homoskedasticity.

Robust standard errors are often reported in applied cross-sectional work, especially when the sample size is large. Sometimes they are reported along with the usual OLS standard errors; sometimes they are presented in place of them. Several regression packages now report these standard errors as an option, so it is easy to obtain heteroskedasticity-robust standard errors.

Sometimes, as a degrees-of-freedom correction, the matrix in equation (4.11) is multiplied by $N/(N-K)$. This procedure guarantees that, if the $\hat{u}_i^2$ were constant across i (an unlikely event in practice, but the strongest evidence of homoskedasticity possible), then the usual OLS standard errors would be obtained. There is some evidence that the degrees-of-freedom adjustment improves finite sample performance. There are other ways to adjust equation (4.11) to improve its small-sample properties—see, for example, MacKinnon and White (1985)—but if N is large relative to K, these adjustments typically make little difference.

Once standard errors are obtained, t statistics are computed in the usual way. These are robust to heteroskedasticity of unknown form, and can be used to test single restrictions. The t statistics computed from heteroskedasticity robust standard errors are **heteroskedasticity-robust *t* statistics**. Confidence intervals are also obtained in the usual way.

When Assumption OLS.3 fails, the usual F statistic is not valid for testing multiple linear restrictions, even asymptotically. Some packages allow robust testing with a simple command, while others do not. If the hypotheses are written as

$$\text{H}_0\colon \mathbf{R}\boldsymbol{\beta} = \mathbf{r} \tag{4.12}$$

where $\mathbf{R}$ is $Q \times K$ and has rank $Q \leq K$, and $\mathbf{r}$ is $Q \times 1$, then the heteroskedasticity-robust Wald statistic for testing equation (4.12) is

$$W = (\mathbf{R}\hat{\boldsymbol{\beta}} - \mathbf{r})'(\mathbf{R}\hat{\mathbf{V}}\mathbf{R}')^{-1}(\mathbf{R}\hat{\boldsymbol{\beta}} - \mathbf{r}) \tag{4.13}$$

where $\hat{\mathbf{V}}$ is given in equation (4.11). Under H_0, $W \overset{a}{\sim} \chi^2_Q$. The Wald statistic can be turned into an approximate $\mathscr{F}_{Q,N-K}$ random variable by dividing it by Q (and usually making the degrees-of-freedom adjustment to $\hat{\mathbf{V}}$). But there is nothing wrong with using equation (4.13) directly.

4.2.4 Lagrange Multiplier (Score) Tests

In the partitioned model

$$y = \mathbf{x}_1\boldsymbol{\beta}_1 + \mathbf{x}_2\boldsymbol{\beta}_2 + u \tag{4.14}$$

under Assumptions OLS.1–OLS.3, where $\mathbf{x}_1$ is $1 \times K_1$ and $\mathbf{x}_2$ is $1 \times K_2$, we know that the hypothesis H_0: $\boldsymbol{\beta}_2 = \mathbf{0}$ is easily tested (asymptotically) using a standard F test. There is another approach to testing such hypotheses that is sometimes useful, especially for computing heteroskedasticity-robust tests and for nonlinear models.

Let $\tilde{\boldsymbol{\beta}}_1$ be the estimator of $\boldsymbol{\beta}_1$ under the null hypothesis H_0: $\boldsymbol{\beta}_2 = \mathbf{0}$; this is called the estimator from the **restricted model**. Define the restricted OLS residuals as $\tilde{u}_i = y_i - \mathbf{x}_{i1}\tilde{\boldsymbol{\beta}}_1$, $i = 1, 2, \ldots, N$. Under H_0, $\mathbf{x}_{i2}$ should be, up to sample variation, uncorrelated with $\tilde{u}_i$ in the sample. The Lagrange multiplier or score principle is based on this observation. It turns out that a valid test statistic is obtained as follows: Run the OLS regression

$$\tilde{u} \text{ on } \mathbf{x}_1, \mathbf{x}_2 \tag{4.15}$$

(where the observation index i has been suppressed). Assuming that $\mathbf{x}_1$ contains a constant (that is, the null model contains a constant), let R_u^2 denote the usual R-squared from the regression (4.15). Then the **Lagrange multiplier (LM)** or **score statistic** is $LM \equiv NR_u^2$. These names come from different features of the constrained optimization problem; see Rao (1948), Aitchison and Silvey (1958), and Chapter 12. Because of its form, LM is also referred to as an **N-R-squared test**. Under H_0, $LM \overset{a}{\sim} \chi^2_{K_2}$, where K_2 is the number of restrictions being tested. If NR_u^2 is sufficiently large, then $\tilde{u}$ is significantly correlated with $\mathbf{x}_2$, and the null hypothesis will be rejected.

It is important to include $\mathbf{x}_1$ along with $\mathbf{x}_2$ in regression (4.15). In other words, the OLS residuals from the null model should be regressed on *all* explanatory variables, even though $\tilde{u}$ is orthogonal to $\mathbf{x}_1$ in the sample. If $\mathbf{x}_1$ is excluded, then the resulting statistic generally does *not* have a chi-square distribution when $\mathbf{x}_2$ and $\mathbf{x}_1$ are correlated. If $\mathrm{E}(\mathbf{x}_1'\mathbf{x}_2) = \mathbf{0}$, then we can exclude $\mathbf{x}_1$ from regression (4.15), but this orthogonality rarely holds in applications. If $\mathbf{x}_1$ does not include a constant, R_u^2 should be the **uncentered R-squared**: the total sum of squares in the denominator is obtained without demeaning the dependent variable, $\tilde{u}$. When $\mathbf{x}_1$ includes a constant, the usual centered R-squared and uncentered R-squared are identical because $\sum_{i=1}^N \tilde{u}_i = 0$.

Example 4.1 (Wage Equation for Married, Working Women): Consider a wage equation for married, working women:

$$\log(wage) = \beta_0 + \beta_1 exper + \beta_2 exper^2 + \beta_3 educ + \beta_4 age + \beta_5 kidslt6 + \beta_6 kidsge6 + u \tag{4.16}$$

where the last three variables are the woman's age, number of children less than six, and number of children at least six years of age, respectively. We can test whether, after the productivity variables experience and education are controlled for, women are paid differently depending on their age and number of children. The F statistic for the hypothesis H_0: $\beta_4 = 0, \beta_5 = 0, \beta_6 = 0$ is $F = [(R_{ur}^2 - R_r^2)/(1 - R_{ur}^2)] \cdot [(N - 7)/3]$, where R_{ur}^2 and R_r^2 are the unrestricted and restricted R-squareds; under H_0 (and homoskedasticity), $F \sim \mathcal{F}_{3,N-7}$. To obtain the LM statistic, we estimate the equation without *age*, *kidslt6*, and *kidsge6*; let $\tilde{u}$ denote the OLS residuals. Then, the LM statistic is NR_u^2 from the regression $\tilde{u}$ on 1, *exper*, *exper*^{2}, *educ*, *age*, *kidslt6*, and *kidsge6*, where the 1 denotes that we include an intercept. Under H_0 and homoskedasticity, $NR_u^2 \overset{a}{\sim} \chi_3^2$.

Using the data on the 428 working, married women in MROZ.RAW (from Mroz, 1987), we obtain the following estimated equation:

$$\begin{aligned}\log(\widehat{wage}) = \; & \underset{\substack{(.317)\\ [.316]}}{-.421} + \underset{\substack{(.013)\\ [.015]}}{.040}\, exper - \underset{\substack{(.00040)\\ [.00041]}}{.00078}\, exper^2 + \underset{\substack{(.014)\\ [.014]}}{.108}\, educ \\ & - \underset{\substack{(.0053)\\ [.0059]}}{.0015}\, age - \underset{\substack{(.089)\\ [.105]}}{.061}\, kidslt6 - \underset{\substack{(.028)\\ [.029]}}{.015}\, kidsge6, \qquad R^2 = .158\end{aligned}$$

where the quantities in brackets are the heteroskedasticity-robust standard errors. The F statistic for joint significance of *age*, *kidslt6*, and *kidsge6* turns out to be about .24, which gives p-value $\approx .87$. Regressing the residuals $\tilde{u}$ from the restricted model on all exogenous variables gives an R-squared of .0017, so $LM = 428(.0017) = .728$, and p-value $\approx .87$. Thus, the F and LM tests give virtually identical results.

The test from regression (4.15) maintains Assumption OLS.3 under H_0, just like the usual F test. It turns out to be easy to obtain a heteroskedasticity-robust LM

statistic. To see how to do so, let us look at the formula for the LM statistic from regression (4.15) in more detail. After some algebra we can write

$$LM = \left(N^{-1/2}\sum_{i=1}^{N}\hat{\mathbf{r}}_i'\tilde{u}_i\right)'\left(\tilde{\sigma}^2 N^{-1}\sum_{i=1}^{N}\hat{\mathbf{r}}_i'\hat{\mathbf{r}}_i\right)^{-1}\left(N^{-1/2}\sum_{i=1}^{N}\hat{\mathbf{r}}_i'\tilde{u}_i\right)$$

where $\tilde{\sigma}^2 \equiv N^{-1}\sum_{i=1}^{N}\tilde{u}_i^2$ and each $\hat{\mathbf{r}}_i$ is a $1 \times K_2$ vector of OLS residuals from the (multivariate) regression of $\mathbf{x}_{i2}$ on $\mathbf{x}_{i1}$, $i = 1, 2, \ldots, N$. This statistic is not robust to heteroskedasticity because the matrix in the middle is not a consistent estimator of the asymptotic variance of $(N^{-1/2}\sum_{i=1}^{N}\hat{\mathbf{r}}_i'\tilde{u}_i)$ under heteroskedasticity. Following the reasoning in Section 4.2.3, a heteroskedasticity-robust statistic is

$$\begin{aligned} LM &= \left(N^{-1/2}\sum_{i=1}^{N}\hat{\mathbf{r}}_i'\tilde{u}_i\right)'\left(N^{-1}\sum_{i=1}^{N}\tilde{u}_i^2\hat{\mathbf{r}}_i'\hat{\mathbf{r}}_i\right)^{-1}\left(N^{-1/2}\sum_{i=1}^{N}\hat{\mathbf{r}}_i'\tilde{u}_i\right) \\ &= \left(\sum_{i=1}^{N}\hat{\mathbf{r}}_i'\tilde{u}_i\right)'\left(\sum_{i=1}^{N}\tilde{u}_i^2\hat{\mathbf{r}}_i'\hat{\mathbf{r}}_i\right)^{-1}\left(\sum_{i=1}^{N}\hat{\mathbf{r}}_i'\tilde{u}_i\right) \end{aligned}$$

Dropping the i subscript, this is easily obtained, as $N - \mathrm{SSR}_0$ from the OLS regression (without an intercept)

$$1 \text{ on } \tilde{u} \cdot \hat{\mathbf{r}} \tag{4.17}$$

where $\tilde{u} \cdot \hat{\mathbf{r}} = (\tilde{u} \cdot \hat{r}_1, \tilde{u} \cdot \hat{r}_2, \ldots, \tilde{u} \cdot \hat{r}_{K_2})$ is the $1 \times K_2$ vector obtained by multiplying $\tilde{u}$ by each element of $\hat{\mathbf{r}}$ and SSR_0 is just the usual sum of squared residuals from regression (4.17). Thus, we first regress each element of $\mathbf{x}_2$ onto all of $\mathbf{x}_1$ and collect the residuals in $\hat{\mathbf{r}}$. Then we form $\tilde{u} \cdot \hat{\mathbf{r}}$ (observation by observation) and run the regression in (4.17); $N - \mathrm{SSR}_0$ from this regression is distributed asymptotically as $\chi^2_{K_2}$. (Do not be thrown off by the fact that the dependent variable in regression (4.17) is unity for each observation; a nonzero sum of squared residuals is reported when you run OLS without an intercept.) For more details, see Davidson and MacKinnon (1985, 1993) or Wooldridge (1991a, 1995b).

Example 4.1 (continued): To obtain the heteroskedasticity-robust LM statistic for H_0: $\beta_4 = 0, \beta_5 = 0, \beta_6 = 0$ in equation (4.16), we estimate the restricted model as before and obtain $\tilde{u}$. Then, we run the regressions (1) *age* on 1, *exper*, *exper*^{2}, *educ*; (2) *kidslt6* on 1, *exper*, *exper*^{2}, *educ*; (3) *kidsge6* on 1, *exper*, *exper*^{2}, *educ*; and obtain the residuals $\hat{r}_1$, $\hat{r}_2$, and $\hat{r}_3$, respectively. The LM statistic is $N - \mathrm{SSR}_0$ from the regression 1 on $\tilde{u} \cdot \hat{r}_1$, $\tilde{u} \cdot \hat{r}_2$, $\tilde{u} \cdot \hat{r}_3$, and $N - \mathrm{SSR}_0 \overset{a}{\sim} \chi^2_3$.

When we apply this result to the data in MROZ.RAW we get $LM = .51$, which is very small for a χ_3^2 random variable: p-value $\approx .92$. For comparison, the heteroskedasticity-robust Wald statistic (scaled by Stata® to have an approximate F distribution) also yields p-value $\approx .92$.

4.3 OLS Solutions to the Omitted Variables Problem

4.3.1 OLS Ignoring the Omitted Variables

Because it is so prevalent in applied work, we now consider the omitted variables problem in more detail. A model that assumes an additive effect of the omitted variable is

$$\mathrm{E}(y \mid x_1, x_2, \ldots, x_K, q) = \beta_0 + \beta_1 x_1 + \beta_2 x_2 + \cdots + \beta_K x_K + \gamma q \tag{4.18}$$

where q is the omitted factor. In particular, we are interested in the β_j, which are the partial effects of the observed explanatory variables holding the other explanatory variables constant, *including* the unobservable q. In the context of this additive model, there is no point in allowing for more than one unobservable; any omitted factors are lumped into q. Henceforth we simply refer to q as the omitted variable.

A good example of equation (4.18) is seen when y is $\log(wage)$ and q includes ability. If x_K denotes a measure of education, β_K in equation (4.18) measures the partial effect of education on wages controlling for—or holding fixed—the level of ability (as well as other observed characteristics). This effect is most interesting from a policy perspective because it provides a causal interpretation of the return to education: β_K is the expected proportionate increase in wage if someone from the working population is exogenously given another year of education.

Viewing equation (4.18) as a structural model, we can always write it in error form as

$$y = \beta_0 + \beta_1 x_1 + \beta_2 x_2 + \cdots + \beta_K x_K + \gamma q + v \tag{4.19}$$

$$\mathrm{E}(v \mid x_1, x_2, \ldots, x_K, q) = 0 \tag{4.20}$$

where v is the **structural error**. One way to handle the nonobservability of q is to put it into the error term. In doing so, nothing is lost by assuming $\mathrm{E}(q) = 0$ because an intercept is included in equation (4.19). Putting q into the error term means we rewrite equation (4.19) as

$$y = \beta_0 + \beta_1 x_1 + \beta_2 x_2 + \cdots + \beta_K x_K + u \tag{4.21}$$

$$u \equiv \gamma q + v \tag{4.22}$$

The error u in equation (4.21) consists of two parts. Under equation (4.20), v has zero mean and is uncorrelated with $x_1, x_2, \ldots, x_K$ (and q). By normalization, q also has zero mean. Thus, $\mathrm{E}(u) = 0$. However, u is uncorrelated with $x_1, x_2, \ldots, x_K$ if and only if q is uncorrelated with each of the observable regressors. If q is correlated with any of the regressors, then so is u, and we have an endogeneity problem. We cannot expect OLS to consistently estimate *any* β_j. Although $\mathrm{E}(u \mid \mathbf{x}) \neq \mathrm{E}(u)$ in equation (4.21), the β_j do have a structural interpretation because they appear in equation (4.19).

It is easy to characterize the plims of the OLS estimators when the omitted variable is ignored; we will call this the **OLS omitted variables inconsistency** or **OLS omitted variables bias** (even though the latter term is not always precise). Write the linear projection of q onto the observable explanatory variables as

$$q = \delta_0 + \delta_1 x_1 + \cdots + \delta_K x_K + r \tag{4.23}$$

where, by definition of a linear projection, $\mathrm{E}(r) = 0$, $\mathrm{Cov}(x_j, r) = 0$, $j = 1, 2, \ldots, K$. Then we can easily infer the plim of the OLS estimators from regressing y onto $1, x_1, \ldots, x_K$ by finding an equation that does satisfy Assumptions OLS.1 and OLS.2. Plugging equation (4.23) into equation (4.19) and doing simple algrebra gives

$$y = (\beta_0 + \gamma\delta_0) + (\beta_1 + \gamma\delta_1)x_1 + (\beta_2 + \gamma\delta_2)x_2 + \cdots + (\beta_K + \gamma\delta_K)x_K + v + \gamma r$$

Now, the error $v + \gamma r$ has zero mean and is uncorrelated with each regressor. It follows that we can just read off the plim of the OLS estimators from the regression of y on $1, x_1, \ldots, x_K$: $\mathrm{plim}\ \hat{\beta}_j = \beta_j + \gamma\delta_j$. Sometimes it is assumed that most of the δ_j are zero. When the correlation between q and a particular variable, say x_K, is the focus, a common (usually implicit) assumption is that all δ_j in equation (4.23) except the intercept and coefficient on x_K are zero. Then $\mathrm{plim}\ \hat{\beta}_j = \beta_j$, $j = 1, \ldots, K-1$, and

$$\mathrm{plim}\ \hat{\beta}_K = \beta_K + \gamma[\mathrm{Cov}(x_K, q)/\mathrm{Var}(x_K)] \tag{4.24}$$

[since $\delta_K = \mathrm{Cov}(x_K, q)/\mathrm{Var}(x_K)$ in this case]. This formula gives us a simple way to determine the sign, and perhaps the magnitude, of the inconsistency in $\hat{\beta}_K$. If $\gamma > 0$ and x_K and q are positively correlated, the asymptotic bias is positive. The other combinations are easily worked out. If x_K has substantial variation in the population relative to the covariance between x_K and q, then the bias can be small. In the general case of equation (4.23), it is difficult to sign δ_K because it measures a partial correlation. It is for this reason that $\delta_j = 0$, $j = 1, \ldots, K-1$ is often maintained for determining the likely asymptotic bias in $\hat{\beta}_K$ when only x_K is endogenous.

Example 4.2 (Wage Equation with Unobserved Ability): Write a structural wage equation explicitly as

$$\log(wage) = \beta_0 + \beta_1 exper + \beta_2 exper^2 + \beta_3 educ + \gamma\, abil + v$$

where v has the structural error property $\mathrm{E}(v \mid exper, educ, abil) = 0$. If *abil* is uncorrelated with *exper* and $exper^2$ once *educ* has been partialed out—that is, $abil = \delta_0 + \delta_3 educ + r$ with r uncorrelated with *exper* and $exper^2$—then $\mathrm{plim}\, \hat{\beta}_3 = \beta_3 + \gamma\delta_3$. Under these assumptions the coefficients on *exper* and $exper^2$ are consistently estimated by the OLS regression that omits ability. If $\delta_3 > 0$ then $\mathrm{plim}\, \hat{\beta}_3 > \beta_3$ (because $\gamma > 0$ by definition), and the return to education is likely to be overestimated in large samples.

4.3.2 The Proxy Variable–OLS Solution

Omitted variables bias can be eliminated, or at least mitigated, if a **proxy variable** is available for the unobserved variable q. There are two formal requirements for a proxy variable for q. The first is that the proxy variable should be **redundant** (sometimes called **ignorable**) in the structural equation. If z is a proxy variable for q, then the most natural statement of redundancy of z in equation (4.18) is

$$\mathrm{E}(y \mid \mathbf{x}, q, z) = \mathrm{E}(y \mid \mathbf{x}, q) \tag{4.25}$$

Condition (4.25) is easy to interpret: z is irrelevant for explaining y, in a conditional mean sense, once $\mathbf{x}$ and q have been controlled for. This assumption on a proxy variable is virtually always made (sometimes only implicitly), and it is rarely controversial: the only reason we bother with z in the first place is that we cannot get data on q. Anyway, we cannot get very far without condition (4.25). In the wage-education example, let q be ability and z be IQ score. By definition it is ability that affects wage: IQ would not matter if true ability were known.

Condition (4.25) is somewhat stronger than needed when unobservables appear additively as in equation (4.18); it suffices to assume that v in equation (4.19) is simply uncorrelated with z. But we will focus on condition (4.25) because it is natural, and because we need it to cover models where q interacts with some observed covariates.

The second requirement of a good proxy variable is more complicated. We require that the correlation between the omitted variable q and each x_j be zero once we *partial out* z. This is easily stated in terms of a linear projection:

$$\mathrm{L}(q \mid 1, x_1, \ldots, x_K, z) = \mathrm{L}(q \mid 1, z) \tag{4.26}$$

It is also helpful to see this relationship in terms of an equation with an unobserved error. Write q as a linear function of z and an error term as

$$q = \theta_0 + \theta_1 z + r \tag{4.27}$$

where, by definition, $\mathrm{E}(r) = 0$ and $\mathrm{Cov}(z, r) = 0$ because $\theta_0 + \theta_1 z$ is the linear projection of q on 1, z. If z is a reasonable proxy for q, $\theta_1 \neq 0$ (and we usually think in terms of $\theta_1 > 0$). But condition (4.26) assumes much more: it is equivalent to

$$\mathrm{Cov}(x_j, r) = 0, \qquad j = 1, 2, \ldots, K$$

This condition requires z to be closely enough related to q so that once it is included in equation (4.27), the x_j are not partially correlated with q.

Before showing why these two proxy variable requirements do the trick, we should head off some possible confusion. The definition of proxy variable here is not universal. While a proxy variable is always assumed to satisfy the redundancy condition (4.25), it is not always assumed to have the second property. In Chapter 5 we will use the notion of an *indicator* of q, which satisfies condition (4.25) but not the second proxy variable assumption.

To obtain an estimable equation, replace q in equation (4.19) with equation (4.27) to get

$$y = (\beta_0 + \gamma\theta_0) + \beta_1 x_1 + \cdots + \beta_K x_K + \gamma\theta_1 z + (\gamma r + v) \tag{4.28}$$

Under the assumptions made, the composite error term $u \equiv \gamma r + v$ is uncorrelated with x_j for all j; redundancy of z in equation (4.18) means that z is uncorrelated with v and, by definition, z is uncorrelated with r. It follows immediately from Theorem 4.1 that the OLS regression y on $1, x_1, x_2, \ldots, x_K$, z produces consistent estimators of $(\beta_0 + \gamma\theta_0), \beta_1, \beta_2, \ldots, \beta_K$, and $\gamma\theta_1$. Thus, we can estimate the partial effect of each of the x_j in equation (4.18) under the proxy variable assumptions.

When z is an **imperfect proxy**, then r in equation (4.27) is correlated with one or more of the x_j. Generally, when we do not impose condition (4.26) and write the linear projection as

$$q = \theta_0 + \rho_1 x_1 + \cdots + \rho_K x_K + \theta_1 z + r$$

the proxy variable regression gives $\operatorname{plim} \hat{\beta}_j = \beta_j + \gamma\rho_j$. Thus, OLS with an imperfect proxy is inconsistent. The hope is that the ρ_j are smaller in magnitude than if z were omitted from the linear projection, and this can usually be argued if z is a reasonable proxy for q.

If including z induces substantial collinearity, it might be better to use OLS without the proxy variable. However, in making these decisions we must recognize that including z reduces the error variance if $\theta_1 \neq 0$: $\mathrm{Var}(\gamma r + v) < \mathrm{Var}(\gamma q + v)$ because $\mathrm{Var}(r) < \mathrm{Var}(q)$, and v is uncorrelated with both r and q. Including a proxy variable can actually reduce asymptotic variances as well as mitigate bias.

Example 4.3 (Using IQ as a Proxy for Ability): We apply the proxy variable method to the data on working men in NLS80.RAW, which was used by Blackburn and Neumark (1992), to estimate the structural model

$$\log(wage) = \beta_0 + \beta_1 exper + \beta_2 tenure + \beta_3 married \\ + \beta_4 south + \beta_5 urban + \beta_6 black + \beta_7 educ + \gamma\, abil + v \tag{4.29}$$

where *exper* is labor market experience, *married* is a dummy variable equal to unity if married, *south* is a dummy variable for the southern region, *urban* is a dummy variable for living in an SMSA, *black* is a race indicator, and *educ* is years of schooling. We assume that *IQ* satisfies the proxy variable assumptions: in the linear projection $abil = \theta_0 + \theta_1 IQ + r$, where r has zero mean and is uncorrelated with *IQ*, we also assume that r is uncorrelated with experience, tenure, education, and other factors appearing in equation (4.29). The estimated equations without and with *IQ* are

$$\begin{aligned}\log(\widehat{wage}) = {} & \underset{(0.11)}{5.40} + \underset{(.003)}{.014}\, exper + \underset{(.002)}{.012}\, tenure + \underset{(.039)}{.199}\, married \\ & - \underset{(.026)}{.091}\, south + \underset{(.027)}{.184}\, urban - \underset{(.038)}{.188}\, black + \underset{(.006)}{.065}\, educ\end{aligned}$$

$N = 935, \qquad R^2 = .253$

$$\begin{aligned}\log(\widehat{wage}) = {} & \underset{(0.13)}{5.18} + \underset{(.003)}{.014}\, exper + \underset{(.002)}{.011}\, tenure + \underset{(.039)}{.200}\, married \\ & - \underset{(.026)}{.080}\, south + \underset{(.027)}{.182}\, urban - \underset{(.039)}{.143}\, black + \underset{(.007)}{.054}\, educ \\ & + \underset{(.0010)}{.0036}\, IQ\end{aligned}$$

$N = 935, \qquad R^2 = .263$

Notice how the return to schooling has fallen from about 6.5 percent to about 5.4 percent when *IQ* is added to the regression. This is what we expect to happen if ability and schooling are (partially) positively correlated. Of course, these are just the findings from one sample. Adding *IQ* explains only one percentage point more of the variation in log(*wage*), and the equation predicts that 15 more *IQ* points (one standard deviation) increases *wage* by about 5.4 percent. The standard error on the return to education has increased, but the 95 percent confidence interval is still fairly tight.

Often the outcome of the dependent variable from an earlier time period can be a useful proxy variable.

Example 4.4 (Effects of Job Training Grants on Worker Productivity): The data in JTRAIN1.RAW are for 157 Michigan manufacturing firms for the years 1987, 1988, and 1989. These data are from Holzer, Block, Cheatham, and Knott (1993). The goal is to determine the effectiveness of job training grants on firm productivity. For this exercise, we use only the 54 firms in 1988 which reported nonmissing values of the scrap rate (number of items out of 100 that must be scrapped). No firms were awarded grants in 1987; in 1988, 19 of the 54 firms were awarded grants. If the training grant has the intended effect, the average scrap rate should be lower among firms receiving a grant. The problem is that the grants were not randomly assigned: whether or not a firm received a grant could be related to other factors unobservable to the econometrician that affect productivity. In the simplest case, we can write (for the 1988 cross section)

$$\log(scrap) = \beta_0 + \beta_1 grant + \gamma q + v$$

where v is orthogonal to *grant* but q contains unobserved productivity factors that might be correlated with *grant*, a binary variable equal to unity if the firm received a job training grant. Since we have the scrap rate in the previous year, we can use $\log(scrap_{-1})$ as a proxy variable for q:

$$q = \theta_0 + \theta_1 \log(scrap_{-1}) + r$$

where r has zero mean and, by definition, is uncorrelated with $\log(scrap_{-1})$. We hope that r has no or little correlation with *grant*. Plugging in for q gives the estimable model

$$\log(scrap) = \delta_0 + \beta_1 grant + \gamma\theta_1 \log(scrap_{-1}) + r + v$$

From this equation, we see that β_1 measures the proportionate difference in scrap rates for two firms having the *same* scrap rates in the previous year, but where one firm received a grant and the other did not. This is intuitively appealing. The estimated equations are

$$\log(\hat{scrap}) = \underset{(.240)}{.409} + \underset{(.406)}{.057}\, grant$$

$$N = 54, \qquad R^2 = .0004$$

$$\log(\hat{scrap}) = \underset{(.089)}{.021} - \underset{(.147)}{.254}\, grant + \underset{(.044)}{.831}\, \log(scrap_{-1})$$

$$N = 54, \qquad R^2 = .873$$

Without the lagged scrap rate, we see that the grant appears, if anything, to reduce productivity (by increasing the scrap rate), although the coefficient is statistically insignificant. When the lagged dependent variable is included, the coefficient on grant changes signs, becomes economically large—firms awarded grants have scrap rates about 25.4 percent less than those not given grants—and the effect is significant at the 5 percent level against a one-sided alternative. [The more accurate estimate of the percentage effect is $100 \cdot [\exp(-.254) - 1] = -22.4\%$; see Problem 4.1(a).]

We can always use more than one proxy for x_K. For example, it might be that $\mathrm{E}(q \mid \mathbf{x}, z_1, z_2) = \mathrm{E}(q \mid z_1, z_2) = \theta_0 + \theta_1 z_1 + \theta_2 z_2$, in which case including both z_1 and z_2 as regressors along with $x_1, \ldots, x_K$ solves the omitted variable problem. The weaker condition that the error r in the equation $q = \theta_0 + \theta_1 z_1 + \theta_2 z_2 + r$ is uncorrelated with $x_1, \ldots, x_K$ also suffices.

The data set NLS80.RAW also contains each man's score on the knowledge of the world of work (KWW) test. Problem 4.11 asks you to reestimate equation (4.29) when KWW and IQ are both used as proxies for ability.

4.3.3 Models with Interactions in Unobservables

In some cases we might be concerned about interactions between unobservables and observable explanatory variables. Obtaining consistent estimators is more difficult in this case, but a good proxy variable can again solve the problem.

Write the structural model with unobservable q as

$$y = \beta_0 + \beta_1 x_1 + \cdots + \beta_K x_K + \gamma_1 q + \gamma_2 x_K q + v \tag{4.30}$$

where we make a zero conditional mean assumption on the structural error v:

$$\mathrm{E}(v \mid \mathbf{x}, q) = 0 \tag{4.31}$$

For simplicity we have interacted q with only one explanatory variable, x_K.

Before discussing estimation of equation (4.30), we should have an interpretation for the parameters in this equation, as the interaction $x_K q$ is unobservable. (We discussed this topic more generally in Section 2.2.5.) If x_K is an essentially continuous variable, the partial effect of x_K on $\mathrm{E}(y \mid \mathbf{x}, q)$ is

$$\frac{\partial \mathrm{E}(y \mid \mathbf{x}, q)}{\partial x_K} = \beta_K + \gamma_2 q \tag{4.32}$$

Thus, the partial effect of x_K actually depends on the level of q. Because q is not observed for anyone in the population, equation (4.32) can never be estimated, even if we could estimate γ_2 (which we cannot, in general). But we can average equation

(4.32) across the population distribution of q. Assuming $\mathrm{E}(q) = 0$, the **average partial effect** (**APE**) of x_K is

$$\mathrm{E}(\beta_K + \gamma_2 q) = \beta_K \tag{4.33}$$

A similar interpretation holds for discrete x_K. For example, if x_K is binary, then $\mathrm{E}(y \mid x_1, \ldots, x_{K-1}, 1, q) - \mathrm{E}(y \mid x_1, \ldots, x_{K-1}, 0, q) = \beta_K + \gamma_2 q$, and β_K is the average of this difference over the distribution of q. In this case, β_K is called the **average treatment effect** (**ATE**). This name derives from the case where x_K represents receiving some "treatment," such as participation in a job training program or participation in an income maintenence program. We will consider the binary treatment case further in Chapter 18, where we introduce a counterfactual framework for estimating average treatment effects.

It turns out that the assumption $\mathrm{E}(q) = 0$ is without loss of generality. Using simple algebra we can show that, if $\mu_q \equiv \mathrm{E}(q) \neq 0$, then we can consistently estimate $\beta_K + \gamma_2 \mu_q$, which is the average partial effect.

If the elements of $\mathbf{x}$ are exogenous in the sense that $\mathrm{E}(q \mid \mathbf{x}) = 0$, then we can consistently estimate each of the β_j by an OLS regression, where q and $x_K q$ are just part of the error term. This result follows from iterated expectations applied to equation (4.30), which shows that $\mathrm{E}(y \mid \mathbf{x}) = \beta_0 + \beta_1 x_1 + \cdots + \beta_K x_K$ if $\mathrm{E}(q \mid \mathbf{x}) = 0$. The resulting equation probably has heteroskedasticity, but this is easily dealt with. Incidentally, this is a case where only assuming that q and $\mathbf{x}$ are uncorrelated would not be enough to ensure consistency of OLS: $x_K q$ and $\mathbf{x}$ can be correlated even if q and $\mathbf{x}$ are uncorrelated.

If q and $\mathbf{x}$ are correlated, we can consistently estimate the β_j by OLS if we have a suitable proxy variable for q. We still assume that the proxy variable, z, satisfies the redundancy condition (4.25). In the current model we must make a stronger proxy variable assumption than we did in Section 4.3.2:

$$\mathrm{E}(q \mid \mathbf{x}, z) = \mathrm{E}(q \mid z) = \theta_1 z \tag{4.34}$$

where now we assume z has a zero mean in the population. Under these two proxy variable assumptions, iterated expectations gives

$$\mathrm{E}(y \mid \mathbf{x}, z) = \beta_0 + \beta_1 x_1 + \cdots + \beta_K x_K + \gamma_1 \theta_1 z + \gamma_2 \theta_1 x_K z \tag{4.35}$$

and the parameters are consistently estimated by OLS.

If we do not define our proxy to have zero mean in the population, then estimating equation (4.35) by OLS does not consistently estimate β_K. If $\mathrm{E}(z) \neq 0$, then we would have to write $\mathrm{E}(q \mid z) = \theta_0 + \theta_1 z$, in which case the coefficient on x_K in equation (4.35) would be $\beta_K + \theta_0 \gamma_2$. In practice, we may not know the population mean of the proxy variable, in which case the proxy variable should be demeaned in the sample before interacting it with x_K.

If we maintain homoskedasticity in the structural model—that is, $\text{Var}(y \mid \mathbf{x}, q, z) = \text{Var}(y \mid \mathbf{x}, q) = \sigma^2$—then there must be heteroskedasticity in $\text{Var}(y \mid \mathbf{x}, z)$. Using Property CV.3 in Appendix 2A, it can be shown that

$$\text{Var}(y \mid \mathbf{x}, z) = \sigma^2 + (\gamma_1 + \gamma_2 x_K)^2 \,\text{Var}(q \mid \mathbf{x}, z)$$

Even if $\text{Var}(q \mid \mathbf{x}, z)$ is constant, $\text{Var}(y \mid \mathbf{x}, z)$ depends on x_K. This situation is most easily dealt with by computing heteroskedasticity-robust statistics, which allows for heteroskedasticity of arbitrary form.

Example 4.5 (Return to Education Depends on Ability): Consider an extension of the wage equation (4.29):

$$\log(wage) = \beta_0 + \beta_1 exper + \beta_2 tenure + \beta_3 married + \beta_4 south + \beta_5 urban + \beta_6 black + \beta_7 educ + \gamma_1 abil + \gamma_2 educ{\cdot}abil + v \tag{4.36}$$

so that *educ* and *abil* have separate effects but also have an interactive effect. In this model the return to a year of schooling depends on *abil*: $\beta_7 + \gamma_2 abil$. Normalizing *abil* to have zero population mean, we see that the average of the return to education is simply β_7. We estimate this equation under the assumption that IQ is redundant in equation (4.36) and $\text{E}(abil \mid \mathbf{x}, IQ) = \text{E}(abil \mid IQ) = \theta_1(IQ - 100) \equiv \theta_1 IQ_0$, where IQ_0 is the population-demeaned IQ (IQ is constructed to have mean 100 in the population). We can estimate the β_j in equation (4.36) by replacing *abil* with IQ_0 and *educ·abil* with $educ{\cdot}IQ_0$ and doing OLS.

Using the sample of men in NLS80.RAW gives the following:

$$\log(\widehat{wage}) = \cdots + \underset{(.007)}{.052}\, educ - \underset{(.00516)}{.00094}\, IQ_0 + \underset{(.00038)}{.00034}\, educ \cdot IQ_0$$

$$N = 935, \qquad R^2 = .263$$

where the usual OLS standard errors are reported (if $\gamma_2 = 0$, homoskedasticity may be reasonable). The interaction term $educ{\cdot}IQ_0$ is not statistically significant, and the return to education at the average IQ, 5.2 percent, is similar to the estimate when the return to education is assumed to be constant. Thus there is little evidence for an interaction between education and ability. Incidentally, the F test for joint significance of IQ_0 and $educ{\cdot}IQ_0$ yields a p-value of about .0011, but the interaction term is not needed.

In this case, we happen to know the population mean of *IQ*, but in most cases we will not know the population mean of a proxy variable. Then, we should use the sample average to demean the proxy before interacting it with x_K; see Problem 4.8. Technically, using the sample average to estimate the population average should be reflected in the OLS standard errors. But, as you are asked to show in Problem 6.10 in Chapter 6, the adjustments generally have very small impacts on the standard errors and can safely be ignored.

In his study on the effects of computer usage on the wage structure in the United States, Krueger (1993) uses computer usage at home as a proxy for unobservables that might be correlated with computer usage at work; he also includes an interaction between the two computer usage dummies. Krueger does not demean the "uses computer at home" dummy before constructing the interaction, so his estimate on "uses a computer at work" does not have an average treatment effect interpretation. However, just as in Example 4.5, Krueger found that the interaction term is insignificant.

4.4 Properties of OLS under Measurement Error

As we saw in Section 4.1, another way that endogenous explanatory variables can arise in economic applications occurs when one or more of the variables in our model contains **measurement error**. In this section, we derive the consequences of measurement error for ordinary least squares estimation.

The measurement error problem has a statistical structure similar to the omitted variable–proxy variable problem discussed in the previous section. However, they are conceptually very different. In the proxy variable case, we are looking for a variable that is somehow associated with the unobserved variable. In the measurement error case, the variable that we do not observe has a well-defined, quantitative meaning (such as a marginal tax rate or annual income), but our measures of it may contain error. For example, reported annual income is a measure of actual annual income, whereas IQ score is a proxy for ability.

Another important difference between the proxy variable and measurement error problems is that, in the latter case, often the mismeasured explanatory variable is the one whose effect is of primary interest. In the proxy variable case, we cannot estimate the effect of the omitted variable.

Before we turn to the analysis, it is important to remember that measurement error is an issue only when the variables on which we can collect data differ from the variables that influence decisions by individuals, families, firms, and so on. For example, suppose we are estimating the effect of peer group behavior on teenage drug usage, where the behavior of one's peer group is self-reported. Self-reporting may be a mismeasure of actual peer group behavior, but so what? We are probably more interested in the effects of how a teenager perceives his or her peer group.

4.4.1 Measurement Error in the Dependent Variable

We begin with the case where the dependent variable is the only variable measured with error. Let y^* denote the variable (in the population, as always) that we would like to explain. For example, y^* could be annual family saving. The regression model has the usual linear form

$$y^* = \beta_0 + \beta_1 x_1 + \cdots + \beta_K x_K + v \tag{4.37}$$

and we assume that it satisfies at least Assumptions OLS.1 and OLS.2. Typically, we are interested in $\mathrm{E}(y^* \mid x_1, \ldots, x_K)$. We let y represent the observable measure of y^* where $y \neq y^*$.

The population measurement error is defined as the difference between the observed value and the actual value:

$$e_0 = y - y^* \tag{4.38}$$

For a random draw i from the population, we can write $e_{i0} = y_i - y_i^*$, but what is important is how the measurement error in the population is related to other factors. To obtain an estimable model, we write $y^* = y - e_0$, plug this into equation (4.37), and rearrange:

$$y = \beta_0 + \beta_1 x_1 + \cdots + \beta_K x_K + v + e_0 \tag{4.39}$$

Since $y, x_1, x_2, \ldots, x_K$ are observed, we can estimate this model by OLS. In effect, we just ignore the fact that y is an imperfect measure of y^* and proceed as usual.

When does OLS with y in place of y^* produce consistent estimators of the β_j? Since the original model (4.37) satisfies Assumption OLS.1, v has zero mean and is uncorrelated with each x_j. It is only natural to assume that the measurement error has zero mean; if it does not, this fact only affects estimation of the intercept, β_0. Much more important is what we assume about the relationship between the measurement error e_0 and the explanatory variables x_j. The usual assumption is that the measurement error in y is statistically independent of each explanatory variable, which implies that e_0 is uncorrelated with $\mathbf{x}$. Then, the OLS estimators from equation (4.39) are consistent (and possibly unbiased as well). Further, the usual OLS inference procedures (t statistics, F statistics, LM statistics) are asymptotically valid under appropriate homoskedasticity assumptions.

If e_0 and v are uncorrelated, as is usually assumed, then $\text{Var}(v + e_0) = \sigma_v^2 + \sigma_0^2 > \sigma_v^2$. Therefore, measurement error in the dependent variable results in a larger error variance than when the dependent variable is not measured with error. This result is hardly surprising and translates into larger asymptotic variances for the OLS estimators than if we could observe y^*. But the larger error variance violates none of the assumptions needed for OLS estimation to have its desirable large-sample properties.

Example 4.6 (Saving Function with Measurement Error): Consider a saving function

$$\text{E}(sav^* \mid inc, size, educ, age) = \beta_0 + \beta_1 inc + \beta_2 size + \beta_3 educ + \beta_4 age$$

but where actual saving (sav^*) may deviate from reported saving (sav). The question is whether the size of the measurement error in sav is systematically related to the other variables. It may be reasonable to assume that the measurement error is not correlated with *inc*, *size*, *educ*, and *age*, but we might expect that families with higher incomes, or more education, report their saving more accurately. Unfortunately, without more information, we cannot know whether the measurement error is correlated with *inc* or *educ*.

When the dependent variable is in logarithmic form, so that $\log(y^*)$ is the dependent variable, a natural measurement error equation is

$$\log(y) = \log(y^*) + e_0 \tag{4.40}$$

This follows from a **multiplicative measurement error** for y: $y = y^* a_0$ where $a_0 > 0$ and $e_0 = \log(a_0)$.

Example 4.7 (Measurement Error in Firm Scrap Rates): In Example 4.4, we might think that the firm scrap rate is mismeasured, leading us to postulate the model $\log(scrap^*) = \beta_0 + \beta_1 grant + v$, where $scrap^*$ is the true scrap rate. The measurement error equation is $\log(scrap) = \log(scrap^*) + e_0$. Is the measurement error e_0 independent of whether the firm receives a grant? Not if a firm receiving a grant is more likely to underreport its scrap rate in order to make it look as if the grant had the intended effect. If underreporting occurs, then, in the estimable equation $\log(scrap) = \beta_0 + \beta_1 grant + v + e_0$, the error $u = v + e_0$ is negatively correlated with *grant*. This result would produce a downward bias in β_1, tending to make the training program look more effective than it actually was.

These examples show that measurement error in the dependent variable *can* cause biases in OLS if the measurement error is systematically related to one or more of the explanatory variables. If the measurement error is uncorrelated with the explanatory variables, OLS is perfectly appropriate.

4.4.2 Measurement Error in an Explanatory Variable

Traditionally, measurement error in an explanatory variable has been considered a much more important problem than measurement error in the response variable. This point was suggested by Example 4.2, and in this subsection we develop the general case.

We consider the model with a single explanatory measured with error:

$$y = \beta_0 + \beta_1 x_1 + \beta_2 x_2 + \cdots + \beta_K x_K^* + v \tag{4.41}$$

where $y, x_1, \ldots, x_{K-1}$ are observable but x_K^* is not. We assume at a minimum that v has zero mean and is uncorrelated with $x_1, x_2, \ldots, x_{K-1}$, x_K^*; in fact, we usually have in mind the structural model $\mathrm{E}(y \mid x_1, \ldots, x_{K-1}, x_K^*) = \beta_0 + \beta_1 x_1 + \beta_2 x_2 + \cdots + \beta_K x_K^*$. If x_K^* were observed, OLS estimation would produce consistent estimators. Instead, we have a measure of x_K^*; call it x_K. A maintained assumption is that v is also uncorrelated with x_K. This follows under the redundancy assumption $\mathrm{E}(y \mid x_1, \ldots, x_{K-1}, x_K^*, x_K) = \mathrm{E}(y \mid x_1, \ldots, x_{K-1}, x_K^*)$, an assumption we used in the proxy variable solution to the omitted variable problem. This means that x_K has no effect on y once the other explanatory variables, including x_K^*, have been controlled for. Since x_K^* is assumed to be the variable that affects y, this assumption is uncontroversial.

The measurement error in the population is simply

$$e_K = x_K - x_K^* \tag{4.42}$$

and this can be positive, negative, or zero. We assume that the average measurement error in the population is zero: $\mathrm{E}(e_K) = 0$, which has no practical consequences because we include an intercept in equation (4.41). Since v is assumed to be uncorrelated with x_K^* and x_K, v is also uncorrelated with e_K.

We want to know the properties of OLS if we simply replace x_K^* with x_K and run the regression of y on $1, x_1, x_2, \ldots, x_K$. These depend crucially on the assumptions we make about the measurement error. An assumption that is almost always maintained is that e_K is uncorrelated with the explanatory variables not measured with error: $\mathrm{E}(x_j e_K) = 0$, $j = 1, \ldots, K-1$.

The key assumptions involve the relationship between the measurement error and x_K^* and x_K. Two assumptions have been the focus in the econometrics literature, and these represent polar extremes. The first assumption is that e_K is uncorrelated with the *observed* measure, x_K:

$$\mathrm{Cov}(x_K, e_K) = 0 \tag{4.43}$$

From equation (4.42), if assumption (4.43) is true, then e_K must be correlated with the unobserved variable x_K^*. To determine the properties of OLS in this case, we write $x_K^* = x_K - e_K$ and plug this into equation (4.41):

$$y = \beta_0 + \beta_1 x_1 + \beta_2 x_2 + \cdots + \beta_K x_K + (v - \beta_K e_K) \tag{4.44}$$

Now, we have assumed that v and e_K both have zero mean and are uncorrelated with each x_j, including x_K; therefore, $v - \beta_K e_K$ has zero mean and is uncorrelated with the x_j. It follows that OLS estimation with x_K in place of x_K^* produces consistent estimators of all of the β_j (assuming the standard rank condition Assumption OLS.2). Since v is uncorrelated with e_K, the variance of the error in equation (4.44) is $\text{Var}(v - \beta_K e_K) = \sigma_v^2 + \beta_K^2 \sigma_{e_K}^2$. Therefore, except when $\beta_K = 0$, measurement error increases the error variance, which is not a surprising finding and violates none of the OLS assumptions.

The assumption that e_K is uncorrelated with x_K is analogous to the proxy variable assumption we made in the Section 4.3.2. Since this assumption implies that OLS has all its nice properties, this is not usually what econometricians have in mind when referring to measurement error in an explanatory variable. The **classical errors-in-variables (CEV)** assumption replaces assumption (4.43) with the assumption that the measurement error is uncorrelated with the *unobserved* explanatory variable:

$$\text{Cov}(x_K^*, e_K) = 0 \tag{4.45}$$

This assumption comes from writing the observed measure as the sum of the true explanatory variable and the measurement error, $x_K = x_K^* + e_K$, and then assuming the two components of x_K are uncorrelated. (This has nothing to do with assumptions about v; we are always maintaining that v is uncorrelated with x_K^* and x_K, and therefore with e_K.)

If assumption (4.45) holds, then x_K and e_K *must* be correlated:

$$\text{Cov}(x_K, e_K) = \text{E}(x_K e_K) = \text{E}(x_K^* e_K) + \text{E}(e_K^2) = \sigma_{e_K}^2 \tag{4.46}$$

Thus, under the CEV assumption, the covariance between x_K and e_K is equal to the variance of the measurement error.

Looking at equation (4.44), we see that correlation between x_K and e_K causes problems for OLS. Because v and x_K are uncorrelated, the covariance between x_K and the composite error $v - \beta_K e_K$ is $\text{Cov}(x_K, v - \beta_K e_K) = -\beta_K \text{Cov}(x_K, e_K) = -\beta_K \sigma_{e_K}^2$. It follows that, in the CEV case, the OLS regression of y on $x_1, x_2, \ldots, x_K$ generally gives inconsistent estimators of *all* of the β_j.

The plims of the $\hat{\beta}_j$ for $j \neq K$ are difficult to characterize except under special assumptions. If x_K^* is uncorrelated with x_j, all $j \neq K$, then so is x_K, and it follows that $\text{plim } \hat{\beta}_j = \beta_j$, all $j \neq K$. The plim of $\hat{\beta}_K$ can be characterized in any case. Problem 4.10 asks you to show that

$$\text{plim}(\hat{\beta}_K) = \beta_K \left(\frac{\sigma_{r_K^*}^2}{\sigma_{r_K^*}^2 + \sigma_{e_K}^2} \right) \tag{4.47}$$

where r_K^* is the linear projection error in

$$x_K^* = \delta_0 + \delta_1 x_1 + \delta_2 x_2 + \cdots + \delta_{K-1} x_{K-1} + r_K^*$$

An important implication of equation (4.47) is that, because the term multiplying β_K is always between zero and one, $|\text{plim}(\hat{\beta}_K)| < |\beta_K|$. This is called the **attenuation bias** in OLS due to classical errors-in-variables: on average (or in large samples), the estimated OLS effect will be *attenuated* as a result of the presence of classical errors-in-variables. If β_K is positive, $\hat{\beta}_K$ will tend to underestimate β_K; if β_K is negative, $\hat{\beta}_K$ will tend to overestimate β_K.

In the case of a single explanatory variable ($K = 1$) measured with error, equation (4.47) becomes

$$\text{plim } \hat{\beta}_1 = \beta_1 \left(\frac{\sigma_{x_1^*}^2}{\sigma_{x_1^*}^2 + \sigma_{e_1}^2} \right) \tag{4.48}$$

The term multiplying β_1 in equation (4.48) is $\text{Var}(x_1^*)/\text{Var}(x_1)$, which is always less than unity under the CEV assumption (4.45). As $\text{Var}(e_1)$ shrinks relative to $\text{Var}(x_1^*)$, the attentuation bias disappears.

In the case with multiple explanatory variables, equation (4.47) shows that it is not $\sigma_{x_K^*}^2$ that affects $\text{plim}(\hat{\beta}_K)$ but the variance in x_K^* after netting out the other explanatory variables. Thus, the more collinear x_K^* is with the other explanatory variables, the worse is the attenuation bias.

Example 4.8 (Measurement Error in Family Income): Consider the problem of estimating the causal effect of family income on college grade point average, after controlling for high school grade point average and SAT score:

$$colGPA = \beta_0 + \beta_1 faminc^* + \beta_2 hsGPA + \beta_3 SAT + v$$

where $faminc^*$ is actual annual family income. Precise data on $colGPA$, $hsGPA$, and SAT are relatively easy to obtain from school records. But family income, especially as reported by students, could be mismeasured. If $faminc = faminc^* + e_1$, and the CEV assumptions hold, then using reported family income in place of actual family income will bias the OLS estimator of β_1 toward zero. One consequence is that a hypothesis test of H_0: $\beta_1 = 0$ will have a higher probability of Type II error.

If measurement error is present in more than one explanatory variable, deriving the inconsistency in the OLS estimators under extensions of the CEV assumptions is complicated and does not lead to very usable results.

In some cases it is clear that the CEV assumption (4.45) cannot be true. For example, suppose that frequency of marijuana usage is to be used as an explanatory variable in a wage equation. Let $smoked^*$ be the number of days, out of the last 30, that a worker has smoked marijuana. The variable *smoked* is the self-reported number of days. Suppose we postulate the standard measurement error model, $smoked = smoked^* + e_1$, and let us even assume that people try to report the truth. It seems very likely that people who do not smoke marijuana at all—so that $smoked^* = 0$—will also report $smoked = 0$. In other words, the measurement error is zero for people who never smoke marijuana. When $smoked^* > 0$ it is more likely that someone miscounts how many days he or she smoked marijuana. Such miscounting almost certainly means that e_1 and $smoked^*$ are correlated, a finding which violates the CEV assumption (4.45).

A general situation where assumption (4.45) is necessarily false occurs when the observed variable x_K has a smaller population variance than the unobserved variable x_K^*. Of course, we can rarely know with certainty whether this is the case, but we can sometimes use introspection. For example, consider actual amount of schooling versus reported schooling. In many cases, reported schooling will be a rounded-off version of actual schooling; therefore, reported schooling is less variable than actual schooling.

Problems

4.1. Consider a standard log(*wage*) equation for men under the assumption that all explanatory variables are exogenous:

$$\log(wage) = \beta_0 + \beta_1 married + \beta_2 educ + \mathbf{z}\gamma + u \tag{4.49}$$

$$\mathrm{E}(u \mid married, educ, \mathbf{z}) = 0$$

where $\mathbf{z}$ contains factors other than marital status and education that can affect wage. When β_1 is small, $100 \cdot \beta_1$ is approximately the ceteris paribus percentage difference in wages between married and unmarried men. When β_1 is large, it is preferable to use the exact percentage difference in $\mathrm{E}(wage \mid married, educ, \mathbf{z})$. Call this θ_1.

a. Show that, if u is independent of all explanatory variables in equation (4.49), then $\theta_1 = 100 \cdot [\exp(\beta_1) - 1]$. [Hint: Find $\mathrm{E}(wage \mid married, educ, \mathbf{z})$ for $married = 1$ and $married = 0$, and find the percentage difference.] A natural, consistent, estimator of θ_1 is $\hat{\theta}_1 = 100 \cdot [\exp(\hat{\beta}_1) - 1]$, where $\hat{\beta}_1$ is the OLS estimator from equation (4.49).

b. Use the delta method (see Section 3.5.2) to show that asymptotic standard error of $\hat{\theta}_1$ is $[100 \cdot \exp(\hat{\beta}_1)] \cdot \mathrm{se}(\hat{\beta}_1)$.

c. Repeat parts a and b by finding the exact percentage change in $\mathrm{E}(wage \mid married, educ, \mathbf{z})$ for any given change in $educ$, $\Delta educ$. Call this θ_2. Explain how to estimate θ_2 and obtain its asymptotic standard error.

d. Use the data in NLS80.RAW to estimate equation (4.49), where $\mathbf{z}$ contains the remaining variables in equation (4.29) (except ability, of course). Find $\hat{\theta}_1$ and its standard error; find $\hat{\theta}_2$ and its standard error when $\Delta educ = 4$.

4.2. a. Show that, under random sampling and the zero conditional mean assumption $\mathrm{E}(u \mid \mathbf{x}) = 0$, $\mathrm{E}(\hat{\boldsymbol{\beta}} \mid \mathbf{X}) = \boldsymbol{\beta}$ if $\mathbf{X}'\mathbf{X}$ is nonsingular. (Hint: Use Property CE.5 in the appendix to Chapter 2.)

b. In addition to the assumptions from part a, assume that $\mathrm{Var}(u \mid \mathbf{x}) = \sigma^2$. Show that $\mathrm{Var}(\hat{\boldsymbol{\beta}} \mid \mathbf{X}) = \sigma^2(\mathbf{X}'\mathbf{X})^{-1}$.

4.3. Suppose that in the linear model (4.5), $\mathrm{E}(\mathbf{x}'u) = \mathbf{0}$ (where $\mathbf{x}$ contains unity), $\mathrm{Var}(u \mid \mathbf{x}) = \sigma^2$, but $\mathrm{E}(u \mid \mathbf{x}) \neq \mathrm{E}(u)$.

a. Is it true that $\mathrm{E}(u^2 \mid \mathbf{x}) = \sigma^2$?

b. What relevance does part a have for OLS estimation?

4.4. Show that the estimator $\hat{\mathbf{B}} \equiv N^{-1} \sum_{i=1}^{N} \hat{u}_i^2 \mathbf{x}_i' \mathbf{x}_i$ is consistent for $\mathbf{B} = \mathrm{E}(u^2 \mathbf{x}' \mathbf{x})$ by showing that $N^{-1} \sum_{i=1}^{N} \hat{u}_i^2 \mathbf{x}_i' \mathbf{x}_i = N^{-1} \sum_{i=1}^{N} u_i^2 \mathbf{x}_i' \mathbf{x}_i + \mathrm{o}_p(1)$. [Hint: Write $\hat{u}_i^2 = u_i^2 - 2\mathbf{x}_i u_i (\hat{\boldsymbol{\beta}} - \boldsymbol{\beta}) + [\mathbf{x}_i(\hat{\boldsymbol{\beta}} - \boldsymbol{\beta})]^2$, and use the facts that sample averages are $\mathrm{O}_p(1)$ when expectations exist and that $\hat{\boldsymbol{\beta}} - \boldsymbol{\beta} = \mathrm{o}_p(1)$. Assume that all necessary expectations exist and are finite.]

4.5. Let y and z be random scalars, and let $\mathbf{x}$ be a $1 \times K$ random vector, where one element of $\mathbf{x}$ can be unity to allow for a nonzero intercept. Consider the population model

$$\mathrm{E}(y \mid \mathbf{x}, z) = \mathbf{x}\boldsymbol{\beta} + \gamma z \tag{4.50}$$

$$\mathrm{Var}(y \mid \mathbf{x}, z) = \sigma^2 \tag{4.51}$$

where interest lies in the $K \times 1$ vector $\boldsymbol{\beta}$. To rule out trivialities, assume that $\gamma \neq 0$. In addition, assume that $\mathbf{x}$ and z are orthogonal in the population: $\mathrm{E}(\mathbf{x}'z) = \mathbf{0}$.

Consider two estimators of $\boldsymbol{\beta}$ based on N independent and identically distributed observations: (1) $\hat{\boldsymbol{\beta}}$ (obtained along with $\hat{\gamma}$) is from the regression of y on $\mathbf{x}$ and z; (2) $\tilde{\boldsymbol{\beta}}$ is from the regression of y on $\mathbf{x}$. Both estimators are consistent for $\boldsymbol{\beta}$ under equation (4.50) and $\mathrm{E}(\mathbf{x}'z) = \mathbf{0}$ (along with the standard rank conditions).

a. Show that, without any additional assumptions (except those needed to apply the law of large numbers and central limit theorem), $\mathrm{Avar}\,\sqrt{N}(\tilde{\boldsymbol{\beta}} - \boldsymbol{\beta}) - \mathrm{Avar}\,\sqrt{N}(\hat{\boldsymbol{\beta}} - \boldsymbol{\beta})$ is always positive semidefinite (and usually positive definite). Therefore—from the standpoint of asymptotic analysis—it is always better under equations (4.50) and (4.51) to include variables in a regression model that are uncorrelated with the variables of interest.

b. Consider the special case where $z = (x_K - \mu_K)^2$, where $\mu_K \equiv \mathrm{E}(x_K)$, and x_K is symetrically distributed: $\mathrm{E}[(x_K - \mu_K)^3] = 0$. Then β_K is the partial effect of x_K on $\mathrm{E}(y \mid \mathbf{x})$ evaluated at $x_K = \mu_K$. Is it better to estimate the average partial effect with or without $(x_K - \mu_K)^2$ included as a regressor?

c. Under the setup in Problem 2.3, with $\mathrm{Var}(y \mid \mathbf{x}) = \sigma^2$, is it better to estimate β_1 and β_2 with or without $x_1 x_2$ in the regression?

4.6. Let the variable *nonwhite* be a binary variable indicating race: *nonwhite* = 1 if the person is a race other than white. Given that race is determined at birth and is beyond an individual's control, explain how *nonwhite* can be an endogenous explanatory variable in a regression model. In particular, consider the three kinds of endogeneity discussed in Section 4.1.

4.7. Consider estimating the effect of personal computer ownership, as represented by a binary variable, *PC*, on college GPA, *colGPA*. With data on SAT scores and high school GPA you postulate the model

$$colGPA = \beta_0 + \beta_1 hsGPA + \beta_2 SAT + \beta_3 PC + u$$

a. Why might u and PC be positively correlated?

b. If the given equation is estimated by OLS using a random sample of college students, is $\hat{\beta}_3$ likely to have an upward or downward asymptotic bias?

c. What are some variables that might be good proxies for the unobservables in u that are correlated with PC?

4.8. Consider a population regression with two explanatory variables, but where they have an interactive effect and x_2 appears as a quadratic:

$$E(y \mid x_1, x_2) = \beta_0 + \beta_1 x_1 + \beta_2 x_2 + \beta_3 x_1 x_2 + \beta_4 x_2^2$$

Let $\mu_1 \equiv E(x_1)$ and $\mu_2 \equiv E(x_2)$ be the population means of the explanatory variables.

a. Let α_1 denote the average partial effect (across the distribution of the explanatory variables) of x_1 on $E(y \mid x_1, x_2)$, and let α_2 be the same for x_2. Find α_1 and α_2 in terms of the β_j and μ_j.

b. Rewrite the regression function so that α_1 and α_2 appear directly. (Note that μ_1 and μ_2 will also appear.)

c. Given a random sample, what regression would you run to estimate α_1 and α_2 directly? What if you do not know μ_1 and μ_2?

d. Apply part c to the data in NLS80.RAW, where $y = \log(wage)$, $x_1 = educ$, and $x_2 = exper$. (You will have to plug in the sample averages of *educ* and *exper*.) Compare coefficients and standard errors when the interaction term is *educ·exper* instead, and discuss.

4.9. Consider a linear model where the dependent variable is in logarithmic form, and the lag of $\log(y)$ is also an explanatory variable:

$$\log(y) = \beta_0 + \mathbf{x}\boldsymbol{\beta} + \alpha_1 \log(y_{-1}) + u, \qquad E(u \mid \mathbf{x}, y_{-1}) = 0$$

where the inclusion of $\log(y_{-1})$ might be to control for correlation between policy variables in $\mathbf{x}$ and a previous value of y; see Example 4.4.

a. For estimating $\boldsymbol{\beta}$, why do we obtain the same estimator if the *growth* in y, $\log(y) - \log(y_{-1})$, is used instead as the dependent variable?

b. Suppose that there are no covariates $\mathbf{x}$ in the equation. Show that, if the distributions of y and y_{-1} are identical, then $|\alpha_1| < 1$. This is the *regression-to-the-mean* phenomenon in a dynamic setting. {Hint: Show that $\alpha_1 = \text{Corr}[\log(y), \log(y_{-1})]$.}

4.10. Use Property LP.7 from Chapter 2 [particularly equation (2.56)] and Problem 2.6 to derive equation (4.47). (Hint: First use Problem 2.6 to show that the population residual r_K, in the linear projection of x_K on $1, x_1, \ldots, x_{K-1}$, is $r_K^* + e_K$. Then find the projection of y on r_K and use Property LP.7.)

4.11. a. In Example 4.3, use *KWW* and *IQ* simultaneously as proxies for ability in equation (4.29). Compare the estimated return to education without a proxy for ability and with *IQ* as the only proxy for ability.

b. Test *KWW* and *IQ* for joint significance in the estimated equation from part a.

c. When *KWW* and *IQ* are used as proxies for *abil*, does the wage differential between nonblacks and blacks disappear? What is the estimated differential?

d. Add the interactions $educ(IQ - 100)$ and $educ(KWW - \overline{KWW})$ to the regression from part a, where $\overline{KWW}$ is the average score in the sample. Are these terms jointly significant using a standard F test? Does adding them affect any important conclusions?

4.12. Redo Example 4.4, adding the variable *union*—a dummy variable indicating whether the workers at the plant are unionized—as an additional explanatory variable.

4.13. Use the data in CORNWELL.RAW (from Cornwell and Trumball, 1994) to estimate a model of county level crime rates, using the year 1987 only.

a. Using logarithms of all variables, estimate a model relating the crime rate to the deterrent variables *prbarr*, *prbconv*, *prbpris*, and *avgsen*.

b. Add $\log(crmrte)$ for 1986 as an additional explanatory variable, and comment on how the estimated elasticities differ from part a.

c. Compute the F statistic for joint significance of all of the wage variables (again in logs), using the restricted model from part b.

d. Redo part c but make the test robust to heteroskedasticity of unknown form.

4.14. Use the data in ATTEND.RAW to answer this question.

a. To determine the effects of attending lecture on final exam performance, estimate a model relating *stndfnl* (the standardized final exam score) to *atndrte* (the percent of lectures attended). Include the binary variables *frosh* and *soph* as explanatory variables. Interpret the coefficient on *atndrte*, and discuss its significance.

b. How confident are you that the OLS estimates from part a are estimating the causal effect of attendence? Explain.

c. As proxy variables for student ability, add to the regression *priGPA* (prior cumulative GPA) and *ACT* (achievement test score). Now what is the effect of *atndrte*? Discuss how the effect differs from that in part a.

d. What happens to the significance of the dummy variables in part c as compared with part a? Explain.

e. Add the squares of *priGPA* and *ACT* to the equation. What happens to the coefficient on *atndrte*? Are the quadratics jointly significant?

f. To test for a nonlinear effect of *atndrte*, add its square to the equation from part e. What do you conclude?

4.15. Assume that y and each x_j have finite second moments, and write the linear projection of y on $(1, x_1, \ldots, x_K)$ as

$$y = \beta_0 + \beta_1 x_1 + \cdots + \beta_K x_K + u = \beta_0 + \mathbf{x}\boldsymbol{\beta} + u$$

$$\mathrm{E}(u) = 0, \qquad \mathrm{E}(x_j u) = 0, \qquad j = 1, 2, \ldots, K$$

a. Show that $\sigma_y^2 = \mathrm{Var}(\mathbf{x}\boldsymbol{\beta}) + \sigma_u^2$.

b. For a random draw i from the population, write $y_i = \beta_0 + \mathbf{x}_i\boldsymbol{\beta} + u_i$. Evaluate the following assumption, which has been known to appear in econometrics textbooks: "$\mathrm{Var}(u_i) = \sigma^2 = \mathrm{Var}(y_i)$ for all i."

c. Define the population R-squared by $\rho^2 \equiv 1 - \sigma_u^2/\sigma_y^2 = \mathrm{Var}(\mathbf{x}\boldsymbol{\beta})/\sigma_y^2$. Show that the R-squared, $R^2 = 1 - \mathrm{SSR}/\mathrm{SST}$, is a consistent estimator of ρ^2, where SSR is the OLS sum of squared residuals and $\mathrm{SST} = \sum_{i=1}^{N} (y_i - \bar{y})^2$ is the total sum of squares.

d. Evaluate the following statement: "In the presence of heteroskedasticity, the R-squared from an OLS regression is meaningless." (This kind of statement also tends to appear in econometrics texts.)

5 Instrumental Variables Estimation of Single-Equation Linear Models

In this chapter we treat instrumental variables estimation, which is probably second only to ordinary least squares in terms of methods used in empirical economic research. The underlying population model is the same as in Chapter 4, but we explicitly allow the unobservable error to be correlated with the explanatory variables.

5.1 Instrumental Variables and Two-Stage Least Squares

5.1.1 Motivation for Instrumental Variables Estimation

To motivate the need for the method of instrumental variables, consider a linear population model

$$y = \beta_0 + \beta_1 x_1 + \beta_2 x_2 + \cdots + \beta_K x_K + u \tag{5.1}$$

$$\mathrm{E}(u) = 0, \qquad \mathrm{Cov}(x_j, u) = 0, \qquad j = 1, 2, \ldots, K-1 \tag{5.2}$$

but where x_K might be correlated with u. In other words, the explanatory variables x_1, $x_2, \ldots, x_{K-1}$ are exogenous, but x_K is potentially endogenous in equation (5.1). The endogeneity can come from any of the sources we discussed in Chapter 4. To fix ideas it might help to think of u as containing an omitted variable that is uncorrelated with all explanatory variables except x_K. So, we may be interested in a conditional expectation as in equation (4.18), but we do not observe q, and q is correlated with x_K.

As we saw in Chapter 4, OLS estimation of equation (5.1) generally results in inconsistent estimators of *all* the β_j if $\mathrm{Cov}(x_K, u) \neq 0$. Further, without more information, we cannot consistently estimate any of the parameters in equation (5.1).

The method of instrumental variables (IV) provides a general solution to the problem of an endogenous explanatory variable. To use the IV approach with x_K endogenous, we need an observable variable, z_1, *not* in equation (5.1) that satisfies two conditions. First, z_1 must be uncorrelated with u:

$$\mathrm{Cov}(z_1, u) = 0 \tag{5.3}$$

In other words, like $x_1, \ldots, x_{K-1}$, z_1 is exogenous in equation (5.1).

The second requirement involves the relationship between z_1 and the endogenous variable, x_K. A precise statement requires the linear projection of x_K onto *all* the exogenous variables:

$$x_K = \delta_0 + \delta_1 x_1 + \delta_2 x_2 + \cdots + \delta_{K-1} x_{K-1} + \theta_1 z_1 + r_K \tag{5.4}$$

where, by definition of a linear projection error, $\mathrm{E}(r_K) = 0$ and r_K is uncorrelated with x_1, $x_2, \ldots, x_{K-1}$, and z_1. The key assumption on this linear projection is that the coefficient on z_1 is nonzero:

$$\theta_1 \neq 0 \tag{5.5}$$

This condition is often loosely described as "z_1 is correlated with x_K," but that statement is not quite correct. The condition $\theta_1 \neq 0$ means that z_1 is *partially* correlated with x_K once the other exogenous variables $x_1, \ldots, x_{K-1}$ have been netted out. If x_K is the only explanatory variable in equation (5.1), then the linear projection is $x_K = \delta_0 + \theta_1 z_1 + r_K$, where $\theta_1 = \text{Cov}(z_1, x_K)/\text{Var}(z_1)$, and so condition (5.5) and $\text{Cov}(z_1, x_K) \neq 0$ are the same.

At this point we should mention that we have put no restrictions on the distribution of x_K or z_1. In many cases x_K and z_1 will be both essentially continuous, but sometimes x_K, z_1, or both are discrete. In fact, one or both of x_K and z_1 can be binary variables, or have continuous and discrete characteristics at the same time. Equation (5.4) is simply a linear projection, and this is always defined when second moments of all variables are finite.

When z_1 satisfies conditions (5.3) and (5.5), then it is said to be an **instrumental variable** (**IV**) candidate for x_K. (Sometimes z_1 is simply called an *instrument* for x_K.) Because $x_1, \ldots, x_{K-1}$ are already uncorrelated with u, they serve as their own instrumental variables in equation (5.1). In other words, the full list of instrumental variables is the same as the list of exogenous variables, but we often just refer to the instrument for the endogenous explanatory variable.

The linear projection in equation (5.4) is called a **reduced form equation** for the endogenous explanatory variable x_K. In the context of single-equation linear models, a reduced form always involves writing an endogenous variable as a linear projection onto all exogenous variables. The "reduced form" terminology comes from simultaneous equations analysis, and it makes more sense in that context. We use it in all IV contexts because it is a concise way of stating that an endogenous variable has been linearly projected onto the exogenous variables. The terminology also conveys that there is nothing necessarily structural about equation (5.4).

From the structural equation (5.1) and the reduced form for x_K, we obtain a reduced form for y by plugging equation (5.4) into equation (5.1) and rearranging:

$$y = \alpha_0 + \alpha_1 x_1 + \cdots + \alpha_{K-1} x_{K-1} + \lambda_1 z_1 + v \tag{5.6}$$

where $v = u + \beta_K r_K$ is the reduced form error, $\alpha_j = \beta_j + \beta_K \delta_j$, and $\lambda_1 = \beta_K \theta_1$. By our assumptions, v is uncorrelated with all explanatory variables in equation (5.6), and so OLS consistently estimates the reduced form parameters, the α_j and λ_1.

Estimates of the reduced form parameters are sometimes of interest in their own right, but estimating the structural parameters is generally more useful. For example, at the firm level, suppose that x_K is job training hours per worker and y is a measure of average worker productivity. Suppose that job training grants were randomly assigned to firms. Then it is natural to use for z_1 either a binary variable indicating whether a firm received a job training grant or the actual amount of the grant per worker (if the amount varies by firm). The parameter β_K in equation (5.1) is the effect of job training on worker productivity. If z_1 is a binary variable for receiving a job training grant, then λ_1 is the effect of receiving this particular job training grant on worker productivity, which is of some interest. But estimating the effect of an hour of general job training is more valuable.

We can now show that the assumptions we have made on the IV z_1 solve the **identification problem** for the β_j in equation (5.1). By identification we mean that we can write the β_j in terms of population moments in observable variables. To see how, write equation (5.1) as

$$y = \mathbf{x}\boldsymbol{\beta} + u \tag{5.7}$$

where the constant is absorbed into $\mathbf{x}$ so that $\mathbf{x} = (1, x_2, \ldots, x_K)$. Write the $1 \times K$ vector of all exogenous variables as

$$\mathbf{z} \equiv (1, x_2, \ldots, x_{K-1}, z_1)$$

Assumptions (5.2) and (5.3) imply the K population orthogonality conditions

$$\mathrm{E}(\mathbf{z}'u) = \mathbf{0} \tag{5.8}$$

Multiplying equation (5.7) through by $\mathbf{z}'$, taking expectations, and using equation (5.8) gives

$$[\mathrm{E}(\mathbf{z}'\mathbf{x})]\boldsymbol{\beta} = \mathrm{E}(\mathbf{z}'y) \tag{5.9}$$

where $\mathrm{E}(\mathbf{z}'\mathbf{x})$ is $K \times K$ and $\mathrm{E}(\mathbf{z}'y)$ is $K \times 1$. Equation (5.9) represents a system of K linear equations in the K unknowns $\beta_1, \beta_2, \ldots, \beta_K$. This system has a unique solution if and only if the $K \times K$ matrix $\mathrm{E}(\mathbf{z}'\mathbf{x})$ has full rank; that is,

$$\text{rank } \mathrm{E}(\mathbf{z}'\mathbf{x}) = K \tag{5.10}$$

in which case the solution is

$$\boldsymbol{\beta} = [\mathrm{E}(\mathbf{z}'\mathbf{x})]^{-1}\mathrm{E}(\mathbf{z}'y) \tag{5.11}$$

The expectations $\mathrm{E}(\mathbf{z}'\mathbf{x})$ and $\mathrm{E}(\mathbf{z}'y)$ can be consistently estimated using a random sample on $(\mathbf{x}, y, z_1)$, and so equation (5.11) identifies the vector $\boldsymbol{\beta}$.

It is clear that condition (5.3) was used to obtain equation (5.11). But where have we used condition (5.5)? Let us maintain that there are no linear dependencies among the exogenous variables, so that $\mathrm{E}(\mathbf{z}'\mathbf{z})$ has full rank K; this simply rules out perfect collinearity in $\mathbf{z}$ in the population. Then, it can be shown that equation (5.10) holds if and only if $\theta_1 \neq 0$. (A more general case, which we cover in Section 5.1.2, is covered in Problem 5.12.) Therefore, along with the exogeneity condition (5.3), assumption (5.5) is the key identification condition. Assumption (5.10) is the **rank condition** for identification, and we return to it more generally in Section 5.2.1.

Given a random sample $\{(\mathbf{x}_i, y_i, \mathbf{z}_{i1}): i = 1, 2, \ldots, N\}$ from the population, the **instrumental variables estimator** of $\boldsymbol{\beta}$ is

$$\hat{\boldsymbol{\beta}} = \left(N^{-1}\sum_{i=1}^{N} \mathbf{z}_i'\mathbf{x}_i\right)^{-1}\left(N^{-1}\sum_{i=1}^{N} \mathbf{z}_i' y_i\right) = (\mathbf{Z}'\mathbf{X})^{-1}\mathbf{Z}'\mathbf{Y}$$

where $\mathbf{Z}$ and $\mathbf{X}$ are $N \times K$ data matrices and $\mathbf{Y}$ is the $N \times 1$ data vector on the y_i. The consistency of this estimator is immediate from equation (5.11) and the law of large numbers. We consider a more general case in Section 5.2.1.

When searching for instruments for an endogenous explanatory variable, conditions (5.3) and (5.5) are equally important in identifying $\boldsymbol{\beta}$. There is, however, one practically important difference between them: condition (5.5) can be tested, whereas condition (5.3) must be maintained. The reason for this disparity is simple: the covariance in condition (5.3) involves the *unobservable* u, and therefore we cannot test anything about $\text{Cov}(z_1, u)$.

Testing condition (5.5) in the reduced form (5.4) is a simple matter of computing a t test after OLS estimation. Nothing guarantees that r_K satisfies the requisite homoskedasticity assumption (Assumption OLS.3), so a heteroskedasticity-robust t statistic for $\hat{\theta}_1$ is often warranted. This statement is especially true if x_K is a binary variable or some other variable with discrete characteristics.

A word of caution is in order here. Econometricians have been known to say that "it is not possible to test for identification." In the model with one endogenous variable and one instrument, we have just seen the sense in which this statement is true: assumption (5.3) cannot be tested. Nevertheless, the fact remains that condition (5.5) can and *should* be tested. In fact, recent work has shown that the strength of the rejection in condition (5.5) (in a p-value sense) is important for determining the finite sample properties, particularly the bias, of the IV estimator. We return to this issue in Section 5.2.6.

In the context of omitted variables, an instrumental variable, like a proxy variable, must be redundant in the structural model [that is, the model that explicitly contains the unobservables; see condition (4.25)]. However, unlike a proxy variable, an IV for x_K should be *uncorrelated* with the omitted variable. Remember, we want a proxy variable to be highly correlated with the omitted variable.

Example 5.1 (Instrumental Variables for Education in a Wage Equation): Consider a wage equation for the U.S. working population

$$\log(wage) = \beta_0 + \beta_1 exper + \beta_2 exper^2 + \beta_3 educ + u \tag{5.12}$$

where u is thought to be correlated with *educ* because of omitted ability, as well as other factors, such as quality of education and family background. Suppose that we can collect data on mother's education, *motheduc*. For this to be a valid instrument for *educ* we must assume that *motheduc* is uncorrelated with u and that $\theta_1 \neq 0$ in the reduced form equation

$$educ = \delta_0 + \delta_1 exper + \delta_2 exper^2 + \theta_1 motheduc + r$$

There is little doubt that *educ* and *motheduc* are partially correlated, and this correlation is easily tested given a random sample from the population. The potential problem with *motheduc* as an instrument for *educ* is that *motheduc* might be correlated with the omitted factors in u: mother's education is likely to be correlated with child's ability and other family background characteristics that might be in u.

A variable such as the last digit of one's social security number makes a poor IV candidate for the opposite reason. Because the last digit is randomly determined, it is independent of other factors that affect earnings. But it is also independent of education. Therefore, while condition (5.3) holds, condition (5.5) does not.

By being clever it is often possible to come up with more convincing instruments. Angrist and Krueger (1991) propose using quarter of birth as an IV for education. In the simplest case, let *frstqrt* be a dummy variable equal to unity for people born in the first quarter of the year and zero otherwise. Quarter of birth is arguably independent of unobserved factors such as ability that affect wage (although there is disagreement on this point; see Bound, Jaeger, and Baker, 1995). In addition, we must have $\theta_1 \neq 0$ in the reduced form

$$educ = \delta_0 + \delta_1 exper + \delta_2 exper^2 + \theta_1 frstqrt + r$$

How can quarter of birth be (partially) correlated with educational attainment? Angrist and Krueger (1991) argue that compulsory school attendence laws induce a relationship between *educ* and *frstqrt*: at least some people are forced, by law, to attend school longer than they otherwise would, and this fact is correlated with quarter of birth. We can determine the strength of this association in a particular sample by estimating the reduced form and obtaining the t statistic for H_0: $\theta_1 = 0$.

This example illustrates that it can be very difficult to find a good instrumental variable for an endogenous explanatory variable because the variable must satisfy two different, often conflicting, criteria. For *motheduc*, the issue in doubt is whether condition (5.3) holds. For *frstqrt*, the initial concern is with condition (5.5). Since condition (5.5) can be tested, *frstqrt* has more appeal as an instrument. However, the partial correlation between *educ* and *frstqrt* is small, and this can lead to finite sample problems (see Section 5.2.6). A more subtle issue concerns the sense in which we are estimating the return to education for the entire population of working people. As we will see in Chapter 18, if the return to education is not constant across people, the IV estimator that uses *frstqrt* as an IV estimates the return to education only for those people induced to obtain more schooling because they were born in the first quarter of the year. These make up a relatively small fraction of the population.

Convincing instruments sometimes arise in the context of program evaluation, where individuals are randomly selected to be eligible for the program. Examples include job training programs and school voucher programs. Actual participation is almost always voluntary, and it may be endogenous because it can depend on unobserved factors that affect the response. However, it is often reasonable to assume that eligibility is exogenous. Because participation and eligibility are correlated, the latter can be used as an IV for the former.

A valid instrumental variable can also come from what is called a **natural experiment**. A natural experiment occurs when some (often unintended) feature of the setup we are studying produces exogenous variation in an otherwise endogenous explanatory variable. The Angrist and Krueger (1991) example seems, at least initially, to be a good natural experiment. Another example is given by Angrist (1990), who studies the effect of serving in the Vietnam war on the earnings of men. Participation in the military is not necessarily exogenous to unobserved factors that affect earnings, even after controlling for education, nonmilitary experience, and so on. Angrist used the following observation to obtain an instrumental variable for the binary Vietnam war participation indicator: men with a lower draft lottery number were more likely to serve in the war. Angrist verifies that the probability of serving in Vietnam is indeed related to draft lottery number. Because the lottery number is randomly determined, it seems like an ideal IV for serving in Vietnam. There are, however, some potential problems. It might be that men who were assigned a low lottery number chose to obtain more education as a way of increasing the chance of obtaining a draft deferment. If we do not control for education in the earnings equation, lottery number could be endogenous. Further, employers may have been willing to invest in job training for men who are unlikely to be drafted. Again, unless we can include measures of job training in the earnings equation, condition (5.3) may be violated. (This reasoning assumes that we are interested in estimating the pure effect of serving in Vietnam, as opposed to including indirect effects such as reduced job training.)

Hoxby (1994) uses topographical features, in particular the natural boundaries created by rivers, as IVs for the concentration of public schools within a school district. She uses these IVs to estimate the effects of competition among public schools on student performance. Cutler and Glaeser (1997) use the Hoxby instruments, as well as others, to estimate the effects of segregation on schooling and employment outcomes for blacks. Levitt (1997) provides another example of obtaining instrumental variables from a natural experiment. He uses the timing of mayoral and gubernatorial elections as instruments for size of the police force in estimating the effects of police on city crime rates. (Levitt actually uses panel data, something we will discuss in Chapter 11.)

Sensible IVs need not come from natural experiments. For example, Evans and Schwab (1995) study the effect of attending a Catholic high school on various outcomes. They use a binary variable for whether a student is Catholic as an IV for attending a Catholic high school, and they spend much effort arguing that religion is exogenous in their versions of equation (5.7). [In this application, condition (5.5) is easy to verify.] Economists often use regional variation in prices or taxes as instruments for endogenous explanatory variables appearing in individual-level equations. For example, in estimating the effects of alcohol consumption on performance in college, the local price of alcohol can be used as an IV for alcohol consumption, provided other regional factors that affect college performance have been appropriately controlled for. The idea is that the price of alcohol, including any taxes, can be assumed to be exogenous to each individual.

Example 5.2 (College Proximity as an IV for Education): Using wage data for 1976, Card (1995) uses a dummy variable that indicates whether a man grew up in the vicinity of a four-year college as an instrumental variable for years of schooling. He also includes several other controls. In the equation with experience and its square, a black indicator, southern and urban indicators, and regional and urban indicators for 1966, the instrumental variables estimate of the return to schooling is .132, or 13.2 percent, while the OLS estimate is 7.5 percent. Thus, for this sample of data, the IV estimate is almost twice as large as the OLS estimate. This result would be counterintuitive if we thought that an OLS analysis suffered from an upward omitted variable bias. One interpretation is that the OLS estimators suffer from the attenuation bias as a result of measurement error, as we discussed in Section 4.4.2. But the classical errors-in-variables assumption for education is questionable. Another interpretation is that the instrumental variable is not exogenous in the wage equation: location is not entirely exogenous. The full set of estimates, including standard errors and t statistics, can be found in Card (1995). Or, you can replicate Card's results in Problem 5.4.

5.1.2 Multiple Instruments: Two-Stage Least Squares

Consider again the model (5.1) and (5.2), where x_K can be correlated with u. Now, however, assume that we have more than one instrumental variable for x_K. Let $z_1, z_2, \dots, z_M$ be variables such that

$$\text{Cov}(z_h, u) = 0, \qquad h = 1, 2, \dots, M \tag{5.13}$$

so that each z_h is exogenous in equation (5.1). If each of these has some partial correlation with x_K, we could have M different IV estimators. Actually, there are many more than this—more than we can count—since any linear combination of $x_1, x_2, \dots, x_{K-1}, z_1, z_2, \dots, z_M$ is uncorrelated with u. So which IV estimator should we use?

In Section 5.2.3 we show that, under certain assumptions, the **two-stage least squares (2SLS) estimator** is the most efficient IV estimator. For now, we rely on intuition.

To illustrate the method of 2SLS, define the vector of exogenous variables again by $\mathbf{z} \equiv (1, x_1, x_2, \dots, x_{K-1}, z_1, \dots, z_M)$, a $1 \times L$ vector $(L = K + M)$. Out of all possible linear combinations of $\mathbf{z}$ that can be used as an instrument for x_K, the method of 2SLS chooses that which is most highly correlated with x_K. If x_K were exogenous, then this choice would imply that the best instrument for x_K is simply itself. Ruling this case out, the linear combination of $\mathbf{z}$ most highly correlated with x_K is given by the linear projection of x_K on $\mathbf{z}$. Write the reduced form for x_K as

$$x_K = \delta_0 + \delta_1 x_1 + \cdots + \delta_{K-1} x_{K-1} + \theta_1 z_1 + \cdots + \theta_M z_M + r_K \tag{5.14}$$

where, by definition, r_K has zero mean and is uncorrelated with each right-hand-side variable. As any linear combination of $\mathbf{z}$ is uncorrelated with u,

$$x_K^* \equiv \delta_0 + \delta_1 x_1 + \cdots + \delta_{K-1} x_{K-1} + \theta_1 z_1 + \cdots + \theta_M z_M \tag{5.15}$$

is uncorrelated with u. In fact, x_K^* is often interpreted as the part of x_K that is uncorrelated with u. If x_K is endogenous, it is because r_K is correlated with u.

If we could observe x_K^*, we would use it as an instrument for x_K in equation (5.1) and use the IV estimator from the previous subsection. Since the δ_j and θ_j are population parameters, x_K^* is not a usable instrument. However, as long as we make the standard assumption that there are no exact linear dependencies among the exogenous variables, we can consistently estimate the parameters in equation (5.14) by OLS. The sample analogues of the x_{iK}^* for each observation i are simply the OLS fitted values:

$$\hat{x}_{iK} = \hat{\delta}_0 + \hat{\delta}_1 x_{i1} + \cdots + \hat{\delta}_{K-1} x_{i,K-1} + \hat{\theta}_1 z_{i1} + \cdots + \hat{\theta}_M z_{iM} \tag{5.16}$$

Now, for each observation i, define the vector $\hat{\mathbf{x}}_i \equiv (1, x_{i1}, \dots, x_{i,K-1}, \hat{x}_{iK})$, $i = 1, 2, \dots, N$. Using $\hat{\mathbf{x}}_i$ as the instruments for $\mathbf{x}_i$ gives the IV estimator

$$\hat{\boldsymbol{\beta}} = \left(\sum_{i=1}^{N} \hat{\mathbf{x}}_i' \mathbf{x}_i\right)^{-1} \left(\sum_{i=1}^{N} \hat{\mathbf{x}}_i' y_i\right) = (\hat{\mathbf{X}}'\mathbf{X})^{-1}\hat{\mathbf{X}}'\mathbf{Y} \tag{5.17}$$

where unity is also the first element of $\mathbf{x}_i$.

The IV estimator in equation (5.17) turns out to be an OLS estimator. To see this fact, note that the $N \times (K+1)$ matrix $\hat{\mathbf{X}}$ can be expressed as $\hat{\mathbf{X}} = \mathbf{Z}(\mathbf{Z}'\mathbf{Z})^{-1}\mathbf{Z}'\mathbf{X} = \mathbf{P}_Z\mathbf{X}$, where the projection matrix $\mathbf{P}_Z = \mathbf{Z}(\mathbf{Z}'\mathbf{Z})^{-1}\mathbf{Z}'$ is idempotent and symmetric. Therefore, $\hat{\mathbf{X}}'\mathbf{X} = \mathbf{X}'\mathbf{P}_Z\mathbf{X} = (\mathbf{P}_Z\mathbf{X})'\mathbf{P}_Z\mathbf{X} = \hat{\mathbf{X}}'\hat{\mathbf{X}}$. Plugging this expression into equation (5.17) shows that the IV estimator that uses instruments $\hat{\mathbf{x}}_i$ can be written as $\hat{\boldsymbol{\beta}} = (\hat{\mathbf{X}}'\hat{\mathbf{X}})^{-1}\hat{\mathbf{X}}'\mathbf{Y}$. The name "two-stage least squares" comes from this procedure.

To summarize, $\hat{\boldsymbol{\beta}}$ can be obtained from the following steps:

1. Obtain the fitted values $\hat{x}_K$ from the regression

$$x_K \text{ on } 1,\ x_1, \dots, x_{K-1}, z_1, \dots, z_M \tag{5.18}$$

where the i subscript is omitted for simplicity. This is called the **first-stage regression.**

2. Run the OLS regression

$$y \text{ on } 1,\ x_1, \dots, x_{K-1}, \hat{x}_K \tag{5.19}$$

This is called the **second-stage regression**, and it produces the $\hat{\beta}_j$.

In practice, it is best to use a software package with a 2SLS command rather than explicitly carry out the two-step procedure. Carrying out the two-step procedure explicitly makes one susceptible to harmful mistakes. For example, the following, seemingly sensible, two-step procedure is generally inconsistent: (1) regress x_K on $1, z_1, \dots, z_M$ and obtain the fitted values, say $\tilde{x}_K$; (2) run the regression in (5.19) with $\tilde{x}_K$ in place of $\hat{x}_K$. Problem 5.11 asks you to show that omitting $x_1, \dots, x_{K-1}$ in the first-stage regression and then explicitly doing the second-stage regression produces inconsistent estimators of the β_j.

Another reason to avoid the two-step procedure is that the OLS standard errors reported with regression (5.19) will be incorrect, something that will become clear later. Sometimes for hypothesis testing we need to carry out the second-stage regression explicitly—see Section 5.2.4.

The 2SLS estimator and the IV estimator from Section 5.1.1 are identical when there is only one instrument for x_K. Unless stated otherwise, we mean 2SLS whenever we talk about IV estimation of a single equation.

What is the analogue of the condition (5.5) when more than one instrument is available with one endogenous explanatory variable? Problem 5.12 asks you to show that $\mathrm{E}(\mathbf{z}'\mathbf{x})$ has full column rank if and only if at least one of the θ_j in equation (5.14) is nonzero. The intuition behind this requirement is pretty clear: we need at least one exogenous variable that does not appear in equation (5.1) to induce variation in x_K that cannot be explained by $x_1, \ldots, x_{K-1}$. Identification of $\boldsymbol{\beta}$ does *not* depend on the values of the δ_h in equation (5.14).

Testing the rank condition with a single endogenous explanatory variable and multiple instruments is straightforward. In equation (5.14) we simply test the null hypothesis

$$\mathrm{H}_0\colon \theta_1 = 0,\ \theta_2 = 0, \ldots, \theta_M = 0 \tag{5.20}$$

against the alternative that at least one of the θ_j is different from zero. This test gives a compelling reason for explicitly running the first-stage regression. If r_K in equation (5.14) satisfies the OLS homoskedasticity assumption OLS.3, a standard F statistic or Lagrange multiplier statistic can be used to test hypothesis (5.20). Often a heteroskedasticity-robust statistic is more appropriate, especially if x_K has discrete characteristics. If we cannot reject hypothesis (5.20) against the alternative that at least one θ_h is different from zero, at a reasonably small significance level, then we should have serious reservations about the proposed 2SLS procedure: the instruments do not pass a minimal requirement.

The model with a single endogenous variable is said to be **overidentified** when $M > 1$ and there are $M - 1$ **overidentifying restrictions**. This terminology comes from the fact that, if each z_h has some partial correlation with x_K, then we have $M - 1$ more exogenous variables than needed to identify the parameters in equation (5.1). For example, if $M = 2$, we could discard one of the instruments and still achieve identification. In Chapter 6 we will show how to test the validity of any overidentifying restrictions.

5.2 General Treatment of 2SLS

5.2.1 Consistency

We now summarize asymptotic results for 2SLS in a single-equation model with perhaps several endogenous variables among the explanatory variables. Write the population model as in equation (5.7), where $\mathbf{x}$ is $1 \times K$ and generally includes unity. Several elements of $\mathbf{x}$ may be correlated with u. As usual, we assume that a random sample is available from the population.

ASSUMPTION 2SLS.1: For some $1 \times L$ vector $\mathbf{z}$, $\mathrm{E}(\mathbf{z}'u) = \mathbf{0}$.

Here we do not specify where the elements of $\mathbf{z}$ come from, but any exogenous elements of $\mathbf{x}$, including a constant, are included in $\mathbf{z}$. Unless every element of $\mathbf{x}$ is exogenous, $\mathbf{z}$ will have to contain variables obtained from outside the model. The zero conditional mean assumption, $\mathrm{E}(u \mid \mathbf{z}) = 0$, implies Assumption 2SLS.1.

The next assumption contains the general rank condition for single-equation analysis.

ASSUMPTION 2SLS.2: (a) rank $\mathrm{E}(\mathbf{z}'\mathbf{z}) = L$; (b) rank $\mathrm{E}(\mathbf{z}'\mathbf{x}) = K$.

Technically, part a of this assumption is needed, but it is not especially important, since the exogenous variables, unless chosen unwisely, will be linearly independent in the population (as well as in a typical sample). Part b is the crucial **rank condition** for identification. In a precise sense it means that $\mathbf{z}$ is sufficiently linearly related to $\mathbf{x}$ so that rank $\mathrm{E}(\mathbf{z}'\mathbf{x})$ has full column rank. We discussed this concept in Section 5.1 for the situation in which $\mathbf{x}$ contains a single endogenous variable. When $\mathbf{x}$ is exogenous, so that $\mathbf{z} = \mathbf{x}$, Assumption 2SLS.1 reduces to Assumption OLS.1 and Assumption 2SLS.2 reduces to Assumption OLS.2.

Necessary for the rank condition is the **order condition**, $L \geq K$. In other words, we must have at least as many instruments as we have explanatory variables. If we do not have as many instruments as right-hand-side variables, then $\boldsymbol{\beta}$ is not identified. However, $L \geq K$ is no guarantee that 2SLS.2b holds: the elements of $\mathbf{z}$ might not be appropriately correlated with the elements of $\mathbf{x}$.

We already know how to test Assumption 2SLS.2b with a single endogenous explanatory variable. In the general case, it is possible to test Assumption 2SLS.2b, given a random sample on $(\mathbf{x}, \mathbf{z})$, essentially by performing tests on the sample analogue of $\mathrm{E}(\mathbf{z}'\mathbf{x})$, $\mathbf{Z}'\mathbf{X}/N$. The tests are somewhat complicated; see, for example Cragg and Donald (1996). Often we estimate the reduced form for each endogenous explanatory variable to make sure that at least one element of $\mathbf{z}$ not in $\mathbf{x}$ is significant. This is not sufficient for the rank condition in general, but it can help us determine if the rank condition fails.

Using linear projections, there is a simple way to see how Assumptions 2SLS.1 and 2SLS.2 identify $\boldsymbol{\beta}$. First, assuming that $\mathrm{E}(\mathbf{z}'\mathbf{z})$ is nonsingular, we can always write the linear projection of $\mathbf{x}$ onto $\mathbf{z}$ as $\mathbf{x}^* = \mathbf{z}\boldsymbol{\Pi}$, where $\boldsymbol{\Pi}$ is the $L \times K$ matrix $\boldsymbol{\Pi} = [\mathrm{E}(\mathbf{z}'\mathbf{z})]^{-1}\mathrm{E}(\mathbf{z}'\mathbf{x})$. Since each column of $\boldsymbol{\Pi}$ can be consistently estimated by regressing the appropriate element of $\mathbf{x}$ onto $\mathbf{z}$, for the purposes of identification of $\boldsymbol{\beta}$, we can treat $\boldsymbol{\Pi}$ as known. Write $\mathbf{x} = \mathbf{x}^* + \mathbf{r}$, where $\mathrm{E}(\mathbf{z}'\mathbf{r}) = \mathbf{0}$ and so $\mathrm{E}(\mathbf{x}^{*\prime}\mathbf{r}) = \mathbf{0}$. Now, the 2SLS estimator is effectively the IV estimator using instruments $\mathbf{x}^*$. Multiplying equation (5.7) by $\mathbf{x}^{*\prime}$, taking expectations, and rearranging gives

$$\mathrm{E}(\mathbf{x}^{*\prime}\mathbf{x})\boldsymbol{\beta} = \mathrm{E}(\mathbf{x}^{*\prime}y) \tag{5.21}$$

since $\mathrm{E}(\mathbf{x}^{*\prime}u) = \mathbf{0}$. Thus, $\boldsymbol{\beta}$ is identified by $\boldsymbol{\beta} = [\mathrm{E}(\mathbf{x}^{*\prime}\mathbf{x})]^{-1}\mathrm{E}(\mathbf{x}^{*\prime}y)$ provided $\mathrm{E}(\mathbf{x}^{*\prime}\mathbf{x})$ is nonsingular. But

$$\mathrm{E}(\mathbf{x}^{*\prime}\mathbf{x}) = \boldsymbol{\Pi}'\mathrm{E}(\mathbf{z}'\mathbf{x}) = \mathrm{E}(\mathbf{x}'\mathbf{z})[\mathrm{E}(\mathbf{z}'\mathbf{z})]^{-1}\mathrm{E}(\mathbf{z}'\mathbf{x})$$

and this matrix is nonsingular if and only if $\mathrm{E}(\mathbf{z}'\mathbf{x})$ has rank K; that is, if and only if Assumption 2SLS.2b holds. If 2SLS.2b fails, then $\mathrm{E}(\mathbf{x}^{*\prime}\mathbf{x})$ is singular and $\boldsymbol{\beta}$ is not identified. [Note that, because $\mathbf{x} = \mathbf{x}^* + \mathbf{r}$ with $\mathrm{E}(\mathbf{x}^{*\prime}\mathbf{r}) = \mathbf{0}$, $\mathrm{E}(\mathbf{x}^{*\prime}\mathbf{x}) = \mathrm{E}(\mathbf{x}^{*\prime}\mathbf{x}^*)$. So $\boldsymbol{\beta}$ is identified if and only if rank $\mathrm{E}(\mathbf{x}^{*\prime}\mathbf{x}^*) = K$.]

The 2SLS estimator can be written as in equation (5.17) or as

$$\hat{\boldsymbol{\beta}} = \left[\left(\sum_{i=1}^{N}\mathbf{x}_i'\mathbf{z}_i\right)\left(\sum_{i=1}^{N}\mathbf{z}_i'\mathbf{z}_i\right)^{-1}\left(\sum_{i=1}^{N}\mathbf{z}_i'\mathbf{x}_i\right)\right]^{-1}\left(\sum_{i=1}^{N}\mathbf{x}_i'\mathbf{z}_i\right)\left(\sum_{i=1}^{N}\mathbf{z}_i'\mathbf{z}_i\right)^{-1}\left(\sum_{i=1}^{N}\mathbf{z}_i'y_i\right) \tag{5.22}$$

We have the following consistency result.

Theorem 5.1 (Consistency of 2SLS): Under Assumptions 2SLS.1 and 2SLS.2, the 2SLS estimator obtained from a random sample is consistent for $\boldsymbol{\beta}$.

Proof: Write

$$\hat{\boldsymbol{\beta}} = \boldsymbol{\beta} + \left[\left(N^{-1}\sum_{i=1}^{N}\mathbf{x}_i'\mathbf{z}_i\right)\left(N^{-1}\sum_{i=1}^{N}\mathbf{z}_i'\mathbf{z}_i\right)^{-1}\left(N^{-1}\sum_{i=1}^{N}\mathbf{z}_i'\mathbf{x}_i\right)\right]^{-1}$$

$$\cdot\left(N^{-1}\sum_{i=1}^{N}\mathbf{x}_i'\mathbf{z}_i\right)\left(N^{-1}\sum_{i=1}^{N}\mathbf{z}_i'\mathbf{z}_i\right)^{-1}\left(N^{-1}\sum_{i=1}^{N}\mathbf{z}_i'u_i\right)$$

and, using Assumptions 2SLS.1 and 2SLS.2, apply the law of large numbers to each term along with Slutsky's theorem.

5.2.2 Asymptotic Normality of 2SLS

The asymptotic normality of $\sqrt{N}(\hat{\boldsymbol{\beta}} - \boldsymbol{\beta})$ follows from the asymptotic normality of $N^{-1/2}\sum_{i=1}^{N}\mathbf{z}_i'u_i$, which follows from the central limit theorem under Assumption 2SLS.1 and mild finite second-moment assumptions. The asymptotic variance is simplest under a homoskedasticity assumption:

ASSUMPTION 2SLS.3: $\mathrm{E}(u^2\mathbf{z}'\mathbf{z}) = \sigma^2\mathrm{E}(\mathbf{z}'\mathbf{z})$, where $\sigma^2 = \mathrm{E}(u^2)$.

This assumption is the same as Assumption OLS.3 except that the vector of instruments appears in place of $\mathbf{x}$. By the usual LIE argument, sufficient for Assumption 2SLS.3 is the assumption

$$\mathrm{E}(u^2 \mid \mathbf{z}) = \sigma^2 \tag{5.23}$$

which is the same as $\mathrm{Var}(u \mid \mathbf{z}) = \sigma^2$ if $\mathrm{E}(u \mid \mathbf{z}) = 0$. [When $\mathbf{x}$ contains endogenous elements, it makes no sense to make assumptions about $\mathrm{Var}(u \mid \mathbf{x})$.]

THEOREM 5.2 (Asymptotic Normality of 2SLS): Under Assumptions 2SLS.1–2SLS.3, $\sqrt{N}(\hat{\boldsymbol{\beta}} - \boldsymbol{\beta})$ is asymptotically normally distributed with mean zero and variance matrix

$$\sigma^2\{\mathrm{E}(\mathbf{x}'\mathbf{z})[\mathrm{E}(\mathbf{z}'\mathbf{z})]^{-1}\mathrm{E}(\mathbf{z}'\mathbf{x})\}^{-1} \tag{5.24}$$

The proof of Theorem 5.2 is similar to Theorem 4.2 for OLS and is therefore omitted.

The matrix in expression (5.24) is easily estimated using sample averages. To estimate σ^2 we will need appropriate estimates of the u_i. Define the **2SLS residuals** as

$$\hat{u}_i = y_i - \mathbf{x}_i\hat{\boldsymbol{\beta}}, \qquad i = 1, 2, \ldots, N \tag{5.25}$$

Note carefully that these residuals are *not* the residuals from the second-stage OLS regression that can be used to obtain the 2SLS estimates. The residuals from the second-stage regression are $y_i - \hat{\mathbf{x}}_i\hat{\boldsymbol{\beta}}$. Any 2SLS software routine will compute equation (5.25) as the 2SLS residuals, and these are what we need to estimate σ^2.

Given the 2SLS residuals, a consistent (though not unbiased) estimator of σ^2 under Assumptions 2SLS.1–2SLS.3 is

$$\hat{\sigma}^2 \equiv (N - K)^{-1} \sum_{i=1}^{N} \hat{u}_i^2 \tag{5.26}$$

Many regression packages use the degrees of freedom adjustment $N - K$ in place of N, but this usage does not affect the consistency of the estimator.

The $K \times K$ matrix

$$\hat{\sigma}^2 \left(\sum_{i=1}^{N} \hat{\mathbf{x}}_i'\hat{\mathbf{x}}_i \right)^{-1} = \hat{\sigma}^2(\hat{\mathbf{X}}'\hat{\mathbf{X}})^{-1} \tag{5.27}$$

is a valid estimator of the asymptotic variance of $\hat{\boldsymbol{\beta}}$ under Assumptions 2SLS.1–2SLS.3. The (asymptotic) standard error of $\hat{\beta}_j$ is just the square root of the jth diagonal element of matrix (5.27). Asymptotic confidence intervals and t statistics are obtained in the usual fashion.

Example 5.3 (Parents' and Husband's Education as IVs): We use the data on the 428 working, married women in MROZ.RAW to estimate the wage equation (5.12). We assume that experience is exogenous, but we allow *educ* to be correlated with u. The instruments we use for *educ* are *motheduc*, *fatheduc*, and *huseduc*. The reduced form for *educ* is

$$educ = \delta_0 + \delta_1 exper + \delta_2 exper^2 + \theta_1 motheduc + \theta_2 fatheduc + \theta_3 huseduc + r$$

Assuming that *motheduc*, *fatheduc*, and *huseduc* are exogenous in the log(*wage*) equation (a tenuous assumption), equation (5.12) is identified if at least one of θ_1, θ_2, and θ_3 is nonzero. We can test this assumption using an F test (under homoskedasticity). The F statistic (with 3 and 422 degrees of freedom) turns out to be 104.29, which implies a p-value of zero to four decimal places. Thus, as expected, *educ* is fairly strongly related to *motheduc*, *fatheduc*, and *huseduc*. (Each of the three t statistics is also very significant.)

When equation (5.12) is estimated by 2SLS, we get the following:

$$\begin{aligned}\log(\widehat{wage}) = \underset{(.285)}{-.187} + \underset{(.013)}{.043}\, exper - \underset{(.00040)}{.00086}\, exper^2 + \underset{(.022)}{.080}\, educ\end{aligned}$$

where standard errors are in parentheses. The 2SLS estimate of the return to education is about 8 percent, and it is statistically significant. For comparison, when equation (5.12) is estimated by OLS, the estimated coefficient on *educ* is about .107 with a standard error of about .014. Thus, the 2SLS estimate is notably below the OLS estimate and has a larger standard error.

5.2.3 Asymptotic Efficiency of 2SLS

The appeal of 2SLS comes from its efficiency in a class of IV estimators:

THEOREM 5.3 (Relative Efficiency of 2SLS): Under Assumptions 2SLS.1–2SLS.3, the 2SLS estimator is efficient in the class of all instrumental variables estimators using instruments linear in $\mathbf{z}$.

Proof: Let $\hat{\boldsymbol{\beta}}$ be the 2SLS estimator, and let $\tilde{\boldsymbol{\beta}}$ be any other IV estimator using instruments linear in $\mathbf{z}$. Let the instruments for $\tilde{\boldsymbol{\beta}}$ be $\tilde{\mathbf{x}} \equiv \mathbf{z}\boldsymbol{\Gamma}$, where $\boldsymbol{\Gamma}$ is an $L \times K$ nonstochastic matrix. (Note that $\mathbf{z}$ is the $1 \times L$ random vector in the population.) We assume that the rank condition holds for $\tilde{\mathbf{x}}$. For 2SLS, the choice of IVs is effectively $\mathbf{x}^* = \mathbf{z}\boldsymbol{\Pi}$, where $\boldsymbol{\Pi} = [\mathrm{E}(\mathbf{z}'\mathbf{z})]^{-1}\mathrm{E}(\mathbf{z}'\mathbf{x}) \equiv \mathbf{D}^{-1}\mathbf{C}$. (In both cases, we can replace $\boldsymbol{\Gamma}$ and $\boldsymbol{\Pi}$ with $\sqrt{N}$-consistent estimators without changing the asymptotic variances.) Now, under Assumptions 2SLS.1–2SLS.3, we know the asymptotic variance of $\sqrt{N}(\hat{\boldsymbol{\beta}} - \boldsymbol{\beta})$ is $\sigma^2[\mathrm{E}(\mathbf{x}^{*\prime}\mathbf{x}^*)]^{-1}$, where $\mathbf{x}^* = \mathbf{z}\boldsymbol{\Pi}$. It is straightforward to show that $\mathrm{Avar}[\sqrt{N}(\tilde{\boldsymbol{\beta}} - \boldsymbol{\beta})] = \sigma^2[\mathrm{E}(\tilde{\mathbf{x}}'\mathbf{x})]^{-1}[\mathrm{E}(\tilde{\mathbf{x}}'\tilde{\mathbf{x}})][\mathrm{E}(\mathbf{x}'\tilde{\mathbf{x}})]^{-1}$. To show that $\mathrm{Avar}[\sqrt{N}(\tilde{\boldsymbol{\beta}} - \boldsymbol{\beta})] - \mathrm{Avar}[\sqrt{N}(\hat{\boldsymbol{\beta}} - \boldsymbol{\beta})]$ is positive semidefinite (p.s.d.), it suffices to show that $\mathrm{E}(\mathbf{x}^{*\prime}\mathbf{x}^*) - \mathrm{E}(\mathbf{x}'\tilde{\mathbf{x}})[\mathrm{E}(\tilde{\mathbf{x}}'\tilde{\mathbf{x}})]^{-1}\mathrm{E}(\tilde{\mathbf{x}}'\mathbf{x})$ is p.s.d. But $\mathbf{x} = \mathbf{x}^* + \mathbf{r}$, where $\mathrm{E}(\mathbf{z}'\mathbf{r}) = \mathbf{0}$, and so $\mathrm{E}(\tilde{\mathbf{x}}'\mathbf{r}) = \mathbf{0}$. It follows that $\mathrm{E}(\tilde{\mathbf{x}}'\mathbf{x}) = \mathrm{E}(\tilde{\mathbf{x}}'\mathbf{x}^*)$, and so

$$\begin{aligned}&\mathrm{E}(\mathbf{x}^{*\prime}\mathbf{x}^*) - \mathrm{E}(\mathbf{x}'\tilde{\mathbf{x}})[\mathrm{E}(\tilde{\mathbf{x}}'\tilde{\mathbf{x}})]^{-1}\mathrm{E}(\tilde{\mathbf{x}}'\mathbf{x})\\ &\quad= \mathrm{E}(\mathbf{x}^{*\prime}\mathbf{x}^*) - \mathrm{E}(\mathbf{x}^{*\prime}\tilde{\mathbf{x}})[\mathrm{E}(\tilde{\mathbf{x}}'\tilde{\mathbf{x}})]^{-1}\mathrm{E}(\tilde{\mathbf{x}}'\mathbf{x}^*) = \mathrm{E}(\mathbf{s}^{*\prime}\mathbf{s}^*)\end{aligned}$$

where $\mathbf{s}^* = \mathbf{x}^* - \mathrm{L}(\mathbf{x}^* \mid \tilde{\mathbf{x}})$ is the population residual from the linear projection of $\mathbf{x}^*$ on $\tilde{\mathbf{x}}$. Because $\mathrm{E}(\mathbf{s}^{*\prime}\mathbf{s}^*)$ is p.s.d, the proof is complete.

Theorem 5.3 is vacuous when $L = K$ because any (nonsingular) choice of $\boldsymbol{\Gamma}$ leads to the same estimator: the IV estimator derived in Section 5.1.1.

When $\mathbf{x}$ is exogenous, Theorem 5.3 implies that, under Assumptions 2SLS.1–2SLS.3, the OLS estimator is efficient in the class of all estimators using instruments linear in exogenous variables $\mathbf{z}$. This statement is true because $\mathbf{x}$ is a subset of $\mathbf{z}$ and so $\mathrm{L}(\mathbf{x} \mid \mathbf{z}) = \mathbf{x}$.

Another important implication of Theorem 5.3 is that, asymptotically, we always do better by using as many instruments as are available, at least under homoskedasticity. This conclusion follows because using a subset of $\mathbf{z}$ as instruments corresponds to using a particular linear combination of $\mathbf{z}$. For certain subsets we might achieve the same efficiency as 2SLS using all of $\mathbf{z}$, but we can do no better. This observation makes it tempting to add many instruments so that L is much larger than K. Unfortunately, 2SLS estimators based on many overidentifying restrictions can cause finite sample problems; see Section 5.2.6.

Since Assumption 2SLS.3 is assumed for Theorem 5.3, it is not surprising that more efficient estimators are available if Assumption 2SLS.3 fails. If $L > K$, a more efficient estimator than 2SLS exists, as shown by Hansen (1982) and White (1982b, 1984). In fact, even if $\mathbf{x}$ is exogenous and Assumption OLS.3 holds, OLS is not generally asymptotically efficient if, for $\mathbf{x} \subset \mathbf{z}$, Assumptions 2SLS.1 and 2SLS.2 hold but Assumption 2SLS.3 does not. Obtaining the efficient estimator falls under the rubric of generalized method of moments estimation, something we cover in Chapter 8.

5.2.4 Hypothesis Testing with 2SLS

We have already seen that testing hypotheses about a single β_j is straightforward using an asymptotic t statistic, which has an asymptotic normal distribution under the null; some prefer to use the t distribution when N is small. Generally, one should be aware that the normal and t approximations can be poor if N is small. Hypotheses about single linear combinations involving the β_j are also easily carried out using a t statistic. The easiest procedure is to define the linear combination of interest, say $\theta \equiv a_1\beta_1 + a_2\beta_2 + \cdots + a_K\beta_K$, and then to write one of the β_j in terms of θ and the other elements of $\boldsymbol{\beta}$. Then, substitute into the equation of interest so that θ appears directly, and estimate the resulting equation by 2SLS to get the standard error of $\hat{\theta}$. See Problem 5.9 for an example.

To test multiple linear restrictions of the form H_0: $\mathbf{R}\boldsymbol{\beta} = \mathbf{r}$, the Wald statistic is just as in equation (4.13), but with $\hat{\mathbf{V}}$ given by equation (5.27). The Wald statistic, as usual, is a limiting null χ^2_Q distribution. Some econometrics packages, such as Stata®, compute the Wald statistic (actually, its F statistic counterpart, obtained by dividing the Wald statistic by Q) after 2SLS estimation using a simple test command.

A valid test of multiple restrictions can be computed using a residual-based method, analogous to the usual F statistic from OLS analysis. Any kind of linear restriction can be recast as exclusion restrictions, and so we explicitly cover exclusion restrictions. Write the model as

$$y = \mathbf{x}_1\boldsymbol{\beta}_1 + \mathbf{x}_2\boldsymbol{\beta}_2 + u \tag{5.28}$$

where $\mathbf{x}_1$ is $1 \times K_1$ and $\mathbf{x}_2$ is $1 \times K_2$, and interest lies in testing the K_2 restrictions

$$\mathrm{H}_0\colon \boldsymbol{\beta}_2 = \mathbf{0} \qquad \text{against} \qquad \mathrm{H}_1\colon \boldsymbol{\beta}_2 \neq \mathbf{0} \tag{5.29}$$

Both $\mathbf{x}_1$ and $\mathbf{x}_2$ can contain endogenous and exogenous variables.

Let $\mathbf{z}$ denote the $L \geq K_1 + K_2$ vector of instruments, and we assume that the rank condition for identification holds. Justification for the following statistic can be found in Wooldridge (1995b).

Let $\hat{u}_i$ be the 2SLS residuals from estimating the unrestricted model using $\mathbf{z}_i$ as instruments. Using these residuals, define the 2SLS unrestricted sum of squared residuals by

$$\mathrm{SSR}_{ur} \equiv \sum_{i=1}^{N} \hat{u}_i^2 \tag{5.30}$$

In order to define the F statistic for 2SLS, we need the sum of squared residuals from the *second*-stage regressions. Thus, let $\hat{\mathbf{x}}_{i1}$ be the $1 \times K_1$ fitted values from the first-stage regression $\mathbf{x}_{i1}$ on $\mathbf{z}_i$. Similarly, $\hat{\mathbf{x}}_{i2}$ are the fitted values from the first-stage regression $\mathbf{x}_{i2}$ on $\mathbf{z}_i$. Define $\widehat{\mathrm{SSR}}_{ur}$ as the usual sum of squared residuals from the unrestricted second-stage regression y on $\hat{\mathbf{x}}_1$, $\hat{\mathbf{x}}_2$. Similarly, $\widehat{\mathrm{SSR}}_r$ is the sum of squared residuals from the restricted second-stage regression, y on $\hat{\mathbf{x}}_1$. It can be shown that, under H_0: $\boldsymbol{\beta}_2 = \mathbf{0}$ (and Assumptions 2SLS.1–2SLS.3), $N \cdot (\hat{\mathrm{SSR}}_r - \hat{\mathrm{SSR}}_{ur})/\mathrm{SSR}_{ur} \overset{a}{\sim} \chi^2_{K_2}$. It is just as legitimate to use an F-type statistic:

$$F \equiv \frac{(\hat{\mathrm{SSR}}_r - \hat{\mathrm{SSR}}_{ur})}{\mathrm{SSR}_{ur}} \cdot \frac{(N-K)}{K_2} \tag{5.31}$$

is distributed approximately as $\mathcal{F}_{K_2, N-K}$.

Note carefully that $\hat{\mathrm{SSR}}_r$ and $\hat{\mathrm{SSR}}_{ur}$ appear in the numerator of (5.31). These quantities typically need to be computed directly from the second-stage regression. In the denominator of F is SSR_{ur}, which is the 2SLS sum of squared residuals. This is what is reported by the 2SLS commands available in popular regression packages.

For 2SLS it is important not to use a form of the statistic that would work for OLS, namely,

$$\frac{(\mathrm{SSR}_r - \mathrm{SSR}_{ur})}{\mathrm{SSR}_{ur}} \cdot \frac{(N-K)}{K_2} \tag{5.32}$$

where SSR_r is the 2SLS restricted sum of squared residuals. Not only does expression (5.32) not have a known limiting distribution, but it can also be negative with positive probability even as the sample size tends to infinity; clearly such a statistic cannot have an approximate F distribution, or any other distribution typically associated with multiple hypothesis testing.

Example 5.4 (Parents' and Husband's Education as IVs, continued): We add the number of young children (*kidslt6*) and older children (*kidsge6*) to equation (5.12) and test for their joint significance using the Mroz (1987) data. The statistic in equation (5.31) is $F = .31$; with two and 422 degrees of freedom, the asymptotic p-value is about .737. There is no evidence that number of children affects the wage for working women.

Rather than equation (5.31), we can compute an LM-type statistic for testing hypothesis (5.29). Let $\tilde{u}_i$ be the 2SLS residuals from the restricted model. That is, obtain $\tilde{\boldsymbol{\beta}}_1$ from the model $y = \mathbf{x}_1\boldsymbol{\beta}_1 + u$ using instruments $\mathbf{z}$, and let $\tilde{u}_i \equiv y_i - \mathbf{x}_{i1}\tilde{\boldsymbol{\beta}}_1$. Letting $\hat{\mathbf{x}}_{i1}$ and $\hat{\mathbf{x}}_{i2}$ be defined as before, the LM statistic is obtained as NR^2_u from the regression

$$\tilde{u}_i \text{ on } \hat{\mathbf{x}}_{i1}, \hat{\mathbf{x}}_{i2}, \qquad i = 1, 2, \ldots, N \tag{5.33}$$

where R^2_u is generally the uncentered R-squared. (That is, the total sum of squares in the denominator of R-squared is not demeaned.) When $\{\tilde{u}_i\}$ has a zero sample average, the uncentered R-squared and the usual R-squared are the same. This is the case when the null explanatory variables $\mathbf{x}_1$ and the instruments $\mathbf{z}$ both contain unity, the typical case. Under H_0 and Assumptions 2SLS.1–2SLS.3, $LM \overset{a}{\sim} \chi^2_{K_2}$. Whether one uses this statistic or the F statistic in equation (5.31) is primarily a matter of taste; asymptotically, there is nothing that distinguishes the two.

5.2.5 Heteroskedasticity-Robust Inference for 2SLS

Assumption 2SLS.3 can be restrictive, so we should have a variance matrix estimator that is robust in the presence of heteroskedasticity of unknown form. As usual, we need to estimate **B** along with **A**. Under Assumptions 2SLS.1 and 2SLS.2 only, $\mathrm{Avar}(\hat{\boldsymbol{\beta}})$ can be estimated as

$$(\hat{\mathbf{X}}'\hat{\mathbf{X}})^{-1}\left(\sum_{i=1}^{N}\hat{u}_i^2\hat{\mathbf{x}}_i'\hat{\mathbf{x}}_i\right)(\hat{\mathbf{X}}'\hat{\mathbf{X}})^{-1} \tag{5.34}$$

Sometimes this matrix is multiplied by $N/(N-K)$ as a degrees-of-freedom adjustment. This heteroskedasticity-robust estimator can be used anywhere the estimator $\hat{\sigma}^2(\hat{\mathbf{X}}'\hat{\mathbf{X}})^{-1}$ is. In particular, the square roots of the diagonal elements of the matrix (5.34) are the heteroskedasticity-robust standard errors for 2SLS. These can be used to construct (asymptotic) t statistics in the usual way. Some packages compute these standard errors using a simple command. For example, using Stata®, rounded to three decimal places the heteroskedasticity-robust standard error for *educ* in Example 5.3 is .022, which is the same as the usual standard error rounded to three decimal places. The robust standard error for *exper* is .015, somewhat higher than the nonrobust one (.013).

Sometimes it is useful to compute a robust standard error that can be computed with any regression package. Wooldridge (1995b) shows how this procedure can be carried out using an auxiliary linear regression for each parameter. Consider computing the robust standard error for $\hat{\beta}_j$. Let "$\mathrm{se}(\hat{\beta}_j)$" denote the standard error computed using the usual variance matrix (5.27); we put this in quotes because it is no longer appropriate if Assumption 2SLS.3 fails. The $\hat{\sigma}$ is obtained from equation (5.26), and $\hat{u}_i$ are the 2SLS residuals from equation (5.25). Let $\hat{r}_{ij}$ be the residuals from the regression

$$\hat{x}_{ij} \text{ on } \hat{x}_{i1}, \hat{x}_{i2}, \ldots, \hat{x}_{i,j-1}, \hat{x}_{i,j+1}, \ldots, \hat{x}_{iK}, \qquad i = 1, 2, \ldots, N$$

and define $\hat{m}_j \equiv \sum_{i=1}^{N}\hat{r}_{ij}\hat{u}_i$. Then, a heteroskedasticity-robust standard error of $\hat{\beta}_j$ can be tabulated as

$$\mathrm{se}(\hat{\beta}_j) = [N/(N-K)]^{1/2}[\text{"}\mathrm{se}(\hat{\beta}_j)\text{"}/\hat{\sigma}]^2/(\hat{m}_j)^{1/2} \tag{5.35}$$

Many econometrics packages compute equation (5.35) for you, but it is also easy to compute directly.

To test multiple linear restrictions using the Wald approach, we can use the usual statistic but with the matrix (5.34) as the estimated variance. For example, the heteroskedasticity-robust version of the test in Example 5.4 gives $F = .25$; asymptotically, F can be treated as an $\mathscr{F}_{2,422}$ variate. The asymptotic p-value is .781.

The Lagrange multiplier test for omitted variables is easily made heteroskedasticity-robust. Again, consider the model (5.28) with the null (5.29), but this time without the homoskedasticity assumptions. Using the notation from before, let $\hat{\mathbf{r}}_i \equiv (\hat{r}_{i1}, \hat{r}_{i2}, \ldots, \hat{r}_{iK_2})$ be the $1 \times K_2$ vectors of residuals from the multivariate regression $\hat{\mathbf{x}}_{i2}$ on $\hat{\mathbf{x}}_{i1}$, $i = 1, 2, \ldots, N$. (Again, this procedure can be carried out by regressing each element of $\hat{\mathbf{x}}_{i2}$ on all of $\hat{\mathbf{x}}_{i1}$.) Then, for each observation, form the $1 \times K_2$ vector $\tilde{u}_i \cdot \hat{\mathbf{r}}_i \equiv (\tilde{u}_i \cdot \hat{r}_{i1}, \ldots, \tilde{u}_i \cdot \hat{r}_{iK_2})$. Then, the robust LM test is $N - \text{SSR}_0$ from the regression 1 on $\tilde{u}_i \cdot \hat{r}_{i1}, \ldots, \tilde{u}_i \cdot \hat{r}_{iK_2}$, $i = 1, 2, \ldots, N$. Under H_0, $N - \text{SSR}_0 \overset{a}{\sim} \chi^2_{K_2}$. This procedure can be justified in a manner similar to the tests in the context of OLS. You are referred to Wooldridge (1995b) for details.

5.2.6 Potential Pitfalls with 2SLS

When properly applied, the method of instrumental variables can be a powerful tool for estimating structural equations using nonexperimental data. Nevertheless, there are some problems that one can encounter when applying IV in practice.

One thing to remember is that, unlike OLS under a zero conditional mean assumption, IV methods are never unbiased when at least one explanatory variable is endogenous in the model. In fact, under standard distributional assumptions, the expected value of the 2SLS estimator does not even exist. As shown by Kinal (1980), in the case when all endogenous variables have homoskedastic normal distributions with expectations linear in the exogenous variables, the number of moments of the 2SLS estimator that exist is one less than the number of overidentifying restrictions. This finding implies that when the number of instruments equals the number of explanatory variables, the IV estimator does not have an expected value. This is one reason we rely on large-sample analysis to justify 2SLS.

Even in large samples IV methods can be ill-behaved if the instruments are weak. Consider the simple model $y = \beta_0 + \beta_1 x_1 + u$, where we use z_1 as an instrument for x_1. Assuming that $\text{Cov}(z_1, x_1) \neq 0$, the plim of the IV estimator is easily shown to be

$$\text{plim}\ \hat{\beta}_1 = \beta_1 + \text{Cov}(z_1, u)/\text{Cov}(z_1, x_1) \tag{5.36}$$

When $\text{Cov}(z_1, u) = 0$ we obtain the consistency result from earlier. However, if z_1 has some correlation with u, the IV estimator is, not surprisingly, inconsistent. Rewrite equation (5.36) as

$$\text{plim}\ \hat{\beta}_1 = \beta_1 + (\sigma_u/\sigma_{x_1})[\text{Corr}(z_1, u)/\text{Corr}(z_1, x_1)] \tag{5.37}$$

where Corr$(\cdot,\cdot)$ denotes correlation. From this equation we see that if z_1 and u are correlated, the inconsistency in the IV estimator gets arbitrarily large as Corr(z_1, x_1) gets close to zero. Thus seemingly small correlations between z_1 and u can cause severe inconsistency—and therefore severe finite sample bias—if z_1 is only weakly correlated with x_1. In such cases it may be better to just use OLS, even if we only focus on the inconsistency in the estimators: the plim of the OLS estimator is generally $\beta_1 + (\sigma_u/\sigma_{x_1})$ Corr(x_1, u). Unfortunately, since we cannot observe u, we can never know the size of the inconsistencies in IV and OLS. But we should be concerned if the correlation between z_1 and x_1 is weak. Similar considerations arise with multiple explanatory variables and instruments.

Another potential problem with applying 2SLS and other IV procedures is that the 2SLS standard errors have a tendency to be "large." What is typically meant by this statement is either that 2SLS coefficients are statistically insignificant or that the 2SLS standard errors are much larger than the OLS standard errors. Not suprisingly, the magnitudes of the 2SLS standard errors depend, among other things, on the quality of the instrument(s) used in estimation.

For the following discussion we maintain the standard 2SLS Assumptions 2SLS.1–2SLS.3 in the model

$$y = \beta_0 + \beta_1 x_1 + \beta_2 x_2 + \cdots + \beta_K x_K + u \tag{5.38}$$

Let $\hat{\boldsymbol{\beta}}$ be the vector of 2SLS estimators using instruments $\mathbf{z}$. For concreteness, we focus on the asymptotic variance of $\hat{\beta}_K$. Technically, we should study Avar $\sqrt{N}(\hat{\beta}_K - \beta_K)$, but it is easier to work with an expression that contains the same information. In particular, we use the fact that

$$\text{Avar}(\hat{\beta}_K) \approx \frac{\sigma^2}{\hat{\text{SSR}}_K} \tag{5.39}$$

where $\hat{\text{SSR}}_K$ is the sum of squared residuals from the regression

$$\hat{x}_K \text{ on } 1,\ \hat{x}_1, \ldots, \hat{x}_{K-1} \tag{5.40}$$

(Remember, if x_j is exogenous for any j, then $\hat{x}_j = x_j$.) If we replace σ^2 in regression (5.39) with $\hat{\sigma}^2$, then expression (5.39) is the usual 2SLS variance estimator. For the current discussion we are interested in the behavior of $\hat{\text{SSR}}_K$.

From the definition of an R-squared, we can write

$$\hat{\text{SSR}}_K = \hat{\text{SST}}_K (1 - \hat{R}_K^2) \tag{5.41}$$

where $\hat{\text{SST}}_K$ is the total sum of squares of $\hat{x}_K$ in the sample, $\hat{\text{SST}}_K = \sum_{i=1}^N (\hat{x}_{iK} - \bar{\hat{x}}_K)$, and $\hat{R}_K^2$ is the R-squared from regression (5.40). In the context of OLS, the term

$(1 - \hat{R}_K^2)$ in equation (5.41) is viewed as a measure of multicollinearity, whereas $\hat{\text{SST}}_K$ measures the total variation in $\hat{x}_K$. We see that, in addition to traditional multicollinearity, 2SLS can have an additional source of large variance: the total variation in $\hat{x}_K$ can be small.

When is $\hat{\text{SST}}_K$ small? Remember, $\hat{x}_K$ denotes the fitted values from the regression

$$x_K \text{ on } \mathbf{z} \tag{5.42}$$

Therefore, $\hat{\text{SST}}_K$ is the *same* as the explained sum of squares from the regression (5.42). If x_K is only weakly related to the IVs, then the explained sum of squares from regression (5.42) can be quite small, causing a large asymptotic variance for $\hat{\beta}_K$. If x_K is highly correlated with $\mathbf{z}$, then $\hat{\text{SST}}_K$ can be almost as large as the total sum of squares of x_K and SST_K, and this fact reduces the 2SLS variance estimate.

When x_K is exogenous—whether or not the other elements of $\mathbf{x}$ are—$\hat{\text{SST}}_K = \text{SST}_K$. While this total variation can be small, it is determined only by the sample variation in $\{x_{iK}\colon i = 1, 2, \ldots, N\}$. Therefore, for exogenous elements appearing among $\mathbf{x}$, the quality of instruments has no bearing on the size of the total sum of squares term in equation (5.41). This fact helps explain why the 2SLS estimates on exogenous explanatory variables are often much more precise than the coefficients on endogenous explanatory variables.

In addition to making the term $\hat{\text{SST}}_K$ small, poor quality of instruments can lead to $\hat{R}_K^2$ close to one. As an illustration, consider a model in which x_K is the only endogenous variable and there is one instrument z_1 in addition to the exogenous variables $(1, x_1, \ldots, x_{K-1})$. Therefore, $\mathbf{z} \equiv (1, x_1, \ldots, x_{K-1}, z_1)$. (The same argument works for multiple instruments.) The fitted values $\hat{x}_K$ come from the regression

$$x_K \text{ on } 1, \; x_1, \ldots, x_{K-1}, z_1 \tag{5.43}$$

Because all other regressors are exogenous (that is, they are included in $\mathbf{z}$), $\hat{R}_K^2$ comes from the regression

$$\hat{x}_K \text{ on } 1, \; x_1, \ldots, x_{K-1} \tag{5.44}$$

Now, from basic least squares mechanics, if the coefficient on z_1 in regression (5.43) is exactly zero, then the R-squared from regression (5.44) is exactly unity, in which case the 2SLS estimator does not even exist. This outcome virtually never happens, but z_1 could have little explanatory value for x_K once $x_1, \ldots, x_{K-1}$ have been controlled for, in which case $\hat{R}_K^2$ can be close to one. Identification, which only has to do with whether we can consistently estimate $\boldsymbol{\beta}$, requires only that z_1 appear with nonzero coefficient in the population analogue of regression (5.43). But if the explanatory power of z_1 is weak, the asymptotic variance of the 2SLS estimator can be quite large. This is another way to illustrate why nonzero correlation between x_K and z_1 is not enough for 2SLS to be effective: the *partial* correlation is what matters for the asymptotic variance.

As always, we must keep in mind that there are no absolute standards for determining when the denominator of equation (5.39) is "large enough." For example, it is quite possible that, say, x_K and $\mathbf{z}$ are only weakly linearly related but the sample size is sufficiently large so that the term $\hat{\mathrm{SST}}_K$ is large enough to produce a small enough standard error (in the sense that confidence intervals are tight enough to reject interesting hypotheses). Provided there is some linear relationship between x_K and $\mathbf{z}$ in the population, $\hat{\mathrm{SST}}_K \xrightarrow{p} \infty$ as $N \to \infty$. Further, in the preceding example, if the coefficent θ_1 on z_1 in the population regression (5.4) is different from zero, then $\hat{R}_K^2$ converges in probability to a number less than one; asymptotically, multicollinearity is not a problem.

We are in a difficult situation when the 2SLS standard errors are so large that nothing is significant. Often we must choose between a possibly inconsistent estimator that has relatively small standard errors (OLS) and a consistent estimator that is so imprecise that nothing interesting can be concluded (2SLS). One approach is to use OLS unless we can reject exogeneity of the explanatory variables. We show how to test for endogeneity of one or more explanatory variables in Section 6.2.1.

There has been some important recent work on the finite sample properties of 2SLS that emphasizes the potentially large *biases* of 2SLS, even when sample sizes seem to be quite large. Remember that the 2SLS estimator is never unbiased (provided one has at least one truly endogenous variable in $\mathbf{x}$). But we hope that, with a very large sample size, we need only weak instruments to get an estimator with small bias. Unfortunately, this hope is not fulfilled. For example, Bound, Jaeger, and Baker (1995) show that in the setting of Angrist and Krueger (1991) the 2SLS estimator can be expected to behave quite poorly, an alarming finding because Angrist and Krueger use 300,000 to 500,000 observations! The problem is that the instruments—representing quarters of birth and various interactions of these with year of birth and state of birth—are very weak, and they are too numerous relative to their contribution in explaining years of education. One lesson is that, even with a very large sample size and zero correlation between the instruments and error, we should not use too many overidentifying restrictions.

Staiger and Stock (1997) provide a theoretical analysis of the 2SLS estimator with weak instruments and conclude that, even with large sample sizes, instruments that have small partial correlation with an endogenous explanatory variable can lead to substantial biases in 2SLS. One lesson that comes out of the Staiger-Stock work is that we should always compute the F statistic from the first-stage regression (or the t statistic with a single instrumental variable). Staiger and Stock (1997) provide some guidelines about how large this F statistic should be (equivalently, how small the p-value should be) for 2SLS to have acceptable properties.

5.3 IV Solutions to the Omitted Variables and Measurement Error Problems

In this section, we briefly survey the different approaches that have been suggested for using IV methods to solve the omitted variables problem. Section 5.3.2 covers an approach that applies to measurement error as well.

5.3.1 Leaving the Omitted Factors in the Error Term

Consider again the omitted variable model

$$y = \beta_0 + \beta_1 x_1 + \cdots + \beta_K x_K + \gamma q + v \tag{5.45}$$

where q represents the omitted variable and $\mathrm{E}(v \mid \mathbf{x}, q) = 0$. The solution that would follow from Section 5.1.1 is to put q in the error term, and then to find instruments for any element of $\mathbf{x}$ that is correlated with q. It is useful to think of the instruments satisfying the following requirements: (1) they are redundant in the structural model $\mathrm{E}(y \mid \mathbf{x}, q)$; (2) they are uncorrelated with the omitted variable, q; and (3) they are sufficiently correlated with the endogenous elements of $\mathbf{x}$ (that is, those elements that are correlated with q). Then 2SLS applied to equation (5.45) with $u \equiv \gamma q + v$ produces consistent and asymptotically normal estimators.

5.3.2 Solutions Using Indicators of the Unobservables

An alternative solution to the omitted variable problem is similar to the OLS proxy variable solution but requires IV rather than OLS estimation. In the OLS proxy variable solution we assume that we have z_1 such that $q = \theta_0 + \theta_1 z_1 + r_1$ where r_1 is uncorrelated with z_1 (by definition) *and* is uncorrelated with $x_1, \ldots, x_K$ (the key proxy variable assumption). Suppose instead that we have two **indicators** of q. Like a proxy variable, an indicator of q must be redundant in equation (5.45). The key difference is that an indicator can be written as

$$q_1 = \delta_0 + \delta_1 q + a_1 \tag{5.46}$$

where

$$\mathrm{Cov}(q, a_1) = 0, \qquad \mathrm{Cov}(\mathbf{x}, a_1) = \mathbf{0} \tag{5.47}$$

This assumption contains the classical errors-in-variables model as a special case, where q is the unobservable, q_1 is the observed measurement, $\delta_0 = 0$, and $\delta_1 = 1$, in which case γ in equation (5.45) can be identified.

Assumption (5.47) is very different from the proxy variable assumption. Assuming that $\delta_1 \neq 0$—otherwise q_1 is not correlated with q—we can rearrange equation (5.46) as

$$q = -(\delta_0/\delta_1) + (1/\delta_1)q_1 - (1/\delta_1)a_1 \tag{5.48}$$

where the error in this equation, $-(1/\delta_1)a_1$, is necessarily correlated with q_1; the OLS–proxy variable solution would be inconsistent.

To use the indicator assumption (5.47), we need some additional information. One possibility is to have a second indicator of q:

$$q_2 = \rho_0 + \rho_1 q + a_2 \tag{5.49}$$

where a_2 satisfies the same assumptions as a_1 and $\rho_1 \neq 0$. We still need one more assumption:

$$\text{Cov}(a_1, a_2) = 0 \tag{5.50}$$

This implies that any correlation between q_1 and q_2 arises through their common dependence on q.

Plugging q_1 in for q and rearranging gives

$$y = \alpha_0 + \mathbf{x}\boldsymbol{\beta} + \gamma_1 q_1 + (v - \gamma_1 a_1) \tag{5.51}$$

where $\gamma_1 = \gamma/\delta_1$. Now, q_2 is uncorrelated with v because it is redundant in equation (5.45). Further, by assumption, q_2 is uncorrelated with a_1 (a_1 is uncorrelated with q and a_2). Since q_1 and q_2 are correlated, q_2 can be used as an IV for q_1 in equation (5.51). Of course the roles of q_2 and q_1 can be reversed. This solution to the omitted variables problem is sometimes called the **multiple indicator solution**.

It is important to see that the multiple indicator IV solution is very different from the IV solution that leaves q in the error term. When we leave q as part of the error, we must decide which elements of $\mathbf{x}$ are correlated with q, and then find IVs for those elements of $\mathbf{x}$. With multiple indicators for q, we need not know which elements of $\mathbf{x}$ are correlated with q; they all might be. In equation (5.51) the elements of $\mathbf{x}$ serve as their own instruments. Under the assumptions we have made, we only need an instrument for q_1, and q_2 serves that purpose.

Example 5.5 (IQ and KWW as Indicators of Ability): We apply the indicator method to the model of Example 4.3, using the 935 observations in NLS80.RAW. In addition to *IQ*, we have a knowledge of the working world (*KWW*) test score. If we write $IQ = \delta_0 + \delta_1 abil + a_1$, $KWW = \rho_0 + \rho_1 abil + a_2$, and the previous assumptions are satisfied in equation (4.29), then we can add IQ to the wage equation and use KWW as an instrument for IQ. We get

$$\begin{aligned}\log(\widehat{wage}) = \ & \underset{(0.33)}{4.59} + \underset{(.003)}{.014}\, exper + \underset{(.003)}{.010}\, tenure + \underset{(.041)}{.201}\, married \\ & - \underset{(.031)}{.051}\, south + \underset{(.028)}{.177}\, urban - \underset{(.074)}{.023}\, black + \underset{(.017)}{.025}\, educ + \underset{(.005)}{.013}\, IQ\end{aligned}$$

The estimated return to education is about 2.5 percent, and it is not statistically significant at the 5 percent level even with a one-sided alternative. If we reverse the roles of KWW and IQ, we get an even smaller return to education: about 1.7 percent with a t statistic of about 1.07. The statistical insignificance is perhaps not too surprising given that we are using IV, but the magnitudes of the estimates are surprisingly small. Perhaps a_1 and a_2 are correlated with each other, or with some elements of $\mathbf{x}$.

In the case of the CEV measurement error model, q_1 and q_2 are measures of q assumed to have uncorrelated measurement errors. Since $\delta_0 = \rho_0 = 0$ and $\delta_1 = \rho_1 = 1$, $\gamma_1 = \gamma$. Therefore, having two measures, where we plug one into the equation and use the other as its instrument, provides consistent estimators of all parameters in the CEV setup.

There are other ways to use indicators of an omitted variable (or a single measurement in the context of measurement error) in an IV approach. Suppose that only one indicator of q is available. Without further information, the parameters in the structural model are not identified. However, suppose we have additional variables that are redundant in the structural equation (uncorrelated with v), are uncorrelated with the error a_1 in the indicator equation, and are correlated with q. Then, as you are asked to show in Problem 5.7, estimating equation (5.51) using this additional set of variables as instruments for q_1 produces consistent estimators. This is the method proposed by Griliches and Mason (1972) and also used by Blackburn and Neumark (1992).

Problems

5.1. In this problem you are to establish the algebraic equivalence between 2SLS and OLS estimation of an equation containing an additional regressor. Although the result is completely general, for simplicity consider a model with a single (suspected) endogenous variable:

$$y_1 = \mathbf{z}_1\boldsymbol{\delta}_1 + \alpha_1 y_2 + u_1$$

$$y_2 = \mathbf{z}\boldsymbol{\pi}_2 + v_2$$

For notational clarity, we use y_2 as the suspected endogenous variable and $\mathbf{z}$ as the vector of all exogenous variables. The second equation is the reduced form for y_2. Assume that $\mathbf{z}$ has at least one more element than $\mathbf{z}_1$.

We know that one estimator of $(\boldsymbol{\delta}_1, \alpha_1)$ is the 2SLS estimator using instruments $\mathbf{x}$. Consider an alternative estimator of $(\boldsymbol{\delta}_1, \alpha_1)$: (a) estimate the reduced form by OLS, and save the residuals $\hat{v}_2$; (b) estimate the following equation by OLS:

$$y_1 = \mathbf{z}_1\boldsymbol{\delta}_1 + \alpha_1 y_2 + \rho_1 \hat{v}_2 + error \tag{5.52}$$

Show that the OLS estimates of $\boldsymbol{\delta}_1$ and α_1 from this regression are identical to the 2SLS estimators. [Hint: Use the partitioned regression algebra of OLS. In particular, if $\hat{y} = \mathbf{x}_1\hat{\boldsymbol{\beta}}_1 + \mathbf{x}_2\hat{\boldsymbol{\beta}}_2$ is an OLS regression, $\hat{\boldsymbol{\beta}}_1$ can be obtained by first regressing $\mathbf{x}_1$ on $\mathbf{x}_2$, getting the residuals, say $\ddot{\mathbf{x}}_1$, and then regressing y on $\ddot{\mathbf{x}}_1$; see, for example, Davidson and MacKinnon (1993, Section 1.4). You must also use the fact that $\mathbf{z}_1$ and $\hat{v}_2$ are orthogonal in the sample.]

5.2. Consider a model for the health of an individual:

$$\begin{aligned} health = {} & \beta_0 + \beta_1 age + \beta_2 weight + \beta_3 height \\ & + \beta_4 male + \beta_5 work + \beta_6 exercise + u_1 \end{aligned} \tag{5.53}$$

where *health* is some quantitative measure of the person's *health*, *age*, *weight*, *height*, and *male* are self-explanatory, *work* is weekly hours worked, and *exercise* is the hours of exercise per week.

a. Why might you be concerned about *exercise* being correlated with the error term u_1?

b. Suppose you can collect data on two additional variables, *disthome* and *distwork*, the distances from home and from work to the nearest health club or gym. Discuss whether these are likely to be uncorrelated with u_1.

c. Now assume that *disthome* and *distwork* are in fact uncorrelated with u_1, as are all variables in equation (5.53) with the exception of *exercise*. Write down the reduced form for *exercise*, and state the conditions under which the parameters of equation (5.53) are identified.

d. How can the identification assumption in part c be tested?

5.3. Consider the following model to estimate the effects of several variables, including cigarette smoking, on the weight of newborns:

$$\log(bwght) = \beta_0 + \beta_1 male + \beta_2 parity + \beta_3 \log(faminc) + \beta_4 packs + u \tag{5.54}$$

where *male* is a binary indicator equal to one if the child is male; *parity* is the birth order of this child; *faminc* is family income; and *packs* is the average number of packs of cigarettes smoked per day during pregnancy.

a. Why might you expect *packs* to be correlated with *u*?

b. Suppose that you have data on average cigarette price in each woman's state of residence. Discuss whether this information is likely to satisfy the properties of a good instrumental variable for packs.

c. Use the data in BWGHT.RAW to estimate equation (5.54). First, use OLS. Then, use 2SLS, where *cigprice* is an instrument for packs. Discuss any important differences in the OLS and 2SLS estimates.

d. Estimate the reduced form for *packs*. What do you conclude about identification of equation (5.54) using *cigprice* as an instrument for *packs*? What bearing does this conclusion have on your answer from part c?

5.4. Use the data in CARD.RAW for this problem.

a. Estimate a log(*wage*) equation by OLS with *educ*, *exper*, $exper^2$, *black*, *south*, *smsa*, *reg661* through *reg668*, and *smsa66* as explanatory variables. Compare your results with Table 2, Column (2) in Card (1995).

b. Estimate a reduced form equation for *educ* containing all explanatory variables from part a and the dummy variable *nearc4*. Do *educ* and *nearc4* have a practically and statistically significant partial correlation? [See also Table 3, Column (1) in Card (1995).]

c. Estimate the log(*wage*) equation by IV, using *nearc4* as an instrument for *educ*. Compare the 95 percent confidence interval for the return to education with that obtained from part a. [See also Table 3, Column (5) in Card (1995).]

d. Now use *nearc2* along with *nearc4* as instruments for *educ*. First estimate the reduced form for *educ*, and comment on whether *nearc2* or *nearc4* is more strongly related to *educ*. How do the 2SLS estimates compare with the earlier estimates?

e. For a subset of the men in the sample, IQ score is available. Regress *iq* on *nearc4*. Is IQ score uncorrelated with *nearc4*?

f. Now regress *iq* on *nearc4* along with *smsa66*, *reg661*, *reg662*, and *reg669*. Are *iq* and *nearc4* partially correlated? What do you conclude about the importance of controlling for the 1966 location and regional dummies in the log(*wage*) equation when using *nearc4* as an IV for *educ*?

5.5. One occasionally sees the following reasoning used in applied work for choosing instrumental variables in the context of omitted variables. The model is

$$y_1 = \mathbf{z}_1 \boldsymbol{\delta}_1 + \alpha_1 y_2 + \gamma q + a_1$$

where q is the omitted factor. We assume that a_1 satisfies the structural error assumption $\mathrm{E}(a_1 \mid \mathbf{z}_1, y_2, q) = 0$, that $\mathbf{z}_1$ is exogenous in the sense that $\mathrm{E}(q \mid \mathbf{z}_1) = 0$, but that y_2 and q may be correlated. Let $\mathbf{z}_2$ be a vector of instrumental variable candidates for y_2. Suppose it is known that $\mathbf{z}_2$ appears in the linear projection of y_2 onto $(\mathbf{z}_1, \mathbf{z}_2)$, and so the requirement that $\mathbf{z}_2$ be partially correlated with y_2 is satisfied. Also, we are willing to assume that $\mathbf{z}_2$ is redundant in the structural equation, so that a_1 is uncorrelated with $\mathbf{z}_2$. What we are unsure of is whether $\mathbf{z}_2$ is correlated with the omitted variable q, in which case $\mathbf{z}_2$ would not contain valid IVs.

To "test" whether $\mathbf{z}_2$ is in fact uncorrelated with q, it has been suggested to use OLS on the equation

$$y_1 = \mathbf{z}_1 \boldsymbol{\delta}_1 + \alpha_1 y_2 + \mathbf{z}_2 \boldsymbol{\psi}_1 + u_1 \tag{5.55}$$

where $u_1 = \gamma q + a_1$, and test H_0: $\boldsymbol{\psi}_1 = \mathbf{0}$. Why does this method not work?

5.6. Refer to the multiple indicator model in Section 5.3.2.

a. Show that if q_2 is uncorrelated with x_j, $j = 1, 2, \ldots, K$, then the reduced form of q_1 depends only on q_2. [Hint: Use the fact that the reduced form of q_1 is the linear projection of q_1 onto $(1, x_1, x_2, \ldots, x_K, q_2)$ and find the coefficient vector on $\mathbf{x}$ using Property LP.7 from Chapter 2.]

b. What happens if q_2 and $\mathbf{x}$ are correlated? In this setting, is it realistic to assume that q_2 and $\mathbf{x}$ are uncorrelated? Explain.

5.7. Consider model (5.45) where v has zero mean and is uncorrelated with $x_1, \ldots, x_K$ and q. The unobservable q is thought to be correlated with at least some of the x_j. Assume without loss of generality that $\mathrm{E}(q) = 0$.

You have a single indicator of q, written as $q_1 = \delta_1 q + a_1$, $\delta_1 \neq 0$, where a_1 has zero mean and is uncorrelated with each of x_j, q, and v. In addition, $z_1, z_2, \ldots, z_M$ is a set of variables that are (1) redundant in the structural equation (5.45) and (2) uncorrelated with a_1.

a. Suggest an IV method for consistently estimating the β_j. Be sure to discuss what is needed for identification.

b. If equation (5.45) is a $\log(wage)$ equation, q is ability, q_1 is IQ or some other test score, and $z_1, \ldots, z_M$ are family background variables, such as parents' education and number of siblings, describe the economic assumptions needed for consistency of the the IV procedure in part a.

c. Carry out this procedure using the data in NLS80.RAW. Include among the explanatory variables *exper*, *tenure*, *educ*, *married*, *south*, *urban*, and *black*. First use *IQ* as q_1 and then *KWW*. Include in the z_h the variables *meduc*, *feduc*, and *sibs*. Discuss the results.

5.8. Consider a model with unobserved heterogeneity (q) and measurement error in an explanatory variable:

$$y = \beta_0 + \beta_1 x_1 + \cdots + \beta_K x_K^* + q + v$$

where $e_K = x_K - x_K^*$ is the measurement error and we set the coefficient on q equal to one without loss of generality. The variable q might be correlated with any of the explanatory variables, but an indicator, $q_1 = \delta_0 + \delta_1 q + a_1$, is available. The measurement error e_K might be correlated with the observed measure, x_K. In addition to q_1, you also have variables $z_1, z_2, \ldots, z_M$, $M \geq 2$, that are uncorrelated with v, a_1, and e_K.

a. Suggest an IV procedure for consistently estimating the β_j. Why is $M \geq 2$ required? (Hint: Plug in q_1 for q and x_K for x_K^*, and go from there.)

b. Apply this method to the model estimated in Example 5.5, where actual education, say *educ**, plays the role of x_K^*. Use *IQ* as the indicator of $q = ability$, and *KWW*, *meduc*, *feduc*, and *sibs* as the elements of $\mathbf{z}$.

5.9. Suppose that the following wage equation is for working high school graduates:

$$\log(wage) = \beta_0 + \beta_1 exper + \beta_2 exper^2 + \beta_3 twoyr + \beta_4 fouryr + u$$

where *twoyr* is years of junior college attended and *fouryr* is years completed at a four-year college. You have distances from each person's home at the time of high school graduation to the nearest two-year and four-year colleges as instruments for *twoyr* and *fouryr*. Show how to rewrite this equation to test $\text{H}_0\colon \beta_3 = \beta_4$ against $\text{H}_0\colon \beta_4 > \beta_3$, and explain how to estimate the equation. See Kane and Rouse (1995) and Rouse (1995), who implement a very similar procedure.

5.10. Consider IV estimation of the simple linear model with a single, possibly endogenous, explanatory variable, and a single instrument:

$$y = \beta_0 + \beta_1 x + u$$

$$\text{E}(u) = 0, \qquad \text{Cov}(z, u) = 0, \qquad \text{Cov}(z, x) \neq 0, \qquad \text{E}(u^2 \mid z) = \sigma^2$$

a. Under the preceding (standard) assumptions, show that Avar $\sqrt{N}(\hat{\beta}_1 - \beta_1)$ can be expressed as $\sigma^2/(\rho_{zx}^2 \sigma_x^2)$, where $\sigma_x^2 = \text{Var}(x)$ and $\rho_{zx} = \text{Corr}(z, x)$. Compare this result with the asymptotic variance of the OLS estimator under Assumptions OLS.1–OLS.3.

b. Comment on how each factor affects the asymptotic variance of the IV estimator. What happens as $\rho_{zx} \to 0$?

5.11. A model with a single endogenous explanatory variable can be written as

$$y_1 = \mathbf{z}_1 \boldsymbol{\delta}_1 + \alpha_1 y_2 + u_1, \qquad \text{E}(\mathbf{z}' u_1) = \mathbf{0}$$

where $\mathbf{z} = (\mathbf{z}_1, \mathbf{z}_2)$. Consider the following two-step method, intended to mimic 2SLS:

a. Regress y_2 on $\mathbf{z}_2$, and obtain fitted values, $\tilde{y}_2$. (That is, $\mathbf{z}_1$ is omitted from the first-stage regression.)

b. Regress y_1 on $\mathbf{z}_1$, $\tilde{y}_2$ to obtain $\tilde{\boldsymbol{\delta}}_1$ and $\tilde{\alpha}_1$. Show that $\tilde{\boldsymbol{\delta}}_1$ and $\tilde{\alpha}_1$ are generally inconsistent. When would $\tilde{\boldsymbol{\delta}}_1$ and $\tilde{\alpha}_1$ be consistent? [Hint: Let y_2^0 be the population linear projection of y_2 on $\mathbf{z}_2$, and let a_2 be the projection error: $y_2^0 = \mathbf{z}_2 \boldsymbol{\lambda}_2 + a_2$, $\text{E}(\mathbf{z}_2' a_2) = \mathbf{0}$. For simplicity, pretend that $\boldsymbol{\lambda}_2$ is known, rather than estimated; that is, assume that $\tilde{y}_2$ is actually y_2^0. Then, write

$$y_1 = \mathbf{z}_1 \boldsymbol{\delta}_1 + \alpha_1 y_2^0 + \alpha_1 a_2 + u_1$$

and check whether the composite error $\alpha_1 a_2 + u_1$ is uncorrelated with the explanatory variables.]

5.12. In the setup of Section 5.1.2 with $\mathbf{x} = (x_1, \ldots, x_K)$ and $\mathbf{z} \equiv (x_1, x_2, \ldots, x_{K-1}, z_1, \ldots, z_M)$ (let $x_1 = 1$ to allow an intercept), assume that $\text{E}(\mathbf{z}'\mathbf{z})$ is nonsingular. Prove that rank $\text{E}(\mathbf{z}'\mathbf{x}) = K$ if and only if at least one θ_j in equation (5.15) is different from zero. [Hint: Write $\mathbf{x}^* = (x_1, \ldots, x_{K-1}, x_K^*)$ as the linear projection of each element of $\mathbf{x}$ on $\mathbf{z}$, where $x_K^* = \delta_1 x_1 + \cdots + \delta_{K-1} x_{K-1} + \theta_1 z_1 + \cdots + \theta_M z_M$. Then $\mathbf{x} = \mathbf{x}^* + \mathbf{r}$, where $\text{E}(\mathbf{z}'\mathbf{r}) = \mathbf{0}$, so that $\text{E}(\mathbf{z}'\mathbf{x}) = \text{E}(\mathbf{z}'\mathbf{x}^*)$. Now $\mathbf{x}^* = \mathbf{z}\boldsymbol{\Pi}$, where $\boldsymbol{\Pi}$ is the $L \times K$ matrix whose first $K-1$ columns are the first $K-1$ unit vectors in $\mathbb{R}^L$—$(1, 0, 0, \ldots, 0)'$, $(0, 1, 0, \ldots, 0)', \ldots, (0, 0, \ldots, 1, 0, \ldots, 0)'$—and whose last column is $(\delta_1, \delta_2, \ldots, \delta_{K-1}, \theta_1, \ldots, \theta_M)$. Write $\text{E}(\mathbf{z}'\mathbf{x}^*) = \text{E}(\mathbf{z}'\mathbf{z})\boldsymbol{\Pi}$, so that, because $\text{E}(\mathbf{z}'\mathbf{z})$ is nonsingular, $\text{E}(\mathbf{z}'\mathbf{x}^*)$ has rank K if and only if $\boldsymbol{\Pi}$ has rank K.]

5.13. Consider the simple regression model

$$y = \beta_0 + \beta_1 x + u$$

and let z be a *binary* instrumental variable for x.

a. Show that the IV estimator $\hat{\beta}_1$ can be written as

$\hat{\beta}_1 = (\bar{y}_1 - \bar{y}_0)/(\bar{x}_1 - \bar{x}_0)$

where $\bar{y}_0$ and $\bar{x}_0$ are the sample averages of y_i and x_i over the part of the sample with $z_i = 0$, and $\bar{y}_1$ and $\bar{x}_1$ are the sample averages of y_i and x_i over the part of the sample with $z_i = 1$. This estimator, known as a **grouping estimator**, was first suggested by Wald (1940).

b. What is the intepretation of $\hat{\beta}_1$ if x is also binary, for example, representing participation in a social program?

5.14. Consider the model in (5.1) and (5.2), where we have additional exogenous variables $z_1, \dots, z_M$. Let $\mathbf{z} = (1, x_1, \dots, x_{K-1}, z_1, \dots, z_M)$ be the vector of all exogenous variables. This problem essentially asks you to obtain the 2SLS estimator using linear projections. Assume that $\mathrm{E}(\mathbf{z}'\mathbf{z})$ is nonsingular.

a. Find $\mathrm{L}(y \mid \mathbf{z})$ in terms of the β_j, $x_1, \dots, x_{K-1}$, and $x_K^* = \mathrm{L}(x_K \mid \mathbf{z})$.

b. Argue that, provided $x_1, \dots, x_{K-1}, x_K^*$ are not perfectly collinear, an OLS regression of y on $1, x_1, \dots, x_{K-1}, x_K^*$—using a random sample—consistently estimates all β_j.

c. State a necessary and sufficient condition for x_K^* not to be a perfect linear combination of $x_1, \dots, x_{K-1}$. What 2SLS assumption is this identical to?

5.15. Consider the model $y = \mathbf{x}\boldsymbol{\beta} + u$, where $x_1, x_2, \dots, x_{K_1}$, $K_1 \le K$, are the (potentially) endogenous explanatory variables. (We assume a zero intercept just to simplify the notation; the following results carry over to models with an unknown intercept.) Let $z_1, \dots, z_{L_1}$ be the instrumental variables available from outside the model. Let $\mathbf{z} = (z_1, \dots, z_{L_1}, x_{K_1+1}, \dots, x_K)$ and assume that $\mathrm{E}(\mathbf{z}'\mathbf{z})$ is nonsingular, so that Assumption 2SLS.2a holds.

a. Show that a necessary condition for the rank condition, Assumption 2SLS.2b, is that for each $j = 1, \dots, K_1$, at least one z_h must appear in the reduced form of x_j.

b. With $K_1 = 2$, give a simple example showing that the condition from part a is not sufficient for the rank condition.

c. If $L_1 = K_1$, show that a sufficient condition for the rank condition is that only z_j appears in the reduced form for x_j, $j = 1, \dots, K_1$. [As in Problem 5.12, it suffices to study the rank of the $L \times K$ matrix $\boldsymbol{\Pi}$ in $\mathrm{L}(\mathbf{x} \mid \mathbf{z}) = \mathbf{z}\boldsymbol{\Pi}$.]

6 Additional Single-Equation Topics

6.1 Estimation with Generated Regressors and Instruments

6.1.1 OLS with Generated Regressors

We often need to draw on results for OLS estimation when one or more of the regressors have been estimated from a first-stage procedure. To illustrate the issues, consider the model

$$y = \beta_0 + \beta_1 x_1 + \cdots + \beta_K x_K + \gamma q + u \tag{6.1}$$

We observe $x_1, \ldots, x_K$, but q is unobserved. However, suppose that q is related to observable data through the function $q = f(\mathbf{w}, \boldsymbol{\delta})$, where f is a known function and $\mathbf{w}$ is a vector of observed variables, but the vector of parameters $\boldsymbol{\delta}$ is unknown (which is why q is not observed). Often, but not always, q will be a linear function of $\mathbf{w}$ and $\boldsymbol{\delta}$. Suppose that we can consistently estimate $\boldsymbol{\delta}$, and let $\hat{\boldsymbol{\delta}}$ be the estimator. For each observation i, $\hat{q}_i = f(\mathbf{w}_i, \hat{\boldsymbol{\delta}})$ effectively estimates q_i. Pagan (1984) calls $\hat{q}_i$ a **generated regressor**. It seems reasonable that, replacing q_i with $\hat{q}_i$ in running the OLS regression

$$y_i \text{ on } 1, x_{i1}, x_{i2}, \ldots, x_{ik}, \hat{q}_i, \qquad i = 1, \ldots, N \tag{6.2}$$

should produce consistent estimates of all parameters, including γ. The question is, What assumptions are sufficient?

While we do not cover the asymptotic theory needed for a careful proof until Chapter 12 (which treats nonlinear estimation), we can provide some intuition here. Because plim $\hat{\boldsymbol{\delta}} = \boldsymbol{\delta}$, by the law of large numbers it is reasonable that

$$N^{-1} \sum_{i=1}^{N} \hat{q}_i u_i \xrightarrow{p} \mathrm{E}(q_i u_i), \qquad N^{-1} \sum_{i=1}^{N} x_{ij} \hat{q}_i \xrightarrow{p} \mathrm{E}(x_{ij} q_i)$$

From this relation it is easily shown that the usual OLS assumption in the population—that u is uncorrelated with $(x_1, x_2, \ldots, x_K, q)$—suffices for the two-step procedure to be consistent (along with the rank condition of Assumption OLS.2 applied to the expanded vector of explanatory variables). In other words, for consistency, replacing q_i with $\hat{q}_i$ in an OLS regression causes no problems.

Things are not so simple when it comes to inference: the standard errors and test statistics obtained from regression (6.2) are generally invalid because they ignore the sampling variation in $\hat{\boldsymbol{\delta}}$. Since $\hat{\boldsymbol{\delta}}$ is also obtained using data—usually the same sample of data—uncertainty in the estimate should be accounted for in the second step. Nevertheless, there is at least one important case where the sampling variation of $\hat{\boldsymbol{\delta}}$ *can* be ignored, at least asymptotically: if

$$\mathrm{E}[\nabla_\delta f(\mathbf{w}, \boldsymbol{\delta})' u] = \mathbf{0} \tag{6.3}$$

$$\gamma = 0 \tag{6.4}$$

then the $\sqrt{N}$-limiting distribution of the OLS estimators from regression (6.2) is the *same* as the OLS estimators when q replaces $\hat{q}$. Condition (6.3) is implied by the zero conditional mean condition

$$\mathrm{E}(u \mid \mathbf{x}, \mathbf{w}) = 0 \tag{6.5}$$

which usually holds in generated regressor contexts.

We often want to test the null hypothesis H_0: $\gamma = 0$ before including $\hat{q}$ in the final regression. Fortunately, the usual t statistic on $\hat{q}$ has a limiting standard normal distribution under H_0, so it can be used to test H_0. It simply requires the usual homoskedasticity assumption, $\mathrm{E}(u^2 \mid \mathbf{x}, q) = \sigma^2$. The heteroskedasticity-robust statistic works if heteroskedasticity is present in u under H_0.

Even if condition (6.3) holds, if $\gamma \neq 0$, then an adjustment is needed for the asymptotic variances of *all* OLS estimators that are due to estimation of $\boldsymbol{\delta}$. Thus, standard t statistics, F statistics, and LM statistics will not be asymptotically valid when $\gamma \neq 0$. Using the methods of Chapter 3, it is not difficult to derive an adjustment to the usual variance matrix estimate that accounts for the variability in $\hat{\boldsymbol{\delta}}$ (and also allows for heteroskedasticity). It is *not* true that replacing q_i with $\hat{q}_i$ simply introduces heteroskedasticity into the error term; this is not the correct way to think about the generated regressors issue. Accounting for the fact that $\hat{\boldsymbol{\delta}}$ depends on the same random sample used in the second-stage estimation is much different from having heteroskedasticity in the error. Of course, we might want to use a heteroskedasticity-robust standard error for testing H_0: $\gamma = 0$ because heteroskedasticity in the population error u can always be a problem. However, just as with the usual OLS standard error, this is generally justified only under H_0: $\gamma = 0$.

A general formula for the asymptotic variance of 2SLS in the presence of generated regressors is given in the appendix to this chapter; this covers OLS with generated regressors as a special case. A general framework for handling these problems is given in Newey (1984) and Newey and McFadden (1994), but we must hold off until Chapter 14 to give a careful treatment.

6.1.2 2SLS with Generated Instruments

In later chapters we will need results on 2SLS estimation when the instruments have been estimated in a preliminary stage. Write the population model as

$$y = \mathbf{x}\boldsymbol{\beta} + u \tag{6.6}$$

$$\mathrm{E}(\mathbf{z}'u) = \mathbf{0} \tag{6.7}$$

where $\mathbf{x}$ is a $1 \times K$ vector of explanatory variables and $\mathbf{z}$ is a $1 \times L$ $(L \geq K)$ vector of intrumental variables. Assume that $\mathbf{z} = \mathbf{g}(\mathbf{w}, \boldsymbol{\lambda})$, where $\mathbf{g}(\cdot\,, \boldsymbol{\lambda})$ is a known function but $\boldsymbol{\lambda}$ needs to be estimated. For each i, define the **generated instruments** $\hat{\mathbf{z}}_i \equiv \mathbf{g}(\mathbf{w}_i, \hat{\boldsymbol{\lambda}})$. What can we say about the 2SLS estimator when the $\hat{\mathbf{z}}_i$ are used as instruments?

By the same reasoning for OLS with generated regressors, consistency follows under weak conditions. Further, under conditions that are met in many applications, we can ignore the fact that the instruments were estimated in using 2SLS for inference. Sufficient are the assumptions that $\hat{\boldsymbol{\lambda}}$ is $\sqrt{N}$-consistent for $\boldsymbol{\lambda}$ and that

$$\mathrm{E}[\nabla_{\lambda}\mathbf{g}(\mathbf{w}, \boldsymbol{\lambda})'u] = \mathbf{0} \tag{6.8}$$

Under condition (6.8), which holds when $\mathrm{E}(u \mid \mathbf{w}) = 0$, the $\sqrt{N}$-asymptotic distribution of $\hat{\boldsymbol{\beta}}$ is the *same* whether we use $\boldsymbol{\lambda}$ or $\hat{\boldsymbol{\lambda}}$ in constructing the instruments. This fact greatly simplifies calculation of asymptotic standard errors and test statistics. Therefore, if we have a choice, there are practical reasons for using 2SLS with generated instruments rather than OLS with generated regressors. We will see some examples in Part IV.

One consequence of this discussion is that, if we add the 2SLS homoskedasticity assumption (2SLS.3), the usual 2SLS standard errors and test statistics are asymptotically valid. If Assumption 2SLS.3 is violated, we simply use the heteroskedasticity-robust standard errors and test statistics. Of course, the finite sample properties of the estimator using $\hat{\mathbf{z}}_i$ as instruments could be notably different from those using $\mathbf{z}_i$ as instruments, especially for small sample sizes. Determining whether this is the case requires either more sophisticated asymptotic approximations or simulations on a case-by-case basis.

6.1.3 Generated Instruments and Regressors

We will encounter examples later where some instruments and some regressors are estimated in a first stage. Generally, the asymptotic variance needs to be adjusted because of the generated regressors, although there are some special cases where the usual variance matrix estimators are valid. As a general example, consider the model

$$y = \mathbf{x}\boldsymbol{\beta} + \gamma f(\mathbf{w}, \boldsymbol{\delta}) + u, \qquad \mathrm{E}(u \mid \mathbf{z}, \mathbf{w}) = 0$$

and we estimate $\boldsymbol{\delta}$ in a first stage. If $\gamma = 0$, then the 2SLS estimator of $(\boldsymbol{\beta}', \gamma)'$ in the equation

$$y_i = \mathbf{x}_i \boldsymbol{\beta} + \gamma \hat{f}_i + error_i$$

using instruments $(\mathbf{z}_i, \hat{f}_i)$, has a limiting distribution that does not depend on the limiting distribution of $\sqrt{N}(\hat{\boldsymbol{\delta}} - \boldsymbol{\delta})$ under conditions (6.3) and (6.8). Therefore, the usual 2SLS t statistic for $\hat{\gamma}$, or its heteroskedsticity-robust version, can be used to test H_0: $\gamma = 0$.

6.2 Some Specification Tests

In Chapters 4 and 5 we covered what is usually called classical hypothesis testing for OLS and 2SLS. In this section we cover some tests of the assumptions underlying either OLS or 2SLS. These are easy to compute and should be routinely reported in applications.

6.2.1 Testing for Endogeneity

We start with the linear model and a single possibly endogenous variable. For notational clarity we now denote the dependent variable by y_1 and the potentially endogenous explanatory variable by y_2. As in all 2SLS contexts, y_2 can be continuous or binary, or it may have continuous and discrete characteristics; there are no restrictions. The population model is

$$y_1 = \mathbf{z}_1 \boldsymbol{\delta}_1 + \alpha_1 y_2 + u_1 \tag{6.9}$$

where $\mathbf{z}_1$ is $1 \times L_1$ (including a constant), $\boldsymbol{\delta}_1$ is $L_1 \times 1$, and u_1 is the unobserved disturbance. The set of all exogenous variables is denoted by the $1 \times L$ vector $\mathbf{z}$, where $\mathbf{z}_1$ is a strict subset of $\mathbf{z}$. The maintained exogeneity assumption is

$$\mathrm{E}(\mathbf{z}' u_1) = \mathbf{0} \tag{6.10}$$

It is important to keep in mind that condition (6.10) is assumed throughout this section. We also assume that equation (6.9) is identified when $\mathrm{E}(y_2 u_1) \neq 0$, which requires that $\mathbf{z}$ have at least one element not in $\mathbf{z}_1$ (the order condition); the rank condition is that at least one element of $\mathbf{z}$ not in $\mathbf{z}_1$ is partially correlated with y_2 (after netting out $\mathbf{z}_1$). Under these assumptions, we now wish to test the null hypothesis that y_2 is actually exogenous.

Hausman (1978) suggested comparing the OLS and 2SLS estimators of $\boldsymbol{\beta}_1 \equiv (\boldsymbol{\delta}_1', \alpha_1)'$ as a formal test of endogeneity: if y_2 is uncorrelated with u_1, the OLS and 2SLS estimators should differ only by sampling error. This reasoning leads to the **Hausman test** for endogeneity.

The original form of the statistic turns out to be cumbersome to compute because the matrix appearing in the quadratic form is singular, except when no exogenous variables are present in equation (6.9). As pointed out by Hausman (1978, 1983), there is a regression-based form of the test that turns out to be asymptotically equivalent to the original form of the Hausman test. In addition, it extends easily to other situations, including some nonlinear models that we cover in Chapters 15, 16, and 19.

To derive the regression-based test, write the linear projection of y_2 on $\mathbf{z}$ in error form as

$$y_2 = \mathbf{z}\boldsymbol{\pi}_2 + v_2 \tag{6.11}$$

$$\mathrm{E}(\mathbf{z}'v_2) = \mathbf{0} \tag{6.12}$$

where $\boldsymbol{\pi}_2$ is $L \times 1$. Since u_1 is uncorrelated with $\mathbf{z}$, it follows from equations (6.11) and (6.12) that y_2 is endogenous if and only if $\mathrm{E}(u_1 v_2) \neq 0$. Thus we can test whether the structural error, u_1, is correlated with the reduced form error, v_2. Write the linear projection of u_1 onto v_2 in error form as

$$u_1 = \rho_1 v_2 + e_1 \tag{6.13}$$

where $\rho_1 = \mathrm{E}(v_2 u_1)/\mathrm{E}(v_2^2)$, $\mathrm{E}(v_2 e_1) = 0$, and $\mathrm{E}(\mathbf{z}'e_1) = \mathbf{0}$ (since u_1 and v_2 are each orthogonal to $\mathbf{z}$). Thus, y_2 is exogenous if and only if $\rho_1 = 0$.

Plugging equation (6.13) into equation (6.9) gives the equation

$$y_1 = \mathbf{z}_1\boldsymbol{\delta}_1 + \alpha_1 y_2 + \rho_1 v_2 + e_1 \tag{6.14}$$

The key is that e_1 is uncorrelated with $\mathbf{z}_1$, y_2, and v_2 by construction. Therefore, a test of H_0: $\rho_1 = 0$ can be done using a standard t test on the variable v_2 in an OLS regression that includes $\mathbf{z}_1$ *and* y_2. The problem is that v_2 is not observed. Nevertheless, the reduced form parameters $\boldsymbol{\pi}_2$ are easily estimated by OLS. Let $\hat{v}_2$ denote the OLS residuals from the first-stage reduced form regression of y_2 on $\mathbf{z}$—remember that $\mathbf{z}$ contains *all* exogenous variables. If we replace v_2 with $\hat{v}_2$ we have the equation

$$y_1 = \mathbf{z}_1\boldsymbol{\delta}_1 + \alpha_1 y_2 + \rho_1 \hat{v}_2 + error \tag{6.15}$$

and $\boldsymbol{\delta}_1$, α_1, and ρ_1 can be consistently estimated by OLS. Now we can use the results on generated regressors in Section 6.1.1: the usual OLS t statistic for $\hat{\rho}_1$ is a valid test of H_0: $\rho_1 = 0$, provided the homoskedasticity assumption $\mathrm{E}(u_1^2 \mid \mathbf{z}, y_2) = \sigma_1^2$ is satisfied under H_0. (Remember, y_2 is exogenous under H_0.) A heteroskedasticity-robust t statistic can be used if heteroskedasticity is suspected under H_0.

As shown in Problem 5.1, the OLS estimates of δ_1 and α_1 from equation (6.15) are in fact *identical* to the 2SLS estimates. This fact is convenient because, along with being computationally simple, regression (6.15) allows us to compare the *magnitudes* of the OLS and 2SLS estimates in order to determine whether the differences are *practically* significant, rather than just finding statistically significant evidence of endogeneity of y_2. It also provides a way to verify that we have computed the statistic correctly.

We should remember that the OLS standard errors that would be reported from equation (6.15) are not valid unless $\rho_1 = 0$, because $\hat{v}_2$ is a generated regressor. In practice, if we reject H_0: $\rho_1 = 0$, then, to get the appropriate standard errors and other test statistics, we estimate equation (6.9) by 2SLS.

Example 6.1 (Testing for Endogeneity of Education in a Wage Equation): Consider the wage equation

$$\log(wage) = \delta_0 + \delta_1 exper + \delta_2 exper^2 + \alpha_1 educ + u_1 \tag{6.16}$$

for working women, where we believe that *educ* and u_1 may be correlated. The instruments for *educ* are parents' education and husband's education. So, we first regress *educ* on 1, *exper*, $exper^2$, *motheduc*, *fatheduc*, and *huseduc* and obtain the residuals, $\hat{v}_2$. Then we simply include $\hat{v}_2$ along with unity, *exper*, $exper^2$, and *educ* in an OLS regression and obtain the t statistic on $\hat{v}_2$. Using the data in MROZ.RAW gives the result $\hat{\rho}_1 = .047$ and $t_{\hat{\rho}_1} = 1.65$. We find evidence of endogeneity of *educ* at the 10 percent significance level against a two-sided alternative, and so 2SLS is probably a good idea (assuming that we trust the instruments). The correct 2SLS standard errors are given in Example 5.3.

Rather than comparing the OLS and 2SLS estimates of a particular linear combination of the parameters—as the original Hausman test does—it often makes sense to compare just the estimates of the parameter of interest, which is usually α_1. If, under H_0, Assumptions 2SLS.1–2SLS.3 hold with $\mathbf{w}$ replacing $\mathbf{z}$, where $\mathbf{w}$ includes all nonredundant elements in $\mathbf{x}$ and $\mathbf{z}$, obtaining the test is straightforward. Under these assumptions it can be shown that $\mathrm{Avar}(\hat{\alpha}_{1,2SLS} - \hat{\alpha}_{1,OLS}) = \mathrm{Avar}(\hat{\alpha}_{1,2SLS}) - \mathrm{Avar}(\hat{\alpha}_{1,OLS})$. [This conclusion essentially holds because of Theorem 5.3; Problem 6.12 asks you to show this result formally. Hausman (1978), Newey and McFadden (1994, Section 5.3), and Section 14.5.1 contain more general treatments.] Therefore, the Hausman t statistic is simply $(\hat{\alpha}_{1,2SLS} - \hat{\alpha}_{1,OLS})/\{[\mathrm{se}(\hat{\alpha}_{1,2SLS})]^2 - [\mathrm{se}(\hat{\alpha}_{1,OLS})]^2\}^{1/2}$, where the standard errors are the usual ones computed under homoskedasticity. The denominator in the t statistic is the standard error of $(\hat{\alpha}_{1,2SLS} - \hat{\alpha}_{1,OLS})$. If there is heteroskedasticity under H_0, this standard error is invalid because the asymptotic variance of the difference is no longer the difference in asymptotic variances.

Extending the regression-based Hausman test to several potentially endogenous explanatory variables is straightforward. Let $\mathbf{y}_2$ denote a $1 \times G_1$ vector of possible endogenous variables in the population model

$$y_1 = \mathbf{z}_1\boldsymbol{\delta}_1 + \mathbf{y}_2\boldsymbol{\alpha}_1 + u_1, \qquad \mathrm{E}(\mathbf{z}'u_1) = \mathbf{0} \tag{6.17}$$

where $\boldsymbol{\alpha}_1$ is now $G_1 \times 1$. Again, we assume the rank condition for 2SLS. Write the reduced form as $\mathbf{y}_2 = \mathbf{z}\boldsymbol{\Pi}_2 + \mathbf{v}_2$, where $\boldsymbol{\Pi}_2$ is $L \times G_1$ and $\mathbf{v}_2$ is the $1 \times G_1$ vector of population reduced form errors. For a generic observation let $\hat{\mathbf{v}}_2$ denote the $1 \times G_1$ vector of OLS residuals obtained from each reduced form. (In other words, take each element of $\mathbf{y}_2$ and regress it on $\mathbf{z}$ to obtain the RF residuals; then collect these in the row vector $\hat{\mathbf{v}}_2$.) Now, estimate the model

$$y_1 = \mathbf{z}_1\boldsymbol{\delta}_1 + \mathbf{y}_2\boldsymbol{\alpha}_1 + \hat{\mathbf{v}}_2\boldsymbol{\rho}_1 + error \tag{6.18}$$

and do a standard F test of H_0: $\boldsymbol{\rho}_1 = \mathbf{0}$, which tests G_1 restrictions in the unrestricted model (6.18). The restricted model is obtained by setting $\boldsymbol{\rho}_1 = \mathbf{0}$, which means we estimate the original model (6.17) by OLS. The test can be made robust to heteroskedasticity in u_1 (since $u_1 = e_1$ under H_0) by applying the heteroskedasticity-robust Wald statistic in Chapter 4. In some regression packages, such as Stata®, the robust test is implemented as an F-type test.

An alternative to the F test is an LM-type test. Let $\hat{u}_1$ be the OLS residuals from the regression y_1 on $\mathbf{z}_1, \mathbf{y}_2$ (the residuals obtained under the null that $\mathbf{y}_2$ is exogenous). Then, obtain the usual R-squared (assuming that $\mathbf{z}_1$ contains a constant), say R_u^2, from the regression

$$\hat{u}_1 \text{ on } \mathbf{z}_1, \mathbf{y}_2, \hat{\mathbf{v}}_2 \tag{6.19}$$

and use NR_u^2 as asymptotically $\chi^2_{G_1}$. This test again maintains homoskedasticity under H_0. The test can be made heteroskedasticity-robust using the method described in equation (4.17): take $\mathbf{x}_1 = (\mathbf{z}_1, \mathbf{y}_2)$ and $\mathbf{x}_2 = \hat{\mathbf{v}}_2$. See also Wooldridge (1995b).

Example 6.2 (Endogeneity of Education in a Wage Equation, continued): We add the interaction term *black·educ* to the log(*wage*) equation estimated by Card (1995); see also Problem 5.4. Write the model as

$$\log(wage) = \alpha_1 educ + \alpha_2 black{\cdot}educ + \mathbf{z}_1\boldsymbol{\delta}_1 + u_1 \tag{6.20}$$

where $\mathbf{z}_1$ contains a constant, *exper*, *exper*^{2}, *black*, *smsa*, 1966 regional dummy variables, and a 1966 SMSA indicator. If *educ* is correlated with u_1, then we also expect *black·educ* to be correlated with u_1. If *nearc4*, a binary indicator for whether a worker grew up near a four-year college, is valid as an instrumental variable for *educ*, then a natural instrumental variable for *black·educ* is *black·nearc4*. Note that *black·nearc4* is uncorrelated with u_1 under the conditional mean assumption $\mathrm{E}(u_1 \mid \mathbf{z}) = 0$, where $\mathbf{z}$ contains all exogenous variables.

The equation estimated by OLS is

$$\log(\widehat{wage}) = \underset{(0.75)}{4.81} + \underset{(.004)}{.071}\, educ + \underset{(.006)}{.018}\, black{\cdot}educ - \underset{(.079)}{.419}\, black + \cdots$$

Therefore, the return to education is estimated to be about 1.8 percentage points higher for blacks than for nonblacks, even though wages are substantially lower for blacks at all but unrealistically high levels of education. (It takes an estimated 23.3 years of education before a black worker earns as much as a nonblack worker.)

To test whether *educ* is exogenous we must test whether *educ* and *black·educ* are uncorrelated with u_1. We do so by first regressing *educ* on all instrumental variables: those elements in $\mathbf{z}_1$ plus *nearc4* and *black·nearc4*. (The interaction *black·nearc4* should be included because it might be partially correlated with *educ*.) Let $\hat{v}_{21}$ be the OLS residuals from this regression. Similarly, regress *black·educ* on $\mathbf{z}_1$, *nearc4*, and *black·nearc4*, and save the residuals $\hat{v}_{22}$. By the way, the fact that the dependent variable in the second reduced form regression, *black·educ*, is zero for a large fraction of the sample has no bearing on how we test for endogeneity.

Adding $\hat{v}_{21}$ and $\hat{v}_{22}$ to the OLS regression and computing the joint F test yields $F = 0.54$ and p-value $= 0.581$; thus we do not reject exogeneity of *educ* and *black·educ*.

Incidentally, the reduced form regressions confirm that *educ* is partially correlated with *nearc4* (but not *black·nearc4*) and *black·educ* is partially correlated with *black·nearc4* (but not *nearc4*). It is easily seen that these findings mean that the rank condition for 2SLS is satisfied—see Problem 5.15c. Even though *educ* does not appear to be endogenous in equation (6.20), we estimate the equation by 2SLS:

$$\log(\widehat{wage}) = \underset{(0.97)}{3.84} + \underset{(.057)}{.127}\, educ + \underset{(.040)}{.011}\, black{\cdot}educ - \underset{(.506)}{.283}\, black + \cdots$$

The 2SLS point estimates certainly differ from the OLS estimates, but the standard errors are so large that the 2SLS and OLS estimates are not statistically different.

6.2.2 Testing Overidentifying Restrictions

When we have more instruments than we need to identify an equation, we can test whether the additional instruments are valid in the sense that they are uncorrelated with u_1. To explain the various procedures, write the equation in the form

$$y_1 = \mathbf{z}_1\delta_1 + \mathbf{y}_2\alpha_1 + u_1 \tag{6.21}$$

where $\mathbf{z}_1$ is $1 \times L_1$ and $\mathbf{y}_2$ is $1 \times G_1$. The $1 \times L$ vector of all exogenous variables is again $\mathbf{z}$; partition this as $\mathbf{z} = (\mathbf{z}_1, \mathbf{z}_2)$ where $\mathbf{z}_2$ is $1 \times L_2$ and $L = L_1 + L_2$. Because the model is overidentified, $L_2 > G_1$. Under the usual identification conditions we could use any $1 \times G_1$ subset of $\mathbf{z}_2$ as instruments for $\mathbf{y}_2$ in estimating equation (6.21) (remember the elements of $\mathbf{z}_1$ act as their own instruments). Following his general principle, Hausman (1978) suggested comparing the 2SLS estimator using all instruments to 2SLS using a subset that just identifies equation (6.21). If all instruments are valid, the estimates should differ only as a result of sampling error. As with testing for endogeneity, constructing the original Hausman statistic is computationally cumbersome. Instead, a simple regression-based procedure is available.

It turns out that, under homoskedasticity, a test for validity of the overidentification restrictions is obtained as NR_u^2 from the OLS regression

$$\hat{u}_1 \text{ on } \mathbf{z} \tag{6.22}$$

where $\hat{u}_1$ are the 2SLS residuals using *all* of the instruments $\mathbf{z}$ and R_u^2 is the usual R-squared (assuming that $\mathbf{z}_1$ and $\mathbf{z}$ contain a constant; otherwise it is the uncentered R-squared). In other words, simply estimate regression (6.21) by 2SLS and obtain the 2SLS residuals, $\hat{u}_1$. Then regress these on all exogenous variables (including a constant). Under the null that $\mathrm{E}(\mathbf{z}'u_1) = \mathbf{0}$ and Assumption 2SLS.3, $NR_u^2 \overset{a}{\sim} \chi^2_{Q_1}$, where $Q_1 \equiv L_2 - G_1$ is the number of overidentifying restrictions.

The usefulness of the Hausman test is that, if we reject the null hypothesis, then our logic for choosing the IVs must be reexamined. If we fail to reject the null, then we can have some confidence in the overall set of instruments used. Of course, it could also be that the test has low power for detecting endogeneity of some of the instruments.

A heteroskedasticity-robust version is a little more complicated but is still easy to obtain. Let $\hat{\mathbf{y}}_2$ denote the fitted values from the first-stage regressions (each element of $\mathbf{y}_2$ onto $\mathbf{z}$). Now, let $\mathbf{h}_2$ be *any* $1 \times Q_1$ subset of $\mathbf{z}_2$. (It does not matter which elements of $\mathbf{z}_2$ we choose, as long as we choose Q_1 of them.) Regress each element of $\mathbf{h}_2$ onto $(\mathbf{z}_1, \hat{\mathbf{y}}_2)$ and collect the residuals, $\hat{\mathbf{r}}_2$ $(1 \times Q_1)$. Then an asymptotic $\chi^2_{Q_1}$ test statistic is obtained as $N - \mathrm{SSR}_0$ from the regression 1 on $\hat{u}_1\hat{\mathbf{r}}_2$. The proof that this method works is very similar to that for the heteroskedasticity-robust test for exclusion restrictions. See Wooldridge (1995b) for details.

Example 6.3 (Overidentifying Restrictions in the Wage Equation): In estimating equation (6.16) by 2SLS, we used (*motheduc, fatheduc, huseduc*) as instruments for *educ*. Therefore, there are two overidentifying restrictions. Letting $\hat{u}_1$ be the 2SLS residuals from equation (6.16) using all instruments, the test statistic is N times the R-squared from the OLS regression

$\hat{u}_1$ on 1, *exper*, $exper^2$, *motheduc*, *fatheduc*, *huseduc*

Under H_0 and homoskedasticity, $NR_u^2 \overset{a}{\sim} \chi_2^2$. Using the data on working women in MROZ.RAW gives $R_u^2 = .0026$, and so the overidentification test statistic is about 1.11. The p-value is about .574, so the overidentifying restrictions are not rejected at any reasonable level.

For the heteroskedasticity-robust version, one approach is to obtain the residuals, $\hat{r}_1$ and $\hat{r}_2$, from the OLS regressions *motheduc* on 1, *exper*, $exper^2$, and $\widehat{educ}$ and *fatheduc* on 1, *exper*, $exper^2$, and $\widehat{educ}$, where $\widehat{educ}$ are the first-stage fitted values from the regression *educ* on 1, *exper*, $exper^2$, *motheduc*, *fatheduc*, and *huseduc*. Then obtain $N - \mathrm{SSR}$ from the OLS regression 1 on $\hat{u}_1 \cdot \hat{r}_1$, $\hat{u}_1 \cdot \hat{r}_2$. Using only the 428 observations on working women to obtain $\hat{r}_1$ and $\hat{r}_2$, the value of the robust test statistic is about 1.04 with p-value $= .595$, which is similar to the p-value for the nonrobust test.

6.2.3 Testing Functional Form

Sometimes we need a test with power for detecting neglected nonlinearities in models estimated by OLS or 2SLS. A useful approach is to add nonlinear functions, such as squares and cross products, to the original model. This approach is easy when all explanatory variables are exogenous: F statistics and LM statistics for exclusion restrictions are easily obtained. It is a little tricky for models with endogenous explanatory variables because we need to choose instruments for the additional nonlinear functions of the endogenous variables. We postpone this topic until Chapter 9 when we discuss simultaneous equation models. See also Wooldridge (1995b).

Putting in squares and cross products of all exogenous variables can consume many degrees of freedom. An alternative is Ramsey's (1969) RESET, which has degrees of freedom that do not depend on K. Write the model as

$$y = \mathbf{x}\boldsymbol{\beta} + u \tag{6.23}$$

$$\mathrm{E}(u \mid \mathbf{x}) = 0 \tag{6.24}$$

[You should convince yourself that it makes no sense to test for functional form if we only assume that $\mathrm{E}(\mathbf{x}'u) = \mathbf{0}$. If equation (6.23) defines a linear projection, then, by definition, functional form is not an issue.] Under condition (6.24) we know that any function of $\mathbf{x}$ is uncorrelated with u (hence the previous suggestion of putting squares and cross products of $\mathbf{x}$ as additional regressors). In particular, if condition (6.24) holds, then $(\mathbf{x}\boldsymbol{\beta})^p$ is uncorrelated with u for any integer p. Since $\boldsymbol{\beta}$ is not observed, we replace it with the OLS estimator, $\hat{\boldsymbol{\beta}}$. Define $\hat{y}_i = \mathbf{x}_i\hat{\boldsymbol{\beta}}$ as the OLS fitted values and $\hat{u}_i$ as the OLS residuals. By definition of OLS, the sample covariance between $\hat{u}_i$ and $\hat{y}_i$ is zero. But we can test whether the $\hat{u}_i$ are sufficiently correlated with low-order polynomials in $\hat{y}_i$, say $\hat{y}_i^2$, $\hat{y}_i^3$, and $\hat{y}_i^4$, as a test for neglected nonlinearity. There are a couple of ways to do so. Ramsey suggests adding these terms to equation (6.23) and doing a standard F test [which would have an approximate $\mathscr{F}_{3,N-K-3}$ distribution under equation (6.23) and the homoskedasticity assumption $\mathrm{E}(u^2 \mid \mathbf{x}) = \sigma^2$]. Another possibility is to use an LM test: Regress $\hat{u}_i$ onto $\mathbf{x}_i$, $\hat{y}_i^2$, $\hat{y}_i^3$, and $\hat{y}_i^4$ and use N times the R-squared from this regression as χ_3^2. The methods discussed in Chapter 4 for obtaining heteroskedasticity-robust statistics can be applied here as well. Ramsey's test uses generated regressors, but the null is that each generated regressor has zero population coefficient, and so the usual limit theory applies. (See Section 6.1.1.)

There is some misunderstanding in the testing literature about the merits of RESET. It has been claimed that RESET can be used to test for a multitude of specification problems, including omitted variables and heteroskedasticity. In fact, RESET is generally a poor test for either of these problems. It is easy to write down models where an omitted variable, say q, is highly correlated with each $\mathbf{x}$, but RESET has the same distribution that it has under H_0. A leading case is seen when $\mathrm{E}(q \mid \mathbf{x})$ is linear in $\mathbf{x}$. Then $\mathrm{E}(y \mid \mathbf{x})$ is linear in $\mathbf{x}$ [even though $\mathrm{E}(y \mid \mathbf{x}) \neq \mathrm{E}(y \mid \mathbf{x}, q)$], and the asymptotic power of RESET equals its asymptotic size. See Wooldridge (1995b) and Problem 6.4a. The following is an empirical illustration.

Example 6.4 (Testing for Neglected Nonlinearities in a Wage Equation): We use OLS and the data in NLS80.RAW to estimate the equation from Example 4.3:

$$\log(wage) = \beta_0 + \beta_1 exper + \beta_2 tenure + \beta_3 married + \beta_4 south$$
$$+ \beta_5 urban + \beta_6 black + \beta_7 educ + u$$

The null hypothesis is that the expected value of u given the explanatory variables in the equation is zero. The R-squared from the regression $\hat{u}$ on $\mathbf{x}$, $\hat{y}^2$, and $\hat{y}^3$ yields $R_u^2 = .0004$, so the chi-square statistic is .374 with p-value $\approx .83$. (Adding $\hat{y}^4$ only increases the p-value.) Therefore, RESET provides no evidence of functional form misspecification.

Even though we already know IQ shows up very significantly in the equation (t statistic $= 3.60$—see Example 4.3), RESET does not, and should not be expected to, detect the omitted variable problem. It can only test whether the expected value of y given the variables actually in the regression is linear in those variables.

6.2.4 Testing for Heteroskedasticity

As we have seen for both OLS and 2SLS, heteroskedasticity does not affect the consistency of the estimators, and it is only a minor nuisance for inference. Nevertheless, sometimes we want to test for the presence of heteroskedasticity in order to justify use of the usual OLS or 2SLS statistics. If heteroskedasticity is present, more efficient estimation is possible.

We begin with the case where the explanatory variables are exogenous in the sense that u has zero mean given $\mathbf{x}$:

$$y = \beta_0 + \mathbf{x}\boldsymbol{\beta} + u, \qquad \mathrm{E}(u \mid \mathbf{x}) = 0$$

The reason we do not assume the weaker assumption $\mathrm{E}(\mathbf{x}'u) = \mathbf{0}$ is that the following class of tests we derive—which encompasses all of the widely used tests for heteroskedasticity—are not valid unless $\mathrm{E}(u \mid \mathbf{x}) = 0$ is maintained under H_0. Thus we maintain that the mean $\mathrm{E}(y \mid \mathbf{x})$ is correctly specified, and then we test the constant conditional variance assumption. If we do not assume correct specification of $\mathrm{E}(y \mid \mathbf{x})$, a significant heteroskedasticity test might just be detecting misspecified functional form in $\mathrm{E}(y \mid \mathbf{x})$; see Problem 6.4c.

Because $\mathrm{E}(u \mid \mathbf{x}) = 0$, the null hypothesis can be stated as H_0: $\mathrm{E}(u^2 \mid \mathbf{x}) = \sigma^2$. Under the alternative, $\mathrm{E}(u^2 \mid \mathbf{x})$ depends on $\mathbf{x}$ in some way. Thus it makes sense to test H_0 by looking at covariances

$$\mathrm{Cov}[\mathbf{h}(\mathbf{x}), u^2] \tag{6.25}$$

for some $1 \times Q$ vector function $\mathbf{h}(\mathbf{x})$. Under H_0, the covariance in expression (6.25) should be zero for any choice of $\mathbf{h}(\cdot)$.

Of course a general way to test zero correlation is to use a regression. Putting i subscripts on the variables, write the model

$$u_i^2 = \delta_0 + \mathbf{h}_i\boldsymbol{\delta} + v_i \tag{6.26}$$

where $\mathbf{h}_i \equiv \mathbf{h}(\mathbf{x}_i)$; we make the standard rank assumption that $\mathrm{Var}(\mathbf{h}_i)$ has rank Q, so that there is no perfect collinearity in $\mathbf{h}_i$. Under H_0, $\mathrm{E}(v_i \mid \mathbf{h}_i) = \mathrm{E}(v_i \mid \mathbf{x}_i) = 0$, $\boldsymbol{\delta} = \mathbf{0}$, and $\delta_0 = \sigma^2$. Thus we can apply an F test or an LM test for the null H_0: $\boldsymbol{\delta} = \mathbf{0}$ in equation (6.26). One thing to notice is that v_i cannot have a normal distribution under H_0: because $v_i = u_i^2 - \sigma^2$, $v_i \geq -\sigma^2$. This does not matter for asymptotic analysis; the OLS regression from equation (6.26) gives a consistent, $\sqrt{N}$-asymptotically normal estimator of $\boldsymbol{\delta}$ whether or not H_0 is true. But to apply a standard F or LM test, we must assume that, under H_0, $\mathrm{E}(v_i^2 \mid \mathbf{x}_i)$ is constant: that is, the errors in equation (6.26) are homoskedastic. In terms of the original error u_i, this assumption implies that

$$\mathrm{E}(u_i^4 \mid \mathbf{x}_i) = \mathit{constant} \equiv \kappa^2 \tag{6.27}$$

under H_0. This is called the **homokurtosis** (constant conditional fourth moment) assumption. Homokurtosis always holds when u is independent of $\mathbf{x}$, but there are conditional distributions for which $\mathrm{E}(u \mid \mathbf{x}) = 0$ and $\mathrm{Var}(u \mid \mathbf{x}) = \sigma^2$ but $\mathrm{E}(u^4 \mid \mathbf{x})$ depends on $\mathbf{x}$.

As a practical matter, we cannot test $\boldsymbol{\delta} = \mathbf{0}$ in equation (6.26) directly because u_i is not observed. Since $u_i = y_i - \mathbf{x}_i\boldsymbol{\beta}$ and we have a consistent estimator of $\boldsymbol{\beta}$, it is natural to replace u_i^2 with $\hat{u}_i^2$, where the $\hat{u}_i$ are the OLS residuals for observation i. Doing this step and applying, say, the LM principle, we obtain NR_c^2 from the regression

$$\hat{u}_i^2 \text{ on } 1, \mathbf{h}_i, \qquad i = 1, 2, \ldots, N \tag{6.28}$$

where R_c^2 is just the usual centered R-squared. Now, if the u_i^2 were used in place of the $\hat{u}_i^2$, we know that, under H_0 and condition (6.27), $NR_c^2 \overset{a}{\sim} \chi_Q^2$, where Q is the dimension of $\mathbf{h}_i$.

What adjustment is needed because we have estimated u_i^2? It turns out that, because of the structure of these tests, no adjustment is needed to the asymptotics. (This statement is not generally true for regressions where the dependent variable has been estimated in a first stage; the current setup is special in that regard.) After tedious algebra, it can be shown that

$$N^{-1/2} \sum_{i=1}^{N} \mathbf{h}_i'(\hat{u}_i^2 - \hat{\sigma}^2) = N^{-1/2} \sum_{i=1}^{N} (\mathbf{h}_i - \boldsymbol{\mu}_h)'(u_i^2 - \sigma^2) + o_p(1) \tag{6.29}$$

see Problem 6.5. Along with condition (6.27), this equation can be shown to justify the NR_c^2 test from regression (6.28).

Two popular tests are special cases. Koenker's (1981) version of the Breusch and Pagan (1979) test is obtained by taking $\mathbf{h}_i \equiv \mathbf{x}_i$, so that $Q = K$. [The original version of the Breusch-Pagan test relies heavily on normality of the u_i, in particular $\kappa^2 = 3\sigma^2$, so that Koenker's version based on NR_c^2 in regression (6.28) is preferred.] White's (1980b) test is obtained by taking $\mathbf{h}_i$ to be all nonconstant, unique elements of $\mathbf{x}_i$ and $\mathbf{x}_i'\mathbf{x}_i$: the levels, squares, and cross products of the regressors in the conditional mean.

The Breusch-Pagan and White tests have degrees of freedom that depend on the number of regressors in $\mathrm{E}(y \mid \mathbf{x})$. Sometimes we want to conserve on degrees of freedom. A test that combines features of the Breusch-Pagan and White tests, but which has only two *df*s, takes $\hat{\mathbf{h}}_i \equiv (\hat{y}_i, \hat{y}_i^2)$, where the $\hat{y}_i$ are the OLS fitted values. (Recall that these are linear functions of the $\mathbf{x}_i$.) To justify this test, we must be able to replace $\mathbf{h}(\mathbf{x}_i)$ with $\mathbf{h}(\mathbf{x}_i, \hat{\boldsymbol{\beta}})$. We discussed the generated regressors problem for OLS in Section 6.1.1 and concluded that, for *testing* purposes, using estimates from earlier stages causes no complications. This is the case here as well: NR_c^2 from $\hat{u}_i^2$ on $1, \hat{y}_i, \hat{y}_i^2$, $i = 1, 2, \ldots, N$ has a limiting χ_2^2 distribution under the null, along with condition (6.27). This is easily seen to be a special case of the White test because $(\hat{y}_i, \hat{y}_i^2)$ contains two linear combinations of the squares and cross products of all elements in $\mathbf{x}_i$.

A simple modification is available for relaxing the auxiliary homokurtosis assumption (6.27). Following the work of Wooldridge (1990)—or, working directly from the representation in equation (6.29), as in Problem 6.5—it can be shown that $N - \mathrm{SSR}_0$ from the regression (without a constant)

$$1 \text{ on } (\mathbf{h}_i - \bar{\mathbf{h}})(\hat{u}_i^2 - \hat{\sigma}^2), \qquad i = 1, 2, \ldots, N \tag{6.30}$$

is distributed asymptotically as χ_Q^2 under H_0 [there are Q regressors in regression (6.30)]. This test is very similar to the heteroskedasticity-robust LM statistics derived in Chapter 4. It is sometimes called a **heterokurtosis-robust test** for heteroskedasticity.

If we allow some elements of $\mathbf{x}_i$ to be endogenous but assume we have instruments $\mathbf{z}_i$ such that $\mathrm{E}(u_i \mid \mathbf{z}_i) = 0$ and the rank condition holds, then we can test H_0: $\mathrm{E}(u_i^2 \mid \mathbf{z}_i) = \sigma^2$ (which implies Assumption 2SLS.3). Let $\mathbf{h}_i \equiv \mathbf{h}(\mathbf{z}_i)$ be a $1 \times Q$ function of the exogenous variables. The statistics are computed as in either regression (6.28) or (6.30), depending on whether the homokurtosis is maintained, where the $\hat{u}_i$ are the 2SLS residuals. There is, however, one caveat. For the validity of the asymptotic variances that these regressions implicitly use, an additional assumption is needed under H_0: $\mathrm{Cov}(\mathbf{x}_i, u_i \mid \mathbf{z}_i)$ must be constant. This covariance is zero when $\mathbf{z}_i = \mathbf{x}_i$, so there is no additional assumption when the regressors are exogenous. Without the assumption of constant conditional covariance, the tests for heteroskedasticity are more complicated. For details, see Wooldridge (1990).

You should remember that $\mathbf{h}_i$ (or $\hat{\mathbf{h}}_i$) must only be a function of exogenous variables and estimated parameters; it should not depend on endogenous elements of $\mathbf{x}_i$. Therefore, when $\mathbf{x}_i$ contains endogenous variables, it is *not* valid to use $\mathbf{x}_i\hat{\boldsymbol{\beta}}$ and $(\mathbf{x}_i\hat{\boldsymbol{\beta}})^2$ as elements of $\hat{\mathbf{h}}_i$. It *is* valid to use, say, $\hat{\mathbf{x}}_i\hat{\boldsymbol{\beta}}$ and $(\hat{\mathbf{x}}_i\hat{\boldsymbol{\beta}})^2$, where the $\hat{\mathbf{x}}_i$ are the first-stage fitted values from regressing $\mathbf{x}_i$ on $\mathbf{z}_i$.

6.3 Single-Equation Methods under Other Sampling Schemes

So far our treatment of OLS and 2SLS has been explicitly for the case of random samples. In this section we briefly discuss some issues that arise for other sampling schemes that are sometimes assumed for cross section data.

6.3.1 Pooled Cross Sections over Time

A data structure that is useful for a variety of purposes, including policy analysis, is what we will call **pooled cross sections over time**. The idea is that during each year a new random sample is taken from the relevant population. Since distributions of variables tend to change over time, the identical distribution assumption is not usually valid, but the independence assumption is. This approach gives rise to **indepen-**

dent, not identically distributed (**i.n.i.d.**) observations. It is important not to confuse a pooling of independent cross sections with a different data structure, panel data, which we treat starting in Chapter 7. Briefly, in a panel data set we follow the same group of individuals, firms, cities, and so on over time. In a pooling of cross sections over time, there is no replicability over time. (Or, if units appear in more than one time period, their recurrence is treated as coincidental and ignored.)

Every method we have learned for pure cross section analysis can be applied to pooled cross sections, including corrections for heteroskedasticity, specification testing, instrumental variables, and so on. But in using pooled cross sections, we should usually include year (or other time period) dummies to account for aggregate changes over time. If year dummies appear in a model, and it is estimated by 2SLS, the year dummies are their own instruments, as the passage of time is exogenous. For an example, see Problem 6.8. Time dummies can also appear in tests for heteroskedasticity to determine whether the unconditional error variance has changed over time.

In some cases we interact some explanatory variables with the time dummies to allow partial effects to change over time. This procedure can be very useful for policy analysis. In fact, much of the recent literature in policy analyis using **natural experiments** can be cast as a pooled cross section analysis with appropriately chosen dummy variables and interactions.

In the simplest case, we have two time periods, say year 1 and year 2. There are also two groups, which we will call a **control group** and an **experimental group** or **treatment group**. In the natural experiment literature, people (or firms, or cities, and so on) find themselves in the treatment group essentially by accident. For example, to study the effects of an unexpected change in unemployment insurance on unemployment duration, we choose the treatment group to be unemployed individuals from a state that has a change in unemployment compensation. The control group could be unemployed workers from a neighboring state. The two time periods chosen would straddle the policy change.

As another example, the treatment group might consist of houses in a city undergoing unexpected property tax reform, and the control group would be houses in a nearby, similar town that is not subject to a property tax change. Again, the two (or more) years of data would include the period of the policy change. Treatment means that a house is in the city undergoing the regime change.

To formalize the discussion, call A the control group, and let B denote the treatment group; the dummy variable dB equals unity for those in the treatment group and is zero otherwise. Letting $d2$ denote a dummy variable for the second (post-policy-change) time period, the simplest equation for analyzing the impact of the policy change is

$$y = \beta_0 + \delta_0 d2 + \beta_1 dB + \delta_1 d2 \cdot dB + u \tag{6.31}$$

where y is the outcome variable of interest. The period dummy *d2* captures aggregate factors that affect y over time in the same way for both groups. The presence of *dB* by itself captures possible differences between the treatment and control groups before the policy change occurs. The coefficient of interest, δ_1, multiplies the interaction term, $d2 \cdot dB$ (which is simply a dummy variable equal to unity for those observations in the treatment group in the second year).

The OLS estimator, $\hat{\delta}_1$, has a very interesting interpretation. Let $\bar{y}_{A,1}$ denote the sample average of y for the control group in the first year, and let $\bar{y}_{A,2}$ be the average of y for the control group in the second year. Define $\bar{y}_{B,1}$ and $\bar{y}_{B,2}$ similarly. Then $\hat{\delta}_1$ can be expressed as

$$\hat{\delta}_1 = (\bar{y}_{B,2} - \bar{y}_{B,1}) - (\bar{y}_{A,2} - \bar{y}_{A,1}) \tag{6.32}$$

This estimator has been labeled the **difference-in-differences (DID)** estimator in the recent program evaluation literature, although it has a long history in analysis of variance.

To see how effective $\hat{\delta}_1$ is for estimating policy effects, we can compare it with some alternative estimators. One possibility is to ignore the control group completely and use the change in the mean over time for the treatment group, $\bar{y}_{B,2} - \bar{y}_{B,1}$, to measure the policy effect. The problem with this estimator is that the mean response can change over time for reasons unrelated to the policy change. Another possibility is to ignore the first time period and compute the difference in means for the treatment and control groups in the second time period, $\bar{y}_{B,2} - \bar{y}_{A,2}$. The problem with this pure cross section approach is that there might be systematic, unmeasured differences in the treatment and control groups that have nothing to do with the treatment; attributing the difference in averages to a particular policy might be misleading.

By comparing the time changes in the means for the treatment and control groups, both group-specific and time-specific effects are allowed for. Nevertheless, unbiasedness of the DID estimator still requires that the policy change not be systematically related to other factors that affect y (and are hidden in u).

In most applications, additional covariates appear in equation (6.31); for example, characteristics of unemployed people or housing characteristics. These account for the possibility that the random samples within a group have systematically different characteristics in the two time periods. The OLS estimator of δ_1 no longer has the simple representation in equation (6.32), but its interpretation is essentially unchanged.

Example 6.5 (Length of Time on Workers' Compensation): Meyer, Viscusi, and Durbin (1995) (hereafter, MVD) study the length of time (in weeks) that an injured worker receives workers' compensation. On July 15, 1980, Kentucky raised the cap on weekly earnings that were covered by workers' compensation. An increase in the cap has no effect on the benefit for low-income workers, but it makes it less costly for a high-income worker to stay on workers' comp. Therefore, the control group is low-income workers, and the treatment group is high-income workers; high-income workers are defined as those for whom the pre-policy-change cap on benefits is binding. Using random samples both before and after the policy change, MVD are able to test whether more generous workers' compensation causes people to stay out of work longer (everything else fixed). MVD start with a difference-in-differences analysis, using log(*durat*) as the dependent variable. The variable *afchnge* is the dummy variable for observations after the policy change, and *highearn* is the dummy variable for high earners. The estimated equation is

$$\begin{aligned} \log(\hat{durat}) = {} & \underset{(0.031)}{1.126} + \underset{(.0447)}{.0077}\, afchnge + \underset{(.047)}{.256}\, highearn \\ & + \underset{(.069)}{.191}\, afchnge \cdot highearn \end{aligned} \tag{6.33}$$

$N = 5{,}626, \qquad R^2 = .021$

Therefore, $\hat{\delta}_1 = .191$ ($t = 2.77$), which implies that the average duration on workers' compensation increased by about 19 percent due to the higher earnings cap. The coefficient on *afchnge* is small and statistically insignificant: as is expected, the increase in the earnings cap had no effect on duration for low-earnings workers. The coefficient on *highearn* shows that, even in the absence of any change in the earnings cap, high earners spent much more time—on the order of $100 \cdot [\exp(.256) - 1] = 29.2$ percent—on workers' compensation.

MVD also add a variety of controls for gender, marital status, age, industry, and type of injury. These allow for the fact that the kind of people and type of injuries differ systematically in the two years. Perhaps not surprisingly, controlling for these factors has little effect on the estimate of δ_1; see the MVD article and Problem 6.9.

Sometimes the two groups consist of people or cities in different states in the United States, often close geographically. For example, to assess the impact of changing alcohol taxes on alcohol consumption, we can obtain random samples on individuals from two states for two years. In state A, the control group, there was no change in alcohol taxes. In state B, taxes increased between the two years. The outcome variable would be a measure of alcohol consumption, and equation (6.31) can be estimated to determine the effect of the tax on alcohol consumption. Other factors, such as age, education, and gender can be controlled for, although this procedure is not necessary for consistency if sampling is random in both years and in both states.

The basic equation (6.31) can be easily modified to allow for continuous, or at least nonbinary, "treatments." An example is given in Problem 6.7, where the "treatment" for a particular home is its distance from a garbage incinerator site. In other words, there is not really a control group: each unit is put somewhere on a continuum of possible treatments. The analysis is similar because the treatment dummy, dB, is simply replaced with the nonbinary treatment.

For a survey on the natural experiment methodology, as well as several additional examples, see Meyer (1995).

6.3.2 Geographically Stratified Samples

Various kinds of stratified sampling, where units in the sample are represented with different frequencies than they are in the population, are also common in the social sciences. We treat general kinds of stratification in Chapter 17. Here, we discuss some issues that arise with geographical stratification, where random samples are taken from separate geographical units.

If the geographically stratified sample can be treated as being independent but not identically distributed, no substantive modifications are needed to apply the previous econometric methods. However, it is prudent to allow different intercepts across strata, and even different slopes in some cases. For example, if people are sampled from states in the United States, it is often important to include state dummy variables to allow for systematic differences in the response and explanatory variables across states.

If we are interested in the effects of variables measured at the strata level, and the individual observations are correlated because of unobserved strata effects, estimation and inference are much more complicated. A model with strata-level covariates and within-strata correlation is

$$y_{is} = \mathbf{x}_{is}\boldsymbol{\beta} + \mathbf{z}_s\boldsymbol{\gamma} + q_s + e_{is} \tag{6.34}$$

where i is for individual and s is for stratum. The covariates in $\mathbf{x}_{is}$ change with the individual, while $\mathbf{z}_s$ changes only at the strata level. That is, there is correlation in the covariates across individuals within the same stratum. The variable q_s is an unobserved stratum effect. We would typically assume that the observations are independently distributed across strata, that the e_{is} are independent across i, and that

$\mathrm{E}(e_{is} \mid \mathbf{X}_s, \mathbf{z}_s, q_s) = 0$ for all i and s—where $\mathbf{X}_s$ is the set of explanatory variables for all units in stratum s—and q_s is an unobserved stratum effect.

The presence of the unobservable q_s induces correlation in the composite error $u_{is} = q_s + e_{is}$ within each stratum. If we are interested in the coefficients on the individual-specific variables, that is, $\boldsymbol{\beta}$, then there is a simple solution: include stratum dummies along with $\mathbf{x}_{is}$. That is, we estimate the model $y_{is} = \alpha_s + \mathbf{x}_{is}\boldsymbol{\beta} + e_{is}$ by OLS, where α_s is the stratum-specific intercept.

Things are more interesting when we want to estimate $\boldsymbol{\gamma}$. The OLS estimators of $\boldsymbol{\beta}$ and $\boldsymbol{\gamma}$ in the regression of y_{is} on $\mathbf{x}_{is}$, $\mathbf{z}_s$ are still unbiased if $\mathrm{E}(q_s \mid \mathbf{X}_s, \mathbf{z}_s) = 0$, but consistency and asymptotic normality are tricky, because, with a small number of strata and many observations within each stratum, the asymptotic analysis makes sense only if the number of observations within each stratum grows, usually with the number of strata fixed. Because the observations within a stratum are correlated, the usual law of large numbers and central limit theorem cannot be applied. By means of a simulation study, Moulton (1990) shows that ignoring the within-group correlation when obtaining standard errors for $\hat{\boldsymbol{\gamma}}$ can be very misleading. Moulton also gives some corrections to the OLS standard errors, but it is not clear what kind of asymptotic analysis justifies them.

If the strata are, say, states in the United States, and we are interested in the effect of state-level policy variables on economic behavior, one way to proceed is to use state-level data on all variables. This avoids the within-stratum correlation in the composite error in equation (6.34). A drawback is that state policies that can be taken as exogenous at the individual level are often endogenous at the aggregate level. However, if $\mathbf{z}_s$ in equation (6.34) contains policy variables, perhaps we should question whether these would be uncorrelated with q_s. If q_s and $\mathbf{z}_s$ are correlated, OLS using individual-level data would be biased and inconsistent.

Related issues arise when aggregate-level variables are used as instruments in equations describing individual behavior. For example, in a birth weight equation, Currie and Cole (1993) use measures of state-level AFDC benefits as instruments for individual women's participation in AFDC. (Therefore, the binary endogenous explanatory variable is at the individual level, while the instruments are at the state level.) If state-level AFDC benefits are exogenous in the birth weight equation, and AFDC participation is sufficiently correlated with state benefit levels—a question that can be checked using the first-stage regression—then the IV approach will yield a consistent estimator of the effect of AFDC participation on birth weight.

Moffitt (1996) discusses assumptions under which using aggregate-level IVs yields consistent estimators. He gives the example of using observations on workers from two cities to estimate the impact of job training programs. In each city, some people received some job training while others did not. The key element in $\mathbf{x}_{is}$ is a job training indicator. If, say, city A exogenously offered more job training slots than city B, a city dummy variable can be used as an IV for whether each worker received training. See Moffitt (1996) and Problem 5.13b for an interpretation of such estimators.

If there are unobserved group effects in the error term, then at a minimum, the usual 2SLS standard errors will be inappropriate. More problematic is that aggregate-level variables might be correlated with q_s. In the birth weight example, the level of AFDC benefits might be correlated with unobserved health care quality variables that are in q_s. In the job training example, city A may have spent more on job training because its workers are, on average, less productive than the workers in city B. Unfortunately, controlling for q_s by putting in strata dummies and applying 2SLS does not work: by definition, the instruments only vary across strata—not within strata—and so $\boldsymbol{\beta}$ in equation (6.34) would be unidentified. In the job training example, we would put in a dummy variable for city of residence as an explanatory variable, and therefore we could not use this dummy variable as an IV for job training participation: we would be short one instrument.

6.3.3 Spatial Dependence

As the previous subsection suggests, cross section data that are not the result of independent sampling can be difficult to handle. **Spatial correlation**, or, more generally, **spatial dependence**, typically occurs when cross section units are large relative to the population, such as when data are collected at the county, state, province, or country level. Outcomes from adjacent units are likely to be correlated. If the correlation arises mainly through the explanatory variables (as opposed to unobservables), then, practically speaking, nothing needs to be done (although the asymptotic analysis can be complicated). In fact, sometimes covariates for one county or state appear as explanatory variables in the equation for neighboring units, as a way of capturing spillover effects. This fact in itself causes no real difficulties.

When the unobservables are correlated across nearby geographical units, OLS can still have desirable properties—often unbiasedness, consistency, and asymptotic normality can be established—but the asymptotic arguments are not nearly as unified as in the random sampling case, and estimating asymptotic variances becomes difficult.

6.3.4 Cluster Samples

Cluster sampling is another case where cross section observations are correlated, but it is somewhat easier to handle. The key is that we randomly sample a large number of clusters, and each cluster consists of relatively few units (compared with the overall sample size). While we allow the units within each cluster to be correlated, we assume independence across clusters. An example is studying teenage peer effects using a large sample of neighborhoods (the clusters) with relatively few teenagers per neighborhood. Or, using siblings in a large sample of families. The asymptotic analysis is with fixed cluster sizes with the number of clusters getting large. As we will see in Section 11.5, handling within-cluster correlation in this context is relatively straightforward. In fact, when the explanatory variables are exogenous, OLS is consistent and asymptotically normal, but the asymptotic variance matrix needs to be adjusted. The same holds for 2SLS.

Problems

6.1. a. In Problem 5.4d, test the null hypothesis that *educ* is exogenous.

b. Test the the single overidentifying restriction in this example.

6.2. In Problem 5.8b, test the null hypothesis that *educ* and *IQ* are exogenous in the equation estimated by 2SLS.

6.3. Consider a model for individual data to test whether nutrition affects productivity (in a developing country):

$$\log(produc) = \delta_0 + \delta_1 exper + \delta_2 exper^2 + \delta_3 educ + \alpha_1 calories + \alpha_2 protein + u_1 \tag{6.35}$$

where *produc* is some measure of worker productivity, *calories* is caloric intake per day, and *protein* is a measure of protein intake per day. Assume here that *exper*, $exper^2$, and *educ* are all exogenous. The variables *calories* and *protein* are possibly correlated with u_1 (see Strauss and Thomas, 1995, for discussion). Possible instrumental variables for *calories* and *protein* are regional prices of various goods such as grains, meats, breads, dairy products, and so on.

a. Under what circumstances do prices make good IVs for *calories* and *proteins*? What if prices reflect quality of food?

b. How many prices are needed to identify equation (6.35)?

c. Suppose we have M prices, $p_1, \ldots, p_M$. Explain how to test the null hypothesis that *calories* and *protein* are exogenous in equation (6.35).

6.4. Consider a structural linear model with unobserved variable q:

$$y = \mathbf{x}\boldsymbol{\beta} + q + v, \qquad \mathrm{E}(v \mid \mathbf{x}, q) = 0$$

Suppose, in addition, that $\mathrm{E}(q \mid \mathbf{x}) = \mathbf{x}\boldsymbol{\delta}$ for some $K \times 1$ vector $\boldsymbol{\delta}$; thus, q and $\mathbf{x}$ are possibly correlated.

a. Show that $\mathrm{E}(y \mid \mathbf{x})$ is linear in $\mathbf{x}$. What consequences does this fact have for tests of functional form to detect the presence of q? Does it matter how strongly q and $\mathbf{x}$ are correlated? Explain.

b. Now add the assumptions $\mathrm{Var}(v \mid \mathbf{x}, q) = \sigma_v^2$ and $\mathrm{Var}(q \mid \mathbf{x}) = \sigma_q^2$. Show that $\mathrm{Var}(y \mid \mathbf{x})$ is constant. [Hint: $\mathrm{E}(qv \mid \mathbf{x}) = 0$ by iterated expectations.] What does this fact imply about using tests for heteroskedasticity to detect omitted variables?

c. Now write the equation as $y = \mathbf{x}\boldsymbol{\beta} + u$, where $\mathrm{E}(\mathbf{x}'u) = \mathbf{0}$ and $\mathrm{Var}(u \mid \mathbf{x}) = \sigma^2$. If $\mathrm{E}(u \mid \mathbf{x}) \neq \mathrm{E}(u)$, argue that an LM test of the form (6.28) will detect "heteroskedasticity" in u, at least in large samples.

6.5. a. Verify equation (6.29) under the assumptions $\mathrm{E}(u \mid \mathbf{x}) = 0$ and $\mathrm{E}(u^2 \mid \mathbf{x}) = \sigma^2$.

b. Show that, under the additional assumption (6.27),

$$\mathrm{E}[(u_i^2 - \sigma^2)^2(\mathbf{h}_i - \boldsymbol{\mu}_h)'(\mathbf{h}_i - \boldsymbol{\mu}_h)] = \eta^2 \mathrm{E}[(\mathbf{h}_i - \boldsymbol{\mu}_h)'(\mathbf{h}_i - \boldsymbol{\mu}_h)]$$

where $\eta^2 = \mathrm{E}[(u^2 - \sigma^2)^2]$.

c. Explain why parts a and b imply that the LM statistic from regression (6.28) has a limiting χ_Q^2 distribution.

d. If condition (6.27) does not hold, obtain a consistent estimator of $\mathrm{E}[(u_i^2 - \sigma^2)^2(\mathbf{h}_i - \boldsymbol{\mu}_h)'(\mathbf{h}_i - \boldsymbol{\mu}_h)]$. Show how this leads to the heterokurtosis-robust test for heteroskedasticity.

6.6. Using the test for heteroskedasticity based on the auxiliary regression $\hat{u}^2$ on $\hat{y}$, $\hat{y}^2$, test the log(*wage*) equation in Example 6.4 for heteroskedasticity. Do you detect heteroskedasticity at the 5 percent level?

6.7. For this problem use the data in HPRICE.RAW, which is a subset of the data used by Kiel and McClain (1995). The file contains housing prices and characteristics for two years, 1978 and 1981, for homes sold in North Andover, Massachusetts. In 1981 construction on a garbage incinerator began. Rumors about the incinerator being built were circulating in 1979, and it is for this reason that 1978 is used as the base year. By 1981 it was very clear that the incinerator would be operating soon.

a. Using the 1981 cross section, estimate a bivariate, constant elasticity model relating housing price to distance from the incinerator. Is this regression appropriate for determining the causal effects of incinerator on housing prices? Explain.

b. Pooling the two years of data, consider the model

$$\log(price) = \delta_0 + \delta_1 y81 + \delta_2 \log(dist) + \delta_3 y81 \cdot \log(dist) + u$$

If the incinerator has a negative effect on housing prices for homes closer to the incinerator, what sign is δ_3? Estimate this model and test the null hypothesis that building the incinerator had no effect on housing prices.

c. Add the variables log(*intst*), $[\log(intst)]^2$, log(*area*), log(*land*), *age*, age^2, *rooms*, *baths* to the model in part b, and test for an incinerator effect. What do you conclude?

6.8. The data in FERTIL1.RAW are a pooled cross section on more than a thousand U.S. women for the even years between 1972 and 1984, inclusive; the data set is similar to the one used by Sander (1992). These data can be used to study the relationship between women's education and fertility.

a. Use OLS to estimate a model relating number of children ever born to a woman (*kids*) to years of education, age, region, race, and type of environment reared in. You should use a quadratic in age and should include year dummies. What is the estimated relationship between fertility and education? Holding other factors fixed, has there been any notable secular change in fertility over the time period?

b. Reestimate the model in part a, but use *motheduc* and *fatheduc* as instruments for *educ*. First check that these instruments are sufficiently partially correlated with *educ*. Test whether *educ* is in fact exogenous in the fertility equation.

c. Now allow the effect of education to change over time by including interaction terms such as *y74·educ*, *y76·educ*, and so on in the model. Use interactions of time dummies and parents' education as instruments for the interaction terms. Test that there has been no change in the relationship between fertility and education over time.

6.9. Use the data in INJURY.RAW for this question.

a. Using the data for Kentucky, reestimate equation (6.33) adding as explanatory variables *male*, *married*, and a full set of industry- and injury-type dummy variables. How does the estimate on *afchnge·highearn* change when these other factors are controlled for? Is the estimate still statistically significant?

b. What do you make of the small R-squared from part a? Does this mean the equation is useless?

c. Estimate equation (6.33) using the data for Michigan. Compare the estimate on the interaction term for Michigan and Kentucky, as well as their statistical significance.

6.10. Consider a regression model with interactions and squares of some explanatory variables: $E(y \mid \mathbf{x}) = \mathbf{z}\boldsymbol{\beta}$, where $\mathbf{z}$ contains a constant, the elements of $\mathbf{x}$, and quadratics and interactions of terms in $\mathbf{x}$.

a. Let $\boldsymbol{\mu} = \mathrm{E}(\mathbf{x})$ be the population mean of $\mathbf{x}$, and let $\bar{\mathbf{x}}$ be the sample average based on the N available observations. Let $\hat{\boldsymbol{\beta}}$ be the OLS estimator of $\boldsymbol{\beta}$ using the N observations on y and $\mathbf{z}$. Show that $\sqrt{N}(\hat{\boldsymbol{\beta}} - \boldsymbol{\beta})$ and $\sqrt{N}(\bar{\mathbf{x}} - \boldsymbol{\mu})$ are asymptotically uncorrelated. [Hint: Write $\sqrt{N}(\hat{\boldsymbol{\beta}} - \boldsymbol{\beta})$ as in equation (4.8), and ignore the $\mathrm{o}_p(1)$ term. You will need to use the fact that $\mathrm{E}(u \mid \mathbf{x}) = 0$.]

b. In the model of Problem 4.8, use part a to argue that

$$\mathrm{Avar}(\hat{\alpha}_1) = \mathrm{Avar}(\tilde{\alpha}_1) + \beta_3^2\ \mathrm{Avar}(\bar{x}_2) = \mathrm{Avar}(\tilde{\alpha}_1) + \beta_3^2(\sigma_2^2/N)$$

where $\alpha_1 = \beta_1 + \beta_3\mu_2$, $\tilde{\alpha}_1$ is the estimator of α_1 *if* we knew μ_2, and $\sigma_2^2 = \mathrm{Var}(x_2)$.

c. How would you obtain the correct asymptotic standard error of $\hat{\alpha}_1$, having run the regression in Problem 4.8d? [Hint: The standard error you get from the regression is really $\mathrm{se}(\tilde{\alpha}_1)$. Thus you can square this to estimate $\mathrm{Avar}(\tilde{\alpha}_1)$, then use the preceding formula. You need to estimate σ_2^2, too.]

d. Apply the result from part c to the model in Problem 4.8; in particular, find the corrected asymptotic standard error for $\hat{\alpha}_1$, and compare it with the uncorrected one from Problem 4.8d. (Both can be nonrobust to heteroskedasticity.) What do you conclude?

6.11. The following wage equation represents the populations of working people in 1978 and 1985:

$$\log(wage) = \beta_0 + \delta_0 y85 + \beta_1 educ + \delta_1 y85{\cdot}educ + \beta_2 exper$$
$$+ \beta_3 exper^2 + \beta_4 union + \beta_5 female + \delta_5 y85{\cdot}female + u$$

where the explanatory variables are standard. The variable *union* is a dummy variable equal to one if the person belongs to a union and zero otherwise. The variable *y85* is a dummy variable equal to one if the observation comes from 1985 and zero if it comes from 1978. In the file CPS78_85.RAW there are 550 workers in the sample in 1978 and a different set of 534 people in 1985.

a. Estimate this equation and test whether the return to education has changed over the seven-year period.

b. What has happened to the gender gap over the period?

c. Wages are measured in nominal dollars. What coefficients would change if we measure *wage* in 1978 dollars in both years? [Hint: Use the fact that for all 1985 observations, $\log(wage_i/P85) = \log(wage_i) - \log(P85)$, where $P85$ is the common deflator; $P85 = 1.65$ according to the Consumer Price Index.]

d. Is there evidence that the variance of the error has changed over time?

e. With wages measured nominally, and holding other factors fixed, what is the estimated increase in nominal wage for a male with 12 years of education? Propose a regression to obtain a confidence interval for this estimate. (Hint: You must replace $y85 \cdot educ$ with something else.)

6.12. In the linear model $y = \mathbf{x}\boldsymbol{\beta} + u$, assume that Assumptions 2SLS.1 and 2SLS.3 hold with $\mathbf{w}$ in place of $\mathbf{z}$, where $\mathbf{w}$ contains all nonredundant elements of $\mathbf{x}$ and $\mathbf{z}$. Further, assume that the rank conditions hold for OLS and 2SLS. Show that

$$\text{Avar}[\sqrt{N}(\hat{\boldsymbol{\beta}}_{\text{2SLS}} - \hat{\boldsymbol{\beta}}_{\text{OLS}})] = \text{Avar}[\sqrt{N}(\hat{\boldsymbol{\beta}}_{\text{2SLS}} - \boldsymbol{\beta})] - \text{Avar}[\sqrt{N}(\hat{\boldsymbol{\beta}}_{\text{OLS}} - \boldsymbol{\beta})]$$

[Hint: First, $\text{Avar}[\sqrt{N}(\hat{\boldsymbol{\beta}}_{\text{2SLS}} - \hat{\boldsymbol{\beta}}_{\text{OLS}})] = \mathbf{V}_1 + \mathbf{V}_2 - (\mathbf{C} + \mathbf{C}')$, where $\mathbf{V}_1 = \text{Avar} \cdot [\sqrt{N}(\hat{\boldsymbol{\beta}}_{\text{2SLS}} - \boldsymbol{\beta})]$, $\mathbf{V}_2 = \text{Avar}[\sqrt{N}(\hat{\boldsymbol{\beta}}_{\text{OLS}} - \boldsymbol{\beta})]$, and $\mathbf{C}$ is the asymptotic covariance between $\sqrt{N}(\hat{\boldsymbol{\beta}}_{\text{2SLS}} - \boldsymbol{\beta})$ and $\sqrt{N}(\hat{\boldsymbol{\beta}}_{\text{OLS}} - \boldsymbol{\beta})$. You can stack the formulas for the 2SLS and OLS estimators and show that $\mathbf{C} = \sigma^2[\text{E}(\mathbf{x}^{*\prime}\mathbf{x}^*)]^{-1}\text{E}(\mathbf{x}^{*\prime}\mathbf{x})[\text{E}(\mathbf{x}'\mathbf{x})]^{-1} = \sigma^2[\text{E}(\mathbf{x}'\mathbf{x})]^{-1} = \mathbf{V}_2$. To show the second equality, it will be helpful to use $\text{E}(\mathbf{x}^{*\prime}\mathbf{x}) = \text{E}(\mathbf{x}^{*\prime}\mathbf{x}^*)$.]

Appendix 6A

We derive the asymptotic distribution of the 2SLS estimator in an equation with generated regressors and generated instruments. The tools needed to make the proof rigorous are introduced in Chapter 12, but the key components of the proof can be given here in the context of the linear model. Write the model as

$$y = \mathbf{x}\boldsymbol{\beta} + u, \qquad \text{E}(u \mid \mathbf{v}) = 0$$

where $\mathbf{x} = \mathbf{f}(\mathbf{w}, \boldsymbol{\delta})$, $\boldsymbol{\delta}$ is a $Q \times 1$ vector, and $\boldsymbol{\beta}$ is $K \times 1$. Let $\hat{\boldsymbol{\delta}}$ be a $\sqrt{N}$-consistent estimator of $\boldsymbol{\delta}$. The instruments for each i are $\hat{\mathbf{z}}_i = \mathbf{g}(\mathbf{v}_i, \hat{\boldsymbol{\lambda}})$ where $\mathbf{g}(\mathbf{v}, \boldsymbol{\lambda})$ is a $1 \times L$ vector, $\boldsymbol{\lambda}$ is an $S \times 1$ vector of parameters, and $\hat{\boldsymbol{\lambda}}$ is $\sqrt{N}$-consistent for $\boldsymbol{\lambda}$. Let $\hat{\boldsymbol{\beta}}$ be the 2SLS estimator from the equation

$$y_i = \hat{\mathbf{x}}_i\boldsymbol{\beta} + error_i$$

where $\hat{\mathbf{x}}_i = \mathbf{f}(\mathbf{w}_i, \hat{\boldsymbol{\delta}})$, using instruments $\hat{\mathbf{z}}_i$:

$$\hat{\boldsymbol{\beta}} = \left[\left(\sum_{i=1}^N \hat{\mathbf{x}}_i'\hat{\mathbf{z}}_i\right)\left(\sum_{i=1}^N \hat{\mathbf{z}}_i'\hat{\mathbf{z}}_i\right)^{-1}\left(\sum_{i=1}^N \hat{\mathbf{z}}_i'\hat{\mathbf{x}}_i\right)\right]^{-1}\left(\sum_{i=1}^N \hat{\mathbf{x}}_i'\hat{\mathbf{z}}_i\right)\left(\sum_{i=1}^N \hat{\mathbf{z}}_i'\hat{\mathbf{z}}_i\right)^{-1}\left(\sum_{i=1}^N \hat{\mathbf{z}}_i' y_i\right)$$

Write $y_i = \hat{\mathbf{x}}_i\boldsymbol{\beta} + (\mathbf{x}_i - \hat{\mathbf{x}}_i)\boldsymbol{\beta} + u_i$, where $\mathbf{x}_i = \mathbf{f}(\mathbf{w}_i, \boldsymbol{\delta})$. Plugging this in and multiplying through by $\sqrt{N}$ gives

$$\sqrt{N}(\hat{\boldsymbol{\beta}} - \boldsymbol{\beta}) = (\hat{\mathbf{C}}'\hat{\mathbf{D}}^{-1}\hat{\mathbf{C}})^{-1}\hat{\mathbf{C}}'\hat{\mathbf{D}}^{-1}\left\{N^{-1/2}\sum_{i=1}^{N}\hat{\mathbf{z}}_i'[(\mathbf{x}_i - \hat{\mathbf{x}}_i)\boldsymbol{\beta} + u_i]\right\}$$

where

$$\hat{\mathbf{C}} \equiv N^{-1}\sum_{i=1}^{N}\hat{\mathbf{z}}_i'\hat{\mathbf{x}}_i \qquad \text{and} \qquad \hat{\mathbf{D}} = N^{-1}\sum_{i=1}^{N}\hat{\mathbf{z}}_i'\hat{\mathbf{z}}_i$$

Now, using Lemma 12.1 in Chapter 12, $\hat{\mathbf{C}} \xrightarrow{p} \mathrm{E}(\mathbf{z}'\mathbf{x})$ and $\hat{\mathbf{D}} \xrightarrow{p} \mathrm{E}(\mathbf{z}'\mathbf{z})$. Further, a mean value expansion of the kind used in Theorem 12.3 gives

$$N^{-1/2}\sum_{i=1}^{N}\hat{\mathbf{z}}_i'u_i = N^{-1/2}\sum_{i=1}^{N}\mathbf{z}_i'u_i + \left[N^{-1}\sum_{i=1}^{N}\nabla_\lambda\mathbf{g}(\mathbf{v}_i,\boldsymbol{\lambda})u_i\right]\sqrt{N}(\hat{\boldsymbol{\lambda}} - \boldsymbol{\lambda}) + \mathrm{o}_p(1)$$

where $\nabla_\lambda\mathbf{g}(\mathbf{v}_i,\boldsymbol{\lambda})$ is the $L \times S$ Jacobian of $\mathbf{g}(\mathbf{v}_i,\boldsymbol{\lambda})'$. Because $\mathrm{E}(u_i \mid \mathbf{v}_i) = 0$, $\mathrm{E}[\nabla_\lambda\mathbf{g}(\mathbf{v}_i,\boldsymbol{\lambda})'u_i] = \mathbf{0}$. It follows that $N^{-1}\sum_{i=1}^{N}\nabla_\lambda\mathbf{g}(\mathbf{v}_i,\boldsymbol{\lambda})u_i = \mathrm{o}_p(1)$ and, since $\sqrt{N}(\hat{\boldsymbol{\lambda}} - \boldsymbol{\lambda}) = \mathrm{O}_p(1)$, it follows that

$$N^{-1/2}\sum_{i=1}^{N}\hat{\mathbf{z}}_i'u_i = N^{-1/2}\sum_{i=1}^{N}\mathbf{z}_i'u_i + \mathrm{o}_p(1)$$

Next, using similar reasoning,

$$\begin{aligned} N^{-1/2}\sum_{i=1}^{N}\hat{\mathbf{z}}_i'(\mathbf{x}_i - \hat{\mathbf{x}}_i)\boldsymbol{\beta} &= -\left[N^{-1}\sum_{i=1}^{N}(\boldsymbol{\beta}\otimes\mathbf{z}_i)'\nabla_\delta\mathbf{f}(\mathbf{w}_i,\boldsymbol{\delta})\right]\sqrt{N}(\hat{\boldsymbol{\delta}} - \boldsymbol{\delta}) + \mathrm{o}_p(1) \\ &= -\mathbf{G}\sqrt{N}(\hat{\boldsymbol{\delta}} - \boldsymbol{\delta}) + \mathrm{o}_p(1) \end{aligned}$$

where $\mathbf{G} = \mathrm{E}[(\boldsymbol{\beta}\otimes\mathbf{z}_i)'\nabla_\delta\mathbf{f}(\mathbf{w}_i,\boldsymbol{\delta})]$ and $\nabla_\delta\mathbf{f}(\mathbf{w}_i,\boldsymbol{\delta})$ is the $K \times Q$ Jacobian of $\mathbf{f}(\mathbf{w}_i,\boldsymbol{\delta})'$. We have used a mean value expansion and $\hat{\mathbf{z}}_i'(\mathbf{x}_i - \hat{\mathbf{x}}_i)\boldsymbol{\beta} = (\boldsymbol{\beta}\otimes\hat{\mathbf{z}}_i)'(\mathbf{x}_i - \hat{\mathbf{x}}_i)'$. Now, assume that

$$\sqrt{N}(\hat{\boldsymbol{\delta}} - \boldsymbol{\delta}) = N^{-1/2}\sum_{i=1}^{N}\mathbf{r}_i(\boldsymbol{\delta}) + \mathrm{o}_p(1)$$

where $\mathrm{E}[\mathbf{r}_i(\boldsymbol{\delta})] = \mathbf{0}$. This assumption holds for all estimators discussed so far, and it also holds for most estimators in nonlinear models; see Chapter 12. Collecting all terms gives

$$\sqrt{N}(\hat{\boldsymbol{\beta}} - \boldsymbol{\beta}) = (\mathbf{C}'\mathbf{D}^{-1}\mathbf{C})^{-1}\mathbf{C}'\mathbf{D}^{-1}\left\{N^{-1/2}\sum_{i=1}^{N}[\mathbf{z}_i'u_i - \mathbf{G}\mathbf{r}_i(\boldsymbol{\delta})]\right\} + \mathrm{o}_p(1)$$

By the central limit theorem,

$$\sqrt{N}(\hat{\boldsymbol{\beta}} - \boldsymbol{\beta}) \overset{a}{\sim} \text{Normal}[\mathbf{0}, (\mathbf{C}'\mathbf{D}^{-1}\mathbf{C})^{-1}\mathbf{C}'\mathbf{D}^{-1}\mathbf{M}\mathbf{D}^{-1}\mathbf{C}(\mathbf{C}'\mathbf{D}^{-1}\mathbf{C})^{-1}]$$

where

$$\mathbf{M} = \text{Var}[\mathbf{z}_i'u_i - \mathbf{G}\mathbf{r}_i(\boldsymbol{\delta})]$$

The asymptotic variance of $\hat{\boldsymbol{\beta}}$ is estimated as

$$(\hat{\mathbf{C}}'\hat{\mathbf{D}}^{-1}\hat{\mathbf{C}})^{-1}\hat{\mathbf{C}}'\hat{\mathbf{D}}^{-1}\hat{\mathbf{M}}\hat{\mathbf{D}}^{-1}\hat{\mathbf{C}}(\hat{\mathbf{C}}'\hat{\mathbf{D}}^{-1}\hat{\mathbf{C}})^{-1}/N, \tag{6.36}$$

where

$$\hat{\mathbf{M}} = N^{-1}\sum_{i=1}^{N}(\hat{\mathbf{z}}_i'\hat{u}_i - \hat{\mathbf{G}}\hat{\mathbf{r}}_i)(\hat{\mathbf{z}}_i'\hat{u}_i - \hat{\mathbf{G}}\hat{\mathbf{r}}_i)' \tag{6.37}$$

$$\hat{\mathbf{G}} = N^{-1}\sum_{i=1}^{N}(\hat{\boldsymbol{\beta}} \otimes \hat{\mathbf{z}}_i)'\nabla_{\delta}\mathbf{f}(\mathbf{w}_i, \hat{\boldsymbol{\delta}}) \tag{6.38}$$

and

$$\hat{\mathbf{r}}_i = \mathbf{r}_i(\hat{\boldsymbol{\delta}}), \qquad \hat{u}_i = y_i - \hat{\mathbf{x}}_i\hat{\boldsymbol{\beta}} \tag{6.39}$$

A few comments are in order. First, estimation of $\boldsymbol{\lambda}$ does not affect the asymptotic distribution of $\hat{\boldsymbol{\beta}}$. Therefore, if there are no generated regressors, the usual 2SLS inference procedures are valid [$\mathbf{G} = \mathbf{0}$ in this case and so $\mathbf{M} = \text{E}(u_i^2\mathbf{z}_i'\mathbf{z}_i)$]. If $\mathbf{G} = \mathbf{0}$ and $\text{E}(u^2\mathbf{z}'\mathbf{z}) = \sigma^2\text{E}(\mathbf{z}'\mathbf{z})$, then the usual 2SLS standard errors and test statistics are valid. If Assumption 2SLS.3 fails, then the heteroskedasticity-robust statistics are valid.

If $\mathbf{G} \neq \mathbf{0}$, then the asymptotic variance of $\hat{\boldsymbol{\beta}}$ depends on that of $\hat{\boldsymbol{\delta}}$ [through the presence of $\mathbf{r}_i(\boldsymbol{\delta})$]. Neither the usual 2SLS variance matrix estimator nor the heteroskedasticity-robust form is valid in this case. The matrix $\hat{\mathbf{M}}$ should be computed as in equation (6.37).

In some cases, $\mathbf{G} = \mathbf{0}$ under the null hypothesis that we wish to test. The jth row of $\mathbf{G}$ can be written as $\text{E}[z_{ij}\boldsymbol{\beta}'\nabla_{\delta}\mathbf{f}(\mathbf{w}_i, \boldsymbol{\delta})]$. Now, suppose that $\hat{x}_{ih}$ is the only generated regressor, so that only the hth row of $\nabla_{\delta}\mathbf{f}(\mathbf{w}_i, \boldsymbol{\delta})$ is nonzero. But then if $\beta_h = 0$, $\boldsymbol{\beta}'\nabla_{\delta}\mathbf{f}(\mathbf{w}_i, \boldsymbol{\delta}) = \mathbf{0}$. It follows that $\mathbf{G} = \mathbf{0}$ and $\mathbf{M} = \text{E}(u_i^2\mathbf{z}_i'\mathbf{z}_i)$, so that no adjustment for the preliminary estimation of $\boldsymbol{\delta}$ is needed. This observation is very useful for a variety of specification tests, including the test for endogeneity in Section 6.2.1. We will also use it in sample selection contexts later on.

7 Estimating Systems of Equations by OLS and GLS

7.1 Introduction

This chapter begins our analysis of linear systems of equations. The first method of estimation we cover is system ordinary least squares, which is a direct extension of OLS for single equations. In some important special cases the system OLS estimator turns out to have a straightforward interpretation in terms of single-equation OLS estimators. But the method is applicable to very general linear systems of equations.

We then turn to a generalized least squares (GLS) analysis. Under certain assumptions, GLS—or its operationalized version, feasible GLS—will turn out to be asymptotically more efficient than system OLS. However, we emphasize in this chapter that the efficiency of GLS comes at a price: it requires stronger assumptions than system OLS in order to be consistent. This is a practically important point that is often overlooked in traditional treatments of linear systems, particularly those which assume that explanatory variables are nonrandom.

As with our single-equation analysis, we assume that a random sample is available from the population. Usually the unit of observation is obvious—such as a worker, a household, a firm, or a city. For example, if we collect consumption data on various commodities for a sample of families, the unit of observation is the family (not a commodity).

The framework of this chapter is general enough to apply to panel data models. Because the asymptotic analysis is done as the cross section dimension tends to infinity, the results are explicitly for the case where the cross section dimension is large relative to the time series dimension. (For example, we may have observations on N firms over the same T time periods for each firm. Then, we assume we have a random sample of firms that have data in each of the T years.) The panel data model covered here, while having many useful applications, does not fully exploit the replicability over time. In Chapters 10 and 11 we explicitly consider panel data models that contain time-invariant, unobserved effects in the error term.

7.2 Some Examples

We begin with two examples of systems of equations. These examples are fairly general, and we will see later that variants of them can also be cast as a general linear system of equations.

Example 7.1 (Seemingly Unrelated Regressions): The population model is a set of G linear equations,

$$
\begin{aligned}
y_1 &= \mathbf{x}_1\boldsymbol{\beta}_1 + u_1 \\
y_2 &= \mathbf{x}_2\boldsymbol{\beta}_2 + u_2 \\
&\vdots \\
y_G &= \mathbf{x}_G\boldsymbol{\beta}_G + u_G
\end{aligned}
\tag{7.1}
$$

where $\mathbf{x}_g$ is $1 \times K_g$ and $\boldsymbol{\beta}_g$ is $K_g \times 1$, $g = 1, 2, \ldots, G$. In many applications $\mathbf{x}_g$ is the same for all g (in which case the $\boldsymbol{\beta}_g$ necessarily have the same dimension), but the general model allows the elements and the dimension of $\mathbf{x}_g$ to vary across equations. Remember, the system (7.1) represents a generic person, firm, city, or whatever from the population. The system (7.1) is often called Zellner's (1962) **seemingly unrelated regressions (SUR) model** (for cross section data in this case). The name comes from the fact that, since each equation in the system (7.1) has its own vector $\boldsymbol{\beta}_g$, it appears that the equations are unrelated. Nevertheless, correlation across the errors in different equations can provide links that can be exploited in estimation; we will see this point later.

As a specific example, the system (7.1) might represent a set of demand functions for the population of families in a country:

$$
\begin{aligned}
housing &= \beta_{10} + \beta_{11} houseprc + \beta_{12} foodprc + \beta_{13} clothprc + \beta_{14} income \\
&\quad + \beta_{15} size + \beta_{16} age + u_1 \\
food &= \beta_{20} + \beta_{21} houseprc + \beta_{22} foodprc + \beta_{23} clothprc + \beta_{24} income \\
&\quad + \beta_{25} size + \beta_{26} age + u_2 \\
clothing &= \beta_{30} + \beta_{31} houseprc + \beta_{32} foodprc + \beta_{33} clothprc + \beta_{34} income \\
&\quad + \beta_{35} size + \beta_{36} age + u_3
\end{aligned}
$$

In this example, $G = 3$ and $\mathbf{x}_g$ (a 1×7 vector) is the same for $g = 1, 2, 3$.

When we need to write the equations for a particular random draw from the population, y_g, $\mathbf{x}_g$, and u_g will also contain an i subscript: equation g becomes $y_{ig} = \mathbf{x}_{ig}\boldsymbol{\beta}_g + u_{ig}$. For the purposes of stating assumptions, it does not matter whether or not we include the i subscript. The system (7.1) has the advantage of being less cluttered while focusing attention on the population, as is appropriate for applications. But for derivations we will often need to indicate the equation for a generic cross section unit i.

When we study the asymptotic properties of various estimators of the $\boldsymbol{\beta}_g$, the asymptotics is done with G fixed and N tending to infinity. In the household demand example, we are interested in a set of three demand functions, and the unit of observation is the family. Therefore, inference is done as the number of families in the sample tends to infinity.

The assumptions that we make about how the unobservables u_g are related to the explanatory variables $(\mathbf{x}_1, \mathbf{x}_2, \ldots, \mathbf{x}_G)$ are crucial for determining which estimators of the $\boldsymbol{\beta}_g$ have acceptable properties. Often, when system (7.1) represents a structural model (without omitted variables, errors-in-variables, or simultaneity), we can assume that

$$\mathrm{E}(u_g \mid \mathbf{x}_1, \mathbf{x}_2, \ldots, \mathbf{x}_G) = 0, \qquad g = 1, \ldots, G \tag{7.2}$$

One important implication of assumption (7.2) is that u_g is uncorrelated with the explanatory variables in *all* equations, as well as all functions of these explanatory variables. When system (7.1) is a system of equations derived from economic theory, assumption (7.2) is often very natural. For example, in the set of demand functions that we have presented, $\mathbf{x}_g \equiv \mathbf{x}$ is the same for all g, and so assumption (7.2) is the same as $\mathrm{E}(u_g \mid \mathbf{x}_g) = \mathrm{E}(u_g \mid \mathbf{x}) = 0$.

If assumption (7.2) is maintained, and if the $\mathbf{x}_g$ are not the same across g, then any explanatory variables excluded from equation g are assumed to have no effect on expected y_g once $\mathbf{x}_g$ has been controlled for. That is,

$$\mathrm{E}(y_g \mid \mathbf{x}_1, \mathbf{x}_2, \ldots \mathbf{x}_G) = \mathrm{E}(y_g \mid \mathbf{x}_g) = \mathbf{x}_g \boldsymbol{\beta}_g, \qquad g = 1, 2, \ldots, G \tag{7.3}$$

There are examples of SUR systems where assumption (7.3) is too strong, but standard SUR analysis either explicitly or implicitly makes this assumption.

Our next example involves panel data.

Example 7.2 (Panel Data Model): Suppose that for each cross section unit we observe data on the same set of variables for T time periods. Let $\mathbf{x}_t$ be a $1 \times K$ vector for $t = 1, 2, \ldots, T$, and let $\boldsymbol{\beta}$ be a $K \times 1$ vector. The model in the population is

$$y_t = \mathbf{x}_t \boldsymbol{\beta} + u_t, \qquad t = 1, 2, \ldots, T \tag{7.4}$$

where y_t is a scalar. For example, a simple equation to explain annual family saving over a five-year span is

$$sav_t = \beta_0 + \beta_1 inc_t + \beta_2 age_t + \beta_3 educ_t + u_t, \qquad t = 1, 2, \ldots, 5$$

where inc_t is annual income, $educ_t$ is years of education of the household head, and age_t is age of the household head. This is an example of a **linear panel data model**. It is a **static model** because all explanatory variables are dated contemporaneously with sav_t.

The panel data setup is conceptually very different from the SUR example. In Example 7.1, each equation explains a different dependent variable for the same cross section unit. Here we only have one dependent variable we are trying to explain—*sav*—but we observe *sav*, and the explanatory variables, over a five-year period. (Therefore, the label "system of equations" is really a misnomer for panel data applications. At this point, we are using the phrase to denote more than one equation in any context.) As we will see in the next section, the statistical properties of estimators in SUR and panel data models can be analyzed within the same structure.

When we need to indicate that an equation is for a particular cross section unit i during a particular time period t, we write $y_{it} = \mathbf{x}_{it}\boldsymbol{\beta} + u_{it}$. We will omit the i subscript whenever its omission does not cause confusion.

What kinds of exogeneity assumptions do we use for panel data analysis? One possibility is to assume that u_t and $\mathbf{x}_t$ are orthogonal in the conditional mean sense:

$$\mathrm{E}(u_t \mid \mathbf{x}_t) = 0, \qquad t = 1, \ldots, T \tag{7.5}$$

We call this **contemporaneous exogeneity** of $\mathbf{x}_t$ because it only restricts the relationship between the disturbance and explanatory variables in the same time period. It is very important to distinguish assumption (7.5) from the stronger assumption

$$\mathrm{E}(u_t \mid \mathbf{x}_1, \mathbf{x}_2, \ldots, \mathbf{x}_T) = 0, \qquad t = 1, \ldots, T \tag{7.6}$$

which, combined with model (7.4), is identical to $\mathrm{E}(y_t \mid \mathbf{x}_1, \mathbf{x}_2, \ldots, \mathbf{x}_T) = \mathrm{E}(y_t \mid \mathbf{x}_t)$. Assumption (7.5) places no restrictions on the relationship between $\mathbf{x}_s$ and u_t for $s \neq t$, while assumption (7.6) implies that each u_t is uncorrelated with the explanatory variables in *all* time periods. When assumption (7.6) holds, we say that the explanatory variables $\{\mathbf{x}_1, \mathbf{x}_2, \ldots, \mathbf{x}_t, \ldots, \mathbf{x}_T\}$ are **strictly exogenous**.

To illustrate the difference between assumptions (7.5) and (7.6), let $\mathbf{x}_t \equiv (1, y_{t-1})$. Then assumption (7.5) holds if $\mathrm{E}(y_t \mid y_{t-1}, y_{t-2}, \ldots, y_0) = \beta_0 + \beta_1 y_{t-1}$, which imposes first-order dynamics in the conditional mean. However, assumption (7.6) *must* fail since $\mathbf{x}_{t+1} = (1, y_t)$, and therefore $\mathrm{E}(u_t \mid \mathbf{x}_1, \mathbf{x}_2, \ldots, \mathbf{x}_T) = \mathrm{E}(u_t \mid y_0, y_1, \ldots, y_{T-1}) = u_t$ for $t = 1, 2, \ldots, T-1$ (because $u_t = y_t - \beta_0 - \beta_1 y_{t-1}$).

Assumption (7.6) can fail even if $\mathbf{x}_t$ does *not* contain a lagged dependent variable. Consider a model relating poverty rates to welfare spending per capita, at the city level. A **finite distributed lag (FDL) model** is

$$poverty_t = \theta_t + \delta_0 welfare_t + \delta_1 welfare_{t-1} + \delta_2 welfare_{t-2} + u_t \tag{7.7}$$

where we assume a two-year effect. The parameter θ_t simply denotes a different aggregate time effect in each year. It is reasonable to think that welfare spending reacts to lagged poverty rates. An equation that captures this feedback is

$$welfare_t = \eta_t + \rho_1 poverty_{t-1} + r_t \tag{7.8}$$

Even if equation (7.7) contains enough lags of welfare spending, assumption (7.6) would be violated if $\rho_1 \neq 0$ in equation (7.8) because $welfare_{t+1}$ depends on u_t and $\mathbf{x}_{t+1}$ includes $welfare_{t+1}$.

How we go about consistently estimating $\boldsymbol{\beta}$ depends crucially on whether we maintain assumption (7.5) or the stronger assumption (7.6). Assuming that the $\mathbf{x}_{it}$ are fixed in repeated samples is effectively the same as making assumption (7.6).

7.3 System OLS Estimation of a Multivariate Linear System

7.3.1 Preliminaries

We now analyze a general multivariate model that contains the examples in Section 7.2, and many others, as special cases. Assume that we have independent, identically distributed cross section observations $\{(\mathbf{X}_i, \mathbf{y}_i): i = 1, 2, \ldots, N\}$, where $\mathbf{X}_i$ is a $G \times K$ matrix and $\mathbf{y}_i$ is a $G \times 1$ vector. Thus, $\mathbf{y}_i$ contains the dependent variables for all G equations (or time periods, in the panel data case). The matrix $\mathbf{X}_i$ contains the explanatory variables appearing anywhere in the system. For notational clarity we include the i subscript for stating the general model and the assumptions.

The multivariate linear model for a random draw from the population can be expressed as

$$\mathbf{y}_i = \mathbf{X}_i \boldsymbol{\beta} + \mathbf{u}_i \tag{7.9}$$

where $\boldsymbol{\beta}$ is the $K \times 1$ parameter vector of interest and $\mathbf{u}_i$ is a $G \times 1$ vector of unobservables. Equation (7.9) explains the G variables $y_{i1}, \ldots, y_{iG}$ in terms of $\mathbf{X}_i$ and the unobservables $\mathbf{u}_i$. Because of the random sampling assumption, we can state all assumptions in terms of a generic observation; in examples, we will often omit the i subscript.

Before stating any assumptions, we show how the two examples introduced in Section 7.2 fit into this framework.

Example 7.1 (SUR, continued): The SUR model (7.1) can be expressed as in equation (7.9) by defining $\mathbf{y}_i = (y_{i1}, y_{i2}, \ldots, y_{iG})'$, $\mathbf{u}_i = (u_{i1}, u_{i2}, \ldots, u_{iG})'$, and

$$\mathbf{X}_i = \begin{pmatrix} \mathbf{x}_{i1} & \mathbf{0} & \mathbf{0} & \cdots & \mathbf{0} \\ \mathbf{0} & \mathbf{x}_{i2} & & & \mathbf{0} \\ \mathbf{0} & \mathbf{0} & & & \vdots \\ \vdots & & & & \mathbf{0} \\ \mathbf{0} & \mathbf{0} & \mathbf{0} & \cdots & \mathbf{x}_{iG} \end{pmatrix}, \qquad \boldsymbol{\beta} = \begin{pmatrix} \boldsymbol{\beta}_1 \\ \boldsymbol{\beta}_2 \\ \vdots \\ \boldsymbol{\beta}_G \end{pmatrix} \tag{7.10}$$

Note that the dimension of $\mathbf{X}_i$ is $G \times (K_1 + K_2 + \cdots + K_G)$, so we define $K \equiv K_1 + \cdots + K_G$.

Example 7.2 (Panel Data, continued): The panel data model (7.6) can be expressed as in equation (7.9) by choosing $\mathbf{X}_i$ to be the $T \times K$ matrix $\mathbf{X}_i = (\mathbf{x}_{i1}', \mathbf{x}_{i2}', \ldots, \mathbf{x}_{iT}')'$.

7.3.2 Asymptotic Properties of System OLS

Given the model in equation (7.9), we can state the key orthogonality condition for consistent estimation of $\boldsymbol{\beta}$ by system ordinary least squares (SOLS).

ASSUMPTION SOLS.1: $\mathrm{E}(\mathbf{X}_i'\mathbf{u}_i) = \mathbf{0}$.

Assumption SOLS.1 appears similar to the orthogonality condition for OLS analysis of single equations. What it implies differs across examples because of the multiple-equation nature of equation (7.9). For most applications, $\mathbf{X}_i$ has a sufficient number of elements equal to unity so that Assumption SOLS.1 implies that $\mathrm{E}(\mathbf{u}_i) = \mathbf{0}$, and we assume zero mean for the sake of discussion.

It is informative to see what Assumption SOLS.1 entails in the previous examples.

Example 7.1 (SUR, continued): In the SUR case, $\mathbf{X}_i'\mathbf{u}_i = (\mathbf{x}_{i1}u_{i1}, \ldots, \mathbf{x}_{iG}u_{iG})'$, and so Assumption SOLS.1 holds if and only if

$$\mathrm{E}(\mathbf{x}_{ig}'u_{ig}) = \mathbf{0}, \qquad g = 1, 2, \ldots, G \tag{7.11}$$

Thus, Assumption SOLS.1 does not require $\mathbf{x}_{ih}$ and u_{ig} to be uncorrelated when $h \neq g$.

Example 7.2 (Panel Data, continued): For the panel data setup, $\mathbf{X}_i'\mathbf{u}_i = \sum_{t=1}^{T} \mathbf{x}_{it}'u_{it}$; therefore, a sufficient, and very natural, condition for Assumption SOLS.1 is

$$\mathrm{E}(\mathbf{x}_{it}'u_{it}) = \mathbf{0}, \qquad t = 1, 2, \ldots, T \tag{7.12}$$

Like assumption (7.5), assumption (7.12) allows $\mathbf{x}_{is}$ and u_{it} to be correlated when $s \neq t$; in fact, assumption (7.12) is weaker than assumption (7.5). Therefore, Assumption SOLS.1 does *not* impose strict exogeneity in panel data contexts.

Assumption SOLS.1 is the weakest assumption we can impose in a regression framework to get consistent estimators of $\boldsymbol{\beta}$. As the previous examples show, Assumption SOLS.1 allows some elements of $\mathbf{X}_i$ to be correlated with elements of $\mathbf{u}_i$. Much stronger is the zero conditional mean assumption

$$\mathrm{E}(\mathbf{u}_i \mid \mathbf{X}_i) = \mathbf{0} \tag{7.13}$$

which implies, among other things, that every element of $\mathbf{X}_i$ and every element of $\mathbf{u}_i$ are uncorrelated. [Of course, assumption (7.13) is not as strong as assuming that $\mathbf{u}_i$ and $\mathbf{X}_i$ are actually *independent*.] Even though assumption (7.13) is stronger than Assumption SOLS.1, it is, nevertheless, reasonable in some applications.

Under Assumption SOLS.1 the vector $\boldsymbol{\beta}$ satisfies

$$\mathrm{E}[\mathbf{X}_i'(\mathbf{y}_i - \mathbf{X}_i\boldsymbol{\beta})] = \mathbf{0} \tag{7.14}$$

or $\mathrm{E}(\mathbf{X}_i'\mathbf{X}_i)\boldsymbol{\beta} = \mathrm{E}(\mathbf{X}_i'\mathbf{y}_i)$. For each i, $\mathbf{X}_i'\mathbf{y}_i$ is a $K \times 1$ random vector and $\mathbf{X}_i'\mathbf{X}_i$ is a $K \times K$ symmetric, positive semidefinite random matrix. Therefore, $\mathrm{E}(\mathbf{X}_i'\mathbf{X}_i)$ is always a $K \times K$ symmetric, positive semidefinite nonrandom matrix (the expectation here is defined over the population distribution of $\mathbf{X}_i$). To be able to estimate $\boldsymbol{\beta}$ we need to assume that it is the only $K \times 1$ vector that satisfies assumption (7.14).

ASSUMPTION SOLS.2: $\mathbf{A} \equiv \mathrm{E}(\mathbf{X}_i'\mathbf{X}_i)$ is nonsingular (has rank K).

Under Assumptions SOLS.1 and SOLS.2 we can write $\boldsymbol{\beta}$ as

$$\boldsymbol{\beta} = [\mathrm{E}(\mathbf{X}_i'\mathbf{X}_i)]^{-1}\mathrm{E}(\mathbf{X}_i'\mathbf{y}_i) \tag{7.15}$$

which shows that Assumptions SOLS.1 and SOLS.2 identify the vector $\boldsymbol{\beta}$. The analogy principle suggests that we estimate $\boldsymbol{\beta}$ by the sample analogue of assumption (7.15). Define the **system ordinary least squares (SOLS) estimator** of $\boldsymbol{\beta}$ as

$$\hat{\boldsymbol{\beta}} = \left(N^{-1}\sum_{i=1}^{N}\mathbf{X}_i'\mathbf{X}_i\right)^{-1}\left(N^{-1}\sum_{i=1}^{N}\mathbf{X}_i'\mathbf{y}_i\right) \tag{7.16}$$

For computing $\hat{\boldsymbol{\beta}}$ using matrix language programming, it is sometimes useful to write $\hat{\boldsymbol{\beta}} = (\mathbf{X}'\mathbf{X})^{-1}\mathbf{X}'\mathbf{Y}$, where $\mathbf{X} \equiv (\mathbf{X}_1', \mathbf{X}_2', \ldots, \mathbf{X}_N')'$ is the $NG \times K$ matrix of stacked $\mathbf{X}$ and $\mathbf{Y} \equiv (\mathbf{y}_1', \mathbf{y}_2', \ldots, \mathbf{y}_N')'$ is the $NG \times 1$ vector of stacked observations on the $\mathbf{y}_i$. For asymptotic derivations, equation (7.16) is much more convenient. In fact, the consistency of $\hat{\boldsymbol{\beta}}$ can be read off of equation (7.16) by taking probability limits. We summarize with a theorem:

THEOREM 7.1 (Consistency of System OLS): Under Assumptions SOLS.1 and SOLS.2, $\hat{\boldsymbol{\beta}} \xrightarrow{p} \boldsymbol{\beta}$.

It is useful to see what the system OLS estimator looks like for the SUR and panel data examples.

Example 7.1 (SUR, continued): For the SUR model,

$$\sum_{i=1}^{N} \mathbf{X}_i'\mathbf{X}_i = \sum_{i=1}^{N} \begin{pmatrix} \mathbf{x}_{i1}'\mathbf{x}_{i1} & \mathbf{0} & \mathbf{0} & \cdots & \mathbf{0} \\ \mathbf{0} & \mathbf{x}_{i2}'\mathbf{x}_{i2} & & & \mathbf{0} \\ \mathbf{0} & \mathbf{0} & & & \vdots \\ \vdots & & & & \mathbf{0} \\ \mathbf{0} & \mathbf{0} & \mathbf{0} & \cdots & \mathbf{x}_{iG}'\mathbf{x}_{iG} \end{pmatrix}; \qquad \sum_{i=1}^{N} \mathbf{X}_i'\mathbf{y}_i = \sum_{i=1}^{N} \begin{pmatrix} \mathbf{x}_{i1}'y_{i1} \\ \mathbf{x}_{i2}'y_{i2} \\ \vdots \\ \mathbf{x}_{iG}'y_{iG} \end{pmatrix}$$

Straightforward inversion of a block diagonal matrix shows that the OLS estimator from equation (7.16) can be written as $\hat{\boldsymbol{\beta}} = (\hat{\boldsymbol{\beta}}_1', \hat{\boldsymbol{\beta}}_2', \ldots, \hat{\boldsymbol{\beta}}_G')'$, where each $\hat{\boldsymbol{\beta}}_g$ is just the single-equation OLS estimator from the gth equation. In other words, system OLS estimation of a SUR model (without restrictions on the parameter vectors $\boldsymbol{\beta}_g$) is equivalent to **OLS equation by equation**. Assumption SOLS.2 is easily seen to hold if $\mathrm{E}(\mathbf{x}_{ig}'\mathbf{x}_{ig})$ is nonsingular for all g.

Example 7.2 (Panel Data, continued): In the panel data case,

$$\sum_{i=1}^{N} \mathbf{X}_i'\mathbf{X}_i = \sum_{i=1}^{N}\sum_{t=1}^{T} \mathbf{x}_{it}'\mathbf{x}_{it}; \qquad \sum_{i=1}^{N} \mathbf{X}_i'\mathbf{y}_i = \sum_{i=1}^{N}\sum_{t=1}^{T} \mathbf{x}_{it}'y_{it}$$

Therefore, we can write $\hat{\boldsymbol{\beta}}$ as

$$\hat{\boldsymbol{\beta}} = \left(\sum_{i=1}^{N}\sum_{t=1}^{T} \mathbf{x}_{it}'\mathbf{x}_{it}\right)^{-1} \left(\sum_{i=1}^{N}\sum_{t=1}^{T} \mathbf{x}_{it}'y_{it}\right) \tag{7.17}$$

This estimator is called the **pooled ordinary least squares (POLS) estimator** because it corresponds to running OLS on the observations pooled across i and t. We mentioned this estimator in the context of *independent* cross sections in Section 6.3. The estimator in equation (7.17) is for the same cross section units sampled at different points in time. Theorem 7.1 shows that the POLS estimator is consistent under the orthogonality conditions in assumption (7.12) and the mild condition rank $\mathrm{E}(\sum_{t=1}^{T} \mathbf{x}_{it}'\mathbf{x}_{it}) = K$.

In the general system (7.9), the system OLS estimator does not necessarily have an interpretation as OLS equation by equation or as pooled OLS. As we will see in Section 7.7 for the SUR setup, sometimes we want to impose cross equation restrictions on the $\boldsymbol{\beta}_g$, in which case the system OLS estimator has no simple interpretation.

While OLS is consistent under Assumptions SOLS.1 and SOLS.2, it is not necessarily unbiased. Assumption (7.13), and the finite sample assumption rank$(\mathbf{X}'\mathbf{X}) = K$, *do* ensure unbiasedness of OLS conditional on $\mathbf{X}$. [This conclusion follows because, under independent sampling, $\mathrm{E}(\mathbf{u}_i \mid \mathbf{X}_1, \mathbf{X}_2, \ldots, \mathbf{X}_N) = \mathrm{E}(\mathbf{u}_i \mid \mathbf{X}_i) = \mathbf{0}$ under assumption (7.13).] We focus on the weaker Assumption SOLS.1 because assumption (7.13) is often violated in economic applications, something we will see especially in our panel data analysis.

For inference, we need to find the asymptotic variance of the OLS estimator under essentially the same two assumptions; technically, the following derivation requires the elements of $\mathbf{X}_i'\mathbf{u}_i\mathbf{u}_i'\mathbf{X}_i$ to have finite expected absolute value. From (7.16) and (7.9) write

$$\sqrt{N}(\hat{\boldsymbol{\beta}} - \boldsymbol{\beta}) = \left(N^{-1}\sum_{i=1}^{N}\mathbf{X}_i'\mathbf{X}_i\right)^{-1}\left(N^{-1/2}\sum_{i=1}^{N}\mathbf{X}_i'\mathbf{u}_i\right)$$

Because $\mathrm{E}(\mathbf{X}_i'\mathbf{u}_i) = \mathbf{0}$ under Assumption SOLS.1, the CLT implies that

$$N^{-1/2}\sum_{i=1}^{N}\mathbf{X}_i'\mathbf{u}_i \xrightarrow{d} \mathrm{Normal}(\mathbf{0}, \mathbf{B}) \tag{7.18}$$

where

$$\mathbf{B} \equiv \mathrm{E}(\mathbf{X}_i'\mathbf{u}_i\mathbf{u}_i'\mathbf{X}_i) \equiv \mathrm{Var}(\mathbf{X}_i'\mathbf{u}_i) \tag{7.19}$$

In particular, $N^{-1/2}\sum_{i=1}^{N}\mathbf{X}_i'\mathbf{u}_i = \mathrm{O}_p(1)$. But $(\mathbf{X}'\mathbf{X}/N)^{-1} = \mathbf{A}^{-1} + \mathrm{o}_p(1)$, so

$$\begin{aligned}\sqrt{N}(\hat{\boldsymbol{\beta}} - \boldsymbol{\beta}) &= \mathbf{A}^{-1}\left(N^{-1/2}\sum_{i=1}^{N}\mathbf{X}_i'\mathbf{u}_i\right) + [(\mathbf{X}'\mathbf{X}/N)^{-1} - \mathbf{A}^{-1}]\left(N^{-1/2}\sum_{i=1}^{N}\mathbf{X}_i'\mathbf{u}_i\right)\\ &= \mathbf{A}^{-1}\left(N^{-1/2}\sum_{i=1}^{N}\mathbf{X}_i'\mathbf{u}_i\right) + \mathrm{o}_p(1)\cdot\mathrm{O}_p(1)\\ &= \mathbf{A}^{-1}\left(N^{-1/2}\sum_{i=1}^{N}\mathbf{X}_i'\mathbf{u}_i\right) + \mathrm{o}_p(1)\end{aligned} \tag{7.20}$$

Therefore, just as with single-equation OLS and 2SLS, we have obtained an asymptotic representation for $\sqrt{N}(\hat{\boldsymbol{\beta}} - \boldsymbol{\beta})$ that is a *nonrandom* linear combination of a partial sum that satisfies the CLT. Equations (7.18) and (7.20) and the asymptotic equivalence lemma imply

$$\sqrt{N}(\hat{\boldsymbol{\beta}} - \boldsymbol{\beta}) \xrightarrow{d} \mathrm{Normal}(\mathbf{0}, \mathbf{A}^{-1}\mathbf{B}\mathbf{A}^{-1}) \tag{7.21}$$

We summarize with a theorem.

THEOREM 7.2 (Asymptotic Normality of SOLS): Under Assumptions SOLS.1 and SOLS.2, equation (7.21) holds.

The asymptotic variance of $\hat{\boldsymbol{\beta}}$ is

$$\text{Avar}(\hat{\boldsymbol{\beta}}) = \mathbf{A}^{-1}\mathbf{B}\mathbf{A}^{-1}/N \tag{7.22}$$

so that $\text{Avar}(\hat{\boldsymbol{\beta}})$ shrinks to zero at the rate $1/N$, as expected. Consistent estimation of $\mathbf{A}$ is simple:

$$\hat{\mathbf{A}} \equiv \mathbf{X}'\mathbf{X}/N = N^{-1}\sum_{i=1}^{N}\mathbf{X}_i'\mathbf{X}_i \tag{7.23}$$

A consistent estimator of $\mathbf{B}$ can be found using the analogy principle. First, because $\mathbf{B} = \text{E}(\mathbf{X}_i'\mathbf{u}_i\mathbf{u}_i'\mathbf{X}_i)$, $N^{-1}\sum_{i=1}^{N}\mathbf{X}_i'\mathbf{u}_i\mathbf{u}_i'\mathbf{X}_i \xrightarrow{p} \mathbf{B}$. Since the $\mathbf{u}_i$ are not observed, we replace them with the SOLS residuals:

$$\hat{\mathbf{u}}_i \equiv \mathbf{y}_i - \mathbf{X}_i\hat{\boldsymbol{\beta}} = \mathbf{u}_i - \mathbf{X}_i(\hat{\boldsymbol{\beta}} - \boldsymbol{\beta}) \tag{7.24}$$

Using matrix algebra and the law of large numbers, it can be shown that

$$\hat{\mathbf{B}} \equiv N^{-1}\sum_{i=1}^{N}\mathbf{X}_i'\hat{\mathbf{u}}_i\hat{\mathbf{u}}_i'\mathbf{X}_i \xrightarrow{p} \mathbf{B} \tag{7.25}$$

[To establish equation (7.25), we need to assume that certain moments involving $\mathbf{X}_i$ and $\mathbf{u}_i$ are finite.] Therefore, Avar $\sqrt{N}(\hat{\boldsymbol{\beta}} - \boldsymbol{\beta})$ is consistently estimated by $\hat{\mathbf{A}}^{-1}\hat{\mathbf{B}}\hat{\mathbf{A}}^{-1}$, and $\text{Avar}(\hat{\boldsymbol{\beta}})$ is estimated as

$$\hat{\mathbf{V}} \equiv \left(\sum_{i=1}^{N}\mathbf{X}_i'\mathbf{X}_i\right)^{-1}\left(\sum_{i=1}^{N}\mathbf{X}_i'\hat{\mathbf{u}}_i\hat{\mathbf{u}}_i'\mathbf{X}_i\right)\left(\sum_{i=1}^{N}\mathbf{X}_i'\mathbf{X}_i\right)^{-1} \tag{7.26}$$

Under Assumptions SOLS.1 and SOLS.2, we perform inference on $\boldsymbol{\beta}$ as if $\hat{\boldsymbol{\beta}}$ is normally distributed with mean $\boldsymbol{\beta}$ and variance matrix (7.26). The square roots of the diagonal elements of the matrix (7.26) are reported as the asymptotic standard errors. The t ratio, $\hat{\beta}_j/\text{se}(\hat{\beta}_j)$, has a limiting normal distribution under the null hypothesis H_0: $\beta_j = 0$. Sometimes the t statistics are treated as being distributed as t_{NG-K}, which is asymptotically valid because $NG - K$ should be large.

The estimator in matrix (7.26) is another example of a **robust variance matrix estimator** because it is valid without *any* second-moment assumptions on the errors $\mathbf{u}_i$ (except, as usual, that the second moments are well defined). In a multivariate setting it is important to know what this robustness allows. First, the $G \times G$ **unconditional variance matrix**, $\boldsymbol{\Omega} \equiv \text{E}(\mathbf{u}_i\mathbf{u}_i')$, is entirely unrestricted. This fact allows **cross equation correlation** in an SUR system as well as different error variances in each equation. In panel data models, an unrestricted $\boldsymbol{\Omega}$ allows for arbitrary **serial correlation** and

time-varying variances in the disturbances. A second kind of robustness is that the **conditional variance matrix**, $\text{Var}(\mathbf{u}_i \mid \mathbf{X}_i)$, can depend on $\mathbf{X}_i$ in an arbitrary, unknown fashion. The generality afforded by formula (7.26) is possible because of the $N \to \infty$ asymptotics.

In special cases it is useful to impose more structure on the conditional and unconditional variance matrix of $\mathbf{u}_i$ in order to simplify estimation of the asymptotic variance. We will cover an important case in Section 7.5.2. Essentially, the key restriction will be that the conditional and unconditional variances of $\mathbf{u}_i$ are the same.

There are also some special assumptions that greatly simplify the analysis of the pooled OLS estimator for panel data; see Section 7.8.

7.3.3 Testing Multiple Hypotheses

Testing multiple hypotheses in a very robust manner is easy once $\hat{\mathbf{V}}$ in matrix (7.26) has been obtained. The robust Wald statistic for testing H_0: $\mathbf{R}\boldsymbol{\beta} = \mathbf{r}$, where $\mathbf{R}$ is $Q \times K$ with rank Q and $\mathbf{r}$ is $Q \times 1$, has its usual form, $W = (\mathbf{R}\hat{\boldsymbol{\beta}} - \mathbf{r})'(\mathbf{R}\hat{\mathbf{V}}\mathbf{R}')^{-1}(\mathbf{R}\hat{\boldsymbol{\beta}} - \mathbf{r})$. Under H_0, $W \overset{a}{\sim} \chi^2_Q$. In the SUR case this is the easiest and most robust way of testing cross equation restrictions on the parameters in different equations using system OLS. In the panel data setting, the robust Wald test provides a way of testing multiple hypotheses about $\boldsymbol{\beta}$ without assuming homoskedasticity or serial independence of the errors.

7.4 Consistency and Asymptotic Normality of Generalized Least Squares

7.4.1 Consistency

System OLS is consistent under fairly weak assumptions, and we have seen how to perform robust inference using OLS. If we strengthen Assumption SOLS.1 and add assumptions on the conditional variance matrix of $\mathbf{u}_i$, we can do better using a generalized least squares procedure. As we will see, GLS is not usually feasible because it requires knowing the variance matrix of the errors up to a multiplicative constant. Nevertheless, deriving the consistency and asymptotic distribution of the GLS estimator is worthwhile because it turns out that the feasible GLS estimator is asymptotically equivalent to GLS.

We start with the model (7.9), but consistency of GLS generally requires a stronger assumption than Assumption SOLS.1. We replace Assumption SOLS.1 with the assumption that each element of $\mathbf{u}_i$ is uncorrelated with each element of $\mathbf{X}_i$. We can state this succinctly using the Kronecker product:

ASSUMPTION SGLS.1: $\mathrm{E}(\mathbf{X}_i \otimes \mathbf{u}_i) = \mathbf{0}$.

Typically, at least one element of $\mathbf{X}_i$ is unity, so in practice Assumption SGLS.1 implies that $\mathrm{E}(\mathbf{u}_i) = \mathbf{0}$. We will assume $\mathbf{u}_i$ has a zero mean for our discussion but not in proving any results.

Assumption SGLS.1 plays a crucial role in establishing consistency of the GLS estimator, so it is important to recognize that it puts more restrictions on the explanatory variables than does Assumption SOLS.1. In other words, when we allow the explanatory variables to be random, GLS requires a stronger assumption than system OLS in order to be consistent. Sufficient for Assumption SGLS.1, but not necessary, is the zero conditional mean assumption (7.13). This conclusion follows from a standard iterated expectations argument.

For GLS estimation of multivariate equations with i.i.d. observations, the second-moment matrix of $\mathbf{u}_i$ plays a key role. Define the $G \times G$ symmetric, positive semi-definite matrix

$$\mathbf{\Omega} \equiv \mathrm{E}(\mathbf{u}_i \mathbf{u}_i') \tag{7.27}$$

As mentioned in Section 7.3.2, we call $\mathbf{\Omega}$ the unconditional variance matrix of $\mathbf{u}_i$. [In the rare case that $\mathrm{E}(\mathbf{u}_i) \neq \mathbf{0}$, $\mathbf{\Omega}$ is not the variance matrix of $\mathbf{u}_i$, but it is always the appropriate matrix for GLS estimation.] It is important to remember that expression (7.27) is *definitional*: because we are using random sampling, the unconditional variance matrix is necessarily the same for all i.

In place of Assumption SOLS.2, we assume that a weighted version of the expected outer product of $\mathbf{X}_i$ is nonsingular.

ASSUMPTION SGLS.2: $\mathbf{\Omega}$ is positive definite and $\mathrm{E}(\mathbf{X}_i' \mathbf{\Omega}^{-1} \mathbf{X}_i)$ is nonsingular.

For the general treatment we assume that $\mathbf{\Omega}$ is positive definite, rather than just positive semidefinite. In applications where the dependent variables across equations satisfy an adding up constraint—such as expenditure shares summing to unity—an equation must be dropped to ensure that $\mathbf{\Omega}$ is nonsingular, a topic we return to in Section 7.7.3. As a practical matter, Assumption SGLS.2 is not very restrictive. The assumption that the $K \times K$ matrix $\mathrm{E}(\mathbf{X}_i' \mathbf{\Omega}^{-1} \mathbf{X}_i)$ has rank K is the analogue of Assumption SOLS.2.

The usual motivation for the GLS estimator is to transform a system of equations where the error has nonscalar variance-covariance matrix into a system where the error vector has a scalar variance-covariance matrix. We obtain this by multiplying equation (7.9) by $\mathbf{\Omega}^{-1/2}$:

$$\boldsymbol{\Omega}^{-1/2}\mathbf{y}_i = (\boldsymbol{\Omega}^{-1/2}\mathbf{X}_i)\boldsymbol{\beta} + \boldsymbol{\Omega}^{-1/2}\mathbf{u}_i, \qquad \text{or} \qquad \mathbf{y}_i^* = \mathbf{X}_i^*\boldsymbol{\beta} + \mathbf{u}_i^* \tag{7.28}$$

Simple algebra shows that $\mathrm{E}(\mathbf{u}_i^*\mathbf{u}_i^{*\prime}) = \mathbf{I}_G$.

Now we estimate equation (7.28) by system OLS. (As yet, we have no real justification for this step, but we know SOLS is consistent under some assumptions.) Call this estimator $\boldsymbol{\beta}^*$. Then

$$\boldsymbol{\beta}^* \equiv \left(\sum_{i=1}^N \mathbf{X}_i^{*\prime}\mathbf{X}_i^*\right)^{-1}\left(\sum_{i=1}^N \mathbf{X}_i^{*\prime}\mathbf{y}_i^*\right) = \left(\sum_{i=1}^N \mathbf{X}_i'\boldsymbol{\Omega}^{-1}\mathbf{X}_i\right)^{-1}\left(\sum_{i=1}^N \mathbf{X}_i'\boldsymbol{\Omega}^{-1}\mathbf{y}_i\right) \tag{7.29}$$

This is the **generalized least squares (GLS) estimator** of $\boldsymbol{\beta}$. Under Assumption SGLS.2, $\boldsymbol{\beta}^*$ exists with probability approaching one as $N \to \infty$.

We can write $\boldsymbol{\beta}^*$ using full matrix notation as $\boldsymbol{\beta}^* = [\mathbf{X}'(\mathbf{I}_N \otimes \boldsymbol{\Omega}^{-1})\mathbf{X}]^{-1} \cdot [\mathbf{X}'(\mathbf{I}_N \otimes \boldsymbol{\Omega}^{-1})\mathbf{Y}]$, where $\mathbf{X}$ and $\mathbf{Y}$ are the data matrices defined in Section 7.3.2 and $\mathbf{I}_N$ is the $N \times N$ identity matrix. But for establishing the asymptotic properties of $\boldsymbol{\beta}^*$, it is most convenient to work with equation (7.29).

We can establish consistency of $\boldsymbol{\beta}^*$ under Assumptions SGLS.1 and SGLS.2 by writing

$$\boldsymbol{\beta}^* = \boldsymbol{\beta} + \left(N^{-1}\sum_{i=1}^N \mathbf{X}_i'\boldsymbol{\Omega}^{-1}\mathbf{X}_i\right)^{-1}\left(N^{-1}\sum_{i=1}^N \mathbf{X}_i'\boldsymbol{\Omega}^{-1}\mathbf{u}_i\right) \tag{7.30}$$

By the weak law of large numbers (WLLN), $N^{-1}\sum_{i=1}^N \mathbf{X}_i'\boldsymbol{\Omega}^{-1}\mathbf{X}_i \xrightarrow{p} \mathrm{E}(\mathbf{X}_i'\boldsymbol{\Omega}^{-1}\mathbf{X}_i)$. By Assumption SGLS.2 and Slutsky's theorem (Lemma 3.4), $\left(N^{-1}\sum_{i=1}^N \mathbf{X}_i'\boldsymbol{\Omega}^{-1}\mathbf{X}_i\right)^{-1} \xrightarrow{p} \mathbf{A}^{-1}$, where $\mathbf{A}$ is now defined as

$$\mathbf{A} \equiv \mathrm{E}(\mathbf{X}_i'\boldsymbol{\Omega}^{-1}\mathbf{X}_i) \tag{7.31}$$

Now we must show that $\mathrm{plim}\ N^{-1}\sum_{i=1}^N \mathbf{X}_i'\boldsymbol{\Omega}^{-1}\mathbf{u}_i = \mathbf{0}$. By the WLLN, it is sufficient that $\mathrm{E}(\mathbf{X}_i'\boldsymbol{\Omega}^{-1}\mathbf{u}_i) = \mathbf{0}$. This is where Assumption SGLS.1 comes in. We can argue this point informally because $\boldsymbol{\Omega}^{-1}\mathbf{X}_i$ is a linear combination of $\mathbf{X}_i$, and since each element of $\mathbf{X}_i$ is uncorrelated with each element of $\mathbf{u}_i$, any linear combination of $\mathbf{X}_i$ is uncorrelated with $\mathbf{u}_i$. We can also show this directly using the algebra of Kronecker products and vectorization. For conformable matrices $\mathbf{D}$, $\mathbf{E}$, and $\mathbf{F}$, recall that $\mathrm{vec}(\mathbf{DEF}) = (\mathbf{F}' \otimes \mathbf{D})\ \mathrm{vec}(\mathbf{E})$, where $\mathrm{vec}(\mathbf{C})$ is the vectorization of the matrix $\mathbf{C}$. [That is, $\mathrm{vec}(\mathbf{C})$ is the column vector obtained by stacking the columns of $\mathbf{C}$ from first to last; see Theil (1983).] Therefore, under Assumption SGLS.1,

$$\mathrm{vec}\ \mathrm{E}(\mathbf{X}_i'\boldsymbol{\Omega}^{-1}\mathbf{u}_i) = \mathrm{E}[(\mathbf{u}_i' \otimes \mathbf{X}_i')]\ \mathrm{vec}(\boldsymbol{\Omega}^{-1}) = \mathrm{E}[(\mathbf{u}_i \otimes \mathbf{X}_i)']\ \mathrm{vec}(\boldsymbol{\Omega}^{-1}) = \mathbf{0}$$

where we have also used the fact that the expectation and vec operators can be interchanged. We can now read the consistency of the GLS estimator off of equation (7.30). We do not state this conclusion as a theorem because the GLS estimator itself is rarely available.

The proof of consistency that we have sketched fails if we only make Assumption SOLS.1: $\mathrm{E}(\mathbf{X}_i'\mathbf{u}_i) = \mathbf{0}$ does not imply $\mathrm{E}(\mathbf{X}_i'\boldsymbol{\Omega}^{-1}\mathbf{u}_i) = \mathbf{0}$, except when $\boldsymbol{\Omega}$ and $\mathbf{X}_i$ have special structures. If Assumption SOLS.1 holds but Assumption SGLS.1 fails, the transformation in equation (7.28) generally induces correlation between $\mathbf{X}_i^*$ and $\mathbf{u}_i^*$. This can be an important point, especially for certain panel data applications. If we are willing to make the zero conditional mean assumption (7.13), $\boldsymbol{\beta}^*$ can be shown to be unbiased conditional on $\mathbf{X}$.

7.4.2 Asymptotic Normality

We now sketch the asymptotic normality of the GLS estimator under Assumptions SGLS.1 and SGLS.2 and some weak moment conditions. The first step is familiar:

$$\sqrt{N}(\boldsymbol{\beta}^* - \boldsymbol{\beta}) = \left(N^{-1}\sum_{i=1}^{N}\mathbf{X}_i'\boldsymbol{\Omega}^{-1}\mathbf{X}_i\right)^{-1}\left(N^{-1/2}\sum_{i=1}^{N}\mathbf{X}_i'\boldsymbol{\Omega}^{-1}\mathbf{u}_i\right) \tag{7.32}$$

By the CLT, $N^{-1/2}\sum_{i=1}^{N}\mathbf{X}_i'\boldsymbol{\Omega}^{-1}\mathbf{u}_i \xrightarrow{d} \mathrm{Normal}(\mathbf{0}, \mathbf{B})$, where

$$\mathbf{B} \equiv \mathrm{E}(\mathbf{X}_i'\boldsymbol{\Omega}^{-1}\mathbf{u}_i\mathbf{u}_i'\boldsymbol{\Omega}^{-1}\mathbf{X}_i) \tag{7.33}$$

Further, since $N^{-1/2}\sum_{i=1}^{N}\mathbf{X}_i'\boldsymbol{\Omega}^{-1}\mathbf{u}_i = \mathrm{O}_p(1)$ and $(N^{-1}\sum_{i=1}^{N}\mathbf{X}_i'\boldsymbol{\Omega}^{-1}\mathbf{X}_i)^{-1} - \mathbf{A}^{-1} = \mathrm{o}_p(1)$, we can write $\sqrt{N}(\boldsymbol{\beta}^* - \boldsymbol{\beta}) = \mathbf{A}^{-1}(N^{-1/2}\sum_{i=1}^{N}\mathbf{x}_i'\boldsymbol{\Omega}^{-1}\mathbf{u}_i) + \mathrm{o}_p(1)$. It follows from the asymptotic equivalence lemma that

$$\sqrt{N}(\boldsymbol{\beta}^* - \boldsymbol{\beta}) \overset{a}{\sim} \mathrm{Normal}(\mathbf{0}, \mathbf{A}^{-1}\mathbf{B}\mathbf{A}^{-1}) \tag{7.34}$$

Thus,

$$\mathrm{Avar}(\hat{\boldsymbol{\beta}}) = \mathbf{A}^{-1}\mathbf{B}\mathbf{A}^{-1}/N \tag{7.35}$$

The asymptotic variance in equation (7.35) is not the asymptotic variance usually derived for GLS estimation of systems of equations. Usually the formula is reported as $\mathbf{A}^{-1}/N$. But equation (7.35) is the appropriate expression under the assumptions made so far. The simpler form, which results when $\mathbf{B} = \mathbf{A}$, is not generally valid under Assumptions SGLS.1 and SGLS.2, because we have assumed nothing about the variance matrix of $\mathbf{u}_i$ conditional on $\mathbf{X}_i$. In Section 7.5.2 we make an assumption that simplifies equation (7.35).

7.5 Feasible GLS

7.5.1 Asymptotic Properties

Obtaining the GLS estimator $\boldsymbol{\beta}^*$ requires knowing $\boldsymbol{\Omega}$ up to scale. That is, we must be able to write $\boldsymbol{\Omega} = \sigma^2\mathbf{C}$ where $\mathbf{C}$ is a *known* $G \times G$ positive definite matrix and σ^2 is allowed to be an unknown constant. Sometimes $\mathbf{C}$ is known (one case is $\mathbf{C} = \mathbf{I}_G$), but much more often it is unknown. Therefore, we now turn to the analysis of feasible GLS (FGLS) estimation.

In FGLS estimation we replace the unknown matrix $\boldsymbol{\Omega}$ with a consistent estimator. Because the estimator of $\boldsymbol{\Omega}$ appears highly nonlinearly in the expression for the FGLS estimator, deriving finite sample properties of FGLS is generally difficult. [However, under essentially assumption (7.13) and some additional assumptions, including symmetry of the distribution of $\mathbf{u}_i$, Kakwani (1967) showed that the distribution of the FGLS is symmetric about $\boldsymbol{\beta}$, a property which means that the FGLS is unbiased *if* its expected value exists; see also Schmidt (1976, Section 2.5).] The asymptotic properties of the FGLS estimator are easily established as $N \to \infty$ because, as we will show, its first-order asymptotic properties are *identical* to those of the GLS estimator under Assumptions SGLS.1 and SGLS.2. It is for this purpose that we spent some time on GLS. After establishing the asymptotic equivalence, we can easily obtain the limiting distribution of the FGLS estimator. Of course, GLS is trivially a special case of FGLS, where there is no first-stage estimation error.

We assume we have a consistent estimator, $\hat{\boldsymbol{\Omega}}$, of $\boldsymbol{\Omega}$:

$$\operatorname*{plim}_{N\to\infty} \hat{\boldsymbol{\Omega}} = \boldsymbol{\Omega} \tag{7.36}$$

[Because the dimension of $\hat{\boldsymbol{\Omega}}$ does not depend on N, equation (7.36) makes sense when defined element by element.] When $\boldsymbol{\Omega}$ is allowed to be a general positive definite matrix, the following estimation approach can be used. First, obtain the system OLS estimator of $\boldsymbol{\beta}$, which we denote $\hat{\hat{\boldsymbol{\beta}}}$ in this section to avoid confusion. We already showed that $\hat{\hat{\boldsymbol{\beta}}}$ is consistent for $\boldsymbol{\beta}$ under Assumptions SOLS.1 and SOLS.2, and therefore under Assumptions SGLS.1 and SOLS.2. (In what follows, we assume that Assumptions SOLS.2 and SGLS.2 both hold.) By the WLLN, $\operatorname{plim}(N^{-1}\sum_{i=1}^N \mathbf{u}_i\mathbf{u}_i') = \boldsymbol{\Omega}$, and so a natural estimator of $\boldsymbol{\Omega}$ is

$$\hat{\boldsymbol{\Omega}} \equiv N^{-1}\sum_{i=1}^N \hat{\hat{\mathbf{u}}}_i\hat{\hat{\mathbf{u}}}_i' \tag{7.37}$$

where $\hat{\hat{\mathbf{u}}}_i \equiv \mathbf{y}_i - \mathbf{X}_i\hat{\hat{\boldsymbol{\beta}}}$ are the SOLS residuals. We can show that this estimator is consistent for $\boldsymbol{\Omega}$ under Assumptions SGLS.1 and SOLS.2 and standard moment conditions. First, write

$$\hat{\hat{\mathbf{u}}}_i = \mathbf{u}_i - \mathbf{X}_i(\hat{\hat{\boldsymbol{\beta}}} - \boldsymbol{\beta}) \tag{7.38}$$

so that

$$\hat{\hat{\mathbf{u}}}_i\hat{\hat{\mathbf{u}}}_i' = \mathbf{u}_i\mathbf{u}_i' - \mathbf{u}_i(\hat{\hat{\boldsymbol{\beta}}} - \boldsymbol{\beta})'\mathbf{X}_i' - \mathbf{X}_i(\hat{\hat{\boldsymbol{\beta}}} - \boldsymbol{\beta})\mathbf{u}_i' + \mathbf{X}_i(\hat{\hat{\boldsymbol{\beta}}} - \boldsymbol{\beta})(\hat{\hat{\boldsymbol{\beta}}} - \boldsymbol{\beta})'\mathbf{X}_i' \tag{7.39}$$

Therefore, it suffices to show that the averages of the last three terms converge in probability to zero. Write the average of the vec of the first term as $N^{-1}\sum_{i=1}^{N}(\mathbf{X}_i \otimes \mathbf{u}_i) \cdot (\hat{\hat{\boldsymbol{\beta}}} - \boldsymbol{\beta})$, which is $o_p(1)$ because $\text{plim}(\hat{\hat{\boldsymbol{\beta}}} - \boldsymbol{\beta}) = \mathbf{0}$ and $N^{-1}\sum_{i=1}^{N}(\mathbf{X}_i \otimes \mathbf{u}_i) \xrightarrow{p} \mathbf{0}$. The third term is the transpose of the second. For the last term in equation (7.39), note that the average of its vec can be written as

$$N^{-1}\sum_{i=1}^{N}(\mathbf{X}_i \otimes \mathbf{X}_i) \cdot \text{vec}\{(\hat{\hat{\boldsymbol{\beta}}} - \boldsymbol{\beta})(\hat{\hat{\boldsymbol{\beta}}} - \boldsymbol{\beta})'\} \tag{7.40}$$

Now $\text{vec}\{(\hat{\hat{\boldsymbol{\beta}}} - \boldsymbol{\beta})(\hat{\hat{\boldsymbol{\beta}}} - \boldsymbol{\beta})'\} = o_p(1)$. Further, assuming that each element of $\mathbf{X}_i$ has finite second moment, $N^{-1}\sum_{i=1}^{N}(\mathbf{X}_i \otimes \mathbf{X}_i) = O_p(1)$ by the WLLN. This step takes care of the last term, since $O_p(1) \cdot o_p(1) = o_p(1)$. We have shown that

$$\hat{\boldsymbol{\Omega}} = N^{-1}\sum_{i=1}^{N}\mathbf{u}_i\mathbf{u}_i' + o_p(1) \tag{7.41}$$

and so equation (7.36) follows immediately. [In fact, a more careful analysis shows that the $o_p(1)$ in equation (7.41) can be replaced by $o_p(N^{-1/2})$; see Problem 7.4.]

Sometimes the elements of $\boldsymbol{\Omega}$ are restricted in some way (an important example is the random effects panel data model that we will cover in Chapter 10). In such cases a different estimator of $\boldsymbol{\Omega}$ is often used that exploits these restrictions. As with $\hat{\boldsymbol{\Omega}}$ in equation (7.37), such estimators typically use the system OLS residuals in some fashion and lead to consistent estimators assuming the structure of $\boldsymbol{\Omega}$ is correctly specified. The advantage of equation (7.37) is that it is consistent for $\boldsymbol{\Omega}$ quite generally. However, if N is not very large relative to G, equation (7.37) can have poor finite sample properties.

Given $\hat{\boldsymbol{\Omega}}$, the **feasible GLS (FGLS) estimator** of $\boldsymbol{\beta}$ is

$$\hat{\boldsymbol{\beta}} = \left(\sum_{i=1}^{N}\mathbf{X}_i'\hat{\boldsymbol{\Omega}}^{-1}\mathbf{X}_i\right)^{-1}\left(\sum_{i=1}^{N}\mathbf{X}_i'\hat{\boldsymbol{\Omega}}^{-1}\mathbf{y}_i\right) \tag{7.42}$$

or, in full matrix notation, $\hat{\boldsymbol{\beta}} = [\mathbf{X}'(\mathbf{I}_N \otimes \hat{\boldsymbol{\Omega}}^{-1})\mathbf{X}]^{-1}[\mathbf{X}'(\mathbf{I}_N \otimes \hat{\boldsymbol{\Omega}}^{-1})\mathbf{Y}]$.

We have already shown that the (infeasible) GLS estimator is consistent under Assumptions SGLS.1 and SGLS.2. Because $\hat{\mathbf{\Omega}}$ converges to $\mathbf{\Omega}$, it is not surprising that FGLS is also consistent. Rather than show this result separately, we verify the stronger result that FGLS has the same limiting distribution as GLS.

The limiting distribution of FGLS is obtained by writing

$$\sqrt{N}(\hat{\boldsymbol{\beta}} - \boldsymbol{\beta}) = \left(N^{-1}\sum_{i=1}^{N}\mathbf{X}_i'\hat{\mathbf{\Omega}}^{-1}\mathbf{X}_i\right)^{-1}\left(N^{-1/2}\sum_{i=1}^{N}\mathbf{X}_i'\hat{\mathbf{\Omega}}^{-1}\mathbf{u}_i\right) \tag{7.43}$$

Now

$$N^{-1/2}\sum_{i=1}^{N}\mathbf{X}_i'\hat{\mathbf{\Omega}}^{-1}\mathbf{u}_i - N^{-1/2}\sum_{i=1}^{N}\mathbf{X}_i'\mathbf{\Omega}^{-1}\mathbf{u}_i = \left[N^{-1/2}\sum_{i=1}^{N}(\mathbf{u}_i \otimes \mathbf{X}_i)'\right] \operatorname{vec}(\hat{\mathbf{\Omega}}^{-1} - \mathbf{\Omega}^{-1})$$

Under Assumption SGLS.1, the CLT implies that $N^{-1/2}\sum_{i=1}^{N}(\mathbf{u}_i \otimes \mathbf{X}_i) = \mathrm{O}_p(1)$. Because $\mathrm{O}_p(1) \cdot \mathrm{o}_p(1) = \mathrm{o}_p(1)$, it follows that

$$N^{-1/2}\sum_{i=1}^{N}\mathbf{X}_i'\hat{\mathbf{\Omega}}^{-1}\mathbf{u}_i = N^{-1/2}\sum_{i=1}^{N}\mathbf{X}_i'\mathbf{\Omega}^{-1}\mathbf{u}_i + \mathrm{o}_p(1)$$

A similar argument shows that $N^{-1}\sum_{i=1}^{N}\mathbf{X}_i'\hat{\mathbf{\Omega}}^{-1}\mathbf{X}_i = N^{-1}\sum_{i=1}^{N}\mathbf{X}_i'\mathbf{\Omega}^{-1}\mathbf{X}_i + \mathrm{o}_p(1)$. Therefore, we have shown that

$$\sqrt{N}(\hat{\boldsymbol{\beta}} - \boldsymbol{\beta}) = \left(N^{-1}\sum_{i=1}^{N}\mathbf{X}_i'\mathbf{\Omega}^{-1}\mathbf{X}_i\right)^{-1}\left(N^{-1/2}\sum_{i=1}^{N}\mathbf{X}_i'\mathbf{\Omega}^{-1}\mathbf{u}_i\right) + \mathrm{o}_p(1) \tag{7.44}$$

The first term in equation (7.44) is just $\sqrt{N}(\boldsymbol{\beta}^* - \boldsymbol{\beta})$, where $\boldsymbol{\beta}^*$ is the GLS estimator. We can write equation (7.44) as

$$\sqrt{N}(\hat{\boldsymbol{\beta}} - \boldsymbol{\beta}^*) = \mathrm{o}_p(1) \tag{7.45}$$

which shows that $\hat{\boldsymbol{\beta}}$ and $\boldsymbol{\beta}^*$ are $\sqrt{N}$-equivalent. Recall from Chapter 3 that this statement is much stronger than simply saying that $\boldsymbol{\beta}^*$ and $\hat{\boldsymbol{\beta}}$ are both consistent for $\boldsymbol{\beta}$. There are many estimators, such as system OLS, that are consistent for $\boldsymbol{\beta}$ but are not $\sqrt{N}$-equivalent to $\boldsymbol{\beta}^*$.

The asymptotic equivalence of $\hat{\boldsymbol{\beta}}$ and $\boldsymbol{\beta}^*$ has practically important consequences. The most important of these is that, for performing asymptotic inference about $\boldsymbol{\beta}$ using $\hat{\boldsymbol{\beta}}$, we do not have to worry that $\hat{\mathbf{\Omega}}$ is an estimator of $\mathbf{\Omega}$. Of course, whether the asymptotic approximation gives a reasonable approximation to the actual distribution of $\hat{\boldsymbol{\beta}}$ is difficult to tell. With large N, the approximation is usually pretty good.

But if N is small relative to G, ignoring estimation of $\mathbf{\Omega}$ in performing inference about $\boldsymbol{\beta}$ can be misleading.

We summarize the limiting distribution of FGLS with a theorem.

THEOREM 7.3 (Asymptotic Normality of FGLS): Under Assumptions SGLS.1 and SGLS.2,

$$\sqrt{N}(\hat{\boldsymbol{\beta}} - \boldsymbol{\beta}) \overset{a}{\sim} \text{Normal}(\mathbf{0}, \mathbf{A}^{-1}\mathbf{B}\mathbf{A}^{-1}) \tag{7.46}$$

where $\mathbf{A}$ is defined in equation (7.31) and $\mathbf{B}$ is defined in equation (7.33).

In the FGLS context a consistent estimator of $\mathbf{A}$ is

$$\hat{\mathbf{A}} \equiv N^{-1} \sum_{i=1}^{N} \mathbf{X}_i' \hat{\mathbf{\Omega}}^{-1} \mathbf{X}_i \tag{7.47}$$

A consistent estimator of $\mathbf{B}$ is also readily available after FGLS estimation. Define the FGLS residuals by

$$\hat{\mathbf{u}}_i \equiv \mathbf{y}_i - \mathbf{X}_i \hat{\boldsymbol{\beta}}, \qquad i = 1, 2, \ldots, N \tag{7.48}$$

[The only difference between the FGLS and SOLS residuals is that the FGLS estimator is inserted in place of the SOLS estimator; in particular, the FGLS residuals are *not* from the transformed equation (7.28).] Using standard arguments, a consistent estimator of $\mathbf{B}$ is

$$\hat{\mathbf{B}} \equiv N^{-1} \sum_{i=1}^{N} \mathbf{X}_i' \hat{\mathbf{\Omega}}^{-1} \hat{\mathbf{u}}_i \hat{\mathbf{u}}_i' \hat{\mathbf{\Omega}}^{-1} \mathbf{X}_i$$

The estimator of $\text{Avar}(\hat{\boldsymbol{\beta}})$ can be written as

$$\hat{\mathbf{A}}^{-1}\hat{\mathbf{B}}\hat{\mathbf{A}}^{-1}/N = \left(\sum_{i=1}^{N} \mathbf{X}_i' \hat{\mathbf{\Omega}}^{-1} \mathbf{X}_i \right)^{-1} \left(\sum_{i=1}^{N} \mathbf{X}_i' \hat{\mathbf{\Omega}}^{-1} \hat{\mathbf{u}}_i \hat{\mathbf{u}}_i' \hat{\mathbf{\Omega}}^{-1} \mathbf{X}_i \right) \left(\sum_{i=1}^{N} \mathbf{X}_i' \hat{\mathbf{\Omega}}^{-1} \mathbf{X}_i \right)^{-1} \tag{7.49}$$

This is the extension of the White (1980b) heteroskedasticity-robust asymptotic variance estimator to the case of systems of equations; see also White (1984). This estimator is valid under Assumptions SGLS.1 and SGLS.2; that is, it is completely robust.

7.5.2 Asymptotic Variance of FGLS under a Standard Assumption

Under the assumptions so far, FGLS really has nothing to offer over SOLS. In addition to being computationally more difficult, FGLS is less robust than SOLS. So why is FGLS used? The answer is that, under an additional assumption, FGLS is asymptotically more efficient than SOLS (and other estimators). First, we state the weakest condition that simplifies estimation of the asymptotic variance for FGLS. For reasons to be seen shortly, we call this a **system homoskedasticity assumption**.

ASSUMPTION SGLS.3: $\mathrm{E}(\mathbf{X}_i'\boldsymbol{\Omega}^{-1}\mathbf{u}_i\mathbf{u}_i'\boldsymbol{\Omega}^{-1}\mathbf{X}_i) = \mathrm{E}(\mathbf{X}_i'\boldsymbol{\Omega}^{-1}\mathbf{X}_i)$, where $\boldsymbol{\Omega} \equiv \mathrm{E}(\mathbf{u}_i\mathbf{u}_i')$.

Another way to state this assumption is, $\mathbf{B} = \mathbf{A}$, which, from expression (7.46), simplifies the asymptotic variance. As stated, Assumption SGLS.3 is somewhat difficult to interpret. When $G = 1$, it reduces to Assumption OLS.3. When $\boldsymbol{\Omega}$ is diagonal and $\mathbf{X}_i$ has either the SUR or panel data structure, Assumption SGLS.3 implies a kind of conditional homoskedasticity in each equation (or time period). Generally, Assumption SGLS.3 puts restrictions on the *conditional* variances and covariances of elements of $\mathbf{u}_i$. A sufficient (though certainly not necessary) condition for Assumption SGLS.3 is easier to interpret:

$$\mathrm{E}(\mathbf{u}_i\mathbf{u}_i' \mid \mathbf{X}_i) = \mathrm{E}(\mathbf{u}_i\mathbf{u}_i') \tag{7.50}$$

If $\mathrm{E}(\mathbf{u}_i \mid \mathbf{X}_i) = \mathbf{0}$, then assumption (7.50) is the same as assuming $\mathrm{Var}(\mathbf{u}_i \mid \mathbf{X}_i) = \mathrm{Var}(\mathbf{u}_i) = \boldsymbol{\Omega}$, which means that each variance and each covariance of elements involving $\mathbf{u}_i$ must be constant conditional on all of $\mathbf{X}_i$. This is a very natural way of stating a system homoskedasticity assumption, but it is sometimes too strong.

When $G = 2$, $\boldsymbol{\Omega}$ contains three distinct elements, $\sigma_1^2 = \mathrm{E}(u_{i1}^2)$, $\sigma_2^2 = \mathrm{E}(u_{i2}^2)$, and $\sigma_{12} = \mathrm{E}(u_{i1}u_{i2})$. These elements are not restricted by the assumptions we have made. (The inequality $|\sigma_{12}| < \sigma_1\sigma_2$ must always hold for $\boldsymbol{\Omega}$ to be a nonsingular covariance matrix.) However, assumption (7.50) requires $\mathrm{E}(u_{i1}^2 \mid \mathbf{X}_i) = \sigma_1^2$, $\mathrm{E}(u_{i2}^2 \mid \mathbf{X}_i) = \sigma_2^2$, and $\mathrm{E}(u_{i1}u_{i2} \mid \mathbf{X}_i) = \sigma_{12}$: the conditional variances and covariance must not depend on $\mathbf{X}_i$.

That assumption (7.50) implies Assumption SGLS.3 is a consequence of iterated expectations:

$$\begin{aligned}\mathrm{E}(\mathbf{X}_i'\boldsymbol{\Omega}^{-1}\mathbf{u}_i\mathbf{u}_i'\boldsymbol{\Omega}^{-1}\mathbf{X}_i) &= \mathrm{E}[\mathrm{E}(\mathbf{X}_i'\boldsymbol{\Omega}^{-1}\mathbf{u}_i\mathbf{u}_i'\boldsymbol{\Omega}^{-1}\mathbf{X}_i \mid \mathbf{X}_i)] \\ &= \mathrm{E}[\mathbf{X}_i'\boldsymbol{\Omega}^{-1}\mathrm{E}(\mathbf{u}_i\mathbf{u}_i' \mid \mathbf{X}_i)\boldsymbol{\Omega}^{-1}\mathbf{X}_i] = \mathrm{E}(\mathbf{X}_i'\boldsymbol{\Omega}^{-1}\boldsymbol{\Omega}\boldsymbol{\Omega}^{-1}\mathbf{X}_i) \\ &= \mathrm{E}(\mathbf{X}_i'\boldsymbol{\Omega}^{-1}\mathbf{X}_i)\end{aligned}$$

While assumption (7.50) is easier to intepret, we use Assumption SGLS.3 for stating the next theorem because there are cases, including some dynamic panel data models, where Assumption SGLS.3 holds but assumption (7.50) does not.

THEOREM 7.4 (Usual Variance Matrix for FGLS): Under Assumptions SGLS.1–SGLS.3, the asymptotic variance of the FGLS estimator is $\mathrm{Avar}(\hat{\boldsymbol{\beta}}) = \mathbf{A}^{-1}/N \equiv [\mathrm{E}(\mathbf{X}_i'\boldsymbol{\Omega}^{-1}\mathbf{X}_i)]^{-1}/N$.

We obtain an estimator of $\operatorname{Avar}(\hat{\boldsymbol{\beta}})$ by using our consistent estimator of $\mathbf{A}$:

$$\operatorname{Av\hat{a}r}(\hat{\boldsymbol{\beta}}) = \hat{\mathbf{A}}^{-1}/N = \left(\sum_{i=1}^{N} \mathbf{X}_i'\hat{\boldsymbol{\Omega}}^{-1}\mathbf{X}_i\right)^{-1} \tag{7.51}$$

Equation (7.51) is the "usual" formula for the asymptotic variance of FGLS. It is nonrobust in the sense that it relies on Assumption SGLS.3 in addition to Assumptions SGLS.1 and SGLS.2. If heteroskedasticity in $\mathbf{u}_i$ is suspected, then the robust estimator (7.49) should be used.

Assumption (7.50) also has important efficiency implications. One consequence of Problem 7.2 is that, under Assumptions SGLS.1, SOLS.2, SGLS.2, and (7.50), the FGLS estimator is more efficient than the system OLS estimator. We can actually say much more: FGLS is more efficient than any other estimator that uses the orthogonality conditions $\mathrm{E}(\mathbf{X}_i \otimes \mathbf{u}_i) = \mathbf{0}$. This conclusion will follow as a special case of Theorem 8.4 in Chapter 8, where we define the class of competing estimators. If we replace Assumption SGLS.1 with the zero conditional mean assumption (7.13), then an even stronger efficiency result holds for FGLS, something we treat in Section 8.6.

7.6 Testing Using FGLS

Asymptotic standard errors are obtained in the usual fashion from the asymptotic variance estimates. We can use the nonrobust version in equation (7.51) or, even better, the robust version in equation (7.49), to construct t statistics and confidence intervals. Testing multiple restrictions is fairly easy using the Wald test, which always has the same general form. The important consideration lies in choosing the asymptotic variance estimate, $\hat{\mathbf{V}}$. Standard Wald statistics use equation (7.51), and this approach produces limiting chi-square statistics under the homoskedasticity assumption SGLS.3. Completely robust Wald statistics are obtained by choosing $\hat{\mathbf{V}}$ as in equation (7.49).

If Assumption SGLS.3 holds under H_0, we can define a statistic based on the weighted sums of squared residuals. To obtain the statistic, we estimate the model with and without the restrictions imposed on $\boldsymbol{\beta}$, where the same estimator of $\boldsymbol{\Omega}$, usually based on the unrestricted SOLS residuals, is used in obtaining the restricted and unrestricted FGLS estimators. Let $\tilde{\mathbf{u}}_i$ denote the residuals from constrained FGLS (with Q restrictions imposed on $\tilde{\boldsymbol{\beta}}$) using variance matrix $\hat{\boldsymbol{\Omega}}$. It can be shown that, under H_0 and Assumptions SGLS.1–SGLS.3,

$$\left(\sum_{i=1}^{N}\tilde{\mathbf{u}}_i'\hat{\boldsymbol{\Omega}}^{-1}\tilde{\mathbf{u}}_i - \sum_{i=1}^{N}\hat{\mathbf{u}}_i'\hat{\boldsymbol{\Omega}}^{-1}\hat{\mathbf{u}}_i\right) \overset{a}{\sim} \chi_Q^2 \tag{7.52}$$

Gallant (1987) shows expression (7.52) for nonlinear models with fixed regressors; essentially the same proof works here under Assumptions SGLS.1–SGLS.3, as we will show more generally in Chapter 12.

The statistic in expression (7.52) is the difference between the *transformed* sum of squared residuals from the restricted and unrestricted models, but it is just as easy to calculate expression (7.52) directly. Gallant (1987, Chapter 5) has found that an F statistic has better finite sample properties. The F statistic in this context is defined as

$$F = \left[\left(\sum_{i=1}^{N}\tilde{\mathbf{u}}_i'\hat{\boldsymbol{\Omega}}^{-1}\tilde{\mathbf{u}}_i - \sum_{i=1}^{N}\hat{\mathbf{u}}_i'\hat{\boldsymbol{\Omega}}^{-1}\hat{\mathbf{u}}_i\right)\Big/\left(\sum_{i=1}^{N}\hat{\mathbf{u}}_i'\hat{\boldsymbol{\Omega}}^{-1}\hat{\mathbf{u}}_i\right)\right][(NG-K)]/Q \tag{7.53}$$

Why can we treat this equation as having an approximate F distribution? First, for $NG-K$ large, $\mathcal{F}_{Q,NG-K} \overset{a}{\sim} \chi_Q^2/Q$. Therefore, dividing expression (7.52) by Q gives us an approximate $\mathcal{F}_{Q,NG-K}$ distribution. The presence of the other two terms in equation (7.53) is to improve the F-approximation. Since $\mathrm{E}(\mathbf{u}_i'\boldsymbol{\Omega}^{-1}\mathbf{u}_i) = \mathrm{tr}\{\mathrm{E}(\boldsymbol{\Omega}^{-1}\mathbf{u}_i\mathbf{u}_i')\} = \mathrm{tr}\{\mathrm{E}(\boldsymbol{\Omega}^{-1}\boldsymbol{\Omega})\} = G$, it follows that $(NG)^{-1}\sum_{i=1}^{N}\mathbf{u}_i'\boldsymbol{\Omega}^{-1}\mathbf{u}_i \xrightarrow{p} 1$; replacing $\mathbf{u}_i'\boldsymbol{\Omega}^{-1}\mathbf{u}_i$ with $\hat{\mathbf{u}}_i'\hat{\boldsymbol{\Omega}}^{-1}\hat{\mathbf{u}}_i$ does not affect this consistency result. Subtracting off K as a degrees-of-freedom adjustment changes nothing asymptotically, and so $(NG-K)^{-1}\sum_{i=1}^{N}\hat{\mathbf{u}}_i'\hat{\boldsymbol{\Omega}}^{-1}\hat{\mathbf{u}}_i \xrightarrow{p} 1$. Multiplying expression (7.52) by the inverse of this quantity does not affect its asymptotic distribution.

7.7 Seemingly Unrelated Regressions, Revisited

We now return to the SUR system in assumption (7.2). We saw in Section 7.3 how to write this system in the form (7.9) if there are no cross equation restrictions on the $\boldsymbol{\beta}_g$. We also showed that the system OLS estimator corresponds to estimating each equation separately by OLS.

As mentioned earlier, in most applications of SUR it is reasonable to assume that $\mathrm{E}(\mathbf{x}_{ig}'u_{ih}) = \mathbf{0}$, $g, h = 1, 2, \ldots, G$, which is just Assumption SGLS.1 for the SUR structure. Under this assumption, FGLS will consistently estimate the $\boldsymbol{\beta}_g$.

OLS equation by equation is simple to use and leads to standard inference for each $\boldsymbol{\beta}_g$ under the OLS homoskedasticity assumption $\mathrm{E}(u_{ig}^2 \mid \mathbf{x}_{ig}) = \sigma_g^2$, which is standard in SUR contexts. So why bother using FGLS in such applications? There are two answers. First, as mentioned in Section 7.5.2, if we can maintain assumption (7.50) in addition to Assumption SGLS.1 (and SGLS.2), FGLS is asymptotically at least as efficient as system OLS. Second, while OLS equation by equation allows us to easily test hypotheses about the coefficients within an equation, it does not provide a convenient way for testing cross equation restrictions. It is possible to use OLS for testing cross equation restrictions by using the variance matrix (7.26), but if we are willing to go through that much trouble, we should just use FGLS.

7.7.1 Comparison between OLS and FGLS for SUR Systems

There are two cases where OLS equation by equation is algebraically equivalent to FGLS. The first case is fairly straightforward to analyze in our setting.

THEOREM 7.5 (Equivalence of FGLS and OLS, I): If $\hat{\mathbf{\Omega}}$ is a diagonal matrix, then OLS equation by equation is identical to FGLS.

Proof: If $\hat{\mathbf{\Omega}}$ is diagonal, then $\hat{\mathbf{\Omega}}^{-1} = \operatorname{diag}(\hat{\sigma}_1^{-2}, \ldots, \hat{\sigma}_G^{-2})$. With $\mathbf{X}_i$ defined as in the matrix (7.10), straightforward algebra shows that

$$\mathbf{X}_i'\hat{\mathbf{\Omega}}^{-1}\mathbf{X}_i = \hat{\mathbf{\Psi}}^{-1}\mathbf{X}_i'\mathbf{X}_i \qquad \text{and} \qquad \mathbf{X}_i'\hat{\mathbf{\Omega}}^{-1}\mathbf{y}_i = \hat{\mathbf{\Psi}}^{-1}\mathbf{X}_i'\mathbf{y}_i$$

where $\hat{\mathbf{\Psi}}$ is the block diagonal matrix with $\hat{\sigma}_g^2\mathbf{I}_{k_g}$ as its gth block. It follows that the FGLS estimator can be written as

$$\hat{\beta} = \left(\sum_{i=1}^{N}\hat{\mathbf{\Psi}}^{-1}\mathbf{X}_i'\mathbf{X}_i\right)^{-1}\left(\sum_{i=1}^{N}\hat{\mathbf{\Psi}}^{-1}\mathbf{X}_i'\mathbf{y}_i\right) = \left(\sum_{i=1}^{N}\mathbf{X}_i'\mathbf{X}_i\right)^{-1}\left(\sum_{i=1}^{N}\mathbf{X}_i'\mathbf{y}_i\right)$$

which is the system OLS estimator.

In applications, $\hat{\mathbf{\Omega}}$ would not be diagonal unless we impose a diagonal structure. Nevertheless, we can use Theorem 7.5 to obtain an *asymptotic* equivalance result when $\mathbf{\Omega}$ is diagonal. If $\mathbf{\Omega}$ is diagonal, then the GLS and OLS are algebraically identical (because GLS uses $\mathbf{\Omega}$). We know that FGLS and GLS are $\sqrt{N}$-asymptotically equivalent for any $\mathbf{\Omega}$. Therefore, OLS and FGLS are $\sqrt{N}$-asymptotically equivalent if $\mathbf{\Omega}$ is diagonal, even though they are not algebraically equivalent (because $\hat{\mathbf{\Omega}}$ is not diagonal).

The second algebraic equivalence result holds without any restrictions on $\hat{\mathbf{\Omega}}$. It is special in that it assumes that the same regressors appear in each equation.

THEOREM 7.6 (Equivalence of FGLS and OLS, II): If $\mathbf{x}_{i1} = \mathbf{x}_{i2} = \cdots = \mathbf{x}_{iG}$ for all i, that is, if the same regressors show up in each equation (for all observations), then OLS equation by equation and FGLS are identical.

In practice, Theorem 7.6 holds when the population model has the same explanatory variables in each equation. The usual proof of this result groups all N observations for the first equation followed by the N observations for the second equation, and so on (see, for example, Greene, 1997, Chapter 17). Problem 7.5 asks you to prove Theorem 7.6 in the current setup, where we have ordered the observations to be amenable to asymptotic analysis.

It is important to know that when every equation contains the same regressors in an SUR system, there is still a good reason to use a SUR software routine in obtaining the estimates: we may be interested in testing joint hypotheses involving parameters in different equations. In order to do so we need to estimate the variance matrix of $\hat{\boldsymbol{\beta}}$ (not just the variance matrix of each $\hat{\boldsymbol{\beta}}_g$, which only allows tests of the coefficients *within* an equation). Estimating each equation by OLS does not directly yield the covariances between the estimators from different equations. Any SUR routine will perform this operation automatically, then compute F statistics as in equation (7.53) (or the chi-square alternative, the Wald statistic).

Example 7.3 (SUR System for Wages and Fringe Benefits): We use the data on wages and fringe benefits in FRINGE.RAW to estimate a two-equation system for hourly wage and hourly benefits. There are 616 workers in the data set. The FGLS estimates are given in Table 7.1, with asymptotic standard errors in parentheses below estimated coefficients.

The estimated coefficients generally have the signs we expect. Other things equal, people with more education have higher hourly wage and benefits, males have higher predicted wages and benefits ($1.79 and 27 cents higher, respectively), and people with more tenure have higher earnings and benefits, although the effect is diminishing in both cases. (The turning point for *hrearn* is at about 10.8 years, while for *hrbens* it is 22.5 years.) The coefficients on experience are interesting. Experience is estimated to have a dimininshing effect for benefits but an increasing effect for earnings, although the estimated upturn for earnings is not until 9.5 years.

Belonging to a union implies higher wages and benefits, with the benefits coefficient being especially statistically significant ($t \approx 7.5$).

The errors across the two equations appear to be positively correlated, with an estimated correlation of about .32. This result is not surprising: the same unobservables, such as ability, that lead to higher earnings, also lead to higher benefits.

Clearly there are significant differences between males and females in both earnings and benefits. But what about between whites and nonwhites, and married and unmarried people? The F-type statistic for joint significance of *married* and *white* in both equations is $F = 1.83$. We are testing four restrictions ($Q = 4$), $N = 616$, $G = 2$, and $K = 2(13) = 26$, so the degrees of freedom in the F distribution are 4 and 1,206. The p-value is about .121, so these variables are jointly insignificant at the 10 percent level.

Table 7.1
An Estimated SUR Model for Hourly Wages and Hourly Benefits

Explanatory Variables	*hrearn*	*hrbens*
educ	.459 (.069)	.077 (.008)
exper	−.076 (.057)	.023 (.007)
exper^2	.0040 (.0012)	−.0005 (.0001)
tenure	.110 (.084)	.054 (.010)
tenure^2	−.0051 (.0033)	−.0012 (.0004)
union	.808 (.408)	.366 (.049)
south	−.457 (.552)	−.023 (.066)
nrtheast	−1.151 (0.606)	−.057 (.072)
nrthcen	−.636 (.556)	−.038 (.066)
married	.642 (.418)	.058 (.050)
white	1.141 (0.612)	.090 (.073)
male	1.785 (0.398)	.268 (.048)
intercept	−2.632 (1.228)	−.890 (.147)

If the regressors are different in different equations, $\mathbf{\Omega}$ is not diagonal, and the conditions in Section 7.5.2 hold, then FGLS is generally asymptotically more efficient than OLS equation by equation. One thing to remember is that the efficiency of FGLS comes at the price of assuming that the regressors in each equation are uncorrelated with the errors in each equation. For SOLS and FGLS to be different, the $\mathbf{x}_g$ must vary across g. If $\mathbf{x}_g$ varies across g, certain explanatory variables have been intentionally omitted from some equations. If we are interested in, say, the first equation, but we make a mistake in specifying the second equation, FGLS will generally produce inconsistent estimators of the parameters in all equations. However, OLS estimation of the first equation is consistent if $\mathrm{E}(\mathbf{x}_1'u_1) = \mathbf{0}$.

The previous discussion reflects the trade-off between efficiency and robustness that we often encounter in estimation problems.

7.7.2 Systems with Cross Equation Restrictions

So far we have studied SUR under the assumption that the $\boldsymbol{\beta}_g$ are unrelated across equations. When systems of equations are used in economics, especially for modeling consumer and producer theory, there are often cross equation restrictions on the parameters. Such models can still be written in the general form we have covered, and so they can be estimated by system OLS and FGLS. We still refer to such systems as SUR systems, even though the equations are now obviously related, and system OLS is no longer OLS equation by equation.

Example 7.4 (SUR with Cross Equation Restrictions): Consider the two-equation population model

$$y_1 = \gamma_{10} + \gamma_{11}x_{11} + \gamma_{12}x_{12} + \alpha_1 x_{13} + \alpha_2 x_{14} + u_1 \tag{7.54}$$

$$y_2 = \gamma_{20} + \gamma_{21}x_{21} + \alpha_1 x_{22} + \alpha_2 x_{23} + \gamma_{24}x_{24} + u_2 \tag{7.55}$$

where we have imposed cross equation restrictions on the parameters in the two equations because α_1 and α_2 show up in each equation. We can put this model into the form of equation (7.9) by appropriately defining $\mathbf{X}_i$ and $\boldsymbol{\beta}$. For example, define $\boldsymbol{\beta} = (\gamma_{10}, \gamma_{11}, \gamma_{12}, \alpha_1, \alpha_2, \gamma_{20}, \gamma_{21}, \gamma_{24})'$, which we know must be an 8×1 vector because there are 8 parameters in this system. The order in which these elements appear in $\boldsymbol{\beta}$ is up to us, but once $\boldsymbol{\beta}$ is defined, $\mathbf{X}_i$ must be chosen accordingly. For each observation i, define the 2×8 matrix

$$\mathbf{X}_i = \begin{pmatrix} 1 & x_{i11} & x_{i12} & x_{i13} & x_{i14} & 0 & 0 & 0 \\ 0 & 0 & 0 & x_{i22} & x_{i23} & 1 & x_{i21} & x_{i24} \end{pmatrix}$$

Multiplying $\mathbf{X}_i$ by $\boldsymbol{\beta}$ gives the equations (7.54) and (7.55).

In applications such as the previous example, it is fairly straightforward to test the cross equation restrictions, especially using the sum of squared residuals statistics [equation (7.52) or (7.53)]. The unrestricted model simply allows each explanatory variable in each equation to have its own coefficient. We would use the unrestricted estimates to obtain $\hat{\boldsymbol{\Omega}}$, and then obtain the restricted estimates using $\hat{\boldsymbol{\Omega}}$.

7.7.3 Singular Variance Matrices in SUR Systems

In our treatment so far we have assumed that the variance matrix $\boldsymbol{\Omega}$ of $\mathbf{u}_i$ is nonsingular. In consumer and producer theory applications this assumption is not always true in the original structural equations, because of additivity constraints.

Example 7.5 (Cost Share Equations): Suppose that, for a given year, each firm in a particular industry uses three inputs, capital (K), labor (L), and materials (M).

Because of regional variation and differential tax concessions, firms across the United States face possibly different prices for these inputs: let p_{iK} denote the price of capital to firm i, p_{iL} be the price of labor for firm i, and s_{iM} denote the price of materials for firm i. For each firm i, let s_{iK} be the cost share for capital, let s_{iL} be the cost share for labor, and let s_{iM} be the cost share for materials. By definition, $s_{iK} + s_{iL} + s_{iM} = 1$.

One popular set of cost share equations is

$$s_{iK} = \gamma_{10} + \gamma_{11}\log(p_{iK}) + \gamma_{12}\log(p_{iL}) + \gamma_{13}\log(p_{iM}) + u_{iK} \tag{7.56}$$

$$s_{iL} = \gamma_{20} + \gamma_{12}\log(p_{iK}) + \gamma_{22}\log(p_{iL}) + \gamma_{23}\log(p_{iM}) + u_{iL} \tag{7.57}$$

$$s_{iM} = \gamma_{30} + \gamma_{13}\log(p_{iK}) + \gamma_{23}\log(p_{iL}) + \gamma_{33}\log(p_{iM}) + u_{iM} \tag{7.58}$$

where the symmetry restrictions from production theory have been imposed. The errors u_{ig} can be viewed as unobservables affecting production that the economist cannot observe. For an SUR analysis we would assume that

$$\mathrm{E}(\mathbf{u}_i \mid \mathbf{p}_i) = \mathbf{0} \tag{7.59}$$

where $\mathbf{u}_i \equiv (u_{iK}, u_{iL}, u_{iM})'$ and $\mathbf{p}_i \equiv (p_{iK}, p_{iL}, p_{iM})$. Because the cost shares must sum to unity for each i, $\gamma_{10} + \gamma_{20} + \gamma_{30} = 1$, $\gamma_{11} + \gamma_{12} + \gamma_{13} = 0$, $\gamma_{12} + \gamma_{22} + \gamma_{23} = 0$, $\gamma_{13} + \gamma_{23} + \gamma_{33} = 0$, and $u_{iK} + u_{iL} + u_{iM} = 0$. This last restriction implies that $\mathbf{\Omega} \equiv \mathrm{Var}(\mathbf{u}_i)$ has rank two. Therefore, we can drop one of the equations—say, the equation for materials—and analyze the equations for labor and capital. We can express the restrictions on the gammas in these first two equations as

$$\gamma_{13} = -\gamma_{11} - \gamma_{12} \tag{7.60}$$

$$\gamma_{23} = -\gamma_{12} - \gamma_{22} \tag{7.61}$$

Using the fact that $\log(a/b) = \log(a) - \log(b)$, we can plug equations (7.60) and (7.61) into equations (7.56) and (7.57) to get

$$s_{iK} = \gamma_{10} + \gamma_{11}\log(p_{iK}/p_{iM}) + \gamma_{12}\log(p_{iL}/p_{iM}) + u_{iK}$$

$$s_{iL} = \gamma_{20} + \gamma_{12}\log(p_{iK}/p_{iM}) + \gamma_{22}\log(p_{iL}/p_{iM}) + u_{iL}$$

We now have a two-equation system with variance matrix of full rank, with unknown parameters $\gamma_{10}, \gamma_{20}, \gamma_{11}, \gamma_{12}$, and γ_{22}. To write this in the form (7.9), redefine $\mathbf{u}_i = (u_{iK}, u_{iL})'$ and $\mathbf{y}_i \equiv (s_{iK}, s_{iL})'$. Take $\boldsymbol{\beta} \equiv (\gamma_{10}, \gamma_{11}, \gamma_{12}, \gamma_{20}, \gamma_{22})'$ and then $\mathbf{X}_i$ must be

$$\mathbf{X}_i \equiv \begin{pmatrix} 1 & \log(p_{iK}/p_{iM}) & \log(p_{iL}/p_{iM}) & 0 & 0 \\ 0 & 0 & \log(p_{iK}/p_{iM}) & 1 & \log(p_{iL}/p_{iM}) \end{pmatrix} \tag{7.62}$$

This formulation imposes all the conditions implied by production theory.

This model could be extended in several ways. The simplest would be to allow the intercepts to depend on firm characteristics. For each firm i, let $\mathbf{z}_i$ be a $1 \times J$ vector of observable firm characteristics, where $\mathbf{z}_{i1} \equiv 1$. Then we can extend the model to

$$s_{iK} = \mathbf{z}_i\boldsymbol{\delta}_1 + \gamma_{11} \log(p_{iK}/p_{iM}) + \gamma_{12} \log(p_{iL}/p_{iM}) + u_{iK} \tag{7.63}$$

$$s_{iL} = \mathbf{z}_i\boldsymbol{\delta}_2 + \gamma_{12} \log(p_{iK}/p_{iM}) + \gamma_{22} \log(p_{iL}/p_{iM}) + u_{iL} \tag{7.64}$$

where

$$\mathrm{E}(u_{ig} \mid \mathbf{z}_i, p_{iK}, p_{iL}, p_{iM}) = 0, \qquad g = K, L \tag{7.65}$$

Because we have already reduced the system to two equations, theory implies no restrictions on $\boldsymbol{\delta}_1$ and $\boldsymbol{\delta}_2$. As an exercise, you should write this system in the form (7.9). For example, if $\boldsymbol{\beta} \equiv (\boldsymbol{\delta}_1', \gamma_{11}, \gamma_{12}, \boldsymbol{\delta}_2', \gamma_{22})'$ is $(2J+3) \times 1$, how should $\mathbf{X}_i$ be defined?

Under condition (7.65), system OLS and FGLS estimators are both consistent. (In this setup system OLS is *not* OLS equation by equation because γ_{12} shows up in both equations). FGLS is asymptotically efficient if $\mathrm{Var}(\mathbf{u}_i \mid \mathbf{z}_i, \mathbf{p}_i)$ is constant. If $\mathrm{Var}(\mathbf{u}_i \mid \mathbf{z}_i, \mathbf{p}_i)$ depends on $(\mathbf{z}_i, \mathbf{p}_i)$—see Brown and Walker (1995) for a discussion of why we should expect it to—then we should at least use the robust variance matrix estimator for FGLS.

We can easily test the symmetry assumption imposed in equations (7.63) and (7.64). One approach is to first estimate the system without *any* restrictions on the parameters, in which case FGLS reduces to OLS estimation of each equation. Then, compute the t statistic of the difference in the estimates on $\log(p_{iL}/p_{iM})$ in equation (7.63) and $\log(p_{iK}/p_{iM})$ in equation (7.64). Or, the F statistic from equation (7.53) can be used; $\hat{\boldsymbol{\Omega}}$ would be obtained from the unrestricted OLS estimation of each equation.

System OLS has no robustness advantages over FGLS in this setup because we cannot relax assumption (7.65) in any useful way.

7.8 The Linear Panel Data Model, Revisited

We now study the linear panel data model in more detail. Having data over time for the same cross section units is useful for several reasons. For one, it allows us to look at dynamic relationships, something we cannot do with a single cross section. A panel data set also allows us to control for unobserved cross section heterogeneity, but we will not exploit this feature of panel data until Chapter 10.

7.8.1 Assumptions for Pooled OLS

We now summarize the properties of pooled OLS and feasible GLS for the linear panel data model

$$y_t = \mathbf{x}_t\boldsymbol{\beta} + u_t, \qquad t = 1, 2, \ldots, T \tag{7.66}$$

As always, when we need to indicate a particular cross section observation we include an i subscript, such as y_{it}.

This model may appear overly restrictive because $\boldsymbol{\beta}$ is the same in each time period. However, by appropriately choosing $\mathbf{x}_{it}$, we can allow for parameters changing over time. Also, even though we write $\mathbf{x}_{it}$, some of the elements of $\mathbf{x}_{it}$ may not be time-varying, such as gender dummies when i indexes individuals, or industry dummies when i indexes firms, or state dummies when i indexes cities.

Example 7.6 (Wage Equation with Panel Data): Suppose we have data for the years 1990, 1991, and 1992 on a cross section of individuals, and we would like to estimate the effect of computer usage on individual wages. One possible static model is

$$\log(wage_{it}) = \theta_0 + \theta_1 d91_t + \theta_2 d92_t + \delta_1 computer_{it} + \delta_2 educ_{it} + \delta_3 exper_{it} + \delta_4 female_i + u_{it} \tag{7.67}$$

where $d91_t$ and $d92_t$ are dummy indicators for the years 1991 and 1992 and $computer_{it}$ is a measure of how much person i used a computer during year t. The inclusion of the year dummies allows for aggregate time effects of the kind discussed in the Section 7.2 examples. This equation contains a variable that is constant across t, $female_i$, as well as variables that can change across i and t, such as $educ_{it}$ and $exper_{it}$. The variable $educ_{it}$ is given a t subscript, which indicates that years of education could change from year to year for at least some people. It could also be the case that $educ_{it}$ is the same for all three years for every person in the sample, in which case we could remove the time subscript. The distinction between variables that are time-constant is not very important here; it becomes much more important in Chapter 10.

As a general rule, with large N and small T it is a good idea to allow for separate intercepts for each time period. Doing so allows for aggregate time effects that have the same influence on y_{it} for all i.

Anything that can be done in a cross section context can also be done in a panel data setting. For example, in equation (7.67) we can interact $female_i$ with the time dummy variables to see whether productivity of females has changed over time, or we can interact $educ_{it}$ and $computer_{it}$ to allow the return to computer usage to depend on level of education.

The two assumptions sufficient for pooled OLS to consistently estimate $\boldsymbol{\beta}$ are as follows:

ASSUMPTION POLS.1: $\mathrm{E}(\mathbf{x}_t' u_t) = 0$, $t = 1, 2, \ldots, T$.

ASSUMPTION POLS.2: $\operatorname{rank}[\sum_{t=1}^{T} \mathrm{E}(\mathbf{x}_t'\mathbf{x}_t)] = K$.

Remember, Assumption POLS.1 says nothing about the relationship between $\mathbf{x}_s$ and u_t for $s \neq t$. Assumption POLS.2 essentially rules out perfect linear dependencies among the explanatory variables.

To apply the usual OLS statistics from the pooled OLS regression across i and t, we need to add homoskedasticity and no serial correlation assumptions. The weakest forms of these assumptions are the following:

ASSUMPTION POLS.3: (a) $\mathrm{E}(u_t^2 \mathbf{x}_t'\mathbf{x}_t) = \sigma^2 \mathrm{E}(\mathbf{x}_t'\mathbf{x}_t)$, $t = 1, 2, \ldots, T$, where $\sigma^2 = \mathrm{E}(u_t^2)$ for all t; (b) $\mathrm{E}(u_t u_s \mathbf{x}_t'\mathbf{x}_s) = \mathbf{0}$, $t \neq s$, $t, s = 1, \ldots, T$.

The first part of Assumption POLS.3 is a fairly strong homoskedasticity assumption; sufficient is $\mathrm{E}(u_t^2 \mid \mathbf{x}_t) = \sigma^2$ for all t. This means not only that the conditional variance does not depend on $\mathbf{x}_t$, but also that the unconditional variance is the same in every time period. Assumption POLS.3b essentially restricts the conditional covariances of the errors across different time periods to be zero. In fact, since $\mathbf{x}_t$ almost always contains a constant, POLS.3b requires *at a minimum* that $\mathrm{E}(u_t u_s) = 0$, $t \neq s$. Sufficient for POLS.3b is $\mathrm{E}(u_t u_s \mid \mathbf{x}_t, \mathbf{x}_s) = 0$, $t \neq s$, $t, s = 1, \ldots, T$.

It is important to remember that Assumption POLS.3 implies more than just a certain form of the *unconditional* variance matrix of $\mathbf{u} \equiv (u_1, \ldots, u_T)'$. Assumption POLS.3 implies $\mathrm{E}(\mathbf{u}_i \mathbf{u}_i') = \sigma^2 \mathbf{I}_T$, which means that the unconditional variances are constant and the unconditional covariances are zero, but it also effectively restricts the *conditional* variances and covariances.

THEOREM 7.7 (Large Sample Properties of Pooled OLS): Under Assumptions POLS.1 and POLS.2, the pooled OLS estimator is consistent and asymptotically normal. If Assumption POLS.3 holds in addition, then $\operatorname{Avar}(\hat{\boldsymbol{\beta}}) = \sigma^2[\mathrm{E}(\mathbf{X}_i'\mathbf{X}_i)]^{-1}/N$, so that the appropriate estimator of $\operatorname{Avar}(\hat{\boldsymbol{\beta}})$ is

$$\hat{\sigma}^2 (\mathbf{X}'\mathbf{X})^{-1} = \hat{\sigma}^2 \left(\sum_{i=1}^{N} \sum_{t=1}^{T} \mathbf{x}_{it}'\mathbf{x}_{it} \right)^{-1} \tag{7.68}$$

where $\hat{\sigma}^2$ is the usual OLS variance estimator from the pooled regression

$$y_{it} \text{ on } \mathbf{x}_{it}, \qquad t = 1, 2, \ldots, T, \ i = 1, \ldots, N \tag{7.69}$$

It follows that the usual t statistics and F statistics from regression (7.69) are approximately valid. Therefore, the F statistic for testing Q linear restrictions on the $K \times 1$ vector $\boldsymbol{\beta}$ is

$$F = \frac{(\text{SSR}_r - \text{SSR}_{ur})}{\text{SSR}_{ur}} \cdot \frac{(NT - K)}{Q} \tag{7.70}$$

where SSR_{ur} is the sum of squared residuals from regression (7.69), and SSR_r is the regression using the NT observations with the restrictions imposed.

Why is a simple pooled OLS analysis valid under Assumption POLS.3? It is easy to show that Assumption POLS.3 implies that $\mathbf{B} = \sigma^2\mathbf{A}$, where $\mathbf{B} \equiv \sum_{t=1}^{T}\sum_{s=1}^{T} \mathrm{E}(u_t u_s \mathbf{x}_t' \mathbf{x}_s)$, and $\mathbf{A} \equiv \sum_{t=1}^{T} \mathrm{E}(\mathbf{x}_t' \mathbf{x}_t)$. For the panel data case, these are the matrices that appear in expression (7.21).

For computing the pooled OLS estimates and standard statistics, it does not matter how the data are ordered. However, if we put lags of any variables in the equation, it is easiest to order the data in the same way as is natural for studying asymptotic properties: the first T observations should be for the first cross section unit (ordered chronologically), the next T observations are for the next cross section unit, and so on. This procedure gives NT rows in the data set ordered in a very specific way.

Example 7.7 (Effects of Job Training Grants on Firm Scrap Rates): Using the data from JTRAIN1.RAW (Holzer, Block, Cheatham, and Knott, 1993), we estimate a model explaining the firm scrap rate in terms of grant receipt. We can estimate the equation for 54 firms and three years of data (1987, 1988, and 1989). The first grants were given in 1988. Some firms in the sample in 1989 received a grant only in 1988, so we allow for a one-year-lagged effect:

$$\begin{aligned}\log(\widehat{scrap}_{it}) = \ & \underset{(.203)}{.597} - \underset{(.311)}{.239}\, d88_t - \underset{(.338)}{.497}\, d89_t + \underset{(.338)}{.200}\, grant_{it} + \underset{(.436)}{.049}\, grant_{i,t-1}\end{aligned}$$

$$N = 54, \qquad T = 3, \qquad R^2 = .0173$$

where we have put i and t subscripts on the variables to emphasize which ones change across firm or time. The R-squared is just the usual one computed from the pooled OLS regression.

In this equation, the estimated grant effect has the wrong sign, and neither the current nor lagged grant variable is statistically significant. When a lag of $\log(scrap_{it})$ is added to the equation, the estimates are notably different. See Problem 7.9.

7.8.2 Dynamic Completeness

While the homoskedasticity assumption, Assumption POLS.3a, can never be guaranteed to hold, there is one important case where Assumption POLS.3b *must* hold. Suppose that the explanatory variables $\mathbf{x}_t$ are such that, for all t,

$$\mathrm{E}(y_t \mid \mathbf{x}_t, y_{t-1}, \mathbf{x}_{t-1}, \ldots, y_1, \mathbf{x}_1) = \mathrm{E}(y_t \mid \mathbf{x}_t) \tag{7.71}$$

This assumption means that $\mathbf{x}_t$ contains sufficient lags of all variables such that additional lagged values have no partial effect on y_t. The inclusion of lagged y in equation (7.71) is important. For example, if $\mathbf{z}_t$ is a vector of contemporaneous variables such that

$$\mathrm{E}(y_t \mid \mathbf{z}_t, \mathbf{z}_{t-1}, \ldots, \mathbf{z}_1) = \mathrm{E}(y_t \mid \mathbf{z}_t, \mathbf{z}_{t-1}, \ldots, \mathbf{z}_{t-L})$$

and we choose $\mathbf{x}_t = (\mathbf{z}_t, \mathbf{z}_{t-1}, \ldots, \mathbf{z}_{t-L})$, then $\mathrm{E}(y_t \mid \mathbf{x}_t, \mathbf{x}_{t-1}, \ldots, \mathbf{x}_1) = \mathrm{E}(y_t \mid \mathbf{x}_t)$. But equation (7.71) need not hold. Generally, in static and FDL models, there is no reason to expect equation (7.71) to hold, even in the absence of specification problems such as omitted variables.

We call equation (7.71) **dynamic completeness of the conditional mean**. Often, we can ensure that equation (7.71) is at least approximately true by putting sufficient lags of $\mathbf{z}_t$ and y_t into $\mathbf{x}_t$.

In terms of the disturbances, equation (7.71) is equivalent to

$$\mathrm{E}(u_t \mid \mathbf{x}_t, u_{t-1}, \mathbf{x}_{t-1}, \ldots, u_1, \mathbf{x}_1) = 0 \tag{7.72}$$

and, by iterated expectations, equation (7.72) implies $\mathrm{E}(u_t u_s \mid \mathbf{x}_t, \mathbf{x}_s) = 0$, $s \neq t$. Therefore, equation (7.71) implies Assumption POLS.3b as well as Assumption POLS.1. If equation (7.71) holds along with the homoskedasticity assumption $\mathrm{Var}(y_t \mid \mathbf{x}_t) = \sigma^2$, then Assumptions POLS.1 and POLS.3 both hold, and standard OLS statistics can be used for inference.

The following example is similar in spirit to an analysis of Maloney and McCormick (1993), who use a large random sample of students (including nonathletes) from Clemson University in a cross section analysis.

Example 7.8 (Effect of Being in Season on Grade Point Average): The data in GPA.RAW are on 366 student-athletes at a large university. There are two semesters of data (fall and spring) for each student. Of primary interest is the "in-season" effect on athletes' GPAs. The model—with i, t subscripts—is

$$\begin{aligned} trmgpa_{it} = {} & \beta_0 + \beta_1 spring_t + \beta_2 cumgpa_{it} + \beta_3 crsgpa_{it} + \beta_4 frstsem_{it} + \beta_5 season_{it} + \beta_6 SAT_i \\ & + \beta_7 verbmath_i + \beta_8 hsperc_i + \beta_9 hssize_i + \beta_{10} black_i + \beta_{11} female_i + u_{it} \end{aligned}$$

The variable $cumgpa_{it}$ is cumulative GPA at the beginning of the term, and this clearly depends on past-term GPAs. In other words, this model has something akin to a lagged dependent variable. In addition, it contains other variables that change over time (such as $season_{it}$) and several variables that do not (such as SAT_i). We assume that the right-hand side (without u_{it}) represents a conditional expectation, so that u_{it} is necessarily uncorrelated with all explanatory variables and any functions of them. It may or may not be that the model is also dynamically complete in the sense of equation (7.71); we will show one way to test this assumption in Section 7.8.5. The estimated equation is

$$\begin{aligned}
\widehat{trmgpa}_{it} = {} & \underset{(0.34)}{-2.07} - \underset{(.046)}{.012}\, spring_t + \underset{(.040)}{.315}\, cumgpa_{it} + \underset{(.096)}{.984}\, crsgpa_{it} \\
& + \underset{(.120)}{.769}\, frstsem_{it} - \underset{(.047)}{.046}\, season_{it} + \underset{(.00015)}{.00141}\, SAT_i - \underset{(.131)}{.113}\, verbmath_i \\
& - \underset{(.0010)}{.0066}\, hsperc_i - \underset{(.000099)}{.000058}\, hssize_i - \underset{(.054)}{.231}\, black_i + \underset{(.051)}{.286}\, female_i
\end{aligned}$$

$N = 366, \qquad T = 2, \qquad R^2 = .519$

The in-season effect is small—an athlete's GPA is estimated to be .046 points lower when the sport is in season—and it is statistically insignificant as well. The other coefficients have reasonable signs and magnitudes.

Often, once we start putting any lagged values of y_t into $\mathbf{x}_t$, then equation (7.71) is an intended assumption. But this generalization is not always true. In the previous example, we can think of the variable *cumgpa* as another control we are using to hold other factors fixed when looking at an in-season effect on GPA for college athletes: *cumgpa* can proxy for omitted factors that make someone successful in college. We may not care that serial correlation is still present in the error, except that, if equation (7.71) fails, we need to estimate the asymptotic variance of the pooled OLS estimator to be robust to serial correlation (and perhaps heteroskedasticity as well).

In introductory econometrics, students are often warned that having serial correlation in a model with a lagged dependent variable causes the OLS estimators to be inconsistent. While this statement is true in the context of a *specific* model of serial correlation, it is not true in general, and therefore it is very misleading. [See Wooldridge (2000a, Chapter 12) for more discussion in the context of the AR(1) model.] Our analysis shows that, whatever is included in $\mathbf{x}_t$, pooled OLS provides consistent estimators of $\boldsymbol{\beta}$ whenever $\mathrm{E}(y_t \mid \mathbf{x}_t) = \mathbf{x}_t\boldsymbol{\beta}$; it does not matter that the u_t might be serially correlated.

7.8.3 A Note on Time Series Persistence

Theorem 7.7 imposes no restrictions on the time series persistence in the data $\{(\mathbf{x}_{it}, y_{it})\colon t = 1, 2, \ldots, T\}$. In light of the explosion of work in time series econometrics on asymptotic theory with persistent processes [often called *unit root processes*—see, for example, Hamilton (1994)], it may appear that we have not been careful in stating our assumptions. However, we do not need to restrict the dynamic behavior of our data in any way because we are doing fixed-T, large-N asymptotics. It is for this reason that the mechanics of the asymptotic analysis is the same for the SUR case and the panel data case. If T is large relative to N, the asymptotics here may be misleading. Fixing N while T grows or letting N and T both grow takes us into the realm of multiple time series analysis: we would have to know about the temporal dependence in the data, and, to have a general treatment, we would have to assume some form of weak dependence (see Wooldridge, 1994, for a discussion of weak dependence). Recently, progress has been made on asymptotics in panel data with large T and N when the data have unit roots; see, for example, Pesaran and Smith (1995) and Phillips and Moon (1999).

As an example, consider the simple AR(1) model

$$y_t = \beta_0 + \beta_1 y_{t-1} + u_t, \qquad \mathrm{E}(u_t \mid y_{t-1}, \ldots, y_0) = 0$$

Assumption POLS.1 holds (provided the appropriate moments exist). Also, Assumption POLS.2 can be maintained. Since this model is dynamically complete, the only potential nuisance is heteroskedasticity in u_t that changes over time or depends on y_{t-1}. In any case, the pooled OLS estimator from the regression y_{it} on 1, $y_{i,t-1}$, $t = 1, \ldots, T$, $i = 1, \ldots, N$, produces consistent, $\sqrt{N}$-asymptotically normal estimators for fixed T as $N \to \infty$, for any values of β_0 and β_1.

In a pure time series case, or in a panel data case with $T \to \infty$ and N fixed, we would have to assume $|\beta_1| < 1$, which is the stability condition for an AR(1) model. Cases where $|\beta_1| \geq 1$ cause considerable complications when the asymptotics is done along the time series dimension (see Hamilton, 1994, Chapter 19). Here, a large cross section and relatively short time series allow us to be agnostic about the amount of temporal persistence.

7.8.4 Robust Asymptotic Variance Matrix

Because Assumption POLS.3 can be restrictive, it is often useful to obtain a robust estimate of $\mathrm{Avar}(\hat{\boldsymbol{\beta}})$ that is valid without Assumption POLS.3. We have already seen the general form of the estimator, given in matrix (7.26). In the case of panel data, this estimator is fully robust to arbitrary heteroskedasticity—conditional or unconditional—and arbitrary serial correlation across time (again, conditional or unconditional). The residuals $\hat{\mathbf{u}}_i$ are the $T \times 1$ pooled OLS residuals for cross section observation i. Some statistical packages compute these very easily, although the command may be disguised. Whether a software package has this capability or whether it must be programmed by you, the data must be stored as described earlier: The $(\mathbf{y}_i, \mathbf{X}_i)$ should be stacked on top of one another for $i = 1, \ldots, N$.

7.8.5 Testing for Serial Correlation and Heteroskedasticity after Pooled OLS

Testing for Serial Correlation It is often useful to have a simple way to detect serial correlation after estimation by pooled OLS. One reason to test for serial correlation is that it should not be present if the model is supposed to be dynamically complete in the conditional mean. A second reason to test for serial correlation is to see whether we should compute a robust variance matrix estimator for the pooled OLS estimator.

One interpretation of serial correlation in the errors of a panel data model is that the error in each time period contains a time-constant omitted factor, a case we cover explicitly in Chapter 10. For now, we are simply interested in knowing whether or not the errors are serially correlated.

We focus on the alternative that the error is a first-order autoregressive process; this will have power against fairly general kinds of serial correlation. Write the AR(1) model as

$$u_t = \rho_1 u_{t-1} + e_t \tag{7.73}$$

where

$$\mathrm{E}(e_t \mid \mathbf{x}_t, u_{t-1}, \mathbf{x}_{t-1}, u_{t-2}, \ldots) = 0 \tag{7.74}$$

Under the null hypothesis of no serial correlation, $\rho_1 = 0$.

One way to proceed is to write the dynamic model under AR(1) serial correlation as

$$y_t = \mathbf{x}_t \boldsymbol{\beta} + \rho_1 u_{t-1} + e_t, \qquad t = 2, \ldots, T \tag{7.75}$$

where we lose the first time period due to the presence of u_{t-1}. If we can observe the u_t, it is clear how we should proceed: simply estimate equation (7.75) by pooled OLS (losing the first time period) and perform a t test on $\hat{\rho}_1$. To operationalize this procedure, we replace the u_t with the pooled OLS residuals. Therefore, we run the regression

$$y_{it} \text{ on } \mathbf{x}_{it}, \hat{u}_{i,t-1}, \qquad t = 2, \ldots, T, \ i = 1, \ldots, N \tag{7.76}$$

and do a standard t test on the coefficient of $\hat{u}_{i,t-1}$. A statistic that is robust to arbitrary heteroskedasticity in $\mathrm{Var}(y_t \mid \mathbf{x}_t, u_{t-1})$ is obtained by the usual heteroskedasticity-robust t statistic in the pooled regression. This includes Engle's (1982) ARCH model and any other form of static or dynamic heteroskedasticity.

Why is a t test from regression (7.76) valid? Under dynamic completeness, equation (7.75) satisfies Assumptions POLS.1–POLS.3 if we also assume that $\text{Var}(y_t \mid \mathbf{x}_t, u_{t-1})$ is constant. Further, the presence of the generated regressor $\hat{u}_{i,t-1}$ does not affect the limiting distribution of $\hat{\rho}_1$ under the null because $\rho_1 = 0$. Verifying this claim is similar to the pure cross section case in Section 6.1.1.

A nice feature of the statistic computed from regression (7.76) is that it works whether or not $\mathbf{x}_t$ is strictly exogenous. A different form of the test is valid if we assume strict exogeneity: use the t statistic on $\hat{u}_{i,t-1}$ in the regression

$$\hat{u}_{it} \text{ on } \hat{u}_{i,t-1}, \qquad t = 2, \ldots, T, \; i = 1, \ldots, N \tag{7.77}$$

or its heteroskedasticity-robust form. That this test is valid follows by applying Problem 7.4 and the assumptions for pooled OLS with a lagged dependent variable.

Example 7.9 (Athletes' Grade Point Averages, continued): We apply the test from regression (7.76) because *cumgpa* cannot be strictly exogenous (GPA this term affects cumulative GPA after this term). We drop the variables *spring* and *frstsem* from regression (7.76), since these are identically unity and zero, respectively, in the spring semester. We obtain $\hat{\rho}_1 = .194$ and $t_{\hat{\rho}_1} = 3.18$, and so the null hypothesis is rejected. Thus there is still some work to do to capture the full dynamics. But, if we assume that we are interested in the conditional expectation implicit in the estimation, we are getting consistent estimators. This result is useful to know because we are primarily interested in the in-season effect, and the other variables are simply acting as controls. The presence of serial correlation means that we should compute standard errors robust to arbitrary serial correlation (and heteroskedasticity); see Problem 7.10.

Testing for Heteroskedasticity The primary reason to test for heteroskedasticity after running pooled OLS is to detect violation of Assumption POLS.3a, which is one of the assumptions needed for the usual statistics accompanying a pooled OLS regression to be valid. We assume throughout this section that $\text{E}(u_t \mid \mathbf{x}_t) = 0$, $t = 1, 2, \ldots, T$, which strengthens Assumption POLS.1 but does not require strict exogeneity. Then the null hypothesis of homoskedasticity can be stated as $\text{E}(u_t^2 \mid \mathbf{x}_t) = \sigma^2$, $t = 1, 2, \ldots, T$.

Under H_0, u_{it}^2 is uncorrelated with any function of $\mathbf{x}_{it}$; let $\mathbf{h}_{it}$ denote a $1 \times Q$ vector of nonconstant functions of $\mathbf{x}_{it}$. In particular, $\mathbf{h}_{it}$ can, and often should, contain dummy variables for the different time periods.

From the tests for heteroskedasticity in Section 6.2.4. the following procedure is natural. Let $\hat{u}_{it}^2$ denote the squared pooled OLS residuals. Then obtain the usual R-squared, R_c^2, from the regression

$$\hat{u}_{it}^2 \text{ on } 1, \mathbf{h}_{it}, \qquad t = 1, \ldots, T, \; i = 1, \ldots, N \tag{7.78}$$

The test statistic is NTR_c^2, which is treated as asymptotically χ_Q^2 under H_0. (Alternatively, we can use the usual F test of joint significance of $\mathbf{h}_{it}$ from the pooled OLS regression. The degrees of freedom are Q and $NT - K$.) When is this procedure valid?

Using arguments very similar to the cross sectional tests from Chapter 6, it can be shown that the statistic has the same distribution if u_{it}^2 replaces $\hat{u}_{it}^2$; this fact is very convenient because it allows us to focus on the other features of the test. Effectively, we are performing a standard LM test of H_0: $\boldsymbol{\delta} = \mathbf{0}$ in the model

$$u_{it}^2 = \delta_0 + \mathbf{h}_{it}\boldsymbol{\delta} + a_{it}, \qquad t = 1, 2, \ldots, T \tag{7.79}$$

This test requires that the errors $\{a_{it}\}$ be appropriately serially uncorrelated and requires homoskedasticity; that is, Assumption POLS.3 must hold in equation (7.79). Therefore, the tests based on nonrobust statistics from regression (7.78) essentially require that $E(a_{it}^2 \mid \mathbf{x}_{it})$ be constant—meaning that $E(u_{it}^4 \mid \mathbf{x}_{it})$ must be constant under H_0. We also need a stronger homoskedasticity assumption; $E(u_{it}^2 \mid \mathbf{x}_{it}, u_{i,t-1}, \mathbf{x}_{i,t-1}, \ldots) = \sigma^2$ is sufficient for the $\{a_{it}\}$ in equation (7.79) to be appropriately serially uncorrelated.

A fully robust test for heteroskedasticity can be computed from the pooled regression (7.78) by obtaining a fully robust variance matrix estimator for $\hat{\boldsymbol{\delta}}$ [see equation (7.26)]; this can be used to form a robust Wald statistic.

Since violation of Assumption POLS.3a is of primary interest, it makes sense to include elements of $\mathbf{x}_{it}$ in $\mathbf{h}_{it}$, and possibly squares and cross products of elements of $\mathbf{x}_{it}$. Another useful choice, covered in Chapter 6, is $\hat{\mathbf{h}}_{it} = (\hat{y}_{it}, \hat{y}_{it}^2)$, the pooled OLS fitted values and their squares. Also, Assumption POLS.3a requires the unconditional variances $E(u_{it}^2)$ to be the same across t. Whether they are can be tested directly by choosing $\mathbf{h}_{it}$ to have $T - 1$ time dummies.

If heteroskedasticity is detected but serial correlation is not, then the usual heteroskedasticity-robust standard errors and test statistics from the pooled OLS regression (7.69) can be used.

7.8.6 Feasible GLS Estimation under Strict Exogeneity

When $E(\mathbf{u}_i\mathbf{u}_i') \neq \sigma^2\mathbf{I}_T$, it is reasonable to consider a feasible GLS analysis rather than a pooled OLS analysis. In Chapter 10 we will cover a particular FGLS analysis after we introduce unobserved components panel data models. With large N and small T, nothing precludes an FGLS analysis in the current setting. However, we must remember that FGLS is not even guaranteed to produce consistent, let alone efficient, estimators under Assumptions POLS.1 and POLS.2. Unless $\boldsymbol{\Omega} = E(\mathbf{u}_i\mathbf{u}_i')$ is a diagonal matrix, Assumption POLS.1 should be replaced with the strict exogeneity assumption (7.6). (Problem 7.7 covers the case when $\boldsymbol{\Omega}$ is diagonal.) Sometimes we are willing to assume strict exogeneity in static and finite distributed lag models. As we saw earlier, it cannot hold in models with lagged y_{it}, and it can fail in static models or distributed lag models if there is feedback from y_{it} to future $\mathbf{z}_{it}$.

Problems

7.1. Provide the details for a proof of Theorem 7.1.

7.2. In model (7.9), maintain Assumptions SOLS.1 and SOLS.2, and assume $\mathrm{E}(\mathbf{X}_i'\mathbf{u}_i\mathbf{u}_i'\mathbf{X}_i) = \mathrm{E}(\mathbf{X}_i'\boldsymbol{\Omega}\mathbf{X}_i)$, where $\boldsymbol{\Omega} \equiv \mathrm{E}(\mathbf{u}_i\mathbf{u}_i')$. [The last assumption is a different way of stating the homoskesdasticity assumption for systems of equations; it always holds if assumption (7.50) holds.] Let $\hat{\boldsymbol{\beta}}_{\mathrm{SOLS}}$ denote the system OLS estimator.

a. Show that $\mathrm{Avar}(\hat{\boldsymbol{\beta}}_{\mathrm{SOLS}}) = [\mathrm{E}(\mathbf{X}_i'\mathbf{X}_i)]^{-1}[\mathrm{E}(\mathbf{X}_i'\boldsymbol{\Omega}\mathbf{X}_i)][\mathrm{E}(\mathbf{X}_i'\mathbf{X}_i)]^{-1}/N$.

b. How would you estimate the asymptotic variance in part a?

c. Now add Assumptions SGLS.1–SGLS.3. Show that $\mathrm{Avar}(\hat{\boldsymbol{\beta}}_{\mathrm{SOLS}}) - \mathrm{Avar}(\hat{\boldsymbol{\beta}}_{\mathrm{FGLS}})$ is positive semidefinite. {Hint: Show that $[\mathrm{Avar}(\hat{\boldsymbol{\beta}}_{\mathrm{FGLS}})]^{-1} - [\mathrm{Avar}(\hat{\boldsymbol{\beta}}_{\mathrm{SOLS}})]^{-1}$ is p.s.d.}

d. If, in addition to the previous assumptions, $\boldsymbol{\Omega} = \sigma^2\mathbf{I}_G$, show that SOLS and FGLS have the same asymptotic variance.

e. Evaluate the following statement: "Under the assumptions of part c, FGLS is never asymptotically worse than SOLS, even if $\boldsymbol{\Omega} = \sigma^2\mathbf{I}_G$."

7.3. Consider the SUR model (7.2) under Assumptions SOLS.1, SOLS.2, and SGLS.3, with $\boldsymbol{\Omega} \equiv \mathrm{diag}(\sigma_1^2, \ldots, \sigma_G^2)$; thus, GLS and OLS estimation equation by equation are the same. (In the SUR model with diagonal $\boldsymbol{\Omega}$, Assumption SOLS.1 is the same as Assumption SGLS.1, and Assumption SOLS.2 is the same as Assumption SGLS.2.)

a. Show that single-equation OLS estimators from any two equations, say, $\hat{\boldsymbol{\beta}}_g$ and $\hat{\boldsymbol{\beta}}_h$, are asymptotically uncorrelated. (That is, show that the asymptotic variance of the system OLS estimator $\hat{\boldsymbol{\beta}}$ is block diagonal.)

b. Under the conditions of part a, assume that $\boldsymbol{\beta}_1$ and $\boldsymbol{\beta}_2$ (the parameter vectors in the first two equations) have the same dimension. Explain how you would test $\mathrm{H}_0\colon \boldsymbol{\beta}_1 = \boldsymbol{\beta}_2$ against $\mathrm{H}_1\colon \boldsymbol{\beta}_1 \neq \boldsymbol{\beta}_2$.

c. Now drop Assumption SGLS.3, maintaining Assumptions SOLS.1 and SOLS.2 and diagonality of $\boldsymbol{\Omega}$. Suppose that $\hat{\boldsymbol{\Omega}}$ is estimated in an unrestricted manner, so that FGLS and OLS are not algebraically equivalent. Show that OLS and FGLS are $\sqrt{N}$-asymptotically equivalent, that is, $\sqrt{N}(\hat{\boldsymbol{\beta}}_{\mathrm{SOLS}} - \hat{\boldsymbol{\beta}}_{\mathrm{FGLS}}) = \mathrm{o}_p(1)$. This is one case where FGLS is consistent under Assumption SOLS.1.

7.4. Using the $\sqrt{N}$-consistency of the system OLS estimator $\hat{\hat{\boldsymbol{\beta}}}$ for $\boldsymbol{\beta}$, for $\hat{\boldsymbol{\Omega}}$ in equation (7.37) show that

$$\text{vec}[\sqrt{N}(\hat{\boldsymbol{\Omega}} - \boldsymbol{\Omega})] = \text{vec}\left[N^{-1/2}\sum_{i=1}^{N}(\mathbf{u}_i\mathbf{u}_i' - \boldsymbol{\Omega})\right] + o_p(1)$$

under Assumptions SGLS.1 and SOLS.2. (Note: This result does not hold when Assumption SGLS.1 is replaced with the weaker Assumption SOLS.1.) Assume that all moment conditions needed to apply the WLLN and CLT are satisfied. The important conclusion is that the asymptotic distribution of vec $\sqrt{N}(\hat{\boldsymbol{\Omega}} - \boldsymbol{\Omega})$ does not depend on that of $\sqrt{N}(\hat{\hat{\boldsymbol{\beta}}} - \boldsymbol{\beta})$, and so any asymptotic tests on the elements of $\boldsymbol{\Omega}$ can ignore the estimation of $\boldsymbol{\beta}$. [Hint: Start from equation (7.39) and use the fact that $\sqrt{N}(\hat{\hat{\boldsymbol{\beta}}} - \boldsymbol{\beta}) = O_p(1)$.]

7.5. Prove Theorem 7.6, using the fact that when $\mathbf{X}_i = \mathbf{I}_G \otimes \mathbf{x}_i$,

$$\sum_{i=1}^{N}\mathbf{X}_i'\hat{\boldsymbol{\Omega}}^{-1}\mathbf{X}_i = \hat{\boldsymbol{\Omega}}^{-1} \otimes \left(\sum_{i=1}^{N}\mathbf{x}_i'\mathbf{x}_i\right) \quad \text{and} \quad \sum_{i=1}^{N}\mathbf{X}_i'\hat{\boldsymbol{\Omega}}^{-1}\mathbf{y}_i = (\hat{\boldsymbol{\Omega}}^{-1} \otimes \mathbf{I}_K)\begin{pmatrix}\sum_{i=1}^{N}\mathbf{x}_i'y_{i1} \\ \vdots \\ \sum_{i=1}^{N}\mathbf{x}_i'y_{iG}\end{pmatrix}$$

7.6. Start with model (7.9). Suppose you wish to impose Q linear restrictions of the form $\mathbf{R}\boldsymbol{\beta} = \mathbf{r}$, where $\mathbf{R}$ is a $Q \times K$ matrix and $\mathbf{r}$ is a $Q \times 1$ vector. Assume that $\mathbf{R}$ is partitioned as $\mathbf{R} \equiv [\mathbf{R}_1 \,|\, \mathbf{R}_2]$, where $\mathbf{R}_1$ is a $Q \times Q$ nonsingular matrix and $\mathbf{R}_2$ is a $Q \times (K - Q)$ matrix. Partition $\mathbf{X}_i$ as $\mathbf{X}_i \equiv [\mathbf{X}_{i1} \,|\, \mathbf{X}_{i2}]$, where $\mathbf{X}_{i1}$ is $G \times Q$ and $\mathbf{X}_{i2}$ is $G \times (K - Q)$, and partition $\boldsymbol{\beta}$ as $\boldsymbol{\beta} \equiv (\boldsymbol{\beta}_1', \boldsymbol{\beta}_2')'$. The restrictions $\mathbf{R}\boldsymbol{\beta} = \mathbf{r}$ can be expressed as $\mathbf{R}_1\boldsymbol{\beta}_1 + \mathbf{R}_2\boldsymbol{\beta}_2 = \mathbf{r}$, or $\boldsymbol{\beta}_1 = \mathbf{R}_1^{-1}(\mathbf{r} - \mathbf{R}_2\boldsymbol{\beta}_2)$. Show that the restricted model can be written as

$$\tilde{\mathbf{y}}_i = \tilde{\mathbf{X}}_{i2}\boldsymbol{\beta}_2 + \mathbf{u}_i$$

where $\tilde{\mathbf{y}}_i = \mathbf{y}_i - \mathbf{X}_{i1}\mathbf{R}_1^{-1}\mathbf{r}$ and $\tilde{\mathbf{X}}_{i2} = \mathbf{X}_{i2} - \mathbf{X}_{i1}\mathbf{R}_1^{-1}\mathbf{R}_2$.

7.7. Consider the panel data model

$$y_{it} = \mathbf{x}_{it}\boldsymbol{\beta} + u_{it}, \qquad t = 1, 2, \ldots, T$$

$$\text{E}(u_{it} \,|\, \mathbf{x}_{it}, u_{i,t-1}, \mathbf{x}_{i,t-1}, \ldots,) = 0 \tag{7.80}$$

$$\text{E}(u_{it}^2 \,|\, \mathbf{x}_{it}) = \text{E}(u_{it}^2) = \sigma_t^2, \qquad t = 1, \ldots, T$$

[Note that $\mathrm{E}(u_{it}^2 \mid \mathbf{x}_{it})$ does not depend on $\mathbf{x}_{it}$, but it is allowed to be a different constant in each time period.]

a. Show that $\mathbf{\Omega} = \mathrm{E}(\mathbf{u}_i\mathbf{u}_i')$ is a diagonal matrix. [Hint: The zero conditional mean assumption (7.80) implies that u_{it} is uncorrelated with u_{is} for $s < t$.]

b. Write down the GLS estimator assuming that $\mathbf{\Omega}$ is known.

c. Argue that Assumption SGLS.1 does not necessarily hold under the assumptions made. (Setting $\mathbf{x}_{it} = y_{i,t-1}$ might help in answering this part.) Nevertheless, show that the GLS estimator from part b *is* consistent for $\boldsymbol{\beta}$ by showing that $\mathrm{E}(\mathbf{X}_i'\mathbf{\Omega}^{-1}\mathbf{u}_i) = \mathbf{0}$. [This proof shows that Assumption SGLS.1 is sufficient, but not necessary, for consistency. Sometimes $\mathrm{E}(\mathbf{X}_i'\mathbf{\Omega}^{-1}\mathbf{u}_i) = \mathbf{0}$ even though Assumption SGLS.1 does not hold.]

d. Show that Assumption SGLS.3 holds under the given assumptions.

e. Explain how to consistently estimate each σ_t^2 (as $N \to \infty$).

f. Argue that, under the assumptions made, valid inference is obtained by weighting each observation $(y_{it}, \mathbf{x}_{it})$ by $1/\hat{\sigma}_t$ and then running pooled OLS.

g. What happens if we assume that $\sigma_t^2 = \sigma^2$ for all $t = 1, \ldots, T$?

7.8. Redo Example 7.3, disaggregating the benefits categories into value of vacation days, value of sick leave, value of employer-provided insurance, and value of pension. Use hourly measures of these along with *hrearn*, and estimate an SUR model. Does marital status appear to affect any form of compensation? Test whether another year of education increases expected pension value and expected insurance by the same amount.

7.9. Redo Example 7.7 but include a single lag of log(*scrap*) in the equation to proxy for omitted variables that may determine grant receipt. Test for AR(1) serial correlation. If you find it, you should also compute the fully robust standard errors that allow for abitrary serial correlation across time and heteroskedasticity.

7.10. In Example 7.9, compute standard errors fully robust to serial correlation and heteroskedasticity. Discuss any important differences between the robust standard errors and the usual standard errors.

7.11. Use the data in CORNWELL.RAW for this question; see Problem 4.13.

a. Using the data for all seven years, and using the logarithms of all variables, estimate a model relating the crime rate to *prbarr*, *prbconv*, *prbpris*, *avgsen*, and *polpc*. Use pooled OLS and include a full set of year dummies. Test for serial correlation assuming that the explanatory variables are strictly exogenous. If there is serial correlation, obtain the fully robust standard errors.

b. Add a one-year lag of log(*crmrte*) to the equation from part a, and compare with the estimates from part a.

c. Test for first-order serial correlation in the errors in the model from part b. If serial correlation is present, compute the fully robust standard errors.

d. Add all of the wage variables (in logarithmic form) to the equation from part c. Which ones are statistically and economically significant? Are they jointly significant? Test for joint significance of the wage variables allowing arbitrary serial correlation and heteroskedasticity.

7.12. If you add wealth at the beginning of year t to the saving equation in Example 7.2, is the strict exogeneity assumption likely to hold? Explain.

8 System Estimation by Instrumental Variables

8.1 Introduction and Examples

In Chapter 7 we covered system estimation of linear equations when the explanatory variables satisfy certain exogeneity conditions. For many applications, even the weakest of these assumptions, Assumption SOLS.1, is violated, in which case instrumental variables procedures are indispensable.

The modern approach to **system instrumental variables (SIV)** estimation is based on the principle of **generalized method of moments (GMM)**. Method of moments estimation has a long history in statistics for obtaining simple parameter estimates when maximum likelihood estimation requires nonlinear optimization. Hansen (1982) and White (1982b) showed how the method of moments can be generalized to apply to a variety of econometric models, and they derived the asymptotic properties of GMM. Hansen (1982), who coined the name "generalized method of moments," treated time series data, and White (1982b) assumed independently sampled observations.

Though the models considered in this chapter are more general than those treated in Chapter 5, the derivations of asymptotic properties of system IV estimators are mechanically similar to the derivations in Chapters 5 and 7. Therefore, the proofs in this chapter will be terse, or omitted altogether.

In econometrics, the most familar application of SIV estimation is to a **simultaneous equations model (SEM)**. We will cover SEMs specifically in Chapter 9, but it is useful to begin with a typical SEM example. System estimation procedures have applications beyond the classical simultaneous equations methods. We will also use the results in this chapter for the analysis of panel data models in Chapter 11.

Example 8.1 (Labor Supply and Wage Offer Functions): Consider the following labor supply function representing the hours of labor supply, h^s, at any wage, w, faced by an individual. As usual, we express this in population form:

$$h^s(w) = \gamma_1 w + \mathbf{z}_1 \boldsymbol{\delta}_1 + u_1 \tag{8.1}$$

where $\mathbf{z}_1$ is a vector of observed labor supply shifters—including such things as education, past experience, age, marital status, number of children, and nonlabor income—and u_1 contains unobservables affecting labor supply. The labor supply function can be derived from individual utility-maximizing behavior, and the notation in equation (8.1) is intended to emphasize that, for given $\mathbf{z}_1$ and u_1, a labor supply function gives the desired hours worked at *any* possible wage (w) facing the worker. As a practical matter, we can only observe *equilibrium* values of hours worked and hourly wage. But the counterfactual reasoning underlying equation (8.1) is the proper way to view labor supply.

A wage offer function gives the hourly wage that the market will offer as a function of hours worked. (It could be that the wage offer does not depend on hours worked, but in general it might.) For observed productivity attributes $\mathbf{z}_2$ (for example, education, experience, and amount of job training) and unobserved attributes u_2, we write the wage offer function as

$$w^o(\mathscr{h}) = \gamma_2 \mathscr{h} + \mathbf{z}_2 \boldsymbol{\delta}_2 + u_2 \tag{8.2}$$

Again, for given $\mathbf{z}_2$ and u_2, $w^o(\mathscr{h})$ gives the wage offer for an individual agreeing to work $\mathscr{h}$ hours.

Equations (8.1) and (8.2) explain different sides of the labor market. However, rarely can we assume that an individual is given an exogenous wage offer and then, at that wage, decides how much to work based on equation (8.1). A reasonable approach is to assume that observed hours and wage are such that equations (8.1) and (8.2) both hold. In other words, letting (h, w) denote the equilibrium values, we have

$$h = \gamma_1 w + \mathbf{z}_1 \boldsymbol{\delta}_1 + u_1 \tag{8.3}$$

$$w = \gamma_2 h + \mathbf{z}_2 \boldsymbol{\delta}_2 + u_2 \tag{8.4}$$

Under weak restrictions on the parameters, these equations can be solved uniquely for (h, w) as functions of $\mathbf{z}_1$, $\mathbf{z}_2$, u_1, u_2, and the parameters; we consider this topic generally in Chapter 9. Further, if $\mathbf{z}_1$ and $\mathbf{z}_2$ are exogenous in the sense that

$$\mathrm{E}(u_1 \mid \mathbf{z}_1, \mathbf{z}_2) = \mathrm{E}(u_2 \mid \mathbf{z}_1, \mathbf{z}_2) = 0$$

then, under identification assumptions, we can consistently estimate the parameters of the labor supply and wage offer functions. We consider identification of SEMs in detail in Chapter 9. We also ignore what is sometimes a practically important issue: the equilibrium hours for an individual might be zero, in which case w is not observed for such people. We deal with missing data issues in Chapter 17.

For a random draw from the population we can write

$$h_i = \gamma_1 w_i + \mathbf{z}_{i1} \boldsymbol{\delta}_1 + u_{i1} \tag{8.5}$$

$$w_i = \gamma_2 h_i + \mathbf{z}_{i2} \boldsymbol{\delta}_2 + u_{i2} \tag{8.6}$$

Except under very special assumptions, u_{i1} will be correlated with w_i, and u_{i2} will be correlated with h_i. In other words, w_i is probably endogenous in equation (8.5), and h_i is probably endogenous in equation (8.6). It is for this reason that we study system instrumental variables methods.

An example with the same statistical structure as Example 8.1, but with an omitted variables interpretation, is motivated by Currie and Thomas (1995).

Example 8.2 (Student Performance and Head Start): Consider an equation to test the effect of Head Start participation on subsequent student performance:

$$score_i = \gamma_1 HeadStart_i + \mathbf{z}_{i1}\boldsymbol{\delta}_1 + u_{i1} \tag{8.7}$$

where $score_i$ is the outcome on a test when the child is enrolled in school and $HeadStart_i$ is a binary indicator equal to one if child i participated in Head Start at an early age. The vector $\mathbf{z}_{i1}$ contains other observed factors, such as income, education, and family background variables. The error term u_{i1} contains unobserved factors that affect *score*—such as child's ability—that may also be correlated with *HeadStart*. To capture the possible endogeneity of *HeadStart*, we write a linear reduced form (linear projection) for $HeadStart_i$:

$$HeadStart_i = \mathbf{z}_i\boldsymbol{\delta}_2 + u_{i2} \tag{8.8}$$

Remember, this projection always exists even though $HeadStart_i$ is a binary variable. The vector $\mathbf{z}_i$ contains $\mathbf{z}_{i1}$ and at least one factor affecting Head Start participation that does not have a direct effect on *score*. One possibility is distance to the nearest Head Start center. In this example we would probably be willing to assume that $\mathrm{E}(u_{i1} \mid \mathbf{z}_i) = 0$—since the test score equation is structural—but we would only want to assume $\mathrm{E}(\mathbf{z}_i' u_{i2}) = \mathbf{0}$, since the Head Start equation is a linear projection involving a binary dependent variable. Correlation between u_1 and u_2 means *HeadStart* is endogenous in equation (8.7).

Both of the previous examples can be written for observation i as

$$y_{i1} = \mathbf{x}_{i1}\boldsymbol{\beta}_1 + u_{i1} \tag{8.9}$$

$$y_{i2} = \mathbf{x}_{i2}\boldsymbol{\beta}_2 + u_{i2} \tag{8.10}$$

which looks just like a two-equation SUR system but where $\mathbf{x}_{i1}$ and $\mathbf{x}_{i2}$ can contain endogenous as well as exogenous variables. Because $\mathbf{x}_{i1}$ and $\mathbf{x}_{i2}$ are generally correlated with u_{i1} and u_{i2}, estimation of these equations by OLS or FGLS, as we studied in Chapter 7, will generally produce inconsistent estimators.

We already know one method for estimating an equation such as equation (8.9): if we have sufficient instruments, apply 2SLS. Often 2SLS produces acceptable results, so why should we go beyond single-equation analysis? Not surprisingly, our interest in system methods with endogenous explanatory variables has to do with efficiency. In many cases we can obtain more efficient estimators by estimating $\boldsymbol{\beta}_1$ and $\boldsymbol{\beta}_2$ *jointly*, that is, by using a system procedure. The efficiency gains are analogous to the gains that can be realized by using feasible GLS rather than OLS in a SUR system.

8.2 A General Linear System of Equations

We now discuss estimation of a general linear model of the form

$$\mathbf{y}_i = \mathbf{X}_i\boldsymbol{\beta} + \mathbf{u}_i \tag{8.11}$$

where $\mathbf{y}_i$ is a $G \times 1$ vector, $\mathbf{X}_i$ is a $G \times K$ matrix, and $\mathbf{u}_i$ is the $G \times 1$ vector of errors. This model is identical to equation (7.9), except that we will use different assumptions. In writing out examples, we will often omit the observation subscript i, but for the general analysis carrying it along is a useful notational device. As in Chapter 7, the rows of $\mathbf{y}_i$, $\mathbf{X}_i$, and $\mathbf{u}_i$ can represent different time periods for the same cross-sectional unit (so $G = T$, the total number of time periods). Therefore, the following analysis applies to panel data models where T is small relative to the cross section sample size, N; for an example, see Problem 8.8. We cover general panel data applications in Chapter 11. (As in Chapter 7, the label "systems of equations" is not especially accurate for basic panel data models because we have only one behavioral equation over T different time periods.)

The following orthogonality condition is the basis for estimating $\boldsymbol{\beta}$:

ASSUMPTION SIV.1: $\mathrm{E}(\mathbf{Z}_i'\mathbf{u}_i) = \mathbf{0}$, where $\mathbf{Z}_i$ is a $G \times L$ matrix of observable instrumental variables.

(The acronym SIV stands for "system instrumental variables.") For the purposes of discussion, we assume that $\mathrm{E}(\mathbf{u}_i) = \mathbf{0}$; this assumption is almost always true in practice anyway.

From what we know about IV and 2SLS for single equations, Assumption SIV.1 cannot be enough to identify the vector $\boldsymbol{\beta}$. An assumption sufficient for identification is the **rank condition**:

ASSUMPTION SIV.2: rank $\mathrm{E}(\mathbf{Z}_i'\mathbf{X}_i) = K$.

Assumption SIV.2 generalizes the rank condition from the single-equation case. (When $G = 1$, Assumption SIV.2 is the same as Assumption 2SLS.2b.) Since $\mathrm{E}(\mathbf{Z}_i'\mathbf{X}_i)$ is an $L \times K$ matrix, Assumption SIV.2 requires the columns of this matrix to be linearly independent. Necessary for the rank condition is the **order condition**: $L \geq K$. We will investigate the rank condition in detail for a broad class of models in Chapter 9. For now, we just assume that it holds.

In what follows, it is useful to carry along a particular example that applies to simultaneous equations models and other models with potentially endogenous explanatory variables. Write a G equation system for the population as

$$
\begin{aligned}
y_1 &= \mathbf{x}_1 \boldsymbol{\beta}_1 + u_1 \\
&\vdots \\
y_G &= \mathbf{x}_G \boldsymbol{\beta}_G + u_G
\end{aligned}
\tag{8.12}
$$

where, for each equation g, $\mathbf{x}_g$ is a $1 \times K_g$ vector that can contain both exogenous and endogenous variables. For each g, $\boldsymbol{\beta}_g$ is $K_g \times 1$. Because this looks just like the SUR system from Chapter 7, we will refer to it as a SUR system, keeping in mind the crucial fact that some elements of $\mathbf{x}_g$ are thought to be correlated with u_g for at least some g.

For each equation we assume that we have a set of instrumental variables, a $1 \times L_g$ vector $\mathbf{z}_g$, that are exogenous in the sense that

$$
\mathrm{E}(\mathbf{z}_g' u_g) = 0, \qquad g = 1, 2, \ldots, G \tag{8.13}
$$

In most applications unity is an element of $\mathbf{z}_g$ for each g, so that $\mathrm{E}(u_g) = 0$, all g. As we will see, and as we already know from single-equation analysis, if $\mathbf{x}_g$ contains some elements correlated with u_g, then $\mathbf{z}_g$ must contain more than just the exogenous variables appearing in equation g. Much of the time the same instruments, which consist of *all* exogenous variables appearing anywhere in the system, are valid for every equation, so that $\mathbf{z}_g = \mathbf{z}$, $g = 1, 2, \ldots, G$. Some applications require us to have different instruments for different equations, so we allow that possibility here.

Putting an i subscript on the variables in equations (8.12), and defining

$$
\underset{G \times 1}{\mathbf{y}_i} \equiv \begin{pmatrix} y_{i1} \\ y_{i2} \\ \vdots \\ y_{iG} \end{pmatrix}, \qquad
\underset{G \times K}{\mathbf{X}_i} \equiv \begin{pmatrix} \mathbf{x}_{i1} & \mathbf{0} & \mathbf{0} & \cdots & \mathbf{0} \\ \mathbf{0} & \mathbf{x}_{i2} & \mathbf{0} & \cdots & \mathbf{0} \\ \vdots & & & & \vdots \\ \mathbf{0} & \mathbf{0} & \mathbf{0} & \cdots & \mathbf{x}_{iG} \end{pmatrix}, \qquad
\underset{G \times 1}{\mathbf{u}_i} \equiv \begin{pmatrix} u_{i1} \\ u_{i2} \\ \vdots \\ u_{iG} \end{pmatrix} \tag{8.14}
$$

and $\boldsymbol{\beta} = (\boldsymbol{\beta}_1', \boldsymbol{\beta}_2', \ldots, \boldsymbol{\beta}_G')'$, we can write equation (8.12) in the form (8.11). Note that $K = K_1 + K_2 + \cdots + K_G$ is the total number of parameters in the system.

The matrix of instruments has a structure similar to $\mathbf{X}_i$:

$$
\mathbf{Z}_i \equiv \begin{pmatrix} \mathbf{z}_{i1} & \mathbf{0} & \mathbf{0} & \cdots & \mathbf{0} \\ \mathbf{0} & \mathbf{z}_{i2} & \mathbf{0} & \cdots & \mathbf{0} \\ \vdots & & & & \vdots \\ \mathbf{0} & \mathbf{0} & \mathbf{0} & \cdots & \mathbf{z}_{iG} \end{pmatrix} \tag{8.15}
$$

which has dimension $G \times L$, where $L = L_1 + L_2 + \cdots + L_G$. Then, for each i,

$$\mathbf{Z}_i'\mathbf{u}_i = (\mathbf{z}_{i1}u_{i1}, \mathbf{z}_{i2}u_{i2}, \ldots, \mathbf{z}_{iG}u_{iG})' \tag{8.16}$$

and so $\mathrm{E}(\mathbf{Z}_i'\mathbf{u}_i) = \mathbf{0}$ reproduces the orthogonality conditions (8.13). Also,

$$\mathrm{E}(\mathbf{Z}_i'\mathbf{X}_i) = \begin{pmatrix} \mathrm{E}(\mathbf{z}_{i1}'\mathbf{x}_{i1}) & \mathbf{0} & \mathbf{0} & \cdots & \mathbf{0} \\ \mathbf{0} & \mathrm{E}(\mathbf{z}_{i2}'\mathbf{x}_{i2}) & \mathbf{0} & \cdots & \mathbf{0} \\ \vdots & & & & \vdots \\ \mathbf{0} & \mathbf{0} & \mathbf{0} & \cdots & \mathrm{E}(\mathbf{z}_{iG}'\mathbf{x}_{iG}) \end{pmatrix} \tag{8.17}$$

where $\mathrm{E}(\mathbf{z}_{ig}'\mathbf{x}_{ig})$ is $L_g \times K_g$. Assumption SIV.2 requires that this matrix have full column rank, where the number of columns is $K = K_1 + K_2 + \cdots + K_G$. A well-known result from linear algebra says that a block diagonal matrix has full column rank if and only if each block in the matrix has full column rank. In other words, Assumption SIV.2 holds in this example if and only if

$$\operatorname{rank} \mathrm{E}(\mathbf{z}_{ig}'\mathbf{x}_{ig}) = K_g, \qquad g = 1, 2, \ldots, G \tag{8.18}$$

This is *exactly* the rank condition needed for estimating each equation by 2SLS, which we know is possible under conditions (8.13) and (8.18). Therefore, identification of the SUR system is equivalent to identification equation by equation. This reasoning assumes that the $\boldsymbol{\beta}_g$ are unrestricted across equations. If some prior restrictions are known, then identification is more complicated, something we cover explicitly in Chapter 9.

In the important special case where the same instruments, $\mathbf{z}_i$, can be used for every equation, we can write definition (8.15) as $\mathbf{Z}_i = \mathbf{I}_G \otimes \mathbf{z}_i$.

8.3 Generalized Method of Moments Estimation

8.3.1 A General Weighting Matrix

The orthogonality conditions in Assumption SIV.1 suggest an estimation strategy. Under Assumptions SIV.1 and SIV.2, $\boldsymbol{\beta}$ is the *unique* $K \times 1$ vector solving the linear set population moment conditions

$$\mathrm{E}[\mathbf{Z}_i'(\mathbf{y}_i - \mathbf{X}_i\boldsymbol{\beta})] = \mathbf{0} \tag{8.19}$$

(That $\boldsymbol{\beta}$ is a solution follows from Assumption SIV.1; that it is unique follows by Assumption SIV.2.) In other words, if $\mathbf{b}$ is any other $K \times 1$ vector (so that at least one element of $\mathbf{b}$ is different from the corresponding element in $\boldsymbol{\beta}$), then

$$\mathrm{E}[\mathbf{Z}_i'(\mathbf{y}_i - \mathbf{X}_i\mathbf{b})] \neq \mathbf{0} \tag{8.20}$$

This formula shows that $\boldsymbol{\beta}$ is identified. Because sample averages are consistent estimators of population moments, the analogy principle applied to condition (8.19) suggests choosing the estimator $\hat{\boldsymbol{\beta}}$ to solve

$$N^{-1}\sum_{i=1}^{N}\mathbf{Z}_i'(\mathbf{y}_i - \mathbf{X}_i\hat{\boldsymbol{\beta}}) = \mathbf{0} \tag{8.21}$$

Equation (8.21) is a set of L linear equations in the K unknowns in $\hat{\boldsymbol{\beta}}$. First consider the case $L = K$, so that we have exactly enough IVs for the explanatory variables in the system. Then, if the $K \times K$ matrix $\sum_{i=1}^{N}\mathbf{Z}_i'\mathbf{X}_i$ is nonsingular, we can solve for $\hat{\boldsymbol{\beta}}$ as

$$\hat{\boldsymbol{\beta}} = \left(N^{-1}\sum_{i=1}^{N}\mathbf{Z}_i'\mathbf{X}_i\right)^{-1}\left(N^{-1}\sum_{i=1}^{N}\mathbf{Z}_i'\mathbf{y}_i\right) \tag{8.22}$$

We can write $\hat{\boldsymbol{\beta}}$ using full matrix notation as $\hat{\boldsymbol{\beta}} = (\mathbf{Z}'\mathbf{X})^{-1}\mathbf{Z}'\mathbf{Y}$, where $\mathbf{Z}$ is the $NG \times L$ matrix obtained by stacking $\mathbf{Z}_i$ from $i = 1, 2, \ldots, N$, $\mathbf{X}$ is the $NG \times K$ matrix obtained by stacking $\mathbf{X}_i$ from $i = 1, 2, \ldots, N$, and $\mathbf{Y}$ is the $NG \times 1$ vector obtained from stacking $\mathbf{y}_i$, $i = 1, 2, \ldots, N$. We call equation (8.22) the **system IV (SIV) estimator**. Application of the law of large numbers shows that the SIV estimator is consistent under Assumptions SIV.1 and SIV.2.

When $L > K$—so that we have more columns in the IV matrix $\mathbf{Z}_i$ than we need for identification—choosing $\hat{\boldsymbol{\beta}}$ is more complicated. Except in special cases, equation (8.21) will not have a solution. Instead, we choose $\hat{\boldsymbol{\beta}}$ to make the vector in equation (8.21) as "small" as possible in the sample. One idea is to minimize the squared Euclidean length of the $L \times 1$ vector in equation (8.21). Dropping the $1/N$, this approach suggests choosing $\hat{\boldsymbol{\beta}}$ to make

$$\left[\sum_{i=1}^{N}\mathbf{Z}_i'(\mathbf{y}_i - \mathbf{X}_i\hat{\boldsymbol{\beta}})\right]'\left[\sum_{i=1}^{N}\mathbf{Z}_i'(\mathbf{y}_i - \mathbf{X}_i\hat{\boldsymbol{\beta}})\right]$$

as small as possible. While this method produces a consistent estimator under Assumptions SIV.1 and SIV.2, it rarely produces the best estimator, for reasons we will see in Section 8.3.3.

A more general class of estimators is obtained by using a **weighting matrix** in the quadratic form. Let $\hat{\mathbf{W}}$ be an $L \times L$ symmetric, positive semidefinite matrix, where the "$\wedge$" is included to emphasize that $\hat{\mathbf{W}}$ is generally an estimator. A **generalized method of moments (GMM) estimator** of $\boldsymbol{\beta}$ is a vector $\hat{\boldsymbol{\beta}}$ that solves the problem

$$\min_{\mathbf{b}} \left[\sum_{i=1}^{N} \mathbf{Z}_i'(\mathbf{y}_i - \mathbf{X}_i\mathbf{b})\right]' \hat{\mathbf{W}} \left[\sum_{i=1}^{N} \mathbf{Z}_i'(\mathbf{y}_i - \mathbf{X}_i\mathbf{b})\right] \tag{8.23}$$

Because expression (8.23) is a quadratic function of $\mathbf{b}$, the solution to it has a closed form. Using multivariable calculus or direct substitution, we can show that the unique solution is

$$\hat{\boldsymbol{\beta}} = (\mathbf{X}'\mathbf{Z}\hat{\mathbf{W}}\mathbf{Z}'\mathbf{X})^{-1}(\mathbf{X}'\mathbf{Z}\hat{\mathbf{W}}\mathbf{Z}'\mathbf{Y}) \tag{8.24}$$

assuming that $\mathbf{X}'\mathbf{Z}\hat{\mathbf{W}}\mathbf{Z}'\mathbf{X}$ is nonsingular. To show that this estimator is consistent, we assume that $\hat{\mathbf{W}}$ has a nonsingular probability limit.

ASSUMPTION SIV.3: $\hat{\mathbf{W}} \xrightarrow{p} \mathbf{W}$ as $N \to \infty$, where $\mathbf{W}$ is a nonrandom, symmetric, $L \times L$ positive definite matrix.

In applications, the convergence in Assumption SIV.3 will follow from the law of large numbers because $\hat{\mathbf{W}}$ will be a function of sample averages. The fact that $\mathbf{W}$ is assumed to be positive definite means that $\hat{\mathbf{W}}$ is positive definite with probability approaching one (see Chapter 3). We could relax the assumption of positive definiteness to positive semidefiniteness at the cost of complicating the assumptions. In most applications, we can assume that $\mathbf{W}$ is positive definite.

THEOREM 8.1 (Consistency of GMM): Under Assumptions SIV.1–SIV.3, $\hat{\boldsymbol{\beta}} \xrightarrow{p} \boldsymbol{\beta}$ as $N \to \infty$.

Proof: Write

$$\hat{\boldsymbol{\beta}} = \left[\left(N^{-1}\sum_{i=1}^{N} \mathbf{X}_i'\mathbf{Z}_i\right)\hat{\mathbf{W}}\left(N^{-1}\sum_{i=1}^{N} \mathbf{Z}_i'\mathbf{X}_i\right)\right]^{-1}\left(N^{-1}\sum_{i=1}^{N} \mathbf{X}_i'\mathbf{Z}_i\right)\hat{\mathbf{W}}\left(N^{-1}\sum_{i=1}^{N} \mathbf{Z}_i'\mathbf{y}_i\right)$$

Plugging in $\mathbf{y}_i = \mathbf{X}_i\boldsymbol{\beta} + \mathbf{u}_i$ and doing a little algebra gives

$$\hat{\boldsymbol{\beta}} = \boldsymbol{\beta} + \left[\left(N^{-1}\sum_{i=1}^{N} \mathbf{X}_i'\mathbf{Z}_i\right)\hat{\mathbf{W}}\left(N^{-1}\sum_{i=1}^{N} \mathbf{Z}_i'\mathbf{X}_i\right)\right]^{-1}\left(N^{-1}\sum_{i=1}^{N} \mathbf{X}_i'\mathbf{Z}_i\right)\hat{\mathbf{W}}\left(N^{-1}\sum_{i=1}^{N} \mathbf{Z}_i'\mathbf{u}_i\right)$$

Under Assumption SIV.2, $\mathbf{C} \equiv \mathrm{E}(\mathbf{Z}_i'\mathbf{X}_i)$ has rank K, and combining this with Assumption SIV.3, $\mathbf{C}'\mathbf{W}\mathbf{C}$ has rank K and is therefore nonsingular. It follows by the law of large numbers that plim $\hat{\boldsymbol{\beta}} = \boldsymbol{\beta} + (\mathbf{C}'\mathbf{W}\mathbf{C})^{-1}\mathbf{C}'\mathbf{W}(\text{plim } N^{-1}\sum_{i=1}^{N} \mathbf{Z}_i'\mathbf{u}_i) = \boldsymbol{\beta} + (\mathbf{C}'\mathbf{W}\mathbf{C})^{-1}\mathbf{C}'\mathbf{W} \cdot \mathbf{0} = \boldsymbol{\beta}$.

Theorem 8.1 shows that a large class of estimators is consistent for $\boldsymbol{\beta}$ under Assumptions SIV.1 and SIV.2, provided that we choose $\hat{\mathbf{W}}$ to satisfy modest restrictions. When $L = K$, the GMM estimator in equation (8.24) becomes equation (8.22), no matter how we choose $\hat{\mathbf{W}}$, because $\mathbf{X}'\mathbf{Z}$ is a $K \times K$ nonsingular matrix.

We can also show that $\hat{\boldsymbol{\beta}}$ is asymptotically normally distributed under these first three assumptions.

THEOREM 8.2 (Asymptotic Normality of GMM): Under Assumptions SIV.1–SIV.3, $\sqrt{N}(\hat{\boldsymbol{\beta}} - \boldsymbol{\beta})$ is asymptotically normally distributed with mean zero and

$$\text{Avar}\,\sqrt{N}(\hat{\boldsymbol{\beta}} - \boldsymbol{\beta}) = (\mathbf{C}'\mathbf{W}\mathbf{C})^{-1}\mathbf{C}'\mathbf{W}\boldsymbol{\Lambda}\mathbf{W}\mathbf{C}(\mathbf{C}'\mathbf{W}\mathbf{C})^{-1} \tag{8.25}$$

where

$$\boldsymbol{\Lambda} \equiv \mathrm{E}(\mathbf{Z}_i'\mathbf{u}_i\mathbf{u}_i'\mathbf{Z}_i) = \mathrm{Var}(\mathbf{Z}_i'\mathbf{u}_i) \tag{8.26}$$

We will not prove this theorem in detail as it can be reasoned from

$$\sqrt{N}(\hat{\boldsymbol{\beta}} - \boldsymbol{\beta})$$

$$= \left[\left(N^{-1}\sum_{i=1}^{N}\mathbf{X}_i'\mathbf{Z}_i\right)\hat{\mathbf{W}}\left(N^{-1}\sum_{i=1}^{N}\mathbf{Z}_i'\mathbf{X}_i\right)\right]^{-1}\left(N^{-1}\sum_{i=1}^{N}\mathbf{X}_i'\mathbf{Z}_i\right)\hat{\mathbf{W}}\left(N^{-1/2}\sum_{i=1}^{N}\mathbf{Z}_i'\mathbf{u}_i\right)$$

where we use the fact that $N^{-1/2}\sum_{i=1}^{N}\mathbf{Z}_i'\mathbf{u}_i \xrightarrow{d} \text{Normal}(\mathbf{0}, \boldsymbol{\Lambda})$. The asymptotic variance matrix in equation (8.25) looks complicated, but it can be consistently estimated. If $\hat{\boldsymbol{\Lambda}}$ is a consistent estimator of $\boldsymbol{\Lambda}$—more on this later—then equation (8.25) is consistently estimated by

$$[(\mathbf{X}'\mathbf{Z}/N)\hat{\mathbf{W}}(\mathbf{Z}'\mathbf{X}/N)]^{-1}(\mathbf{X}'\mathbf{Z}/N)\hat{\mathbf{W}}\hat{\boldsymbol{\Lambda}}\hat{\mathbf{W}}(\mathbf{Z}'\mathbf{X}/N)[(\mathbf{X}'\mathbf{Z}/N)\hat{\mathbf{W}}(\mathbf{Z}'\mathbf{X}/N)]^{-1} \tag{8.27}$$

As usual, we estimate $\text{Avar}(\hat{\boldsymbol{\beta}})$ by dividing expression (8.27) by N.

While the general formula (8.27) is occasionally useful, it turns out that it is greatly simplified by choosing $\hat{\mathbf{W}}$ appropriately. Since this choice also (and not coincidentally) gives the asymptotically efficient estimator, we hold off discussing asymptotic variances further until we cover the optimal choice of $\hat{\mathbf{W}}$ in Section 8.3.3.

8.3.2 The System 2SLS Estimator

A choice of $\hat{\mathbf{W}}$ that leads to a useful and familiar-looking estimator is

$$\hat{\mathbf{W}} = \left(N^{-1}\sum_{i=1}^{N}\mathbf{Z}_i'\mathbf{Z}_i\right)^{-1} = (\mathbf{Z}'\mathbf{Z}/N)^{-1} \tag{8.28}$$

which is a consistent estimator of $[\mathrm{E}(\mathbf{Z}_i'\mathbf{Z}_i)]^{-1}$. Assumption SIV.3 simply requires that $\mathrm{E}(\mathbf{Z}_i'\mathbf{Z}_i)$ exist and be nonsingular, and these requirements are not very restrictive.

When we plug equation (8.28) into equation (8.24) and cancel N everywhere, we get

$$\hat{\boldsymbol{\beta}} = [\mathbf{X}'\mathbf{Z}(\mathbf{Z}'\mathbf{Z})^{-1}\mathbf{Z}'\mathbf{X}]^{-1}\mathbf{X}'\mathbf{Z}(\mathbf{Z}'\mathbf{Z})^{-1}\mathbf{Z}'\mathbf{Y} \tag{8.29}$$

This looks just like the single-equation 2SLS estimator, and so we call it the **system 2SLS estimator**.

When we apply equation (8.29) to the system of equations (8.12), with definitions (8.14) and (8.15), we get something very familiar. As an exercise, you should show that $\hat{\boldsymbol{\beta}}$ produces **2SLS equation by equation**. (The proof relies on the block diagonal structures of $\mathbf{Z}_i'\mathbf{Z}_i$ and $\mathbf{Z}_i'\mathbf{X}_i$ for each i.) In other words, we estimate the first equation by 2SLS using instruments $\mathbf{z}_{i1}$, the second equation by 2SLS using instruments $\mathbf{z}_{i2}$, and so on. When we stack these into one long vector, we get equation (8.29).

Problem 8.8 asks you to show that, in panel data applications, a natural choice of $\mathbf{Z}_i$ makes the system 2SLS estimator a **pooled 2SLS estimator**.

In the next subsection we will see that the system 2SLS estimator is not necessarily the asymptotically efficient estimator. Still, it is $\sqrt{N}$-consistent and easy to compute given the data matrices $\mathbf{X}$, $\mathbf{Y}$, and $\mathbf{Z}$. This latter feature is important because we need a preliminary estimator of $\boldsymbol{\beta}$ to obtain the asymptotically efficient estimator.

8.3.3 The Optimal Weighting Matrix

Given that a GMM estimator exists for any positive definite weighting matrix, it is important to have a way of choosing among all of the possibilities. It turns out that there is a choice of $\mathbf{W}$ that produces the GMM estimator with the smallest asymptotic variance.

We can appeal to expression (8.25) for a hint as to the optimal choice of $\mathbf{W}$. It is this expression we are trying to make as small as possible, in the matrix sense. (See Definition 3.11 for the definition of relative asymptotic efficiency.) The expression (8.25) simplifies to $(\mathbf{C}'\boldsymbol{\Lambda}^{-1}\mathbf{C})^{-1}$ if we set $\mathbf{W} \equiv \boldsymbol{\Lambda}^{-1}$. Using standard arguments from matrix algebra, it can be shown that $(\mathbf{C}'\mathbf{W}\mathbf{C})^{-1}\mathbf{C}'\mathbf{W}\boldsymbol{\Lambda}\mathbf{W}\mathbf{C}(\mathbf{C}'\mathbf{W}\mathbf{C})^{-1} - (\mathbf{C}'\boldsymbol{\Lambda}^{-1}\mathbf{C})^{-1}$ is positive semidefinite for any $L \times L$ positive definite matrix $\mathbf{W}$. The easiest way to prove this point is to show that

$$(\mathbf{C}'\boldsymbol{\Lambda}^{-1}\mathbf{C}) - (\mathbf{C}'\mathbf{W}\mathbf{C})(\mathbf{C}'\mathbf{W}\boldsymbol{\Lambda}\mathbf{W}\mathbf{C})^{-1}(\mathbf{C}'\mathbf{W}\mathbf{C}) \tag{8.30}$$

is positive semidefinite, and we leave this proof as an exercise (see Problem 8.5). This discussion motivates the following assumption and theorem.

ASSUMPTION SIV.4: $\mathbf{W} = \boldsymbol{\Lambda}^{-1}$, where $\boldsymbol{\Lambda}$ is defined by expression (8.26).

THEOREM 8.3 (Optimal Weighting Matrix): Under Assumptions SIV.1–SIV.4, the resulting GMM estimator is efficient among all GMM estimators of the form (8.24).

Provided that we can consistently estimate $\mathbf{\Lambda}$, we can obtain the asymptotically efficient GMM estimator. Any consistent estimator of $\mathbf{\Lambda}$ delivers the efficient GMM estimator, but one estimator is commonly used that imposes no structure on $\mathbf{\Lambda}$.

Procedure 8.1 (GMM with Optimal Weighting Matrix):

a. Let $\hat{\hat{\boldsymbol{\beta}}}$ be an initial consistent estimator of $\boldsymbol{\beta}$. In most cases this is the system 2SLS estimator.

b. Obtain the $G \times 1$ residual vectors

$$\hat{\hat{\mathbf{u}}}_i = \mathbf{y}_i - \mathbf{X}_i\hat{\hat{\boldsymbol{\beta}}}, \qquad i = 1, 2, \ldots, N \tag{8.31}$$

c. A generally consistent estimator of $\mathbf{\Lambda}$ is $\hat{\mathbf{\Lambda}} = N^{-1}\sum_{i=1}^{N} \mathbf{Z}_i'\hat{\hat{\mathbf{u}}}_i\hat{\hat{\mathbf{u}}}_i'\mathbf{Z}_i$.

d. Choose

$$\hat{\mathbf{W}} \equiv \hat{\mathbf{\Lambda}}^{-1} = \left(N^{-1}\sum_{i=1}^{N} \mathbf{Z}_i'\hat{\hat{\mathbf{u}}}_i\hat{\hat{\mathbf{u}}}_i'\mathbf{Z}_i\right)^{-1} \tag{8.32}$$

and use this matrix to obtain the asymptotically optimal GMM estimator.

The estimator of $\mathbf{\Lambda}$ in part c of Procedure 8.1 is consistent for $\mathrm{E}(\mathbf{Z}_i'\mathbf{u}_i\mathbf{u}_i'\mathbf{Z}_i)$ under general conditions. When each row of $\mathbf{Z}_i$ and $\mathbf{u}_i$ represent different time periods—so that we have a single-equation panel data model—the estimator $\hat{\mathbf{\Lambda}}$ allows for arbitrary heteroskedasticity (conditional or unconditional) as well as arbitrary serial dependence (conditional or unconditional). The reason we can allow this generality is that we fix the row dimension of $\mathbf{Z}_i$ and $\mathbf{u}_i$ and let $N \to \infty$. Therefore, we are assuming that N, the size of the cross section, is large enough relative to T to make fixed T asymptotics sensible. (This is the same approach we took in Chapter 7.) With N very large relative to T, there is no need to downweight correlations between time periods that are far apart, as in the Newey and West (1987) estimator applied to time series problems. Ziliak and Kniesner (1998) do use a Newey-West type procedure in a panel data application with large N. Theoretically, this is not required, and it is not completely general because it assumes that the underlying time series are weakly dependent. (See Wooldridge, 1994, for discussion of weak dependence in time series contexts.) A Newey-West type estimator might improve the finite-sample performance of the GMM estimator.

The asymptotic variance of the optimal GMM estimator is estimated as

$$\left[(\mathbf{X}'\mathbf{Z})\left(\sum_{i=1}^{N} \mathbf{Z}_i'\hat{\mathbf{u}}_i\hat{\mathbf{u}}_i'\mathbf{Z}_i\right)^{-1}(\mathbf{Z}'\mathbf{X})\right]^{-1} \tag{8.33}$$

where $\hat{\mathbf{u}}_i \equiv \mathbf{y}_i - \mathbf{X}_i\hat{\boldsymbol{\beta}}$; asymptotically, it makes no difference whether the first-stage residuals $\hat{\hat{\mathbf{u}}}_i$ are used in place of $\hat{\mathbf{u}}_i$. The square roots of diagonal elements of this matrix are the asymptotic standard errors of the optimal GMM estimator. This estimator is called a **minimum chi-square estimator**, for reasons that will become clear in Section 8.5.2.

When $\mathbf{Z}_i = \mathbf{X}_i$ and the $\hat{\mathbf{u}}_i$ are the system OLS residuals, expression (8.33) becomes the robust variance matrix estimator for SOLS [see expression (7.26)]. This expression reduces to the robust variance matrix estimator for FGLS when $\mathbf{Z}_i = \hat{\boldsymbol{\Omega}}^{-1}\mathbf{X}_i$ and the $\hat{\mathbf{u}}_i$ are the FGLS residuals [see equation (7.49)].

8.3.4 The Three-Stage Least Squares Estimator

The GMM estimator using weighting matrix (8.32) places no restrictions on either the unconditional or conditional (on $\mathbf{Z}_i$) variance matrix of $\mathbf{u}_i$: we can obtain the asymptotically efficient estimator without making additional assumptions. Nevertheless, it is still common, especially in traditional simultaneous equations analysis, to assume that the conditional variance matrix of $\mathbf{u}_i$ given $\mathbf{Z}_i$ is constant. This assumption leads to a system estimator that is a middle ground between system 2SLS and the always-efficient minimum chi-square estimator.

The **three-stage least squares (3SLS) estimator** is a GMM estimator that uses a particular weighting matrix. To define the 3SLS estimator, let $\hat{\hat{\mathbf{u}}}_i = \mathbf{y}_i - \mathbf{X}_i\hat{\hat{\boldsymbol{\beta}}}$ be the residuals from an initial estimation, usually system 2SLS. Define the $G \times G$ matrix

$$\hat{\boldsymbol{\Omega}} \equiv N^{-1}\sum_{i=1}^{N}\hat{\hat{\mathbf{u}}}_i\hat{\hat{\mathbf{u}}}_i' \tag{8.34}$$

Using the same arguments as in the FGLS case in Section 7.5.1, $\hat{\boldsymbol{\Omega}} \xrightarrow{p} \boldsymbol{\Omega} = \mathrm{E}(\mathbf{u}_i\mathbf{u}_i')$. The weighting matrix used by 3SLS is

$$\hat{\mathbf{W}} = \left(N^{-1}\sum_{i=1}^{N}\mathbf{Z}_i'\hat{\boldsymbol{\Omega}}\mathbf{Z}_i\right)^{-1} = [\mathbf{Z}'(\mathbf{I}_N \otimes \hat{\boldsymbol{\Omega}})\mathbf{Z}/N]^{-1} \tag{8.35}$$

where $\mathbf{I}_N$ is the $N \times N$ identity matrix. Plugging this into equation (8.24) gives the 3SLS estimator

$$\hat{\boldsymbol{\beta}} = [\mathbf{X}'\mathbf{Z}\{\mathbf{Z}'(\mathbf{I}_N \otimes \hat{\boldsymbol{\Omega}})\mathbf{Z}\}^{-1}\mathbf{Z}'\mathbf{X}]^{-1}\mathbf{X}'\mathbf{Z}\{\mathbf{Z}'(\mathbf{I}_N \otimes \hat{\boldsymbol{\Omega}})\mathbf{Z}\}^{-1}\mathbf{Z}'\mathbf{Y} \tag{8.36}$$

By Theorems 8.1 and 8.2, $\hat{\boldsymbol{\beta}}$ is consistent and asymptotically normal under Assumptions SIV.1–SIV.3. Assumption SIV.3 requires $\mathrm{E}(\mathbf{Z}_i'\boldsymbol{\Omega}\mathbf{Z}_i)$ to be nonsingular, a standard assumption.

When is 3SLS asymptotically efficient? First, note that equation (8.35) always consistently estimates $[\mathrm{E}(\mathbf{Z}_i'\boldsymbol{\Omega}\mathbf{Z}_i)]^{-1}$. Therefore, from Theorem 8.3, equation (8.35) is an efficient weighting matrix provided $\mathrm{E}(\mathbf{Z}_i'\boldsymbol{\Omega}\mathbf{Z}_i) = \boldsymbol{\Lambda} = \mathrm{E}(\mathbf{Z}_i'\mathbf{u}_i\mathbf{u}_i'\mathbf{Z}_i)$.

ASSUMPTION SIV.5: $\mathrm{E}(\mathbf{Z}_i'\mathbf{u}_i\mathbf{u}_i'\mathbf{Z}_i) = \mathrm{E}(\mathbf{Z}_i'\boldsymbol{\Omega}\mathbf{Z}_i)$, where $\boldsymbol{\Omega} \equiv \mathrm{E}(\mathbf{u}_i\mathbf{u}_i')$.

Assumption SIV.5 is the system extension of the homoskedasticity assumption for 2SLS estimation of a single equation. A sufficient condition for Assumption SIV.5, and one that is easier to interpret, is

$$\mathrm{E}(\mathbf{u}_i\mathbf{u}_i' \mid \mathbf{Z}_i) = \mathrm{E}(\mathbf{u}_i\mathbf{u}_i') \tag{8.37}$$

We do not take equation (8.37) as the homoskedasticity assumption because there are interesting applications where Assumption SIV.5 holds but equation (8.37) does not (more on this topic in Chapters 9 and 11). When

$$\mathrm{E}(\mathbf{u}_i \mid \mathbf{Z}_i) = \mathbf{0} \tag{8.38}$$

is assumed in place of Assumption SIV.1, then equation (8.37) is equivalent to $\mathrm{Var}(\mathbf{u}_i \mid \mathbf{Z}_i) = \mathrm{Var}(\mathbf{u}_i)$. Whether we state the assumption as in equation (8.37) or use the weaker form, Assumption SIV.5, it is important to see that the elements of the unconditional variance matrix $\boldsymbol{\Omega}$ are *not* restricted: $\sigma_g^2 = \mathrm{Var}(u_g)$ can change across g, and $\sigma_{gh} = \mathrm{Cov}(u_g, u_h)$ can differ across g and h.

The system homoskedasticity assumption (8.37) necessarily holds when the instruments $\mathbf{Z}_i$ are treated as nonrandom and $\mathrm{Var}(\mathbf{u}_i)$ is constant across i. Because we are assuming random sampling, we are forced to properly focus attention on the variance of $\mathbf{u}_i$ *conditional* on $\mathbf{Z}_i$.

For the system of equations (8.12) with instruments defined in the matrix (8.15), Assumption SIV.5 reduces to (without the i subscript)

$$\mathrm{E}(u_g u_h \mathbf{z}_g'\mathbf{z}_h) = \mathrm{E}(u_g u_h)\mathrm{E}(\mathbf{z}_g'\mathbf{z}_h), \qquad g, h = 1, 2, \ldots, G \tag{8.39}$$

Therefore, $u_g u_h$ must be uncorrelated with each of the elements of $\mathbf{z}_g'\mathbf{z}_h$. When $g = h$, assumption (8.39) becomes

$$\mathrm{E}(u_g^2\mathbf{z}_g'\mathbf{z}_g) = \mathrm{E}(u_g^2)\mathrm{E}(\mathbf{z}_g'\mathbf{z}_g) \tag{8.40}$$

so that u_g^2 is uncorrelated with each element of $\mathbf{z}_g$ along with the squares and cross products of the $\mathbf{z}_g$ elements. This is exactly the homoskedasticity assumption for single-equation IV analysis (Assumption 2SLS.3). For $g \neq h$, assumption (8.39) is new because it involves covariances across different equations.

Assumption SIV.5 implies that Assumption SIV.4 holds [because the matrix (8.35) consistently estimates $\boldsymbol{\Lambda}^{-1}$ under Assumption SIV.5]. Therefore, we have the following theorem:

THEOREM 8.4 (Optimality of 3SLS): Under Assumptions SIV.1, SIV.2, SIV.3, and SIV.5, the 3SLS estimator is an optimal GMM estimator. Further, the appropriate estimator of Avar($\hat{\boldsymbol{\beta}}$) is

$$\left[(\mathbf{X}'\mathbf{Z})\left(\sum_{i=1}^{N}\mathbf{Z}_i'\hat{\boldsymbol{\Omega}}\mathbf{Z}_i\right)^{-1}(\mathbf{Z}'\mathbf{X})\right]^{-1} = [\mathbf{X}'\mathbf{Z}\{\mathbf{Z}'(\mathbf{I}_N \otimes \hat{\boldsymbol{\Omega}})\mathbf{Z}\}^{-1}\mathbf{Z}'\mathbf{X}]^{-1} \tag{8.41}$$

It is important to understand the implications of this theorem. First, without Assumption SIV.5, the 3SLS estimator is generally less efficient, asymptotically, than the minimum chi-square estimator, and the asymptotic variance estimator for 3SLS in equation (8.41) is inappropriate. Second, even with Assumption SIV.5, the 3SLS estimator is no more asymptotically efficient than the minimum chi-square estimator: expressions (8.32) and (8.35) are both consistent estimators of $\boldsymbol{\Lambda}^{-1}$ under Assumption SIV.5. In other words, the estimators based on these two different choices for $\hat{\mathbf{W}}$ are $\sqrt{N}$-equivalent under Assumption SIV.5.

Given the fact that the GMM estimator using expression (8.32) as the weighting matrix is never worse, asymptotically, than 3SLS, and in some important cases is strictly better, why is 3SLS ever used? There are at least two reasons. First, 3SLS has a long history in simultaneous equations models, whereas the GMM approach has been around only since the early 1980s, starting with the work of Hansen (1982) and White (1982b). Second, the 3SLS estimator might have better finite sample properties than the optimal GMM estimator when Assumption SIV.5 holds. However, whether it does or not must be determined on a case-by-case basis.

There is an interesting corollary to Theorem 8.4. Suppose that in the system (8.11) we can assume $\mathrm{E}(\mathbf{X}_i \otimes \mathbf{u}_i) = \mathbf{0}$, which is Assumption SGLS.1 from Chapter 7. We can use a method of moments approach to estimating $\boldsymbol{\beta}$, where the instruments for each equation, $\mathbf{x}_i^o$, is the row vector containing every row of $\mathbf{X}_i$. As shown by Im, Ahn, Schmidt, and Wooldridge (1999), the 3SLS estimator using instruments $\mathbf{Z}_i \equiv \mathbf{I}_G \otimes \mathbf{x}_i^o$ is equal to the feasible GLS estimator that uses the same $\hat{\boldsymbol{\Omega}}$. Therefore, if Assumption SIV.5 holds with $\mathbf{Z}_i \equiv \mathbf{I}_G \otimes \mathbf{x}_i^o$, FGLS is asymptotically efficient in the class of GMM estimators that use the orthogonality condition in Assumption SGLS.1. Sufficient for Assumption SIV.5 in the GLS context is the homoskedasticity assumption $\mathrm{E}(\mathbf{u}_i\mathbf{u}_i' \mid \mathbf{X}_i) = \boldsymbol{\Omega}$.

8.3.5 Comparison between GMM 3SLS and Traditional 3SLS

The definition of the GMM 3SLS estimator in equation (8.36) differs from the definition of the 3SLS estimator in most textbooks. Using our notation, the expression for the **traditional 3SLS estimator** is

$$\hat{\boldsymbol{\beta}} = \left(\sum_{i=1}^{N} \hat{\mathbf{X}}_i' \hat{\boldsymbol{\Omega}}^{-1} \hat{\mathbf{X}}_i\right)^{-1} \left(\sum_{i=1}^{N} \hat{\mathbf{X}}_i' \hat{\boldsymbol{\Omega}}^{-1} \mathbf{y}_i\right)$$

$$= [\hat{\mathbf{X}}'(\mathbf{I}_N \otimes \hat{\boldsymbol{\Omega}}^{-1})\hat{\mathbf{X}}]^{-1} \hat{\mathbf{X}}'(\mathbf{I}_N \otimes \hat{\boldsymbol{\Omega}}^{-1})\mathbf{Y} \tag{8.42}$$

where $\hat{\boldsymbol{\Omega}}$ is given in expression (8.34), $\hat{\mathbf{X}}_i \equiv \mathbf{Z}_i\hat{\boldsymbol{\Pi}}$, and $\hat{\boldsymbol{\Pi}} = (\mathbf{Z}'\mathbf{Z})^{-1}\mathbf{Z}'\mathbf{X}$. Comparing equations (8.36) and (8.42) shows that, in general, these are different estimators. To study equation (8.42) more closely, write it as

$$\hat{\boldsymbol{\beta}} = \boldsymbol{\beta} + \left(N^{-1} \sum_{i=1}^{N} \hat{\mathbf{X}}_i' \hat{\boldsymbol{\Omega}}^{-1} \hat{\mathbf{X}}_i\right)^{-1} \left(N^{-1} \sum_{i=1}^{N} \hat{\mathbf{X}}_i' \hat{\boldsymbol{\Omega}}^{-1} \mathbf{u}_i\right)$$

Because $\hat{\boldsymbol{\Pi}} \xrightarrow{p} \boldsymbol{\Pi} \equiv [\mathrm{E}(\mathbf{Z}_i'\mathbf{Z}_i)]^{-1}\mathrm{E}(\mathbf{Z}_i'\mathbf{X}_i)$ and $\hat{\boldsymbol{\Omega}} \xrightarrow{p} \boldsymbol{\Omega}$, the probability limit of the second term is the same as

$$\operatorname{plim}\left[N^{-1} \sum_{i=1}^{N} (\mathbf{Z}_i\boldsymbol{\Pi})' \boldsymbol{\Omega}^{-1} (\mathbf{Z}_i\boldsymbol{\Pi})\right]^{-1} \left[N^{-1} \sum_{i=1}^{N} (\mathbf{Z}_i\boldsymbol{\Pi})' \boldsymbol{\Omega}^{-1} \mathbf{u}_i\right] \tag{8.43}$$

The first factor in expression (8.43) generally converges to a positive definite matrix. Therefore, if equation (8.42) is to be consistent for $\boldsymbol{\beta}$, we need

$$\mathrm{E}[(\mathbf{Z}_i\boldsymbol{\Pi})'\boldsymbol{\Omega}^{-1}\mathbf{u}_i] = \boldsymbol{\Pi}'\mathrm{E}[(\boldsymbol{\Omega}^{-1}\mathbf{Z}_i)'\mathbf{u}_i] = \mathbf{0}$$

Without assuming a special structure for $\boldsymbol{\Pi}$, we should have that $\boldsymbol{\Omega}^{-1}\mathbf{Z}_i$ is uncorrelated with $\mathbf{u}_i$, an assumption that is *not* generally implied by Assumption SIV.1. In other words, the traditional 3SLS estimator generally uses a different set of orthogonality conditions than the GMM 3SLS estimator. The GMM 3SLS estimator is guaranteed to be consistent under Assumptions SIV.1–SIV.3, while the traditional 3SLS estimator is not.

The best way to illustrate this point is with model (8.12) where $\mathbf{Z}_i$ is given in matrix (8.15) and we assume $\mathrm{E}(\mathbf{z}_{ig}'u_{ig}) = \mathbf{0}$, $g = 1, 2, \ldots, G$. Now, unless $\boldsymbol{\Omega}$ is diagonal, $\mathrm{E}[(\boldsymbol{\Omega}^{-1}\mathbf{Z}_i)'\mathbf{u}_i] \neq \mathbf{0}$ unless $\mathbf{z}_{ig}$ is uncorrelated with each u_{ih} for *all* $g, h = 1, 2, \ldots, G$. If $\mathbf{z}_{ig}$ is correlated with u_{ih} for some $g \neq h$, the transformation of the instruments in equation (8.42) results in inconsistency. The GMM 3SLS estimator is based on the original orthogonality conditions, while the traditional 3SLS estimator is not. See Problem 8.6 for the $G = 2$ case.

Why, then, does equation (8.42) usually appear as the definition of the 3SLS estimator? The reason is that the 3SLS estimator is typically introduced in simultaneous equations models where any variable exogenous in one equation is assumed to be exogenous in all equations. Consider the model (8.12) again, but assume that the instrument matrix is $\mathbf{Z}_i = \mathbf{I}_G \otimes \mathbf{z}_i$, where $\mathbf{z}_i$ contains the exogenous variables appearing anywhere in the system. With this choice of $\mathbf{Z}_i$, Assumption SIV.1 is equivalent to $\mathrm{E}(\mathbf{z}_i' u_{ig}) = \mathbf{0}$, $g = 1, 2, \ldots, G$. It follows that *any* linear combination of $\mathbf{Z}_i$ is orthogonal to $\mathbf{u}_i$, including $\boldsymbol{\Omega}^{-1}\mathbf{Z}_i$. In this important special case, traditional 3SLS is a consistent estimator. In fact, as shown by Schmidt (1990), the GMM 3SLS estimator and the traditional 3SLS estimator are algebraically identical.

Because we will encounter cases where we need different instruments for different equations, the GMM definition of 3SLS in equation (8.36) is preferred: it is more generally valid, and it reduces to the standard definition in the traditional simultaneous equations setting.

8.4 Some Considerations When Choosing an Estimator

We have already discussed the assumptions under which the 3SLS estimator is an efficient GMM estimator. It follows that, under the assumptions of Theorem 8.4, 3SLS is as efficient asymptotically as the system 2SLS estimator. Nevertheless, it is useful to know that there are some situations where the system 2SLS and 3SLS estimators are equivalent. First, when the general system (8.11) is just identified, that is, $L = K$, all GMM estimators reduce to the instrumental variables estimator in equation (8.22). In the special (but still fairly general) case of the SUR system (8.12), the system is just identified if and only if each equation is just identified: $L_g = K_g$, $g = 1, 2, \ldots, G$ and the rank condition holds for each equation. When each equation is just identified, the system IV estimator is IV equation by equation.

For the remaining discussion, we consider model (8.12) when at least one equation is overidentified. When $\hat{\boldsymbol{\Omega}}$ is a diagonal matrix, that is, $\hat{\boldsymbol{\Omega}} = \mathrm{diag}(\hat{\sigma}_1^2, \ldots, \hat{\sigma}_G^2)$, 2SLS equation by equation is algebraically equivalent to 3SLS, regardless of the degree of overidentification (see Problem 8.7). Therefore, if we force our estimator $\hat{\boldsymbol{\Omega}}$ to be diagonal, we obtain 2SLS equation by equation.

The algebraic equivalance between system 2SLS and 3SLS when $\hat{\boldsymbol{\Omega}}$ is diagonal allows us to conclude that 2SLS and 3SLS are *asymptotically* equivalent if $\boldsymbol{\Omega}$ is diagonal. The reason is simple. If we could use $\boldsymbol{\Omega}$ in the 3SLS estimator, 3SLS would be identical to 2SLS. The actual 3SLS estimator, which uses $\hat{\boldsymbol{\Omega}}$, is $\sqrt{N}$-equivalent to the hypothetical 3SLS estimator that uses $\boldsymbol{\Omega}$. Therefore, 3SLS and 2SLS are $\sqrt{N}$-equivalent.

Even in cases where the 2SLS estimator is not algebraically or asympotically equivalent to 3SLS, it is not necessarily true that we should prefer 3SLS (or the minimum chi-square estimator more generally). Why? Suppose that primary interest lies in estimating the parameters in the first equation, $\boldsymbol{\beta}_1$. On the one hand, we know that 2SLS estimation of this equation produces consistent estimators under the orthogonality condition $\mathrm{E}(\mathbf{z}_1' u_1) = \mathbf{0}$ and the condition rank $\mathrm{E}(\mathbf{z}_1'\mathbf{x}_1) = K_1$. We do not care what is happening elsewhere in the system as long as these two assumptions hold. On the other hand, the system-based 3SLS and minimum chi-square estimators of $\boldsymbol{\beta}_1$ are generally inconsistent unless $\mathrm{E}(\mathbf{z}_g' u_g) = \mathbf{0}$ for all g. Therefore, in using a system method to consistently estimate $\boldsymbol{\beta}_1$, all equations in the system must be properly specified, which means their instruments must be exogenous. Such is the nature of system estimation procedures. As with system OLS and FGLS, there is a trade-off between robustness and efficiency.

8.5 Testing Using GMM

8.5.1 Testing Classical Hypotheses

Testing hypotheses after GMM estimation is straightforward. Let $\hat{\boldsymbol{\beta}}$ denote a GMM estimator, and let $\hat{\mathbf{V}}$ denote its estimated asymptotic variance. Although the following analysis can be made more general, in most applications we use an optimal GMM estimator. Without Assumption SIV.5, the weighting matrix would be expression (8.32) and $\hat{\mathbf{V}}$ would be as in expression (8.33). This can be used for computing t statistics by obtaining the asymptotic standard errors (square roots of the diagonal elements of $\hat{\mathbf{V}}$). Wald statistics of linear hypotheses of the form H_0: $\mathbf{R}\boldsymbol{\beta} = \mathbf{r}$, where $\mathbf{R}$ is a $Q \times K$ matrix with rank Q, are obtained using the same statistic we have already seen several times. Under Assumption SIV.5 we can use the 3SLS estimator and its asymptotic variance estimate in equation (8.41). For testing general system hypotheses we would probably not use the 2SLS estimator because its asymptotic variance is more complicated unless we make very restrictive assumptions.

An alternative method for testing linear restrictions uses a statistic based on the difference in the GMM objective function with and without the restrictions imposed. To apply this statistic, we must assume that the GMM estimator uses the optimal weighting matrix, so that $\hat{\mathbf{W}}$ consistently estimates $[\mathrm{Var}(\mathbf{Z}_i'\mathbf{u}_i)]^{-1}$. Then, from Lemma 3.8,

$$\left(N^{-1/2}\sum_{i=1}^{N}\mathbf{Z}_i'\mathbf{u}_i\right)'\hat{\mathbf{W}}\left(N^{-1/2}\sum_{i=1}^{N}\mathbf{Z}_i'\mathbf{u}_i\right) \overset{a}{\sim} \chi_L^2 \tag{8.44}$$

since $\mathbf{Z}_i'\mathbf{u}_i$ is an $L \times 1$ vector with zero mean and variance $\boldsymbol{\Lambda}$. If $\hat{\mathbf{W}}$ does not consistently estimate $[\mathrm{Var}(\mathbf{Z}_i'\mathbf{u}_i)]^{-1}$, then result (8.44) is false, and the following method does not produce an asymptotically chi-square statistic.

Let $\hat{\boldsymbol{\beta}}$ again be the GMM estimator, using optimal weighting matrix $\hat{\mathbf{W}}$, obtained without imposing the restrictions. Let $\tilde{\boldsymbol{\beta}}$ be the GMM estimator using the *same* weighting matrix $\hat{\mathbf{W}}$ but obtained with the Q linear restrictions imposed. The restricted estimator can always be obtained by estimating a linear model with $K - Q$ rather than K parameters. Define the unrestricted and restricted residuals as $\hat{\mathbf{u}}_i \equiv \mathbf{y}_i - \mathbf{X}_i\hat{\boldsymbol{\beta}}$ and $\tilde{\mathbf{u}}_i \equiv \mathbf{y}_i - \mathbf{X}_i\tilde{\boldsymbol{\beta}}$, respectively. It can be shown that, under H_0, the **GMM distance statistic** has a limiting chi-square distribution:

$$\left[\left(\sum_{i=1}^{N} \mathbf{Z}_i'\tilde{\mathbf{u}}_i\right)' \hat{\mathbf{W}} \left(\sum_{i=1}^{N} \mathbf{Z}_i'\tilde{\mathbf{u}}_i\right) - \left(\sum_{i=1}^{N} \mathbf{Z}_i'\hat{\mathbf{u}}_i\right)' \hat{\mathbf{W}} \left(\sum_{i=1}^{N} \mathbf{Z}_i'\hat{\mathbf{u}}_i\right)\right] \Big/ N \overset{a}{\sim} \chi_Q^2 \tag{8.45}$$

See, for example, Hansen (1982) and Gallant (1987). The GMM distance statistic is simply the difference in the criterion function (8.23) evaluated at the restricted and unrestricted estimates, divided by the sample size, N. For this reason, expression (8.45) is called a **criterion function statistic**. Because constrained minimization cannot result in a smaller objective function than unconstrained minimization, expression (8.45) is always nonnegative and usually strictly positive.

Under Assumption SIV.5 we can use the 3SLS estimator, in which case expression (8.45) becomes

$$\left(\sum_{i=1}^{N} \mathbf{Z}_i'\tilde{\mathbf{u}}_i\right)' \left(\sum_{i=1}^{N} \mathbf{Z}_i'\hat{\boldsymbol{\Omega}}\mathbf{Z}_i\right)^{-1} \left(\sum_{i=1}^{N} \mathbf{Z}_i'\tilde{\mathbf{u}}_i\right) - \left(\sum_{i=1}^{N} \mathbf{Z}_i'\hat{\mathbf{u}}_i\right)' \left(\sum_{i=1}^{N} \mathbf{Z}_i'\hat{\boldsymbol{\Omega}}\mathbf{Z}_i\right)^{-1} \left(\sum_{i=1}^{N} \mathbf{Z}_i'\hat{\mathbf{u}}_i\right) \tag{8.46}$$

where $\hat{\boldsymbol{\Omega}}$ would probably be computed using the 2SLS residuals from estimating the unrestricted model. The division by N has disappeared because of the definition of $\hat{\mathbf{W}}$; see equation (8.35).

Testing nonlinear hypotheses is easy once the unrestricted estimator $\hat{\boldsymbol{\beta}}$ has been obtained. Write the null hypothesis as

$$\mathrm{H}_0\colon \mathbf{c}(\boldsymbol{\beta}) = \mathbf{0} \tag{8.47}$$

where $\mathbf{c}(\boldsymbol{\beta}) \equiv [c_1(\boldsymbol{\beta}), c_2(\boldsymbol{\beta}), \ldots, c_Q(\boldsymbol{\beta})]'$ is a $Q \times 1$ vector of functions. Let $\mathbf{C}(\boldsymbol{\beta})$ denote the $Q \times K$ Jacobian of $\mathbf{c}(\boldsymbol{\beta})$. Assuming that rank $\mathbf{C}(\boldsymbol{\beta}) = Q$, the Wald statistic is

$$W = \mathbf{c}(\hat{\boldsymbol{\beta}})'(\hat{\mathbf{C}}\hat{\mathbf{V}}\hat{\mathbf{C}}')^{-1}\mathbf{c}(\hat{\boldsymbol{\beta}}) \tag{8.48}$$

where $\hat{\mathbf{C}} \equiv \mathbf{C}(\hat{\boldsymbol{\beta}})$ is the Jacobian evaluated at the GMM estimate $\hat{\boldsymbol{\beta}}$. Under H_0, the Wald statistic has an asymptotic χ_Q^2 distribution.

8.5.2 Testing Overidentification Restrictions

Just as in the case of single-equation analysis with more exogenous variables than explanatory variables, we can test whether overidentifying restrictions are valid in a system context. In the model (8.11) with instrument matrix $\mathbf{Z}_i$, where $\mathbf{X}_i$ is $G \times K$ and $\mathbf{Z}_i$ is $G \times L$, there are overidentifying restrictions if $L > K$. Assuming that $\hat{\mathbf{W}}$ is an optimal weighting matrix, it can be shown that

$$\left(N^{-1/2}\sum_{i=1}^{N}\mathbf{Z}_i'\hat{\mathbf{u}}_i\right)'\hat{\mathbf{W}}\left(N^{-1/2}\sum_{i=1}^{N}\mathbf{Z}_i'\hat{\mathbf{u}}_i\right) \overset{a}{\sim} \chi^2_{L-K} \tag{8.49}$$

under the null hypothesis H_0: $\mathrm{E}(\mathbf{Z}_i'\mathbf{u}_i) = \mathbf{0}$. The asymptotic χ^2_{L-K} distribution is similar to result (8.44), but expression (8.44) contains the unobserved errors, $\mathbf{u}_i$, whereas expression (8.49) contains the residuals, $\hat{\mathbf{u}}_i$. Replacing $\mathbf{u}_i$ with $\hat{\mathbf{u}}_i$ causes the degrees of freedom to fall from L to $L - K$: in effect, K orthogonality conditions have been used to compute $\hat{\boldsymbol{\beta}}$, and $L - K$ are left over for testing.

The **overidentification test statistic** in expression (8.49) is just the objective function (8.23) evaluated at the solution $\hat{\boldsymbol{\beta}}$ and divided by N. It is because of expression (8.49) that the GMM estimator using the optimal weighting matrix is called the minimum chi-square estimator: $\hat{\boldsymbol{\beta}}$ is chosen to make the minimum of the objective function have an asymptotic chi-square distribution. If $\hat{\mathbf{W}}$ is not optimal, expression (8.49) fails to hold, making it much more difficult to test the overidentifying restrictions. When $L = K$, the left-hand side of expression (8.49) is identically zero; there are no overidentifying restrictions to be tested.

Under Assumption SIV.5, the 3SLS estimator is a minimum chi-square estimator, and the overidentification statistic in equation (8.49) can be written as

$$\left(\sum_{i=1}^{N}\mathbf{Z}_i'\hat{\mathbf{u}}_i\right)'\left(\sum_{i=1}^{N}\mathbf{Z}_i'\hat{\mathbf{\Omega}}\mathbf{Z}_i\right)^{-1}\left(\sum_{i=1}^{N}\mathbf{Z}_i'\hat{\mathbf{u}}_i\right) \tag{8.50}$$

Without Assumption SIV.5, the limiting distribution of this statistic is not chi square.

In the case where the model has the form (8.12), overidentification test statistics can be used to choose between a systems and a single-equation method. For example, if the test statistic (8.50) rejects the overidentifying restrictions in the entire system, then the 3SLS estimators of the first equation are generally inconsistent. Assuming that the single-equation 2SLS estimation passes the overidentification test discussed in Chapter 6, 2SLS would be preferred. However, in making this judgment it is, as always, important to compare the magnitudes of the two sets of estimates in addition to the statistical significance of test statistics. Hausman (1983, p. 435) shows how to construct a statistic based directly on the 3SLS and 2SLS estimates of a particular equation (assuming that 3SLS is asymptotically more efficient under the null), and this discussion can be extended to allow for the more general minimum chi-square estimator.

8.6 More Efficient Estimation and Optimal Instruments

In Section 8.3.3 we characterized the optimal weighting matrix given the matrix $\mathbf{Z}_i$ of instruments. But this discussion begs the question of how we can best choose $\mathbf{Z}_i$. In this section we briefly discuss two efficiency results. The first has to do with adding valid instruments.

To be precise, let $\mathbf{Z}_{i1}$ be a $G \times L_1$ submatrix of the $G \times L$ matrix $\mathbf{Z}_i$, where $\mathbf{Z}_i$ satisfies Assumptions SIV.1 and SIV.2. We also assume that $\mathbf{Z}_{i1}$ satisfies Assumption SIV.2; that is, $\mathrm{E}(\mathbf{Z}_{i1}'\mathbf{X}_i)$ has rank K. This assumption ensures that $\boldsymbol{\beta}$ is identified using the smaller set of instruments. (Necessary is $L_1 \geq K$.) Given $\mathbf{Z}_{i1}$, we know that the efficient GMM estimator uses a weighting matrix that is consistent for $\boldsymbol{\Lambda}_1^{-1}$, where $\boldsymbol{\Lambda}_1 = \mathrm{E}(\mathbf{Z}_{i1}'\mathbf{u}_i\mathbf{u}_i'\mathbf{Z}_{i1})$. When we use the full set of instruments $\mathbf{Z}_i = (\mathbf{Z}_{i1}, \mathbf{Z}_{i2})$, the optimal weighting matrix is a consistent estimator of $\boldsymbol{\Lambda}$ given in expression (8.26). The question is, Can we say that using the full set of instruments (with the optimal weighting matrix) is better than using the reduced set of instruments (with the optimal weighting matrix)? The answer is that, asymptotically, we can do no worse, and often we can do better, using a larger set of valid instruments.

The proof that adding orthogonality conditions generally improves efficiency proceeds by comparing the asymptotic variances of $\sqrt{N}(\tilde{\boldsymbol{\beta}} - \boldsymbol{\beta})$ and $\sqrt{N}(\hat{\boldsymbol{\beta}} - \boldsymbol{\beta})$, where the former estimator uses the restricted set of IVs and the latter uses the full set. Then

$$\text{Avar } \sqrt{N}(\tilde{\boldsymbol{\beta}} - \boldsymbol{\beta}) - \text{Avar } \sqrt{N}(\hat{\boldsymbol{\beta}} - \boldsymbol{\beta}) = (\mathbf{C}_1'\boldsymbol{\Lambda}_1^{-1}\mathbf{C}_1)^{-1} - (\mathbf{C}'\boldsymbol{\Lambda}^{-1}\mathbf{C})^{-1} \tag{8.51}$$

where $\mathbf{C}_1 = \mathrm{E}(\mathbf{Z}_{i1}'\mathbf{X}_i)$. The difference in equation (8.51) is positive semidefinite if and only if $\mathbf{C}'\boldsymbol{\Lambda}^{-1}\mathbf{C} - \mathbf{C}_1'\boldsymbol{\Lambda}_1^{-1}\mathbf{C}_1$ is p.s.d. The latter result is shown by White (1984, Proposition 4.49) using the formula for partitioned inverse; we will not reproduce it here.

The previous argument shows that we can never do worse asymptotically by adding instruments and computing the minimum chi-square estimator. But we need not always do better. The proof in White (1984) shows that the asymptotic variances of $\tilde{\boldsymbol{\beta}}$ and $\hat{\boldsymbol{\beta}}$ are identical if and only if

$$\mathbf{C}_2 = \mathrm{E}(\mathbf{Z}_{i2}'\mathbf{u}_i\mathbf{u}_i'\mathbf{Z}_{i1})\boldsymbol{\Lambda}_1^{-1}\mathbf{C}_1 \tag{8.52}$$

where $\mathbf{C}_2 = \mathrm{E}(\mathbf{Z}_{i2}'\mathbf{X}_i)$. Generally, this condition is difficult to check. However, if we assume that $\mathrm{E}(\mathbf{Z}_i'\mathbf{u}_i\mathbf{u}_i'\mathbf{Z}_i) = \sigma^2\mathrm{E}(\mathbf{Z}_i'\mathbf{Z}_i)$—the ideal assumption for system 2SLS—then condition (8.52) becomes

$$\mathrm{E}(\mathbf{Z}_{i2}'\mathbf{X}_i) = \mathrm{E}(\mathbf{Z}_{i2}'\mathbf{Z}_{i1})[\mathrm{E}(\mathbf{Z}_{i1}'\mathbf{Z}_{i1})]^{-1}\mathrm{E}(\mathbf{Z}_{i1}'\mathbf{X}_i)$$

Straightforward algebra shows that this condition is equivalent to

$$\mathrm{E}[(\mathbf{Z}_{i2} - \mathbf{Z}_{i1}\mathbf{D}_1)'\mathbf{X}_i] = \mathbf{0} \tag{8.53}$$

where $\mathbf{D}_1 = [\mathrm{E}(\mathbf{Z}_{i1}'\mathbf{Z}_{i1})]^{-1}\mathrm{E}(\mathbf{Z}_{i1}'\mathbf{Z}_{i2})$ is the $L_1 \times L_2$ matrix of coefficients from the population regression of $\mathbf{Z}_{i1}$ on $\mathbf{Z}_{i2}$. Therefore, condition (8.53) has a simple interpretation: $\mathbf{X}_i$ is orthogonal to the part of $\mathbf{Z}_{i2}$ that is left after netting out $\mathbf{Z}_{i1}$. This statement means that $\mathbf{Z}_{i2}$ is not *partially* correlated with $\mathbf{X}_i$, and so it is not useful as instruments once $\mathbf{Z}_{i1}$ has been included.

Condition (8.53) is very intuitive in the context of 2SLS estimation of a single equation. Under $\mathrm{E}(u_i^2\mathbf{z}_i'\mathbf{z}_i) = \sigma^2\mathrm{E}(\mathbf{z}_i'\mathbf{z}_i)$, 2SLS is the minimum chi-square estimator. The elements of $\mathbf{z}_i$ would include all exogenous elements of $\mathbf{x}_i$, and then some. If, say, x_{iK} is the only endogenous element of $\mathbf{x}_i$, condition (8.53) becomes

$$\mathrm{L}(x_{iK} \mid \mathbf{z}_{i1}, \mathbf{z}_{i2}) = \mathrm{L}(x_{iK} \mid \mathbf{z}_{i1}) \tag{8.54}$$

so that the linear projection of x_{iK} onto $\mathbf{z}_i$ depends only on $\mathbf{z}_{i1}$. If you recall how the IVs for 2SLS are obtained—by estimating the linear projection of x_{iK} on $\mathbf{z}_i$ in the first stage—it makes perfectly good sense that $\mathbf{z}_{i2}$ can be omitted under condition (8.54) without affecting efficiency of 2SLS.

In the general case, if the error vector $\mathbf{u}_i$ contains conditional heteroskedasticity, or correlation across its elements (conditional or otherwise), condition (8.52) is unlikely to be true. As a result, we can keep improving asymptotic efficiency by adding more valid instruments. Whenever the error term satisfies a zero conditional mean assumption, unlimited IVs are available. For example, consider the linear model $\mathrm{E}(y \mid \mathbf{x}) = \mathbf{x}\boldsymbol{\beta}$, so that the error $u = y - \mathbf{x}\boldsymbol{\beta}$ has a zero mean given $\mathbf{x}$. The OLS estimator is the IV estimator using IVs $\mathbf{z}_1 = \mathbf{x}$. The preceding efficiency result implies that, if $\mathrm{Var}(u \mid \mathbf{x}) \neq \mathrm{Var}(u)$, there are unlimited minimum chi-square estimators that are asymptotically more efficient than OLS. Because $\mathrm{E}(u \mid \mathbf{x}) = 0$, $\mathbf{h}(\mathbf{x})$ is a valid set of IVs for any vector function $\mathbf{h}(\cdot)$. (Assuming, as always, that the appropriate moments exist.) Then, the minimum chi-square estimate using IVs $\mathbf{z} = [\mathbf{x}, \mathbf{h}(\mathbf{x})]$ is generally more asymptotically efficient than OLS. (Chamberlain, 1982, and Cragg, 1983, independently obtained this result.) If $\mathrm{Var}(y \mid \mathbf{x})$ is constant, adding functions of $\mathbf{x}$ to the IV list results in no asymptotic improvement because the linear projection of $\mathbf{x}$ onto $\mathbf{x}$ and $\mathbf{h}(\mathbf{x})$ obviously does not depend on $\mathbf{h}(\mathbf{x})$.

Under homoskedasticity, adding moment conditions does not reduce the asymptotic efficiency of the minimum chi-square estimator. Therefore, it may seem that, when we have a linear model that represents a conditional expectation, we cannot lose by adding IVs and performing minimum chi-square. [Plus, we can then test the functional form $\mathrm{E}(y \mid \mathbf{x}) = \mathbf{x}\boldsymbol{\beta}$ by testing the overidentifying restrictions.] Unfortunately, as shown by several authors, including Tauchen (1986), Altonji and Segal (1996), and Ziliak (1997), GMM estimators that use many overidentifying restrictions can have very poor finite sample properties.

The previous discussion raises the following possibility: rather than adding more and more orthogonality conditions to improve on inefficient estimators, can we find a small set of optimal IVs? The answer is yes, provided we replace Assumption SIV.1 with a zero conditional mean assumption.

ASSUMPTION SIV.1′: $\mathrm{E}(u_{ig} \mid \mathbf{z}_i) = 0$, $g = 1, \ldots, G$ for some vector $\mathbf{z}_i$.

Assumption SIV.1′ implies that $\mathbf{z}_i$ is exogenous in *every* equation, and each element of the instrument matrix $\mathbf{Z}_i$ can be *any* function of $\mathbf{z}_i$.

THEOREM 8.5 (Optimal Instruments): Under Assumption SIV.1′ (and sufficient regularity conditions), the optimal choice of instruments is $\mathbf{Z}_i^* = \boldsymbol{\Omega}(\mathbf{z}_i)^{-1}\mathrm{E}(\mathbf{X}_i \mid \mathbf{z}_i)$, where $\boldsymbol{\Omega}(\mathbf{z}_i) \equiv \mathrm{E}(\mathbf{u}_i'\mathbf{u}_i \mid \mathbf{z}_i)$, provided that rank $\mathrm{E}(\mathbf{Z}_i^{*\prime}\mathbf{X}_i) = K$.

We will not prove Theorem 8.5 here. We discuss a more general case in Section 14.5; see also Newey and McFadden (1994, Section 5.4). Theorem 8.5 implies that, if the $G \times K$ matrix $\mathbf{Z}_i^*$ were available, we would use it in equation (8.22) in place of $\mathbf{Z}_i$ to obtain the SIV estimator with the smallest asymptotic variance. This would take the arbitrariness out of choosing additional functions of $\mathbf{z}_i$ to add to the IV list: once we have $\mathbf{Z}_i^*$, all other functions of $\mathbf{z}_i$ are redundant.

Theorem 8.5 implies that, if the errors in the system satisfy SIV.1′, the homoskedasticity assumption (8.37), *and* $\mathrm{E}(\mathbf{X}_i \mid \mathbf{z}_i) = \mathbf{Z}_i\boldsymbol{\Pi}$ for some $G \times L$ matrix $\mathbf{Z}_i$ and an $L \times K$ unknown matrix $\boldsymbol{\Pi}$, then the 3SLS estimator is the efficient estimator based on the orthogonality conditions SIV.1′. Showing this result is easy given the traditional form of the 3SLS estimator in equation (8.41).

If $\mathrm{E}(\mathbf{u}_i \mid \mathbf{X}_i) = \mathbf{0}$ and $\mathrm{E}(\mathbf{u}_i\mathbf{u}_i' \mid \mathbf{X}_i) = \boldsymbol{\Omega}$, then the optimal instruments are $\boldsymbol{\Omega}^{-1}\mathbf{X}_i$, which gives the GLS estimator. Replacing $\boldsymbol{\Omega}$ by $\hat{\boldsymbol{\Omega}}$ has no effect asymptotically, and so the FGLS is the SIV estimator with optimal choice of instruments.

Without further assumptions, both $\boldsymbol{\Omega}(\mathbf{z}_i)$ and $\mathrm{E}(\mathbf{X}_i \mid \mathbf{z}_i)$ can be arbitrary functions of $\mathbf{z}_i$, in which case the optimal SIV estimator is not easily obtainable. It is possible to find an estimator that is asymptotically efficient using *nonparametric* estimation methods to estimate $\mathbf{\Omega}(\mathbf{z}_i)$ and $\mathrm{E}(\mathbf{X}_i \mid \mathbf{z}_i)$, but there are many practical hurdles to overcome in applying such procedures. See Newey (1990) for an approach that approximates $\mathrm{E}(\mathbf{X}_i \mid \mathbf{z}_i)$ by parametric functional forms, where the approximation gets better as the sample size grows.

Problems

8.1. Show that the GMM estimator that solves the problem (8.23) satisfies the first-order condition

$$\left(\sum_{i=1}^{N} \mathbf{Z}_i'\mathbf{X}_i\right)'\hat{\mathbf{W}}\left(\sum_{i=1}^{N} \mathbf{Z}_i'(\mathbf{y}_i - \mathbf{X}_i\hat{\boldsymbol{\beta}})\right) = \mathbf{0}$$

Use this expression to obtain formula (8.24).

8.2. Consider the system of equations

$$\mathbf{y}_i = \mathbf{X}_i\boldsymbol{\beta} + \mathbf{u}_i$$

where i indexes the cross section observation, $\mathbf{y}_i$ and $\mathbf{u}_i$ are $G \times 1$, $\mathbf{X}_i$ is $G \times K$, $\mathbf{Z}_i$ is the $G \times L$ matrix of instruments, and $\boldsymbol{\beta}$ is $K \times 1$. Let $\mathbf{\Omega} = \mathrm{E}(\mathbf{u}_i\mathbf{u}_i')$. Make the following four assumptions: (1) $\mathrm{E}(\mathbf{Z}_i'\mathbf{u}_i) = \mathbf{0}$; (2) rank $\mathrm{E}(\mathbf{Z}_i'\mathbf{X}_i) = K$; (3) $\mathrm{E}(\mathbf{Z}_i'\mathbf{Z}_i)$ is nonsingular; and (4) $\mathrm{E}(\mathbf{Z}_i'\mathbf{\Omega}\mathbf{Z}_i)$ is nonsingular.

a. What are the properties of the 3SLS estimator?

b. Find the asymptotic variance matrix of $\sqrt{N}(\hat{\boldsymbol{\beta}}_{3SLS} - \boldsymbol{\beta})$.

c. How would you estimate $\mathrm{Avar}(\hat{\boldsymbol{\beta}}_{3SLS})$?

8.3. Let $\mathbf{x}$ be a $1 \times K$ random vector and let $\mathbf{z}$ be a $1 \times M$ random vector. Suppose that $\mathrm{E}(\mathbf{x} \mid \mathbf{z}) = \mathrm{L}(\mathbf{x} \mid \mathbf{z}) = \mathbf{z}\mathbf{\Pi}$, where $\mathbf{\Pi}$ is an $M \times K$ matrix; in other words, the expectation of $\mathbf{x}$ given $\mathbf{z}$ is linear in $\mathbf{z}$. Let $\mathbf{h}(\mathbf{z})$ be any $1 \times Q$ nonlinear function of $\mathbf{z}$, and define an expanded instrument list as $\mathbf{w} \equiv [\mathbf{z}, \mathbf{h}(\mathbf{z})]$.

Show that rank $\mathrm{E}(\mathbf{z}'\mathbf{x}) =$ rank $\mathrm{E}(\mathbf{w}'\mathbf{x})$. {Hint: First show that rank $\mathrm{E}(\mathbf{z}'\mathbf{x}) =$ rank $\mathrm{E}(\mathbf{z}'\mathbf{x}^*)$, where $\mathbf{x}^*$ is the linear projection of $\mathbf{x}$ onto $\mathbf{z}$; the same holds with $\mathbf{z}$ replaced by $\mathbf{w}$. Next, show that when $\mathrm{E}(\mathbf{x} \mid \mathbf{z}) = \mathrm{L}(\mathbf{x} \mid \mathbf{z})$, $\mathrm{L}[\mathbf{x} \mid \mathbf{z}, \mathbf{h}(\mathbf{z})] = \mathrm{L}(\mathbf{x} \mid \mathbf{z})$ for any function $\mathbf{h}(\mathbf{z})$ of $\mathbf{z}$.}

8.4. Consider the system of equations (8.12), and let $\mathbf{z}$ be a row vector of variables exogenous in every equation. Assume that the exogeneity assumption takes the stronger form $\mathrm{E}(u_g \mid \mathbf{z}) = 0$, $g = 1, 2, \ldots, G$. This assumption means that $\mathbf{z}$ and nonlinear functions of $\mathbf{z}$ are valid instruments in every equation.

a. Suppose that $\mathrm{E}(\mathbf{x}_g \mid \mathbf{z})$ is linear in $\mathbf{z}$ for all g. Show that adding nonlinear functions of $\mathbf{z}$ to the instrument list cannot help in satisfying the rank condition. (Hint: Apply Problem 8.3.)

b. What happens if $\mathrm{E}(\mathbf{x}_g \mid \mathbf{z})$ is a nonlinear function of $\mathbf{z}$ for some g?

8.5. Verify that the difference $(\mathbf{C}'\mathbf{\Lambda}^{-1}\mathbf{C}) - (\mathbf{C}'\mathbf{W}\mathbf{C})(\mathbf{C}'\mathbf{W}\mathbf{\Lambda}\mathbf{W}\mathbf{C})^{-1}(\mathbf{C}'\mathbf{W}\mathbf{C})$ in expression (8.30) is positive semidefinite for any symmetric positive definite matrices $\mathbf{W}$ and $\mathbf{\Lambda}$. {Hint: Show that the difference can be expressed as

$$\mathbf{C}'\mathbf{\Lambda}^{-1/2}[\mathbf{I}_L - \mathbf{D}(\mathbf{D}'\mathbf{D})^{-1}\mathbf{D}']\mathbf{\Lambda}^{-1/2}\mathbf{C}$$

where $\mathbf{D} \equiv \mathbf{\Lambda}^{1/2}\mathbf{W}\mathbf{C}$. Then, note that for any $L \times K$ matrix $\mathbf{D}$, $\mathbf{I}_L - \mathbf{D}(\mathbf{D}'\mathbf{D})^{-1}\mathbf{D}'$ is a symmetric, idempotent matrix, and therefore positive semidefinite.}

8.6. Consider the system (8.12) in the $G = 2$ case, with an i subscript added:

$$y_{i1} = \mathbf{x}_{i1}\boldsymbol{\beta}_1 + u_{i1}$$

$$y_{i2} = \mathbf{x}_{i2}\boldsymbol{\beta}_2 + u_{i2}$$

The instrument matrix is

$$\mathbf{Z}_i = \begin{pmatrix} \mathbf{z}_{i1} & \mathbf{0} \\ \mathbf{0} & \mathbf{z}_{i2} \end{pmatrix}$$

Let $\mathbf{\Omega}$ be the 2×2 variance matrix of $\mathbf{u}_i \equiv (u_{i1}, u_{i2})'$, and write

$$\mathbf{\Omega}^{-1} = \begin{pmatrix} \sigma^{11} & \sigma^{12} \\ \sigma^{12} & \sigma^{22} \end{pmatrix}$$

a. Find $\mathrm{E}(\mathbf{Z}_i'\mathbf{\Omega}^{-1}\mathbf{u}_i)$ and show that it is not necessarily zero under the orthogonality conditions $\mathrm{E}(\mathbf{z}_{i1}'u_{i1}) = \mathbf{0}$ and $\mathrm{E}(\mathbf{z}_{i2}'u_{i2}) = \mathbf{0}$.

b. What happens if $\mathbf{\Omega}$ is diagonal (so that $\mathbf{\Omega}^{-1}$ is diagonal)?

c. What if $\mathbf{z}_{i1} = \mathbf{z}_{i2}$ (without restrictions on $\mathbf{\Omega}$)?

8.7. With definitions (8.14) and (8.15), show that system 2SLS and 3SLS are numerically identical whenever $\hat{\mathbf{\Omega}}$ is a diagonal matrix.

8.8. Consider the standard panel data model introduced in Chapter 7:

$$y_{it} = \mathbf{x}_{it}\boldsymbol{\beta} + u_{it} \tag{8.55}$$

where the $1 \times K$ vector $\mathbf{x}_{it}$ might have some elements correlated with u_{it}. Let $\mathbf{z}_{it}$ be a $1 \times L$ vector of instruments, $L \geq K$, such that $\mathrm{E}(\mathbf{z}_{it}'u_{it}) = \mathbf{0}$, $t = 1, 2, \ldots, T$. (In practice, $\mathbf{z}_{it}$ would contain some elements of $\mathbf{x}_{it}$, including a constant and possibly time dummies.)

a. Write down the system 2SLS estimator if the instrument matrix is $\mathbf{Z}_i = (\mathbf{z}_{i1}', \mathbf{z}_{i2}', \ldots, \mathbf{z}_{iT}')'$ (a $T \times L$ matrix). Show that this estimator is a pooled 2SLS estimator. That is, it is the estimator obtained by 2SLS estimation of equation (8.55) using instruments $\mathbf{z}_{it}$, pooled across all i and t.

b. What is the rank condition for the pooled 2SLS estimator?

c. Without further assumptions, show how to estimate the asymptotic variance of the pooled 2SLS estimator.

d. Show that the assumptions

$$\mathrm{E}(u_{it} \mid \mathbf{z}_{it}, u_{i,t-1}, \mathbf{z}_{i,t-1}, \ldots, u_{i1}, \mathbf{z}_{i1}) = 0, \qquad t = 1, \ldots, T \tag{8.56}$$

$$\mathrm{E}(u_{it}^2 \mid \mathbf{z}_{it}) = \sigma^2, \qquad t = 1, \ldots, T \tag{8.57}$$

imply that the usual standard errors and test statistics reported from the pooled 2SLS estimation are valid. These assumptions make implementing 2SLS for panel data very simple.

e. What estimator would you use under condition (8.56) but where we relax condition (8.57) to $\mathrm{E}(u_{it}^2 \mid \mathbf{z}_{it}) = \mathrm{E}(u_{it}^2) \equiv \sigma_t^2$, $t = 1, \ldots, T$? This approach will involve an initial pooled 2SLS estimation.

8.9. Consider the single-equation linear model from Chapter 5: $y = \mathbf{x}\boldsymbol{\beta} + u$. Strengthen Assumption 2SLS.1 to $\mathrm{E}(u \mid \mathbf{z}) = 0$ and Assumption 2SLS.3 to $\mathrm{E}(u^2 \mid \mathbf{z}) = \sigma^2$, and keep the rank condition 2SLS.2. Show that if $\mathrm{E}(\mathbf{x} \mid \mathbf{z}) = \mathbf{z}\boldsymbol{\Pi}$ for some $L \times K$ matrix $\boldsymbol{\Pi}$, the 2SLS estimator uses the optimal instruments based on the orthogonality condition $\mathrm{E}(u \mid \mathbf{z}) = 0$. What does this result imply about OLS if $\mathrm{E}(u \mid \mathbf{x}) = 0$ and $\mathrm{Var}(u \mid \mathbf{x}) = \sigma^2$?

8.10. In the model from Problem 8.8, let $\hat{u}_{it} \equiv y_{it} - \mathbf{x}_{it}\hat{\boldsymbol{\beta}}$ be the residuals after pooled 2SLS estimation.

a. Consider the following test for AR(1) serial correlation in $\{u_{it}\colon t = 1, \ldots, T\}$: estimate the auxiliary equation

$$y_{it} = \mathbf{x}_{it}\boldsymbol{\beta} + \rho\hat{u}_{i,t-1} + error_{it}, \qquad t = 2, \ldots, T,\ i = 1, \ldots, N$$

by 2SLS using instruments $(\mathbf{z}_{it}, \hat{u}_{i,t-1})$, and use the t statistic on $\hat{\rho}$. Argue that, if we strengthen (8.56) to $\mathrm{E}(u_{it} \mid \mathbf{z}_{it}, \mathbf{x}_{i,t-1}, u_{i,t-1}, \mathbf{z}_{i,t-1}, \mathbf{x}_{i,t-2}, \ldots, \mathbf{x}_{i1}, u_{i1}, \mathbf{z}_{i1}) = 0$, then the heteroskedasticity-robust t statistic for $\hat{\rho}$ is asymptotically valid as a test for serial correlation. [Hint: Under the dynamic completeness assumption (8.56), which is effectively the null hypothesis, the fact that $\hat{u}_{i,t-1}$ is used in place of $u_{i,t-1}$ does not affect the limiting distribution of $\hat{\rho}$; see Section 6.1.3.] What is the homoskedasticity assumption that justifies the usual t statistic?

b. What should be done to obtain a heteroskedasticity-robust test?

8.11. a. Use Theorem 8.5 to show that, in the single-equation model

$$y_1 = \mathbf{z}_1\boldsymbol{\delta}_1 + \alpha_1 y_2 + u_1$$

with $\mathrm{E}(u_1 \mid \mathbf{z}) = 0$—where $\mathbf{z}_1$ is a strict subset of $\mathbf{z}$—and $\mathrm{Var}(u_1 \mid \mathbf{z}) = \sigma_1^2$, the optimal instrumental variables are $[\mathbf{z}_1, \mathrm{E}(y_2 \mid \mathbf{z})]$.

b. If y_2 is a binary variable with $\mathrm{P}(y_2 = 1 \mid \mathbf{z}) = F(\mathbf{z})$ for some known function $F(\cdot)$, $0 \le F(\mathbf{z}) \le 1$, what are the optimal IVs?

9 Simultaneous Equations Models

9.1 The Scope of Simultaneous Equations Models

The emphasis in this chapter is on situations where two or more variables are jointly determined by a system of equations. Nevertheless, the population model, the identification analysis, and the estimation methods apply to a much broader range of problems. In Chapter 8, we saw that the omitted variables problem described in Example 8.2 has the same statistical structure as the true simultaneous equations model in Example 8.1. In fact, any or all of simultaneity, omitted variables, and measurement error can be present in a system of equations. Because the omitted variable and measurement error problems are conceptually easier—and it was for this reason that we discussed them in single-equation contexts in Chapters 4 and 5—our examples and discussion in this chapter are geared mostly toward true **simultaneous equations models (SEMs)**.

For effective application of true SEMs, we must understand the kinds of situations suitable for SEM analysis. The labor supply and wage offer example, Example 8.1, is a legitimate SEM application. The labor supply function describes individual behavior, and it is derivable from basic economic principles of individual utility maximization. Holding other factors fixed, the labor supply function gives the hours of labor supply at *any* potential wage facing the individual. The wage offer function describes firm behavior, and, like the labor supply function, the wage offer function is self-contained.

When an equation in an SEM has economic meaning in isolation from the other equations in the system, we say that the equation is **autonomous**. One way to think about autonomy is in terms of counterfactual reasoning, as in Example 8.1. If we know the parameters of the labor supply function, then, for any individual, we can find labor hours given any value of the potential wage (and values of the other observed and unobserved factors affecting labor supply). In other words, we could, in principle, trace out the individual labor supply function for given levels of the other observed and unobserved variables.

Causality is closely tied to the autonomy requirement. An equation in an SEM should represent a causal relationship; therefore, we should be interested in varying each of the explanatory variables—including any that are endogenous—while holding *all* the others fixed. Put another way, each equation in an SEM should represent *some* underlying conditional expectation that has a causal structure. What complicates matters is that the conditional expectations are in terms of counterfactual variables. In the labor supply example, *if* we could run a controlled experiment, where we exogenously vary the wage offer across individuals, then the labor supply function could be estimated without ever considering the wage offer function. In fact, in the absence of omitted variables or measurement error, ordinary least squares would be an appropriate estimation method.

Generally, supply and demand examples satisfy the autonomy requirement, regardless of the level of aggregation (individual, household, firm, city, and so on), and simultaneous equations systems were originally developed for such applications. [See, for example, Haavelmo (1943) and Kiefer's (1989) interview of Arthur S. Goldberger.] Unfortunately, many recent applications of simultaneous equations methods fail the autonomy requirement; as a result, it is difficult to interpret what has actually been estimated. Examples that fail the autonomy requirement often have the same feature: the endogenous variables in the system are all choice variables of the *same* economic unit.

As an example, consider an individual's choice of weekly hours spent in legal market activities and hours spent in criminal behavior. An economic model of crime can be derived from utility maximization; for simplicity, suppose the choice is only between hours working legally (*work*) and hours involved in crime (*crime*). The factors assumed to be exogenous to the individual's choice are things like wage in legal activities, other income sources, probability of arrest, expected punishment, and so on. The utility function can depend on education, work experience, gender, race, and other demographic variables.

Two structural equations fall out of the individual's optimization problem: one has *work* as a function of the exogenous factors, demographics, and unobservables; the other has *crime* as a function of these same factors. Of course, it is always possible that factors treated as exogenous by the individual cannot be treated as exogenous by the econometrician: unobservables that affect the choice of *work* and *crime* could be correlated with the observable factors. But this possibility is an omitted variables problem. (Measurement error could also be an important issue in this example.) Whether or not omitted variables or measurement error are problems, each equation has a causal interpretation.

In the crime example, and many similar examples, it may be tempting to stop before completely solving the model—or to circumvent economic theory altogether—and specify a simultaneous equations system consisting of two equations. The first equation would describe *work* in terms of *crime*, while the second would have *crime* as a function of *work* (with other factors appearing in both equations). While it is often possible to write the first-order conditions for an optimization problem in this way, these equations are *not* the structural equations of interest. Neither equation can stand on its own, and neither has a causal interpretation. For example, what would it mean to study the effect of changing the market wage on hours spent in criminal activity, holding hours spent in legal employment fixed? An individual will generally adjust the time spent in both activities to a change in the market wage.

Often it *is* useful to determine how one endogenous choice variable trades off against another, but in such cases the goal is not—and should not be—to infer causality. For example, Biddle and Hamermesh (1990) present OLS regressions of minutes spent per week sleeping on minutes per week working (controlling for education, age, and other demographic and health factors). Biddle and Hamermesh recognize that there is nothing "structural" about such an analysis. (In fact, the choice of the dependent variable is largely arbitrary.) Biddle and Hamermesh (1990) *do* derive a structural model of the demand for sleep (along with a labor supply function) where a key explanatory variable is the wage offer. The demand for sleep has a causal interpretation, and it does *not* include labor supply on the right-hand side.

Why are SEM applications that do not satisfy the autonomy requirement so prevalent in applied work? One possibility is that there appears to be a general misperception that "structural" and "simultaneous" are synonymous. However, we already know that structural models need not be systems of simultaneous equations. And, as the crime/work example shows, a simultaneous system is not necessarily structural.

9.2 Identification in a Linear System

9.2.1 Exclusion Restrictions and Reduced Forms

Write a system of linear simultaneous equations for the population as

$$\begin{aligned} y_1 &= \mathbf{y}_{(1)}\gamma_{(1)} + \mathbf{z}_{(1)}\delta_{(1)} + u_1 \\ &\vdots \\ y_G &= \mathbf{y}_{(G)}\gamma_{(G)} + \mathbf{z}_{(G)}\delta_{(G)} + u_G \end{aligned} \tag{9.1}$$

where $\mathbf{y}_{(h)}$ is $1 \times G_h$, $\gamma_{(h)}$ is $G_h \times 1$, $\mathbf{z}_{(h)}$ is $1 \times M_h$, and $\delta_{(h)}$ is $M_h \times 1$, $h = 1, 2, \ldots, G$. These are **structural equations** for the **endogenous variables** $y_1, y_2, \ldots, y_G$. We will assume that, if the system (9.1) represents a true simultaneous equations model, then equilibrium conditions have been imposed. Hopefully, each equation is autonomous, but, of course, they do not need to be for the statistical analysis.

The vector $\mathbf{y}_{(h)}$ denotes endogenous variables that appear on the right-hand side of the hth structural equation. By convention, $\mathbf{y}_{(h)}$ can contain any of the endogenous variables $y_1, y_2, \ldots, y_G$ *except* for y_h. The variables in $\mathbf{z}_{(h)}$ are the **exogenous variables** appearing in equation h. Usually there is some overlap in the exogenous variables across different equations; for example, except in special circumstances each $\mathbf{z}_{(h)}$ would contain unity to allow for nonzero intercepts. The restrictions imposed in system (9.1) are called **exclusion restrictions** because certain endogenous and exogenous variables are excluded from some equations.

The $1 \times M$ vector of all exogenous variables $\mathbf{z}$ is assumed to satisfy

$$\mathrm{E}(\mathbf{z}'u_g) = \mathbf{0}, \qquad g = 1, 2, \ldots, G \tag{9.2}$$

When all of the equations in system (9.1) are truly structural, we are usually willing to assume

$$\mathrm{E}(u_g \mid \mathbf{z}) = 0, \qquad g = 1, 2, \ldots, G \tag{9.3}$$

However, we know from Chapters 5 and 8 that assumption (9.2) is sufficient for consistent estimation. Sometimes, especially in omitted variables and measurement error applications, one or more of the equations in system (9.1) will simply represent a linear projection onto exogenous variables, as in Example 8.2. It is for this reason that we use assumption (9.2) for most of our identification and estimation analysis. We assume throughout that $\mathrm{E}(\mathbf{z}'\mathbf{z})$ is nonsingular, so that there are no exact linear dependencies among the exogenous variables in the population.

Assumption (9.2) implies that the exogenous variables appearing anywhere in the system are orthogonal to *all* the structural errors. If some elements in, say, $\mathbf{z}_{(1)}$, do not appear in the second equation, then we are explicitly assuming that they do not enter the structural equation for y_2. If there are no reasonable exclusion restrictions in an SEM, it may be that the system fails the autonomy requirement.

Generally, in the system (9.1), the error u_g in equation g will be correlated with $\mathbf{y}_{(g)}$ (we show this correlation explicitly later), and so OLS and GLS will be inconsistent. Nevertheless, under certain identification assumptions, we can estimate this system using the instrumental variables procedures covered in Chapter 8.

In addition to the exclusion restrictions in system (9.1), another possible source of identifying information is on the $G \times G$ variance matrix $\boldsymbol{\Sigma} \equiv \mathrm{Var}(\mathbf{u})$. For now, $\boldsymbol{\Sigma}$ is unrestricted and therefore contains no identifying information.

To motivate the general analysis, consider specific labor supply and demand functions for some population:

$$h^s(\omega) = \gamma_1 \log(\omega) + \mathbf{z}_{(1)}\boldsymbol{\delta}_{(1)} + u_1$$

$$h^d(\omega) = \gamma_2 \log(\omega) + \mathbf{z}_{(2)}\boldsymbol{\delta}_{(2)} + u_2$$

where ω is the dummy argument in the labor supply and labor demand functions. We assume that observed hours, h, and observed wage, w, equate supply and demand:

$$h = h^s(w) = h^d(w)$$

The variables in $\mathbf{z}_{(1)}$ shift the labor supply curve, and $\mathbf{z}_{(2)}$ contains labor demand shifters. By defining $y_1 = h$ and $y_2 = \log(w)$ we can write the equations in equilibrium as a linear simultaneous equations model:

$$y_1 = \gamma_1 y_2 + \mathbf{z}_{(1)}\boldsymbol{\delta}_{(1)} + u_1 \tag{9.4}$$

$$y_1 = \gamma_2 y_2 + \mathbf{z}_{(2)}\boldsymbol{\delta}_{(2)} + u_2 \tag{9.5}$$

Nothing about the general system (9.1) rules out having the same variable on the left-hand side of more than one equation.

What is needed to identify the parameters in, say, the supply curve? Intuitively, since we observe only the equilibrium quantities of hours and wages, we cannot distinguish the supply function from the demand function if $\mathbf{z}_{(1)}$ and $\mathbf{z}_{(2)}$ contain exactly the same elements. If, however, $\mathbf{z}_{(2)}$ contains an element *not* in $\mathbf{z}_{(1)}$—that is, if there is some factor that exogenously shifts the demand curve but not the supply curve—then we can hope to estimate the parameters of the supply curve. To identify the demand curve, we need at least one element in $\mathbf{z}_{(1)}$ that is not also in $\mathbf{z}_{(2)}$.

To formally study identification, assume that $\gamma_1 \neq \gamma_2$; this assumption just means that the supply and demand curves have different slopes. Subtracting equation (9.5) from equation (9.4), dividing by $\gamma_2 - \gamma_1$, and rearranging gives

$$y_2 = \mathbf{z}_{(1)}\boldsymbol{\pi}_{21} + \mathbf{z}_{(2)}\boldsymbol{\pi}_{22} + v_2 \tag{9.6}$$

where $\boldsymbol{\pi}_{21} \equiv \boldsymbol{\delta}_{(1)}/(\gamma_2 - \gamma_1)$, $\boldsymbol{\pi}_{22} = -\boldsymbol{\delta}_{(2)}/(\gamma_2 - \gamma_1)$, and $v_2 \equiv (u_1 - u_2)/(\gamma_2 - \gamma_1)$. This is the **reduced form** for y_2 because it expresses y_2 as a linear function of all of the exogenous variables and an error v_2 which, by assumption (9.2), is orthogonal to all exogenous variables: $\mathrm{E}(\mathbf{z}'v_2) = \mathbf{0}$. Importantly, the reduced form for y_2 is obtained from the two structural equations (9.4) and (9.5).

Given equation (9.4) and the reduced form (9.6), we can now use the identification condition from Chapter 5 for a linear model with a single right-hand-side endogenous variable. This condition is easy to state: the reduced form for y_2 must contain at least one exogenous variable not also in equation (9.4). This means there must be at least one element of $\mathbf{z}_{(2)}$ not in $\mathbf{z}_{(1)}$ with coefficient in equation (9.6) different from zero. Now we use the structural equations. Because $\boldsymbol{\pi}_{22}$ is proportional to $\boldsymbol{\delta}_{(2)}$, the condition is easily restated in terms of the *structural* parameters: in equation (9.5) at least one element of $\mathbf{z}_{(2)}$ not in $\mathbf{z}_{(1)}$ must have nonzero coefficient. In the supply and demand example, identification of the supply function requires at least one exogenous variable appearing in the demand function that does not also appear in the supply function; this conclusion corresponds exactly with our earlier intuition.

The condition for identifying equation (9.5) is just the mirror image: there must be at least one element of $\mathbf{z}_{(1)}$ actually appearing in equation (9.4) that is not also an element of $\mathbf{z}_{(2)}$.

Example 9.1 (Labor Supply for Married Women): Consider labor supply and demand equations for married women, with the equilibrium condition imposed:

$$hours = \gamma_1 \log(wage) + \delta_{10} + \delta_{11} educ + \delta_{12} age + \delta_{13} kids + \delta_{14} othinc + u_1$$

$$hours = \gamma_2 \log(wage) + \delta_{20} + \delta_{21} educ + \delta_{22} exper + u_2$$

The supply equation is identified because, by assumption, *exper* appears in the demand function (assuming $\delta_{22} \neq 0$) but not in the supply equation. The assumption that past experience has no direct affect on labor supply can be questioned, but it has been used by labor economists. The demand equation is identified provided that at least one of the three variables *age*, *kids*, and *othinc* actually appears in the supply equation.

We now extend this analysis to the general system (9.1). For concreteness, we study identification of the first equation:

$$y_1 = \mathbf{y}_{(1)}\boldsymbol{\gamma}_{(1)} + \mathbf{z}_{(1)}\boldsymbol{\delta}_{(1)} + u_1 = \mathbf{x}_{(1)}\boldsymbol{\beta}_{(1)} + u_1 \tag{9.7}$$

where the notation used for the subscripts is needed to distinguish an equation with exclusion restrictions from a general equation that we will study in Section 9.2.2. Assuming that the reduced forms exist, write the reduced form for $\mathbf{y}_{(1)}$ as

$$\mathbf{y}_{(1)} = \mathbf{z}\boldsymbol{\Pi}_{(1)} + \mathbf{v}_{(1)} \tag{9.8}$$

where $\mathrm{E}[\mathbf{z}'\mathbf{v}_{(1)}] = \mathbf{0}$. Further, define the $M \times M_1$ matrix *selection matrix* $\mathbf{S}_{(1)}$, which consists of zeros and ones, such that $\mathbf{z}_{(1)} = \mathbf{z}\mathbf{S}_{(1)}$. The rank condition from Chapter 5, Assumption 2SLS.2b, can be stated as

$$\operatorname{rank} \mathrm{E}[\mathbf{z}'\mathbf{x}_{(1)}] = K_1 \tag{9.9}$$

where $K_1 \equiv G_1 + M_1$. But $\mathrm{E}[\mathbf{z}'\mathbf{x}_{(1)}] = \mathrm{E}[\mathbf{z}'(\mathbf{z}\boldsymbol{\Pi}_{(1)}, \mathbf{z}\mathbf{S}_{(1)})] = \mathrm{E}(\mathbf{z}'\mathbf{z})[\boldsymbol{\Pi}_{(1)} \mid \mathbf{S}_{(1)}]$. Since we always assume that $\mathrm{E}(\mathbf{z}'\mathbf{z})$ has full rank M, assumption (9.9) is the same as

$$\operatorname{rank}[\boldsymbol{\Pi}_{(1)} \mid \mathbf{S}_{(1)}] = G_1 + M_1 \tag{9.10}$$

In other words, $[\boldsymbol{\Pi}_{(1)} \mid \mathbf{S}_{(1)}]$ must have full column rank. If the reduced form for $\mathbf{y}_{(1)}$ has been found, this condition can be checked directly. But there is one thing we can conclude immediately: because $[\boldsymbol{\Pi}_{(1)} \mid \mathbf{S}_{(1)}]$ is an $M \times (G_1 + M_1)$ matrix, a *necessary* condition for assumption (9.10) is $M \geq G_1 + M_1$, or

$$M - M_1 \geq G_1 \tag{9.11}$$

We have already encountered condition (9.11) in Chapter 5: the number of exogenous variables not appearing in the first equation, $M - M_1$, must be at least as great as the number of endogenous variables appearing on the right-hand side of the first equation, G_1. This is the **order condition** for identification of equation one. We have proven the following theorem:

THEOREM 9.1 (Order Condition with Exclusion Restrictions): In a linear system of equations with exclusion restrictions, a *necessary* condition for identifying any particular equation is that the number of excluded exogenous variables from the equation must be at least as large as the number of included right-hand-side endogenous variables in the equation.

It is important to remember that the order condition is only necessary, not sufficient, for identification. If the order condition fails for a particular equation, there is no hope of estimating the parameters in that equation. If the order condition is met, the equation *might* be identified.

9.2.2 General Linear Restrictions and Structural Equations

The identification analysis of the preceding subsection is useful when reduced forms are appended to structural equations. When an entire structural system has been specified, it is best to study identification entirely in terms of the structural parameters.

To this end, we now write the G equations in the population as

$$\begin{aligned} \mathbf{y}\gamma_1 + \mathbf{z}\delta_1 + u_1 &= 0 \\ &\vdots \\ \mathbf{y}\gamma_G + \mathbf{z}\delta_G + u_G &= 0 \end{aligned} \tag{9.12}$$

where $\mathbf{y} \equiv (y_1, y_2, \ldots, y_G)$ is the $1 \times G$ vector of *all* endogenous variables and $\mathbf{z} \equiv (z_1, \ldots, z_M)$ is still the $1 \times M$ vector of all exogenous variables, and probably contains unity. We maintain assumption (9.2) throughout this section and also assume that $\mathrm{E}(\mathbf{z}'\mathbf{z})$ is nonsingular. The notation here differs from that in Section 9.2.1. Here, γ_g is $G \times 1$ and δ_g is $M \times 1$ for all $g = 1, 2, \ldots, G$, so that the system (9.12) is the general linear system without *any* restrictions on the structural parameters.

We can write this system compactly as

$$\mathbf{y\Gamma} + \mathbf{z\Delta} + \mathbf{u} = \mathbf{0} \tag{9.13}$$

where $\mathbf{u} \equiv (u_1, \ldots, u_G)$ is the $1 \times G$ vector of structural errors, $\mathbf{\Gamma}$ is the $G \times G$ matrix with gth column γ_g, and $\mathbf{\Delta}$ is the $M \times G$ matrix with gth column δ_g. So that a reduced form exists, we assume that $\mathbf{\Gamma}$ is nonsingular. Let $\mathbf{\Sigma} \equiv \mathrm{E}(\mathbf{u}'\mathbf{u})$ denote the $G \times G$ variance matrix of $\mathbf{u}$, which we assume to be nonsingular. At this point, we have placed no other restrictions on $\mathbf{\Gamma}$, $\mathbf{\Delta}$, or $\mathbf{\Sigma}$.

The reduced form is easily expressed as

$$\mathbf{y} = \mathbf{z}(-\mathbf{\Delta}\mathbf{\Gamma}^{-1}) + \mathbf{u}(-\mathbf{\Gamma}^{-1}) \equiv \mathbf{z}\mathbf{\Pi} + \mathbf{v} \tag{9.14}$$

where $\mathbf{\Pi} \equiv (-\mathbf{\Delta}\mathbf{\Gamma}^{-1})$ and $\mathbf{v} \equiv \mathbf{u}(-\mathbf{\Gamma}^{-1})$. Define $\mathbf{\Lambda} \equiv \mathrm{E}(\mathbf{v}'\mathbf{v}) = \mathbf{\Gamma}^{-1\prime}\mathbf{\Sigma}\mathbf{\Gamma}^{-1}$ as the reduced form variance matrix. Because $\mathrm{E}(\mathbf{z}'\mathbf{v}) = \mathbf{0}$ and $\mathrm{E}(\mathbf{z}'\mathbf{z})$ is nonsingular, $\mathbf{\Pi}$ and $\mathbf{\Lambda}$ are identified because they can be consistently estimated given a random sample on $\mathbf{y}$ and $\mathbf{z}$ by OLS equation by equation. The question is, Under what assumptions can we recover the structural parameters $\mathbf{\Gamma}$, $\mathbf{\Delta}$, and $\mathbf{\Sigma}$ from the reduced form parameters?

It is easy to see that, without some restrictions, we will not be able to identify any of the parameters in the structural system. Let $\mathbf{F}$ be any $G \times G$ nonsingular matrix, and postmultiply equation (9.13) by $\mathbf{F}$:

$$\mathbf{y}\mathbf{\Gamma}\mathbf{F} + \mathbf{z}\mathbf{\Delta}\mathbf{F} + \mathbf{u}\mathbf{F} = \mathbf{0} \qquad \text{or} \qquad \mathbf{y}\mathbf{\Gamma}^* + \mathbf{z}\mathbf{\Delta}^* + \mathbf{u}^* = \mathbf{0} \tag{9.15}$$

where $\mathbf{\Gamma}^* \equiv \mathbf{\Gamma}\mathbf{F}$, $\mathbf{\Delta}^* \equiv \mathbf{\Delta}\mathbf{F}$, and $\mathbf{u}^* \equiv \mathbf{u}\mathbf{F}$; note that $\mathrm{Var}(\mathbf{u}^*) = \mathbf{F}'\mathbf{\Sigma}\mathbf{F}$. Simple algebra shows that equations (9.15) and (9.13) have *identical* reduced forms. This result means that, without restrictions on the structural parameters, there are many **equivalent structures** in the sense that they lead to the same reduced form. In fact, there is an equivalent structure for each nonsingular $\mathbf{F}$.

Let $\mathbf{B} \equiv \begin{pmatrix} \mathbf{\Gamma} \\ \mathbf{\Delta} \end{pmatrix}$ be the $(G + M) \times G$ matrix of structural parameters in equation (9.13). If $\mathbf{F}$ is any nonsingular $G \times G$ matrix, then $\mathbf{F}$ represents an **admissible linear transformation** if

1. $\mathbf{BF}$ satisfies all restrictions on $\mathbf{B}$.
2. $\mathbf{F}'\mathbf{\Sigma}\mathbf{F}$ satisfies all restrictions on $\mathbf{\Sigma}$.

To identify the system, we need enough prior information on the structural parameters $(\mathbf{B}, \mathbf{\Sigma})$ so that $\mathbf{F} = \mathbf{I}_G$ is the only admissible linear transformation.

In most applications identification of $\mathbf{B}$ is of primary interest, and this identification is achieved by putting restrictions directly on $\mathbf{B}$. As we will touch on in Section 9.4.2, it is possible to put restrictions on $\mathbf{\Sigma}$ in order to identify $\mathbf{B}$, but this approach is somewhat rare in practice. Until we come to Section 9.4.2, $\mathbf{\Sigma}$ is an unrestricted $G \times G$ positive definite matrix.

As before, we consider identification of the first equation:

$$\mathbf{y}\boldsymbol{\gamma}_1 + \mathbf{z}\boldsymbol{\delta}_1 + u_1 = 0 \tag{9.16}$$

or $\gamma_{11}y_1 + \gamma_{12}y_2 + \cdots + \gamma_{1G}y_G + \delta_{11}z_1 + \delta_{12}z_2 + \cdots + \delta_{1M}z_M + u_1 = 0$. The first restriction we make on the parameters in equation (9.16) is the **normalization restriction** that one element of $\boldsymbol{\gamma}_1$ is -1. Each equation in the system (9.1) has a normalization restriction because one variable is taken to be the left-hand-side explained variable. In applications, there is usually a natural normalization for each equation. If there is not, we should ask whether the system satisfies the autonomy requirement discussed in Section 9.1. (Even in models that satisfy the autonomy requirement, we often have to choose between reasonable normalization conditions. For example, in Example 9.1, we could have specified the second equation to be a wage offer equation rather than a labor demand equation.)

Let $\boldsymbol{\beta}_1 \equiv (\boldsymbol{\gamma}_1', \boldsymbol{\delta}_1')'$ be the $(G+M) \times 1$ vector of structural parameters in the first equation. With a normalization restriction there are $(G+M) - 1$ unknown elements in $\boldsymbol{\beta}_1$. Assume that prior knowledge about $\boldsymbol{\beta}_1$ can be expressed as

$$\mathbf{R}_1\boldsymbol{\beta}_1 = \mathbf{0} \tag{9.17}$$

where $\mathbf{R}_1$ is a $J_1 \times (G+M)$ matrix of known constants, and J_1 is the number of restrictions on $\boldsymbol{\beta}_1$ (in addition to the normalization restriction). We assume that rank $\mathbf{R}_1 = J_1$, so that there are no redundant restrictions. The restrictions in assumption (9.17) are sometimes called **homogeneous linear restrictions**, but, when coupled with a normalization assumption, equation (9.17) actually allows for nonhomogeneous restrictions.

Example 9.2 (A Three-Equation System): Consider the first equation in a system with $G = 3$ and $M = 4$:

$$y_1 = \gamma_{12}y_2 + \gamma_{13}y_3 + \delta_{11}z_1 + \delta_{12}z_2 + \delta_{13}z_3 + \delta_{14}z_4 + u_1$$

so that $\boldsymbol{\gamma}_1 = (-1, \gamma_{12}, \gamma_{13})'$, $\boldsymbol{\delta}_1 = (\delta_{11}, \delta_{12}, \delta_{13}, \delta_{14})'$, and $\boldsymbol{\beta}_1 = (-1, \gamma_{12}, \gamma_{13}, \delta_{11}, \delta_{12}, \delta_{13}, \delta_{14})'$. (We can set $z_1 = 1$ to allow an intercept.) Suppose the restrictions on the structural parameters are $\gamma_{12} = 0$ and $\delta_{13} + \delta_{14} = 3$. Then $J_1 = 2$ and

$$\mathbf{R}_1 = \begin{pmatrix} 0 & 1 & 0 & 0 & 0 & 0 & 0 \\ 3 & 0 & 0 & 0 & 0 & 1 & 1 \end{pmatrix}$$

Straightforward multiplication gives $\mathbf{R}_1\boldsymbol{\beta}_1 = (\gamma_{12}, \delta_{13} + \delta_{14} - 3)'$, and setting this vector to zero as in equation (9.17) incorporates the restrictions on $\boldsymbol{\beta}_1$.

Given the linear restrictions in equation (9.17), when are these and the normalization restriction enough to identify $\boldsymbol{\beta}_1$? Let $\mathbf{F}$ again be any $G \times G$ nonsingular matrix, and write it in terms of its columns as $\mathbf{F} = (\mathbf{f}_1, \mathbf{f}_2, \ldots, \mathbf{f}_G)$. Define a linear transformation of $\mathbf{B}$ as $\mathbf{B}^* = \mathbf{BF}$, so that the first column of $\mathbf{B}^*$ is $\boldsymbol{\beta}_1^* \equiv \mathbf{Bf}_1$. We need to find a condition so that equation (9.17) allows us to distinguish $\boldsymbol{\beta}_1$ from any other $\boldsymbol{\beta}_1^*$. For the moment, ignore the normalization condition. The vector $\boldsymbol{\beta}_1^*$ satisfies the linear restrictions embodied by $\mathbf{R}_1$ if and only if

$$\mathbf{R}_1\boldsymbol{\beta}_1^* = \mathbf{R}_1(\mathbf{Bf}_1) = (\mathbf{R}_1\mathbf{B})\mathbf{f}_1 = \mathbf{0} \tag{9.18}$$

Naturally, $(\mathbf{R}_1\mathbf{B})\mathbf{f}_1 = \mathbf{0}$ is true for $\mathbf{f}_1 = \mathbf{e}_1 \equiv (1, 0, 0, \ldots, 0)'$, since then $\boldsymbol{\beta}_1^* = \mathbf{Bf}_1 = \boldsymbol{\beta}_1$. Since assumption (9.18) holds for $\mathbf{f}_1 = \mathbf{e}_1$ it clearly holds for any scalar multiple of $\mathbf{e}_1$. The key to identification is that vectors of the form $c_1\mathbf{e}_1$, for some constant c_1, are the *only* vectors $\mathbf{f}_1$ satisfying condition (9.18). If condition (9.18) holds for vectors $\mathbf{f}_1$ other than scalar multiples of $\mathbf{e}_1$ then we have no hope of identifying $\boldsymbol{\beta}_1$.

Stating that condition (9.18) holds only for vectors of the form $c_1\mathbf{e}_1$ just means that the null space of $\mathbf{R}_1\mathbf{B}$ has dimension unity. Equivalently, because $\mathbf{R}_1\mathbf{B}$ has G columns,

$$\text{rank } \mathbf{R}_1\mathbf{B} = G - 1 \tag{9.19}$$

This is the **rank condition** for identification of $\boldsymbol{\beta}_1$ in the first structural equation under general linear restrictions. Once condition (9.19) is known to hold, the normalization restriction allows us to distinguish $\boldsymbol{\beta}_1$ from any other scalar multiple of $\boldsymbol{\beta}_1$.

THEOREM 9.2 (Rank Condition for Identification): Let $\boldsymbol{\beta}_1$ be the $(G + M) \times 1$ vector of structural parameters in the first equation, with the normalization restriction that one of the coefficients on an endogenous variable is -1. Let the additional information on $\boldsymbol{\beta}_1$ be given by restriction (9.17). Then $\boldsymbol{\beta}_1$ is identified if and only if the rank condition (9.19) holds.

As promised earlier, the rank condition in this subsection depends on the *structural* parameters, $\mathbf{B}$. We can determine whether the first equation is identified by studying the matrix $\mathbf{R}_1\mathbf{B}$. Since this matrix can depend on *all* structural parameters, we must generally specify the entire structural model.

The $J_1 \times G$ matrix $\mathbf{R}_1\mathbf{B}$ can be written as $\mathbf{R}_1\mathbf{B} = [\mathbf{R}_1\boldsymbol{\beta}_1, \mathbf{R}_1\boldsymbol{\beta}_2, \ldots, \mathbf{R}_1\boldsymbol{\beta}_G]$, where $\boldsymbol{\beta}_g$ is the $(G + M) \times 1$ vector of structural parameters in equation g. By assumption (9.17), the first column of $\mathbf{R}_1\mathbf{B}$ is the zero vector. Therefore, $\mathbf{R}_1\mathbf{B}$ cannot have rank larger than $G - 1$. What we must check is whether the columns of $\mathbf{R}_1\mathbf{B}$ other than the first form a linearly independent set.

Using condition (9.19) we can get a more general form of the order condition. Because $\boldsymbol{\Gamma}$ is nonsingular, $\mathbf{B}$ necessarily has rank G (full column rank). Therefore, for condition (9.19) to hold, we must have rank $\mathbf{R}_1 \geq G - 1$. But we have assumed that rank $\mathbf{R}_1 = J_1$, which is the row dimension of $\mathbf{R}_1$.

THEOREM 9.3 (Order Condition for Identification): In system (9.12) under assumption (9.17), a *necessary* condition for the first equation to be identified is

$$J_1 \geq G - 1 \tag{9.20}$$

where J_1 is the row dimension of $\mathbf{R}_1$. Equation (9.20) is the general form of the order condition.

We can summarize the steps for checking whether the first equation in the system is identified.

1. Set one element of γ_1 to -1 as a normalization.
2. Define the $J_1 \times (G + M)$ matrix $\mathbf{R}_1$ such that equation (9.17) captures all restrictions on $\boldsymbol{\beta}_1$.
3. If $J_1 < G - 1$, the first equation is not identified.
4. If $J_1 \geq G - 1$, the equation might be identified. Let $\mathbf{B}$ be the matrix of all structural parameters with only the normalization restrictions imposed, and compute $\mathbf{R}_1\mathbf{B}$. Now impose the restrictions in the entire system and check the rank condition (9.19).

The simplicity of the order condition makes it attractive as a tool for studying identification. Nevertheless, it is not difficult to write down examples where the order condition is satisfied but the rank condition fails.

Example 9.3 (Failure of the Rank Condition): Consider the following three-equation structural model in the population ($G = 3$, $M = 4$):

$$y_1 = \gamma_{12} y_2 + \gamma_{13} y_3 + \delta_{11} z_1 + \delta_{13} z_3 + u_1 \tag{9.21}$$

$$y_2 = \gamma_{21} y_1 + \delta_{21} z_1 + u_2 \tag{9.22}$$

$$y_3 = \delta_{31} z_1 + \delta_{32} z_2 + \delta_{33} z_3 + \delta_{34} z_4 + u_3 \tag{9.23}$$

where $z_1 \equiv 1$, $\mathrm{E}(u_g) = 0$, $g = 1, 2, 3$, and each z_j is uncorrelated with each u_g. Note that the third equation is already a reduced form equation (although it may also have a structural interpretation). In equation (9.21) we have set $\gamma_{11} = -1$, $\delta_{12} = 0$, and $\delta_{14} = 0$. Since this equation contains two right-hand-side endogenous variables and there are two excluded exogenous variables, it passes the order condition.

To check the rank condition, let $\boldsymbol{\beta}_1$ denote the 7×1 vector of parameters in the first equation with only the normalization restriction imposed: $\boldsymbol{\beta}_1 = (-1, \gamma_{12}, \gamma_{13}, \delta_{11}, \delta_{12}, \delta_{13}, \delta_{14})'$. The restrictions $\delta_{12} = 0$ and $\delta_{14} = 0$ are obtained by choosing

$$\mathbf{R}_1 = \begin{pmatrix} 0 & 0 & 0 & 0 & 1 & 0 & 0 \\ 0 & 0 & 0 & 0 & 0 & 0 & 1 \end{pmatrix}$$

Let $\mathbf{B}$ be the full 7×3 matrix of parameters with only the three normalizations imposed [so that $\boldsymbol{\beta}_2 = (\gamma_{21}, -1, \gamma_{23}, \delta_{21}, \delta_{22}, \delta_{23}, \delta_{24})'$ and $\boldsymbol{\beta}_3 = (\gamma_{31}, \gamma_{32}, -1, \delta_{31}, \delta_{32}, \delta_{33}, \delta_{34})'$]. Matrix multiplication gives

$$\mathbf{R}_1\mathbf{B} = \begin{pmatrix} \delta_{12} & \delta_{22} & \delta_{32} \\ \delta_{14} & \delta_{24} & \delta_{34} \end{pmatrix}$$

Now we impose all of the restrictions in the system. In addition to the restrictions $\delta_{12} = 0$ and $\delta_{14} = 0$ from equation (9.21), we also have $\delta_{22} = 0$ and $\delta_{24} = 0$ from equation (9.22). Therefore, with all restrictions imposed,

$$\mathbf{R}_1\mathbf{B} = \begin{pmatrix} 0 & 0 & \delta_{32} \\ 0 & 0 & \delta_{34} \end{pmatrix} \tag{9.24}$$

The rank of this matrix is at most unity, and so the rank condition fails because $G - 1 = 2$.

Equation (9.22) easily passes the order condition. It is left to you to show that the rank condition holds if and only if $\delta_{13} \neq 0$ and at least one of δ_{32} and δ_{34} is different from zero. The third equation is identified because it contains no endogenous explanatory variables.

When the restrictions on $\boldsymbol{\beta}_1$ consist entirely of normalization and exclusion restrictions, the order condition (9.20) reduces to the order condition (9.11), as can be seen by the following argument. When all restrictions are exclusion restrictions, the matrix $\mathbf{R}_1$ consists only of zeros and ones, and the number of rows in $\mathbf{R}_1$ equals the number of excluded right-hand-side endogenous variables, $G - G_1 - 1$, plus the number of excluded exogenous variables, $M - M_1$. In other words, $J_1 = (G - G_1 - 1) + (M - M_1)$, and so the order condition (9.20) becomes $(G - G_1 - 1) + (M - M_1) \geq G - 1$, which, upon rearrangement, becomes condition (9.11).

9.2.3 Unidentified, Just Identified, and Overidentified Equations

We have seen that, for identifying a single equation the rank condition (9.19) is necessary and sufficient. When condition (9.19) fails, we say that the equation is **unidentified**.

When the rank condition holds, it is useful to refine the sense in which the equation is identified. If $J_1 = G - 1$, then we have just enough identifying information. If we were to drop one restriction in $\mathbf{R}_1$, we would necessarily lose identification of the first equation because the order condition would fail. Therefore, when $J_1 = G - 1$, we say that the equation is **just identified**.

If $J_1 > G - 1$, it is often possible to drop one or more restrictions on the parameters of the first equation and still achieve identification. In this case we say the equation is **overidentified**. Necessary but not sufficient for overidentification is $J_1 > G - 1$. It is possible that J_1 is strictly greater than $G - 1$ but the restrictions are such that dropping one restriction loses identification, in which case the equation is not overidentified.

In practice, we often appeal to the order condition to determine the degree of overidentification. While in special circumstances this approach can fail to be accurate, for most applications it is reasonable. Thus, for the first equation, $J_1 - (G - 1)$ is usually intepreted as the number of **overidentifying restrictions**.

Example 9.4 (Overidentifying Restrictions): Consider the two-equation system

$$y_1 = \gamma_{12} y_2 + \delta_{11} z_1 + \delta_{12} z_2 + \delta_{13} z_3 + \delta_{14} z_4 + u_1 \tag{9.25}$$

$$y_2 = \gamma_{21} y_1 + \delta_{21} z_1 + \delta_{22} z_2 + u_2 \tag{9.26}$$

where $\mathrm{E}(z_j u_g) = 0$, all j and g. Without further restrictions, equation (9.25) fails the order condition because every exogenous variable appears on the right-hand side, and the equation contains an endogenous variable. Using the order condition, equation (9.26) is overidentified, with one overidentifying restriction. If z_3 does not actually appear in equation (9.25), then equation (9.26) is just identified, assuming that $\delta_{14} \neq 0$.

9.3 Estimation after Identification

9.3.1 The Robustness-Efficiency Trade-off

All SEMs with linearly homogeneous restrictions within each equation can be written with exclusion restrictions as in the system (9.1); doing so may require redefining some of the variables. If we let $\mathbf{x}_{(g)} = (\mathbf{y}_{(g)}, \mathbf{z}_{(g)})$ and $\boldsymbol{\beta}_{(g)} = (\boldsymbol{\gamma}'_{(g)}, \boldsymbol{\delta}'_{(g)})'$, then the system (9.1) is in the general form (8.11) with the slight change in notation. Under assumption (9.2) the matrix of instruments for observation i is the $G \times GM$ matrix

$$\mathbf{Z}_i \equiv \mathbf{I}_G \otimes \mathbf{z}_i \tag{9.27}$$

If every equation in the system passes the rank condition, a system estimation procedure—such as 3SLS or the more general minimum chi-square estimator—can be used. Alternatively, the equations of interest can be estimated by 2SLS. The bottom line is that the methods studied in Chapters 5 and 8 are directly applicable. All of the tests we have covered apply, including the tests of overidentifying restrictions in Chapters 6 and 8, and the single-equation tests for endogeneity in Chapter 6.

When estimating a simultaneous equations system, it is important to remember the pros and cons of full system estimation. If all equations are correctly specified, system procedures are asymptotically more efficient than a single-equation procedure such as 2SLS. But single-equation methods are more robust. If interest lies, say, in the first equation of a system, 2SLS is consistent and asymptotically normal provided the first equation is correctly specified and the instruments are exogenous. However, if one equation in a system is misspecified, the 3SLS or GMM estimates of all the parameters are generally inconsistent.

Example 9.5 (Labor Supply for Married, Working Women): Using the data in MROZ.RAW, we estimate a labor supply function for working, married women. Rather than specify a demand function, we specify the second equation as a wage offer function and impose the equilibrium condition:

$$hours = \gamma_{12} \log(wage) + \delta_{10} + \delta_{11} educ + \delta_{12} age + \delta_{13} kidslt6 + \delta_{14} kidsge6 + \delta_{15} nwifeinc + u_1 \tag{9.28}$$

$$\log(wage) = \gamma_{21} hours + \delta_{20} + \delta_{21} educ + \delta_{22} exper + \delta_{23} exper^2 + u_2 \tag{9.29}$$

where *kidslt6* is number of children less than 6, *kidsge6* is number of children between 6 and 18, and *nwifeinc* is income other than the woman's labor income. We assume that u_1 and u_2 have zero mean conditional on *educ*, *age*, *kidslt6*, *kidsge6*, *nwifeinc*, and *exper*.

The key restriction on the labor supply function is that *exper* (and $exper^2$) have no direct effect on current annual hours. This identifies the labor supply function with one overidentifying restriction, as used by Mroz (1987). We estimate the labor supply function first by OLS [to see what ignoring the endogeneity of log(*wage*) does] and then by 2SLS, using as instruments all exogenous variables in equations (9.28) and (9.29).

There are 428 women who worked at some time during the survey year, 1975. The average annual hours are about 1,303 with a minimum of 12 and a maximum of 4,950.

We first estimate the labor supply function by OLS:

$$\underset{}{\widehat{hours}} = \underset{(340.1)}{2{,}114.7} - \underset{(54.22)}{17.41} \log(wage) - \underset{(17.97)}{14.44}\, educ - \underset{(5.53)}{7.73}\, age$$

$$- \underset{(100.01)}{342.50}\, kidslt6 - \underset{(30.83)}{115.02}\, kidsge6 - \underset{(3.66)}{4.35}\, nwifeinc$$

The OLS estimates indicate a downward-sloping labor supply function, although the estimate on log(*wage*) is statistically insignificant.

The estimates are much different when we use 2SLS:

$$\widehat{hours} = \underset{(594.2)}{2{,}432.2} + \underset{(480.74)}{1{,}544.82}\ \log(wage) - \underset{(58.14)}{177.45}\ educ - \underset{(9.58)}{10.78}\ age$$

$$- \underset{(176.93)}{210.83}\ kidslt6 - \underset{(56.92)}{47.56}\ kidsge6 - \underset{(6.48)}{9.25}\ nwifeinc$$

The estimated labor supply elasticity is 1,544.82/*hours*. At the mean *hours* for working women, 1,303, the estimated elasticity is about 1.2, which is quite large.

The supply equation has a single overidentifying restriction. The regression of the 2SLS residuals $\hat{u}_1$ on all exogenous variables produces $R_u^2 = .002$, and so the test statistic is $428(.002) \approx .856$ with p-value $\approx .355$; the overidentifying restriction is not rejected.

Under the exclusion restrictions we have imposed, the wage offer function (9.29) is also identified. Before estimating the equation by 2SLS, we first estimate the reduced form for *hours* to ensure that the exogenous variables excluded from equation (9.29) are jointly significant. The p-value for the F test of joint significance of *age*, *kidslt6*, *kidsge6*, and *nwifeinc* is about .0009. Therefore, we can proceed with 2SLS estimation of the wage offer equation. The coefficient on *hours* is about .00016 (standard error $\approx .00022$), and so the wage offer does not appear to differ by hours worked. The remaining coefficients are similar to what is obtained by dropping *hours* from equation (9.29) and estimating the equation by OLS. (For example, the 2SLS coefficient on education is about .111 with se $\approx .015$.)

Interestingly, while the wage offer function (9.29) is identified, the analogous labor demand function is apparently unidentified. (This finding shows that choosing the normalization—that is, choosing between a labor demand function and a wage offer function—is not innocuous.) The labor demand function, written in equilibrium, would look like this:

$$hours = \gamma_{22} \log(wage) + \delta_{20} + \delta_{21} educ + \delta_{22} exper + \delta_{23} exper^2 + u_2 \tag{9.30}$$

Estimating the reduced form for log(*wage*) and testing for joint significance of *age*, *kidslt6*, *kidsge6*, and *nwifeinc* yields a p-value of about .46, and so the exogenous variables excluded from equation (9.30) would not seem to appear in the reduced form for log(*wage*). Estimation of equation (9.30) by 2SLS would be pointless. [You are invited to estimate equation (9.30) by 2SLS to see what happens.]

It would be more efficient to estimate equations (9.28) and (9.29) by 3SLS, since each equation is overidentified (assuming the homoskedasticity assumption SIV.5). If heteroskedasticity is suspected, we could use the general minimum chi-square estimator. A system procedure is more efficient for estimating the labor supply function because it uses the information that *age*, *kidslt6*, *kidsge6*, and *nwifeinc* do not appear in the log(*wage*) equation. If these exclusion restrictions are wrong, the 3SLS estimators of parameters in *both* equations are generally inconsistent. Problem 9.9 asks you to obtain the 3SLS estimates for this example.

9.3.2 When Are 2SLS and 3SLS Equivalent?

In Section 8.4 we discussed the relationship between 2SLS and 3SLS for a general linear system. Applying that discussion to linear SEMs, we can immediately draw the following conclusions: (1) if each equation is just identified, 2SLS equation by equation is algebraically identical to 3SLS, which is the same as the IV estimator in equation (8.22); (2) regardless of the degree of overidentification, 2SLS equation by equation and 3SLS are identical if $\hat{\boldsymbol{\Sigma}}$ is diagonal.

Another useful equivalence result in the context of linear SEMs is as follows. Suppose that the first equation in a system is overidentified but every other equation is just identified. (A special case occurs when the first equation is a structural equation and all remaining equations are unrestricted reduced forms.) Then the 2SLS estimator of the first equation is the same as the 3SLS estimator. This result follows as a special case of Schmidt (1976, Theorem 5.2.13).

9.3.3 Estimating the Reduced Form Parameters

So far, we have discussed estimation of the structural parameters. The usual justifications for focusing on the structural parameters are as follows: (1) we are interested in estimates of "economic parameters" (such as labor supply elasticities) for curiosity's sake; (2) estimates of structural parameters allow us to obtain the effects of a variety of policy interventions (such as changes in tax rates); and (3) even if we want to estimate the reduced form parameters, we often can do so more efficiently by first estimating the structural parameters. Concerning the second reason, if the goal is to estimate, say, the equilibrium change in hours worked given an exogenous change in a marginal tax rate, we must ultimately estimate the reduced form.

As another example, we might want to estimate the effect on county-level alcohol consumption due to an increase in exogenous alcohol taxes. In other words, we are interested in $\partial \mathrm{E}(y_g \mid \mathbf{z})/\partial z_j = \pi_{gj}$, where y_g is alcohol consumption and z_j is the tax on alcohol. Under weak assumptions, reduced form equations exist, and each equation of the reduced form can be estimated by ordinary least squares. Without placing any restrictions on the reduced form, OLS equation by equation is identical to SUR estimation (see Section 7.7). In other words, we do not need to analyze the structural equations at all in order to consistently estimate the reduced form parameters. Ordinary least squares estimates of the reduced form parameters are robust in the sense that they do not rely on any identification assumptions imposed on the structural system.

If the structural model is correctly specified and at least one equation is overidentified, we obtain asymptotically more efficient estimators of the reduced form parameters by deriving the estimates from the structural parameter estimates. In particular, given the structural parameter estimates $\hat{\mathbf{\Delta}}$ and $\hat{\mathbf{\Gamma}}$, we can obtain the reduced form estimates as $\hat{\mathbf{\Pi}} = -\hat{\mathbf{\Delta}}\hat{\mathbf{\Gamma}}^{-1}$ [see equation (9.14)]. These are consistent, $\sqrt{N}$-asymptotically normal estimators (although the asymptotic variance matrix is somewhat complicated). From Problem 3.9, we obtain the most efficient estimator of $\mathbf{\Pi}$ by using the most efficient estimators of $\mathbf{\Delta}$ and $\mathbf{\Gamma}$ (minimum chi-square or, under system homoskedasticity, 3SLS).

Just as in estimating the structural parameters, there is a robustness-efficiency trade-off in estimating the π_{gj}. As mentioned earlier, the OLS estimators of each reduced form are robust to misspecification of any restrictions on the structural equations (although, as always, each element of $\mathbf{z}$ should be exogenous for OLS to be consistent). The estimators of the π_{gj} derived from estimators of $\mathbf{\Delta}$ and $\mathbf{\Gamma}$—whether the latter are 2SLS or system estimators—are generally nonrobust to incorrect restrictions on the structural system. See Problem 9.11 for a simple illustration.

9.4 Additional Topics in Linear SEMs

9.4.1 Using Cross Equation Restrictions to Achieve Identification

So far we have discussed identification of a single equation using only within-equation parameter restrictions [see assumption (9.17)]. This is by far the leading case, especially when the system represents a simultaneous equations model with truly autonomous equations. Nevertheless, occasionally economic theory implies parameter restrictions across different equations in a system that contains endogenous variables. Not surprisingly, such **cross equation restrictions** are generally useful for identifying equations. A general treatment is beyond the scope of our analysis. Here we just give an example to show how identification and estimation work.

Consider the two-equation system

$$y_1 = \gamma_{12} y_2 + \delta_{11} z_1 + \delta_{12} z_2 + \delta_{13} z_3 + u_1 \tag{9.31}$$

$$y_2 = \gamma_{21} y_1 + \delta_{21} z_1 + \delta_{22} z_2 + u_2 \tag{9.32}$$

where each z_j is uncorrelated with u_1 and u_2 (z_1 can be unity to allow for an intercept). Without further information, equation (9.31) is unidentified, and equation (9.32) is just identified if and only if $\delta_{13} \neq 0$. We maintain these assumptions in what follows.

Now suppose that $\delta_{12} = \delta_{22}$. Because δ_{22} is identified in equation (9.32) we can treat it as known for studying identification of equation (9.31). But $\delta_{12} = \delta_{22}$, and so we can write

$$y_1 - \delta_{12} z_2 = \gamma_{12} y_2 + \delta_{11} z_1 + \delta_{13} z_3 + u_1 \tag{9.33}$$

where $y_1 - \delta_{12} z_2$ is effectively known. Now the right-hand side of equation (9.33) has one endogenous variable, y_2, and the two exogenous variables z_1 and z_3. Because z_2 is excluded from the right-hand side, we can use z_2 as an instrument for y_2, as long as z_2 appears in the reduced form for y_2. This is the case provided $\delta_{12} = \delta_{22} \neq 0$.

This approach to showing that equation (9.31) is identified also suggests a consistent estimation procedure: first, estimate equation (9.32) by 2SLS using (z_1, z_2, z_3) as instruments, and let $\hat{\delta}_{22}$ be the estimator of δ_{22}. Then, estimate

$$y_1 - \hat{\delta}_{22} z_2 = \gamma_{12} y_2 + \delta_{11} z_1 + \delta_{13} z_3 + error$$

by 2SLS using (z_1, z_2, z_3) as instruments. Since $\hat{\delta}_{22} \xrightarrow{p} \delta_{12}$ when $\delta_{12} = \delta_{22} \neq 0$, this last step produces consistent estimators of γ_{12}, δ_{11}, and δ_{13}. Unfortunately, the usual 2SLS standard errors obtained from the final estimation would not be valid because of the preliminary estimation of δ_{22}.

It is easier to use a system procedure when cross equation restrictions are present because the asymptotic variance can be obtained directly. We can always rewrite the system in a linear form with the restrictions imposed. For this example, one way to do so is to write the system as

$$\begin{pmatrix} y_1 \\ y_2 \end{pmatrix} = \begin{pmatrix} y_2 & z_1 & z_2 & z_3 & 0 & 0 \\ 0 & 0 & z_2 & 0 & y_1 & z_1 \end{pmatrix} \boldsymbol{\beta} + \begin{pmatrix} u_1 \\ u_2 \end{pmatrix} \tag{9.34}$$

where $\boldsymbol{\beta} = (\gamma_{12}, \delta_{11}, \delta_{12}, \delta_{13}, \gamma_{21}, \delta_{21})'$. The parameter δ_{22} does not show up in $\boldsymbol{\beta}$ because we have imposed the restriction $\delta_{12} = \delta_{22}$ by appropriate choice of the matrix of explanatory variables.

The matrix of instruments is $\mathbf{I}_2 \otimes \mathbf{z}$, meaning that we just use all exogenous variables as instruments in each equation. Since $\mathbf{I}_2 \otimes \mathbf{z}$ has six columns, the order condition is exactly satisfied (there are six elements of $\boldsymbol{\beta}$), and we have already seen when the rank condition holds. The system can be consistently estimated using GMM or 3SLS.

9.4.2 Using Covariance Restrictions to Achieve Identification

In most applications of linear SEMs, identification is obtained by putting restrictions on the matrix of structural parameters **B**. Occasionally, we are willing to put restrictions on the variance matrix $\mathbf{\Sigma}$ of the structural errors. Such restrictions, which are almost always zero covariance assumptions, can help identify the structural parameters in some equations. For general treatments see Hausman (1983) and Hausman, Newey, and Taylor (1987). We give a couple of examples to show how identification with covariance restrictions works.

The first example is the two-equation system

$$y_1 = \gamma_{12} y_2 + \delta_{11} z_1 + \delta_{13} z_3 + u_1 \tag{9.35}$$

$$y_2 = \gamma_{21} y_1 + \delta_{21} z_1 + \delta_{22} z_2 + \delta_{23} z_3 + u_2 \tag{9.36}$$

Equation (9.35) is just identified if $\delta_{22} \neq 0$, which we assume, while equation (9.36) is unidentified without more information. Suppose that we have one piece of additional information in terms of a covariance restriction:

$$\mathrm{Cov}(u_1, u_2) = \mathrm{E}(u_1 u_2) = 0 \tag{9.37}$$

In other words, if $\mathbf{\Sigma}$ is the 2×2 structural variance matrix, we are assuming that $\mathbf{\Sigma}$ is diagonal. Assumption (9.37), along with $\delta_{22} \neq 0$, is enough to identify equation (9.36).

Here is a simple way to see how assumption (9.37) identifies equation (9.36). First, because γ_{12}, δ_{11}, and δ_{13} are identified, we can treat them as known when studying identification of equation (9.36). But if the parameters in equation (9.35) are known, u_1 is effectively known. By assumption (9.37), u_1 is uncorrelated with u_2, and u_1 is certainly partially correlated with y_1. Thus, we effectively have (z_1, z_2, z_3, u_1) as instruments available for estimating equation (9.36), and this result shows that equation (9.36) is identified.

We can use this method for verifying identification to obtain consistent estimators. First, estimate equation (9.35) by 2SLS using instruments (z_1, z_2, z_3) and save the 2SLS residuals, $\hat{u}_1$. Then estimate equation (9.36) by 2SLS using instruments $(z_1, z_2, z_3, \hat{u}_1)$. The fact that $\hat{u}_1$ depends on estimates from a prior stage does not affect consistency. But inference is complicated because of the estimation of u_1: condition (6.8) does not hold because u_1 depends on y_2, which is correlated with u_2.

The most efficient way to use covariance restrictions is to write the entire set of orthogonality conditions as $\mathrm{E}[\mathbf{z}' u_1(\boldsymbol{\beta}_1)] = \mathbf{0}$, $\mathrm{E}[\mathbf{z}' u_2(\boldsymbol{\beta}_2)] = \mathbf{0}$, and

$$\mathrm{E}[u_1(\boldsymbol{\beta}_1) u_2(\boldsymbol{\beta}_2)] = 0 \tag{9.38}$$

where the notation $u_1(\boldsymbol{\beta}_1)$ emphasizes that the errors are functions of the structural parameters $\boldsymbol{\beta}_1$—with normalization and exclusion restrictions imposed—and similarly for $u_2(\boldsymbol{\beta}_2)$. For example, from equation (9.35), $u_1(\boldsymbol{\beta}_1) = y_1 - \gamma_{12}y_2 - \delta_{11}z_1 - \delta_{13}z_3$. Equation (9.38), because it is nonlinear in $\boldsymbol{\beta}_1$ and $\boldsymbol{\beta}_2$, takes us outside the realm of linear moment restrictions. In Chapter 14 we will use nonlinear moment conditions in GMM estimation.

A general example with covariance restrictions is a **fully recursive system**. First, a **recursive system** can be written as

$$\begin{aligned} y_1 &= \mathbf{z}\boldsymbol{\delta}_1 + u_1 \\ y_2 &= \gamma_{21}y_1 + \mathbf{z}\boldsymbol{\delta}_2 + u_2 \\ y_3 &= \gamma_{31}y_1 + \gamma_{32}y_2 + \mathbf{z}\boldsymbol{\delta}_3 + u_3 \\ &\vdots \\ y_G &= \gamma_{G1}y_1 + \cdots + \gamma_{G,G-1}y_{G-1} + \mathbf{z}\boldsymbol{\delta}_G + u_G \end{aligned} \tag{9.39}$$

so that in each equation only endogenous variables from previous equations appear on the right-hand side. We have allowed all exogenous variables to appear in each equation, and we maintain assumption (9.2).

The first equation in the system (9.39) is clearly identified and can be estimated by OLS. Without further exclusion restrictions none of the remaining equations is identified, but each is identified if we assume that the structural errors are pairwise uncorrelated:

$$\mathrm{Cov}(u_g, u_h) = 0, \qquad g \neq h \tag{9.40}$$

This assumption means that $\boldsymbol{\Sigma}$ is a $G \times G$ diagonal matrix. Equations (9.39) and (9.40) define a fully recursive system. Under these assumptions, the right-hand-side variables in equation g are each uncorrelated with u_g; this fact is easily seen by starting with the first equation and noting that y_1 is a linear function of $\mathbf{z}$ and u_1. Then, in the second equation, y_1 is uncorrelated with u_2 under assumption (9.40). But y_2 is a linear function of $\mathbf{z}$, u_1, and u_2, and so y_2 and y_1 are both uncorrelated with u_3 in the third equation. And so on. It follows that each equation in the system is consistently estimated by ordinary least squares.

It turns out that OLS equation by equation is not necessarily the most efficient estimator in fully recursive systems, even though $\boldsymbol{\Sigma}$ is a diagonal matrix. Generally, efficiency can be improved by adding the zero covariance restrictions to the orthogonality conditions, as in equation (9.38), and applying nonlinear GMM estimation. See Lahiri and Schmidt (1978) and Hausman, Newey, and Taylor (1987).

9.4.3 Subtleties Concerning Identification and Efficiency in Linear Systems

So far we have discussed identification and estimation under the assumption that each exogenous variable appearing in the system, z_j, is *uncorrelated* with each structural error, u_g. It is important to assume only zero correlation in the general treatment because we often add a reduced form equation for an endogenous variable to a structural system, and zero correlation is all we should impose in linear reduced forms.

For entirely structural systems, it is often natural to assume that the structural errors satisfy the zero conditional mean assumption

$$\mathrm{E}(u_g \mid \mathbf{z}) = 0, \qquad g = 1, 2, \ldots, G \tag{9.41}$$

In addition to giving the parameters in the structural equations the appropriate partial effect interpretations, assumption (9.41) has some interesting statistical implications: *any* function of $\mathbf{z}$ is uncorrelated with each error u_g. Therefore, in the labor supply example (9.28), age^2, $\log(age)$, $educ \cdot exper$, and so on (there are too many functions to list) are all uncorrelated with u_1 and u_2. Realizing this fact, we might ask, Why not use nonlinear functions of $\mathbf{z}$ as additional instruments in estimation?

We need to break the answer to this question into two parts. The first concerns identification, and the second concerns efficiency. For identification, the bottom line is this: adding nonlinear functions of $\mathbf{z}$ to the instrument list *cannot* help with identification in linear systems. You were asked to show this generally in Problem 8.4, but the main points can be illustrated with a simple model:

$$y_1 = \gamma_{12} y_2 + \delta_{11} z_1 + \delta_{12} z_2 + u_1 \tag{9.42}$$

$$y_2 = \gamma_{21} y_1 + \delta_{21} z_1 + u_2 \tag{9.43}$$

$$\mathrm{E}(u_1 \mid \mathbf{z}) = \mathrm{E}(u_2 \mid \mathbf{z}) = 0 \tag{9.44}$$

From the order condition in Section 9.2.2, equation (9.42) is not identified, and equation (9.43) is identified if and only if $\delta_{12} \neq 0$. Knowing properties of conditional expectations, we might try something clever to identify equation (9.42): since, say, z_1^2 is uncorrelated with u_1 under assumption (9.41), and z_1^2 would appear to be correlated with y_2, we can use it as an instrument for y_2 in equation (9.42). Under this reasoning, we would have enough instruments—z_1, z_2, z_1^2—to identify equation (9.42). In fact, any number of functions of z_1 and z_2 can be added to the instrument list.

The fact that this argument is faulty is fortunate because our identification analysis in Section 9.2.2 says that equation (9.42) is not identified. In this example it is clear that z_1^2 cannot appear in the reduced form for y_2 because z_1^2 appears nowhere in the system. Technically, because $E(y_2 \mid \mathbf{z})$ is linear in z_1 and z_2 under assumption (9.44), the linear projection of y_2 onto (z_1, z_2, z_1^2) does not depend on z_1^2:

$$L(y_2 \mid z_1, z_2, z_1^2) = L(y_2 \mid z_1, z_2) = \pi_{21} z_1 + \pi_{22} z_2 \tag{9.45}$$

In other words, there is no *partial* correlation between y_2 and z_1^2 once z_1 and z_2 are included in the projection.

The zero conditional mean assumptions (9.41) can have some relevance for choosing an efficient estimator, although not always. If assumption (9.41) holds and $\text{Var}(\mathbf{u} \mid \mathbf{z}) = \text{Var}(\mathbf{u}) = \boldsymbol{\Sigma}$, 3SLS using instruments $\mathbf{z}$ for each equation is the asymptotically efficient estimator that uses the orthogonality conditions in assumption (9.41); this conclusion follows from Theorem 8.5. In other words, if $\text{Var}(\mathbf{u} \mid \mathbf{z})$ is constant, it does not help to expand the instrument list beyond the functions of the exogenous variables actually appearing in the system.

However, if assumption (9.41) holds but $\text{Var}(\mathbf{u} \mid \mathbf{z})$ is not constant, we can do better (asymptotically) than 3SLS. If $\mathbf{h}(\mathbf{z})$ is some additional functions of the exogenous variables, the minimum chi-square estimator using $[\mathbf{z}, \mathbf{h}(\mathbf{z})]$ as instruments in each equation is, generally, more efficient than 3SLS or minimum chi-square using only $\mathbf{z}$ as IVs. This result was discovered independently by Hansen (1982) and White (1982b), and it follows from the discussion in Section 8.6. Expanding the IV list to arbitrary functions of $\mathbf{z}$ and applying full GMM is not used very much in practice: it is usually not clear how to choose $\mathbf{h}(\mathbf{z})$, and, if we use too many additional instruments, the finite sample properties of the GMM estimator can be poor, as we discussed in Section 8.6.

For SEMs linear in the parameters but nonlinear in endogenous variables (in a sense to be made precise), adding nonlinear functions of the exogenous variables to the instruments not only is desirable, but is often needed to achieve identification. We turn to this topic next.

9.5 SEMs Nonlinear in Endogenous Variables

We now study models that are nonlinear in some endogenous variables. While the general estimation methods we have covered are still applicable, identification and choice of instruments require special attention.

9.5.1 Identification

The issues that arise in identifying models nonlinear in endogenous variables are most easily illustrated with a simple example. Suppose that supply and demand are given by

$$\log(q) = \gamma_{12} \log(p) + \gamma_{13}[\log(p)]^2 + \delta_{11} z_1 + u_1 \tag{9.46}$$

$$\log(q) = \gamma_{22} \log(p) + \delta_{22} z_2 + u_2 \tag{9.47}$$

$$\mathrm{E}(u_1 \mid \mathbf{z}) = \mathrm{E}(u_2 \mid \mathbf{z}) = 0 \tag{9.48}$$

where the first equation is the supply equation, the second equation is the demand equation, and the equilibrium condition that supply equals demand has been imposed. For simplicity, we do not include an intercept in either equation, but no important conclusions hinge on this omission. The exogenous variable z_1 shifts the supply function but not the demand function; z_2 shifts the demand function but not the supply function. The vector of exogenous variables appearing somewhere in the system is $\mathbf{z} = (z_1, z_2)$.

It is important to understand why equations (9.46) and (9.47) constitute a "nonlinear" system. This system is still linear in *parameters*, which is important because it means that the IV procedures we have learned up to this point are still applicable. Further, it is *not* the presence of the logarithmic transformations of q and p that makes the system nonlinear. In fact, if we set $\gamma_{13} = 0$, then the model *is* linear for the purposes of identification and estimation: defining $y_1 \equiv \log(q)$ and $y_2 \equiv \log(p)$, we can write equations (9.46) and (9.47) as a standard two-equation system.

When we include $[\log(p)]^2$ we have the model

$$y_1 = \gamma_{12} y_2 + \gamma_{13} y_2^2 + \delta_{11} z_1 + u_1 \tag{9.49}$$

$$y_1 = \gamma_{22} y_2 + \delta_{22} z_2 + u_2 \tag{9.50}$$

With this system there is no way to define *two* endogenous variables such that the system is a two-equation system in two endogenous variables. The presence of y_2^2 in equation (9.49) makes this model different from those we have studied up until now. We say that this is a system **nonlinear in endogenous variables**. What this statement really means is that, while the system is still linear in parameters, identification needs to be treated differently.

If we used equations (9.49) and (9.50) to obtain y_2 as a function of the z_1, z_2, u_1, u_2, and the parameters, the result would not be linear in $\mathbf{z}$ and $\mathbf{u}$. In this particular case we can find the solution for y_2 using the quadratic formula (assuming a real solution exists). However, $\mathrm{E}(y_2 \mid \mathbf{z})$ would not be linear in $\mathbf{z}$ unless $\gamma_{13} = 0$, and $\mathrm{E}(y_2^2 \mid \mathbf{z})$ would not be linear in $\mathbf{z}$ regardless of the value of γ_{13}. These observations have important implications for identification of equation (9.49) and for choosing instruments.

Before considering equations (9.49) and (9.50) further, consider a second example where closed form expressions for the endogenous variables in terms of the exogenous variables and structural errors do not even exist. Suppose that a system describing crime rates in terms of law enforcement spending is

$$crime = \gamma_{12} \log(spending) + \mathbf{z}_{(1)}\boldsymbol{\delta}_{(1)} + u_1 \tag{9.51}$$

$$spending = \gamma_{21} crime + \gamma_{22} crime^2 + \mathbf{z}_{(2)}\boldsymbol{\delta}_{(2)} + u_2 \tag{9.52}$$

where the errors have zero mean given $\mathbf{z}$. Here, we cannot solve for either *crime* or *spending* (or any other transformation of them) in terms of $\mathbf{z}$, u_1, u_2, and the parameters. And there is no way to define y_1 and y_2 to yield a linear SEM in two endogenous variables. The model is still linear in parameters, but $\mathrm{E}(crime \mid \mathbf{z})$, $\mathrm{E}[\log(spending) \mid \mathbf{z}]$, and $\mathrm{E}(spending \mid \mathbf{z})$ are not linear in $\mathbf{z}$ (nor can we find closed forms for these expectations).

One possible approach to identification in nonlinear SEMs is to ignore the fact that the same endogenous variables show up differently in different equations. In the supply and demand example, define $y_3 \equiv y_2^2$ and rewrite equation (9.49) as

$$y_1 = \gamma_{12} y_2 + \gamma_{13} y_3 + \delta_{11} z_1 + u_1 \tag{9.53}$$

Or, in equations (9.51) and (9.52) define $y_1 = crime$, $y_2 = spending$, $y_3 = \log(spending)$, and $y_4 = crime^2$, and write

$$y_1 = \gamma_{12} y_3 + \mathbf{z}_{(1)}\boldsymbol{\delta}_{(1)} + u_1 \tag{9.54}$$

$$y_2 = \gamma_{21} y_1 + \gamma_{22} y_4 + \mathbf{z}_{(2)}\boldsymbol{\delta}_{(2)} + u_2 \tag{9.55}$$

Defining nonlinear functions of endogenous variables as new endogenous variables turns out to work fairly generally, *provided* we apply the rank and order conditions properly. The key question is, What kinds of equations do we add to the system for the newly defined endogenous variables?

If we add linear projections of the newly defined endogenous variables in terms of the *original* exogenous variables appearing somewhere in the system—that is, the linear projection onto $\mathbf{z}$—then we are being much too restrictive. For example, suppose to equations (9.53) and (9.50) we add the linear equation

$$y_3 = \pi_{31} z_1 + \pi_{32} z_2 + v_3 \tag{9.56}$$

where, by definition, $\mathrm{E}(z_1 v_3) = \mathrm{E}(z_2 v_3) = 0$. With equation (9.56) to round out the system, the order condition for identification of equation (9.53) clearly fails: we have two endogenous variables in equation (9.53) but only one excluded exogenous variable, z_2.

The conclusion that equation (9.53) is not identified is too pessimistic. There are many other possible instruments available for y_2^2. Because $\mathrm{E}(y_2^2 \mid \mathbf{z})$ is not linear in z_1 and z_2 (even if $\gamma_{13} = 0$), other functions of z_1 and z_2 will appear in a linear projection involving y_2^2 as the dependent variable. To see what the most useful of these are likely to be, suppose that the structural system actually is linear, so that $\gamma_{13} = 0$. Then $y_2 = \pi_{21} z_1 + \pi_{22} z_2 + v_2$, where v_2 is a linear combination of u_1 and u_2. Squaring this reduced form and using $\mathrm{E}(v_2 \mid \mathbf{z}) = 0$ gives

$$\mathrm{E}(y_2^2 \mid \mathbf{z}) = \pi_{21}^2 z_1^2 + \pi_{22}^2 z_2^2 + 2\pi_{21}\pi_{22} z_1 z_2 + \mathrm{E}(v_2^2 \mid \mathbf{z}) \tag{9.57}$$

If $\mathrm{E}(v_2^2 \mid \mathbf{z})$ is constant, an assumption that holds under homoskedasticity of the structural errors, then equation (9.57) shows that y_2^2 is correlated with z_1^2, z_2^2, and $z_1 z_2$, which makes these functions natural instruments for y_2^2. The only case where no functions of $\mathbf{z}$ are correlated with y_2^2 occurs when both π_{21} and π_{22} equal zero, in which case the linear version of equation (9.49) (with $\gamma_{13} = 0$) is also unidentified.

Because we derived equation (9.57) under the restrictive assumptions $\gamma_{13} = 0$ and homoskedasticity of v_2, we would not want our linear projection for y_2^2 to omit the exogenous variables that originally appear in the system. In practice, we would augment equations (9.53) and (9.50) with the linear projection

$$y_3 = \pi_{31} z_1 + \pi_{32} z_2 + \pi_{33} z_1^2 + \pi_{34} z_2^2 + \pi_{35} z_1 z_2 + v_3 \tag{9.58}$$

where v_3 is, by definition, uncorrelated with z_1, z_2, z_1^2, z_2^2, and $z_1 z_2$. The system (9.53), (9.50), and (9.58) can now be studied using the usual rank condition.

Adding equation (9.58) to the original system and then studying the rank condition of the first two equations is equivalent to studying the rank condition in the smaller system (9.53) and (9.50). What we mean by this statement is that we do not explicitly add an equation for $y_3 = y_2^2$, but we *do* include y_3 in equation (9.53). Therefore, when applying the rank condition to equation (9.53), we use $G = 2$ (not $G = 3$). The reason this approach is the same as studying the rank condition in the three-equation system (9.53), (9.50), and (9.58) is that adding the third equation increases the rank of $\mathbf{R}_1\mathbf{B}$ by one whenever at least one additional nonlinear function of $\mathbf{z}$ appears in equation (9.58). (The functions z_1^2, z_2^2, and $z_1 z_2$ appear nowhere else in the system.)

As a general approach to identification in models where the nonlinear functions of the endogenous variables depend only on a single endogenous variable—such as the two examples that we have already covered—Fisher (1965) argues that the following method is sufficient for identification:

1. Relabel the nonredundant functions of the endogenous variables to be new endogenous variables, as in equation (9.53) or (9.54) and equation (9.55).

2. Apply the rank condition to the original system *without* increasing the number of equations. If the equation of interest satisfies the rank condition, then it is identified.

The proof that this method works is complicated, and it requires more assumptions than we have made (such as $\mathbf{u}$ being *independent* of $\mathbf{z}$). Intuitively, we can expect each additional nonlinear function of the endogenous variables to have a linear projection that depends on new functions of the exogenous variables. Each time we add another function of an endogenous variable, it effectively comes with its own instruments.

Fisher's method can be expected to work in all but the most pathological cases. One case where it does not work is if $\mathrm{E}(v_2^2 \mid \mathbf{z})$ in equation (9.57) is heteroskedastic in such a way as to cancel out the squares and cross product terms in z_1 and z_2; then $\mathrm{E}(y_2^2 \mid \mathbf{z})$ would be constant. Such unfortunate coincidences are not practically important.

It is tempting to think that Fisher's rank condition is also necessary for identification, but this is not the case. To see why, consider the two-equation system

$$y_1 = \gamma_{12} y_2 + \gamma_{13} y_2^2 + \delta_{11} z_1 + \delta_{12} z_2 + u_1 \tag{9.59}$$

$$y_2 = \gamma_{21} y_1 + \delta_{21} z_1 + u_2 \tag{9.60}$$

The first equation cleary fails the modified rank condition because it fails the order condition: there are no restrictions on the first equation except the normalization restriction. However, if $\gamma_{13} \neq 0$ and $\gamma_{21} \neq 0$, then $\mathrm{E}(y_2 \mid \mathbf{z})$ is a nonlinear function of $\mathbf{z}$ (which we cannot obtain in closed form). The result is that functions such as z_1^2, z_2^2, and $z_1 z_2$ (and others) will appear in the linear projections of y_2 and y_2^2 even after z_1 and z_2 have been included, and these can then be used as instruments for y_2 and y_2^2. But if $\gamma_{13} = 0$, the first equation cannot be identified by adding nonlinear functions of z_1 and z_2 to the instrument list: the linear projection of y_2 on z_1, z_2, and any function of (z_1, z_2) will only depend on z_1 and z_2.

Equation (9.59) is an example of a **poorly identified model** because, when it is identified, it is **identified due to a nonlinearity** ($\gamma_{13} \neq 0$ in this case). Such identification is especially tenuous because the hypothesis H_0: $\gamma_{13} = 0$ cannot be tested by estimating the structural equation (since the structural equation is not identified when H_0 holds).

There are other models where identification can be verified using reasoning similar to that used in the labor supply example. Models with interactions between exogenous variables and endogenous variables can be shown to be identified when the model without the interactions is identified (see Example 6.2 and Problem 9.6). Models with interactions among endogenous variables are also fairly easy to handle. Generally, it is good practice to check whether the most general *linear* version of the model would be identified. If it is, then the nonlinear version of the model is probably identified. We saw this result in equation (9.46): if this equation is identified when $\gamma_{13} = 0$, then it is identified for any value of γ_{13}. If the most general linear version of a nonlinear model is not identified, we should be very wary about proceeding, since identification hinges on the presence of nonlinearities that we usually will not be able to test.

9.5.2 Estimation

In practice, it is difficult to know which additional functions we should add to the instrument list for nonlinear SEMs. Naturally, we must always include the exogenous variables appearing somewhere in the system instruments in every equation. After that, the choice is somewhat arbitrary, although the functional forms appearing in the structural equations can be helpful.

A general approach is to always use some squares and cross products of the exogenous variables appearing somewhere in the system. If something like $exper^2$ appears in the system, additional terms such as $exper^3$ and $exper^4$ would be added to the instrument list.

Once we decide on a set of instruments, any equation in a nonlinear SEM can be estimated by 2SLS. Because each equation satisfies the assumptions of single-equation analysis, we can use everything we have learned up to now for inference and specification testing for 2SLS. A system method can also be used, where linear projections for the functions of endogenous variables are explicitly added to the system. Then, all exogenous variables included in these linear projections can be used as the instruments for every equation. The minimum chi-square estimator is generally more appropriate than 3SLS because the homoskedasticity assumption will rarely be satisfied in the linear projections.

It is important to apply the instrumental variables procedures directly to the structural equation or equations. In other words, we should directly use the formulas for 2SLS, 3SLS, or GMM. Trying to mimic 2SLS or 3SLS by substituting fitted values for some of the endogenous variables inside the nonlinear functions is usually a mistake: neither the conditional expectation nor the linear projection operator passes through nonlinear functions, and so such attempts rarely produce consistent estimators in nonlinear systems.

Example 9.6 (Nonlinear Labor Supply Function): We add $[\log(wage)]^2$ to the labor supply function in Example 9.5:

$$hours = \gamma_{12} \log(wage) + \gamma_{13}[\log(wage)]^2 + \delta_{10} + \delta_{11} educ + \delta_{12} age + \delta_{13} kidslt6 + \delta_{14} kidsge6 + \delta_{15} nwifeinc + u_1 \tag{9.61}$$

$$\log(wage) = \delta_{20} + \delta_{21} educ + \delta_{22} exper + \delta_{23} exper^2 + u_2 \tag{9.62}$$

where we have dropped *hours* from the wage offer function because it was insignificant in Example 9.5. The natural assumptions in this system are $\mathrm{E}(u_1 \mid \mathbf{z}) = \mathrm{E}(u_2 \mid \mathbf{z}) = 0$, where $\mathbf{z}$ contains all variables other than *hours* and $\log(wage)$.

There are many possibilities as additional instruments for $[\log(wage)]^2$. Here, we add three quadratic terms to the list—age^2, $educ^2$, and $nwifeinc^2$—and we estimate equation (9.61) by 2SLS. We obtain $\hat{\gamma}_{12} = 1{,}873.62$ (se $= 635.99$) and $\hat{\gamma}_{13} = -437.29$ (se $= 350.08$). The t statistic on $[\log(wage)]^2$ is about -1.25, so we would be justified in dropping it from the labor supply function. Regressing the 2SLS residuals $\hat{u}_1$ on all variables used as instruments in the supply equation gives R-squared $= .0061$, and so the N-R-squared statistic is 2.61. With a χ_3^2 distribution this gives p-value $= .456$. Thus, we fail to reject the overidentifying restrictions.

In the previous example we may be tempted to estimate the labor supply function using a two-step procedure that appears to mimic 2SLS:

1. Regress $\log(wage)$ on all exogenous variables appearing in the system and obtain the predicted values. For emphasis, call these $\hat{y}_2$.
2. Estimate the labor supply function from the OLS regression *hours* on $1, \hat{y}_2, (\hat{y}_2)^2, educ, \ldots, nwifeinc$.

This two-step procedure is *not* the same as estimating equation (9.61) by 2SLS, and, except in special circumstances, it does *not* produce consistent estimators of the structural parameters. The regression in step 2 is an example of what is sometimes called a **forbidden regression**, a phrase that describes replacing a nonlinear function of an endogenous explanatory variable with the same nonlinear function of fitted values from a first-stage estimation. In plugging fitted values into equation (9.61), our mistake is in thinking that the linear projection of the square is the square of the linear projection. What the 2SLS estimator does in the first stage is project each of y_2 and y_2^2 onto the original exogenous variables and the additional nonlinear functions of these that we have chosen. The fitted values from the reduced form regression for y_2^2, say $\hat{y}_3$, are not the same as the squared fitted values from the reduced form regression for y_2, $(\hat{y}_2)^2$. This distinction is the difference between a consistent estimator and an inconsistent estimator.

If we apply the forbidden regression to equation (9.61), some of the estimates are very different from the 2SLS estimates. For example, the coefficient on *educ*, when equation (9.61) is properly estimated by 2SLS, is about -87.85 with a t statistic of -1.32. The forbidden regression gives a coefficient on *educ* of about -176.68 with a t statistic of -5.36. Unfortunately, the t statistic from the forbidden regression is generally invalid, even asymptotically. (The forbidden regression will produce consistent estimators in the special case $\gamma_{13} = 0$, if $\mathrm{E}(u_1 \mid \mathbf{z}) = 0$; see Problem 9.12.)

Many more functions of the exogenous variables could be added to the instrument list in estimating the labor supply function. From Chapter 8, we know that efficiency of GMM never falls by adding more nonlinear functions of the exogenous variables to the instrument list (even under the homoskedasticity assumption). This statement is true whether we use a single-equation or system method. Unfortunately, the fact that we do no worse asymptotically by adding instruments is of limited practical help, since we do not want to use too many instruments for a given data set. In Example 9.6, rather than using a long list of additional nonlinear functions, we might use $(\hat{y}_2)^2$ as a single IV for y_2^2. (This method is not the same as the forbidden regression!) If it happens that $\gamma_{13} = 0$ and the structural errors are homoskedastic, this would be the optimal IV. (See Problem 9.12.)

A general system linear in parameters can be written as

$$
\begin{aligned}
y_1 &= \mathbf{q}_1(\mathbf{y}, \mathbf{z})\boldsymbol{\beta}_1 + u_1 \\
&\vdots \\
y_G &= \mathbf{q}_G(\mathbf{y}, \mathbf{z})\boldsymbol{\beta}_G + u_G
\end{aligned}
\tag{9.63}
$$

where $\mathrm{E}(u_g \mid \mathbf{z}) = 0$, $g = 1, 2, \ldots, G$. Among other things this system allows for complicated interactions among endogenous and exogenous variables. We will not give a general analysis of such systems because identification and choice of instruments are too abstract to be very useful. Either single-equation or system methods can be used for estimation.

9.6 Different Instruments for Different Equations

There are general classes of SEMs where the same instruments cannot be used for every equation. We already encountered one such example, the fully recursive system. Another general class of models is SEMs where, in addition to simultaneous determination of some variables, some equations contain variables that are endogenous as a result of omitted variables or measurement error.

As an example, reconsider the labor supply and wage offer equations (9.28) and (9.62), respectively. On the one hand, in the supply function it is not unreasonable to assume that variables other than $\log(wage)$ are uncorrelated with u_1. On the other hand, ability is a variable omitted from the $\log(wage)$ equation, and so *educ* might be correlated with u_2. This is an omitted variable, not a simultaneity, issue, but the statistical problem is the same: correlation between the error and an explanatory variable.

Equation (9.28) is still identified as it was before, because *educ* is exogenous in equation (9.28). What about equation (9.62)? It satisfies the order condition because we have excluded four exogenous variables from equation (9.62): *age*, *kidslt6*, *kidsge6*, and *nwifeinc*. How can we analyze the rank condition for this equation? We need to add to the system the linear projection of *educ* on all exogenous variables:

$$educ = \delta_{30} + \delta_{31} exper + \delta_{32} exper^2 + \delta_{33} age + \delta_{34} kidslt6 + \delta_{35} kidsge6 + \delta_{36} nwifeinc + u_3 \tag{9.64}$$

Provided the variables other than *exper* and $exper^2$ are sufficiently partially correlated with *educ*, the log(*wage*) equation is identified. However, the 2SLS estimators might be poorly behaved if the instruments are not very good. If possible, we would add other exogenous factors to equation (9.64) that are partially correlated with *educ*, such as mother's and father's education. In a system procedure, because we have assumed that *educ* is uncorrelated with u_1, *educ* can, and should, be included in the list of instruments for estimating equation (9.28).

This example shows that having different instruments for different equations changes nothing for single-equation analysis: we simply determine the valid list of instruments for the endogenous variables in the equation of interest and then estimate the equations separately by 2SLS. Instruments may be required to deal with simultaneity, omitted variables, or measurement error, in any combination.

Estimation is more complicated for system methods. First, if 3SLS is to be used, then the GMM 3SLS version must be used to produce consistent estimators of any equation; the more traditional 3SLS estimator discussed in Section 8.3.5 is generally valid only when all instruments are uncorrelated with all errors. When we have different instruments for different equations, the instrument matrix has the form in equation (8.15).

There is a more subtle issue that arises in system analysis with different instruments for different equations. While it is still popular to use 3SLS methods for such problems, it turns out that the key assumption that makes 3SLS the efficient GMM estimator, Assumption SIV.5, is often violated. In such cases the GMM estimator with general weighting matrix enhances asymptotic efficiency and simplifies inference.

As a simple example, consider a two-equation system

$$y_1 = \delta_{10} + \gamma_{12} y_2 + \delta_{11} z_1 + u_1 \tag{9.65}$$

$$y_2 = \delta_{20} + \gamma_{21} y_1 + \delta_{22} z_2 + \delta_{23} z_3 + u_2 \tag{9.66}$$

where (u_1, u_2) has mean zero and variance matrix $\mathbf{\Sigma}$. Suppose that z_1, z_2, and z_3 are uncorrelated with u_2 but we can only assume that z_1 and z_3 are uncorrelated with u_1.

In other words, z_2 is not exogenous in equation (9.65). Each equation is still identified by the order condition, and we just assume that the rank conditions also hold. The instruments for equation (9.65) are $(1, z_1, z_3)$, and the instruments for equation (9.66) are $(1, z_1, z_2, z_3)$. Write these as $\mathbf{z}_1 \equiv (1, z_1, z_3)$ and $\mathbf{z}_2 \equiv (1, z_1, z_2, z_3)$. Assumption SIV.5 requires the following three conditions:

$$\mathrm{E}(u_1^2 \mathbf{z}_1' \mathbf{z}_1) = \sigma_1^2 \mathrm{E}(\mathbf{z}_1' \mathbf{z}_1) \tag{9.67}$$

$$\mathrm{E}(u_2^2 \mathbf{z}_2' \mathbf{z}_2) = \sigma_2^2 \mathrm{E}(\mathbf{z}_2' \mathbf{z}_2) \tag{9.68}$$

$$\mathrm{E}(u_1 u_2 \mathbf{z}_1' \mathbf{z}_2) = \sigma_{12} \mathrm{E}(\mathbf{z}_1' \mathbf{z}_2) \tag{9.69}$$

The first two conditions hold if $\mathrm{E}(u_1 \mid \mathbf{z}_1) = \mathrm{E}(u_2 \mid \mathbf{z}_2) = 0$ and $\mathrm{Var}(u_1 \mid \mathbf{z}_1) = \sigma_1^2$, $\mathrm{Var}(u_2 \mid \mathbf{z}_2) = \sigma_2^2$. These are standard zero conditional mean and homoskedasticity assumptions. The potential problem comes with condition (9.69). Since u_1 is correlated with one of the elements in $\mathbf{z}_2$, we can hardly just assume condition (9.69). Generally, there is no conditioning argument that implies condition (9.69). One case where condition (9.69) holds is if $\mathrm{E}(u_2 \mid u_1, z_1, z_2, z_3) = 0$, which implies that u_2 and u_1 are uncorrelated. The left-hand side of condition (9.69) is also easily shown to equal zero. But 3SLS with $\sigma_{12} = 0$ imposed is just 2SLS equation by equation. If u_1 and u_2 are correlated, we should not expect condition (9.69) to hold, and therefore the general minimum chi-square estimator should be used for estimation and inference.

Wooldridge (1996) provides a general discussion and contains other examples of cases in which Assumption SIV.5 can and cannot be expected to hold. Whenever a system contains linear projections for nonlinear functions of endogenous variables, we should expect Assumption SIV.5 to fail.

Problems

9.1. Discuss whether each example satisfies the autonomy requirement for true simultaneous equations analysis. The specification of y_1 and y_2 means that each is to be written as a function of the other in a two-equation system.

a. For an employee, $y_1 =$ hourly wage, $y_2 =$ hourly fringe benefits.

b. At the city level, $y_1 =$ per capita crime rate, $y_2 =$ per capita law enforcement expenditures.

c. For a firm operating in a developing country, $y_1 =$ firm research and development expenditures, $y_2 =$ firm foreign technology purchases.

d. For an individual, $y_1 =$ hourly wage, $y_2 =$ alcohol consumption.

e. For a family, $y_1 =$ annual housing expenditures, $y_2 =$ annual savings.

f. For a profit maximizing firm, $y_1 =$ price markup, $y_2 =$ advertising expenditures.

g. For a single-output firm, $y_1 =$ quantity demanded of its good, $y_2 =$ advertising expenditure.

h. At the city level, $y_1 =$ incidence of HIV, $y_2 =$ per capita condom sales.

9.2. Write a two-equation system in the form

$$y_1 = \gamma_1 y_2 + \mathbf{z}_{(1)}\boldsymbol{\delta}_{(1)} + u_1$$

$$y_2 = \gamma_2 y_1 + \mathbf{z}_{(2)}\boldsymbol{\delta}_{(2)} + u_2$$

a. Show that reduced forms exist if and only if $\gamma_1\gamma_2 \neq 1$.

b. State in words the rank condition for identifying each equation.

9.3. The following model jointly determines monthly child support payments and monthly visitation rights for divorced couples with children:

$$support = \delta_{10} + \gamma_{12} visits + \delta_{11} finc + \delta_{12} fremarr + \delta_{13} dist + u_1$$

$$visits = \delta_{20} + \gamma_{21} support + \delta_{21} mremarr + \delta_{22} dist + u_2.$$

For expository purposes, assume that children live with their mothers, so that fathers pay child support. Thus, the first equation is the father's "reaction function": it describes the amount of child support paid for any given level of visitation rights and the other exogenous variables *finc* (father's income), *fremarr* (binary indicator if father remarried), and *dist* (miles currently between the mother and father). Similarly, the second equation is the mother's reaction function: it describes visitation rights for a given amount of child support; *mremarr* is a binary indicator for whether the mother is remarried.

a. Discuss identification of each equation.

b. How would you estimate each equation using a single-equation method?

c. How would you test for endogeneity of *visits* in the father's reaction function?

d. How many overidentification restrictions are there in the mother's reaction function? Explain how to test the overidentifying restriction(s).

9.4. Consider the following three-equation structural model:

$$y_1 = \gamma_{12} y_2 + \delta_{11} z_1 + \delta_{12} z_2 + \delta_{13} z_3 + u_1$$

$$y_1 = \gamma_{22} y_2 + \gamma_{23} y_3 + \delta_{21} z_1 + u_2$$

$$y_3 = \delta_{31}z_1 + \delta_{32}z_2 + \delta_{33}z_3 + u_3$$

where $z_1 \equiv 1$ (to allow an intercept), $E(u_g) = 0$, all g, and each z_j is uncorrelated with each u_g. You might think of the first two equations as demand and supply equations, where the supply equation depends on a possibly endogenous variable y_3 (such as wage costs) that might be correlated with u_2. For example, u_2 might contain managerial quality.

a. Show that a well-defined reduced form exists as long as $\gamma_{12} \neq \gamma_{22}$.

b. Allowing for the structural errors to be arbitrarily correlated, determine which of these equations is identified. First consider the order condition, and then the rank condition.

9.5. The following three-equation structural model describes a population:

$$y_1 = \gamma_{12}y_2 + \gamma_{13}y_3 + \delta_{11}z_1 + \delta_{13}z_3 + \delta_{14}z_4 + u_1$$

$$y_2 = \gamma_{21}y_1 + \delta_{21}z_1 + u_2$$

$$y_3 = \delta_{31}z_1 + \delta_{32}z_2 + \delta_{33}z_3 + \delta_{34}z_4 + u_3$$

where you may set $z_1 = 1$ to allow an intercept. Make the usual assumptions that $E(u_g) = 0$, $g = 1, 2, 3$, and that each z_j is uncorrelated with each u_g. In addition to the exclusion restrictions that have already been imposed, assume that $\delta_{13} + \delta_{14} = 1$.

a. Check the order and rank conditions for the first equation. Determine necessary and sufficient conditions for the rank condition to hold.

b. Assuming that the first equation is identified, propose a single-equation estimation method with all restrictions imposed. Be very precise.

9.6. The following two-equation model contains an interaction between an endogenous and exogenous variable (see Example 6.2 for such a model in an omitted variable context):

$$y_1 = \delta_{10} + \gamma_{12}y_2 + \gamma_{13}y_2z_1 + \delta_{11}z_1 + \delta_{12}z_2 + u_1$$

$$y_2 = \delta_{20} + \gamma_{21}y_1 + \delta_{21}z_1 + \delta_{23}z_3 + u_2$$

a. Initially, assume that $\gamma_{13} = 0$, so that the model is a linear SEM. Discuss identification of each equation in this case.

b. For any value of γ_{13}, find the reduced form for y_1 (assuming it exists) in terms of the z_j, the u_g, and the parameters.

c. Assuming that $E(u_1 \mid \mathbf{z}) = E(u_2 \mid \mathbf{z}) = 0$, find $E(y_1 \mid \mathbf{z})$.

d. Argue that, under the conditions in part a, the model is identified regardless of the value of γ_{13}.

e. Suggest a 2SLS procedure for estimating the first equation.

f. Define a matrix of instruments suitable for 3SLS estimation.

g. Suppose that $\delta_{23} = 0$, but we also known that $\gamma_{13} \neq 0$. Can the parameters in the first equation be consistently estimated? If so, how? Can H_0: $\gamma_{13} = 0$ be tested?

9.7. Assume that wage and alcohol consumption are determined by the system

$$wage = \gamma_{12} alcohol + \gamma_{13} educ + \mathbf{z}_{(1)} \boldsymbol{\delta}_{(1)} + u_1$$

$$alcohol = \gamma_{21} wage + \gamma_{23} educ + \mathbf{z}_{(2)} \boldsymbol{\delta}_{(2)} + u_2$$

$$educ = \mathbf{z}_{(3)} \boldsymbol{\delta}_{(3)} + u_3$$

The third equation is a reduced form for years of education.

Elements in $\mathbf{z}_{(1)}$ include a constant, experience, gender, marital status, and amount of job training. The vector $\mathbf{z}_{(2)}$ contains a constant, experience, gender, marital status, and local prices (including taxes) on various alcoholic beverages. The vector $\mathbf{z}_{(3)}$ can contain elements in $\mathbf{z}_{(1)}$ and $\mathbf{z}_{(2)}$ and, in addition, exogenous factors affecting education; for concreteness, suppose one element of $\mathbf{z}_{(3)}$ is distance to nearest college at age 16. Let $\mathbf{z}$ denote the vector containing all nonredundant elements of $\mathbf{z}_{(1)}$, $\mathbf{z}_{(2)}$, and $\mathbf{z}_{(3)}$. In addition to assuming that $\mathbf{z}$ is uncorrelated with each of u_1, u_2, and u_3, assume that educ is uncorrelated with u_2, but *educ* might be correlated with u_1.

a. When does the order condition hold for the first equation?

b. State carefully how you would estimate the first equation using a single-equation method.

c. For each observation i define the matrix of instruments for system estimation of all three equations.

d. In a system procedure, how should you choose $\mathbf{z}_{(3)}$ to make the analysis as robust as possible to factors appearing in the reduced form for *educ*?

9.8. a. Extend Problem 5.4b using CARD.RAW to allow $educ^2$ to appear in the $\log(wage)$ equation, without using *nearc2* as an instrument. Specifically, use interactions of *nearc4* with some or all of the other exogenous variables in the $\log(wage)$ equation as instruments for $educ^2$. Compute a heteroskedasticity-robust test to be sure that at least one of these additional instruments appears in the linear projection of $educ^2$ onto your entire list of instruments. Test whether $educ^2$ needs to be in the $\log(wage)$ equation.

b. Start again with the model estimated in Problem 5.4b, but suppose we add the interaction *black·educ*. Explain why $black \cdot z_j$ is a potential IV for *black·educ*, where z_j is any exogenous variable in the system (including *nearc4*).

c. In Example 6.2 we used *black·nearc4* as the IV for *black·educ*. Now use 2SLS with $black \cdot \widehat{educ}$ as the IV for *black·educ*, where $\widehat{educ}$ are the fitted values from the first-stage regression of *educ* on all exogenous variables (including *nearc4*). What do you find?

d. If $\mathrm{E}(educ \mid \mathbf{z})$ is linear and $\mathrm{Var}(u_1 \mid \mathbf{z}) = \sigma_1^2$, where $\mathbf{z}$ is the set of all exogenous variables and u_1 is the error in the $\log(wage)$ equation, explain why the estimator using $black \cdot \widehat{educ}$ as the IV is asymptotically more efficient than the estimator using *black·nearc4* as the IV.

9.9. Use the data in MROZ.RAW for this question.

a. Estimate equations (9.28) and (9.29) jointly by 3SLS, and compare the 3SLS estimates with the 2SLS estimates for equations (9.28) and (9.29).

b. Now allow *educ* to be endogenous in equation (9.29), but assume it is exogenous in equation (9.28). Estimate a three-equation system using different instruments for different equations, where *motheduc*, *fatheduc*, and *huseduc* are assumed exogenous in equations (9.28) and (9.29).

9.10. Consider a two-equation system of the form

$$y_1 = \gamma_1 y_2 + \mathbf{z}_1 \boldsymbol{\delta}_1 + u_1$$

$$y_2 = \mathbf{z}_2 \boldsymbol{\delta}_2 + u_2$$

Assume that $\mathbf{z}_1$ contains at least one element not also in $\mathbf{z}_2$, and $\mathbf{z}_2$ contains at least one element not in $\mathbf{z}_1$. The second equation is also the reduced form for y_2, but restrictions have been imposed to make it a structural equation. (For example, it could be a wage offer equation with exclusion restrictions imposed, whereas the first equation is a labor supply function.)

a. If we estimate the first equation by 2SLS using all exogenous variables as IVs, are we imposing the exclusion restrictions in the second equation? (Hint: Does the first-stage regression in 2SLS impose any restrictions on the reduced form?)

b. Will the 3SLS estimates of the first equation be the same as the 2SLS estimates? Explain.

c. Explain why 2SLS is more robust than 3SLS for estimating the parameters of the first equation.

9.11. Consider a two-equation SEM:

$$y_1 = \gamma_{12} y_2 + \delta_{11} z_1 + u_1$$

$$y_2 = \gamma_{21} y_1 + \delta_{22} z_2 + \delta_{23} z_3 + u_2$$

$$\mathrm{E}(u_1 \mid z_1, z_2, z_3) = \mathrm{E}(u_2 \mid z_1, z_2, z_3) = 0$$

where, for simplicity, we omit intercepts. The exogenous variable z_1 is a policy variable, such as a tax rate. Assume that $\gamma_{12}\gamma_{21} \neq 1$. The structural errors, u_1 and u_2, may be correlated.

a. Under what assumptions is each equation identified?

b. The reduced form for y_1 can be written in conditional expectation form as $\mathrm{E}(y_1 \mid \mathbf{z}) = \pi_{11} z_1 + \pi_{12} z_2 + \pi_{13} z_3$, where $\mathbf{z} = (z_1, z_2, z_3)$. Find the π_{11} in terms of the γ_{gj} and δ_{gj}.

c. How would you estimate the structural parameters? How would you obtain $\hat{\pi}_{11}$ in terms of the structural parameter estimates?

d. Suppose that z_2 should be in the first equation, but it is left out in the estimation from part c. What effect does this omission have on estimating $\partial \mathrm{E}(y_1 \mid \mathbf{z})/\partial z_1$? Does it matter whether you use single-equation or system estimators of the structural parameters?

e. If you are only interested in $\partial \mathrm{E}(y_1 \mid \mathbf{z})/\partial z_1$, what could you do instead of estimating an SEM?

f. Would you say estimating a simultaneous equations model is a robust method for estimating $\partial \mathrm{E}(y_1 \mid \mathbf{z})/\partial z_1$? Explain.

9.12. The following is a two-equation, nonlinear SEM:

$$y_1 = \delta_{10} + \gamma_{12} y_2 + \gamma_{13} y_2^2 + \mathbf{z}_1 \boldsymbol{\delta}_1 + u_1$$

$$y_2 = \delta_{20} + \gamma_{12} y_1 + \mathbf{z}_2 \boldsymbol{\delta}_2 + u_2$$

where u_1 and u_2 have zero means conditional on all exogenous variables, $\mathbf{z}$. (For emphasis, we have included separate intercepts.) Assume that both equations are identified when $\gamma_{13} = 0$.

a. When $\gamma_{13} = 0$, $\mathrm{E}(y_2 \mid \mathbf{z}) = \pi_{20} + \mathbf{z}\boldsymbol{\pi}_2$. What is $\mathrm{E}(y_2^2 \mid \mathbf{z})$ under homoskedasticity assumptions for u_1 and u_2?

b. Use part a to find $\mathrm{E}(y_1 \mid \mathbf{z})$ when $\gamma_{13} = 0$.

c. Use part b to argue that, when $\gamma_{13} = 0$, the forbidden regression consistently estimates the parameters in the first equation, including $\gamma_{13} = 0$.

d. If u_1 and u_2 have constant variances conditional on $\mathbf{z}$, and γ_{13} happens to be zero, show that the optimal instrumental variables for estimating the first equation are $\{1, \mathbf{z}, [\mathrm{E}(y_2 \mid \mathbf{z})]^2\}$. (Hint: Use Theorem 8.5; for a similar problem, see Problem 8.11.)

e. Reestimate equation (9.61) using IVs $[1, \mathbf{z}, (\hat{y}_2)^2]$, where $\mathbf{z}$ is all exogenous variables appearing in equations (9.61) and (9.62) and $\hat{y}_2$ denotes the fitted values from regressing log(*wage*) on 1, $\mathbf{z}$. Discuss the results.

9.13. For this question use the data in OPENNESS.RAW, taken from Romer (1993).

a. A simple simultaneous equations model to test whether "openness" (*open*) leads to lower inflation rates (*inf*) is

$$inf = \delta_{10} + \gamma_{12} open + \delta_{11} \log(pcinc) + u_1$$

$$open = \delta_{20} + \gamma_{21} inf + \delta_{21} \log(pcinc) + \delta_{22} \log(land) + u_2$$

Assuming that *pcinc* (per capita income) and *land* (land area) are exogenous, under what assumption is the first equation identified?

b. Estimate the reduced form for *open* to verify that log(*land*) is statistically significant.

c. Estimate the first equation from part a by 2SLS. Compare the estimate of γ_{12} with the OLS estimate.

d. Add the term $\gamma_{13} open^2$ to the first equation, and propose a way to test whether it is statistically significant. (Use only one more IV than you used in part c.)

e. With $\gamma_{13} open^2$ in the first equation, use the following method to estimate δ_{10}, γ_{12}, γ_{13}, and δ_{11}: (1) Regress *open* on 1, log(*pcinc*) and log(*land*), and obtain the fitted values, $\widehat{open}$. (2) Regress *inf* on 1, $\widehat{open}$, $(\widehat{open})^2$, and log(*pcinc*). Compare the results with those from part d. Which estimates do you prefer?

10 Basic Linear Unobserved Effects Panel Data Models

In Chapter 7 we covered a class of linear panel data models where, at a minimum, the error in each time period was assumed to be uncorrelated with the explanatory variables in the same time period. For certain panel data applications this assumption is too strong. In fact, a primary motivation for using panel data is to solve the omitted variables problem.

In this chapter we study population models that explicitly contain a time-constant, unobserved effect. The treatment in this chapter is "modern" in the sense that unobserved effects are treated as random variables, drawn from the population along with the observed explained and explanatory variables, as opposed to parameters to be estimated. In this framework, the key issue is whether the unobserved effect is uncorrelated with the explanatory variables.

10.1 Motivation: The Omitted Variables Problem

It is easy to see how panel data can be used, at least under certain assumptions, to obtain consistent estimators in the presence of omitted variables. Let y and $\mathbf{x} \equiv (x_1, x_2, \ldots, x_K)$ be observable random variables, and let c be an unobservable random variable; the vector $(y, x_1, x_2, \ldots, x_K, c)$ represents the population of interest. As is often the case in applied econometrics, we are interested in the partial effects of the observable explanatory variables x_j in the population regression function

$$\mathrm{E}(y \mid x_1, x_2, \ldots, x_K, c) \tag{10.1}$$

In words, we would like to hold c constant when obtaining partial effects of the observable explanatory variables. We follow Chamberlain (1984) in using c to denote the unobserved variable. Much of the panel data literature uses a Greek letter, such as α or ϕ, but we want to emphasize that the unobservable is a random variable, not a parameter to be estimated. (We discuss this point further in Section 10.2.1.)

Assuming a linear model, with c entering additively along with the x_j, we have

$$\mathrm{E}(y \mid \mathbf{x}, c) = \beta_0 + \mathbf{x}\boldsymbol{\beta} + c \tag{10.2}$$

where interest lies in the $K \times 1$ vector $\boldsymbol{\beta}$. On the one hand, if c is uncorrelated with each x_j, then c is just another unobserved factor affecting y that is not systematically related to the observable explanatory variables whose effects are of interest. On the other hand, if $\mathrm{Cov}(x_j, c) \neq 0$ for some j, putting c into the error term can cause serious problems. Without additional information we cannot consistently estimate $\boldsymbol{\beta}$, nor will we be able to determine whether there is a problem (except by introspection, or by concluding that the estimates of $\boldsymbol{\beta}$ are somehow "unreasonable").

Under additional assumptions there are ways to address the problem $\text{Cov}(\mathbf{x}, c) \neq \mathbf{0}$. We have covered at least three possibilities in the context of cross section analysis: (1) we might be able to find a suitable proxy variable for c, in which case we can estimate an equation by OLS where the proxy is plugged in for c; (2) we may be able to find instruments for the elements of $\mathbf{x}$ that are correlated with c and use an instrumental variables method, such as 2SLS; or (3) we may be able to find indicators of c that can then be used in multiple indicator instrumental variables procedure. These solutions are covered in Chapters 4 and 5.

If we have access to only a single cross section of observations, then the three remedies listed, or slight variants of them, largely exhaust the possibilities. However, if we can observe the *same* cross section units at different points in time—that is, if we can collect a panel data set—then other possibilties arise.

For illustration, suppose we can observe y and $\mathbf{x}$ at two different time periods; call these y_t, $\mathbf{x}_t$ for $t = 1, 2$. The population now represents two time periods on the same unit. Also, suppose that the omitted variable c is *time constant*. Then we are interested in the population regression function

$$\text{E}(y_t \mid \mathbf{x}_t, c) = \beta_0 + \mathbf{x}_t\boldsymbol{\beta} + c, \qquad t = 1, 2 \tag{10.3}$$

where $\mathbf{x}_t\boldsymbol{\beta} = \beta_1 x_{t1} + \cdots + \beta_K x_{tK}$ and x_{tj} indicates variable j at time t. Model (10.3) assumes that c has the same effect on the mean response in each time period. Without loss of generality, we set the coefficient on c equal to one. (Because c is unobserved and virtually never has a natural unit of measurement, it would be meaningless to try to estimate its partial effect.)

The assumption that c is constant over time (and has a constant partial effect over time) is crucial to the following analysis. An unobserved, time-constant variable is called an **unobserved effect** in panel data analysis. When t represents different time periods for the same individual, the unobserved effect is often interpreted as capturing features of an individual, such as cognitive ability, motivation, or early family upbringing, that are given and do not change over time. Similarly, if the unit of observation is the firm, c contains unobserved firm characteristics—such as managerial quality or structure—that can be viewed as being (roughly) constant over the period in question. We cover several specific examples of unobserved effects models in Section 10.2.

To discuss the additional assumptions sufficient to estimate $\boldsymbol{\beta}$, it is useful to write model (10.3) in error form as

$$y_t = \beta_0 + \mathbf{x}_t\boldsymbol{\beta} + c + u_t \tag{10.4}$$

where, by definition,

$$\mathrm{E}(u_t \mid \mathbf{x}_t, c) = 0, \qquad t = 1, 2 \tag{10.5}$$

One implication of condition (10.5) is

$$\mathrm{E}(\mathbf{x}_t' u_t) = \mathbf{0}, \qquad t = 1, 2 \tag{10.6}$$

If we were to assume $\mathrm{E}(\mathbf{x}_t' c) = \mathbf{0}$, we could apply pooled OLS, as we covered in Section 7.8. If c is correlated with any element of $\mathbf{x}_t$, then pooled OLS is biased and inconsistent.

With two years of data we can difference equation (10.4) across the two time periods to eliminate the time-constant unobservable, c. Define $\Delta y = y_2 - y_1$, $\Delta \mathbf{x} = \mathbf{x}_2 - \mathbf{x}_1$, and $\Delta u = u_2 - u_1$. Then, differencing equation (10.4) gives

$$\Delta y = \Delta \mathbf{x} \boldsymbol{\beta} + \Delta u \tag{10.7}$$

which is just a standard linear model in the differences of all variables (although the intercept has dropped out). Importantly, the parameter vector of interest, $\boldsymbol{\beta}$, appears directly in equation (10.7), and its presence suggests estimating equation (10.7) by OLS. Given a panel data set with two time periods, equation (10.7) is just a standard cross section equation. Under what assumptions will the OLS estimator from equation (10.7) be consistent?

Because we assume a random sample from the population, we can apply the results in Chapter 4 directly to equation (10.7). The key conditions for OLS to consistently estimate $\boldsymbol{\beta}$ are the orthogonality condition (Assumption OLS.1)

$$\mathrm{E}(\Delta \mathbf{x}' \Delta u) = \mathbf{0} \tag{10.8}$$

and the rank condition (Assumption OLS.2)

$$\operatorname{rank} \mathrm{E}(\Delta \mathbf{x}' \Delta \mathbf{x}) = K \tag{10.9}$$

Consider condition (10.8) first. It is equivalent to $\mathrm{E}[(\mathbf{x}_2 - \mathbf{x}_1)'(u_2 - u_1)] = \mathbf{0}$ or, after simple algebra,

$$\mathrm{E}(\mathbf{x}_2' u_2) + \mathrm{E}(\mathbf{x}_1' u_1) - \mathrm{E}(\mathbf{x}_1' u_2) - \mathrm{E}(\mathbf{x}_2' u_1) = \mathbf{0} \tag{10.10}$$

The first two terms in equation (10.10) are zero by condition (10.6), which holds for $t = 1, 2$. But condition (10.5) does *not* guarantee that $\mathbf{x}_1$ and u_2 are uncorrelated or that $\mathbf{x}_2$ and u_1 are uncorrelated. It might be reasonable to *assume* that condition (10.8) holds, but we must recognize that it does not follow from condition (10.5). Assuming that the error u_t is uncorrelated with $\mathbf{x}_1$ and $\mathbf{x}_2$ for $t = 1, 2$ is an example of a strict exogeneity assumption in unobserved components panel data models. We discuss strict exogeneity assumptions generally in Section 10.2. For now, we emphasize that assuming $\mathrm{Cov}(\mathbf{x}_t, u_s) = \mathbf{0}$ for all t and s puts no restrictions on the correlation between $\mathbf{x}_t$ and the unobserved effect, c.

The second assumption, condition (10.9), also deserves some attention now because the elements of $\mathbf{x}_t$ appearing in structural equation (10.3) have been differenced across time. If $\mathbf{x}_t$ contains a variable that is constant across time for every member of the population, then $\Delta\mathbf{x}$ contains an entry that is identically zero, and condition (10.9) fails. This outcome is not surprising: if c is allowed to be arbitrarily correlated with the elements of $\mathbf{x}_t$, the effect of any variable that is constant across time cannot be distinguished from the effect of c. Therefore, we can consistently estimate β_j only if there is some variation in x_{tj} over time.

In the remainder of this chapter, we cover various ways of dealing with the presence of unobserved effects under different sets of assumptions. We assume we have repeated observations on a cross section of N individuals, families, firms, school districts, cities, or some other economic unit. As in Chapter 7, we assume in this chapter that we have the same time periods, denoted $t = 1, 2, \ldots, T$, for each cross section observation. Such a data set is usually called a **balanced panel** because the same time periods are available for all cross section units. While the mechanics of the unbalanced case are similar to the balanced case, a careful treatment of the unbalanced case requires a formal description of why the panel may be unbalanced, and the sample selection issues can be somewhat subtle. Therefore, we hold off covering unbalanced panels until Chapter 17, where we discuss sample selection and attrition issues.

We still focus on asymptotic properties of estimators, where the time dimension, T, is fixed and the cross section dimension, N, grows without bound. With large-N asymptotics it is convenient to view the cross section observations as independent, identically distributed draws from the population. For any cross section observation i—denoting a single individual, firm, city, and so on—we denote the observable variables for all T time periods by $\{(y_{it}, \mathbf{x}_{it}): t = 1, 2, \ldots, T\}$. Because of the fixed T assumption, the asymptotic analysis is valid for arbitrary time dependence and distributional heterogeneity across t.

When applying asymptotic analysis to panel data methods it is important to remember that asymptotics are useful insofar as they provide a reasonable approximation to the finite sample properties of estimators and statistics. For example, a priori it is difficult to know whether $N \to \infty$ asymptotics works well with, say, $N = 50$ states in the United States and $T = 8$ years. But we can be pretty confident that $N \to \infty$ asymptotics are more appropriate than $T \to \infty$ asymptotics, even though N is practically fixed while T can grow. With large geographical regions, the random sampling assumption in the cross section dimension is conceptually flawed.

Nevertheless, if N is sufficiently large relative to T, and we can assume rough independence in the cross section, then our asymptotic analysis should provide suitable approximations.

If T is of the same order as N—for example, $N = 60$ countries and $T = 55$ post–World War II years—an asymptotic analysis that makes explicit assumptions about the nature of the time series dependence is needed. (In special cases, the conclusions about consistent estimation and approximate normality of t statistics will be the same, but not generally.) This area is just beginning to receive careful attention. If T is much larger than N, say $N = 5$ companies and $T = 40$ years, the framework becomes multiple time series analysis: N can be held fixed while $T \to \infty$.

10.2 Assumptions about the Unobserved Effects and Explanatory Variables

Before analyzing panel data estimation methods in more detail, it is useful to generally discuss the nature of the unobserved effects and certain features of the observed explanatory variables.

10.2.1 Random or Fixed Effects?

The basic **unobserved effects model (UEM)** can be written, for a randomly drawn cross section observation i, as

$$y_{it} = \mathbf{x}_{it}\boldsymbol{\beta} + c_i + u_{it}, \qquad t = 1, 2, \ldots, T \tag{10.11}$$

where $\mathbf{x}_{it}$ is $1 \times K$ and can contain observable variables that change across t but not i, variables that change across i but not t, and variables that change across i and t. In addition to unobserved effect, there are many other names given to c_i in applications: **unobserved component, latent variable,** and **unobserved heterogeneity** are common. If i indexes individuals, then c_i is sometimes called an **individual effect** or **individual heterogeneity**; analogous terms apply to families, firms, cities, and other cross-sectional units. The u_{it} are called the **idiosyncratic errors** or **idiosyncratic disturbances** because these change across t as well as across i.

Especially in methodological papers, but also in applications, one often sees a discussion about whether c_i will be treated as a *random effect* or a *fixed effect*. Originally, such discussions centered on whether c_i is properly viewed as a random variable or as a parameter to be estimated. In the traditional approach to panel data models, c_i is called a "random effect" when it is treated as a random variable and a "fixed effect" when it is treated as a parameter to be estimated for each cross section observation i. Our view is that discussions about whether the c_i should be treated as random variables or as parameters to be estimated are wrongheaded for microeconometric panel data applications. With a large number of random draws from the cross section, it almost always makes sense to treat the unobserved effects, c_i, as random draws from the population, along with y_{it} and $\mathbf{x}_{it}$. This approach is certainly appropriate from an omitted variables or neglected heterogeneity perspective. As our discussion in Section 10.1 suggests, the key issue involving c_i is whether or not it is uncorrelated with the observed explanatory variables $\mathbf{x}_{it}$, $t = 1, 2, \ldots, T$. Mundlak (1978) made this argument many years ago, and it still is persuasive.

In modern econometric parlance, "random effect" is synonymous with zero correlation between the observed explanatory variables and the unobserved effect: $\text{Cov}(\mathbf{x}_{it}, c_i) = \mathbf{0}$, $t = 1, 2, \ldots, T$. [Actually, a stronger conditional mean independence assumption, $\text{E}(c_i \mid \mathbf{x}_{i1}, \ldots, \mathbf{x}_{iT}) = \text{E}(c_i)$, will be needed to fully justify statistical inference; more on this subject in Section 10.4.] In applied papers, when c_i is referred to as, say, an "individual random effect," then c_i is probably being assumed to be uncorrelated with the $\mathbf{x}_{it}$.

In microeconometric applications, the term "fixed effect" does not usually mean that c_i is being treated as nonrandom; rather, it means that one is allowing for arbitrary correlation between the unobserved effect c_i and the observed explanatory variables $\mathbf{x}_{it}$. So, if c_i is called an "individual fixed effect" or a "firm fixed effect," then, for practical purposes, this terminology means that c_i is allowed to be correlated with $\mathbf{x}_{it}$. In this book, we avoid referring to c_i as a random effect or a fixed effect. Instead, we will refer to c_i as unobserved effect, unobserved heterogeneity, and so on. Nevertheless, later we will label two different estimation methods **random effects estimation** and **fixed effects estimation**. This terminology is so ingrained that it is pointless to try to change it now.

10.2.2 Strict Exogeneity Assumptions on the Explanatory Variables

Traditional unobserved components panel data models take the $\mathbf{x}_{it}$ as fixed. We will never assume the $\mathbf{x}_{it}$ are nonrandom because potential feedback from y_{it} to $\mathbf{x}_{is}$ for $s > t$ needs to be addressed explicitly.

In Chapter 7 we discussed strict exogeneity assumptions in panel data models that did not explicitly contain unobserved effects. We now provide strict exogeneity assumptions for models with unobserved effects.

In Section 10.1 we stated the strict exogeneity assumption in terms of zero correlation. For inference and efficiency discussions, we need to state the strict exogeneity assumption in terms of conditional expectations, and this statement also gives the assumption a clear meaning. With an unobserved effect, the most revealing form of the strict exogeneity assumption is

$$\mathrm{E}(y_{it} \mid \mathbf{x}_{i1}, \mathbf{x}_{i2}, \ldots, \mathbf{x}_{iT}, c_i) = \mathrm{E}(y_{it} \mid \mathbf{x}_{it}, c_i) = \mathbf{x}_{it}\boldsymbol{\beta} + c_i \tag{10.12}$$

for $t = 1, 2, \ldots, T$. The second equality is the functional form assumption on $\mathrm{E}(y_{it} \mid \mathbf{x}_{it}, c_i)$. It is the first equality that gives the strict exogeneity its interpretation. It means that, once $\mathbf{x}_{it}$ *and* c_i are controlled for, $\mathbf{x}_{is}$ has no partial effect on y_{it} for $s \neq t$.

When assumption (10.12) holds, we say that the $\{\mathbf{x}_{it}: t = 1, 2, \ldots, T\}$ are **strictly exogenous conditional on the unobserved effect** c_i. Assumption (10.12) and the corresponding terminology were introduced and used by Chamberlain (1982). We will explicitly cover Chamberlain's approach to estimating unobserved effects models in the next chapter, but his manner of stating assumptions is instructive even for traditional panel data analysis.

Assumption (10.12) restricts how the expected value of y_{it} can depend on explanatory variables in other time periods, but it is more reasonable than strict exogeneity without conditioning on the unobserved effect. Without conditioning on an unobserved effect, the strict exogeneity assumption is

$$\mathrm{E}(y_{it} \mid \mathbf{x}_{i1}, \mathbf{x}_{i2}, \ldots, \mathbf{x}_{iT}) = \mathrm{E}(y_{it} \mid \mathbf{x}_{it}) = \mathbf{x}_{it}\boldsymbol{\beta} \tag{10.13}$$

$t = 1, \ldots, T$. To see that assumption (10.13) is less likely to hold than assumption (10.12), first consider an example. Suppose that y_{it} is output of soybeans for farm i during year t, and $\mathbf{x}_{it}$ contains capital, labor, materials (such as fertilizer), rainfall, and other observable inputs. The unobserved effect, c_i, can capture average quality of land, managerial ability of the family running the farm, and other unobserved, time-constant factors. A natural assumption is that, once current inputs have been controlled for *along with* c_i, inputs used in other years have no effect on output during the current year. However, since the optimal choice of inputs in every year generally depends on c_i, it is likely that some partial correlation between output in year t and inputs in other years will exist if c_i is not controlled for: assumption (10.12) is reasonable while assumption (10.13) is not.

More generally, it is easy to see that assumption (10.13) fails whenever assumption (10.12) holds *and* the expected value of c_i depends on $(\mathbf{x}_{i1}, \ldots, \mathbf{x}_{iT})$. From the law of iterated expectations, if assumption (10.12) holds, then

$$\mathrm{E}(y_{it} \mid \mathbf{x}_{i1}, \ldots, \mathbf{x}_{iT}) = \mathbf{x}_{it}\boldsymbol{\beta} + \mathrm{E}(c_i \mid \mathbf{x}_{i1}, \ldots, \mathbf{x}_{iT})$$

and so assumption (10.13) fails if $\mathrm{E}(c_i \mid \mathbf{x}_{i1}, \ldots, \mathbf{x}_{iT}) \neq \mathrm{E}(c_i)$. In particular, assumption (10.13) fails if c_i is correlated with any of the $\mathbf{x}_{it}$.

Given equation (10.11), the strict exogeneity assumption can be stated in terms of the idiosyncratic errors as

$$\mathrm{E}(u_{it} \mid \mathbf{x}_{i1}, \ldots, \mathbf{x}_{iT}, c_i) = 0, \qquad t = 1, 2, \ldots, T \tag{10.14}$$

This assumption, in turn, implies that explanatory variables in each time period are uncorrelated with the idiosyncratic error in each time period:

$$\mathrm{E}(\mathbf{x}_{is}'u_{it}) = \mathbf{0}, \qquad s,t = 1,\ldots,T \tag{10.15}$$

This assumption is much stronger than assuming zero *contemporaneous* correlation: $\mathrm{E}(\mathbf{x}_{it}'u_{it}) = \mathbf{0}$, $t = 1,\ldots,T$. Nevertheless, assumption (10.15) does allow arbitary correlation between c_i and $\mathbf{x}_{it}$ for all t, something we ruled out in Section 7.8. Later, we will use the fact that assumption (10.14) implies that u_{it} and c_i are uncorrelated.

For examining consistency of panel data estimators, the zero correlation assumption (10.15) generally suffices. Further, assumption (10.15) is often the easiest way to think about whether strict exogeneity is likely to hold in a particular application. But standard forms of statistical inference, as well as the efficiency properties of standard estimators, rely on the stronger conditional mean formulation in assumption (10.14). Therefore, we focus on assumption (10.14).

10.2.3 Some Examples of Unobserved Effects Panel Data Models

Our discussions in Sections 10.2.1 and 10.2.2 emphasize that in any panel data application we should initially focus on two questions: (1) Is the unobserved effect, c_i, uncorrelated with $\mathbf{x}_{it}$ for all t? (2) Is the strict exogeneity assumption (conditional on c_i) reasonable? The following examples illustrate how we might organize our thinking on these two questions.

Example 10.1 (Program Evaluation): A standard model for estimating the effects of job training or other programs on subsequent wages is

$$\log(wage_{it}) = \theta_t + \mathbf{z}_{it}\gamma + \delta_1 prog_{it} + c_i + u_{it} \tag{10.16}$$

where i indexes individual and t indexes time period. The parameter θ_t denotes a time-varying intercept, and $\mathbf{z}_{it}$ is a set of observable characteristics that affect wage and may also be correlated with program participation.

Evaluation data sets are often collected at two points in time. At $t = 1$, no one has participated in the program, so that $prog_{i1} = 0$ for all i. Then, a subgroup is chosen to participate in the program (or the individuals choose to participate), and subsequent wages are observed for the control and treatment groups in $t = 2$. Model (10.16) allows for any number of time periods and general patterns of program participation.

The reason for including the individual effect, c_i, is the usual omitted ability story: if individuals choose whether or not to participate in the program, that choice could be correlated with ability. This possibility is often called the **self-selection problem**. Alternatively, administrators might assign people based on characteristics that the econometrician cannot observe.

The other issue is the strict exogeneity assumption of the explanatory variables, particularly $prog_{it}$. Typically, we feel comfortable with assuming that u_{it} is uncorrelated with $prog_{it}$. But what about correlation between u_{it} and, say, $prog_{i,t+1}$? Future program participation could depend on u_{it} if people choose to participate in the future based on shocks to their wage in the past, or if administrators choose people as participants at time $t+1$ who had a low u_{it}. Such feedback might not be very important, since c_i is being allowed for, but it could be. See, for example, Bassi (1984) and Ham and Lalonde (1996). Another issue, which is more easily dealt with, is that the training program could have lasting effects. If so, then we should include lags of $prog_{it}$ in model (10.16). Or, the program itself might last more than one period, in which case $prog_{it}$ can be replaced by a series of dummy variables for how long unit i at time t has been subject to the program.

Example 10.2 (Distributed Lag Model): Hausman, Hall, and Griliches (1984) estimate nonlinear distributed lag models to study the relationship between patents awarded to a firm and current and past levels of R&D spending. A linear, five-lag version of their model is

$$patents_{it} = \theta_t + \mathbf{z}_{it}\gamma + \delta_0 RD_{it} + \delta_1 RD_{i,t-1} + \cdots + \delta_5 RD_{i,t-5} + c_i + u_{it} \tag{10.17}$$

where RD_{it} is spending on R&D for firm i at time t and $\mathbf{z}_{it}$ contains variables such as firm size (as measured by sales or employees). The variable c_i is a firm heterogeneity term that may influence $patents_{it}$ and that may be correlated with current, past, and future R&D expenditures. Interest lies in the pattern of the δ_j coefficients. As with the other examples, we must decide whether R&D spending is likely to be correlated with c_i. In addition, if shocks to patents today (changes in u_{it}) influence R&D spending at future dates, then strict exogeneity can fail, and the methods in this chapter will not apply.

The next example presents a case where the strict exogeneity assumption is necessarily false, and the unobserved effect and the explanatory variable must be correlated.

Example 10.3 (Lagged Dependent Variable): A simple dynamic model of wage determination with unobserved heterogeneity is

$$\log(wage_{it}) = \beta_1 \log(wage_{i,t-1}) + c_i + u_{it}, \qquad t = 1, 2, \ldots, T \tag{10.18}$$

Often, interest lies in how persistent wages are (as measured by the size of β_1) *after* controlling for unobserved heterogeneity (individual productivity), c_i. Letting $y_{it} = \log(wage_{it})$, a standard assumption would be

$$\mathrm{E}(u_{it} \mid y_{i,t-1}, \ldots, y_{i0}, c_i) = 0 \tag{10.19}$$

which means that all of the dynamics are captured by the first lag. Let $x_{it} = y_{i,t-1}$. Then, under assumption (10.19), u_{it} is uncorrelated with $(x_{it}, x_{i,t-1}, \ldots, x_{i1})$, but u_{it} cannot be uncorrelated with $(x_{i,t+1}, \ldots, x_{iT})$, as $x_{i,t+1} = y_{it}$. In fact,

$$\mathrm{E}(y_{it}u_{it}) = \beta_1 \mathrm{E}(y_{i,t-1}u_{it}) + \mathrm{E}(c_i u_{it}) + \mathrm{E}(u_{it}^2) = \mathrm{E}(u_{it}^2) > 0 \tag{10.20}$$

because $\mathrm{E}(y_{i,t-1}u_{it}) = 0$ and $\mathrm{E}(c_i u_{it}) = 0$ under assumption (10.19). Therefore, the strict exogeneity assumption never holds in unobserved effects models with lagged dependent variables.

In addition, $y_{i,t-1}$ and c_i are necessarily correlated (since at time $t-1$, $y_{i,t-1}$ is the left-hand-side variable). Not only must strict exogeneity fail in this model, but the exogeneity assumption required for pooled OLS estimation of model (10.18) is also violated. We will study estimation of such models in Chapter 11.

10.3 Estimating Unobserved Effects Models by Pooled OLS

Under certain assumptions, the pooled OLS estimator can be used to obtain a consistent estimator of $\boldsymbol{\beta}$ in model (10.11). Write the model as

$$y_{it} = \mathbf{x}_{it}\boldsymbol{\beta} + v_{it}, \qquad t = 1, 2, \ldots, T \tag{10.21}$$

where $v_{it} \equiv c_i + u_{it}$, $t = 1, \ldots, T$ are the **composite errors**. For each t, v_{it} is the sum of the unobserved effect and an idiosyncratic error. From Section 7.8, we know that pooled OLS estimation of this equation is consistent if $\mathrm{E}(\mathbf{x}_{it}'v_{it}) = \mathbf{0}$, $t = 1, 2, \ldots, T$. Practically speaking, no correlation between x_{it} and v_{it} means that we are assuming $\mathrm{E}(\mathbf{x}_{it}'u_{it}) = \mathbf{0}$ and

$$\mathrm{E}(\mathbf{x}_{it}'c_i) = \mathbf{0}, \qquad t = 1, 2, \ldots, T \tag{10.22}$$

Equation (10.22) is the restrictive assumption, since $\mathrm{E}(\mathbf{x}_{it}'u_{it}) = \mathbf{0}$ holds if we have successfully modeled $\mathrm{E}(y_{it} \mid \mathbf{x}_{it}, c_i)$.

In static and finite distributed lag models we are sometimes willing to make the assumption (10.22); in fact, we will do so in the next section on random effects estimation. As seen in Example 10.3, models with lagged dependent variables in $\mathbf{x}_{it}$ *must* violate assumption (10.22) because $y_{i,t-1}$ and c_i must be correlated.

Even if assumption (10.22) holds, the composite errors will be serially correlated due to the presence of c_i in each time period. Therefore, inference using pooled OLS requires the robust variance matrix estimator and robust test statistics from Chapter 7. Because v_{it} depends on c_i for all t, the correlation between v_{it} and v_{is} does not generally decrease as the distance $|t-s|$ increases; in time-series parlance, the v_{it} are not weakly dependent across time. (We show this fact explicitly in the next section when $\{u_{it}: t = 1, \ldots, T\}$ is homoskedastic and serially uncorrelated.) Therefore, it is important that we be able to do large-N and fixed-T asymptotics when applying pooled OLS.

As we discussed in Chapter 7, each $(\mathbf{y}_i, \mathbf{X}_i)$ has T rows and should be ordered chronologically, and the $(\mathbf{y}_i, \mathbf{X}_i)$ should be stacked from $i = 1, \ldots, N$. The order of the cross section observations is, as usual, irrelevant.

10.4 Random Effects Methods

10.4.1 Estimation and Inference under the Basic Random Effects Assumptions

As with pooled OLS, a **random effects analysis** puts c_i into the error term. In fact, random effects analysis imposes more assumptions than those needed for pooled OLS: strict exogeneity in addition to orthogonality between c_i and $\mathbf{x}_{it}$. Stating the assumption in terms of conditional means, we have

ASSUMPTION RE.1:
(a) $\mathrm{E}(u_{it} \mid \mathbf{x}_i, c_i) = 0$, $t = 1, \ldots, T$.
(b) $\mathrm{E}(c_i \mid \mathbf{x}_i) = \mathrm{E}(c_i) = 0$

where $\mathbf{x}_i \equiv (\mathbf{x}_{i1}, \mathbf{x}_{i2}, \ldots, \mathbf{x}_{iT})$.

In Section 10.2 we discussed the meaning of the strict exogeneity Assumption RE.1a. Assumption RE.1b is how we will state the orthogonality between c_i and each $\mathbf{x}_{it}$. For obtaining consistent results, we could relax RE.1b to assumption (10.22), but in practice this approach affords little more generality, and we will use Assumption RE.1b later to derive the traditional asymptotic variance for the random effects estimator. Assumption RE.1b is always implied by the assumption that the $\mathbf{x}_{it}$ are fixed and $\mathrm{E}(c_i) = 0$, or by the assumption that c_i is independent of $\mathbf{x}_i$. The important part is $\mathrm{E}(c_i \mid \mathbf{x}_i) = \mathrm{E}(c_i)$; the assumption $\mathrm{E}(c_i) = 0$ is without loss of generality, provided an intercept is included in $\mathbf{x}_{it}$, as should almost always be the case.

Why do we maintain Assumption RE.1 when it is more restrictive than needed for a pooled OLS analysis? The random effects approach exploits the serial correlation in the composite error, $v_{it} = c_i + u_{it}$, in a generalized least squares (GLS) framework. In order to ensure that feasible GLS is consistent, we need some form of strict exogeneity between the explanatory variables and the composite error. Under Assumption RE.1 we can write

$$y_{it} = \mathbf{x}_{it}\boldsymbol{\beta} + v_{it} \tag{10.23}$$

$$\mathrm{E}(v_{it} \mid \mathbf{x}_i) = 0, \qquad t = 1, 2, \ldots, T \tag{10.24}$$

where

$$v_{it} = c_i + u_{it} \tag{10.25}$$

Equation (10.24) shows that $\{\mathbf{x}_{it}: t = 1, \ldots, T\}$ satisfies the strict exogeneity assumption SGLS.1 (see Chapter 7) in the model (10.23). Therefore, we can apply GLS methods that account for the particular error structure in equation (10.25).

Write the model (10.23) for all T time periods as

$$\mathbf{y}_i = \mathbf{X}_i \boldsymbol{\beta} + \mathbf{v}_i \tag{10.26}$$

and $\mathbf{v}_i$ can be written as $\mathbf{v}_i = c_i \mathbf{j}_T + \mathbf{u}_i$, where $\mathbf{j}_T$ is the $T \times 1$ vector of ones. Define the (unconditional) variance matrix of $\mathbf{v}_i$ as

$$\boldsymbol{\Omega} \equiv \mathrm{E}(\mathbf{v}_i \mathbf{v}_i') \tag{10.27}$$

a $T \times T$ matrix that we assume to be positive definite. Remember, this matrix is necessarily the same for all i because of the random sampling assumption in the cross section.

For consistency of GLS, we need the usual rank condition for GLS:

ASSUMPTION RE.2: rank $\mathrm{E}(\mathbf{X}_i' \boldsymbol{\Omega}^{-1} \mathbf{X}_i) = K$.

Applying the results from Chapter 7, we know that GLS and feasible GLS are consistent under Assumptions RE.1 and RE.2. A general FGLS analysis, using an unrestricted variance estimator $\boldsymbol{\Omega}$, is consistent and $\sqrt{N}$-asymptotically normal as $N \to \infty$. But we would not be exploiting the unobserved effects structure of v_{it}. A standard random effects analysis adds assumptions on the idiosyncratic errors that give $\boldsymbol{\Omega}$ a special form. The first assumption is that the idiosyncratic errors u_{it} have a constant unconditional variance across t:

$$\mathrm{E}(u_{it}^2) = \sigma_u^2, \qquad t = 1, 2, \ldots, T \tag{10.28}$$

The second assumption is that the idiosyncratic errors are serially uncorrelated:

$$\mathrm{E}(u_{it} u_{is}) = 0, \qquad \text{all } t \neq s \tag{10.29}$$

Under these two assumptions, we can derive the variances and covariances of the elements of $\mathbf{v}_i$. Under Assumption RE.1a, $\mathrm{E}(c_i u_{it}) = 0$, $t = 1, 2, \ldots, T$, and so

$$\mathrm{E}(v_{it}^2) = \mathrm{E}(c_i^2) + 2\mathrm{E}(c_i u_{it}) + \mathrm{E}(u_{it}^2) = \sigma_c^2 + \sigma_u^2$$

where $\sigma_c^2 = \mathrm{E}(c_i^2)$. Also, for all $t \neq s$,

$$\mathrm{E}(v_{it}v_{is}) = \mathrm{E}[(c_i + u_{it})(c_i + u_{is})] = \mathrm{E}(c_i^2) = \sigma_c^2$$

Therefore, under assumptions RE.1, (10.28), and (10.29), $\boldsymbol{\Omega}$ takes the special form

$$\boldsymbol{\Omega} = \mathrm{E}(\mathbf{v}_i\mathbf{v}_i') = \begin{pmatrix} \sigma_c^2 + \sigma_u^2 & \sigma_c^2 & \cdots & \sigma_c^2 \\ \sigma_c^2 & \sigma_c^2 + \sigma_u^2 & \cdots & \vdots \\ \vdots & & \ddots & \sigma_c^2 \\ \sigma_c^2 & & & \sigma_c^2 + \sigma_u^2 \end{pmatrix} \tag{10.30}$$

Because $\mathbf{j}_T\mathbf{j}_T'$ is the $T \times T$ matrix with unity in every element, we can write the matrix (10.30) as

$$\boldsymbol{\Omega} = \sigma_u^2\mathbf{I}_T + \sigma_c^2\mathbf{j}_T\mathbf{j}_T' \tag{10.31}$$

When $\boldsymbol{\Omega}$ has the form (10.31), we say it has the **random effects structure**. Rather than depending on $T(T+1)/2$ unrestricted variances and covariances, as would be the case in a general GLS analysis, $\boldsymbol{\Omega}$ depends only on two parameters, σ_c^2 and σ_u^2, regardless of the size of T. The correlation between the composite errors v_{it} and v_{is} does not depend on the difference between t and s: $\mathrm{Corr}(v_{is}, v_{it}) = \sigma_c^2/(\sigma_c^2 + \sigma_u^2) \geq 0$, $s \neq t$. This correlation is also the ratio of the variance of c_i to the variance of the composite error, and it is useful as a measure of the relative importance of the unobserved effect c_i.

Assumptions (10.28) and (10.29) are special to random effects. For efficiency of feasible GLS, we assume that the variance matrix of $\mathbf{v}_i$ conditional on $\mathbf{x}_i$ is constant:

$$\mathrm{E}(\mathbf{v}_i\mathbf{v}_i' \mid \mathbf{x}_i) = \mathrm{E}(\mathbf{v}_i\mathbf{v}_i') \tag{10.32}$$

Assumptions (10.28), (10.29), and (10.32) are implied by our third random effects assumption:

ASSUMPTION RE.3: (a) $\mathrm{E}(\mathbf{u}_i\mathbf{u}_i' \mid \mathbf{x}_i, c_i) = \sigma_u^2\mathbf{I}_T$. (b) $\mathrm{E}(c_i^2 \mid \mathbf{x}_i) = \sigma_c^2$.

Under Assumption RE.3a, $\mathrm{E}(u_{it}^2 \mid \mathbf{x}_i, c_i) = \sigma_u^2$, $t = 1, \ldots, T$, which implies assumption (10.28), and $\mathrm{E}(u_{it}u_{is} \mid \mathbf{x}_i, c_i) = 0$, $t \neq s$, $t, s = 1, \ldots, T$, which implies assumption (10.29) (both by the usual iterated expectations argument). But Assumption RE.3a is stronger because it assumes that the *conditional* variances are constant and the *conditional* covariances are zero. Along with Assumption RE.1b, Assumption RE.3b is the same as $\mathrm{Var}(c_i \mid \mathbf{x}_i) = \mathrm{Var}(c_i)$, which is a homoskedasticity assumption on the unobserved effect c_i. Under Assumption RE.3, assumption (10.32) holds and $\boldsymbol{\Omega}$ has the form (10.30).

To implement an FGLS procedure, define $\sigma_v^2 = \sigma_c^2 + \sigma_u^2$. For now, assume that we have consistent estimators of σ_u^2 and σ_c^2. Then we can form

$$\hat{\mathbf{\Omega}} \equiv \hat{\sigma}_u^2 \mathbf{I}_T + \hat{\sigma}_c^2 \mathbf{j}_T \mathbf{j}_T' \tag{10.33}$$

a $T \times T$ matrix that we assume to be positive definite. In a panel data context, the FGLS estimator that uses the variance matrix (10.33) is what is known as the **random effects estimator**:

$$\hat{\boldsymbol{\beta}}_{RE} = \left(\sum_{i=1}^{N} \mathbf{X}_i' \hat{\mathbf{\Omega}}^{-1} \mathbf{X}_i\right)^{-1} \left(\sum_{i=1}^{N} \mathbf{X}_i' \hat{\mathbf{\Omega}}^{-1} \mathbf{y}_i\right) \tag{10.34}$$

The random effects estimator is clearly motivated by Assumption RE.3. Nevertheless, $\hat{\boldsymbol{\beta}}_{RE}$ is consistent whether or not Assumption RE.3 holds. As long as Assumption RE.1 and the appropriate rank condition hold, $\hat{\boldsymbol{\beta}}_{RE} \xrightarrow{p} \boldsymbol{\beta}$ as $N \to \infty$. The argument is almost the same as showing that consistency of the FGLS estimator does not rely on $\mathrm{E}(\mathbf{v}_i\mathbf{v}_i' \mid \mathbf{X}_i) = \mathbf{\Omega}$. The only difference is that, even if $\mathbf{\Omega}$ does not have the special form in equation (10.31), $\hat{\mathbf{\Omega}}$ still has a well-defined probability limit. The fact that it does not necessarily converge to $\mathrm{E}(\mathbf{v}_i\mathbf{v}_i')$ does not affect the consistency of the random effects procedure. (Technically, we need to replace $\mathbf{\Omega}$ with $\mathrm{plim}(\hat{\mathbf{\Omega}})$ in stating Assumption RE.2.)

Under Assumption RE.3 the random effects estimator is efficient in the class of estimators consistent under $\mathrm{E}(\mathbf{v}_i \mid \mathbf{x}_i) = \mathbf{0}$, including pooled OLS and a variety of weighted least squares estimators, because RE is asymptotically equivalent to GLS under Assumptions RE.1–RE.3. The usual feasible GLS variance matrix—see equation (7.51)—is valid under Assumptions RE.1–RE.3. The only difference from the general analysis is that $\hat{\mathbf{\Omega}}$ is chosen as in expression (10.33).

In order to implement the RE procedure, we need to obtain $\hat{\sigma}_c^2$ and $\hat{\sigma}_u^2$. Actually, it is easiest to first find $\hat{\sigma}_v^2 = \hat{\sigma}_c^2 + \hat{\sigma}_u^2$. Under Assumption RE.3a, $\sigma_v^2 = T^{-1} \sum_{t=1}^{T} \mathrm{E}(v_{it}^2)$ for all i; therefore, averaging v_{it}^2 across all i and t would give a consistent estimator of σ_v^2. But we need to estimate $\boldsymbol{\beta}$ to make this method operational. A convenient initial estimator of $\boldsymbol{\beta}$ is the pooled OLS estimator, denoted here by $\hat{\hat{\boldsymbol{\beta}}}$. Let $\hat{\hat{v}}_{it}$ denote the pooled OLS residuals. A consistent estimator of σ_v^2 is

$$\hat{\sigma}_v^2 = \frac{1}{(NT - K)} \sum_{i=1}^{N} \sum_{t=1}^{T} \hat{\hat{v}}_{it}^2 \tag{10.35}$$

which is the usual variance estimator from the OLS regression on the pooled data. The degrees-of-freedom correction in equation (10.35)—that is, the use of $NT - K$

rather than NT—has no effect asymptotically. Under Assumptions RE.1–RE.3, equation (10.35) is a consistent estimator of σ_v^2.

To find a consistent estimator of σ_c^2, recall that $\sigma_c^2 = \mathrm{E}(v_{it}v_{is})$, all $t \neq s$. Therefore, for each i, there are $T(T-1)/2$ nonredundant error products that can be used to estimate σ_c^2. If we sum all these combinations and take the expectation, we get, for each i,

$$\mathrm{E}\left(\sum_{t=1}^{T-1}\sum_{s=t+1}^{T} v_{it}v_{is}\right) = \sum_{t=1}^{T-1}\sum_{s=t+1}^{T} \mathrm{E}(v_{it}v_{is}) = \sum_{t=1}^{T-1}\sum_{s=t+1}^{T} \sigma_c^2 = \sigma_c^2 \sum_{t=1}^{T-1}(T-t)$$
$$= \sigma_c^2((T-1)+(T-2)+\cdots+2+1) = \sigma_c^2 T(T-1)/2 \qquad (10.36)$$

where we have used the fact that the sum of the first $T-1$ positive integers is $T(T-1)/2$. As usual, a consistent estimator is obtained by replacing the expectation with an average (across i) and replacing v_{it} with its pooled OLS residual. We also make a degrees-of-freedom adjustment as a small-sample correction:

$$\hat{\sigma}_c^2 = \frac{1}{[NT(T-1)/2 - K]}\sum_{i=1}^{N}\sum_{t=1}^{T-1}\sum_{s=t+1}^{T} \hat{\hat{v}}_{it}\hat{\hat{v}}_{is} \qquad (10.37)$$

is a consistent estimator of σ_c^2 under Assumptions RE.1–RE.3. Given $\hat{\sigma}_v^2$ and $\hat{\sigma}_c^2$, we can form $\hat{\sigma}_u^2 = \hat{\sigma}_v^2 - \hat{\sigma}_c^2$. [The idiosyncratic error variance, σ_u^2, can also be estimated using the fixed effects method, which we discuss in Section 10.5. Also, there are other methods of estimating σ_c^2. A common estimator of σ_c^2 is based on the between estimator of $\boldsymbol{\beta}$, which we touch on in Section 10.5; see Hsiao (1986, Section 3.3) and Baltagi (1995, Section 2.3). Because the RE estimator is a feasible GLS estimator, all that we need are consistent estimators of σ_c^2 and σ_u^2 in order to obtain a $\sqrt{N}$-efficient estimator of $\boldsymbol{\beta}$.]

As a practical matter, equation (10.37) is not guaranteed to be positive, although it is in the vast majority of applications. A negative value for $\hat{\sigma}_c^2$ is indicative of negative serial correlation in u_{it}, probably a substantial amount, which means that Assumption RE.3a is violated. Alternatively, some other assumption in the model can be false. We should make sure that time dummies are included in the model if they are significant; omitting them can induce serial correlation in the implied u_{it}. If $\hat{\sigma}_c^2$ is negative, unrestricted FGLS may be called for; see Section 10.4.3.

Example 10.4 (RE Estimation of the Effects of Job Training Grants): We now use the data in JTRAIN1.RAW to estimate the effect of job training grants on firm scrap rates, using a random effects analysis. There are 54 firms that reported scrap rates for each of the years 1987, 1988, and 1989. Grants were not awarded in 1987. Some firms received grants in 1988, others received grants in 1989, and a firm could not receive a grant twice. Since there are firms in 1989 that received a grant only in 1988, it is important to allow the grant effect to persist one period. The estimated equation is

$$\begin{aligned}\log(\widehat{scrap}) = \underset{(.243)}{.415} - \underset{(.109)}{.093}\ d88 - \underset{(.132)}{.270}\ d89 + \underset{(.411)}{.548}\ union \\ - \underset{(.148)}{.215}\ grant - \underset{(.205)}{.377}\ grant_{-1}\end{aligned}$$

The lagged value of *grant* has the larger impact and is statistically significant at the 5 percent level against a one-sided alternative. You are invited to estimate the equation without $grant_{-1}$ to verify that the estimated grant effect is much smaller (on the order of 6.7 percent) and statistically insignificant.

Multiple hypotheses tests are carried out as in any FGLS analysis; see Section 7.6, where $G = T$. In computing an F-type statistic based on weighted sums of squared residuals, $\hat{\mathbf{\Omega}}$ in expression (10.33) should be based on the pooled OLS residuals from the unrestricted model. Then, obtain the residuals from the unrestricted random effects estimation as $\hat{\mathbf{v}}_i \equiv \mathbf{y}_i - \mathbf{X}_i\hat{\boldsymbol{\beta}}_{RE}$. Let $\tilde{\boldsymbol{\beta}}_{RE}$ denote the random effects estimator with the Q linear restrictions imposed, and define the restricted random effects residuals as $\tilde{\mathbf{v}}_i \equiv \mathbf{y}_i - \mathbf{X}_i\tilde{\boldsymbol{\beta}}_{RE}$. Insert these into equation (7.52) in place of $\hat{\mathbf{u}}_i$ and $\tilde{\mathbf{u}}_i$ for a chi-square statistic or into equation (7.53) for an F-type statistic.

In Example 10.4, the Wald test for joint significance of *grant* and $grant_{-1}$ (against a two-sided alternative) yields a χ^2_2 statistic equal to 3.66, with p-value $= .16$. (This test comes from Stata®.)

10.4.2 Robust Variance Matrix Estimator

Because failure of Assumption RE.3 does not cause inconsistency in the RE estimator, it is very useful to be able to conduct statistical inference without this assumption. Assumption RE.3 can fail for two reasons. First, $\mathrm{E}(\mathbf{v}_i\mathbf{v}_i' \mid \mathbf{x}_i)$ may not be constant, so that $\mathrm{E}(\mathbf{v}_i\mathbf{v}_i' \mid \mathbf{x}_i) \neq \mathrm{E}(\mathbf{v}_i\mathbf{v}_i')$. This outcome is always a possibility with GLS analysis. Second, $\mathrm{E}(\mathbf{v}_i\mathbf{v}_i')$ may not have the random effects structure: the idiosyncratic errors u_{it} may have variances that change over time, or they could be serially correlated. In either case a robust variance matrix is available from the analysis in Chapter 7. We simply use equation (7.49) with $\hat{\mathbf{u}}_i$ replaced by $\hat{\mathbf{v}}_i = \mathbf{y}_i - \mathbf{X}_i\hat{\boldsymbol{\beta}}_{RE}$, $i = 1, 2, \ldots, N$, the $T \times 1$ vectors of RE residuals.

Robust standard errors are obtained in the usual way from the robust variance matrix estimator, and robust Wald statistics are obtained by the usual formula $W =$

$(\mathbf{R}\hat{\boldsymbol{\beta}} - \mathbf{r})'(\mathbf{R}\hat{\mathbf{V}}\mathbf{R}')^{-1}(\mathbf{R}\hat{\boldsymbol{\beta}} - \mathbf{r})$, where $\hat{\mathbf{V}}$ is the robust variance matrix estimator. Remember, if Assumption RE.3 is violated, the sum of squared residuals form of the F statistic is not valid.

The idea behind using a robust variance matrix is the following. Assumptions RE.1–RE.3 lead to a well-known estimation technique whose properties are understood under these assumptions. But it is always a good idea to make the analysis robust whenever feasible. With fixed T and large N asymptotics, we lose nothing in using the robust standard errors and test statistics even if Assumption RE.3 holds. In Section 10.7.2, we show how the RE estimator can be obtained from a particular pooled OLS regression, which makes obtaining robust standard errors and t and F statistics especially easy.

10.4.3 A General FGLS Analysis

If the idiosyncratic errors $\{u_{it}\colon t = 1, 2, \ldots, T\}$ are generally heteroskedastic and serially correlated across t, a more general estimator of $\boldsymbol{\Omega}$ can be used in FGLS:

$$\hat{\boldsymbol{\Omega}} = N^{-1} \sum_{i=1}^{N} \hat{\hat{\mathbf{v}}}_i \hat{\hat{\mathbf{v}}}_i' \tag{10.38}$$

where the $\hat{\hat{\mathbf{v}}}_i$ would be the pooled OLS residuals. The FGLS estimator is consistent under Assumptions RE.1 and RE.2, and, if we assume that $\mathrm{E}(\mathbf{v}_i\mathbf{v}_i' \mid \mathbf{x}_i) = \boldsymbol{\Omega}$, then the FGLS estimator is asymptotically efficient and its asymptotic variance estimator takes the usual form.

Using equation (10.38) is more general than the RE analysis. In fact, with large N asymptotics, the general FGLS estimator is just as efficient as the random effects estimator under Assumptions RE.1–RE.3. Using equation (10.38) is asymptotically more efficient if $\mathrm{E}(\mathbf{v}_i\mathbf{v}_i' \mid \mathbf{x}_i) = \boldsymbol{\Omega}$, but $\boldsymbol{\Omega}$ does not have the random effects form. So why not always use FGLS with $\hat{\boldsymbol{\Omega}}$ given in equation (10.38)? There are historical reasons for using random effects methods rather than a general FGLS analysis. The structure of $\boldsymbol{\Omega}$ in the matrix (10.30) was once synonomous with unobserved effects models: any correlation in the composite errors $\{v_{it}\colon t = 1, 2, \ldots, T\}$ was assumed to be caused by the presence of c_i. The idiosyncratic errors, u_{it}, were, by definition, taken to be serially uncorrelated and homoskedastic.

If N is not several times larger than T, an unrestricted FGLS analysis can have poor finite sample properties because $\hat{\boldsymbol{\Omega}}$ has $T(T+1)/2$ estimated elements. Even though estimation of $\boldsymbol{\Omega}$ does not affect the asymptotic distribution of the FGLS estimator, it certainly affects its finite sample properties. Random effects estimation requires estimation of only two variance parameters for any T.

With very large N, using the general estimate of $\boldsymbol{\Omega}$ is an attractive alternative, especially if the estimate in equation (10.38) appears to have a pattern different from the random effects pattern. As a middle ground between a traditional random effects analysis and a full-blown FGLS analysis, we might specify a particular structure for the idiosyncratic error variance matrix $\mathrm{E}(\mathbf{u}_i\mathbf{u}_i')$. For example, if $\{u_{it}\}$ follows a stable first-order autoregressive process with autocorrelation coefficient ρ and variance σ_u^2, then $\boldsymbol{\Omega} = \mathrm{E}(\mathbf{u}_i\mathbf{u}_i') + \sigma_c^2\mathbf{j}_T\mathbf{j}_T'$ depends in a known way on only three parameters, σ_u^2, σ_c^2, and ρ. These parameters can be estimated after initial pooled OLS estimation, and then an FGLS procedure using the particular structure of $\boldsymbol{\Omega}$ is easy to implement. We do not cover such possibilities explicitly; see, for example, MaCurdy (1982).

10.4.4 Testing for the Presence of an Unobserved Effect

If the standard random effects assumptions RE.1–RE.3 hold but the model does not actually contain an unobserved effect, pooled OLS is efficient and all associated pooled OLS statistics are asymptotically valid. The absence of an unobserved effect is statistically equivalent to H_0: $\sigma_c^2 = 0$.

To test H_0: $\sigma_c^2 = 0$, we can use the simple test for AR(1) serial correlation covered in Chapter 7 [see equation (7.77)]. The AR(1) test is valid because the errors v_{it} are serially uncorrelated under the null H_0: $\sigma_c^2 = 0$ (and we are assuming that $\{\mathbf{x}_{it}\}$ is strictly exogenous). However, a better test is based directly on the estimator of σ_c^2 in equation (10.37).

Breusch and Pagan (1980) derive a statistic using the Lagrange multiplier principle in a likelihood setting (something we cover in Chapter 13). We will not derive the Breusch and Pagan statistic because we are not assuming any particular distribution for the v_{it}. Instead, we derive a similar test that has the advantage of being valid for *any* distribution of $\mathbf{v}_i$ and only states that the v_{it} are uncorrelated under the null. (In particular, the statistic is valid for heteroskedasticity in the v_{it}.)

From equation (10.37), we base a test of H_0: $\sigma_c^2 = 0$ on the null asymptotic distribution of

$$N^{-1/2}\sum_{i=1}^{N}\sum_{t=1}^{T-1}\sum_{s=t+1}^{T}\hat{v}_{it}\hat{v}_{is} \tag{10.39}$$

which is essentially the estimator $\hat{\sigma}_c^2$ scaled up by $\sqrt{N}$. Because of strict exogeneity, this statistic has the same limiting distribution (as $N \to \infty$ with fixed T) when we replace the pooled OLS residuals $\hat{v}_{it}$ with the errors v_{it} (see Problem 7.4). For any distribution of the v_{it}, $N^{-1/2}\sum_{i=1}^{N}\sum_{t=1}^{T-1}\sum_{s=t+1}^{T} v_{it}v_{is}$ has a limiting normal distribution (under the null that the v_{it} are serially uncorrelated) with variance

$\mathrm{E}(\sum_{t=1}^{T-1}\sum_{s=t+1}^{T} v_{it}v_{is})^2$. We can estimate this variance in the usual way (take away the expectation, average across i, and replace v_{it} with $\hat{v}_{it}$). When we put expression (10.39) over its asymptotic standard error we get the statistic

$$\frac{\sum_{i=1}^{N}\sum_{t=1}^{T-1}\sum_{s=t+1}^{T}\hat{v}_{it}\hat{v}_{is}}{\left[\sum_{i=1}^{N}\left(\sum_{t=1}^{T-1}\sum_{s=t+1}^{T}\hat{v}_{it}\hat{v}_{is}\right)^2\right]^{1/2}} \tag{10.40}$$

Under the null hypothesis that the v_{it} are serially uncorrelated, this statistic is distributed asymptotically as standard normal. Unlike the Breusch-Pagan statistic, with expression (10.40) we can reject H_0 for *negative* estimates of σ_c^2, although negative estimates are rare in practice (unless we have already differenced the data, something we discuss in Section 10.6).

The statistic in expression (10.40) can detect many kinds of serial correlation in the composite error v_{it}, and so a rejection of the null should not be interpreted as implying that the random effects error structure *must* be true. Finding that the v_{it} are serially uncorrelated is not very surprising in applications, especially since $\mathbf{x}_{it}$ cannot contain lagged dependent variables for the methods in this chapter.

It is probably more interesting to test for serial correlation in the $\{u_{it}\}$, as this is a test of the random effects form of $\mathbf{\Omega}$. Baltagi and Li (1995) obtain a test under normality of c_i and $\{u_{it}\}$, based on the Lagrange multiplier principle. In Section 10.7.2, we discuss a simpler test for serial correlation in $\{u_{it}\}$ using a pooled OLS regression on transformed data, which does not rely on normality.

10.5 Fixed Effects Methods

10.5.1 Consistency of the Fixed Effects Estimator

Again consider the linear unobserved effects model for T time periods:

$$y_{it} = \mathbf{x}_{it}\boldsymbol{\beta} + c_i + u_{it}, \qquad t = 1, \ldots, T \tag{10.41}$$

The random effects approach to estimating $\boldsymbol{\beta}$ effectively puts c_i into the error term, under the assumption that c_i is orthogonal to $\mathbf{x}_{it}$, and then accounts for the implied serial correlation in the composite error $v_{it} = c_i + u_{it}$ using a GLS analysis. In many applications the whole point of using panel data is to allow for c_i to be arbitrarily correlated with the $\mathbf{x}_{it}$. A fixed effects analysis achieves this purpose explicitly.

The T equations in the model (10.41) can be written as

$$\mathbf{y}_i = \mathbf{X}_i\boldsymbol{\beta} + c_i\mathbf{j}_T + \mathbf{u}_i \tag{10.42}$$

where $\mathbf{j}_T$ is still the $T \times 1$ vector of ones. As usual, equation (10.42) represents a single random draw from the cross section.

The first fixed effects (FE) assumption is strict exogeneity of the explanatory variables conditional on c_i:

ASSUMPTION FE.1: $\mathrm{E}(u_{it} \mid \mathbf{x}_i, c_i) = 0$, $t = 1, 2, \ldots, T$.

This assumption is *identical* to the first part of Assumption RE.1. Thus, we maintain strict exogeneity of $\{\mathbf{x}_{it}: t = 1, \ldots, T\}$ conditional on the unobserved effect. The key difference is that we do not assume RE.1b. In other words, for fixed effects analysis, $\mathrm{E}(c_i \mid \mathbf{x}_i)$ is allowed to be any function of $\mathbf{x}_i$.

By relaxing RE.1b we can consistently estimate partial effects in the presence of time-constant omitted variables that can be arbitrarily related to the observables $\mathbf{x}_{it}$. Therefore, fixed effects analysis is more robust than random effects analysis. As we suggested in Section 10.1, this robustness comes at a price: without further assumptions, we cannot include time-constant factors in $\mathbf{x}_{it}$. The reason is simple: if c_i can be arbitrarily correlated with each element of $\mathbf{x}_{it}$, there is no way to distinguish the effects of time-constant observables from the time-constant unobservable c_i. When analyzing individuals, factors such as gender or race cannot be included in $\mathbf{x}_{it}$. For analyzing firms, industry cannot be included in $\mathbf{x}_{it}$ unless industry designation changes over time for at least some firms. For cities, variables describing fixed city attributes, such as whether or not the city is near a river, cannot be included in $\mathbf{x}_{it}$.

The fact that $\mathbf{x}_{it}$ cannot include time-constant explanatory variables is a drawback in certain applications, but when the interest is only on time-varying explanatory variables, it is convenient not to have to worry about modeling time-constant factors that are not of direct interest.

In panel data analysis the term "time-varying explanatory variables" means that each element of $\mathbf{x}_{it}$ varies over time for *some* cross section units. Often there are elements of $\mathbf{x}_{it}$ that are constant across time for a subset of the cross section. For example, if we have a panel of adults and one element of $\mathbf{x}_{it}$ is education, we can allow education to be constant for some part of the sample. But we must have education changing for some people in the sample.

As a general specification, let $d2_t, \ldots, dT_t$ denote time period dummies so that $ds_t = 1$ if $s = t$, and zero otherwise (often these are defined in terms of specific years, such as $d88_t$, but at this level we call them time period dummies). Let $\mathbf{z}_i$ be a vector of time-constant observables, and let $\mathbf{w}_{it}$ be a vector of time-varying variables. Suppose y_{it} is determined by

$$y_{it} = \theta_1 + \theta_2 d2_t + \cdots + \theta_T dT_t + \mathbf{z}_i \gamma_1 + d2_t \mathbf{z}_i \gamma_2 + \cdots + dT_t \mathbf{z}_i \gamma_T + \mathbf{w}_{it} \boldsymbol{\delta} + c_i + u_{it} \tag{10.43}$$

$$\mathrm{E}(u_{it} \mid \mathbf{z}_i, \mathbf{w}_{i1}, \mathbf{w}_{i2}, \ldots, \mathbf{w}_{iT}, c_i) = 0, \qquad t = 1, 2, \ldots, T \tag{10.44}$$

We hope that this model represents a causal relationship, where the conditioning on c_i allows us to control for unobserved factors that are time constant. Without further assumptions, the intercept θ_1 cannot be identified and the vector γ_1 on $\mathbf{z}_i$ cannot be identified, because $\theta_1 + \mathbf{z}_i \gamma_1$ cannot be distinguished from c_i. Note that θ_1 is the intercept for the base time period, $t = 1$, and γ_1 measures the effects of $\mathbf{z}_i$ on y_{it} in period $t = 1$. Even though we cannot identify the effects of the $\mathbf{z}_i$ in any particular time period, $\gamma_2, \gamma_3, \ldots, \gamma_T$ *are* identified, and therefore we can estimate the *differences* in the partial effects on time-constant variables relative to a base period. In particular, we can test whether the effects of time-constant variables have changed over time. As a specific example, if $y_{it} = \log(wage_{it})$ and one element of $\mathbf{z}_i$ is a female binary variable, then we can estimate how the gender gap has changed over time, even though we cannot estimate the gap in any particular time period.

The idea for estimating $\boldsymbol{\beta}$ under Assumption FE.1 is to transform the equations to eliminate the unobserved effect c_i. When at least two time periods are available, there are several transformations that accomplish this purpose. In this section we study the **fixed effects transformation**, also called the **within transformation**. The FE transformation is obtained by first averaging equation (10.41) over $t = 1, \ldots, T$ to get the cross section equation

$$\bar{y}_i = \bar{\mathbf{x}}_i \boldsymbol{\beta} + c_i + \bar{u}_i \tag{10.45}$$

where $\bar{y}_i = T^{-1} \sum_{t=1}^{T} y_{it}$, $\bar{\mathbf{x}}_i = T^{-1} \sum_{t=1}^{T} \mathbf{x}_{it}$, and $\bar{u}_i = T^{-1} \sum_{t=1}^{T} u_{it}$. Subtracting equation (10.45) from equation (10.41) for each t gives the FE transformed equation,

$$y_{it} - \bar{y}_i = (\mathbf{x}_{it} - \bar{\mathbf{x}}_i)\boldsymbol{\beta} + u_{it} - \bar{u}_i$$

or

$$\ddot{y}_{it} = \ddot{\mathbf{x}}_{it} \boldsymbol{\beta} + \ddot{u}_{it}, \qquad t = 1, 2, \ldots, T \tag{10.46}$$

where $\ddot{y}_{it} \equiv y_{it} - \bar{y}_i$, $\ddot{\mathbf{x}}_{it} \equiv \mathbf{x}_{it} - \bar{\mathbf{x}}_i$, and $\ddot{u}_{it} \equiv u_{it} - \bar{u}_i$. The time demeaning of the original equation has removed the individual specific effect c_i.

With c_i out of the picture, it is natural to think of estimating equation (10.46) by pooled OLS. Before investigating this possibility, we must remember that equation (10.46) is an *estimating* equation: the interpretation of $\boldsymbol{\beta}$ comes from the (structural) conditional expectation $\mathrm{E}(y_{it} \mid \mathbf{x}_i, c_i) = \mathrm{E}(y_{it} \mid \mathbf{x}_{it}, c_i) = \mathbf{x}_{it} \boldsymbol{\beta} + c_i$.

To see whether pooled OLS estimation of equation (10.46) will be consistent, we need to show that the key pooled OLS assumption (Assumption POLS.1 from Chapter 7) holds in equation (10.46). That is,

$$\mathrm{E}(\ddot{\mathbf{x}}_{it}'\ddot{u}_{it}) = \mathbf{0}, \qquad t = 1, 2, \ldots, T \tag{10.47}$$

For each t, the left-hand side of equation (10.47) can be written as $\mathrm{E}[(\mathbf{x}_{it} - \bar{\mathbf{x}}_i)'(u_{it} - \bar{u}_i)]$. Now, under Assumption FE.1, u_{it} is uncorrelated with $\mathbf{x}_{is}$, for all $s, t = 1, 2, \ldots, T$. It follows that u_{it} and $\bar{u}_i$ are uncorrelated with $\mathbf{x}_{it}$ and $\bar{\mathbf{x}}_i$ for $t = 1, 2, \ldots, T$. Therefore, assumption (10.47) holds under Assumption FE.1, and so pooled OLS applied to equation (10.46) can be expected to produce consistent estimators. We can actually say a lot more than condition (10.47): under Assumption FE.1, $\mathrm{E}(\ddot{u}_{it} \mid \mathbf{x}_i) = \mathrm{E}(u_{it} \mid \mathbf{x}_i) - \mathrm{E}(\bar{u}_i \mid \mathbf{x}_i) = 0$, which in turn implies that $\mathrm{E}(\ddot{u}_{it} \mid \ddot{\mathbf{x}}_{i1}, \ldots, \ddot{\mathbf{x}}_{iT}) = 0$, since each $\ddot{\mathbf{x}}_{it}$ is just a function of $\mathbf{x}_i = (\mathbf{x}_{i1}, \ldots, \mathbf{x}_{iT})$. This result shows that the $\ddot{\mathbf{x}}_{it}$ satisfy the conditional expectation form of the strict exogeneity assumption in the model (10.46). Among other things, this conclusion implies that the fixed effects estimator of $\boldsymbol{\beta}$ that we will derive is actually unbiased under Assumption FE.1.

It is important to see that assumption (10.47) fails if we try to relax the strict exogeneity assumption to something weaker, such as $\mathrm{E}(\mathbf{x}_{it}'u_{it}) = \mathbf{0}$, all t, because this assumption does not ensure that $\mathbf{x}_{is}$ is uncorrelated with u_{it}, $s \neq t$.

The **fixed effects (FE) estimator**, denoted by $\hat{\boldsymbol{\beta}}_{FE}$, is the pooled OLS estimator from the regression

$$\ddot{y}_{it} \text{ on } \ddot{\mathbf{x}}_{it}, \qquad t = 1, 2, \ldots, T; i = 1, 2, \ldots, N \tag{10.48}$$

The FE estimator is simple to compute once the time demeaning has been carried out. Some econometrics packages have special commands to carry out fixed effects estimation (and commands to carry out the time demeaning for all i). It is also fairly easy to program this estimator in matrix-oriented languages.

To study the FE estimator a little more closely, write equation (10.46) for all time periods as

$$\ddot{\mathbf{y}}_i = \ddot{\mathbf{X}}_i\boldsymbol{\beta} + \ddot{\mathbf{u}}_i \tag{10.49}$$

where $\ddot{\mathbf{y}}_i$ is $T \times 1$, $\ddot{\mathbf{X}}_i$ is $T \times K$, and $\ddot{\mathbf{u}}_i$ is $T \times 1$. This set of equations can be obtained by premultiplying equation (10.42) by a **time-demeaning matrix**. Define $\mathbf{Q}_T \equiv \mathbf{I}_T - \mathbf{j}_T(\mathbf{j}_T'\mathbf{j}_T)^{-1}\mathbf{j}_T'$, which is easily seen to be a $T \times T$ symmetric, idempotent matrix with rank $T - 1$. Further, $\mathbf{Q}_T\mathbf{j}_T = \mathbf{0}$, $\mathbf{Q}_T\mathbf{y}_i = \ddot{\mathbf{y}}_i$, $\mathbf{Q}_T\mathbf{X}_i = \ddot{\mathbf{X}}_i$, and $\mathbf{Q}_T\mathbf{u}_i = \ddot{\mathbf{u}}_i$, and so premultiplying equation (10.42) by $\mathbf{Q}_T$ gives the demeaned equations (10.49).

In order to ensure that the FE estimator is well behaved asymptotically, we need a standard rank condition on the matrix of time-demeaned explanatory variables:

ASSUMPTION FE.2: $\operatorname{rank}\left(\sum_{t=1}^{T} \mathrm{E}(\ddot{\mathbf{x}}_{it}'\ddot{\mathbf{x}}_{it})\right) = \operatorname{rank}[\mathrm{E}(\ddot{\mathbf{X}}_i'\ddot{\mathbf{X}}_i)] = K$.

If $\mathbf{x}_{it}$ contains an element that does not vary over time for any i, then the corresponding element in $\ddot{\mathbf{x}}_{it}$ is identically zero for all t and any draw from the cross section. Since $\ddot{\mathbf{X}}_i$ would contain a column of zeros for all i, Assumption FE.2 could not be true. Assumption FE.2 shows explicitly why time-constant variables are not allowed in fixed effects analysis (unless they are interacted with time-varying variables, such as time dummies).

The fixed effects estimator can be expressed as

$$\hat{\boldsymbol{\beta}}_{FE} = \left(\sum_{i=1}^{N} \ddot{\mathbf{X}}_i'\ddot{\mathbf{X}}_i\right)^{-1} \left(\sum_{i=1}^{N} \ddot{\mathbf{X}}_i'\ddot{\mathbf{y}}_i\right) = \left(\sum_{i=1}^{N}\sum_{t=1}^{T} \ddot{\mathbf{x}}_{it}'\ddot{\mathbf{x}}_{it}\right)^{-1} \left(\sum_{i=1}^{N}\sum_{t=1}^{T} \ddot{\mathbf{x}}_{it}'\ddot{y}_{it}\right) \tag{10.50}$$

It is also called the **within estimator** because it uses the time variation within each cross section. The **between estimator**, which uses only variation between the cross section observations, is the OLS estimator applied to the time-averaged equation (10.45). This estimator is not consistent under Assumption FE.1 because $\mathrm{E}(\bar{\mathbf{x}}_i'c_i)$ is not necessarily zero. The between estimator is consistent under Assumption RE.1 and a standard rank condition, but it effectively discards the time series information in the data set. It is more efficient to use the random effects estimator.

Under Assumption FE.1 and the finite sample version of Assumption FE.2, namely, $\operatorname{rank}(\ddot{\mathbf{X}}'\ddot{\mathbf{X}}) = K$, $\hat{\boldsymbol{\beta}}_{FE}$ can be shown to be *unbiased* conditional on $\mathbf{X}$.

10.5.2 Asymptotic Inference with Fixed Effects

Without further assumptions the FE estimator is not necessarily the most efficient estimator based on Assumption FE.1. The next assumption ensures that FE is efficient.

ASSUMPTION FE.3: $\mathrm{E}(\mathbf{u}_i\mathbf{u}_i' \mid \mathbf{x}_i, c_i) = \sigma_u^2\mathbf{I}_T$.

Assumption FE.3 is identical to Assumption RE.3a. Since $\mathrm{E}(\mathbf{u}_i \mid \mathbf{x}_i, c_i) = \mathbf{0}$ by Assumption FE.1, Assumption FE.3 is the same as saying $\operatorname{Var}(\mathbf{u}_i \mid \mathbf{x}_i, c_i) = \sigma_u^2\mathbf{I}_T$ if Assumption FE.1 also holds. As with Assumption RE.3a, it is useful to think of Assumption FE.3 as having two parts. The first is that $\mathrm{E}(\mathbf{u}_i\mathbf{u}_i' \mid \mathbf{x}_i, c_i) = \mathrm{E}(\mathbf{u}_i\mathbf{u}_i')$, which is standard in system estimation contexts [see equation (7.50)]. The second is that the unconditional variance matrix $\mathrm{E}(\mathbf{u}_i\mathbf{u}_i')$ has the special form $\sigma_u^2\mathbf{I}_T$. This implies that the idiosyncratic errors u_{it} have a constant variance across t and are serially uncorrelated, just as in assumptions (10.28) and (10.29).

Assumption FE.3, along with Assumption FE.1, implies that the *unconditional* variance matrix of the composite error $\mathbf{v}_i = c_i \mathbf{j}_T + \mathbf{u}_i$ has the random effects form. However, without Assumption RE.3b, $\mathrm{E}(\mathbf{v}_i \mathbf{v}_i' \mid \mathbf{x}_i) \neq \mathrm{E}(\mathbf{v}_i \mathbf{v}_i')$. While this result matters for inference with the RE estimator, it has no bearing on a fixed effects analysis.

It is not obvious that Assumption FE.3 has the desired consequences of ensuring efficiency of fixed effects and leading to simple computation of standard errors and test statistics. Consider the demeaned equation (10.46). Normally, for pooled OLS to be relatively efficient, we require that the $\{\ddot{u}_{it}: t = 1, 2, \ldots, T\}$ be homoskedastic across t and serially uncorrelated. The variance of $\ddot{u}_{it}$ can be computed as

$$\begin{aligned} \mathrm{E}(\ddot{u}_{it}^2) &= \mathrm{E}[(u_{it} - \bar{u}_i)^2] = \mathrm{E}(u_{it}^2) + \mathrm{E}(\bar{u}_i^2) - 2\mathrm{E}(u_{it}\bar{u}_i) \\ &= \sigma_u^2 + \sigma_u^2/T - 2\sigma_u^2/T = \sigma_u^2(1 - 1/T) \end{aligned} \tag{10.51}$$

which verifies (unconditional) homoskedasticity across t. However, for $t \neq s$, the covariance between $\ddot{u}_{it}$ and $\ddot{u}_{is}$ is

$$\begin{aligned} \mathrm{E}(\ddot{u}_{it}\ddot{u}_{is}) &= \mathrm{E}[(u_{it} - \bar{u}_i)(u_{is} - \bar{u}_i)] = \mathrm{E}(u_{it}u_{is}) - \mathrm{E}(u_{it}\bar{u}_i) - \mathrm{E}(u_{is}\bar{u}_i) + \mathrm{E}(\bar{u}_i^2) \\ &= 0 - \sigma_u^2/T - \sigma_u^2/T + \sigma_u^2/T = -\sigma_u^2/T < 0 \end{aligned}$$

Combining this expression with the variance in equation (10.51) gives, for all $t \neq s$,

$$\mathrm{Corr}(\ddot{u}_{it}, \ddot{u}_{is}) = -1/(T - 1) \tag{10.52}$$

which shows that the time-demeaned errors $\ddot{u}_{it}$ are negatively serially correlated. (As T gets large, the correlation tends to zero.)

It turns out that, because of the nature of time demeaning, the serial correlation in the $\ddot{u}_{it}$ under Assumption FE.3 causes only minor complications. To find the asymptotic variance of $\hat{\boldsymbol{\beta}}_{FE}$, write

$$\sqrt{N}(\hat{\boldsymbol{\beta}}_{FE} - \boldsymbol{\beta}) = \left(N^{-1}\sum_{i=1}^{N} \ddot{\mathbf{X}}_i'\ddot{\mathbf{X}}_i\right)^{-1} \left(N^{-1/2}\sum_{i=1}^{N} \ddot{\mathbf{X}}_i'\mathbf{u}_i\right)$$

where we have used the important fact that $\ddot{\mathbf{X}}_i'\ddot{\mathbf{u}}_i = \mathbf{X}_i'\mathbf{Q}_T\mathbf{u}_i = \ddot{\mathbf{X}}_i'\mathbf{u}_i$. Under Assumption FE.3, $\mathrm{E}(\mathbf{u}_i\mathbf{u}_i' \mid \ddot{\mathbf{X}}_i) = \sigma_u^2 \mathbf{I}_T$. From the system OLS analysis in Chapter 7 it follows that

$$\sqrt{N}(\hat{\boldsymbol{\beta}}_{FE} - \boldsymbol{\beta}) \sim \mathrm{Normal}(\mathbf{0}, \sigma_u^2[\mathrm{E}(\ddot{\mathbf{X}}_i'\ddot{\mathbf{X}}_i)]^{-1})$$

and so

$$\mathrm{Avar}(\hat{\boldsymbol{\beta}}_{FE}) = \sigma_u^2[\mathrm{E}(\ddot{\mathbf{X}}_i'\ddot{\mathbf{X}}_i)]^{-1}/N \tag{10.53}$$

Given a consistent estimator $\hat{\sigma}_u^2$ of σ_u^2, equation (10.53) is easily estimated by also replacing $\mathrm{E}(\ddot{\mathbf{X}}_i'\ddot{\mathbf{X}}_i)$ with its sample analogue $N^{-1}\sum_{i=1}^N \ddot{\mathbf{X}}_i'\ddot{\mathbf{X}}_i$:

$$\mathrm{Av\hat{a}r}(\hat{\boldsymbol{\beta}}_{FE}) = \hat{\sigma}_u^2\left(\sum_{i=1}^N \ddot{\mathbf{X}}_i'\ddot{\mathbf{X}}_i\right)^{-1} = \hat{\sigma}_u^2\left(\sum_{i=1}^N\sum_{t=1}^T \ddot{\mathbf{x}}_{it}'\ddot{\mathbf{x}}_{it}\right)^{-1} \tag{10.54}$$

The asymptotic standard errors of the fixed effects estimates are obtained as the square roots of the diagonal elements of the matrix (10.54).

Expression (10.54) is very convenient because it looks just like the usual OLS variance matrix estimator that would be reported from the pooled OLS regression (10.48). However, there is one catch, and this comes in obtaining the estimator $\hat{\sigma}_u^2$ of σ_u^2. The errors in the transformed model are $\ddot{u}_{it}$, and these errors are what the OLS residuals from regression (10.48) estimate. Since σ_u^2 is the variance of u_{it}, we must use a little care.

To see how to estimate σ_u^2, we use equation (10.51) summed across t: $\sum_{t=1}^T \mathrm{E}(\ddot{u}_{it}^2) = (T-1)\sigma_u^2$, and so $[N(T-1)]^{-1}\sum_{i=1}^N\sum_{t=1}^T \mathrm{E}(\ddot{u}_{it}^2) = \sigma_u^2$. Now, define the **fixed effects residuals** as

$$\hat{u}_{it} = \ddot{y}_{it} - \ddot{\mathbf{x}}_{it}\hat{\boldsymbol{\beta}}_{FE}, \qquad t = 1,2,\ldots,T;\, i = 1,2,\ldots,N \tag{10.55}$$

which are simply the OLS residuals from the pooled regression (10.48). Then a consistent estimator of σ_u^2 under Assumptions FE.1–FE.3 is

$$\hat{\sigma}_u^2 = \mathrm{SSR}/[N(T-1)-K] \tag{10.56}$$

where $\mathrm{SSR} = \sum_{i=1}^N\sum_{t=1}^T \hat{u}_{it}^2$. The subtraction of K in the denominator of equation (10.56) does not matter asymptotically, but it is standard to make such a correction. In fact, under Assumptions FE.1–FE.3, it can be shown that $\hat{\sigma}_u^2$ is actually an unbiased estimator of σ_u^2 conditional on $\mathbf{X}$ (and therefore unconditionally as well).

Pay careful attention to the denominator in equation (10.56). This is not the degrees of freedom that would be obtained from regression (10.48). In fact, the usual variance estimate from regression (10.48) would be $\mathrm{SSR}/(NT-K)$, which has a probability limit less than σ_u^2 as N gets large. The difference between $\mathrm{SSR}/(NT-K)$ and equation (10.56) can be substantial when T is small.

The upshot of all this is that the usual standard errors reported from the regression (10.48) will be too small on average because they use the incorrect estimate of σ_u^2. Of course, computing equation (10.56) directly is pretty trivial. But, if a standard regression package is used after time demeaning, it is perhaps easiest to adjust the usual standard errors directly. Since $\hat{\sigma}_u$ appears in the standard errors, each standard error is simply multiplied by the factor $\{(NT-K)/[N(T-1)-K]\}^{1/2}$. As an example, if $N=500$, $T=3$, and $K=10$, the correction factor is about 1.227.

If an econometrics package has an option for explicitly obtaining fixed effects estimates using panel data, σ_u^2 will be properly estimated, and you do not have to worry about adjusting the standard errors. Many software packages also compute an estimate of σ_c^2, which is useful to determine how large the variance of the unobserved component is to the variance of the idiosyncratic component. Given $\hat{\boldsymbol{\beta}}_{FE}$, $\hat{\sigma}_v^2 = (NT-K^{-1})\sum_{i=1}^{N}\sum_{t=1}^{T}(y_{it}-\mathbf{x}_{it}\hat{\boldsymbol{\beta}}_{FE})^2$ is a consistent estimator of $\sigma_v^2=\sigma_c^2+\sigma_u^2$, and so a consistent estimator of σ_c^2 is $\hat{\sigma}_v^2-\hat{\sigma}_u^2$. (See Problem 10.14 for a discussion of why the estimated variance of the unobserved effect in a fixed effects analysis is generally larger than that for a random effects analysis.)

Example 10.5 (FE Estimation of the Effects of Job Training Grants): Using the data in JTRAIN1.RAW, we estimate the effect of job training grants using the fixed effects estimator. The variable *union* has been dropped because it does not vary over time for any of the firms in the sample. The estimated equation with standard errors is

$$\log(\widehat{scrap}) = \underset{(.109)}{-.080}\ d88 - \underset{(.133)}{.247}\ d89 - \underset{(.151)}{.252}\ grant - \underset{(.210)}{.422}\ grant_{-1}$$

Compared with the random effects, the grant is estimated to have a larger effect, both contemporaneously and lagged one year. The t statistics are also somewhat more significant with fixed effects.

Under Assumptions FE.1–FE.3, multiple restrictions are most easily tested using an F statistic, provided the degrees of freedom are appropriately computed. Let SSR_{ur} be the unrestricted SSR from regression (10.48), and let SSR_r denote the restricted sum of squared residuals from a similar regression, but with Q restrictions imposed on $\boldsymbol{\beta}$. Then

$$F = \frac{(\text{SSR}_r - \text{SSR}_{ur})}{\text{SSR}_{ur}} \cdot \frac{[N(T-1)-K]}{Q}$$

is approximately F distributed with Q and $N(T-1)-K$ degrees of freedom. (The precise statement is that $Q\cdot F \sim \chi_Q^2$ as $N\to\infty$ under H_0.) When this equation is applied to Example 10.5, the F statistic for joint significance of *grant* and $grant_{-1}$ is $F=2.23$, with p-value $=.113$.

10.5.3 The Dummy Variable Regression

So far we have viewed the c_i as being unobservable random variables, and for most applications this approach gives the appropriate interpretation of $\boldsymbol{\beta}$. Traditional approaches to fixed effects estimation view the c_i as *parameters* to be estimated along with $\boldsymbol{\beta}$. In fact, if Assumption FE.2 is changed to its finite sample version, $\text{rank}(\ddot{\mathbf{X}}'\ddot{\mathbf{X}}) = K$, then the model under Assumptions FE.1–FE.3 satisfies the Gauss-Markov assumptions conditional on $\mathbf{X}$.

If the c_i are parameters to estimate, how would we estimate each c_i along with $\boldsymbol{\beta}$? One possibility is to define N dummy variables, one for each cross section observation: $dn_i = 1$ if $n = i$, $dn_i = 0$ if $n \neq i$. Then, run the pooled OLS regression

$$y_{it} \text{ on } d1_i, d2_i, \ldots, dN_i, \mathbf{x}_{it}, \qquad t = 1, 2, \ldots, T; i = 1, 2, \ldots, N \tag{10.57}$$

Then, $\hat{c}_1$ is the coefficient on $d1_i$, $\hat{c}_2$ is the coefficient on $d2_i$, and so on.

It is a nice exercise in least squares mechanics—in particular, partitioned regression (see Davidson and MacKinnon, 1993, Section 1.4)—to show that the estimator of $\boldsymbol{\beta}$ obtained from regression (10.57) is, in fact, the fixed effects estimator. This is why $\hat{\boldsymbol{\beta}}_{FE}$ is sometimes referred to as the **dummy variable estimator**. Also, the residuals from regression (10.57) are identical to the residuals from regression (10.48). One benefit of regression (10.57) is that it produces the appropriate estimate of σ_u^2 because it uses $NT - N - K = N(T - 1) - K$ as the degrees of freedom. Therefore, if it can be done, regression (10.57) is a convenient way to carry out fixed effects analysis under Assumptions FE.1–FE.3.

There is an important difference between the $\hat{c}_i$ and $\hat{\boldsymbol{\beta}}_{FE}$. We already know that $\hat{\boldsymbol{\beta}}_{FE}$ is consistent with fixed T as $N \to \infty$. This is not the case with the $\hat{c}_i$. Each time a new cross section observation is added, another c_i is added, and information does not accumulate on the c_i as $N \to \infty$. Each $\hat{c}_i$ *is* an unbiased estimator of c_i when the c_i are treated as parameters, at least if we maintain Assumption FE.1 and the finite sample analogue of Assumption FE.2. When we add Assumption FE.3, the Gauss-Markov assumptions hold (conditional on $\mathbf{X}$), and $\hat{c}_1, \hat{c}_2, \ldots, \hat{c}_N$ are best linear unbiased conditional on $\mathbf{X}$. (The $\hat{c}_i$ give practical examples of estimators that are unbiased but not consistent.)

Econometric software that employs fixed effects usually suppresses the "estimates" of the c_i, although an overall intercept is often reported. The overall intercept is either for an arbitrary cross section unit or, more commonly, for the average of the $\hat{c}_i$ across i.

Sometimes it is useful to obtain the $\hat{c}_i$ even when regression (10.57) is infeasible. Using the OLS first-order conditions, each $\hat{c}_i$ can be shown to be

$$\hat{c}_i = \bar{y}_i - \bar{\mathbf{x}}_i\hat{\boldsymbol{\beta}}_{FE}, \qquad i = 1, 2, \ldots, N \tag{10.58}$$

After obtaining the $\hat{c}_i$, the sample average, sample standard deviation, and quantiles can be obtained to get some idea of how much heterogeneity is in the population.

(For example: Is the population distribution of c_i spread out or tightly centered about its mean? Is the distribution symmetric?) With large T, the $\hat{c}_i$ can be precise enough to learn something about the distribution of c_i. With small T, the $\hat{c}_i$ can contain substantial noise. Under the classical linear model assumptions (which require, in addition to Assumptions FE.1–FE.3, normality of the u_{it}), we can test the equality of the c_i using a standard F test for T of any size. [The degrees of freedom are $N - 1$ and $N(T-1) - K$.] Unfortunately, the properties of this test as $N \to \infty$ with T fixed are unknown without the normality assumption.

Generally, we should view the fact that the dummy variable regression (10.57) produces $\hat{\boldsymbol{\beta}}_{FE}$ as the coefficient vector on $\mathbf{x}_{it}$ as a coincidence. While there are other unobserved effects models where "estimating" the unobserved effects along with the vector $\boldsymbol{\beta}$ results in a consistent estimator of $\boldsymbol{\beta}$, there are many cases where this approach leads to trouble. As we will see in Part IV, many nonlinear panel data models with unobserved effects suffer from an incidental parameters problem, where estimating the incidental parameters, c_i, along with $\boldsymbol{\beta}$ produces an inconsistent estimator of $\boldsymbol{\beta}$.

10.5.4 Serial Correlation and the Robust Variance Matrix Estimator

Recall that the FE estimator is consistent and asymptotically normal under Assumptions FE.1 and FE.2. But without Assumption FE.3, expression (10.54) gives an improper variance matrix estimator. While heteroskedasticity in u_{it} is always a potential problem, serial correlation is likely to be more important in certain applications. When applying the FE estimator, it is important to remember that nothing rules out serial correlation in $\{u_{it}: t = 1, \dots, T\}$. While it is true that the observed serial correlation in the composite errors, $v_{it} = c_i + u_{it}$, is dominated by the presence of c_i, there can also be serial correlation that dies out over time. Sometimes, $\{u_{it}\}$ can have very strong serial dependence, in which case the usual FE standard errors obtained from expression (10.54) can be very misleading. This possibility tends to be a bigger problem with large T. (As we will see, there is no reason to worry about serial correlation in u_{it} when $T = 2$.)

Testing the idiosyncratic errors, $\{u_{it}\}$, for serial correlation is somewhat tricky. A key point is that we cannot estimate the u_{it}; because of the time demeaning used in FE, we can only estimate the time-demeaned errors, $\ddot{u}_{it}$. As shown in equation (10.52), the time-demeaned errors are negatively correlated if the u_{it} are uncorrelated. When $T = 2$, $\ddot{u}_{i1} = -\ddot{u}_{i2}$ for all i, and so there is perfect negative correlation. This result shows that for $T = 2$ it is pointless to use the $\ddot{u}_{it}$ to test for any kind of serial correlation pattern.

When $T \geq 3$, we can use equation (10.52) to determine if there is serial correlation in $\{u_{it}\}$. Naturally, we use the fixed effects residuals, $\hat{u}_{it}$. One simplification is obtained by applying Problem 7.4: we can ignore the estimation error in $\boldsymbol{\beta}$ in obtaining the asymptotic distribution of any test statistic based on sample covariances and variances. In other words, it is as if we are using the $\ddot{u}_{it}$, rather than the $\hat{u}_{it}$. The test is complicated by the fact that the $\{\ddot{u}_{it}\}$ are serially correlated under the null hypothesis. There are two simple possibilities for dealing with this. First, we can just use any two time periods (say, the last two), to test equation (10.52) using a simple regression. In other words, run the regression

$$\hat{u}_{iT} \text{ on } \hat{u}_{i,T-1}, \qquad i = 1, \dots, N$$

and use $\hat{\delta}$, the coefficient on $\hat{u}_{i,T-1}$, along with its standard error, to test H_0: $\delta = -1/(T-1)$, where $\delta = \mathrm{Corr}(\ddot{u}_{i,T-1}, \ddot{u}_{iT})$. Under Assumptions FE.1–FE.3, the usual t statistic has an asymptotic normal distribution. (It is trivial to make this test robust to heteroskedasticity.)

Alternatively, we can use more time periods if we make the t statistic robust to arbitrary serial correlation. In other words, run the pooled OLS regression

$$\hat{u}_{it} \text{ on } \hat{u}_{i,t-1}, \qquad t = 3, \dots, T; i = 1, \dots, N$$

and use the fully robust standard error for pooled OLS; see equation (7.26). It may seem a little odd that we make a test for serial correlation robust to serial correlation, but this need arises because the null hypothesis is that the time-demeaned errors are serially correlated. This approach clearly does not produce an optimal test against, say, AR(1) correlation in the u_{it}, but it is very simple and may be good enough to indicate a problem.

If we find serial correlation, we should, at a minimum, adjust the asymptotic variance matrix estimator and test statistics. Fortunately, we can apply the results from Chapter 7 directly to obtain a fully robust asymptotic variance matrix estimator. Let $\hat{\mathbf{u}}_i \equiv \ddot{\mathbf{y}}_i - \ddot{\mathbf{X}}_i\hat{\boldsymbol{\beta}}_{FE}$, $i = 1, 2, \dots, N$ denote the $T \times 1$ vectors fixed effects residuals. Applying equation (7.26), the robust variance matrix estimator of $\hat{\boldsymbol{\beta}}_{FE}$ is

$$\mathrm{Av\hat{a}r}(\hat{\boldsymbol{\beta}}_{FE}) = (\ddot{\mathbf{X}}'\ddot{\mathbf{X}})^{-1}\left(\sum_{i=1}^{N} \ddot{\mathbf{X}}_i'\hat{\mathbf{u}}_i\hat{\mathbf{u}}_i'\ddot{\mathbf{X}}_i\right)(\ddot{\mathbf{X}}'\ddot{\mathbf{X}})^{-1} \tag{10.59}$$

which was suggested by Arellano (1987) and follows from the general results of White (1984, Chapter 6). The robust variance matrix estimator is valid in the presence of any heteroskedasticity or serial correlation in $\{u_{it}: t = 1, \dots, T\}$, provided that T is small relative to N. [Remember, equation (7.26) is justified for fixed T, $N \to \infty$ asymptotics.] The robust standard errors are obtained as the square roots of the diagonal elements of the matrix (10.59), and matrix (10.59) can be used as the $\hat{\mathbf{V}}$ matrix in constructing Wald statistics. Unfortunately, the sum of squared residuals form of the F statistic is no longer asymptotically valid when Assumption FE.3 fails.

Example 10.5 (continued): We now report the robust standard errors for the log(*scrap*) equation along with the usual FE standard errors:

$$
\begin{aligned}
\log(\widehat{scrap}) = {} & -.080\ d88 - .247\ d89 - .252\ grant - .422\ grant_{-1} \\
& \quad (.109) \qquad\quad (.133) \qquad\quad (.151) \qquad\qquad (.210) \\
& \quad [.096] \qquad\quad [.193] \qquad\quad [.140] \qquad\qquad [.276]
\end{aligned}
$$

The robust standard error on *grant* is actually smaller than the usual standard error, while the robust standard error on $grant_{-1}$ is larger than the usual one. As a result, the absolute value of the t statistic on $grant_{-1}$ drops from about 2 to just over 1.5.

Remember, with fixed T as $N \to \infty$, the robust standard errors are just as valid asymptotically as the nonrobust ones when Assumptions FE.1–FE.3 hold. But the usual standard errors and test statistics may be better behaved under Assumptions FE.1–FE.3 if N is not very large relative to T, especially if u_{it} is normally distributed.

10.5.5 Fixed Effects GLS

Recall that Assumption FE.3 can fail for two reasons. The first is that the conditional variance matrix does not equal the unconditional variance matrix: $\mathrm{E}(\mathbf{u}_i\mathbf{u}_i' \mid \mathbf{x}_i, c_i) \neq \mathrm{E}(\mathbf{u}_i\mathbf{u}_i')$. Even if $\mathrm{E}(\mathbf{u}_i\mathbf{u}_i' \mid \mathbf{x}_i, c_i) = \mathrm{E}(\mathbf{u}_i\mathbf{u}_i')$, the unconditional variance matrix may not be scalar: $\mathrm{E}(\mathbf{u}_i\mathbf{u}_i') \neq \sigma_u^2\mathbf{I}_T$, which means either that the variance of u_{it} changes with t or, probably more importantly, that there is serial correlation in the idiosyncratic errors. The robust variance matrix (10.59) is valid in any case.

Rather than compute a robust variance matrix for the FE estimator, we can instead relax Assumption FE.3 to allow for an unrestricted, albeit constant, conditional covariance matrix. This is a natural route to follow if the robust standard errors of the fixed effects estimator are too large to be useful and if there is evidence of serial dependence or a time-varying variance in the u_{it}.

ASSUMPTION FEGLS.3: $\mathrm{E}(\mathbf{u}_i\mathbf{u}_i' \mid \mathbf{x}_i, c_i) = \mathbf{\Lambda}$, a $T \times T$ positive definite matrix.

Under Assumption FEGLS.3, $\mathrm{E}(\ddot{\mathbf{u}}_i\ddot{\mathbf{u}}_i' \mid \ddot{\mathbf{x}}_i) = \mathrm{E}(\ddot{\mathbf{u}}_i\ddot{\mathbf{u}}_i')$. Further, using $\ddot{\mathbf{u}}_i = \mathbf{Q}_T\mathbf{u}_i$,

$$
\mathrm{E}(\ddot{\mathbf{u}}_i\ddot{\mathbf{u}}_i') = \mathbf{Q}_T\mathrm{E}(\mathbf{u}_i\mathbf{u}_i')\mathbf{Q}_T = \mathbf{Q}_T\mathbf{\Lambda}\mathbf{Q}_T \tag{10.60}
$$

which has rank $T-1$. The deficient rank in expression (10.60) causes problems for the usual approach to GLS, because the variance matrix cannot be inverted. One way to proceed is to use a *generalized inverse*. A much easier approach—and one that turns out to be algebraically identical—is to drop one of the time periods from the analysis. It can be shown (see Im, Ahn, Schmidt, and Wooldridge, 1999) that it does not matter which of these time periods is dropped: the resulting GLS estimator is the same.

For concreteness, suppose we drop time period T, leaving the equations

$$\begin{aligned} \ddot{y}_{i1} &= \ddot{\mathbf{x}}_{i1}\boldsymbol{\beta} + \ddot{u}_{i1} \\ &\vdots \\ \ddot{y}_{i,T-1} &= \ddot{\mathbf{x}}_{i,T-1}\boldsymbol{\beta} + \ddot{u}_{i,T-1} \end{aligned} \tag{10.61}$$

So that we do not have to introduce new notation, we write the system (10.61) as equation (10.49), with the understanding that now $\ddot{\mathbf{y}}_i$ is $(T-1)\times 1$, $\ddot{\mathbf{X}}_i$ is $(T-1)\times K$, and $\ddot{\mathbf{u}}_i$ is $(T-1)\times 1$. Define the $(T-1)\times(T-1)$ positive definite matrix $\boldsymbol{\Omega} \equiv \mathrm{E}(\ddot{\mathbf{u}}_i\ddot{\mathbf{u}}_i')$. We do not need to make the dependence of $\boldsymbol{\Omega}$ on $\boldsymbol{\Lambda}$ and $\mathbf{Q}_T$ explicit; the key point is that, if no restrictions are made on $\boldsymbol{\Lambda}$, then $\boldsymbol{\Omega}$ is also unrestricted.

To estimate $\boldsymbol{\Omega}$, we estimate $\boldsymbol{\beta}$ by fixed effects in the first stage. After dropping the last time period for each i, define the $(T-1)\times 1$ residuals $\hat{\ddot{\mathbf{u}}}_i = \ddot{\mathbf{y}}_i - \ddot{\mathbf{X}}_i\hat{\boldsymbol{\beta}}_{FE}$, $i = 1, 2, \ldots, N$. A consistent estimator of $\boldsymbol{\Omega}$ is

$$\hat{\boldsymbol{\Omega}} = N^{-1}\sum_{i=1}^{N}\hat{\ddot{\mathbf{u}}}_i\hat{\ddot{\mathbf{u}}}_i' \tag{10.62}$$

The **fixed effects GLS (FEGLS)** estimator is defined by

$$\hat{\boldsymbol{\beta}}_{FEGLS} = \left(\sum_{i=1}^{N}\ddot{\mathbf{X}}_i'\hat{\boldsymbol{\Omega}}^{-1}\ddot{\mathbf{X}}_i\right)^{-1}\left(\sum_{i=1}^{N}\ddot{\mathbf{X}}_i'\hat{\boldsymbol{\Omega}}^{-1}\ddot{\mathbf{y}}_i\right)$$

where $\ddot{\mathbf{X}}_i$ and $\ddot{\mathbf{y}}_i$ are defined with the last time period dropped. For consistency of FEGLS, we replace Assumption FE.2 with a new rank condition:

ASSUMPTION FEGLS.2: rank $\mathrm{E}(\ddot{\mathbf{X}}_i'\boldsymbol{\Omega}^{-1}\ddot{\mathbf{X}}_i) = K$.

Under Assumptions FE.1 and FEGLS.2, the FEGLS estimator is consistent. When we add Assumption FEGLS.3, the asymptotic variance is easy to estimate:

$$\mathrm{Av\hat{a}r}(\hat{\boldsymbol{\beta}}_{FEGLS}) = \left(\sum_{i=1}^{N}\ddot{\mathbf{X}}_i'\hat{\boldsymbol{\Omega}}^{-1}\ddot{\mathbf{X}}_i\right)^{-1}$$

The sum of squared residual statistics from FGLS can be used to test multiple restrictions. Note that $G = T - 1$ in the F statistic in equation (7.53).

The FEGLS estimator was proposed by Kiefer (1980) when the c_i are treated as parameters. As we just showed, the procedure consistently estimates $\boldsymbol{\beta}$ when we view c_i as random and allow it to be arbitrarily correlated with $\mathbf{x}_{it}$.

The FEGLS estimator is asymptotically no less efficient than the FE estimator under Assumption FEGLS.3, even when $\boldsymbol{\Lambda} = \sigma_u^2 \mathbf{I}_T$. Generally, if $\boldsymbol{\Lambda} \neq \sigma_u^2 \mathbf{I}_T$, FEGLS is more efficient than FE, but this conclusion relies on the large-N, fixed-T asymptotics. Unfortunately, because FEGLS still uses the fixed effects transformation to remove c_i, it can have large asymptotic standard errors if the matrices $\ddot{\mathbf{X}}_i$ have columns close to zero.

Rather than allowing $\boldsymbol{\Omega}$ to be an unrestricted matrix, we can impose restrictions on $\boldsymbol{\Lambda}$ that imply $\boldsymbol{\Omega}$ has a restricted form. For example, Bhargava, Franzini, and Narendranatahn (1982) (BFN) assume that $\{u_{it}\}$ follows a stable, homoskedastic AR(1) model. This assumption implies that $\boldsymbol{\Omega}$ depends on only three parameters, σ_c^2, σ_u^2, and the AR coefficient, ρ, no matter how large T is. BFN obtain a transformation that eliminates the unobserved effect, c_i, and removes the serial correlation in u_{it}. They also propose estimators of ρ, so that feasible GLS is possible. Modeling $\{u_{it}\}$ as a specific time series process is attractive when N is not very large relative to T, as estimating an unrestricted covariance matrix for $\ddot{\mathbf{u}}_i$ [the $(T-1) \times 1$ vector of time-demeaned errors] without large N can lead to poor finite-sample performance of the FGLS estimator. However, the only general statements we can make concern fixed-T, $N \to \infty$ asymptotics. In this scenario, the FGLS estimator that uses unrestricted $\boldsymbol{\Omega}$ is no less asymptotically efficient than an FGLS estimator that puts restrictions on $\boldsymbol{\Omega}$. And, if the restrictions on $\boldsymbol{\Omega}$ are incorrect, the estimator that imposes the restrictions is less asymptotically efficient. Therefore, on theoretical grounds, we prefer an estimator of the type in equation (10.62).

10.5.6 Using Fixed Effects Estimation for Policy Analysis

There are other ways to interpret the fixed effects transformation to illustrate why fixed effects is useful for policy analysis and program evaluation. Consider the model

$$y_{it} = \mathbf{x}_{it}\boldsymbol{\beta} + v_{it} = \mathbf{z}_{it}\boldsymbol{\gamma} + \delta w_{it} + v_{it}$$

where v_{it} may or may not contain an unobserved effect. Let w_{it} be the policy variable of interest; it could be continuous or discrete. The vector $\mathbf{z}_{it}$ contains other controls that might be correlated with w_{it}, including time-period dummy variables.

As an exercise, you can show that sufficient for consistency of fixed effects, along with the rank condition FE.2, is

$$\mathrm{E}[\mathbf{x}_{it}'(v_{it} - \bar{v}_i)] = \mathbf{0}, \qquad t = 1, 2, \ldots, T$$

This assumption shows that each element of $\mathbf{x}_{it}$, and in particular the policy variable w_{it}, can be correlated with $\bar{v}_i$. What fixed effects requires for consistency is that w_{it} be uncorrelated with deviations of v_{it} from the average over the time period. So a policy variable, such as program participation, can be systematically related to the *persistent* component in the error v_{it} as measured by $\bar{v}_i$. It is for this reason that FE is often superior to be pooled OLS or random effects for applications where participation in a program is determined by preprogram attributes that also affect y_{it}.

10.6 First Differencing Methods

10.6.1 Inference

In Section 10.1 we used differencing to eliminate the unobserved effect c_i with $T = 2$. We now study the differencing transformation in the general case of model (10.41). For completeness, we state the first assumption as follows:

ASSUMPTION FD.1: Same as Assumption FE.1.

We emphasize that the model and the interpretation of $\boldsymbol{\beta}$ are *exactly* as in Section 10.5. What differs is our method for estimating $\boldsymbol{\beta}$.

Lagging the model (10.41) one period and subtracting gives

$$\Delta y_{it} = \Delta \mathbf{x}_{it}\boldsymbol{\beta} + \Delta u_{it}, \qquad t = 2, 3, \ldots, T \tag{10.63}$$

where $\Delta y_{it} = y_{it} - y_{i,t-1}$, $\Delta \mathbf{x}_{it} = \mathbf{x}_{it} - \mathbf{x}_{i,t-1}$, and $\Delta u_{it} = u_{it} - u_{i,t-1}$. As with the FE transformation, this **first-differencing transformation** eliminates the unobserved effect c_i. In differencing we lose the first time period for each cross section: we now have $T - 1$ time periods for each i, rather than T. If we start with $T = 2$, then, after differencing, we arrive at one time period for each cross section: $\Delta y_{i2} = \Delta \mathbf{x}_{i2}\boldsymbol{\beta} + \Delta u_{i2}$.

Equation (10.63) makes it clear that the elements of $\mathbf{x}_{it}$ must be time varying (for at least some cross section units); otherwise $\Delta \mathbf{x}_{it}$ has elements that are identically zero for all i and t. Also, while the intercept in the original equation gets differenced away, equation (10.63) contains changes in time dummies if $\mathbf{x}_{it}$ contains time dummies. In the $T = 2$ case, the coefficient on the second-period time dummy becomes the intercept in the differenced equation. If we difference the general equation (10.43) we get

$$\begin{aligned} \Delta y_{it} = {} & \theta_2(\Delta d2_t) + \cdots + \theta_T(\Delta dT_t) + (\Delta d2_t)\mathbf{z}_i\boldsymbol{\gamma}_2 \\ & + \cdots + (\Delta dT_t)\mathbf{z}_i\boldsymbol{\gamma}_T + \Delta \mathbf{w}_{it}\boldsymbol{\delta} + \Delta u_{it} \end{aligned} \tag{10.64}$$

The parameters θ_1 and γ_1 are not identified because they disappear from the transformed equation, just as with fixed effects.

The **first-difference (FD) estimator**, $\hat{\boldsymbol{\beta}}_{FD}$, is the pooled OLS estimator from the regression

$$\Delta y_{it} \text{ on } \Delta \mathbf{x}_{it}, \qquad t = 2, \ldots, T; i = 1, 2, \ldots, N \tag{10.65}$$

Under Assumption FD.1, pooled OLS estimation of the first-differenced equations will be consistent because

$$\mathrm{E}(\Delta \mathbf{x}_{it}' \Delta u_{it}) = 0, \qquad t = 2, 3, \ldots, T \tag{10.66}$$

Therefore, Assumption POLS.1 from Section 7.8 holds. In fact, strict exogeneity holds in the first-differenced equation:

$$\mathrm{E}(\Delta u_{it} \mid \Delta \mathbf{x}_{i2}, \Delta \mathbf{x}_{i3}, \ldots, \Delta \mathbf{x}_{iT}) = 0, \qquad t = 2, 3, \ldots, T$$

which means the FD estimator is actually unbiased conditional on $\mathbf{X}$.

To arrive at assumption (10.66) we clearly can get by with an assumption weaker than Assumption FD.1. The key point is that assumption (10.66) fails if u_{it} is correlated with $\mathbf{x}_{i,t-1}$, $\mathbf{x}_{it}$, or $\mathbf{x}_{i,t+1}$, and so we just assume that $\mathbf{x}_{is}$ is uncorrelated with u_{it} for all t and s.

For completeness, we state the rank condition for the FD estimator:

ASSUMPTION FD.2: $\operatorname{rank}\left(\sum_{t=2}^{T} \mathrm{E}(\Delta \mathbf{x}_{it}' \Delta \mathbf{x}_{it})\right) = K$.

In practice, Assumption FD.2 rules out time-constant explanatory variables and perfect collinearity among the time-varying variables.

Assuming the data have been ordered as we discussed earlier, first differencing is easy to implement provided we keep track of which transformed observations are valid and which are not. Differences for observation numbers 1, $T+1$, $2T+1$, $3T+1, \ldots,$ and $(N-1)T+1$ should be set to missing. These observations correspond to the first time period for every cross section unit in the original data set; by definition, there is no first difference for the $t = 1$ observations. A little care is needed so that differences between the first time period for unit $i+1$ and the last time period for unit i are not treated as valid observations. Making sure these are set to missing is easy when a year variable or time period dummies have been included in the data set.

One reason to prefer the FD estimator to the FE estimator is that FD is easier to implement without special software. Are there statistical reasons to prefer FD to FE? Recall that, under Assumptions FE.1–FE.3, the fixed effects estimator is asymptotically efficient in the class of estimators using the strict exogeneity assumption FE.1. Therefore, the first difference estimator is less efficient than fixed effects under Assumptions FE.1–FE.3. Assumption FE.3 is key to the efficiency of FE. It assumes homoskedasticity and no serial correlation in u_{it}. Assuming that the $\{u_{it}: t = 1, 2, \ldots T\}$ are serially uncorrelated may be too strong. An alternative assumption is that the first difference of the idiosyncratic errors, $\{e_{it} \equiv \Delta u_{it}, t = 2, \ldots, T\}$, are serially uncorrelated (and have constant variance):

ASSUMPTION FD.3: $\mathrm{E}(\mathbf{e}_i \mathbf{e}_i' \mid \mathbf{x}_{i1}, \ldots, \mathbf{x}_{iT}, c_i) = \sigma_e^2 \mathbf{I}_{T-1}$, where $\mathbf{e}_i$ is the $(T-1) \times 1$ vector containing e_{it}, $t = 2, \ldots, T$.

Under Assumption FD.3 we can write $u_{it} = u_{i,t-1} + e_{it}$, so that no serial correlation in the e_{it} implies that u_{it} is a random walk. A random walk has substantial serial dependence, and so Assumption FD.3 represents an opposite extreme from Assumption FE.3.

Under Assumptions FD.1–FD.3 it can be shown that the FD estimator is most efficient in the class of estimators using the strict exogeneity assumption FE.1. Further, from the pooled OLS analysis in Section 7.8,

$$\mathrm{Av\hat{a}r}(\hat{\boldsymbol{\beta}}_{FD}) = \hat{\sigma}_e^2 (\Delta \mathbf{X}' \Delta \mathbf{X})^{-1} \tag{10.67}$$

where $\hat{\sigma}_e^2$ is a consistent estimator of σ_e^2. The simplest estimator is obtained by computing the OLS residuals

$$\hat{e}_{it} = \Delta y_{it} - \Delta \mathbf{x}_{it} \hat{\boldsymbol{\beta}}_{FD} \tag{10.68}$$

from the pooled regression (10.65). A consistent estimator of σ_e^2 is

$$\hat{\sigma}_e^2 = [N(T-1) - K]^{-1} \sum_{i=1}^{N} \sum_{t=2}^{T} \hat{e}_{it}^2 \tag{10.69}$$

which is the usual error variance estimator from regression (10.65). These equations show that, under Assumptions FD.1–FD.3, the usual OLS standard errors from the first difference regression (10.65) are asymptotically valid.

Unlike in the FE regression (10.48), the denominator in equation (10.69) is correctly obtained from regression (10.65). Dropping the first time period appropriately captures the lost degrees of freedom (N of them).

Under Assumption FD.3, all statistics reported from the pooled regression on the first-differenced data are asymptotically valid, including F statistics based on sums of squared residuals.

10.6.2 Robust Variance Matrix

If Assumption FD.3 is violated, then, as usual, we can compute a robust variance matrix. The estimator in equation (7.26) applied in this context is

$$\mathrm{Av\hat{a}r}(\hat{\boldsymbol{\beta}}_{FD}) = (\Delta\mathbf{X}'\Delta\mathbf{X})^{-1}\left(\sum_{i=1}^{N}\Delta\mathbf{X}_i'\hat{\mathbf{e}}_i\hat{\mathbf{e}}_i'\Delta\mathbf{X}_i\right)(\Delta\mathbf{X}'\Delta\mathbf{X})^{-1} \tag{10.70}$$

where $\Delta\mathbf{X}$ denotes the $N(T-1)\times K$ matrix of stacked first differences of $\mathbf{x}_{it}$.

Example 10.6 (FD Estimation of the Effects of Job Training Grants): We now estimate the effect of job training grants on log(*scrap*) using first differencing. Specifically, we use pooled OLS on

$$\Delta\log(scrap_{it}) = \delta_1 + \delta_2 d89_t + \beta_1 \Delta grant_{it} + \beta_2 \Delta grant_{i,t-1} + \Delta u_{it}$$

Rather than difference the year dummies and omit the intercept, we simply include an intercept and a dummy variable for 1989 to capture the aggregate time effects. If we were specifically interested in the year effects from the structural model (in levels), then we should difference those as well.

The estimated equation is

$$\begin{aligned}\Delta\log(\widehat{scrap}) = \ & -.091 \ - \ .096\ d89 - \ .223\ \Delta grant - \ .351\ \Delta grant_{-1}\\ & (.091) \quad (.125) \qquad\quad (.131) \qquad\qquad (.235)\\ & [.088] \quad [.111] \qquad\quad [.128] \qquad\qquad [.265]\end{aligned}$$

$$R^2 = .037$$

where the usual standard errors are in parentheses and the robust standard errors are in brackets. We report R^2 here because it has a useful interpretation: it measures the amount of variation in the growth in the scrap rate that is explained by $\Delta grant$ and $\Delta grant_{-1}$ (and *d89*). The estimates on *grant* and $grant_{-1}$ are fairly similar to the fixed effects estimates, although *grant* is now statistically more significant than $grant_{-1}$. The usual F test for joint significance of $\Delta grant$ and $\Delta grant_{-1}$ is 1.53 with p-value $= .222$.

10.6.3 Testing for Serial Correlation

Under Assumption FD.3, the errors $e_{it} \equiv \Delta u_{it}$ should be serially uncorrelated. We can easily test this assumption given the pooled OLS residuals from regression (10.65). Since the strict exogeneity assumption holds, we can apply the simple form of the test in Section 7.8. The regression is based on $T-2$ time periods:

$$\hat{e}_{it} = \hat{\rho}_1 \hat{e}_{i,t-1} + error_{it}, \qquad t = 3, 4, \ldots, T; i = 1, 2, \ldots, N \tag{10.71}$$

The test statistic is the usual t statistic on $\hat{\rho}_1$. With $T = 2$ this test is not available, nor is it necessary. With $T = 3$, regression (10.71) is just a cross section regression because we lose the $t = 1$ and $t = 2$ time periods.

If the idiosyncratic errors $\{u_{it}: t = 1, 2, \ldots, T\}$ are uncorrelated to begin with, $\{e_{it}: t = 2, 3, \ldots, T\}$ will be autocorrelated. In fact, under Assumption FE.3 it is easily shown that $\text{Corr}(e_{it}, e_{i,t-1}) = -.5$. In any case, a finding of significant serial correlation in the e_{it} warrants computing the robust variance matrix for the FD estimator.

Example 10.6 (continued): We test for AR(1) serial correlation in the first-differenced equation by regressing $\hat{e}_{it}$ on $\hat{e}_{i,t-1}$ using the year 1989. We get $\hat{\rho}_1 = .237$ with t statistic $= 1.76$. There is marginal evidence of positive serial correlation in the first differences Δu_{it}. Further, $\hat{\rho}_1 = .237$ is very different from $\rho_1 = -.5$, which is implied by the standard random and fixed effects assumption that the u_{it} are serially uncorrelated.

An alternative to computing robust standard errors and test statistics is to use an FDGLS analysis under the assumption that $\text{E}(\mathbf{e}_i\mathbf{e}_i' \mid \mathbf{x}_i)$ is a constant $(T-1) \times (T-1)$ matrix. We omit the details, as they are similar to the FEGLS case in Section 10.5.5. As with FEGLS, we could impose structure on $\text{E}(\mathbf{u}_i\mathbf{u}_i')$, such as a stable, homoskedastic AR(1) model, and then derive $\text{E}(\mathbf{e}_i\mathbf{e}_i')$ in terms of a small set of parameters.

10.6.4 Policy Analysis Using First Differencing

First differencing a structural equation with an unobserved effect is a simple yet powerful method of program evaluation. Many questions can be addressed by having a two-year panel data set with control and treatment groups available at two points in time.

In applying first differencing, we should difference all variables appearing in the structural equation to obtain the estimating equation, including any binary indicators indicating participation in the program. The estimates should be interpreted in the orginal equation because it allows us to think of comparing different units in the cross section at any point in time, where one unit receives the treatment and the other does not.

In one special case it does not matter whether the policy variable is differenced. Assume that $T = 2$, and let $prog_{it}$ denote a binary indicator set to one if person i was in the program at time t. For many programs, $prog_{i1} = 0$ for all i: no one participated in the program in the initial time period. In the second time period, $prog_{i2}$ is unity for those who participate in the program and zero for those who do not. In this one case, $\Delta prog_i = prog_{i2}$, and the first-differenced equation can be written as

$$\Delta y_{i2} = \theta_2 + \Delta \mathbf{z}_{i2}\gamma + \delta_1 prog_{i2} + \Delta u_{i2} \tag{10.72}$$

The effect of the policy can be obtained by regressing the change in y on the change in $\mathbf{z}$ and the policy indicator. When $\Delta \mathbf{z}_{i2}$ is omitted, the estimate of δ_1 from equation (10.72) is the **difference-in-differences (DID)** estimator (see Problem 10.4): $\hat{\delta}_1 = \overline{\Delta y}_{treat} - \overline{\Delta y}_{control}$. This is similar to the DID estimator from Section 6.3—see equation (6.32)—but there is an important difference: with panel data, the differences over time are for the *same* cross section units.

If some people participated in the program in the first time period, or if more than two periods are involved, equation (10.72) can give misleading answers. In general, the equation that should be estimated is

$$\Delta y_{it} = \xi_t + \Delta \mathbf{z}_{it}\gamma + \delta_1 \Delta prog_{it} + \Delta u_{it} \tag{10.73}$$

where the program participation indicator is differenced along with everything else, and the ξ_t are new period intercepts. Example 10.6 is one such case. Extensions of the model, where $prog_{it}$ appears in other forms, are discussed in Chapter 11.

10.7 Comparison of Estimators

10.7.1 Fixed Effects versus First Differencing

When we have only two time periods, fixed effects estimation and first differencing produce *identical* estimates and inference, as you are asked to show in Problem 10.3. First differencing is easier to implement, and all procedures that can be applied to a single cross section—such as heteroskedasticity-robust inference—can be applied directly.

When $T > 2$, the choice between FD and FE hinges on the assumptions about the idiosyncratic errors, u_{it}. In particular, the FE estimator is more efficient under Assumption FE.3—the u_{it} are serially uncorrelated—while the FD estimator is more efficient when u_{it} follows a random walk. In many cases, the truth is likely to lie somewhere in between.

If FE and FD estimates differ in ways that cannot be attributed to sampling error, we should worry about the strict exogeneity assumption. If u_{it} is correlated with $\mathbf{x}_{is}$ for any t and s, FE and FD generally have different probability limits. Any of the standard endogeneity problems, including measurement error, time-varying omitted variables, and simultaneity, generally cause correlation between $\mathbf{x}_{it}$ and u_{it}—that is, contemporaneous correlation—which then causes both FD and FE to be inconsistent and to have different probability limits. (We explicitly consider these problems in

Chapter 11.) In addition, correlation between u_{it} and $\mathbf{x}_{is}$ for $s \neq t$ causes FD and FE to be inconsistent. When lagged $\mathbf{x}_{it}$ is correlated with u_{it}, we can solve lack of strict exogeneity by including lags and interpreting the equation as a distributed lag model. More problematical is when u_{it} is correlated with *future* $\mathbf{x}_{it}$: only rarely does putting future values of explanatory variables in an equation lead to an interesting economic model. In Chapter 11 we show how to estimate the parameters consistently when there is feedback from u_{it} to $\mathbf{x}_{is}$, $s > t$.

We can formally test the assumptions underlying the consistency of the FE and FD estimators by using a Hausman test. It might be important to use a robust form of the Hausman test that maintains neither Assumption FE.3 nor Assumption FD.3 under the null hypothesis. This approach is not difficult—see Problem 10.6—but we focus here on regression-based tests, which are easier to compute.

If $T = 2$, it is easy to test for strict exogeneity. In the equation $\Delta y_i = \Delta \mathbf{x}_i \boldsymbol{\beta} + \Delta u_i$, neither $\mathbf{x}_{i1}$ nor $\mathbf{x}_{i2}$ should be significant as additional explanatory variables in the first-differenced equation. We simply add, say, $\mathbf{x}_{i2}$ to the FD equation and carry out an F test for significance of $\mathbf{x}_{i2}$. With more than two time periods, a test of strict exogeneity is a test of H_0: $\boldsymbol{\gamma} = \mathbf{0}$ in the expanded equation

$$\Delta y_t = \Delta \mathbf{x}_t \boldsymbol{\beta} + \mathbf{w}_t \boldsymbol{\gamma} + \Delta u_t, \qquad t = 2, \ldots, T$$

where $\mathbf{w}_t$ is a subset of $\mathbf{x}_t$ (that would exclude time dummies). Using the Wald approach, this test can be made robust to arbitrary serial correlation or heteroskedasticity; under Assumptions FD.1–FD.3 the usual F statistic is asymptotically valid.

A test of strict exogeneity using fixed effects, when $T > 2$, is obtained by specifying the equation

$$y_{it} = \mathbf{x}_{it} \boldsymbol{\beta} + \mathbf{w}_{i,t+1} \boldsymbol{\delta} + c_i + u_{it}, \qquad t = 1, 2, \ldots, T-1$$

where $\mathbf{w}_{i,t+1}$ is again a subset of $\mathbf{x}_{i,t+1}$. Under strict exogeneity, $\boldsymbol{\delta} = \mathbf{0}$, and we can carry out the test using fixed effects estimation. (We lose the last time period by leading $\mathbf{w}_{it}$.) An example is given in Problem 10.12.

Under strict exogeneity, we can use a GLS procedure on either the time-demeaned equation or the first-differenced equation. If the variance matrix of $\mathbf{u}_i$ is unrestricted, it does not matter which transformation we use. Intuitively, this point is pretty clear, since allowing $\mathrm{E}(\mathbf{u}_i \mathbf{u}_i')$ to be unrestricted places no restrictions on $\mathrm{E}(\ddot{\mathbf{u}}_i \ddot{\mathbf{u}}_i')$ or $\mathrm{E}(\Delta \mathbf{u}_i \Delta \mathbf{u}_i')$. Im, Ahn, Schmidt, and Wooldridge (1999) show formally that the FEGLS and FDGLS estimators are asymptotically equivalent under Assumptions FE.1 and FEGLS.3 and the appropriate rank conditions.

10.7.2 The Relationship between the Random Effects and Fixed Effects Estimators

In cases where the key variables in $\mathbf{x}_t$ do not vary much over time, fixed effects and first-differencing methods can lead to imprecise estimates. We may be forced to use random effects estimation in order to learn anything about the population parameters. If a random effects analysis is appropriate—that is, if c_i is orthogonal to $\mathbf{x}_{it}$—then the random effects estimators can have much smaller variances than the FE or FD estimators. We now obtain an expression for the RE estimator that allows us to compare it with the FE estimator.

Using the fact that $\mathbf{j}_T'\mathbf{j}_T = T$, we can write $\boldsymbol{\Omega}$ under the random effects structure as

$$\begin{aligned}\boldsymbol{\Omega} &= \sigma_u^2\mathbf{I}_T + \sigma_c^2\mathbf{j}_T\mathbf{j}_T' = \sigma_u^2\mathbf{I}_T + T\sigma_c^2\mathbf{j}_T(\mathbf{j}_T'\mathbf{j}_T)^{-1}\mathbf{j}_T' \\ &= \sigma_u^2\mathbf{I}_T + T\sigma_c^2\mathbf{P}_T = (\sigma_u^2 + T\sigma_c^2)(\mathbf{P}_T + \eta\mathbf{Q}_T)\end{aligned}$$

where $\mathbf{P}_T \equiv \mathbf{I}_T - \mathbf{Q}_T = \mathbf{j}_T(\mathbf{j}_T'\mathbf{j}_T)^{-1}\mathbf{j}_T'$ and $\eta \equiv \sigma_u^2/(\sigma_u^2 + T\sigma_c^2)$. Next, define $\mathbf{S}_T \equiv \mathbf{P}_T + \eta\mathbf{Q}_T$. Then $\mathbf{S}_T^{-1} = \mathbf{P}_T + (1/\eta)\mathbf{Q}_T$, as can be seen by direct matrix multiplication. Further, $\mathbf{S}_T^{-1/2} = \mathbf{P}_T + (1/\sqrt{\eta})\mathbf{Q}_T$, because multiplying this matrix by itself gives $\mathbf{S}_T^{-1}$ (the matrix is clearly symmetric, since $\mathbf{P}_T$ and $\mathbf{Q}_T$ are symmetric). After simple algebra, it can be shown that $\mathbf{S}_T^{-1/2} = (1-\lambda)^{-1}[\mathbf{I}_T - \lambda\mathbf{P}_T]$, where $\lambda = 1 - \sqrt{\eta}$. Therefore,

$$\boldsymbol{\Omega}^{-1/2} = (\sigma_u^2 + T\sigma_c^2)^{-1/2}(1-\lambda)^{-1}[\mathbf{I}_T - \lambda\mathbf{P}_T] = (1/\sigma_u)[\mathbf{I}_T - \lambda\mathbf{P}_T]$$

where $\lambda = 1 - [\sigma_u^2/(\sigma_u^2 + T\sigma_c^2)]^{1/2}$. Assume for the moment that we know λ. Then the RE estimator is obtained by estimating the transformed equation $\mathbf{C}_T\mathbf{y}_i = \mathbf{C}_T\mathbf{X}_i\boldsymbol{\beta} + \mathbf{C}_T\mathbf{v}_i$ by system OLS, where $\mathbf{C}_T \equiv [\mathbf{I}_T - \lambda\mathbf{P}_T]$. Write the transformed equation as

$$\check{\mathbf{y}}_i = \check{\mathbf{X}}_i\boldsymbol{\beta} + \check{\mathbf{v}}_i \tag{10.74}$$

The variance matrix of $\check{\mathbf{v}}_i$ is $\mathrm{E}(\check{\mathbf{v}}_i\check{\mathbf{v}}_i') = \mathbf{C}_T\boldsymbol{\Omega}\mathbf{C}_T = \sigma_u^2\mathbf{I}_T$, which verifies that $\check{\mathbf{v}}_i$ has variance matrix ideal for system OLS estimation.

The tth element of $\check{\mathbf{y}}_i$ is easily seen to be $y_{it} - \lambda\bar{y}_i$, and similarly for $\check{\mathbf{X}}_i$. Therefore, system OLS estimation of equation (10.74) is just pooled OLS estimation of

$$y_{it} - \lambda\bar{y}_i = (\mathbf{x}_{it} - \lambda\bar{\mathbf{x}}_i)\boldsymbol{\beta} + (v_{it} - \lambda\bar{v}_i)$$

over all t and i. The errors in this equation are serially uncorrelated and homoskedastic under Assumption RE.3; therefore, they satisfy the key conditions for pooled OLS analysis. The feasible RE estimator replaces the unknown λ with its estimator, $\hat{\lambda}$, so that $\hat{\boldsymbol{\beta}}_{RE}$ can be computed from the pooled OLS regression

$$\check{y}_{it} \text{ on } \check{\mathbf{x}}_{it}, \qquad t = 1, \ldots, T;\ i = 1, \ldots, N \tag{10.75}$$

where now $\check{\mathbf{x}}_{it} = \mathbf{x}_{it} - \hat{\lambda}\bar{\mathbf{x}}_i$ and $\check{y}_{it} = y_{it} - \hat{\lambda}\bar{y}_i$, all t and i. Therefore, we can write

$$\hat{\boldsymbol{\beta}}_{RE} = \left(\sum_{i=1}^{N}\sum_{t=1}^{T}\check{\mathbf{x}}_{it}'\check{\mathbf{x}}_{it}\right)^{-1}\left(\sum_{i=1}^{N}\sum_{t=1}^{T}\check{\mathbf{x}}_{it}'\check{y}_{it}\right) \tag{10.76}$$

The usual variance estimate from the pooled OLS regression (10.75), $\mathrm{SSR}/(NT-K)$, is a consistent estimator of σ_u^2. The usual t statistics and F statistics from the pooled regression are asymptotically valid under Assumptions RE.1–RE.3. For F tests, we obtain $\hat{\lambda}$ from the unrestricted model.

Equation (10.76) shows that the random effects estimator is obtained by a **quasi-time demeaning**: rather than removing the time average from the explanatory and dependent variables at each t, random effects removes a fraction of the time average. If $\hat{\lambda}$ is close to unity, the random effects and fixed effects estimates tend to be close. To see when this result occurs, write $\hat{\lambda}$ as

$$\hat{\lambda} = 1 - \{1/[1 + T(\hat{\sigma}_c^2/\hat{\sigma}_u^2)]\}^{1/2} \tag{10.77}$$

where $\hat{\sigma}_u^2$ and $\hat{\sigma}_c^2$ are consistent estimators of σ_u^2 and σ_c^2 (see Section 10.4). When $T(\hat{\sigma}_c^2/\hat{\sigma}_u^2)$ is large, the second term in $\hat{\lambda}$ is small, in which case $\hat{\lambda}$ is close to unity. In fact, $\hat{\lambda} \to 1$ as $T \to \infty$ or as $\hat{\sigma}_c^2/\hat{\sigma}_u^2 \to \infty$. For large T, it is not surprising to find similar estimates from fixed effects and random effects. Even with small T, random effects can be close to fixed effects if the estimated variance of c_i is large relative to the estimated variance of u_{it}, a case often relevant for applications. (As λ approaches unity, the precision of the random effects estimator approaches that of the fixed effects estimator, and the effects of time-constant explanatory variables become harder to estimate.)

Example 10.7 (Job Training Grants): In Example 10.4, $T = 3$, $\hat{\sigma}_u^2 \approx .248$, and $\hat{\sigma}_c^2 \approx 1.932$, which gives $\hat{\lambda} \approx .797$. This helps explain why the RE and FE estimates are reasonably close.

Equations (10.76) and (10.77) also show how random effects and pooled OLS are related. Pooled OLS is obtained by setting $\hat{\lambda} = 0$, which is never exactly true but could be close. In practice, $\hat{\lambda}$ is not usually close to zero because this outcome would require $\hat{\sigma}_u^2$ to be large relative to $\hat{\sigma}_c^2$.

In Section 10.4 we emphasized that consistency of random effects hinges on the orthogonality between c_i and $\mathbf{x}_{it}$. In fact, Assumption POLS.1 is weaker than Assumption RE.1. We now see, because of the particular transformation used by the RE estimator, that its inconsistency when Assumption RE.1b is violated can be small relative to pooled OLS if σ_c^2 is large relative to σ_u^2 or if T is large.

If we are primarily interested in the effect of a time-constant variable in a panel data study, the robustness of the FE estimator to correlation between the unobserved effect and the $\mathbf{x}_{it}$ is practically useless. Without using an instrumental variables approach—something we take up in Chapter 11—random effects is probably our only choice. Sometimes, applications of the RE estimator attempt to control for the part of c_i correlated with $\mathbf{x}_{it}$ by including dummy variables for various groups, assuming that we have many observations within each group. For example, if we have panel data on a group of working people, we might include city dummy variables in a wage equation. Or, if we have panel data at the student level, we might include school dummy variables. Including dummy variables for groups controls for a certain amount of heterogeneity that might be correlated with the (time-constant) elements of $\mathbf{x}_{it}$. By using RE, we can efficiently account for any remaining serial correlation due to unobserved time-constant factors. (Unfortunately, the language used in empirical work can be confusing. It is not uncommon to see school dummy variables referred to as "school fixed effects" even though they appear in a random effects analysis at the individual level.)

Regression (10.75) using the quasi-time-demeaned data has several other practical uses. Since it is just a pooled OLS regression that is asymptotically the same as using λ in place of $\hat{\lambda}$, we can easily obtain standard errors that are robust to arbitrary heteroskedasticity in c_i and u_{it} as well as arbitrary serial correlation in the $\{u_{it}\}$. All that is required is an econometrics package that computes robust standard errors, t, and F statistics for pooled OLS regression, such as Stata®. Further, we can use the residuals from regression (10.75), say $\hat{r}_{it}$, to test for serial correlation in $r_{it} \equiv v_{it} - \lambda \bar{v}_i$, which are serially uncorrelated under Assumption RE.3a. If we detect serial correlation in $\{r_{it}\}$, we conclude that Assumption RE.3a is false, and this result means that the u_{it} are serially correlated. Although the arguments are tedious, it can be shown that estimation of λ and $\boldsymbol{\beta}$ has no effect on the null limiting distribution of the usual (or heteroskedasticity-robust) t statistic from the pooled OLS regression $\hat{r}_{it}$ on $\hat{r}_{i,t-1}$, $t = 2, \ldots, T, i = 1, \ldots, N$.

10.7.3 The Hausman Test Comparing the RE and FE Estimators

Since the key consideration in choosing between a random effects and fixed effects approach is whether c_i and $\mathbf{x}_{it}$ are correlated, it is important to have a method for testing this assumption. Hausman (1978) proposed a test based on the difference between the random effects and fixed effects estimates. Since FE is consistent when c_i and $\mathbf{x}_{it}$ are correlated, but RE is inconsistent, a statistically significant difference is interpreted as evidence against the random effects assumption RE.1b.

Before we obtain the Hausman test, there are two caveats. First, strict exogeneity, Assumption RE.1a, is maintained under the null and the alternative. Correlation between $\mathbf{x}_{is}$ and u_{it} for any s and t causes both FE and RE to be inconsistent, and generally their plims will differ.

A second caveat is that the test is usually implemented assuming that Assumption RE.3 holds under the null. As we will see, this setup implies that the random effects estimator is more efficient than the FE estimator, and it simplifies computation of the test statistic. But we must emphasize that Assumption RE.3 is an auxiliary assumption, and it is *not* being tested by the Hausman statistic: the Hausman test has no systematic power against the alternative that Assumption RE.1 is true but Assumption RE.3 is false. Failure of Assumption RE.3 causes the usual Hausman test to have a nonstandard limiting distribution, which means the resulting test could have asymptotic size larger or smaller than the nominal size.

Assuming that Assumptions RE.1–RE.3 hold, consider the case where $\mathbf{x}_{it}$ contains only time-varying elements, since these are the only coefficients that we can estimate using fixed effects. Then

$$\text{Avar}(\hat{\boldsymbol{\beta}}_{FE}) = \sigma_u^2[\text{E}(\ddot{\mathbf{X}}_i'\ddot{\mathbf{X}}_i)]^{-1}/N \qquad \text{and} \qquad \text{Avar}(\hat{\boldsymbol{\beta}}_{RE}) = \sigma_u^2[\text{E}(\check{\mathbf{X}}_i'\check{\mathbf{X}}_i)]^{-1}/N$$

where the tth row of $\ddot{\mathbf{X}}_i$ is $\mathbf{x}_{it} - \bar{\mathbf{x}}_i$ and the tth row of $\check{\mathbf{X}}_i$ is $\mathbf{x}_{it} - \lambda\bar{\mathbf{x}}_i$. Now

$$\begin{aligned}\text{E}(\check{\mathbf{X}}_i'\check{\mathbf{X}}_i) - \text{E}(\ddot{\mathbf{X}}_i'\ddot{\mathbf{X}}_i) &= \text{E}[\mathbf{X}_i'(\mathbf{I}_T - \lambda\mathbf{P}_T)\mathbf{X}_i] - \text{E}[\mathbf{X}_i'(\mathbf{I}_T - \mathbf{P}_T)\mathbf{X}_i] \\ &= (1-\lambda)\text{E}(\mathbf{X}_i'\mathbf{P}_T\mathbf{X}_i) = (1-\lambda)T\text{E}(\bar{\mathbf{x}}_i'\bar{\mathbf{x}}_i)\end{aligned}$$

from which it follows that $[\text{Avar}(\hat{\boldsymbol{\beta}}_{RE})]^{-1} - [\text{Avar}(\hat{\boldsymbol{\beta}}_{FE})]^{-1}$ is positive definite, implying that $\text{Avar}(\hat{\boldsymbol{\beta}}_{FE}) - \text{Avar}(\hat{\boldsymbol{\beta}}_{RE})$ is positive definite. Since $\lambda \to 1$ as $T \to \infty$, these expressions show that the asymptotic variance of the RE estimator tends to that of FE as T gets large.

The original form of the Hausman statistic can be computed as follows. Let $\hat{\boldsymbol{\delta}}_{RE}$ denote the vector of random effects estimates without the coefficients on time-constant variables or aggregate time variables, and let $\hat{\boldsymbol{\delta}}_{FE}$ denote the corresponding fixed effects estimates; let these each be $M \times 1$ vectors. Then

$$H = (\hat{\boldsymbol{\delta}}_{FE} - \hat{\boldsymbol{\delta}}_{RE})'[\text{Av\^ar}(\hat{\boldsymbol{\delta}}_{FE}) - \text{Av\^ar}(\hat{\boldsymbol{\delta}}_{RE})]^{-1}(\hat{\boldsymbol{\delta}}_{FE} - \hat{\boldsymbol{\delta}}_{RE}) \tag{10.78}$$

is distributed asymptotically as χ_M^2 under Assumptions RE.1–RE.3. A key to establishing the limiting chi-square distribution of H is to show that $\text{Avar}[\sqrt{N}(\hat{\boldsymbol{\delta}}_{FE} - \hat{\boldsymbol{\delta}}_{RE})] = \text{Avar}[\sqrt{N}(\hat{\boldsymbol{\delta}}_{FE} - \boldsymbol{\delta})] - \text{Avar}[\sqrt{N}(\hat{\boldsymbol{\delta}}_{RE} - \boldsymbol{\delta})]$. Newey and McFadden (1994, Section 5.3) provide general sufficient conditions, which are met by the FE and RE estimators under Assumptions RE.1–RE.3. (We cover these conditions in Chapter 14 in our discussion of general efficiency issues; see Lemma 14.1 and the surrounding discussion.) The usual estimators of $\text{Avar}(\hat{\boldsymbol{\delta}}_{FE})$ and $\text{Avar}(\hat{\boldsymbol{\delta}}_{RE})$ can be used in equation (10.78), but if different estimates of σ_u^2 are used, the matrix $\widehat{\text{Avar}}(\hat{\boldsymbol{\delta}}_{FE}) - \widehat{\text{Avar}}(\hat{\boldsymbol{\delta}}_{RE})$ need not be positive definite. Thus it is best to use either the fixed effects estimate or the random effects estimate of σ_u^2 in both places.

Often, we are primarly interested in a single parameter, in which case we can use a t statistic that ignores the other parameters. (For example, if one element of $\mathbf{x}_{it}$ is a policy variable, and the other elements of $\mathbf{x}_{it}$ are just controls or aggregrate time dummies, we may only care about the coefficient on the policy variable.) Let δ be the element of $\boldsymbol{\beta}$ that we wish to use in the test. The Hausman test can be computed as a t statistic version of (10.78), $(\hat{\delta}_{FE} - \hat{\delta}_{RE})/\{[\text{se}(\hat{\delta}_{FE})]^2 - [\text{se}(\hat{\delta}_{RE})]^2\}^{1/2}$, where the standard errors are computed under the usual assumptions. Under Assumptions RE.1–RE.3, the t statistic has an asymptotic standard normal distribution.

For testing more than one parameter, it is often easier to use an F statistic version of the Hausman test. Let $\check{\mathbf{x}}_{it}$ and $\check{y}_{it}$ be the quasi-demeaned data defined previously. Let $\mathbf{w}_{it}$ denote a $1 \times M$ subset of time-varying elements of $\mathbf{x}_{it}$ (excluding time dummies); one can include all elements of $\mathbf{x}_{it}$ that vary across i and t or a subset. Let $\ddot{\mathbf{w}}_{it}$ denote the time-demeaned version of $\mathbf{w}_{it}$, and consider the extended model

$$\check{y}_{it} = \check{\mathbf{x}}_{it}\boldsymbol{\beta} + \ddot{\mathbf{w}}_{it}\boldsymbol{\xi} + error_{it}, \qquad t = 1, \dots, T; i = 1, \dots, N \tag{10.79}$$

where $\boldsymbol{\xi}$ is an $M \times 1$ vector. The error terms are complicated because $\hat{\lambda}$ replaces λ in obtaining the quasi-demeaned data, but they can be treated as being homoskedastic and serially uncorrelated because replacing λ with $\hat{\lambda}$ does not matter asymptotically. (This comment is just the usual observation that, in feasible GLS analysis, replacing $\boldsymbol{\Omega}$ with $\hat{\boldsymbol{\Omega}}$ has no effect on the asymptotic distribution of the feasible GLS estimator as $N \to \infty$ under strict exogeneity.) Now, the Hausman test can be implemented by testing H_0: $\boldsymbol{\xi} = \mathbf{0}$ using standard pooled OLS analysis. The simplest approach is to compute the F statistic. The restricted SSR is obtained from the pooled regression that can be used to obtain $\hat{\boldsymbol{\beta}}_{RE}$, namely regression (10.75). Call this sum of squared residuals SSR_r. The unrestricted SSR comes from the pooled estimation of (10.79). Then the F statistic is

$$F = \frac{(\text{SSR}_r - \text{SSR}_{ur})}{\text{SSR}_{ur}} \cdot \frac{(NT - K - M)}{M} \tag{10.80}$$

Under H_0 (which is Assumptions RE.1–RE.3 in this case), F can be treated as an $\mathcal{F}_{M,NT-K-M}$ random variable (because $M \cdot F \overset{a}{\sim} \chi_M^2$).

This statistic turns out to be identical to a statistic derived by Mundlak (1978), who suggested putting $\overline{\mathbf{w}}_i$ in place of $\ddot{\mathbf{w}}_{it}$. Mundlak's motivation is to test an alternative to

Assumption RE.1b of the form $\mathrm{E}(c_i \mid \mathbf{x}_i) = \mathrm{E}(c_i \mid \mathbf{w}_i) = \gamma_0 + \overline{\mathbf{w}}_i \gamma$. The equivalence of the two approaches follows because the regressors $(\check{\mathbf{x}}_{it}, \ddot{\mathbf{w}}_{it})$ are just a nonsingular linear transformation of the regressors $(\check{\mathbf{x}}_{it}, \overline{\mathbf{w}}_i)$, and so the SSRs in the unrestricted regression are the same; the restricted SSRs are clearly the same.

If Assumption RE.3 fails, then a robust form of the Hausman statistic is needed. Probably the easiest approach is to test $\mathrm{H}_0\colon \boldsymbol{\xi} = \mathbf{0}$ via a robust Wald statistic in the context of pooled OLS estimation of (10.79), or with $\overline{\mathbf{w}}_i$ in place of $\ddot{\mathbf{w}}_i$. The robust test should account for serial correlation across time as well as general heteroskedasticity.

As in any other context that uses statistical inference, it is possible to get a statistical rejection of RE.1b (say, at the 5 percent level) with the differences between the RE and FE estimates being practically small. The opposite case is also possible: there can be seemingly large differences between the random effects and fixed effects estimates but, due to large standard errors, the Hausman statistic fails to reject. What should be done in this case? A typical response is to conclude that the random effects assumptions hold and to focus on the RE estimates. Unfortunately, we may be committing a Type II error: failing to reject Assumption RE.1b when it is false.

Problems

10.1. Consider a model for new capital investment in a particular industry (say, manufacturing), where the cross section observations are at the county level and there are T years of data for each county:

$$\log(invest_{it}) = \theta_t + \mathbf{z}_{it}\gamma + \delta_1 tax_{it} + \delta_2 disaster_{it} + c_i + u_{it}$$

The variable tax_{it} is a measure of the marginal tax rate on capital in the county, and $disaster_{it}$ is a dummy indicator equal to one if there was a significant natural disaster in county i at time period t (for example, a major flood, a hurricane, or an earthquake). The variables in $\mathbf{z}_{it}$ are other factors affecting capital investment, and the θ_t represent different time intercepts.

a. Why is allowing for aggregate time effects in the equation important?

b. What kinds of variables are captured in c_i?

c. Interpreting the equation in a causal fashion, what sign does economic reasoning suggest for δ_1?

d. Explain in detail how you would estimate this model; be specific about the assumptions you are making.

e. Discuss whether strict exogeneity is reasonable for the two variables tax_{it} and $disaster_{it}$; assume that neither of these variables has a lagged effect on capital investment.

10.2. Suppose you have $T = 2$ years of data on the same group of N working individuals. Consider the following model of wage determination:

$$\log(wage_{it}) = \theta_1 + \theta_2 d2_t + \mathbf{z}_{it}\gamma + \delta_1 female_i + \delta_2 d2_t \cdot female_i + c_i + u_{it}$$

The unobserved effect c_i is allowed to be correlated with $\mathbf{z}_{it}$ and $female_i$. The variable $d2_t$ is a time period indicator, where $d2_t = 1$ if $t = 2$ and $d2_t = 0$ if $t = 1$. In what follows, assume that

$$\mathrm{E}(u_{it} \mid female_i, \mathbf{z}_{i1}, \mathbf{z}_{i2}, c_i) = 0, \qquad t = 1, 2$$

a. Without further assumptions, what parameters in the log wage equation can be consistently estimated?

b. Interpret the coefficients θ_2 and δ_2.

c. Write the log wage equation explicitly for the two time periods. Show that the differenced equation can be written as

$$\Delta\log(wage_i) = \theta_2 + \Delta\mathbf{z}_i\gamma + \delta_2 female_i + \Delta u_i$$

where $\Delta\log(wage_i) = \log(wage_{i2}) - \log(wage_{i1})$, and so on.

10.3. For $T = 2$ consider the standard unoberved effects model

$$y_{it} = \mathbf{x}_{it}\boldsymbol{\beta} + c_i + u_{it}, \qquad t = 1, 2$$

Let $\hat{\boldsymbol{\beta}}_{FE}$ and $\hat{\boldsymbol{\beta}}_{FD}$ denote the fixed effects and first difference estimators, respectively.

a. Show that the FE and FD estimates are numerically identical.

b. Show that the error variance estimates from the FE and FD methods are numerically identical.

10.4. A common setup for program evaluation with two periods of panel data is the following. Let y_{it} denote the outcome of interest for unit i in period t. At $t = 1$, no one is in the program; at $t = 2$, some units are in the control group, and others are in the experimental group. Let $prog_{it}$ be a binary indicator equal to one if unit i is in the program in period t; by the program design, $prog_{i1} = 0$ for all i. An unobserved effects model without additional covariates is

$$y_{it} = \theta_1 + \theta_2 d2_t + \delta_1 prog_{it} + c_i + u_{it}, \qquad \mathrm{E}(u_{it} \mid prog_{i2}, c_i) = 0$$

where $d2_t$ is a dummy variable equal to unity if $t = 2$, and zero if $t = 1$, and c_i is the unobserved effect.

a. Explain why including $d2_t$ is important in these contexts. In particular, what problems might be caused by leaving it out?

b. Why is it important to include c_i in the equation?

c. Using the first differencing method, show that $\hat{\theta}_2 = \overline{\Delta y}_{control}$ and $\hat{\delta}_1 = \overline{\Delta y}_{treat} - \overline{\Delta y}_{control}$, where $\overline{\Delta y}_{control}$ is the average change in y over the two periods for the group with $prog_{i2} = 0$, and $\overline{\Delta y}_{treat}$ is the average change in y for the group where $prog_{i2} = 1$. This formula shows that $\hat{\delta}_1$, the difference-in-differences estimator, arises out of an unobserved effects panel data model.

d. Write down the extension of the model for T time periods.

e. A common way to obtain the DID estimator for two years of panel data is from the model

$$y_{it} = \alpha_1 + \alpha_2 start_t + \alpha_3 prog_i + \delta_1 start_t prog_i + u_{it} \tag{10.81}$$

where $\mathrm{E}(u_{it} \mid start_t, prog_i) = 0$, $prog_i$ denotes whether unit i is in the program in the second period, and $start_t$ is a binary variable indicating when the program starts. In the two-period setup, $start_t = d2_t$ and $prog_{it} = start_t prog_i$. The pooled OLS estimator of δ_1 is the DID estimator from part c. With $T > 2$, the unobserved effects model from part d and pooled estimation of equation (10.81) no longer generally give the same estimate of the program effect. Which approach do you prefer, and why?

10.5. Assume that Assumptions RE.1 and RE.3a hold, but $\mathrm{Var}(c_i \mid \mathbf{x}_i) \neq \mathrm{Var}(c_i)$.

a. Describe the general nature of $\mathrm{E}(\mathbf{v}_i \mathbf{v}_i' \mid \mathbf{x}_i)$.

b. What are the asymptotic properties of the random effects estimator and the associated test statistics? How should the random effects statistics be modified?

10.6. Define the $K \times K$ symmetric matrices $\mathbf{A}_1 \equiv \mathrm{E}(\Delta\mathbf{X}_i' \Delta\mathbf{X}_i)$ and $\mathbf{A}_2 \equiv \mathrm{E}(\ddot{\mathbf{X}}_i' \ddot{\mathbf{X}}_i)$, and assume both are positive definite. Define $\hat{\boldsymbol{\theta}} \equiv (\hat{\boldsymbol{\beta}}_{FD}', \hat{\boldsymbol{\beta}}_{FE}')'$ and $\boldsymbol{\theta} \equiv (\boldsymbol{\beta}', \boldsymbol{\beta}')'$, both $2K \times 1$ vectors.

a. Under Assumption FE.1 (and the rank conditions we have given), find $\sqrt{N}(\hat{\boldsymbol{\theta}} - \boldsymbol{\theta})$ in terms of $\mathbf{A}_1, \mathbf{A}_2$, $N^{-1/2} \sum_{i=1}^N \Delta\mathbf{X}_i' \Delta\mathbf{u}_i$, and $N^{-1/2} \sum_{i=1}^N \ddot{\mathbf{X}}_i' \ddot{\mathbf{u}}_i$ [with a $o_p(1)$ remainder].

b. Explain how to consistently estimate Avar $\sqrt{N}(\hat{\boldsymbol{\theta}} - \boldsymbol{\theta})$ without further assumptions.

c. Use parts a and b to obtain a robust Hausman statistic comparing the FD and FE estimators. What is the limiting distribution of your statistic under H_0?

10.7. Use the two terms of data in GPA.RAW to estimate an unobserved effects version of the model in Example 7.8. You should drop the variable *cumgpa* (since this variable violates strict exogeneity).

a. Estimate the model by random effects, and interpret the coefficient on the in-season variable.

b. Estimate the model by fixed effects; informally compare the estimates to the RE estimates, in particular that on the in-season effect.

c. Construct the nonrobust Hausman test comparing RE and FE. Include all variables in $\mathbf{w}_{it}$ that have some variation across i and t, except for the term dummy.

10.8. Use the data in NORWAY.RAW for the years 1972 and 1978 for a two-year panel data analysis. The model is a simple distributed lag model:

$$\log(crime_{it}) = \theta_0 + \theta_1 d78_t + \beta_1 clrprc_{i,t-1} + \beta_2 clrprc_{i,t-2} + c_i + u_{it}$$

The variable *clrprc* is the clear-up percentage (the percentage of crimes solved). The data are stored for two years, with the needed lags given as variables for each year.

a. First estimate this equation using a pooled OLS analysis. Comment on the deterrent effect of the clear-up percentage, including interpreting the size of the coefficients. Test for serial correlation in the composite error v_{it} assuming strict exogeneity (see Section 7.8).

b. Estimate the equation by fixed effects, and compare the estimates with the pooled OLS estimates. Is there any reason to test for serial correlation? Obtain heteroskedasticity-robust standard errors for the FE estimates.

c. Using FE analysis, test the hypothesis H_0: $\beta_1 = \beta_2$. What do you conclude? If the hypothesis is not rejected, what would be a more parsimonious model? Estimate this model.

10.9. Use the data in CORNWELL.RAW for this problem.

a. Estimate both a random effects and a fixed effects version of the model in Problem 7.11a. Compute the regression-based version of the Hausman test comparing RE and FE.

b. Add the wage variables (in logarithmic form), and test for joint significance after estimation by fixed effects.

c. Estimate the equation by first differencing, and comment on any notable changes. Do the standard errors change much between fixed effects and first differencing?

d. Test the first-differenced equation for AR(1) serial correlation.

10.10. An unobserved effects model explaining current murder rates in terms of the number of executions in the last three years is

$$mrdrte_{it} = \theta_t + \beta_1 exec_{it} + \beta_2 unem_{it} + c_i + u_{it}$$

where $mrdrte_{it}$ is the number of murders in state i during year t, per 10,000 people; $exec_{it}$ is the total number of executions for the current and prior two years; and $unem_{it}$ is the current unemployment rate, included as a control.

a. Using the data in MURDER.RAW, estimate this model by first differencing. Notice that you should allow different year intercepts. Test the errors in the first-differenced equation for serial correlation.

b. Estimate the model by fixed effects. Are there any important differences from the FD estimates?

c. Under what circumstances would $exec_{it}$ not be strictly exogenous (conditional on c_i)?

10.11. Use the data in LOWBIRTH.RAW for this question.

a. For 1987 and 1990, consider the state-level equation

$$\begin{aligned} lowbrth_{it} = {} & \theta_1 + \theta_2 d90_t + \beta_1 afdcprc_{it} + \beta_2 \log(phypc_{it}) \\ & + \beta_3 \log(bedspc_{it}) + \beta_4 \log(pcinc_{it}) + \beta_5 \log(popul_{it}) + c_i + u_{it} \end{aligned}$$

where the dependent variable is percentage of births that are classified as low birth weight and the key explanatory variable is *afdcprc*, the percentage of the population in the welfare program, Aid to Families with Dependent Children (AFDC). The other variables, which act as controls for quality of health care and income levels, are physicians per capita, hospital beds per capita, per capita income, and population. Interpretating the equation causally, what sign should each β_j have? (Note: Participation in AFDC makes poor women eligible for nutritional programs and prenatal care.)

b. Estimate the preceding equation by pooled OLS, and discuss the results. You should report the usual standard errors and serial correlation–robust standard errors.

c. Difference the equation to eliminate the state fixed effects, c_i, and reestimate the equation. Interpret the estimate of β_1 and compare it to the estimate from part b. What do you make of $\hat{\beta}_2$?

d. Add $afdcprc^2$ to the model, and estimate it by FD. Are the estimates on *afdcprc* and $afdcprc^2$ sensible? What is the estimated turning point in the quadratic?

10.12. The data in WAGEPAN.RAW are from Vella and Verbeek (1998) for 545 men who worked every year from 1980 to 1987. Consider the wage equation

$$\log(wage_{it}) = \theta_t + \beta_1 educ_i + \beta_2 black_i + \beta_3 hispan_i + \beta_4 exper_{it} + \beta_5 exper_{it}^2 + \beta_6 married_{it} + \beta_7 union_{it} + c_i + u_{it}$$

The variables are described in the data set. Notice that education does not change over time.

a. Estimate this equation by pooled OLS, and report the results in standard form. Are the usual OLS standard errors reliable, even if c_i is uncorrelated with all explanatory variables? Explain. Compute appropriate standard errors.

b. Estimate the wage equation by random effects. Compare your estimates with the pooled OLS estimates.

c. Now estimate the equation by fixed effects. Why is $exper_{it}$ redundant in the model even though it changes over time? What happens to the marriage and union premiums as compared with the random effects estimates?

d. Now add interactions of the form $d81 \cdot educ, d82 \cdot educ, \ldots, d87 \cdot educ$ and estimate the equation by fixed effects. Has the return to education increased over time?

e. Return to the original model estimated by fixed effects in part c. Add a *lead* of the union variable, $union_{i,t+1}$ to the equation, and estimate the model by fixed effects (note that you lose the data for 1987). Is $union_{i,t+1}$ significant? What does this result say about strict exogeneity of union membership?

10.13. Consider the standard linear unobserved effects model (10.11), under the assumptions

$$\mathrm{E}(u_{it} \mid \mathbf{x}_i, \mathbf{h}_i, c_i) = 0, \; \mathrm{Var}(u_{it} \mid \mathbf{x}_i, \mathbf{h}_i, c_i) = \sigma_u^2 h_{it}, \qquad t = 1, \ldots, T$$

where $\mathbf{h}_i = (h_{i1}, \ldots, h_{iT})$. In other words, the errors display heteroskedasticity that depends on h_{it}. (In the leading case, h_{it} is a function of $\mathbf{x}_{it}$.) Suppose you estimate $\boldsymbol{\beta}$ by minimizing the weighted sum of squared residuals

$$\sum_{i=1}^{N} \sum_{t=1}^{T} (y_{it} - a_1 d1_i - \cdots - a_N dN_i - \mathbf{x}_{it}\mathbf{b})^2 / h_{it}$$

with respect to the a_i, $i = 1, \ldots, N$ and $\mathbf{b}$, where $dn_i = 1$ if $i = n$. (This would seem to be the natural analogue of the dummy variable regression, modified for known heteroskedasticity.) Can you justify this procedure with fixed T as $N \to \infty$?

10.14. Suppose that we have the unobserved effects model

$$y_{it} = \alpha + \mathbf{x}_{it}\boldsymbol{\beta} + \mathbf{z}_i\boldsymbol{\gamma} + h_i + u_{it}$$

where the $\mathbf{x}_{it}(1 \times K)$ are time-varying, the $\mathbf{z}_i(1 \times M)$ are time-constant, $\mathrm{E}(u_{it} \mid \mathbf{x}_i, \mathbf{z}_i, h_i) = 0$, $t = 1, \ldots, T$, and $\mathrm{E}(h_i \mid \mathbf{x}_i, \mathbf{z}_i) = 0$. Let $\sigma_h^2 = \mathrm{Var}(h_i)$ and $\sigma_u^2 = \mathrm{Var}(u_{it})$. If we estimate $\boldsymbol{\beta}$ by fixed effects, we are estimating the equation $y_{it} = \mathbf{x}_{it}\boldsymbol{\beta} + c_i + u_{it}$, where $c_i = \alpha + \mathbf{z}_i\boldsymbol{\gamma} + h_i$.

a. Find $\sigma_c^2 \equiv \mathrm{Var}(c_i)$. Show that σ_c^2 is at least as large as σ_h^2, and usually strictly larger.

b. Explain why estimation of the model by fixed effects will lead to a larger estimated variance of the unobserved effect than if we estimate the model by random effects. Does this result make intuitive sense?

11 More Topics in Linear Unobserved Effects Models

This chapter continues our treatment of linear, unobserved effects panel data models. We first cover estimation of models where the strict exogeneity Assumption FE.1 fails but sequential moment conditions hold. A simple approach to consistent estimation involves differencing combined with instrumental variables methods. We also cover models with individual slopes, where unobservables can interact with explanatory variables, and models where some of the explanatory variables are assumed to be orthogonal to the unobserved effect while others are not.

The final section in this chapter briefly covers some non-panel-data settings where unobserved effects models and panel data estimation methods can be used.

11.1 Unobserved Effects Models without the Strict Exogeneity Assumption

11.1.1 Models under Sequential Moment Restrictions

In Chapter 10 all the estimation methods we studied assumed that the explanatory variables were strictly exogenous (conditional on an unobserved effect in the case of fixed effects and first differencing). As we saw in the examples in Section 10.2.3, strict exogeneity rules out certain kinds of feedback from y_{it} to future values of $\mathbf{x}_{it}$. Generally, random effects, fixed effects, and first differencing are inconsistent if an explanatory variable in some time period is correlated with u_{it}. While the size of the inconsistency might be small—something we will investigate further—in other cases it can be substantial. Therefore, we should have general ways of obtaining consistent estimators as $N \to \infty$ with T fixed when the explanatory variables are not strictly exogenous.

The model of interest can still be written as

$$y_{it} = \mathbf{x}_{it}\boldsymbol{\beta} + c_i + u_{it}, \qquad t = 1, 2, \ldots, T \tag{11.1}$$

but, in addition to allowing c_i and $\mathbf{x}_{it}$ to be arbitrarily correlated, we now allow u_{it} to be correlated with *future* values of the explanatory variables, $(\mathbf{x}_{i,t+1}, \mathbf{x}_{i,t+2}, \ldots, \mathbf{x}_{iT})$. We saw in Example 10.3 that u_{it} and $x_{i,t+1}$ must be correlated because $x_{i,t+1} = y_{it}$. Nevertheless, there are many models, including the AR(1) model, for which it is reasonable to assume that u_{it} is uncorrelated with current *and* past values of $\mathbf{x}_{it}$. Following Chamberlain (1992b), we introduce **sequential moment restrictions**:

$$\mathrm{E}(u_{it} \mid \mathbf{x}_{it}, \mathbf{x}_{i,t-1}, \ldots, \mathbf{x}_{i1}, c_i) = 0, \qquad t = 1, 2, \ldots, T \tag{11.2}$$

When assumption (11.2) holds, we will say that the $\mathbf{x}_{it}$ are **sequentially exogenous conditional on the unobserved effect**.

Given model (11.1), assumption (11.2) is equivalent to

$$\mathrm{E}(y_{it} \mid \mathbf{x}_{it}, \mathbf{x}_{i,t-1}, \ldots, \mathbf{x}_{i1}, c_i) = \mathrm{E}(y_{it} \mid \mathbf{x}_{it}, c_i) = \mathbf{x}_{it}\boldsymbol{\beta} + c_i \tag{11.3}$$

which makes it clear what sequential exogeneity implies about the explanatory variables: after $\mathbf{x}_{it}$ and c_i have been controlled for, no *past* values of $\mathbf{x}_{it}$ affect the expected value of y_{it}. This condition is more natural than the strict exogeneity assumption, which requires conditioning on future values of $\mathbf{x}_{it}$ as well.

Example 11.1 (Dynamic Unobserved Effects Model): An AR(1) model with additional explanatory variables is

$$y_{it} = \mathbf{z}_{it}\boldsymbol{\gamma} + \rho_1 y_{i,t-1} + c_i + u_{it} \tag{11.4}$$

and so $\mathbf{x}_{it} \equiv (\mathbf{z}_{it}, y_{i,t-1})$. Therefore, $(\mathbf{x}_{it}, \mathbf{x}_{i,t-1}, \ldots, \mathbf{x}_{i1}) = (\mathbf{z}_{it}, y_{i,t-1}, \mathbf{z}_{i,t-1}, \ldots, \mathbf{z}_{i1}, y_{i0})$, and the sequential exogeneity assumption (11.3) requires

$$\begin{aligned}\mathrm{E}(y_{it} \mid \mathbf{z}_{it}, y_{i,t-1}, \mathbf{z}_{i,t-1}, \ldots, \mathbf{z}_{i1}, y_{i0}, c_i) &= \mathrm{E}(y_{it} \mid \mathbf{z}_{it}, y_{i,t-1}, c_i) \\ &= \mathbf{z}_{it}\boldsymbol{\gamma} + \rho_1 y_{i,t-1} + c_i \end{aligned} \tag{11.5}$$

An interesting hypothesis in this model is H_0: $\rho_1 = 0$, which means that, after unobserved heterogeneity, c_i, has been controlled for (along with current and past $\mathbf{z}_{it}$), $y_{i,t-1}$ does not help to predict y_{it}. When $\rho_1 \neq 0$, we say that $\{y_{it}\}$ exhibits **state dependence**: the current state depends on last period's state, even after controlling for c_i and $(\mathbf{z}_{it}, \ldots, \mathbf{z}_{i1})$.

In this example, assumption (11.5) is an example of **dynamic completeness conditional on** c_i; we covered the unconditional version of dynamic completeness in Section 7.8.2. It means that one lag of y_{it} is sufficient to capture the dynamics in the conditional expectation; neither further lags of y_{it} nor lags of $\mathbf{z}_{it}$ are important once $(\mathbf{z}_{it}, y_{i,t-1}, c_i)$ have been controlled for. In general, if $\mathbf{x}_{it}$ contains $y_{i,t-1}$, then assumption (11.3) implies dynamic completeness conditional on c_i.

Assumption (11.3) does not require that $\mathbf{z}_{i,t+1} \ldots, \mathbf{z}_{iT}$ be uncorrelated with u_{it}, so that feedback is allowed from y_{it} to $(\mathbf{z}_{i,t+1}, \ldots, \mathbf{z}_{iT})$. If we think that $\mathbf{z}_{is}$ is uncorrelated with u_{it} for all s, then additional orthogonality conditions can be used. Finally, we do not need to restrict the value of ρ_1 in any way because we are doing fixed-T asymptotics; the arguments from Section 7.8.3 are also valid here.

Example 11.2 (Static Model with Feedback): Consider a static panel data model

$$y_{it} = \mathbf{z}_{it}\boldsymbol{\gamma} + \delta w_{it} + c_i + u_{it} \tag{11.6}$$

where $\mathbf{z}_{it}$ is strictly exogenous and w_{it} is sequentially exogenous:

$$\mathrm{E}(u_{it} \mid \mathbf{z}_i, w_{it}, w_{i,t-1}, \ldots, w_{i1}, c_i) = 0 \tag{11.7}$$

However, w_{it} is influenced by past y_{it}, as in this case:

$$w_{it} = \mathbf{z}_{it}\xi + \rho_1 y_{i,t-1} + \psi c_i + r_{it} \tag{11.8}$$

For example, let y_{it} be per capita condom sales in city i during year t, and let w_{it} be the HIV infection rate for year t. Model (11.6) can be used to test whether condom usage is influenced by the spread of HIV. The unobserved effect c_i contains city-specific unobserved factors that can affect sexual conduct, as well as the incidence of HIV. Equation (11.8) is one way of capturing the fact that the spread of HIV is influenced by past condom usage. Generally, if $\mathrm{E}(r_{i,t+1}u_{it}) = 0$, it is easy to show that $\mathrm{E}(w_{i,t+1}u_{it}) = \rho_1 \mathrm{E}(y_{it}u_{it}) = \rho_1 \mathrm{E}(u_{it}^2) > 0$ under equations (11.7) and (11.8), and so strict exogeneity fails unless $\rho_1 = 0$.

Lagging variables that are thought to violate strict exogeneity can mitigate but does not usually solve the problem. Suppose we use $w_{i,t-1}$ in place of w_{it} in equation (11.6) because we think w_{it} might be correlated with u_{it}. For example, let y_{it} be the percentage of flights canceled by airline i during year t, and let $w_{i,t-1}$ be airline profits during the previous year. In this case $\mathbf{x}_{i,t+1} = (\mathbf{z}_{i,t+1}, w_{it})$, and so $\mathbf{x}_{i,t+1}$ is correlated with u_{it}; this fact results in failure of strict exogeneity. In the airline example this issue may be important: poor airline performance this year (as measured by canceled flights) can affect profits in subsequent years. Nevertheless, the sequential exogeneity condition (11.2) is reasonable.

Keane and Runkle (1992) argue that panel data models for testing rational expectations using individual-level data generally do not satisfy the strict exogeneity requirement. But they do satisfy sequential exogeneity: in fact, in the conditioning set in assumption (11.2), we can include all variables observed at time $t-1$.

What happens if we apply the standard fixed effects estimator when the strict exogeneity assumption fails? Generally,

$$\mathrm{plim}(\hat{\boldsymbol{\beta}}_{FE}) = \boldsymbol{\beta} + \left[T^{-1}\sum_{t=1}^{T}\mathrm{E}(\ddot{\mathbf{x}}_{it}'\ddot{\mathbf{x}}_{it})\right]^{-1}\left[T^{-1}\sum_{t=1}^{T}\mathrm{E}(\ddot{\mathbf{x}}_{it}'u_{it})\right]$$

where $\ddot{\mathbf{x}}_{it} = \mathbf{x}_{it} - \overline{\mathbf{x}}_i$, as in Chapter 10 ($i$ is a random draw from the cross section). Now, under sequential exogeneity, $\mathrm{E}(\ddot{\mathbf{x}}_{it}'u_{it}) = \mathrm{E}[(\mathbf{x}_{it} - \overline{\mathbf{x}}_i)'u_{it}] = -\mathrm{E}(\overline{\mathbf{x}}_i'u_{it})$ because $\mathrm{E}(\mathbf{x}_{it}'u_{it}) = \mathbf{0}$, and so $T^{-1}\sum_{t=1}^{T}\mathrm{E}(\ddot{\mathbf{x}}_{it}'u_{it}) = -T^{-1}\sum_{t=1}^{T}\mathrm{E}(\overline{\mathbf{x}}_i u_{it}) = -\mathrm{E}(\overline{\mathbf{x}}_i'\bar{u}_i)$. We can bound the size of the inconsistency as a function of T if we assume that the time series process is appropriately stable and weakly dependent. Under such assumptions, $T^{-1}\sum_{t=1}^{T}\mathrm{E}(\ddot{\mathbf{x}}_{it}'\ddot{\mathbf{x}}_{it})$ is bounded. Further, $\mathrm{Var}(\overline{\mathbf{x}}_i)$ and $\mathrm{Var}(\bar{u}_i)$ are of order T^{-1}. By the

Cauchy-Schwartz inequality (for example, Davidson, 1994, Chapter 9), $|\mathrm{E}(\bar{x}_{ij}\bar{u}_i)| \le [\mathrm{Var}(\bar{x}_{ij})\mathrm{Var}(\bar{u}_i)]^{1/2} = \mathrm{O}(T^{-1})$. Therefore, under bounded moments and weak dependence assumptions, the inconsistency from using fixed effects when the strict exogeneity assumption fails is of order T^{-1}. With large T the bias may be minimal. See Hamilton (1994) and Wooldridge (1994) for general discussions of weak dependence for time series processes.

Hsiao (1986, Section 4.2) works out the inconsistency in the FE estimator for the AR(1) model. The key stability condition sufficient for the bias to be of order T^{-1} is $|\rho_1| < 1$. However, for ρ_1 close to unity, the bias in the FE estimator can be sizable, even with fairly large T. Generally, if the process $\{\mathbf{x}_{it}\}$ has very persistent elements—which is often the case in panel data sets—the FE estimator can have substantial bias.

If our choice were between fixed effects and first differencing, we would tend to prefer fixed effects because, when $T > 2$, FE can have less bias as $N \to \infty$. To see this point, write

$$\mathrm{plim}(\hat{\boldsymbol{\beta}}_{FD}) = \boldsymbol{\beta} + \left[T^{-1}\sum_{t=1}^{T}\mathrm{E}(\Delta\mathbf{x}_{it}'\Delta\mathbf{x}_{it})\right]^{-1}\left[T^{-1}\sum_{t=1}^{T}\mathrm{E}(\Delta\mathbf{x}_{it}'\Delta u_{it})\right] \tag{11.9}$$

If $\{\mathbf{x}_{it}\}$ is weakly dependent, so is $\{\Delta\mathbf{x}_{it}\}$, and so the first average in equation (11.9) is bounded as a function of T. (In fact, under stationarity, this average does not depend on T.) Under assumption (11.2), we have

$$\mathrm{E}(\Delta\mathbf{x}_{it}'\Delta u_{it}) = \mathrm{E}(\mathbf{x}_{it}'u_{it}) + \mathrm{E}(\mathbf{x}_{i,t-1}'u_{i,t-1}) - \mathrm{E}(\mathbf{x}_{i,t-1}'u_{it}) - \mathrm{E}(\mathbf{x}_{it}'u_{i,t-1}) = -\mathrm{E}(\mathbf{x}_{it}'u_{i,t-1})$$

which is generally different from zero. Under stationarity, $\mathrm{E}(\mathbf{x}_{it}'u_{i,t-1})$ does not depend on t, and so the second average in equation (11.9) is constant. This result shows not only that the FD estimator is inconsistent, but also that its inconsistency does not depend on T. As we showed previously, the time demeaning underlying FE results in its bias being on the order of T^{-1}. But we should caution that this analysis assumes that the original series, $\{(\mathbf{x}_{it}, y_{it})\colon t = 1, \ldots, T\}$, is weakly dependent. Without this assumption, the inconsistency in the FE estimator cannot be shown to be of order T^{-1}.

If we make certain assumptions, we do not have to settle for estimators that are inconsistent with fixed T. A general approach to estimating equation (11.1) under assumption (11.2) is to use a transformation to remove c_i, but then search for instrumental variables. The FE transformation can be used provided that strictly exogenous instruments are available (see Problem 11.9). For models under sequential exogeneity assumptions, first differencing is more attractive.

First differencing equation (11.1) gives

$$\Delta y_{it} = \Delta \mathbf{x}_{it}\boldsymbol{\beta} + \Delta u_{it}, \qquad t = 2, 3, \ldots, T \tag{11.10}$$

Now, under assumption (11.2),

$$\mathrm{E}(\mathbf{x}_{is}'u_{it}) = 0, \qquad s = 1, 2, \ldots, t \tag{11.11}$$

Assumption (11.11) implies the orthogonality conditions

$$\mathrm{E}(\mathbf{x}_{is}'\Delta u_{it}) = 0, \qquad s = 1, 2, \ldots, t-1 \tag{11.12}$$

so at time t we can use $\mathbf{x}_{i,t-1}^o$ as potential instruments for $\Delta \mathbf{x}_{it}$, where

$$\mathbf{x}_{it}^o \equiv (\mathbf{x}_{i1}, \mathbf{x}_{i2}, \ldots, \mathbf{x}_{it}) \tag{11.13}$$

The fact that $\mathbf{x}_{i,t-1}^o$ is uncorrelated with Δu_{it} opens up a variety of estimation procedures. For example, a simple estimator uses $\Delta \mathbf{x}_{i,t-1}$ as the instruments for $\Delta \mathbf{x}_{it}$: $\mathrm{E}(\Delta \mathbf{x}_{i,t-1}'\Delta u_{it}) = \mathbf{0}$ under assumption (11.12), and the rank condition rank $\mathrm{E}(\Delta \mathbf{x}_{i,t-1}'\Delta \mathbf{x}_{it}) = K$ is usually reasonable. Then, the equation

$$\Delta y_{it} = \Delta \mathbf{x}_{it}\boldsymbol{\beta} + \Delta u_{it}, \qquad t = 3, \ldots, T \tag{11.14}$$

can be estimated by pooled 2SLS using instruments $\Delta \mathbf{x}_{i,t-1}$. This choice of instruments loses an additional time period. If $T = 3$, estimation of equation (11.14) becomes 2SLS on a cross section: $(\mathbf{x}_{i2} - \mathbf{x}_{i1})$ is used as instruments for $(\mathbf{x}_{i3} - \mathbf{x}_{i2})$. When $T > 3$, equation (11.14) is a pooled 2SLS procedure. There is a set of assumptions—the sequential exogeneity analogues of Assumptions FD.1–FD.3—under which the usual 2SLS statistics obtained from the pooled 2SLS estimation are valid; see Problem 11.8 for details. With $\Delta \mathbf{x}_{i,t-1}$ as the instruments, equation (11.14) is just identified.

Rather than use changes in lagged $\mathbf{x}_{it}$ as instruments, we can use lagged levels of $\mathbf{x}_{it}$. For example, choosing $(\mathbf{x}_{i,t-1}, \mathbf{x}_{i,t-2})$ as instruments at time t is no less efficient than the procedure that uses $\Delta \mathbf{x}_{i,t-1}$, as the latter is a linear combination of the former. It also gives K overidentifying restrictions that can be used to test assumption (11.2). (There will be fewer than K if $\mathbf{x}_{it}$ contains time dummies.)

When $T = 2$, $\boldsymbol{\beta}$ may be poorly identified. The equation is $\Delta y_{i2} = \Delta \mathbf{x}_{i2}\boldsymbol{\beta} + \Delta u_{i2}$, and, under assumption (11.2), $\mathbf{x}_{i1}$ is uncorrelated with Δu_{i2}. This is a cross section equation that can be estimated by 2SLS using $\mathbf{x}_{i1}$ as instruments for $\Delta \mathbf{x}_{i2}$. The estimator in this case may have a large asymptotic variance because the correlations between $\mathbf{x}_{i1}$, the levels of the explanatory variables, and the differences $\Delta \mathbf{x}_{i2} = \mathbf{x}_{i2} - \mathbf{x}_{i1}$ are often small. Of course, whether the correlation is sufficient to yield small enough standard errors depends on the application.

Even with large T, the available IVs may be poor in the sense that they are not highly correlated with $\Delta \mathbf{x}_{it}$. As an example, consider the AR(1) model (11.4) without $\mathbf{z}_{it}$: $y_{it} = \rho_1 y_{i,t-1} + c_i + u_{it}, \mathrm{E}(u_{it} \mid y_{i,t-1}, \ldots, y_{i0}, c_i) = 0,\ t = 1, 2, \ldots, T$. Differencing to eliminate c_i gives $\Delta y_{it} = \rho_1 \Delta y_{i,t-1} + \Delta u_{it}$, $t \geq 2$. At time t, all elements of $(y_{i,t-2}, \ldots, y_{i0})$ are IV candidates because Δu_{it} is uncorrelated with $y_{i,t-h}$, $h \geq 2$. Anderson and Hsiao (1982) suggested pooled IV with instruments $y_{i,t-2}$ or $\Delta y_{i,t-2}$, whereas Arellano and Bond (1991) proposed using the entire set of instruments in a GMM procedure. Now, suppose that $\rho_1 = 1$ and, in fact, there is no unobserved effect. Then $\Delta y_{i,t-1}$ is uncorrelated with any variable dated at time $t-2$ or earlier, and so the elements of $(y_{i,t-2}, \ldots, y_{i0})$ cannot be used as IVs for $\Delta y_{i,t-1}$. What this conclusion shows is that we cannot use IV methods to test H_0: $\rho_1 = 1$ in the absence of an unobserved effect.

Even if $\rho_1 < 1$, IVs from $(y_{i,t-2}, \ldots, y_{i0})$ tend to be weak if ρ_1 is close to one. Recently, Arellano and Bover (1995) and Ahn and Schmidt (1995) suggested additional orthogonality conditions that improve the efficiency of the GMM estimator, but these are nonlinear in the parameters. (In Chapter 14 we will see how to use these kinds of moment restrictions.) Blundell and Bond (1998) obtained additional linear moment restrictions in the levels equation $y_{it} = \rho_1 y_{i,t-1} + v_{it}$, $v_{it} = c_i + u_{it}$. The additional restrictions are based on y_{i0} being drawn from a steady-state distribution, and they are especially helpful in improving the efficiency of GMM for ρ_1 close to one. (Actually, the Blundell-Bond orthogonality conditions are valid under weaker assumptions.) See also Hahn (1999). Of course, when $\rho_1 = 1$, it makes no sense to assume that there is a steady-state distribution. In Chapter 13 we cover conditional maximum likelihood methods that can be applied to the AR(1) model.

A general feature of pooled 2SLS procedures where the dimension of the IVs is constant across t is that they do not use all the instruments available in each time period; therefore, they cannot be expected to be efficient. The optimal procedure is to use expression (11.13) as the instruments at time t in a GMM procedure. Write the system of equations as

$$\Delta \mathbf{y}_i = \Delta \mathbf{X}_i \boldsymbol{\beta} + \Delta \mathbf{u}_i \tag{11.15}$$

using the same definitions as in Section 10.6. Define the matrix of instruments as

$$\mathbf{Z}_i = \begin{pmatrix} \mathbf{x}_{i1}^o & \mathbf{0} & \mathbf{0} & \cdots & \mathbf{0} \\ \mathbf{0} & \mathbf{x}_{i2}^o & \mathbf{0} & \cdots & \mathbf{0} \\ \vdots & & & & \vdots \\ \mathbf{0} & \mathbf{0} & \mathbf{0} & \cdots & \mathbf{x}_{i,T-1}^o \end{pmatrix} \tag{11.16}$$

where $\mathbf{x}_{it}^o$ is defined in expression (11.13). Note that $\mathbf{Z}_i$ has $T-1$ rows to correspond with the $T - 1$ time periods in the system (11.15). Since each row contains different instruments, different instruments are used for different time periods.

Efficient estimation of $\boldsymbol{\beta}$ now proceeds in the GMM framework from Chapter 8 with instruments (11.16). Without further assumptions, the unrestricted weighting matrix should be used. In most applications there is a reasonable set of assumptions under which

$$\mathrm{E}(\mathbf{Z}_i'\mathbf{e}_i\mathbf{e}_i'\mathbf{Z}_i) = \mathrm{E}(\mathbf{Z}_i'\Omega\mathbf{Z}_i) \tag{11.17}$$

where $\mathbf{e}_i \equiv \Delta\mathbf{u}_i$ and $\Omega \equiv \mathrm{E}(\mathbf{e}_i\mathbf{e}_i')$. Recall from Chapter 8 that assumption (11.17) is the assumption under which the GMM 3SLS estimator is the asymptotically efficient GMM estimator (see Assumption SIV.5). The full GMM analysis is not much more difficult. The traditional form of 3SLS estimator that first transforms the instruments should not be used because it is not consistent under assumption (11.2).

As a practical matter, the column dimension of $\mathbf{Z}_i$ can be very large, making GMM estimation difficult. In addition, GMM estimators—including 2SLS and 3SLS—using many overidentifying restrictions are known to have poor finite sample properties (see, for example, Tauchen, 1986; Altonji and Segal, 1996; and Ziliak, 1997). In practice, it may be better to use a couple of lags rather than lags back to $t = 1$.

Example 11.3 (Testing for Persistence in County Crime Rates): We use the data in CORNWELL.RAW to test for state dependence in county crime rates, after allowing for unobserved county effects. Thus, the model is equation (11.4) with $y_{it} \equiv \log(crmrte_{it})$ but without any other explanatory variables. As instruments for $\Delta y_{i,t-1}$, we use $(y_{i,t-2}, y_{i,t-3})$. Further, so that we do not have to worry about correcting the standard error for possible serial correlation in Δu_{it}, we use just the 1986–1987 differenced equation. The F statistic for joint significance of $y_{i,t-2}, y_{i,t-3}$ in the reduced form for $\Delta y_{i,t-1}$ yields p-value $= .023$, although the R-squared is only .083. The 2SLS estimates of the first-differenced equation are

$$\begin{aligned} \Delta\log(\widehat{crmrte}) = {} & \underset{(.040)}{.065} + \underset{(.497)}{.212}\,\Delta\log(crmrte)_{-1}, \qquad N = 90 \end{aligned}$$

so that we cannot reject H_0: $\rho_1 = 0$ ($t = .427$).

11.1.2 Models with Strictly and Sequentially Exogenous Explanatory Variables

Estimating models with both strictly exogenous and sequentially exogenous variables is not difficult. For $t = 1, 2, \ldots, T$, suppose that

$$y_{it} = \mathbf{z}_{it}\boldsymbol{\gamma} + \mathbf{w}_{it}\boldsymbol{\delta} + c_i + u_{it} \tag{11.18}$$

Assume that $\mathbf{z}_{is}$ is uncorrelated with u_{it} for all s and t, but that u_{it} is uncorrelated with

$\mathbf{w}_{is}$ only for $s \leq t$; sufficient is $\mathrm{E}(u_{it} \mid \mathbf{z}_i, \mathbf{w}_{it}, \mathbf{w}_{i,t-1}, \ldots, \mathbf{w}_{i1}) = 0$. This model covers many cases of interest, including when $\mathbf{w}_{it}$ contains a lagged dependent variable.

After first differencing we have

$$\Delta y_{it} = \Delta \mathbf{z}_{it}\gamma + \Delta \mathbf{w}_{it}\delta + \Delta u_{it} \tag{11.19}$$

and the instruments available at time t are $(\mathbf{z}_i, \mathbf{w}_{i,t-1}, \ldots, \mathbf{w}_{i1})$. In practice, so that there are not so many overidentifying restrictions, we might replace $\mathbf{z}_i$ with $\Delta \mathbf{z}_{it}$ and choose something like $(\Delta \mathbf{z}_{it}, \mathbf{w}_{i,t-1}, \mathbf{w}_{i,t-2})$ as the instruments at time t. Or, $\mathbf{z}_{it}$ and a couple of lags of $\mathbf{z}_{it}$ can be used. In the AR(1) model (11.4), this approach would mean something like $(\mathbf{z}_{it}, \mathbf{z}_{i,t-1}, \mathbf{z}_{i,t-2}, y_{i,t-2}, y_{i,t-3})$. We can even use leads of $\mathbf{z}_{it}$, such as $\mathbf{z}_{i,t+1}$, when $\mathbf{z}_{it}$ is strictly exogenous. Such choices are amenable to a pooled 2SLS procedure to estimate γ and δ. Of course, whether or not the usual 2SLS standard errors are valid depends on serial correlation and variance properties of Δu_{it}. Nevertheless, assuming that the changes in the errors are (conditionally) homoskedastic and serially uncorrelated is a reasonable start.

Example 11.4 (Effects of Enterprise Zones): Papke (1994) uses several different panel data models to determine the effect of enterprise zone designation on economic outcomes for 22 communities in Indiana. One model she uses is

$$y_{it} = \theta_t + \rho_1 y_{i,t-1} + \delta_1 ez_{it} + c_i + u_{it} \tag{11.20}$$

where y_{it} is the log of unemployment claims. The coefficient of interest is on the binary indicator ez_{it}, which is unity if community i in year t was designated as an enterprise zone. The model holds for the years 1981 to 1988, with y_{i0} corresponding to 1980, the first year of data. Differencing gives

$$\Delta y_{it} = \xi_t + \rho_1 \Delta y_{i,t-1} + \delta_1 \Delta ez_{it} + \Delta u_{it} \tag{11.21}$$

The differenced equation has new time intercepts, but as we are not particularly interested in these, we just include year dummies in equation (11.21).

Papke estimates equation (11.21) by 2SLS, using $\Delta y_{i,t-2}$ as an instrument for $\Delta y_{i,t-1}$; because of the lags used, equation (11.21) can be estimated for six years of data. The enterprise zone indicator is assumed to be strictly exogenous in equation (11.20), and so Δez_{it} acts as its own instrument. Strict exogeneity of ez_{it} is valid because, over the years in question, each community was a zone in every year following initial designation: future zone designation did not depend on past performance.

The estimated equation in first differences is

$$\Delta \log(\widehat{uclms}) = \hat{\xi}_t + \underset{(.288)}{.165}\, \Delta \log(uclms)_{-1} - \underset{(.106)}{.219}\, \Delta ez$$

where the intercept and year dummies are supressed for brevity. Based on the usual pooled 2SLS standard errors, $\hat{\rho}_1$ is not significant (or practially very large), while $\hat{\delta}_1$ is economically large and statistically significant at the 5 percent level.

If the u_{it} in equation (11.20) are serially uncorrelated, then, as we saw in Chapter 10, Δu_{it} must be serially correlated. Papke found no important differences when the standard error for $\hat{\delta}_1$ was adjusted for serial correlation and heteroskedasticity.

In the pure AR(1) model, using lags of y_{it} as an instrument for $\Delta y_{i,t-1}$ means that we are assuming the AR(1) model captures all of the dynamics. If further lags of y_{it} are added to the structural model, then we must go back even further to obtain instruments. If strictly exogenous variables appear in the model along with $y_{i,t-1}$—such as in equation (11.4)—then lags of $\mathbf{z}_{it}$ are good candidates as instruments for $\Delta y_{i,t-1}$. Much of the time inclusion of $y_{i,t-1}$ (or additional lags) in a model with other explanatory variables is intended to simply control for another source of omitted variables bias; Example 11.4 falls into this class.

Things are even trickier in finite distributed lag models. Consider the patents-R&D model of Example 10.2: after first differencing, we have

$$\Delta patents_{it} = \Delta\theta_t + \Delta\mathbf{z}_{it}\boldsymbol{\gamma} + \delta_0 \Delta RD_{it} + \cdots + \delta_5 \Delta RD_{i,t-5} + \Delta u_{it} \tag{11.22}$$

If we are concerned that strict exogeneity fails because of feedback from u_{it} to future R&D expenditures, then ΔRD_{it} and Δu_{it} are potentially correlated (because $u_{i,t-1}$ and RD_{it} are correlated). Assuming that the distributed lag dynamics are correct—and assuming strict exogeneity of $\mathbf{z}_{it}$—all other explanatory variables in equation (11.22) are uncorrelated with Δu_{it}. What can we use as an instrument for ΔRD_{it} in equation (11.22)? We can include $RD_{i,t-1}, RD_{i,t-2}, \ldots$ in the instrument list at time t (along with all of $\mathbf{z}_i$).

This approach identifies the parameters under the assumptions made, but it is problematic. What if we have the distributed lag dynamics wrong, so that six lags, rather than five, belong in the structural model? Then choosing additional lags of RD_{it} as instruments fails. If ΔRD_{it} is sufficiently correlated with the elements of $\mathbf{z}_{is}$ for some s, then using all of $\mathbf{z}_i$ as instruments can help. Generally, some exogenous factors either in $\mathbf{z}_{it}$ or from outside the structural equation are needed for a convincing analysis.

11.1.3 Models with Contemporaneous Correlation between Some Explanatory Variables and the Idiosyncratic Error

Consider again model (11.18), where $\mathbf{z}_{it}$ is strictly exogenous in the sense that

$$\mathrm{E}(\mathbf{z}_{is}' u_{it}) = \mathbf{0}, \qquad \text{all } s, t \tag{11.23}$$

but where we allow $\mathbf{w}_{it}$ to be *contemporaneously* correlated with u_{it}. This correlation can be due to any of the three problems that we studied earlier: omission of an important time-varying explanatory variable, measurement error in some elements of $\mathbf{w}_{it}$, or simultaneity between y_{it} and one or more elements of $\mathbf{w}_{it}$. We assume that equation (11.18) is the equation of interest. In a simultaneous equations model with panel data, equation (11.18) represents a single equation. A system approach is also possible. See, for example, Baltagi (1981); Cornwell, Schmidt, and Wyhowski (1992); and Kinal and Lahiri (1993).

Example 11.5 (Effects of Smoking on Earnings): A panel data model to examine the effects of cigarette smoking on earnings is

$$\log(wage_{it}) = \mathbf{z}_{it}\gamma + \delta_1 cigs_{it} + c_i + u_{it} \tag{11.24}$$

(For an empirical analysis, see Levine, Gustafson, and Velenchik, 1997.) As always, we would like to know the causal effect of smoking on hourly wage. For concreteness, assume $cigs_{it}$ is measured as average packs per day. This equation has a causal interpretation: holding fixed the factors in $\mathbf{z}_{it}$ *and* c_i, what is the effect of an exogenous change in cigarette smoking on wages? Thus equation (11.24) is a structural equation.

The presence of the individual heterogeneity, c_i, in equation (11.24) recognizes that cigarette smoking might be correlated with individual characteristics that also affect wage. An additional problem is that $cigs_{it}$ might also be correlated with u_{it}, something we have not allowed so far. In this example the correlation could be from a variety of sources, but simultaneity is one possibility: if cigarettes are a normal good, then, as income increases—holding everything else fixed—cigarette consumption increases. Therefore, we might add another equation to equation (11.24) that reflects that $cigs_{it}$ may depend on income, which clearly depends on wage. If equation (11.24) is of interest, we do not need to add equations explicitly, but we must find some instrumental variables.

To get an estimable model, we must first deal with the presence of c_i, since it might be correlated with $\mathbf{z}_{it}$ as well as $cigs_{it}$. In the general model (11.18), either the FE or FD transformations can be used to eliminate c_i before addressing the correlation between $\mathbf{w}_{it}$ and u_{it}. If we first difference, as in equation (11.19), we can use the entire vector $\mathbf{z}_i$ as valid instruments in equation (11.19) because $\mathbf{z}_{it}$ is strictly exogenous. Neither $\mathbf{w}_{it}$ nor $\mathbf{w}_{i,t-1}$ is valid as instruments at time t, but it could be that $\mathbf{w}_{i,t-2}$ is valid, provided we assume that u_{it} is uncorrelated with $\mathbf{w}_{is}$ for $s < t$. This assumption means that $\mathbf{w}_{it}$ has only a contemporaneous effect on y_{it}, something that is likely to be false in example 11.5. [If smoking affects wages, the effects are likely to be determined by prior smoking behavior as well as current smoking behavior. If we include a measure of past smoking behavior in equation (11.24), then this must act as its own instrument in a differenced equation, and so using $cigs_{is}$ for $s < t$ as IVs becomes untenable.]

Another thought is to use lagged values of y_{it} as instruments, but this approach effectively rules out serial correlation in u_{it}. In the wage equation (11.24), it would mean that lagged wage does not predict current wage, once c_i and the other variables are controlled for. If this assumption is false, using lags of y_{it} is not a valid way of identifying the parameters.

If $\mathbf{z}_i$ is the only valid set of instruments for equation (11.18), the analysis probably will not be convincing: it relies on $\Delta \mathbf{w}_{it}$ being correlated with some linear combination of $\mathbf{z}_i$ other than $\Delta \mathbf{z}_{it}$. Such partial correlation is likely to be small, resulting in poor IV estimators; see Problem 11.2.

Perhaps the most convincing possibility for obtaining additional instruments is to follow the standard SEM approach from Chapter 9: use exclusion restrictions in the structural equations. For example, we can hope to find exogenous variables that do not appear in equation (11.24) but that do affect cigarette smoking. The local price of cigarettes (or level of cigarette taxes) is one possibility. Such variables can usually be considered strictly exogenous, unless we think people change their residence based on the price of cigarettes.

If we difference equation (11.24) we get

$$\Delta \log(wage_{it}) = \Delta \mathbf{z}_{it}\gamma + \delta_1 \Delta cigs_{it} + \Delta u_{it} \tag{11.25}$$

Now, for each t, we can study identification of this equation just as in the cross sectional case: we must first make sure the order condition holds, and then argue (or test) that the rank condition holds. Equation (11.25) can be estimated using a pooled 2SLS analysis, where corrections to standard errors and test statistics for heteroskedasticity or serial correlation might be warranted. With a large cross section, a GMM system procedure that exploits general heteroskedasticity and serial correlation in Δu_{it} can be used instead.

Example 11.6 (Effects of Prison Population on Crime Rates): In order to estimate the causal effect of prison population increases on crime rates at the state level, Levitt (1996) uses instances of prison overcrowding litigation as instruments for the growth in prison population. The equation Levitt estimates is in first differences. We can write an underlying unobserved effects model as

$$\log(crime_{it}) = \theta_t + \beta_1 \log(prison_{it}) + \mathbf{x}_{it}\gamma + c_i + u_{it} \tag{11.26}$$

where θ_t denotes different time intercepts and *crime* and *prison* are measured per 100,000 people. (The prison population variable is measured on the last day of the previous year.) The vector $\mathbf{x}_{it}$ contains other controls listed in Levitt, including measures of police per capita, income per capita, unemployment rate, and race, metropolitan, and age distribution proportions.

Differencing equation (11.26) gives the equation estimated by Levitt:

$$\Delta\log(crime_{it}) = \xi_t + \beta_1 \Delta\log(prison_{it}) + \Delta\mathbf{x}_{it}\gamma + \Delta u_{it} \tag{11.27}$$

Simultaneity between crime rates and prison population, or, more precisely, in the growth rates, makes OLS estimation of equation (11.27) generally inconsistent. Using the violent crime rate and a subset of the data from Levitt (in PRISON.RAW, for the years 1980 to 1993, for $51 \cdot 14 = 714$ total observations), the OLS estimate of β_1 is $-.181$ (se $= .048$). We also estimate the equation by 2SLS, where the instruments for $\Delta\log(prison)$ are two binary variables, one for whether a final decision was reached on overcrowding litigation in the current year and one for whether a final decision was reached in the previous two years. The 2SLS estimate of β_1 is -1.032 (se $= .370$). Therefore, the 2SLS estimated effect is much larger; not surprisingly, it is much less precise, too. Levitt (1996) found similar results when using a longer time period and more instruments.

A different approach to estimating SEMs with panel data is to use the fixed effects transformation and then to apply an IV technique such as pooled 2SLS. A simple procedure is to estimate the time-demeaned equation (10.46) by pooled 2SLS, where the instruments are also time demeaned. This is equivalent to using 2SLS in the dummy variable formulation, where the unit-specific dummy variables act as their own instruments. See Problem 11.9 for a careful analysis of this approach. Foster and Rosenzweig (1995) use the within transformation along with IV to estimate household-level profit functions for adoption of high-yielding seed varieties in rural India. Ayres and Levitt (1998) apply 2SLS to a time-demeaned equation to estimate the effect of Lojack electronic theft prevention devices on city car-theft rates.

The FE transformation precludes the use of lagged values of $\mathbf{w}_{it}$ among the instruments, for essentially the same reasons discussed for models with sequentially exogenous explanatory variables: u_{it} will be correlated with the time-demeaned instruments. Therefore, if we make assumptions on the dynamics in the model that ensure that u_{it} is uncorrelated with $\mathbf{w}_{is}$, $s < t$, differencing is preferred in order to use the extra instruments.

Differencing or time demeaning followed by some sort of IV procedure is useful when u_{it} contains an important, time-varying omitted variable that is correlated with

u_{it}. The same considerations for choosing instruments in the simultaneity context are relevant in the omitted variables case as well. In some cases, $\mathbf{w}_{is}$, $s < t - 1$, can be used as instruments at time t in a first-differenced equation (11.18); in other cases, we might not want identification to hinge on using lagged exploratory variables as IVs. For example, suppose that we wish to study the effects of per student spending on test scores, using three years of data, say 1980, 1985, and 1990. A structural model at the school level is

$$avgscore_{it} = \theta_t + \mathbf{z}_{it}\gamma + \delta_1 spending_{it} + c_i + u_{it} \tag{11.28}$$

where $\mathbf{z}_{it}$ contains other school and student characteristics. In addition to worrying about the school fixed effect c_i, u_{it} contains average family income for school i at time t (unless we are able to collect data on income); average family income is likely to be correlated with $spending_{it}$. After differencing away c_i, we need an instrument for $\Delta spending_{it}$. One possibility is to use exogenous changes in property taxes that arose because of an unexpected change in the tax laws. [Such changes occurred in California in 1978 (Proposition 13) and in Michigan in 1994 (Proposal A).] Using lagged spending changes as IVs is probably not a good idea, as spending might affect test scores with a lag.

The third form of endogeneity, measurement error, can also be solved by eliminating c_i and finding appropriate IVs. Measurement error in panel data was studied by Solon (1985) and Griliches and Hausman (1986). It is widely believed in econometrics that the differencing and FE transformations exacerbate measurement error bias (even though they eliminate heterogeneity bias). However, it is important to know that this conclusion rests on the classical errors-in-variables model under strict exogeneity, as well as on other assumptions.

To illustrate, consider a model with a single explanatory variable,

$$y_{it} = \beta x_{it}^* + c_i + u_{it} \tag{11.29}$$

under the strict exogeneity assumption

$$\mathrm{E}(u_{it} \mid \mathbf{x}_i^*, \mathbf{x}_i, c_i) = 0, \qquad t = 1, 2, \ldots, T \tag{11.30}$$

where x_{it} denotes the observed measure of the unobservable x_{it}^*. Condition (11.30) embodies the standard redundancy condition—that x_{it} does not matter once x_{it}^* is controlled for—in addition to strict exogeneity of the unmeasured and measured regressors. Denote the measurement error as $r_{it} = x_{it} - x_{it}^*$. Assuming that r_{it} is uncorrelated with x_{it}^*—the key CEV assumption—and that variances and covariances are all constant across t, it is easily shown that, as $N \to \infty$, the plim of the pooled OLS estimator is

$$\underset{N\to\infty}{\text{plim}}\ \hat{\beta}_{POLS} = \beta + \frac{\text{Cov}(x_{it}, c_i + u_{it} - \beta r_{it})}{\text{Var}(x_{it})}$$

$$= \beta + \frac{\text{Cov}(x_{it}, c_i) - \beta\sigma_r^2}{\text{Var}(x_{it})} \tag{11.31}$$

where $\sigma_r^2 = \text{Var}(r_{it}) = \text{Cov}(x_{it}, r_{it})$; this is essentially the formula derived by Solon (1985).

From equation (11.31), we see that there are two sources of asymptotic bias in the POLS estimator: correlation between x_{it} and the unobserved effect, c_i, and a measurement error bias term, $-\beta\sigma_r^2$. If x_{it} and c_i are positively correlated and $\beta > 0$, the two sources of bias tend to cancel each other out.

Now assume that r_{is} is uncorrelated with x_{it}^* for all t and s, and for simplicity suppose that $T = 2$. If we first difference to remove c_i before performing OLS we obtain

$$\underset{N\to\infty}{\text{plim}}\ \hat{\beta}_{FD} = \beta + \frac{\text{Cov}(\Delta x_{it}, \Delta u_{it} - \beta\Delta r_{it})}{\text{Var}(\Delta x_{it})} = \beta - \beta\frac{\text{Cov}(\Delta x_{it}, \Delta r_{it})}{\text{Var}(\Delta x_{it})}$$

$$= \beta - 2\beta\frac{[\sigma_r^2 - \text{Cov}(r_{it}, r_{i,t-1})]}{\text{Var}(\Delta x_{it})}$$

$$= \beta\left(1 - \frac{\sigma_r^2(1-\rho_r)}{\sigma_{x^*}^2(1-\rho_{x^*}) + \sigma_r^2(1-\rho_r)}\right) \tag{11.32}$$

where $\rho_{x^*} = \text{Corr}(x_{it}^*, x_{i,t-1}^*)$ and $\rho_r = \text{Corr}(r_{it}, r_{i,t-1})$, where we have used the fact that $\text{Cov}(r_{it}, r_{i,t-1}) = \sigma_r^2\rho_r$ and $\text{Var}(\Delta x_{it}) = 2[\sigma_{x^*}^2(1-\rho_{x^*}) + \sigma_r^2(1-\rho_r)]$; see also Solon (1985) and Hsiao (1986, p. 64). Equation (11.32) shows that, in addition to the ratio $\sigma_r^2/\sigma_{x^*}^2$ being important in determining the size of the measurement error bias, the ratio $(1-\rho_r)/(1-\rho_{x^*})$ is also important. As the autocorrelation in x_{it}^* increases relative to that in r_{it}, the measurement error bias in $\hat{\beta}_{FD}$ increases. In fact, as $\rho_{x^*} \to 1$, the measurement error bias approaches $-\beta$.

Of course, we can never know whether the bias in equation (11.31) is larger than that in equation (11.32), or vice versa. Also, both expressions are based on the CEV assumptions, and then some. If there is little correlation between Δx_{it} and Δr_{it}, the measurement error bias from first differencing may be small, but the small correlation is offset by the fact that differencing can considerably reduce the variation in the explanatory variables.

Consistent estimation in the presence of measurement error is possible under certain assumptions. Consider the more general model

$$y_{it} = \mathbf{z}_{it}\gamma + \delta w_{it}^* + c_i + u_{it}, \qquad t = 1, 2, \ldots, T \tag{11.33}$$

where w_{it}^* is measured with error. Write $r_{it} = w_{it} - w_{it}^*$, and assume strict exogeneity along with redundancy of w_{it}:

$$E(u_{it} \mid \mathbf{z}_i, \mathbf{w}_i^*, \mathbf{w}_i, c_i) = 0, \qquad t = 1, 2, \ldots, T \tag{11.34}$$

Replacing w_{it}^* with w_{it} and first differencing gives

$$\Delta y_{it} = \Delta \mathbf{z}_{it}\gamma + \delta \Delta w_{it} + \Delta u_{it} - \delta \Delta r_{it} \tag{11.35}$$

The standard CEV assumption in the current context can be stated as

$$E(r_{it} \mid \mathbf{z}_i, \mathbf{w}_i^*, c_i) = 0, \qquad t = 1, 2, \ldots, T \tag{11.36}$$

which implies that r_{it} is uncorrelated with $\mathbf{z}_{is}$, w_{is}^* for all t and s. (As always in the context of linear models, assuming zero correlation is sufficient for consistency, but not for usual standard errors and test statistics to be valid.) Under assumption (11.36) (and other measurement error assumptions), Δr_{it} is correlated with Δw_{it}. To apply an IV method to equation (11.35), we need at least one instrument for Δw_{it}. As in the omitted variables and simultaneity contexts, we may have additional variables outside the model that can be used as instruments. Analogous to the cross section case (as in Chapter 5), one possibility is to use another measure on w_{it}^*, say h_{it}. If the measurement error in h_{it} is orthogonal to the measurement error in w_{is}, all t and s, then Δh_{it} is a natural instrument for Δw_{it} in equation (11.35). Of course, we can use many more instruments in equation (11.35), as any linear combination of $\mathbf{z}_i$ and $\mathbf{h}_i$ is uncorrelated with the composite error under the given assumptions.

Alternatively, a vector of variables $\mathbf{h}_{it}$ may exist that are known to be redundant in equation (11.33), strictly exogenous, and uncorrelated with r_{is} for all s. If $\Delta \mathbf{h}_{it}$ is correlated with Δw_{it}, then an IV procedure, such as pooled 2SLS, is easy to apply. It may be that in applying something like pooled 2SLS to equation (11.35) results in asymptotically valid statistics; this imposes serial independence and homoskedasticity assumptions on Δu_{it}. Generally, however, it is a good idea to use standard errors and test statistics robust to arbitrary serial correlation and heteroskedasticity, or to use a full GMM approach that efficiently accounts for these. An alternative is to use the FE transformation, as explained in Problem 11.9. Ziliak, Wilson, and Stone (1999) find that, for a model explaining cyclicality of real wages, the FD and FE estimates are different in important ways. The differences largely disappear when IV methods are used to account for measurement error in the local unemployment rate.

So far, the solutions to measurement error in the context of panel data have assumed nothing about the serial correlation in r_{it}. Suppose that, in addition to assumption (11.34), we assume that the measurement error is serially uncorrelated:

$$E(r_{it} r_{is}) = 0, \qquad s \neq t \tag{11.37}$$

Assumption (11.37) opens up a solution to the measurement error problem with panel data that is not available with a single cross section or independently pooled cross sections. Under assumption (11.36), r_{it} is uncorrelated with w_{is}^* for all t and s. Thus, if we assume that the measurement error r_{it} is serially uncorrelated, then r_{it} is uncorrelated with w_{is} for all $t \neq s$. Since, by the strict exogeneity assumption, Δu_{it} is uncorrelated with all leads and lags of $\mathbf{z}_{it}$ and w_{it}, we have instruments readily available. For example, $w_{i,t-2}$ and $w_{i,t-3}$ are valid as instruments for Δw_{it} in equation (11.35); so is $w_{i,t+1}$. Again, pooled 2SLS or some other IV procedure can be used once the list of instruments is specified for each time period. However, it is important to remember that this approach requires the r_{it} to be serially uncorrelated, in addition to the other CEV assumptions.

The methods just covered for solving measurement error problems all assume strict exogeneity of all explanatory variables. Naturally, things get harder when measurement error is combined with models with only sequentially exogenous explanatory variables. Nevertheless, differencing away the unobserved effect and then selecting instruments—based on the maintained assumptions—generally works in models with a variety of problems.

11.1.4 Summary of Models without Strictly Exogenous Explanatory Variables

Before leaving this section, it is useful to summarize the general approach we have taken to estimate models that do not satisfy strict exogeneity: first, a transformation is used to eliminate the unobserved effect; next, instruments are chosen for the endogenous variables in the transformed equation. In the previous subsections we have stated various assumptions, but we have not catalogued them as in Chapter 10, largely because there are so many variants. For example, in Section 11.1.3 we saw that different assumptions lead to different sets of instruments. The importance of carefully stating assumptions—such as (11.2), (11.34), (11.36), and (11.37)—cannot be overstated.

First differencing, which allows for more general violations of strict exogeneity than the within transformation, has an additional benefit: it is easy to test the first-differenced equation for serial correlation after pooled 2SLS estimation. The test suggested in Problem 8.10 is immediately applicable with the change in notation that all variables are in first differences. Arellano and Bond (1991) propose tests for serial correlation in the original errors, $\{u_{it}: t = 1, \ldots, T\}$; the tests are based on GMM estimation. When the original model has a lagged dependent variable, it makes more sense to test for serial correlation in $\{u_{it}\}$: models with lagged dependent variables are usually taken to have errors that are serially uncorrelated, in which case the first-differenced errors must be serially correlated. As Arellano and Bond point out, serial correlation in $\{u_{it}\}$ generally invalidates using lags of y_{it} as IVs in the first-differenced equation. Of course, one might ask why we would be interested in ρ_1 in model (11.4) if $\{u_{it}\}$ is generally serially correlated.

11.2 Models with Individual-Specific Slopes

The unobserved effects models we have studied up to this point all have an additive unobserved effect that has the same partial effect on y_{it} in all time periods. This assumption may be too strong for some applications. We now turn to models that allow for individual-specific slopes.

11.2.1 A Random Trend Model

Consider the following extension of the standard unobserved effects model:

$$y_{it} = c_i + g_i t + \mathbf{x}_{it}\boldsymbol{\beta} + u_{it}, \qquad t = 1, 2, \ldots, T \tag{11.38}$$

This is sometimes called a **random trend model**, as each individual, firm, city, and so on is allowed to have its own time trend. The individual-specific trend is an additional source of heterogeneity. If y_{it} is the natural log of a variable, as is often the case in economic studies, then g_i is (roughly) the average growth rate over a period (holding the explanatory variables fixed). Then equation (11.38) is referred to a **random growth model**; see, for example, Heckman and Hotz (1989).

In many applications of equation (11.38) we want to allow (c_i, g_i) to be arbitrarily correlated with $\mathbf{x}_{it}$. (Unfortunately, allowing this correlation makes the name "random trend model" conflict with our previous usage of random versus fixed effects.) For example, if one element of $\mathbf{x}_{it}$ is an indicator of program participation, equation (11.38) allows program participation to depend on individual-specific trends (or growth rates) in addition to the level effect, c_i. We proceed without imposing restrictions on correlations among $(c_i, g_i, \mathbf{x}_{it})$, so that our analysis is of the fixed effects variety. A random effects approach is also possible, but it is more cumbersome; see Problem 11.5.

For the random trend model, the strict exogeneity assumption on the explanatory variables is

$$\mathrm{E}(u_{it} \mid \mathbf{x}_{i1}, \ldots, \mathbf{x}_{iT}, c_i, g_i) = 0 \tag{11.39}$$

which follows definitionally from the conditional mean specification

$$\mathrm{E}(y_{it} \mid \mathbf{x}_{i1}, \ldots, \mathbf{x}_{iT}, c_i, g_i) = \mathrm{E}(y_{it} \mid \mathbf{x}_{it}, c_i, g_i) = c_i + g_i t + \mathbf{x}_{it}\boldsymbol{\beta} \tag{11.40}$$

We are still primarily interested in consistently estimating $\boldsymbol{\beta}$.

One approach to estimating $\boldsymbol{\beta}$ is to difference away c_i:

$$\Delta y_{it} = g_i + \Delta \mathbf{x}_{it}\boldsymbol{\beta} + \Delta u_{it}, \qquad t = 2, 3, \ldots, T \tag{11.41}$$

where we have used the fact that $g_i t - g_i(t-1) = g_i$. Now equation (11.41) is just the standard unobserved effects model we studied in Chapter 10. The key strict exogeneity assumption, $\mathrm{E}(\Delta u_{it} \mid g_i, \Delta \mathbf{x}_{i2}, \ldots, \Delta \mathbf{x}_{iT}) = 0$, $t = 2, 3, \ldots, T$, holds under assumption (11.39). Therefore, we can apply fixed effects or first-differencing methods to equation (11.41) in order to estimate $\boldsymbol{\beta}$.

In differencing the equation to eliminate c_i we lose one time period, so that equation (11.41) applies to $T - 1$ time periods. To apply FE or FD methods to equation (11.41) we must have $T - 1 \geq 2$, or $T \geq 3$. In other words, $\boldsymbol{\beta}$ can be estimated consistently in the random trend model only if $T \geq 3$.

Whether we prefer FE or FD estimation of equation (11.41) depends on the properties of $\{\Delta u_{it}\colon t = 2, 3, \ldots, T\}$. As we argued in Section 10.6, in some cases it is reasonable to assume that the first difference of $\{u_{it}\}$ is serially uncorrelated, in which case the FE method applied to equation (11.41) is attractive. If we make the assumption that the u_{it} are serially uncorrelated and homoskedastic (conditional on $\mathbf{x}_i$, c_i, g_i), then FE applied to equation (11.41) is still consistent and asymptotically normal, but not efficient. The next subsection covers that case explicitly.

Example 11.7 (Random Growth Model for Analyzing Enterprise Zones): Papke (1994) estimates a random growth model to examine the effects of enterprise zones on unemployment claims:

$$\log(uclms_{it}) = \theta_t + c_i + g_i t + \delta_1 ez_{it} + u_{it}$$

so that aggregate time effects are allowed in addition to a jurisdiction-specific growth rate, g_i. She first differences the equation to eliminate c_i and then applies fixed effects to the differences. The estimate of δ_1 is $\hat{\delta}_1 = -.192$ with $\mathrm{se}(\hat{\delta}_1) = .085$. Thus enterprise zone designation is predicted to lower unemployment claims by about 19.2 percent, and the effect is statistically significant at the 5 percent level.

Friedberg (1998) provides an example, using state-level panel data on divorce rates and divorce laws, that shows how important it can be to allow for state-specific trends. Without state-specific trends, she finds no effect of unilateral divorce laws on divorce rates; with state-specific trends, the estimated effect is large and statistically significant. The estimation method Friedberg uses is the one we discuss in the next subsection.

In using the random trend or random growth model for program evaluation, it may make sense to allow the trend or growth rate to depend on program participation: in addition to shifting the level of y, program participation may also affect the rate of change. In addition to $prog_{it}$, we would include $prog_{it} \cdot t$ in the model:

$$y_{it} = \theta_t + c_i + g_i t + \mathbf{z}_{it}\gamma + \delta_1 prog_{it} + \delta_2 prog_{it} \cdot t + u_{it}$$

Differencing once, as before, removes c_i,

$$\Delta y_{it} = \xi_t + g_i + \Delta\mathbf{z}_{it}\gamma + \delta_1 \Delta prog_{it} + \delta_2 \Delta(prog_{it} \cdot t) + \Delta u_{it}$$

We can estimate this differenced equation by fixed effects. An even more flexible specification is to replace $prog_{it}$ and $prog_{it} \cdot t$ with a series of program indicators, $prog1_{it}, \ldots, progM_{it}$, where $progj_{it}$ is one if unit i in time t has been in the program exactly j years, and M is the maximum number of years the program has been around.

If $\{u_{it}\}$ contains substantial serial correlation—more than a random walk—then differencing equation (11.41) might be more attractive. Denote the second difference of y_{it} by

$$\Delta^2 y_{it} \equiv \Delta y_{it} - \Delta y_{i,t-1} = y_{it} - 2y_{i,t-1} + y_{i,t-2}$$

with similar expressions for $\Delta^2 \mathbf{x}_{it}$ and $\Delta^2 u_{it}$. Then

$$\Delta^2 y_{it} = \Delta^2 \mathbf{x}_{it}\boldsymbol{\beta} + \Delta^2 u_{it}, \qquad t = 3, \ldots, T \tag{11.42}$$

As with the FE transformation applied to equation (11.41), second differencing also eliminates g_i. Because $\Delta^2 u_{it}$ is uncorrelated with $\Delta^2 \mathbf{x}_{is}$, for all t and s, we can estimate equation (11.42) by pooled OLS or a GLS procedure.

When $T = 3$, second differencing is the same as first differencing and then applying fixed effects. Second differencing results in a single cross section on the second-differenced data, so that if the second-difference error is homoskedastic conditional on $\mathbf{x}_i$, the standard OLS analysis on the cross section of second differences is appropriate. Hoxby (1996) uses this method to estimate the effect of teachers' unions on education production using three years of census data.

If $\mathbf{x}_{it}$ contains a time trend, then $\Delta\mathbf{x}_{it}$ contains the same constant for $t = 2, 3, \ldots, T$, which then gets swept away in the FE or FD transformation applied to equation (11.41). Therefore, $\mathbf{x}_{it}$ cannot have time-constant variables *or* variables that have exact linear time trends for all cross section units.

11.2.2 General Models with Individual-Specific Slopes

We now consider a more general model with interactions between time-varying explanatory variables and some unobservable, time-constant variables:

$$y_{it} = \mathbf{z}_{it}\mathbf{a}_i + \mathbf{x}_{it}\boldsymbol{\beta} + u_{it}, \qquad t = 1, 2, \ldots, T \tag{11.43}$$

where $\mathbf{z}_{it}$ is $1 \times J$, $\mathbf{a}_i$ is $J \times 1$, $\mathbf{x}_{it}$ is $1 \times K$, and $\boldsymbol{\beta}$ is $K \times 1$. The standard unobserved effects model is a special case with $\mathbf{z}_{it} \equiv 1$; the random trend model is a special case with $\mathbf{z}_{it} = \mathbf{z}_t = (1, t)$.

Equation (11.43) allows some time-constant unobserved heterogeneity, contained in the vector $\mathbf{a}_i$, to interact with some of the observable explanatory variables. For example, suppose that $prog_{it}$ is a program participation indicator and y_{it} is an outcome variable. The model

$$y_{it} = \mathbf{x}_{it}\boldsymbol{\beta} + a_{i1} + a_{i2} \cdot prog_{it} + u_{it}$$

allows the effect of the program to depend on the unobserved effect a_{i2} (which may or may not be tied to a_{i1}). While we are interested in estimating $\boldsymbol{\beta}$, we are also interested in the average effect of the program, $\mu_2 = \mathrm{E}(a_{i2})$. We cannot hope to get good estimators of the a_{i2} in the usual case of small T. Polachek and Kim (1994) study such models, where the return to experience is allowed to be person-specific. Lemieux (1998) estimates a model where unobserved heterogeneity is rewarded differently in the union and nonunion sectors.

In the general model, we initially focus on estimating $\boldsymbol{\beta}$ and then turn to estimation of $\boldsymbol{\alpha} = \mathrm{E}(\mathbf{a}_i)$, which is the vector of average partial effects for the covariates $\mathbf{z}_{it}$. The strict exogeneity assumption is the natural extension of assumption (11.39):

ASSUMPTION FE.1′: $\mathrm{E}(u_{it} \mid \mathbf{z}_i, \mathbf{x}_i, \mathbf{a}_i) = 0, \; t = 1, 2, \ldots, T.$

Along with equation (11.43), Assumption FE.1′ is equivalent to

$$\mathrm{E}(y_{it} \mid \mathbf{z}_{i1}, \ldots, \mathbf{z}_{iT}, \mathbf{x}_{i1}, \ldots, \mathbf{x}_{iT}, \mathbf{a}_i) = \mathrm{E}(y_{it} \mid \mathbf{z}_{it}, \mathbf{x}_{it}, \mathbf{a}_i) = \mathbf{z}_{it}\mathbf{a}_i + \mathbf{x}_{it}\boldsymbol{\beta}$$

which says that, once $\mathbf{z}_{it}$, $\mathbf{x}_{it}$, and $\mathbf{a}_i$ have been controlled for, $(\mathbf{z}_{is}, \mathbf{x}_{is})$ for $s \neq t$ do not help to explain y_{it}.

Define $\mathbf{Z}_i$ as the $T \times J$ matrix with tth row $\mathbf{z}_{it}$, and similarly for the $T \times K$ matrix $\mathbf{X}_i$. Then equation (11.43) can be written as

$$\mathbf{y}_i = \mathbf{Z}_i\mathbf{a}_i + \mathbf{X}_i\boldsymbol{\beta} + \mathbf{u}_i \tag{11.44}$$

Assuming that $\mathbf{Z}_i'\mathbf{Z}_i$ is nonsingular (technically, with probability one), define

$$\mathbf{M}_i \equiv \mathbf{I}_T - \mathbf{Z}_i(\mathbf{Z}_i'\mathbf{Z}_i)^{-1}\mathbf{Z}_i' \tag{11.45}$$

the projection matrix onto the null space of $\mathbf{Z}_i$ [the matrix $\mathbf{Z}_i(\mathbf{Z}_i'\mathbf{Z}_i)^{-1}\mathbf{Z}_i'$ is the projection matrix onto the column space of $\mathbf{Z}_i$]. In other words, for each cross section observation i, $\mathbf{M}_i\mathbf{y}_i$ is the $T \times 1$ vector of residuals from the time series regression

$$y_{it} \text{ on } \mathbf{z}_{it}, \qquad t = 1, 2, \ldots, T \tag{11.46}$$

In the basic fixed effects case, regression (11.46) is the regression y_{it} on 1, $t = 1, 2, \ldots, T$, and the residuals are simply the time-demeaned variables. In the random trend case, the regression is y_{it} on 1, t, $t = 1, 2, \ldots, T$, which linearly detrends y_{it} for each i.

The $T \times K$ matrix $\mathbf{M}_i\mathbf{X}_i$ contains as its rows the $1 \times K$ vectors of residuals from the regression $\mathbf{x}_{it}$ on $\mathbf{z}_{it}$, $t = 1, 2, \ldots, T$. The usefulness of premultiplying by $\mathbf{M}_i$ is that it allows us to eliminate the unobserved effect $\mathbf{a}_i$ by premultiplying equation (11.44) through by $\mathbf{M}_i$ and noting that $\mathbf{M}_i\mathbf{Z}_i = \mathbf{0}$:

$$\ddot{\mathbf{y}}_i = \ddot{\mathbf{X}}_i\boldsymbol{\beta} + \ddot{\mathbf{u}}_i \tag{11.47}$$

where $\ddot{\mathbf{y}}_i = \mathbf{M}_i\mathbf{y}_i$, $\ddot{\mathbf{X}}_i = \mathbf{M}_i\mathbf{X}_i$, and $\ddot{\mathbf{u}}_i = \mathbf{M}_i\mathbf{u}_i$. This is an extension of the within transformation used in basic fixed effects estimation.

To consistently estimate $\boldsymbol{\beta}$ by system OLS on equation (11.47), we make the following assumption:

ASSUMPTION FE.2$'$: rank $\mathrm{E}(\ddot{\mathbf{X}}_i'\ddot{\mathbf{X}}_i) = K$, where $\ddot{\mathbf{X}}_i = \mathbf{M}_i\mathbf{X}_i$.

The rank of $\mathbf{M}_i$ is $T - J$, so a necessary condition for Assumption FE.2$'$ is $J < T$. In other words, we must have at least one more time period than the number of elements in $\mathbf{a}_i$. In the basic unobserved effects model, $J = 1$, and we know that $T \geq 2$ is needed. In the random trend model, $J = 2$, and we need $T \geq 3$ to estimate $\boldsymbol{\beta}$.

The system OLS estimator of equation (11.47) is

$$\hat{\boldsymbol{\beta}}_{FE} = \left(\sum_{i=1}^{N} \ddot{\mathbf{X}}_i'\ddot{\mathbf{X}}_i\right)^{-1}\left(\sum_{i=1}^{N} \ddot{\mathbf{X}}_i'\ddot{\mathbf{y}}_i\right) = \boldsymbol{\beta} + \left(N^{-1}\sum_{i=1}^{N} \ddot{\mathbf{X}}_i'\ddot{\mathbf{X}}_i\right)^{-1}\left(N^{-1}\sum_{i=1}^{N} \ddot{\mathbf{X}}_i'\mathbf{u}_i\right)$$

Under Assumption FE.1$'$, $\mathrm{E}(\ddot{\mathbf{X}}_i'\mathbf{u}_i) = \mathbf{0}$, and under Assumption FE.2$'$, rank $\mathrm{E}(\ddot{\mathbf{X}}_i'\ddot{\mathbf{X}}_i) = K$, and so the usual consistency argument goes through. Generally, it is possible that for some observations, $\ddot{\mathbf{X}}_i'\ddot{\mathbf{X}}_i$ has rank less than K. For example, this result occurs in the standard fixed effects case when $\mathbf{x}_{it}$ does not vary over time for unit i. However, under Assumption FE.2$'$, $\hat{\boldsymbol{\beta}}_{FE}$ should be well defined unless our cross section sample size is small or we are unlucky in obtaining the sample.

Naturally, the FE estimator is $\sqrt{N}$-asymptotically normally distributed. To obtain the simplest expression for its asymptotic variance, we add the assumptions of constant conditional variance and no (conditional) serial correlation on the idiosyncratic errors $\{u_{it}: t = 1, 2, \ldots, T\}$.

ASSUMPTION FE.3$'$: $\mathrm{E}(\mathbf{u}_i\mathbf{u}_i' \mid \mathbf{z}_i, \mathbf{x}_i, \mathbf{a}_i) = \sigma_u^2\mathbf{I}_T$.

Under Assumption FE.3′, iterated expectations implies

$$\mathrm{E}(\ddot{\mathbf{X}}_i'\mathbf{u}_i\mathbf{u}_i'\ddot{\mathbf{X}}_i) = \mathrm{E}[\ddot{\mathbf{X}}_i'\mathrm{E}(\mathbf{u}_i\mathbf{u}_i' \mid \mathbf{Z}_i, \mathbf{X}_i)\ddot{\mathbf{X}}_i] = \sigma_u^2\mathrm{E}(\ddot{\mathbf{X}}_i'\ddot{\mathbf{X}}_i)$$

Using essentially the same argument as in Section 10.5.2, under Assumptions FE.1′, FE.2′, and FE.3′, Avar $\sqrt{N}(\hat{\boldsymbol{\beta}}_{FE} - \boldsymbol{\beta}) = \sigma_u^2[\mathrm{E}(\ddot{\mathbf{X}}_i'\ddot{\mathbf{X}}_i)]^{-1}$, and so $\mathrm{Avar}(\hat{\boldsymbol{\beta}}_{FE})$ is consistently estimated by

$$\mathrm{Av\hat{a}r}(\hat{\boldsymbol{\beta}}_{FE}) = \hat{\sigma}_u^2\left(\sum_{i=1}^{N}\ddot{\mathbf{X}}_i'\ddot{\mathbf{X}}_i\right)^{-1} \tag{11.48}$$

where $\hat{\sigma}_u^2$ is a consistent estimator for σ_u^2. As with the standard FE analysis, we must use some care in obtaining $\hat{\sigma}_u^2$. We have

$$\begin{aligned}\sum_{t=1}^{T}\mathrm{E}(\ddot{u}_{it}^2) &= \mathrm{E}(\ddot{\mathbf{u}}_i'\ddot{\mathbf{u}}_i) = \mathrm{E}[\mathrm{E}(\mathbf{u}_i'\mathbf{M}_i\mathbf{u}_i \mid \mathbf{Z}_i, \mathbf{X}_i)] = \mathrm{E}\{\mathrm{tr}[\mathrm{E}(\mathbf{u}_i'\mathbf{u}_i\mathbf{M}_i \mid \mathbf{Z}_i, \mathbf{X}_i)]\} \\ &= \mathrm{E}\{\mathrm{tr}[\mathrm{E}(\mathbf{u}_i'\mathbf{u}_i \mid \mathbf{Z}_i, \mathbf{X}_i)\mathbf{M}_i]\} = \mathrm{E}[\mathrm{tr}(\sigma_u^2\mathbf{M}_i)] = (T - J)\sigma_u^2 \end{aligned} \tag{11.49}$$

since $\mathrm{tr}(\mathbf{M}_i) = T - J$. Let $\hat{u}_{it} = \ddot{y}_{it} - \ddot{\mathbf{x}}_{it}\hat{\boldsymbol{\beta}}_{FE}$. Then equation (11.49) and standard arguments imply that an unbiased and consistent estimator of σ_u^2 is

$$\hat{\sigma}_u^2 = [N(T - J) - K]^{-1}\sum_{i=1}^{N}\sum_{t=1}^{T}\hat{u}_{it}^2 = \mathrm{SSR}/[N(T - J) - K] \tag{11.50}$$

The SSR in equation (11.50) is from the pooled regression

$$\ddot{y}_{it} \text{ on } \ddot{\mathbf{x}}_{it}, \qquad t = 1, 2, \ldots, T; i = 1, 2, \ldots, N \tag{11.51}$$

which can be used to obtain $\hat{\boldsymbol{\beta}}_{FE}$. Division of the SSR from regression (11.51) by $N(T - J) - K$ produces $\hat{\sigma}_u^2$. The standard errors reported from regression (11.51) will be off because the SSR is only divided by $NT - K$; the adjustment factor is $\{(NT - K)/[N(T - J) - K]\}^{1/2}$.

A standard F statistic for testing hypotheses about $\boldsymbol{\beta}$ is also asymptotically valid. Let Q be the number of restrictions on $\boldsymbol{\beta}$ under H_0, and let SSR_r be the restricted sum of squared residuals from a regression like regression (11.51) but with the restrictions on $\boldsymbol{\beta}$ imposed. Let SSR_{ur} be the unrestricted sum of squared residuals. Then

$$F = \frac{(\mathrm{SSR}_r - \mathrm{SSR}_{ur})}{\mathrm{SSR}_{ur}} \cdot \frac{[N(T - J) - K]}{Q} \tag{11.52}$$

can be treated as having an F distribution with Q and $N(T - J) - K$ degrees of freedom. Unless we add a (conditional) normality assumption on $\mathbf{u}_i$, equation (11.52) does not have an exact F distribution, but it is asymptotically valid because $Q \cdot F \overset{a}{\sim} \chi^2_Q$.

Without Assumption FE.3′, equation (11.48) is no longer valid as the variance estimator and equation (11.52) is not a valid test statistic. But the robust variance matrix estimator (10.59) can be used with the new definitions for $\ddot{\mathbf{X}}_i$ and $\hat{\mathbf{u}}_i$. This step leads directly to robust Wald statistics for multiple restrictions.

To obtain a consistent estimator of $\boldsymbol{\alpha} = \mathrm{E}(\mathbf{a}_i)$, premultiply equation (11.44) by $(\mathbf{Z}_i'\mathbf{Z}_i)^{-1}\mathbf{Z}_i'$ and rearrange to get

$$\mathbf{a}_i = (\mathbf{Z}_i'\mathbf{Z}_i)^{-1}\mathbf{Z}_i'(\mathbf{y}_i - \mathbf{X}_i\boldsymbol{\beta}) - (\mathbf{Z}_i'\mathbf{Z}_i)^{-1}\mathbf{Z}_i'\mathbf{u}_i \tag{11.53}$$

Under Assumption FE.1′, $\mathrm{E}(\mathbf{u}_i \mid \mathbf{Z}_i) = \mathbf{0}$, and so the second term in equation (11.53) has a zero expected value. Therefore, assuming that the expected value exists,

$$\boldsymbol{\alpha} = \mathrm{E}[(\mathbf{Z}_i'\mathbf{Z}_i)^{-1}\mathbf{Z}_i'(\mathbf{y}_i - \mathbf{X}_i\boldsymbol{\beta})]$$

So a consistent, $\sqrt{N}$-asymptotically normal estimator of $\boldsymbol{\alpha}$ is

$$\hat{\boldsymbol{\alpha}} = N^{-1}\sum_{i=1}^{N}(\mathbf{Z}_i'\mathbf{Z}_i)^{-1}\mathbf{Z}_i'(\mathbf{y}_i - \mathbf{X}_i\hat{\boldsymbol{\beta}}_{FE}) \tag{11.54}$$

With fixed T we cannot consistently estimate the $\mathbf{a}_i$ when they are viewed as parameters. However, for each i, the term in the summand in equation (11.54), call it $\hat{\mathbf{a}}_i$, is an *unbiased* estimator of $\mathbf{a}_i$ under Assumptions FE.1′ and FE.2′. This conclusion is easy to show: $\mathrm{E}(\hat{\mathbf{a}}_i \mid \mathbf{Z}, \mathbf{X}) = (\mathbf{Z}_i'\mathbf{Z}_i)^{-1}\mathbf{Z}_i'[\mathrm{E}(\mathbf{y}_i \mid \mathbf{Z}, \mathbf{X}) - \mathbf{X}_i\mathrm{E}(\hat{\boldsymbol{\beta}}_{FE} \mid \mathbf{Z}, \mathbf{X})] = (\mathbf{Z}_i'\mathbf{Z}_i)^{-1}\mathbf{Z}_i'[\mathbf{Z}_i\mathbf{a}_i + \mathbf{X}_i\boldsymbol{\beta} - \mathbf{X}_i\boldsymbol{\beta}] = \mathbf{a}_i$, where we have used the fact that $\mathrm{E}(\hat{\boldsymbol{\beta}}_{FE} \mid \mathbf{Z}, \mathbf{X}) = \boldsymbol{\beta}$. The estimator $\hat{\boldsymbol{\alpha}}$ simply averages the $\hat{\mathbf{a}}_i$ over all cross section observations.

The asymptotic variance of $\sqrt{N}(\hat{\boldsymbol{\alpha}} - \boldsymbol{\alpha})$ can be obtained by expanding equation (11.54) and plugging in $\sqrt{N}(\hat{\boldsymbol{\beta}}_{FE} - \boldsymbol{\beta}) = [\mathrm{E}(\ddot{\mathbf{X}}_i'\ddot{\mathbf{X}}_i)]^{-1}(N^{-1/2}\sum_{i=1}^{N}\ddot{\mathbf{X}}_i'\mathbf{u}_i) + \mathrm{o}_p(1)$. A consistent estimator of Avar $\sqrt{N}(\hat{\boldsymbol{\alpha}} - \boldsymbol{\alpha})$ can be shown to be

$$N^{-1}\sum_{i=1}^{N}[(\hat{\mathbf{s}}_i - \hat{\boldsymbol{\alpha}}) - \hat{\mathbf{C}}\hat{\mathbf{A}}^{-1}\ddot{\mathbf{X}}_i'\hat{\mathbf{u}}_i][(\hat{\mathbf{s}}_i - \hat{\boldsymbol{\alpha}}) - \hat{\mathbf{C}}\hat{\mathbf{A}}^{-1}\ddot{\mathbf{X}}_i'\hat{\mathbf{u}}_i]' \tag{11.55}$$

where $\hat{\mathbf{s}}_i \equiv (\mathbf{Z}_i'\mathbf{Z}_i)^{-1}\mathbf{Z}_i'(\mathbf{y}_i - \mathbf{X}_i\hat{\boldsymbol{\beta}}_{FE})$, $\hat{\mathbf{C}} \equiv N^{-1}\sum_{i=1}^{N}(\mathbf{Z}_i'\mathbf{Z}_i)^{-1}\mathbf{Z}_i'\mathbf{X}_i$, $\hat{\mathbf{A}} \equiv N^{-1}\sum_{i=1}^{N}\ddot{\mathbf{X}}_i'\ddot{\mathbf{X}}_i$, and $\hat{\mathbf{u}}_i \equiv \ddot{\mathbf{y}}_i - \ddot{\mathbf{X}}_i\hat{\boldsymbol{\beta}}_{FE}$. This estimator is fully robust in the sense that it does not rely on Assumption FE.3′. As usual, asymptotic standard errors of the elements of $\hat{\boldsymbol{\alpha}}$ are obtained by multiplying expression (11.55) by N and taking the square roots of the diagonal elements. As special cases, expression (11.55) can be applied to the traditional unobserved effects and random trend models.

The estimator $\hat{\alpha}$ in equation (11.54) is not necessarily the most efficient. A better approach is to use the moment conditions for $\hat{\boldsymbol{\beta}}_{FE}$ and $\hat{\alpha}$ simultaneously. This leads to nonlinear instrumental variables methods, something we take up in Chapter 14. Chamberlain (1992a) covers the efficient method of moments approach to estimating $\boldsymbol{\alpha}$ and $\boldsymbol{\beta}$; see also Lemieux (1998).

11.3 GMM Approaches to Linear Unobserved Effects Models

11.3.1 Equivalence between 3SLS and Standard Panel Data Estimators

Random effects, fixed effects, and first differencing are still the most popular approaches to estimating unobserved effects panel data models under strict exogeneity of the explanatory variables. As we saw in Chapter 10, each of these is efficient under a particular set of assumptions. If these assumptions fail, we can do worse than using an optimal GMM approach. We have already seen how to generalize Assumption RE.3, FE.3, or FD.3 by allowing the idiosyncratic error variance matrix, $\text{Var}(\mathbf{u}_i)$, to be unrestricted. But we still assumed that either $\text{Var}(c_i \mathbf{j}_T + \mathbf{u}_i \mid \mathbf{x}_i)$ (random effects) or $\text{Var}(\mathbf{u}_i \mid \mathbf{x}_i, c_i)$ was constant.

Suppose first that Assumption RE.1 holds, so that $\text{E}(c_i \mid \mathbf{x}_i) = 0$. Write the model in composite error form as

$$\mathbf{y}_i = \mathbf{X}_i \boldsymbol{\beta} + \mathbf{v}_i \tag{11.56}$$

Under Assumption RE.1, $\mathbf{x}_{is}$ is uncorrelated with v_{it} for all s and t. [In fact, any function of $\mathbf{x}_i \equiv (\mathbf{x}_{i1}, \ldots, \mathbf{x}_{iT})$ is uncorrelated with v_{it} for all t, but we will only use the $\mathbf{x}_{is}$ themselves.] Let $\mathbf{x}_i^o$ denote the row vector of nonredundant elements of $\mathbf{x}_i$, so that any time constant element appears only once in $\mathbf{x}_i^o$. Then $\text{E}(\mathbf{x}_i^{o\prime} v_{it}) = \mathbf{0}$, $t = 1, 2, \ldots, T$. This orthogonality condition suggests a system instrumental variables procedure, with matrix of instruments

$$\mathbf{Z}_i \equiv \mathbf{I}_T \otimes \mathbf{x}_i^o \tag{11.57}$$

In other words, use instruments $\mathbf{Z}_i$ to estimate equation (11.56) by 3SLS or, more generally, by minimum chi-square.

The matrix (11.57) can contain many instruments. If $\mathbf{x}_{it}$ contains only time-varying variables, then $\mathbf{Z}_i$ is $T \times TK$. With only K parameters to estimate, this choice of instruments implies many overidentifying restrictions even for moderately sized T. Even if computation is not an issue, using many overidentifying restrictions can result in poor finite sample properties.

In some cases, we can reduce the number of moment conditions without sacrificing efficiency. Im, Ahn, Schmidt, and Wooldridge (1999) (IASW) show the following result. If $\hat{\boldsymbol{\Omega}}$ has the random effects structure—which means we impose the RE structure in estimating $\boldsymbol{\Omega}$—then 3SLS applied to equation (11.56), using instruments

$$\mathbf{Z}_i \equiv (\mathbf{P}_T \mathbf{X}_i, \mathbf{Q}_T \mathbf{W}_i) \tag{11.58}$$

where $\mathbf{P}_T = \mathbf{j}_T(\mathbf{j}_T'\mathbf{j}_T)^{-1}\mathbf{j}_T'$, $\mathbf{Q}_T \equiv \mathbf{I}_T - \mathbf{P}_T$, $\mathbf{j}_T \equiv (1, 1, \ldots, 1)'$, and $\mathbf{W}_i$ is the $T \times M$ submatrix of $\mathbf{X}_i$ obtained by removing the time-constant variables, is identical to the random effects estimator. The column dimension of matrix (11.58) is only $K + M$, so there are only M overidentifying restrictions in using the 3SLS estimator.

The algebraic equivalence between 3SLS and random effects has some useful applications. First, it provides a different way of testing the orthogonality between c_i and $\mathbf{x}_{it}$ for all t: after 3SLS estimation, we simply apply the GMM overidentification statistic from Chapter 8. (We discussed regression-based tests in Section 10.7.3.) Second, it provides a way to obtain a more efficient estimator when Assumption RE.3 does not hold. If $\boldsymbol{\Omega}$ does not have the random effects structure [see equation (10.30)], then the 3SLS estimator that imposes this structure is inefficient; an unrestricted estimator of $\boldsymbol{\Omega}$ should be used instead. Because an unrestricted estimator of $\boldsymbol{\Omega}$ is consistent with or without the random effects structure, 3SLS with unrestricted $\hat{\boldsymbol{\Omega}}$ and IVs in matrix (11.58) is no less efficient than the RE estimator. Further, if $\mathrm{E}(\mathbf{v}_i\mathbf{v}_i \mid \mathbf{x}_i) \neq \mathrm{E}(\mathbf{v}_i\mathbf{v}_i')$, any 3SLS estimator is inefficient relative to GMM with the optimal weighting matrix. Therefore, if Assumption RE.3 fails, minimum chi-square estimation with IVs in matrix (11.58) generally improves on the random effects estimator. In other words, we can gain asymptotic efficiency by using only $M \leq K$ additional moment conditions.

A different 3SLS estimator can be shown to be equivalent to the fixed effects estimator. In particular, IASW (1999, Theorem 4.1) verify an assertion of Arellano and Bover (1995): when $\hat{\boldsymbol{\Omega}}$ has the random effects form, the 3SLS estimator applied to equation (11.56) using instruments $\mathbf{L}_T \otimes \mathbf{x}_i^o$—where $\mathbf{L}_T$ is the $T \times (T-1)$ differencing matrix defined in IASW [1999, equation (4.1)]—is identical to the fixed effects estimator. Therefore, we might as well use fixed effects.

11.3.2 Chamberlain's Approach to Unobserved Effects Models

We now study an approach to estimating the linear unobserved effects model (11.1) due to Chamberlain (1982, 1984) and related to Mundlak (1978). We maintain the strict exogeneity assumption on $\mathbf{x}_{it}$ conditional on c_i (see Assumption FE.1), but we allow arbitrary correlation between c_i and $\mathbf{x}_{it}$. Thus we are in the fixed effects environment, and $\mathbf{x}_{it}$ contains only time-varying explanatory variables.

In Chapter 10 we saw that the FE and FD transformations eliminate c_i and produce consistent estimators under strict exogeneity. Chamberlain's approach is to replace the unobserved effect c_i with its linear projection onto the explanatory variables in all time periods (plus the projection error). Assuming c_i and all elements of $\mathbf{x}_i$ have finite second moments, we can always write

$$c_i = \psi + \mathbf{x}_{i1}\boldsymbol{\lambda}_1 + \mathbf{x}_{i2}\boldsymbol{\lambda}_2 + \cdots + \mathbf{x}_{iT}\boldsymbol{\lambda}_T + a_i \tag{11.59}$$

where ψ is a scalar and $\boldsymbol{\lambda}_1, \ldots, \boldsymbol{\lambda}_T$ are $1 \times K$ vectors. The projection error a_i, by definition, has zero mean and is uncorrelated with $\mathbf{x}_{i1}, \ldots, \mathbf{x}_{iT}$. This equation assumes nothing about the conditional distribution of c_i given $\mathbf{x}_i$. In particular, $\mathrm{E}(c_i \mid \mathbf{x}_i)$ is unrestricted, as in the usual fixed effects analysis.

Plugging equation (11.59) into equation (11.1) gives, for each t,

$$y_{it} = \psi + \mathbf{x}_{i1}\boldsymbol{\lambda}_1 + \cdots + \mathbf{x}_{it}(\boldsymbol{\beta} + \boldsymbol{\lambda}_t) + \cdots + \mathbf{x}_{iT}\boldsymbol{\lambda}_T + r_{it} \tag{11.60}$$

where, under Assumption FE.1, the errors $r_{it} \equiv a_i + u_{it}$ satisfy

$$\mathrm{E}(r_{it}) = 0, \ \mathrm{E}(\mathbf{x}_i' r_{it}) = \mathbf{0}, \qquad t = 1, 2, \ldots, T \tag{11.61}$$

However, unless we assume that $\mathrm{E}(c_i \mid \mathbf{x}_i)$ is linear, it is *not* the case that $\mathrm{E}(r_{it} \mid \mathbf{x}_i) = 0$. Nevertheless, assumption (11.61) suggests a variety of methods for estimating $\boldsymbol{\beta}$ (along with $\psi, \boldsymbol{\lambda}_1, \ldots, \boldsymbol{\lambda}_T$).

Write the system (11.60) for all time periods t as

$$\begin{pmatrix} y_{i1} \\ y_{i2} \\ \vdots \\ y_{iT} \end{pmatrix} = \begin{pmatrix} 1 & \mathbf{x}_{i1} & \mathbf{x}_{i2} & \cdots & \mathbf{x}_{iT} & \mathbf{x}_{i1} \\ 1 & \mathbf{x}_{i1} & \mathbf{x}_{i2} & \cdots & \mathbf{x}_{iT} & \mathbf{x}_{i2} \\ & & & \vdots & & \\ 1 & \mathbf{x}_{i1} & \mathbf{x}_{i2} & \cdots & \mathbf{x}_{iT} & \mathbf{x}_{iT} \end{pmatrix} \begin{pmatrix} \psi \\ \boldsymbol{\lambda}_1 \\ \boldsymbol{\lambda}_2 \\ \vdots \\ \boldsymbol{\lambda}_T \\ \boldsymbol{\beta} \end{pmatrix} + \begin{pmatrix} r_{i1} \\ r_{i2} \\ \vdots \\ r_{iT} \end{pmatrix} \tag{11.62}$$

or

$$\mathbf{y}_i = \mathbf{W}_i\boldsymbol{\theta} + \mathbf{r}_i \tag{11.63}$$

where $\mathbf{W}_i$ is $T \times (1 + TK + K)$ and $\boldsymbol{\theta}$ is $(1 + TK + K) \times 1$. From equation (11.61), $\mathrm{E}(\mathbf{W}_i'\mathbf{r}_i) = \mathbf{0}$, and so system OLS is one way to consistently estimate $\boldsymbol{\theta}$. The rank condition requires that rank $\mathrm{E}(\mathbf{W}_i'\mathbf{W}_i) = 1 + TK + K$; essentially, it suffices that the elements of $\mathbf{x}_{it}$ are not collinear and that they vary sufficiently over time. While system OLS is consistent, it is very unlikely to be the most efficient estimator. Not only is the scalar variance assumption $\mathrm{E}(\mathbf{r}_i\mathbf{r}_i') = \sigma_r^2\mathbf{I}_T$ highly unlikely, but also the homoskedasticity assumption

$$\mathrm{E}(\mathbf{r}_i\mathbf{r}_i' \mid \mathbf{x}_i) = \mathrm{E}(\mathbf{r}_i\mathbf{r}_i') \tag{11.64}$$

fails unless we impose further assumptions. Generally, assumption (11.64) is violated if $\mathrm{E}(\mathbf{u}_i\mathbf{u}_i' \mid c_i, \mathbf{x}_i) \neq \mathrm{E}(\mathbf{u}_i\mathbf{u}_i')$, if $\mathrm{E}(c_i \mid \mathbf{x}_i)$ is not linear in $\mathbf{x}_i$, or if $\mathrm{Var}(c_i \mid \mathbf{x}_i)$ is not constant.

If assumption (11.64) does happen to hold, feasible GLS is a natural approach. The matrix $\boldsymbol{\Omega} = \mathrm{E}(\mathbf{r}_i\mathbf{r}_i')$ can be consistently estimated by first estimating $\boldsymbol{\theta}$ by system OLS, and then proceeding with FGLS as in Section 7.5.

If assumption (11.64) fails, a more efficient estimator is obtained by applying GMM to equation (11.63) with the optimal weighting matrix. Because r_{it} is orthogonal to $\mathbf{x}_i^o = (1, \mathbf{x}_{i1}, \ldots, \mathbf{x}_{iT})$, $\mathbf{x}_i^o$ can be used as instruments for each time period, and so we choose the matrix of instruments (11.57). Interestingly, the 3SLS estimator, which uses $[\mathbf{Z}'(\mathbf{I}_N \otimes \hat{\boldsymbol{\Omega}})\mathbf{Z}/N]^{-1}$ as the weighting matrix—see Section 8.3.4—is numerically identical to FGLS with the same $\hat{\boldsymbol{\Omega}}$. Arellano and Bover (1995) showed this result in the special case that $\hat{\boldsymbol{\Omega}}$ has the random effects structure, and IASW (1999, Theorem 3.1) obtained the general case.

In expression (11.63) there are $1 + TK + K$ parameters, and the matrix of instruments is $T \times T(1 + TK)$; there are $T(1 + TK) - (1 + TK + K) = (T - 1)(1 + TK) - K$ overidentifying restrictions. Testing these restrictions is precisely a test of the strict exogeneity Assumption FE.1, and it is a fully robust test when full GMM is used because no additional assumptions are used.

Chamberlain (1982) works from the system (11.62) under assumption (11.61), but he uses a different estimation approach, known as minimum distance estimation. We cover this approach to estimation in Chapter 14.

11.4 Hausman and Taylor-Type Models

In the panel data methods we covered in Chapter 10, and so far in this chapter, coefficients on time-constant explanatory variables are not identified unless we make Assumption RE.1. In some cases the explanatory variable of primary interest is time constant, yet we are worried that c_i is correlated with some explanatory variables. Random effects will produce inconsistent estimators of all parameters if such correlation exists, while fixed effects or first differencing eliminates the time-constant variables.

When all time-constant variables are assumed to be uncorrelated with the unobserved effect, but the time-varying variables are possibly correlated with c_i, consistent estimation is fairly simple. Write the model as

$$y_{it} = \mathbf{z}_i\boldsymbol{\gamma} + \mathbf{x}_{it}\boldsymbol{\beta} + c_i + u_{it}, \qquad t = 1, 2, \ldots, T \tag{11.65}$$

where all elements of $\mathbf{x}_{it}$ display some time variation, and it is convenient to include unity in $\mathbf{z}_i$ and assume that $\mathrm{E}(c_i) = 0$. We assume strict exogeneity conditional on c_i:

$$\mathrm{E}(u_{it} \mid \mathbf{z}_i, \mathbf{x}_{i1}, \ldots, \mathbf{x}_{iT}, c_i) = 0, \qquad t = 1, \ldots, T \tag{11.66}$$

Estimation of $\boldsymbol{\beta}$ can proceed by fixed effects: the FE transformation eliminates $\mathbf{z}_i\boldsymbol{\gamma}$ and c_i. As usual, this approach places no restrictions on the correlation between c_i and $(\mathbf{z}_i, \mathbf{x}_{it})$.

What about estimation of $\boldsymbol{\gamma}$? If, in addition to assumption (11.66) we assume

$$\mathrm{E}(\mathbf{z}_i'c_i) = \mathbf{0} \tag{11.67}$$

then a $\sqrt{N}$-consistent estimator is easy to obtain: average equation (11.65) across t, premultiply by $\mathbf{z}_i'$, take expectations, use the fact that $\mathrm{E}[\mathbf{z}_i'(c_i + \bar{u}_i)] = \mathbf{0}$, and rearrange to get

$$\mathrm{E}(\mathbf{z}_i'\mathbf{z}_i)\boldsymbol{\gamma} = \mathrm{E}[\mathbf{z}_i'(\bar{y}_i - \bar{\mathbf{x}}_i\boldsymbol{\beta})]$$

Now, making the standard assumption that $\mathrm{E}(\mathbf{z}_i'\mathbf{z}_i)$ is nonsingular, it follows by the usual analogy principle argument that

$$\hat{\boldsymbol{\gamma}} = \left(N^{-1}\sum_{i=1}^{N}\mathbf{z}_i'\mathbf{z}_i\right)^{-1}\left[N^{-1}\sum_{i=1}^{N}\mathbf{z}_i'(\bar{y}_i - \bar{\mathbf{x}}_i\hat{\boldsymbol{\beta}}_{FE})\right]$$

is consistent for $\boldsymbol{\gamma}$. The asymptotic variance of $\sqrt{N}(\hat{\boldsymbol{\gamma}} - \boldsymbol{\gamma})$ can be obtained by standard arguments for two-step estimators. Rather than derive this asymptotic variance, we turn to a more general model.

Hausman and Taylor (1981) (HT) partition $\mathbf{z}_i$ and $\mathbf{x}_{it}$ as $\mathbf{z}_i = (\mathbf{z}_{i1}, \mathbf{z}_{i2})$, $\mathbf{x}_{it} = (\mathbf{x}_{it1}, \mathbf{x}_{it2})$—where $\mathbf{z}_{i1}$ is $1 \times J_1$, $\mathbf{z}_{i2}$ is $1 \times J_2$, $\mathbf{x}_{it1}$ is $1 \times K_1$, $\mathbf{x}_{it2}$ is $1 \times K_2$—and assume that

$$\mathrm{E}(\mathbf{z}_{i1}'c_i) = \mathbf{0} \qquad \text{and} \qquad \mathrm{E}(\mathbf{x}_{it1}'c_i) = \mathbf{0}, \qquad \text{all } t \tag{11.68}$$

We still maintain assumption (11.66), so that $\mathbf{z}_i$ and $\mathbf{x}_{is}$ are uncorrelated with u_{it} for all t and s.

Assumptions (11.66) and (11.68) provide orthogonality conditions that can be used in a method of moments procedure. HT actually imposed enough assumptions so that the variance matrix $\boldsymbol{\Omega}$ of the composite error $\mathbf{v}_i = c_i\mathbf{j}_T + \mathbf{u}_i$ has the random effects structure *and* Assumption SIV.5 from Section 8.3.4 holds. Neither of these is necessary, but together they afford some simplifications.

Write equation (11.65) for all T time periods as

$$\mathbf{y}_i = \mathbf{Z}_i\boldsymbol{\gamma} + \mathbf{X}_i\boldsymbol{\beta} + \mathbf{v}_i \tag{11.69}$$

Since $\mathbf{x}_{it}$ is strictly exogenous and $\mathbf{Q}_T\mathbf{v}_i = \mathbf{Q}_T\mathbf{u}_i$ [where $\mathbf{Q}_T \equiv \mathbf{I}_T - \mathbf{j}_T(\mathbf{j}_T'\mathbf{j}_T)^{-1}\mathbf{j}_T'$ is again the $T \times T$ time-demeaning matrix], it follows that $\mathrm{E}[(\mathbf{Q}_T\mathbf{X}_i)'\mathbf{v}_i] = \mathbf{0}$. Thus, the

$T \times K$ matrix $\mathbf{Q}_T\mathbf{X}_i$ can be used as instruments in estimating equation (11.69). If these were the only instruments available, then we would be back to fixed effects estimation of $\boldsymbol{\beta}$ without being able to estimate $\boldsymbol{\gamma}$.

Additional instruments come from assumption (11.68). In particular, $\mathbf{z}_{i1}$ is orthogonal to v_{it} for all t, and so is $\mathbf{x}_{i1}^o$, the $1 \times TK_1$ vector containing $\mathbf{x}_{it1}$ for all $t = 1, \ldots, T$. Thus, define a set of instruments for equation (11.69) by

$$[\mathbf{Q}_T\mathbf{X}_i, \mathbf{j}_T \otimes (\mathbf{z}_{i1}, \mathbf{x}_{i1}^o)] \tag{11.70}$$

which is a $T \times (K + J_1 + TK_1)$ matrix. Simply put, the vector of IVs for time period t is $(\ddot{\mathbf{x}}_{it}, \mathbf{z}_{i1}, \mathbf{x}_{i1}^o)$. With this set of instruments, the order condition for identification of $(\boldsymbol{\gamma}, \boldsymbol{\beta})$ is that $K + J_1 + TK_1 \geq J + K$, or $TK_1 \geq J_2$. In effect, we must have a sufficient number of elements in $\mathbf{x}_{i1}^o$ to act as instruments for $\mathbf{z}_{i2}$. ($\ddot{\mathbf{x}}_{it}$ are the IVs for $\mathbf{x}_{it}$, and $\mathbf{z}_{i1}$ act as their own IVs.) Whether we do depends on the number of time periods, as well as on K_1.

Actually, matrix (11.70) does not include all possible instruments under assumptions (11.66) and (11.68), even when we only focus on zero covariances. However, under the full set of Hausman-Taylor assumptions mentioned earlier—including the assumption that $\boldsymbol{\Omega}$ has the random effects structure—it can be shown that all instruments other than those in matrix (11.70) are redundant in the sense of Section 8.6; see IASW (1999, Theorem 4.4) for details. In fact, a very simple estimation strategy is available. First, estimate equation (11.65) by pooled 2SLS, using IVs $(\ddot{\mathbf{x}}_{it}, \mathbf{z}_{i1}, \mathbf{x}_{i1}^o)$. Use the pooled 2SLS residuals, say $\hat{\hat{v}}_{it}$, in the formulas from Section 10.4.1, namely, equations (10.35) and (10.37), to obtain $\hat{\sigma}_c^2$ and $\hat{\sigma}_u^2$, which can then be used to obtain $\hat{\lambda}$ in equation (10.77). Then, perform quasi–time demeaning on all the dependent variables, explanatory variables, and IVs, and use these in a pooled 2SLS estimation. Under the Hausman-Taylor assumptions, this estimator—sometimes called a **generalized IV (GIV) estimator**—is the efficient GMM estimator, and all statistics from pooled 2SLS on the quasi-demeaned data are asymptotically valid.

If $\boldsymbol{\Omega}$ is not of the random effects form, or if Assumption SIV.5 fails, many more instruments than are in matrix (11.70) can help improve efficiency. Unfortunately, the value of these additional IVs is unclear. For practical purposes, 3SLS with $\hat{\boldsymbol{\Omega}}$ of the RE form, 3SLS with $\hat{\boldsymbol{\Omega}}$ unrestricted, or GMM with optimal weighting matrix—using the instruments in matrix (11.70)—should be sufficient, with the latter being the most efficient in the presence of conditional heteroskedasticity. The first-stage estimator can be the system 2SLS estimator using matrix (11.70) as instruments. The GMM overidentification test statistic can be used to test the $TK_1 - J_2$ overidentifying restrictions.

In cases where $K_1 \geq J_2$, we can reduce the instrument list even further and still achieve identification: we use $\bar{\mathbf{x}}_{i1}$ as the instruments for $\mathbf{z}_{i2}$. Then, the IVs at time t are

$(\ddot{\mathbf{x}}_{it}, \mathbf{z}_{i1}, \overline{\mathbf{x}}_{i1})$. We can then use the pooled 2SLS estimators described previously with this new set of IVs. Quasi-demeaning leads to an especially simple analysis. Although it generally reduces asymptotic efficiency, replacing $\mathbf{x}_{i1}^o$ with $\overline{\mathbf{x}}_{i1}$ is a reasonable way to reduce the instrument list because much of the partial correlation between $\mathbf{z}_{i2}$ and $\mathbf{x}_{i1}^o$ is likely to be through the time average, $\overline{\mathbf{x}}_{i1}$.

HT provide an application of their model to estimating the return to education, where education levels do not vary over the two years in their sample. Initially, HT include as the elements of $\mathbf{x}_{it1}$ all time-varying explanatory variables: experience, an indicator for bad health, and a previous-year unemployment indicator. Race and union status are assumed to be uncorrelated with c_i, and, because these do not change over time, they comprise $\mathbf{z}_{i1}$. The only element of z_{i2} is years of schooling. HT apply the GIV estimator and obtain a return to schooling that is almost twice as large as the pooled OLS estimate. When they allow some of the time-varying explanatory variables to be correlated with c_i, the estimated return to schooling gets even larger. It is difficult to know what to conclude, as the identifying assumptions are not especially convincing. For example, assuming that experience and union status are uncorrelated with the unobserved effect and then using this information to identify the return to schooling seems tenuous.

Breusch, Mizon, and Schmidt (1989) studied the Hausman-Taylor model under the additional assumption that $\mathrm{E}(\mathbf{x}_{it2}'c_i)$ is constant across t. This adds more orthogonality conditions that can be exploited in estimation. See IASW (1999) for a recent analysis.

It is easy to bring in outside, exogenous variables in the Hausman-Taylor framework. For example, if the model (11.65) is an equation in a simultaneous equations model, and if elements of $\mathbf{x}_{it2}$ are simultaneously determined with y_{it}, then we can use exogenous variables appearing elsewhere in the system as IVs. If such variables do not vary over time, we need to assume that they are uncorrelated with c_i as well as with u_{it} for all t. If they do vary over time and are correlated with c_i, we can use their deviations from means as IVs, provided these instruments are strictly exogenous with respect to u_{it}. The time averages can be added to the instrument list if the external variables are uncorrelated with c_i. For example, in a wage equation containing alcohol consumption, which is determined simultaneously with the wage, we can, under reasonable assumptions, use the time-demeaned local price of alcohol as an IV for alcohol consumption.

11.5 Applying Panel Data Methods to Matched Pairs and Cluster Samples

Unobserved effects structures arise in contexts other than repeated cross sections over time. One simple data structure is a **matched pairs sample**. To illustrate, we consider the case of sibling data, which are often used in the social sciences in order to control for the effect of unobserved family background variables. For each family i in the population, there are two siblings, described by

$$y_{i1} = \mathbf{x}_{i1}\boldsymbol{\beta} + f_i + u_{i1} \tag{11.71}$$

$$y_{i2} = \mathbf{x}_{i2}\boldsymbol{\beta} + f_i + u_{i2} \tag{11.72}$$

where the equations are for siblings 1 and 2, respectively, and f_i is an unobserved *family effect*. The strict exogeneity assumption now means that the idiosyncratic error u_{is} in each sibling's equation is uncorrelated with the explanatory variables in *both* equations. For example, if y denotes log(*wage*) and $\mathbf{x}$ contains years of schooling as an explanatory variable, then we must assume that sibling's schooling has no effect on wage after controlling for the family effect, own schooling, and other observed covariates. Such assumptions are often reasonable, although the condition should be studied in each application.

If f_i is assumed to be uncorrelated with $\mathbf{x}_{i1}$ and $\mathbf{x}_{i2}$, then a random effects analysis can be used. The mechanics of random effects for matched pairs are identical to the case of two time periods.

More commonly, f_i is allowed to be arbitrarily correlated with the observed factors in $\mathbf{x}_{i1}$ and $\mathbf{x}_{i2}$, in which case differencing across siblings to remove f_i is the appropriate strategy. Under this strategy, $\mathbf{x}$ cannot contain common observable family background variables, as these are indistinguishable from f_i. The IV methods developed in Section 11.1 to account for omitted variables, measurement error, and simultaneity, can be applied directly to the differenced equation. Examples of where sibling (in some cases twin) differences have been used in economics include Geronimus and Korenman (1992), Ashenfelter and Krueger (1994), Bronars and Grogger (1994), and Ashenfelter and Rouse (1998).

A matched pairs sample is a special case of a **cluster sample**, which we touched on in Section 6.3.4. A cluster sample is typically a cross section on individuals (or families, firms, and so on), where each individual is part of a cluster. For example, students may be clustered by the high school they attend, or workers may be clustered by employer. Observations within a cluster are thought to be correlated as a result of an unobserved cluster effect.

The unobserved effects model

$$y_{is} = \mathbf{x}_{is}\boldsymbol{\beta} + c_i + u_{is} \tag{11.73}$$

is often reasonable, where i indexes the group or cluster and s indexes units within a cluster. In some fields, an unobserved effects model for a cluster sample is called a **hierarchical model**.

One complication that arises in cluster samples, which we have not yet addressed, is that the number of observations within a cluster usually differs across clusters. Nevertheless, for cluster i, we can write

$$\mathbf{y}_i = \mathbf{X}_i\boldsymbol{\beta} + c_i\mathbf{j}_{G_i} + \mathbf{u}_i \tag{11.74}$$

where the row dimension of $\mathbf{y}_i$, $\mathbf{X}_i$, $\mathbf{j}_{G_i}$, and $\mathbf{u}_i$ is G_i, the number of units in cluster i. The dimension of $\boldsymbol{\beta}$ is $K \times 1$.

To apply the panel data methods we have discussed so far, we assume that the number of clusters, N, is large, because we fix the number of units within each cluster in analyzing the asymptotic properties of the estimators. Because the dimension of the vectors and matrix in equation (11.74) changes with i, we cannot assume an identical distribution across i. However, in most cases it is reasonable to assume that the observations are independent across cluster. The fact that they are not also identically distributed makes the theory more complicated but has no practical consequences.

The strict exogeneity assumption in the model (11.73) requires that the error u_{is} be uncorrelated with the explanatory variables for *all* units within cluster i. This assumption is often reasonable when a cluster effect c_i is explicitly included. (In other words, we assume strict exogeneity conditional on c_i.) If we also assume that c_i is uncorrelated with $\mathbf{x}_{is}$ for all $s = 1, \ldots, G_i$, then pooled OLS across all clusters and units is consistent as $N \to \infty$. However, the composite error will be correlated within cluster, just as in a random effects analysis. Even with different cluster sizes a valid variance matrix for pooled OLS is easy to obtain: just use formula (7.26) but where $\hat{\mathbf{v}}_i$, the $G_i \times 1$ vector of pooled OLS residuals for cluster i, replaces $\hat{\mathbf{u}}_i$. The resulting variance matrix estimator is robust to any kind of intracluster correlation and arbitrary heteroskedasticity, provided N is large relative to the G_i.

In the hierarchical models literature, c_i is often allowed to depend on cluster-level covariates, for example, $c_i = \delta_0 + \mathbf{w}_i\boldsymbol{\delta} + a_i$, where a_i is assumed to be independent of (or at least uncorrelated with) $\mathbf{w}_i$ and $\mathbf{x}_{is}$, $s = 1, \ldots, G_i$. But this is equivalent to simply adding cluster-level observables to the original model and relabeling the unobserved cluster effect.

The fixed effects transformation can be used to eliminate c_i in equation (11.74) when c_i is thought to be correlated with $\mathbf{x}_{is}$. The different cluster sizes cause no problems here: demeaning is done within each cluster. Any explanatory variable that is constant within each cluster for all clusters—for example, the gender of the teacher if the clusters are elementary school classrooms—is eliminated, just as in the panel data case. Pooled OLS can be applied to the demeaned data, just as with panel data. Under the immediate generalizations of Assumptions FE.1–FE.3 to allow for different cluster sizes, the variance matrix of the FE estimator for cluster samples can be estimated as in expression (10.54), but σ_u^2 must be estimated with care. A consistent estimator is $\hat{\sigma}_u^2 = \text{SSR}/[\sum_{i=1}^N (G_i - 1) - K]$, which is exactly the estimator that would be obtained from the pooled regression that includes a dummy variable for each cluster. The robust variance matrix (10.59) is valid very generally, where $\hat{\mathbf{u}}_i = \ddot{\mathbf{y}}_i - \ddot{\mathbf{X}}_i\hat{\boldsymbol{\beta}}_{FE}$, as usual.

The 2SLS estimator described in Section 11.1.3 can also be applied to cluster samples, once we adjust for different cluster sizes in doing the within-cluster demeaning.

Rather than include a cluster effect, c_i, sometimes the goal is to see whether person s within cluster i is affected by the characteristics of other people within the cluster. One way to estimate the importance of **peer effects** is to specify

$$y_{is} = \mathbf{x}_{is}\boldsymbol{\beta} + \overline{\mathbf{w}}_{i(s)}\boldsymbol{\delta} + v_{is} \tag{11.75}$$

where $\overline{\mathbf{w}}_{i(s)}$ indicates averages of a subset of elements of $\mathbf{x}_{is}$ across all other people in the cluster. If equation (11.75) represents $\mathrm{E}(y_{is} \mid \mathbf{x}_i) = \mathrm{E}(y_{is} \mid \mathbf{x}_{is}, \overline{\mathbf{w}}_{i(s)})$ for each s, then the strict exogeneity assumption $\mathrm{E}(v_{is} \mid \mathbf{x}_i) = 0$, $s = 1, \ldots, G_i$, necessarily holds. Pooled OLS will consistently estimate $\boldsymbol{\beta}$ and $\boldsymbol{\delta}$, although a robust variance matrix may be needed to account for correlation in v_{is} across s, and possibly for heteroskedasticity. If $\mathrm{Cov}(v_{is}, v_{ir} \mid \mathbf{x}_i) = 0$, $s \neq r$, and $\mathrm{Var}(v_{is} \mid \mathbf{x}_i) = \sigma_v^2$ are assumed, then pooled OLS is efficient, and the usual test standard errors and test statistics are valid. It is also easy to allow the unconditional variance to change across cluster using a simple weighting; for a similar example, see Problem 7.7.

We can also apply the more general models from Section 11.2.2, where unobserved cluster effects interact with some of the explanatory variables. If we allow arbitrary dependence between the cluster effects and the explanatory variables, the transformations in Section 11.2.2 should be used. In the hierarchical models literature, the unobserved cluster effects are assumed to be either independent of the covariates $\mathbf{x}_{is}$ or independent of the covariates after netting out observed cluster covariates. This assumption results in a particular form of heteroskedasticity that can be exploited for efficiency. However, it makes as much sense to include cluster-level covariates, individual-level covariates, and possibly interactions of these in an initial model, and then to make inference in pooled OLS robust to arbitrary heteroskedasticity and cluster correlation. (See Problem 11.5 for a related analysis in the context of panel data.)

We should remember that the methods described in this section are known to have good properties only when the number of clusters is large relative to the number of units within a cluster. Case and Katz (1991) and Evans, Oates, and Schwab (1992) apply cluster-sampling methods to the problem of estimating peer effects.

Problems

11.1. Let y_{it} denote the unemployment rate for city i at time t. You are interested in studying the effects of a federally funded job training program on city unemployment rates. Let $\mathbf{z}_i$ denote a vector of time-constant city-specific variables that may influence the unemployment rate (these could include things like geographic location). Let $\mathbf{x}_{it}$ be a vector of time-varying factors that can affect the unemployment rate. The variable $prog_{it}$ is the dummy indicator for program participation: $prog_{it} = 1$ if city i participated at time t. Any sequence of program participation is possible, so that a city may participate in one year but not the next.

a. Discuss the merits of including $y_{i,t-1}$ in the model

$$y_{it} = \theta_t + \mathbf{z}_i\gamma + \mathbf{x}_{it}\boldsymbol{\beta} + \rho_1 y_{i,t-1} + \delta_1 prog_{it} + u_{it}, \qquad t = 1, 2, \ldots, T$$

State an assumption that allows you to consistently estimate the parameters by pooled OLS.

b. Evaluate the following statement: "The model in part a is of limited value because the pooled OLS estimators are inconsistent if the $\{u_{it}\}$ are serially correlated."

c. Suppose that it is more realistic to assume that program participation depends on time-constant, unobservable city heterogeneity, but not directly on past unemployment. Write down a model that allows you to estimate the effectiveness of the program in this case. Explain how to estimate the parameters, describing any minimal assumptions you need.

d. Write down a model that allows the features in parts a and c. In other words, $prog_{it}$ can depend on unobserved city heterogeneity as well as the past unemployment history. Explain how to consistently estimate the effect of the program, again stating minimal assumptions.

11.2. Consider the following unobserved components model:

$$y_{it} = \mathbf{z}_{it}\gamma + \delta w_{it} + c_i + u_{it}, \qquad t = 1, 2, \ldots, T$$

where $\mathbf{z}_{it}$ is a $1 \times K$ vector of time-varying variables (which could include time-period dummies), w_{it} is a time-varying scalar, c_i is a time-constant unobserved effect, and u_{it} is the idiosyncratic error. The $\mathbf{z}_{it}$ are strictly exogenous in the sense that

$$\mathrm{E}(\mathbf{z}_{is}'u_{it}) = \mathbf{0}, \qquad \text{all } s,\ t = 1, 2, \ldots, T \tag{11.76}$$

but c_i is allowed to be arbitrarily correlated with each $\mathbf{z}_{it}$. The variable w_{it} is endogenous in the sense that it can be correlated with u_{it} (as well as with c_i).

a. Suppose that $T = 2$, and that assumption (11.76) contains the only available orthogonality conditions. What are the properties of the OLS estimators of γ and δ on the differenced data? Support your claim (but do not include asymptotic derivations).

b. Under assumption (11.76), still with $T = 2$, write the linear reduced form for the difference Δw_i as $\Delta w_i = \mathbf{z}_{i1}\boldsymbol{\pi}_1 + \mathbf{z}_{i2}\boldsymbol{\pi}_2 + r_i$, where, by construction, r_i is uncorrelated with both $\mathbf{z}_{i1}$ and $\mathbf{z}_{i2}$. What condition on $(\boldsymbol{\pi}_1, \boldsymbol{\pi}_2)$ is needed to identify γ and δ? (Hint: It is useful to rewrite the reduced form of Δw_i in terms of $\Delta \mathbf{z}_i$ and, say, $\mathbf{z}_{i1}$.) How can you test this condition?

c. Now consider the general T case, where we add to assumption (11.76) the assumption $\mathrm{E}(w_{is}u_{it}) = 0$, $s < t$, so that previous values of w_{it} are uncorrelated with u_{it}. Explain carefully, including equations where appropriate, how you would estimate γ and δ.

d. Again consider the general T case, but now use the fixed effects transformation to eliminate c_i:

$$\ddot{y}_{it} = \ddot{\mathbf{z}}_{it}\gamma + \delta\ddot{w}_{it} + \ddot{u}_{it}$$

What are the properties of the IV estimators if you use $\ddot{\mathbf{z}}_{it}$ and $w_{i,t-p}$, $p \geq 1$, as instruments in estimating this equation by pooled IV? (You can only use time periods $p + 1, \ldots, T$ after the initial demeaning.)

11.3. Show that, in the simple model (11.29) with $T > 2$, under the assumptions (11.30), $\mathrm{E}(r_{it} \mid \mathbf{x}_i^*, c_i) = 0$ for all t, and $\mathrm{Var}(r_{it} - \bar{r}_i)$ and $\mathrm{Var}(x_{it}^* - \bar{x}_i^*)$ constant across t, the plim of the FE estimator is

$$\operatorname*{plim}_{N\to\infty} \hat{\beta}_{FE} = \beta\left\{1 - \frac{\mathrm{Var}(r_{it} - \bar{r}_i)}{[\mathrm{Var}(x_{it}^* - \bar{x}_i^*) + \mathrm{Var}(r_{it} - \bar{r}_i)]}\right\}$$

Thus, there is attenuation bias in the FE estimator under these assumptions.

11.4. a. Show that, in the fixed effects model, a consistent estimator of $\mu_c \equiv \mathrm{E}(c_i)$ is $\hat{\mu}_c = N^{-1}\sum_{i=1}^{N}(\bar{y}_i - \bar{\mathbf{x}}_i\hat{\boldsymbol{\beta}}_{FE})$.

b. In the random trend model, how would you estimate $\mu_g = \mathrm{E}(g_i)$?

11.5. A random effects analysis of model (11.43) would add $\mathrm{E}(\mathbf{a}_i \mid \mathbf{z}_i, \mathbf{x}_i) = \mathrm{E}(\mathbf{a}_i) = \boldsymbol{\alpha}$ to Assumption FE.1′ and, to Assumption FE.3′, $\mathrm{Var}(\mathbf{a}_i \mid \mathbf{z}_i, \mathbf{x}_i) = \boldsymbol{\Lambda}$, where $\boldsymbol{\Lambda}$ is a $J \times J$ positive semidefinite matrix. (This approach allows the elements of $\mathbf{a}_i$ to be arbitrarily correlated.)

a. Define the $T \times 1$ composite error vector $\mathbf{v}_i \equiv \mathbf{Z}_i(\mathbf{a}_i - \boldsymbol{\alpha}) + \mathbf{u}_i$. Find $\mathrm{E}(\mathbf{v}_i \mid \mathbf{z}_i, \mathbf{x}_i)$ and $\mathrm{Var}(\mathbf{v}_i \mid \mathbf{z}_i, \mathbf{x}_i)$. Comment on the conditional variance.

b. If you apply the usual RE procedure to the equation

$$y_{it} = \mathbf{z}_{it}\boldsymbol{\alpha} + \mathbf{x}_{it}\boldsymbol{\beta} + v_{it}, \qquad t = 1, 2, \ldots, T$$

what are the asymptotic properties of the RE estimator and the usual RE standard errors and test statistics?

c. How could you modify your inference from part b to be asymptotically valid?

11.6. Does the measurement error model in equations (11.33) to (11.37) apply when w_{it}^* is a lagged dependent variable? Explain.

11.7. In the Chamberlain model in Section 11.3.2, suppose that $\lambda_t = \lambda/T$ for all t. Show that the pooled OLS coefficient on $\mathbf{x}_{it}$ in the regression y_{it} on 1, $\mathbf{x}_{it}$, $\bar{\mathbf{x}}_i$, $t = 1, \ldots, T$; $i = 1, \ldots, N$, is the FE estimator. (Hint: Use partitioned regression.)

11.8. In model (11.1), first difference to remove c_i:

$$\Delta y_{it} = \Delta \mathbf{x}_{it}\boldsymbol{\beta} + \Delta u_{it}, \qquad t = 2, \ldots, T \tag{11.77}$$

Assume that a vector of instruments, $\mathbf{z}_{it}$, satisfies $\mathrm{E}(\Delta u_{it} \mid \mathbf{z}_{it}) = 0$, $t = 2, \ldots, T$. Typically, several elements in $\Delta \mathbf{x}_{it}$ would be included in $\mathbf{z}_{it}$, provided they are appropriately exogenous. Of course the elements of $\mathbf{z}_{it}$ can be arbitrarily correlated with c_i.

a. State the rank condition that is necessary and sufficient for pooled 2SLS estimation of equation (11.77) using instruments $\mathbf{z}_{it}$ to be consistent (for fixed T).

b. Under what additional assumptions are the usual pooled 2SLS standard errors and test statistics asymptotically valid? (Hint: See Problem 8.8.)

c. How would you test for first-order serial correlation in Δu_{it}? (Hint: See Problem 8.10.)

11.9. Consider model (11.1) under the assumption

$$\mathrm{E}(u_{it} \mid \mathbf{z}_i, c_i) = 0, \qquad t = 1, 2, \ldots, T \tag{11.78}$$

where $\mathbf{z}_i = (\mathbf{z}_{i1}, \ldots, \mathbf{z}_{iT})$ and each $\mathbf{z}_{it}$ is $1 \times L$. Typically, $\mathbf{z}_{it}$ would contain some elements of $\mathbf{x}_{it}$. However, $\{\mathbf{z}_{it}\colon t = 1, 2, \ldots, T\}$ is assumed to be strictly exogenous (conditional on c_i). All elements of $\mathbf{z}_{it}$ are allowed to be correlated with c_i.

a. Use the fixed effects transformation to eliminate c_i:

$$\ddot{y}_{it} = \ddot{\mathbf{x}}_{it}\boldsymbol{\beta} + \ddot{u}_{it}, \qquad t = 1, \ldots, T; i = 1, \ldots, N \tag{11.79}$$

Let $\ddot{\mathbf{z}}_{it}$ denote the time-demeaned IVs. State the rank condition that is necessary and sufficient for pooled 2SLS estimation of equation (11.79) using instruments $\ddot{\mathbf{z}}_{it}$ to be consistent (for fixed T).

b. Show that, under the additional assumption

$$\mathrm{E}(\mathbf{u}_i \mathbf{u}_i' \mid \mathbf{z}_i, c_i) = \sigma_u^2 \mathbf{I}_T \tag{11.80}$$

the asymptotic variance of $\sqrt{N}(\hat{\boldsymbol{\beta}} - \boldsymbol{\beta})$ is

$$\sigma_u^2 \{\mathrm{E}(\ddot{\mathbf{X}}_i' \ddot{\mathbf{Z}}_i)[\mathrm{E}(\ddot{\mathbf{Z}}_i' \ddot{\mathbf{Z}}_i)]^{-1} \mathrm{E}(\ddot{\mathbf{Z}}_i' \ddot{\mathbf{X}}_i)\}^{-1}$$

where the notation should be clear from Chapter 10.

c. Propose a consistent estimator of σ_u^2.

d. Show that the 2SLS estimator of $\boldsymbol{\beta}$ from part a can be obtained by means of a dummy variable approach: estimate

$$y_{it} = c_1 \, d1_i + \cdots + c_N \, dN_i + \mathbf{x}_{it}\boldsymbol{\beta} + u_{it} \tag{11.81}$$

by pooled 2SLS, using instruments $(d1_i, d2_i, \ldots, dN_i, \mathbf{z}_{it})$. (Hint: Use the obvious extension of Problem 5.1 to pooled 2SLS, and repeatedly apply the algebra of partial regression.) This is another case where, even though we cannot estimate the c_i consistently with fixed T, we still get a consistent estimator of $\boldsymbol{\beta}$.

e. In using the 2SLS approach from part d, explain why the usually reported standard errors are valid under assumption (11.80).

f. How would you obtain valid standard errors for 2SLS without assumption (11.80)?

g. If some elements of $\mathbf{z}_{it}$ are not strictly exogenous, but we perform the procedure in part c, what are the asymptotic ($N \to \infty$, T fixed) properties of $\hat{\boldsymbol{\beta}}$?

11.10. Consider the general model (11.43) where unobserved heterogeneity interacts with possibly several variables. Show that the fixed effects estimator of $\boldsymbol{\beta}$ is also obtained by running the regression

$$y_{it} \text{ on } d1_i\mathbf{z}_{it}, d2_i\mathbf{z}_{it}, \ldots, dN_i\mathbf{z}_{it}, \mathbf{x}_{it}, \qquad t = 1, 2, \ldots, T; i = 1, 2, \ldots, N \tag{11.82}$$

where $dn_i = 1$ if and only if $n = i$. In other words, we interact $\mathbf{z}_{it}$ in each time period with a full set of cross section dummies, and then include all of these terms in a pooled OLS regression with $\mathbf{x}_{it}$. You should also verify that the residuals from regression (11.82) are identical to those from regression (11.51), and that regression (11.82) yields equation (11.50) directly. This proof extends the material on the basic dummy variable regression from Section 10.5.3.

11.11. Apply the random growth model to the data in JTRAIN1.RAW (see Example 10.6):

$$\log(scrap_{it}) = \theta_t + c_i + g_i t + \beta_1 grant_{it} + \beta_2 grant_{i,t-1} + u_{it}$$

Specifically, difference once and then either difference again or apply fixed effects to the first-differenced equation. Discuss the results.

11.12. An unobserved effects model explaining current murder rates in terms of the number of executions in the last three years is

$$mrdrte_{it} = \theta_t + \beta_1 exec_{it} + \beta_2 unem_{it} + c_i + u_{it}$$

where $mrdrte_{it}$ is the number of murders in state i during year t, per 10,000 people; $exec_{it}$ is the total number of executions for the current and prior two years; and $unem_{it}$ is the current unemployment rate, included as a control.

a. Using the data for 1990 and 1993 in MURDER.RAW, estimate this model by first differencing. Notice that you should allow different year intercepts.

b. Under what circumstances would $exec_{it}$ *not* be strictly exogenous (conditional on c_i)? Assuming that no further lags of *exec* appear in the model and that *unem* is strictly exogenous, propose a method for consistently estimating $\boldsymbol{\beta}$ when *exec* is not strictly exogenous.

c. Apply the method from part b to the data in MURDER.RAW. Be sure to also test the rank condition. Do your results differ much from those in part a?

d. What happens to the estimates from parts a and c if Texas is dropped from the analysis?

11.13. Use the data in PRISON.RAW for this question to estimate model (11.26).

a. Estimate the reduced form equation for $\Delta\log(prison)$ to ensure that *final1* and *final2* are partially correlated with $\Delta\log(prison)$. Test whether the parameters on *final1* and *final2* are equal. What does this finding say about choosing an IV for $\Delta\log(prison)$? The elements of $\Delta\mathbf{x}$ should be the changes in the following variables: $\log(polpc)$, $\log(incpc)$, *unem*, *black*, *metro*, *ag0_14*, *ag15_17*, *ag18_24*, and *ag25_34*. Is there serial correlation in this reduced form?

b. Use Problem 11.8c to test for serial correlation in Δu_{it}. What do you conclude?

c. Add a fixed effect to equation (11.27). [This procedure is appropriate if we add a random growth term to equation (11.26).] Estimate the equation in first differences using the method of Problem 11.9. (Since N is only 51, you might be able to include 51 state dummies and use them as their own IVs.)

d. Estimate equation (11.26) using the property crime rate, and test for serial correlation in Δu_{it}. Are there important differences compared with the violent crime rate?

11.14. An extension of the model in Example 11.7 that allows enterprise zone designation to affect the *growth* of unemployment claims is

$$\log(uclms_{it}) = \theta_t + c_i + g_i t + \delta_1 ez_{it} + \delta_2 ez_{it} \cdot t + u_{it}$$

Notice that each jurisdiction also has a separate growth rate g_i.

a. Use the data in EZUNEM.RAW to estimate this model by first differencing followed by fixed effects on the differenced equation. Interpret your estimate of $\hat{\delta}_2$. Is it statistically significant?

b. Reestimate the model setting $\delta_1 = 0$. Does this model fit better than the basic model in Example 11.7?

c. Let w_i be an observed, time-constant variable, and suppose we add $\beta_1 w_i + \beta_2 w_i \cdot t$ to the random growth model. Can either β_1 or β_2 be estimated? Explain.

11.15. Use the data in JTRAIN1.RAW for this question.

a. Consider the simple equation

$$\log(scrap_{it}) = \theta_t + \beta_1 hrsemp_{it} + c_i + u_{it}$$

where $scrap_{it}$ is the scrap rate for firm i in year t, and $hrsemp_{it}$ is hours of training per employee. Suppose that you difference to remove c_i, but you still think that $\Delta hrsemp_{it}$ and $\Delta\log(scrap_{it})$ are simultaneously determined. Under what assumption is $\Delta grant_{it}$ a valid IV for $\Delta hrsemp_{it}$?

b. Using the differences from 1987 to 1988 only, test the rank condition for identification for the method described in part a.

c. Estimate the first-differenced equation by IV, and discuss the results.

d. Compare the IV estimates on the first differences with the OLS estimates on the first differences.

e. Use the IV method described in part a, but use all three years of data. How does the estimate of β_1 compare with only using two years of data?

11.16. Consider a Hausman and Taylor–type model with a single time-constant explanatory variable:

$$y_{it} = \gamma z_i + \mathbf{x}_{it}\boldsymbol{\beta} + c_i + u_{it}$$

$$\mathrm{E}(u_{it} \mid z_i, \mathbf{x}_i, c_i) = 0, \qquad t = 1, \ldots, T$$

where $\mathbf{x}_{it}$ is $1 \times K$ vector of time-varying explanatory variables.

a. If we are interested only in estimating $\boldsymbol{\beta}$, how should we proceed, without making additional assumptions (other than a standard rank assumption)?

b. Let w_i be a time-constant proxy variable for c_i in the sense that

$$\mathrm{E}(c_i \mid w_i, z_i, \mathbf{x}_i) = \mathrm{E}(c_i \mid w_i, \mathbf{x}_i) = \delta_0 + \delta_1 w_i + \bar{\mathbf{x}}_i \boldsymbol{\delta}_2$$

The key assumption is that, once we condition on w_i and $\mathbf{x}_i$, z_i is not partially related to c_i. Assuming the standard proxy variable redundancy assumption $\mathrm{E}(u_{it} \mid z_i, \mathbf{x}_i, c_i, w_i) = 0$, find $\mathrm{E}(y_{it} \mid z_i, \mathbf{x}_i, w_i)$.

c. Using part b, argue that γ is identified. Suggest a pooled OLS estimator.

d. Assume now that (1) $\mathrm{Var}(u_{it} \mid z_i, \mathbf{x}_i, c_i, w_i) = \sigma_u^2$, $t = 1, \ldots, T$; (2) $\mathrm{Cov}(u_{it}, u_{is} \mid z_i, \mathbf{x}_i, c_i, w_i) = 0$, all $t \neq s$; (3) $\mathrm{Var}(c_i \mid z_i, \mathbf{x}_i, w_i) = \sigma_a^2$. How would you efficiently estimate γ (along with $\boldsymbol{\beta}$, δ_0, δ_1, and $\boldsymbol{\delta}_2$)? [Hint: It might be helpful to write $c_i = \delta_0 + \delta_1 w_i + \bar{\mathbf{x}}_i \boldsymbol{\delta}_2 + a_i$, where $\mathrm{E}(a_i \mid z_i, \mathbf{x}_i, w_i) = 0$ and $\mathrm{Var}(a_i \mid z_i, \mathbf{x}_i, w_i) = \sigma_a^2$.]

11.17. Derive equation (11.55).

III GENERAL APPROACHES TO NONLINEAR ESTIMATION

In this part we begin our study of nonlinear econometric methods. What we mean by nonlinear needs some explanation because it does not necessarily mean that the underlying model is what we would think of as nonlinear. For example, suppose the population model of interest can be written as $y = \mathbf{x}\boldsymbol{\beta} + u$, but, rather than assuming $\mathrm{E}(u \mid \mathbf{x}) = 0$, we assume that the *median* of u given $\mathbf{x}$ is zero for all $\mathbf{x}$. This assumption implies $\mathrm{Med}(y \mid \mathbf{x}) = \mathbf{x}\boldsymbol{\beta}$, which is a linear model for the conditional median of y given $\mathbf{x}$. [The conditional mean, $\mathrm{E}(y \mid \mathbf{x})$, may or may not be linear in $\mathbf{x}$.] The standard estimator for a conditional median turns out to be least absolute deviations (LAD), not ordinary least squares. Like OLS, the LAD estimator solves a minimization problem: it minimizes the sum of absolute residuals. However, there is a key difference between LAD and OLS: the LAD estimator cannot be obtained in closed form. The lack of a closed-form expression for LAD has implications not only for obtaining the LAD estimates from a sample of data, but also for the asymptotic theory of LAD.

All the estimators we studied in Part II were obtained in closed form, a fact which greatly facilitates asymptotic analysis: we needed nothing more than the weak law of large numbers, the central limit theorem, and the basic algebra of probability limits. When an estimation method does not deliver closed-form solutions, we need to use more advanced asymptotic theory. In what follows, "nonlinear" describes any problem in which the estimators cannot be obtained in closed form.

The three chapters in this part provide the foundation for asymptotic analysis of most nonlinear models encountered in applications with cross section or panel data. We will make certain assumptions concerning continuity and differentiability, and so problems violating these conditions will not be covered. In the general development of M-estimators in Chapter 12, we will mention some of the applications that are ruled out and provide references.

This part of the book is by far the most technical. We will not dwell on the sometimes intricate arguments used to establish consistency and asymptotic normality in nonlinear contexts. For completeness, we do provide some general results on consistency and asymptotic normality for general classes of estimators. However, for specific estimation methods, such as nonlinear least squares, we will only state assumptions that have real impact for performing inference. Unless the underlying *regularity conditions*—which involve assuming that certain moments of the population random variables are finite, as well as assuming continuity and differentiability of the regression function or log-likelihood function—are obviously false, they are usually just assumed. Where possible, the assumptions will correspond closely with those given previously for linear models.

The analysis of maximum likelihood methods in Chapter 13 is greatly simplified once we have given a general treatment of M-estimators. Chapter 14 contains results for generalized method of moments estimators for models nonlinear in parameters. We also briefly discuss the related topic of minimum distance estimation in Chapter 14.

Readers who are not interested in general approaches to nonlinear estimation might use these chapters only when needed for reference in Part IV.

12 M-Estimation

12.1 Introduction

We begin our study of nonlinear estimation with a general class of estimators known as M-estimators, a term introduced by Huber (1967). (You might think of the "M" as standing for minimization or maximization.) M-estimation methods include maximum likelihood, nonlinear least squares, least absolute deviations, quasi-maximum likelihood, and many other procedures used by econometricians.

This chapter is somewhat abstract and technical, but it is useful to develop a unified theory early on so that it can be applied in a variety of situations. We will carry along the example of nonlinear least squares for cross section data to motivate the general approach.

In a **nonlinear regression model**, we have a random variable, y, and we would like to model $\mathrm{E}(y \mid \mathbf{x})$ as a function of the explanatory variables $\mathbf{x}$, a K-vector. We already know how to estimate models of $\mathrm{E}(y \mid \mathbf{x})$ when the model is linear in its parameters: OLS produces consistent, asymptotically normal estimators. What happens if the regression function is nonlinear in its parameters?

Generally, let $m(\mathbf{x}, \boldsymbol{\theta})$ be a **parametric model** for $\mathrm{E}(y \mid \mathbf{x})$, where m is a *known* function of $\mathbf{x}$ and $\boldsymbol{\theta}$, and $\boldsymbol{\theta}$ is a $P \times 1$ parameter vector. [This is a parametric model because $m(\cdot, \boldsymbol{\theta})$ is assumed to be known up to a *finite* number of parameters.] The dimension of the parameters, P, can be less than or greater than K. The **parameter space**, $\boldsymbol{\Theta}$, is a subset of $\mathbb{R}^P$. This is the set of values of $\boldsymbol{\theta}$ that we are willing to consider in the regression function. Unlike in linear models, for nonlinear models the asymptotic analysis requires explicit assumptions on the parameter space.

An example of a nonlinear regression function is the **exponential regression function**, $m(\mathbf{x}, \boldsymbol{\theta}) = \exp(\mathbf{x}\boldsymbol{\theta})$, where $\mathbf{x}$ is a row vector and contains unity as its first element. This is a useful functional form whenever $y \geq 0$. A regression model suitable when the response y is restricted to the unit interval is the **logistic function**, $m(\mathbf{x}, \boldsymbol{\theta}) = \exp(\mathbf{x}\boldsymbol{\theta})/[1 + \exp(\mathbf{x}\boldsymbol{\theta})]$. Both the exponential and logistic functions are nonlinear in $\boldsymbol{\theta}$.

In any application, there is no guarantee that our chosen model is adequate for $\mathrm{E}(y \mid \mathbf{x})$. We say that we have a **correctly specified model for the conditional mean**, $\mathrm{E}(y \mid \mathbf{x})$, if, for some $\boldsymbol{\theta}_o \in \boldsymbol{\Theta}$,

$$\mathrm{E}(y \mid \mathbf{x}) = m(\mathbf{x}, \boldsymbol{\theta}_o) \tag{12.1}$$

We introduce the subscript "o" on theta to distinguish the parameter vector appearing in $\mathrm{E}(y \mid \mathbf{x})$ from other candidates for that vector. (Often, the value $\boldsymbol{\theta}_o$ is called "the true value of theta," a phrase that is somewhat loose but still useful as shorthand.) As an example, for $y \geq 0$ and a single explanatory variable x, consider the model $m(x, \boldsymbol{\theta}) = \theta_1 x^{\theta_2}$. If the population regression function is $\mathrm{E}(y \mid x) = 4x^{1.5}$, then

$\theta_{o1} = 4$ and $\theta_{o2} = 1.5$. We will never know the actual θ_{o1} and θ_{o2} (unless we somehow control the way the data have been generated), but, if the model is correctly specified, then these values exist, and we would like to estimate them. Generic candidates for θ_{o1} and θ_{o2} are labeled θ_1 and θ_2, and, without further information, θ_1 is any positive number and θ_2 is any real number: the parameter space is $\boldsymbol{\Theta} \equiv \{(\theta_1, \theta_2): \theta_1 > 0, \theta_2 \in \mathbb{R}\}$. For an exponential regression model, $m(\mathbf{x}, \boldsymbol{\theta}) = \exp(\mathbf{x}\boldsymbol{\theta})$ is a correctly specified model for $\mathrm{E}(y \mid \mathbf{x})$ if and only if there is some K-vector $\boldsymbol{\theta}_o$ such that $\mathrm{E}(y \mid \mathbf{x}) = \exp(\mathbf{x}\boldsymbol{\theta}_o)$.

In our analysis of linear models, there was no need to make the distinction between the parameter vector in the population regression function and other candidates for this vector, because the estimators in linear contexts are obtained in closed form, and so their asymptotic properties can be studied directly. As we will see, in our theoretical development we need to distinguish the vector appearing in $\mathrm{E}(y \mid \mathbf{x})$ from a generic element of $\boldsymbol{\Theta}$. We will often drop the subscripting by "o" when studying particular applications because the notation can be cumbersome.

Equation (12.1) is the most general way of thinking about what nonlinear least squares is intended to do: estimate models of conditional expectations. But, as a statistical matter, equation (12.1) is equivalent to a model with an additive, unobservable error with a zero conditional mean:

$$y = m(\mathbf{x}, \boldsymbol{\theta}_o) + u, \qquad \mathrm{E}(u \mid \mathbf{x}) = 0 \tag{12.2}$$

Given equation (12.2), equation (12.1) clearly holds. Conversely, given equation (12.1), we obtain equation (12.2) by *defining* the error to be $u \equiv y - m(\mathbf{x}, \boldsymbol{\theta}_o)$. In interpreting the model and deciding on appropriate estimation methods, we should not focus on the error form in equation (12.2) because, evidently, the additivity of u has some unintended connotations. In particular, we must remember that, in writing the model in error form, the *only* thing implied by equation (12.1) is $\mathrm{E}(u \mid \mathbf{x}) = 0$. Depending on the nature of y, the error u may have some unusual properties. For example, if $y \geq 0$ then $u \geq -m(\mathbf{x}, \boldsymbol{\theta}_o)$, in which case u and $\mathbf{x}$ cannot be independent. Heteroskedasticity in the error—that is, $\mathrm{Var}(u \mid \mathbf{x}) \neq \mathrm{Var}(u)$—is present whenever $\mathrm{Var}(y \mid \mathbf{x})$ depends on $\mathbf{x}$, as is very common when y takes on a restricted range of values. Plus, when we introduce randomly sampled observations $\{(\mathbf{x}_i, y_i): i = 1, 2, \ldots, N\}$, it is too tempting to write the model and its assumptions as "$y_i = m(\mathbf{x}_i, \boldsymbol{\theta}_o) + u_i$ where the u_i are i.i.d. errors." As we discussed in Section 1.4 for the linear model, under random sampling the $\{u_i\}$ are always i.i.d. What is usually meant is that u_i and $\mathbf{x}_i$ are independent, but, for the reasons we just gave, this assumption is often much too strong. The error form of the model does turn out to be useful for defining estimators of asymptotic variances and for obtaining test statistics.

For later reference, we formalize the first **nonlinear least squares (NLS)** assumption as follows:

ASSUMPTION NLS.1: For some $\boldsymbol{\theta}_{\mathrm{o}} \in \boldsymbol{\Theta}$, $\mathrm{E}(y \mid \mathbf{x}) = m(\mathbf{x}, \boldsymbol{\theta}_{\mathrm{o}})$.

This form of presentation represents the level at which we will state assumptions for particular econometric methods. In our general development of M-estimators that follows, we will need to add conditions involving moments of $m(\mathbf{x}, \boldsymbol{\theta})$ and y, as well as continuity assumptions on $m(\mathbf{x}, \cdot)$.

If we let $\mathbf{w} \equiv (\mathbf{x}, y)$, then $\boldsymbol{\theta}_{\mathrm{o}}$ indexes a feature of the population distribution of $\mathbf{w}$, namely, the conditional mean of y given $\mathbf{x}$. More generally, let $\mathbf{w}$ be an M-vector of random variables with some distribution in the population. We let $\mathscr{W}$ denote the subset of $\mathbb{R}^M$ representing the possible values of $\mathbf{w}$. Let $\boldsymbol{\theta}_{\mathrm{o}}$ denote a parameter vector describing some feature of the distribution of $\mathbf{w}$. This could be a conditional mean, a conditional mean and conditional variance, a conditional median, or a conditional distribution. As shorthand, we call $\boldsymbol{\theta}_{\mathrm{o}}$ "the true parameter" or "the true value of theta." These phrases simply mean that $\boldsymbol{\theta}_{\mathrm{o}}$ is the parameter vector describing the underlying population, something we will make precise later. We assume that $\boldsymbol{\theta}_{\mathrm{o}}$ belongs to a known parameter space $\boldsymbol{\Theta} \subset \mathbb{R}^P$.

We assume that our data come as a random sample of size N from the population; we label this random sample $\{\mathbf{w}_i : i = 1, 2, \ldots\}$, where each $\mathbf{w}_i$ is an M-vector. This assumption is much more general than it may initially seem. It covers cross section models with many equations, and it also covers panel data settings with small time series dimension. The extension to independently pooled cross sections is almost immediate. In the NLS example, $\mathbf{w}_i$ consists of $\mathbf{x}_i$ and y_i, the ith draw from the population on $\mathbf{x}$ and y.

What allows us to estimate $\boldsymbol{\theta}_{\mathrm{o}}$ when it indexes $\mathrm{E}(y \mid \mathbf{x})$? It is the fact that $\boldsymbol{\theta}_{\mathrm{o}}$ is the value of $\boldsymbol{\theta}$ that minimizes the expected squared error between y and $m(\mathbf{x}, \boldsymbol{\theta})$. That is, $\boldsymbol{\theta}_{\mathrm{o}}$ solves the population problem

$$\min_{\boldsymbol{\theta} \in \boldsymbol{\Theta}} \mathrm{E}\{[y - m(\mathbf{x}, \boldsymbol{\theta})]^2\} \tag{12.3}$$

where the expectation is over the joint distribution of $(\mathbf{x}, y)$. This conclusion follows immediately from basic properties of conditional expectations (in particular, condition CE.8 in Chapter 2). We will give a slightly different argument here. Write

$$\begin{aligned}[y - m(\mathbf{x}, \boldsymbol{\theta})]^2 = {} & [y - m(\mathbf{x}, \boldsymbol{\theta}_{\mathrm{o}})]^2 + 2[m(\mathbf{x}, \boldsymbol{\theta}_{\mathrm{o}}) - m(\mathbf{x}, \boldsymbol{\theta})]u \\ & + [m(\mathbf{x}, \boldsymbol{\theta}_{\mathrm{o}}) - m(\mathbf{x}, \boldsymbol{\theta})]^2 \end{aligned} \tag{12.4}$$

where u is defined in equation (12.2). Now, since $\mathrm{E}(u \mid \mathbf{x}) = 0$, u is uncorrelated with *any* function of $\mathbf{x}$, including $m(\mathbf{x}, \boldsymbol{\theta}_o) - m(\mathbf{x}, \boldsymbol{\theta})$. Thus, taking the expected value of equation (12.4) gives

$$\mathrm{E}\{[y - m(\mathbf{x}, \boldsymbol{\theta})]^2\} = \mathrm{E}\{[y - m(\mathbf{x}, \boldsymbol{\theta}_o)]^2\} + \mathrm{E}\{[m(\mathbf{x}, \boldsymbol{\theta}_o) - m(\mathbf{x}, \boldsymbol{\theta})]^2\} \tag{12.5}$$

Since the last term in equation (12.5) is nonnegative, it follows that

$$\mathrm{E}\{[y - m(\mathbf{x}, \boldsymbol{\theta})]^2\} \geq \mathrm{E}\{[y - m(\mathbf{x}, \boldsymbol{\theta}_o)]^2\}, \qquad \text{all } \boldsymbol{\theta} \in \boldsymbol{\Theta} \tag{12.6}$$

The inequality is strict when $\boldsymbol{\theta} \neq \boldsymbol{\theta}_o$ unless $\mathrm{E}\{[m(\mathbf{x}, \boldsymbol{\theta}_o) - m(\mathbf{x}, \boldsymbol{\theta})]^2\} = 0$; for $\boldsymbol{\theta}_o$ to be identified, we will have to rule this possibility out.

Because $\boldsymbol{\theta}_o$ solves the population problem in expression (12.3), the analogy principle—which we introduced in Chapter 4—suggests estimating $\boldsymbol{\theta}_o$ by solving the sample analogue. In other words, we replace the population moment $\mathrm{E}\{[(y - m(\mathbf{x}, \boldsymbol{\theta})]^2\}$ with the sample average. The **nonlinear least squares (NLS) estimator** of $\boldsymbol{\theta}_o$, $\hat{\boldsymbol{\theta}}$, solves

$$\min_{\boldsymbol{\theta} \in \boldsymbol{\Theta}} N^{-1} \sum_{i=1}^{N} [y_i - m(\mathbf{x}_i, \boldsymbol{\theta})]^2 \tag{12.7}$$

For now, we assume that a solution to this problem exists.

The NLS objective function in expression (12.7) is a special case of a more general class of estimators. Let $q(\mathbf{w}, \boldsymbol{\theta})$ be a function of the random vector $\mathbf{w}$ and the parameter vector $\boldsymbol{\theta}$. An **M-estimator** of $\boldsymbol{\theta}_o$ solves the problem

$$\min_{\boldsymbol{\theta} \in \boldsymbol{\Theta}} N^{-1} \sum_{i=1}^{N} q(\mathbf{w}_i, \boldsymbol{\theta}) \tag{12.8}$$

assuming that a solution, call it $\hat{\boldsymbol{\theta}}$, exists. The estimator clearly depends on the sample $\{\mathbf{w}_i\colon i = 1, 2, \ldots, N\}$, but we suppress that fact in the notation.

The objective function for an M-estimator is a sample average of a function of $\mathbf{w}_i$ and $\boldsymbol{\theta}$. The division by N, while needed for the theoretical development, does not affect the minimization problem. Also, the focus on minimization, rather than maximization, is without loss of generality because maximiziation can be trivially turned into minimization.

The parameter vector $\boldsymbol{\theta}_o$ is assumed to uniquely solve the population problem

$$\min_{\boldsymbol{\theta} \in \boldsymbol{\Theta}} \mathrm{E}[q(\mathbf{w}, \boldsymbol{\theta})] \tag{12.9}$$

Comparing equations (12.8) and (12.9), we see that M-estimators are based on the analogy principle. Once $\boldsymbol{\theta}_o$ has been defined, finding an appropriate function q that delivers $\boldsymbol{\theta}_o$ as the solution to problem (12.9) requires basic results from probability theory. Usually there is more than one choice of q such that $\boldsymbol{\theta}_o$ solves problem (12.9), in which case the choice depends on efficiency or computational issues. In this chapter we carry along the NLS example; we treat maximum likelihood estimation in Chapter 13.

How do we translate the fact that $\boldsymbol{\theta}_o$ solves the population problem (12.9) into consistency of the M-estimator $\hat{\boldsymbol{\theta}}$ that solves problem (12.8)? Heuristically, the argument is as follows. Since for each $\boldsymbol{\theta} \in \boldsymbol{\Theta}$ $\{q(\mathbf{w}_i, \boldsymbol{\theta}): i = 1, 2, \ldots\}$ is just an i.i.d. sequence, the law of large numbers implies that

$$N^{-1} \sum_{i=1}^{N} q(\mathbf{w}_i, \boldsymbol{\theta}) \xrightarrow{p} \mathrm{E}[q(\mathbf{w}, \boldsymbol{\theta})] \tag{12.10}$$

under very weak finite moment assumptions. Since $\hat{\boldsymbol{\theta}}$ minimizes the function on the left side of equation (12.10) and $\boldsymbol{\theta}_o$ minimizes the function on the right, it seems plausible that $\hat{\boldsymbol{\theta}} \xrightarrow{p} \boldsymbol{\theta}_o$. This informal argument turns out to be correct, except in pathological cases. There are essentially two issues to address. The first is identifiability of $\boldsymbol{\theta}_o$, which is purely a population issue. The second is the sense in which the convergence in equation (12.10) happens across different values of $\boldsymbol{\theta}$ in $\boldsymbol{\Theta}$.

12.2 Identification, Uniform Convergence, and Consistency

We now present a formal consistency result for M-estimators under fairly weak assumptions. As mentioned previously, the conditions can be broken down into two parts. The first part is the **identification** or **identifiability** of $\boldsymbol{\theta}_o$. For nonlinear regression, we showed how $\boldsymbol{\theta}_o$ solves the population problem (12.3). However, we did not argue that $\boldsymbol{\theta}_o$ is always the *unique* solution to problem (12.3). Whether or not this is the case depends on the distribution of $\mathbf{x}$ and the nature of the regression function:

ASSUMPTION NLS.2: $\mathrm{E}\{[m(\mathbf{x}, \boldsymbol{\theta}_o) - m(\mathbf{x}, \boldsymbol{\theta})]^2\} > 0$, all $\boldsymbol{\theta} \in \boldsymbol{\Theta}$, $\boldsymbol{\theta} \neq \boldsymbol{\theta}_o$.

Assumption NLS.2 plays the same role as Assumption OLS.2 in Chapter 4. It can fail if the explanatory variables $\mathbf{x}$ do not have sufficient variation in the population. In fact, in the linear case $m(\mathbf{x}, \boldsymbol{\theta}) = \mathbf{x}\boldsymbol{\theta}$, Assumption NLS.2 holds if and only if rank $\mathrm{E}(\mathbf{x}'\mathbf{x}) = K$, which is just Assumption OLS.2 from Chapter 4. In nonlinear models, Assumption NLS.2 can fail if $m(\mathbf{x}, \boldsymbol{\theta}_o)$ depends on fewer parameters than are actually in $\boldsymbol{\theta}$. For example, suppose that we choose as our model $m(\mathbf{x}, \boldsymbol{\theta}) = \theta_1 + \theta_2 x_2 + \theta_3 x_3^{\theta_4}$, but the true model is linear: $\theta_{o3} = 0$. Then $\mathrm{E}[(y - m(\mathbf{x}, \boldsymbol{\theta}))]^2$ is minimized for any $\boldsymbol{\theta}$ with $\theta_1 = \theta_{o1}$, $\theta_2 = \theta_{o2}$, $\theta_3 = 0$, and θ_4 any value. If $\theta_{o3} \neq 0$, Assumption NLS.2

would typically hold provided there is sufficient variation in x_2 and x_3. Because identification fails for certain values of $\boldsymbol{\theta}_o$, this is an example of a **poorly identified model**. (See Section 9.5 for other examples of poorly identified models.)

Identification in commonly used nonlinear regression models, such as exponential and logistic regression functions, holds under weak conditions, provided perfect collinearity in $\mathbf{x}$ can be ruled out. For the most part, we will just assume that, when the model is correctly specified, $\boldsymbol{\theta}_o$ is the unique solution to problem (12.3). For the general M-estimation case, we assume that $q(\mathbf{w}, \boldsymbol{\theta})$ has been chosen so that $\boldsymbol{\theta}_o$ is a solution to problem (12.9). Identification requires that $\boldsymbol{\theta}_o$ be the unique solution:

$$\mathrm{E}[q(\mathbf{w}, \boldsymbol{\theta}_o)] < \mathrm{E}[q(\mathbf{w}, \boldsymbol{\theta})], \qquad \text{all } \boldsymbol{\theta} \in \boldsymbol{\Theta}, \quad \boldsymbol{\theta} \neq \boldsymbol{\theta}_o \tag{12.11}$$

The second component for consistency of the M-estimator is convergence of the sample average $N^{-1}\sum_{i=1}^{N} q(\mathbf{w}_i, \boldsymbol{\theta})$ to its expected value. It turns out that **pointwise convergence in probability**, as stated in equation (12.10), is not sufficient for consistency. That is, it is not enough to simply invoke the usual weak law of large numbers at each $\boldsymbol{\theta} \in \boldsymbol{\Theta}$. Instead, **uniform convergence in probability** is sufficient. Mathematically,

$$\max_{\boldsymbol{\theta} \in \boldsymbol{\Theta}} \left| N^{-1} \sum_{i=1}^{N} q(\mathbf{w}_i, \boldsymbol{\theta}) - \mathrm{E}[q(\mathbf{w}, \boldsymbol{\theta})] \right| \xrightarrow{p} 0 \tag{12.12}$$

Uniform convergence clearly implies pointwise convergence, but the converse is not true: it is possible for equation (12.10) to hold but equation (12.12) to fail. Nevertheless, under certain regularity conditions, the pointwise convergence in equation (12.10) translates into the uniform convergence in equation (12.12).

To state a formal result concerning uniform convergence, we need to be more careful in stating assumptions about the function $q(\cdot, \cdot)$ and the parameter space $\boldsymbol{\Theta}$. Since we are taking expected values of $q(\mathbf{w}, \boldsymbol{\theta})$ with respect to the distribution of $\mathbf{w}$, $q(\mathbf{w}, \boldsymbol{\theta})$ must be a random variable for each $\boldsymbol{\theta} \in \boldsymbol{\Theta}$. Technically, we should assume that $q(\cdot, \boldsymbol{\theta})$ is a *Borel measurable function* on $\mathcal{W}$ for each $\boldsymbol{\theta} \in \boldsymbol{\Theta}$. Since it is very difficult to write down a function that is not Borel measurable, we spend no further time on it. Rest assured that any objective function that arises in econometrics is Borel measurable. You are referred to Billingsley (1979) and Davidson (1994, Chapter 3).

The next assumption concerning q is practically more important. We assume that, for each $\mathbf{w} \in \mathcal{W}$, $q(\mathbf{w}, \cdot)$ is a *continuous function* over the parameter space $\boldsymbol{\Theta}$. All of the problems we treat in detail have objective functions that are continuous in the parameters, but these do not cover all cases of interest. For example, Manski's (1975) maximum score estimator for binary response models has an objective function that is not continuous in $\boldsymbol{\theta}$. (We cover binary response models in Chapter 15.) It is possible to somewhat relax the continuity assumption in order to handle such cases, but we will not need that generality. See Manski (1988, Section 7.3) and Newey and McFadden (1994).

Obtaining uniform convergence is generally difficult for unbounded parameter sets, such as $\boldsymbol{\Theta} = \mathbb{R}^P$. It is easiest to assume that $\boldsymbol{\Theta}$ is a *compact subset* of $\mathbb{R}^P$, which means that $\boldsymbol{\Theta}$ is closed and bounded (see Rudin, 1976, Theorem 2.41). Because the natural parameter spaces in most applications are not bounded (and sometimes not closed), the compactness assumption is unattractive for developing a general theory of estimation. However, for most applications it is not an assumption to worry about: $\boldsymbol{\Theta}$ can be defined to be such a large closed and bounded set as to always contain $\boldsymbol{\theta}_o$. Some consistency results for nonlinear estimation without compact parameter spaces are available; see the discussion and references in Newey and McFadden (1994).

We can now state a theorem concerning uniform convergence appropriate for the random sampling environment. This result, known as the **uniform weak law of large numbers (UWLLN)**, dates back to LeCam (1953). See also Newey and McFadden (1994, Lemma 2.4).

THEOREM 12.1 (Uniform Weak Law of Large Numbers): Let $\mathbf{w}$ be a random vector taking values in $\mathcal{W} \subset \mathbb{R}^M$, let $\boldsymbol{\Theta}$ be a subset of $\mathbb{R}^P$, and let $q: \mathcal{W} \times \boldsymbol{\Theta} \to \mathbb{R}$ be a real-valued function. Assume that (a) $\boldsymbol{\Theta}$ is compact; (b) for each $\boldsymbol{\theta} \in \boldsymbol{\Theta}$, $q(\cdot, \boldsymbol{\theta})$ is Borel measurable on $\mathcal{W}$; (c) for each $\mathbf{w} \in \mathcal{W}$, $q(\mathbf{w}, \cdot)$ is continuous on $\boldsymbol{\Theta}$; and (d) $|q(\mathbf{w}, \boldsymbol{\theta})| \leq b(\mathbf{w})$ for all $\boldsymbol{\theta} \in \boldsymbol{\Theta}$, where b is a nonnegative function on $\mathcal{W}$ such that $\mathrm{E}[b(\mathbf{w})] < \infty$. Then equation (12.12) holds.

The only assumption we have not discussed is assumption d, which requires the expected absolute value of $q(\mathbf{w}, \boldsymbol{\theta})$ to be bounded across $\boldsymbol{\theta}$. This kind of moment condition is rarely verified in practice, although, with some work, it can be; see Newey and McFadden (1994) for examples.

The continuity and compactness assumptions are important for establishing uniform convergence, and they also ensure that both the sample minimization problem (12.8) and the population minimization problem (12.9) actually have solutions. Consider problem (12.8) first. Under the assumptions of Theorem 12.1, the sample average is a continuous function of $\boldsymbol{\theta}$, since $q(\mathbf{w}_i, \boldsymbol{\theta})$ is continuous for each $\mathbf{w}_i$. Since a continuous function on a compact space always achieves its minimum, the M-estimation problem is well defined (there could be more than one solution). As a technical matter, it can be shown that $\hat{\boldsymbol{\theta}}$ is actually a random variable under the measurability assumption on $q(\cdot, \boldsymbol{\theta})$. See, for example, Gallant and White (1988).

It can also be shown that, under the assumptions of Theorem 12.1, the function $\mathrm{E}[q(\mathbf{w}, \boldsymbol{\theta})]$ is continuous as a function of $\boldsymbol{\theta}$. Therefore, problem (12.9) also has at least one solution; identifiability ensures that it has only one solution, and this fact implies consistency of the M-estimator.

THEOREM 12.2 (Consistency of M-Estimators): Under the assumptions of Theorem 12.1, assume that the identification assumption (12.11) holds. Then a random vector, $\hat{\boldsymbol{\theta}}$, solves problem (12.8), and $\hat{\boldsymbol{\theta}} \xrightarrow{p} \boldsymbol{\theta}_o$.

A proof of Theorem 12.2 is given in Newey and McFadden (1994). For nonlinear least squares, once Assumptions NLS.1 and NLS.2 are maintained, the practical requirement is that $m(\mathbf{x}, \cdot)$ be a continuous function over $\boldsymbol{\Theta}$. Since this assumption is almost always true in applications of NLS, we do not list it as a separate assumption. Noncompactness of $\boldsymbol{\Theta}$ is not much of a concern for most applications.

Theorem 12.2 also applies to **median regression**. Suppose that the conditional median of y given $\mathbf{x}$ is $\mathrm{Med}(y \mid \mathbf{x}) = m(\mathbf{x}, \boldsymbol{\theta}_o)$, where $m(\mathbf{x}, \boldsymbol{\theta})$ is a known function of $\mathbf{x}$ and $\boldsymbol{\theta}$. The leading case is a linear model, $m(\mathbf{x}, \boldsymbol{\theta}) = \mathbf{x}\boldsymbol{\theta}$, where $\mathbf{x}$ contains unity. The **least absolute deviations (LAD) estimator** of $\boldsymbol{\theta}_o$ solves

$$\min_{\boldsymbol{\theta} \in \boldsymbol{\Theta}} N^{-1} \sum_{i=1}^{N} |y_i - m(\mathbf{x}_i, \boldsymbol{\theta})|$$

If $\boldsymbol{\Theta}$ is compact and $m(\mathbf{x}, \cdot)$ is continuous over $\boldsymbol{\Theta}$ for each $\mathbf{x}$, a solution always exists. The LAD estimator is motivated by the fact that $\boldsymbol{\theta}_o$ minimizes $\mathrm{E}[|y - m(\mathbf{x}, \boldsymbol{\theta})|]$ over the parameter space $\boldsymbol{\Theta}$; this follows by the fact that for each $\mathbf{x}$, the conditional median is the minimum absolute loss predictor conditional on $\mathbf{x}$. (See, for example, Bassett and Koenker, 1978, and Manski, 1988, Section 4.2.2.) If we assume that $\boldsymbol{\theta}_o$ is the unique solution—a standard identification assumption—then the LAD estimator is consistent very generally. In addition to the continuity, compactness, and identification assumptions, it suffices that $\mathrm{E}[|y|] < \infty$ and $|m(\mathbf{x}, \boldsymbol{\theta})| \leq a(\mathbf{x})$ for some function $a(\cdot)$ such that $\mathrm{E}[a(\mathbf{x})] < \infty$. [To see this point, take $b(\mathbf{w}) \equiv |y| + a(\mathbf{x})$ in Theorem 12.2.]

Median regression is a special case of **quantile regression**, where we model quantiles in the distribution of y given $\mathbf{x}$. For example, in addition to the median, we can estimate how the first and third quartiles in the distribution of y given $\mathbf{x}$ change with $\mathbf{x}$. Except for the median (which leads to LAD), the objective function that identifies a conditional quantile is asymmetric about zero. See, for example, Koenker and Bassett (1978) and Manski (1988, Section 4.2.4). Buchinsky (1994) applies quantile regression methods to examine factors affecting the distribution of wages in the United States over time.

We end this section with a lemma that we use repeatedly in the rest of this chapter. It follows from Lemma 4.3 in Newey and McFadden (1994).

LEMMA 12.1: Suppose that $\hat{\boldsymbol{\theta}} \xrightarrow{p} \boldsymbol{\theta}_{\mathrm{o}}$, and assume that $r(\mathbf{w}, \boldsymbol{\theta})$ satisfies the same assumptions on $q(\mathbf{w}, \boldsymbol{\theta})$ in Theorem 12.2. Then

$$N^{-1} \sum_{i=1}^{N} r(\mathbf{w}_i, \hat{\boldsymbol{\theta}}) \xrightarrow{p} \mathrm{E}[r(\mathbf{w}, \boldsymbol{\theta}_{\mathrm{o}})] \tag{12.13}$$

That is, $N^{-1} \sum_{i=1}^{N} r(\mathbf{w}_i, \hat{\boldsymbol{\theta}})$ is a consistent estimator of $\mathrm{E}[r(\mathbf{w}, \boldsymbol{\theta}_{\mathrm{o}})]$.

Intuitively, Lemma 12.1 is quite reasonable. We know that $N^{-1} \sum_{i=1}^{N} r(\mathbf{w}_i, \boldsymbol{\theta}_{\mathrm{o}})$ generally converges in probability to $\mathrm{E}[r(\mathbf{w}, \boldsymbol{\theta}_{\mathrm{o}})]$ by the law of large numbers. Lemma 12.1 shows that, if we replace $\boldsymbol{\theta}_{\mathrm{o}}$ with a consistent estimator, the convergence still holds, at least under standard regularity conditions.

12.3 Asymptotic Normality

Under additional assumptions on the objective function, we can also show that M-estimators are asymptotically normally distributed (and converge at the rate $\sqrt{N}$). It turns out that continuity over the parameter space does not ensure asymptotic normality. We will assume more than is needed because all of the problems we cover in this book have objective functions with many continuous derivatives.

The simplest asymptotic normality proof proceeds as follows. Assume that $\boldsymbol{\theta}_{\mathrm{o}}$ is in the interior of $\boldsymbol{\Theta}$, which means that $\boldsymbol{\Theta}$ must have nonempty interior; this assumption is true in most applications. Then, since $\hat{\boldsymbol{\theta}} \xrightarrow{p} \boldsymbol{\theta}_{\mathrm{o}}$, $\hat{\boldsymbol{\theta}}$ is in the interior of $\boldsymbol{\Theta}$ with probability approaching one. If $q(\mathbf{w}, \cdot)$ is continuously differentiable on the interior of $\boldsymbol{\Theta}$, then (with probability approaching one) $\hat{\boldsymbol{\theta}}$ solves the first-order condition

$$\sum_{i=1}^{N} \mathbf{s}(\mathbf{w}_i, \hat{\boldsymbol{\theta}}) = \mathbf{0} \tag{12.14}$$

where $\mathbf{s}(\mathbf{w}, \boldsymbol{\theta})$ is the $P \times 1$ vector of partial derivatives of $q(\mathbf{w}, \boldsymbol{\theta})$: $\mathbf{s}(\mathbf{w}, \boldsymbol{\theta})' = [\partial q(\mathbf{w}, \boldsymbol{\theta})/\partial \theta_1, \partial q(\mathbf{w}, \boldsymbol{\theta})/\partial \theta_2, \ldots, \partial q(\mathbf{w}, \boldsymbol{\theta})/\partial \theta_P]$. [Or, $\mathbf{s}(\mathbf{w}, \boldsymbol{\theta})$ is the transpose of the gradient of $q(\mathbf{w}, \boldsymbol{\theta})$.] We call $\mathbf{s}(\mathbf{w}, \boldsymbol{\theta})$ the **score of the objective function**, $q(\mathbf{w}, \boldsymbol{\theta})$. While condition (12.14) can only be guaranteed to hold with probability approaching one, usually it holds exactly; at any rate, we will drop the qualifier, as it does not affect the derivation of the limiting distribution.

If $q(\mathbf{w}, \cdot)$ is twice continuously differentiable, then each row of the left-hand side of equation (12.14) can be expanded about $\boldsymbol{\theta}_{\mathrm{o}}$ in a mean-value expansion:

$$\sum_{i=1}^{N} \mathbf{s}(\mathbf{w}_i, \hat{\boldsymbol{\theta}}) = \sum_{i=1}^{N} \mathbf{s}(\mathbf{w}_i, \boldsymbol{\theta}_{\mathrm{o}}) + \left(\sum_{i=1}^{N} \ddot{\mathbf{H}}_i \right) (\hat{\boldsymbol{\theta}} - \boldsymbol{\theta}_{\mathrm{o}}) \tag{12.15}$$

The notation $\ddot{\mathbf{H}}_i$ denotes the $P \times P$ **Hessian of the objective function**, $q(\mathbf{w}_i, \boldsymbol{\theta})$, with respect to $\boldsymbol{\theta}$, but with each row of $\mathbf{H}(\mathbf{w}_i, \boldsymbol{\theta}) \equiv \partial^2 q(\mathbf{w}_i, \boldsymbol{\theta})/\partial\boldsymbol{\theta}\partial\boldsymbol{\theta}' \equiv \nabla_{\theta}^2 q(\mathbf{w}_i, \boldsymbol{\theta})$ evaluated at a different mean value. Each of the P mean values is on the line segment between $\boldsymbol{\theta}_o$ and $\hat{\boldsymbol{\theta}}$. We cannot know what these mean values are, but we do know that each must converge in probability to $\boldsymbol{\theta}_o$ (since each is "trapped" between $\hat{\boldsymbol{\theta}}$ and $\boldsymbol{\theta}_o$).

Combining equations (12.14) and (12.15) and multiplying through by $1/\sqrt{N}$ gives

$$\mathbf{0} = N^{-1/2} \sum_{i=1}^{N} \mathbf{s}(\mathbf{w}_i, \boldsymbol{\theta}_o) + \left(N^{-1} \sum_{i=1}^{N} \ddot{\mathbf{H}}_i \right) \sqrt{N}(\hat{\boldsymbol{\theta}} - \boldsymbol{\theta}_o)$$

Now, we can apply Lemma 12.1 to get $N^{-1} \sum_{i=1}^{N} \ddot{\mathbf{H}}_i \xrightarrow{p} \mathrm{E}[\mathbf{H}(\mathbf{w}, \boldsymbol{\theta}_o)]$ (under some moment conditions). If $\mathbf{A}_o \equiv \mathrm{E}[\mathbf{H}(\mathbf{w}, \boldsymbol{\theta}_o)]$ is nonsingular, then $N^{-1} \sum_{i=1}^{N} \ddot{\mathbf{H}}_i$ is nonsingular w.p.a.1 and $(N^{-1} \sum_{i=1}^{N} \ddot{\mathbf{H}}_i)^{-1} \xrightarrow{p} \mathbf{A}_o^{-1}$. Therefore, we can write

$$\sqrt{N}(\hat{\boldsymbol{\theta}} - \boldsymbol{\theta}_o) = \left(N^{-1} \sum_{i=1}^{N} \ddot{\mathbf{H}}_i \right)^{-1} \left[-N^{-1/2} \sum_{i=1}^{N} \mathbf{s}_i(\boldsymbol{\theta}_o) \right]$$

where $\mathbf{s}_i(\boldsymbol{\theta}_o) \equiv \mathbf{s}(\mathbf{w}_i, \boldsymbol{\theta}_o)$. As we will show, $\mathrm{E}[\mathbf{s}_i(\boldsymbol{\theta}_o)] = \mathbf{0}$. Therefore, $N^{-1/2} \sum_{i=1}^{N} \mathbf{s}_i(\boldsymbol{\theta}_o)$ generally satisfies the central limit theorem because it is the average of i.i.d. random vectors with zero mean, multiplied by the usual $\sqrt{N}$. Since $\mathrm{o}_p(1) \cdot \mathrm{O}_p(1) = \mathrm{o}_p(1)$, we have

$$\sqrt{N}(\hat{\boldsymbol{\theta}} - \boldsymbol{\theta}_o) = \mathbf{A}_o^{-1} \left[-N^{-1/2} \sum_{i=1}^{N} \mathbf{s}_i(\boldsymbol{\theta}_o) \right] + \mathrm{o}_p(1) \tag{12.16}$$

This is an important equation. It shows that $\sqrt{N}(\hat{\boldsymbol{\theta}} - \boldsymbol{\theta}_o)$ inherits its limiting distribution from the average of the scores, evaluated at $\boldsymbol{\theta}_o$. The matrix $\mathbf{A}_o^{-1}$ simply acts as a linear transformation. If we absorb this linear transformation into $\mathbf{s}_i(\boldsymbol{\theta}_o)$, we can write

$$\sqrt{N}(\hat{\boldsymbol{\theta}} - \boldsymbol{\theta}_o) = N^{-1/2} \sum_{i=1}^{N} \mathbf{r}_i(\boldsymbol{\theta}_o) + \mathrm{o}_p(1) \tag{12.17}$$

where $\mathbf{r}_i(\boldsymbol{\theta}_o) \equiv -\mathbf{A}_o^{-1}\mathbf{s}_i(\boldsymbol{\theta}_o)$; this is sometimes called the **influence function representation** of $\hat{\boldsymbol{\theta}}$, where $\mathbf{r}(\mathbf{w}, \boldsymbol{\theta})$ is the influence function.

Equation (12.16) [or (12.17)] allows us to derive the **first-order asymptotic distribution** of $\hat{\boldsymbol{\theta}}$. Higher order representations attempt to reduce the error in the $\mathrm{o}_p(1)$ term in equation (12.16); such derivations are much more complicated than equation (12.16) and are beyond the scope of this book.

We have essentially proven the following result:

THEOREM 12.3 (Asymptotic Normality of M-estimators): In addition to the assumptions in Theorem 12.2, assume (a) $\boldsymbol{\theta}_o$ is in the interior of $\boldsymbol{\Theta}$; (b) $\mathbf{s}(\mathbf{w}, \cdot)$ is continuously differentiable on the interior of $\boldsymbol{\Theta}$ for all $\mathbf{w} \in \mathcal{W}$; (c) Each element of $\mathbf{H}(\mathbf{w}, \boldsymbol{\theta})$ is bounded in absolute value by a function $b(\mathbf{w})$, where $\mathrm{E}[b(\mathbf{w})] < \infty$; (d) $\mathbf{A}_o \equiv \mathrm{E}[\mathbf{H}(\mathbf{w}, \boldsymbol{\theta}_o)]$ is positive definite; (e) $\mathrm{E}[\mathbf{s}(\mathbf{w}, \boldsymbol{\theta}_o)] = \mathbf{0}$; and (f) each element of $\mathbf{s}(\mathbf{w}, \boldsymbol{\theta}_o)$ has finite second moment.

Then

$$\sqrt{N}(\hat{\boldsymbol{\theta}} - \boldsymbol{\theta}_o) \xrightarrow{d} \mathrm{Normal}(0, \mathbf{A}_o^{-1}\mathbf{B}_o\mathbf{A}_o^{-1}) \tag{12.18}$$

where

$$\mathbf{A}_o \equiv \mathrm{E}[\mathbf{H}(\mathbf{w}, \boldsymbol{\theta}_o)] \tag{12.19}$$

and

$$\mathbf{B}_o \equiv \mathrm{E}[\mathbf{s}(\mathbf{w}, \boldsymbol{\theta}_o)\mathbf{s}(\mathbf{w}, \boldsymbol{\theta}_o)'] = \mathrm{Var}[\mathbf{s}(\mathbf{w}, \boldsymbol{\theta}_o)] \tag{12.20}$$

Thus,

$$\mathrm{Avar}\ \hat{\boldsymbol{\theta}} = \mathbf{A}_o^{-1}\mathbf{B}_o\mathbf{A}_o^{-1}/N \tag{12.21}$$

Theorem 12.3 implies asymptotic normality of most of the estimators we study in the remainder of the book. A leading example that is not covered by Theorem 12.3 is the LAD estimator. Even if $m(\mathbf{x}, \boldsymbol{\theta})$ is twice continuously differentiable in $\boldsymbol{\theta}$, the objective function for each i, $q(\mathbf{w}_i, \boldsymbol{\theta}) \equiv |y_i - m(\mathbf{x}_i, \boldsymbol{\theta})|$, is not twice continuously differentiable because the absolute value function is nondifferentiable at zero. By itself, this limitation is a minor nuisance. More importantly, by any reasonable definition, the Hessian of the LAD objective function is the zero matrix in the leading case of a linear conditional median function, and this fact violates assumption d of Theorem 12.3. It turns out that the LAD estimator *is* generally $\sqrt{N}$-asymptotically normal, but Theorem 12.3 cannot be applied. Newey and McFadden (1994) contains results that can be used.

A key component of Theorem 12.3 is that the score evaluated at $\boldsymbol{\theta}_o$ has expected value zero. In many applications, including NLS, we can show this result directly. But it is also useful to know that it holds in the abstract M-estimation framework, at least if we can interchange the expectation and the derivative. To see this point, note that, if $\boldsymbol{\theta}_o$ is in the interior of $\boldsymbol{\Theta}$, and $\mathrm{E}[q(\mathbf{w}, \boldsymbol{\theta})]$ is differentiable for $\boldsymbol{\theta} \in \mathrm{int}\ \boldsymbol{\Theta}$, then

$$\nabla_{\theta}\mathrm{E}[q(\mathbf{w}, \boldsymbol{\theta})]|_{\boldsymbol{\theta}=\boldsymbol{\theta}_o} = \mathbf{0} \tag{12.22}$$

where ∇_θ denotes the gradient with respect to $\boldsymbol{\theta}$. Now, if the derivative and expectations operator can be interchanged (which is the case quite generally), then equation (12.22) implies

$$\mathrm{E}[\nabla_\theta q(\mathbf{w}, \boldsymbol{\theta}_o)] = \mathrm{E}[\mathbf{s}(\mathbf{w}, \boldsymbol{\theta}_o)] = \mathbf{0} \tag{12.23}$$

A similar argument shows that, in general, $\mathrm{E}[\mathbf{H}(\mathbf{w}, \boldsymbol{\theta}_o)]$ is positive semidefinite. If $\boldsymbol{\theta}_o$ is identified, $\mathrm{E}[\mathbf{H}(\mathbf{w}, \boldsymbol{\theta}_o)]$ is positive definite.

For the remainder of this chapter, it is convenient to divide the original NLS objective function by two:

$$q(\mathbf{w}, \boldsymbol{\theta}) = [y - m(\mathbf{x}, \boldsymbol{\theta})]^2/2 \tag{12.24}$$

The score of equation (12.24) can be written as

$$\mathbf{s}(\mathbf{w}, \boldsymbol{\theta}) = -\nabla_\theta m(\mathbf{x}, \boldsymbol{\theta})'[y - m(\mathbf{x}, \boldsymbol{\theta})] \tag{12.25}$$

where $\nabla_\theta m(\mathbf{x}, \boldsymbol{\theta})$ is the $1 \times P$ gradient of $m(\mathbf{x}, \boldsymbol{\theta})$, and therefore $\nabla_\theta m(\mathbf{x}, \boldsymbol{\theta})'$ is $P \times 1$. We can show directly that this expression has an expected value of zero at $\boldsymbol{\theta} = \boldsymbol{\theta}_o$ by showing that expected value of $\mathbf{s}(\mathbf{w}, \boldsymbol{\theta}_o)$ conditional on $\mathbf{x}$ is zero:

$$\mathrm{E}[\mathbf{s}(\mathbf{w}, \boldsymbol{\theta}_o) \mid \mathbf{x}] = -\nabla_\theta m(\mathbf{x}, \boldsymbol{\theta})'[\mathrm{E}(y \mid \mathbf{x}) - m(\mathbf{x}, \boldsymbol{\theta}_o)] = \mathbf{0} \tag{12.26}$$

The variance of $\mathbf{s}(\mathbf{w}, \boldsymbol{\theta}_o)$ is

$$\mathbf{B}_o \equiv \mathrm{E}[\mathbf{s}(\mathbf{w}, \boldsymbol{\theta}_o)\mathbf{s}(\mathbf{w}, \boldsymbol{\theta}_o)'] = \mathrm{E}[u^2 \nabla_\theta m(\mathbf{x}, \boldsymbol{\theta}_o)' \nabla_\theta m(\mathbf{x}, \boldsymbol{\theta}_o)] \tag{12.27}$$

where the error $u \equiv y - m(\mathbf{x}, \boldsymbol{\theta}_o)$ is the difference between y and $\mathrm{E}(y \mid \mathbf{x})$.

The Hessian of $q(\mathbf{w}, \boldsymbol{\theta})$ is

$$\mathbf{H}(\mathbf{w}, \boldsymbol{\theta}) = \nabla_\theta m(\mathbf{x}, \boldsymbol{\theta})' \nabla_\theta m(\mathbf{x}, \boldsymbol{\theta}) - \nabla_\theta^2 m(\mathbf{x}, \boldsymbol{\theta})[y - m(\mathbf{x}, \boldsymbol{\theta})] \tag{12.28}$$

where $\nabla_\theta^2 m(\mathbf{x}, \boldsymbol{\theta})$ is the $P \times P$ Hessian of $m(\mathbf{x}, \boldsymbol{\theta})$ with respect to $\boldsymbol{\theta}$. To find the expected value of $\mathbf{H}(\mathbf{w}, \boldsymbol{\theta})$ at $\boldsymbol{\theta} = \boldsymbol{\theta}_o$, we first find the expectation conditional on $\mathbf{x}$. When evaluated at $\boldsymbol{\theta}_o$, the second term in equation (12.28) is $\nabla_\theta^2 m(\mathbf{x}, \boldsymbol{\theta}_o)u$, and it therefore has a zero mean conditional on $\mathbf{x}$ [since $\mathrm{E}(u \mid \mathbf{x}) = 0$]. Therefore,

$$\mathrm{E}[\mathbf{H}(\mathbf{w}, \boldsymbol{\theta}_o) \mid \mathbf{x}] = \nabla_\theta m(\mathbf{x}, \boldsymbol{\theta}_o)' \nabla_\theta m(\mathbf{x}, \boldsymbol{\theta}_o) \tag{12.29}$$

Taking the expected value of equation (12.29) over the distribution of $\mathbf{x}$ gives

$$\mathbf{A}_o = \mathrm{E}[\nabla_\theta m(\mathbf{x}, \boldsymbol{\theta}_o)' \nabla_\theta m(\mathbf{x}, \boldsymbol{\theta}_o)] \tag{12.30}$$

This matrix plays a fundamental role in nonlinear regression. When $\boldsymbol{\theta}_o$ is identified, $\mathbf{A}_o$ is generally positive definite. In the linear case $m(\mathbf{x}, \boldsymbol{\theta}) = \mathbf{x}\boldsymbol{\theta}$, $\mathbf{A}_o = \mathrm{E}(\mathbf{x}'\mathbf{x})$. In the exponential case $m(\mathbf{x}, \boldsymbol{\theta}) = \exp(\mathbf{x}\boldsymbol{\theta})$, $\mathbf{A}_o = \mathrm{E}[\exp(2\mathbf{x}\boldsymbol{\theta}_o)\mathbf{x}'\mathbf{x}]$, which is generally positive definite whenever $\mathrm{E}(\mathbf{x}'\mathbf{x})$ is. In the example $m(\mathbf{x}, \boldsymbol{\theta}) = \theta_1 + \theta_2 x_2 + \theta_3 x_3^{\theta_4}$ with $\theta_{o3} = 0$, it is easy to show that matrix (12.30) has rank less than four.

For nonlinear regression, $\mathbf{A}_o$ and $\mathbf{B}_o$ are similar in that they both depend on $\nabla_\theta m(\mathbf{x}, \boldsymbol{\theta}_o)' \nabla_\theta m(\mathbf{x}, \boldsymbol{\theta}_o)$. Generally, though, there is no simple relationship between $\mathbf{A}_o$ and $\mathbf{B}_o$ because the latter depends on the distribution of u^2, the squared population error. In Section 12.5 we will show that a homoskedasticity assumption implies that $\mathbf{B}_o$ is proportional to $\mathbf{A}_o$.

12.4 Two-Step M-Estimators

Sometimes applications of M-estimators involve a first-stage estimation (an example is OLS with generated regressors, as in Chapter 6). Let $\hat{\gamma}$ be a preliminary estimator, usually based on the random sample $\{\mathbf{w}_i\colon i = 1, 2, \ldots, N\}$. Where this estimator comes from must be vague at this point.

A **two-step M-estimator** $\hat{\theta}$ of θ_o solves the problem

$$\min_{\theta \in \Theta} \sum_{i=1}^{N} q(\mathbf{w}_i, \theta; \hat{\gamma}) \tag{12.31}$$

where q is now defined on $\mathcal{W} \times \boldsymbol{\Theta} \times \boldsymbol{\Gamma}$, and $\boldsymbol{\Gamma}$ is a subset of $\mathbb{R}^J$. We will see several examples of two-step M-estimators in the applications in Part IV. An example of a two-step M-estimator is the **weighted nonlinear least squares (WNLS) estimator**, where the weights are estimated in a first stage. The WNLS estimator solves

$$\min_{\theta \in \Theta} \tfrac{1}{2} \sum_{i=1}^{N} [y_i - m(\mathbf{x}_i, \theta)]^2 / h(\mathbf{x}_i, \hat{\gamma}) \tag{12.32}$$

where the weighting function, $h(\mathbf{x}, \gamma)$, depends on the explanatory variables and a parameter vector. As with NLS, $m(\mathbf{x}, \theta)$ is a model of $\mathrm{E}(y \mid \mathbf{x})$. The function $h(\mathbf{x}, \gamma)$ is chosen to be a model of $\mathrm{Var}(y \mid \mathbf{x})$. The estimator $\hat{\gamma}$ comes from a problem used to estimate the conditional variance. We list the key assumptions needed for WNLS to have desirable properties here, but several of the derivations are left for the problems.

ASSUMPTION WNLS.1: Same as Assumption NLS.1.

12.4.1 Consistency

For the general two-step M-estimator, when will $\hat{\theta}$ be consistent for θ_o? In practice, the important condition is the identification assumption. To state the identification condition, we need to know about the asymptotic behavior of $\hat{\gamma}$. A general assumption is that $\hat{\gamma} \xrightarrow{p} \gamma^*$, where γ^* is some element in $\mathbf{\Gamma}$. We label this value γ^* to allow for the possibility that $\hat{\gamma}$ does not converge to a parameter indexing some interesting feature of the distribution of $\mathbf{w}$. In some cases, the plim of $\hat{\gamma}$ will be of direct interest. In the weighted regression case, if we assume that $h(\mathbf{x}, \gamma)$ is a correctly specified model for $\mathrm{Var}(y \mid \mathbf{x})$, then it is possible to choose an estimator such that $\hat{\gamma} \xrightarrow{p} \gamma_o$, where $\mathrm{Var}(y \mid \mathbf{x}) = h(\mathbf{x}, \gamma_o)$. (For an example, see Problem 12.2.) If the variance model is misspecified, plim $\hat{\gamma}$ is generally well defined, but $\mathrm{Var}(y \mid \mathbf{x}) \neq h(\mathbf{x}, \gamma^*)$; it is for this reason that we use the notation γ^*.

The identification condition for the two-step M-estimator is

$$\mathrm{E}[q(\mathbf{w}, \boldsymbol{\theta}_o; \gamma^*)] < \mathrm{E}[q(\mathbf{w}, \boldsymbol{\theta}; \gamma^*)], \qquad \text{all } \boldsymbol{\theta} \in \boldsymbol{\Theta}, \quad \boldsymbol{\theta} \neq \boldsymbol{\theta}_o$$

The consistency argument is essentially the same as that underlying Theorem 12.2. If $q(\mathbf{w}_i, \boldsymbol{\theta}; \gamma)$ satisfies the UWLLN over $\boldsymbol{\Theta} \times \mathbf{\Gamma}$ then expression (12.31) can be shown to converge to $\mathrm{E}[q(\mathbf{w}, \boldsymbol{\theta}; \gamma^*)]$ uniformly over $\boldsymbol{\Theta}$. Along with identification, this result can be shown to imply consistency of $\hat{\boldsymbol{\theta}}$ for $\boldsymbol{\theta}_o$.

In some applications of two-step M-estimation, identification of $\boldsymbol{\theta}_o$ holds for *any* $\gamma \in \mathbf{\Gamma}$. This result can be shown for the WNLS estimator (see Problem 12.4). It is for this reason that WNLS is still consistent even if the function $h(\mathbf{x}, \gamma)$ is not correctly specified for $\mathrm{Var}(y \mid \mathbf{x})$. The weakest version of the identification assumption for WNLS is the following:

ASSUMPTION WNLS.2: $\mathrm{E}\{[m(\mathbf{x}, \boldsymbol{\theta}_o) - m(\mathbf{x}, \boldsymbol{\theta})]^2 / h(\mathbf{x}, \gamma^*)\} > 0$, all $\boldsymbol{\theta} \in \boldsymbol{\Theta}$, $\boldsymbol{\theta} \neq \boldsymbol{\theta}_o$, where $\gamma^* = \text{plim } \hat{\gamma}$.

As with the case of NLS, we know that weak inequality holds in Assumption WNLS.2 under Assumption WNLS.1. The strict inequality in Assumption WNLS.2 puts restrictions on the distribution of $\mathbf{x}$ and the functional forms of m and h.

In other cases, including several two-step maximum likelihood estimators we encounter in Part IV, the identification condition for $\boldsymbol{\theta}_o$ holds only for $\gamma = \gamma^* = \gamma_o$, where γ_o also indexes some feature of the distribution of $\mathbf{w}$.

12.4.2 Asymptotic Normality

With the two-step M-estimator, there are two cases worth distinguishing. The first occurs when the asymptotic variance of $\sqrt{N}(\hat{\boldsymbol{\theta}} - \boldsymbol{\theta}_o)$ does not depend on the asymptotic variance of $\sqrt{N}(\hat{\gamma} - \gamma^*)$, and the second occurs when the asymptotic variance of $\sqrt{N}(\hat{\boldsymbol{\theta}} - \boldsymbol{\theta}_o)$ must be adjusted to account for the first-stage estimation of γ^*. We first derive conditions under which we can ignore the first-stage estimation error.

Using arguments similar to those in Section 12.3, it can be shown that, under standard regularity conditions,

$$\sqrt{N}(\hat{\boldsymbol{\theta}} - \boldsymbol{\theta}_o) = \mathbf{A}_o^{-1}\left(-N^{-1/2}\sum_{i=1}^{N}\mathbf{s}_i(\boldsymbol{\theta}_o;\hat{\gamma})\right) + o_p(1) \tag{12.33}$$

where now $\mathbf{A}_o = \mathrm{E}[\mathbf{H}(\mathbf{w}, \boldsymbol{\theta}_o; \gamma^*)]$. In obtaining the score and the Hessian, we take derivatives only with respect to $\boldsymbol{\theta}$; γ^* simply appears as an extra argument. Now, if

$$N^{-1/2}\sum_{i=1}^{N}\mathbf{s}_i(\boldsymbol{\theta}_o;\hat{\gamma}) = N^{-1/2}\sum_{i=1}^{N}\mathbf{s}_i(\boldsymbol{\theta}_o;\gamma^*) + o_p(1) \tag{12.34}$$

then $\sqrt{N}(\hat{\boldsymbol{\theta}} - \boldsymbol{\theta}_o)$ behaves the same asymptotically whether we used $\hat{\gamma}$ or its plim in defining the M-estimator.

When does equation (12.34) hold? Assuming that $\sqrt{N}(\hat{\gamma} - \gamma^*) = O_p(1)$, which is standard, a mean value expansion similar to the one in Section 12.3 gives

$$N^{-1/2}\sum_{i=1}^{N}\mathbf{s}_i(\boldsymbol{\theta}_o;\hat{\gamma}) = N^{-1/2}\sum_{i=1}^{N}\mathbf{s}_i(\boldsymbol{\theta}_o;\gamma^*) + \mathbf{F}_o\sqrt{N}(\hat{\gamma} - \gamma^*) + o_p(1) \tag{12.35}$$

where $\mathbf{F}_o$ is the $P \times J$ matrix

$$\mathbf{F}_o \equiv \mathrm{E}[\nabla_\gamma \mathbf{s}(\mathbf{w}, \boldsymbol{\theta}_o; \gamma^*)] \tag{12.36}$$

(Remember, J is the dimension of γ.) Therefore, if

$$\mathrm{E}[\nabla_\gamma \mathbf{s}(\mathbf{w}, \boldsymbol{\theta}_o; \gamma^*)] = \mathbf{0} \tag{12.37}$$

then equation (12.34) holds, and the asymptotic variance of the two-step M-estimator is the same as if γ^* were plugged in. In other words, under assumption (12.37), we conclude that equation (12.18) holds, where $\mathbf{A}_o$ and $\mathbf{B}_o$ are given in expressions (12.19) and (12.20), respectively, except that γ^* appears as an argument in the score and Hessian. For deriving the asymptotic distribution of $\sqrt{N}(\hat{\boldsymbol{\theta}} - \boldsymbol{\theta}_o)$, we can ignore the fact that $\hat{\gamma}$ was obtained in a first-stage estimation.

One case where assumption (12.37) holds is weighted nonlinear least squares, something you are asked to show in Problem 12.4. Naturally, we must assume that the conditional mean is correctly specified, but, interestingly, assumption (12.37) holds whether or not the conditional variance is correctly specified.

There are many problems for which assumption (12.37) does not hold, including some of the methods for correcting for endogeneity in probit and Tobit models in Part IV. In Chapter 17 we will see that two-step methods for correcting sample selection bias are two-step M-estimators, but assumption (12.37) fails. In such cases we need to make an adjustment to the asymptotic variance of $\sqrt{N}(\hat{\boldsymbol{\theta}} - \boldsymbol{\theta}_o)$. The adjustment is easily obtained from equation (12.35), once we have a first-order representation for $\sqrt{N}(\hat{\gamma} - \gamma^*)$. We assume that

$$\sqrt{N}(\hat{\gamma} - \gamma^*) = N^{-1/2} \sum_{i=1}^{N} \mathbf{r}_i(\gamma^*) + o_p(1) \tag{12.38}$$

where $\mathbf{r}_i(\gamma^*)$ is a $J \times 1$ vector with $\mathrm{E}[\mathbf{r}_i(\gamma^*)] = \mathbf{0}$ (in practice, $\mathbf{r}_i$ depends on parameters other than γ^*, but we suppress those here for simplicity). Therefore, $\hat{\gamma}$ could itself be an M-estimator or, as we will see in Chapter 14, a generalized method of moments estimator. In fact, every estimator considered in this book has a representation as in equation (12.38).

Now we can write

$$\sqrt{N}(\hat{\boldsymbol{\theta}} - \boldsymbol{\theta}_o) = \mathbf{A}_o^{-1} N^{-1/2} \sum_{i=1}^{N} [-\mathbf{g}_i(\boldsymbol{\theta}_o; \gamma^*)] + o_p(1) \tag{12.39}$$

where $\mathbf{g}_i(\boldsymbol{\theta}_o; \gamma^*) \equiv \mathbf{s}_i(\boldsymbol{\theta}_o; \gamma^*) + \mathbf{F}_o \mathbf{r}_i(\gamma^*)$. Since $\mathbf{g}_i(\boldsymbol{\theta}_o; \gamma^*)$ has zero mean, the standardized partial sum in equation (12.39) can be assumed to satisfy the central limit theorem. Define the $P \times P$ matrix

$$\mathbf{D}_o \equiv \mathrm{E}[\mathbf{g}_i(\boldsymbol{\theta}_o; \gamma^*) \mathbf{g}_i(\boldsymbol{\theta}_o; \gamma^*)'] = \mathrm{Var}[\mathbf{g}_i(\boldsymbol{\theta}_o; \gamma^*)] \tag{12.40}$$

Then

$$\mathrm{Avar}\ \sqrt{N}(\hat{\boldsymbol{\theta}} - \boldsymbol{\theta}_o) = \mathbf{A}_o^{-1} \mathbf{D}_o \mathbf{A}_o^{-1} \tag{12.41}$$

We will discuss estimation of this matrix in the next section.

12.5 Estimating the Asymptotic Variance

12.5.1 Estimation without Nuisance Parameters

We first consider estimating the asymptotic variance of $\hat{\boldsymbol{\theta}}$ in the case where there are no nuisance parameters. This task requires consistently estimating the matrices $\mathbf{A}_o$ and $\mathbf{B}_o$. One thought is to solve for the expected values of $\mathbf{H}(\mathbf{w}, \boldsymbol{\theta}_o)$ and $\mathbf{s}(\mathbf{w}, \boldsymbol{\theta}_o) \cdot \mathbf{s}(\mathbf{w}, \boldsymbol{\theta}_o)'$ over the distribution of $\mathbf{w}$, and then to plug in $\hat{\boldsymbol{\theta}}$ for $\boldsymbol{\theta}_o$. When we have completely specified the distribution of $\mathbf{w}$, obtaining closed-form expressions for $\mathbf{A}_o$ and $\mathbf{B}_o$ is, in principle, possible. However, except in simple cases, it would be difficult. More importantly, we rarely specify the entire distribution of $\mathbf{w}$. Even in a maximum likelihood setting, $\mathbf{w}$ is almost always partitioned into two parts: a set of endogenous variables, $\mathbf{y}$, and conditioning variables, $\mathbf{x}$. Rarely do we wish to specify the distribution of $\mathbf{x}$, and so the expected values needed to obtain $\mathbf{A}_o$ and $\mathbf{B}_o$ are not available.

We can always estimate $\mathbf{A}_o$ consistently by taking away the expectation and replacing $\boldsymbol{\theta}_o$ with $\hat{\boldsymbol{\theta}}$. Under regularity conditions that ensure uniform converge of the Hessian, the estimator

$$N^{-1}\sum_{i=1}^{N}\mathbf{H}(\mathbf{w}_i, \hat{\boldsymbol{\theta}}) \equiv N^{-1}\sum_{i=1}^{N}\hat{\mathbf{H}}_i \tag{12.42}$$

is consistent for $\mathbf{A}_o$, by Lemma 12.1. The advantage of the estimator (12.42) is that it is always available in problems with a twice continuously differentiable objective function. The drawbacks are that it requires calculation of the second derivatives—a nontrivial task for some problems—and it is not guaranteed to be positive definite, or even positive semidefinite, for the particular sample we are working with. As we will see shortly, in some cases the asymptotic variance of $\sqrt{N}(\hat{\boldsymbol{\theta}} - \boldsymbol{\theta}_o)$ is proportional to $\mathbf{A}_o^{-1}$, in which case using the estimator (12.42) to estimate $\mathbf{A}_o$ can result in a nonpositive definite variance matrix estimator. Without a positive definite variance matrix estimator, some asymptotic standard errors need not even be defined, and test statistics that have limiting chi-square distributions could actually be negative.

In most econometric applications, more structure is available that allows a different estimator. Suppose we can partition $\mathbf{w}$ into $\mathbf{x}$ and $\mathbf{y}$, and that $\boldsymbol{\theta}_o$ indexes some feature of the distribution of $\mathbf{y}$ given $\mathbf{x}$ (such as the conditional mean or, in the case of maximum likelihood, the conditional distribution). Define

$$\mathbf{A}(\mathbf{x}, \boldsymbol{\theta}_o) \equiv \mathrm{E}[\mathbf{H}(\mathbf{w}, \boldsymbol{\theta}_o) \mid \mathbf{x}] \tag{12.43}$$

While $\mathbf{H}(\mathbf{w}, \boldsymbol{\theta}_o)$ is generally a function of $\mathbf{x}$ and $\mathbf{y}$, $\mathbf{A}(\mathbf{x}, \boldsymbol{\theta}_o)$ is a function only of $\mathbf{x}$. By the law of iterated expectations, $\mathrm{E}[\mathbf{A}(\mathbf{x}, \boldsymbol{\theta}_o)] = \mathrm{E}[\mathbf{H}(\mathbf{w}, \boldsymbol{\theta}_o)] = \mathbf{A}_o$. From Lemma 12.1 and standard regularity conditions it follows that

$$N^{-1}\sum_{i=1}^{N}\mathbf{A}(\mathbf{x}_i, \hat{\boldsymbol{\theta}}) \equiv N^{-1}\sum_{i=1}^{N}\hat{\mathbf{A}}_i \xrightarrow{p} \mathbf{A}_o \tag{12.44}$$

The estimator (12.44) of $\mathbf{A}_o$ is useful in cases where $\mathrm{E}[\mathbf{H}(\mathbf{w}, \boldsymbol{\theta}_o) \mid \mathbf{x}]$ can be obtained in closed form or is easily approximated. In some leading cases, including NLS and certain maximum likelihood problems, $\mathbf{A}(\mathbf{x}, \boldsymbol{\theta}_o)$ depends only on the first derivatives of the conditional mean function.

When the estimator (12.44) is available, it is usually the case that $\boldsymbol{\theta}_o$ actually minimizes $\mathrm{E}[q(\mathbf{w}, \boldsymbol{\theta}) \mid \mathbf{x}]$ for any value of $\mathbf{x}$; this is easily seen to be the case for NLS from equation (12.4). Under assumptions that allow the interchange of derivative and expectation, this result implies that $\mathbf{A}(\mathbf{x}, \boldsymbol{\theta}_o)$ is positive semidefinite. The expected value of $\mathbf{A}(\mathbf{x}, \boldsymbol{\theta}_o)$ over the distribution of $\mathbf{x}$ is positive definite provided $\boldsymbol{\theta}_o$ is identified. Therefore, the estimator (12.44) is usually positive definite in the sample; as a result, it is more attractive than the estimator (12.42).

Obtaining a positive semidefinite estimator of $\mathbf{B}_o$ is straightforward. By Lemma 12.1, under standard regularity conditions we have

$$N^{-1} \sum_{i=1}^{N} \mathbf{s}(\mathbf{w}_i, \hat{\boldsymbol{\theta}}) \mathbf{s}(\mathbf{w}_i, \hat{\boldsymbol{\theta}})' \equiv N^{-1} \sum_{i=1}^{N} \hat{\mathbf{s}}_i \hat{\mathbf{s}}_i' \xrightarrow{p} \mathbf{B}_o \tag{12.45}$$

Combining the estimator (12.45) with the consistent estimators for $\mathbf{A}_o$, we can consistently estimate Avar $\sqrt{N}(\hat{\boldsymbol{\theta}} - \boldsymbol{\theta}_o)$ by

$$\text{Av}\hat{\text{a}}\text{r } \sqrt{N}(\hat{\boldsymbol{\theta}} - \boldsymbol{\theta}_o) = \hat{\mathbf{A}}^{-1} \hat{\mathbf{B}} \hat{\mathbf{A}}^{-1} \tag{12.46}$$

where $\hat{\mathbf{A}}$ is one of the estimators (12.42) or (12.44). The asymptotic standard errors are obtained from the matrix

$$\hat{\mathbf{V}} \equiv \text{Av}\hat{\text{a}}\text{r}(\hat{\boldsymbol{\theta}}) = \hat{\mathbf{A}}^{-1} \hat{\mathbf{B}} \hat{\mathbf{A}}^{-1}/N \tag{12.47}$$

which can be expressed as

$$\left(\sum_{i=1}^{N} \hat{\mathbf{H}}_i \right)^{-1} \left(\sum_{i=1}^{N} \hat{\mathbf{s}}_i \hat{\mathbf{s}}_i' \right) \left(\sum_{i=1}^{N} \hat{\mathbf{H}}_i \right)^{-1} \tag{12.48}$$

or

$$\left(\sum_{i=1}^{N} \hat{\mathbf{A}}_i \right)^{-1} \left(\sum_{i=1}^{N} \hat{\mathbf{s}}_i \hat{\mathbf{s}}_i' \right) \left(\sum_{i=1}^{N} \hat{\mathbf{A}}_i \right)^{-1} \tag{12.49}$$

depending on the estimator used for $\mathbf{A}_o$. Expressions (12.48) and (12.49) are both at least positive semidefinite when they are well defined.

In the case of nonlinear least squares, the estimator of $\mathbf{A}_o$ in equation (12.44) is always available and always used:

$$\sum_{i=1}^{N} \hat{\mathbf{A}}_i = \sum_{i=1}^{N} \nabla_\theta \hat{m}_i' \nabla_\theta \hat{m}_i$$

where $\nabla_\theta \hat{m}_i \equiv \nabla_\theta m(\mathbf{x}_i, \hat{\boldsymbol{\theta}})$ for every observation i. Also, the estimated score for NLS can be written as

$$\hat{\mathbf{s}}_i = -\nabla_\theta \hat{m}_i'[y_i - m(\mathbf{x}_i, \hat{\boldsymbol{\theta}})] = -\nabla_\theta \hat{m}_i' \hat{u}_i \tag{12.50}$$

where the **nonlinear least squares residuals**, $\hat{u}_i$, are defined as

$$\hat{u}_i \equiv y_i - m(\mathbf{x}_i, \hat{\boldsymbol{\theta}}) \tag{12.51}$$

The estimated asymptotic variance of the NLS estimator is

$$\text{A}\hat{\text{va}}\text{r}(\hat{\boldsymbol{\theta}}) = \left(\sum_{i=1}^{N} \nabla_\theta \hat{m}_i' \nabla_\theta \hat{m}_i\right)^{-1} \left(\sum_{i=1}^{N} \hat{u}_i^2 \nabla_\theta \hat{m}_i' \nabla_\theta \hat{m}_i\right) \left(\sum_{i=1}^{N} \nabla_\theta \hat{m}_i' \nabla_\theta \hat{m}_i\right)^{-1} \tag{12.52}$$

This is called the **heteroskedasticity-robust variance matrix estimator for NLS** because it places no restrictions on $\text{Var}(y \mid \mathbf{x})$. It was first proposed by White (1980a). [Sometimes the expression is multiplied by $N/(N-P)$ as a degrees-of-freedom adjustment, where P is the dimension of $\boldsymbol{\theta}$.] As always, the asymptotic standard error of each element of $\hat{\boldsymbol{\theta}}$ is the square root of the appropriate diagonal element of matrix (12.52).

As a specific example, suppose that $m(\mathbf{x}, \boldsymbol{\theta}) = \exp(\mathbf{x}\boldsymbol{\theta})$. Then $\nabla_\theta \hat{m}_i' \nabla_\theta \hat{m}_i = \exp(2\mathbf{x}_i\hat{\boldsymbol{\theta}})\mathbf{x}_i'\mathbf{x}_i$, which has dimension $K \times K$. We can plug this equation into expression (12.52) along with $\hat{u}_i = y_i - \exp(\mathbf{x}_i\hat{\boldsymbol{\theta}})$.

In many contexts, including nonlinear least squares and certain quasi-likelihood methods, the asymptotic variance estimator can be simplified under additional assumptions. For our purposes, we state the assumption as follows: For some $\sigma_o^2 > 0$,

$$\text{E}[\mathbf{s}(\mathbf{w}, \boldsymbol{\theta}_o)\mathbf{s}(\mathbf{w}, \boldsymbol{\theta}_o)'] = \sigma_o^2 \text{E}[\mathbf{H}(\mathbf{w}, \boldsymbol{\theta}_o)] \tag{12.53}$$

This assumption simply says that the expected outer product of the score, evaluated at $\boldsymbol{\theta}_o$, is proportional to the expected value of the Hessian (evaluated at $\boldsymbol{\theta}_o$): $\mathbf{B}_o = \sigma_o^2 \mathbf{A}_o$. Shortly we will provide an assumption under which assumption (12.53) holds for NLS. In the next chapter we will show that assumption (12.53) holds for $\sigma_o^2 = 1$ in the context of maximum likelihood with a correctly specified conditional density. For reasons we will see in Chapter 13, we refer to assumption (12.53) as the **generalized information matrix equality (GIME)**.

LEMMA 12.2: Under regularity conditions of the type contained in Theorem 12.3 and assumption (12.53), $\text{Avar}(\hat{\boldsymbol{\theta}}) = \sigma_o^2 \mathbf{A}_o^{-1}/N$. Therefore, under assumption (12.53), the asymptotic variance of $\hat{\boldsymbol{\theta}}$ can be estimated as

$$\hat{\mathbf{V}} = \hat{\sigma}^2 \left(\sum_{i=1}^{N} \hat{\mathbf{H}}_i\right)^{-1} \tag{12.54}$$

or

$$\hat{\mathbf{V}} = \hat{\sigma}^2 \left(\sum_{i=1}^{N} \hat{\mathbf{A}}_i \right)^{-1} \tag{12.55}$$

where $\hat{\mathbf{H}}_i$ and $\hat{\mathbf{A}}_i$ are defined as before, and $\hat{\sigma}^2 \xrightarrow{p} \sigma_o^2$.

In the case of nonlinear regression, the parameter σ_o^2 is the variance of y given $\mathbf{x}$, or equivalently $\mathrm{Var}(u \mid \mathbf{x})$, under homoskedasticity:

ASSUMPTION NLS.3: $\mathrm{Var}(y \mid \mathbf{x}) = \mathrm{Var}(u \mid \mathbf{x}) = \sigma_o^2$.

Under Assumption NLS.3, we can show that assumption (12.53) holds with $\sigma_o^2 = \mathrm{Var}(y \mid \mathbf{x})$. First, since $\mathbf{s}(\mathbf{w}, \boldsymbol{\theta}_o)\mathbf{s}(\mathbf{w}, \boldsymbol{\theta}_o)' = u^2 \nabla_\theta m(\mathbf{x}, \boldsymbol{\theta}_o)' \nabla_\theta m(\mathbf{x}, \boldsymbol{\theta}_o)$, it follows that

$$\begin{aligned} \mathrm{E}[\mathbf{s}(\mathbf{w}, \boldsymbol{\theta}_o)\mathbf{s}(\mathbf{w}, \boldsymbol{\theta}_o)' \mid \mathbf{x}] &= \mathrm{E}(u^2 \mid \mathbf{x}) \nabla_\theta m(\mathbf{x}, \boldsymbol{\theta}_o)' \nabla_\theta m(\mathbf{x}, \boldsymbol{\theta}_o) \\ &= \sigma_o^2 \nabla_\theta m(\mathbf{x}, \boldsymbol{\theta}_o)' \nabla_\theta m(\mathbf{x}, \boldsymbol{\theta}_o) \end{aligned} \tag{12.56}$$

under Assumptions NLS.1 and NLS.3. Taking the expected value with respect to $\mathbf{x}$ gives equation (12.53).

Under Assumption NLS.3, a simplified estimator of the asymptotic variance of the NLS estimator exists from equation (12.55). Let

$$\hat{\sigma}^2 = \frac{1}{(N-P)} \sum_{i=1}^{N} \hat{u}_i^2 = \mathrm{SSR}/(N-P) \tag{12.57}$$

where the $\hat{u}_i$ are the NLS residuals (12.51) and SSR is the sum of squared NLS residuals. Using Lemma 12.1, $\hat{\sigma}^2$ can be shown to be consistent very generally. The subtraction of P in the denominator of equation (12.57) is an adjustment that is thought to improve the small sample properties of $\hat{\sigma}^2$.

Under Assumptions NLS.1–NLS.3, the asymptotic variance of the NLS estimator is estimated as

$$\hat{\sigma}^2 \left(\sum_{i=1}^{N} \nabla_\theta \hat{m}_i' \nabla_\theta \hat{m}_i \right)^{-1} \tag{12.58}$$

This is the default asymptotic variance estimator for NLS, but it is valid only under homoskedasticity; the estimator (12.52) is valid with or without Assumption NLS.3. For an exponential regression function, expression (12.58) becomes $\hat{\sigma}^2 (\sum_{i=1}^{N} \exp(2\mathbf{x}_i \hat{\boldsymbol{\theta}}) \mathbf{x}_i' \mathbf{x}_i)^{-1}$.

12.5.2 Adjustments for Two-Step Estimation

In the case of the two-step M-estimator, we may or may not need to adjust the asymptotic variance. If assumption (12.37) holds, estimation is very simple. The most general estimators are expressions (12.48) and (12.49), where $\hat{\mathbf{s}}_i$, $\hat{\mathbf{H}}_i$, and $\hat{\mathbf{A}}_i$ depend on $\hat{\gamma}$, but we only compute derivatives with respect to $\boldsymbol{\theta}$.

In some cases under assumption (12.37), the analogue of assumption (12.53) holds (with $\gamma_o = \text{plim}\ \hat{\gamma}$ appearing in $\mathbf{H}$ and $\mathbf{s}$). If so, the simpler estimators (12.54) and (12.55) are available. In Problem 12.4 you are asked to show this result for weighted NLS when $\text{Var}(y \mid \mathbf{x}) = \sigma_o^2 h(\mathbf{x}, \gamma_o)$ and $\gamma_o = \text{plim}\ \hat{\gamma}$. The natural third assumption for WNLS is that the variance function is correctly specified:

ASSUMPTION WNLS.3: For some $\gamma_o \in \boldsymbol{\Gamma}$ and σ_o^2, $\text{Var}(y \mid \mathbf{x}) = \sigma_o^2 h(\mathbf{x}, \gamma_o)$. Further, $\sqrt{N}(\hat{\gamma} - \gamma_o) = \text{O}_p(1)$.

Under Assumption WNLS.3, the asymptotic variance of the WNLS estimator is estimated as

$$\hat{\sigma}^2 \left(\sum_{i=1}^{N} (\nabla_\theta \hat{m}_i' \nabla_\theta \hat{m}_i)/\hat{h}_i \right)^{-1} \tag{12.59}$$

where $\hat{h}_i = h(\mathbf{x}_i, \hat{\gamma})$ and $\hat{\sigma}^2$ is as in equation (12.57) except that the residual $\hat{u}_i$ is replaced with the **standardized residual**, $\hat{u}_i/\sqrt{\hat{h}_i}$. The sum in expression (12.59) is simply the outer product of the weighted gradients, $\nabla_\theta \hat{m}_i/\sqrt{\hat{h}_i}$. Thus the NLS formulas can be used but with all quantities weighted by $1/\sqrt{\hat{h}_i}$. It is important to remember that expression (12.59) is not valid without Assumption WNLS.3.

When assumption (12.37) is violated, the asymptotic variance estimator of $\hat{\boldsymbol{\theta}}$ must account for the asymptotic variance of $\hat{\gamma}$; we must estimate equation (12.41). We already know how to consistently estimate $\mathbf{A}_o$: use expression (12.42) or (12.44) where $\hat{\gamma}$ is also plugged in. Estimation of $\mathbf{D}_o$ is also straightforward. First, we need to estimate $\mathbf{F}_o$. An estimator that is always available is

$$\hat{\mathbf{F}} = N^{-1} \sum_{i=1}^{N} \nabla_\gamma \mathbf{s}_i(\hat{\boldsymbol{\theta}}; \hat{\gamma}) \tag{12.60}$$

In cases with conditioning variables, such as nonlinear least squares, a simpler estimator can be obtained by computing $\text{E}[\nabla_\gamma \mathbf{s}(\mathbf{w}_i, \boldsymbol{\theta}_o, \gamma^*) \mid \mathbf{x}_i]$, replacing $(\boldsymbol{\theta}_o, \gamma^*)$ with $(\hat{\boldsymbol{\theta}}, \hat{\gamma})$, and using this in place of $\nabla_\gamma \mathbf{s}_i(\hat{\boldsymbol{\theta}}; \hat{\gamma})$. Next, replace $\mathbf{r}_i(\gamma^*)$ with $\hat{\mathbf{r}}_i \equiv \mathbf{r}_i(\hat{\gamma})$. Then

$$\hat{\mathbf{D}} \equiv N^{-1} \sum_{i=1}^{N} \hat{\mathbf{g}}_i \hat{\mathbf{g}}_i' \tag{12.61}$$

is consistent for $\mathbf{D}_o$, where $\hat{\mathbf{g}}_i = \hat{\mathbf{s}}_i + \hat{\mathbf{F}}\hat{\mathbf{r}}_i$. The asymptotic variance of the two-step M-estimator can be obtained as in expression (12.48) or (12.49), but where $\hat{\mathbf{s}}_i$ is replaced with $\hat{\mathbf{g}}_i$.

12.6 Hypothesis Testing

12.6.1 Wald Tests

Wald tests are easily obtained once we choose a form of the asymptotic variance. To test the Q restrictions

$$\text{H}_0\text{: } \mathbf{c}(\boldsymbol{\theta}_o) = \mathbf{0} \tag{12.62}$$

we can form the Wald statistic

$$W \equiv \mathbf{c}(\hat{\boldsymbol{\theta}})'(\hat{\mathbf{C}}\hat{\mathbf{V}}\hat{\mathbf{C}}')^{-1}\mathbf{c}(\hat{\boldsymbol{\theta}}) \tag{12.63}$$

where $\hat{\mathbf{V}}$ is an asymptotic variance matrix estimator of $\hat{\boldsymbol{\theta}}$, $\hat{\mathbf{C}} \equiv \mathbf{C}(\hat{\boldsymbol{\theta}})$, and $\mathbf{C}(\boldsymbol{\theta})$ is the $Q \times P$ Jacobian of $\mathbf{c}(\boldsymbol{\theta})$. The estimator $\hat{\mathbf{V}}$ can be chosen to be fully robust, as in expression (12.48) or (12.49); under assumption (12.53), the simpler forms in Lemma 12.2 are available. Also, $\hat{\mathbf{V}}$ can be chosen to account for two-step estimation, when necessary. Provided $\hat{\mathbf{V}}$ has been chosen appropriately, $W \overset{a}{\sim} \chi^2_Q$ under H_0.

A couple of practical restrictions are needed for W to have a limiting χ^2_Q distribution. First, $\boldsymbol{\theta}_o$ must be in the interior of $\boldsymbol{\Theta}$; that is, $\boldsymbol{\theta}_o$ cannot be on the boundary. If, for example, the first element of $\boldsymbol{\theta}$ must be nonnegative—and we impose this restriction in the estimation—then expression (12.63) does not have a limiting chi-square distribution under H_0: $\theta_{o1} = 0$. The second condition is that $\mathbf{C}(\boldsymbol{\theta}_o) = \nabla_\theta \mathbf{c}(\boldsymbol{\theta}_o)$ must have rank Q. This rules out cases where $\boldsymbol{\theta}_o$ is unidentified under the null hypothesis, such as the NLS example where $m(\mathbf{x}, \boldsymbol{\theta}) = \theta_1 + \theta_2 x_2 + \theta_3 x_3^{\theta_4}$ and $\theta_{o3} = 0$ under H_0.

One drawback to the Wald statistic is that it is not invariant to how the nonlinear restrictions are imposed. We can change the outcome of a hypothesis test by redefining the constraint function, $\mathbf{c}(\cdot)$. We can illustrate the lack of invariance by studying an asymptotic t statistic (since a t statistic is a special case of a Wald statistic). Suppose that for a parameter $\theta_1 > 0$, the null hypothesis is H_0: $\theta_{o1} = 1$. The asymptotic t statistic is $(\hat{\theta}_1 - 1)/\text{se}(\hat{\theta}_1)$, where $\text{se}(\hat{\theta}_1)$ is the asymptotic standard error of $\hat{\theta}_1$. Now define $\phi_1 = \log(\theta_1)$, so that $\phi_{o1} = \log(\theta_{o1})$ and $\hat{\phi}_1 = \log(\hat{\theta}_1)$. The null hypothesis can be stated as $\text{H}_0 : \phi_{o1} = 0$. Using the delta method (see Chapter 3), $\text{se}(\hat{\phi}_1) =$

$\hat{\theta}_1^{-1}\,\text{se}(\hat{\theta}_1)$, and so the t statistic based on $\hat{\phi}_1$ is $\hat{\phi}_1/\text{se}(\hat{\phi}_1) = \log(\hat{\theta}_1)\hat{\theta}_1/\text{se}(\hat{\theta}_1) \neq (\hat{\theta}_1 - 1)/\text{se}(\hat{\theta}_1)$.

The lack of invariance of the Wald statistic is discussed in more detail by Gregory and Veall (1985), Phillips and Park (1988), and Davidson and MacKinnon (1993, Section 13.6). The lack of invariance is a cause for concern because it suggests that the Wald statistic can have poor finite sample properties for testing nonlinear hypotheses. What is much less clear is that the lack of invariance has led empirical researchers to search over different statements of the null hypothesis in order to obtain a desired result.

12.6.2 Score (or Lagrange Multiplier) Tests

In cases where the unrestricted model is difficult to estimate but the restricted model is relatively simple to estimate, it is convenient to have a statistic that only requires estimation under the null. Such a statistic is Rao's (1948) **score statistic**, also called the **Lagrange multiplier statistic** in econometrics, based on the work of Aitchison and Silvey (1958). We will focus on Rao's original motivation for the statistic because it leads more directly to test statistics that are used in econometrics. An important point is that, even though Rao, Aitchison and Silvey, Engle (1984), and many others focused on the maximum likelihood setup, the score principle is applicable to any problem where the estimators solve a first-order condition, including the general class of M-estimators.

The score approach is ideally suited for **specification testing**. Typically, the first step in specification testing is to begin with a popular model—one that is relatively easy to estimate and interpret—and nest it within a more complicated model. Then the popular model is tested against the more general alternative to determine if the original model is misspecified. We do not want to estimate the more complicated model unless there is significant evidence against the restricted form of the model. In stating the null and alternative hypotheses, there is no difference between specification testing and classical tests of parameter restrictions. However, in practice, specification testing gives primary importance to the restricted model, and we may have no intention of actually estimating the general model even if the null model is rejected.

We will derive the score test only in the case where no correction is needed for preliminary estimation of nuisance parameters: either there are no such parameters present, or assumption (12.37) holds under H_0. If nuisance parameters are present, we do not explicitly show the score and Hessian depending on $\hat{\gamma}$.

We again assume that there are Q continuously differentiable restrictions imposed on $\boldsymbol{\theta}_{\text{o}}$ under H_0, as in expression (12.62). However, we must also assume that the restrictions define a mapping from $\mathbb{R}^{P-Q}$ to $\mathbb{R}^P$, say, $\mathbf{d}$: $\mathbb{R}^{P-Q} \to \mathbb{R}^P$. In particular, under the null hypothesis, we can write $\boldsymbol{\theta}_o = \mathbf{d}(\boldsymbol{\lambda}_o)$, where $\boldsymbol{\lambda}_o$ is a $(P - Q) \times 1$ vector. We must assume that $\boldsymbol{\lambda}_o$ is in the interior of its parameter space, $\boldsymbol{\Lambda}$, under H_0. We also assume that $\mathbf{d}$ is twice continuously differentiable on the interior of $\boldsymbol{\Lambda}$.

Let $\tilde{\boldsymbol{\lambda}}$ be the solution to the constrained minimization problem

$$\min_{\boldsymbol{\lambda} \in \boldsymbol{\Lambda}} \sum_{i=1}^{N} q[\mathbf{w}_i, \mathbf{d}(\boldsymbol{\lambda})] \tag{12.64}$$

The constrained estimator of $\boldsymbol{\theta}_o$ is simply $\tilde{\boldsymbol{\theta}} \equiv \mathbf{d}(\tilde{\boldsymbol{\lambda}})$. In practice, we do not have to explicitly find the function $\mathbf{d}$; solving problem (12.64) is easily done just by directly imposing the restrictions, especially when the restrictions set certain parameters to hypothesized values (such as zero). Then, we just minimize the resulting objective function over the free parameters.

As an example, consider the nonlinear regression model

$$m(\mathbf{x}, \boldsymbol{\theta}) = \exp[\mathbf{x}\boldsymbol{\beta} + \delta_1(\mathbf{x}\boldsymbol{\beta})^2 + \delta_2(\mathbf{x}\boldsymbol{\beta})^3]$$

where $\mathbf{x}$ is $1 \times K$ and contains unity as its first element. The null hypthosis is H_0: $\delta_1 = \delta_2 = 0$, so that the model with the restrictions imposed is just an exponential regression function, $m(\mathbf{x}, \boldsymbol{\beta}) = \exp(\mathbf{x}\boldsymbol{\beta})$.

The simplest method for deriving the LM test is to use Rao's score principle extended to the M-estimator case. The LM statistic is based on the limiting distribution of

$$N^{-1/2} \sum_{i=1}^{N} \mathbf{s}_i(\tilde{\boldsymbol{\theta}}) \tag{12.65}$$

under H_0. This is the score with respect to the entire vector $\boldsymbol{\theta}$, but we are evaluating it at the restricted estimates. If $\tilde{\boldsymbol{\theta}}$ were replaced by $\hat{\boldsymbol{\theta}}$, then expression (12.65) would be identically zero, which would make it useless as a test statistic. If the restrictions imposed by the null hypothesis are true, then expression (12.65) will not be statistically different from zero.

Assume initially that $\boldsymbol{\theta}_o$ is in the interior of $\boldsymbol{\Theta}$ under H_0; we will discuss how to relax this assumption later. Now $\sqrt{N}(\tilde{\boldsymbol{\theta}} - \boldsymbol{\theta}_o) = \mathrm{O}_p(1)$ by the delta method because $\sqrt{N}(\tilde{\boldsymbol{\lambda}} - \boldsymbol{\lambda}_o) = \mathrm{O}_p(1)$ under the given assumptions. A standard mean value expansion yields

$$N^{-1/2} \sum_{i=1}^{N} \mathbf{s}_i(\tilde{\boldsymbol{\theta}}) = N^{-1/2} \sum_{i=1}^{N} \mathbf{s}_i(\boldsymbol{\theta}_o) + \mathbf{A}_o \sqrt{N}(\tilde{\boldsymbol{\theta}} - \boldsymbol{\theta}_o) + \mathrm{o}_p(1) \tag{12.66}$$

under H_0, where $\mathbf{A}_o$ is given in expression (12.19). But $\mathbf{0} = \sqrt{N}\mathbf{c}(\tilde{\boldsymbol{\theta}}) = \sqrt{N}\mathbf{c}(\boldsymbol{\theta}_o) + \ddot{\mathbf{C}}\sqrt{N}(\tilde{\boldsymbol{\theta}} - \boldsymbol{\theta}_o)$, where $\ddot{\mathbf{C}}$ is the $Q \times P$ Jacobian matrix $\mathbf{C}(\boldsymbol{\theta})$ with rows evaluated at mean values between $\tilde{\boldsymbol{\theta}}$ and $\boldsymbol{\theta}_o$. Under H_0, $\mathbf{c}(\boldsymbol{\theta}_o) = \mathbf{0}$, and plim $\ddot{\mathbf{C}} = \mathbf{C}(\boldsymbol{\theta}_o) \equiv \mathbf{C}_o$. Therefore, under H_0, $\mathbf{C}_o\sqrt{N}(\tilde{\boldsymbol{\theta}} - \boldsymbol{\theta}_o) = o_p(1)$, and so multiplying equation (12.66) through by $\mathbf{C}_o\mathbf{A}_o^{-1}$ gives

$$\mathbf{C}_o\mathbf{A}_o^{-1}N^{-1/2}\sum_{i=1}^{N}\mathbf{s}_i(\tilde{\boldsymbol{\theta}}) = \mathbf{C}_o\mathbf{A}_o^{-1}N^{-1/2}\sum_{i=1}^{N}\mathbf{s}_i(\boldsymbol{\theta}_o) + o_p(1) \tag{12.67}$$

By the CLT, $\mathbf{C}_o\mathbf{A}_o^{-1}N^{-1/2}\sum_{i=1}^{N}\mathbf{s}_i(\boldsymbol{\theta}_o) \xrightarrow{d} \text{Normal}(\mathbf{0}, \mathbf{C}_o\mathbf{A}_o^{-1}\mathbf{B}_o\mathbf{A}_o^{-1}\mathbf{C}_o')$, where $\mathbf{B}_o$ is defined in expression (12.20). Under our assumptions, $\mathbf{C}_o\mathbf{A}_o^{-1}\mathbf{B}_o\mathbf{A}_o^{-1}\mathbf{C}_o'$ has full rank Q, and so

$$\left[N^{-1/2}\sum_{i=1}^{N}\mathbf{s}_i(\tilde{\boldsymbol{\theta}})\right]'\mathbf{A}_o^{-1}\mathbf{C}_o'[\mathbf{C}_o\mathbf{A}_o^{-1}\mathbf{B}_o\mathbf{A}_o^{-1}\mathbf{C}_o']^{-1}\mathbf{C}_o\mathbf{A}_o^{-1}\left[N^{-1/2}\sum_{i=1}^{N}\mathbf{s}_i(\tilde{\boldsymbol{\theta}})\right] \xrightarrow{d} \chi_Q^2$$

The score or LM statistic is given by

$$LM \equiv \left(\sum_{i=1}^{N}\tilde{\mathbf{s}}_i\right)'\tilde{\mathbf{A}}^{-1}\tilde{\mathbf{C}}'(\tilde{\mathbf{C}}\tilde{\mathbf{A}}^{-1}\tilde{\mathbf{B}}\tilde{\mathbf{A}}^{-1}\tilde{\mathbf{C}}')^{-1}\tilde{\mathbf{C}}\tilde{\mathbf{A}}^{-1}\left(\sum_{i=1}^{N}\tilde{\mathbf{s}}_i\right)\Big/N \tag{12.68}$$

where all quantities are evaluated at $\tilde{\boldsymbol{\theta}}$. For example, $\tilde{\mathbf{C}} \equiv \mathbf{C}(\tilde{\boldsymbol{\theta}})$, $\tilde{\mathbf{B}}$ is given in expression (12.45) but with $\tilde{\boldsymbol{\theta}}$ in place of $\hat{\boldsymbol{\theta}}$, and $\tilde{\mathbf{A}}$ is one of the estimators in expression (12.42) or (12.44), again evaluated at $\tilde{\boldsymbol{\theta}}$. Under H_0, $LM \xrightarrow{d} \chi_Q^2$.

For the Wald statistic we assumed that $\boldsymbol{\theta}_o \in \text{int}(\boldsymbol{\Theta})$ under H_0; this assumption is crucial for the statistic to have a limiting chi-square distribution. We will not consider the Wald statistic when $\boldsymbol{\theta}_o$ is on the boundary of $\boldsymbol{\Theta}$ under H_0; see Wolak (1991) for some results. The general derivation of the LM statistic also assumed that $\boldsymbol{\theta}_o \in \text{int}(\boldsymbol{\Theta})$ under H_0. Nevertheless, for certain applications of the LM test we can drop the requirement that $\boldsymbol{\theta}_o$ is in the interior of $\boldsymbol{\Theta}$ under H_0. A leading case occurs when $\boldsymbol{\theta}$ can be partitioned as $\boldsymbol{\theta} \equiv (\boldsymbol{\theta}_1', \boldsymbol{\theta}_2')'$, where $\boldsymbol{\theta}_1$ is $(P - Q) \times 1$ and $\boldsymbol{\theta}_2$ is $Q \times 1$. The null hypothesis is H_0: $\boldsymbol{\theta}_{o2} = \mathbf{0}$, so that $\mathbf{c}(\boldsymbol{\theta}) \equiv \boldsymbol{\theta}_2$. It is easy to see that the mean value expansion used to derive the LM statistic is valid provided $\boldsymbol{\lambda}_o \equiv \boldsymbol{\theta}_{o1}$ is in the interior of its parameter space under H_0; $\boldsymbol{\theta}_o \equiv (\boldsymbol{\theta}_{o1}', \mathbf{0})'$ can be on the boundary of $\boldsymbol{\Theta}$. This observation is useful especially when testing hypotheses about parameters that must be either nonnegative or nonpositive.

If we assume the generalized information matrix equality (12.53) with $\sigma_o^2 = 1$, the LM statistic simplifies. The simplification results from the following reasoning: (1) $\tilde{\mathbf{C}}\tilde{\mathbf{D}} = \mathbf{0}$ by the chain rule, where $\tilde{\mathbf{D}} \equiv \nabla_\lambda \mathbf{d}(\tilde{\boldsymbol{\lambda}})$, since $\mathbf{c}[\mathbf{d}(\boldsymbol{\lambda})] \equiv \mathbf{0}$ for $\boldsymbol{\lambda}$ in $\boldsymbol{\Lambda}$. (2) If $\mathbf{E}$ is a $P \times Q$ matrix $\mathbf{E}$ with rank Q, $\mathbf{F}$ is a $P \times (P - Q)$ matrix with rank $P - Q$, and $\mathbf{E}'\mathbf{F} = \mathbf{0}$, then $\mathbf{E}(\mathbf{E}'\mathbf{E})^{-1}\mathbf{E}' = \mathbf{I}_P - \mathbf{F}(\mathbf{F}'\mathbf{F})^{-1}\mathbf{F}'$. (This is simply a statement about projections onto orthogonal subspaces.) Choosing $\mathbf{E} \equiv \tilde{\mathbf{A}}^{-1/2}\tilde{\mathbf{C}}'$ and $\mathbf{F} \equiv \tilde{\mathbf{A}}^{1/2}\tilde{\mathbf{D}}$ gives $\tilde{\mathbf{A}}^{-1/2}\tilde{\mathbf{C}}'(\tilde{\mathbf{C}}\tilde{\mathbf{A}}^{-1}\tilde{\mathbf{C}}')^{-1}\tilde{\mathbf{C}}\tilde{\mathbf{A}}^{-1/2} = \mathbf{I}_P - \tilde{\mathbf{A}}^{1/2}\tilde{\mathbf{D}}(\tilde{\mathbf{D}}'\tilde{\mathbf{A}}\tilde{\mathbf{D}})^{-1}\tilde{\mathbf{D}}'\tilde{\mathbf{A}}^{1/2}$. Now, pre- and post-multiply this equality by $\tilde{\mathbf{A}}^{-1/2}$ to get $\tilde{\mathbf{A}}^{-1}\tilde{\mathbf{C}}'(\tilde{\mathbf{C}}\tilde{\mathbf{A}}^{-1}\tilde{\mathbf{C}}')^{-1}\tilde{\mathbf{C}}\tilde{\mathbf{A}}^{-1} = \tilde{\mathbf{A}}^{-1} - \tilde{\mathbf{D}}(\tilde{\mathbf{D}}'\tilde{\mathbf{A}}\tilde{\mathbf{D}})^{-1}\tilde{\mathbf{D}}'$. (3) Plug $\tilde{\mathbf{B}} = \tilde{\mathbf{A}}$ into expression (12.68) and use step 2, along with the first-order condition $\tilde{\mathbf{D}}'(\sum_{i=1}^N \tilde{\mathbf{s}}_i) = \mathbf{0}$, to get

$$LM = \left(\sum_{i=1}^N \tilde{\mathbf{s}}_i\right)' \tilde{\mathbf{M}}^{-1} \left(\sum_{i=1}^N \tilde{\mathbf{s}}_i\right) \tag{12.69}$$

where $\tilde{\mathbf{M}}$ can be chosen as $\sum_{i=1}^N \tilde{\mathbf{A}}_i$, $\sum_{i=1}^N \tilde{\mathbf{H}}_i$, or $\sum_{i=1}^N \tilde{\mathbf{s}}_i\tilde{\mathbf{s}}_i'$. (Each of these expressions consistently estimates $\mathbf{A}_o = \mathbf{B}_o$ when divided by N.) The last choice of $\tilde{\mathbf{M}}$ results in a statistic that is N times the uncentered R-squared, say R_0^2, from the regression

$$1 \text{ on } \tilde{\mathbf{s}}_i', \qquad i = 1, 2, \ldots, N \tag{12.70}$$

(Recall that $\tilde{\mathbf{s}}_i'$ is a $1 \times P$ vector.) Because the dependent variable in regression (12.70) is unity, NR_0^2 is equivalent to $N - \text{SSR}_0$, where SSR_0 is the sum of squared residuals from regression (12.70). This is often called the **outer product of the score LM statistic** because of the estimator it uses for $\mathbf{A}_o$. While this statistic is simple to compute, there is ample evidence that it can have severe size distortions (typically, the null hypothesis is rejected much more often than the nominal size of the test). See, for example, Davidson and MacKinnon (1993), Bera and McKenzie (1986), Orme (1990), and Chesher and Spady (1991).

The **Hessian form of the LM statistic** uses $\tilde{\mathbf{M}} = \sum_{i=1}^N \tilde{\mathbf{H}}_i$, and it has a few drawbacks: (1) the LM statistic can be negative if the average estimated Hessian is not positive definite; (2) it requires computation of the second derivatives; and (3) it is not invariant to reparameterizations. We will discuss the last problem later.

A statistic that always avoids the first problem, and often the second and third problems, is based on $\mathrm{E}[\mathbf{H}(\mathbf{w}, \boldsymbol{\theta}_o) \mid \mathbf{x}]$, assuming that $\mathbf{w}$ partitions into endogenous variables $\mathbf{y}$ and exogenous variables $\mathbf{x}$. We call the LM statistic that uses $\tilde{\mathbf{M}} = \sum_{i=1}^N \tilde{\mathbf{A}}_i$ the **expected Hessian form of the LM statistic**. This name comes from the fact that the statistic is based on the *conditional* expectation of $\mathbf{H}(\mathbf{w}, \boldsymbol{\theta}_o)$ given $\mathbf{x}$. When it can be computed, the expected Hessian form is usually preferred because it tends to have the best small sample properties.

The LM statistic in equation (12.69) is valid only when $\mathbf{B}_o = \mathbf{A}_o$, and therefore it is not robust to failures of auxiliary assumptions in some important models. If $\mathbf{B}_o \neq \mathbf{A}_o$, the limiting distribution of equation (12.69) is not chi-square and is not suitable for testing.

In the context of NLS, the expected Hessian form of the LM statistic needs to be modified for the presence of σ_o^2, assuming that Assumption NLS.3 holds under H_0. Let $\tilde{\sigma}^2 \equiv N^{-1}\sum_{i=1}^N \tilde{u}_i^2$ be the estimate of σ_o^2 using the restricted estimator of $\boldsymbol{\theta}_o$: $\tilde{u}_i \equiv y_i - m(\mathbf{x}_i, \tilde{\boldsymbol{\theta}})$, $i = 1, 2, \ldots, N$. It is customary not to make a degrees-of-freedom adjustment when estimating the variance using the null estimates, partly because the sum of squared residuals for the restricted model is always larger than for the unrestricted model. The score evaluated at the restricted estimates can be written as $\tilde{\mathbf{s}}_i = \nabla_\theta \tilde{m}_i' \tilde{u}_i$. Thus the LM statistic that imposes homoskedasticity is

$$LM = \left(\sum_{i=1}^N \nabla_\theta \tilde{m}_i' \tilde{u}_i\right)' \left(\sum_{i=1}^N \nabla_\theta \tilde{m}_i' \nabla_\theta \tilde{m}_i\right)^{-1} \left(\sum_{i=1}^N \nabla_\theta \tilde{m}_i' \tilde{u}_i\right) / \tilde{\sigma}^2 \tag{12.71}$$

A little algebra shows that this expression is identical to N times the uncentered R-squared, R_u^2, from the auxiliary regression

$$\tilde{u}_i \text{ on } \nabla_\theta \tilde{m}_i, \qquad i = 1, 2, \ldots, N \tag{12.72}$$

In other words, just regress the residuals from the restricted model on the gradient with respect to the *unrestricted* mean function but evaluated at the *restricted* estimates. Under H_0 and Assumption NLS.3, $LM = NR_u^2 \overset{a}{\sim} \chi_Q^2$.

In the nonlinear regression example with $m(\mathbf{x}, \boldsymbol{\theta}) = \exp[\mathbf{x}\boldsymbol{\beta} + \delta_1(\mathbf{x}\boldsymbol{\beta})^2 + \delta_2(\mathbf{x}\boldsymbol{\beta})^3]$, let $\tilde{\boldsymbol{\beta}}$ be the restricted NLS estimator with $\delta_1 = 0$ and $\delta_2 = 0$; in other words, $\tilde{\boldsymbol{\beta}}$ is from a nonlinear regression with an exponential regression function. The restricted residuals are $\tilde{u}_i = y_i - \exp(\mathbf{x}_i\tilde{\boldsymbol{\beta}})$, and the gradient of $m(\mathbf{x}, \boldsymbol{\theta})$ with respect to all parameters, evaluated at the null, is

$$\nabla_\theta m(\mathbf{x}_i, \boldsymbol{\beta}_o, \mathbf{0}) = \{\mathbf{x}_i \exp(\mathbf{x}_i\boldsymbol{\beta}_o), (\mathbf{x}_i\boldsymbol{\beta}_o)^2 \exp(\mathbf{x}_i\boldsymbol{\beta}_o), (\mathbf{x}_i\boldsymbol{\beta}_o)^3 \exp(\mathbf{x}_i\boldsymbol{\beta}_o)\}$$

Plugging in $\tilde{\boldsymbol{\beta}}$ gives $\nabla_\theta \tilde{m}_i = [\mathbf{x}_i\tilde{m}_i, (\mathbf{x}_i\tilde{\boldsymbol{\beta}})^2\tilde{m}_i, (\mathbf{x}_i\tilde{\boldsymbol{\beta}})^3\tilde{m}_i]$, where $\tilde{m}_i \equiv \exp(\mathbf{x}_i\tilde{\boldsymbol{\beta}})$. Regression (12.72) becomes

$$\tilde{u}_i \text{ on } \mathbf{x}_i\tilde{m}_i, \; (\mathbf{x}_i\tilde{\boldsymbol{\beta}})^2\tilde{m}_i, \; (\mathbf{x}_i\tilde{\boldsymbol{\beta}})^3\tilde{m}_i, \qquad i = 1, 2, \ldots, N \tag{12.73}$$

Under H_0 and homoskedasticity, $NR_u^2 \sim \chi_2^2$, since there are two restrictions being tested. This is a fairly simple way to test the exponential functional form without ever estimating the more complicated alternative model. Other models that nest the exponential model are discussed in Wooldridge (1992).

This example illustrates an important point: even though $\sum_{i=1}^N (\mathbf{x}_i\tilde{m}_i)'\tilde{u}_i$ is identically zero by the first-order condition for NLS, the term $\mathbf{x}_i\tilde{m}_i$ must generally be included in regression (12.73). The R-squared from the regression without $\mathbf{x}_i\tilde{m}_i$ will be different because the remaining regressors in regression (12.73) are usually correlated with $\mathbf{x}_i\tilde{m}_i$ in the sample. [More importantly, for $h = 2$ and 3, $(\mathbf{x}_i\boldsymbol{\beta})^h \exp(\mathbf{x}_i\boldsymbol{\beta})$ is probably correlated with $\mathbf{x}_i\boldsymbol{\beta}$ in the population.] As a general rule, the entire gradient $\nabla_\theta \tilde{m}_i$ must appear in the auxiliary regression.

In order to be robust against failure of Assumption NLS.3, the more general form of the statistic in expression (12.68) should be used. Fortunately, this statistic also can be easily computed for most hypotheses. Partition $\boldsymbol{\theta}$ into the $(P - Q) \times 1$ vector $\boldsymbol{\beta}$ and the Q vector $\boldsymbol{\delta}$. Assume that the null hypothesis is H_0: $\boldsymbol{\delta}_{\mathrm{o}} = \bar{\boldsymbol{\delta}}$, where $\bar{\boldsymbol{\delta}}$ is a prespecified vector (often containing all zeros, but not always). Let $\nabla_\beta \tilde{m}_i$ $[1 \times (P - Q)]$ and $\nabla_\delta \tilde{m}_i$ $(1 \times Q)$ denote the gradients with respect to $\boldsymbol{\beta}$ and $\boldsymbol{\delta}$, respectively, evaluated at $\tilde{\boldsymbol{\beta}}$ and $\bar{\boldsymbol{\delta}}$. After tedious algebra, and using the special structure $\mathbf{C}(\boldsymbol{\theta}) = [\mathbf{0} \,|\, \mathbf{I}_Q]$, where $\mathbf{0}$ is a $Q \times (P - Q)$ matrix of zero, the following procedure can be shown to produce expression (12.68):

1. Run a multivariate regression

$$\nabla_\delta \tilde{m}_i \text{ on } \nabla_\beta \tilde{m}_i, \qquad i = 1, 2, \ldots, N \tag{12.74}$$

and save the $1 \times Q$ vector residuals, say $\tilde{\mathbf{r}}_i$. Then, for each i, form $\tilde{u}_i \tilde{\mathbf{r}}_i$. (That is, multiply $\tilde{u}_i$ by each element of $\tilde{\mathbf{r}}_i$.)

2. $LM = N - \mathrm{SSR}_0 = NR_0^2$ from the regression

$$1 \text{ on } \tilde{u}_i \tilde{\mathbf{r}}_i, \qquad i = 1, 2, \ldots, N \tag{12.75}$$

where SSR_0 is the usual sum of squared residuals. This step produces a statistic that has a limiting χ_Q^2 distribution whether or not Assumption NLS.3 holds. See Wooldridge (1991a) for more discussion.

We can illustrate the heteroskedasticity-robust test using the preceding exponential model. Regression (12.74) is the same as regressing each of $(\mathbf{x}_i\tilde{\boldsymbol{\beta}})^2 \tilde{m}_i$ and $(\mathbf{x}_i\tilde{\boldsymbol{\beta}})^3 \tilde{m}_i$ onto $\mathbf{x}_i \tilde{m}_i$, and saving the residuals $\tilde{r}_{i1}$ and $\tilde{r}_{i2}$, respectively (N each). Then, regression (12.75) is simply 1 on $\tilde{u}_i \tilde{r}_{i1}$, $\tilde{u}_i \tilde{r}_{i2}$. The number of regressors in the final regression of the robust test is always the same as the degrees of freedom of the test.

Finally, these procedures are easily modified for WNLS. Simply multiply both $\tilde{u}_i$ and $\nabla_\theta \tilde{m}_i$ by $1/\sqrt{\tilde{h}_i}$, where the variance estimates $\tilde{h}_i$ are based on the null model (so we use a $\sim$ rather than a $\wedge$). The nonrobust LM statistic that maintains Assumption WNLS.3 is obtained as in regression (12.72). The robust form, which allows $\mathrm{Var}(y \,|\, \mathbf{x}) \neq \sigma_{\mathrm{o}}^2 h(\mathbf{x}, \boldsymbol{\gamma}_{\mathrm{o}})$, follows exactly as in regressions (12.74) and (12.75).

The invariance issue for the score statistic is somewhat complicated, but several results are known. First, it is easy to see that the outer product form of the statistic is invariant to differentiable reparameterizations. Write $\boldsymbol{\phi} = \mathbf{g}(\boldsymbol{\theta})$ as a twice continuously differentiable, invertible reparameterization; thus the $P \times P$ Jacobian of $\mathbf{g}$,

$\mathbf{G}(\boldsymbol{\theta})$, is nonsingular for all $\boldsymbol{\theta} \in \boldsymbol{\Theta}$. The objective function in terms of $\boldsymbol{\phi}$ is $q^g(\mathbf{w}, \boldsymbol{\phi})$, and we must have $q^g[\mathbf{w}, \mathbf{g}(\boldsymbol{\theta})] = q(\mathbf{w}, \boldsymbol{\theta})$ for all $\boldsymbol{\theta} \in \boldsymbol{\Theta}$. Differentiating and transposing gives $\mathbf{s}(\mathbf{w}, \boldsymbol{\theta}) = \mathbf{G}(\boldsymbol{\theta})'\mathbf{s}^g[\mathbf{w}, \mathbf{g}(\boldsymbol{\theta})]$, where $\mathbf{s}^g(\mathbf{w}, \boldsymbol{\phi})$ is the score of $q^g[\mathbf{w}, \boldsymbol{\phi}]$. If $\tilde{\boldsymbol{\phi}}$ is the restricted estimator of $\boldsymbol{\phi}$, then $\tilde{\boldsymbol{\phi}} = \mathbf{g}(\tilde{\boldsymbol{\theta}})$, and so, for each observation i, $\tilde{\mathbf{s}}_i^g = (\tilde{\mathbf{G}}')^{-1}\tilde{\mathbf{s}}_i$. Plugging this equation into the LM statistic in equation (12.69), with $\tilde{\mathbf{M}}$ chosen as the outer product form, shows that the statistic based on $\tilde{\mathbf{s}}_i^g$ is identical to that based on $\tilde{\mathbf{s}}_i$.

Score statistics based on the estimated Hessian are not generally invariant to reparameterization because they can involve second derivatives of the function $\mathbf{g}(\boldsymbol{\theta})$; see Davidson and MacKinnon (1993, Section 13.6) for details. However, when $\mathbf{w}$ partitions as $(\mathbf{x}, \mathbf{y})$, score statistics based on the expected Hessian (conditional on $\mathbf{x}$), $\mathbf{A}(\mathbf{x}, \boldsymbol{\theta})$, *are* often invariant. In Chapter 13 we will see that this is always the case for conditional maximum likelihood estimation. Invariance also holds for NLS and WNLS for both the usual and robust LM statistics because any reparameterization comes through the conditional mean. Predicted values and residuals are invariant to reparameterization, and the statistics obtained from regressions (12.72) and (12.75) only involve the residuals and first derivatives of the conditional mean function. As in the usual outer product LM statistic, the Jacobian in the first derivative cancels out.

12.6.3 Tests Based on the Change in the Objective Function

When both the restricted and unrestricted models are easy to estimate, a test based on the change in the objective function can greatly simplify the mechanics of obtaining a test statistic: we only need to obtain the value of the objective function with and without the restrictions imposed. However, the computational simplicity comes at a price in terms of robustness. Unlike the Wald and score tests, a test based on the change in the objective function *cannot* be made robust to general failure of assumption (12.53). Therefore, throughout this subsection we assume that the generalized information matrix equality holds. Because the minimized objective function is invariant with respect to any reparameterization, the test statistic is invariant.

In the context of two-step estimators, we must also assume that $\hat{\gamma}$ has no effect on the asymptotic distribution of the M-estimator. That is, we maintain assumption (12.37) when nuisance parameter estimates appear in the objective function (see Problem 12.8).

We first consider the case where $\sigma_o^2 = 1$, so that $\mathbf{B}_o = \mathbf{A}_o$. Using a second-order Taylor expansion,

$$\sum_{i=1}^{N} q(\mathbf{w}_i, \tilde{\boldsymbol{\theta}}) - \sum_{i=1}^{N} q(\mathbf{w}_i, \hat{\boldsymbol{\theta}}) = \sum_{i=1}^{N} \mathbf{s}_i(\hat{\boldsymbol{\theta}}) + (1/2)(\tilde{\boldsymbol{\theta}} - \hat{\boldsymbol{\theta}})' \left(\sum_{i=1}^{N} \ddot{\mathbf{H}}_i \right) (\tilde{\boldsymbol{\theta}} - \hat{\boldsymbol{\theta}})$$

where $\ddot{\mathbf{H}}_i$ is the $P \times P$ Hessian evaluate at mean values between $\tilde{\boldsymbol{\theta}}$ and $\hat{\boldsymbol{\theta}}$. Therefore, under H_0 (using the first-order condition for $\hat{\boldsymbol{\theta}}$), we have

$$2\left[\sum_{i=1}^{N} q(\mathbf{w}_i, \tilde{\boldsymbol{\theta}}) - \sum_{i=1}^{N} q(\mathbf{w}_i, \hat{\boldsymbol{\theta}})\right] = [\sqrt{N}(\tilde{\boldsymbol{\theta}} - \hat{\boldsymbol{\theta}})]'\mathbf{A}_0[\sqrt{N}(\tilde{\boldsymbol{\theta}} - \hat{\boldsymbol{\theta}})] + \mathrm{o}_p(1) \tag{12.76}$$

since $N^{-1}\sum_{i=1}^{N} \ddot{\mathbf{H}}_i = \mathbf{A}_\mathrm{o} + o_p\ (1)$ and $\sqrt{N}(\tilde{\boldsymbol{\theta}} - \hat{\boldsymbol{\theta}}) = \mathrm{O}_p(1)$. In fact, it follows from equations (12.33) (without $\hat{\gamma}$) and (12.66) that $\sqrt{N}(\tilde{\boldsymbol{\theta}} - \hat{\boldsymbol{\theta}}) = \mathbf{A}_\mathrm{o}^{-1} N^{-1/2} \sum_{i=1}^{N} \mathbf{s}_i(\tilde{\boldsymbol{\theta}}) + \mathrm{o}_p(1)$. Plugging this equation into equation (12.76) shows that

$$\begin{aligned} QLR &\equiv 2\left[\sum_{i=1}^{N} q(\mathbf{w}_i, \tilde{\boldsymbol{\theta}}) - \sum_{i=1}^{N} q(\mathbf{w}_i, \hat{\boldsymbol{\theta}})\right] \\ &= \left(N^{-1/2}\sum_{i=1}^{N} \tilde{\mathbf{s}}_i\right)' \mathbf{A}_\mathrm{o}^{-1} \left(N^{-1/2}\sum_{i=1}^{N} \tilde{\mathbf{s}}_i\right) + \mathrm{o}_p(1) \end{aligned} \tag{12.77}$$

so that QLR has the same limiting distribution, χ^2_Q, as the LM statistic under H_0. [See equation (12.69), remembering that $\mathrm{plim}(\tilde{\mathbf{M}}/N) = \mathbf{A}_\mathrm{o}$.] We call statistic (12.77) the **quasi-likelihood ratio (QLR) statistic**, which comes from the fact that the leading example of equation (12.77) is the likelihood ratio statistic in the context of maximum likelihood estimation, as we will see in Chapter 13. We could also call equation (12.77) a **criterion function statistic**, as it is based on the difference in the criterion or objective function with and without the restrictions imposed.

When nuisance parameters are present, the same estimate, say $\hat{\gamma}$, should be used in obtaining the restricted and unrestricted estimates. This is to ensure that QLR is nonnegative given any sample. Typically, $\hat{\gamma}$ would be based on initial estimation of the unrestricted model.

If $\sigma_\mathrm{o}^2 \neq 1$, we simply divide QLR by $\hat{\sigma}^2$, which is a consistent estimator of σ_o^2 obtained from the unrestricted estimation. For example, consider NLS under Assumptions NLS.1–NLS.3. When equation (12.77) is divided by $\hat{\sigma}^2$ in equation (12.57), we obtain $(\mathrm{SSR}_r - \mathrm{SSR}_{ur})/[\mathrm{SSR}_{ur}/(N - P)]$, where SSR_r and SSR_{ur} are the restricted and unrestricted sums of squared residuals. Sometimes an F version of this statistic is used instead, which is obtained by dividing the chi-square version by Q:

$$F = \frac{(\mathrm{SSR}_r - \mathrm{SSR}_{ur})}{\mathrm{SSR}_{ur}} \cdot \frac{(N - P)}{Q} \tag{12.78}$$

This has exactly the same form as the F statistic from classical linear regression analysis. Under the null hypothesis and homoskedasticity, F can be treated as having an approximate $\mathscr{F}_{Q,N-P}$ distribution. (As always, this treatment is justified because $Q \cdot \mathscr{F}_{Q,N-P} \overset{a}{\sim} \chi^2_Q$ as $N - P \to \infty$.) Some authors (for example, Gallant, 1987) have found that F has better finite sample properties than the chi-square version of the statistic.

For weighted NLS, the same statistic works under Assumption WNLS.3 provided the residuals (both restricted and unrestricted) are weighted by $1/\sqrt{\hat{h}_i}$, where the $\hat{h}_i$ are obtained from estimation of the unrestricted model.

12.6.4 Behavior of the Statistics under Alternatives

To keep the notation and assumptions as simple as possible, and to focus on the computation of valid test statistics under various assumptions, we have only derived the limiting distribution of the classical test statistics under the null hypothesis. It is also important to know how the tests behave under alternative hypotheses in order to choose a test with the highest power.

All the tests we have discussed are consistent against the alternatives they are specifically designed against. While this consistency is desirable, it tells us nothing about the likely finite sample power that a statistic will have against particular alternatives. A framework that allows us to say more uses the notion of a sequence of **local alternatives**. Specifying a local alternative is a device that can approximate the finite sample power of test statistics for alternatives "close" to H_0. If the null hypothesis is H_0: $\mathbf{c}(\boldsymbol{\theta}_\mathrm{o}) = \mathbf{0}$ then a sequence of local alternatives is

$$\mathrm{H}_1^N\colon \mathbf{c}(\boldsymbol{\theta}_{\mathrm{o},N}) = \boldsymbol{\delta}_\mathrm{o}/\sqrt{N} \tag{12.79}$$

where $\boldsymbol{\delta}_\mathrm{o}$ is a given $Q \times 1$ vector. As $N \to \infty$, H_1^N approaches H_0, since $\boldsymbol{\delta}_\mathrm{o}/\sqrt{N} \to \mathbf{0}$. The division by $\sqrt{N}$ means that the alternatives are local: for given N, equation (12.79) is an alternative to H_0, but as $N \to \infty$, the alternative gets closer to H_0. Dividing $\boldsymbol{\delta}_\mathrm{o}$ by $\sqrt{N}$ ensures that each of the statistics has a well-defined limiting distribution under the alternative that differs from the limiting distribution under H_0.

It can be shown that, under equation (12.79), the general forms of the Wald and LM statistics have a limiting *noncentral* chi-square distribution with Q degrees of freedom under the regularity conditions used to obtain their null limiting distributions. The noncentrality parameter depends on $\mathbf{A}_\mathrm{o}$, $\mathbf{B}_\mathrm{o}$, $\mathbf{C}_\mathrm{o}$, and $\boldsymbol{\delta}_\mathrm{o}$, and can be estimated by using consistent estimators of $\mathbf{A}_\mathrm{o}$, $\mathbf{B}_\mathrm{o}$, and $\mathbf{C}_\mathrm{o}$. When we add assumption (12.53), then the special versions of the Wald and LM statistics and the QLR statistics have limiting noncentral chi-square distributions. For various $\boldsymbol{\delta}_\mathrm{o}$, we can estimate what is known as the **asymptotic local power** of the test statistics by computing probabilities from noncentral chi-square distributions.

Consider the Wald statistic where $\mathbf{B}_o = \mathbf{A}_o$. Denote by $\boldsymbol{\theta}_o$ the limit of $\boldsymbol{\theta}_{o,N}$ as $N \to \infty$. The usual mean value expansion under H_1^N gives

$$\sqrt{N}\mathbf{c}(\hat{\boldsymbol{\theta}}) = \boldsymbol{\delta}_o + \mathbf{C}(\boldsymbol{\theta}_o)\sqrt{N}(\hat{\boldsymbol{\theta}} - \boldsymbol{\theta}_{o,N}) + o_p(1)$$

and, under standard assumptions, $\sqrt{N}(\hat{\boldsymbol{\theta}} - \boldsymbol{\theta}_{o,N}) \overset{a}{\sim} \mathrm{Normal}(\mathbf{0}, \mathbf{A}_o^{-1})$. Therefore, $\sqrt{N}\mathbf{c}(\hat{\boldsymbol{\theta}}) \overset{a}{\sim} \mathrm{Normal}(\boldsymbol{\delta}_o, \mathbf{C}_o\mathbf{A}_o^{-1}\mathbf{C}_o')$ under the sequence (12.79). This result implies that the Wald statistic has a limiting noncentral chi-square distribution with Q degrees of freedom and noncentrality parameter $\boldsymbol{\delta}_o'(\mathbf{C}_o\mathbf{A}_o^{-1}\mathbf{C}_o')^{-1}\boldsymbol{\delta}_o$. This turns out to be the same noncentrality parameter for the LM and QLR statistics when $\mathbf{B}_o = \mathbf{A}_o$. The details are similar to those under H_0; see, for example, Gallant (1987, Section 3.6).

The statistic with the largest noncentrality parameter has the largest asymptotic local power. For choosing among the Wald, LM, and QLR statistics, this criterion does not help: they all have the same noncentrality parameters under equation (12.79). [For the QLR statistic, assumption (12.53) must also be maintained.]

The notion of local alternatives is useful when choosing among statistics based on different *estimators*. Not surprisingly, the more efficient estimator produces tests with the best asymptotic local power under standard assumptions. But we should keep in mind the efficiency–robustness trade-off, especially when efficient test statistics are computed under tenuous assumptions.

General analyses under local alternatives are available in Gallant (1987), Gallant and White (1988), and White (1994). See Andrews (1989) for innovative suggestions for using local power analysis in applied work.

12.7 Optimization Methods

In this section we briefly discuss three iterative schemes that can be used to solve the general minimization problem (12.8) or (12.31). In the latter case, the minimization is only over $\boldsymbol{\theta}$, so the presence of $\hat{\gamma}$ changes nothing. If $\hat{\gamma}$ is present, the score and Hessian with respect to $\boldsymbol{\theta}$ are simply evaluated at $\hat{\gamma}$. These methods are closely related to the asymptotic variance matrix estimators and test statistics we discussed in Sections 12.5 and 12.6.

12.7.1 The Newton-Raphson Method

Iterative methods are defined by an algorithm for going from one iteration to the next. Let $\boldsymbol{\theta}^{\{g\}}$ be the $P \times 1$ vector on the gth iteration, and let $\boldsymbol{\theta}^{\{g+1\}}$ be the value on the next iteration. To motivate how we get from $\boldsymbol{\theta}^{\{g\}}$ to $\boldsymbol{\theta}^{\{g+1\}}$, use a mean value expansion (row by row) to write

$$\sum_{i=1}^{N} \mathbf{s}_i(\boldsymbol{\theta}^{\{g+1\}}) = \sum_{i=1}^{N} \mathbf{s}_i(\boldsymbol{\theta}^{\{g\}}) + \left[\sum_{i=1}^{N} \mathbf{H}_i(\boldsymbol{\theta}^{\{g\}})\right](\boldsymbol{\theta}^{\{g+1\}} - \boldsymbol{\theta}^{\{g\}}) + \mathbf{r}^{\{g\}} \tag{12.80}$$

where $\mathbf{s}_i(\boldsymbol{\theta})$ is the $P \times 1$ score with respect to $\boldsymbol{\theta}$, evaluated at observation i, $\mathbf{H}_i(\boldsymbol{\theta})$ is the $P \times P$ Hessian, and $\mathbf{r}^{\{g\}}$ is a $P \times 1$ vector of remainder terms. We are trying to find the solution $\hat{\boldsymbol{\theta}}$ to equation (12.14). *If* $\boldsymbol{\theta}^{\{g+1\}} = \hat{\boldsymbol{\theta}}$, then the left-hand side of equation (12.80) is zero. Setting the left-hand side to zero, ignoring $\mathbf{r}^{\{g\}}$, and assuming that the Hessian evaluated at $\boldsymbol{\theta}^{\{g\}}$ is nonsingular, we can write

$$\boldsymbol{\theta}^{\{g+1\}} = \boldsymbol{\theta}^{\{g\}} - \left[\sum_{i=1}^{N} \mathbf{H}_i(\boldsymbol{\theta}^{\{g\}})\right]^{-1} \left[\sum_{i=1}^{N} \mathbf{s}_i(\boldsymbol{\theta}^{\{g\}})\right] \tag{12.81}$$

Equation (12.81) provides an iterative method for finding $\hat{\boldsymbol{\theta}}$. To begin the iterations we must choose a vector of starting values; call this vector $\boldsymbol{\theta}^{\{0\}}$. Good starting values are often difficult to come by, and sometimes we must experiment with several choices before the problem converges. Ideally, the iterations wind up at the same place regardless of the starting values, but this outcome is not guaranteed. Given the starting values, we plug $\boldsymbol{\theta}^{\{0\}}$ into the right-hand side of equation (12.81) to get $\boldsymbol{\theta}^{\{1\}}$. Then, we plug $\boldsymbol{\theta}^{\{1\}}$ into equation (12.81) to get $\boldsymbol{\theta}^{\{2\}}$, and so on.

If the iterations are proceeding toward the minimum, the increments $\boldsymbol{\theta}^{\{g+1\}} - \boldsymbol{\theta}^{\{g\}}$ will eventually become very small: as we near the solution, $\sum_{i=1}^{N} \mathbf{s}_i(\boldsymbol{\theta}^{\{g\}})$ gets close to zero. Some use as a stopping rule the requirement that the largest absolute change $|\theta_j^{\{g+1\}} - \theta_j^{\{g\}}|$, for $j = 1, 2, \ldots, P$, is smaller than some small constant; others prefer to look at the largest *percentage* change in the parameter values.

Another popular stopping rule is based on the quadratic form

$$\left[\sum_{i=1}^{N} \mathbf{s}_i(\boldsymbol{\theta}^{\{g\}})\right]' \left[\sum_{i=1}^{N} \mathbf{H}_i(\boldsymbol{\theta}^{\{g\}})\right]^{-1} \left[\sum_{i=1}^{N} \mathbf{s}_i(\boldsymbol{\theta}^{\{g\}})\right] \tag{12.82}$$

where the iterations stop when expression (12.82) is less than some suitably small number, say .0001.

The iterative scheme just outlined is usually called the **Newton-Raphson method**. It is known to work in a variety of circumstances. Our motivation here has been heuristic, and we will not investigate situations under which the Newton-Raphson method does not work well. (See, for example, Quandt, 1983, for some theoretical results.) The Newton-Raphson method has some drawbacks. First, it requires computing the second derivatives of the objective function at every iteration. These calculations are not very taxing if closed forms for the second partials are available, but in many cases they are not. A second problem is that, as we saw for the case of nonlinear least squares, the sum of the Hessians evaluated at a particular value of $\boldsymbol{\theta}$ may not be positive definite. If the inverted Hessian in expression (12.81) is not positive definite, the procedure may head in the wrong direction.

We should always check that progress is being made from one iteration to the next by computing the difference in the values of the objective function from one iteration to the next:

$$\sum_{i=1}^{N} q_i(\boldsymbol{\theta}^{\{g+1\}}) - \sum_{i=1}^{N} q_i(\boldsymbol{\theta}^{\{g\}}) \tag{12.83}$$

Because we are minimizing the objective function, we should not take the step from g to $g+1$ unless expression (12.83) is negative. [If we are maximizing the function, the iterations in equation (12.81) can still be used because the expansion in equation (12.80) is still appropriate, but then we want expression (12.83) to be positive.]

A slight modification of the Newton-Raphson method is sometimes useful to speed up convergence: multiply the Hessian term in expression (12.81) by a positive number, say r, known as the *step size*. Sometimes the step size $r = 1$ produces too large a change in the parameters. If the objective function does not decrease using $r = 1$, then try, say, $r = \frac{1}{2}$. Again, check the value of the objective function. If it has now decreased, go on to the next iteration (where $r = 1$ is usually used at the beginning of each iteration); if the objective function still has not decreased, replace r with, say, $\frac{1}{4}$. Continue halving r until the objective function decreases. If you have not succeeded in decreasing the objective function after several choices of r, new starting values might be needed. Or, a different optimization method might be needed.

12.7.2 The Berndt, Hall, Hall, and Hausman Algorithm

In the context of maximum likelihood estimation, Berndt, Hall, Hall, and Hausman (1974) (hereafter, BHHH) proposed using the outer product of the score in place of the Hessian. This method can be applied in the general M-estimation case [even though the information matrix equality (12.53) that motivates the method need not hold]. The BHHH iteration for a minimization problem is

$$\boldsymbol{\theta}^{\{g+1\}} = \boldsymbol{\theta}^{\{g\}} - r\left[\sum_{i=1}^{N} \mathbf{s}_i(\boldsymbol{\theta}^{\{g\}})\mathbf{s}_i(\boldsymbol{\theta}^{\{g\}})'\right]^{-1}\left[\sum_{i=1}^{N} \mathbf{s}_i(\boldsymbol{\theta}^{\{g\}})\right] \tag{12.84}$$

where r is the step size. [If we want to maximize $\sum_{i=1}^{N} q(\mathbf{w}_i, \boldsymbol{\theta})$, the minus sign in equation (12.84) should be replaced with a plus sign.] The term multiplying r, sometimes called the *direction* for the next iteration, can be obtained as the $P \times 1$ OLS coefficients from the regression

$$1 \text{ on } \mathbf{s}_i(\boldsymbol{\theta}^{\{g\}})', \qquad i = 1, 2, \ldots, N \tag{12.85}$$

The BHHH procedure is easy to implement because it requires computation of the score only; second derivatives are not needed. Further, since the sum of the outer product of the scores is always at least positive semidefinite, it does not suffer from the potential nonpositive definiteness of the Hessian.

A convenient stopping rule for the BHHH method is obtained as in expression (12.82), but with the sum of the outer products of the score replacing the sum of the Hessians. This is identical to N times the uncentered R-squared from regression (12.85). Interestingly, this is the same regression used to obtain the outer product of the score form of the LM statistic when $\mathbf{B}_o = \mathbf{A}_o$, and this fact suggests a natural method for estimating a complicated model after a simpler version of the model has been estimated. Set the starting value, $\boldsymbol{\theta}^{\{0\}}$, equal to the vector of restricted estimates, $\tilde{\boldsymbol{\theta}}$. Then NR_0^2 from the regression used to obtain the first iteration can be used to test the restricted model against the more general model to be estimated; if the restrictions are not rejected, we could just stop the iterations. Of course, as we discussed in Section 12.6.2, this form of the LM statistic is often ill-behaved even with fairly large sample sizes.

12.7.3 The Generalized Gauss-Newton Method

The final iteration scheme we cover is closely related to the estimator of the expected value of the Hessian in expression (12.44). Let $\mathbf{A}(\mathbf{x}, \boldsymbol{\theta}_o)$ be the expected value of $\mathbf{H}(\mathbf{w}, \boldsymbol{\theta}_o)$ conditional on $\mathbf{x}$, where $\mathbf{w}$ is partitioned into $\mathbf{y}$ and $\mathbf{x}$. Then the **generalized Gauss-Newton method** uses the updating equation

$$\boldsymbol{\theta}^{\{g+1\}} = \boldsymbol{\theta}^{\{g\}} - r\left[\sum_{i=1}^{N} \mathbf{A}_i(\boldsymbol{\theta}^{\{g\}})\right]^{-1}\left[\sum_{i=1}^{N} \mathbf{s}_i(\boldsymbol{\theta}^{\{g\}})\right] \tag{12.86}$$

where $\boldsymbol{\theta}^{\{g\}}$ replaces $\boldsymbol{\theta}_o$ in $\mathbf{A}(\mathbf{x}_i, \boldsymbol{\theta}_o)$. (As before, $\mathbf{A}_i$ and $\mathbf{s}_i$ might also depend on $\hat{\gamma}$.) This scheme works well when $\mathbf{A}(\mathbf{x}, \boldsymbol{\theta}_o)$ can be obtained in closed form.

In the special case of nonlinear least squares, we obtain what is traditionally called the **Gauss-Newton method** (for example, Quandt, 1983). Since $\mathbf{s}_i(\boldsymbol{\theta}) = -\nabla_\theta m_i(\boldsymbol{\theta})'[y_i - m_i(\boldsymbol{\theta})]$, the iteration step is

$$\boldsymbol{\theta}^{\{g+1\}} = \boldsymbol{\theta}^{\{g\}} + r\left(\sum_{i=1}^{N} \nabla_\theta m_i^{\{g\}\prime} \nabla_\theta m_i^{\{g\}}\right)^{-1}\left(\sum_{i=1}^{N} \nabla_\theta m_i^{\{g\}\prime} u_i^{\{g\}}\right)$$

The term multiplying the step size r is obtained as the OLS coefficients of the regression of the resididuals on the gradient, both evaluated at $\boldsymbol{\theta}^{\{g\}}$. The stopping rule can be based on N times the uncentered R-squared from this regression. Note how closely the Gauss-Newton method of optimization is related to the regression used to obtain the nonrobust LM statistic [see regression (12.72)].

12.7.4 Concentrating Parameters out of the Objective Function

In some cases, it is computationally convenient to *concentrate* one set of parameters out of the objective function. Partition $\boldsymbol{\theta}$ into the vectors $\boldsymbol{\beta}$ and $\boldsymbol{\gamma}$. Then the first-order conditions that define $\hat{\boldsymbol{\theta}}$ are

$$\sum_{i=1}^{N} \nabla_{\beta} q(\mathbf{w}_i, \boldsymbol{\beta}, \boldsymbol{\gamma}) = \mathbf{0}, \qquad \sum_{i=1}^{N} \nabla_{\gamma} q(\mathbf{w}_i, \boldsymbol{\beta}, \boldsymbol{\gamma}) = \mathbf{0} \tag{12.87}$$

Rather than solving these for $\hat{\boldsymbol{\beta}}$ and $\hat{\boldsymbol{\gamma}}$, suppose that the second set of equations can be solved for $\boldsymbol{\gamma}$ as a function of $\mathbf{W} \equiv (\mathbf{w}_1, \mathbf{w}_2, \ldots, \mathbf{w}_N)$ and $\boldsymbol{\beta}$ for any outcomes $\mathbf{W}$ and any $\boldsymbol{\beta}$ in the parameter set $\boldsymbol{\gamma} = \mathbf{g}(\mathbf{W}, \boldsymbol{\beta})$. Then, by construction,

$$\sum_{i=1}^{N} \nabla_{\gamma} q[\mathbf{w}_i, \boldsymbol{\beta}, \mathbf{g}(\mathbf{W}, \boldsymbol{\beta})] = \mathbf{0} \tag{12.88}$$

When we plug $\mathbf{g}(\mathbf{W}, \boldsymbol{\beta})$ into the original objective function, we obtain the **concentrated objective function**,

$$Q^c(\mathbf{W}, \boldsymbol{\beta}) = \sum_{i=1}^{N} q[\mathbf{w}_i, \boldsymbol{\beta}, \mathbf{g}(\mathbf{W}, \boldsymbol{\beta})] \tag{12.89}$$

Under standard differentiability assumptions, the minimizer of equation (12.89) is identical to the $\hat{\boldsymbol{\beta}}$ that solves equations (12.87) (along with $\hat{\boldsymbol{\gamma}}$), as can be seen by differentiating equation (12.89) with respect to $\boldsymbol{\beta}$ using the chain rule, setting the result to zero, and using equation (12.88); then $\hat{\boldsymbol{\gamma}}$ can be obtained as $\mathbf{g}(\mathbf{W}, \hat{\boldsymbol{\beta}})$.

As a device for studying asymptotic properties, the concentrated objective function is of limited value because $\mathbf{g}(\mathbf{W}, \boldsymbol{\beta})$ generally depends on all of $\mathbf{W}$, in which case the objective function cannot be written as the sum of independent, identically distributed summands. One setting where equation (12.89) is a sum of i.i.d. functions occurs when we concentrate out individual-specific effects from certain nonlinear panel data models. In addition, the concentrated objective function can be useful for establishing the equivalence of seemingly different estimation approaches.

12.8 Simulation and Resampling Methods

So far we have focused on the asymptotic properties of M-estimators, as these provide a unified framework for inference. But there are a few good reasons to go beyond asymptotic results, at least in some cases. First, the asymptotic approximations need not be very good, especially with small sample sizes, highly nonlinear models, or unusual features of the population distribution of $\mathbf{w}_i$. Simulation methods, while always special, can help determine how well the asymptotic approximations work. Resampling methods can allow us to improve on the asymptotic distribution approximations.

Even if we feel comfortable with asymptotic approximations to the distribution of $\hat{\boldsymbol{\theta}}$, we may not be as confident in the approximations for estimating a nonlinear function of the parameters, say $\gamma_o = \mathbf{g}(\boldsymbol{\theta}_o)$. Under the assumptions in Section 3.5.2, we can use the delta method to approximate the variance of $\hat{\gamma} = \mathbf{g}(\hat{\boldsymbol{\theta}})$. Depending on the nature of $\mathbf{g}(\cdot)$, applying the delta method might be difficult, and it might not result in a very good approximation. Resampling methods can simplify the calculation of standard errors, confidence intervals, and p-values for test statistics, and we can get a good idea of the amount of finite-sample bias in the estimation method. In addition, under certain assumptions and for certain statistics, resampling methods can provide quantifiable improvements to the usual asymptotics.

12.8.1 Monte Carlo Simulation

In a **Monte Carlo simulation**, we attempt to estimate the mean and variance—assuming that these exist—and possibly other features of the distribution of the M-estimator, $\hat{\boldsymbol{\theta}}$. The idea is usually to determine how much bias $\hat{\boldsymbol{\theta}}$ has for estimating $\boldsymbol{\theta}_o$, or to determine the efficiency of $\hat{\boldsymbol{\theta}}$ compared with other estimators of $\boldsymbol{\theta}_o$. In addition, we often want to know how well the asymptotic standard errors approximate the standard deviations of the $\hat{\theta}_j$.

To conduct a simulation, we must choose a population distribution for $\mathbf{w}$, which depends on the finite dimensional vector $\boldsymbol{\theta}_o$. We must set the values of $\boldsymbol{\theta}_o$, and decide on a sample size, N. We then draw a random sample of size N from this distribution and use the sample to obtain an estimate of $\boldsymbol{\theta}_o$. We draw a new random sample and compute another estimate of $\boldsymbol{\theta}_o$. We repeat the process for several iterations, say M. Let $\hat{\boldsymbol{\theta}}^{(m)}$ be the estimate of $\boldsymbol{\theta}_o$ based on the mth iteration. Given $\{\hat{\boldsymbol{\theta}}^{(m)}: m = 1, 2, \ldots, M\}$, we can compute the sample average and sample variance to estimate $\mathrm{E}(\hat{\boldsymbol{\theta}})$ and $\mathrm{Var}(\hat{\boldsymbol{\theta}})$, respectively. We might also form t statistics or other test statistics to see how well the asymptotic distributions approximate the finite sample distributions.

We can also see how well asymptotic confidence intervals cover the population parameter relative to the nominal confidence level.

A good Monte Carlo study varies the value of $\boldsymbol{\theta}_{\mathrm{o}}$, the sample size, and even the general form of the distribution of $\mathbf{w}$. Obtaining a thorough study can be very challenging, especially for a complicated, nonlinear model. First, to get good estimates of the distribution of $\hat{\boldsymbol{\theta}}$, we would like M to be large (perhaps several thousand). But for each Monte Carlo iteration, we must obtain $\hat{\boldsymbol{\theta}}^{(m)}$, and this step can be computationally expensive because it often requires the iterative methods we discussed in Section 12.7. Repeating the simulations for many different sample sizes N, values of $\boldsymbol{\theta}_{\mathrm{o}}$, and distributional shapes can be very time-consuming.

In most economic applications, $\mathbf{w}_i$ is partitioned as $(\mathbf{x}_i, \mathbf{y}_i)$. While we can draw the full vector $\mathbf{w}_i$ randomly in the Monte Carlo iterations, more often the $\mathbf{x}_i$ are fixed at the beginning of the iterations, and then $\mathbf{y}_i$ is drawn from the conditional distribution given $\mathbf{x}_i$. This method simplifies the simulations because we do not need to vary the distribution of $\mathbf{x}_i$ along with the distribution of interest, the distribution of $\mathbf{y}_i$ given $\mathbf{x}_i$. If we fix the $\mathbf{x}_i$ at the beginning of the simulations, the distributional features of $\hat{\boldsymbol{\theta}}$ that we estimate from the Monte Carlo simulations are conditional on $\{\mathbf{x}_1, \mathbf{x}_2, \ldots, \mathbf{x}_N\}$. This conditional approach is especially common in linear and nonlinear regression contexts, as well as conditional maximum likelihood.

It is important not to rely too much on Monte Carlo simulations. Many estimation methods, including OLS, IV, and panel data estimators, have asymptotic properties that do not depend on underlying distributions. In the nonlinear regression model, the NLS estimator is $\sqrt{N}$-asymptotically normal, and the usual asymptotic variance matrix (12.58) is valid under Assumptions NLS.1–NLS.3. However, in a typical Monte Carlo simulation, the implied error, u, is assumed to be independent of $\mathbf{x}$, and the distribution of u must be specified. The Monte Carlo results then pertain to this distribution, and it can be misleading to extrapolate to different settings. In addition, we can never try more than just a small part of the parameter space. Since we never know the population value $\boldsymbol{\theta}_{\mathrm{o}}$, we can never be sure how well our Monte Carlo study describes the underlying population. Hendry (1984) discusses how **response surface analysis** can be used to reduce the specificity of Monte Carlo studies. See also Davidson and MacKinnon (1993, Chapter 21).

12.8.2 Bootstrapping

A Monte Carlo simulation, although it is informative about how well the asymptotic approximations can be expected to work in specific situations, does not generally help us refine our inference given a particular sample. (Since we do not know $\boldsymbol{\theta}_{\mathrm{o}}$, we cannot know whether our Monte Carlo findings apply to the population we are studying. Nevertheless, researchers sometimes use the results of a Monte Carlo simulation to obtain rules of thumb for adjusting standard errors or for adjusting critical values for test statistics.) The method of **bootstrapping**, which is a popular **resampling method**, can be used as an alternative to asymptotic approximations for obtaining standard errors, confidence intervals, and p-values for test statistics.

Though there are several variants of the bootstrap, we begin with one that can be applied to general M-estimation. The goal is to approximate the distribution of $\hat{\boldsymbol{\theta}}$ without relying on the usual first-order asymptotic theory. Let $\{\mathbf{w}_1, \mathbf{w}_2, \ldots, \mathbf{w}_N\}$ denote the outcome of the random sample used to obtain the estimate. The **nonparametric bootstrap** is essentially a Monte Carlo simulation where the observed sample is treated as the population. In other words, at each bootstrap iteration, b, a random sample of size N is drawn from $\{\mathbf{w}_1, \mathbf{w}_2, \ldots, \mathbf{w}_N\}$. (That is, we sample *with replacement*.) In practice, we use a random number generator to obtain N integers from the set $\{1, 2, \ldots, N\}$; in the vast majority of iterations some integers will be repeated at least once. These integers index the elements that we draw from $\{\mathbf{w}_1, \mathbf{w}_2, \ldots, \mathbf{w}_N\}$; call these $\{\mathbf{w}_1^{(b)}, \mathbf{w}_2^{(b)}, \ldots, \mathbf{w}_N^{(b)}\}$. Next, we use this bootstrap sample to obtain the M-estimate $\hat{\boldsymbol{\theta}}^{(b)}$ by solving

$$\min_{\boldsymbol{\theta} \in \boldsymbol{\Theta}} \sum_{i=1}^{N} q(\mathbf{w}_i^{(b)}, \boldsymbol{\theta})$$

We iterate the process B times, obtaining $\hat{\boldsymbol{\theta}}^{(b)}$, $b = 1, \ldots, B$. These estimates can now be used as in a Monte Carlo simulation. Computing the average of the $\hat{\boldsymbol{\theta}}^{(b)}$, say $\bar{\hat{\boldsymbol{\theta}}}$, allows us to estimate the bias in $\hat{\boldsymbol{\theta}}$. The sample variance, $(B-1)^{-1} \sum_{b=1}^{B} [\hat{\boldsymbol{\theta}}^{(b)} - \bar{\hat{\boldsymbol{\theta}}}] \cdot [\hat{\boldsymbol{\theta}}^{(b)} - \bar{\hat{\boldsymbol{\theta}}}]'$, can be used to obtain standard errors for the $\hat{\theta}_j$—the estimates from the original sample. A 95 percent bootstrapped confidence interval for θ_{oj} can be obtained by finding the 2.5 and 97.5 percentiles in the list of values $\{\hat{\theta}_j^{(b)}: b = 1, \ldots, B\}$. The p-value for a test statistic is approximated as the fraction of times the bootstrapped test statistic exceeds the statistic computed from the original sample.

The **parametric bootstrap** is even more similar to a standard Monte Carlo simulation because we assume that the distribution of $\mathbf{w}$ is known up to the parameters $\boldsymbol{\theta}_o$. Let $f(\cdot, \boldsymbol{\theta})$ denote the parametric density. Then, on each bootstrap iteration, we draw a random sample of size N from $f(\cdot, \hat{\boldsymbol{\theta}})$; this gives $\{\mathbf{w}_1^{(b)}, \mathbf{w}_2^{(b)}, \ldots, \mathbf{w}_N^{(b)}\}$ and the rest of the calculations are the same as in the nonparametric bootstrap. [With the parametric bootstrap when $f(\cdot, \boldsymbol{\theta})$ is a continuous density, only rarely would we find repeated values among the $\mathbf{w}_i^{(b)}$.]

When $\mathbf{w}_i$ is partitioned into $(\mathbf{x}_i, \mathbf{y}_i)$, where the $\mathbf{x}_i$ are conditioning variables, other resampling schemes are sometimes preferred. For example, in a regression model where the error u_i is *independent* of $\mathbf{x}_i$, we first compute the NLS estimate $\hat{\boldsymbol{\theta}}$ and the NLS residuals, $\hat{u}_i = y_i - m(\mathbf{x}_i, \hat{\boldsymbol{\theta}})$, $i = 1, 2, \ldots, N$. Then, using the procedure described for the nonparametric bootstrap, a bootstrap sample of residuals, $\{\hat{u}_i^{(b)}: i = 1, 2, \ldots, N\}$, is obtained, and we compute $y_i^{(b)} = m(\mathbf{x}_i, \hat{\boldsymbol{\theta}}) + \hat{u}_i^{(b)}$. Using the generated data $\{(\mathbf{x}_i, y_i^{(b)}): i = 1, 2, \ldots, N\}$, we compute the NLS estimate, $\hat{\boldsymbol{\theta}}^{(b)}$. This procedure is called the **nonparametric residual bootstrap**. (We resample the residuals and use these to generate a sample on the dependent variable, but we do not resample the conditioning variables, $\mathbf{x}_i$.) If the model is nonlinear in $\boldsymbol{\theta}$, this method can be computationally demanding because we want B to be several hundred, if not several thousand. Nonetheless, such procedures are becoming more and more feasible as computational speed increases. When u_i has zero conditional mean $[\mathrm{E}(u_i \mid \mathbf{x}_i) = 0]$ but is heteroskedastic $[\mathrm{Var}(u_i \mid \mathbf{x}_i)$ depends on $\mathbf{x}_i]$, alternative sampling methods, in particular the **wild bootstrap**, can be used to obtain heteroskedastic-consistent standard errors. See, for example, Horowitz (in press).

For certain test statistics, the bootstrap can be shown to improve upon the approximation provided by the first-order asymptotic theory that we treat in this book. A detailed treatment of the bootstrap, including discussions of when it works and when it does not, is given in Horowitz (in press).

Problems

12.1. Use equation (12.4) to show that $\boldsymbol{\theta}_{\mathrm{o}}$ minimizes $\mathrm{E}\{[y - m(\mathbf{x}, \boldsymbol{\theta})]^2 \mid \mathbf{x}\}$ over Θ for any $\mathbf{x}$. Explain why this result is stronger than stating that $\boldsymbol{\theta}_{\mathrm{o}}$ solves problem (12.3).

12.2. Consider the model

$$\mathrm{E}(y \mid \mathbf{x}) = m(\mathbf{x}, \boldsymbol{\theta}_{\mathrm{o}})$$

$$\mathrm{Var}(y \mid \mathbf{x}) = \exp(\alpha_{\mathrm{o}} + \mathbf{x}\boldsymbol{\gamma}_{\mathrm{o}})$$

where $\mathbf{x}$ is $1 \times K$. The vector $\boldsymbol{\theta}_{\mathrm{o}}$ is $P \times 1$ and $\boldsymbol{\gamma}_{\mathrm{o}}$ is $K \times 1$.

a. Define $u \equiv y - \mathrm{E}(y \mid \mathbf{x})$. Show that $\mathrm{E}(u^2 \mid \mathbf{x}) = \exp(\alpha_{\mathrm{o}} + \mathbf{x}\boldsymbol{\gamma}_{\mathrm{o}})$.

b. Let $\hat{u}_i$ denote the residuals from estimating the conditional mean by NLS. Argue that α_{o} and $\boldsymbol{\gamma}_{\mathrm{o}}$ can be consistently estimated by a nonlinear regression where $\hat{u}_i^2$ is the dependent variable and the regression function is $\exp(\alpha_{\mathrm{o}} + \mathbf{x}\boldsymbol{\gamma}_{\mathrm{o}})$. (Hint: Use the results on two-step estimation.)

c. Using part b, propose a (feasible) weighted least squares procedure for estimating $\boldsymbol{\theta}_{\mathrm{o}}$.

d. If the error u is divided by $[\text{Var}(u \mid \mathbf{x})]^{1/2}$, we obtain $v \equiv \exp[-(\alpha_o + \mathbf{x}\gamma_o)/2]u$. Argue that if v is independent of $\mathbf{x}$, then γ_o is consistently estimated from the regression $\log(\hat{u}_i^2)$ on 1, $\mathbf{x}_i$, $i = 1, 2, \ldots, N$. [The intercept from this regression will not consistently estimate α_o, but this fact does not matter, since $\exp(\alpha_o + \mathbf{x}\gamma_o) = \sigma_o^2 \exp(\mathbf{x}\gamma_o)$, and σ_o^2 can be estimated from the WNLS regression.]

e. What would you do after running WNLS if you suspect the variance function is misspecified?

12.3. Consider the exponential regression function $m(\mathbf{x}, \boldsymbol{\theta}) = \exp(\mathbf{x}\boldsymbol{\theta})$, where $\mathbf{x}$ is $1 \times K$.

a. Suppose you have estimated a special case of the model, $\hat{\text{E}}(y \mid \mathbf{z}) = \exp[\hat{\theta}_1 + \hat{\theta}_2 \log(z_1) + \hat{\theta}_3 z_2]$, where z_1 and z_2 are the conditioning variables. Show that $\hat{\theta}_2$ is approximately the elasticity of $\hat{\text{E}}(y \mid \mathbf{z})$ with respect to z_1.

b. In the same estimated model from part a, how would you approximate the percentage change in $\hat{\text{E}}(y \mid \mathbf{z})$ given $\Delta z_2 = 1$?

c. Now suppose a square of z_2 is added: $\hat{\text{E}}(y \mid \mathbf{z}) = \exp[\hat{\theta}_1 + \hat{\theta}_2 \log(z_1) + \hat{\theta}_3 z_2 + \hat{\theta}_4 z_2^2]$, where $\hat{\theta}_3 > 0$ and $\hat{\theta}_4 < 0$. How would you compute the value of z_2 where the partial effect of z_2 on $\hat{\text{E}}(y \mid \mathbf{z})$ becomes negative?

d. Now write the general model as $\exp(\mathbf{x}\boldsymbol{\theta}) = \exp(\mathbf{x}_1\boldsymbol{\theta}_1 + \mathbf{x}_2\boldsymbol{\theta}_2)$, where $\mathbf{x}_1$ is $1 \times K_1$ (and probably contains unity as an element) and $\mathbf{x}_2$ is $1 \times K_2$. Derive the usual (nonrobust) and heteroskedasticity-robust LM tests of H_0: $\boldsymbol{\theta}_{o2} = \mathbf{0}$, where $\boldsymbol{\theta}_o$ indexes $\text{E}(y \mid \mathbf{x})$.

12.4. a. Show that the score for WNLS is $\mathbf{s}_i(\boldsymbol{\theta}; \gamma) = -\nabla_\theta m(\mathbf{x}_i, \boldsymbol{\theta})' u_i(\boldsymbol{\theta}) / h(\mathbf{x}_i, \gamma)$.

b. Show that, under Assumption WNLS.1, $\text{E}[\mathbf{s}_i(\boldsymbol{\theta}_o; \gamma) \mid \mathbf{x}_i] = \mathbf{0}$ for any value of γ.

c. Show that, under Assumption WNLS.1, $\text{E}[\nabla_\gamma \mathbf{s}_i(\boldsymbol{\theta}_o; \gamma)] = \mathbf{0}$ for any value of γ.

d. How would you estimate $\text{Avar}(\hat{\boldsymbol{\theta}})$ without Assumption WNLS.3?

12.5. For the regression model

$$m(\mathbf{x}, \boldsymbol{\theta}) = G[\mathbf{x}\boldsymbol{\beta} + \delta_1(\mathbf{x}\boldsymbol{\beta})^2 + \delta_2(\mathbf{x}\boldsymbol{\beta})^3]$$

where $G(\cdot)$ is a known, twice continuously differentiable function with derivative $g(\cdot)$, derive the standard LM test of H_0: $\delta_{o2} = 0$, $\delta_{o3} = 0$ using NLS. Show that, when $G(\cdot)$ is the identify function, the test reduces to RESET from Section 6.2.3.

12.6. Consider a panel data model for a random draw i from the population:

$$y_{it} = m(\mathbf{x}_{it}, \boldsymbol{\theta}_o) + u_{it}, \qquad \text{E}(u_{it} \mid \mathbf{x}_{it}) = 0, \qquad t = 1, \ldots, T$$

a. If you apply **pooled nonlinear least squares** to estimate $\boldsymbol{\theta}_o$, how would you estimate its asymptotic variance without further assumptions?

b. Suppose that the model is dynamically complete in the conditional mean, so that $\mathrm{E}(u_{it} \mid \mathbf{x}_{it}, u_{i,t-1}, \mathbf{x}_{i,t-1}, \ldots) = 0$ for all t. In addition, $\mathrm{E}(u_{it}^2 \mid \mathbf{x}_{it}) = \sigma_o^2$. Show that the usual statistics from a pooled NLS regression are valid. {Hint: The objective function for each i is $q_i(\boldsymbol{\theta}) = \sum_{t=1}^{T} [y_{it} - m(\mathbf{x}_{it}, \boldsymbol{\theta})]^2/2$ and the score is $\mathbf{s}_i(\boldsymbol{\theta}) = -\sum_{t=1}^{T} \nabla_\theta m(\mathbf{x}_{it}, \boldsymbol{\theta})' u_{it}(\boldsymbol{\theta})$. Now show that $\mathbf{B}_o = \sigma_o^2 \mathbf{A}_o$ and that σ_o^2 is consistently estimated by $(NT - P)^{-1} \sum_{i=1}^{N} \sum_{t=1}^{T} \hat{u}_{it}^2$.}

12.7. Consider a nonlinear analogue of the SUR system from Chapter 7:

$$\mathrm{E}(y_{ig} \mid \mathbf{x}_i) = \mathrm{E}(y_{ig} \mid \mathbf{x}_{ig}) = m_g(\mathbf{x}_{ig}, \boldsymbol{\theta}_{og}), \qquad g = 1, \ldots, G$$

Thus, each $\boldsymbol{\theta}_{og}$ can be estimated by NLS using only equation g; call these $\hat{\hat{\boldsymbol{\theta}}}_g$. Suppose also that $\mathrm{Var}(\mathbf{y}_i \mid \mathbf{x}_i) = \boldsymbol{\Omega}_o$, where $\boldsymbol{\Omega}_o$ is $G \times G$ and positive definite.

a. Explain how to consistently estimate $\boldsymbol{\Omega}_o$ (as usual, with G fixed and $N \to \infty$). Call this estimator $\hat{\boldsymbol{\Omega}}$.

b. Let $\hat{\boldsymbol{\theta}}$ solve the problem

$$\min_{\boldsymbol{\theta}} \sum_{i=1}^{N} [\mathbf{y}_i - \mathbf{m}(\mathbf{x}_i, \boldsymbol{\theta})]' \hat{\boldsymbol{\Omega}}^{-1} [\mathbf{y}_i - \mathbf{m}(\mathbf{x}_i, \boldsymbol{\theta})]/2$$

where $\mathbf{m}(\mathbf{x}_i, \boldsymbol{\theta})$ is the $G \times 1$ vector of conditional mean functions and $\mathbf{y}_i$ is $G \times 1$; this is sometimes called the **nonlinear SUR estimator**. Show that

$$\mathrm{Avar}\, \sqrt{N}(\hat{\boldsymbol{\theta}} - \boldsymbol{\theta}_o) = \{\mathrm{E}[\nabla_\theta \mathbf{m}(\mathbf{x}_i, \boldsymbol{\theta}_o)' \boldsymbol{\Omega}_o^{-1} \nabla_\theta \mathbf{m}(\mathbf{x}_i, \boldsymbol{\theta}_o)]\}^{-1}$$

{Hint: Under standard regularity conditions, $N^{-1/2} \sum_{i=1}^{N} \nabla_\theta \mathbf{m}(\mathbf{x}_i, \boldsymbol{\theta}_o)' \hat{\boldsymbol{\Omega}}^{-1} [\mathbf{y}_i - \mathbf{m}(\mathbf{x}_i, \boldsymbol{\theta}_o)] = N^{-1/2} \sum_{i=1}^{N} \nabla_\theta \mathbf{m}(\mathbf{x}_i, \boldsymbol{\theta}_o)' \boldsymbol{\Omega}_o^{-1} [\mathbf{y}_i - \mathbf{m}(\mathbf{x}_i, \boldsymbol{\theta}_o)] + o_p(1)$.}

c. How would you estimate $\mathrm{Avar}(\hat{\boldsymbol{\theta}})$?

d. If $\boldsymbol{\Omega}_o$ is diagonal and if the assumptions stated previously hold, show that nonlinear least squares equation by equation is just as asymptotically efficient as the nonlinear SUR estimator.

e. Is there a nonlinear analogue of Theorem 7.7 for linear systems in the sense that nonlinear SUR and NLS equation by equation are asymptotically equivalent when the same explanatory variables appear in each equation? [Hint: When would $\nabla_\theta \mathbf{m}(\mathbf{x}_i, \boldsymbol{\theta}_o)$ have the form needed to apply the hint in Problem 7.5? You might try $\mathrm{E}(y_g \mid \mathbf{x}) = \exp(\mathbf{x}\boldsymbol{\theta}_{og})$ for all g as an example.]

12.8. Consider the M-estimator with estimated nuisance parameter $\hat{\gamma}$, where $\sqrt{N}(\hat{\gamma} - \gamma_o) = O_p(1)$. If assumption (12.37) holds under the null hypothesis, show that the QLR statistic still has a limiting chi-square distribution, assuming also that $\mathbf{A}_o = \mathbf{B}_o$. [Hint: Start from equation (12.76) but where $\sqrt{N}(\tilde{\boldsymbol{\theta}} - \hat{\boldsymbol{\theta}}) = \mathbf{A}_o^{-1} N^{-1/2} \cdot \sum_{i=1}^N \mathbf{s}_i(\tilde{\boldsymbol{\theta}}; \hat{\gamma}) + o_p(1)$. Now use a mean value expansion of the score about $(\tilde{\boldsymbol{\theta}}, \gamma_o)$ to show that $\sqrt{N}(\tilde{\boldsymbol{\theta}} - \hat{\boldsymbol{\theta}}) = \mathbf{A}_o^{-1} N^{-1/2} \sum_{i=1}^N \mathbf{s}_i(\tilde{\boldsymbol{\theta}}; \gamma_o) + o_p(1)$.]

12.9. For scalar y, suppose that $y = m(\mathbf{x}, \boldsymbol{\beta}_o) + u$, where $\mathbf{x}$ is a $1 \times K$ vector.

a. If $\mathrm{E}(u \mid \mathbf{x}) = 0$, what can you say about $\mathrm{Med}(y \mid \mathbf{x})$?

b. Suppose that u and $\mathbf{x}$ are independent. Show that $\mathrm{E}(y \mid \mathbf{x}) - \mathrm{Med}(y \mid \mathbf{x})$ does not depend on $\mathbf{x}$.

c. What does part b imply about $\partial \mathrm{E}(y \mid \mathbf{x})/\partial x_j$ and $\partial\, \mathrm{Med}(y \mid \mathbf{x})/\partial x_j$?

12.10. For each i, let y_i be a nonnegative integer with a conditional binomial distribution with upper bound n_i (a positive integer) and probability of success $p(\mathbf{x}_i, \boldsymbol{\beta}_o)$, where $0 < p(\mathbf{x}, \boldsymbol{\beta}) < 1$ for all $\mathbf{x}$ and $\boldsymbol{\beta}$. (A leading case is the logistic function.) Therefore, $\mathrm{E}(y_i \mid \mathbf{x}_i, n_i) = n_i p(\mathbf{x}_i, \boldsymbol{\beta}_o)$ and $\mathrm{Var}(y_i \mid \mathbf{x}_i, n_i) = n_i p(\mathbf{x}_i, \boldsymbol{\beta}_o)[1 - p(\mathbf{x}_i, \boldsymbol{\beta}_o)]$. Explain in detail how to obtain the weighted nonlinear least squares estimator of $\boldsymbol{\beta}_o$.

12.11. Let $\mathbf{y}_i$ be a $G \times 1$ vector (where G could be T, the number of time periods in a panel data application), and let $\mathbf{x}_i$ be a vector of covariates. Let $\mathbf{m}(\mathbf{x}, \boldsymbol{\beta})$ be a model of $\mathrm{E}(\mathbf{y} \mid \mathbf{x})$, where $m_g(\mathbf{x}, \boldsymbol{\beta})$ is a model for $\mathrm{E}(y_g \mid \mathbf{x})$. Assume that the model is correctly specified, and let $\boldsymbol{\beta}_o$ denote the true value. Assume that $\mathbf{m}(\mathbf{x}, \cdot)$ has many continuous derivatives.

a. Argue that the **multivariate nonlinear least squares (MNLS) estimator**, which minimizes

$$\sum_{i=1}^N [\mathbf{y}_i - \mathbf{m}(\mathbf{x}_i, \boldsymbol{\beta})]'[\mathbf{y}_i - \mathbf{m}(\mathbf{x}_i, \boldsymbol{\beta})]/2$$

is generally consistent and $\sqrt{N}$-asymptotically normal. Use Theorems 12.2 and 12.3. What is the identification assumption?

b. Let $\mathbf{W}(\mathbf{x}, \boldsymbol{\delta})$ be a model for $\mathrm{Var}(\mathbf{y} \mid \mathbf{x})$, and suppose that this model is correctly specified. Let $\hat{\boldsymbol{\delta}}$ be a $\sqrt{N}$-consistent estimator of $\boldsymbol{\delta}_o$. Argue that the **multivariate weighted nonlinear least squares (MWNLS) estimator**, which solves

$$\sum_{i=1}^N [\mathbf{y}_i - \mathbf{m}(\mathbf{x}_i, \boldsymbol{\beta})]'[\mathbf{W}_i(\hat{\boldsymbol{\delta}})]^{-1}[\mathbf{y}_i - \mathbf{m}(\mathbf{x}_i, \boldsymbol{\beta})]/2$$

is generally consistent and $\sqrt{N}$-asymptotically normal. Find Avar $\sqrt{N}(\hat{\boldsymbol{\beta}} - \boldsymbol{\beta}_o)$ and show how to consistently estimate it.

c. Argue that, even if the variance model for $\mathbf{y}$ given $\mathbf{x}$ is misspecified, the MWNLS estimator is still consistent and $\sqrt{N}$-asymptotically normal. How would you estimate its asymptotic variance if you suspect the variance model is misspecified?

13 Maximum Likelihood Methods

13.1 Introduction

This chapter contains a general treatment of maximum likelihood estimation (MLE) under random sampling. All the models we considered in Part I could be estimated without making full distributional assumptions about the endogenous variables conditional on the exogenous variables: maximum likelihood methods were not needed. Instead, we focused primarily on zero-covariance and zero-conditional-mean assumptions, and secondarily on assumptions about conditional variances and covariances. These assumptions were sufficient for obtaining consistent, asymptotically normal estimators, some of which were shown to be efficient within certain classes of estimators.

Some texts on advanced econometrics take maximum likelihood estimation as the unifying theme, and then most models are estimated by maximum likelihood. In addition to providing a unified approach to estimation, MLE has some desirable efficiency properties: it is generally the most efficient estimation procedure in the class of estimators that use information on the distribution of the endogenous variables given the exogenous variables. (We formalize the efficiency of MLE in Section 14.5.) So why not always use MLE?

As we saw in Part I, efficiency usually comes at the price of nonrobustness, and this is certainly the case for maximum likelihood. Maximum likelihood estimators are generally inconsistent if some part of the specified distribution is misspecified. As an example, consider from Section 9.5 a simultaneous equations model that is linear in its parameters but nonlinear in some endogenous variables. There, we discussed estimation by instrumental variables methods. We could estimate SEMs nonlinear in endogenous variables by maximum likelihood if we assumed independence between the structural errors and the exogenous variables and if we assumed a particular distribution for the structural errors, say, multivariate normal. The MLE would be asymptotically more efficient than the best GMM estimator, but failure of normality generally results in inconsistent estimators of all parameters.

As a second example, suppose we wish to estimate $\mathrm{E}(y \mid \mathbf{x})$, where y is bounded between zero and one. The logistic function, $\exp(\mathbf{x}\boldsymbol{\beta})/[1+\exp(\mathbf{x}\boldsymbol{\beta})]$, is a reasonable model for $\mathrm{E}(y \mid \mathbf{x})$, and, as we discussed in Section 12.2, nonlinear least squares provides consistent, $\sqrt{N}$-asymptotically normal estimators under weak regularity conditions. We can easily make inference robust to arbitrary heteroskedasticity in $\mathrm{Var}(y \mid \mathbf{x})$. An alternative approach is to model the density of y given $\mathbf{x}$—which, of course, implies a particular model for $\mathrm{E}(y \mid \mathbf{x})$—and use maximum likelihood estimation. As we will see, the strength of MLE is that, under correct specification of the density, we would have the asymptotically efficient estimators, and we would be able to estimate any feature of the conditional distribution, such as $P(y = 1 \mid \mathbf{x})$. The drawback is that, except in special cases, if we have misspecified the density in any way, we will not be able to consistently estimate the conditional mean.

In most applications, specifying the distribution of the endogenous variables conditional on exogenous variables must have a component of arbitrariness, as economic theory rarely provides guidance. Our perspective is that, for robustness reasons, it is desirable to make as few assumptions as possible—at least until relaxing them becomes practically difficult. There *are* cases in which MLE turns out to be robust to failure of certain assumptions, but these must be examined on a case-by-case basis, a process that detracts from the unifying theme provided by the MLE approach. (One such example is nonlinear regression under a homoskedastic normal assumption; the MLE of the parameters $\boldsymbol{\beta}_o$ is identical to the NLS estimator, and we know the latter is consistent and asymptotically normal quite generally. We will cover some other leading cases in Chapter 19.)

Maximum likelihood plays an important role in modern econometric analysis, for good reason. There are many problems for which it is indispensable. For example, in Chapters 15 and 16 we study various limited dependent variable models, and MLE plays a central role.

13.2 Preliminaries and Examples

Traditional maximum likelihood theory for independent, identically distributed observations $\{\mathbf{y}_i \in \mathbb{R}^G : i = 1, 2, \ldots\}$ starts by specifying a family of densities for $\mathbf{y}_i$. This is the framework used in introductory statistics courses, where $\mathbf{y}_i$ is a scalar with a normal or Poisson distribution. But in almost all economic applications, we are interested in estimating parameters in *conditional* distributions. Therefore, we assume that each random draw is partitioned as $(\mathbf{x}_i, \mathbf{y}_i)$, where $\mathbf{x}_i \in \mathbb{R}^K$ and $\mathbf{y}_i \in \mathbb{R}^G$, and we are interested in estimating a model for the conditional distribution of $\mathbf{y}_i$ given $\mathbf{x}_i$. We are not interested in the distribution of $\mathbf{x}_i$, so we will not specify a model for it. Consequently, the method of this chapter is properly called **conditional maximum likelihood estimation (CMLE)**. By taking $\mathbf{x}_i$ to be null we cover unconditional MLE as a special case.

An alternative to viewing $(\mathbf{x}_i, \mathbf{y}_i)$ as a random draw from the population is to treat the conditioning variables $\mathbf{x}_i$ as *nonrandom* vectors that are set ahead of time and that appear in the unconditional distribution of $\mathbf{y}_i$. (This is analogous to the fixed regressor assumption in classical regression analysis.) Then, the $\mathbf{y}_i$ cannot be identically distributed, and this fact complicates the asymptotic analysis. More importantly, treating the $\mathbf{x}_i$ as nonrandom is much too restrictive for all uses of maximum likelihood. In fact, later on we will cover methods where $\mathbf{x}_i$ contains what are endogenous variables in a structural model, but where it is convenient to obtain the distribution of one set of endogenous variables conditional on another set. Once we know how to analyze the general CMLE case, applications follow fairly directly.

It is important to understand that the subsequent results apply any time we have random sampling in the cross section dimension. Thus, the general theory applies to system estimation, as in Chapters 7 and 9, provided we are willing to assume a distribution for $\mathbf{y}_i$ given $\mathbf{x}_i$. In addition, panel data settings with large cross sections and relatively small time periods are encompassed, since the appropriate asymptotic analysis is with the time dimension fixed and the cross section dimension tending to infinity.

In order to perform maximum likelihood analysis we need to specify, or derive from an underlying (structural) model, the density of $\mathbf{y}_i$ given $\mathbf{x}_i$. We assume this density is known up to a finite number of unknown parameters, with the result that we have a **parametric model** of a conditional density. The vector $\mathbf{y}_i$ can be continuous or discrete, or it can have both discrete and continuous characteristics. In many of our applications, $\mathbf{y}_i$ is a scalar, but this fact does not simplify the general treatment.

We will carry along two examples in this chapter to illustrate the general theory of conditional maximum likelihood. The first example is a **binary response model**, specifically the **probit model**. We postpone the uses and interepretation of binary response models until Chapter 15.

Example 13.1 (Probit): Suppose that the **latent variable** y_i^* follows

$$y_i^* = \mathbf{x}_i\boldsymbol{\theta} + e_i \tag{13.1}$$

where e_i is *independent* of $\mathbf{x}_i$ (which is a $1 \times K$ vector with first element equal to unity for all i), $\boldsymbol{\theta}$ is a $K \times 1$ vector of parameters, and $e_i \sim \text{Normal}(0,1)$. Instead of observing y_i^* we observe only a binary variable indicating the sign of y_i^*:

$$y_i = \begin{cases} 1 & \text{if } y_i^* > 0 \quad (13.2) \\ 0 & \text{if } y_i^* \leq 0 \quad (13.3) \end{cases}$$

To be succinct, it is useful to write equations (13.2) and (13.3) in terms of the **indicator function**, denoted $1[\cdot]$. This function is unity whenever the statement in brackets is true, and zero otherwise. Thus, equations (13.2) and (13.3) are equivalently written as $y_i = 1[y_i^* > 0]$. Because e_i is normally distributed, it is irrelevant whether the strict inequality is in equation (13.2) or (13.3).

We can easily obtain the distribution of y_i given $\mathbf{x}_i$:

$$\begin{aligned}\mathrm{P}(y_i = 1 \mid \mathbf{x}_i) &= \mathrm{P}(y_i^* > 0 \mid \mathbf{x}_i) = \mathrm{P}(\mathbf{x}_i\boldsymbol{\theta} + e_i > 0 \mid \mathbf{x}_i) \\ &= \mathrm{P}(e_i > -\mathbf{x}_i\boldsymbol{\theta} \mid \mathbf{x}_i) = 1 - \Phi(-\mathbf{x}_i\boldsymbol{\theta}) = \Phi(\mathbf{x}_i\boldsymbol{\theta}) \end{aligned} \tag{13.4}$$

where $\Phi(\cdot)$ denotes the standard normal cumulative distribution function (cdf). We have used Property CD.4 in the chapter appendix along with the symmetry of the normal distribution. Therefore,

$$\mathrm{P}(y_i = 0 \mid \mathbf{x}_i) = 1 - \Phi(\mathbf{x}_i\boldsymbol{\theta}) \tag{13.5}$$

We can combine equations (13.4) and (13.5) into the density of y_i given $\mathbf{x}_i$:

$$f(y \mid \mathbf{x}_i) = [\Phi(\mathbf{x}_i\boldsymbol{\theta})]^y[1 - \Phi(\mathbf{x}_i\boldsymbol{\theta})]^{1-y}, \qquad y = 0, 1 \tag{13.6}$$

The fact that $f(y \mid \mathbf{x}_i)$ is zero when $y \notin \{0, 1\}$ is obvious, so we will not be explicit about this in the future.

Our second example is useful when the variable to be explained takes on nonnegative integer values. Such a variable is called a **count variable**. We will discuss the use and interpretation of count data models in Chapter 19. For now, it suffices to note that a linear model for $\mathrm{E}(y \mid \mathbf{x})$ when y takes on nonnegative integer values is not ideal because it can lead to negative predicted values. Further, since y can take on the value zero with positive probability, the transformation $\log(y)$ cannot be used to obtain a model with constant elasticities or constant semielasticities. A functional form well suited for $\mathrm{E}(y \mid \mathbf{x})$ is $\exp(\mathbf{x}\boldsymbol{\theta})$. We could estimate $\boldsymbol{\theta}$ by using nonlinear least squares, but all of the standard distributions for count variables imply heteroskedasticity (see Chapter 19). Thus, we can hope to do better. A traditional approach to regression models with count data is to assume that y_i given $\mathbf{x}_i$ has a Poisson distribution.

Example 13.2 (Poisson Regression): Let y_i be a nonnegative count variable; that is, y_i can take on integer values $0, 1, 2, \ldots$. Denote the conditional mean of y_i given the vector $\mathbf{x}_i$ as $\mathrm{E}(y_i \mid \mathbf{x}_i) = \mu(\mathbf{x}_i)$. A natural distribution for y_i given $\mathbf{x}_i$ is the Poisson distribution:

$$f(y \mid \mathbf{x}_i) = \exp[-\mu(\mathbf{x}_i)]\{\mu(\mathbf{x}_i)\}^y/y!, \qquad y = 0, 1, 2, \ldots \tag{13.7}$$

(We use y as the dummy argument in the density, not to be confused with the random variable y_i.) Once we choose a form for the conditional mean function, we have completely determined the distribution of y_i given $\mathbf{x}_i$. For example, from equation (13.7), $\mathrm{P}(y_i = 0 \mid \mathbf{x}_i) = \exp[-\mu(\mathbf{x}_i)]$. An important feature of the Poisson distribution is that the variance equals the mean: $\mathrm{Var}(y_i \mid \mathbf{x}_i) = \mathrm{E}(y_i \mid \mathbf{x}_i) = \mu(\mathbf{x}_i)$. The usual choice for $\mu(\cdot)$ is $\mu(\mathbf{x}) = \exp(\mathbf{x}\boldsymbol{\theta})$, where $\boldsymbol{\theta}$ is $K \times 1$ and $\mathbf{x}$ is $1 \times K$ with first element unity.

13.3 General Framework for Conditional MLE

Let $p_o(\mathbf{y} \mid \mathbf{x})$ denote the conditional density of $\mathbf{y}_i$ given $\mathbf{x}_i = \mathbf{x}$, where $\mathbf{y}$ and $\mathbf{x}$ are dummy arguments. We index this density by "o" to emphasize that it is the true density of $\mathbf{y}_i$ given $\mathbf{x}_i$, and not just one of many candidates. It will be useful to let $\mathscr{X} \subset \mathbb{R}^K$ denote the possible values for $\mathbf{x}_i$ and $\mathscr{Y}$ denote the possible values of $\mathbf{y}_i$; $\mathscr{X}$ and $\mathscr{Y}$ are called the *supports* of the random vectors $\mathbf{x}_i$ and $\mathbf{y}_i$, respectively.

For a general treatment, we assume that, for all $\mathbf{x} \in \mathscr{X}$, $p_o(\cdot \mid \mathbf{x})$ is a density with respect to a *σ-finite measure*, denoted $\nu(d\mathbf{y})$. Defining a σ-finite measure would take us too far afield. We will say little more about the measure $\nu(d\mathbf{y})$ because it does not play a crucial role in applications. It suffices to know that $\nu(d\mathbf{y})$ can be chosen to allow $\mathbf{y}_i$ to be discrete, continuous, or some mixture of the two. When $\mathbf{y}_i$ is discrete, the measure $\nu(d\mathbf{y})$ simply turns all integrals into sums; when $\mathbf{y}_i$ is purely continuous, we obtain the usual Riemann integrals. Even in more complicated cases—where, say, $\mathbf{y}_i$ has both discrete and continuous characteristics—we can get by with tools from basic probability without ever explicitly defining $\nu(d\mathbf{y})$. For more on measures and general integrals, you are referred to Billingsley (1979) and Davidson (1994, Chapters 3 and 4).

In Chapter 12 we saw how nonlinear least squares can be motivated by the fact that $\mu_o(\mathbf{x}) \equiv \mathrm{E}(y \mid \mathbf{x})$ minimizes $\mathrm{E}\{[y - m(\mathbf{x})]^2\}$ for all other functions $m(\mathbf{x})$ with $\mathrm{E}\{[m(\mathbf{x})]^2\} < \infty$. Conditional maximum likelihood has a similar motivation. The result from probability that is crucial for applying the analogy principle is the **conditional Kullback-Leibler information inequality.** Although there are more general statements of this inequality, the following suffices for our purpose: for any nonnegative function $f(\cdot \mid \mathbf{x})$ such that

$$\int_{\mathscr{Y}} f(\mathbf{y} \mid \mathbf{x})\nu(d\mathbf{y}) = 1, \qquad \text{all } \mathbf{x} \in \mathscr{X} \tag{13.8}$$

Property CD.1 in the chapter appendix implies that

$$\mathscr{K}(f; \mathbf{x}) \equiv \int_{\mathscr{Y}} \log[p_o(\mathbf{y} \mid \mathbf{x})/f(\mathbf{y} \mid \mathbf{x})]p_o(\mathbf{y} \mid \mathbf{x})\nu(d\mathbf{y}) \geq 0, \qquad \text{all } \mathbf{x} \in \mathscr{X} \tag{13.9}$$

Because the integral is identically zero for $f = p_o$, expression (13.9) says that, for each $\mathbf{x}$, $\mathscr{K}(f; \mathbf{x})$ is minimized at $f = p_o$.

We can apply inequality (13.9) to a parametric model for $p_o(\cdot \mid \mathbf{x})$,

$$\{f(\cdot \mid \mathbf{x}; \boldsymbol{\theta}),\ \boldsymbol{\theta} \in \boldsymbol{\Theta},\ \boldsymbol{\Theta} \subset \mathbb{R}^P\} \tag{13.10}$$

which we assume satisfies condition (13.8) for each $\mathbf{x} \in \mathscr{X}$ and each $\boldsymbol{\theta} \in \boldsymbol{\Theta}$; if it does not, then $f(\cdot \mid \mathbf{x}; \boldsymbol{\theta})$ does not integrate to unity (with respect to the measure ν), and as a result it is a very poor candidate for $p_o(\mathbf{y} \mid \mathbf{x})$. Model (13.10) is a **correctly specified model of the conditional density**, $p_o(\cdot \mid \cdot)$, if, for some $\boldsymbol{\theta}_o \in \boldsymbol{\Theta}$,

$$f(\cdot \mid \mathbf{x}; \boldsymbol{\theta}_o) = p_o(\cdot \mid \mathbf{x}), \qquad \text{all } \mathbf{x} \in \mathscr{X} \tag{13.11}$$

As we discussed in Chapter 12, it is useful to use $\boldsymbol{\theta}_o$ to distinguish the true value of the parameter from a generic element of $\boldsymbol{\Theta}$. In particular examples, we will not bother making this distinction unless it is needed to make a point.

For each $\mathbf{x} \in \mathscr{X}$, $\mathscr{K}(f, \mathbf{x})$ can be written as $\mathrm{E}\{\log[p_o(\mathbf{y}_i \mid \mathbf{x}_i)] \mid \mathbf{x}_i = \mathbf{x}\} - \mathrm{E}\{\log[f(\mathbf{y}_i \mid \mathbf{x}_i)] \mid \mathbf{x}_i = \mathbf{x}\}$. Therefore, if the parametric model is correctly specified, then $\mathrm{E}\{\log[f(\mathbf{y}_i \mid \mathbf{x}_i; \boldsymbol{\theta}_o)] \mid \mathbf{x}_i\} \geq \mathrm{E}\{\log[f(\mathbf{y}_i \mid \mathbf{x}_i; \boldsymbol{\theta})] \mid \mathbf{x}_i\}$, or

$$\mathrm{E}[\ell_i(\boldsymbol{\theta}_o) \mid \mathbf{x}_i] \geq \mathrm{E}[\ell_i(\boldsymbol{\theta}) \mid \mathbf{x}_i], \qquad \boldsymbol{\theta} \in \boldsymbol{\Theta} \tag{13.12}$$

where

$$\ell_i(\boldsymbol{\theta}) \equiv \ell(\mathbf{y}_i, \mathbf{x}_i, \boldsymbol{\theta}) \equiv \log f(\mathbf{y}_i \mid \mathbf{x}_i; \boldsymbol{\theta}) \tag{13.13}$$

is the **conditional log likelihood for observation i**. Note that $\ell_i(\boldsymbol{\theta})$ is a *random* function of $\boldsymbol{\theta}$, since it depends on the random vector $(\mathbf{x}_i, \mathbf{y}_i)$. By taking the expected value of expression (13.12) and using iterated expectations, we see that $\boldsymbol{\theta}_o$ solves

$$\max_{\boldsymbol{\theta} \in \boldsymbol{\Theta}} \mathrm{E}[\ell_i(\boldsymbol{\theta})] \tag{13.14}$$

where the expectation is with respect to the joint distribution of $(\mathbf{x}_i, \mathbf{y}_i)$. The sample analogue of expression (13.14) is

$$\max_{\boldsymbol{\theta} \in \boldsymbol{\Theta}} N^{-1} \sum_{i=1}^{N} \log f(\mathbf{y}_i \mid \mathbf{x}_i; \boldsymbol{\theta}) \tag{13.15}$$

A solution to problem (13.15), assuming that one exists, is the **conditional maximum likelihood estimator (CMLE)** of $\boldsymbol{\theta}_o$, which we denote as $\hat{\boldsymbol{\theta}}$. We will sometimes drop "conditional" when it is not needed for clarity.

The CMLE is clearly an M-estimator, since a maximization problem is easily turned into a minimization problem: in the notation of Chapter 12, take $\mathbf{w}_i \equiv (\mathbf{x}_i, \mathbf{y}_i)$ and $q(\mathbf{w}_i, \boldsymbol{\theta}) \equiv -\log f(\mathbf{y}_i \mid \mathbf{x}_i; \boldsymbol{\theta})$. As long as we keep track of the minus sign in front of the log likelihood, we can apply the results in Chapter 12 directly.

The motivation for the conditional MLE as a solution to problem (13.15) may appear backward if you learned about maximum likelihood estimation in an introductory statistics course. In a traditional framework, we would treat the $\mathbf{x}_i$ as constants appearing in the distribution of $\mathbf{y}_i$, and we would define $\hat{\theta}$ as the solution to

$$\max_{\theta \in \Theta} \prod_{i=1}^{N} f(\mathbf{y}_i \mid \mathbf{x}_i; \boldsymbol{\theta}) \tag{13.16}$$

Under independence, the product in expression (13.16) is the model for the joint density of $(\mathbf{y}_1, \ldots, \mathbf{y}_N)$, evaluated at the data. Because maximizing the function in (13.16) is the same as maximizing its natural log, we are led to problem (13.15). However, the arguments explaining why solving (13.16) should lead to a good estimator of $\boldsymbol{\theta}_o$ are necessarily heuristic. By contrast, the analogy principle applies directly to problem (13.15), and we need not assume that the $\mathbf{x}_i$ are fixed.

In our two examples, the conditional log likelihoods are fairly simple.

Example 13.1 (continued): In the probit example, the log likelihood for observation i is $\ell_i(\boldsymbol{\theta}) = y_i \log \Phi(\mathbf{x}_i\boldsymbol{\theta}) + (1 - y_i) \log[1 - \Phi(\mathbf{x}_i\boldsymbol{\theta})]$.

Example 13.2 (continued): In the Poisson example, $\ell_i(\boldsymbol{\theta}) = -\exp(\mathbf{x}_i\boldsymbol{\theta}) + y_i\mathbf{x}_i\boldsymbol{\theta} - \log(y_i!)$. Normally, we would drop the last term in defining $\ell_i(\boldsymbol{\theta})$ because it does not affect the maximization problem.

13.4 Consistency of Conditional MLE

In this section we state a formal consistency result for the CMLE, which is a special case of the M-estimator consistency result Theorem 12.2.

THEOREM 13.1 (Consistency of CMLE): Let $\{(\mathbf{x}_i, \mathbf{y}_i): i = 1, 2, \ldots\}$ be a random sample with $\mathbf{x}_i \in \mathcal{X} \subset \mathbb{R}^K$, $\mathbf{y}_i \in \mathcal{Y} \subset \mathbb{R}^G$. Let $\boldsymbol{\Theta} \subset \mathbb{R}^P$ be the parameter set and denote the parametric model of the conditional density as $\{f(\cdot \mid \mathbf{x}; \boldsymbol{\theta}): \mathbf{x} \in \mathcal{X}, \boldsymbol{\theta} \in \boldsymbol{\Theta}\}$. Assume that (a) $f(\cdot \mid \mathbf{x}; \boldsymbol{\theta})$ is a true density with respect to the measure $v(d\mathbf{y})$ for all $\mathbf{x}$ and $\boldsymbol{\theta}$, so that condition (13.8) holds; (b) for some $\boldsymbol{\theta}_o \in \boldsymbol{\Theta}$, $p_o(\cdot \mid \mathbf{x}) = f(\cdot \mid \mathbf{x}; \boldsymbol{\theta}_o)$, all $\mathbf{x} \in \mathcal{X}$, and $\boldsymbol{\theta}_o$ is the *unique* solution to problem (13.14); (c) $\boldsymbol{\Theta}$ is a compact set; (d) for each $\boldsymbol{\theta} \in \boldsymbol{\Theta}$, $\ell(\cdot, \boldsymbol{\theta})$ is a Borel measurable function on $\mathcal{Y} \times \mathcal{X}$; (e) for each $(\mathbf{y}, \mathbf{x}) \in \mathcal{Y} \times \mathcal{X}$, $\ell(\mathbf{y}, \mathbf{x}, \cdot)$ is a continuous function on $\boldsymbol{\Theta}$; and (f) $|\ell(\mathbf{w}, \boldsymbol{\theta})| \leq b(\mathbf{w})$, all $\boldsymbol{\theta} \in \boldsymbol{\Theta}$, and $\mathrm{E}[b(\mathbf{w})] < \infty$. Then there exists a solution to problem (13.15), the CMLE $\hat{\boldsymbol{\theta}}$, and plim $\hat{\boldsymbol{\theta}} = \boldsymbol{\theta}_o$.

As we discussed in Chapter 12, the measurability assumption in part d is purely technical and does not need to be checked in practice. Compactness of $\boldsymbol{\Theta}$ can be relaxed, but doing so usually requires considerable work. The continuity assumption holds in most econometric applications, but there are cases where it fails, such as when estimating certain models of auctions—see Donald and Paarsch (1996). The moment assumption in part f typically restricts the distribution of $\mathbf{x}_i$ in some way, but such restrictions are rarely a serious concern. For the most part, the key assumptions are that the parametric model is correctly specified, that $\boldsymbol{\theta}_o$ is identified, and that the log-likelihood function is continuous in $\boldsymbol{\theta}$.

For the probit and Poisson examples, the log likelihoods are clearly continuous in $\boldsymbol{\theta}$. We can verify the moment condition (f) if we bound certain moments of $\mathbf{x}_i$ and make the parameter space compact. But our primary concern is that densities are correctly specified. For example, in the probit case, the density for y_i given $\mathbf{x}_i$ will be incorrect if the latent error e_i is not independent of $\mathbf{x}_i$ and normally distributed, or if the latent variable model is not linear to begin with. For identification we must rule out perfect collinearity in $\mathbf{x}_i$. The Poisson CMLE turns out to have desirable properties even if the Poisson distributional assumption does not hold, but we postpone a discussion of the robustness of the Poisson CMLE until Chapter 19.

13.5 Asymptotic Normality and Asymptotic Variance Estimation

Under the differentiability and moment assumptions that allow us to apply the theorems in Chapter 12, we can show that the MLE is generally asymptotically normal. Naturally, the computational methods discussed in Section 12.7, including concentrating parameters out of the log likelihood, apply directly.

13.5.1 Asymptotic Normality

We can derive the limiting distribution of the MLE by applying Theorem 12.3. We will have to assume the regularity conditions there; in particular, we assume that $\boldsymbol{\theta}_o$ is in the interior of $\boldsymbol{\Theta}$, and $\ell_i(\boldsymbol{\theta})$ is twice continuously differentiable on the interior of $\boldsymbol{\Theta}$.

The **score of the log likelihood** for observation i is simply

$$\mathbf{s}_i(\boldsymbol{\theta}) \equiv \nabla_{\theta}\ell_i(\boldsymbol{\theta})' = \left(\frac{\partial \ell_i}{\partial \theta_1}(\boldsymbol{\theta}), \frac{\partial \ell_i}{\partial \theta_2}(\boldsymbol{\theta}), \ldots, \frac{\partial \ell_i}{\partial \theta_P}(\boldsymbol{\theta})\right)' \tag{13.17}$$

a $P \times 1$ vector as in Chapter 12.

Example 13.1 (continued): For the probit case, $\boldsymbol{\theta}$ is $K \times 1$ and

$$\nabla_{\theta}\ell_i(\boldsymbol{\theta}) = y_i\left[\frac{\phi(\mathbf{x}_i\boldsymbol{\theta})\mathbf{x}_i}{\Phi(\mathbf{x}_i\boldsymbol{\theta})}\right] - (1 - y_i)\left\{\frac{\phi(\mathbf{x}_i\boldsymbol{\theta})\mathbf{x}_i}{[1 - \Phi(\mathbf{x}_i\boldsymbol{\theta})]}\right\}$$

Transposing this equation, and using a little algebra, gives

$$\mathbf{s}_i(\boldsymbol{\theta}) = \frac{\phi(\mathbf{x}_i\boldsymbol{\theta})\mathbf{x}_i'[y_i - \Phi(\mathbf{x}_i\boldsymbol{\theta})]}{\Phi(\mathbf{x}_i\boldsymbol{\theta})[1 - \Phi(\mathbf{x}_i\boldsymbol{\theta})]} \tag{13.18}$$

Recall that $\mathbf{x}_i'$ is a $K \times 1$ vector.

Example 13.2 (continued): The score for the Poisson case, where $\boldsymbol{\theta}$ is again $K \times 1$, is

$$\mathbf{s}_i(\boldsymbol{\theta}) = -\exp(\mathbf{x}_i\boldsymbol{\theta})\mathbf{x}_i' + y_i\mathbf{x}_i' = \mathbf{x}_i'[y_i - \exp(\mathbf{x}_i\boldsymbol{\theta})] \tag{13.19}$$

In the vast majority of cases, the score of the log-likelihood function has an important zero conditional mean property:

$$\mathrm{E}[\mathbf{s}_i(\boldsymbol{\theta}_o) \mid \mathbf{x}_i] = \mathbf{0} \tag{13.20}$$

In other words, when we evaluate the $P \times 1$ score at $\boldsymbol{\theta}_o$, and take its expectation with respect to $f(\cdot \mid \mathbf{x}_i; \boldsymbol{\theta}_o)$, the expectation is zero. Under condition (13.20), $\mathrm{E}[\mathbf{s}_i(\boldsymbol{\theta}_o)] = \mathbf{0}$, which was a key condition in deriving the asymptotic normality of the M-estimator in Chapter 12.

To show condition (13.20) generally, let $\mathrm{E}_{\theta}[\cdot \mid \mathbf{x}_i]$ denote conditional expectation with respect to the density $f(\cdot \mid \mathbf{x}_i; \boldsymbol{\theta})$ for any $\boldsymbol{\theta} \in \boldsymbol{\Theta}$. Then, by definition,

$$\mathrm{E}_{\theta}[\mathbf{s}_i(\boldsymbol{\theta}) \mid \mathbf{x}_i] = \int_{\mathcal{Y}} \mathbf{s}(\mathbf{y}, \mathbf{x}_i, \boldsymbol{\theta}) f(\mathbf{y} \mid \mathbf{x}_i; \boldsymbol{\theta}) \nu(d\mathbf{y})$$

If integration and differentation can be interchanged on $\mathrm{int}(\boldsymbol{\Theta})$—that is, if

$$\nabla_{\theta}\left(\int_{\mathcal{Y}} f(\mathbf{y} \mid \mathbf{x}_i; \boldsymbol{\theta}) \nu(d\mathbf{y})\right) = \int_{\mathcal{Y}} \nabla_{\theta} f(\mathbf{y} \mid \mathbf{x}_i; \boldsymbol{\theta}) \nu(d\mathbf{y}) \tag{13.21}$$

for all $\mathbf{x}_i \in \mathcal{X}$, $\boldsymbol{\theta} \in \mathrm{int}(\boldsymbol{\Theta})$—then

$$\mathbf{0} = \int_{\mathcal{Y}} \nabla_{\theta} f(\mathbf{y} \mid \mathbf{x}_i; \boldsymbol{\theta}) \nu(d\mathbf{y}) \tag{13.22}$$

since $\int_{\mathcal{Y}} f(\mathbf{y} \mid \mathbf{x}_i; \boldsymbol{\theta}) \nu(d\mathbf{y})$ is unity for all $\boldsymbol{\theta}$, and therefore the partial derivatives with respect to $\boldsymbol{\theta}$ must be identically zero. But the right-hand side of equation (13.22) can be written as $\int_{\mathcal{Y}} [\nabla_{\theta} \ell(\mathbf{y}, \mathbf{x}_i, \boldsymbol{\theta})] f(\mathbf{y} \mid \mathbf{x}_i; \boldsymbol{\theta}) \nu(d\mathbf{y})$. Putting in $\boldsymbol{\theta}_o$ for $\boldsymbol{\theta}$ and transposing yields condition (13.20).

Example 13.1 (continued): Define $u_i \equiv y_i - \Phi(\mathbf{x}_i\boldsymbol{\theta}_o) = y_i - \mathrm{E}(y_i \mid \mathbf{x}_i)$. Then

$$\mathbf{s}_i(\boldsymbol{\theta}_o) = \frac{\phi(\mathbf{x}_i\boldsymbol{\theta}_o)\mathbf{x}_i' u_i}{\Phi(\mathbf{x}_i\boldsymbol{\theta}_o)[1 - \Phi(\mathbf{x}_i\boldsymbol{\theta}_o)]}$$

and, since $\mathrm{E}(u_i \mid \mathbf{x}_i) = 0$, it follows that $\mathrm{E}[\mathbf{s}_i(\boldsymbol{\theta}_o) \mid \mathbf{x}_i] = \mathbf{0}$.

Example 13.2 (continued): Define $u_i \equiv y_i - \exp(\mathbf{x}_i\boldsymbol{\theta}_o)$. Then $\mathbf{s}_i(\boldsymbol{\theta}_o) = \mathbf{x}_i'u_i$ and so $\mathrm{E}[\mathbf{s}_i(\boldsymbol{\theta}_o) \mid \mathbf{x}_i] = \mathbf{0}$.

Assuming that $\ell_i(\boldsymbol{\theta})$ is twice continuously differentiable on the interior of $\boldsymbol{\Theta}$, let the Hessian for observation i be the $P \times P$ matrix of second partial derivatives of $\ell_i(\boldsymbol{\theta})$:

$$\mathbf{H}_i(\boldsymbol{\theta}) \equiv \nabla_\theta \mathbf{s}_i(\boldsymbol{\theta}) = \nabla_\theta^2 \ell_i(\boldsymbol{\theta}) \tag{13.23}$$

The Hessian is a symmetric matrix that generally depends on $(\mathbf{x}_i, \mathbf{y}_i)$. Since MLE is a maximization problem, the expected value of $\mathbf{H}_i(\boldsymbol{\theta}_o)$ is negative definite. Thus, to apply the theory in Chapter 12, we define

$$\mathbf{A}_o \equiv -\mathrm{E}[\mathbf{H}_i(\boldsymbol{\theta}_o)] \tag{13.24}$$

which is generally a positive definite matrix when $\boldsymbol{\theta}_o$ is identified. Under standard regularity conditions, the asymptotic normality of the CMLE follows from Theorem 12.3: $\sqrt{N}(\hat{\boldsymbol{\theta}} - \boldsymbol{\theta}_o) \stackrel{a}{\sim} \mathrm{Normal}(\mathbf{0}, \mathbf{A}_o^{-1}\mathbf{B}_o\mathbf{A}_o^{-1})$, where $\mathbf{B}_o \equiv \mathrm{Var}[\mathbf{s}_i(\boldsymbol{\theta}_o)] \equiv \mathrm{E}[\mathbf{s}_i(\boldsymbol{\theta}_o)\mathbf{s}_i(\boldsymbol{\theta}_o)']$. It turns out that this general form of the asymptotic variance matrix is too complicated. We now show that $\mathbf{B}_o = \mathbf{A}_o$.

We must assume enough smoothness such that the following interchange of integral and derivative is valid (see Newey and McFadden, 1994, Section 5.1, for the case of unconditional MLE):

$$\nabla_\theta\left(\int_{\mathcal{Y}} \mathbf{s}_i(\boldsymbol{\theta}) f(\mathbf{y} \mid \mathbf{x}_i; \boldsymbol{\theta}) \nu(d\mathbf{y})\right) = \int_{\mathcal{Y}} \nabla_\theta[\mathbf{s}_i(\boldsymbol{\theta}) f(\mathbf{y} \mid \mathbf{x}_i; \boldsymbol{\theta})] \nu(d\mathbf{y}) \tag{13.25}$$

Then, taking the derivative of the identity

$$\int_{\mathcal{Y}} \mathbf{s}_i(\boldsymbol{\theta}) f(\mathbf{y} \mid \mathbf{x}_i; \boldsymbol{\theta}) \nu(d\mathbf{y}) \equiv \mathrm{E}_\theta[\mathbf{s}_i(\boldsymbol{\theta}) \mid \mathbf{x}_i] = \mathbf{0}, \qquad \boldsymbol{\theta} \in \mathrm{int}(\boldsymbol{\Theta})$$

and using equation (13.25), gives, for all $\boldsymbol{\theta} \in \mathrm{int}(\boldsymbol{\Theta})$,

$$-\mathrm{E}_\theta[\mathbf{H}_i(\boldsymbol{\theta}) \mid \mathbf{x}_i] = \mathrm{Var}_\theta[\mathbf{s}_i(\boldsymbol{\theta}) \mid \mathbf{x}_i]$$

where the indexing by $\boldsymbol{\theta}$ denotes expectation and variance when $f(\cdot \mid \mathbf{x}_i; \boldsymbol{\theta})$ is the density of $\mathbf{y}_i$ given $\mathbf{x}_i$. When evaluated at $\boldsymbol{\theta} = \boldsymbol{\theta}_o$ we get a very important equality:

$$-\mathrm{E}[\mathbf{H}_i(\boldsymbol{\theta}_o) \mid \mathbf{x}_i] = \mathrm{E}[\mathbf{s}_i(\boldsymbol{\theta}_o)\mathbf{s}_i(\boldsymbol{\theta}_o)' \mid \mathbf{x}_i] \tag{13.26}$$

where the expectation and variance are with respect to the true conditional distribution of $\mathbf{y}_i$ given $\mathbf{x}_i$. Equation (13.26) is called the **conditional information matrix equality (CIME)**. Taking the expectation of equation (13.26) (with respect to the distribution of $\mathbf{x}_i$) and using the law of iterated expectations gives

$$-\mathrm{E}[\mathbf{H}_i(\theta_o)] = \mathrm{E}[\mathbf{s}_i(\theta_o)\mathbf{s}_i(\theta_o)'] \tag{13.27}$$

or $\mathbf{A}_o = \mathbf{B}_o$. This relationship is best thought of as the **unconditional information matrix equality (UIME).**

THEOREM 13.2 (Asymptotic Normality of CMLE): Let the conditions of Theorem 13.1 hold. In addition, assume that (a) $\theta_o \in \operatorname{int}(\Theta)$; (b) for each $(\mathbf{y},\mathbf{x}) \in \mathcal{Y} \times \mathcal{X}$, $\ell(\mathbf{y},\mathbf{x},\cdot)$ is twice continuously differentiable on $\operatorname{int}(\Theta)$; (c) the interchanges of derivative and integral in equations (13.21) and (13.25) hold for all $\theta \in \operatorname{int}(\Theta)$; (d) the elements of $\nabla_\theta^2 \ell(\mathbf{y},\mathbf{x},\theta)$ are bounded in absolute value by a function $b(\mathbf{y},\mathbf{x})$ with finite expectation; and (e) $\mathbf{A}_o$ defined by expression (13.24) is positive definite. Then

$$\sqrt{N}(\hat{\theta} - \theta_o) \xrightarrow{d} \mathrm{Normal}(\mathbf{0}, \mathbf{A}_o^{-1}) \tag{13.28}$$

and therefore

$$\mathrm{Avar}(\hat{\theta}) = \mathbf{A}_o^{-1}/N \tag{13.29}$$

In standard applications, the log likelihood has many continuous partial derivatives, although there are examples where it does not. Some examples also violate the interchange of the integral and derivative in equation (13.21) or (13.25), such as when the conditional support of $\mathbf{y}_i$ depends on the parameters θ_o. In such cases we cannot expect the CMLE to have a limiting normal distribution; it may not even converge at the rate $\sqrt{N}$. Some progress has been made for specific models when the support of the distribution depends on unknown parameters; see, for example, Donald and Paarsch (1996).

13.5.2 Estimating the Asymptotic Variance

Estimating $\mathrm{Avar}(\hat{\theta})$ requires estimating $\mathbf{A}_o$. From the equalities derived previously, there are at least three possible estimators of $\mathbf{A}_o$ in the CMLE context. In fact, under slight extensions of the regularity conditions in Theorem 13.2, each of the matrices

$$N^{-1}\sum_{i=1}^{N} -\mathbf{H}_i(\hat{\theta}), \qquad N^{-1}\sum_{i=1}^{N} \mathbf{s}_i(\hat{\theta})\mathbf{s}_i(\hat{\theta})', \qquad \text{and} \qquad N^{-1}\sum_{i=1}^{N} \mathbf{A}(\mathbf{x}_i, \hat{\theta}) \tag{13.30}$$

converges to $\mathbf{A}_o = \mathbf{B}_o$, where

$$\mathbf{A}(\mathbf{x}_i, \theta_o) \equiv -\mathrm{E}[\mathbf{H}(\mathbf{y}_i, \mathbf{x}_i, \theta_o) \,|\, \mathbf{x}_i] \tag{13.31}$$

Thus, $\text{Av\^{a}r}(\hat{\boldsymbol{\theta}})$ can be taken to be any of the three matrices

$$\left[-\sum_{i=1}^{N}\mathbf{H}_i(\hat{\boldsymbol{\theta}})\right]^{-1}, \qquad \left[\sum_{i=1}^{N}\mathbf{s}_i(\hat{\boldsymbol{\theta}})\mathbf{s}_i(\hat{\boldsymbol{\theta}})'\right]^{-1}, \qquad \text{or} \qquad \left[\sum_{i=1}^{N}\mathbf{A}(\mathbf{x}_i,\hat{\boldsymbol{\theta}})\right]^{-1} \tag{13.32}$$

and the asymptotic standard errors are the square roots of the diagonal elements of any of the matrices. We discussed each of these estimators in the general M-estimator case in Chapter 12, but a brief review is in order. The first estimator, based on the Hessian of the log likelihood, requires computing second derivatives and is not guaranteed to be positive definite. If the estimator is not positive definite, standard errors of some linear combinations of the parameters will not be well defined.

The second estimator in equation (13.32), based on the outer product of the score, is always positive definite (whenever the inverse exists). This simple estimator was proposed by Berndt, Hall, Hall, and Hausman (1974). Its primary drawback is that it can be poorly behaved in even moderate sample sizes, as we discussed in Section 12.6.2.

If the conditional expectation $\mathbf{A}(\mathbf{x}_i,\boldsymbol{\theta}_o)$ is in closed form (as it is in some leading cases) or can be simulated—as discussed in Porter (1999)—then the estimator based on $\mathbf{A}(\mathbf{x}_i,\hat{\boldsymbol{\theta}})$ has some attractive features. First, it often depends only on first derivatives of a conditional mean or conditional variance function. Second, it is positive definite when it exists because of the conditional information matrix equality (13.26). Third, this estimator has been found to have significantly better finite sample properties than the outer product of the score estimator in some situations where $\mathbf{A}(\mathbf{x}_i,\boldsymbol{\theta}_o)$ can be obtained in closed form.

Example 13.1 (continued): The Hessian for the probit log-likelihood is a mess. Fortunately, $\mathrm{E}[\mathbf{H}_i(\boldsymbol{\theta}_o)\,|\,\mathbf{x}_i]$ has a fairly simple form. Taking the derivative of equation (13.18) and using the product rule gives

$$\mathbf{H}_i(\boldsymbol{\theta}) = -\frac{\{\phi(\mathbf{x}_i\boldsymbol{\theta})\}^2\mathbf{x}_i'\mathbf{x}_i}{\Phi(\mathbf{x}_i\boldsymbol{\theta})[1-\Phi(\mathbf{x}_i\boldsymbol{\theta})]} + [y_i - \Phi(\mathbf{x}_i\boldsymbol{\theta})]\mathbf{L}(\mathbf{x}_i\boldsymbol{\theta})$$

where $\mathbf{L}(\mathbf{x}_i\boldsymbol{\theta})$ is a $K \times K$ complicated function of $\mathbf{x}_i\boldsymbol{\theta}$ that we need not find explicitly. Now, when we evaluate this expression at $\boldsymbol{\theta}_o$ and note that $E\{[y_i - \Phi(\mathbf{x}_i\boldsymbol{\theta}_o)]\mathbf{L}(\mathbf{x}_i\boldsymbol{\theta}_o)\,|\,\mathbf{x}_i\} = [\mathrm{E}(y_i\,|\,\mathbf{x}_i) - \Phi(\mathbf{x}_i\boldsymbol{\theta}_o)]\mathbf{L}(\mathbf{x}_i\boldsymbol{\theta}_o) = \mathbf{0}$, we have

$$-\mathrm{E}[\mathbf{H}_i(\boldsymbol{\theta}_o)\,|\,\mathbf{x}_i] = \mathbf{A}_i(\boldsymbol{\theta}_o) = \frac{\{\phi(\mathbf{x}_i\boldsymbol{\theta}_o)\}^2\mathbf{x}_i'\mathbf{x}_i}{\Phi(\mathbf{x}_i\boldsymbol{\theta}_o)[1-\Phi(\mathbf{x}_i\boldsymbol{\theta}_o)]}$$

Thus, $\text{Av\^{a}r}(\hat{\boldsymbol{\theta}})$ in probit analysis is

$$\left(\sum_{i=1}^{N} \frac{\{\phi(\mathbf{x}_i\hat{\boldsymbol{\theta}})\}^2 \mathbf{x}_i'\mathbf{x}_i}{\Phi(\mathbf{x}_i\hat{\boldsymbol{\theta}})[1 - \Phi(\mathbf{x}_i\hat{\boldsymbol{\theta}})]}\right)^{-1} \tag{13.33}$$

which is always positive definite when the inverse exists. Note that $\mathbf{x}_i'\mathbf{x}_i$ is a $K \times K$ matrix for each i.

Example 13.2 (continued): For the Poisson model with exponential conditional mean, $\mathbf{H}_i(\boldsymbol{\theta}) = -\exp(\mathbf{x}_i\boldsymbol{\theta})\mathbf{x}_i'\mathbf{x}_i$. In this example, the Hessian does not depend on y_i, so there is no distinction between $\mathbf{H}_i(\boldsymbol{\theta}_o)$ and $\mathrm{E}[\mathbf{H}_i(\boldsymbol{\theta}_o) \mid \mathbf{x}_i]$. The positive definite estimate of $\widehat{\mathrm{Avar}}(\hat{\boldsymbol{\theta}})$ is simply

$$\left[\sum_{i=1}^{N} \exp(\mathbf{x}_i\hat{\boldsymbol{\theta}})\mathbf{x}_i'\mathbf{x}_i\right]^{-1} \tag{13.34}$$

13.6 Hypothesis Testing

Given the asymptotic standard errors, it is easy to form asymptotic t statistics for testing single hypotheses. These t statistics are asymptotically distributed as standard normal.

The three tests covered in Chapter 12 are immediately applicable to the MLE case. Since the information matrix equality holds when the density is correctly specified, we need only consider the simplest forms of the test statistics. The Wald statistic is given in equation (12.63), and the conditions sufficient for it to have a limiting chi-square distribution are discussed in Section 12.6.1.

Define the log-likelihood function for the entire sample by $\mathscr{L}(\boldsymbol{\theta}) \equiv \sum_{i=1}^{N} \ell_i(\boldsymbol{\theta})$. Let $\hat{\boldsymbol{\theta}}$ be the unrestricted estimator, and let $\tilde{\boldsymbol{\theta}}$ be the estimator with the Q nonredundant constraints imposed. Then, under the regularity conditions discussed in Section 12.6.3, the **likelihood ratio (LR) statistic**,

$$LR \equiv 2[\mathscr{L}(\hat{\boldsymbol{\theta}}) - \mathscr{L}(\tilde{\boldsymbol{\theta}})] \tag{13.35}$$

is distributed asymptotically as χ_Q^2 under H_0. As with the Wald statistic, we cannot use LR as approximately χ_Q^2 when $\boldsymbol{\theta}_o$ is on the boundary of the parameter set. The LR statistic is very easy to compute once the restricted and unrestricted models have been estimated, and the LR statistic is invariant to reparameterizing the conditional density.

The score or LM test is based on the restricted estimation only. Let $\mathbf{s}_i(\tilde{\boldsymbol{\theta}})$ be the $P \times 1$ score of $\ell_i(\boldsymbol{\theta})$ evaluated at the restricted estimates $\tilde{\boldsymbol{\theta}}$. That is, we compute the partial derivatives of $\ell_i(\boldsymbol{\theta})$ with respect to each of the P parameters, but then we evaluate this vector of partials at the restricted estimates. Then, from Section 12.6.2 and the information matrix equality, the statistics

$$\left(\sum_{i=1}^{N}\tilde{\mathbf{s}}_i\right)'\left(-\sum_{i=1}^{N}\tilde{\mathbf{H}}_i\right)^{-1}\left(\sum_{i=1}^{N}\tilde{\mathbf{s}}_i\right), \quad \left(\sum_{i=1}^{N}\tilde{\mathbf{s}}_i\right)'\left(\sum_{i=1}^{N}\tilde{\mathbf{A}}_i\right)^{-1}\left(\sum_{i=1}^{N}\tilde{\mathbf{s}}_i\right), \quad \text{and}$$

$$\left(\sum_{i=1}^{N}\tilde{\mathbf{s}}_i\right)'\left(\sum_{i=1}^{N}\tilde{\mathbf{s}}_i\tilde{\mathbf{s}}_i'\right)^{-1}\left(\sum_{i=1}^{N}\tilde{\mathbf{s}}_i\right) \tag{13.36}$$

have limiting χ^2_Q distributions under H_0. As we know from Section 12.6.2, the first statistic is not invariant to reparameterizations, but the outer product statistic is. In addition, using the conditional information matrix equality, it can be shown that the LM statistic based on $\tilde{\mathbf{A}}_i$ is invariant to reparameterization. Davidson and MacKinnon (1993, Section 13.6) show invariance in the case of unconditional maximum likelihood. Invariance holds in the more general conditional ML setup, with $\mathbf{x}_i$ containing any conditioning variables; see Problem 13.5. We have already used the expected Hessian form of the LM statistic for nonlinear regression in Section 12.6.2. We will use it in several applications in Part IV, including binary response models and Poisson regression models. In these examples, the statistic can be computed conveniently using auxiliary regressions based on weighted residuals.

Because the unconditional information matrix equality holds, we know from Section 12.6.4 that the three classical statistics have the same limiting distribution under local alternatives. Therefore, either small-sample considerations, invariance, or computational issues must be used to choose among the statistics.

13.7 Specification Testing

Since MLE generally relies on its distributional assumptions, it is useful to have available a general class of specification tests that are simple to compute. One general approach is to nest the model of interest within a more general model (which may be much harder to estimate) and obtain the score test against the more general alternative. RESET in a linear model and its extension to exponential regression models in Section 12.6.2 are examples of this approach, albeit in a non-maximum-likelihood setting.

In the context of MLE, it makes sense to test moment conditions implied by the conditional density specification. Let $\mathbf{w}_i = (\mathbf{x}_i, \mathbf{y}_i)$ and suppose that, when $f(\cdot \mid \mathbf{x}; \boldsymbol{\theta})$ is correctly specified,

$$\mathrm{H}_0\colon \mathrm{E}[\mathbf{g}(\mathbf{w}_i, \boldsymbol{\theta}_{\mathrm{o}})] = \mathbf{0} \tag{13.37}$$

where $\mathbf{g}(\mathbf{w}, \boldsymbol{\theta})$ is a $Q \times 1$ vector. Any application implies innumerable choices for the function $\mathbf{g}$. Since the MLE $\hat{\boldsymbol{\theta}}$ sets the sum of the score to zero, $\mathbf{g}(\mathbf{w}, \boldsymbol{\theta})$ cannot contain elements of $\mathbf{s}(\mathbf{w}, \boldsymbol{\theta})$. Generally, $\mathbf{g}$ should be chosen to test features of a model that are of primary interest, such as first and second conditional moments, or various conditional probabilities.

A test of hypothesis (13.37) is based on how far the sample average of $\mathbf{g}(\mathbf{w}_i, \hat{\boldsymbol{\theta}})$ is from zero. To derive the asymptotic distribution, note that

$$N^{-1/2} \sum_{i=1}^{N} \mathbf{g}_i(\hat{\boldsymbol{\theta}}) = N^{-1/2} \sum_{i=1}^{N} [\mathbf{g}_i(\hat{\boldsymbol{\theta}}) - \mathbf{s}_i(\hat{\boldsymbol{\theta}})\boldsymbol{\Pi}_o]$$

holds trivially because $\sum_{i=1}^{N} \mathbf{s}_i(\hat{\boldsymbol{\theta}}) = \mathbf{0}$, where

$$\boldsymbol{\Pi}_o \equiv \{\mathrm{E}[\mathbf{s}_i(\boldsymbol{\theta}_o)\mathbf{s}_i(\boldsymbol{\theta}_o)']\}^{-1}\{\mathrm{E}[\mathbf{s}_i(\boldsymbol{\theta}_o)\mathbf{g}_i(\boldsymbol{\theta}_o)']\}$$

is the $P \times Q$ matrix of population regression coefficients from regressing $\mathbf{g}_i(\boldsymbol{\theta}_o)'$ on $\mathbf{s}_i(\boldsymbol{\theta}_o)'$. Using a mean-value expansion about $\boldsymbol{\theta}_o$ and algebra similar to that in Chapter 12, we can write

$$N^{-1/2} \sum_{i=1}^{N} [\mathbf{g}_i(\hat{\boldsymbol{\theta}}) - \mathbf{s}_i(\hat{\boldsymbol{\theta}})\boldsymbol{\Pi}_o] = N^{-1/2} \sum_{i=1}^{N} [\mathbf{g}_i(\boldsymbol{\theta}_o) - \mathbf{s}_i(\boldsymbol{\theta}_o)\boldsymbol{\Pi}_o] + \mathrm{E}[\nabla_\theta \mathbf{g}_i(\boldsymbol{\theta}_o) - \nabla_\theta \mathbf{s}_i(\boldsymbol{\theta}_o)\boldsymbol{\Pi}_o]\sqrt{N}(\hat{\boldsymbol{\theta}} - \boldsymbol{\theta}_o) + o_p(1) \tag{13.38}$$

The key is that, when the density is correctly specified, the second term on the right-hand side of equation (13.38) is identically zero. Here is the reason: First, equation (13.27) implies that $[\mathrm{E}\nabla_\theta \mathbf{s}_i(\boldsymbol{\theta}_o)]\{\mathrm{E}[\mathbf{s}_i(\boldsymbol{\theta}_o)\mathbf{s}_i(\boldsymbol{\theta}_o)']\}^{-1} = -\mathbf{I}_P$. Second, an extension of the conditional information matrix equality (Newey, 1985; Tauchen, 1985) implies that

$$-\mathrm{E}[\nabla_\theta \mathbf{g}_i(\boldsymbol{\theta}_o) \mid \mathbf{x}_i] = \mathrm{E}[\mathbf{g}_i(\boldsymbol{\theta}_o)\mathbf{s}_i(\boldsymbol{\theta}_o)' \mid \mathbf{x}_i]. \tag{13.39}$$

To show equation (13.39), write

$$\mathrm{E}_\theta[\mathbf{g}_i(\boldsymbol{\theta}) \mid \mathbf{x}_i] = \int_{\mathscr{Y}} \mathbf{g}(\mathbf{y}, \mathbf{x}_i, \boldsymbol{\theta}) f(\mathbf{y} \mid \mathbf{x}_i; \boldsymbol{\theta}) \nu(d\mathbf{y}) = \mathbf{0} \tag{13.40}$$

for all $\boldsymbol{\theta}$. Now, if we take the derivative with respect to $\boldsymbol{\theta}$ and assume that the integrals and derivative can be interchanged, equation (13.40) implies that

$$\int_{\mathscr{Y}} \nabla_\theta \mathbf{g}(\mathbf{y}, \mathbf{x}_i, \boldsymbol{\theta}) f(\mathbf{y} \mid \mathbf{x}_i; \boldsymbol{\theta}) \nu(d\mathbf{y}) + \int_{\mathscr{Y}} \mathbf{g}(\mathbf{y}, \mathbf{x}_i, \boldsymbol{\theta}) \nabla_\theta f(\mathbf{y} \mid \mathbf{x}_i; \boldsymbol{\theta}) \nu(d\mathbf{y}) = \mathbf{0}$$

or $\mathrm{E}_{\theta}[\nabla_{\theta}\mathbf{g}_i(\boldsymbol{\theta}) \mid \mathbf{x}_i] + \mathrm{E}_{\theta}[\mathbf{g}_i(\boldsymbol{\theta})\mathbf{s}_i(\boldsymbol{\theta})' \mid \mathbf{x}_i] = \mathbf{0}$, where we use the fact that $\nabla_{\theta} f(\mathbf{y} \mid \mathbf{x}; \boldsymbol{\theta}) = \mathbf{s}(\mathbf{y}, \mathbf{x}, \boldsymbol{\theta})' f(\mathbf{y} \mid \mathbf{x}; \boldsymbol{\theta})$. Plugging in $\boldsymbol{\theta} = \boldsymbol{\theta}_{\mathrm{o}}$ and rearranging gives equation (13.39).

What we have shown is that

$$N^{-1/2} \sum_{i=1}^{N} [\mathbf{g}_i(\hat{\boldsymbol{\theta}}) - \mathbf{s}_i(\hat{\boldsymbol{\theta}})\boldsymbol{\Pi}_{\mathrm{o}}] = N^{-1/2} \sum_{i=1}^{N} [\mathbf{g}_i(\boldsymbol{\theta}_{\mathrm{o}}) - \mathbf{s}_i(\boldsymbol{\theta}_{\mathrm{o}})\boldsymbol{\Pi}_{\mathrm{o}}] + o_p(1)$$

which means these standardized partial sums have the same asymptotic distribution. Letting

$$\hat{\boldsymbol{\Pi}} \equiv \left(\sum_{i=1}^{N} \hat{\mathbf{s}}_i \hat{\mathbf{s}}_i'\right)^{-1} \left(\sum_{i=1}^{N} \hat{\mathbf{s}}_i \hat{\mathbf{g}}_i'\right)$$

it is easily seen that plim $\hat{\boldsymbol{\Pi}} = \boldsymbol{\Pi}_{\mathrm{o}}$ under standard regularity conditions. Therefore, the asymptotic variance of $N^{-1/2} \sum_{i=1}^{N} [\mathbf{g}_i(\hat{\boldsymbol{\theta}}) - \mathbf{s}_i(\hat{\boldsymbol{\theta}})\boldsymbol{\Pi}_{\mathrm{o}}] = N^{-1/2} \sum_{i=1}^{N} \mathbf{g}_i(\hat{\boldsymbol{\theta}})$ is consistently estimated by $N^{-1} \sum_{i=1}^{N} (\hat{\mathbf{g}}_i - \hat{\mathbf{s}}_i\hat{\boldsymbol{\Pi}})(\hat{\mathbf{g}}_i - \hat{\mathbf{s}}_i\hat{\boldsymbol{\Pi}})'$. When we construct the quadratic form, we get the **Newey-Tauchen-White (NTW) statistic**,

$$NTW = \left[\sum_{i=1}^{N} \mathbf{g}_i(\hat{\boldsymbol{\theta}})\right]' \left[\sum_{i=1}^{N} (\hat{\mathbf{g}}_i - \hat{\mathbf{s}}_i\hat{\boldsymbol{\Pi}})(\hat{\mathbf{g}}_i - \hat{\mathbf{s}}_i\hat{\boldsymbol{\Pi}})'\right]^{-1} \left[\sum_{i=1}^{N} \mathbf{g}_i(\hat{\boldsymbol{\theta}})\right] \tag{13.41}$$

This statistic was proposed independently by Newey (1985) and Tauchen (1985), and is an extension of White's (1982a) information matrix (IM) test statistic.

For computational purposes it is useful to note that equation (13.41) is identical to $N - \mathrm{SSR}_0 = NR_0^2$ from the regression

$$1 \text{ on } \hat{\mathbf{s}}_i', \hat{\mathbf{g}}_i', \qquad i = 1, 2, \ldots, N \tag{13.42}$$

where SSR_0 is the usual sum of squared residuals. Under the null that the density is correctly specified, NTW is distributed asymptotically as χ_Q^2, assuming that $\mathbf{g}(\mathbf{w}, \boldsymbol{\theta})$ contains Q nonredundant moment conditions. Unfortunately, the outer product form of regression (13.42) means that the statistic can have poor finite sample properties. In particular applications—such as nonlinear least squares, binary response analysis, and Poisson regression, to name a few—it is best to use forms of test statistics based on the expected Hessian. We gave the regression-based test for NLS in equation (12.72), and we will see other examples in later chapters. For the information matrix test statistic, Davidson and MacKinnon (1992) have suggested an alternative form of the IM statistic that appears to have better finite sample properties.

Example 13.2 (continued): To test the specification of the conditional mean for Poission regression, we might take $\mathbf{g}(\mathbf{w}, \boldsymbol{\theta}) = \exp(\mathbf{x}\boldsymbol{\theta})\mathbf{x}'[y - \exp(\mathbf{x}\boldsymbol{\theta})] = \exp(\mathbf{x}\boldsymbol{\theta})\mathbf{s}(\mathbf{w}, \boldsymbol{\theta})$, where the score is given by equation (13.19). If $E(y \mid \mathbf{x}) = \exp(\mathbf{x}\boldsymbol{\theta}_o)$ then $\mathrm{E}[\mathbf{g}(\mathbf{w}, \boldsymbol{\theta}_o) \mid \mathbf{x}] = \exp(\mathbf{x}\boldsymbol{\theta}_o)\mathrm{E}[\mathbf{s}(\mathbf{w}, \boldsymbol{\theta}_o) \mid \mathbf{x}] = \mathbf{0}$. To test the Poisson variance assumption, $\mathrm{Var}(y \mid \mathbf{x}) = \mathrm{E}(y \mid \mathbf{x}) = \exp(\mathbf{x}\boldsymbol{\theta}_o)$, $\mathbf{g}$ can be of the form $\mathbf{g}(\mathbf{w}, \boldsymbol{\theta}) = \mathbf{a}(\mathbf{x}, \boldsymbol{\theta})\{[y - \exp(\mathbf{x}\boldsymbol{\theta})]^2 - \exp(\mathbf{x}\boldsymbol{\theta})\}$, where $\mathbf{a}(\mathbf{x}, \boldsymbol{\theta})$ is a $Q \times 1$ vector. If the Poisson assumption is true, then $u = y - \exp(\mathbf{x}\boldsymbol{\theta}_o)$ has a zero conditional mean and $\mathrm{E}(u^2 \mid \mathbf{x}) = \mathrm{Var}(y \mid \mathbf{x}) = \exp(\mathbf{x}\boldsymbol{\theta}_o)$. It follows that $\mathrm{E}[\mathbf{g}(\mathbf{w}, \boldsymbol{\theta}_o) \mid \mathbf{x}] = \mathbf{0}$.

Example 13.2 contains examples of what are known as **conditional moment tests**. As the name suggests, the idea is to form orthogonality conditions based on some key conditional moments, usually the conditional mean or conditional variance, but sometimes conditional probabilities or higher order moments. The tests for nonlinear regression in Chapter 12 can be viewed as conditional moment tests, and we will see several other examples in Part IV. For reasons discussed earlier, we will avoid computing the tests using regression (13.42) whenever possible. See Newey (1985), Tauchen (1985), and Pagan and Vella (1989) for general treatments and applications of conditional moment tests. White's (1982a) information matrix test can often be viewed as a conditional moment test; see Hall (1987) for the linear regression model and White (1994) for a general treatment.

13.8 Partial Likelihood Methods for Panel Data and Cluster Samples

Up to this point we have assumed that the parametric model for the density of $\mathbf{y}$ given $\mathbf{x}$ is correctly specified. This assumption is fairly general because $\mathbf{x}$ can contain any observable variable. The leading case occurs when $\mathbf{x}$ contains variables we view as exogenous in a structural model. In other cases, $\mathbf{x}$ will contain variables that are endogenous in a structural model, but putting them in the conditioning set and finding the new conditional density makes estimation of the structural parameters easier.

For studying various panel data models, for estimation using cluster samples, and for various other applications, we need to relax the assumption that the full conditional density of $\mathbf{y}$ given $\mathbf{x}$ is correctly specified. In some examples, such a model is too complicated. Or, for robustness reasons, we do not wish to fully specify the density of $\mathbf{y}$ given $\mathbf{x}$.

13.8.1 Setup for Panel Data

For panel data applications we let $\mathbf{y}$ denote a $T \times 1$ vector, with generic element y_t. Thus, $\mathbf{y}_i$ is a $T \times 1$ random draw vector from the cross section, with tth element y_{it}. As always, we are thinking of T small relative to the cross section sample size. With a slight notational change we can replace y_{it} with, say, a G-vector for each t, an extension that allows us to cover general systems of equations with panel data.

For some vector $\mathbf{x}_t$ containing any set of observable variables, let $\mathrm{D}(y_t \mid \mathbf{x}_t)$ denote the distribution of y_t given $\mathbf{x}_t$. The key assumption is that we have a correctly specified model for the density of y_t given $\mathbf{x}_t$; call it $f_t(y_t \mid \mathbf{x}_t; \boldsymbol{\theta})$, $t = 1, 2, \ldots, T$. The vector $\mathbf{x}_t$ can contain anything, including conditioning variables $\mathbf{z}_t$, lags of these, and lagged values of y. The vector $\boldsymbol{\theta}$ consists of all parameters appearing in f_t for any t; some or all of these may appear in the density for every t, and some may appear only in the density for a single time period.

What distinguishes partial likelihood from maximum likelihood is that we do *not* assume that

$$\prod_{t=1}^{T} \mathrm{D}(y_{it} \mid \mathbf{x}_{it}) \tag{13.43}$$

is a conditional distribution of the vector $\mathbf{y}_i$ given some set of conditioning variables. In other words, even though $f_t(y_t \mid \mathbf{x}_t; \boldsymbol{\theta}_o)$ is the correct density for y_{it} given $\mathbf{x}_{it}$ for each t, the product of these is not (necessarily) the density of $\mathbf{y}_i$ given some conditioning variables. Usually, we specify $f_t(y_t \mid \mathbf{x}_t; \boldsymbol{\theta})$ because it is the density of interest for each t.

We define the **partial log likelihood** for each observation i as

$$\ell_i(\boldsymbol{\theta}) \equiv \sum_{t=1}^{T} \log f_t(y_{it} \mid \mathbf{x}_{it}; \boldsymbol{\theta}) \tag{13.44}$$

which is the sum of the log likelihoods across t. What makes partial likelihood methods work is that $\boldsymbol{\theta}_o$ maximizes the expected value of equation (13.44) provided we have the densities $f_t(y_t \mid \mathbf{x}_t; \boldsymbol{\theta})$ correctly specified.

By the Kullback-Leibler information inequality, $\boldsymbol{\theta}_o$ maximizes $\mathrm{E}[\log f_t(y_{it} \mid \mathbf{x}_{it}; \boldsymbol{\theta})]$ over $\boldsymbol{\Theta}$ for each t, so $\boldsymbol{\theta}_o$ also maximizes the sum of these over t. As usual, identification requires that $\boldsymbol{\theta}_o$ be the unique maximizer of the expected value of equation (13.44). It is sufficient that $\boldsymbol{\theta}_o$ uniquely maximizes $\mathrm{E}[\log f_t(y_{it} \mid \mathbf{x}_{it}; \boldsymbol{\theta})]$ for each t, but this assumption is not necessary.

The **partial maximum likelihood estimator (PMLE)** $\hat{\boldsymbol{\theta}}$ solves

$$\max_{\boldsymbol{\theta} \in \boldsymbol{\Theta}} \sum_{i=1}^{N} \sum_{t=1}^{T} \log f_t(y_{it} \mid \mathbf{x}_{it}; \boldsymbol{\theta}) \tag{13.45}$$

and this problem is clearly an M-estimator problem (where the asymptotics are with fixed T and $N \to \infty$). Therefore, from Theorem 12.2, the partial MLE is generally consistent provided $\boldsymbol{\theta}_o$ is identified.

It is also clear that the partial MLE will be asymptotically normal by Theorem 12.3 in Section 12.3. However, unless

$$p_o(\mathbf{y} \mid \mathbf{z}) = \prod_{t=1}^{T} f_t(y_t \mid \mathbf{x}_t; \boldsymbol{\theta}_o) \tag{13.46}$$

for some subvector $\mathbf{z}$ of $\mathbf{x}$, we cannot apply the conditional information matrix equality. A more general asymptotic variance estimator of the type covered in Section 12.5.1 is needed, and we provide such estimators in the next two subsections.

It is useful to discuss at a general level why equation (13.46) does not necessarily hold in a panel data setting. First, suppose $\mathbf{x}_t$ contains only contemporaneous conditioning variables, $\mathbf{z}_t$; in particular, $\mathbf{x}_t$ contains no lagged dependent variables. Then we can always write

$$p_o(\mathbf{y} \mid \mathbf{z}) = p_1^o(y_1 \mid \mathbf{z}) \cdot p_2^o(y_2 \mid y_1, \mathbf{z}) \cdots p_t^o(y_t \mid y_{t-1}, y_{t-2}, \ldots, y_1, \mathbf{z}) \cdots$$
$$p_T^o(y_T \mid y_{T-1}, y_{T-2}, \ldots, y_1, \mathbf{z})$$

where $p_t^o(y_t \mid y_{t-1}, y_{t-2}, \ldots, y_1, \mathbf{z})$ is the true conditional density of y_t given y_{t-1}, $y_{t-2}, \ldots, y_1$ and $\mathbf{z} \equiv (\mathbf{z}_1, \ldots, \mathbf{z}_T)$. (For $t = 1$, p_1^o is the density of y_1 given $\mathbf{z}$.) For equation (13.46) to hold, we should have

$$p_t^o(y_t \mid y_{t-1}, y_{t-2}, \ldots, y_1, \mathbf{z}) = f_t(y_t \mid \mathbf{z}_t; \boldsymbol{\theta}_o), \qquad t = 1, \ldots, T$$

which requires that, once $\mathbf{z}_t$ is conditioned on, neither past lags of y_t nor elements of $\mathbf{z}$ from any other time period—past or future—appear in the conditional density $p_t^o(y_t \mid y_{t-1}, y_{t-2}, \ldots, y_1, \mathbf{z})$. Generally, this requirement is very strong, as it requires a combination of strict exogeneity of $\mathbf{z}_t$ and the absense of dynamics in p_t^o.

Equation (13.46) is more likely to hold when $\mathbf{x}_t$ contains lagged dependent variables. In fact, if $\mathbf{x}_t$ contains only lagged values of y_t, then

$$p_o(\mathbf{y}) = \prod_{t=1}^{T} f_t(y_t \mid \mathbf{x}_t; \boldsymbol{\theta}_o)$$

holds if $f_t(y_t \mid \mathbf{x}_t; \boldsymbol{\theta}_o) = p_t^o(y_t \mid y_{t-1}, y_{t-2}, \ldots, y_1)$ for all t (where p_1^o is the unconditional density of y_1), so that all dynamics are captured by f_t. When $\mathbf{x}_t$ contains some variables $\mathbf{z}_t$ in addition to lagged y_t, equation (13.46) requires that the parametric density captures all of the dynamics—that is, that all lags of y_t and $\mathbf{z}_t$ have been properly accounted for in $f(y_t \mid \mathbf{x}_t, \boldsymbol{\theta}_o)$—and strict exogeneity of $\mathbf{z}_t$.

In most treatments of maximum likelihood estimation of dynamic models containing additional exogenous variables, the strict exogeneity assumption is maintained, often implicitly by taking $\mathbf{z}_t$ to be nonrandom. In Chapter 7 we saw that strict exogeneity played no role in getting consistent, asymptotically normal estimators in linear panel data models by pooled OLS, and the same is true here. We also allow models where the dynamics have been incompletely specified.

Example 13.3 (Probit with Panel Data): To illustrate the previous discussion, we consider estimation of a panel data binary choice model. The idea is that, for each unit i in the population (individual, firm, and so on) we have a binary outcome, y_{it}, for each of T time periods. For example, if t represents a year, then y_{it} might indicate whether a person was arrested for a crime during year t.

Consider the model in latent variable form:

$$\begin{aligned} y_{it}^* &= \mathbf{x}_{it}\boldsymbol{\theta}_o + e_{it} \\ y_{it} &= 1[y_{it}^* > 0] \\ e_{it} \mid \mathbf{x}_{it} &\sim \text{Normal}(0, 1) \end{aligned} \tag{13.47}$$

The vector $\mathbf{x}_{it}$ might contain exogenous variables $\mathbf{z}_{it}$, lags of these, and even lagged y_{it} (not lagged y_{it}^*). Under the assumptions in model (13.47), we have, for each t, $P(y_{it} = 1 \mid \mathbf{x}_{it}) = \Phi(\mathbf{x}_{it}\boldsymbol{\theta}_o)$, and the density of y_{it} given $\mathbf{x}_{it} = \mathbf{x}_t$ is $f(y_t \mid \mathbf{x}_t) = [\Phi(\mathbf{x}_t\boldsymbol{\theta}_o)]^{y_t}[1 - \Phi(\mathbf{x}_t\boldsymbol{\theta}_o)]^{1-y_t}$.

The partial log likelihood for a cross section observation i is

$$\ell_i(\boldsymbol{\theta}) = \sum_{t=1}^{T} \{y_{it} \log \Phi(\mathbf{x}_{it}\boldsymbol{\theta}) + (1 - y_{it}) \log[1 - \Phi(\mathbf{x}_{it}\boldsymbol{\theta})]\} \tag{13.48}$$

and the partial MLE in this case—which simply maximizes $\ell_i(\boldsymbol{\theta})$ summed across all i—is the **pooled probit estimator**. With T fixed and $N \to \infty$, this estimator is consistent and $\sqrt{N}$-asymptotically normal without any assumptions other than identification and standard regularity conditions.

It is very important to know that the pooled probit estimator works without imposing additional assumptions on $\mathbf{e}_i = (e_{i1}, \ldots, e_{iT})'$. When $\mathbf{x}_{it}$ contains only exogenous variables $\mathbf{z}_{it}$, it would be standard to assume that

$$e_{it} \text{ is independent of } \mathbf{z}_i \equiv (\mathbf{z}_{i1}, \mathbf{z}_{i2}, \ldots, \mathbf{z}_{iT}), \qquad t = 1, \ldots, T \tag{13.49}$$

This is the natural strict exogeneity assumption (and is much stronger than simply assuming that e_{it} and $\mathbf{z}_{it}$ are independent for each t). The crime example can illustrate how strict exogeneity might fail. For example, suppose that $\mathbf{z}_{it}$ measures the amount of time the person has spent in prison prior to the current year. An arrest this year ($y_{it} = 1$) certainly has an effect on expected future values of $\mathbf{z}_{it}$, so that assumption

(13.49) is almost certainly false. Fortunately, we do *not* need assumption (13.49) to apply partial likelihood methods.

A second standard assumption is that the e_{it}, $t = 1, 2, \ldots, T$ are serially independent. This is especially restrictive in a static model. If we maintain this assumption in addition to assumption (13.49), then equation (13.46) holds (because the y_{it} are then independent conditional on $\mathbf{z}_i$) and the partial MLE is a conditional MLE.

To relax the assumption that the y_{it} are conditionally independent, we can allow the e_{it} to be correlated across t (still assuming that no lagged dependent variables appear). A common assumption is that $\mathbf{e}_i$ has a multivariate normal distribution with a general correlation matrix. Under this assumption, we can write down the joint distribution of $\mathbf{y}_i$ given $\mathbf{z}_i$, but it is complicated, and estimation is very computationally intensive (for recent discussions, see Keane, 1993, and Hajivassilou and Ruud, 1994). We will cover a special case, the random effects probit model, in Chapter 15.

A nice feature of the partial MLE is that $\hat{\theta}$ will be consistent and asymptotically normal even if the e_{it} are arbitrarily serially correlated. This result is entirely analogous to using pooled OLS in linear panel data models when the errors have arbitrary serial correlation.

When $\mathbf{x}_{it}$ contains lagged dependent variables, model (13.47) provides a way of examining dynamic behavior. Or, perhaps $y_{i,t-1}$ is included in $\mathbf{x}_{it}$ as a proxy for unobserved factors, and our focus is on on policy variables in $\mathbf{z}_{it}$. For example, if y_{it} is a binary indicator of employment, $y_{i,t-1}$ might be included as a control when studying the effect of a job training program (which may be a binary element of $\mathbf{z}_{it}$) on the employment probability; this method controls for the fact that participation in job training this year might depend on employment last year, and it captures the fact that employment status is persistent. In any case, provided $\mathrm{P}(y_{it} = 1 \mid \mathbf{x}_{it})$ follows a probit, the pooled probit estimator is consistent and asymptotically normal. The dynamics may or may not be correctly specified (more on this topic later), and the $\mathbf{z}_{it}$ need not be strictly exogenous (so that whether someone participates in job training in year t can depend on the past employment history).

13.8.2 Asymptotic Inference

The most important practical difference between conditional MLE and partial MLE is in the computation of asymptotic standard errors and test statistics. In many cases, including the pooled probit estimator, the pooled Poisson estimator (see Problem 13.6), and many other pooled procedures, standard econometrics packages can be used to compute the partial MLEs. However, except under certain assumptions, the usual standard errors and test statistics reported from a pooled analysis are not valid.

This situation is entirely analogous to the linear model case in Section 7.8 when the errors are serially correlated.

Estimation of the asymptotic variance of the partial MLE is not difficult. In fact, we can combine the M-estimation results from Section 12.5.1 and the results of Section 13.5 to obtain valid estimators.

From Theorem 12.3, we have Avar $\sqrt{N}(\hat{\boldsymbol{\theta}} - \boldsymbol{\theta}_o) = \mathbf{A}_o^{-1}\mathbf{B}_o\mathbf{A}_o^{-1}$, where

$$\mathbf{A}_o = -\mathrm{E}[\nabla_\theta^2 \ell_i(\boldsymbol{\theta}_o)] = -\sum_{t=1}^{T} \mathrm{E}[\nabla_\theta^2 \ell_{it}(\boldsymbol{\theta}_o)] = \sum_{t=1}^{T} \mathrm{E}[\mathbf{A}_{it}(\boldsymbol{\theta}_o)]$$

$$\mathbf{B}_o = \mathrm{E}[\mathbf{s}_i(\boldsymbol{\theta}_o)\mathbf{s}_i(\boldsymbol{\theta}_o)'] = \mathrm{E}\left\{\left[\sum_{t=1}^{T} \mathbf{s}_{it}(\boldsymbol{\theta}_o)\right]\left[\sum_{t=1}^{T} \mathbf{s}_{it}(\boldsymbol{\theta}_o)\right]'\right\}$$

$$\mathbf{A}_{it}(\boldsymbol{\theta}_o) = -\mathrm{E}[\nabla_\theta^2 \ell_{it}(\boldsymbol{\theta}_o) \mid \mathbf{x}_{it}]$$

$$\mathbf{s}_{it}(\boldsymbol{\theta}) = \nabla_\theta \ell_{it}(\boldsymbol{\theta})'$$

There are several important features of these formulas. First, the matrix $\mathbf{A}_o$ is just the sum across t of minus the expected Hessian. Second, the matrix $\mathbf{B}_o$ generally depends on the correlation between the scores at different time periods: $\mathrm{E}[\mathbf{s}_{it}(\boldsymbol{\theta}_o)\mathbf{s}_{ir}(\boldsymbol{\theta}_o)']$, $t \neq r$. Third, for each t, the conditional information matrix equality holds:

$$\mathbf{A}_{it}(\boldsymbol{\theta}_o) = \mathrm{E}[\mathbf{s}_{it}(\boldsymbol{\theta}_o)\mathbf{s}_{it}(\boldsymbol{\theta}_o)' \mid \mathbf{x}_{it}]$$

However, in general, $-\mathrm{E}[\mathbf{H}_i(\boldsymbol{\theta}_o) \mid \mathbf{x}_i] \neq \mathrm{E}[\mathbf{s}_i(\boldsymbol{\theta}_o)\mathbf{s}_i(\boldsymbol{\theta}_o)' \mid \mathbf{x}_i]$ and, more importantly, $\mathbf{B}_o \neq \mathbf{A}_o$. Thus, to perform inference in the context of partial MLE, we generally need separate estimates of $\mathbf{A}_o$ and $\mathbf{B}_o$. Given the structure of the partial MLE, these are easy to obtain. Three possibilities for $\mathbf{A}_o$ are

$$N^{-1}\sum_{i=1}^{N}\sum_{t=1}^{T} -\nabla_\theta^2 \ell_{it}(\hat{\boldsymbol{\theta}}), \qquad N^{-1}\sum_{i=1}^{N}\sum_{t=1}^{T} \mathbf{A}_{it}(\hat{\boldsymbol{\theta}}), \qquad \text{and}$$

$$N^{-1}\sum_{i=1}^{N}\sum_{t=1}^{T} \mathbf{s}_{it}(\hat{\boldsymbol{\theta}})\mathbf{s}_{it}(\hat{\boldsymbol{\theta}})' \tag{13.50}$$

The validity of the second of these follows from a standard iterated expectations argument, and the last of these follows from the conditional information matrix equality for each t. In most cases, the second estimator is preferred when it is easy to compute.

Since $\mathbf{B}_o$ depends on $\mathrm{E}[\mathbf{s}_{it}(\boldsymbol{\theta}_o)\mathbf{s}_{it}(\boldsymbol{\theta}_o)']$ as well as cross product terms, there are also at least three estimators available for $\mathbf{B}_o$. The simplest is

$$N^{-1}\sum_{i=1}^{N}\hat{\mathbf{s}}_i\hat{\mathbf{s}}_i' = N^{-1}\sum_{i=1}^{N}\sum_{t=1}^{T}\hat{\mathbf{s}}_{it}\hat{\mathbf{s}}_{it}' + N^{-1}\sum_{i=1}^{N}\sum_{t=1}^{T}\sum_{r\neq t}\hat{\mathbf{s}}_{ir}\hat{\mathbf{s}}_{it}' \tag{13.51}$$

where the second term on the right-hand side accounts for possible serial correlation in the score. The first term on the right-hand side of equation (13.51) can be replaced by one of the other two estimators in equation (13.50). The asymptotic variance of $\hat{\boldsymbol{\theta}}$ is estimated, as usual, by $\hat{\mathbf{A}}^{-1}\hat{\mathbf{B}}\hat{\mathbf{A}}^{-1}/N$ for the chosen estimators $\hat{\mathbf{A}}$ and $\hat{\mathbf{B}}$. The asymptotic standard errors come directly from this matrix, and Wald tests for linear and nonlinear hypotheses can be obtained directly. The robust score statistic discussed in Section 12.6.2 can also be used. When $\mathbf{B}_o \neq \mathbf{A}_o$, the likelihood ratio statistic computed after pooled estimation is *not* valid.

Because the CIME holds for each t, $\mathbf{B}_o = \mathbf{A}_o$ when the scores evaluated at $\boldsymbol{\theta}_o$ are serially uncorrelated, that is, when

$$\mathrm{E}[\mathbf{s}_{it}(\boldsymbol{\theta}_o)\mathbf{s}_{ir}(\boldsymbol{\theta}_o)'] = \mathbf{0}, \qquad t \neq r \tag{13.52}$$

When the score is serially uncorrelated, inference is very easy: the usual MLE statistics computed from the pooled estimation, including likelihood ratio statistics, are asymptotically valid. Effectively, we can ignore the fact that a time dimension is present. The estimator of $\mathrm{Avar}(\hat{\boldsymbol{\theta}})$ is just $\hat{\mathbf{A}}^{-1}/N$, where $\hat{\mathbf{A}}$ is one of the matrices in equation (13.50).

Example 13.3 (continued): For the pooled probit example, a simple, general estimator of the asymptotic variance is

$$\left[\sum_{i=1}^{N}\sum_{t=1}^{T}\mathbf{A}_{it}(\hat{\boldsymbol{\theta}})\right]^{-1}\left[\sum_{i=1}^{N}\mathbf{s}_i(\hat{\boldsymbol{\theta}})\mathbf{s}_i(\hat{\boldsymbol{\theta}})'\right]\left[\sum_{i=1}^{N}\sum_{t=1}^{T}\mathbf{A}_{it}(\hat{\boldsymbol{\theta}})\right]^{-1} \tag{13.53}$$

where

$$\mathbf{A}_{it}(\hat{\boldsymbol{\theta}}) = \frac{\{\phi(\mathbf{x}_{it}\hat{\boldsymbol{\theta}})\}^2\mathbf{x}_{it}'\mathbf{x}_{it}}{\Phi(\mathbf{x}_{it}\hat{\boldsymbol{\theta}})[1-\Phi(\mathbf{x}_{it}\hat{\boldsymbol{\theta}})]}$$

and

$$\mathbf{s}_i(\boldsymbol{\theta}) = \sum_{t=1}^{T}\mathbf{s}_{it}(\boldsymbol{\theta}) = \sum_{t=1}^{T}\frac{\phi(\mathbf{x}_{it}\boldsymbol{\theta})\mathbf{x}_{it}'[y_{it}-\Phi(\mathbf{x}_{it}\boldsymbol{\theta})]}{\Phi(\mathbf{x}_{it}\boldsymbol{\theta})[1-\Phi(\mathbf{x}_{it}\boldsymbol{\theta})]}$$

The estimator (13.53) contains cross product terms of the form $\mathbf{s}_{it}(\hat{\boldsymbol{\theta}})\mathbf{s}_{ir}(\hat{\boldsymbol{\theta}})'$, $t \neq r$, and so it is fully robust. If the score is serially uncorrelated, then the usual probit standard errors and test statistics from the pooled estimation are valid. We will discuss a sufficient condition for the scores to be serially uncorrelated in the next subsection.

13.8.3 Inference with Dynamically Complete Models

There is a very important case where condition (13.52) holds, in which case all statistics obtained by treating $\ell_i(\boldsymbol{\theta})$ as a standard log likelihood are valid. For any definition of $\mathbf{x}_t$, we say that $\{f_t(y_t \mid \mathbf{x}_t; \boldsymbol{\theta}_o): t = 1, \ldots, T\}$ is a **dynamically complete conditional density** if

$$f_t(y_t \mid \mathbf{x}_t; \boldsymbol{\theta}_o) = p_t^o(y_t \mid \mathbf{x}_t, y_{t-1}, \mathbf{x}_{t-1}, y_{t-2}, \ldots, y_1, \mathbf{x}_1), \qquad t = 1, \ldots, T \tag{13.54}$$

In other words, $f_t(y_t \mid \mathbf{x}_t; \boldsymbol{\theta}_o)$ must be the conditional density of y_t given $\mathbf{x}_t$ *and* the entire past of $(\mathbf{x}_t, y_t)$.

When $\mathbf{x}_t = \mathbf{z}_t$ for contemporaneous exogenous variables, equation (13.54) is very strong: it means that, once $\mathbf{z}_t$ is controlled for, no past values of $\mathbf{z}_t$ *or* y_t appear in the conditional density $p_t^o(y_t \mid \mathbf{z}_t, y_{t-1}, \mathbf{z}_{t-1}, y_{t-2}, \ldots, y_1, \mathbf{z}_1)$. When $\mathbf{x}_t$ contains $\mathbf{z}_t$ and some lags—similar to a finite distributed lag model—then equation (13.54) is perhaps more reasonable, but it still assumes that lagged y_t has no effect on y_t once current and lagged $\mathbf{z}_t$ are controlled for. That assumption (13.54) can be false is analogous to the omnipresence of serial correlation in static and finite distributed lag regression models. One important feature of dynamic completeness is that it does not require strict exogeneity of $\mathbf{z}_t$ [since only current and lagged $\mathbf{x}_t$ appear in equation (13.54)].

Dynamic completeness is more likely to hold when $\mathbf{x}_t$ contains lagged dependent variables. The issue, then, is whether enough lags of y_t (and $\mathbf{z}_t$) have been included in $\mathbf{x}_t$ to fully capture the dynamics. For example, if $\mathbf{x}_t \equiv (\mathbf{z}_t, y_{t-1})$, then equation (13.54) means that, along with $\mathbf{z}_t$, only one lag of y_t is needed to capture all of the dynamics.

Showing that condition (13.52) holds under dynamic completeness is easy. First, for each t, $\mathrm{E}[\mathbf{s}_{it}(\boldsymbol{\theta}_o) \mid \mathbf{x}_{it}] = \mathbf{0}$, since $f_t(y_t \mid \mathbf{x}_t; \boldsymbol{\theta}_o)$ is a correctly specified conditional density. But then, under assumption (13.54),

$$\mathrm{E}[\mathbf{s}_{it}(\boldsymbol{\theta}_o) \mid \mathbf{x}_{it}, y_{i,t-1}, \ldots, y_{i1}, \mathbf{x}_{i1}] = \mathbf{0} \tag{13.55}$$

Now consider the expected value in condition (13.52) for $r < t$. Since $\mathbf{s}_{ir}(\boldsymbol{\theta}_o)$ is a function of $(\mathbf{x}_{ir}, y_{ir})$, which is in the conditioning set (13.55), the usual iterated expectations argument shows that condition (13.52) holds. It follows that, under dynamic completeness, the usual maximum likelihood statistics from the pooled estimation are asymptotically valid. This result is completely analogous to pooled OLS under dynamic completeness of the conditional mean and homoskedasticity (see Section 7.8).

If the panel data probit model is dynamically complete, any software package that does standard probit can be used to obtain valid standard errors and test statistics, provided the response probability satisfies $\mathrm{P}(y_{it} = 1 \mid \mathbf{x}_{it}) = \mathrm{P}(y_{it} = 1 \mid \mathbf{x}_{it}, y_{i,t-1}, \mathbf{x}_{i,t-1}, \ldots)$. Without dynamic completeness the standard errors and test statistics generally need to be adjusted for serial dependence.

Since dynamic completeness affords nontrivial simplifications, does this fact mean that we should always include lagged values of exogenous and dependent variables until equation (13.54) appears to be satisfied? Not necessarily. Static models are sometimes desirable even if they neglect dynamics. For example, suppose that we have panel data on individuals in an occupation where pay is determined partly by cumulative productivity. (Professional athletes and college professors are two examples.) An equation relating salary to the productivity measures, and possibly demographic variables, is appropriate. Nothing implies that the equation would be dynamically complete; in fact, past salary could help predict current salary, even after controlling for observed productivity. But it does not make much sense to include past salary in the regression equation. As we know from Chapter 10, a reasonable approach is to include an unobserved effect in the equation, and this does not lead to a model with complete dynamics. See also Section 13.9.

We may wish to test the null hypothesis that the density is dynamically complete. White (1994) shows how to test whether the score is serially correlated in a pure time series setting. A similar approach can be used with panel data. A general test for dynamic misspecification can be based on the limiting distribution of (the vectorization of)

$$N^{-1/2} \sum_{i=1}^{N} \sum_{t=2}^{T} \hat{\mathbf{s}}_{it} \hat{\mathbf{s}}_{i,t-1}'$$

where the scores are evaluated at the partial MLE. Rather than derive a general statistic here, we will study tests of dynamic completeness in particular applications later (see particularly Chapters 15, 16, and 19).

13.8.4 Inference under Cluster Sampling

Partial MLE methods are also useful when using cluster samples. Suppose that, for each group or cluster g, $f(y_g \mid \mathbf{x}_g; \boldsymbol{\theta})$ is a correctly specified conditional density of y_g given $\mathbf{x}_g$. Here, i indexes the cluster, and as before we assume a large number of clusters N and relatively small group sizes, G_i. The primary issue is that the y_{ig} might be correlated within a cluster, possibly through unobserved cluster effects. A partial MLE of $\boldsymbol{\theta}_o$ is defined exactly as in the panel data case, except that t is replaced with g and T is replaced with G_i for each i; for example, equation (13.44) becomes $\ell_i(\boldsymbol{\theta}) \equiv \sum_{g=1}^{G_i} \log f(y_{ig} \mid \mathbf{x}_{ig}; \boldsymbol{\theta})$. Obtaining the partial MLE is usually much easier than specifying (or deriving) the joint distribution of $\mathbf{y}_i$ conditional on $\mathbf{x}_i$ for each cluster i and employing MLE (which must recognize that the cluster observations cannot be identically distributed if the cluster sizes differ).

In addition to allowing the y_{ig} to be arbitrarily dependent within a cluster, the partial MLE does not require $\mathrm{D}(y_{ig} \mid \mathbf{x}_{i1}, \ldots, \mathbf{x}_{iG_i}) = \mathrm{D}(y_{ig} \mid \mathbf{x}_{ig})$. But we need to compute the robust variance matrix estimator as in Section 13.8.2, along with robust test statistics. The quasi-likelihood ratio statistic is not valid unless $\mathrm{D}(y_{ig} \mid \mathbf{x}_i) = \mathrm{D}(y_{ig} \mid \mathbf{x}_{ig})$ and the y_{ig} are independent within each cluster, conditional on $\mathbf{x}_i$.

We can use partial MLE analysis to test for peer effects in cluster samples, as discussed briefly in Section 11.5 for linear models. For example, some elements of $\mathbf{x}_{ig}$ might be averages of explanatory variables for other units (say, people) in the cluster. Therefore, we might specify a model $f_g(y_g \mid \mathbf{z}_g, \overline{\mathbf{w}}_{(g)}; \boldsymbol{\theta})$ (for example, a probit model), where $\overline{\mathbf{w}}_{(g)}$ represents average characteristics of other people (or units) in the same cluster. The pooled partial MLE analysis is consistent and asymptotically normal, but the variance matrix must be corrected for additional within-cluster dependence.

13.9 Panel Data Models with Unobserved Effects

As we saw in Chapters 10 and 11, linear unobserved effects panel data models play an important role in modern empirical research. Nonlinear unobserved effects panel data models are becoming increasingly more important. Although we will cover particular models in Chapters 15, 16, and 19, it is useful to have a general treatment.

13.9.1 Models with Strictly Exogenous Explanatory Variables

For each i, let $\{(\mathbf{y}_{it}, \mathbf{x}_{it})\colon t = 1, 2, \ldots, T\}$ be a random draw from the cross section, where $\mathbf{y}_{it}$ and $\mathbf{x}_{it}$ can both be vectors. Associated with each cross section unit i is unobserved heterogeneity, $\mathbf{c}_i$, which could be a vector. We assume interest lies in the distribution of $\mathbf{y}_{it}$ given $(\mathbf{x}_{it}, \mathbf{c}_i)$. The vector $\mathbf{x}_{it}$ can contain lags of contemporaneous variables, say $\mathbf{z}_{it}$ [for example, $\mathbf{x}_{it} = (\mathbf{z}_{it}, \mathbf{z}_{i,t-1}, \mathbf{z}_{i,t-2})$], or even leads of $\mathbf{z}_{it}$ [for example, $\mathbf{x}_{it} = (\mathbf{z}_{it}, \mathbf{z}_{i,t+1})$], but not lags of y_{it}. Whatever the lag structure, we let $t = 1$ denote the first time period available for estimation.

Let $f_t(\mathbf{y}_t \mid \mathbf{x}_t, \mathbf{c}; \boldsymbol{\theta})$ denote a correctly specified density for each t. A key assumption on $\mathbf{x}_{it}$ is analogous to the strict exogeneity assumption for linear unobserved effects models: $\mathrm{D}(\mathbf{y}_{it} \mid \mathbf{x}_i, \mathbf{c}_i) = \mathrm{D}(\mathbf{y}_{it} \mid \mathbf{x}_{it}, \mathbf{c}_i)$, which means that only contemporaneous $\mathbf{x}_{it}$ matters once $\mathbf{c}_i$ is also conditioned on. (Whether or not $\mathbf{x}_{it}$ contains lagged $\mathbf{z}_{it}$, strict exogeneity conditonal on $\mathbf{c}_i$ rules out certain kinds of feedback from y_{it} to $\mathbf{z}_{i,t+h}$, $h > 0$.)

In many cases we want to allow $\mathbf{c}_i$ and $\mathbf{x}_i$ to be dependent. A general approach to estimating $\boldsymbol{\theta}_o$ (and other quantities of interest) is to model the distribution of $\mathbf{c}_i$ given $\mathbf{x}_i$. [In Chapters 15 and 19 we cover some important models where $\boldsymbol{\theta}_o$ can be consistently estimated without making any assumptions about $\mathrm{D}(\mathbf{c}_i \mid \mathbf{x}_i)$.] Let $h(\mathbf{c} \mid \mathbf{x}; \boldsymbol{\delta})$ be a correctly specified density for $\mathbf{c}_i$ given $\mathbf{x}_i = \mathbf{x}$.

There are two common ways to proceed. First, we can make the additional assumption that, conditional on $(\mathbf{x}_i, \mathbf{c}_i)$, the $\mathbf{y}_{it}$ are independent. Then, the joint density of $(\mathbf{y}_{i1}, \ldots, \mathbf{y}_{iT})$, given $(\mathbf{x}_i, \mathbf{c}_i)$, is

$$\prod_{t=1}^{T} f_t(\mathbf{y}_t \mid \mathbf{x}_{it}, \mathbf{c}_i; \boldsymbol{\theta})$$

We cannot use this density directly to estimate $\boldsymbol{\theta}_o$ because we do not observe the outcomes $\mathbf{c}_i$. Instead, we can use the density of $\mathbf{c}_i$ given $\mathbf{x}_i$ to integrate out the dependence on $\mathbf{c}$. The density of $\mathbf{y}_i$ given $\mathbf{x}_i$ is

$$\int_{\mathbb{R}^J} \left[\prod_{t=1}^{T} f_t(\mathbf{y}_t \mid \mathbf{x}_{it}, \mathbf{c}; \boldsymbol{\theta}_o) \right] h(\mathbf{c} \mid \mathbf{x}_i; \boldsymbol{\delta}_o) \, d\mathbf{c} \tag{13.56}$$

where J is the dimension of $\mathbf{c}$ and $h(\mathbf{c} \mid \mathbf{x}; \boldsymbol{\delta})$ is the correctly specified model for the density of $\mathbf{c}_i$ given $\mathbf{x}_i = \mathbf{x}$. For concreteness, we assume that $\mathbf{c}$ is a continuous random vector. For each i, the log-likelihood function is

$$\log\left\{ \int_{\mathbb{R}^J} \left[\prod_{t=1}^{T} f_t(\mathbf{y}_{it} \mid \mathbf{x}_{it}, \mathbf{c}; \boldsymbol{\theta}_o) \right] h(\mathbf{c} \mid \mathbf{x}_i; \boldsymbol{\delta}_o) \, d\mathbf{c} \right\} \tag{13.57}$$

[It is important to see that expression (13.57) does not depend on the $\mathbf{c}_i$; $\mathbf{c}$ has been integrated out.] Assuming identification and standard regularity conditions, we can consistently estimate $\boldsymbol{\theta}_o$ and $\boldsymbol{\delta}_o$ by conditional MLE, where the asymptotics are for fixed T and $N \to \infty$. The CMLE is $\sqrt{N}$-asymptotically normal.

Another approach is often simpler and places no restrictions on the joint distribution of the $\mathbf{y}_{it}$ [conditional on $(\mathbf{x}_i, \mathbf{c}_i)$]. For each t, we can obtain the density of $\mathbf{y}_{it}$ given $\mathbf{x}_i$:

$$\int_{\mathbb{R}^J} [f_t(\mathbf{y}_t \mid \mathbf{x}_{it}, \mathbf{c}; \boldsymbol{\theta}_o)] h(\mathbf{c} \mid \mathbf{x}_i; \boldsymbol{\delta}_o) \, d\mathbf{c}$$

Now the problem becomes one of partial MLE. We estimate θ_o and δ_o by maximizing

$$\sum_{i=1}^{N}\sum_{t=1}^{T} \log\left\{\int_{\mathbb{R}^J} [f_t(\mathbf{y}_{it} \mid \mathbf{x}_{it}, \mathbf{c}; \boldsymbol{\theta})] h(\mathbf{c} \mid \mathbf{x}_i; \boldsymbol{\delta})\, d\mathbf{c}\right\} \tag{13.58}$$

(Actually, using PMLE, θ_o and δ_o are not always separately identified, although interesting functions of them are. We will see examples in Chapters 15 and 16.) Across time, the scores for each i will necessarily be serially correlated because the $\mathbf{y}_{it}$ are dependent when we condition only on $\mathbf{x}_i$, and not also on $\mathbf{c}_i$. Therefore, we must make inference robust to serial dependence, as in Section 13.8.2. In Chapter 15, we will study both the conditional MLE and partial MLE approaches for unobserved effects probit models.

13.9.2 Models with Lagged Dependent Variables

Now assume that we are interested in modeling $\mathrm{D}(\mathbf{y}_{it} \mid \mathbf{z}_{it}, \mathbf{y}_{i,t-1}, \mathbf{c}_i)$ where, for simplicity, we include only contemporaneous conditioning variables, $\mathbf{z}_{it}$, and only one lag of $\mathbf{y}_{it}$. Adding lags (or even leads) of $\mathbf{z}_{it}$ or more lags of $\mathbf{y}_{it}$ requires only a notational change.

A key assumption is that we have the dynamics correctly specified and that $\mathbf{z}_i = \{\mathbf{z}_{i1}, \ldots, \mathbf{z}_{iT}\}$ is appropriately strictly exogenous (conditional on $\mathbf{c}_i$). These assumptions are both captured by

$$\mathrm{D}(\mathbf{y}_{it} \mid \mathbf{z}_{it}, \mathbf{y}_{i,t-1}, \mathbf{c}_i) = \mathrm{D}(\mathbf{y}_{it} \mid \mathbf{z}_i, \mathbf{y}_{i,t-1}, \ldots, \mathbf{y}_{i0}, \mathbf{c}_i) \tag{13.59}$$

We assume that $f_t(\mathbf{y}_t \mid \mathbf{z}_t, \mathbf{y}_{t-1}, \mathbf{c}; \boldsymbol{\theta})$ is a correctly specified density for the conditional distribution on the left-hand side of equation (13.59). Given strict exogeneity of $\{\mathbf{z}_{it}: t = 1, \ldots, T\}$ and dynamic completeness, the density of $(\mathbf{y}_{i1}, \ldots, \mathbf{y}_{iT})$ given $(\mathbf{z}_i = \mathbf{z}, \mathbf{y}_{i0} = \mathbf{y}_0, \mathbf{c}_i = \mathbf{c})$ is

$$\prod_{t=1}^{T} f_t(\mathbf{y}_t \mid \mathbf{z}_t, \mathbf{y}_{t-1}, \mathbf{c}; \boldsymbol{\theta}_o) \tag{13.60}$$

(By convention, $\mathbf{y}_{i0}$ is the first observation on $\mathbf{y}_{it}$.) Again, to estimate θ_o, we integrate $\mathbf{c}$ out of this density. To do so, we specify a density for $\mathbf{c}_i$ given $\mathbf{z}_i$ *and* the initial value $\mathbf{y}_{i0}$ (sometimes called the **initial condition**). Let $h(\mathbf{c} \mid \mathbf{z}, \mathbf{y}_0; \boldsymbol{\delta})$ denote the model for this conditional density. Then, assuming that we have this model correctly specifed, the density of $(\mathbf{y}_{i1}, \ldots, \mathbf{y}_{iT})$ given $(\mathbf{z}_i = \mathbf{z}, \mathbf{y}_{i0} = \mathbf{y}_0)$ is

$$\int_{\mathbb{R}^J} \left[\prod_{t=1}^{T} f_t(\mathbf{y}_t \mid \mathbf{z}_t, \mathbf{y}_{t-1}, \mathbf{c}; \boldsymbol{\theta}_o)\right] h(\mathbf{c} \mid \mathbf{z}, \mathbf{y}_0; \boldsymbol{\delta}_o)\, d\mathbf{c} \tag{13.61}$$

which, for each i, leads to the log-likelihood function conditional on $(\mathbf{z}_i, \mathbf{y}_{i0})$:

$$\log\left\{\int_{\mathbb{R}^J}\left[\prod_{t=1}^{T} f_t(\mathbf{y}_{it} \mid \mathbf{z}_{it}, \mathbf{y}_{i,t-1}, \mathbf{c}; \boldsymbol{\theta})\right] h(\mathbf{c} \mid \mathbf{z}_i, \mathbf{y}_{i0}; \boldsymbol{\delta})\, d\mathbf{c}\right\} \tag{13.62}$$

We sum expression (13.62) across $i = 1, \ldots, N$ and maximize with respect to $\boldsymbol{\theta}$ and $\boldsymbol{\delta}$ to obtain the CMLEs. Provided all functions are sufficiently differentiable and identification holds, the conditional MLEs are consistent and $\sqrt{N}$-asymptotically normal, as usual. Because we have fully specified the conditional density of $(\mathbf{y}_{i1}, \ldots, \mathbf{y}_{iT})$ given $(\mathbf{z}_i, \mathbf{y}_{i0})$, the general theory of conditional MLE applies directly. [The fact that the distribution of $\mathbf{y}_{i0}$ given $\mathbf{z}_i$ would typically depend on $\boldsymbol{\theta}_o$ has no bearing on the consistency of the CMLE. The fact that we are conditioning on $\mathbf{y}_{i0}$, rather than basing the analysis on $\mathrm{D}(\mathbf{y}_{i0}, \mathbf{y}_{i1}, \ldots, \mathbf{y}_{iT} \mid \mathbf{z}_i)$, means that we are generally sacrificing efficiency. But by conditioning on $\mathbf{y}_{i0}$ we do not have to find $\mathrm{D}(\mathbf{y}_{i0} \mid \mathbf{z}_i)$, something which is very difficult if not impossible.] The asymptotic variance of $(\hat{\boldsymbol{\theta}}', \hat{\boldsymbol{\delta}}')'$ can be estimated by any of the formulas in equation (13.32) (properly modified to account for estimation of $\boldsymbol{\theta}_o$ and $\boldsymbol{\delta}_o$).

A weakness of the CMLE approach is that we must specify a density for $\mathbf{c}_i$ given $(\mathbf{z}_i, \mathbf{y}_{i0})$, but this is a price we pay for estimating dynamic, nonlinear models with unobserved effects. The alternative of treating the $\mathbf{c}_i$ as parameters to estimate—which is, unfortunately, often labeled the "fixed effects" approach—does not lead to consistent estimation of $\boldsymbol{\theta}_o$.

In any application, several issues need to be addressed. First, when are the parameters identified? Second, what quantities are we interested in? As we cannot observe $\mathbf{c}_i$, we typically want to average out $\mathbf{c}_i$ when obtaining partial effects. Wooldridge (2000e) shows that average partial effects are generally identified under the assumptions that we have made. Finally, obtaining the CMLE can be very difficult computationally, as can be obtaining the asymptotic variance estimates in equation (13.32). If $\mathbf{c}_i$ is a scalar, estimation is easier, but there is still a one-dimensional integral to approximate for each i. In Chapters 15, 16, and 19 we will see that, under reasonable assumptions, standard software can be used to estimate dynamic models with unobserved effects, including effects that are averaged across the distribution of heterogeneity. See also Problem 13.11 for application to a dynamic linear model.

13.10 Two-Step MLE

Consistency and asymptotic normality results are also available for **two-step maximum likelihood estimators** and **two-step partial maximum likelihood estimators**; we focus on the former for concreteness. Let the conditional density be $f(\cdot \mid \mathbf{x}_i; \boldsymbol{\theta}_o, \boldsymbol{\gamma}_o)$, where $\boldsymbol{\gamma}_o$ is an $R \times 1$ vector of additional parameters. A preliminary estimator of $\boldsymbol{\gamma}_o$, say $\hat{\boldsymbol{\gamma}}$, is plugged into the log-likelihood function, and $\hat{\boldsymbol{\theta}}$ solves

$$\max_{\boldsymbol{\theta} \in \boldsymbol{\Theta}} \sum_{i=1}^{N} \log f(\mathbf{y}_i \mid \mathbf{x}_i; \boldsymbol{\theta}, \hat{\boldsymbol{\gamma}})$$

Consistency follow from results for two-step M-estimators. The practical limitation is that $\log f(\mathbf{y}_i \mid \mathbf{x}_i; \boldsymbol{\theta}, \boldsymbol{\gamma})$ is continuous on $\boldsymbol{\Theta} \times \boldsymbol{\Gamma}$ and that $\boldsymbol{\theta}_o$ and $\boldsymbol{\gamma}_o$ are identified.

Asymptotic normality of the two-step MLE follows directly from the results on two-step M-estimation in Chapter 12. As we saw there, in general the asymptotic variance of $\sqrt{N}(\hat{\boldsymbol{\theta}} - \boldsymbol{\theta}_o)$ depends on the asymptotic variance of $\sqrt{N}(\hat{\boldsymbol{\gamma}} - \boldsymbol{\gamma}_o)$ [see equation (12.41)], so we need to know the estimation problem solved by $\hat{\boldsymbol{\gamma}}$. In some cases estimation of $\boldsymbol{\gamma}_o$ can be ignored. An important case is where the expected Hessian, defined with respect to $\boldsymbol{\theta}$ and $\boldsymbol{\gamma}$, is block diagonal [the matrix $\mathbf{F}_o$ in equation (12.36) is zero in this case]. It can also hold for some values of $\boldsymbol{\theta}_o$, which is important for testing certain hypotheses. We will encounter several examples in Part IV.

Problems

13.1. If $f(\mathbf{y} \mid \mathbf{x}; \boldsymbol{\theta})$ is a correctly specified model for the density of $\mathbf{y}_i$ given $\mathbf{x}_i$, does $\boldsymbol{\theta}_o$ solve $\max_{\boldsymbol{\theta} \in \boldsymbol{\Theta}} \mathrm{E}[f(\mathbf{y}_i \mid \mathbf{x}_i; \boldsymbol{\theta})]$?

13.2. Suppose that for a random sample, $y_i \mid \mathbf{x}_i \sim \text{Normal}[m(\mathbf{x}_i, \boldsymbol{\beta}_o), \sigma_o^2]$, where $m(\mathbf{x}, \boldsymbol{\beta})$ is a function of the K-vector of explanatory variables $\mathbf{x}$ and the $P \times 1$ parameter vector $\boldsymbol{\beta}$. Recall that $\mathrm{E}(y_i \mid \mathbf{x}_i) = m(\mathbf{x}_i, \boldsymbol{\beta}_o)$ and $\mathrm{Var}(y_i \mid \mathbf{x}_i) = \sigma_o^2$.

a. Write down the conditional log-likelihood function for observation i. Show that the CMLE of $\boldsymbol{\beta}_o$, $\hat{\boldsymbol{\beta}}$, solves the problem $\min_{\boldsymbol{\beta}} \sum_{i=1}^{N} [y_i - m(\mathbf{x}_i, \boldsymbol{\beta})]^2$. In other words, the CMLE for $\boldsymbol{\beta}_o$ is the nonlinear least squares estimator.

b. Let $\boldsymbol{\theta} \equiv (\boldsymbol{\beta}' \sigma^2)'$ denote the $(P+1) \times 1$ vector of parameters. Find the score of the log likelihood for a generic i. Show directly that $\mathrm{E}[\mathbf{s}_i(\boldsymbol{\theta}_o) \mid \mathbf{x}_i] = \mathbf{0}$. What features of the normal distribution do you need in order to show that the conditional expectation of the score is zero?

c. Use the first-order condition to find $\hat{\sigma}^2$ in terms of $\hat{\boldsymbol{\beta}}$.

d. Find the Hessian of the log-likelihood function with respect to $\boldsymbol{\theta}$.

e. Show directly that $-\mathrm{E}[\mathbf{H}_i(\boldsymbol{\theta}_o) \mid \mathbf{x}_i] = \mathrm{E}[\mathbf{s}_i(\boldsymbol{\theta}_o)\mathbf{s}_i(\boldsymbol{\theta}_o)' \mid \mathbf{x}_i]$.

f. Write down the estimated asymptotic variance of $\hat{\beta}$, and explain how to obtain the asymptotic standard errors.

13.3. Consider a general binary response model $P(y_i = 1 \mid \mathbf{x}_i) = G(\mathbf{x}_i, \boldsymbol{\theta}_o)$, where $G(\mathbf{x}, \boldsymbol{\theta})$ is strictly between zero and one for all $\mathbf{x}$ and $\boldsymbol{\theta}$. Here, $\mathbf{x}$ and $\boldsymbol{\theta}$ need not have the same dimension; let $\mathbf{x}$ be a K-vector and $\boldsymbol{\theta}$ a P-vector.

a. Write down the log likelihood for observation i.

b. Find the score for each i. Show directly that $E[\mathbf{s}_i(\boldsymbol{\theta}_o) \mid \mathbf{x}_i] = \mathbf{0}$.

c. When $G(\mathbf{x}, \boldsymbol{\theta}) = \Phi[\mathbf{x}\boldsymbol{\beta} + \delta_1(\mathbf{x}\boldsymbol{\beta})^2 + \delta_2(\mathbf{x}\boldsymbol{\beta})^3]$, find the LM statistic for testing H_0: $\delta_{o1} = 0, \delta_{o2} = 0$.

13.4. In the Newey-Tauchen-White specification-testing context, explain why we can take $\mathbf{g}(\mathbf{w}, \boldsymbol{\theta}) = a(\mathbf{x}, \boldsymbol{\theta})\mathbf{s}(\mathbf{w}, \boldsymbol{\theta})$, where $a(\mathbf{x}, \boldsymbol{\theta})$ is essentially any scalar function of $\mathbf{x}$ and $\boldsymbol{\theta}$.

13.5. In the context of CMLE, consider a reparameterization of the kind in Section 12.6.2: $\boldsymbol{\phi} = \mathbf{g}(\boldsymbol{\theta})$, where the Jacobian of $\mathbf{g}$, $\mathbf{G}(\boldsymbol{\theta})$, is continuous and nonsingular for all $\boldsymbol{\theta} \in \boldsymbol{\Theta}$. Let $\mathbf{s}_i^g(\boldsymbol{\phi}) = \mathbf{s}_i^g[\mathbf{g}(\boldsymbol{\theta})]$ denote the score of the log likelihood in the reparameterized model; thus, from Section 12.6.2, $\mathbf{s}_i^g(\boldsymbol{\phi}) = [\mathbf{G}(\boldsymbol{\theta})']^{-1}\mathbf{s}_i(\boldsymbol{\theta})$.

a. Using the conditional information matrix equality, find $\mathbf{A}_i^g(\boldsymbol{\phi}_o) \equiv E[\mathbf{s}_i^g(\boldsymbol{\phi}_o)\mathbf{s}_i^g(\boldsymbol{\phi}_o)' \mid \mathbf{x}_i]$ in terms of $\mathbf{G}(\boldsymbol{\theta}_o)$ and $\mathbf{A}_i(\boldsymbol{\theta}_o) \equiv E[\mathbf{s}_i(\boldsymbol{\theta}_o)\mathbf{s}_i(\boldsymbol{\theta}_o)' \mid \mathbf{x}_i]$.

b. Show that $\tilde{\mathbf{A}}_i^g = \tilde{\mathbf{G}}'^{-1}\tilde{\mathbf{A}}_i\tilde{\mathbf{G}}^{-1}$, where these are all evaluated at the restricted estimate, $\tilde{\boldsymbol{\theta}}$.

c. Use part b to show that the expected Hessian form of the LM statistic is invariant to reparameterization.

13.6. Suppose that for a panel data set with T time periods, y_{it} given $\mathbf{x}_{it}$ has a Poisson distribution with mean $\exp(\mathbf{x}_{it}\boldsymbol{\theta}_o)$, $t = 1, \ldots, T$.

a. Do you have enough information to construct the joint distribution of $\mathbf{y}_i$ given $\mathbf{x}_i$? Explain.

b. Write down the partial log likelihood for each i and find the score, $\mathbf{s}_i(\boldsymbol{\theta})$.

c. Show how to estimate $\text{Avar}(\hat{\boldsymbol{\theta}})$; it should be of the form (13.53).

d. How does the estimator of $\text{Avar}(\hat{\boldsymbol{\theta}})$ simplify if the conditional mean is dynamically complete?

13.7. Suppose that you have two parametric models for conditional densities: $g(y_1 \mid y_2, \mathbf{x}; \boldsymbol{\theta})$ and $h(y_2 \mid \mathbf{x}; \boldsymbol{\theta})$; not all elements of $\boldsymbol{\theta}$ need to appear in both densities. Denote the true value of $\boldsymbol{\theta}$ by $\boldsymbol{\theta}_o$.

a. What is the joint density of (y_1, y_2) given $\mathbf{x}$? How would you estimate $\boldsymbol{\theta}_o$ given a random sample on $(\mathbf{x}, y_1, y_2)$?

b. Suppose now that a random sample is not available on all variables. In particular, y_1 is observed only when $(\mathbf{x}, y_2)$ satisfies a known rule. For example, when y_2 is binary, y_1 is observed only when $y_2 = 1$. We assume $(\mathbf{x}, y_2)$ is always observed. Let r_2 be a binary variable equal to one if y_1 is observed and zero otherwise. A partial MLE is obtained by defining

$$\ell_i(\boldsymbol{\theta}) = r_{i2} \log g(y_{i1} \mid y_{i2}, \mathbf{x}_i; \boldsymbol{\theta}) + \log h(y_{i2} \mid \mathbf{x}_i; \boldsymbol{\theta}) \equiv r_{i2}\ell_{i1}(\boldsymbol{\theta}) + \ell_{i2}(\boldsymbol{\theta})$$

for each i. This formulation ensures that first part of ℓ_i only enters the estimation when y_{i1} is observed. Verify that $\boldsymbol{\theta}_o$ maximizes $\mathrm{E}[\ell_i(\boldsymbol{\theta})]$ over $\boldsymbol{\Theta}$.

c. Show that $-\mathrm{E}[\mathbf{H}_i(\boldsymbol{\theta}_o)] = \mathrm{E}[\mathbf{s}_i(\boldsymbol{\theta}_o)\mathbf{s}_i(\boldsymbol{\theta}_o)']$, even though the problem is not a true conditional MLE problem (and therefore a conditional information matrix equality does not hold).

d. Argue that a consistent estimator of Avar $\sqrt{N}(\hat{\boldsymbol{\theta}} - \boldsymbol{\theta}_o)$ is

$$\left[N^{-1}\sum_{i=1}^{N}(r_{i2}\hat{\mathbf{A}}_{i1} + \hat{\mathbf{A}}_{i2})\right]^{-1}$$

where $\mathbf{A}_{i1}(\boldsymbol{\theta}_o) = -\mathrm{E}[\nabla_{\theta}^2 \ell_{i1}(\boldsymbol{\theta}_o) \mid y_{i2}, \mathbf{x}_i]$, $\mathbf{A}_{i2}(\boldsymbol{\theta}_o) = -\mathrm{E}[\nabla_{\theta}^2 \ell_{i2}(\boldsymbol{\theta}_o) \mid \mathbf{x}_i]$, and $\hat{\boldsymbol{\theta}}$ replaces $\boldsymbol{\theta}_o$ in obtaining the estimates.

13.8. Consider a probit model with an unobserved explanatory variable v,

$$\mathrm{P}(y = 1 \mid \mathbf{x}, \mathbf{z}, v) = \Phi(\mathbf{x}\boldsymbol{\delta}_o + \rho_o v)$$

but where v depends on observable variables w and $\mathbf{z}$ and a vector of parameters $\boldsymbol{\gamma}_o$: $v = w - \mathbf{z}\boldsymbol{\gamma}_o$. Assume that $\mathrm{E}(v \mid \mathbf{x}, \mathbf{z}) = \mathbf{0}$; this assumption implies, among other things, that $\boldsymbol{\gamma}_o$ can be consistently estimated by the OLS regression of w_i on $\mathbf{z}_i$, using a random sample. Define $\hat{v}_i \equiv w_i - \mathbf{z}_i\hat{\boldsymbol{\gamma}}$. Let $\hat{\boldsymbol{\theta}} = (\hat{\boldsymbol{\delta}}', \hat{\rho})'$ be the **two-step probit estimator** from probit of y_i on $\mathbf{x}_i$, $\hat{v}_i$.

a. Using the results from Section 12.5.2, show how to consistently estimate Avar $\sqrt{N}(\hat{\boldsymbol{\theta}} - \boldsymbol{\theta}_o)$.

b. Show that, when $\rho_o = 0$, the usual probit asymptotic variance estimator is valid. That is, valid inference is obtained for $(\boldsymbol{\delta}_o', \rho_o)'$ by ignoring the first-stage estimation.

c. How would you test H_0: $\rho_o = 0$?

13.9. Let $\{y_t: t = 0, 1, \ldots, T\}$ be an observable time series representing a population, where we use the convention that $t = 0$ is the first time period for which y is observed. Assume that the sequence follows a *Markov process*: $D(y_t \mid y_{t-1}, y_{t-2}, \ldots y_0) = D(y_t \mid y_{t-1})$ for all $t \geq 1$. Let $f_t(y_t \mid y_{t-1}; \boldsymbol{\theta})$ denote a correctly specified model for the density of y_t given y_{t-1}, $t \geq 1$, where $\boldsymbol{\theta}_o$ is the true value of $\boldsymbol{\theta}$.

a. Show that, to obtain the joint distribution of $(y_0, y_2, \ldots, y_T)$, you need to correctly model the density of y_0.

b. Given a random sample of size N from the population, that is, $(y_{i0}, y_{i1}, \ldots, y_{iT})$ for each i, explain how to consistently etimate $\boldsymbol{\theta}_o$ without modeling $D(y_0)$.

c. How would you estimate the asymptotic variance of the estimator from part b? Be specific.

13.10. Let $\mathbf{y}$ be a $G \times 1$ random vector with elements y_g, $g = 1, 2, \ldots, G$. These could be different response variables for the same cross section unit or responses at different points in time. Let $\mathbf{x}$ be a K-vector of observed conditioning variables, and let c be an unobserved conditioning variable. Let $f_g(\cdot \mid \mathbf{x}, c)$ denote the density of y_g given $(\mathbf{x}, c)$. Further, assume that the $y_1, y_2, \ldots, y_G$ are independent conditional on $(\mathbf{x}, c)$.

a. Write down the joint density of $\mathbf{y}$ given $(\mathbf{x}, c)$.

b. Let $h(\cdot \mid \mathbf{x})$ be the density of c given $\mathbf{x}$. Find the joint density of $\mathbf{y}$ given $\mathbf{x}$.

c. If each $f_g(\cdot \mid \mathbf{x}, c)$ is known up to a P_g-vector of parameters γ_o^g and $h(\cdot \mid \mathbf{x})$ is known up to an M-vector $\boldsymbol{\delta}_o$, find the log likelihood for any random draw $(\mathbf{x}_i, \mathbf{y}_i)$ from the population.

d. Is there a relationship between this setup and a linear SUR model?

13.11. Consider the dynamic, linear unobserved effects model

$$y_{it} = \rho y_{i,t-1} + c_i + e_{it}, \qquad t = 1, 2, \ldots, T$$

$$E(e_{it} \mid y_{i,t-1}, y_{i,t-2}, \ldots, y_{i0}, c_i) = 0$$

In Section 11.1.1 we discussed estimation of ρ by instrumental variables methods after differencing. The deficiencies of the IV approach for large ρ may be overcome by applying the conditional MLE methods in Section 13.9.2.

a. Make the stronger assumption that $y_{it} \mid (y_{i,t-1}, y_{i,t-2}, \ldots, y_{i0}, c_i)$ is normally distributed with mean $\rho y_{i,t-1} + c_i$ and variance σ_e^2. Find the density of $(y_{i1}, \ldots, y_{iT})$ given (y_{i0}, c_i). Is it a good idea to use the log of this density, summed across i, to estimate ρ and σ_e^2 along with the "fixed effects" c_i?

b. If $c_i \mid y_{i0} \sim \text{Normal}(\alpha_0 + \alpha_1 y_{i0}, \sigma_a^2)$, where $\sigma_a^2 \equiv \text{Var}(a_i)$ and $a_i \equiv c_i - \alpha_0 - \alpha_1 y_{i0}$, write down the density of $(y_{i1}, \ldots, y_{iT})$ given y_{i0}. How would you estimate ρ, α_0, α_1, σ_e^2, and σ_a^2?

c. Under the same assumptions in parts a and b, extend the model to $y_{it} = \rho y_{i,t-1} + c_i + \delta c_i y_{i,t-1} + e_{it}$. Explain how to estimate the parameters of this model, and propose a consistent estimator of the average partial effect of the lag, $\rho + \delta \mathrm{E}(c_i)$.

d. Now extend part b to the case where $\mathbf{z}_{it}\boldsymbol{\beta}$ is added to the conditional mean function, where the $\mathbf{z}_{it}$ are strictly exogenous conditional on c_i. Assume that $c_i \mid y_{i0}, \mathbf{z}_i \sim \mathrm{Normal}(\alpha_0 + \alpha_1 y_{i0} + \bar{\mathbf{z}}_i \boldsymbol{\delta}, \sigma_a^2)$, where $\bar{\mathbf{z}}_i$ is the vector of time averages.

Appendix 13A

In this appendix we cover some important properties of conditional distributions and conditional densities. Billingsley (1979) is a good reference for this material. For random vectors $\mathbf{y} \in \mathcal{Y} \subset \mathbb{R}^G$ and $\mathbf{x} \in \mathcal{X} \subset \mathbb{R}^K$, the **conditional distribution** of $\mathbf{y}$ given $\mathbf{x}$ always exists and is denoted $\mathrm{D}(\mathbf{y} \mid \mathbf{x})$. For each $\mathbf{x}$ this distribution is a probability measure and completely describes the behavior of the random vector $\mathbf{y}$ once $\mathbf{x}$ takes on a particular value. In econometrics, we almost always assume that this distribution is described by a **conditional density**, which we denote by $p(\cdot \mid \mathbf{x})$. The density is with respect to a **measure** defined on the support $\mathcal{Y}$ of $\mathbf{y}$. A conditional density makes sense only when this measure does not change with the value of $\mathbf{x}$. In practice, this assumption is not very restrictive, as it means that the nature of $\mathbf{y}$ is not dramatically different for different values of $\mathbf{x}$. Let ν be this measure on $\mathbb{R}^J$. If $\mathrm{D}(\mathbf{y} \mid \mathbf{x})$ is discrete, ν can be the counting measure and all integrals are sums. If $\mathrm{D}(\mathbf{y} \mid \mathbf{x})$ is **absolutely continuous**, then ν is the familiar Lebesgue measure appearing in elementary integration theory. In some cases, $\mathrm{D}(\mathbf{y} \mid \mathbf{x})$ has both discrete and continuous characteristics.

The important point is that all conditional probabilities can be obtained by integration:

$$\mathrm{P}(\mathbf{y} \in \mathcal{A} \mid \mathbf{x} = x) = \int_A p(y \mid x) \nu(\mathrm{d}y)$$

where y is the dummy argument of integration. When $\mathbf{y}$ is discrete, taking on the values $y_1, y_2, \ldots$, then $p(\cdot \mid x)$ is a probability mass function and $\mathrm{P}(\mathbf{y} = y_j \mid \mathbf{x} = x) = p(y_j \mid x)$, $j = 1, 2, \ldots$.

Suppose that f and g are nonnegative functions on $\mathbb{R}^M$, and define $\mathcal{S}_f \equiv \{z \in \mathbb{R}^M : f(z) > 0\}$. Assume that

$$1 = \int_{\mathcal{S}_f} f(z) \nu(dz) \geq \int_{\mathcal{S}_f} g(z) \nu(\mathrm{d}z) \tag{13.63}$$

where ν is a measure on $\mathbb{R}^M$. The equality in expression (13.63) implies that f is a density on $\mathbb{R}^M$, while the inequality holds if g is also a density on $\mathbb{R}^M$. An important result is that

$$\mathscr{I}(f;g) \equiv \int_{\mathscr{S}_f} \log[f(z)/g(z)]f(z)\nu(\mathrm{d}z) \geq 0 \tag{13.64}$$

[Note that $\mathscr{I}(f;g) = \infty$ is allowed; one case where this result can occur is $f(z) > 0$ but $g(z) = 0$ for some z. Also, the integrand is not defined when $f(z) = g(z) = 0$, but such values of z have no effect because the integrand receives zero weight in the integration.] The quantity $\mathscr{I}(f;g)$ is called the **Kullback-Leibler information criterion (KLIC)**. Another way to state expression (13.64) is

$$\mathrm{E}\{\log[f(\mathbf{z})]\} \geq \mathrm{E}\{\log[g(\mathbf{z})]\} \tag{13.65}$$

where $\mathbf{z} \in \mathscr{Z} \subset \mathbb{R}^M$ is a random vector with density f.

Conditional MLE relies on a conditional version of inequality (13.63):

PROPERTY CD.1: Let $\mathbf{y} \in \mathscr{Y} \subset \mathbb{R}^G$ and $\mathbf{x} \in \mathscr{X} \subset \mathbb{R}^K$ be random vectors. Let $p(\cdot\,|\,\cdot)$ denote the conditional density of $\mathbf{y}$ given $\mathbf{x}$. For each $\mathbf{x}$, let $\mathscr{Y}(\mathbf{x}) \equiv \{y\colon p(y\,|\,\mathbf{x}) > 0\}$ be the *conditional support* of $\mathbf{y}$, and let ν be a measure that does not depend on $\mathbf{x}$. Then for any other function $g(\cdot\,|\,\mathbf{x}) \geq 0$ such that

$$1 = \int_{\mathscr{Y}(\mathbf{x})} p(y\,|\,\mathbf{x})\nu(\mathrm{d}y) \geq \int_{\mathscr{Y}(\mathbf{x})} g(y\,|\,\mathbf{x})\nu(\mathrm{d}y)$$

the conditional KLIC is nonnegative:

$$\mathscr{I}_{\mathbf{x}}(p;g) \equiv \int_{\mathscr{Y}(\mathbf{x})} \log[p(y\,|\,\mathbf{x})/g(y\,|\,\mathbf{x})]p(y\,|\,\mathbf{x})\nu(\mathrm{d}y) \geq 0$$

That is,

$$\mathrm{E}\{\log[p(\mathbf{y}\,|\,\mathbf{x})]\,|\,\mathbf{x}\} \geq \mathrm{E}\{\log[g(\mathbf{y}\,|\,\mathbf{x})]\,|\,\mathbf{x}\}$$

for any $\mathbf{x} \in \mathscr{X}$. The proof uses the conditional Jensen's inequality (Property CE.7 in Chapter 2). See Manski (1988, Section 5.1).

PROPERTY CD.2: For random vectors $\mathbf{y}$, $\mathbf{x}$, and $\mathbf{z}$, let $p(y\,|\,\mathbf{x},\mathbf{z})$ be the conditional density of $\mathbf{y}$ given $(\mathbf{x},\mathbf{z})$ and let $p(x\,|\,\mathbf{z})$ denote the conditional density of $\mathbf{x}$ given $\mathbf{z}$. Then the density of $(\mathbf{y},\mathbf{x})$ given $\mathbf{z}$ is

$$p(y,x\,|\,\mathbf{z}) = p(y\,|\,x,\mathbf{z})p(x\,|\,\mathbf{z})$$

where the script variables are placeholders.

PROPERTY CD.3: For random vectors $\mathbf{y}$, $\mathbf{x}$, and $\mathbf{z}$, let $p(\mathscr{y} \mid \mathbf{x}, \mathbf{z})$ be the conditional density of $\mathbf{y}$ given $(\mathbf{x}, \mathbf{z})$, let $p(\mathscr{y} \mid \mathbf{x})$ be the conditional density of $\mathbf{y}$ given $\mathbf{x}$, and let $p(\mathscr{z} \mid \mathbf{x})$ denote the conditional density of $\mathbf{z}$ given $\mathbf{x}$ with respect to the measure $\nu(d\mathscr{z})$. Then

$$p(\mathscr{y} \mid \mathbf{x}) = \int_{\mathscr{Z}} p(\mathscr{y} \mid \mathbf{x}, \mathscr{z}) p(\mathscr{z} \mid \mathbf{x}) \nu(d\mathscr{z})$$

In other words, we can obtain the density of $\mathbf{y}$ given $\mathbf{x}$ by integrating the density of $\mathbf{y}$ given the larger conditioning set, $(\mathbf{x}, \mathbf{z})$, against the density of $\mathbf{z}$ given $\mathbf{x}$.

PROPERTY CD.4: Suppose that the random variable, u, with cdf, F, is independent of the random vector $\mathbf{x}$. Then, for any function $a(\mathbf{x})$ of $\mathbf{x}$,

$$\mathrm{P}[u \leq a(\mathbf{x}) \mid \mathbf{x}] = F[a(\mathbf{x})].$$

14 Generalized Method of Moments and Minimum Distance Estimation

In Chapter 8 we saw how the generalized method of moments (GMM) approach to estimation can be applied to multiple-equation linear models, including systems of equations, with exogenous or endogenous explanatory variables, and to panel data models. In this chapter we extend GMM to nonlinear estimation problems. This setup allows us to treat various efficiency issues that we have glossed over until now. We also cover the related method of minimum distance estimation. Because the asymptotic analysis has many features in common with Chapters 8 and 12, the analysis is not quite as detailed here as in previous chapters. A good reference for this material, which fills in most of the gaps left here, is Newey and McFadden (1994).

14.1 Asymptotic Properties of GMM

Let $\{\mathbf{w}_i \in \mathbb{R}^M : i = 1, 2, \ldots\}$ denote a set of independent, identically distributed random vectors, where some feature of the distribution of $\mathbf{w}_i$ is indexed by the $P \times 1$ parameter vector $\boldsymbol{\theta}$. The assumption of identical distribution is mostly for notational convenience; the following methods apply to independently pooled cross sections without modification.

We assume that for some function $\mathbf{g}(\mathbf{w}_i, \boldsymbol{\theta}) \in \mathbb{R}^L$, the parameter $\boldsymbol{\theta}_o \in \boldsymbol{\Theta} \subset \mathbb{R}^P$ satisfies the moment assumptions

$$\mathrm{E}[\mathbf{g}(\mathbf{w}_i, \boldsymbol{\theta}_o)] = 0 \tag{14.1}$$

As we saw in the linear case, where $\mathbf{g}(\mathbf{w}_i, \boldsymbol{\theta})$ was of the form $\mathbf{Z}_i'(\mathbf{y}_i - \mathbf{X}_i\boldsymbol{\theta})$, a minimal requirement for these moment conditions to identify $\boldsymbol{\theta}_o$ is $L \geq P$. If $L = P$, then the analogy principle suggests estimating $\boldsymbol{\theta}_o$ by setting the sample counterpart, $N^{-1}\sum_{i=1}^N \mathbf{g}(\mathbf{w}_i, \boldsymbol{\theta})$, to zero. In the linear case, this step leads to the instrumental variables estimator [see equation (8.22)]. When $L > P$, we can choose $\hat{\boldsymbol{\theta}}$ to make the sample average close to zero in an appropriate metric. A **generalized method of moments (GMM)** estimator, $\hat{\boldsymbol{\theta}}$, minimizes a quadratic form in $\sum_{i=1}^N \mathbf{g}(\mathbf{w}_i, \boldsymbol{\theta})$:

$$\min_{\boldsymbol{\theta} \in \boldsymbol{\Theta}} \left[\sum_{i=1}^N \mathbf{g}(\mathbf{w}_i, \boldsymbol{\theta})\right]' \hat{\boldsymbol{\Xi}} \left[\sum_{i=1}^N \mathbf{g}(\mathbf{w}_i, \boldsymbol{\theta})\right] \tag{14.2}$$

where $\hat{\boldsymbol{\Xi}}$ is an $L \times L$ symmetric, positive semidefinite weighting matrix.

Consistency of the GMM estimator follows along the lines of consistency of the M-estimator in Chapter 12. Under standard moment conditions, $N^{-1}\sum_{i=1}^N \mathbf{g}(\mathbf{w}_i, \boldsymbol{\theta})$ satisfies the uniform law of large numbers (see Theorem 12.1). If, $\hat{\boldsymbol{\Xi}} \xrightarrow{p} \boldsymbol{\Xi}_o$, where $\boldsymbol{\Xi}_o$ is an $L \times L$ positive definite matrix, then the random function

$$Q_N(\boldsymbol{\theta}) \equiv \left[N^{-1}\sum_{i=1}^{N}\mathbf{g}(\mathbf{w}_i,\boldsymbol{\theta})\right]'\hat{\boldsymbol{\Xi}}\left[N^{-1}\sum_{i=1}^{N}\mathbf{g}(\mathbf{w}_i,\boldsymbol{\theta})\right] \tag{14.3}$$

converges uniformly in probability to

$$\{\mathrm{E}[\mathbf{g}(\mathbf{w}_i,\boldsymbol{\theta})]\}'\boldsymbol{\Xi}_{\mathrm{o}}\{\mathrm{E}[\mathbf{g}(\mathbf{w}_i,\boldsymbol{\theta})]\} \tag{14.4}$$

Because $\boldsymbol{\Xi}_{\mathrm{o}}$ is positive definite, $\boldsymbol{\theta}_{\mathrm{o}}$ *uniquely* minimizes expression (14.4). For completeness, we summarize with a theorem containing regularity conditions:

THEOREM 14.1 (Consistency of GMM): Assume that (a) $\boldsymbol{\Theta}$ is compact; (b) for each $\boldsymbol{\theta} \in \boldsymbol{\Theta}$, $\mathbf{g}(\cdot,\boldsymbol{\theta})$ is Borel measurable on $\mathcal{W}$; (c) for each $\mathbf{w} \in \mathcal{W}$, $\mathbf{g}(\mathbf{w},\cdot)$ is continuous on $\boldsymbol{\Theta}$; (d) $|g_j(\mathbf{w},\boldsymbol{\theta})| \le b(\mathbf{w})$ for all $\boldsymbol{\theta} \in \boldsymbol{\Theta}$ and $j = 1,\ldots,L$, where $b(\cdot)$ is a nonnegative function on $\mathcal{W}$ such that $\mathrm{E}[b(\mathbf{w})] < \infty$; (e) $\hat{\boldsymbol{\Xi}} \xrightarrow{p} \boldsymbol{\Xi}_{\mathrm{o}}$, an $L \times L$ positive definite matrix; and (f) $\boldsymbol{\theta}_{\mathrm{o}}$ is the unique solution to equation (14.1). Then a random vector $\hat{\boldsymbol{\theta}}$ exists that solves problem (14.2), and $\hat{\boldsymbol{\theta}} \xrightarrow{p} \boldsymbol{\theta}_{\mathrm{o}}$.

If we assume only that $\boldsymbol{\Xi}_{\mathrm{o}}$ is positive semidefinite, then we must directly assume that $\boldsymbol{\theta}_{\mathrm{o}}$ is the unique minimizer of expression (14.4). Occasionally this generality is useful, but we will not need it.

Under the assumption that $\mathbf{g}(\mathbf{w},\cdot)$ is continuously differentiable on $\mathrm{int}(\boldsymbol{\Theta})$, $\boldsymbol{\theta}_{\mathrm{o}} \in \mathrm{int}(\boldsymbol{\Theta})$, and other standard regularity conditions, we can easily derive the limiting distribution of the GMM estimator. The first-order condition for $\hat{\boldsymbol{\theta}}$ can be written as

$$\left[\sum_{i=1}^{N}\nabla_{\theta}\mathbf{g}(\mathbf{w}_i,\hat{\boldsymbol{\theta}})\right]'\hat{\boldsymbol{\Xi}}\left[\sum_{i=1}^{N}\mathbf{g}(\mathbf{w}_i,\hat{\boldsymbol{\theta}})\right] \equiv \mathbf{0} \tag{14.5}$$

Define the $L \times P$ matrix

$$\mathbf{G}_{\mathrm{o}} \equiv \mathrm{E}[\nabla_{\theta}\mathbf{g}(\mathbf{w}_i,\boldsymbol{\theta}_{\mathrm{o}})] \tag{14.6}$$

which we assume to have full rank P. This assumption essentially means that the moment conditions (14.1) are nonredundant. Then, by the WLLN and CLT,

$$N^{-1}\sum_{i=1}^{N}\nabla_{\theta}\mathbf{g}(\mathbf{w}_i,\boldsymbol{\theta}_{\mathrm{o}}) \xrightarrow{p} \mathbf{G}_{\mathrm{o}} \qquad \text{and} \qquad N^{-1/2}\sum_{i=1}^{N}\mathbf{g}(\mathbf{w}_i,\boldsymbol{\theta}_{\mathrm{o}}) = \mathrm{O}_p(1) \tag{14.7}$$

respectively. Let $\mathbf{g}_i(\boldsymbol{\theta}) \equiv \mathbf{g}(\mathbf{w}_i,\boldsymbol{\theta})$. A mean value expansion of $\sum_{i=1}^{N}\mathbf{g}(\mathbf{w}_i,\hat{\boldsymbol{\theta}})$ about $\boldsymbol{\theta}_{\mathrm{o}}$, appropriate standardizations by the sample size, and replacing random averages with their plims gives

$$\mathbf{0} = \mathbf{G}_{\mathrm{o}}'\boldsymbol{\Xi}_{\mathrm{o}}N^{-1/2}\sum_{i=1}^{N}\mathbf{g}_i(\boldsymbol{\theta}_{\mathrm{o}}) + \mathbf{A}_{\mathrm{o}}\sqrt{N}(\hat{\boldsymbol{\theta}} - \boldsymbol{\theta}_{\mathrm{o}}) + \mathrm{o}_p(1) \tag{14.8}$$

where

$$\mathbf{A}_o \equiv \mathbf{G}_o' \boldsymbol{\Xi}_o \mathbf{G}_o \tag{14.9}$$

Since $\mathbf{A}_o$ is positive definite under the given assumptions, we have

$$\sqrt{N}(\hat{\boldsymbol{\theta}} - \boldsymbol{\theta}_o) = -\mathbf{A}_o^{-1}\mathbf{G}_o'\boldsymbol{\Xi}_o N^{-1/2}\sum_{i=1}^{N}\mathbf{g}_i(\boldsymbol{\theta}_o) + o_p(1) \xrightarrow{d} \text{Normal}(\mathbf{0}, \mathbf{A}_o^{-1}\mathbf{B}_o\mathbf{A}_o^{-1}) \tag{14.10}$$

where

$$\mathbf{B}_o \equiv \mathbf{G}_o'\boldsymbol{\Xi}_o\boldsymbol{\Lambda}_o\boldsymbol{\Xi}_o\mathbf{G}_o \tag{14.11}$$

and

$$\boldsymbol{\Lambda}_o \equiv \mathrm{E}[\mathbf{g}_i(\boldsymbol{\theta}_o)\mathbf{g}_i(\boldsymbol{\theta}_o)'] = \mathrm{Var}[\mathbf{g}_i(\boldsymbol{\theta}_o)] \tag{14.12}$$

Expression (14.10) gives the influence function representation for the GMM estimator, and it also gives the limiting distribution of the GMM estimator. We summarize with a theorem, which is essentially given by Newey and McFadden (1994, Theorem 3.4):

THEOREM 14.2 (Asymptotic Normality of GMM): In addition to the assumptions in Theorem 14.1, assume that (a) $\boldsymbol{\theta}_o$ is in the interior of $\boldsymbol{\Theta}$; (b) $\mathbf{g}(\mathbf{w}, \cdot)$ is continuously differentiable on the interior of $\boldsymbol{\Theta}$ for all $\mathbf{w} \in \mathscr{W}$; (c) each element of $\mathbf{g}(\mathbf{w}, \boldsymbol{\theta}_o)$ has finite second moment; (d) each element of $\nabla_\theta \mathbf{g}(\mathbf{w}, \boldsymbol{\theta})$ is bounded in absolute value by a function $b(\mathbf{w})$, where $\mathrm{E}[b(\mathbf{w})] < \infty$; and (e) $\mathbf{G}_o$ in expression (14.6) has rank P. Then expression (14.10) holds, and so $\mathrm{Avar}(\hat{\boldsymbol{\theta}}) = \mathbf{A}_o^{-1}\mathbf{B}_o\mathbf{A}_o^{-1}/N$.

Estimating the asymptotic variance of the GMM estimator is easy once $\hat{\boldsymbol{\theta}}$ has been obtained. A consistent estimator of $\boldsymbol{\Lambda}_o$ is given by

$$\hat{\boldsymbol{\Lambda}} \equiv N^{-1}\sum_{i=1}^{N}\mathbf{g}_i(\hat{\boldsymbol{\theta}})\mathbf{g}_i(\hat{\boldsymbol{\theta}})' \tag{14.13}$$

and $\mathrm{Avar}(\hat{\boldsymbol{\theta}})$ is estimated as $\hat{\mathbf{A}}^{-1}\hat{\mathbf{B}}\hat{\mathbf{A}}^{-1}/N$, where

$$\hat{\mathbf{A}} \equiv \hat{\mathbf{G}}'\hat{\boldsymbol{\Xi}}\hat{\mathbf{G}}, \qquad \hat{\mathbf{B}} \equiv \hat{\mathbf{G}}'\hat{\boldsymbol{\Xi}}\hat{\boldsymbol{\Lambda}}\hat{\boldsymbol{\Xi}}\hat{\mathbf{G}} \tag{14.14}$$

and

$$\hat{\mathbf{G}} \equiv N^{-1}\sum_{i=1}^{N}\nabla_\theta \mathbf{g}_i(\hat{\boldsymbol{\theta}}) \tag{14.15}$$

As in the linear case in Section 8.3.3, an optimal weighting matrix exists for the given moment conditions: $\hat{\boldsymbol{\Xi}}$ should be a consistent estimator of $\boldsymbol{\Lambda}_o^{-1}$. When $\boldsymbol{\Xi}_o = \boldsymbol{\Lambda}_o^{-1}$, $\mathbf{B}_o = \mathbf{A}_o$ and Avar $\sqrt{N}(\hat{\boldsymbol{\theta}} - \boldsymbol{\theta}_o) = (\mathbf{G}_o'\boldsymbol{\Lambda}_o^{-1}\mathbf{G}_o)^{-1}$. Thus the difference in asymptotic variances between the general GMM estimator and the estimator with plim $\hat{\boldsymbol{\Xi}} = \boldsymbol{\Lambda}_o^{-1}$ is

$$(\mathbf{G}_o'\boldsymbol{\Xi}_o\mathbf{G}_o)^{-1}(\mathbf{G}_o'\boldsymbol{\Xi}_o\boldsymbol{\Lambda}_o\boldsymbol{\Xi}_o\mathbf{G}_o)(\mathbf{G}_o'\boldsymbol{\Xi}_o\mathbf{G}_o)^{-1} - (\mathbf{G}_o'\boldsymbol{\Lambda}_o^{-1}\mathbf{G}_o)^{-1} \tag{14.16}$$

This expression can be shown to be positive semidefinite using the same argument as in Chapter 8 (see Problem 8.5).

In order to obtain an asymptotically efficient GMM estimator we need a preliminary estimator of $\boldsymbol{\theta}_o$ in order to obtain $\hat{\boldsymbol{\Lambda}}$. Let $\hat{\hat{\boldsymbol{\theta}}}$ be such an estimator, and define $\hat{\boldsymbol{\Lambda}}$ as in expression (14.13) but with $\hat{\hat{\boldsymbol{\theta}}}$ in place of $\hat{\boldsymbol{\theta}}$. Then, an efficient GMM estimator [given the function $\mathbf{g}(\mathbf{w}, \boldsymbol{\theta})$] solves

$$\min_{\boldsymbol{\theta} \in \boldsymbol{\Theta}} \left[\sum_{i=1}^{N} \mathbf{g}(\mathbf{w}_i, \boldsymbol{\theta})\right]' \hat{\boldsymbol{\Lambda}}^{-1} \left[\sum_{i=1}^{N} \mathbf{g}(\mathbf{w}_i, \boldsymbol{\theta})\right] \tag{14.17}$$

and its asymptotic variance is estimated as

$$\text{Av}\hat{\text{a}}\text{r}(\hat{\boldsymbol{\theta}}) = (\hat{\mathbf{G}}'\hat{\boldsymbol{\Lambda}}^{-1}\hat{\mathbf{G}})^{-1}/N \tag{14.18}$$

As in the linear case, an optimal GMM estimator is called the **minimum chi-square estimator** because

$$\left[N^{-1/2}\sum_{i=1}^{N} \mathbf{g}_i(\hat{\boldsymbol{\theta}})\right]' \hat{\boldsymbol{\Lambda}}^{-1} \left[\sum_{i=1}^{N} N^{-1/2}\mathbf{g}_i(\hat{\boldsymbol{\theta}})\right] \tag{14.19}$$

has a limiting chi-square distribution with $L - P$ degrees of freedom under the conditions of Theorem 14.2. Therefore, the value of the objective function (properly standardized by the sample size) can be used as a test of any overidentifying restrictions in equation (14.1) when $L > P$. If statistic (14.19) exceeds the relevant critical value in a χ^2_{L-P} distribution, then equation (14.1) must be rejected: at least some of the moment conditions are not supported by the data. For the linear model, this is the same statistic given in equation (8.49).

As always, we can test hypotheses of the form H_0: $\mathbf{c}(\boldsymbol{\theta}_o) = \mathbf{0}$, where $\mathbf{c}(\boldsymbol{\theta})$ is a $Q \times 1$ vector, $Q \leq P$, by using the Wald approach and the appropriate variance matrix estimator. A statistic based on the difference in objective functions is also available if the minimum chi-square estimator is used so that $\mathbf{B}_o = \mathbf{A}_o$. Let $\tilde{\boldsymbol{\theta}}$ denote the solution to problem (14.17) subject to the restrictions $\mathbf{c}(\boldsymbol{\theta}) = \mathbf{0}$, and let $\hat{\boldsymbol{\theta}}$ denote the unrestricted estimator solving problem (14.17); importantly, these both use the same weighting matrix $\hat{\mathbf{\Lambda}}^{-1}$. Typically, $\hat{\mathbf{\Lambda}}$ is obtained from a first-stage, unrestricted estimator. Assuming that the constraints can be written in implicit form and satisfy the conditions discussed in Section 12.6.2, the **GMM distance statistic** (or **GMM criterion function statistic**) has a limiting χ^2_Q distribution:

$$\left\{\left[\sum_{i=1}^{N} \mathbf{g}_i(\tilde{\boldsymbol{\theta}})\right]' \hat{\mathbf{\Lambda}}^{-1} \left[\sum_{i=1}^{N} \mathbf{g}_i(\tilde{\boldsymbol{\theta}})\right] - \left[\sum_{i=1}^{N} \mathbf{g}_i(\hat{\boldsymbol{\theta}})\right]' \hat{\mathbf{\Lambda}}^{-1} \left[\sum_{i=1}^{N} \mathbf{g}_i(\hat{\boldsymbol{\theta}})\right]\right\} / N \xrightarrow{d} \chi^2_Q \qquad (14.20)$$

When applied to linear GMM problems, we obtain the statistic in equation (8.45). One nice feature of expression (14.20) is that it is invariant to reparameterization of the null hypothesis, just as the quasi-LR statistic is invariant for M-estimation. Therefore, we might prefer statistic (14.20) over the Wald statistic (8.48) for testing nonlinear restrictions in linear models. Of course, the computation of expression (14.20) is more difficult because we would actually need to carry out estimation subject to nonlinear restrictions.

A nice application of the GMM methods discussed in this section is two-step estimation procedures, which arose in Chapters 6, 12, and 13. Suppose that the estimator $\hat{\boldsymbol{\theta}}$—it could be an M-estimator or a GMM estimator—depends on a first-stage estimator, $\hat{\boldsymbol{\gamma}}$. A unified approach to obtaining the asymptotic variance of $\hat{\boldsymbol{\theta}}$ is to stack the first-order conditions for $\hat{\boldsymbol{\theta}}$ *and* $\hat{\boldsymbol{\gamma}}$ into the same function $\mathbf{g}(\cdot)$. This is always possible for the estimators encountered in this book. For example, if $\hat{\boldsymbol{\gamma}}$ is an M-estimator solving $\sum_{i=1}^{N} \mathbf{s}(\mathbf{w}_i, \hat{\boldsymbol{\gamma}}) = \mathbf{0}$, and $\hat{\boldsymbol{\theta}}$ is a two-step M-estimator solving

$$\sum_{i=1}^{N} \mathbf{h}(\mathbf{w}_i, \hat{\boldsymbol{\theta}}; \hat{\boldsymbol{\gamma}})] = \mathbf{0} \qquad (14.21)$$

then we can obtain the asymptotic variance of $\hat{\boldsymbol{\theta}}$ by defining

$$\mathbf{g}(\mathbf{w}, \boldsymbol{\theta}, \boldsymbol{\gamma}) = \begin{bmatrix} \mathbf{h}(\mathbf{w}, \boldsymbol{\theta}; \boldsymbol{\gamma}) \\ \mathbf{s}(\mathbf{w}, \boldsymbol{\gamma}) \end{bmatrix}$$

and applying the GMM formulas. The first-order condition for the full GMM problem reproduces the first-order conditions for each estimator separately.

In general, either $\hat{\boldsymbol{\gamma}}$, $\hat{\boldsymbol{\theta}}$, or both might themselves be GMM estimators. Then, stacking the orthogonality conditions into one vector can simplify the derivation of the asymptotic variance of the second-step estimator $\hat{\boldsymbol{\theta}}$ while also ensuring efficient estimation when the optimal weighting matrix is used.

Finally, sometimes we want to know whether adding additional moment conditions does not improve the efficiency of the minimum chi-square estimator. (Adding additional moment conditions can never reduce asymptotic efficiency, provided an efficient weighting matrix is used.) In other words, if we start with equation (14.1) but add new moments of the form $\mathrm{E}[\mathbf{h}(\mathbf{w}, \boldsymbol{\theta}_o)] = 0$, when does using the extra moment conditions yield the same asymptotic variance as the original moment conditions? Breusch, Qian, Schmidt, and Wyhowski (1999) prove some general redundancy results for the minimum chi-square estimator. Qian and Schmidt (1999) study the problem of adding moment conditions that do not depend on unknown parameters, and they characterize when such moment conditions improve efficiency.

14.2 Estimation under Orthogonality Conditions

In Chapter 8 we saw how linear systems of equations can be estimated by GMM under certain orthogonality conditions. In general applications, the moment conditions (14.1) almost always arise from assumptions that disturbances are uncorrelated with exogenous variables. For a $G \times 1$ vector $\mathbf{r}(\mathbf{w}_i, \boldsymbol{\theta})$ and a $G \times L$ matrix $\mathbf{Z}_i$, assume that $\boldsymbol{\theta}_o$ satisfies

$$\mathrm{E}[\mathbf{Z}_i'\mathbf{r}(\mathbf{w}_i, \boldsymbol{\theta}_o)] = \mathbf{0} \tag{14.22}$$

The vector function $\mathbf{r}(\mathbf{w}_i, \boldsymbol{\theta})$ can be thought of as a **generalized residual function**. The matrix $\mathbf{Z}_i$ is usually called the **matrix of instruments**. Equation (14.22) is a special case of equation (14.1) with $\mathbf{g}(\mathbf{w}_i, \boldsymbol{\theta}) \equiv \mathbf{Z}_i'\mathbf{r}(\mathbf{w}_i, \boldsymbol{\theta})$. In what follows, write $\mathbf{r}_i(\boldsymbol{\theta}) \equiv \mathbf{r}(\mathbf{w}_i, \boldsymbol{\theta})$.

Identification requires that $\boldsymbol{\theta}_o$ be the only $\boldsymbol{\theta} \in \boldsymbol{\Theta}$ such that equation (14.22) holds. Condition e of the asymptotic normality result Theorem 14.2 requires that rank $\mathrm{E}[\mathbf{Z}_i'\nabla_\theta \mathbf{r}_i(\boldsymbol{\theta}_o)] = P$ (necessary is $L \geq P$). Thus, while $\mathbf{Z}_i$ must be orthogonal to $\mathbf{r}_i(\boldsymbol{\theta}_o)$, $\mathbf{Z}_i$ must be sufficiently correlated with the $G \times P$ Jacobian, $\nabla_\theta \mathbf{r}_i(\boldsymbol{\theta}_o)$. In the linear case where $\mathbf{r}(\mathbf{w}_i, \boldsymbol{\theta}) = \mathbf{y}_i - \mathbf{X}_i\boldsymbol{\theta}$, this requirement reduces to $\mathrm{E}(\mathbf{Z}_i'\mathbf{X}_i)$ having full column rank, which is simply Assumption SIV.2 in Chapter 8.

Given the instruments $\mathbf{Z}_i$, the efficient estimator can be obtained as in Section 14.1. A preliminary estimator $\hat{\hat{\boldsymbol{\theta}}}$ is usually obtained with

$$\hat{\boldsymbol{\Xi}} \equiv \left(N^{-1}\sum_{i=1}^{N} \mathbf{Z}_i'\mathbf{Z}_i\right)^{-1} \tag{14.23}$$

so that $\hat{\hat{\boldsymbol{\theta}}}$ solves

$$\min_{\boldsymbol{\theta} \in \boldsymbol{\Theta}} \left[\sum_{i=1}^{N} \mathbf{Z}_i'\mathbf{r}_i(\boldsymbol{\theta})\right]' \left[N^{-1}\sum_{i=1}^{N} \mathbf{Z}_i'\mathbf{Z}_i\right]^{-1} \left[\sum_{i=1}^{N} \mathbf{Z}_i'\mathbf{r}_i(\boldsymbol{\theta})\right] \tag{14.24}$$

The solution to problem (14.24) is called the **nonlinear system 2SLS estimator**; it is an example of a **nonlinear instrumental variables estimator**.

From Section 14.1, we know that the nonlinear system 2SLS estimator is guaranteed to be the efficient GMM estimator if for some $\sigma_o^2 > 0$,

$$\mathrm{E}[\mathbf{Z}_i'\mathbf{r}_i(\boldsymbol{\theta}_o)\mathbf{r}_i(\boldsymbol{\theta}_o)'\mathbf{Z}_i] = \sigma_o^2 \mathrm{E}(\mathbf{Z}_i'\mathbf{Z}_i)$$

Generally, this is a strong assumption. Instead, we can obtain the minimum chi-square estimator by obtaining

$$\hat{\boldsymbol{\Lambda}} = N^{-1} \sum_{i=1}^{N} \mathbf{Z}_i'\mathbf{r}_i(\hat{\hat{\boldsymbol{\theta}}})\mathbf{r}_i(\hat{\hat{\boldsymbol{\theta}}})'\mathbf{Z}_i \tag{14.25}$$

and using this in expression (14.17).

In some cases more structure is available that leads to a three-stage least squares estimator. In particular, suppose that

$$\mathrm{E}[\mathbf{Z}_i'\mathbf{r}_i(\boldsymbol{\theta}_o)\mathbf{r}_i(\boldsymbol{\theta}_o)'\mathbf{Z}_i] = \mathrm{E}(\mathbf{Z}_i'\boldsymbol{\Omega}_o\mathbf{Z}_i) \tag{14.26}$$

where $\boldsymbol{\Omega}_o$ is the $G \times G$ matrix

$$\boldsymbol{\Omega}_o = \mathrm{E}[\mathbf{r}_i(\boldsymbol{\theta}_o)\mathbf{r}_i(\boldsymbol{\theta}_o)'] \tag{14.27}$$

When $\mathrm{E}[\mathbf{r}_i(\boldsymbol{\theta}_o)] = \mathbf{0}$, as is almost always the case under assumption (14.22), $\boldsymbol{\Omega}_o$ is the variance matrix of $\mathbf{r}_i(\boldsymbol{\theta}_o)$. As in Chapter 8, assumption (14.26) is a kind of system homoskedasticity assumption.

By iterated expectations, a sufficient condition for assumption (14.26) is

$$\mathrm{E}[\mathbf{r}_i(\boldsymbol{\theta}_o)\mathbf{r}_i(\boldsymbol{\theta}_o)' \mid \mathbf{Z}_i] = \boldsymbol{\Omega}_o \tag{14.28}$$

However, assumption (14.26) can hold in cases where assumption (14.28) does not.

If assumption (14.26) holds, then $\boldsymbol{\Lambda}_o$ can be estimated as

$$\hat{\boldsymbol{\Lambda}} = N^{-1} \sum_{i=1}^{N} \mathbf{Z}_i'\hat{\boldsymbol{\Omega}}\mathbf{Z}_i \tag{14.29}$$

where

$$\hat{\boldsymbol{\Omega}} = N^{-1} \sum_{i=1}^{N} \mathbf{r}_i(\hat{\hat{\boldsymbol{\theta}}})\mathbf{r}_i(\hat{\hat{\boldsymbol{\theta}}}) \tag{14.30}$$

and $\hat{\hat{\boldsymbol{\theta}}}$ is a preliminary estimator. The resulting GMM estimator is usually called the **nonlinear 3SLS (N3SLS) estimator**. The name is a holdover from the traditional

3SLS estimator in linear systems of equations; there are not really three estimation steps. We should remember that nonlinear 3SLS is generally inefficient when assumption (14.26) fails.

The Wald statistic and the QLR statistic can be computed as in Section 14.1. In addition, a score statistic is sometimes useful. Let $\tilde{\tilde{\boldsymbol{\theta}}}$ be a preliminary inefficient estimator with Q restrictions imposed. The estimator $\tilde{\tilde{\boldsymbol{\theta}}}$ would usually come from problem (14.24) subject to the restrictions $\mathbf{c}(\boldsymbol{\theta}) = \mathbf{0}$. Let $\tilde{\boldsymbol{\Lambda}}$ be the estimated weighting matrix from equation (14.25) or (14.29), based on $\tilde{\tilde{\boldsymbol{\theta}}}$. Let $\tilde{\boldsymbol{\theta}}$ be the minimum chi-square estimator using weighting matrix $\tilde{\boldsymbol{\Lambda}}^{-1}$. Then the score statistic is based on the limiting distribution of the score of the unrestricted objective function evaluated at the restricted estimates, properly standardized:

$$\left[N^{-1}\sum_{i=1}^{N}\mathbf{Z}_i'\nabla_{\theta}\mathbf{r}_i(\tilde{\boldsymbol{\theta}})\right]'\tilde{\boldsymbol{\Lambda}}^{-1}\left[N^{-1/2}\sum_{i=1}^{N}\mathbf{Z}_i'\mathbf{r}_i(\tilde{\boldsymbol{\theta}})\right] \tag{14.31}$$

Let $\tilde{\mathbf{s}}_i \equiv \tilde{\mathbf{G}}'\tilde{\boldsymbol{\Lambda}}^{-1}\mathbf{Z}_i'\tilde{\mathbf{r}}_i$, where $\tilde{\mathbf{G}}$ is the first matrix in expression (14.31), and let $\mathbf{s}_i^{\mathrm{o}} \equiv \mathbf{G}_{\mathrm{o}}'\boldsymbol{\Lambda}_{\mathrm{o}}^{-1}\mathbf{Z}_i'\mathbf{r}_i^{\mathrm{o}}$. Then, following the proof in Section 12.6.2, it can be shown that equation (12.67) holds with $\mathbf{A}_{\mathrm{o}} \equiv \mathbf{G}_{\mathrm{o}}'\boldsymbol{\Lambda}_{\mathrm{o}}^{-1}\mathbf{G}_{\mathrm{o}}$. Further, since $\mathbf{B}_{\mathrm{o}} = \mathbf{A}_{\mathrm{o}}$ for the minimum chi-square estimator, we obtain

$$LM = \left(\sum_{i=1}^{N}\tilde{\mathbf{s}}_i\right)'\tilde{\mathbf{A}}^{-1}\left(\sum_{i=1}^{N}\tilde{\mathbf{s}}_i\right)\Big/N \tag{14.32}$$

where $\tilde{\mathbf{A}} = \tilde{\mathbf{G}}'\tilde{\boldsymbol{\Lambda}}^{-1}\tilde{\mathbf{G}}$. Under H_0 and the usual regularity conditions, LM has a limiting χ_Q^2 distribution.

14.3 Systems of Nonlinear Equations

A leading application of the results in Section 14.2 is to estimation of the parameters in an implicit set of nonlinear equations, such as a nonlinear simultaneous equations model. Partition $\mathbf{w}_i$ as $\mathbf{y}_i \in \mathbb{R}^J$, $\mathbf{x}_i \in \mathbb{R}^K$ and, for $h = 1, \ldots, G$, suppose we have

$$\begin{aligned} q_1(\mathbf{y}_i, \mathbf{x}_i, \boldsymbol{\theta}_{\mathrm{o}1}) &= u_{i1} \\ &\vdots \\ q_G(\mathbf{y}_i, \mathbf{x}_i, \boldsymbol{\theta}_{\mathrm{o}G}) &= u_{iG} \end{aligned} \tag{14.33}$$

where $\boldsymbol{\theta}_{\mathrm{o}h}$ is a $P_h \times 1$ vector of parameters. As an example, write a two-equation SEM in the population as

$$y_1 = \mathbf{x}_1\boldsymbol{\delta}_1 + \gamma_1 y_2^{\gamma_2} + u_1 \tag{14.34}$$

$$y_2 = \mathbf{x}_2\boldsymbol{\delta}_2 + \gamma_3 y_1 + u_2 \tag{14.35}$$

(where we drop "o" to index the parameters). This model, unlike those covered in Section 9.5, is nonlinear in the *parameters* as well as the endogenous variables. Nevertheless, assuming that $\mathrm{E}(u_g \mid \mathbf{x}) = 0$, $g = 1, 2$, the parameters in the system can be estimated by GMM by defining $q_1(\mathbf{y}, \mathbf{x}, \boldsymbol{\theta}_1) = y_1 - \mathbf{x}_1\boldsymbol{\delta}_1 - \gamma_1 y_2^{\gamma_2}$ and $q_2(\mathbf{y}, \mathbf{x}, \boldsymbol{\theta}_2) = y_2 - \mathbf{x}_2\boldsymbol{\delta}_2 - \gamma_3 y_1$.

Generally, the equations (14.33) need not actually determine $\mathbf{y}_i$ given the exogenous variables and disturbances; in fact, nothing requires $J = G$. Sometimes equations (14.33) represent a system of orthogonality conditions of the form $\mathrm{E}[q_g(\mathbf{y}, \mathbf{x}, \boldsymbol{\theta}_{og}) \mid \mathbf{x}] = 0$, $g = 1, \ldots, G$. We will see an example later.

Denote the $P \times 1$ vector of all parameters by $\boldsymbol{\theta}_o$, and the parameter space by $\boldsymbol{\Theta} \subset \mathbb{R}^P$. To identify the parameters we need the errors u_{ih} to satisfy some orthogonality conditions. A general assumption is, for some subvector $\mathbf{x}_{ih}$ of $\mathbf{x}_i$,

$$\mathrm{E}(u_{ih} \mid \mathbf{x}_{ih}) = \mathbf{0}, \qquad h = 1, 2, \ldots, G \tag{14.36}$$

This allows elements of $\mathbf{x}_i$ to be correlated with some errors, a situation that sometimes arises in practice (see, for example, Chapter 9 and Wooldridge, 1996). Under assumption (14.36), let $\mathbf{z}_{ih} \equiv \mathbf{f}_h(\mathbf{x}_{ih})$ be a $1 \times L_h$ vector of possibly nonlinear functions of $\mathbf{x}_i$. If there are no restrictions on the $\boldsymbol{\theta}_{oh}$ across equations we should have $L_h \geq P_h$ so that each $\boldsymbol{\theta}_{oh}$ is identified. By iterated expectations, for all $h = 1, \ldots, G$,

$$\mathrm{E}(\mathbf{z}_{ih}' u_{ih}) = \mathbf{0} \tag{14.37}$$

provided appropriate moments exist. Therefore, we obtain a set of orthogonality conditions by defining the $G \times L$ matrix $\mathbf{Z}_i$ as the block diagonal matrix with $\mathbf{z}_{ig}$ in the gth block:

$$\mathbf{Z}_i \equiv \begin{bmatrix} \mathbf{z}_{i1} & \mathbf{0} & \mathbf{0} & \cdots & \mathbf{0} \\ \mathbf{0} & \mathbf{z}_{i2} & \mathbf{0} & \cdots & \mathbf{0} \\ \vdots & & & & \vdots \\ \mathbf{0} & \mathbf{0} & \mathbf{0} & \cdots & \mathbf{z}_{iG} \end{bmatrix} \tag{14.38}$$

where $L \equiv L_1 + L_2 + \cdots + L_G$. Letting $\mathbf{r}(\mathbf{w}_i, \boldsymbol{\theta}) \equiv \mathbf{q}(\mathbf{y}_i, \mathbf{x}_i, \boldsymbol{\theta}) \equiv [q_{i1}(\boldsymbol{\theta}_1), \ldots, q_{iG}(\boldsymbol{\theta}_G)]'$, equation (14.22) holds under assumption (14.36).

When there are no restrictions on the $\boldsymbol{\theta}_g$ across equations and $\mathbf{Z}_i$ is chosen as in matrix (14.38), the system 2SLS estimator reduces to the **nonlinear 2SLS (N2SLS) estimator** (Amemiya, 1974) equation by equation. That is, for each h, the N2SLS estimator solves

$$\min_{\boldsymbol{\theta}_h} \left[\sum_{i=1}^{N} \mathbf{z}'_{ih} q_{ih}(\boldsymbol{\theta}_h)\right]' \left(N^{-1} \sum_{i=1}^{N} \mathbf{z}'_{ih}\mathbf{z}_{ih}\right)^{-1} \left[\sum_{i=1}^{N} \mathbf{z}'_{ih} q_{ih}(\boldsymbol{\theta}_h)\right] \tag{14.39}$$

Given only the orthogonality conditions (14.37), the N2SLS estimator is the efficient estimator of $\boldsymbol{\theta}_{\text{o}h}$ if

$$\mathrm{E}(u_{ih}^2 \mathbf{z}'_{ih}\mathbf{z}_{ih}) = \sigma_{\text{o}h}^2 \mathrm{E}(\mathbf{z}'_{ih}\mathbf{z}_{ih}) \tag{14.40}$$

where $\sigma_{\text{o}h}^2 \equiv \mathrm{E}(u_{ih}^2)$; sufficient for condition (14.40) is $\mathrm{E}(u_{ih}^2 \mid \mathbf{x}_{ih}) = \sigma_{\text{o}h}^2$. Let $\hat{\hat{\boldsymbol{\theta}}}_h$ denote the N2SLS estimator. Then a consistent estimator of $\sigma_{\text{o}h}^2$ is

$$\hat{\sigma}_h^2 \equiv N^{-1} \sum_{i=1}^{N} \hat{\hat{u}}_{ih}^2 \tag{14.41}$$

where $\hat{\hat{u}}_{ih} \equiv q_h(\mathbf{y}_i, \mathbf{x}_i, \hat{\hat{\boldsymbol{\theta}}}_h)$ are the N2SLS residuals. Under assumptions (14.37) and (14.40), the asymptotic variance of $\hat{\hat{\boldsymbol{\theta}}}_h$ is estimated as

$$\hat{\sigma}_h^2 \left\{ \left[\sum_{i=1}^{N} \mathbf{z}'_{ih} \nabla_{\theta_h} q_{ih}(\hat{\hat{\boldsymbol{\theta}}}_h)\right]' \left(\sum_{i=1}^{N} \mathbf{z}'_{ih}\mathbf{z}_{ih}\right)^{-1} \left[\sum_{i=1}^{N} \mathbf{z}'_{ih} \nabla_{\theta_h} q_{ih}(\hat{\hat{\boldsymbol{\theta}}}_h)\right] \right\}^{-1} \tag{14.42}$$

where $\nabla_{\theta_h} q_{ih}(\hat{\hat{\boldsymbol{\theta}}}_h)$ is the $1 \times P_h$ gradient.

If assumption (14.37) holds but assumption (14.40) does not, the N2SLS estimator is still $\sqrt{N}$-consistent, but it is not the efficient estimator that uses the orthogonality condition (14.37) whenever $L_h > P_h$ [and expression (14.42) is no longer valid]. A more efficient estimator is obtained by solving

$$\min_{\boldsymbol{\theta}_h} \left[\sum_{i=1}^{N} \mathbf{z}'_{ih} q_{ih}(\boldsymbol{\theta}_h)\right]' \left(N^{-1} \sum_{i=1}^{N} \hat{\hat{u}}_{ih}^2 \mathbf{z}'_{ih}\mathbf{z}_{ih}\right)^{-1} \left[\sum_{i=1}^{N} \mathbf{z}'_{ih} q_{ih}(\boldsymbol{\theta}_h)\right]$$

with asymptotic variance estimated as

$$\left\{ \left[\sum_{i=1}^{N} \mathbf{z}'_{ih} \nabla_{\theta_h} q_{ih}(\hat{\hat{\boldsymbol{\theta}}}_h)\right]' \left(\sum_{i=1}^{N} \hat{\hat{u}}_{ih}^2 \mathbf{z}'_{ih}\mathbf{z}_{ih}\right)^{-1} \left[\sum_{i=1}^{N} \mathbf{z}'_{ih} \nabla_{\theta_h} q_{ih}(\hat{\hat{\boldsymbol{\theta}}}_h)\right] \right\}^{-1}$$

This estimator is asymptotically equivalent to the N2SLS estimator if assumption (14.40) happens to hold.

Rather than focus on one equation at a time, we can increase efficiency if we estimate the equations simultaneously. One reason for doing so is to impose cross equation restrictions on the $\boldsymbol{\theta}_{\text{o}h}$. The system 2SLS estimator can be used for these purposes, where $\mathbf{Z}_i$ generally has the form (14.38). But this estimator does not exploit correlation in the errors u_{ig} and u_{ih} in different equations.

The efficient estimator that uses all orthogonality conditions in equation (14.37) is just the GMM estimator with $\hat{\boldsymbol{\Lambda}}$ given by equation (14.25), where $\mathbf{r}_i(\hat{\hat{\boldsymbol{\theta}}})$ is the $G \times 1$ vector of system 2SLS residuals, $\hat{\mathbf{u}}_i$. In other words, the efficient GMM estimator solves

$$\min_{\theta \in \Theta} \left[\sum_{i=1}^{N} \mathbf{Z}_i'\mathbf{q}_i(\theta)\right]' \left(N^{-1}\sum_{i=1}^{N} \mathbf{Z}_i'\hat{\mathbf{u}}_i\hat{\mathbf{u}}_i'\mathbf{Z}_i\right)^{-1} \left[\sum_{i=1}^{N} \mathbf{Z}_i'\mathbf{q}_i(\theta)\right] \tag{14.43}$$

The asymptotic variance of $\hat{\theta}$ is estimated as

$$\left\{\left[\sum_{i=1}^{N} \mathbf{Z}_i'\nabla_\theta\mathbf{q}_i(\hat{\theta})\right]' \left(\sum_{i=1}^{N} \mathbf{Z}_i'\hat{\mathbf{u}}_i\hat{\mathbf{u}}_i'\mathbf{Z}_i\right)^{-1} \left[\sum_{i=1}^{N} \mathbf{Z}_i'\nabla_\theta\mathbf{q}_i(\hat{\theta})\right]\right\}^{-1}$$

Because this is the efficient GMM estimator, the QLR statistic can be used to test hypotheses about θ_o. The Wald statistic can also be applied.

Under the homoskedasticity assumption (14.26) with $\mathbf{r}_i(\theta_o) = \mathbf{u}_i$, the nonlinear 3SLS estimator, which solves

$$\min_{\theta \in \Theta} \left[\sum_{i=1}^{N} \mathbf{Z}_i'\mathbf{q}_i(\theta)\right]' \left(N^{-1}\sum_{i=1}^{N} \mathbf{Z}_i'\hat{\boldsymbol{\Omega}}\mathbf{Z}_i\right)^{-1} \left[\sum_{i=1}^{N} \mathbf{Z}_i'\mathbf{q}_i(\theta)\right]$$

is efficient, and its asymptotic variance is estimated as

$$\left\{\left[\sum_{i=1}^{N} \mathbf{Z}_i'\nabla_\theta\mathbf{r}_i(\hat{\theta})\right]' \left(\sum_{i=1}^{N} \mathbf{Z}_i'\hat{\boldsymbol{\Omega}}\mathbf{Z}_i\right)^{-1} \left[\sum_{i=1}^{N} \mathbf{Z}_i'\nabla_\theta\mathbf{r}_i(\hat{\theta})\right]\right\}^{-1}$$

The N3SLS estimator is used widely for systems of the form (14.33), but, as we discussed in Section 9.6, there are many cases where assumption (14.26) must fail when different instruments are needed for different equations.

As an example, we show how a **hedonic price system** fits into this framework. Consider a linear demand and supply system for G attributes of a good or service (see Epple, 1987; Kahn and Lang, 1988; and Wooldridge, 1996). The demand and supply system is written as

$$demand_g = \eta_{1g} + \mathbf{w}\boldsymbol{\alpha}_{1g} + \mathbf{x}_1\boldsymbol{\beta}_{1g} + u_{1g}, \qquad g = 1, \ldots, G$$

$$supply_g = \eta_{2g} + \mathbf{w}\boldsymbol{\alpha}_{2g} + \mathbf{x}_2\boldsymbol{\beta}_{2g} + u_{2g}, \qquad g = 1, \ldots, G$$

where $\mathbf{w} = (w_1, \ldots, w_G)$ is the $1 \times G$ vector of attribute prices. The demand equations usually represent an individual or household; the supply equations can represent an individual, firm, or employer.

There are several tricky issues in estimating either the demand or supply function for a particular g. First, the attribute prices w_g are not directly observed. What is usually observed are the equilibrium quantities for each attribute and each cross section unit i; call these q_{ig}, $g = 1, \ldots, G$. (In the hedonic systems literature these are often denoted z_{ig}, but we use q_{ig} here because they are endogenous variables, and we have been using $\mathbf{z}_i$ to denote exogenous variables.) For example, the q_{ig} can be features of a house, such as size, number of bathrooms, and so on. Along with these features we observe the equilibrium price of the good, p_i, which we assume follows a quadratic hedonic price function:

$$p_i = \gamma + \mathbf{q}_i\boldsymbol{\psi} + \mathbf{q}_i\boldsymbol{\Pi}\mathbf{q}_i'/2 + \mathbf{x}_{i3}\boldsymbol{\delta} + \mathbf{x}_{i3}\boldsymbol{\Gamma}\mathbf{q}_i' + u_{i3} \tag{14.44}$$

where $\mathbf{x}_{i3}$ is a vector of variables that affect p_i, $\boldsymbol{\Pi}$ is a $G \times G$ symmetric matrix, and $\boldsymbol{\Gamma}$ is a $G \times G$ matrix.

A key point for identifying the demand and supply functions is that $\mathbf{w}_i = \partial p_i/\partial \mathbf{q}_i$, which, under equation (14.44), becomes $\mathbf{w}_i = \mathbf{q}_i\boldsymbol{\Pi} + \mathbf{x}_{i3}\boldsymbol{\Gamma}$, or $w_{ig} = \mathbf{q}_i\boldsymbol{\pi}_g + \mathbf{x}_{i3}\boldsymbol{\gamma}_g$ for each g. By substitution, the equilibrium estimating equations can be written as equation (14.44) plus

$$q_{ig} = \eta_{1g} + (\mathbf{q}_i\boldsymbol{\Pi} + \mathbf{x}_{i3}\boldsymbol{\Gamma})\boldsymbol{\alpha}_{1g} + \mathbf{x}_{i1}\boldsymbol{\beta}_{1g} + u_{i1g}, \qquad g = 1, \ldots, G \tag{14.45}$$

$$q_{ig} = \eta_{2g} + (\mathbf{q}_i\boldsymbol{\Pi} + \mathbf{x}_{i3}\boldsymbol{\Gamma})\boldsymbol{\alpha}_{2g} + \mathbf{x}_{i2}\boldsymbol{\beta}_{2g} + u_{i2g}, \qquad g = 1, \ldots, G \tag{14.46}$$

These two equations are linear in $\mathbf{q}_i, \mathbf{x}_{i1}, \mathbf{x}_{i2}$, and $\mathbf{x}_{i3}$ but nonlinear in the parameters.

Let $\mathbf{u}_{i1}$ be the $G \times 1$ vector of attribute demand disturbances and $\mathbf{u}_{i2}$ the $G \times 1$ vector of attribute supply disturbances. What are reasonable assumptions about $\mathbf{u}_{i1}, \mathbf{u}_{i2}$, and u_{i3}? It is almost always assumed that equation (14.44) represents a conditional expectation with no important unobserved factors; this assumption means $\mathrm{E}(u_{i3} \mid \mathbf{q}_i, \mathbf{x}_i) = 0$, where $\mathbf{x}_i$ contains all elements in $\mathbf{x}_{i1}, \mathbf{x}_{i2}$, and $\mathbf{x}_{i3}$. The properties of $\mathbf{u}_{i1}$ and $\mathbf{u}_{i2}$ are more subtle. It is clear that these cannot be uncorrelated with $\mathbf{q}_i$, and so equations (14.45) and (14.46) contain endogenous explanatory variables if $\boldsymbol{\Pi} \neq \mathbf{0}$. But there is another problem, pointed out by Bartik (1987), Epple (1987), and Kahn and Lang (1988): because of matching that happens between individual buyers and sellers, $\mathbf{x}_{i2}$ is correlated with u_{i1}, and $\mathbf{x}_{i1}$ is correlated with u_{i2}. Consequently, what would seem to be the obvious IVs for the demand equations (14.45)—the factors shifting the supply curve—are endogenous to equation (14.45). Fortunately, all is not lost: if $\mathbf{x}_{i3}$ contains exogenous factors that affect p_i but do not appear in the structural demand and supply functions, we can use these as instruments in both the demand and supply equations. Specifically, we assume

$$\mathrm{E}(\mathbf{u}_{i1} \mid \mathbf{x}_{i1}, \mathbf{x}_{i3}) = \mathbf{0}, \qquad \mathrm{E}(\mathbf{u}_{i2} \mid \mathbf{x}_{i2}, \mathbf{x}_{i3}) = \mathbf{0}, \qquad \mathrm{E}(u_{i3} \mid \mathbf{q}_i, \mathbf{x}_i) = 0 \tag{14.47}$$

Common choices for $\mathbf{x}_{i3}$ are geographical or industry dummy indicators (for example, Montgomery, Shaw, and Benedict, 1992; Hagy, 1998), where the assumption is that the demand and supply functions do not change across region or industry but the type of matching does, and therefore p_i can differ systematically across region or industry. Bartik (1987) discusses how a randomized experiment can be used to create the elements of $\mathbf{x}_{i3}$.

For concreteness, let us focus on estimating the set of demand functions. If $\mathbf{\Pi} = \mathbf{0}$, so that the quadratic in $\mathbf{q}_i$ does not appear in equation (14.44), a simple two-step procedure is available: (1) estimate equation (14.44) by OLS, and obtain $\hat{w}_{ig} = \hat{\psi}_g + \mathbf{x}_{i3}\hat{\gamma}_g$ for each i and g; (2) run the regression q_{ig} on $1, \hat{\mathbf{w}}_i, \mathbf{x}_{i1}, i = 1, \ldots, N$. Under assumptions (14.47) and identification assumptions, this method produces $\sqrt{N}$-consistent, asymptotically normal estimators of the parameters in demand equation g. Because the second regression involves generated regressors, the standard errors and test statistics should be adjusted.

It is clear that, without restrictions on $\boldsymbol{\alpha}_{1g}$, the order condition necessary for identifying the demand parameters is that the dimension of $\mathbf{x}_{i3}$, say K_3, must exceed G. If $K_3 < G$ then $\mathrm{E}[(\mathbf{w}_i, \mathbf{x}_{i1})'(\mathbf{w}_i, \mathbf{x}_{i1})]$ has less than full rank, and the OLS rank condition fails. If we make exclusion restrictions on $\boldsymbol{\alpha}_{1g}$, fewer elements are needed in $\mathbf{x}_{i3}$. In the case that only w_{ig} appears in the demand equation for attribute g, $\mathbf{x}_{i3}$ can be a scalar, provided its interaction with q_{ig} in the hedonic price system is significant ($\gamma_{gg} \neq 0$). Checking the analogue of the rank condition in general is somewhat complicated; see Epple (1987) for discussion.

When $\mathbf{w}_i = \mathbf{q}_i\mathbf{\Pi} + \mathbf{x}_{i3}\mathbf{\Gamma}$, $\mathbf{w}_i$ is correlated with u_{i1g}, so we must modify the two-step procedure. In the second step, we can use instruments for $\hat{\mathbf{w}}_i$ and perform 2SLS rather than OLS. Assuming that $\mathbf{x}_{i3}$ has enough elements, the demand equations are still identified. If only w_{ig} appears in $demand_{ig}$, sufficient for identification is that an element of $\mathbf{x}_{i3}$ appears in the linear projection of w_{ig} on $\mathbf{x}_{i1}$, $\mathbf{x}_{i3}$. This assumption can hold even if $\mathbf{x}_{i3}$ has only a single element. For the matching reasons we discussed previously, $\mathbf{x}_{i2}$ cannot be used as instruments for $\hat{\mathbf{w}}_i$ in the demand equation.

Whether $\mathbf{\Pi} = \mathbf{0}$ or not, more efficient estimators are obtained from the full demand system and the hedonic price function. Write

$$\mathbf{q}_i' = \boldsymbol{\eta}_1 + (\mathbf{q}_i\mathbf{\Pi} + \mathbf{x}_{i3}\mathbf{\Gamma})\mathbf{A}_1 + \mathbf{x}_{i1}\mathbf{B}_1 + \mathbf{u}_{i1}$$

along with equation (14.44). Then $(\mathbf{x}_{i1}, \mathbf{x}_{i3})$ (and functions of these) can be used as instruments in any of the G demand equations, and $(\mathbf{q}_i, \mathbf{x}_i)$ act as IVs in equation (14.44). (It may be that the supply function is not even specified, in which case $\mathbf{x}_i$ contains only $\mathbf{x}_{i1}$ and $\mathbf{x}_{i3}$.) A first-stage estimator is the nonlinear system 2SLS estimator. Then the system can be estimated by the minimum chi-square estimator that solves problem (14.43). When restricting attention to demand equations plus the hedonic price equation, or supply equations plus the hedonic price equation, nonlinear 3SLS is efficient under certain assumptions. If the demand and supply equations are estimated together, the key assumption (14.26) that makes nonlinear 3SLS asymptotically efficient cannot be expected to hold; see Wooldridge (1996) for discussion.

If one of the demand functions is of primary interest, it may make sense to estimate it along with equation (14.44), by GMM or nonlinear 3SLS. If the demand functions are written in inverse form, the resulting system is linear in the parameters, as shown in Wooldridge (1996).

14.4 Panel Data Applications

As we saw in Chapter 11, system IV methods are needed in certain panel data contexts. In the current case, our interest is in nonlinear panel data models that cannot be estimated using linear methods. We hold off on discussing nonlinear panel data models explicitly containing unobserved effects until Part IV.

One increasingly popular use of panel data is to test rationality in economic models of individual, family, or firm behavior (see, for example, Shapiro, 1984; Zeldes, 1989; Keane and Runkle, 1992; Shea, 1995). For a random draw from the population we assume that T time periods are available. Suppose that an economic theory implies that

$$\mathrm{E}[r_t(\mathbf{w}_t, \boldsymbol{\theta}_o) \mid \mathbf{w}_{t-1}, \ldots, \mathbf{w}_1) = 0, \qquad t = 1, \ldots, T \tag{14.48}$$

where, for simplicity, r_t is a scalar. These conditional moment restrictions are often implied by rational expectations, under the assumption that the decision horizon is the same length as the sampling period. For example, consider a standard life-cycle model of consumption. Let c_{it} denote consumption of family i at time t, let $\mathbf{h}_{it}$ denote taste shifters, let δ_o denote the common rate of time preference, and let a_{it}^j denote the return for family i from holding asset j from period $t-1$ to t. Under the assumption that utility is given by

$$\mathrm{u}(c_{it}, \theta_{it}) = \exp(\mathbf{h}_{it}\boldsymbol{\beta}_o) c_{it}^{1-\lambda_o}/(1-\lambda_o) \tag{14.49}$$

the Euler equation is

$$E[(1 + a_{it}^j)(c_{it}/c_{i,t-1})^{-\lambda_o} \mid \mathscr{I}_{i,t-1}] = (1 + \delta_o)^{-1} \exp(\mathbf{x}_{it}\boldsymbol{\beta}_o) \tag{14.50}$$

where $\mathscr{I}_{it}$ is family i's information set at time t and $\mathbf{x}_{it} \equiv \mathbf{h}_{i,t-1} - \mathbf{h}_{it}$; equation (14.50) assumes that $\mathbf{h}_{it} - \mathbf{h}_{i,t-1} \in \mathscr{I}_{i,t-1}$, an assumption which is often reasonable. Given equation (14.50), we can define a residual function for each t:

$$r_{it}(\boldsymbol{\theta}) = (1 + a_{it}^j)(c_{it}/c_{i,t-1})^{-\lambda} - \exp(\mathbf{x}_{it}\boldsymbol{\beta}) \tag{14.51}$$

where $(1 + \delta)^{-1}$ is absorbed in an intercept in $\mathbf{x}_{it}$. Let $\mathbf{w}_{it}$ contain c_{it}, $c_{i,t-1}$, a_{it}, and $\mathbf{x}_{it}$. Then condition (14.48) holds, and λ_o and $\boldsymbol{\beta}_o$ can be estimated by GMM.

Returning to condition (14.48), valid instruments at time t are functions of information known at time $t - 1$:

$$\mathbf{z}_t = \mathbf{f}_t(\mathbf{w}_{t-1}, \ldots, \mathbf{w}_1) \tag{14.52}$$

The $T \times 1$ residual vector is $\mathbf{r}(\mathbf{w}, \boldsymbol{\theta}) = [r_1(\mathbf{w}_1, \boldsymbol{\theta}), \ldots, r_T(\mathbf{w}_T, \boldsymbol{\theta})]'$, and the matrix of instruments has the same form as matrix (14.38) for each i (with $G = T$). Then, the minimum chi-square estimator can be obtained after using the system 2SLS estimator, although the choice of instruments is a nontrivial matter. A common choice is linear and quadratic functions of variables lagged one or two time periods.

Estimation of the optimal weighting matrix is somewhat simplified under the conditional moment restrictions (14.48). Recall from Section 14.2 that the optimal estimator uses the inverse of a consistent estimator of $\boldsymbol{\Lambda}_o = E[\mathbf{Z}_i'\mathbf{r}_i(\boldsymbol{\theta}_o)\mathbf{r}_i(\boldsymbol{\theta}_o)'\mathbf{Z}_i]$. Under condition (14.48), this matrix is block diagonal. Dropping the i subscript, the (s, t) block is $E[r_s(\boldsymbol{\theta}_o)r_t(\boldsymbol{\theta}_o)\mathbf{z}_s'\mathbf{z}_t]$. For concreteness, assume that $s < t$. Then $\mathbf{z}_t, \mathbf{z}_s$, and $r_s(\boldsymbol{\theta}_o)$ are all functions of $\mathbf{w}_{t-1}, \mathbf{w}_{t-2}, \ldots, \mathbf{w}_1$. By iterated expectations it follows that

$$E[r_s(\boldsymbol{\theta}_o)r_t(\boldsymbol{\theta}_o)\mathbf{z}_s'\mathbf{z}_t] = E\{r_s(\boldsymbol{\theta}_o)\mathbf{z}_s'\mathbf{z}_t E[r_t(\boldsymbol{\theta}_o) \mid \mathbf{w}_{t-1}, \ldots, \mathbf{w}_1]\} = 0$$

and so we only need to estimate the diagonal blocks of $E[\mathbf{Z}_i'\mathbf{r}_i(\boldsymbol{\theta}_o)\mathbf{r}_i(\boldsymbol{\theta}_o)'\mathbf{Z}_i]$:

$$N^{-1} \sum_{i=1}^{N} \hat{\breve{r}}_{it}^2 \mathbf{z}_{it}'\mathbf{z}_{it} \tag{14.53}$$

is a consistent estimator of the tth block, where the $\hat{\breve{r}}_{it}$ are obtained from an inefficient GMM estimator.

In cases where the data frequency does not match the horizon relevant for decision making, the optimal matrix does not have the block diagonal form: some off-diagonal blocks will be nonzero. See Hansen (1982) for the pure time series case.

Ahn and Schmidt (1995) apply nonlinear GMM methods to estimate the linear, unobserved effects AR(1) model. Some of the orthogonality restrictions they use are nonlinear in the parameters of interest. In Part IV we will cover nonlinear panel data models with unobserved effects. For the consumption example, we would like to allow for a family-specific rate of time preference, as well as unobserved family tastes. Orthogonality conditions can often be obtained in such cases, but they are not as straightforward to obtain as in the previous example.

14.5 Efficient Estimation

In Chapter 8 we obtained the efficient weighting matrix for GMM estimation of linear models, and we extended that to nonlinear models in Section 14.1. In Chapter 13 we asserted that maximum likelihood estimation has some important efficiency properties. We are now in a position to study a framework that allows us to show the efficiency of an estimator within a particular class of estimators, and also to find efficient estimators within a stated class. Our approach is essentially that in Newey and McFadden (1994, Section 5.3), although we will not use the weakest possible assumptions. Bates and White (1993) proposed a very similar framework and also considered time series problems.

14.5.1 A General Efficiency Framework

Most estimators in econometrics—and all of the ones we have studied—are $\sqrt{N}$-asymptotically normal, with variance matrices of the form

$$\mathbf{V} = \mathbf{A}^{-1}\mathrm{E}[\mathbf{s}(\mathbf{w})\mathbf{s}(\mathbf{w})'](\mathbf{A}')^{-1} \tag{14.54}$$

where, in most cases, $\mathbf{s}(\mathbf{w})$ is the score of an objective function (evaluated at $\boldsymbol{\theta}_o$) and $\mathbf{A}$ is the expected value of the Jacobian of the score, again evaluated at $\boldsymbol{\theta}_o$. (We suppress an "o" subscript here, as the value of the true parameter is irrelevant.) All M-estimators with twice continuously differentiable objective functions (and even some without) have variance matrices of this form, as do GMM estimators. The following lemma is a useful sufficient condition for showing that one estimator is more efficient than another.

LEMMA 14.1 (Relative Efficiency): Let $\hat{\boldsymbol{\theta}}_1$ and $\hat{\boldsymbol{\theta}}_2$ be two $\sqrt{N}$-asymptotically normal estimators of the $P \times 1$ parameter vector $\boldsymbol{\theta}_o$, with asymptotic variances of the form (14.54) (with appropriate subscripts on $\mathbf{A}$, $\mathbf{s}$, and $\mathbf{V}$). If for some $\rho > 0$,

$$\mathrm{E}[\mathbf{s}_1(\mathbf{w})\mathbf{s}_1(\mathbf{w})'] = \rho\mathbf{A}_1 \tag{14.55}$$

$$\mathrm{E}[\mathbf{s}_2(\mathbf{w})\mathbf{s}_1(\mathbf{w})'] = \rho\mathbf{A}_2 \tag{14.56}$$

then $\mathbf{V}_2 - \mathbf{V}_1$ is positive semidefinite.

The proof of Lemma 14.1 is given in the chapter appendix.

Condition (14.55) is essentially the generalized information matrix equality (GIME) we introduced in Section 12.5.1 for the estimator $\hat{\theta}_1$. Notice that $\mathbf{A}_1$ is necessarily symmetric and positive definite under condition (14.55). Condition (14.56) is new. In most cases, it says that the expected outer product of the scores $\mathbf{s}_2$ and $\mathbf{s}_1$ equals the expected Jacobian of $\mathbf{s}_2$ (evaluated at $\boldsymbol{\theta}_o$). In Section 12.5.1 we claimed that the GIME plays a role in efficiency, and Lemma 14.1 shows that it does so.

Verifying the conditions of Lemma 14.1 is also very convenient for constructing simple forms of the Hausman (1978) statistic in a variety of contexts. Provided that the two estimators are jointly asymptotically normally distributed—something that is almost always true when each is $\sqrt{N}$-asymptotically normal, and that can be verified by stacking the first-order representations of the estimators—assumptions (14.55) and (14.56) imply that the asymptotic covariance between $\sqrt{N}(\hat{\boldsymbol{\theta}}_2 - \boldsymbol{\theta}_o)$ and $\sqrt{N}(\hat{\boldsymbol{\theta}}_1 - \boldsymbol{\theta}_o)$ is $\mathbf{A}_2^{-1}\mathrm{E}(\mathbf{s}_2\mathbf{s}_1')\mathbf{A}_1^{-1} = \mathbf{A}_2^{-1}(\rho\mathbf{A}_2)\mathbf{A}_1^{-1} = \rho\mathbf{A}_1^{-1} = \mathrm{Avar}[\sqrt{N}(\hat{\boldsymbol{\theta}}_1 - \boldsymbol{\theta}_o)]$. In other words, the asymptotic covariance between the ($\sqrt{N}$-scaled) estimators is equal to the asymptotic variance of the efficient estimator. This equality implies that $\mathrm{Avar}[\sqrt{N}(\hat{\boldsymbol{\theta}}_2 - \hat{\boldsymbol{\theta}}_1)] = \mathbf{V}_2 + \mathbf{V}_1 - \mathbf{C} - \mathbf{C}' = \mathbf{V}_2 + \mathbf{V}_1 - 2\mathbf{V}_1 = \mathbf{V}_2 - \mathbf{V}_1$, where $\mathbf{C}$ is the asymptotic covariance. If $\mathbf{V}_2 - \mathbf{V}_1$ is actually positive definite (rather than just positive semidefinite), then $[\sqrt{N}(\hat{\boldsymbol{\theta}}_2 - \hat{\boldsymbol{\theta}}_1)]'(\hat{\mathbf{V}}_2 - \hat{\mathbf{V}}_1)^{-1}[\sqrt{N}(\hat{\boldsymbol{\theta}}_2 - \hat{\boldsymbol{\theta}}_1)] \overset{a}{\sim} \chi^2_P$ under the assumptions of Lemma 14.1, where $\hat{\mathbf{V}}_g$ is a consistent estimator of $\mathbf{V}_g$, $g = 1, 2$. Statistically significant differences between $\hat{\boldsymbol{\theta}}_2$ and $\hat{\boldsymbol{\theta}}_1$ signal some sort of model misspecification. (See Section 6.2.1, where we discussed this form of the Hausman test for comparing 2SLS and OLS to test whether the explanatory variables are exogenous.) If assumptions (14.55) and (14.56) do not hold, this standard form of the Hausman statistic is invalid.

Given Lemma 14.1, we can state a condition that implies efficiency of an estimator in an entire *class* of estimators. It is useful to be somewhat formal in defining the relevant class of estimators. We do so by introducing an index, τ. For each τ in an index set, say, $\mathscr{T}$, the estimator $\hat{\boldsymbol{\theta}}_\tau$ has an associated $\mathbf{s}_\tau$ and $\mathbf{A}_\tau$ such that the asymptotic variance of $\sqrt{N}(\hat{\boldsymbol{\theta}}_\tau - \boldsymbol{\theta}_o)$ has the form (14.54). The index can be very abstract; it simply serves to distinguish different $\sqrt{N}$-asymptotically normal estimators of $\boldsymbol{\theta}_o$. For example, in the class of M-estimators, the set $\mathscr{T}$ consists of objective functions $q(\cdot,\cdot)$ such that $\boldsymbol{\theta}_o$ uniquely minimizes $\mathrm{E}[q(\mathbf{w},\boldsymbol{\theta})]$ over $\boldsymbol{\Theta}$, and q satisfies the twice continuously differentiable and bounded moment assumptions imposed for asymptotic normality. For GMM with *given* moment conditions, $\mathscr{T}$ is the set of all $L \times L$ positive definite matrices. We will see another example in Section 14.5.3.

Lemma 14.1 immediately implies the following theorem.

THEOREM 14.3 (Efficiency in a Class of Estimators): Let $\{\hat{\boldsymbol{\theta}}_\tau : \tau \in \mathscr{T}\}$ be a class of $\sqrt{N}$-asymptotically normal estimators with variance matrices of the form (14.54). If for some $\tau^* \in \mathscr{T}$ and $\rho > 0$

$$\mathrm{E}[\mathbf{s}_\tau(\mathbf{w})\mathbf{s}_{\tau^*}(\mathbf{w})'] = \rho\mathbf{A}_\tau, \qquad \text{all } \tau \in \mathscr{T} \tag{14.57}$$

then $\hat{\boldsymbol{\theta}}_{\tau^*}$ is asymptotically relatively efficient in the class $\{\hat{\boldsymbol{\theta}}_\tau\colon \tau \in \mathscr{T}\}$.

This theorem has many applications. If we specify a class of estimators by defining the index set $\mathscr{T}$, then the estimator $\hat{\boldsymbol{\theta}}_{\tau^*}$ is more efficient than all other estimators in the class if we can show condition (14.57). [A partial converse to Theorem 14.3 also holds; see Newey and McFadden (1994, Section 5.3).] This is not to say that $\hat{\boldsymbol{\theta}}_{\tau^*}$ is necessarily more efficient than *all* possible $\sqrt{N}$-asymptotically normal estimators. If there is an estimator that falls outside of the specified class, then Theorem 14.3 does not help us to compare it with $\hat{\boldsymbol{\theta}}_{\tau^*}$. In this sense, Theorem 14.3 is a more general (and asymptotic) version of the Gauss-Markov theorem from linear regression analysis: while the Gauss-Markov theorem states that OLS has the smallest variance in the class of linear, unbiased estimators, it does not allow us to compare OLS to unbiased estimators that are not linear in the vector of observations on the dependent variable.

14.5.2 Efficiency of MLE

Students of econometrics are often told that the maximum likelihood estimator is "efficient." Unfortunately, in the context of conditional MLE from Chapter 13, the statement of efficiency is usually ambiguous; Manski (1988, Chapter 8) is a notable exception. Theorem 14.3 allows us to state precisely the class of estimators in which the conditional MLE is relatively efficient. As in Chapter 13, we let $\mathrm{E}_\theta(\cdot \mid \mathbf{x})$ denote the expectation with respect to the conditional density $f(\mathbf{y} \mid \mathbf{x}; \boldsymbol{\theta})$.

Consider the class of estimators solving the first-order condition

$$N^{-1}\sum_{i=1}^{N}\mathbf{g}(\mathbf{w}_i, \hat{\boldsymbol{\theta}}) \equiv \mathbf{0} \tag{14.58}$$

where the $P \times 1$ function $\mathbf{g}(\mathbf{w}, \boldsymbol{\theta})$ such that

$$\mathrm{E}_\theta[\mathbf{g}(\mathbf{w}, \boldsymbol{\theta}) \mid \mathbf{x}] = \mathbf{0}, \qquad \text{all } \mathbf{x} \in \mathscr{X}, \quad \text{all } \boldsymbol{\theta} \in \boldsymbol{\Theta} \tag{14.59}$$

In other words, the class of estimators is indexed by functions $\mathbf{g}$ satisfying a zero conditional moment restriction. We assume the standard regularity conditions from Chapter 12; in particular, $\mathbf{g}(\mathbf{w}, \cdot)$ is continuously differentiably on the interior of $\boldsymbol{\Theta}$.

As we showed in Section 13.7, functions $\mathbf{g}$ satisfying condition (14.59) generally have the property

$$-\mathrm{E}[\nabla_\theta \mathbf{g}(\mathbf{w}, \boldsymbol{\theta}_o) \mid \mathbf{x}] = \mathrm{E}[\mathbf{g}(\mathbf{w}, \boldsymbol{\theta}_o)\mathbf{s}(\mathbf{w}, \boldsymbol{\theta}_o)' \mid \mathbf{x}]$$

where $\mathbf{s}(\mathbf{w}, \boldsymbol{\theta})$ is the score of $\log f(\mathbf{y} \mid \mathbf{x}; \boldsymbol{\theta})$ (as always, we must impose certain regularity conditons on $\mathbf{g}$ and $\log f$). If we take the expectation of both sides with respect to $\mathbf{x}$, we obtain condition (14.57) with $\rho = 1$, $\mathbf{A}_\tau = \mathrm{E}[\nabla_\theta \mathbf{g}(\mathbf{w}, \boldsymbol{\theta}_o)]$, and $\mathbf{s}_{\tau^*}(\mathbf{w}) = -\mathbf{s}(\mathbf{w}, \boldsymbol{\theta}_o)$. It follows from Theorem 14.3 that the conditional MLE is efficient in the class of estimators solving equation (14.58), where $\mathbf{g}(\cdot)$ satisfies condition (14.59) and appropriate regularity conditions. Recall from Section 13.5.1 that the asymptotic variance of the (centered and standardized) CMLE is $\{\mathrm{E}[\mathbf{s}(\mathbf{w}, \boldsymbol{\theta}_o)\mathbf{s}(\mathbf{w}, \boldsymbol{\theta}_o)']\}^{-1}$. This is an example of an **efficiency bound** because no estimator of the form (14.58) under condition (14.59) can have an asymptotic variance smaller than $\{\mathrm{E}[\mathbf{s}(\mathbf{w}, \boldsymbol{\theta}_o)\mathbf{s}(\mathbf{w}, \boldsymbol{\theta}_o)']\}^{-1}$ (in the matrix sense). When an estimator from this class has the same asymptotic variance as the CMLE, we way it *achieves the efficiency bound.*

It is important to see that the efficiency of the conditional MLE in the class of estimators solving equation (14.58) under condition (14.59) does *not* require $\mathbf{x}$ to be ancillary for $\boldsymbol{\theta}_o$: except for regularity conditions, the distribution of $\mathbf{x}$ is essentially unrestricted, and could depend on $\boldsymbol{\theta}_o$. Conditional MLE simply ignores information on $\boldsymbol{\theta}_o$ that might be contained in the distribution of $\mathbf{x}$, but so do all other estimators that are based on condition (14.59).

By choosing $\mathbf{x}$ to be empty, we conclude that the unconditional MLE is efficient in the class of estimators based on equation (14.58) with $\mathrm{E}_\theta[\mathbf{g}(\mathbf{w}, \boldsymbol{\theta})] = \mathbf{0}$, all $\boldsymbol{\theta} \in \boldsymbol{\Theta}$. This is a very broad class of estimators, including all of the estimators requiring condition (14.59): if a function $\mathbf{g}$ satisfies condition (14.59), it has zero unconditional mean, too. Consequently, the unconditional MLE is generally more efficient than the conditional MLE. This efficiency comes at the price of having to model the joint density of $(\mathbf{y}, \mathbf{x})$, rather than just the conditional density of $\mathbf{y}$ given $\mathbf{x}$. And, if our model for the density of $\mathbf{x}$ is incorrect, the unconditional MLE generally would be inconsistent.

When is CMLE as efficient as unconditional MLE for estimating $\boldsymbol{\theta}_o$? Assume that the model for the joint density of $(\mathbf{x}, \mathbf{y})$ can be expressed as $f(\mathbf{y} \mid \mathbf{x}; \boldsymbol{\theta})h(\mathbf{x}; \boldsymbol{\delta})$, where $\boldsymbol{\theta}$ is the parameter vector of interest, and $h(\mathbf{x}, \boldsymbol{\delta}_o)$ is the marginal density of $\mathbf{x}$ for some vector $\boldsymbol{\delta}_o$. Then, if $\boldsymbol{\delta}$ does not depend on $\boldsymbol{\theta}$ in the sense that $\nabla_\theta h(\mathbf{x}; \boldsymbol{\delta}) = \mathbf{0}$ for all $\mathbf{x}$ and $\boldsymbol{\delta}$, $\mathbf{x}$ is ancillary for $\boldsymbol{\theta}_o$. In fact, the CMLE is identical to the unconditional MLE. If $\boldsymbol{\delta}$ depends on $\boldsymbol{\theta}$, the term $\nabla_\theta \log[h(\mathbf{x}; \boldsymbol{\delta})]$ generally contains information for estimating $\boldsymbol{\theta}_o$, and unconditional MLE will be more efficient than CMLE.

14.5.3 Efficient Choice of Instruments under Conditional Moment Restrictions

We can also apply Theorem 14.3 to find the optimal set of instrumental variables under general **conditional moment restrictions**. For a $G \times 1$ vector $\mathbf{r}(\mathbf{w}_i, \boldsymbol{\theta})$, where $\mathbf{w}_i \in \mathbb{R}^M$, $\boldsymbol{\theta}_o$ is said to satisfy conditional moment restrictions if

$$\mathrm{E}[\mathbf{r}(\mathbf{w}_i, \boldsymbol{\theta}_o) \mid \mathbf{x}_i] = \mathbf{0} \tag{14.60}$$

where $\mathbf{x}_i \in \mathbb{R}^K$ is a subvector of $\mathbf{w}_i$. Under assumption (14.60), the matrix $\mathbf{Z}_i$ appearing in equation (14.22) can be any function of $\mathbf{x}_i$. For a *given* matrix $\mathbf{Z}_i$, we obtain the efficient GMM estimator by using the efficient weighting matrix. However, unless $\mathbf{Z}_i$ is the optimal set of instruments, we can generally obtain a more efficient estimator by adding any nonlinear function of $\mathbf{x}_i$ to $\mathbf{Z}_i$. Because the list of potential IVs is endless, it is useful to characterize the optimal choice of $\mathbf{Z}_i$.

The solution to this problem is now pretty well known, and it can be obtained by applying Theorem 14.3. Let

$$\boldsymbol{\Omega}_o(\mathbf{x}_i) \equiv \mathrm{Var}[\mathbf{r}(\mathbf{w}_i, \boldsymbol{\theta}_o) \mid \mathbf{x}_i] \tag{14.61}$$

be the $G \times G$ conditional variance of $\mathbf{r}_i(\boldsymbol{\theta}_o)$ given $\mathbf{x}_i$, and define

$$\mathbf{R}_o(\mathbf{x}_i) \equiv \mathrm{E}[\nabla_\theta \mathbf{r}(\mathbf{w}_i, \boldsymbol{\theta}_o) \mid \mathbf{x}_i] \tag{14.62}$$

Problem 14.3 asks you to verify that the optimal choice of instruments is

$$\mathbf{Z}^*(\mathbf{x}_i) \equiv \boldsymbol{\Omega}_o(\mathbf{x}_i)^{-1}\mathbf{R}_o(\mathbf{x}_i) \tag{14.63}$$

The optimal instrument matrix is always $G \times P$, and so the efficient method of moments estimator solves

$$\sum_{i=1}^{N} \mathbf{Z}^*(\mathbf{x}_i)'\mathbf{r}_i(\hat{\boldsymbol{\theta}}) = \mathbf{0}$$

There is no need to use a weighting matrix. Incidentally, by taking $\mathbf{g}(\mathbf{w}, \boldsymbol{\theta}) \equiv \mathbf{Z}^*(\mathbf{x})'\mathbf{r}(\mathbf{w}, \boldsymbol{\theta})$, we obtain a function $\mathbf{g}$ satisfying condition (14.59). From our discussion in Section 14.5.2, it follows immediately that the conditional MLE is no less efficient than the optimal IV estimator.

In practice, $\mathbf{Z}^*(\mathbf{x}_i)$ is never a known function of $\mathbf{x}_i$. In some cases the function $\mathbf{R}_o(\mathbf{x}_i)$ is a known function of $\mathbf{x}_i$ and $\boldsymbol{\theta}_o$ and can be easily estimated; this statement is true of linear SEMs under conditional mean assumptions (see Chapters 8 and 9) and of multivariate nonlinear regression, which we cover later in this subsection. Rarely do moment conditions imply a parametric form for $\boldsymbol{\Omega}_o(\mathbf{x}_i)$, but sometimes homoskedasticity is assumed:

$$\mathrm{E}[\mathbf{r}_i(\boldsymbol{\theta}_o)\mathbf{r}_i(\boldsymbol{\theta}_o) \mid \mathbf{x}_i] = \boldsymbol{\Omega}_o \tag{14.64}$$

and $\boldsymbol{\Omega}_o$ is easily estimated as in equation (14.30) given a preliminary estimate of $\boldsymbol{\theta}_o$.

Since both $\boldsymbol{\Omega}_o(\mathbf{x}_i)$ and $\mathbf{R}_o(\mathbf{x}_i)$ must be estimated, we must know the asymptotic properties of **GMM with generated instruments**. Under conditional moment restrictions, generated instruments have *no* effect on the asymptotic variance of the GMM estimator. Thus, if the matrix of instruments is $\mathbf{Z}(\mathbf{x}_i, \boldsymbol{\gamma}_o)$ for some unknown parameter vector γ_o, and $\hat{\gamma}$ is an estimator such that $\sqrt{N}(\hat{\gamma} - \gamma_o) = O_p(1)$, then the GMM estimator using the generated instruments $\hat{\mathbf{Z}}_i \equiv \mathbf{Z}(\mathbf{x}_i, \hat{\gamma})$ has the same limiting distribution as the GMM estimator using instruments $\mathbf{Z}(\mathbf{x}_i, \gamma_o)$ (using any weighting matrix). This result follows from a mean value expansion, using the fact that the derivative of each element of $\mathbf{Z}(\mathbf{x}_i, \gamma)$ with respect to γ is orthogonal to $\mathbf{r}_i(\boldsymbol{\theta}_o)$ under condition (14.60):

$$N^{-1/2} \sum_{i=1}^{N} \hat{\mathbf{Z}}_i' \mathbf{r}_i(\hat{\boldsymbol{\theta}}) = N^{-1/2} \sum_{i=1}^{N} \mathbf{Z}_i(\gamma_o)' \mathbf{r}_i(\boldsymbol{\theta}_o) + \mathrm{E}[\mathbf{Z}_i(\gamma_o)' \mathbf{R}_o(\mathbf{x}_i)] \sqrt{N}(\hat{\boldsymbol{\theta}} - \boldsymbol{\theta}_o) + o_p(1) \tag{14.65}$$

The right-hand side of equation (14.65) is identical to the expansion with $\hat{\mathbf{Z}}_i$ replaced with $\mathbf{Z}_i(\gamma_o)$.

Assuming now that $\mathbf{Z}_i(\gamma_o)$ is the matrix of efficient instruments, the asymptotic variance of the efficient estimator is

$$\text{Avar}\, \sqrt{N}(\hat{\boldsymbol{\theta}} - \boldsymbol{\theta}_o) = \{\mathrm{E}[\mathbf{R}_o(\mathbf{x}_i)' \boldsymbol{\Omega}_o(\mathbf{x}_i)^{-1} \mathbf{R}_o(\mathbf{x}_i)]\}^{-1} \tag{14.66}$$

as can be seen from Section 14.1 by noting that $\mathbf{G}_o = \mathrm{E}[\mathbf{R}_o(\mathbf{x}_i)' \boldsymbol{\Omega}_o(\mathbf{x}_i)^{-1} \mathbf{R}_o(\mathbf{x}_i)]$ and $\boldsymbol{\Lambda}_o = \mathbf{G}_o^{-1}$ when the instruments are given by equation (14.63).

Equation (14.66) is another example of an efficiency bound, this time under the conditional moment restrictions (14.54). What we have shown is that any GMM estimator has variance matrix that differs from equation (14.66) by a positive semi-definite matrix. Chamberlain (1987) has shown more: *any* estimator that uses only condition (14.60) and satisfies regularity conditions has variance matrix no smaller than equation (14.66).

Estimation of $\mathbf{R}_o(\mathbf{x}_i)$ generally requires nonparametric methods. Newey (1990) describes one approach. Essentially, regress the elements of $\nabla_\theta \mathbf{r}_i(\hat{\hat{\boldsymbol{\theta}}})$ on polynomial functions of $\mathbf{x}_i$ (or other functions with good approximating properties), where $\hat{\hat{\boldsymbol{\theta}}}$ is an initial estimate of $\boldsymbol{\theta}_o$. The fitted values from these regressions can be used as the elements of $\hat{\mathbf{R}}_i$. Other nonparametric approaches are available. See Newey (1990, 1993) for details. Unfortunately, we need a fairly large sample size in order to apply such methods effectively.

As an example of finding the optimal instruments, consider the problem of estimating a conditional mean for a vector $\mathbf{y}_i$:

$$\mathrm{E}(\mathbf{y}_i \mid \mathbf{x}_i) = \mathbf{m}(\mathbf{x}_i, \boldsymbol{\theta}_o) \tag{14.67}$$

Then the residual function is $\mathbf{r}(\mathbf{w}_i, \boldsymbol{\theta}) \equiv \mathbf{y}_i - \mathbf{m}(\mathbf{x}_i, \boldsymbol{\theta})$ and $\boldsymbol{\Omega}_o(\mathbf{x}_i) = \mathrm{Var}(\mathbf{y}_i \mid \mathbf{x}_i)$; therefore, the optimal instruments are $\mathbf{Z}_o(\mathbf{x}_i) \equiv \boldsymbol{\Omega}_o(\mathbf{x}_i)^{-1} \nabla_\theta \mathbf{m}(\mathbf{x}_i, \boldsymbol{\theta}_o)$. This is an important example where $\mathbf{R}_o(\mathbf{x}_i) = -\nabla_\theta \mathbf{m}(\mathbf{x}_i, \boldsymbol{\theta}_o)$ is a known function of $\mathbf{x}_i$ and $\boldsymbol{\theta}_o$. If the homoskedasticity assumption

$$\text{Var}(\mathbf{y}_i \mid \mathbf{x}_i) = \boldsymbol{\Omega}_o \tag{14.68}$$

holds, then the efficient estimator is easy to obtain. First, let $\hat{\hat{\boldsymbol{\theta}}}$ be the multivariate nonlinear least squares (MNLS) estimator, which solves $\min_{\boldsymbol{\theta} \in \Theta} \sum_{i=1}^N [\mathbf{y}_i - \mathbf{m}(\mathbf{x}_i, \boldsymbol{\theta})]' \cdot [\mathbf{y}_i - \mathbf{m}(\mathbf{x}_i, \boldsymbol{\theta})]$. As discussed in Problem 12.11, the MNLS estimator is generally consistent and $\sqrt{N}$-asymptotic normal. Define the residuals $\hat{\hat{\mathbf{u}}}_i \equiv \mathbf{y}_i - \mathbf{m}(\mathbf{x}_i, \hat{\hat{\boldsymbol{\theta}}})$, and define a consistent estimator of $\boldsymbol{\Omega}_o$ by $\hat{\boldsymbol{\Omega}} = N^{-1} \sum_{i=1}^N \hat{\hat{\mathbf{u}}}_i \hat{\hat{\mathbf{u}}}_i'$. An efficient estimator, $\hat{\boldsymbol{\theta}}$, solves

$$\sum_{i=1}^N \nabla_\theta \mathbf{m}(\mathbf{x}_i, \hat{\hat{\boldsymbol{\theta}}})' \hat{\boldsymbol{\Omega}}^{-1} [\mathbf{y}_i - \mathbf{m}(\mathbf{x}_i, \hat{\boldsymbol{\theta}})] = \mathbf{0}$$

and the asymptotic variance of $\sqrt{N}(\hat{\boldsymbol{\theta}} - \boldsymbol{\theta}_o)$ is $\{\text{E}[\nabla_\theta \mathbf{m}_i(\boldsymbol{\theta}_o)' \boldsymbol{\Omega}_o^{-1} \nabla_\theta \mathbf{m}_i(\boldsymbol{\theta}_o)]\}^{-1}$. An asymptotically equivalent estimator is the nonlinear SUR estimator described in Problem 12.7. In either case, the estimator of $\text{Avar}(\hat{\boldsymbol{\theta}})$ under assumption (14.68) is

$$\text{Av\hat{a}r}(\hat{\boldsymbol{\theta}}) = \left[\sum_{i=1}^N \nabla_\theta \mathbf{m}_i(\hat{\boldsymbol{\theta}})' \hat{\boldsymbol{\Omega}}^{-1} \nabla_\theta \mathbf{m}_i(\hat{\boldsymbol{\theta}})\right]^{-1}$$

Because the nonlinear SUR estimator is a two-step M-estimator and $\mathbf{B}_o = \mathbf{A}_o$ (in the notation of Chapter 12), the simplest forms of tests statistics are valid. If assumption (14.68) fails, the nonlinear SUR estimator is consistent, but robust inference should be used because $\mathbf{A}_o \neq \mathbf{B}_o$. And, the estimator is no longer efficient.

14.6 Classical Minimum Distance Estimation

We end this chapter with a brief treatment of **classical minimum distance (CMD) estimation**. This method has features in common with GMM, and often it is a convenient substitute for GMM.

Suppose that the $P \times 1$ parameter vector of interest, $\boldsymbol{\theta}_o$, which often consists of parameters from a structural model, is known to be related to an $S \times 1$ vector of reduced form parameters, $\boldsymbol{\pi}_o$, where $S > P$. In particular, $\boldsymbol{\pi}_o = \mathbf{h}(\boldsymbol{\theta}_o)$ for a known, continuously differentiable function $\mathbf{h}$: $\mathbb{R}^P \to \mathbb{R}^S$, so that $\mathbf{h}$ maps the structural parameters into the reduced form parameters.

CMD estimation of $\boldsymbol{\theta}_o$ entails first estimating $\boldsymbol{\pi}_o$ by $\hat{\boldsymbol{\pi}}$, and then choosing an estimator $\hat{\boldsymbol{\theta}}$ of $\boldsymbol{\theta}_o$ by making the distance between $\hat{\boldsymbol{\pi}}$ and $\mathbf{h}(\hat{\boldsymbol{\theta}})$ as small as possible. As with GMM estimation, we use a weighted Euclidean measure of distance. While a

CMD estimator can be defined for any positive semidefinite weighting matrix, we consider only the efficient CMD estimator given our choice of $\hat{\boldsymbol{\pi}}$. As with efficient GMM, the CMD estimator that uses the efficient weighting matrix is also called the **minimum chi-square estimator**.

Assuming that for an $S \times S$ positive definite matrix $\boldsymbol{\Xi}_o$

$$\sqrt{N}(\hat{\boldsymbol{\pi}} - \boldsymbol{\pi}_o) \overset{a}{\sim} \text{Normal}(\mathbf{0}, \boldsymbol{\Xi}_o) \tag{14.69}$$

it turns out that an efficient CMD estimator solves

$$\min_{\theta \in \Theta} \{\hat{\boldsymbol{\pi}} - \mathbf{h}(\boldsymbol{\theta})\}' \hat{\boldsymbol{\Xi}}^{-1} \{\hat{\boldsymbol{\pi}} - \mathbf{h}(\boldsymbol{\theta})\} \tag{14.70}$$

where $\text{plim}_{N \to \infty} \hat{\boldsymbol{\Xi}} = \boldsymbol{\Xi}_o$. In other words, an efficient weighting matrix is the inverse of any consistent estimator of Avar $\sqrt{N}(\hat{\boldsymbol{\pi}} - \boldsymbol{\pi}_o)$.

We can easily derive the asymptotic variance of $\sqrt{N}(\hat{\boldsymbol{\theta}} - \boldsymbol{\theta}_o)$. The first-order condition for $\hat{\boldsymbol{\theta}}$ is

$$\mathbf{H}(\hat{\boldsymbol{\theta}})' \hat{\boldsymbol{\Xi}}^{-1} \{\hat{\boldsymbol{\pi}} - \mathbf{h}(\hat{\boldsymbol{\theta}})\} \equiv \mathbf{0} \tag{14.71}$$

where $\mathbf{H}(\boldsymbol{\theta}) \equiv \nabla_\theta \mathbf{h}(\boldsymbol{\theta})$ is the $S \times P$ Jacobian of $\mathbf{h}(\boldsymbol{\theta})$. Since $\mathbf{h}(\boldsymbol{\theta}_o) = \boldsymbol{\pi}_o$ and

$$\sqrt{N}\{\mathbf{h}(\hat{\boldsymbol{\theta}}) - \mathbf{h}(\boldsymbol{\theta}_o)\} = \mathbf{H}(\boldsymbol{\theta}_o)\sqrt{N}(\hat{\boldsymbol{\theta}} - \boldsymbol{\theta}_o) + o_p(1)$$

by a standard mean value expansion about $\boldsymbol{\theta}_o$, we have

$$\mathbf{0} = \mathbf{H}(\hat{\boldsymbol{\theta}})' \hat{\boldsymbol{\Xi}}^{-1} \{\sqrt{N}(\hat{\boldsymbol{\pi}} - \boldsymbol{\pi}_o) - \mathbf{H}(\boldsymbol{\theta}_o)\sqrt{N}(\hat{\boldsymbol{\theta}} - \boldsymbol{\theta}_o)\} + o_p(1) \tag{14.72}$$

Because $\mathbf{H}(\cdot)$ is continuous and $\hat{\boldsymbol{\theta}} \overset{p}{\to} \boldsymbol{\theta}_o$, $\mathbf{H}(\hat{\boldsymbol{\theta}}) = \mathbf{H}(\boldsymbol{\theta}_o) + o_p(1)$; by assumption $\hat{\boldsymbol{\Xi}} = \boldsymbol{\Xi}_o + o_p(1)$. Therefore,

$$\mathbf{H}(\boldsymbol{\theta}_o)' \boldsymbol{\Xi}_o^{-1} \mathbf{H}(\boldsymbol{\theta}_o)\sqrt{N}(\hat{\boldsymbol{\theta}} - \boldsymbol{\theta}_o) = \mathbf{H}(\boldsymbol{\theta}_o)' \boldsymbol{\Xi}_o^{-1} \sqrt{N}(\hat{\boldsymbol{\pi}} - \boldsymbol{\pi}_o) + o_p(1)$$

By assumption (14.69) and the asymptotic equivalence lemma,

$$\mathbf{H}(\boldsymbol{\theta}_o)' \boldsymbol{\Xi}_o^{-1} \mathbf{H}(\boldsymbol{\theta}_o)\sqrt{N}(\hat{\boldsymbol{\theta}} - \boldsymbol{\theta}_o) \overset{a}{\sim} \text{Normal}[\mathbf{0}, \mathbf{H}(\boldsymbol{\theta}_o)' \boldsymbol{\Xi}_o^{-1} \mathbf{H}(\boldsymbol{\theta}_o)]$$

and so

$$\sqrt{N}(\hat{\boldsymbol{\theta}} - \boldsymbol{\theta}_o) \overset{a}{\sim} \text{Normal}[\mathbf{0}, (\mathbf{H}_o' \boldsymbol{\Xi}_o^{-1} \mathbf{H}_o)^{-1}] \tag{14.73}$$

provided that $\mathbf{H}_o \equiv \mathbf{H}(\boldsymbol{\theta}_o)$ has full-column rank P, as will generally be the case when $\boldsymbol{\theta}_o$ is identified and $\mathbf{h}(\cdot)$ contains no redundancies. The appropriate estimator of $\widehat{\text{Avar}}(\hat{\boldsymbol{\theta}})$ is

$$\widehat{\text{Avar}}(\hat{\boldsymbol{\theta}}) \equiv (\hat{\mathbf{H}}' \hat{\boldsymbol{\Xi}}^{-1} \hat{\mathbf{H}})^{-1}/N = (\hat{\mathbf{H}}' [\widehat{\text{Avar}}(\hat{\boldsymbol{\pi}})]^{-1} \hat{\mathbf{H}})^{-1} \tag{14.74}$$

The proof that $\hat{\boldsymbol{\Xi}}^{-1}$ is the optimal weighting matrix in expression (14.70) is very similar to the derivation of the optimal weighting matrix for GMM. (It can also be shown by applying Theorem 14.3.) We will simply call the efficient estimator the CMD estimator, where it is understood that we are using the efficient weighting matrix.

There is another efficiency issue that arises when more than one $\sqrt{N}$-asymptotically normal estimator for $\boldsymbol{\pi}_o$ is available: Which estimator of $\boldsymbol{\pi}_o$ should be used? Let $\hat{\boldsymbol{\theta}}$ be the estimator based on $\hat{\boldsymbol{\pi}}$, and let $\tilde{\boldsymbol{\theta}}$ be the estimator based on another estimator, $\tilde{\boldsymbol{\pi}}$. You are asked to show in Problem 14.6 that Avar $\sqrt{N}(\tilde{\boldsymbol{\theta}} - \boldsymbol{\theta}_o)$ − Avar $\sqrt{N}(\hat{\boldsymbol{\theta}} - \boldsymbol{\theta}_o)$ is p.s.d. whenever Avar $\sqrt{N}(\tilde{\boldsymbol{\pi}} - \boldsymbol{\pi}_o)$ − Avar $\sqrt{N}(\hat{\boldsymbol{\pi}} - \boldsymbol{\pi}_o)$ is p.s.d. In other words, we should use the most efficient estimator of $\boldsymbol{\pi}_o$ to obtain the most efficient estimator of $\boldsymbol{\theta}_o$.

A test of overidentifying restrictions is immediately available after estimation, because, under the null hypothesis $\boldsymbol{\pi}_o = \mathbf{h}(\boldsymbol{\theta}_o)$,

$$N[\hat{\boldsymbol{\pi}} - \mathbf{h}(\hat{\boldsymbol{\theta}})]'\hat{\boldsymbol{\Xi}}^{-1}[\hat{\boldsymbol{\pi}} - \mathbf{h}(\hat{\boldsymbol{\theta}})] \overset{a}{\sim} \chi^2_{S-P} \tag{14.75}$$

To show this result, we use

$$\begin{aligned}\sqrt{N}[\hat{\boldsymbol{\pi}} - \mathbf{h}(\hat{\boldsymbol{\theta}})] &= \sqrt{N}(\hat{\boldsymbol{\pi}} - \boldsymbol{\pi}_o) - \mathbf{H}_o\sqrt{N}(\hat{\boldsymbol{\theta}} - \boldsymbol{\theta}_o) + o_p(1)\\ &= \sqrt{N}(\hat{\boldsymbol{\pi}} - \boldsymbol{\pi}_o) - \mathbf{H}_o(\mathbf{H}_o'\boldsymbol{\Xi}_o^{-1}\mathbf{H}_o)^{-1}\mathbf{H}_o'\boldsymbol{\Xi}_o^{-1}\sqrt{N}(\hat{\boldsymbol{\pi}} - \boldsymbol{\pi}_o) + o_p(1)\\ &= [\mathbf{I}_S - \mathbf{H}_o(\mathbf{H}_o'\boldsymbol{\Xi}_o^{-1}\mathbf{H}_o)^{-1}\mathbf{H}_o'\boldsymbol{\Xi}_o^{-1}]\sqrt{N}(\hat{\boldsymbol{\pi}} - \boldsymbol{\pi}_o) + o_p(1)\end{aligned}$$

Therefore, up to $o_p(1)$,

$$\boldsymbol{\Xi}_o^{-1/2}\sqrt{N}\{\hat{\boldsymbol{\pi}} - \mathbf{h}(\hat{\boldsymbol{\theta}})\} = [\mathbf{I}_S - \boldsymbol{\Xi}_o^{-1/2}\mathbf{H}_o(\mathbf{H}_o'\boldsymbol{\Xi}_o^{-1}\mathbf{H}_o)^{-1}\mathbf{H}_o'\boldsymbol{\Xi}_o^{-1/2}]\mathscr{Z} \equiv \mathbf{M}_o\mathscr{Z}$$

where $\mathscr{Z} \equiv \boldsymbol{\Xi}_o^{-1/2}\sqrt{N}(\hat{\boldsymbol{\pi}} - \boldsymbol{\pi}_o) \xrightarrow{d} \text{Normal}(\mathbf{0}, \mathbf{I}_S)$. But $\mathbf{M}_o$ is a symmetric idempotent matrix with rank $S - P$, so $\{\sqrt{N}[\hat{\boldsymbol{\pi}} - \mathbf{h}(\hat{\boldsymbol{\theta}})]\}'\boldsymbol{\Xi}_o^{-1}\{\sqrt{N}[\hat{\boldsymbol{\pi}} - \mathbf{h}(\hat{\boldsymbol{\theta}})]\} \overset{a}{\sim} \chi^2_{S-P}$. Because $\hat{\boldsymbol{\Xi}}$ is consistent for $\boldsymbol{\Xi}_o$, expression (14.75) follows from the asymptotic equivalence lemma. The statistic can also be expressed as

$$\{\hat{\boldsymbol{\pi}} - \mathbf{h}(\hat{\boldsymbol{\theta}})\}'[\text{Av}\hat{\text{a}}\text{r}(\hat{\boldsymbol{\pi}})]^{-1}\{\hat{\boldsymbol{\pi}} - \mathbf{h}(\hat{\boldsymbol{\theta}})\} \tag{14.76}$$

Testing restrictions on $\boldsymbol{\theta}_o$ is also straightforward, assuming that we can express the restrictions as $\boldsymbol{\theta}_o = \mathbf{d}(\boldsymbol{\alpha}_o)$ for an $R \times 1$ vector $\boldsymbol{\alpha}_o$, $R < P$. Under these restrictions, $\boldsymbol{\pi}_o = \mathbf{h}[\mathbf{d}(\boldsymbol{\alpha}_o)] \equiv \mathbf{g}(\boldsymbol{\alpha}_o)$. Thus, $\boldsymbol{\alpha}_o$ can be estimated by minimum distance by solving problem (14.70) with $\boldsymbol{\alpha}$ in place of $\boldsymbol{\theta}$ and $\mathbf{g}(\boldsymbol{\alpha})$ in place of $\mathbf{h}(\boldsymbol{\theta})$. The *same* estimator $\hat{\boldsymbol{\Xi}}$ should be used in both minimization problems. Then it can be shown (under interiority and differentiability) that

$$N[\hat{\boldsymbol{\pi}} - \mathbf{g}(\hat{\boldsymbol{\alpha}})]'\hat{\boldsymbol{\Xi}}^{-1}[\hat{\boldsymbol{\pi}} - \mathbf{g}(\hat{\boldsymbol{\alpha}})] - N[\hat{\boldsymbol{\pi}} - \mathbf{h}(\hat{\boldsymbol{\theta}})]'\hat{\boldsymbol{\Xi}}^{-1}[\hat{\boldsymbol{\pi}} - \mathbf{h}(\hat{\boldsymbol{\theta}})] \overset{a}{\sim} \chi^2_{P-R} \tag{14.77}$$

when the restrictions on $\boldsymbol{\theta}_{\mathrm{o}}$ are true.

To illustrate the application of CMD estimation, we reconsider Chamberlain's (1982, 1984) approach to linear, unobserved effects panel data models. (See Section 11.3.2 for the GMM approach.) The key equations are

$$y_{it} = \psi + \mathbf{x}_{i1}\boldsymbol{\lambda}_1 + \cdots + \mathbf{x}_{it}(\boldsymbol{\beta} + \boldsymbol{\lambda}_t) + \cdots + \mathbf{x}_{iT}\boldsymbol{\lambda}_T + v_{it} \tag{14.78}$$

where

$$\mathrm{E}(v_{it}) = 0, \quad \mathrm{E}(\mathbf{x}_i'v_{it}) = \mathbf{0}, \qquad t = 1, 2, \ldots, T \tag{14.79}$$

(For notational simplicity we do not index the true parameters by "o".) Equation (14.78) embodies the restrictions on the "structural" parameters $\boldsymbol{\theta} \equiv (\psi, \boldsymbol{\lambda}_1', \ldots, \boldsymbol{\lambda}_T', \boldsymbol{\beta}')'$, a $(1 + TK + K) \times 1$ vector. To apply CMD, write

$$y_{it} = \pi_{t0} + \mathbf{x}_i\boldsymbol{\pi}_t + v_{it}, \qquad t = 1, \ldots, T$$

so that the vector $\boldsymbol{\pi}$ is $T(1 + TK) \times 1$. When we impose the restrictions,

$$\boldsymbol{\pi}_{t0} = \psi, \ \boldsymbol{\pi}_t = [\boldsymbol{\lambda}_1', \boldsymbol{\lambda}_2', \ldots, (\boldsymbol{\beta} + \boldsymbol{\lambda}_t)', \ldots, \boldsymbol{\lambda}_T']', \qquad t = 1, \ldots, T$$

Therefore, we can write $\boldsymbol{\pi} = \mathbf{H}\boldsymbol{\theta}$ for a $(T + T^2K) \times (1 + TK + K)$ matrix $\mathbf{H}$. When $T = 2$, $\boldsymbol{\pi}$ can be written with restrictions imposed as $\boldsymbol{\pi} = (\psi, \boldsymbol{\beta}' + \boldsymbol{\lambda}_1', \boldsymbol{\lambda}_2', \psi, \boldsymbol{\lambda}_1', \boldsymbol{\beta}' + \boldsymbol{\lambda}_2')'$, and so

$$\mathbf{H} = \begin{bmatrix} 1 & \mathbf{0} & \mathbf{0} & \mathbf{0} \\ \mathbf{0} & \mathbf{I}_K & \mathbf{0} & \mathbf{I}_K \\ \mathbf{0} & \mathbf{0} & \mathbf{I}_K & \mathbf{0} \\ 1 & \mathbf{0} & \mathbf{0} & \mathbf{0} \\ \mathbf{0} & \mathbf{I}_K & \mathbf{0} & \mathbf{0} \\ \mathbf{0} & \mathbf{0} & \mathbf{I}_K & \mathbf{I}_K \end{bmatrix}$$

The CMD estimator can be obtained in closed form, once we have $\hat{\boldsymbol{\pi}}$; see Problem 14.7 for the general case.

How should we obtain $\hat{\boldsymbol{\pi}}$, the vector of estimates without the restrictions imposed? There is really only one way, and that is OLS for each time period. Condition (14.79) ensures that OLS is consistent and $\sqrt{N}$-asymptotically normal. Why not use a system method, in particular, SUR? For one thing, we cannot generally assume that $\mathbf{v}_i$ satisfies the requisite homoskedasticity assumption that ensures that SUR is more efficient than OLS equation by equation; see Section 11.3.2. Anyway, because the same regressors appear in each equation and no restrictions are imposed on the $\boldsymbol{\pi}_t$, OLS and SUR are identical. Procedures that might use nonlinear functions of $\mathbf{x}_i$ as instruments are not allowed under condition (14.79).

The estimator $\hat{\boldsymbol{\Xi}}$ of Avar $\sqrt{N}(\hat{\boldsymbol{\pi}} - \boldsymbol{\pi})$ is the robust asymptotic variance for system OLS from Chapter 7:

$$\hat{\boldsymbol{\Xi}} \equiv \left(N^{-1}\sum_{i=1}^{N}\mathbf{X}_i'\mathbf{X}_i\right)^{-1}\left(N^{-1}\sum_{i=1}^{N}\mathbf{X}_i'\hat{\mathbf{v}}_i\hat{\mathbf{v}}_i'\mathbf{X}_i\right)\left(N^{-1}\sum_{i=1}^{N}\mathbf{X}_i'\mathbf{X}_i\right)^{-1} \tag{14.80}$$

where $\mathbf{X}_i = \mathbf{I}_T \otimes (1, \mathbf{x}_i)$ is $T \times (T + T^2K)$ and $\hat{\mathbf{v}}_i$ is the vector of OLS residuals; see also equation (7.26).

Given the linear model with an additive unobserved effect, the overidentification test statistic (14.75) in Chamberlain's setup is a test of the strict exogeneity assumption. Essentially, it is a test of whether the leads and lags of $\mathbf{x}_t$ appearing in each time period are due to a time-constant unobserved effect c_i. The number of overidentifying restrictions is $(T + T^2K) - (1 + TK + K)$. Perhaps not surprisingly, the minimum distance approach to estimating $\boldsymbol{\theta}$ is asymptotically equivalent to the GMM procedure we described in Section 11.3.2, as can be reasoned from the work of Angrist and Newey (1991).

One hypothesis of interest concerning $\boldsymbol{\theta}$ is that $\boldsymbol{\lambda}_t = 0$, $t = 1, \dots, T$. Under this hypothesis, the random effects assumption that the unobserved effect c_i is uncorrelated with $\mathbf{x}_{it}$ for all t holds. We discussed a test of this assumption in Chapter 10. A more general test is available in the minimum distance setting. First, estimate $\boldsymbol{\alpha} \equiv (\psi, \boldsymbol{\beta}')'$ by minimum distance, using $\hat{\boldsymbol{\pi}}$ and $\hat{\boldsymbol{\Xi}}$ in equation (14.80). Second, compute the test statistic (14.77). Chamberlain (1984) gives an empirical example.

Minimum distance methods can be applied to more complicated panel data models, including some of the duration models that we cover in Chapter 20. (See Han and Hausman, 1990.) Van der Klaauw (1996) uses minimum distance estimation in a complicated dynamic model of labor force participation and marital status.

Problems

14.1. Consider the system in equations (14.34) and (14.35).

a. How would you estimate equation (14.35) using single-equation methods? Give a few possibilities, ranging from simple to more complicated. State any additional assumptions relevant for estimating asymptotic variances or for efficiency of the various estimators.

b. Is equation (14.34) identified if $\gamma_1 = 0$?

c. Now suppose that $\gamma_3 = 0$, so that the parameters in equation (14.35) can be consistently estimated by OLS. Let $\hat{y}_2$ be the OLS fitted values. Explain why nonlinear least squares estimation of

$$y_1 = \mathbf{x}_1\boldsymbol{\delta}_1 + \gamma_1\hat{y}_2^{\gamma_2} + error$$

does not consistently estimate $\boldsymbol{\delta}_1$, γ_1, and γ_2 when $\gamma_1 \neq 0$ and $\gamma_2 \neq 1$.

14.2. Consider the following labor supply function nonlinear in parameters:

$$hours = \mathbf{z}_1\boldsymbol{\delta}_1 + \gamma_1(wage^{\rho_1} - 1)/\rho_1 + u_1, \qquad \mathrm{E}(u_1 \mid \mathbf{z}) = 0$$

where $\mathbf{z}_1$ contains unity and $\mathbf{z}$ is the full set of exogenous variables.

a. Show that this model contains the level-level and level-log models as special cases. [Hint: For $w > 0$, $(w^{\rho} - 1)/\rho \to \log(w)$ as $\rho \to 0$.]

b. How would you test H_0: $\gamma_1 = 0$? (Be careful here; ρ_1 cannot be consistently estimated under H_0.)

c. Assuming that $\gamma_1 \neq 0$, how would you estimate this equation if $\mathrm{Var}(u_1 \mid \mathbf{z}) = \sigma_1^2$? What if $\mathrm{Var}(u_1 \mid \mathbf{z})$ is not constant?

d. Find the gradient of the residual function with respect to $\boldsymbol{\delta}_1$, γ_1, and ρ_1. [Hint: Recall that the derivative of w^{ρ} with respect to ρ is $w^{\rho}\log(w)$.]

e. Explain how to obtain the score test of H_0: $\rho_1 = 1$.

14.3. Use Theorem 14.3 to show that the optimal instrumental variables based on the conditional moment restrictions (14.60) are given by equation (14.63).

14.4. a. Show that, under Assumptions WNLS.1–WNLS.3 in Chapter 12, the weighted NLS estimator has asymptotic variance equal to that of the efficient IV estimator based on the orthogonality condition $\mathrm{E}[(y_i - m(\mathbf{x}_i, \boldsymbol{\beta}_o)) \mid \mathbf{x}_i] = 0$.

b. When does the nonlinear least squares estimator of $\boldsymbol{\beta}_o$ achieve the efficiency bound derived in part a?

c. Suppose that, in addition to $\mathrm{E}(y \mid \mathbf{x}) = m(\mathbf{x}, \boldsymbol{\beta}_o)$, you use the restriction $\mathrm{Var}(y \mid \mathbf{x}) = \sigma_o^2$ for some $\sigma_o^2 > 0$. Write down the two conditional moment restrictions for estimating $\boldsymbol{\beta}_o$ and σ_o^2. What are the efficient instrumental variables?

14.5. Write down $\boldsymbol{\theta}$, $\boldsymbol{\pi}$, and the matrix $\mathbf{H}$ such that $\boldsymbol{\pi} = \mathbf{H}\boldsymbol{\theta}$ in Chamberlain's approach to unobserved effects panel data models when $T = 3$.

14.6. Let $\hat{\boldsymbol{\pi}}$ and $\tilde{\boldsymbol{\pi}}$ be two consistent estimators of $\boldsymbol{\pi}_o$, with $\mathrm{Avar}\,\sqrt{N}(\hat{\boldsymbol{\pi}} - \boldsymbol{\pi}_o) = \boldsymbol{\Xi}_o$ and $\mathrm{Avar}\,\sqrt{N}(\tilde{\boldsymbol{\pi}} - \boldsymbol{\pi}_o) = \boldsymbol{\Lambda}_o$. Let $\hat{\boldsymbol{\theta}}$ be the CMD estimator based on $\hat{\boldsymbol{\pi}}$, and let $\tilde{\boldsymbol{\theta}}$ be the CMD estimator based on $\tilde{\boldsymbol{\pi}}$, where $\boldsymbol{\pi}_o = \mathbf{h}(\boldsymbol{\theta}_o)$. Show that, if $\boldsymbol{\Lambda}_o - \boldsymbol{\Xi}_o$ is positive semidefinite, then so is Avar $\sqrt{N}(\tilde{\boldsymbol{\theta}} - \boldsymbol{\theta}_o)$ – Avar $\sqrt{N}(\hat{\boldsymbol{\theta}} - \boldsymbol{\theta}_o)$. (Hint: Twice use the fact that, for two positive definite matrices $\mathbf{A}$ and $\mathbf{B}$, $\mathbf{A} - \mathbf{B}$ is p.s.d. if and only if $\mathbf{B}^{-1} - \mathbf{A}^{-1}$ is p.s.d.)

14.7. Show that when the mapping from $\boldsymbol{\theta}_o$ to $\boldsymbol{\pi}_o$ is linear, $\boldsymbol{\pi}_o = \mathbf{H}\boldsymbol{\theta}_o$ for a known $S \times P$ matrix $\mathbf{H}$ with rank$(\mathbf{H}) = P$, the CMD estimator $\hat{\boldsymbol{\theta}}$ is

$$\hat{\boldsymbol{\theta}} = (\mathbf{H}'\hat{\boldsymbol{\Xi}}^{-1}\mathbf{H})^{-1}\mathbf{H}'\hat{\boldsymbol{\Xi}}^{-1}\hat{\boldsymbol{\pi}} \tag{14.81}$$

Equation (14.81) *looks* like a generalized least squares (GLS) estimator of $\hat{\boldsymbol{\pi}}$ on $\mathbf{H}$ using variance matrix $\hat{\boldsymbol{\Xi}}$, and this apparent similarity has prompted some to call the minimum chi-square estimator a "generalized least squares" (GLS) estimator. Unfortunately, the association between CMD and GLS is misleading because $\hat{\boldsymbol{\pi}}$ and $\mathbf{H}$ are not data vectors whose row dimension, S, grows with N. The asymptotic properties of the minimum chi-square estimator do *not* follow from those of GLS.

14.8. In Problem 13.9, suppose you model the unconditional distribution of y_0 as $f_0(y_0; \boldsymbol{\theta})$, which depends on at least some elements of $\boldsymbol{\theta}$ appearing in $f_t(y_t \mid y_{t-1}; \boldsymbol{\theta})$. Discuss the pros and cons of using $f_0(y_0; \boldsymbol{\theta})$ in a maximum likelihood analysis along with $f_t(y_t \mid y_{t-1}; \boldsymbol{\theta})$, $t = 1, 2, \ldots, T$.

14.9. Verify that, for the linear unobserved effects model under Assumptions RE.1–RE.3, the conditions of Lemma 14.1 hold for the fixed effects ($\hat{\boldsymbol{\theta}}_2$) and the random effects ($\hat{\boldsymbol{\theta}}_1$) estimators, with $\rho = \sigma_u^2$. [Hint: For clarity, it helps to introduce a cross section subscript, i. Then $\mathbf{A}_1 = \mathrm{E}(\check{\mathbf{X}}_i'\check{\mathbf{X}}_i)$, where $\check{\mathbf{X}}_i = \mathbf{X}_i - \lambda \mathbf{j}_T \bar{\mathbf{x}}_i$; $\mathbf{A}_2 = \mathrm{E}(\ddot{\mathbf{X}}_i'\ddot{\mathbf{X}}_i)$, where $\ddot{\mathbf{X}}_i = \mathbf{X}_i - \mathbf{j}_T \bar{\mathbf{x}}_i$; $\mathbf{s}_{i1} = \check{\mathbf{X}}_i'\mathbf{r}_i$, where $\mathbf{r}_i = \mathbf{v}_i - \lambda \mathbf{j}_T \bar{v}_i$; and $\mathbf{s}_{i2} = \ddot{\mathbf{X}}_i'\mathbf{u}_i$; see Chapter 10 for further notation. You should show that $\ddot{\mathbf{X}}_i'\mathbf{u}_i = \ddot{\mathbf{X}}_i'\mathbf{r}_i$ and then $\ddot{\mathbf{X}}_i'\check{\mathbf{X}}_i = \ddot{\mathbf{X}}_i'\ddot{\mathbf{X}}_i$.]

Appendix 14A

Proof of Lemma 14.1: Given condition (14.55), $\mathbf{A}_1 = (1/\rho)\mathrm{E}(\mathbf{s}_1\mathbf{s}_1')$, a $P \times P$ symmetric matrix, and

$$\mathbf{V}_1 = \mathbf{A}_1^{-1}\mathrm{E}(\mathbf{s}_1\mathbf{s}_1')\mathbf{A}_1^{-1} = \rho^2[\mathrm{E}(\mathbf{s}_1\mathbf{s}_1')]^{-1}$$

where we drop the argument $\mathbf{w}$ for notational simplicity. Next, under condition (14.56), $\mathbf{A}_2 = (1/\rho)\mathrm{E}(\mathbf{s}_2'\mathbf{s}_1)$, and so

$$\mathbf{V}_2 = \mathbf{A}_2^{-1}\mathrm{E}(\mathbf{s}_2\mathbf{s}_2')(\mathbf{A}_2')^{-1} = \rho^2[\mathrm{E}(\mathbf{s}_2\mathbf{s}_1')]^{-1}\mathrm{E}(\mathbf{s}_2\mathbf{s}_2')[\mathrm{E}(\mathbf{s}_1\mathbf{s}_2')]^{-1}$$

Now we use the standard result that $\mathbf{V}_2 - \mathbf{V}_1$ is positive semidefinite if and only if $\mathbf{V}_1^{-1} - \mathbf{V}_2^{-1}$ is p.s.d. But, dropping the term ρ^2 (which is simply a positive constant), we have

$$\mathbf{V}_1^{-1} - \mathbf{V}_2^{-1} = \mathrm{E}(\mathbf{s}_1\mathbf{s}_1') - \mathrm{E}(\mathbf{s}_1\mathbf{s}_2')[\mathrm{E}(\mathbf{s}_2\mathbf{s}_2')]^{-1}\mathrm{E}(\mathbf{s}_2\mathbf{s}_1') \equiv \mathrm{E}(\mathbf{r}_1\mathbf{r}_1')$$

where $\mathbf{r}_1$ is the $P \times 1$ population residual from the population regression $\mathbf{s}_1$ on $\mathbf{s}_2$. As $\mathrm{E}(\mathbf{r}_1\mathbf{r}_1')$ is necessarily p.s.d., this step completes the proof.

IV NONLINEAR MODELS AND RELATED TOPICS

We now apply the general methods of Part III to study specific nonlinear models that often arise in applications. Many nonlinear econometric models are intended to explain limited dependent variables. Roughly, a **limited dependent variable** is a variable whose range is restricted in some important way. Most variables encountered in economics are limited in range, but not all require special treatment. For example, many variables—wage, population, and food consumption, to name just a few—can only take on positive values. If a strictly positive variable takes on numerous values, special econometric methods are rarely called for. Often, taking the log of the variable and then using a linear model suffices.

When the variable to be explained, y, is discrete and takes on a finite number of values, it makes little sense to treat it as an approximately continuous variable. Discreteness of y does not in itself mean that a linear model for $\mathrm{E}(y \mid \mathbf{x})$ is inappropriate. However, in Chapter 15 we will see that linear models have certain drawbacks for modeling binary responses, and we will treat nonlinear models such as probit and logit. We also cover basic multinomial response models in Chapter 15, including the case when the response has a natural ordering.

Other kinds of limited dependent variables arise in econometric analysis, especially when modeling choices by individuals, families, or firms. Optimizing behavior often leads to corner solutions for some nontrivial fraction of the population. For example, during any given time, a fairly large fraction of the working age population does not work outside the home. Annual hours worked has a population distribution spread out over a range of values, but with a pileup at the value zero. While it could be that a linear model is appropriate for modeling expected hours worked, a linear model will likely lead to negative predicted hours worked for some people. Taking the natural log is not possible because of the corner solution at zero. In Chapter 16 we will discuss econometric models that are better suited for describing these kinds of limited dependent variables.

We treat the problem of sample selection in Chapter 17. In many sample selection contexts the underlying population model is linear, but nonlinear econometric methods are required in order to correct for nonrandom sampling. Chapter 17 also covers testing and correcting for attrition in panel data models, as well as methods for dealing with stratified samples.

In Chapter 18 we provide a modern treatment of switching regression models and, more generally, random coefficient models with endogenous explanatory variables. We focus on estimating average treatment effects.

We treat methods for count-dependent variables, which take on nonnegative integer values, in Chapter 19. An introduction to modern duration analysis is given in Chapter 20.

15 Discrete Response Models

15.1 Introduction

In qualitative response models, the variable to be explained, y, is a random variable taking on a finite number of outcomes; in practice, the number of outcomes is usually small. The leading case occurs where y is a binary response, taking on the values zero and one, which indicate whether or not a certain event has occurred. For example, $y = 1$ if a person is employed, $y = 0$ otherwise; $y = 1$ if a family contributes to charity during a particular year, $y = 0$ otherwise; $y = 1$ if a firm has a particular type of pension plan, $y = 0$ otherwise. Regardless of the definition of y, it is traditional to refer to $y = 1$ as a *success* and $y = 0$ as a *failure*.

As in the case of linear models, we often call y the explained variable, the response variable, the dependent variable, or the endogenous variable; $\mathbf{x} \equiv (x_1, x_2, \ldots, x_K)$ is the vector of explanatory variables, regressors, independent variables, exogenous variables, or covariates.

In binary response models, interest lies primarily in the **response probability**,

$$p(\mathbf{x}) \equiv \mathrm{P}(y = 1 \mid \mathbf{x}) = \mathrm{P}(y = 1 \mid x_1, x_2, \ldots, x_K) \tag{15.1}$$

for various values of $\mathbf{x}$. For example, when y is an employment indicator, $\mathbf{x}$ might contain various individual characteristics such as education, age, marital status, and other factors that affect employment status, such as a binary indicator variable for participation in a recent job training program, or measures of past criminal behavior.

For a continuous variable, x_j, the partial effect of x_j on the response probability is

$$\frac{\partial \mathrm{P}(y = 1 \mid \mathbf{x})}{\partial x_j} = \frac{\partial p(\mathbf{x})}{\partial x_j} \tag{15.2}$$

When multiplied by Δx_j, equation (15.2) gives the approximate change in $\mathrm{P}(y = 1 \mid \mathbf{x})$ when x_j increases by Δx_j, holding all other variables fixed (for "small" Δx_j). Of course if, say, $x_1 \equiv z$ and $x_2 \equiv z^2$ for some variable z (for example, z could be work experience), we would be interested in $\partial p(\mathbf{x})/\partial z$.

If x_K is a binary variable, interest lies in

$$p(x_1, x_2, \ldots, x_{K-1}, 1) - p(x_1, x_2, \ldots, x_{K-1}, 0) \tag{15.3}$$

which is the difference in response probabilities when $x_K = 1$ and $x_K = 0$. For most of the models we consider, whether a variable x_j is continuous or discrete, the partial effect of x_j on $p(\mathbf{x})$ depends on all of $\mathbf{x}$.

In studying binary response models, we need to recall some basic facts about Bernoulli (zero-one) random variables. The only difference between the setup here and that in basic statistics is the conditioning on $\mathbf{x}$. If $\mathrm{P}(y = 1 \mid \mathbf{x}) = p(\mathbf{x})$ then $\mathrm{P}(y = 0 \mid \mathbf{x}) = 1 - p(\mathbf{x})$, $\mathrm{E}(y \mid \mathbf{x}) = p(\mathbf{x})$, and $\mathrm{Var}(y \mid \mathbf{x}) = p(\mathbf{x})[1 - p(\mathbf{x})]$.

15.2 The Linear Probability Model for Binary Response

The **linear probability model (LPM)** for binary response y is specified as

$$\mathrm{P}(y = 1 \mid \mathbf{x}) = \beta_0 + \beta_1 x_1 + \beta_2 x_2 + \cdots + \beta_K x_K \tag{15.4}$$

As usual, the x_j can be functions of underlying explanatory variables, which would simply change the interpretations of the β_j. Assuming that x_1 is not functionally related to the other explanatory variables, $\beta_1 = \partial \mathrm{P}(y = 1 \mid \mathbf{x})/\partial x_1$. Therefore, β_1 is the change in the probability of success given a one-unit increase in x_1. If x_1 is a binary explanatory variable, β_1 is just the difference in the probability of success when $x_1 = 1$ and $x_1 = 0$, holding the other x_j fixed.

Using functions such as quadratics, logarithms, and so on among the independent variables causes no new difficulties. The important point is that the β_j now measure the effects of the explanatory variables x_j on a particular probability.

Unless the range of $\mathbf{x}$ is severely restricted, the linear probability model cannot be a good description of the population response probability $\mathrm{P}(y = 1 \mid \mathbf{x})$. For given values of the population parameters β_j, there would usually be feasible values of $x_1, \ldots, x_K$ such that $\beta_0 + \mathbf{x}\boldsymbol{\beta}$ is outside the unit interval. Therefore, the LPM should be seen as a convenient approximation to the underlying response probability. What we hope is that the linear probability approximates the response probability for common values of the covariates. Fortunately, this often turns out to be the case.

In deciding on an appropriate estimation technique, it is useful to derive the conditional mean and variance of y. Since y is a Bernoulli random variable, these are simply

$$\mathrm{E}(y \mid \mathbf{x}) = \beta_0 + \beta_1 x_1 + \beta_2 x_2 + \cdots + \beta_K x_K \tag{15.5}$$

$$\mathrm{Var}(y \mid \mathbf{x}) = \mathbf{x}\boldsymbol{\beta}(1 - \mathbf{x}\boldsymbol{\beta}) \tag{15.6}$$

where $\mathbf{x}\boldsymbol{\beta}$ is shorthand for the right-hand side of equation (15.5).

Equation (15.5) implies that, given a random sample, the OLS regression of y on $1, x_1, x_2, \ldots, x_K$ produces consistent and even unbiased estimators of the β_j. Equation (15.6) means that heteroskedasticity is present unless all of the slope coefficients $\beta_1, \ldots, \beta_K$ are zero. A nice way to deal with this issue is to use standard heteroskedasticity-robust standard errors and t statistics. Further, robust tests of multiple restrictions should also be used. There is one case where the usual F statistic can be used, and that is to test for joint significance of all variables (leaving the constant unrestricted). This test is asymptotically valid because $\text{Var}(y \mid \mathbf{x})$ is constant under this particular null hypothesis.

Since the form of the variance is determined by the model for $\text{P}(y = 1 \mid \mathbf{x})$, an asymptotically more efficient method is weighted least squares (WLS). Let $\hat{\boldsymbol{\beta}}$ be the OLS estimator, and let $\hat{y}_i$ denote the OLS fitted values. Then, provided $0 < \hat{y}_i < 1$ for *all* observations i, define the estimated standard deviation as $\hat{\sigma}_i \equiv [\hat{y}_i(1 - \hat{y}_i)]^{1/2}$. Then the WLS estimator, $\boldsymbol{\beta}^*$, is obtained from the OLS regression

$$y_i/\hat{\sigma}_i \text{ on } 1/\hat{\sigma}_i, x_{i1}/\hat{\sigma}_i, \ldots, x_{iK}/\hat{\sigma}_i, \qquad i = 1, 2, \ldots, N \tag{15.7}$$

The usual standard errors from this regression are valid, as follows from the treatment of weighted least squares in Chapter 12. In addition, all other testing can be done using F statistics or LM statistics using weighted regressions.

If some of the OLS fitted values are not between zero and one, WLS analysis is not possible without ad hoc adjustments to bring deviant fitted values into the unit interval. Further, since the OLS fitted value $\hat{y}_i$ is an estimate of the conditional probability $\text{P}(y_i = 1 \mid \mathbf{x}_i)$, it is somewhat awkward if the predicted probability is negative or above unity.

Aside from the issue of fitted values being outside the unit interval, the LPM implies that a ceteris paribus unit increase in x_j always changes $\text{P}(y = 1 \mid \mathbf{x})$ by the same amount, regardless of the initial value of x_j. This implication cannot literally be true because continually increasing one of the x_j would eventually drive $\text{P}(y = 1 \mid \mathbf{x})$ to be less than zero or greater than one.

Even with these weaknesses, the LPM often seems to give good estimates of the partial effects on the response probability near the center of the distribution of $\mathbf{x}$. (How good they are can be determined by comparing the coefficients from the LPM with the partial effects estimated from the nonlinear models we cover in Section 15.3.) If the main purpose is to estimate the partial effect of x_j on the response probability, averaged across the distribution of $\mathbf{x}$, then the fact that some predicted values are outside the unit interval may not be very important. The LPM need not provide very good estimates of partial effects at extreme values of $\mathbf{x}$.

Example 15.1 (Married Women's Labor Force Participation): We use the data from MROZ.RAW to estimate a linear probability model for labor force participation (*inlf*) of married women. Of the 753 women in the sample, 428 report working nonzero hours during the year. The variables we use to explain labor force participation are age, education, experience, nonwife income in thousands (*nwifeinc*), number of children less than six years of age (*kidslt6*), and number of kids between 6 and 18 inclusive (*kidsge6*); 606 women report having no young children, while 118 report having exactly one young child. The usual OLS standard errors are in parentheses, while the heteroskedasticity-robust standard errors are in brackets:

$$\begin{aligned}
\widehat{inlf} = {} & \underset{\substack{(.154)\\ [.151]}}{.586} - \underset{\substack{(.0014)\\ [.0015]}}{.0034}\, nwifeinc + \underset{\substack{(.007)\\ [.007]}}{.038}\, educ + \underset{\substack{(.006)\\ [.006]}}{.039}\, exper - \underset{\substack{(.00018)\\ [.00019]}}{.00060}\, exper^2 \\
& - \underset{\substack{(.002)\\ [.002]}}{.016}\, age - \underset{\substack{(.034)\\ [.032]}}{.262}\, kidslt6 + \underset{\substack{(.013)\\ [.013]}}{.013}\, kidsge6
\end{aligned}$$

$N = 753, \qquad R^2 = .264$

With the exception of *kidsge6*, all coefficients have sensible signs and are statistically significant; *kidsge6* is neither statistically significant nor practically important. The coefficient on *nwifeinc* means that if nonwife income increases by 10 (\$10,000), the probability of being in the labor force is predicted to fall by .034. This is a small effect given that an increase in income by \$10,000 in 1975 dollars is very large in this sample. (The average of *nwifeinc* is about \$20,129 with standard deviation \$11,635.) Having one more small child is estimated to reduce the probability of $inlf = 1$ by about .262, which is a fairly large effect.

Of the 753 fitted probabilities, 33 are outside the unit interval. Rather than using some adjustment to those 33 fitted values and applying weighted least squares, we just use OLS and report heteroskedasticity-robust standard errors. Interestingly, these differ in practically unimportant ways from the usual OLS standard errors.

The case for the LPM is even stronger if most of the x_j are discrete and take on only a few values. In the previous example, to allow a diminishing effect of young children on the probability of labor force participation, we can break *kidslt6* into three binary indicators: no young children, one young child, and two or more young children. The last two indicators can be used in place of *kidslt6* to allow the first young child to have a larger effect than subsequent young children. (Interestingly, when this method is used, the marginal effects of the first and second young children are virtually the same. The estimated effect of the first child is about $-.263$, and the additional reduction in the probability of labor force participation for the next child is about $-.274$.)

In the extreme case where the model is *saturated*—that is, $\mathbf{x}$ contains dummy variables for mutually exclusive and exhaustive categories—the linear probability model is completely general. The fitted probabilities are simply the average y_i within each cell defined by the different values of $\mathbf{x}$; we need not worry about fitted probabilities less than zero or greater than one. See Problem 15.1.

15.3 Index Models for Binary Response: Probit and Logit

We now study binary response models of the form

$$\mathrm{P}(y = 1 \mid \mathbf{x}) = G(\mathbf{x}\boldsymbol{\beta}) \equiv p(\mathbf{x}) \tag{15.8}$$

where $\mathbf{x}$ is $1 \times K$, $\boldsymbol{\beta}$ is $K \times 1$, and we take the first element of $\mathbf{x}$ to be unity. Examples where $\mathbf{x}$ does not contain unity are rare in practice. For the linear probability model, $G(z) = z$ is the identity function, which means that the response probabilities cannot be between 0 and 1 for all $\mathbf{x}$ and $\boldsymbol{\beta}$. In this section we assume that $G(\cdot)$ takes on values in the open unit interval: $0 < G(z) < 1$ for all $z \in \mathbb{R}$.

The model in equation (15.8) is generally called an **index model** because it restricts the way in which the response probability depends on $\mathbf{x}$: $p(\mathbf{x})$ is a function of $\mathbf{x}$ only through the *index* $\mathbf{x}\boldsymbol{\beta} = \beta_1 + \beta_2 x_2 + \cdots + \beta_K x_K$. The function G maps the index into the response probability.

In most applications, G is a cumulative distribution function (cdf), whose specific form can sometimes be derived from an underlying economic model. For example, in Problem 15.2 you are asked to derive an index model from a utility-based model of charitable giving. The binary indicator y equals unity if a family contributes to charity and zero otherwise. The vector $\mathbf{x}$ contains family characteristics, income, and the price of a charitable contribution (as determined by marginal tax rates). Under a normality assumption on a particular unobservable taste variable, G is the standard normal cdf.

Index models where G is a cdf can be derived more generally from an underlying **latent variable model**, as in Example 13.1:

$$y^* = \mathbf{x}\boldsymbol{\beta} + e, \qquad y = 1[y^* > 0] \tag{15.9}$$

where e is a continuously distributed variable independent of $\mathbf{x}$ and the distribution of e is symmetric about zero; recall from Chapter 13 that $1[\cdot]$ is the indicator function. If G is the cdf of e, then, because the pdf of e is symmetric about zero, $1 - G(-z) = G(z)$ for all real numbers z. Therefore,

$$\mathrm{P}(y = 1 \mid \mathbf{x}) = \mathrm{P}(y^* > 0 \mid \mathbf{x}) = \mathrm{P}(e > -\mathbf{x}\boldsymbol{\beta} \mid \mathbf{x}) = 1 - G(-\mathbf{x}\boldsymbol{\beta}) = G(\mathbf{x}\boldsymbol{\beta})$$

which is exactly equation (15.8).

There is no particular reason for requiring e to be symmetrically distributed in the latent variable model, but this happens to be the case for the binary response models applied most often.

In most applications of binary response models, the primary goal is to explain the effects of the x_j on the response probability $\mathrm{P}(y = 1 \mid \mathbf{x})$. The latent variable formulation tends to give the impression that we are primarily interested in the effects of each x_j on y^*. As we will see, the *direction* of the effects of x_j on $\mathrm{E}(y^* \mid \mathbf{x}) = \mathbf{x}\boldsymbol{\beta}$ and on $\mathrm{E}(y \mid \mathbf{x}) = \mathrm{P}(y = 1 \mid \mathbf{x}) = G(\mathbf{x}\boldsymbol{\beta})$ are the same. But the latent variable y^* rarely has a well-defined unit of measurement (for example, y^* might be measured in utility units). Therefore, the magnitude of β_j is not especially meaningful except in special cases.

The **probit model** is the special case of equation (15.8) with

$$G(z) \equiv \Phi(z) \equiv \int_{-\infty}^{z} \phi(v)\, \mathrm{d}v \tag{15.10}$$

where $\phi(z)$ is the standard normal density

$$\phi(z) = (2\pi)^{-1/2} \exp(-z^2/2) \tag{15.11}$$

The probit model can be derived from the latent variable formulation when e has a standard normal distribution.

The **logit model** is a special case of equation (15.8) with

$$G(z) = \Lambda(z) \equiv \exp(z)/[1 + \exp(z)] \tag{15.12}$$

This model arises from the model (15.9) when e has a standard logistic distribution.

The general specification (15.8) allows us to cover probit, logit, and a number of other binary choice models in one framework. In fact, in what follows we do not even need G to be a cdf, but we do assume that $G(z)$ is strictly between zero and unity for all real numbers z.

In order to successfully apply probit and logit models, it is important to know how to interpret the β_j on both continuous and discrete explanatory variables. First, if x_j is continuous,

$$\frac{\partial p(\mathbf{x})}{\partial x_j} = g(\mathbf{x}\boldsymbol{\beta})\beta_j, \qquad \text{where } g(z) \equiv \frac{\mathrm{d}G}{\mathrm{d}z}(z) \tag{15.13}$$

Therefore, the partial effect of x_j on $p(\mathbf{x})$ depends on $\mathbf{x}$ through $g(\mathbf{x}\boldsymbol{\beta})$. If $G(\cdot)$ is a strictly increasing cdf, as in the probit and logit cases, $g(z) > 0$ for all z. Therefore, the sign of the effect is given by the sign of β_j. Also, the *relative* effects do not depend on $\mathbf{x}$: for continuous variables x_j and x_h, the ratio of the partial effects is constant and given by the ratio of the corresponding coefficients: $\dfrac{\partial p(\mathbf{x})/\partial x_j}{\partial p(\mathbf{x})/\partial x_h} = \beta_j/\beta_h$. In the typical case that g is a symmetric density about zero, with unique mode at zero, the largest effect is when $\mathbf{x}\boldsymbol{\beta} = 0$. For example, in the probit case with $g(z) = \phi(z)$, $g(0) = \phi(0) = 1/\sqrt{2\pi} \approx .399$. In the logit case, $g(z) = \exp(z)/[1 + \exp(z)]^2$, and so $g(0) = .25$.

If x_K is a binary explanatory variable, then the partial effect from changing x_K from zero to one, holding all other variables fixed, is simply

$$G(\beta_1 + \beta_2 x_2 + \cdots + \beta_{K-1}x_{K-1} + \beta_K) - G(\beta_1 + \beta_2 x_2 + \cdots + \beta_{K-1}x_{K-1}) \tag{15.14}$$

Again, this expression depends on all other values of the other x_j. For example, if y is an employment indicator and x_j is a dummy variable indicating participation in a job training program, then expression (15.14) is the change in the probability of employment due to the job training program; this depends on other characteristics that affect employability, such as education and experience. Knowing the sign of β_K is enough to determine whether the program had a positive or negative effect. But to find the *magnitude* of the effect, we have to estimate expression (15.14).

We can also use the difference in expression (15.14) for other kinds of discrete variables (such as number of children). If x_K denotes this variable, then the effect on the probability of x_K going from c_K to $c_K + 1$ is simply

$$\begin{aligned} &G[\beta_1 + \beta_2 x_2 + \cdots + \beta_{K-1}x_{K-1} + \beta_K(c_K + 1)] \\ &\quad - G(\beta_1 + \beta_2 x_2 + \cdots + \beta_{K-1}x_{K-1} + \beta_K c_K) \end{aligned} \tag{15.15}$$

It is straightforward to include standard functional forms among the explanatory variables. For example, in the model

$$\mathrm{P}(y = 1 \mid \mathbf{z}) = G[\beta_0 + \beta_1 z_1 + \beta_2 z_1^2 + \beta_3 \log(z_2) + \beta_4 z_3]$$

the partial effect of z_1 on $\mathrm{P}(y = 1 \mid \mathbf{z})$ is $\partial \mathrm{P}(y = 1 \mid \mathbf{z})/\partial z_1 = g(\mathbf{x}\boldsymbol{\beta})(\beta_1 + 2\beta_2 z_1)$, where $\mathbf{x}\boldsymbol{\beta} = \beta_0 + \beta_1 z_1 + \beta_2 z_1^2 + \beta_3 \log(z_2) + \beta_4 z_3$. It follows that if the quadratic in z_1 has a hump shape or a **U** shape, the turning point in the response probability is $|\beta_1/(2\beta_2)|$ [because $g(\mathbf{x}\boldsymbol{\beta}) > 0$]. Also, $\partial \mathrm{P}(y = 1 \mid \mathbf{z})/\partial \log(z_2) = g(\mathbf{x}\boldsymbol{\beta})\beta_3$, and so $g(\mathbf{x}\boldsymbol{\beta})(\beta_3/100)$ is the approximate change in $\mathrm{P}(y = 1 \mid \mathbf{z})$ given a 1 *percent* increase in z_2. Models with interactions among explanatory variables, including interactions between discrete and continuous variables, are handled similarly. When measuring effects of discrete variables, we should use expression (15.15).

15.4 Maximum Likelihood Estimation of Binary Response Index Models

Assume we have N independent, identically distributed observations following the model (15.8). Since we essentially covered the case of probit in Chapter 13, the discussion here will be brief. To estimate the model by (conditional) maximum likelihood, we need the log-likelihood function for each i. The density of y_i given $\mathbf{x}_i$ can be written as

$$f(y \mid \mathbf{x}_i; \boldsymbol{\beta}) = [G(\mathbf{x}_i\boldsymbol{\beta})]^y [1 - G(\mathbf{x}_i\boldsymbol{\beta})]^{1-y}, \qquad y = 0, 1 \tag{15.16}$$

The log-likelihood for observation i is a function of the $K \times 1$ vector of parameters and the data $(\mathbf{x}_i, y_i)$:

$$\ell_i(\boldsymbol{\beta}) = y_i \log[G(\mathbf{x}_i\boldsymbol{\beta})] + (1 - y_i) \log[1 - G(\mathbf{x}_i\boldsymbol{\beta})] \tag{15.17}$$

(Recall from Chapter 13 that, technically speaking, we should distinguish the "true" value of beta, $\boldsymbol{\beta}_{\mathrm{o}}$, from a generic value. For conciseness we do not do so here.) Restricting $G(\cdot)$ to be strictly between zero and one ensures that $\ell_i(\boldsymbol{\beta})$ is well defined for all values of $\boldsymbol{\beta}$.

As usual, the log likelihood for a sample size of N is $\mathscr{L}(\boldsymbol{\beta}) = \sum_{i=1}^{N} \ell_i(\boldsymbol{\beta})$, and the MLE of $\boldsymbol{\beta}$, denoted $\hat{\boldsymbol{\beta}}$, maximizes this log likelihood. If $G(\cdot)$ is the standard normal cdf, then $\hat{\boldsymbol{\beta}}$ is the **probit estimator**; if $G(\cdot)$ is the logistic cdf, then $\hat{\boldsymbol{\beta}}$ is the **logit estimator**. From the general maximum likelihood results we know that $\hat{\boldsymbol{\beta}}$ is consistent and asymptotically normal. We can also easily estimate the asymptotic variance $\hat{\boldsymbol{\beta}}$.

We assume that $G(\cdot)$ is twice continuously differentiable, an assumption that is usually satisfied in applications (and, in particular, for probit and logit). As before, the function $g(z)$ is the derivative of $G(z)$. For the probit model, $g(z) = \phi(z)$, and for the logit model, $g(z) = \exp(z)/[1 + \exp(z)]^2$.

Using the same calculations for the probit example as in Chapter 13, the score of the conditional log likelihood for observation i can be shown to be

$$\mathbf{s}_i(\boldsymbol{\beta}) \equiv \frac{g(\mathbf{x}_i\boldsymbol{\beta})\mathbf{x}_i'[y_i - G(\mathbf{x}_i\boldsymbol{\beta})]}{G(\mathbf{x}_i\boldsymbol{\beta})[1 - G(\mathbf{x}_i\boldsymbol{\beta})]} \tag{15.18}$$

Similarly, the expected value of the Hessian conditional on $\mathbf{x}_i$ is

$$-\mathrm{E}[\mathbf{H}_i(\boldsymbol{\beta}) \mid \mathbf{x}_i] = \frac{[g(\mathbf{x}_i\boldsymbol{\beta})]^2 \mathbf{x}_i'\mathbf{x}_i}{\{G(\mathbf{x}_i\boldsymbol{\beta})[1 - G(\mathbf{x}_i\boldsymbol{\beta})]\}} \equiv \mathbf{A}(\mathbf{x}_i, \boldsymbol{\beta}) \tag{15.19}$$

which is a $K \times K$ positive semidefinite matrix for each i. From the general conditional MLE results in Chapter 13, $\mathrm{Avar}(\hat{\boldsymbol{\beta}})$ is estimated as

$$\text{Av\^{a}r}(\hat{\boldsymbol{\beta}}) \equiv \left\{ \sum_{i=1}^{N} \frac{[g(\mathbf{x}_i\hat{\boldsymbol{\beta}})]^2 \mathbf{x}_i'\mathbf{x}_i}{G(\mathbf{x}_i\hat{\boldsymbol{\beta}})[1 - G(\mathbf{x}_i\hat{\boldsymbol{\beta}})]} \right\}^{-1} \equiv \hat{\mathbf{V}} \tag{15.20}$$

In most cases the inverse exists, and when it does, $\hat{\mathbf{V}}$ is positive definite. If the matrix in equation (15.20) is not invertible, then perfect collinearity probably exists among the regressors.

As usual, we treat $\hat{\boldsymbol{\beta}}$ as being normally distributed with mean zero and variance matrix in equation (15.20). The (asymptotic) standard error of $\hat{\beta}_j$ is the square root of the jth diagonal element of $\hat{\mathbf{V}}$. These can be used to construct t statistics, which have a limiting standard normal distribution, and to construct approximate confidence intervals for each population parameter. These are reported with the estimates for packages that perform logit and probit. We discuss multiple hypothesis testing in the next section.

Some packages also compute Huber-White standard errors as an option for probit and logit analysis, using the general M-estimator formulas; see, in particular, equation (12.49). While the robust variance matrix is consistent, using it in place of the usual estimator means we must think that the binary response model is incorrectly specified. Unlike with nonlinear regression, in a binary response model it is not possible to correctly specify $\mathrm{E}(y \mid \mathbf{x})$ but to misspecify $\mathrm{Var}(y \mid \mathbf{x})$. Once we have specified $\mathrm{P}(y = 1 \mid \mathbf{x})$, we have specified all conditional moments of y given $\mathbf{x}$.

In Section 15.8 we will see that, when using binary response models with panel data or cluster samples, it is sometimes important to compute variance matrix estimators that are robust to either serial dependence or within-group correlation. But this need arises as a result of dependence across time or subgroup, and not because the response probability is misspecified.

15.5 Testing in Binary Response Index Models

Any of the three tests from general MLE analysis—the Wald, LR, or LM test—can be used to test hypotheses in binary response contexts. Since the tests are all asymptotically equivalent under local alternatives, the choice of statistic usually depends on computational simplicity (since finite sample comparisons must be limited in scope). In the following subsections we discuss some testing situations that often arise in binary choice analysis, and we recommend particular tests for their computational advantages.

15.5.1 Testing Multiple Exclusion Restrictions

Consider the model

$$\mathrm{P}(y = 1 \mid \mathbf{x}, \mathbf{z}) = G(\mathbf{x}\boldsymbol{\beta} + \mathbf{z}\boldsymbol{\gamma}) \tag{15.21}$$

where $\mathbf{x}$ is $1 \times K$ and $\mathbf{z}$ is $1 \times Q$. We wish to test the null hypothesis H_0: $\boldsymbol{\gamma} = \mathbf{0}$, so we are testing Q exclusion restrictions. The elements of $\mathbf{z}$ can be functions of $\mathbf{x}$, such as quadratics and interactions—in which case the test is a pure functional form test. Or, the $\mathbf{z}$ can be additional explanatory variables. For example, $\mathbf{z}$ could contain dummy variables for occupation or region. In any case, the form of the test is the same.

Some packages, such as Stata, compute the Wald statistic for exclusion restrictions using a simple command following estimation of the general model. This capability makes it very easy to test multiple exclusion restrictions, provided the dimension of $(\mathbf{x}, \mathbf{z})$ is not so large as to make probit estimation difficult.

The likelihood ratio statistic is also easy to use. Let $\mathscr{L}_{ur}$ denote the value of the log-likelihood function from probit of y on $\mathbf{x}$ and $\mathbf{z}$ (the unrestricted model), and let $\mathscr{L}_r$ denote the value of the likelihood function from probit of y on $\mathbf{x}$ (the restricted model). Then the likelihood ratio test of H_0: $\boldsymbol{\gamma} = \mathbf{0}$ is simply $2(\mathscr{L}_{ur} - \mathscr{L}_r)$, which has an asymptotic χ^2_Q distribution under H_0. This is analogous to the usual F statistic in OLS analysis of a linear model.

The score or LM test is attractive if the unrestricted model is difficult to estimate. In this section, let $\hat{\boldsymbol{\beta}}$ denote the *restricted* estimator of $\boldsymbol{\beta}$, that is, the probit or logit estimator with $\mathbf{z}$ excluded from the model. The LM statistic using the estimated expected hessian, $\hat{\mathbf{A}}_i$ [see equation (15.20) and Section 12.6.2], can be shown to be numerically identical to the following: (1) Define $\hat{u}_i \equiv y_i - G(\mathbf{x}_i\hat{\boldsymbol{\beta}})$, $\hat{G}_i \equiv G(\mathbf{x}_i\hat{\boldsymbol{\beta}})$, and $\hat{g}_i \equiv g(\mathbf{x}_i\hat{\boldsymbol{\beta}})$. These are all obtainable after estimating the model without $\mathbf{z}$. (2) Use all N observations to run the auxiliary OLS regression

$$\frac{\hat{u}_i}{\sqrt{\hat{G}_i(1-\hat{G}_i)}} \quad \text{on} \quad \frac{\hat{g}_i}{\sqrt{\hat{G}_i(1-\hat{G}_i)}}\mathbf{x}_i, \qquad \frac{\hat{g}_i}{\sqrt{\hat{G}_i(1-\hat{G}_i)}}\mathbf{z}_i \tag{15.22}$$

The LM statistic is equal to the explained sum of squares from this regression. A test that is asymptotically (but not numerically) equivalent is NR^2_u, where R^2_u is the uncentered R-squared from regression (15.22).

The LM procedure is rather easy to remember. The term $\hat{g}_i\mathbf{x}_i$ is the gradient of the mean function $G(\mathbf{x}_i\boldsymbol{\beta} + \mathbf{z}_i\boldsymbol{\gamma})$ with respect to $\boldsymbol{\beta}$, evaluated at $\boldsymbol{\beta} = \hat{\boldsymbol{\beta}}$ and $\boldsymbol{\gamma} = \mathbf{0}$. Similarly, $\hat{g}_i\mathbf{z}_i$ is the gradient of $G(\mathbf{x}_i\boldsymbol{\beta} + \mathbf{z}_i\boldsymbol{\gamma})$ with respect to $\boldsymbol{\gamma}$, again evaluated at $\boldsymbol{\beta} = \hat{\boldsymbol{\beta}}$ and $\boldsymbol{\gamma} = \mathbf{0}$. Finally, under H_0: $\boldsymbol{\gamma} = \mathbf{0}$, the conditional variance of u_i given $(\mathbf{x}_i, \mathbf{z}_i)$ is $G(\mathbf{x}_i\boldsymbol{\beta})[1 - G(\mathbf{x}_i\boldsymbol{\beta})]$; therefore, $[\hat{G}_i(1-\hat{G}_i)]^{1/2}$ is an estimate of the conditional standard deviation of u_i. The dependent variable in regression (15.22) is often called a **standardized residual** because it is an estimate of $u_i/[G_i(1-G_i)]^{1/2}$, which has unit conditional (and unconditional) variance. The regressors are simply the gradient of the conditional mean function with respect to both sets of parameters, evaluated under

H_0, and weighted by the estimated inverse conditional standard deviation. The first set of regressors in regression (15.22) is $1 \times K$ and the second set is $1 \times Q$.

Under H_0, $LM \sim \chi^2_Q$. The LM approach can be an attractive alternative to the LR statistic if $\mathbf{z}$ has large dimension, since with many explanatory variables probit can be difficult to estimate.

15.5.2 Testing Nonlinear Hypotheses about $\boldsymbol{\beta}$

For testing nonlinear restrictions on $\boldsymbol{\beta}$ in equation (15.8), the Wald statistic is computationally the easiest because the unrestricted estimator of $\boldsymbol{\beta}$, which is just probit or logit, is easy to obtain. Actually imposing nonlinear restrictions in estimation—which is required to apply the score or likelihood ratio methods—can be difficult. However, we must also remember that the Wald statistic for testing nonlinear restrictions is not invariant to reparameterizations, whereas the LM and LR statistics are. (See Sections 12.6 and 13.6; for the LM statistic, we would always use the expected Hessian.)

Let the restictions on $\boldsymbol{\beta}$ be given by H_0: $\mathbf{c}(\boldsymbol{\beta}) = \mathbf{0}$, where $\mathbf{c}(\boldsymbol{\beta})$ is a $Q \times 1$ vector of possibly nonlinear functions satisfying the differentiability and rank requirements from Chapter 13. Then, from the general MLE analysis, the Wald statistic is simply

$$W = \mathbf{c}(\hat{\boldsymbol{\beta}})'[\nabla_\beta \mathbf{c}(\hat{\boldsymbol{\beta}})\hat{\mathbf{V}}\nabla_\beta \mathbf{c}(\hat{\boldsymbol{\beta}})']^{-1}\mathbf{c}(\hat{\boldsymbol{\beta}}) \tag{15.23}$$

where $\hat{\mathbf{V}}$ is given in equation (15.20) and $\nabla_\beta \mathbf{c}(\hat{\boldsymbol{\beta}})$ is the $Q \times K$ Jacobian of $\mathbf{c}(\boldsymbol{\beta})$ evaluated at $\hat{\boldsymbol{\beta}}$.

15.5.3 Tests against More General Alternatives

In addition to testing for omitted variables, sometimes we wish to test the probit or logit model against a more general functional form. When the alternatives are not standard binary response models, the Wald and LR statistics are cumbersome to apply, whereas the LM approach is convenient because it only requires estimation of the null model.

As an example of a more complicated binary choice model, consider the latent variable model (15.9) but assume that $e \mid \mathbf{x} \sim \text{Normal}[0, \exp(2\mathbf{x}_1\boldsymbol{\delta})]$, where $\mathbf{x}_1$ is $1 \times K_1$ subset of $\mathbf{x}$ that excludes a constant and $\boldsymbol{\delta}$ is a $K_1 \times 1$ vector of additional parameters. (In many cases we would take $\mathbf{x}_1$ to be all nonconstant elements of $\mathbf{x}$.) Therefore, there is heteroskedasticity in the latent variable model, so that e is no longer independent of $\mathbf{x}$. The standard deviation of e given $\mathbf{x}$ is simply $\exp(\mathbf{x}_1\boldsymbol{\delta})$. Define $r = e/\exp(\mathbf{x}_1\boldsymbol{\delta})$, so that r is independent of $\mathbf{x}$ with a standard normal distribution. Then

$$\mathrm{P}(y = 1 \mid \mathbf{x}) = \mathrm{P}(e > -\mathbf{x}\boldsymbol{\beta} \mid \mathbf{x}) = \mathrm{P}[\exp(-\mathbf{x}_1\boldsymbol{\delta})e > -\exp(-\mathbf{x}_1\boldsymbol{\delta})\mathbf{x}\boldsymbol{\beta}]$$
$$= \mathrm{P}[r > -\exp(-\mathbf{x}_1\boldsymbol{\delta})\mathbf{x}\boldsymbol{\beta}] = \Phi[\exp(-\mathbf{x}_1\boldsymbol{\delta})\mathbf{x}\boldsymbol{\beta}] \tag{15.24}$$

The partial effects of x_j on $\mathrm{P}(y = 1 \mid \mathbf{x})$ are much more complicated in equation (15.24) than in equation (15.8). When $\boldsymbol{\delta} = \mathbf{0}$, we obtain the standard probit model. Therefore, a test of the probit functional form for the response probability is a test of H_0: $\boldsymbol{\delta} = \mathbf{0}$.

To obtain the LM test of $\boldsymbol{\delta} = \mathbf{0}$ in equation (15.24), it is useful to derive the LM test for an index model against a more general alternative. Consider

$$\mathrm{P}(y = 1 \mid \mathbf{x}) = m(\mathbf{x}\boldsymbol{\beta}, \mathbf{x}, \boldsymbol{\delta}) \tag{15.25}$$

where $\boldsymbol{\delta}$ is a $Q \times 1$ vector of parameters. We wish to test H_0: $\boldsymbol{\delta} = \boldsymbol{\delta}_0$, where $\boldsymbol{\delta}_0$ is often (but not always) a vector of zeros. We assume that, under the null, we obtain a standard index model (probit or logit, usually):

$$G(\mathbf{x}\boldsymbol{\beta}) = m(\mathbf{x}\boldsymbol{\beta}, \mathbf{x}, \boldsymbol{\delta}_0) \tag{15.26}$$

In the previous example, $G(\cdot) = \Phi(\cdot)$, $\boldsymbol{\delta}_0 = \mathbf{0}$, and $m(\mathbf{x}\boldsymbol{\beta}, \mathbf{x}, \boldsymbol{\delta}) = \Phi[\exp(-\mathbf{x}_1\boldsymbol{\delta})\mathbf{x}\boldsymbol{\beta}]$.

Let $\hat{\boldsymbol{\beta}}$ be the probit or logit estimator of $\boldsymbol{\beta}$ obtained under $\boldsymbol{\delta} = \boldsymbol{\delta}_0$. Define $\hat{u}_i \equiv y_i - G(\mathbf{x}_i\hat{\boldsymbol{\beta}})$, $\hat{G}_i \equiv G(\mathbf{x}_i\hat{\boldsymbol{\beta}})$, and $\hat{g}_i \equiv g(\mathbf{x}_i\hat{\boldsymbol{\beta}})$. The gradient of the mean function $m(\mathbf{x}_i\boldsymbol{\beta}, \mathbf{x}_i, \boldsymbol{\delta})$ with respect to $\boldsymbol{\beta}$, evaluated at $\boldsymbol{\delta}_0$, is simply $g(\mathbf{x}_i\boldsymbol{\beta})\mathbf{x}_i$. The only other piece we need is the gradient of $m(\mathbf{x}_i\boldsymbol{\beta}, \mathbf{x}_i, \boldsymbol{\delta})$ with respect to $\boldsymbol{\delta}$, evaluated at $\boldsymbol{\delta}_0$. Denote this $1 \times Q$ vector as $\nabla_\delta m(\mathbf{x}_i\boldsymbol{\beta}, \mathbf{x}_i, \boldsymbol{\delta}_0)$. Further, set $\nabla_\delta \hat{m}_i \equiv \nabla_\delta m(\mathbf{x}_i\hat{\boldsymbol{\beta}}, \mathbf{x}_i, \boldsymbol{\delta}_0)$. The LM statistic can be obtained as the explained sum of squares or NR_u^2 from the regression

$$\frac{\hat{u}_i}{\sqrt{\hat{G}_i(1 - \hat{G}_i)}} \quad \text{on} \quad \frac{\hat{g}_i}{\sqrt{\hat{G}_i(1 - \hat{G}_i)}}\mathbf{x}_i, \qquad \frac{\nabla_\delta \hat{m}_i}{\sqrt{\hat{G}_i(1 - \hat{G}_i)}} \tag{15.27}$$

which is quite similar to regression (15.22). The null distribution of the LM statistic is χ_Q^2, where Q is the dimension of $\boldsymbol{\delta}$.

When applying this test to the preceding probit example, we have only $\nabla_\delta \hat{m}_i$ left to compute. But $m(\mathbf{x}_i\boldsymbol{\beta}, \mathbf{x}_i, \boldsymbol{\delta}) = \Phi[\exp(-\mathbf{x}_{i1}\boldsymbol{\delta})\mathbf{x}_i\boldsymbol{\beta}]$, and so

$$\nabla_\delta m(\mathbf{x}_i\boldsymbol{\beta}, \mathbf{x}_i, \boldsymbol{\delta}) = -(\mathbf{x}_i\boldsymbol{\beta}) \exp(-\mathbf{x}_{i1}\boldsymbol{\delta})\mathbf{x}_{i1}\phi[\exp(-\mathbf{x}_{i1}\boldsymbol{\delta})\mathbf{x}_i\boldsymbol{\beta}]$$

When evaluated at $\boldsymbol{\beta} = \hat{\boldsymbol{\beta}}$ and $\boldsymbol{\delta} = \mathbf{0}$ (the null value), we get $\nabla_\delta \hat{m}_i = -(\mathbf{x}_i\hat{\boldsymbol{\beta}})\phi(\mathbf{x}_i\hat{\boldsymbol{\beta}})\mathbf{x}_{i1} \equiv -(\mathbf{x}_i\hat{\boldsymbol{\beta}})\hat{\phi}_i\mathbf{x}_{i1}$, a $1 \times K_1$ vector. Regression (15.27) becomes

$$\frac{\hat{u}_i}{\sqrt{\hat{\Phi}_i(1 - \hat{\Phi}_i)}} \quad \text{on} \quad \frac{\hat{\phi}_i}{\sqrt{\hat{\Phi}_i(1 - \hat{\Phi}_i)}}\mathbf{x}_i, \qquad \frac{(\mathbf{x}_i\hat{\boldsymbol{\beta}})\hat{\phi}_i}{\sqrt{\hat{\Phi}_i(1 - \hat{\Phi}_i)}}\mathbf{x}_{i1} \tag{15.28}$$

(We drop the minus sign because it does not affect the value of the explained sum of squares or R_u^2.) Under the null hypothesis that the probit model is correctly specified, $LM \sim \chi^2_{K_1}$. This statistic is easy to compute after estimation by probit.

For a one-degree-of-freedom test regardless of the dimension of $\mathbf{x}_i$, replace the last term in regression (15.28) with $(\mathbf{x}_i\hat{\boldsymbol{\beta}})^2\hat{\phi}_i/\sqrt{\hat{\Phi}_i(1-\hat{\Phi}_i)}$, and then the explained sum of squares is distributed asymptotically as χ^2_1. See Davidson and MacKinnon (1984) for further examples.

15.6 Reporting the Results for Probit and Logit

Several statistics should be reported routinely in any probit or logit (or other binary choice) analysis. The $\hat{\beta}_j$, their standard errors, and the value of the likelihood function are reported by all software packages that do binary response analysis. The $\hat{\beta}_j$ give the signs of the partial effects of each x_j on the response probability, and the statistical significance of x_j is determined by whether we can reject H_0: $\beta_j = 0$.

One measure of goodness of fit that is usually reported is the **percent correctly predicted**. For each i, we compute the predicted probability that $y_i = 1$, given the explanatory variables, $\mathbf{x}_i$. If $G(\mathbf{x}_i\hat{\boldsymbol{\beta}}) > .5$, we predict y_i to be unity; if $G(\mathbf{x}_i\hat{\boldsymbol{\beta}}) \leq .5$, y_i is predicted to be zero. The percentage of times the predicted y_i matches the actual y_i is the percent correctly predicted. In many cases it is easy to predict one of the outcomes and much harder to predict another outcome, in which case the percent correctly predicted can be misleading as a goodness-of-fit statistic. More informative is to compute the percent correctly predicted for each outcome, $y = 0$ and $y = 1$. The overall percent correctly predicted is a weighted average of the two, with the weights being the fractions of zero and one outcomes, respectively. Problem 15.7 provides an illustration.

Various **pseudo R-squared** measures have been proposed for binary response. McFadden (1974) suggests the measure $1 - \mathscr{L}_{ur}/\mathscr{L}_o$, where $\mathscr{L}_{ur}$ is the log-likelihood function for the estimated model and $\mathscr{L}_o$ is the log-likelihood function in the model with only an intercept. Because the log likelihood for a binary response model is always negative, $|\mathscr{L}_{ur}| \leq |\mathscr{L}_o|$, and so the pseudo R-squared is always between zero and one. Alternatively, we can use a sum of squared residuals measure: $1 - \mathrm{SSR}_{ur}/\mathrm{SSR}_o$, where SSR_{ur} is the sum of squared residuals $\hat{u}_i = y_i - G(\mathbf{x}_i\hat{\boldsymbol{\beta}})$ and SSR_o is the total sum of squares of y_i. Several other measures have been suggested (see, for example, Maddala, 1983, Chapter 2), but goodness of fit is not as important as statistical and economic significance of the explanatory variables. Estrella (1998) contains a recent comparison of goodness-of-fit measures for binary response.

Often we want to estimate the effects of the variables x_j on the response probabilities $\mathrm{P}(y = 1 \mid \mathbf{x})$. If x_j is (roughly) continuous then

$$\Delta\hat{\mathrm{P}}(y = 1 \mid \mathbf{x}) \approx [g(\mathbf{x}\hat{\boldsymbol{\beta}})\hat{\beta}_j]\Delta x_j \tag{15.29}$$

for small changes in x_j. (As usual when using calculus, the notion of "small" here is somewhat vague.) Since $g(\mathbf{x}\hat{\boldsymbol{\beta}})$ depends on $\mathbf{x}$, we must compute $g(\mathbf{x}\hat{\boldsymbol{\beta}})$ at interesting values of $\mathbf{x}$. Often the sample averages of the x_j's are plugged in to get $g(\overline{\mathbf{x}}\hat{\boldsymbol{\beta}})$. This factor can then be used to adjust each of the $\hat{\beta}_j$ (at least those on continuous variables) to obtain the effect of a one-unit increase in x_j. If $\mathbf{x}$ contains nonlinear functions of some explanatory variables, such as natural logs or quadratics, there is the issue of using the log of the average versus the average of the log (and similarly with quadratics). To get the effect for the "average" person, it makes more sense to plug the averages into the nonlinear functions, rather than average the nonlinear functions. Software packages (such as Stata with the *dprobit* command) necessarily average the nonlinear functions. Sometimes minimum and maximum values of key variables are used in obtaining $g(\mathbf{x}\hat{\boldsymbol{\beta}})$, so that we can see how the partial effects change as some elements of $\mathbf{x}$ get large or small.

Equation (15.29) also suggests how to roughly compare magnitudes of the probit and logit estimates. If $\overline{\mathbf{x}}\hat{\boldsymbol{\beta}}$ is close to zero for logit and probit, the scale factor we use can be $g(0)$. For probit, $g(0) \approx .4$, and for logit, $g(0) = .25$. Thus the logit estimates can be expected to be larger by a factor of about $.4/.25 = 1.6$. Alternatively, multiply the logit estimates by .625 to make them comparable to the probit estimates. In the linear probability model, $g(0)$ is unity, and so logit estimates should be divided by four to compare them with LPM estimates, while probit estimates should be divided by 2.5 to make them roughly comparable to LPM estimates. More accurate comparisons are obtained by using the scale factors $g(\overline{\mathbf{x}}\hat{\boldsymbol{\beta}})$ for probit and logit. Of course, one of the potential advantages of using probit or logit is that the partial effects vary with $\mathbf{x}$, and it is of some interest to compute $g(\mathbf{x}\hat{\boldsymbol{\beta}})$ at values of $\mathbf{x}$ other than the sample averages.

If, say, x_2 is a binary variable, it perhaps makes more sense to plug in zero or one for x_2, rather than $\bar{x}_2$ (which is the fraction of ones in the sample). Putting in the averages for the binary variables means that the effect does not really correspond to a particular individual. But often the results are similar, and the choice is really based on taste.

To obtain standard errors of the partial effects in equation (15.29) we use the delta method. Consider the case $j = K$ for notational simplicity, and for given $\mathbf{x}$, define $\delta_K = \beta_K g(\mathbf{x}\boldsymbol{\beta}) = \partial \mathrm{P}(y = 1 \mid \mathbf{x})/\partial x_K$. Write this relation as $\delta_K = h(\boldsymbol{\beta})$ to denote that this is a (nonlinear) function of the vector $\boldsymbol{\beta}$. We assume $x_1 = 1$. The gradient of $h(\boldsymbol{\beta})$ is

$$\nabla_\beta h(\boldsymbol{\beta}) = \left[\beta_K \frac{dg}{dz}(\mathbf{x}\boldsymbol{\beta}), \beta_K x_2 \frac{dg}{dz}(\mathbf{x}\boldsymbol{\beta}), \ldots, \beta_K x_{K-1} \frac{dg}{dz}(\mathbf{x}\boldsymbol{\beta}), \beta_K x_K \frac{dg}{dz}(\mathbf{x}\boldsymbol{\beta}) + g(\mathbf{x}\boldsymbol{\beta})\right]$$

where dg/dz is simply the derivative of g with respect to its argument. The delta method implies that the asymptotic variance of $\hat{\delta}_K$ is estimated as

$$[\nabla_\beta h(\hat{\boldsymbol{\beta}})]\hat{\mathbf{V}}[\nabla_\beta h(\hat{\boldsymbol{\beta}})]' \tag{15.30}$$

where $\hat{\mathbf{V}}$ is the asymptotic variance estimate of $\hat{\boldsymbol{\beta}}$. The asymptotic standard error of $\hat{\delta}_K$ is simply the square root of expression (15.30). This calculation allows us to obtain a large-sample confidence interval for $\hat{\delta}_K$. The program Stata does this calculation for the probit model using the *dprobit* command.

If x_K is a discrete variable, then we can estimate the change in the predicted probability in going from c_K to $c_K + 1$ as

$$\begin{aligned}\hat{\delta}_K = {} & G[\hat{\beta}_1 + \hat{\beta}_2 \bar{x}_2 + \cdots + \hat{\beta}_{K-1}\bar{x}_{K-1} + \hat{\beta}_K(c_K + 1)] \\ & - G(\hat{\beta}_1 + \hat{\beta}_2 \bar{x}_2 + \cdots + \hat{\beta}_{K-1}\bar{x}_{K-1} + \hat{\beta}_K c_K)\end{aligned} \tag{15.31}$$

In particular, when x_K is a binary variable, set $c_K = 0$. Of course, the other x_j's can be evaluated anywhere, but the use of sample averages is typical. The delta method can be used to obtain a standard error of equation (15.31). For probit, Stata does this calculation when x_K is a binary variable. Usually the calculations ignore the fact that $\bar{x}_j$ is an estimate of $\mathrm{E}(x_j)$ in applying the delta method. If we are truly interested in $\beta_K g(\boldsymbol{\mu}_x \boldsymbol{\beta})$, the estimation error in $\bar{\mathbf{x}}$ can be accounted for, but it makes the calculation more complicated, and it is unlikely to have a large effect.

An alternative way to summarize the estimated marginal effects is to estimate the average value of $\beta_K g(\mathbf{x}\boldsymbol{\beta})$ across the population, or $\beta_K \mathrm{E}[g(\mathbf{x}\boldsymbol{\beta})]$. A consistent estimator is

$$\hat{\beta}_K \left[N^{-1} \sum_{i=1}^{N} g(\mathbf{x}_i \hat{\boldsymbol{\beta}})\right] \tag{15.32}$$

when x_K is continuous or

$$N^{-1} \sum_{i=1}^{N} [G(\hat{\beta}_1 + \hat{\beta}_2 x_{i2} + \cdots + \hat{\beta}_{K-1} x_{i,K-1} + \hat{\beta}_K) - G(\hat{\beta}_1 + \hat{\beta}_2 x_{i2} + \cdots + \hat{\beta}_{K-1} x_{i,K-1})] \tag{15.33}$$

if x_K is binary. The delta method can be used to obtain an asymptotic standard error of expression (15.32) or (15.33). Costa (1995) is a recent example of average effects obtained from expression (15.33).

Table 15.1
LPM, Logit, and Probit Estimates of Labor Force Participation

Dependent Variable: *inlf*

Independent Variable	LPM (OLS)	Logit (MLE)	Probit (MLE)
nwifeinc	−.0034 (.0015)	−.021 (.008)	−.012 (.005)
educ	.038 (.007)	.221 (.043)	.131 (.025)
exper	.039 (.006)	.206 (.032)	.123 (.019)
$exper^2$	−.00060 (.00019)	−.0032 (.0010)	−.0019 (.0006)
age	−.016 (.002)	−.088 (.015)	−.053 (.008)
kidslt6	−.262 (.032)	−1.443 (0.204)	−.868 (.119)
kidsge6	.013 (.013)	.060 (.075)	.036 (.043)
constant	.586 (.151)	.425 (.860)	.270 (.509)
Number of observations	753	753	753
Percent correctly predicted	73.4	73.6	73.4
Log-likelihood value	—	−401.77	−401.30
Pseudo *R*-squared	.264	.220	.221

Example 15.2 (Married Women's Labor Force Participation): We now estimate logit and probit models for women's labor force participation. For comparison we report the linear probability estimates. The results, with standard errors in parentheses, are given in Table 15.1 (for the LPM, these are heteroskedasticity-robust).

The estimates from the three models tell a consistent story. The signs of the coefficients are the same across models, and the same variables are statistically significant in each model. The pseudo *R*-squared for the LPM is just the usual *R*-squared reported for OLS; for logit and probit the pseudo *R*-squared is the measure based on the log likelihoods described previously. In terms of overall percent correctly predicted, the models do equally well. For the probit model, it correctly predicts "out of the labor force" about 63.1 percent of the time, and it correctly predicts "in the labor force" about 81.3 percent of the time. The LPM has the same overall percent correctly predicted, but there are slight differences within each outcome.

As we emphasized earlier, the *magnitudes* of the coefficients are not directly comparable across the models. Using the rough rule of thumb discussed earlier, we can divide the logit estimates by four and the probit estimates by 2.5 to make all estimates comparable to the LPM estimates. For example, for the coefficients on *kidslt6*, the scaled logit estimate is about $-.361$, and the scaled probit estimate is about $-.347$. These are larger in magnitude than the LPM estimate (for reasons we will soon discuss). The scaled coefficient on *educ* is .055 for logit and .052 for probit.

If we evaluate the standard normal probability density function, $\phi(\hat{\beta}_0 + \hat{\beta}_1 x_1 + \cdots + \hat{\beta}_k x_k)$, at the average values of the independent variables in the sample (including the average of $exper^2$), we obtain about .391; this value is close enough to .4 to make the rough rule of thumb for scaling the probit coefficients useful in obtaining the effects on the response probability. In other words, to estimate the change in the response probability given a one-unit increase in any independent variable, we multiply the corresponding probit coefficient by .4.

The biggest difference between the LPM model on one hand, and the logit and probit models on the other, is that the LPM assumes *constant* marginal effects for *educ*, *kidslt6*, and so on, while the logit and probit models imply diminishing marginal magnitudes of the partial effects. In the LPM, one more small child is estimated to reduce the probability of labor force participation by about .262, regardless of how many young children the woman already has (and regardless of the levels of the other dependent variables). We can contrast this finding with the estimated marginal effect from probit. For concreteness, take a woman with $nwifeinc = 20.13$, $educ = 12.3$, $exper = 10.6$, $age = 42.5$—which are roughly the sample averages—and $kidsge6 = 1$. What is the estimated fall in the probability of working in going from zero to one small child? We evaluate the standard normal cdf, $\Phi(\hat{\beta}_0 + \hat{\beta}_1 x_1 + \cdots + \hat{\beta}_k x_k)$ with $kidslt6 = 1$ and $kidslt6 = 0$, and the other independent variables set at the values given. We get roughly $.373 - .707 = -.334$, which means that the labor force participation probability is about .334 lower when a woman has one young child. This is not much different from the scaled probit coefficient of $-.347$. If the woman goes from one to two young children, the probability falls even more, but the marginal effect is not as large: $.117 - .373 = -.256$. Interestingly, the estimate from the linear probability model, which we think can provide a good estimate near the average values of the covariates, is in fact between the probit estimated partial effects starting from zero and one children.

Binary response models apply with little modification to independently pooled cross sections or to other data sets where the observations are independent but not necessarily identically distributed. Often year or other time-period dummy variables are included to account for aggregate time effects. Just as with linear models, probit can be used to evaluate the impact of certain policies in the context of a natural experiment; see Problem 15.13. An application is given in Gruber and Poterba (1994).

15.7 Specification Issues in Binary Response Models

We now turn to several issues that can arise in applying binary response models to economic data. All of these topics are relevant for general index models, but features of the normal distribution allow us to obtain concrete results in the context of probit models. Therefore, our primary focus is on probit models.

15.7.1 Neglected Heterogeneity

We begin by studying the consequences of omitting variables when those omitted variables are *independent* of the included explanatory variables. This is also called the **neglected heterogeneity** problem. The (structural) model of interest is

$$\mathrm{P}(y = 1 \mid \mathbf{x}, c) = \Phi(\mathbf{x}\boldsymbol{\beta} + \gamma c) \tag{15.34}$$

where $\mathbf{x}$ is $1 \times K$ with $x_1 \equiv 1$ and c is a scalar. We are interested in the partial effects of the x_j on the probability of success, holding c (and the other elements of $\mathbf{x}$) fixed. We can write equation (15.34) in latent variable form as $y^* = \mathbf{x}\boldsymbol{\beta} + \gamma c + e$, where $y = 1[y^* > 0]$ and $e \mid \mathbf{x}, c \sim \mathrm{Normal}(0, 1)$. Because $x_1 = 1$, $\mathrm{E}(c) = 0$ without loss of generality.

Now suppose that c is independent of $\mathbf{x}$ and $c \sim \mathrm{Normal}(0, \tau^2)$. [Remember, this assumption is much stronger than $\mathrm{Cov}(\mathbf{x}, c) = \mathbf{0}$ or even $\mathrm{E}(c \mid \mathbf{x}) = 0$: under independence, the distribution of c given $\mathbf{x}$ does not depend on $\mathbf{x}$.] Given these assumptions, the composite term, $\gamma c + e$, is independent of $\mathbf{x}$ and has a $\mathrm{Normal}(0, \gamma^2\tau^2 + 1)$ distribution. Therefore,

$$\mathrm{P}(y = 1 \mid \mathbf{x}) = \mathrm{P}(\gamma c + e > -\mathbf{x}\boldsymbol{\beta} \mid \mathbf{x}) = \Phi(\mathbf{x}\boldsymbol{\beta}/\sigma) \tag{15.35}$$

where $\sigma^2 \equiv \gamma^2\tau^2 + 1$. It follows immediately from equation (15.35) that probit of y on $\mathbf{x}$ consistently estimates $\boldsymbol{\beta}/\sigma$. In other words, if $\hat{\boldsymbol{\beta}}$ is the estimator from a probit of y on $\mathbf{x}$, then $\mathrm{plim}\, \hat{\beta}_j = \beta_j/\sigma$. Because $\sigma = (\gamma^2\tau^2 + 1)^{1/2} > 1$ (unless $\gamma = 0$ or $\tau^2 = 0$), $|\beta_j/\sigma| < |\beta_j|$.

The attenuation bias in estimating β_j in the presence of neglected heterogeneity has prompted statements of the following kind: "In probit analysis, neglected heterogeneity is a much more serious problem than in linear models because, even if the omitted heterogeneity is independent of $\mathbf{x}$, the probit coefficients are inconsistent." We just derived that probit of y on $\mathbf{x}$ consistently estimates $\boldsymbol{\beta}/\sigma$ rather than $\boldsymbol{\beta}$, so the statement is technically correct. However, we should remember that, in nonlinear models, we usually want to estimate partial effects and not just parameters. For the purposes of obtaining the directions of the effects or the relative effects of the explanatory variables, estimating $\boldsymbol{\beta}/\sigma$ is just as good as estimating $\boldsymbol{\beta}$.

For continuous x_j, we would like to estimate

$$\partial \mathrm{P}(y = 1 \mid \mathbf{x}, c)/\partial x_j = \beta_j \phi(\mathbf{x}\boldsymbol{\beta} + \gamma c) \tag{15.36}$$

for various values of $\mathbf{x}$ and c. Because c is not observed, we cannot estimate γ. Even if we could estimate γ, c almost never has meaningful units of measurement—for example, c might be "ability," "health," or "taste for saving"—so it is not obvious what values of c we should plug into equation (15.36). Nevertheless, c is normalized so that $\mathrm{E}(c) = 0$, so we may be interested in equation (15.36) evaluated at $c = 0$, which is simply $\beta_j \phi(\mathbf{x}\boldsymbol{\beta})$. What we consistently estimate from the probit of y on $\mathbf{x}$ is

$$(\beta_j/\sigma)\phi(\mathbf{x}\boldsymbol{\beta}/\sigma) \tag{15.37}$$

This expression shows that, if we are interested in the partial effects evaluated at $c = 0$, then probit of y on $\mathbf{x}$ does not do the trick. An interesting fact about expression (15.37) is that, even though β_j/σ is closer to zero than β_j, $\phi(\mathbf{x}\boldsymbol{\beta}/\sigma)$ is larger than $\phi(\mathbf{x}\boldsymbol{\beta})$ because $\phi(z)$ increases as $|z| \to 0$, and $\sigma > 1$. Therefore, for estimating the partial effects in equation (15.36) at $c = 0$, it is not clear for what values of $\mathbf{x}$ an attenuation bias exists.

With c having a normal distribution in the population, the partial effect evaluated at $c = 0$ describes only a small fraction of the population. [Technically, $\mathrm{P}(c = 0) = 0$.] Instead, we can estimate the **average partial effect (APE)**, which we introduced in Section 2.2.5. The APE is obtained, for given $\mathbf{x}$, by averaging equation (15.36) across the distribution of c in the population. For emphasis, let $\mathbf{x}^{\mathrm{o}}$ be a given value of the explanatory variables (which could be, but need not be, the mean value). When we plug $\mathbf{x}^{\mathrm{o}}$ into equation (15.36) and take the expected value with respect to the distribution of c, we get

$$\mathrm{E}[\beta_j \phi(\mathbf{x}^{\mathrm{o}}\boldsymbol{\beta} + \gamma c)] = (\beta_j/\sigma)\phi(\mathbf{x}^{\mathrm{o}}\boldsymbol{\beta}/\sigma) \tag{15.38}$$

In other words, probit of y on $\mathbf{x}$ consistently estimates the average partial effects, which is usually what we want.

The result in equation (15.38) follows from the general treatment of average partial effects in Section 2.2.5. In the current setup, there are no extra conditioning variables, $\mathbf{w}$, and the unobserved heterogeneity is independent of $\mathbf{x}$. It follows from equation (2.35) that the APE with respect to x_j, evaluated at $\mathbf{x}^{\mathrm{o}}$, is simply $\partial \mathrm{E}(y \mid \mathbf{x}^{\mathrm{o}})/\partial x_j$. But from the law of iterated expectations, $\mathrm{E}(y \mid \mathbf{x}) = \mathrm{E}_c[\Phi(\mathbf{x}\boldsymbol{\beta} + \gamma c)] = \Phi(\mathbf{x}\boldsymbol{\beta}/\sigma)$, where $\mathrm{E}_c(\cdot)$ denotes the expectation with respect to the distribution of c. The derivative of $\Phi(\mathbf{x}\boldsymbol{\beta}/\sigma)$ with respect to x_j is $(\beta_j/\sigma)\phi(\mathbf{x}\boldsymbol{\beta}/\sigma)$, which is what we wanted to show.

The bottom line is that, except in cases where the magnitudes of the β_j in equation (15.34) have some meaning, omitted heterogeneity in probit models is not a problem when it is independent of $\mathbf{x}$: ignoring it consistently estimates the average partial effects. Of course, the previous arguments hinge on the normality of c and the probit structural equation. If the structural model (15.34) were, say, logit and if c were normally distributed, we would not get a probit or logit for the distribution of y given $\mathbf{x}$; the response probability is more complicated. The lesson from Section 2.2.5 is that we might as well work directly with models for $\mathrm{P}(y = 1 \mid \mathbf{x})$ because partial effects of $\mathrm{P}(y = 1 \mid \mathbf{x})$ are always the average of the partial effects of $\mathrm{P}(y = 1 \mid \mathbf{x}, c)$ over the distribution of c.

If c is correlated with $\mathbf{x}$ or is otherwise dependent on $\mathbf{x}$ [for example, if $\mathrm{Var}(c \mid \mathbf{x})$ depends on $\mathbf{x}$], then omission of c is serious. In this case we cannot get consistent estimates of the average partial effects. For example, if $c \mid \mathbf{x} \sim \mathrm{Normal}(\mathbf{x}\boldsymbol{\delta}, \eta^2)$, then probit of y on $\mathbf{x}$ gives consistent estimates of $(\boldsymbol{\beta} + \gamma\boldsymbol{\delta})/\rho$, where $\rho^2 = \gamma^2\eta^2 + 1$. Unless $\gamma = 0$ or $\boldsymbol{\delta} = \mathbf{0}$, we do not consistently estimate $\boldsymbol{\beta}/\sigma$. This result is not surprising given what we know from the linear case with omitted variables correlated with the x_j. We now study what can be done to account for endogenous variables in probit models.

15.7.2 Continuous Endogenous Explanatory Variables

We now explicitly allow for the case where one of the explanatory variables is correlated with the error term in the latent variable model. One possibility is to estimate a linear probability model by 2SLS. This procedure is relatively easy and might provide a good estimate of the average effect.

If we want to estimate a probit model with an endogenous explanatory variables, we must make some fairly strong assumptions. In this section we consider the case of a continuous endogenous explanatory variable.

Write the model as

$$y_1^* = \mathbf{z}_1\boldsymbol{\delta}_1 + \alpha_1 y_2 + u_1 \tag{15.39}$$

$$y_2 = \mathbf{z}_1\boldsymbol{\delta}_{21} + \mathbf{z}_2\boldsymbol{\delta}_{22} + v_2 = \mathbf{z}\boldsymbol{\delta}_2 + v_2 \tag{15.40}$$

$$y_1 = 1[y_1^* > 0] \tag{15.41}$$

where (u_1, v_2) has a zero mean, bivariate normal distribution and is independent of $\mathbf{z}$. Equation (15.39), along with equation (15.41), is the structural equation; equation (15.40) is a reduced form for y_2, which is endogenous if u_1 and v_2 are correlated. If u_1 and v_2 are independent, there is no endogeneity problem. Because v_2 is normally distributed, we are assuming that y_2 given $\mathbf{z}$ is normal; thus y_2 should have features of a normal random variable. (For example, y_2 should not be a discrete variable.)

The model is applicable when y_2 is correlated with u_1 because of omitted variables or measurement error. It can also be applied to the case where y_2 is determined jointly with y_1, but with a caveat. If y_1 appears on the right-hand side in a linear structural equation for y_2, then the reduced form for y_2 cannot be found with v_2 having the stated properties. However, if y_1^* appears in a linear structural equation for y_2, then y_2 has the reduced form given by equation (15.40); see Maddala (1983, Chapter 7) for further discussion.

The normalization that gives the parameters in equation (15.39) an average partial effect interpretation, at least in the omitted variable and simultaneity contexts, is $\mathrm{Var}(u_1) = 1$, just as in a probit model with all explanatory variables exogenous. To see this point, consider the outcome on y_1 at two different outcomes of y_2, say $\bar{y}_2$ and $\bar{y}_2 + 1$. Holding the observed exogenous factors fixed at $\bar{\mathbf{z}}_1$, and holding u_1 fixed, the difference in responses is

$$1[\bar{\mathbf{z}}_1\boldsymbol{\delta}_1 + \alpha_1(\bar{y}_2 + 1) + u_1 \geq 0] - 1[\bar{\mathbf{z}}_1\boldsymbol{\delta}_1 + \alpha_1\bar{y}_2 + u_1 \geq 0]$$

(This difference can take on the values -1, 0, and 1.) Because u_1 is unobserved, we cannot estimate the difference in responses for a given population unit. Nevertheless, if we average across the distribution of u_1, which is Normal(0, 1), we obtain

$$\Phi[\bar{\mathbf{z}}_1\boldsymbol{\delta}_1 + \alpha_1(\bar{y}_2 + 1)] - \Phi(\bar{\mathbf{z}}_1\boldsymbol{\delta}_1 + \alpha_1\bar{y}_2)$$

Therefore, $\boldsymbol{\delta}_1$ and α_1 are the parameters appearing in the APE. [Alternatively, if we begin by allowing $\sigma_1^2 = \mathrm{Var}(u_1) > 0$ to be unrestricted, the APE would depend on $\boldsymbol{\delta}_1/\sigma_1$ and α_1/σ_1, and so we should just rescale u_1 to have unit variance. The variance and slope parameters are not separately identified, anyway.] The proper normalization for $\mathrm{Var}(u_1)$ should be kept in mind, as two-step procedures, which we cover in the following paragraphs, only consistently estimate $\boldsymbol{\delta}_1$ and α_1 up to scale; we have to do a little more work to obtain estimates of the APE. If y_2 is a mismeasured variable, we apparently cannot estimate the APE of interest: we would like to estimate the change in the response probability due to a change in y_2^*, but, without further assumptions, we can only estimate the effect of changing y_2.

The most useful two-step approach is due to Rivers and Vuong (1988), as it leads to a simple test for endogeneity of y_2. To derive the procedure, first note that, under joint normality of (u_1, v_2), with $\mathrm{Var}(u_1) = 1$, we can write

$$u_1 = \theta_1 v_2 + e_1 \tag{15.42}$$

where $\theta_1 = \eta_1/\tau_2^2$, $\eta_1 = \mathrm{Cov}(v_2, u_1)$, $\tau_2^2 = \mathrm{Var}(v_2)$, and e_1 is independent of $\mathbf{z}$ *and* v_2 (and therefore of y_2). Because of joint normality of (u_1, v_2), e_1 is also normally distributed with $\mathrm{E}(e_1) = 0$ and $\mathrm{Var}(e_1) = \mathrm{Var}(u_1) - \eta_1^2/\tau_2^2 = 1 - \rho_1^2$, where $\rho_1 = \mathrm{Corr}(v_2, u_1)$. We can now write

$$y_1^* = \mathbf{z}_1\boldsymbol{\delta}_1 + \alpha_1 y_2 + \theta_1 v_2 + e_1 \tag{15.43}$$

$$e_1 \mid \mathbf{z}, y_2, v_2 \sim \mathrm{Normal}(0, 1 - \rho_1^2) \tag{15.44}$$

A standard calculation shows that

$$\mathrm{P}(y_1 = 1 \mid \mathbf{z}, y_2, v_2) = \Phi[(\mathbf{z}_1\boldsymbol{\delta}_1 + \alpha_1 y_2 + \theta_1 v_2)/(1 - \rho_1^2)^{1/2}]$$

Assuming for the moment that we observe v_2, then probit of y_1 on $\mathbf{z}_1$, y_2, and v_2 consistently estimates $\boldsymbol{\delta}_{\rho 1} \equiv \boldsymbol{\delta}_1/(1-\rho_1^2)^{1/2}$, $\alpha_{\rho 1} \equiv \alpha_1/(1-\rho_1^2)^{1/2}$, and $\theta_{\rho 1} \equiv \theta_1/(1-\rho_1^2)^{1/2}$. Notice that because $\rho_1^2 < 1$, each scaled coefficient is greater than its unscaled counterpart unless y_2 is exogenous ($\rho_1 = 0$).

Since we do not know $\boldsymbol{\delta}_2$, we must first estimate it, as in the following procedure:

Procedure 15.1: (a) Run the OLS regression y_2 on $\mathbf{z}$ and save the residuals $\hat{v}_2$.

(b) Run the probit y_1 on $\mathbf{z}_1$, y_2, $\hat{v}_2$ to get consistent estimators of the scaled coefficients $\boldsymbol{\delta}_{\rho 1}$, $\alpha_{\rho 1}$, and $\theta_{\rho 1}$.

A nice feature of Procedure 15.1 is that the usual probit t statistic on $\hat{v}_2$ is a valid test of the null hypothesis that y_2 is exogenous, that is, H_0: $\theta_1 = 0$. If $\theta_1 \neq 0$, the usual probit standard errors and test statistics are not strictly valid, and we have only estimated $\boldsymbol{\delta}_1$ and α_1 up to scale. The asymptotic variance of the two-step estimator can be derived using the M-estimator results in Section 12.5.2; see also Rivers and Vuong (1988).

Under H_0: $\theta_1 = 0$, $e_1 = u_1$, and so the distribution of v_2 plays no role under the null. Therefore, the *test* of exogeneity is valid without assuming normality or homoskedasticity of v_2, and it can be applied very broadly, even if y_2 is a binary variable. Unfortunately, if y_2 and u_1 are correlated, normality of v_2 is crucial.

Example 15.3 (Testing for Exogeneity of Education in the Women's LFP Model): We test the null hypothesis that *educ* is exogenous in the married women's labor force participation equation. We first obtain the reduced form residuals, $\hat{v}_2$, from regressing *educ* on all exogenous variables, including *motheduc*, *fatheduc*, and *huseduc*. Then, we add $\hat{v}_2$ to the probit from Example 15.2. The t statistic on $\hat{v}_2$ is only .867, which is weak evidence against the null hypothesis that *educ* is exogenous. As always, this conclusion hinges on the assumption that the instruments for *educ* are themselves exogenous.

Even when $\theta_1 \neq 0$, it turns out that we can consistently estimate the average partial effects after the two-stage estimation. We simply apply the results from Section 2.2.5.

To see how, write $y_1 = 1[\mathbf{z}_1\boldsymbol{\delta}_1 + \alpha_1 y_2 + u_1 > 0]$, where, in the notation of Section 2.2.5, $q \equiv u_1$, $\mathbf{x} \equiv (\mathbf{z}_1, y_2)$, and $\mathbf{w} \equiv v_2$ (a scalar in this case). Because y_1 is a deterministic function of $(\mathbf{z}_1, y_2, u_1)$, v_2 is trivially redundant in $\mathrm{E}(y_1 \mid \mathbf{z}_1, y_2, u_1)$, and so equation (2.34) holds. Further, as we have already used, u_1 given $(\mathbf{z}_1, y_2, v_2)$ is independent of $(\mathbf{z}_1, y_2)$, and so equation (2.33) holds as well. It follows from Section 2.2.5 that the APEs are obtained by taking derivatives (or differences) of

$$\mathrm{E}_{v_2}[\Phi(\mathbf{z}_1\boldsymbol{\delta}_{\rho 1} + \alpha_{\rho 1} y_2 + \theta_{\rho 1} v_2)] \tag{15.45}$$

where we still use the ρ subscript to denote the scaled coefficients. But we computed exactly this kind of expectation in Section 15.7.1. The same reasoning gives

$$\mathrm{E}_{v_2}[\Phi(\mathbf{z}_1\boldsymbol{\delta}_{\rho 1} + \alpha_{\rho 1} y_2 + \theta_{\rho 1} v_2)] = \Phi(\mathbf{z}_1\boldsymbol{\delta}_{\theta 1} + \alpha_{\theta 1} y_2)$$

where $\boldsymbol{\delta}_{\theta 1} \equiv \boldsymbol{\delta}_{\rho 1}/(\theta_{\rho 1}^2\tau_2^2 + 1)^{1/2}$ and $\alpha_{\theta 1} \equiv \alpha_{\rho 1}/(\theta_{\rho 1}^2\tau_2^2 + 1)^{1/2}$, where $\tau_2^2 = \mathrm{Var}(v_2)$. Therefore, for any $(\mathbf{z}_1, y_2)$, a consistent estimator of expression (15.45) is

$$\Phi(\mathbf{z}_1\hat{\boldsymbol{\delta}}_{\theta 1} + \hat{\alpha}_{\theta 1} y_2) \tag{15.46}$$

where $\hat{\boldsymbol{\delta}}_{\theta 1} \equiv \hat{\boldsymbol{\delta}}_{\rho 1}/(\hat{\theta}_{\rho 1}^2\hat{\tau}_2^2 + 1)^{1/2}$ and $\hat{\alpha}_{\theta 1} \equiv \hat{\alpha}_{\rho 1}/(\hat{\theta}_{\rho 1}^2\hat{\tau}_2^2 + 1)^{1/2}$. Note that $\hat{\tau}_2^2$ is the usual error variance estimator from the first-stage regression of y_2 on $\mathbf{z}$. Expression (15.46) implies a very simple way to obtain the estimated APEs after the second-stage probit. We simply divide each coefficient by the factor $(\hat{\theta}_{\rho 1}^2\hat{\tau}_2^2 + 1)^{1/2}$ before computing derivatives or differences with respect to the elements of $(\mathbf{z}_1, y_2)$. Unfortunately, because the APEs depend on the parameters in a complicated way—and the asymptotic variance of $(\hat{\boldsymbol{\delta}}_{\rho 1}', \hat{\alpha}_{\rho 1}, \hat{\theta}_{\rho 1})'$ is already complicated because of the two-step estimation—standard errors for the APEs would be very difficult to come by using the delta method.

An alternative method for estimating the APEs does not exploit the normality assumption for v_2. By the usual uniform weak law of large numbers argument—see Lemma 12.1—a consistent estimator of expression (15.45) for any $(\mathbf{z}_1, y_2)$ is obtained by replacing unknown parameters by consistent estimators:

$$N^{-1}\sum_{i=1}^{N}\Phi(\mathbf{z}_1\hat{\boldsymbol{\delta}}_{\rho 1} + \hat{\alpha}_{\rho 1} y_2 + \hat{\theta}_{\rho 1}\hat{v}_{i2}) \tag{15.47}$$

where the $\hat{v}_{i2}$ are the first-stage OLS residuals from regressing y_{i2} on $\mathbf{z}_i$, $i = 1, \ldots, N$. This approach provides a different strategy for estimating APEs: simply compute partial effects with respect to $\mathbf{z}_1$ and y_2 after the second-stage estimation, but then average these across the $\hat{v}_{i2}$ in the sample.

Rather than use a two-step procedure, we can estimate equations (15.39)–(15.41) by conditional maximum likelihood. To obtain the joint distribution of (y_1, y_2), conditional on $\mathbf{z}$, recall that

$$f(y_1, y_2 \mid \mathbf{z}) = f(y_1 \mid y_2, \mathbf{z}) f(y_2 \mid \mathbf{z}) \tag{15.48}$$

(see Property CD.2 in Appendix 13A). Since $y_2 \mid \mathbf{z} \sim \text{Normal}(\mathbf{z}\boldsymbol{\delta}_2, \tau_2^2)$, the density $f(y_2 \mid \mathbf{z})$ is easy to write down. We can also derive the conditional density of y_1 given $(y_2, \mathbf{z})$. Since $v_2 = y_2 - \mathbf{z}\boldsymbol{\delta}_2$ and $y_1 = 1[y_1^* > 0]$,

$$\mathrm{P}(y_1 = 1 \mid y_2, \mathbf{z}) = \Phi\left[\frac{\mathbf{z}_1\boldsymbol{\delta}_1 + \alpha_1 y_2 + (\rho_1/\tau_2)(y_2 - \mathbf{z}\boldsymbol{\delta}_2)}{(1 - \rho_1^2)^{1/2}}\right] \tag{15.49}$$

where we have used the fact that $\theta_1 = \rho_1/\tau_2$.

Let w denote the term in inside $\Phi(\cdot)$ in equation (15.49). Then we have derived

$$f(y_1, y_2 \mid \mathbf{z}) = \{\Phi(w)\}^{y_1}\{1 - \Phi(w)\}^{1-y_1}(1/\tau_2)\phi[(y_2 - \mathbf{z}\boldsymbol{\delta}_2)/\tau_2]$$

and so the log likelihood for observation i (apart from terms not depending on the parameters) is

$$y_{i1} \log \Phi(w_i) + (1 - y_{i1}) \log[1 - \Phi(w_i)] - \tfrac{1}{2} \log(\tau_2^2) - \tfrac{1}{2}(y_{i2} - \mathbf{z}_i\boldsymbol{\delta}_2)^2/\tau_2^2 \tag{15.50}$$

where we understand that w_i depends on the parameters $(\boldsymbol{\delta}_1, \alpha_1, \rho_1, \boldsymbol{\delta}_2, \tau_2)$:

$$w_i \equiv [\mathbf{z}_{i1}\boldsymbol{\delta}_1 + \alpha_1 y_{i2} + (\rho_1/\tau_2)(y_{i2} - \mathbf{z}_i\boldsymbol{\delta}_2)]/(1 - \rho_1^2)^{1/2}$$

Summing expression (15.50) across all i and maximizing with respect to all parameters gives the MLEs of $\boldsymbol{\delta}_1$, α_1, ρ_1, $\boldsymbol{\delta}_2$, τ_2^2. The general theory of conditional MLE applies, and so standard errors can be obtained using the estimated Hessian, the estimated expected Hessian, or the outer product of the score.

Maximum likelihood estimation has some decided advantages over two-step procedures. First, MLE is more efficient than any two-step procedure. Second, we get direct estimates of $\boldsymbol{\delta}_1$ and α_1, the parameters of interest for computing partial effects. Evans, Oates, and Schwab (1992) study peer effects on teenage behavior using the full MLE.

Testing that y_2 is exogenous is easy once the MLE has been obtained: just test $\mathrm{H}_0\colon \rho_1 = 0$ using an asymptotic t test. We could also use a likelihood ratio test.

The drawback with the MLE is computational. Sometimes it can be difficult to get the iterations to converge, as $\hat{\rho}_1$ sometimes tends toward 1 or -1.

Comparing the Rivers-Vuong approach to the MLE shows that the former is a **limited information procedure**. Essentially, Rivers and Vuong focus on $f(y_1 \mid y_2, \mathbf{z})$, where they replace the unknown $\boldsymbol{\delta}_2$ with the OLS estimator $\hat{\boldsymbol{\delta}}_2$ (and they ignore the rescaling problem by taking e_1 in equation (15.43) to have unit variance). MLE estimates the parameters using the information in $f(y_1 \mid y_2, \mathbf{z})$ and $f(y_2 \mid \mathbf{z})$ simultaneously. For the initial test of whether y_2 is exogenous, the Rivers-Vuong approach has significant computational advantages. If exogeneity is rejected, it is probably worth doing MLE.

Another benefit of the maximum likelihood approach for this and related problems is that it forces discipline on us in coming up with consistent estimation procedures and correct standard errors. It is easy to abuse two-step procedures if we are not careful in deriving estimating equations. With MLE, although it can be difficult to derive joint distributions of the endogenous variables given the exogenous variables, we know that, if the underlying distributional assumptions hold, consistent and efficient estimators are obtained.

15.7.3 A Binary Endogenous Explanatory Variable

We now consider the case where the probit model contains a *binary* explanatory variable that is endogenous. The model is

$$y_1 = 1[\mathbf{z}_1\boldsymbol{\delta}_1 + \alpha_1 y_2 + u_1 > 0] \tag{15.51}$$

$$y_2 = 1[\mathbf{z}\boldsymbol{\delta}_2 + v_2 > 0] \tag{15.52}$$

where (u_1, v_2) is independent of $\mathbf{z}$ and distributed as bivariate normal with mean zero, each has unit variance, and $\rho_1 = \text{Corr}(u_1, v_2)$. If $\rho_1 \neq 0$, then u_1 and y_2 are correlated, and probit estimation of equation (15.51) is inconsistent for $\boldsymbol{\delta}_1$ and α_1.

As discussed in Section 15.7.2, the normalization $\text{Var}(u_1) = 1$ is the proper one for computing average partial effects. Often, the effect of y_2 is of primary interest, especially when y_2 indicates participation in some sort of program, such as job training, and the binary outcome y_1 might denote employment status. The average treatment effect (for a given value of $\mathbf{z}_1$) is $\Phi(\mathbf{z}_1\boldsymbol{\delta}_1 + \alpha_1) - \Phi(\mathbf{z}_1\boldsymbol{\delta}_1)$.

To derive the likelihood function, we again need the joint distribution of (y_1, y_2) given $\mathbf{z}$, which we obtain from equation (15.48). To obtain $\text{P}(y_1 = 1 \mid y_2, \mathbf{z})$, first note that

$$\text{P}(y_1 = 1 \mid v_2, \mathbf{z}) = \Phi[(\mathbf{z}_1\boldsymbol{\delta}_1 + \alpha_1 y_2 + \rho_1 v_2)/(1 - \rho_1^2)^{1/2}] \tag{15.53}$$

Since $y_2 = 1$ if and only if $v_2 > -\mathbf{z}\boldsymbol{\delta}_2$, we need a basic fact about truncated normal distributions: If v_2 has a standard normal distribution and is independent of $\mathbf{z}$, then the density of v_2 given $v_2 > -\mathbf{z}\boldsymbol{\delta}_2$ is

$$\phi(v_2)/\text{P}(v_2 > -\mathbf{z}\boldsymbol{\delta}_2) = \phi(v_2)/\Phi(\mathbf{z}\boldsymbol{\delta}_2) \tag{15.54}$$

Therefore,

$$\mathrm{P}(y_1 = 1 \mid y_2 = 1, \mathbf{z}) = \mathrm{E}[\mathrm{P}(y_1 = 1 \mid v_2, \mathbf{z}) \mid y_2 = 1, \mathbf{z}]$$
$$= \mathrm{E}\{\Phi[(\mathbf{z}_1\boldsymbol{\delta}_1 + \alpha_1 y_2 + \rho_1 v_2)/(1-\rho_1^2)^{1/2}] \mid y_2 = 1, \mathbf{z}\}$$
$$= \frac{1}{\Phi(\mathbf{z}\boldsymbol{\delta}_2)} \int_{-\mathbf{z}\boldsymbol{\delta}_2}^{\infty} \Phi[(\mathbf{z}_1\boldsymbol{\delta}_1 + \alpha_1 y_2 + \rho_1 v_2)/(1-\rho_1^2)^{1/2}]\phi(v_2)\,\mathrm{d}v_2 \tag{15.55}$$

where v_2 in the integral is a dummy argument of integration. Of course $\mathrm{P}(y_1 = 0 \mid y_2 = 1, \mathbf{z})$ is just one minus equation (15.55).

Similarly, $\mathrm{P}(y_1 = 1 \mid y_2 = 0, \mathbf{z})$ is

$$\frac{1}{1-\Phi(\mathbf{z}\boldsymbol{\delta}_2)} \int_{-\infty}^{-\mathbf{z}\boldsymbol{\delta}_2} \Phi[(\mathbf{z}_1\boldsymbol{\delta}_1 + \alpha_1 y_2 + \rho_1 v_2)/(1-\rho_1^2)^{1/2}]\phi(v_2)\,\mathrm{d}v_2 \tag{15.56}$$

Combining the four possible outcomes of (y_1, y_2), along with the probit model for y_2, and taking the log gives the log-likelihood function for maximum likelihood analysis. It is messy but certainly doable. Evans and Schwab (1995) use the MLE approach to study the causal effects of attending a Catholic high school on the probability of attending college, allowing the Catholic high school indicator to be correlated with unobserved factors that affect college attendence. As an IV they use a binary variable indicating whether a student is Catholic.

Because the MLE is nontrivial to compute, it is tempting to use some seemingly "obvious" two-step procedures. As an example, we might try to inappropriately mimic 2SLS. Since $\mathrm{E}(y_2 \mid \mathbf{z}) = \Phi(\mathbf{z}\boldsymbol{\delta}_2)$ and $\boldsymbol{\delta}_2$ is consistently estimated by probit of y_2 on $\mathbf{z}$, it is tempting to estimate $\boldsymbol{\delta}_1$ and α_1 from the probit of y_1 on $\mathbf{z}$, $\hat{\Phi}_2$, where $\hat{\Phi}_2 \equiv \Phi(\mathbf{z}\hat{\boldsymbol{\delta}}_2)$. This approach does not produce consistent estimators, for the same reasons the forbidden regression discussed in Section 9.5 for nonlinear simultaneous equations models does not. For this two-step procedure to work, we would have to have $\mathrm{P}(y_1 = 1 \mid \mathbf{z}) = \Phi[\mathbf{z}_1\boldsymbol{\delta}_1 + \alpha_1\Phi(\mathbf{z}\boldsymbol{\delta}_2)]$. But $\mathrm{P}(y_1 = 1 \mid \mathbf{z}) = \mathrm{E}(y_1 \mid \mathbf{z}) = \mathrm{E}(1[\mathbf{z}_1\boldsymbol{\delta}_1 + \alpha_1 y_2 + u_1 > 0] \mid \mathbf{z})$, and since the indicator function $1[\cdot]$ is nonlinear, we cannot pass the expected value through. If we were to compute the correct (complicated) formula for $\mathrm{P}(y_1 = 1 \mid \mathbf{z})$, plug in $\hat{\boldsymbol{\delta}}_2$, and then maximize the resulting binary response log likelihood, then the two-step approach would produce consistent estimators. But full maximum likelihood is easier and more efficient.

As mentioned in the previous subsection, we can use the Rivers-Vuong approach to *test* for exogeneity of y_2. This has the virtue of being simple, and, if the test fails to reject, we may not need to compute the MLE. A more efficient test is the score test of H_0: $\rho_1 = 0$, and this does not require estimation of the full MLE.

15.7.4 Heteroskedasticity and Nonnormality in the Latent Variable Model

In applying the probit model it is easy to become confused about the problems of heteroskedasticity and nonnormality. The confusion stems from a failure to distinguish between the underlying latent variable formulation, as in the model (15.9), and the response probability in equation (15.8). As we have emphasized throughout this chapter, for most purposes we want to estimate $\mathrm{P}(y = 1 \mid \mathbf{x})$. The latent variable formulation is convenient for certain manipulations, but we are rarely interested in $\mathrm{E}(y^* \mid \mathbf{x})$. [One case in which $\mathrm{E}(y^* \mid \mathbf{x})$ is of interest is covered in Problem 15.16.]

Once we focus on $\mathrm{P}(y = 1 \mid \mathbf{x})$, we can easily see why we should not attempt to compare heteroskedasticity in the latent variable model (15.9) with the consequences of heteroskedasticity in a standard linear regression model. Heteroskedasticity in $\mathrm{Var}(e \mid \mathbf{x})$ entirely changes the functional form for $\mathrm{P}(y = 1 \mid \mathbf{x}) = \mathrm{E}(y \mid \mathbf{x})$. While the statement "probit will be inconsistent for $\boldsymbol{\beta}$ when e is heteroskedastic" is correct, it largely misses the point. In most probit applications, it makes little sense to care about consistent estimation of $\boldsymbol{\beta}$ when $\mathrm{P}(y = 1 \mid \mathbf{x}) \neq \Phi(\mathbf{x}\boldsymbol{\beta})$. (Section 15.7.5 contains a different perspective.)

It is easy to construct examples where the partial effect of a variable on $\mathrm{P}(y = 1 \mid \mathbf{x})$ has the sign opposite to that of its coefficient in the latent variable formulation. For example, let x_1 be a positive, continuous variable, and write the latent variable model as $y^* = \beta_0 + \beta_1 x_1 + e$, $e \mid x_1 \sim \mathrm{Normal}(0, x_1^2)$. The binary response is defined as $y = 1[y^* > 0]$. A simple calculation shows that $\mathrm{P}(y = 1 \mid x_1) = \Phi(\beta_0/x_1 + \beta_1)$, and so $\partial\mathrm{P}(y = 1 \mid \mathbf{x}_1)/\partial x_1 = -(\beta_0/x_1^2)\phi(\beta_0/x_1 + \beta_1)$. If $\beta_0 > 0$ and $\beta_1 > 0$, then $\partial\mathrm{P}(y = 1 \mid x_1)/\partial x_1$ and β_1 have opposite signs. The problem is fairly clear: while the latent variable model has a conditional mean that is linear in x_1, the response probability depends on $1/x_1$. If the latent variable model is correct, we should just do probit of y on 1 and $1/x_1$.

Nonnormality in the latent error e means that $G(z) \neq \Phi(z)$, and therefore $\mathrm{P}(y = 1 \mid \mathbf{x}) \neq \Phi(\mathbf{x}\boldsymbol{\beta})$. Again, this is a functional form problem in the response probability, and it should be treated as such. As an example, suppose that the true model is logit, but we estimate probit. We are not going to consistently estimate $\boldsymbol{\beta}$ in $\mathrm{P}(y = 1 \mid \mathbf{x}) = \Lambda(\mathbf{x}\boldsymbol{\beta})$—in fact, Table 15.1 shows that the logit estimates are generally much larger (roughly 1.6 times as large)—because of the different scalings inherent in the probit and logit functions. But inconsistent estimation of $\boldsymbol{\beta}$ is practically irrelevant: probit might provide very good estimates of the partial effects, $\partial\mathrm{P}(y = 1 \mid \mathbf{x})/\partial x_j$, even though logit is the correct model. In Example 15.2, the estimated partial effects are very similar for logit and probit.

Relaxing distributional assumptions on e in the model (15.9) can be useful for obtaining more flexible functional forms for $\mathrm{P}(y = 1 \mid \mathbf{x})$, as we saw in equation (15.24). Replacing $\Phi(z)$ with some function $G(z; \gamma)$, where γ is a vector of parameters, is a good idea, especially when it nests the standard normal cdf. [Moon (1988) covers some interesting possibilities in the context of logit models, including asymmetric cumulative distribution functions.] But it is important to remember that these are just ways of generalizing functional form, and they may be no better than directly specifying a more flexible functional form for the response probability, as in McDonald (1996). When different functional forms are used, parameter estimates across different models should not be the basis for comparison: in most cases, it makes sense only to compare the estimated response probabilities at various values of $\mathbf{x}$ and goodness of fit, such as the values of the log-likelihood function. (For an exception, see Problem 15.16.)

15.7.5 Estimation under Weaker Assumptions

Probit, logit, and the extensions of these mentioned in the previous subsection are all parametric models: $\mathrm{P}(y = 1 \mid \mathbf{x})$ depends on a finite number of parameters. There have been many recent advances in estimation of binary response models that relax parametric assumptions on $\mathrm{P}(y = 1 \mid \mathbf{x})$. We briefly discuss some of those here.

If we are interested in estimating the directions and relative sizes of the partial effects, and not the response probabilities, several approaches are possible. Ruud (1983) obtains conditions under which we can estimate the slope parameters, call these $\boldsymbol{\beta}$, up to scale—that is, we can consistently estimate $\tau\boldsymbol{\beta}$ for some unknown constant τ—even though we misspecify the function $G(\cdot)$. Ruud (1986) shows how to exploit these results to consistently estimate the slope parameters up to scale fairly generally.

An alternative approach is to recognize that we do not know the function $G(\cdot)$, but the response probability has the index form in equation (15.8). This arises from the latent variable formulation (15.9) when e is independent of $\mathbf{x}$ but the distribution of e is not known. There are several **semiparametric estimators** of the slope parameters, up to scale, that do not require knowledge of G. Under certain restrictions on the function G and the distribution of $\mathbf{x}$, the semiparametric estimators are consistent and $\sqrt{N}$-asymptotically normal. See, for example, Stoker (1986); Powell, Stock, and Stoker (1989); Ichimura (1993); Klein and Spady (1993); and Ai (1997). Powell (1994) contains a recent survey of these methods.

Once $\hat{\boldsymbol{\beta}}$ is obtained, the function G can be consistently estimated (in a sense we cannot make precise here, as G is part of an infinite dimensional space). Thus, the response probabilities, as well as the partial effects on these probabilities, can be consistently estimated for unknown G. Obtaining $\hat{G}$ requires **nonparametric regression** of y_i on $\mathbf{x}_i\hat{\boldsymbol{\beta}}$, where $\hat{\boldsymbol{\beta}}$ are the scaled slope estimators. Accessible treatments of the methods used are contained in Stoker (1992), Powell (1994), and Härdle and Linton (1994).

Remarkably, it is possible to estimate $\boldsymbol{\beta}$ up to scale without assuming that e and $\mathbf{x}$ are independent in the model (15.9). In the specification $y = 1[\mathbf{x}\boldsymbol{\beta} + e > 0]$, Manski (1975, 1988) shows how to consistently estimate $\boldsymbol{\beta}$, subject to a scaling, under the assumption that the median of e given $\mathbf{x}$ is zero. Some mild restrictions are needed on the distribution of $\mathbf{x}$; the most important of these is that at least one element of $\mathbf{x}$ with nonzero coefficient is essentially continuous. This allows e to have any distribution, and e and $\mathbf{x}$ can be dependent; for example, $\mathrm{Var}(e \mid \mathbf{x})$ is unrestricted. Manski's estimator, called the **maximum score estimator**, is a least absolute deviations estimator. Since the median of y given $\mathbf{x}$ is $1[\mathbf{x}\boldsymbol{\beta} > 0]$, the maximum score estimator solves

$$\min_{\boldsymbol{\beta}} \sum_{i=1}^{N} |y_i - 1[\mathbf{x}_i\boldsymbol{\beta} > 0]|$$

over all $\boldsymbol{\beta}$ with, say, $\boldsymbol{\beta}'\boldsymbol{\beta} = 1$, or with some element of $\boldsymbol{\beta}$ fixed at unity if the corresponding x_j is known to appear in $\mathrm{Med}(y \mid \mathbf{x})$. {A normalization is needed because if $\mathrm{Med}(y \mid \mathbf{x}) = 1[\mathbf{x}\boldsymbol{\beta} > 0]$ then $\mathrm{Med}(y \mid \mathbf{x}) = 1[\mathbf{x}(\tau\boldsymbol{\beta}) > 0]$ for any $\tau > 0$.} The resulting estimator is consistent—for a recent proof see Newey and McFadden (1994)—but its limiting distribution is nonnormal. In fact, it converges to its limiting distribution at rate $N^{1/3}$. Horowitz (1992) proposes a smoothed version of the maximum score estimator that converges at a rate close to $\sqrt{N}$.

The maximum score estimator's strength is that it consistently estimates $\boldsymbol{\beta}$ up to scale in cases where the index model (15.8) does not hold. In a sense, this is also the estimator's weakness, because it is not intended to deliver estimates of the response probabilities $\mathrm{P}(y = 1 \mid \mathbf{x})$. In some cases we might only want to know the relative effects of each x_j on an underlying utility difference or unobserved willingness to pay (y^*), and the maximum score estimator is well suited for that purpose. However, for most policy purposes we want to know the magnitude of the change in $\mathrm{P}(y = 1 \mid \mathbf{x})$ for a given change in x_j. As illustrated by the heteroskedasticity example in the previous subsection, where $\mathrm{Var}(e \mid x_1) = x_1^2$, it is possible for β_j and $\partial \mathrm{P}(y = 1 \mid \mathbf{x})/\partial x_j$ to have opposite signs. More generally, for any variable y, it is possible that x_j has a positive effect on $\mathrm{Med}(y \mid \mathbf{x})$ but a negative effect on $\mathrm{E}(y \mid \mathbf{x})$, or vice versa. This possibility raises the issue of what should be the focus, the median or the mean. For binary response, the conditional mean is the response probability.

It is also possible to estimate the parameters in a binary response model with endogenous explanatory variables without knowledge of $G(\cdot)$. Lewbel (1998) contains some recent results. Apparently, methods for estimating average partial effects with endogenous explanatory variables and unknown $G(\cdot)$ are not yet available.

15.8 Binary Response Models for Panel Data and Cluster Samples

When analyzing binary responses in the context of panel data, it is often useful to begin with a linear model with an additive, unobserved effect, and then, just as in Chapters 10 and 11, use the within transformation or first differencing to remove the unobserved effect. A linear probability model for binary outcomes has the same problems as in the cross section case. In fact, it is probably less appealing for unobserved effects models, as it implies the unnatural restrictions $\mathbf{x}_{it}\boldsymbol{\beta} \leq c_i \leq 1 - \mathbf{x}_{it}\boldsymbol{\beta}, t = 1, \ldots, T$, on the unobserved effects. In this section we discuss probit and logit models that can incorporate unobserved effects.

15.8.1 Pooled Probit and Logit

In Section 13.8 we used a probit model to illustrate partial likelihood methods with panel data. Naturally, we can use logit or any other binary response function as well. Suppose the model is

$$\mathrm{P}(y_{it} = 1 \mid \mathbf{x}_{it}) = G(\mathbf{x}_{it}\boldsymbol{\beta}), \qquad t = 1, 2, \ldots, T \tag{15.57}$$

where $G(\cdot)$ is a known function taking on values in the open unit interval. As we discussed in Chapter 13, $\mathbf{x}_{it}$ can contain a variety of factors, including time dummies, interactions of time dummies with time-constant or time-varying variables, and lagged dependent variables.

In specifying the model (15.57) we have not assumed nearly enough to obtain the distribution of $\mathbf{y}_i \equiv (y_{i1}, \ldots, y_{iT})$ given $\mathbf{x}_i = (\mathbf{x}_{i1}, \ldots, \mathbf{x}_{iT})$. Nevertheless, we can obtain a $\sqrt{N}$-consistent estimator of $\boldsymbol{\beta}$ by maximizing the partial log-likelihood function

$$\sum_{i=1}^{N}\sum_{t=1}^{T}\{y_{it} \log G(\mathbf{x}_{it}\boldsymbol{\beta}) + (1 - y_{it}) \log[1 - G(\mathbf{x}_{it}\boldsymbol{\beta})]\}$$

which is simply an exercise in pooled estimation. Without further assumptions, a robust variance matrix estimator is needed to account for serial correlation in the scores across t; see equation (13.53) with $\hat{\boldsymbol{\beta}}$ in place of $\hat{\boldsymbol{\theta}}$ and G in place of Φ. Wald and score statistics can be computed as in Chapter 12.

In the case that the model (15.57) is dynamically complete, that is,

$$\mathrm{P}(y_{it} = 1 \mid \mathbf{x}_{it}, y_{i,t-1}, \mathbf{x}_{i,t-1}, \ldots) = \mathrm{P}(y_{it} = 1 \mid \mathbf{x}_{it}) \tag{15.58}$$

inference is considerably easier: all the usual statistics from a probit or logit that pools observations and treats the sample as a long independent cross section of size NT are valid, including likelihood ratio statistics. Remember, we are definitely *not* assuming independence across t (for example, $\mathbf{x}_{it}$ can contain lagged dependent variables). Dynamic completeness implies that the scores are serially uncorrelated across t, which is the key condition for the standard inference procedures to be valid. (See the general treatment in Section 13.8.)

To test for dynamic completeness, we can always add a lagged dependent variable and possibly lagged explanatory variables. As an alternative, we can derive a simple one-degree-of-freedom test that works regardless of what is in $\mathbf{x}_{it}$. For concreteness, we focus on the probit case; other index models are handled similarly. Define $u_{it} \equiv y_{it} - \Phi(\mathbf{x}_{it}\boldsymbol{\beta})$, so that, under assumption (15.58), $\mathrm{E}(u_{it} \mid \mathbf{x}_{it}, y_{i,t-1}, \mathbf{x}_{i,t-1}, \ldots) = 0$, all t. It follows that u_{it} is uncorrelated with any function of the variables $(\mathbf{x}_{it}, y_{i,t-1}, \mathbf{x}_{i,t-1}, \ldots)$, including $u_{i,t-1}$. By studying equation (13.53), we can see that it is serial correlation in the u_{it} that makes the usual inference procedures invalid. Let $\hat{u}_{it} = y_{it} - \Phi(\mathbf{x}_{it}\hat{\boldsymbol{\beta}})$. Then a simple test is available by using pooled probit to estimate the artificial model

$$\text{“}\mathrm{P}(y_{it} = 1 \mid \mathbf{x}_{it}, \hat{u}_{i,t-1}) = \Phi(\mathbf{x}_{it}\boldsymbol{\beta} + \gamma_1 \hat{u}_{i,t-1})\text{”} \tag{15.59}$$

using time periods $t = 2, \ldots, T$. The null hypothesis is H_0: $\gamma_1 = 0$. If H_0 is rejected, then so is assumption (15.58). This is a case where under the null hypothesis, the estimation of $\boldsymbol{\beta}$ required to obtain $\hat{u}_{i,t-1}$ does not affect the limiting distribution of any of the usual test statistics, Wald, LR, or LM, of H_0: $\gamma_1 = 0$. The Wald statistic, that is, the t statistic on $\hat{\gamma}_1$, is the easiest to obtain. For the LM and LR statistics we must be sure to drop the first time period in estimating the restricted model ($\gamma_1 = 0$).

15.8.2 Unobserved Effects Probit Models under Strict Exogeneity

A popular model for binary outcomes with panel data is the **unobserved effects probit model**. The main assumption of this model is

$$\mathrm{P}(y_{it} = 1 \mid \mathbf{x}_i, c_i) = \mathrm{P}(y_{it} = 1 \mid \mathbf{x}_{it}, c_i) = \Phi(\mathbf{x}_{it}\boldsymbol{\beta} + c_i), \qquad t = 1, \ldots, T \tag{15.60}$$

where c_i is the unobserved effect and $\mathbf{x}_i$ contains $\mathbf{x}_{it}$ for all t. The first equality says that $\mathbf{x}_{it}$ is strictly exogenous conditional on c_i: once c_i is conditioned on, only $\mathbf{x}_{it}$ appears in the response probability at time t. This rules out lagged dependent variables in $\mathbf{x}_{it}$, as well as certain kinds of explanatory variables whose future movements depend on current and past outcomes on y. (Strict exogeneity also requires that we have enough lags of explanatory variables if there are distributed lag effects.) The second equality is the standard probit assumption, with c_i appearing additively in the index inside $\Phi(\cdot)$. Many analyses are not convincing unless $\mathbf{x}_{it}$ contains a full set of time dummies.

In addition to assumption (15.60), a standard assumption is that the outcomes are independent conditional on $(\mathbf{x}_i, c_i)$:

$$y_{i1}, \ldots, y_{iT} \text{ are independent conditional on } (\mathbf{x}_i, c_i) \tag{15.61}$$

Because of the presence of c_i, the y_{it} are dependent across t conditional only on the observables, $\mathbf{x}_i$. [Assumption (15.61) is analogous to the linear model assumption that, conditional on $(\mathbf{x}_i, c_i)$, the y_{it} are serially uncorrelated; see Assumption FE.3 in Chapter 10.] Under assumptions (15.60) and (15.61), we can derive the density of $(y_{i1}, \ldots, y_{iT})$ conditional on $(\mathbf{x}_i, c_i)$:

$$f(y_1, \ldots, y_T \mid \mathbf{x}_i, c_i; \boldsymbol{\beta}) = \prod_{t=1}^{T} f(y_t \mid \mathbf{x}_{it}, c_i; \boldsymbol{\beta}) \tag{15.62}$$

where $f(y_t \mid \mathbf{x}_t, c; \boldsymbol{\beta}) = \Phi(\mathbf{x}_t\boldsymbol{\beta} + c)^{y_t}[1 - \Phi(\mathbf{x}_t\boldsymbol{\beta} + c)]^{1-y_t}$. Ideally, we could estimate the quantities of interest without restricting the relationship between c_i and the $\mathbf{x}_{it}$. In this spirit, a **fixed effects probit analysis** treats the c_i as parameters to be estimated along with $\boldsymbol{\beta}$, as this treatment obviates the need to make assumptions about the distribution of c_i given $\mathbf{x}_i$. The log-likelihood function is $\sum_{i=1}^{N} \ell_i(c_i, \boldsymbol{\beta})$, where $\ell_i(c_i, \boldsymbol{\beta})$ is the log of equation (15.62) evaluated at the y_{it}. Unfortunately, in addition to being computationally difficult, estimation of the c_i along with $\boldsymbol{\beta}$ introduces an **incidental parameters problem**. Unlike in the linear case, where estimating the c_i along with $\boldsymbol{\beta}$ leads to the $\sqrt{N}$-consistent fixed effects estimator of $\boldsymbol{\beta}$, in the present case estimating the c_i (N of them) along with $\boldsymbol{\beta}$ leads to inconsistent estimation of $\boldsymbol{\beta}$ with T fixed and $N \to \infty$. We discuss the incidental parameters problem in more detail for the unobserved effects logit model in Section 15.8.3.

The name "fixed effects probit" to describe the model where the c_i are fixed parameters is somewhat unfortunate. As we saw with linear models, and, as we will see with the logit model in the next subsection and with count data models in Chapter 19, in some cases we can consistently estimate the parameters $\boldsymbol{\beta}$ without specifying a distribution for c_i given $\mathbf{x}_i$. This ability is the hallmark of a fixed effects analysis for most microeconometric applications. By contrast, treating the c_i as parameters to estimate can lead to potentially serious biases.

Here we follow the same approach adopted for linear models: we *always* treat c_i as an unobservable random variable drawn along with $(\mathbf{x}_i, \mathbf{y}_i)$. The question is, Under what additional assumptions can we consistently estimate parameters, as well as interesting partial effects? Unfortunately, for the unobserved effects probit model, we must make an assumption about the relationship between c_i and $\mathbf{x}_i$. The **traditional random effects probit model** adds, to assumptions (15.60) and (15.61), the assumption

$$c_i \mid \mathbf{x}_i \sim \text{Normal}(0, \sigma_c^2) \tag{15.63}$$

This is a strong assumption, as it implies that c_i and $\mathbf{x}_i$ are independent and that c_i has a normal distribution. It is not enough to assume that c_i and $\mathbf{x}_i$ are uncorrelated, or even that $\text{E}(c_i \mid \mathbf{x}_i) = 0$. The assumption $\text{E}(c_i) = 0$ is without loss of generality provided $\mathbf{x}_{it}$ contains an intercept, as it always should.

Before we discuss estimation of the random effects probit model, we should be sure we know what we want to estimate. As in Section 15.7.1, consistent estimation of $\boldsymbol{\beta}$ means that we can consistently estimate the partial effects of the elements of $\mathbf{x}_t$ on the response probability $\text{P}(y_t = 1 \mid \mathbf{x}_t, c)$ at the average value of c in the population, $c = 0$. (We can also estimate the relative effects of any two elements of $\mathbf{x}_t$ for any value of c, as the relative effects do not depend on c.) For the reasons discussed in Section 15.7.1, average partial effects (APEs) are at least as useful. Since $c_i \sim \text{Normal}(0, \sigma_c^2)$, the APE for a continuous x_{tj} is $[\beta_j/(1+\sigma_c^2)^{1/2}]\phi[\mathbf{x}_t\boldsymbol{\beta}/(1+\sigma_c^2)^{1/2}]$, just as in equation (15.38). Therefore, we only need to estimate $\boldsymbol{\beta}_c \equiv \boldsymbol{\beta}/(1+\sigma_c^2)^{1/2}$ to estimate the APEs, for either continuous or discrete explanatory variables. (In other branches of applied statistics, such as biostatistics and education, the coefficients indexing the APEs—$\boldsymbol{\beta}_c$ in our notation—are called the **population-averaged parameters**.)

Under assumptions (15.60), (15.61), and (15.63), a conditional maximum likelihood approach is available for estimating $\boldsymbol{\beta}$ and σ_c^2. This is a special case of the approach in Section 13.9. Because the c_i are not observed, they cannot appear in the likelihood function. Instead, we find the joint distribution of $(y_{i1}, \ldots, y_{iT})$ conditional on $\mathbf{x}_i$, a step that requires us to *integrate out* c_i. Since c_i has a $\text{Normal}(0, \sigma_c^2)$ distribution,

$$f(y_1, \ldots, y_T \mid \mathbf{x}_i; \boldsymbol{\theta}) = \int_{-\infty}^{\infty} \left[\prod_{t=1}^{T} f(y_t \mid \mathbf{x}_{it}, c; \boldsymbol{\beta}) \right] (1/\sigma_c)\phi(c/\sigma_c)\, dc \tag{15.64}$$

where $f(y_t \mid \mathbf{x}_t, c; \boldsymbol{\beta}) = \Phi(\mathbf{x}_t\boldsymbol{\beta} + c)^{y_t}[1 - \Phi(\mathbf{x}_t\boldsymbol{\beta} + c)]^{1-y_t}$ and $\boldsymbol{\theta}$ contains $\boldsymbol{\beta}$ and σ_c^2. Plugging in y_{it} for all t and taking the log of equation (15.64) gives the conditional log likelihood $\ell_i(\boldsymbol{\theta})$ for each i. The log-likelihood function for the entire sample of size N can be maximized with respect to $\boldsymbol{\beta}$ and σ_c^2 (or $\boldsymbol{\beta}$ and σ_c) to obtain $\sqrt{N}$-consistent asymptotically normal estimators; Butler and Moffitt (1982) describe a procedure for approximating the integral in equation (15.64). The conditional MLE in this context is typically called the **random effects probit estimator**, and the theory in Section 13.9 can be applied directly to obtain asymptotic standard errors and test statistics. Since $\boldsymbol{\beta}$ and σ_c^2 can be estimated, the partial effects at $c = 0$ as well as the average partial effects can be estimated. Since the variance of the idiosyncratic error in the latent variable model is unity, the relative importance of the unobserved effect is measured as $\rho = \sigma_c^2/(\sigma_c^2 + 1)$, which is also the correlation between the composite latent error, say, $c_i + e_{it}$, across any two time periods. Many random effects probit routines report $\hat{\rho}$ and its standard error; these statistics lead to an easy test for the presence of the unobserved effect.

Assumptions (15.61) and (15.63) are fairly strong, and it is possible to relax them. First consider relaxing assumption (15.61). One useful observation is that, under assumptions (15.60) and (15.63) only,

$$\mathrm{P}(y_{it} = 1 \mid \mathbf{x}_i) = \mathrm{P}(y_{it} = 1 \mid \mathbf{x}_{it}) = \Phi(\mathbf{x}_{it}\boldsymbol{\beta}_c) \tag{15.65}$$

where $\boldsymbol{\beta}_c = \boldsymbol{\beta}/(1 + \sigma_c^2)^{1/2}$. Therefore, just as in Section 15.8.1, we can estimate $\boldsymbol{\beta}_c$ from pooled probit of y_{it} on $\mathbf{x}_{it}$, $t = 1, \ldots, T$, $i = 1, \ldots, N$, meaning that we directly estimate the average partial effects. If c_i is truly present, $\{y_{it}: t = 1, \ldots, T\}$ will not be independent conditional on $\mathbf{x}_i$. Robust inference is needed to account for the serial dependence, as discussed in Section 15.8.1.

An alternative to simply calculating robust standard errors for $\hat{\boldsymbol{\beta}}_c$ after pooled probit, or using the full random effects assumptions and obtaining the MLE, is what is called the **generalized estimating equations (GEE)** approach (see Zeger, Liang, and Albert, 1988). In the GEE approach to unobserved effects binary response models, the response probabilities are specified conditional only on $\mathbf{x}_i$, with the result that we have $\mathrm{E}(y_{it} \mid \mathbf{x}_{it}) = \mathrm{E}(y_{it} \mid \mathbf{x}_i)$ for all t. [Unfortunately, the model is then called a **population-averaged model**. As we just saw, we can estimate the population-averaged parameters, or APEs, even if we have used random effects probit estimation. It is best to think of assumption (15.60) as the unobserved effects model of interest. The relevant question is, What effects are we interested in, and how can we consistently estimate them under various assumptions? We are usually interested in averaging across the distribution of c_i, but the basic model has not changed.] Next, a model for the $T \times T$ matrix $\mathbf{W}_i \equiv \mathrm{Var}(\mathbf{y}_i \mid \mathbf{x}_i)$ is specified, and this depends on $\boldsymbol{\beta}$ as well as some additional parameters, say $\boldsymbol{\delta}$. After estimating $\boldsymbol{\beta}$ and $\boldsymbol{\delta}$ in a first step, $\hat{\mathbf{W}}_i$ is obtained, and the GEE estimate of $\boldsymbol{\beta}$ is a multivariate weighted nonlinear least squares (MWNLS) estimator. (See Problem 12.11.) As the model for $\mathrm{Var}(\mathbf{y}_i \mid \mathbf{x}_i)$ is often chosen for convenience, it can be misspecified. The MWNLS estimator is still consistent and asymptotically normal because $\mathrm{E}(\mathbf{y}_i \mid \mathbf{x}_i)$ is correctly specified under assumptions (15.60) and (15.63)—we do not need assumption (15.61)—but a robust variance matrix is needed (see Problem 12.11). Even with a misspecified variance function, the MWNLS estimator is likely to be more efficient than pooled probit but less efficient than the random effects MLE under the full set of random effects assumptions.

Another way to relax assumption (15.61) is to assume a particular correlation structure and then use full conditional maximum likelihood. For example, for each t write the latent variable model as

$$y_{it}^* = \mathbf{x}_{it}\boldsymbol{\beta} + c_i + e_{it}, \qquad y_{it} = 1[y_{it}^* > 0] \tag{15.66}$$

and assume that the $T \times 1$ vector $\mathbf{e}_i$ is multivariate normal, with unit variances, but unrestricted correlation matrix. This assumption, along with assumptions (15.60) and (15.63), fully characterizes the distribution of $\mathbf{y}_i$ given $\mathbf{x}_i$. However, even for moderate T the computation of the CMLE can be very difficult. Recent advances in simulation methods of estimation make it possible to estimate such models for fairly large T; see, for example, Keane (1993) and Geweke and Keane (in press). The pooled probit procedure that we have described is valid for estimating $\boldsymbol{\beta}_c$, the vector that indexes the average partial effects, regardless of the serial dependence in $\{e_{it}\}$, but it is inefficient relative to the full CMLE.

As in the linear case, in many applications the point of introducing the unobserved effect, c_i, is to explicitly allow unobservables to be correlated with some elements of $\mathbf{x}_{it}$. Chamberlain (1980) allowed for correlation between c_i and $\mathbf{x}_i$ by assuming a conditional normal distribution with linear expectation and constant variance. A Mundlak (1978) version of Chamberlain's assumption is

$$c_i \mid \mathbf{x}_i \sim \mathrm{Normal}(\psi + \bar{\mathbf{x}}_i\xi, \sigma_a^2) \tag{15.67}$$

where $\bar{\mathbf{x}}_i$ is the average of $\mathbf{x}_{it}$, $t = 1, \ldots, T$ and σ_a^2 is the variance of a_i in the equation $c_i = \psi + \bar{\mathbf{x}}_i\boldsymbol{\xi} + a_i$. (In other words, σ_a^2 is the conditional variance of c_i, which is assumed not to depend on $\mathbf{x}_i$.) Chamberlain (1980) allowed more generality by having $\mathbf{x}_i$, the vector of all explanatory variables across all time periods, in place of $\bar{\mathbf{x}}_i$. We will work with assumption (15.67), as it conserves on parameters; the more general model requires a simple notational change. Chamberlain (1980) called model (15.60) under assumption (15.67) a *random effects probit model*, so we refer to the model as **Chamberlain's random effects probit model**. While assumption (15.67) is restrictive in that it specifies a distribution for c_i given $\mathbf{x}_i$, it at least allows for some dependence between c_i and $\mathbf{x}_i$.

As in the linear case, we can only estimate the effects of time-varying elements in $\mathbf{x}_{it}$. In particular, $\mathbf{x}_{it}$ should no longer contain a constant, as that would be indistinguishable from ψ in assumption (15.67). If our original model contains a time-constant explanatory variable, say w_i, it can be included among the explanatory variables, but we cannot distinguish its effect from c_i unless we assume that the coefficient for w_i in ξ is zero. (That is, unless we assume that c_i is partially uncorrelated with w_i.) Time dummies, which do not vary across i, are omitted from $\bar{\mathbf{x}}_i$.

If assumptions (15.60), (15.61), and (15.67) hold, estimation of $\boldsymbol{\beta}$, ψ, ξ, and σ_a^2 is straightforward because we can write the latent variable as $y_{it}^* = \psi + \mathbf{x}_{it}\boldsymbol{\beta} + \bar{\mathbf{x}}_i\xi + a_i + e_{it}$, where the e_{it} are independent Normal(0, 1) variates [conditional on $(\mathbf{x}_i, a_i)$], and $a_i \mid \mathbf{x}_i \sim \text{Normal}(0, \sigma_a^2)$. In other words, by adding $\bar{\mathbf{x}}_i$ to the equation for each time period, we arrive at a traditional random effects probit model. (The variance we estimate is σ_a^2 rather than σ_c^2, but, as we will see, this suits our purposes nicely.) Adding $\bar{\mathbf{x}}_i$ as a set of controls for unobserved heterogeneity is very intuitive: we are estimating the effect of changing x_{itj} but holding the time average fixed. A test of the usual RE probit model is easily obtained as a test of H_0: $\xi = \mathbf{0}$. Estimation can be carried out using standard random effects probit software. Given estimates of ψ and ξ, we can estimate $\mathrm{E}(c_i) = \psi + \mathrm{E}(\bar{\mathbf{x}}_i)\xi$ by $\hat{\psi} + \bar{\mathbf{x}}\hat{\xi}$, where $\bar{\mathbf{x}}$ is the sample average of $\bar{\mathbf{x}}_i$. Therefore, for any vector $\mathbf{x}_t$, we can estimate the response probability at $\mathrm{E}(c_i)$ as $\Phi(\hat{\psi} + \mathbf{x}_t\hat{\boldsymbol{\beta}} + \bar{\mathbf{x}}\hat{\xi})$. Taking differences or derivatives (with respect to the elements of $\mathbf{x}_t$) allows us to estimate the partial effects on the response probabilities for any value of $\mathbf{x}_t$. (We will show how to estimate the average partial effects shortly.)

If we drop assumption (15.61), we can still estimate scaled versions of ψ, $\boldsymbol{\beta}$, and ξ. Under assumptions (15.60) and (15.67) we have

$$\begin{aligned} \mathrm{P}(y_{it} = 1 \mid \mathbf{x}_i) &= \Phi[(\psi + \mathbf{x}_{it}\boldsymbol{\beta} + \bar{\mathbf{x}}_i\xi) \cdot (1 + \sigma_a^2)^{-1/2}] \\ &\equiv \Phi(\psi_a + \mathbf{x}_{it}\boldsymbol{\beta}_a + \bar{\mathbf{x}}_i\xi_a) \end{aligned} \tag{15.68}$$

where the a subscript means that a parameter vector has been multiplied by $(1 + \sigma_a^2)^{-1/2}$. It follows immediately that ψ_a, $\boldsymbol{\beta}_a$, and ξ_a can be consistently estimated using a pooled probit analysis of y_{it} on 1, $\mathbf{x}_{it}$, $\bar{\mathbf{x}}_i$, $t = 1, \ldots, T$, $i = 1, \ldots, N$. Because the y_{it} will be dependent condition on $\mathbf{x}_i$, inference that is robust to arbitrary time dependence is required.

Conveniently, once we have estimated ψ_a, $\boldsymbol{\beta}_a$, and ξ_a, we can estimate the average partial effects. (We could apply the results from Section 2.2.5 here, but a direct argument is instructive.) To see how, we need to average $\mathrm{P}(y_t = 1 \mid \mathbf{x}_t = \mathbf{x}^o, c_i)$ across the distribution of c_i; that is, we need to find $\mathrm{E}[\mathrm{P}(y_t = 1 \mid \mathbf{x}_t = \mathbf{x}^o, c_i)] = \mathrm{E}[\Phi(\mathbf{x}^o\boldsymbol{\beta} + c_i)]$ for any given value $\mathbf{x}^o$ of the explanatory variables. (In what follows, $\mathbf{x}^o$ is a nonrandom vector of numbers that we choose as interesting values of the explanatory variables. For emphasis, we include an i subscript on the random variables appearing in the expectations.) Writing $c_i = \psi + \bar{\mathbf{x}}_i\xi + a_i$ and using iterated expectations, we have $\mathrm{E}[\Phi(\psi + \mathbf{x}^{\mathrm{o}}\boldsymbol{\beta} + \bar{\mathbf{x}}_i\xi + a_i)] = \mathrm{E}[\mathrm{E}\{\Phi(\psi + \mathbf{x}^{\mathrm{o}}\boldsymbol{\beta} + \bar{\mathbf{x}}_i\xi + a_i) \mid \mathbf{x}_i\}]$ [where the first expectation is with respect to $(\mathbf{x}_i, a_i)$]. Using the same argument from Section 15.7.1, $\mathrm{E}[\Phi(\psi + \mathbf{x}^{\mathrm{o}}\boldsymbol{\beta} + \bar{\mathbf{x}}_i\xi + a_i) \mid \mathbf{x}_i] = \Phi[\{\psi + \mathbf{x}^{\mathrm{o}}\boldsymbol{\beta} + \bar{\mathbf{x}}_i\xi\} \cdot (1 + \sigma_a^2)^{-1/2}] = \Phi(\psi_a + \mathbf{x}^{\mathrm{o}}\boldsymbol{\beta}_a + \bar{\mathbf{x}}_i\xi_a)$, and so

$$\mathrm{E}[\Phi(\mathbf{x}^{\mathrm{o}}\boldsymbol{\beta} + c_i)] = \mathrm{E}[\Phi(\psi_a + \mathbf{x}^{\mathrm{o}}\boldsymbol{\beta}_a + \bar{\mathbf{x}}_i\xi_a)] \tag{15.69}$$

Because the only random variable in the right-hand-side expectation is $\bar{\mathbf{x}}_i$, a consistent estimator of the right-hand side of equation (15.66) is simply

$$N^{-1}\sum_{i=1}^{N}\Phi(\hat{\psi}_a + \mathbf{x}^{\mathrm{o}}\hat{\boldsymbol{\beta}}_a + \bar{\mathbf{x}}_i\hat{\xi}_a) \tag{15.70}$$

Average partial effects can be estimated by evaluating expression (15.70) at two different values for $\mathbf{x}^{\mathrm{o}}$ and forming the difference, or, for continuous variable x_j, by using the average across i of $\hat{\beta}_{aj}\phi(\hat{\psi}_a + \mathbf{x}^{\mathrm{o}}\hat{\boldsymbol{\beta}}_a + \bar{\mathbf{x}}_i\hat{\xi}_a)$ to get the approximate APE of a one-unit increase in x_j. See also Chamberlain [1984, equation (3.4)]. If we use Chamberlain's more general version of assumption (15.67), $\mathbf{x}_i$ replaces $\bar{\mathbf{x}}_i$ everywhere. [Incidentally, the focus on the APEs raises an interesting, and apparently open, question: How does treating the c_i's as parameters to estimate—in a "fixed effects probit" analysis—affect estimation of the APEs? Given $\hat{c}_i$, $i = 1, \ldots, N$ and $\hat{\boldsymbol{\beta}}$, the APEs could be based on $N^{-1}\sum_{i=1}^{N}\Phi(\hat{c}_i + \mathbf{x}^{\mathrm{o}}\hat{\boldsymbol{\beta}})$. Even though $\hat{\boldsymbol{\beta}}$ does not consistently estimate $\boldsymbol{\beta}$ and the $\hat{c}_i$ are estimates of the incidental parameters, it could be that the resulting estimates of the APEs have reasonable properties.]

Under assumption (15.60) and the more general version of assumption (15.67), Chamberlain (1980) suggested a minimum distance approach analogous to the linear case (see Section 14.6). Namely, obtain $\hat{\boldsymbol{\pi}}_t$ for each t by running a cross-sectional probit of y_{it} on 1, $\mathbf{x}_i$, $i = 1, \ldots, N$. The mapping from the structural parameters $\boldsymbol{\theta}_a \equiv (\psi_a, \boldsymbol{\beta}_a', \xi_a')'$ to the vector $\boldsymbol{\pi}$ is exactly as in the linear case (see Section 14.6). The variance matrix estimator for $\hat{\boldsymbol{\pi}}$ is obtained by pooling all T probits and computing the robust variance matrix estimator in equation (13.53), with $\hat{\boldsymbol{\theta}}$ replaced by $\hat{\boldsymbol{\pi}}$; see also Chamberlain (1984, Section 4.5). The minimum distance approach leads to a straightforward test of H_0: $\xi_a = \mathbf{0}$, which is a test of assumption (15.63) that does not impose assumption (15.61).

All of the previous estimation methods hinge crucially on the strict exogeneity of $\{\mathbf{x}_{it}: t = 1, \ldots, T\}$, conditional on c_i. As mentioned earlier, this assumption rules out lagged dependent variables, a case we consider explicitly in Section 15.8.4. But there are other cases where strict exogeneity is questionable. For example, suppose that y_{it} is an employment indicator for person i in period t and w_{it} is measure of recent arrests. It is possible that whether someone is employed this period has an effect on future arrests. If so, then shocks that affect employment status could be correlated with future arrests, and such correlation would violate strict exogeneity. Whether this situation is empirically important is largely unknown.

On the one hand, correcting for an explanatory variable that is not strictly exogenous is quite difficult in nonlinear models; Wooldridge (2000c) suggests one possible approach. On the other hand, obtaining a test of strict exogeneity is fairly easy. Let $\mathbf{w}_{it}$ denote a $1 \times G$ subset of $\mathbf{x}_{it}$ that we suspect of failing the strict exogeneity requirement. Then a simple test is to add $\mathbf{w}_{i,t+1}$ as an additional set of covariates; under the null hypothesis, $\mathbf{w}_{i,t+1}$ should be insignificant. In implementing this test, we can use either random effects probit or pooled probit, where, in either case, we lose the last time period. (In the pooled probit case, we should use a fully robust Wald or score test.) We should still obtain $\bar{\mathbf{x}}_i$ from all T time periods, as the test is either based on the distribution of $(y_{i1}, \ldots, y_{i,T-1})$ given $(\mathbf{x}_{i1}, \ldots, \mathbf{x}_{iT})$ (random effects probit) or on the marginal distributions of y_{it} given $(\mathbf{x}_{i1}, \ldots, \mathbf{x}_{iT})$, $t = 1, \ldots, T-1$ (pooled probit). If the test does not reject, it provides at least some justification for the strict exogeneity assumption.

15.8.3 Unobserved Effects Logit Models under Strict Exogeneity

The unobserved effects probit models of the previous subsection have logit counterparts. If we replace the standard normal cdf Φ in assumption (15.60) with the logistic function Λ, and also maintain assumptions (15.61) and (15.63), we arrive at what is usually called the **random effects logit model**. This model is not as attractive as the random effects probit model because there are no simple estimators available. The normal distribution, with its property that linear combinations of normals are normally distributed, facilitates the pooled probit, random effects, and minimum distance estimation approaches. By contrast, in the random effects logit model, $\mathrm{P}(y_{it} = 1 \mid \mathbf{x}_i)$ has no simple form: integrating the logit response $\Lambda(\mathbf{x}_t\boldsymbol{\beta} + c)$ with respect to the normal density $(1/\sigma_c)\phi(c/\sigma_c)$ yields no simple functional form. This statement is also true of other popular continuous distributions for c.

There is one important advantage of the unobserved effects logit model over the probit model: under assumptions (15.60) (with Φ replaced by Λ) and (15.61), it is possible to obtain a $\sqrt{N}$-consistent estimator of $\boldsymbol{\beta}$ without *any* assumptions about how c_i is related to $\mathbf{x}_i$.

How can we allow c_i and $\mathbf{x}_i$ to be arbitrarily related in the unobserved effects logit model? In the linear case we used the FE or FD transformation to eliminate c_i from the estimating equation. It turns out that a similar strategy works in the logit case, although the argument is more subtle. What we do is find the joint distribution of $\mathbf{y}_i \equiv (y_{i1}, \ldots, y_{iT})'$ conditional on $\mathbf{x}_i, c_i,$ *and* $n_i \equiv \sum_{t=1}^{T} y_{it}$. It turns out that this conditional distribution does not depend on c_i, so that it is also the distribution of $\mathbf{y}_i$ given $\mathbf{x}_i$ and n_i. Therefore, we can use standard conditional maximum likelihood methods to estimate $\boldsymbol{\beta}$. (The fact that we can find a conditional distribution that does not depend on the c_i is a feature of the logit functional form. Unfortunately, the same argument does not work for the unobserved effects probit model.)

First consider the $T = 2$ case, where n_i takes a value in $\{0, 1, 2\}$. Intuitively, the conditional distribution of $(y_{i1}, y_{i2})'$ given n_i cannot be informative for $\boldsymbol{\beta}$ when $n_i = 0$ or $n_i = 2$ because these values completely determine the outcome on $\mathbf{y}_i$. However, for $n_i = 1$,

$$
\begin{aligned}
\mathrm{P}(y_{i2} = 1 \mid \mathbf{x}_i, c_i, n_i = 1) &= \mathrm{P}(y_{i2} = 1, n_i = 1 \mid \mathbf{x}_i, c_i)/\mathrm{P}(n_i = 1 \mid \mathbf{x}_i, c_i) \\
&= \mathrm{P}(y_{i2} = 1 \mid \mathbf{x}_i, c_i)\mathrm{P}(y_{i1} = 0 \mid \mathbf{x}_i, c_i)/\{\mathrm{P}(y_{i1} = 0, y_{i2} = 1 \mid \mathbf{x}_i, c_i) \\
&\quad + \mathrm{P}(y_{i1} = 1, y_{i2} = 0 \mid \mathbf{x}_i, c_i)\} \\
&= \Lambda(\mathbf{x}_{i2}\boldsymbol{\beta} + c_i)[1 - \Lambda(\mathbf{x}_{i1}\boldsymbol{\beta} + c_i)]/\{[1 - \Lambda(\mathbf{x}_{i1}\boldsymbol{\beta} + c_i)]\Lambda(\mathbf{x}_{i2}\boldsymbol{\beta} + c_i) \\
&\quad + \Lambda(\mathbf{x}_{i1}\boldsymbol{\beta} + c_i)[1 - \Lambda(\mathbf{x}_{i2}\boldsymbol{\beta} + c_i)]\} = \Lambda[(\mathbf{x}_{i2} - \mathbf{x}_{i1})\boldsymbol{\beta}]
\end{aligned}
$$

Similarly, $\mathrm{P}(y_{i1} = 1 \mid \mathbf{x}_i, c_i, n_i = 1) = \Lambda[-(\mathbf{x}_{i2} - \mathbf{x}_{i1})\boldsymbol{\beta}] = 1 - \Lambda[(\mathbf{x}_{i2} - \mathbf{x}_{i1})\boldsymbol{\beta}]$. The conditional log likelihood for observation i is

$$
\ell_i(\boldsymbol{\beta}) = 1[n_i = 1](w_i \log \Lambda[(\mathbf{x}_{i2} - \mathbf{x}_{i1})\boldsymbol{\beta}] + (1 - w_i) \log\{1 - \Lambda[(\mathbf{x}_{i2} - \mathbf{x}_{i1})\boldsymbol{\beta}]\}) \quad (15.71)
$$

where $w_i = 1$ if $(y_{i1} = 0, y_{i2} = 1)$ and $w_i = 0$ if $(y_{i1} = 1, y_{i2} = 0)$. The conditional MLE is obtained by maximizing the sum of the $\ell_i(\boldsymbol{\beta})$ across i. The indicator function $1[n_i = 1]$ selects out the observations for which $n_i = 1$; as stated earlier, observations for which $n_i = 0$ or $n_i = 2$ do not contribute to the log likelihood. Interestingly, equation (15.71) is just a standard cross-sectional logit of w_i on $(\mathbf{x}_{i2} - \mathbf{x}_{i1})$ using the observations for which $n_i = 1$. (This approach is analogous to differencing in the linear case with $T = 2$.)

The conditional MLE from equation (15.71) is usually called the **fixed effects logit estimator**. We must emphasize that the FE logit estimator does *not* arise by treating the c_i as parameters to be estimated along with $\boldsymbol{\beta}$. (This fact is confusing, as the FE probit estimator *does* estimate the c_i along with $\boldsymbol{\beta}$.) As shown recently by Abrevaya

(1997), the MLE of $\boldsymbol{\beta}$ that is obtained by maximizing the log likelihood over $\boldsymbol{\beta}$ and the c_i has probability limit $2\boldsymbol{\beta}$. (This finding extends a simple example due to Andersen, 1970; see also Hsiao, 1986, Section 7.3.)

Sometimes the conditional MLE is described as "conditioning on the unobserved effects in the sample." This description is misleading. What we have done is found a conditional density—which describes the subpopulation with $n_i = 1$—that depends only on observable data and the parameter $\boldsymbol{\beta}$.

For general T the log likelihood is more complicated, but it is tractable. First,

$$\mathrm{P}(y_{i1} = y_1, \ldots, y_{iT} = y_T \mid \mathbf{x}_i, c_i, n_i = n)$$
$$= \mathrm{P}(y_{i1} = y_1, \ldots, y_{iT} = y_T \mid \mathbf{x}_i, c_i)/\mathrm{P}(n_i = n \mid \mathbf{x}_i, c_i) \tag{15.72}$$

and the numerator factors as $\mathrm{P}(y_{i1} = y_1 \mid \mathbf{x}_i, c_i) \cdots \mathrm{P}(y_{iT} = y_T \mid \mathbf{x}_i, c_i)$ by the conditional independence assumption. The denominator is the complicated part, but it is easy to describe: $\mathrm{P}(n_i = n \mid \mathbf{x}_i, c_i)$ is the sum of the probabilities of all possible outcomes of $\mathbf{y}_i$ such that $n_i = n$. Using the specific form of the logit function we can write

$$\ell_i(\boldsymbol{\beta}) = \log\left\{\exp\left(\sum_{t=1}^{T} y_{it}\mathbf{x}_{it}\boldsymbol{\beta}\right)\left[\sum_{\mathbf{a} \in R_i} \exp\left(\sum_{t=1}^{T} a_t\mathbf{x}_{it}\boldsymbol{\beta}\right)\right]^{-1}\right\} \tag{15.73}$$

where R_i is the subset of $\mathbb{R}^T$ defined as $\{\mathbf{a} \in \mathbb{R}^T: a_t \in \{0, 1\} \text{ and } \sum_{t=1}^{T} a_t = n_i\}$. The log likelihood summed across i can be used to obtain a $\sqrt{N}$-asymptotically normal estimator of $\boldsymbol{\beta}$, and all inference follows from conditional MLE theory. Observations for which equation (15.72) is zero or unity—and which therefore do not depend on $\boldsymbol{\beta}$—drop out of $\mathscr{L}(\boldsymbol{\beta})$. See Chamberlain (1984).

The fixed effects logit estimator $\hat{\boldsymbol{\beta}}$ immediately gives us the effect of each element of $\mathbf{x}_t$ on the log-odds ratio, $\log\{\Lambda(\mathbf{x}_t\boldsymbol{\beta} + c)/[1 - \Lambda(\mathbf{x}_t\boldsymbol{\beta} + c)]\} = \mathbf{x}_t\boldsymbol{\beta} + c$. Unfortunately, we cannot estimate the partial effects on the response probabilities unless we plug in a value for c. Because the distribution of c_i is unrestricted—in particular, $\mathrm{E}(c_i)$ is not necessarily zero—it is hard to know what to plug in for c. In addition, we cannot estimate average partial effects, as doing so would require finding $\mathrm{E}[\Lambda(\mathbf{x}_t\boldsymbol{\beta} + c_i)]$, a task that apparently requires specifying a distribution for c_i.

The conditional logit approach also has the drawback of apparently requiring the conditional independence assumption (15.61) for consistency. As we saw in Section 15.8.2, if we are willing to make the normality assumption (15.67), the probit approach allows unrestricted serial dependence in y_{it} even after conditioning on $\mathbf{x}_i$ and c_i. This possibility may be especially important when several time periods are available.

15.8.4 Dynamic Unobserved Effects Models

Dynamic models that also contain unobserved effects are important in testing theories and evaluating policies. Here we cover one class of models that illustrates the important points for general dynamic models and is of considerable interest in its own right.

Suppose we date our observations starting at $t = 0$, so that y_{i0} is the first observation on y. For $t = 1, \ldots, T$ we are interested in the dynamic unobserved effects model

$$\mathrm{P}(y_{it} = 1 \mid y_{i,t-1}, \ldots, y_{i0}, \mathbf{z}_i, c_i) = G(\mathbf{z}_{it}\boldsymbol{\delta} + \rho y_{i,t-1} + c_i) \tag{15.74}$$

where $\mathbf{z}_{it}$ is a vector of contemporaneous explanatory variables, $\mathbf{z}_i = (\mathbf{z}_{i1}, \ldots, \mathbf{z}_{iT})$, and G can be the probit or logit function. There are several important points about this model. First, the $\mathbf{z}_{it}$ are assumed to satisfy a strict exogeneity assumption (conditional on c_i), since $\mathbf{z}_i$ appears in the conditioning set on the left-hand side of equation (15.74), but only $\mathbf{z}_{it}$ appears on the right-hand side. Second, the probability of success at time t is allowed to depend on the outcome in $t - 1$ as well as unobserved heterogeneity, c_i. We saw the linear version in Section 11.1.1. Of particular interest is the hypothesis H_0: $\rho = 0$. Under this null, the response probability at time t does not depend on past outcomes once c_i (and $\mathbf{z}_i$) have been controlled for. Even if $\rho = 0$, $\mathrm{P}(y_{it} = 1 \mid y_{i,t-1}, \mathbf{z}_i) \neq \mathrm{P}(y_{it} = 1 \mid \mathbf{z}_i)$ owing to the presence of c_i. But economists are interested in whether there is **state dependence**—that is, $\rho \neq 0$ in equation (15.74)—*after* controlling for the unobserved heterogeneity, c_i.

We might also be interested in the effects of $\mathbf{z}_t$, as it may contain policy variables. Then, equation (15.74) simply captures the fact that, in addition to an unobserved effect, behavior may depend on past observed behavior.

How can we estimate $\boldsymbol{\delta}$ and ρ in equation (15.74), in addition to quantities such as average partial effects? First, we can always write

$$\begin{aligned} f(y_1, y_2, \ldots, y_T \mid y_0, \mathbf{z}, c; \boldsymbol{\beta}) &= \prod_{t=1}^{T} f(y_t \mid y_{t-1}, \ldots y_1, y_0, \mathbf{z}_t, c; \boldsymbol{\beta}) \\ &= \prod_{t=1}^{T} G(\mathbf{z}_t\boldsymbol{\delta} + \rho y_{t-1} + c)^{y_t}[1 - G(\mathbf{z}_t\boldsymbol{\delta} + \rho y_{t-1} + c)]^{1-y_t} \end{aligned} \tag{15.75}$$

With fixed-T asymptotics, this density, because of the unobserved effect c, does not allow us to construct a log-likelihood function that can be used to estimate $\boldsymbol{\beta}$ consistently. Just as in the case with strictly exogenous explanatory variables, treating the

c_i as parameters to be estimated does not result in consistent estimators of $\boldsymbol{\delta}$ and ρ as $N \to \infty$. In fact, the simulations in Heckman (1981) show that the incidental parameters problem is even more severe in dynamic models. What we should do is integrate out the unobserved effect c, as we discussed generally in Section 13.9.2.

Our need to integrate c out of the distribution raises the issue of how we treat the initial observations, y_{i0}; this is usually called the **initial conditions problem**. One possibility is to treat each y_{i0} as a nonstochastic starting position for each i. Then, if c_i is assumed to be independent of $\mathbf{z}_i$ (as in a pure random effects environment), equation (15.75) can be integrated against the density of c to obtain the density of $(y_1, y_2, \ldots, y_T)$ given $\mathbf{z}$; this density also depends on y_0 through $f(y_1 \mid y_0, c, \mathbf{z}_1; \boldsymbol{\beta})$. We can then apply conditional MLE. Although treating the y_{i0} as nonrandom simplifies estimation, it is undesirable because it effectively means that c_i and y_{i0} are independent, a very strong assumption.

Another possibility is to first specify a density for y_{i0} given $(\mathbf{z}_i, c_i)$ and to multiply this density by equation (15.75) to obtain $f(y_0, y_1, y_2, \ldots, y_T \mid \mathbf{z}, c; \boldsymbol{\beta}, \gamma)$. Next, a density for c_i given $\mathbf{z}_i$ can be specified. Finally, $f(y_0, y_1, y_2, \ldots, y_T \mid \mathbf{z}, c; \boldsymbol{\beta}, \gamma)$ is integrated against the density $h(c \mid \mathbf{z}; \boldsymbol{\alpha})$ to obtain the density of $(y_{i0}, y_{i1}, y_{i2}, \ldots, y_{iT})$ given $\mathbf{z}_i$. This density can then be used in an MLE analysis. The problem with this approach is that finding the density of y_{i0} given $(\mathbf{z}_i, c_i)$ is very difficult, if not impossible, even if the process is assumed to be in equilibrium. For discussion, see Hsiao (1986, Section 7.4).

Heckman (1981) suggests approximating the conditional density of y_{i0} given $(\mathbf{z}_i, c_i)$ and then specifying a density for c_i given $\mathbf{z}_i$. For example, we might assume that y_{i0} follows a probit model with success probability $\Phi(\eta + \mathbf{z}_i\boldsymbol{\pi} + \gamma c_i)$ and specify the density of c_i given $\mathbf{z}_i$ as normal. Once these two densities are given, they can be multiplied by equation (15.75), and c can be integrated out to approximate the density of $(y_{i0}, y_{i1}, y_{i2}, \ldots, y_{iT})$ given $\mathbf{z}_i$; see Hsiao (1986, Section 7.4).

Heckman's (1981) approach attempts to find or approximate the joint distribution of $(y_{i0}, y_{i1}, y_{i2}, \ldots, y_{iT})$ given $\mathbf{z}_i$. We discussed an alternative approach in Section 13.9.2: obtain the joint distribution of $(y_{i1}, y_{i2}, \ldots, y_{iT})$ conditional on $(y_{i0}, \mathbf{z}_i)$. This allows us to remain agnostic about the distribution of y_{i0} given $(\mathbf{z}_i, c_i)$, which is the primary source of difficulty in Heckman's approach. If we can find the density of $(y_{i1}, y_{i2}, \ldots, y_{iT})$ given $(y_{i0}, \mathbf{z}_i)$, in terms of $\boldsymbol{\beta}$ and other parameters, then we can use standard conditional maximum likelihood methods: we are simply conditioning on y_{i0} in addition to $\mathbf{z}_i$. It is important to see that using the density of $(y_{i1}, y_{i2}, \ldots, y_{iT})$ given $(y_{i0}, \mathbf{z}_i)$ is *not* the same as treating y_{i0} as nonrandom. Indeed, the model with c_i independent of y_{i0}, given $\mathbf{z}_i$, is a special case.

To obtain $f(y_1, y_2, \ldots, y_T \mid y_{i0}, \mathbf{z}_i)$, we need to propose a density for c_i given $(y_{i0}, \mathbf{z}_i)$. This approach is very much like Chamberlain's (1980) approach to static probit models with unobserved effects, except that we now condition on y_{i0} as well. [Since the density of c_i given $\mathbf{z}_i$ is not restricted by the specification (15.75), our choice of the density of c_i given $(y_{i0}, \mathbf{z}_i)$ is not logically restricted in any way.] Given a density $h(c \mid y_0, \mathbf{z}; \gamma)$, which depends on a vector of parameters γ, we have

$$f(y_1, y_2, \ldots, y_T \mid y_0, \mathbf{z}, \boldsymbol{\theta}) = \int_{-\infty}^{\infty} f(y_1, y_2, \ldots, y_T \mid y_0, \mathbf{z}, c; \boldsymbol{\beta}) h(c \mid y_0, \mathbf{z}; \gamma)\, \mathrm{d}c$$

See Property CD.2 in Chapter 13. The integral can be replaced with a weighted average if the distribution of c is discrete. When $G = \Phi$ in the model (15.74)—the leading case—a very convenient choice for $h(c \mid y_0, \mathbf{z}; \gamma)$ is $\text{Normal}(\psi + \xi_0 y_{i0} + \mathbf{z}_i \xi, \sigma_a^2)$, which follows by writing $c_i = \psi + \xi_0 y_{i0} + \mathbf{z}_i \xi + a_i$, where $a_i \sim \text{Normal}(0, \sigma_a^2)$ and independent of $(y_{i0}, \mathbf{z}_i)$. Then we can write

$$y_{it} = 1[\psi + \mathbf{z}_{it}\boldsymbol{\delta} + \rho y_{i,t-1} + \xi_0 y_{i0} + \mathbf{z}_i \xi + a_i + e_{it} > 0]$$

so that y_{it} given $(y_{i,t-1}, \ldots, y_{i0}, \mathbf{z}_i, a_i)$ follows a probit model and a_i given $(y_{i0}, \mathbf{z}_i)$ is distributed as $\text{Normal}(0, \sigma_a^2)$. Therefore, the density of $(y_{i1}, \ldots, y_{iT})$ given $(y_{i0}, \mathbf{z}_i)$ has exactly the form in equation (15.64), where $\mathbf{x}_{it} = (1, \mathbf{z}_{it}, y_{i,t-1}, y_{i0}, \mathbf{z}_i)$ and with a and σ_a replacing c and σ_c, respectively. Conveniently, this result means that we can use standard random effects probit software to estimate ψ, $\boldsymbol{\delta}$, ρ, ξ_0, ξ, and σ_a^2: we simply expand the list of explanatory variables to include y_{i0} and $\mathbf{z}_i$ in *each* time period. (The approach that treats y_{i0} and $\mathbf{z}_i$ as fixed omits y_{i0} and $\mathbf{z}_i$ in each time period.) It is simple to test H_0: $\rho = 0$, which means there is no state dependence once we control for an unobserved effect.

Average partial effects can be estimated as in Chamberlain's unobserved effects probit model: for given values of $\mathbf{z}_t(\mathbf{z}^{\text{o}})$ and $y_{t-1}(y_{-1}^{\text{o}})$, $\text{E}[\Phi(\mathbf{z}^{\text{o}}\boldsymbol{\delta} + \rho y_{-1}^{\text{o}} + c_i)]$ is consistently estimated by $N^{-1}\sum_{i=1}^{N} \Phi(\hat{\psi}_a + \mathbf{z}^{\text{o}}\hat{\boldsymbol{\delta}}_a + \hat{\rho}_a y_{-1}^{\text{o}} + \hat{\xi}_{a0} y_{i0} + \mathbf{z}_i \hat{\xi}_a)$, where the a subscript denotes multiplication by $(1 + \hat{\sigma}_a^2)^{-1/2}$, and $\hat{\psi}$, $\hat{\boldsymbol{\delta}}$, $\hat{\rho}$, $\hat{\xi}_0$, $\hat{\xi}$, and $\hat{\sigma}_a^2$ are the conditional MLEs. See Wooldridge (2000e) for additional details. A mean value expansion can be used to obtain asymptotic standard errors for the APEs, or a bootstrapping approach, as described in Section 12.8.2, can be used.

15.8.5 Semiparametric Approaches

Under strict exogeneity of the explanatory variables, it is possible to consistently estimate $\boldsymbol{\beta}$ up to scale under very weak assumptions. Manski (1987) derives an objective function that identifies $\boldsymbol{\beta}$ up to scale in the $T = 2$ case when e_{i1} and e_{i2} in the model (15.66) are identically distributed conditional on $(\mathbf{x}_{i1}, \mathbf{x}_{i2}, c_i)$ and $\mathbf{x}_{it}$ is strictly exogenous. The estimator is the maximum score estimator applied to the differences Δy_i and $\Delta \mathbf{x}_i$. As in the cross-sectional case, it is not known how to estimate the average response probabilities.

Honoré and Kyriazidou (2000a) show how to estimate the parameters in the unobserved effects logit model with a lagged dependent variable and strictly exogenous explanatory variables without making distributional assumptions about the unobserved effect. Unfortunately, the estimators, which are consistent and asymptotically normal, do not generally converge at the usual $\sqrt{N}$ rate. In addition, as with many semiparametric approaches, discrete explanatory variables such as time dummies are ruled out, and it is not possible to estimate the average partial effects. See also Arellano and Honoré (in press).

15.8.6 Cluster Samples

In Section 13.8 we noted how partial MLE methods can be applied to cluster samples, and binary choice models are no exception. For cluster i and unit g, we might specify $\mathrm{P}(y_{ig} = 1 \mid \mathbf{x}_{ig}) = \Phi(\mathbf{x}_{ig}\boldsymbol{\beta})$, and then estimate $\boldsymbol{\beta}$ using a pooled probit analysis. (Replacing Φ with Λ gives pooled logit.) A robust variance matrix is needed to account for any within-cluster correlation due, say, to unobserved cluster effects. The formula is given in equation (13.53), except that g replaces t, and G_i, the size of cluster i, replaces T everywhere. This estimator is valid as $N \to \infty$ with G_i fixed.

We can also test for peer group effects by including among $\mathbf{x}_{ig}$ the average (or other summary statistics) of variables within the same cluster. In this scenario there are almost certainly unobserved cluster effects, so statistics robust to intercluster correlation should be computed.

An alternative to pooled probit or logit is to use an unobserved effect framework explicitly. For example, we might have $\mathrm{P}(y_{ig} = 1 \mid \mathbf{x}_i, c_i) = \Phi(\mathbf{x}_{ig}\boldsymbol{\beta} + c_i)$, where c_i is an unobserved cluster effect. If observations are assumed independent within cluster conditional on $(\mathbf{x}_i, c_i)$, and if c_i is independent of $\mathbf{x}_i$, then the random effects probit MLE is easily modified: just use equation (15.64) with $t = g$ and $T = G_i$. The fact that the observations are no longer identically distributed across i has no practical implications. Allowing c_i and $\mathbf{x}_i$ to be correlated in the context of cluster sampling is easy if we maintain assumption (15.67) regardless of the cluster size. The details are essentially the same as the panel data case.

When $G_i = 2$ for all i, the fixed effects logit approach is straightforward. Geronimus and Korenman (1992) use sister pairs to determine the effects of teenage motherhood on subsequent economic outcomes. When the outcome is binary (such as an employment indicator), Geronimus and Korenman allow for an unobserved family effect by applying fixed effects logit.

15.9 Multinomial Response Models

15.9.1 Multinomial Logit

The logit model for binary outcomes extends to the case where the **unordered response** has more than two outcomes. Examples of unordered multinomial responses include occupational choice, choice of health plan, and transportation mode for commuting to work. In each case, an individual chooses one alternative from the group of choices, and the labeling of the choices is arbitrary. Let y denote a random variable taking on the values $\{0, 1, \ldots, J\}$ for J a positive integer, and let $\mathbf{x}$ denote a set of conditioning variables. For example, if y denotes occupational choice, $\mathbf{x}$ can contain things like education, age, gender, race, and marital status. As usual, $(\mathbf{x}_i, y_i)$ is a random draw from the population.

As in the binary response case, we are interested in how ceteris paribus changes in the elements of $\mathbf{x}$ affect the response probabilities, $\mathrm{P}(y = j \mid \mathbf{x})$, $j = 0, 1, 2, \ldots, J$. Since the probabilities must sum to unity, $\mathrm{P}(y = 0 \mid \mathbf{x})$ is determined once we know the probabilities for $j = 1, \ldots, J$.

Let $\mathbf{x}$ be a $1 \times K$ vector with first-element unity. The **multinomial logit (MNL) model** has response probabilities

$$\mathrm{P}(y = j \mid \mathbf{x}) = \exp(\mathbf{x}\boldsymbol{\beta}_j) \bigg/ \left[1 + \sum_{h=1}^{J} \exp(\mathbf{x}\boldsymbol{\beta}_h)\right], \qquad j = 1, \ldots, J \tag{15.76}$$

where $\boldsymbol{\beta}_j$ is $K \times 1$, $j = 1, \ldots, J$. Because the response probabilities must sum to unity,

$$\mathrm{P}(y = 0 \mid \mathbf{x}) = 1 \bigg/ \left[1 + \sum_{h=1}^{J} \exp(\mathbf{x}\boldsymbol{\beta}_h)\right]$$

When $J = 1$, $\boldsymbol{\beta}_1$ is the $K \times 1$ vector of unknown parameters, and we get the binary logit model.

The partial effects for this model are complicated. For continuous x_k, we can write

$$\frac{\partial \mathrm{P}(y = j \mid \mathbf{x})}{\partial x_k} = \mathrm{P}(y = j \mid \mathbf{x}) \left\{ \beta_{jk} - \left[\sum_{h=1}^{J} \beta_{hk} \exp(\mathbf{x}\boldsymbol{\beta}_h)\right] \bigg/ g(\mathbf{x}, \boldsymbol{\beta}) \right\} \tag{15.77}$$

where β_{hk} is the kth element of $\boldsymbol{\beta}_h$ and $g(\mathbf{x}, \boldsymbol{\beta}) = 1 + \sum_{h=1}^{J} \exp(\mathbf{x}\boldsymbol{\beta}_h)$. Equation

(15.77) shows that even the direction of the effect is not determined entirely by β_{jk}. A simpler interpretation of $\boldsymbol{\beta}_j$ is given by

$$p_j(\mathbf{x}, \boldsymbol{\beta})/p_0(\mathbf{x}, \boldsymbol{\beta}) = \exp(\mathbf{x}\boldsymbol{\beta}_j), \qquad j = 1, 2, \ldots, J \tag{15.78}$$

where $p_j(\mathbf{x}, \boldsymbol{\beta})$ denotes the response probability in equation (15.76). Thus the change in $p_j(\mathbf{x}, \boldsymbol{\beta})/p_0(\mathbf{x}, \boldsymbol{\beta})$ is approximately $\beta_{jk} \exp(\mathbf{x}\boldsymbol{\beta}_j)\Delta x_k$ for roughly continuous x_k. Equivalently, the log-odds ratio is linear in $\mathbf{x}$: $\log[p_j(\mathbf{x}, \boldsymbol{\beta})/p_0(\mathbf{x}, \boldsymbol{\beta})] = \mathbf{x}\boldsymbol{\beta}_j$. This result extends to general j and h: $\log[p_j(\mathbf{x}, \boldsymbol{\beta})/p_h(\mathbf{x}, \boldsymbol{\beta})] = \mathbf{x}(\boldsymbol{\beta}_j - \boldsymbol{\beta}_h)$.

Here is another useful fact about the multinomial logit model. Since $\mathrm{P}(y = j$ or $y = h \mid \mathbf{x}) = p_j(\mathbf{x}, \boldsymbol{\beta}) + p_h(\mathbf{x}, \boldsymbol{\beta})$,

$$\mathrm{P}(y = j \mid y = j \text{ or } y = h, \mathbf{x}) = p_j(\mathbf{x}, \boldsymbol{\beta})/[p_j(\mathbf{x}, \boldsymbol{\beta}) + p_h(\mathbf{x}, \boldsymbol{\beta})] = \Lambda[\mathbf{x}(\boldsymbol{\beta}_j - \boldsymbol{\beta}_h)]$$

where $\Lambda(\cdot)$ is the logistic function. In other words, conditional on the choice being either j or h, the probability that the outcome is j follows a standard logit model with parameter vector $\boldsymbol{\beta}_j - \boldsymbol{\beta}_h$.

Since we have fully specified the density of y given $\mathbf{x}$, estimation of the MNL model is best carried out by maximum likelihood. For each i the conditional log likelihood can be written as

$$\ell_i(\boldsymbol{\beta}) = \sum_{j=0}^{J} 1[y_i = j] \log[p_j(\mathbf{x}_i, \boldsymbol{\beta})]$$

where the indicator function selects out the appropriate response probability for each observation i. As usual, we estimate $\boldsymbol{\beta}$ by maximizing $\sum_{i=1}^{N} \ell_i(\boldsymbol{\beta})$. McFadden (1974) has shown that the log-likelihood function is globally concave, and this fact makes the maximization problem straightforward. The conditions needed to apply Theorems 13.1 and 13.2 for consistency and asymptotic normality are broadly applicable; see McFadden (1984).

Example 15.4 (School and Employment Decisions for Young Men): The data KEANE.RAW (a subset from Keane and Wolpin, 1997) contains employment and schooling history for a sample of men for the years 1981 to 1987. We use the data for 1987. The three possible outcomes are enrolled in school ($status = 0$), not in school and not working ($status = 1$), and working ($status = 2$). The explanatory variables are education, a quadratic in past work experience, and a black binary indicator. The base category is enrolled in school. Out of 1,717 observations, 99 are enrolled in school, 332 are at home, and 1,286 are working. The results are given in Table 15.2.

Another year of education reduces the log-odds between at home and enrolled in school by $-.674$, and the log-odds between at home and enrolled in school is .813

Table 15.2
Multinomial Logit Estimates of School and Labor Market Decisions

Dependent Variable: *status*

Explanatory Variable	*home* (*status* = 1)	*work* (*status* = 2)
educ	−.674 (.070)	−.315 (.065)
exper	−.106 (.173)	.849 (.157)
$exper^2$	−.013 (.025)	−.077 (.023)
black	.813 (.303)	.311 (.282)
constant	10.28 (1.13)	5.54 (1.09)
Number of observations	1,717	
Percent correctly predicted	79.6	
Log-likelihood value	−907.86	
Pseudo R-squared	.243	

higher for black men. The magnitudes of these coefficients are difficult to interpret. Instead, we can either compute partial effects, as in equation (15.77), or compute differences in probabilities. For example, consider two black men, each with five years of experience. A black man with 16 years of education has an employment probability that is .042 higher than a man with 12 years of education, and the at-home probability is .072 lower. (Necessarily, the in-school probability is .030 higher for the man with 16 years of education.) These results are easily obtained by comparing fitted probabilities after multinomial logit estimation.

The experience terms are each insignificant in the *home* column, but the Wald test for joint significance of *exper* and $exper^2$ gives p-value = .047, and so they are jointly significant at the 5 percent level. We would probably leave their coefficients unrestricted in $\boldsymbol{\beta}_1$ rather than setting them to zero.

The fitted probabilities can be used for prediction purposes: for each observation i, the outcome with the highest estimated probability is the predicted outcome. This can be used to obtain a percent correctly predicted, by category if desired. For the previous example, the overall percent correctly predicted is almost 80 percent, but the model does a much better job of predicting that a man is employed (95.2 percent correct) than in school (12.1 percent) or at home (39.2 percent).

15.9.2 Probabilistic Choice Models

McFadden (1974) showed that a model closely related to the multinomial logit model can be obtained from an underlying utility comparison. Suppose that, for a random draw i from the underlying population (usually, but not necessarily, individuals), the utility from choosing alternative j is

$$y_{ij}^* = \mathbf{x}_{ij}\boldsymbol{\beta} + a_{ij}, \qquad j = 0, \ldots, J \tag{15.79}$$

where a_{ij}, $j = 0, 1, 2, \ldots, J$ are unobservables affecting tastes. Here, $\mathbf{x}_{ij}$ is a $1 \times K$ vector that differs across alternatives and possibly across individuals as well. For example, $\mathbf{x}_{ij}$ might contain the commute time for individual i using transportation mode j, or the co-payment required by health insurance plan j (which may or may not differ by individual). For reasons we will see, $\mathbf{x}_{ij}$ cannot contain elements that vary only across i and not j; in particular, $\mathbf{x}_{ij}$ does not contain unity. We assume that the $(J+1)$-vector $\mathbf{a}_i$ is independent of $\mathbf{x}_i$, which contains $\{\mathbf{x}_{ij}\colon j = 0, \ldots, J\}$.

Let y_i denote the choice of individual i that maximizes utility:

$$y_i = \operatorname{argmax}(y_{i0}^*, y_{i2}^*, \ldots, y_{iJ}^*)$$

so that y_i takes on a value in $\{0, 1, \ldots, J\}$. As shown by McFadden (1974), if the a_{ij}, $j = 0, \ldots, J$ are independently distributed with cdf $F(a) = \exp[-\exp(-a)]$—the **type I extreme value distribution**—then

$$\mathrm{P}(y_i = j \mid \mathbf{x}_i) = \exp(\mathbf{x}_{ij}\boldsymbol{\beta}) \Big/ \left[\sum_{h=0}^{J} \exp(\mathbf{x}_{ih}\boldsymbol{\beta})\right], \qquad j = 0, \ldots, J \tag{15.80}$$

The response probabilities in equation (15.80) constitute what is usually called the **conditional logit model**. Dropping the subscript i and differentiating shows that the marginal effects are given by

$$\partial p_j(\mathbf{x})/\partial x_{jk} = p_j(\mathbf{x})[1 - p_j(\mathbf{x})]\beta_k, \qquad j = 0, \ldots, J, \; k = 1, \ldots, K \tag{15.81}$$

and

$$\partial p_j(\mathbf{x})/\partial x_{hk} = -p_j(\mathbf{x})p_h(\mathbf{x})\beta_k, \qquad j \neq h, \; k = 1, \ldots, K \tag{15.82}$$

where $p_j(\mathbf{x})$ is the response probability in equation (15.80) and β_k is the kth element of $\boldsymbol{\beta}$. As usual, if the $\mathbf{x}_j$ contain nonlinear functions of underlying explanatory variables, this fact will be reflected in the partial derivatives.

The conditional logit and multinomial logit models have similar response probabilities, but they differ in some important respects. In the MNL model, the conditioning variables do not change across alternative: for each i, $\mathbf{x}_i$ contains variables specific to the individual but not to the alternatives. This model is appropriate for problems where characteristics of the alternatives are unimportant or are not of interest, or where the data are simply not available. For example, in a model of occupational choice, we do not usually know how much someone could make in every occupation. What we can usually collect data on are things that affect individual productivity and tastes, such as education and past experience. The MNL model allows these characteristics to have different effects on the relative probabilities between any two choices.

The conditional logit model is intended specifically for problems where consumer or firm choices are at least partly made based on observable attributes of each alternative. The utility level of each choice is assumed to be a linear function in choice attributes, $\mathbf{x}_{ij}$, with common parameter vector $\boldsymbol{\beta}$. This turns out to actually contain the MNL model as a special case by appropriately choosing $\mathbf{x}_{ij}$. Suppose that $\mathbf{w}_i$ is a vector of individual characteristics and that $\mathrm{P}(y_i = j \mid \mathbf{w}_i)$ follows the MNL in equation (15.76) with parameters $\boldsymbol{\delta}_j$, $j = 1, \ldots, J$. We can cast this model as the conditional logit model by defining $\mathbf{x}_{ij} = (d1_j\mathbf{w}_i, d2_j\mathbf{w}_i, \ldots, dJ_j\mathbf{w}_i)$, where dj_h is a dummy variable equal to unity when $j = h$, and $\boldsymbol{\beta} = (\boldsymbol{\delta}_1', \ldots, \boldsymbol{\delta}_J')'$. Consequently, some authors refer to the conditional logit model as the multinomial logit model, with the understanding that alternative-specific characteristics are allowed in the response probability.

Empirical applications of the conditional logit model often include individual-specific variables by allowing them to have separate effects on the latent utilities. A general model is

$$y_{ij}^* = \mathbf{z}_{ij}\boldsymbol{\gamma} + \mathbf{w}_i\boldsymbol{\delta}_j + a_{ij}, \qquad j = 0, 1, \ldots, J$$

with $\boldsymbol{\delta}_0 = \mathbf{0}$ as a normalization, where $\mathbf{z}_{ij}$ varies across j and possibly i. If $\boldsymbol{\delta}_j = \boldsymbol{\delta}$ for all j, then $\mathbf{w}_i\boldsymbol{\delta}$ drops out of all response probabilities.

The conditional logit model is very convenient for modeling probabilistic choice, but it has some limitations. An important restriction is

$$p_j(\mathbf{x}_j)/p_h(\mathbf{x}_h) = \exp(\mathbf{x}_j\boldsymbol{\beta})/\exp(\mathbf{x}_h\boldsymbol{\beta}) = \exp[(\mathbf{x}_j - \mathbf{x}_h)\boldsymbol{\beta}] \tag{15.83}$$

so that relative probabilities for any two alternatives depend only on the attributes of those two alternatives. This is called the **independence from irrelevant alternatives (IIA) assumption** because it implies that adding another alernative or changing the characteristics of a third alternative does not affect the relative odds between alternatives j and h. This implication is implausible for applications with similar alternatives. A well-known example is due to McFadden (1974). Consider commuters initially choosing between two modes of transportation, car and red bus. Suppose that a consumer chooses between the buses with equal probability, .5, so that the ratio in equation (15.83) is unity. Now suppose a third mode, blue bus, is added. Assuming bus commuters do not care about the color of the bus, consumers will choose between these with equal probability. But then IIA implies that the probability of each mode is $\frac{1}{3}$; therefore, the fraction of commuters taking a car would fall from $\frac{1}{2}$ to $\frac{1}{3}$, a result that is not very realistic. This example is admittedly extreme—in practice, we would lump the blue bus and red bus into the same category, provided there are no other differences—but it indicates that the IIA property can impose unwanted restrictions in the conditional logit model.

Hausman and McFadden (1984) offer tests of the IIA assumption based on the observation that, if the conditional logit model is true, $\boldsymbol{\beta}$ can be consistently estimated by conditional logit by focusing on any subset of alternatives. They apply the Hausman principle that compares the estimate of $\boldsymbol{\beta}$ using all alternatives to the estimate using a subset of alternatives.

Several models that relax the IIA assumption have been suggested. In the context of the random utility model the IIA assumption comes about because the $\{a_{ij}: j = 0, 1, \ldots, J\}$ are assumed to be independent Wiebull random variables. A more flexible assumption is that $\mathbf{a}_i$ has a multivariate normal distribution with arbitrary correlations between a_{ij} and a_{ih}, all $j \neq h$. The resulting model is called the **multinomial probit model**. [In keeping with the spirit of the previous names, **conditional probit model** is a better name, which is used by Hausman and Wise (1978) but not by many others.]

Theoretically, the multinomial probit model is attractive, but it has some practical limitations. The response probabilities are very complicated, involving a $(J + 1)$-dimensional integral. This complexity not only makes it difficult to obtain the partial effects on the response probabilities, but also makes maximum likelihood infeasible for more than about five alternatives. For details, see Maddala (1983, Chapter 3) and Amemiya (1985, Chapter 9). Hausman and Wise (1978) contain an application to transportation mode for three alternatives.

Recent advances on estimation through simulation make multinomial probit estimation feasible for many alternatives. See Hajivassilou and Ruud (1994) and Keane (1993) for recent surveys of simulation estimation. Keane and Moffitt (1998) apply simulation methods to structural multinomial response models, where the econometric model is obtained from utility maximization subject to constraints. Keane and Moffitt study the tax effects of labor force participation allowing for participation in multiple welfare programs.

A different approach to relaxing IIA is to specify a **hierarchical model**. The most popular of these is called the **nested logit model**. McFadden (1984) gives a detailed treatment of these and other models; here we illustrate the basic approach where there are only two hierarchies.

Suppose that the total number of alternatives can be put into S groups of similar alternatives, and let G_s denote the number of alternatives within group s. Thus the first hierarchy corresponds to which of the S groups y falls into, and the second corresponds to the actual alternative within each group. McFadden (1981) studied the model

$$P(y \in G_s \mid \mathbf{x}) = \left\{ \alpha_s \left[\sum_{j \in G_s} \exp(\rho_s^{-1} \mathbf{x}_j \boldsymbol{\beta}) \right]^{\rho_s} \right\} \Big/ \left\{ \sum_{r=1}^{S} \alpha_r \left[\sum_{j \in G_r} \exp(\rho_r^{-1} \mathbf{x}_j \boldsymbol{\beta}) \right]^{\rho_r} \right\} \tag{15.84}$$

and

$$P(y = j \mid y \in G_s, \mathbf{x}) = \exp(\rho_s^{-1} \mathbf{x}_j \boldsymbol{\beta}) \Big/ \left[\sum_{h \in G_s} \exp(\rho_s^{-1} \mathbf{x}_h \boldsymbol{\beta}) \right] \tag{15.85}$$

where equation (15.84) is defined for $s = 1, 2, \ldots, S$ while equation (15.85) is defined for $j \in G_s$ and $s = 1, 2, \ldots, S$; of course, if $j \notin G_s$, $P(y = j \mid y \in G_s, \mathbf{x}) = 0$. This model requires a normalization restriction, usually $\alpha_1 = 1$. Equation (15.84) gives the probability that the outcome is in group s (conditional on $\mathbf{x}$); then, conditional on $y \in G_s$, equation (15.85) gives the probability of choosing alternative j within G_s. The response probability $P(y = j \mid \mathbf{x})$, which is ultimately of interest, is obtained by multiplying equations (15.84) and (15.85). This model can be derived by specifying a particular joint distribution for $\mathbf{a}_i$ in equation (15.79); see Amemiya (1985, p. 303).

Equation (15.85) implies that, conditional on choosing group s, the response probabilities take a conditional logit form with parameter vector $\rho_s^{-1}\boldsymbol{\beta}$. This suggests a natural two-step estimation procedure. First, estimate $\boldsymbol{\lambda}_s \equiv \rho_s^{-1}\boldsymbol{\beta}$, $s = 1, 2, \ldots, S$, by applying conditional logit analysis separately to each of the groups. Then, plug the $\hat{\boldsymbol{\lambda}}_s$ into equation (15.84) and estimate α_s, $s = 2, \ldots, S$ and ρ_s, $s = 1, \ldots, S$ by maximizing the log-likelihood function

$$\sum_{i=1}^{N} \sum_{s=1}^{S} 1[y_i \in G_s] \log[q_s(\mathbf{x}_i; \hat{\boldsymbol{\lambda}}, \boldsymbol{\alpha}, \boldsymbol{\rho})]$$

where $q_s(\mathbf{x}; \boldsymbol{\lambda}, \boldsymbol{\alpha}, \boldsymbol{\rho})$ is the probability in equation (15.84) with $\boldsymbol{\lambda}_s = \rho_s^{-1}\boldsymbol{\beta}$. This two-step conditional MLE is consistent and $\sqrt{N}$-asymptotically normal under general conditions, but the asymptotic variance needs to be adjusted for the first-stage estimation of the λ_s; see Chapters 12 and 13 for more on two-step estimators.

Of course, we can also use full maximum likelihood. The log likelihood for observation i can be written as

$$\ell_i(\boldsymbol{\beta}, \boldsymbol{\alpha}, \boldsymbol{\rho}) = \sum_{s=1}^{S} (1[y_i \in G_s]\{\log[q_s(\mathbf{x}_i; \boldsymbol{\beta}, \boldsymbol{\alpha}, \boldsymbol{\rho})] + 1[y_i = j] \log[p_{sj}(\mathbf{x}_i; \boldsymbol{\beta}, \rho_s)]\}) \tag{15.86}$$

where $q_s(\mathbf{x}_i; \boldsymbol{\beta}, \boldsymbol{\alpha}, \boldsymbol{\rho})$ is the probability in equation (15.84) and $p_{sj}(\mathbf{x}_i; \boldsymbol{\beta}, \rho_s)$ is the probability in equation (15.85). The regularity conditions for MLE are satisfied under weak assumptions.

When $\alpha_s = 1$ and $\rho_s = 1$ for all s, the nested logit model reduces to the conditional logit model. Thus, a test of IIA (as well as the other assumptions underlying the CL model) is a test of H_0: $\alpha_2 = \cdots = \alpha_S = \rho_1 = \cdots = \rho_S = 1$. McFadden (1987) suggests a score test, which only requires estimation of the conditional logit model.

Often special cases of the model are used, such as setting each α_s to unity and estimating the ρ_s. In his study of community choice and type of dwelling within a community, McFadden (1978) imposes this restriction along with $\rho_s = \rho$ for all s, so that the model has only one more parameter than the conditional logit model. This approach allows for correlation among the a_j for j belonging to the same community group, but the correlation is assumed to be the same for all communities.

Higher-level nested-logit models are covered in McFadden (1984) and Amemiya (1985, Chapter 9).

15.10 Ordered Response Models

15.10.1 Ordered Logit and Ordered Probit

Another kind of multinomial response is an **ordered response**. As the name suggests, if y is an ordered response, then the values we assign to each outcome are no longer arbitrary. For example, y might be a credit rating on a scale from zero to six, with $y = 6$ representing the highest rating and $y = 0$ the lowest rating. The fact that six is a better rating than five conveys useful information, even though the credit rating itself only has ordinal meaning. For example, we cannot say that the difference between four and two is somehow twice as important as the difference between one and zero.

Let y be an ordered response taking on the values $\{0, 1, 2, \ldots, J\}$ for some known integer J. The **ordered probit model** for y (conditional on explanatory variables $\mathbf{x}$) can be derived from a latent variable model. Assume that a latent variable y^* is determined by

$$y^* = \mathbf{x}\boldsymbol{\beta} + e, \qquad e \mid \mathbf{x} \sim \text{Normal}(0, 1) \tag{15.87}$$

where $\boldsymbol{\beta}$ is $K \times 1$ and, for reasons to be seen, $\mathbf{x}$ does not contain a constant. Let $\alpha_1 < \alpha_2 < \cdots < \alpha_J$ be unknown **cut points** (or **threshold parameters**), and define

$$\begin{aligned}
y &= 0 \quad \text{if } y^* \leq \alpha_1 \\
y &= 1 \quad \text{if } \alpha_1 < y^* \leq \alpha_2 \\
&\;\;\vdots \\
y &= J \quad \text{if } y^* > \alpha_J
\end{aligned} \tag{15.88}$$

For example, if y takes on the values 0, 1, and 2, then there are two cut points, α_1 and α_2.

Given the standard normal assumption for e, it is straightforward to derive the conditional distribution of y given $\mathbf{x}$; we simply compute each response probability:

$$\begin{aligned}
&\mathrm{P}(y = 0 \mid \mathbf{x}) = \mathrm{P}(y^* \leq \alpha_1 \mid \mathbf{x}) = \mathrm{P}(\mathbf{x}\boldsymbol{\beta} + e \leq \alpha_1 \mid \mathbf{x}) = \Phi(\alpha_1 - \mathbf{x}\boldsymbol{\beta}) \\
&\mathrm{P}(y = 1 \mid \mathbf{x}) = \mathrm{P}(\alpha_1 < y^* \leq \alpha_2 \mid \mathbf{x}) = \Phi(\alpha_2 - \mathbf{x}\boldsymbol{\beta}) - \Phi(\alpha_1 - \mathbf{x}\boldsymbol{\beta}) \\
&\;\;\vdots \\
&\mathrm{P}(y = J-1 \mid \mathbf{x}) = \mathrm{P}(\alpha_{J-1} < y^* \leq \alpha_J \mid \mathbf{x}) = \Phi(\alpha_J - \mathbf{x}\boldsymbol{\beta}) - \Phi(\alpha_{J-1} - \mathbf{x}\boldsymbol{\beta}) \\
&\mathrm{P}(y = J \mid \mathbf{x}) = \mathrm{P}(y^* > \alpha_J \mid \mathbf{x}) = 1 - \Phi(\alpha_J - \mathbf{x}\boldsymbol{\beta})
\end{aligned}$$

You can easily verify that these sum to unity. When $J = 1$ we get the binary probit model: $\mathrm{P}(y = 1 \mid \mathbf{x}) = 1 - \mathrm{P}(y = 0 \mid \mathbf{x}) = 1 - \Phi(\alpha_1 - \mathbf{x}\boldsymbol{\beta}) = \Phi(\mathbf{x}\boldsymbol{\beta} - \alpha_1)$, and so $-\alpha_1$ is the intercept inside Φ. It is for this reason that $\mathbf{x}$ does not contain an intercept in this formulation of the ordered probit model. (When there are only two outcomes, zero and one, we set the single cut point to zero and estimate the intercept; this approach leads to the standard probit model.)

The parameters $\boldsymbol{\alpha}$ and $\boldsymbol{\beta}$ can be estimated by maximum likelihood. For each i, the log-likelihood function is

$$\begin{aligned}
\ell_i(\boldsymbol{\alpha}, \boldsymbol{\beta}) = {} & 1[y_i = 0] \log[\Phi(\alpha_1 - \mathbf{x}_i\boldsymbol{\beta})] + 1[y_i = 1] \log[\Phi(\alpha_2 - \mathbf{x}_i\boldsymbol{\beta}) \\
& - \Phi(\alpha_1 - \mathbf{x}_i\boldsymbol{\beta})] + \cdots + 1[y_i = J] \log[1 - \Phi(\alpha_J - \mathbf{x}_i\boldsymbol{\beta})]
\end{aligned} \tag{15.89}$$

This log-likelihood function is well behaved, and many statistical packages routinely estimate ordered probit models.

Other distribution functions can be used in place of Φ. Replacing Φ with the logit function, Λ, gives the **ordered logit model**. In either case we must remember that $\boldsymbol{\beta}$, by itself, is of limited interest. In most cases we are not interested in $E(y^* \mid \mathbf{x}) = \mathbf{x}\boldsymbol{\beta}$, as y^* is an abstract construct. Instead, we are interested in the response probabilities $P(y = j \mid \mathbf{x})$, just as in the ordered response case. For the ordered probit model

$$\partial p_0(\mathbf{x})/\partial x_k = -\beta_k \phi(\alpha_1 - \mathbf{x}\boldsymbol{\beta}), \; \partial p_J(\mathbf{x})/\partial x_k = \beta_k \phi(\alpha_J - \mathbf{x}\boldsymbol{\beta})$$

$$\partial p_j(\mathbf{x})/\partial x_k = \beta_k[\phi(\alpha_{j-1} - \mathbf{x}\boldsymbol{\beta}) - \phi(\alpha_j - \mathbf{x}\boldsymbol{\beta})], \qquad 0 < j < J$$

and the formulas for the ordered logit model are similar. In making comparisons across different models—in particular, comparing ordered probit and ordered logit—we must remember to compare estimated response probabilities at various values of $\mathbf{x}$, such as $\bar{\mathbf{x}}$; the $\hat{\boldsymbol{\beta}}$ are not directly comparable. In particular, the $\hat{\alpha}_j$ are important determinants of the magnitudes of the estimated probabilities and partial effects. (Therefore, treatments of ordered probit that refer to the α_j as ancillary, or secondary, parameters are misleading.)

While the direction of the effect of x_k on the probabilities $P(y = 0 \mid \mathbf{x})$ and $P(y = J \mid \mathbf{x})$ is unambiguously determined by the sign of β_k, the sign of β_k does not always determine the direction of the effect for the intermediate outcomes, $1, 2, \ldots, J - 1$. To see this point, suppose there are three possible outcomes, 0, 1, and 2, and that $\beta_k > 0$. Then $\partial p_0(\mathbf{x})/\partial x_k < 0$ and $\partial p_2(\mathbf{x})/\partial x_k > 0$, but $\partial p_1(\mathbf{x})/\partial x_k$ could be either sign. If $|\alpha_1 - \mathbf{x}\boldsymbol{\beta}| < |\alpha_2 - \mathbf{x}\boldsymbol{\beta}|$, the scale factor, $\phi(\alpha_1 - \mathbf{x}\boldsymbol{\beta}) - \phi(\alpha_2 - \mathbf{x}\boldsymbol{\beta})$, is positive; otherwise it is negative. (This conclusion follows because the standard normal pdf is symmetric about zero, reaches its maximum at zero, and declines monotonically as its argument increases in absolute value.)

As with multinomial logit, for ordered responses we can compute the percent correctly predicted, for each outcome as well as overall: our prediction for y is simply the outcome with the highest probability.

Ordered probit and logit can also be applied when y is given quantitative meaning but we wish to acknowledge the discrete, ordered nature of the response. For example, suppose that individuals are asked to give one of three responses on how their pension funds are invested: "mostly bonds," "mixed," and "mostly stocks." One possibility is to assign these outcomes as 0, 1, 2 and apply ordered probit or ordered logit to estimate the effects of various factors on the probability of each outcome. Instead, we could assign the percent invested in stocks as, say 0, 50, and 100, or 25, 50, and 75. For estimating the probabilities of each category it is irrelevant how we assign the percentages as long as the order is preserved. However, if we give quantitative meaning to y, the expected value of y has meaning. We have

$$E(y \mid \mathbf{x}) = a_0 P(y = a_0 \mid \mathbf{x}) + a_1 P(y = a_1 \mid \mathbf{x}) + \cdots + a_J P(y = a_J \mid \mathbf{x})$$

where $a_0 < a_1 < \cdots < a_J$ are the J values taken on by y. Once we have estimated the response probabilities by ordered probit or ordered logit, we can easily estimate $\mathrm{E}(y \mid \mathbf{x})$ for any value of $\mathbf{x}$, for example, $\bar{\mathbf{x}}$. Estimates of the expected values can be compared at different values of the explanatory variables to obtain partial effects for discrete x_j.

Example 15.5 (Asset Allocation in Pension Plans): The data in PENSION.RAW are a subset of data used by Papke (1998) in assessing the impact of allowing individuals to choose their own allocations on asset allocation in pension plans. Initially, Papke codes the responses "mostly bonds," "mixed," and "mostly stocks" as 0, 50, and 100, and uses a linear regression model estimated by OLS. The binary explanatory variable *choice* is unity if the person has choice in how his or her pension fund is invested. Controlling for age, education, gender, race, marital status, income (via a set of dummy variables), wealth, and whether the plan is profit sharing, gives the OLS estimate $\hat{\beta}_{\text{choice}} = 12.05$ (se $= 6.30$), where $N = 194$. This result means that, other things equal, a person having choice has about 12 percentage points more assets in stocks.

The ordered probit coefficient on *choice* is .371 (se $=$ .184). The magnitude of the ordered probit coefficient does not have a simple interpretation, but its sign and statistical significance agree with the linear regression results. (The estimated cut points are $\hat{\alpha}_1 = -3.087$ and $\hat{\alpha}_2 = -2.054$.) To get an idea of the magnitude of the estimated effect of choice on the expected percent in stocks, we can estimate $\mathrm{E}(y \mid \mathbf{x})$ with $choice = 1$ and $choice = 0$, and obtain the difference. However, we need to choose values for the other regressors. For illustration, suppose the person is 60 years old, has 13.5 years of education (roughly the averages in the sample), is a single, nonblack male, has annual income between \$50,000 and \$75,000, and had wealth in 1989 of \$200,000 (also close to the sample average). Then, for $choice = 1$, $\hat{\mathrm{E}}(pctstck \mid \mathbf{x}) \approx 50.4$, and with $choice = 0$, $\hat{\mathrm{E}}(pctstck \mid \mathbf{x}) \approx 37.6$. The difference, 12.8, is remarkably close to the linear model estimate of the effect on choice.

For ordered probit, the percentages correctly predicted for each category are 51.6 (mostly bonds), 43.1 (mixed), and 37.9 (mostly stocks). The overall percentage correctly predicted is about 44.3.

The specification issues discussed in Section 15.7 for binary probit have analogues for ordered probit. The presence of normally distributed unobserved heterogeneity that is independent of $\mathbf{x}$ does not cause any problems when average partial effects are the focus. We can test for continuous endogenous variables in a manner very similar to the Rivers and Vuong (1988) procedure for binary probit, and maximum likelihood estimation is possible if we make a distributional assumption for the endogenous explanatory variable.

Heteroskedasticity in the latent error e in equation (15.87) changes the form of the response probabilities and, therefore, $\mathrm{E}(y \mid \mathbf{x})$ when y has quantitative meaning. If the heteroskedasticity is modeled, for example, as $\exp(\mathbf{x}_1\boldsymbol{\delta}_1)$ where $\mathbf{x}_1$ is a subset of $\mathbf{x}$, then maximum likelihood can be used to estimate $\boldsymbol{\beta}$, $\boldsymbol{\alpha}$ and $\boldsymbol{\delta}_1$. However, as with the probit case, we must compute the partial effects on the response probabilities in comparing different models. It does not make sense to compare estimates of $\boldsymbol{\beta}$ with and without heteroskedasticity. Score tests for heteroskedasticity are also easily derived along the lines of Section 15.5.3. Similar comments hold for deviations from normality in the latent variable model.

Unobserved effects ordered probit models can be handled by adapting Chamberlain's approach for binary probit in Section 15.8.2. The latent variable model can be written as

$$y_{it}^* = \mathbf{x}_{it}\boldsymbol{\beta} + c_i + e_{it}, e_{it} \mid \mathbf{x}_i \sim \mathrm{Normal}(0, 1), \qquad t = 1, \ldots, T$$

and $y_{it} = 0$ if $y_{it}^* \leq \alpha_1$, $y_{it} = 1$ if $\alpha_1 < y_{it}^* \leq \alpha_2$, and so on. Certain embellishments are possible, such as letting the α_j change over time. Assumption (15.67) allows estimation of the average partial effects by using a pooled ordered probit of y_{it} on 1, $\mathbf{x}_{it}$, $\bar{\mathbf{x}}_i$. A full conditional MLE analysis is possible when we add assumption (15.61). The details are very similar to the probit case and are omitted.

15.10.2 Applying Ordered Probit to Interval-Coded Data

The ordered probit model can be modified to apply to a very different situation. When the *quantitative* outcome we would like to explain is grouped into intervals, we say that we have **interval-coded data**. Specifically, suppose that y^* is a variable with quantitative meaning, such as family wealth, and we are interested in estimating the model $\mathrm{E}(y^* \mid \mathbf{x}) = \mathbf{x}\boldsymbol{\beta}$, where $x_1 = 1$. (Therefore, y^* is no longer a vague, latent variable.) If we observed y^* we would just use OLS to estimate $\boldsymbol{\beta}$. However, because we only observe whether, say, wealth falls into one of several cells, we have a **data-coding problem**. We can still consistently estimate $\boldsymbol{\beta}$ if we make a distributional assumption.

Let $a_1 < a_2 < \cdots < a_J$ denote the known cell limits, and define y as in equations (15.88), but with a_j replacing the unknown parameter α_j. Because our interest is now in the linear model for $\mathrm{E}(y^* \mid \mathbf{x})$, we replace the standard normal assumption in equation (15.87) with the assumption $y^* \mid \mathbf{x} \sim \mathrm{Normal}(\mathbf{x}\boldsymbol{\beta}, \sigma^2)$, where $\sigma^2 = \mathrm{Var}(y^* \mid \mathbf{x})$ is assumed not to depend on $\mathbf{x}$. The parameters of $\boldsymbol{\beta}$ and σ^2 can be estimated by maximum likelihood by defining the log likelihood for observation i as in equation (15.89), but with $(\boldsymbol{\beta}, \sigma^2)$ replacing $(\boldsymbol{\alpha}, \boldsymbol{\beta})$, and $(a_j - \mathbf{x}\boldsymbol{\beta})/\sigma$ replacing $(\alpha_j - \mathbf{x}\boldsymbol{\beta})$.

(Remember, now we do not estimate the cut points, as these are set by the data collection scheme.)

Many ordered probit software routines assume that our purpose in estimating an ordered probit model is to model a qualitative, ordered response. This assumption means that the cut points are always estimated and that σ^2 is normalized to be one, but these characteristics are not what we want in interval coding applications. Fortunately, some econometrics packages have a feature for **interval regression**, which is exactly ordered probit with the cut points fixed and with $\boldsymbol{\beta}$ and σ^2 estimated by maximum likelihood.

When applying ordered probit to interval regression, it is important to remember that the β_j are interpretable *as if* we had observed y_i^* for each i and estimated $\mathrm{E}(y^* \mid \mathbf{x}) = \mathbf{x}\boldsymbol{\beta}$ by OLS. Our ability to estimate the partial effects of the x_j is due to the strong assumption that y^* given $\mathbf{x}$ satisfies the classical linear model assumptions; without these assumptions, the ordered probit estimator of $\boldsymbol{\beta}$ would be inconsistent. A simpler method, which sometimes works well for approximating the partial effects on y^*, is to define an artificial dependent variable. For each observation i, w_i is the midpoint of the reported interval. If all we know is that $y_i^* > a_J$, so that the response is in the cell unbounded from above, we might set w_i equal to a_J, or some value above a_J, perhaps based on an estimated cell average from aggregate data or other data sets. (For example, if $a_J = 250{,}000$ and we are modeling wealth, we might be able to find from a separate data source the average wealth for people with wealth above \$250,000.) Once we have defined w_i for each observation i, an OLS regression of w_i on $\mathbf{x}_i$ might approximately estimate the β_j.

If the variable we would like to explain, y^*, is strictly positive, it often makes sense to estimate the model $\log(y^*) = \mathbf{x}\boldsymbol{\beta} + u$. Of course, this transformation changes the cell limits to $\log(a_j)$.

Problems

15.1. Suppose that y is a binary outcome and $d1, d2, \ldots, dM$ are dummy variables for exhaustive and mutually exclusive categories; that is, each person in the population falls into one and only one category.

a. Show that the fitted values from the regression (without an intercept)

$$y_i \text{ on } d1_i, d2_i, \ldots, dM_i, \qquad i = 1, 2, \ldots, N$$

are always in the unit interval. In particular, carefully describe the coefficient on each dummy variable and the fitted value for each i.

b. What happens if y_i is regressed on M linearly independent, linear combinations of $d1_i, \ldots, dM_i$, for example, $1, d2_i, d3_i, \ldots, dM_i$?

15.2. Suppose that family i chooses annual consumption c_i (in dollars) and charitable contributions q_i (in dollars) to solve the problem

$$\max_{c,q} \; c + a_i \log(1+q)$$

$$\text{subject to } c + p_i q \leq m_i, \qquad c, q \geq 0$$

where m_i is income of family i, p_i is the price of one dollar of charitable contributions —where $p_i < 1$ because of the tax deductability of charitable contributions, and this price differs across families because of different marginal tax rates and different state tax codes—and $a_i \geq 0$ determines the marginal utility of charitable contributions. Take m_i and p_i as exogenous to the family in this problem.

a. Show that the optimal solution is $q_i = 0$ if $a_i \leq p_i$, and $q_i = a_i/p_i - 1$ if $a_i > p_i$.

b. Define $y_i = 1$ if $q_i > 0$ and $y_i = 0$ if $q_i = 0$, and suppose that $a_i = \exp(\mathbf{z}_i\gamma + v_i)$, where $\mathbf{z}_i$ is a J-vector of observable family traits and v_i is unobservable. Assume that v_i is independent of $(\mathbf{z}_i, m_i, p_i)$ and v_i/σ has symmetric distribution function $G(\cdot)$, where $\sigma^2 = \text{Var}(v_i)$. Show that

$$\text{P}(y_i = 1 \mid \mathbf{z}_i, m_i, p_i) = G[(\mathbf{z}_i\gamma - \log p_i)/\sigma]$$

so that y_i follows an index model.

15.3. Let $\mathbf{z}_1$ be a vector of variables, let z_2 be a continuous variable, and let d_1 be a dummy variable.

a. In the model

$$\text{P}(y = 1 \mid \mathbf{z}_1, z_2) = \Phi(\mathbf{z}_1\delta_1 + \gamma_1 z_2 + \gamma_2 z_2^2)$$

find the partial effect of z_2 on the response probability. How would you estimate this partial effect?

b. In the model

$$\text{P}(y = 1 \mid \mathbf{z}_1, z_2, d_1) = \Phi(\mathbf{z}_1\delta_1 + \gamma_1 z_2 + \gamma_2 d_1 + \gamma_3 z_2 d_1)$$

find the partial effect of z_2. How would you measure the effect of d_1 on the response probability? How would you estimate these effects?

c. Describe how you would obtain the standard errors of the estimated partial effects from parts a and b.

15.4. Evaluate the following statement: "Estimation of a linear probability model is more robust than probit or logit because the LPM does not assume homoskedasticity or a distributional assumption."

15.5. Consider the probit model

$$P(y = 1 \mid \mathbf{z}, q) = \Phi(\mathbf{z}_1\boldsymbol{\delta}_1 + \gamma_1 z_2 q)$$

where q is independent of $\mathbf{z}$ and distributed as Normal$(0, 1)$; the vector $\mathbf{z}$ is observed but the scalar q is not.

a. Find the partial effect of z_2 on the response probability, namely,

$$\frac{\partial P(y = 1 \mid \mathbf{z}, q)}{\partial z_2}$$

b. Show that $P(y = 1 \mid \mathbf{z}) = \Phi[\mathbf{z}_1\boldsymbol{\delta}_1/(1 + \gamma_1^2 z_2^2)^{1/2}]$.

c. Define $\rho_1 \equiv \gamma_1^2$. How would you test H_0: $\rho_1 = 0$?

d. If you have reason to believe $\rho_1 > 0$, how would you estimate $\boldsymbol{\delta}_1$ along with ρ_1?

15.6. Consider taking a large random sample of workers at a given point in time. Let $sick_i = 1$ if person i called in sick during the last 90 days, and zero otherwise. Let $\mathbf{z}_i$ be a vector of individual and employer characteristics. Let $cigs_i$ be the number of cigarettes individual i smokes per day (on average).

a. Explain the underlying experiment of interest when we want to examine the effects of cigarette smoking on workdays lost.

b. Why might $cigs_i$ be correlated with unobservables affecting $sick_i$?

c. One way to write the model of interest is

$$P(sick = 1 \mid \mathbf{z}, cigs, q_1) = \Phi(\mathbf{z}_1\boldsymbol{\delta}_1 + \gamma_1 cigs + q_1)$$

where $\mathbf{z}_1$ is a subset of $\mathbf{z}$ and q_1 is an unobservable variable that is possibly correlated with *cigs*. What happens if q_1 is ignored and you estimate the probit of *sick* on $\mathbf{z}_1$, *cigs*?

d. Can *cigs* have a conditional normal distribution in the population? Explain.

e. Explain how to test whether *cigs* is exogenous. Does this test rely on *cigs* having a conditional normal distribution?

f. Suppose that some of the workers live in states that recently implemented no-smoking laws in the workplace. Does the presence of the new laws suggest a good IV candidate for *cigs*?

15.7. Use the data in GROGGER.RAW for this question.

a. Define a binary variable, say *arr86*, equal to unity if a man was arrested at least once during 1986, and zero otherwise. Estimate a linear probability model relating *arr86* to *pcnv*, *avgsen*, *tottime*, *ptime86*, *inc86*, *black*, *hispan*, and *born60*. Report the usual and heteroskedasticity-robust standard errors. What is the estimated effect on the probability of arrest if *pcnv* goes from .25 to .75?

b. Test the joint significance of *avgsen* and *tottime*, using a nonrobust and robust test.

c. Now estimate the model by probit. At the average values of *avgsen*, *tottime*, *inc86*, and *ptime86* in the sample, and with $black = 1$, $hispan = 0$, and $born60 = 1$, what is the estimated effect on the probability of arrest if *pcnv* goes from .25 to .75? Compare this result with the answer from part a.

d. For the probit model estimated in part c, obtain the percent correctly predicted. What is the percent correctly predicted when $narr86 = 0$? When $narr86 = 1$? What do you make of these findings?

e. In the probit model, add the terms $pcnv^2$, $ptime86^2$, and $inc86^2$ to the model. Are these individually or jointly significant? Describe the estimated relationship between the probability of arrest and *pcnv*. In particular, at what point does the probability of conviction have a negative effect on probability of arrest?

15.8. Use the data set BWGHT.RAW for this problem.

a. Define a binary variable, *smokes*, if the woman smokes during pregnancy. Estimate a probit model relating *smokes* to *motheduc*, *white*, and $\log(faminc)$. At $white = 0$ and *faminc* evaluated at the average in the sample, what is the estimated difference in the probability of smoking for a woman with 16 years of education and one with 12 years of education?

b. Do you think *faminc* is exogenous in the smoking equation? What about *motheduc*?

c. Assume that *motheduc* and *white* are exogenous in the probit from part a. Also assume that *fatheduc* is exogenous to this equation. Estimate the reduced form for $\log(faminc)$ to see if *fatheduc* is partially correlated with $\log(faminc)$.

d. Test the null hypothesis that $\log(faminc)$ is exogenous in the probit from part a.

15.9. Assume that the binary variable y follows a linear probability model.

a. Write down the log-likelihood function for observation i.

b. Why might maximum likelihood estimation of the LPM be difficult?

c. Assuming that you can estimate the LPM by MLE, explain why it is valid, as a model selection device, to compare the log likelihood from the LPM with that from logit or probit.

15.10. Suppose you wish to use goodness-of-fit measures to compare the LPM with a model such as logit or probit, after estimating the LPM by ordinary least squares. The usual R-squared from OLS estimation measures the proportion of the variance in y that is explained by $\hat{\mathrm{P}}(y = 1 \mid \mathbf{x}) = \mathbf{x}\hat{\boldsymbol{\beta}}$.

a. Explain how to obtain a comparable R-squared measured for the general index model $\mathrm{P}(y = 1 \mid \mathbf{x}) = G(\mathbf{x}\boldsymbol{\beta})$.

b. Compute the R-squared measures using the data in CRIME.RAW, where the dependent variable is *arr86* and the explanatory variables are *pcnv*, $pcnv^2$, *avgsen*, *tottime*, *ptime86*, $ptime86^2$, *inc86*, $inc86^2$, *black*, *hispan*, and *born60*. Are the R-squareds substantially different?

15.11. List assumptions under which the pooled probit estimator is a conditional MLE based on the distribution of $\mathbf{y}_i$ given $\mathbf{x}_i$, where $\mathbf{y}_i$ is the $T \times 1$ vector of binary outcomes and $\mathbf{x}_i$ is the vector of all explanatory variables across all T time periods.

15.12. Find $\mathrm{P}(y_{i1} = 1, y_{i2} = 0, y_{i3} = 0 \mid \mathbf{x}_i, c_i, n_i = 1)$ in the fixed effects logit model with $T = 3$.

15.13. Suppose that you have a control group, A, and a treatment group, B, and two periods of data. Between the two years, a new policy is implemented that affects group B; see Section 6.3.1.

a. If your outcome variable is binary (for example, an employment indicator), and you have no covariates, how would you estimate the effect of the policy?

b. If you have covariates, write down a probit model that allows you to estimate the effect of the policy change. Explain in detail how you would estimate this effect.

c. How would you get an asymptotic 95 percent confidence interval for the estimate in part b?

15.14. Use the data in PENSION.RAW for this example.

a. Estimate a linear model for *pctstck*, where the explanatory variables are *choice*, *age*, *educ*, *female*, *black*, *married*, *finc25*, ..., *finc101*, *wealth89*, and *prftshr*. Why might you compute heteroskedasticity-robust standard errors?

b. The sample contains separate observations for some husband-wife pairs. Compute standard errors of the estimates from the model in part a that account for the cluster correlation within family. (These should also be heteroskedasticity-robust.) Do the standard errors differ much from the usual OLS standard errors, or from the heteroskedasticity-robust standard errors?

c. Estimate the model from part a by ordered probit. Estimate $\mathrm{E}(pctstck \mid \mathbf{x})$ for a single, nonblack female with 12 years of education who is 60 years old. Assume she has net worth (in 1989) equal to \$150,000 and earns \$45,000 a year, and her plan is not profit sharing. Compare this with the estimate of $\mathrm{E}(pctstck \mid \mathbf{x})$ from the linear model.

d. If you want to choose between the linear model and ordered probit based on how well each estimates $\mathrm{E}(y \mid \mathbf{x})$, how would you proceed?

15.15. Suppose that you are hired by a university to estimate the effect of drug usage on college grade point average of undergraduates. The survey data given to you had students choose a range of grade point averages: less than 1.0, 1.0 to 1.5, and so on, with the last interval being 3.5 to 4.0. You have data on family background variables, drug usage, and standardized test scores such as the SAT or ACT. What approach would you use? Provide enough detail so that someone can implement your suggested method.

15.16. Let wtp_i denote the willingness of person i from a population to pay for a new public project, such as a new park or the widening of an existing highway. You are interested in the effects of various socioeconomic variables on wtp, and you specify the population model $wtp = \mathbf{x}\boldsymbol{\beta} + u$, where $\mathbf{x}$ is $1 \times K$ and $\mathrm{E}(u \mid \mathbf{x}) = 0$. Rather than observe wtp_i, each person in the sample is presented with a cost of the project, r_i. At this cost the person either favors or does not favor the project. Let $y_i = 1$ if person i favors the project and zero otherwise.

a. Assume that $y_i = 1$ if and only if $wtp_i > r_i$. If u_i is independent of $(\mathbf{x}_i, r_i)$ and is distributed as $\mathrm{Normal}(0, \sigma^2)$, find $\mathrm{P}(y_i = 1 \mid \mathbf{x}_i, r_i)$. In particular, show that this probability follows a probit model with parameters depending on $\boldsymbol{\beta}$ and σ.

b. Let $\hat{\gamma}$ be the $K \times 1$ vector of estimates on $\mathbf{x}$, and let $\hat{\delta}$ be the coefficient on r_i, from the probit of y_i on $\mathbf{x}_i$, r_i. Given these estimates, how would you estimate $\boldsymbol{\beta}$ and σ?

c. How would you estimate $\boldsymbol{\beta}$ and σ directly?

d. Now suppose u_i is independent of $(\mathbf{x}_i, r_i)$ with cdf $G(\cdot\,; \boldsymbol{\delta})$, where $\boldsymbol{\delta}$ is an $R \times 1$ vector of parameters. Write down the log likelihood for observation i as a function of $\boldsymbol{\beta}$ and $\boldsymbol{\delta}$.

e. Does it make sense to compare the estimates of $\boldsymbol{\beta}$ for different choices of $G(\cdot\,; \boldsymbol{\delta})$ in part d? Explain.

15.17. Let $y_1, y_2, \ldots, y_G$ be a set of discrete outcomes representing a population. These could be outcomes for the same individual, family, firm, and so on. Some entries could be binary outcomes, others might be ordered outcomes. For a vector of conditioning variables $\mathbf{x}$ and unobserved heterogeneity c, assume that $y_1, y_2, \ldots, y_G$ are independent conditional on $(\mathbf{x}, c)$, where $f_g(\cdot \mid \mathbf{x}, c; \gamma_o^g)$ is the density of y_g given $(\mathbf{x}, c)$, where γ_o^g is a P_g-vector of parameters. For example, if y_1 is a binary outcome, $f_1(\cdot \mid \mathbf{x}, c; \gamma_o^1)$ might represent a probit model with response probability $\Phi(\mathbf{x}\gamma_o^1 + c)$.

a. Write down the density of $\mathbf{y} = (y_1, y_2, \ldots, y_G)$ given $(\mathbf{x}, c)$.

b. Let $h(\cdot \mid \mathbf{x}; \boldsymbol{\delta}_o)$ be the density of c given $\mathbf{x}$, where $\boldsymbol{\delta}_o$ is a vector of parameters. Find the density of $\mathbf{y}$ given $\mathbf{x}$. Are the y_g independent conditional on $\mathbf{x}$? Explain.

c. Find the log likelihood for any random draw $(\mathbf{x}_i, \mathbf{y}_i)$.

15.18. Consider Chamberlain's random effects probit model under assumptions (15.60) and (15.61), but replace assumption (15.67) with

$$c_i \mid \mathbf{x}_i \sim \text{Normal}[\psi + \bar{\mathbf{x}}_i \xi, \sigma_a^2 \exp(\bar{\mathbf{x}}_i \boldsymbol{\lambda})]$$

so that c_i given $\bar{\mathbf{x}}_i$ has exponential heteroskedasticity.

a. Find $\mathrm{P}(y_{it} = 1 \mid \mathbf{x}_i, a_i)$, where $a_i = c_i - \mathrm{E}(c_i \mid \mathbf{x}_i)$. Does this probability differ from the probability under assumption (15.67)? Explain.

b. Derive the log-likelihood function by first finding the density of $(y_{i1}, \ldots, y_{iT})$ given $\mathbf{x}_i$. Does it have similarities with the log-likelihood function under assumption (15.67)?

c. Assuming you have estimated $\boldsymbol{\beta}$, ψ, ξ, σ_a^2, and $\boldsymbol{\lambda}$ by CMLE, how would you estimate the average partial effects? {Hint: First show that $\mathrm{E}[\Phi(\mathbf{x}^o\boldsymbol{\beta} + \psi + \bar{\mathbf{x}}_i\xi + a_i) \mid \mathbf{x}_i] = \Phi(\{\mathbf{x}^o\boldsymbol{\beta} + \psi + \bar{\mathbf{x}}_i\xi\}/\{1 + \sigma_a^2 \exp(\bar{\mathbf{x}}_i\boldsymbol{\lambda})\}^{1/2})$, and then use the appropriate average across i.}

15.19. Use the data in KEANE.RAW for this question, and restrict your attention to black men who are in the sample all 11 years.

a. Use pooled probit to estimate the model $\mathrm{P}(employ_{it} = 1 \mid employ_{i,t-1}) = \Phi(\delta_0 + \rho employ_{i,t-1})$. What assumption is needed to ensure that the usual standard errors and test statistics from pooled probit are asymptotically valid?

b. Estimate $\mathrm{P}(employ_t = 1 \mid employ_{t-1} = 1)$ and $\mathrm{P}(employ_t = 1 \mid employ_{t-1} = 0)$. Explain how you would obtain standard errors of these estimates.

c. Add a full set of year dummies to the analysis in part a, and estimate the probabilities in part b for 1987. Are there important differences with the estimates in part b?

d. Now estimate a dynamic unobserved effects model using the method described in Section 15.8.4. In particular, add $employ_{i,81}$ as an additional explanatory variable, and use random effects probit software. Use a full set of year dummies.

e. Is there evidence of state dependence, conditional on c_i? Explain.

f. Average the estimated probabilities across $employ_{i,81}$ to get the average partial effect for 1987. Compare the estimates with the effects estimated in part c.

15.20. A nice feature of the Rivers and Vuong (1988) approach to estimating probit models with endogenous explanatory variables—see Section 15.7.2—is that it immediately extends to models containing any nonlinear functions of the endogenous explanatory variables. Suppose that the model is

$$y_1^* = \mathbf{z}_1\boldsymbol{\delta}_1 + \mathbf{g}(y_2)\boldsymbol{\alpha}_1 + u_1$$

along with equations (15.40) and (15.41) and the assumption that (u_1, v_2) is independent of $\mathbf{z}$ and bivariate normal. Here, $\mathbf{g}(y_2)$ is a row vector of functions of y_2; for example, $\mathbf{g}(y_2) = (y_2, y_2^2)$. Show that

$$\mathrm{P}(y_1 = 1 \mid \mathbf{z}, v_2) = \Phi\{[\mathbf{z}_1\boldsymbol{\delta}_1 + \mathbf{g}(y_2)\boldsymbol{\alpha}_1 + \theta_1 v_2]/(1 - \rho_1^2)^{1/2}\}$$

so that Procedure 15.1 goes through with the minor notational change that $\mathbf{g}(y_2)$ replaces y_2 in step b; step a is unchanged.

16 Corner Solution Outcomes and Censored Regression Models

16.1 Introduction and Motivation

In this chapter we cover a class of models traditionally called **censored regression models**. Censored regression models generally apply when the variable to be explained is partly continuous but has positive probability mass at one or more points. In order to apply these methods effectively, we must understand that the statistical model underlying censored regression analysis applies to problems that are conceptually very different.

For the most part, censored regression applications can be put into one of two categories. In the first case there is a variable with quantitative meaning, call it y^*, and we are interested in the population regression $\mathrm{E}(y^* \mid \mathbf{x})$. If y^* and $\mathbf{x}$ were observed for everyone in the population, there would be nothing new: we could use standard regression methods (ordinary or nonlinear least squares). But a data problem arises because y^* is censored above or below some value; that is, it is not observable for part of the population. An example is **top coding** in survey data. For example, assume that y^* is family wealth, and, for a randomly drawn family, the actual value of wealth is recorded up to some threshold, say, \$200,000, but above that level only the fact that wealth was more than \$200,000 is recorded. Top coding is an example of **data censoring**, and is analogous to the data-coding problem we discussed in Section 15.10.2 in connection with interval regression.

Example 16.1 (Top Coding of Wealth): In the population of all families in the United States, let $wealth^*$ denote actual family wealth, measured in thousands of dollars. Suppose that $wealth^*$ follows the linear regression model $\mathrm{E}(wealth^* \mid \mathbf{x}) = \mathbf{x}\boldsymbol{\beta}$, where $\mathbf{x}$ is a $1 \times K$ vector of conditioning variables. However, we observe $wealth^*$ only when $wealth^* \leq 200$. When $wealth^*$ is greater than 200 we know that it is, but we do not know the actual value of wealth. Define observed wealth as

$$wealth = \min(wealth^*, 200)$$

The definition $wealth = 200$ when $wealth^* > 200$ is arbitrary, but it is useful for defining the statistical model that follows. To estimate $\boldsymbol{\beta}$ we might assume that $wealth^*$ given $\mathbf{x}$ has a homoskedastic normal distribution. In error form,

$$wealth^* = \mathbf{x}\boldsymbol{\beta} + u, \qquad u \mid \mathbf{x} \sim \mathrm{Normal}(0, \sigma^2)$$

This is a strong assumption about the conditional distribution of $wealth^*$, something we could avoid entirely if $wealth^*$ were not censored above 200. Under these assumptions we can write recorded wealth as

$$wealth = \min(200, \mathbf{x}\boldsymbol{\beta} + u) \tag{16.1}$$

Data censoring also arises in the analysis of duration models, a topic we treat in Chapter 20.

A second kind of application of censored regression models appears more often in econometrics and, unfortunately, is where the label "censored regression" is least appropriate. To describe the situation, let y be an observable choice or outcome describing some economic agent, such as an individual or a firm, with the following characteristics: y takes on the value zero with positive probability but is a continuous random variable over strictly positive values. There are many examples of variables that, at least approximately, have these features. Just a few examples include amount of life insurance coverage chosen by an individual, family contributions to an individual retirement account, and firm expenditures on research and development. In each of these examples we can imagine economic agents solving an optimization problem, and for some agents the optimal choice will be the corner solution, $y = 0$. We will call this kind of response variable a **corner solution outcome**. For corner solution outcomes, it makes more sense to call the resulting model a **corner solution model**. Unfortunately, the name "censored regression model" appears to be firmly entrenched.

For corner solution applications, we must understand that the issue is *not* data observability: we are interested in features of the distribution of y given $\mathbf{x}$, such as $\mathrm{E}(y \mid \mathbf{x})$ and $\mathrm{P}(y = 0 \mid \mathbf{x})$. If we are interested only in the effect of the x_j on the mean response, $\mathrm{E}(y \mid \mathbf{x})$, it is natural to ask, Why not just assume $\mathrm{E}(y \mid \mathbf{x}) = \mathbf{x}\boldsymbol{\beta}$ and apply OLS on a random sample? Theoretically, the problem is that, when $y \geq 0$, $\mathrm{E}(y \mid \mathbf{x})$ cannot be linear in $\mathbf{x}$ unless the range of $\mathbf{x}$ is fairly limited. A related weakness is that the model implies constant partial effects. Further, for the sample at hand, predicted values for y can be negative for many combinations of $\mathbf{x}$ and $\boldsymbol{\beta}$. These are very similar to the shortcomings of the linear probability model for binary responses.

We have already seen functional forms that ensure that $\mathrm{E}(y \mid \mathbf{x})$ is positive for all values of $\mathbf{x}$ and parameters, the leading case being the exponential function, $\mathrm{E}(y \mid \mathbf{x}) = \exp(\mathbf{x}\boldsymbol{\beta})$. [We cannot use $\log(y)$ as the dependent variable in a linear regression because $\log(0)$ is undefined.] We could then estimate $\boldsymbol{\beta}$ using nonlinear least squares (NLS), as in Chapter 12. Using an exponential conditional mean function is a reasonable strategy to follow, as it ensures that predicted values are positive and that the parameters are easy to interpret. However, it also has limitations. First, if y is a corner solution outcome, $\mathrm{Var}(y \mid \mathbf{x})$ is probably heteroskedastic, and so NLS could be inefficient. While we may be able to partly solve this problem using weighted NLS, any model for the conditional variance would be arbitrary. Probably a more important criticism is that we would not be able to measure the effect of each x_j on other features of the distribution of y given $\mathbf{x}$. Two that are commonly of interest are $\mathrm{P}(y = 0 \mid \mathbf{x})$ and $\mathrm{E}(y \mid \mathbf{x}, y > 0)$. By definition, a model for $\mathrm{E}(y \mid \mathbf{x})$ does not allow us to estimate other features of the distribution. If we make a full distributional assumption for y given $\mathbf{x}$, we can estimate any feature of the conditional distribution. In addition, we will obtain efficient estimates of quantities such as $\mathrm{E}(y \mid \mathbf{x})$.

The following example shows how a simple economic model leads to an econometric model where y can be zero with positive probability and where the conditional expectation $\mathrm{E}(y \mid \mathbf{x})$ is not a linear function of parameters.

Example 16.2 (Charitable Contributions): Problem 15.1 shows how to derive a probit model from a utility maximization problem for charitable giving, using utility function $util_i(c, q) = c + a_i \log(1 + q)$, where c is annual consumption, in dollars, and q is annual charitable giving. The variable a_i determines the marginal utility of giving for family i. Maximizing subject to the budget constraint $c_i + p_i q_i = m_i$ (where m_i is family income and p_i is the price of a dollar of charitable contributions) and the inequality constraint $c,\ q \geq 0$, the solution q_i is easily shown to be $q_i = 0$ if $a_i/p_i \leq 1$ and $q_i = a_i/p_i - 1$ if $a_i/p_i > 1$. We can write this relation as $1 + q_i = \max(1, a_i/p_i)$. If $a_i = \exp(\mathbf{z}_i\gamma + u_i)$, where u_i is an unobservable independent of $(\mathbf{z}_i, p_i, m_i)$ and normally distributed, then charitable contributions are determined by the equation

$$\log(1 + q_i) = \max[0, \mathbf{z}_i\gamma - \log(p_i) + u_i] \tag{16.2}$$

Comparing equations (16.2) and (16.1) shows that they have similar statistical structures. In equation (16.2) we are taking a maximum, and the lower threshold is zero, whereas in equation (16.1) we are taking a minimum with an upper threshold of 200. Each problem can be transformed into the same statistical model: for a randomly drawn observation i from the population,

$$y_i^* = \mathbf{x}_i\boldsymbol{\beta} + u_i, \qquad u_i \mid \mathbf{x}_i \sim \mathrm{Normal}(0, \sigma^2) \tag{16.3}$$

$$y_i = \max(0, y_i^*) \tag{16.4}$$

These equations constitute what is known as the **standard censored Tobit model** (after Tobin, 1956) or **type I Tobit model** (which is from Amemiya's 1985 taxonomy). This is the canonical form of the model in the sense that it is the form usually studied in methodological papers, and it is the default model estimated by many software packages.

The charitable contributions example immediately fits into the standard censored Tobit framework by defining $\mathbf{x}_i = [\mathrm{z}_i, \log(p_i)]$ and $y_i = \log(1 + q_i)$. This particular transformation of q_i and the restriction that the coefficient on $\log(p_i)$ is -1 depend critically on the utility function used in the example. In practice, we would probably take $y_i = q_i$ and allow all parameters to be unrestricted.

The wealth example can be cast as equations (16.3) and (16.4) after a simple transformation:

$$-(wealth_i - 200) = \max(0, -200 - \mathbf{x}_i\boldsymbol{\beta} - u_i)$$

and so the intercept changes, and all slope coefficients have the opposite sign from equation (16.1). For data-censoring problems, it is easier to study the censoring scheme directly, and many econometrics packages support various kinds of data censoring. Problem 16.3 asks you to consider general forms of data censoring, including the case when the censoring point can change with observation, in which case the model is often called the **censored normal regression model**. (This label properly emphasizes the data-censoring aspect.)

For the population, we write the standard censored Tobit model as

$$y^* = \mathbf{x}\boldsymbol{\beta} + u, \qquad u \mid \mathbf{x} \sim \text{Normal}(0, \sigma^2) \tag{16.5}$$

$$y = \max(0, y^*) \tag{16.6}$$

where, except in rare cases, $\mathbf{x}$ contains unity. As we saw from the two previous examples, different features of this model are of interest depending on the type of application. In examples with true data censoring, such as Example 16.1, the vector $\boldsymbol{\beta}$ tells us everything we want to know because $\mathrm{E}(y^* \mid \mathbf{x}) = \mathbf{x}\boldsymbol{\beta}$ is of interest. For corner solution outcomes, such as Example 16.2, $\boldsymbol{\beta}$ does not give the entire story. Usually, we are interested in $\mathrm{E}(y \mid \mathbf{x})$ or $\mathrm{E}(y \mid \mathbf{x}, y > 0)$. These certainly depend on $\boldsymbol{\beta}$, but in a nonlinear fashion.

For the statistical model (16.5) and (16.6) to make sense, the variable y^* should have characteristics of a normal random variable. In data censoring cases this requirement means that the variable of interest y^* should have a homoskedastic normal distribution. In some cases the logarithmic transformation can be used to make this assumption more plausible. Example 16.1 might be one such case if wealth is positive for all families. See also Problems 16.1 and 16.2.

In corner solution examples, the variable y should be (roughly) continuous when $y > 0$. Thus the Tobit model is not appropriate for ordered responses, as in Section 15.10. Similarly, Tobit should not be applied to count variables, especially when the count variable takes on only a small number of values (such as number of patents awarded annually to a firm or the number of times someone is arrested during a year). Poisson regression models, a topic we cover in Chapter 19, are better suited for analyzing count data.

For corner solution outcomes, we must avoid placing too much emphasis on the latent variable y^*. Most of the time y^* is an artificial construct, and we are not interested in $\mathrm{E}(y^* \mid \mathbf{x})$. In Example 16.2 we derived the model for charitable contributions using utility maximization, and a latent variable never appeared. Viewing y^* as something like "desired charitable contributions" can only sow confusion: the variable of interest, y, is observed charitable contributions.

16.2 Derivations of Expected Values

In corner solution applications such as the charitable contributions example, interest centers on probabilities or expectations involving y. Most of the time we focus on the expected values $\mathrm{E}(y \mid \mathbf{x}, y > 0)$ and $\mathrm{E}(y \mid \mathbf{x})$.

Before deriving these expectations for the Tobit model, it is interesting to derive an inequality that bounds $\mathrm{E}(y \mid \mathbf{x})$ from below. Since the function $g(z) \equiv \max(0, z)$ is convex, it follows from the conditional Jensen's inequality (see Appendix 2A) that $\mathrm{E}(y \mid \mathbf{x}) \geq \max[0, \mathrm{E}(y^* \mid \mathbf{x})]$. This condition holds when y^* has any distribution and for any form of $\mathrm{E}(y^* \mid \mathbf{x})$. If $\mathrm{E}(y^* \mid \mathbf{x}) = \mathbf{x}\boldsymbol{\beta}$, then

$$\mathrm{E}(y \mid \mathbf{x}) \geq \max(0, \mathbf{x}\boldsymbol{\beta}) \tag{16.7}$$

which is always nonnegative. Equation (16.7) shows that $\mathrm{E}(y \mid \mathbf{x})$ is bounded from below by the larger of zero and $\mathbf{x}\boldsymbol{\beta}$.

When u is independent of $\mathbf{x}$ and has a normal distribution, we can find an explicit expression for $\mathrm{E}(y \mid \mathbf{x})$. We first derive $\mathrm{P}(y > 0 \mid \mathbf{x})$ and $\mathrm{E}(y \mid \mathbf{x}, y > 0)$, which are of interest in their own right. Then, we use the law of iterated expectations to obtain $\mathrm{E}(y \mid \mathbf{x})$:

$$\begin{aligned} \mathrm{E}(y \mid \mathbf{x}) &= \mathrm{P}(y = 0 \mid \mathbf{x}) \cdot 0 + \mathrm{P}(y > 0 \mid \mathbf{x}) \cdot \mathrm{E}(y \mid \mathbf{x}, y > 0) \\ &= \mathrm{P}(y > 0 \mid \mathbf{x}) \cdot \mathrm{E}(y \mid \mathbf{x}, y > 0) \end{aligned} \tag{16.8}$$

Deriving $\mathrm{P}(y > 0 \mid \mathbf{x})$ is easy. Define the binary variable $w = 1$ if $y > 0$, $w = 0$ if $y = 0$. Then w follows a probit model:

$$\begin{aligned} \mathrm{P}(w = 1 \mid \mathbf{x}) &= \mathrm{P}(y^* > 0 \mid \mathbf{x}) = \mathrm{P}(u > -\mathbf{x}\boldsymbol{\beta} \mid \mathbf{x}) \\ &= \mathrm{P}(u/\sigma > -\mathbf{x}\boldsymbol{\beta}/\sigma) = \Phi(\mathbf{x}\boldsymbol{\beta}/\sigma) \end{aligned} \tag{16.9}$$

One implication of equation (16.9) is that $\boldsymbol{\gamma} \equiv \boldsymbol{\beta}/\sigma$, but not $\boldsymbol{\beta}$ and σ separately, can be consistently estimated from a probit of w on $\mathbf{x}$.

To derive $\mathrm{E}(y \mid \mathbf{x}, y > 0)$, we need the following fact about the normal distribution: if $z \sim \mathrm{Normal}(0, 1)$, then, for any constant c,

$$\mathrm{E}(z \mid z > c) = \frac{\phi(c)}{1 - \Phi(c)}$$

where $\phi(\cdot)$ is the standard normal density function. {This is easily shown by noting that the density of z given $z > c$ is $\phi(z)/[1 - \Phi(c)]$, $z > c$, and then integrating $z\phi(z)$ from c to ∞.} Therefore, if $u \sim \text{Normal}(0, \sigma^2)$, then

$$\mathrm{E}(u \mid u > c) = \sigma \mathrm{E}\left(\frac{u}{\sigma} \,\middle|\, \frac{u}{\sigma} > \frac{c}{\sigma}\right) = \sigma\left[\frac{\phi(c/\sigma)}{1 - \Phi(c/\sigma)}\right]$$

We can use this equation to find $\mathrm{E}(y \mid \mathbf{x}, y > 0)$ when y follows a Tobit model:

$$\mathrm{E}(y \mid \mathbf{x}, y > 0) = \mathbf{x}\boldsymbol{\beta} + \mathrm{E}(u \mid u > -\mathbf{x}\boldsymbol{\beta}) = \mathbf{x}\boldsymbol{\beta} + \sigma\left[\frac{\phi(\mathbf{x}\boldsymbol{\beta}/\sigma)}{\Phi(\mathbf{x}\boldsymbol{\beta}/\sigma)}\right] \tag{16.10}$$

since $1 - \Phi(-\mathbf{x}\boldsymbol{\beta}/\sigma) = \Phi(\mathbf{x}\boldsymbol{\beta}/\sigma)$. Although it is not obvious from looking at equation (16.10), the right-hand side is positive for any values of $\mathbf{x}$ and $\boldsymbol{\beta}$; this statement must be true by equations (16.7) and (16.8).

For any c the quantity $\lambda(c) \equiv \phi(c)/\Phi(c)$ is called the **inverse Mills ratio**. Thus, $\mathrm{E}(y \mid \mathbf{x}, y > 0)$ is the sum of $\mathbf{x}\boldsymbol{\beta}$ and σ times the inverse Mills ratio evaluated at $\mathbf{x}\boldsymbol{\beta}/\sigma$.

If x_j is a continuous explanatory variable, then

$$\frac{\partial \mathrm{E}(y \mid \mathbf{x}, y > 0)}{\partial x_j} = \beta_j + \beta_j\left[\frac{\mathrm{d}\lambda}{\mathrm{d}c}(\mathbf{x}\boldsymbol{\beta}/\sigma)\right]$$

assuming that x_j is not functionally related to other regressors. By differentiating $\lambda(c) = \phi(c)/\Phi(c)$, it can be shown that $\dfrac{\mathrm{d}\lambda}{\mathrm{d}c}(c) = -\lambda(c)[c + \lambda(c)]$, and therefore

$$\frac{\partial \mathrm{E}(y \mid \mathbf{x}, y > 0)}{\partial x_j} = \beta_j\{1 - \lambda(\mathbf{x}\boldsymbol{\beta}/\sigma)[\mathbf{x}\boldsymbol{\beta}/\sigma + \lambda(\mathbf{x}\boldsymbol{\beta}/\sigma)]\} \tag{16.11}$$

This equation shows that the partial effect of x_j on $\mathrm{E}(y \mid \mathbf{x}, y > 0)$ is not entirely determined by β_j; there is an adjustment factor multiplying β_j, the term in $\{\cdot\}$, that depends on $\mathbf{x}$ through the index $\mathbf{x}\boldsymbol{\beta}/\sigma$. We can use the fact that if $z \sim \text{Normal}(0, 1)$, then $\mathrm{Var}(z \mid z > -c) = 1 - \lambda(c)[c + \lambda(c)]$ for any $c \in \mathbb{R}$, which implies that the adjustment factor in equation (16.11), call it $\theta(\mathbf{x}\boldsymbol{\beta}/\sigma) = \{1 - \lambda(\mathbf{x}\boldsymbol{\beta}/\sigma)[\mathbf{x}\boldsymbol{\beta}/\sigma + \lambda(\mathbf{x}\boldsymbol{\beta}/\sigma)]\}$, is strictly between zero and one. Therefore, the sign of β_j is the same as the sign of the partial effect of x_j.

Other functional forms are easily handled. Suppose that $x_1 = \log(z_1)$ (and that this is the only place z_1 appears in $\mathbf{x}$). Then

$$\frac{\partial \mathrm{E}(y \mid \mathbf{x}, y > 0)}{\partial z_1} = (\beta_1/z_1)\theta(\mathbf{x}\boldsymbol{\beta}/\sigma) \tag{16.12}$$

where β_1 now denotes the coefficient on $\log(z_1)$. Or, suppose that $x_1 = z_1$ and $x_2 = z_1^2$. Then

$$\frac{\partial \mathrm{E}(y \mid \mathbf{x}, y > 0)}{\partial z_1} = (\beta_1 + 2\beta_2 z_1)\theta(\mathbf{x}\boldsymbol{\beta}/\sigma)$$

where β_1 is the coefficient on z_1 and β_2 is the coefficient on z_1^2. Interaction terms are handled similarly. Generally, we compute the partial effect of $\mathbf{x}\boldsymbol{\beta}$ with respect to the variable of interest and multiply this by the factor $\theta(\mathbf{x}\boldsymbol{\beta}/\sigma)$.

All of the usual economic quantities such as elasticities can be computed. The elasticity of y with respect to x_1, conditional on $y > 0$, is

$$\frac{\partial \mathrm{E}(y \mid \mathbf{x}, y > 0)}{\partial x_1} \cdot \frac{x_1}{\mathrm{E}(y \mid \mathbf{x}, y > 0)} \tag{16.13}$$

and equations (16.11) and (16.10) can be used to find the elasticity when x_1 appears in levels form. If z_1 appears in logarithmic form, the elasticity is obtained simply as $\partial \log \mathrm{E}(y \mid \mathbf{x}, y > 0)/\partial \log(z_1)$.

If x_1 is a binary variable, the effect of interest is obtained as the difference between $\mathrm{E}(y \mid \mathbf{x}, y > 0)$ with $x_1 = 1$ and $x_1 = 0$. Other discrete variables (such as number of children) can be handled similarly.

We can also compute $\mathrm{E}(y \mid \mathbf{x})$ from equation (16.8):

$$\begin{aligned} \mathrm{E}(y \mid \mathbf{x}) &= \mathrm{P}(y > 0 \mid \mathbf{x}) \cdot \mathrm{E}(y \mid \mathbf{x}, y > 0) \\ &= \Phi(\mathbf{x}\boldsymbol{\beta}/\sigma)[\mathbf{x}\boldsymbol{\beta} + \sigma\lambda(\mathbf{x}\boldsymbol{\beta}/\sigma)] = \Phi(\mathbf{x}\boldsymbol{\beta}/\sigma)\mathbf{x}\boldsymbol{\beta} + \sigma\phi(\mathbf{x}\boldsymbol{\beta}/\sigma) \end{aligned} \tag{16.14}$$

We can find the partial derivatives of $\mathrm{E}(y \mid \mathbf{x})$ with respect to continuous x_j using the chain rule. In examples where y is some quantity chosen by individuals (labor supply, charitable contributions, life insurance), this derivative accounts for the fact that some people who start at $y = 0$ may switch to $y > 0$ when x_j changes. Formally,

$$\frac{\partial \mathrm{E}(y \mid \mathbf{x})}{\partial x_j} = \frac{\partial \mathrm{P}(y > 0 \mid \mathbf{x})}{\partial x_j} \cdot \mathrm{E}(y \mid \mathbf{x}, y > 0) + \mathrm{P}(y > 0 \mid \mathbf{x}) \cdot \frac{\partial \mathrm{E}(y \mid \mathbf{x}, y > 0)}{\partial x_j} \tag{16.15}$$

This decomposition is attributed to McDonald and Moffitt (1980). Because $\mathrm{P}(y > 0 \mid \mathbf{x}) = \Phi(\mathbf{x}\boldsymbol{\beta}/\sigma)$, $\partial \mathrm{P}(y > 0 \mid \mathbf{x})/\partial x_j = (\beta_j/\sigma)\phi(\mathbf{x}\boldsymbol{\beta}/\sigma)$. If we plug this along with equation (16.11) into equation (16.15), we get a remarkable simplification:

$$\frac{\partial \mathrm{E}(y \mid \mathbf{x})}{\partial x_j} = \Phi(\mathbf{x}\boldsymbol{\beta}/\sigma)\beta_j \tag{16.16}$$

The estimated scale factor for a given $\mathbf{x}$ is $\Phi(\mathbf{x}\hat{\boldsymbol{\beta}}/\hat{\sigma})$. This scale factor has a very interesting interpretation: $\Phi(\mathbf{x}\hat{\boldsymbol{\beta}}/\hat{\sigma}) = \hat{\mathrm{P}}(y > 0 \mid \mathbf{x})$; that is, $\Phi(\mathbf{x}\hat{\boldsymbol{\beta}}/\hat{\sigma})$ is the estimated probability of observing a positive response given $\mathbf{x}$. If $\Phi(\mathbf{x}\hat{\boldsymbol{\beta}}/\hat{\sigma})$ is close to one, then it is unlikely we observe $y_i = 0$ when $\mathbf{x}_i = \mathbf{x}$, and the adjustment factor becomes unimportant. In practice, a single adjustment factor is obtained as $\Phi(\bar{\mathbf{x}}\hat{\boldsymbol{\beta}}/\hat{\sigma})$, where $\bar{\mathbf{x}}$ denotes the vector of mean values. If the estimated probability of a positive response is close to one at the sample means of the covariates, the adjustment factor can be ignored. In most interesting Tobit applications, $\Phi(\bar{\mathbf{x}}\hat{\boldsymbol{\beta}}/\hat{\sigma})$ is notably less than unity.

For discrete variables or for large changes in continuous variables, we can compute the difference in $\mathrm{E}(y \mid \mathbf{x})$ at different values of $\mathbf{x}$. [Incidentally, equations (16.11) and (16.16) show that σ is not a "nuisance parameter," as it is sometimes called in Tobit applications: σ plays a crucial role in estimating the partial effects of interest in corner solution applications.]

Equations (16.9), (16.11), and (16.14) show that, for continuous variables x_j and x_h, the *relative* partial effects on $\mathrm{P}(y > 0 \mid \mathbf{x})$, $\mathrm{E}(y \mid \mathbf{x}, y > 0)$, and $\mathrm{E}(y \mid \mathbf{x})$ are all equal to β_j/β_h (assuming that $\beta_h \neq 0$). This fact can be a limitation of the Tobit model, something we take up further in Section 16.7.

By taking the log of equation (16.8) and differentiating, we see that the elasticity (or semielasticity) of $\mathrm{E}(y \mid \mathbf{x})$ with respect to any x_j is simply the sum of the elasticities (or semielasticities) of $\Phi(\mathbf{x}\boldsymbol{\beta}/\sigma)$ and $\mathrm{E}(y \mid \mathbf{x}, y > 0)$, each with respect to x_j.

16.3 Inconsistency of OLS

We can use the previous expectation calculations to show that OLS using the entire sample or OLS using the subsample for which $y_i > 0$ are both (generally) inconsistent estimators of $\boldsymbol{\beta}$. First consider OLS using the subsample with strictly positive y_i. From equation (16.10) we can write

$$y_i = \mathbf{x}_i\boldsymbol{\beta} + \sigma\lambda(\mathbf{x}_i\boldsymbol{\beta}/\sigma) + e_i \tag{16.17}$$

$$\mathrm{E}(e_i \mid \mathbf{x}_i, y_i > 0) = 0 \tag{16.18}$$

which implies that $\mathrm{E}(e_i \mid \mathbf{x}_i, \lambda_i, y_i > 0) = 0$, where $\lambda_i \equiv \lambda(\mathbf{x}_i\boldsymbol{\beta}/\sigma)$. It follows that if we run OLS of y_i on $\mathbf{x}_i$ using the sample for which $y_i > 0$, we effectively omit the variable λ_i. Correlation between λ_i and $\mathbf{x}_i$ in the selected subpopulation results in inconsistent estimation of $\boldsymbol{\beta}$.

The inconsistency of OLS restricted to the subsample with $y_i > 0$ is especially unfortunate in the case of true data censoring. Restricting the sample to $y_i > 0$ means we are only using the data on uncensored observations. In the wealth top coding example, this restriction means we drop all people whose wealth is at least \$200,000. In a duration application—see Problem 16.1 and Chapter 20—it would mean using only observations with uncensored durations. It would be convenient if OLS using only the uncensored observations were consistent for $\boldsymbol{\beta}$, but such is not the case.

From equation (16.14) it is also pretty clear that regressing y_i on $\mathbf{x}_i$ using all of the data will not consistently estimate $\boldsymbol{\beta}$: $\mathrm{E}(y \mid \mathbf{x})$ is nonlinear in $\mathbf{x}$, $\boldsymbol{\beta}$, and σ, so it would be a fluke if a linear regression consistently estimated $\boldsymbol{\beta}$.

There are some interesting theoretical results about how the slope coefficients in $\boldsymbol{\beta}$ can be estimated up to scale using one of the two OLS regressions that we have discussed. Therefore, each OLS coefficient is inconsistent by the *same* multiplicative factor. This fact allows us—both in data-censoring applications and corner solution applications—to estimate the relative effects of any two explanatory variables. The assumptions made to derive such results are very restrictive, and they generally rule out discrete and other discontinuous regressors. [Multivariate normality of $(\mathbf{x}, y^*)$ is sufficient.] The arguments, which rely on linear projections, are elegant—see, for example, Chung and Goldberger (1984)—but such results have questionable practical value.

The previous discussion does not mean a linear regression of y_i on $\mathbf{x}_i$ is uninformative. Remember that, whether or not the Tobit model holds, we can always write the linear projection of y on $\mathbf{x}$ as $\mathrm{L}(y \mid \mathbf{x}) = \mathbf{x}\boldsymbol{\gamma}$ for $\boldsymbol{\gamma} = [\mathrm{E}(\mathbf{x}'\mathbf{x})]^{-1}\mathrm{E}(\mathbf{x}'y)$, under the mild restriction that all second moments are finite. It is possible that γ_j approximates the effect of x_j on $\mathrm{E}(y \mid \mathbf{x})$ when $\mathbf{x}$ is near its population mean. Similarly, a linear regression of y_i on $\mathbf{x}_i$, using only observations with $y_i > 0$, might approximate the partial effects on $\mathrm{E}(y \mid \mathbf{x}, y > 0)$ near the mean values of the x_j. Such issues have not been fully explored in corner solution applications of the Tobit model.

16.4 Estimation and Inference with Censored Tobit

Let $\{(\mathbf{x}_i, y_i): i = 1, 2, \ldots N\}$ be a random sample following the censored Tobit model. To use maximum likelihood, we need to derive the density of y_i given $\mathbf{x}_i$. We have already shown that $f(0 \mid \mathbf{x}_i) = \mathrm{P}(y_i = 0 \mid \mathbf{x}_i) = 1 - \Phi(\mathbf{x}_i\boldsymbol{\beta}/\sigma)$. Further, for $\mathscr{y} > 0$, $\mathrm{P}(y_i \le \mathscr{y} \mid \mathbf{x}_i) = \mathrm{P}(y_i^* \le \mathscr{y} \mid \mathbf{x}_i)$, which implies that

$$f(\mathscr{y} \mid \mathbf{x}_i) = f^*(\mathscr{y} \mid \mathbf{x}_i), \qquad \text{all } \mathscr{y} > 0$$

where $f^*(\cdot \mid \mathbf{x}_i)$ denotes the density of y_i^* given $\mathbf{x}_i$. (We use $\mathscr{y}$ as the dummy argument in the density.) By assumption, $y_i^* \mid \mathbf{x}_i \sim \mathrm{Normal}(\mathbf{x}_i\boldsymbol{\beta}, \sigma^2)$, so

$$f^*(\mathscr{y} \mid \mathbf{x}_i) = \frac{1}{\sigma}\phi[(\mathscr{y} - \mathbf{x}_i\boldsymbol{\beta})/\sigma], \qquad -\infty < \mathscr{y} < \infty$$

(As in recent chapters, we will use $\boldsymbol{\beta}$ and σ^2 to denote the true values as well as dummy arguments in the log-likelihood function and its derivatives.) We can write the density for y_i given $\mathbf{x}_i$ compactly using the indicator function $1[\cdot]$ as

$$f(y \mid \mathbf{x}_i) = \{1 - \Phi(\mathbf{x}_i\boldsymbol{\beta}/\sigma)\}^{1[y=0]}\{(1/\sigma)\phi[(y - \mathbf{x}_i\boldsymbol{\beta})/\sigma]\}^{1[y>0]} \tag{16.19}$$

where the density is zero for $y < 0$. Let $\boldsymbol{\theta} \equiv (\boldsymbol{\beta}', \sigma^2)'$ denote the $(K+1) \times 1$ vector of parameters. The conditional log likelihood is

$$\ell_i(\boldsymbol{\theta}) = 1[y_i = 0] \log[1 - \Phi(\mathbf{x}_i\boldsymbol{\beta}/\sigma)] + 1[y_i > 0]\{\log \phi[(y_i - \mathbf{x}_i\boldsymbol{\beta})/\sigma] - \log(\sigma^2)/2\} \tag{16.20}$$

Apart from a constant that does not affect the maximization, equation (16.20) can be written as

$$1[y_i = 0] \log[1 - \Phi(\mathbf{x}_i\boldsymbol{\beta}/\sigma)] - 1[y_i > 0]\{(y_i - \mathbf{x}_i\boldsymbol{\beta})^2/2\sigma^2 + \log(\sigma^2)/2\}$$

Therefore,

$$\partial\ell_i(\boldsymbol{\theta})/\partial\boldsymbol{\beta} = -1[y_i = 0]\phi(\mathbf{x}_i\boldsymbol{\beta}/\sigma)\mathbf{x}_i/[1 - \Phi(\mathbf{x}_i\boldsymbol{\beta}/\sigma)] + 1[y_i > 0](y_i - \mathbf{x}_i\boldsymbol{\beta})\mathbf{x}_i/\sigma^2 \tag{16.21}$$

$$\begin{aligned}\partial\ell_i(\boldsymbol{\theta})/\partial\sigma^2 = {} & 1[y_i = 0]\phi(\mathbf{x}_i\boldsymbol{\beta}/\sigma)(\mathbf{x}_i\boldsymbol{\beta})/\{2\sigma^2[1 - \Phi(\mathbf{x}_i\boldsymbol{\beta}/\sigma)]\} \\ & + 1[y_i > 0]\{(y_i - \mathbf{x}_i\boldsymbol{\beta})^2/(2\sigma^4) - 1/(2\sigma^2)\}\end{aligned} \tag{16.22}$$

The second derivatives are complicated, but all we need is $\mathbf{A}(\mathbf{x}_i, \boldsymbol{\theta}) \equiv -\mathrm{E}[\mathbf{H}_i(\boldsymbol{\theta}) \mid \mathbf{x}_i]$. After tedious calculations it can be shown that

$$\mathbf{A}(\mathbf{x}_i, \boldsymbol{\theta}) = \begin{bmatrix} a_i\mathbf{x}_i'\mathbf{x}_i & b_i\mathbf{x}_i' \\ b_i\mathbf{x}_i & c_i \end{bmatrix} \tag{16.23}$$

where

$$a_i = -\sigma^{-2}\{\mathbf{x}_i\gamma\phi_i - [\phi_i^2/(1 - \Phi_i)] - \Phi_i\}$$

$$b_i = \sigma^{-3}\{(\mathbf{x}_i\gamma)^2\phi_i + \phi_i - [(\mathbf{x}_i\gamma)\phi_i^2/(1 - \Phi_i)]\}/2$$

$$c_i = -\sigma^{-4}\{(\mathbf{x}_i\gamma)^3\phi_i + (\mathbf{x}_i\gamma)\phi_i - [(\mathbf{x}_i\gamma)\phi_i^2/(1 - \Phi_i)] - 2\Phi_i\}/4$$

$\gamma = \boldsymbol{\beta}/\sigma$, and ϕ_i and Φ_i are evaluated at $\mathbf{x}_i\gamma$. This matrix is used in equation (13.32) to obtain the estimate of $\mathrm{Avar}(\hat{\boldsymbol{\theta}})$. See Amemiya (1973) for details.

Testing is easily carried out in a standard MLE framework. Single exclusion restrictions are tested using asymptotic t statistics once $\hat{\beta}_j$ and its asymptotic standard error have been obtained. Multiple exclusion restrictions are easily tested using the LR statistic, and some econometrics packages routinely compute the Wald statistic.

If the unrestricted model has so many variables that computation becomes an issue, the LM statistic is an attractive alternative.

The Wald statistic is the easiest to compute for testing nonlinear restrictions on $\boldsymbol{\beta}$, just as in binary response analysis, because the unrestricted model is just standard Tobit.

16.5 Reporting the Results

For data censoring applications, the quantities of interest are the $\hat{\beta}_j$ and their standard errors. (We might use these to compute elasticities, and so on.) We interpret the estimated model *as if* there were no data-censoring problem, because the population model is a linear conditional mean. The value of the log-likelihood function should be reported for any estimated model because of its role in obtaining likelihood ratio statistics. We can test for omitted variables, including nonlinear functions of already included variables, using either t tests or LR tests. All of these rely on the homoskedastic normal assumption in the underlying population.

For corner solution applications, the same statistics can be reported, and, in addition, we should report estimated partial effects on $\mathrm{E}(y \mid \mathbf{x}, y > 0)$ and $\mathrm{E}(y \mid \mathbf{x})$. The formulas for these are given in Section 16.2, where $\boldsymbol{\beta}$ and σ are replaced with their MLEs. Because these estimates depend on $\mathbf{x}$, we must decide at what values of $\mathbf{x}$ to report the partial effects or elasticities. As with probit, the average values of $\mathbf{x}$ can be used, or, if some elements of $\mathbf{x}$ are qualitative variables, we can assign them values of particular interest. For the important elements of $\mathbf{x}$, the partial effects or elasticities can be estimated at a range of values, holding the other elements fixed. For example, if x_1 is price, then we can compute equation (16.11) or (16.16), or the corresponding elasticities, for low, medium, and high prices, while keeping all other elements fixed. If x_1 is a dummy variable, then we can obtain the difference in estimates with $x_1 = 1$ and $x_1 = 0$, holding all other elements of $\mathbf{x}$ fixed. Standard errors of these estimates can be obtained by the delta method, although the calculations can be tedious.

Example 16.3 (Annual Hours Equation for Married Women): We use the Mroz (1987) data (MROZ.RAW) to estimate a reduced form annual hours equation for married women. The equation is a reduced form because we do not include hourly wage offer as an explanatory variable. The hourly wage offer is unlikely to be exogenous, and, just as importantly, we cannot observe it when *hours* $= 0$. We will show how to deal with both these issues in Chapter 17. For now, the explanatory variables are the same ones appearing in the labor force participation probit in Example 15.2.

Of the 753 women in the sample, 428 worked for a wage outside the home during the year; 325 of the women worked zero hours. For the women who worked positive

Table 16.1
OLS and Tobit Estimation of Annual Hours Worked

Dependent Variable: *hours*		
Independent Variable	Linear (OLS)	Tobit (MLE)
nwifeinc	−3.45 (2.54)	−8.81 (4.46)
educ	28.76 (12.95)	80.65 (21.58)
exper	65.67 (9.96)	131.56 (17.28)
$exper^2$	−.700 (.325)	−1.86 (0.54)
age	−30.51 (4.36)	−54.41 (7.42)
kidslt6	−442.09 (58.85)	−894.02 (111.88)
kidsge6	−32.78 (23.18)	−16.22 (38.64)
constant	1,330.48 (270.78)	965.31 (446.44)
Log-likelihood value	—	−3,819.09
R-squared	.266	.275
$\hat{\sigma}$	750.18	1,122.02

hours, the range is fairly broad, ranging from 12 to 4,950. Thus, annual hours worked is a reasonable candidate for a Tobit model. We also estimate a linear model (using all 753 observations) by OLS. The results are in Table 16.1.

Not surprisingly, the Tobit coefficient estimates are the same sign as the corresponding OLS estimates, and the statistical significance of the estimates is similar. (Possible exceptions are the coefficients on *nwifeinc* and *kidsge6*, but the t statistics have similar magnitudes.) Second, though it is tempting to compare the magnitudes of the OLS estimates and the Tobit estimates, such comparisons are not very informative. We must not think that, because the Tobit coefficient on *kidslt6* is roughly twice that of the OLS coefficient, the Tobit model somehow implies a much greater response of hours worked to young children.

We can multiply the Tobit estimates by the adjustment factors in equations (16.11) and (16.16), evaluated at the estimates and the mean values of the x_j (but where we square $\overline{exper}$ rather than use the average of the $exper_i^2$), to obtain the partial effects on the conditional expectations. The factor in equation (16.11) is about .451. For example, conditional on *hours* being positive, a year of education (starting from the mean values of all variables) is estimated to increase expected hours by about

$.451(80.65) \approx 36.4$ hours. Using the approximation for one more young child gives a fall in expected hours by about $(.451)(894.02) \approx 403.2$. Of course, this figure does not make sense for a woman working less than 403.2 hours. It would be better to estimate the expected values at two different values of *kidslt6* and form the difference, rather than using the calculus approximation.

The factor in equation (16.16), again evaluated at the mean values of the x_j, is about .645. This result means that the estimated probability of a woman being in the workforce, at the mean values of the covariates, is about .645. Therefore, the magnitudes of the effects of each x_j on expected *hours*—that is, when we account for people who initially do not work, as well as those who are initially working—is larger than when we condition on $hours > 0$. We can multiply the Tobit coefficients, at least those on roughly continuous explanatory variables, by .645 to make them roughly comparable to the OLS estimates in the first column. In most cases the estimated Tobit effect at the mean values are significantly above the corresponding OLS estimate. For example, the Tobit effect of one more year of education is about $.645(80.65) \approx 52.02$, which is well above the OLS estimate of 28.76.

We have reported an *R*-squared for both the linear regression model and the Tobit model. The *R*-squared for OLS is the usual one. For Tobit, the *R*-squared is the square of the correlation coefficient between y_i and $\hat{y}_i$, where $\hat{y}_i = \Phi(\mathbf{x}_i\hat{\boldsymbol{\beta}}/\hat{\sigma})\mathbf{x}_i\hat{\boldsymbol{\beta}} + \hat{\sigma}\phi(\mathbf{x}_i\hat{\boldsymbol{\beta}}/\hat{\sigma})$ is the estimate of $\mathrm{E}(y \mid \mathbf{x} = \mathbf{x}_i)$. This statistic is motivated by the fact that the usual *R*-squared for OLS is equal to the squared correlation between the y_i and the OLS fitted values.

Based on the *R*-squared measures, the Tobit conditional mean function fits the hours data somewhat better, although the difference is not overwhelming. However, we should remember that the Tobit estimates are not chosen to maximize an *R*-squared—they maximize the log-likelihood function—whereas the OLS estimates produce the highest *R*-squared given the linear functional form for the conditional mean.

When two additional variables, the local unemployment rate and a binary city indicator, are included, the log likelihood becomes about $-3{,}817.89$. The likelihood ratio statistic is about $2(3{,}819.09 - 3{,}817.89) = 2.40$. This is the outcome of a χ_2^2 variate under H_0, and so the *p*-value is about .30. Therefore, these two variables are jointly insignificant.

16.6 Specification Issues in Tobit Models

16.6.1 Neglected Heterogeneity

Suppose that we are initially interested in the model

$$y = \max(0, \mathbf{x}\boldsymbol{\beta} + \gamma q + u), \qquad u \mid \mathbf{x}, q \sim \mathrm{Normal}(0, \sigma^2) \tag{16.24}$$

where q is an unobserved variable that is assumed to be independent of $\mathbf{x}$ and has a Normal$(0, \tau^2)$ distribution. It follows immediately that

$$y = \max(0, \mathbf{x}\boldsymbol{\beta} + v), \qquad v \mid \mathbf{x} \sim \text{Normal}(0, \sigma^2 + \gamma^2\tau^2) \tag{16.25}$$

Thus, y conditional on $\mathbf{x}$ follows a Tobit model, and Tobit of y on $\mathbf{x}$ consistently estimates $\boldsymbol{\beta}$ and $\eta^2 \equiv \sigma^2 + \gamma^2\tau^2$. In data-censoring cases we are interested in $\boldsymbol{\beta}$; γ is of no use without observing q, and γ cannot be estimated anyway. We have shown that heterogeneity independent of $\mathbf{x}$ and normally distributed has no important consequences in data-censoring examples.

Things are more complicated in corner solution examples because, at least initially, we are interested in $\text{E}(y \mid \mathbf{x}, q)$ or $\text{E}(y \mid \mathbf{x}, q, y > 0)$. As we discussed in Sections 2.2.5 and 15.7.1, we are often interested in the average partial effects (APEs), where, say, $\text{E}(y \mid \mathbf{x}, q)$ is averaged over the population distribution of q, and then derivatives or differences with respect to elements of $\mathbf{x}$ are obtained. From Section 2.2.5 we know that when the heterogeneity is independent of $\mathbf{x}$, the APEs are obtained by finding $\text{E}(y \mid \mathbf{x})$ [or $\text{E}(y \mid \mathbf{x}, y > 0)$]. Naturally, these conditional means come from the distribution of y given $\mathbf{x}$. Under the preceding assumptions, it is exactly this distribution that Tobit of y on $\mathbf{x}$ estimates. In other words, we estimate the desired quantities—the APEs—by simply ignoring the heterogeneity. This is the same conclusion we reached for the probit model in Section 15.7.1.

If q is not normal, then these arguments do not carry over because y given $\mathbf{x}$ does not follow a Tobit model. But the flavor of the argument does. A more difficult issue arises when q and $\mathbf{x}$ are correlated, and we address this in the next subsection.

16.6.2 Endogenous Explanatory Variables

Suppose we now allow one of the variables in the Tobit model to be endogenous. The model is

$$y_1 = \max(0, \mathbf{z}_1\boldsymbol{\delta}_1 + \alpha_1 y_2 + u_1) \tag{16.26}$$

$$y_2 = \mathbf{z}\boldsymbol{\delta}_2 + v_2 = \mathbf{z}_1\boldsymbol{\delta}_{21} + \mathbf{z}_2\boldsymbol{\delta}_{22} + v_2 \tag{16.27}$$

where (u_1, v_2) are zero-mean normally distributed, independent of $\mathbf{z}$. If u_1 and v_2 are correlated, then y_2 is endogenous. For identification we need the usual rank condition $\boldsymbol{\delta}_{22} \neq \mathbf{0}$; $\text{E}(\mathbf{z}'\mathbf{z})$ is assumed to have full rank, as always.

If equation (16.26) represents a data-censoring problem, we are interested, as always, in the parameters, $\boldsymbol{\delta}_1$ and α_1, as these are the parameters of interest in the uncensored population model. For corner solution outcomes, the quantities of interest are more subtle. However, when the endogeneity of y_2 is due to omitted variables or simultaneity, the parameters we need to estimate to obtain average partial effects are $\boldsymbol{\delta}_1$, α_1, and $\sigma_1^2 = \mathrm{Var}(u_1)$. The reasoning is just as for the probit model in Section 15.7.2. Holding other factors fixed, the difference in y_1 when y_2 changes from $\bar{y}_2$ to $\bar{y}_2 + 1$ is

$$\max[0, \bar{\mathbf{z}}_1 \boldsymbol{\delta}_1 + \alpha_1(\bar{y}_2 + 1) + u_1] - \max[0, \bar{\mathbf{z}}_1 \boldsymbol{\delta}_1 + \alpha_1 \bar{y}_2 + u_1]$$

Averaging this expression across the distribution of u_1 gives differences in expectations that have the form (16.14), with $\mathbf{x} = [\bar{\mathbf{z}}_1, (\bar{y}_2 + 1)]$ in the first case, $\mathbf{x} = (\bar{\mathbf{z}}_1, \bar{y}_2)$ in the second, and $\sigma = \sigma_1$. Importantly, unlike in the data censoring case, we need to estimate σ_1^2 in order to estimate the partial effects of interest (the APEs).

Before estimating this model by maximum likelihood, a procedure that requires obtaining the distribution of (y_1, y_2) given $\mathbf{z}$, it is convenient to have a two-step procedure that also delivers a simple test for the endogeneity of y_2. Smith and Blundell (1986) propose a two-step procedure that is analogous to the Rivers-Vuong method (see Section 15.7.2) for binary response models. Under bivariate normality of (u_1, v_2), we can write

$$u_1 = \theta_1 v_2 + e_1 \tag{16.28}$$

where $\theta_1 = \eta_1/\tau_2^2$, $\eta_1 = \mathrm{Cov}(u_1, v_2)$, $\tau_2^2 = \mathrm{Var}(v_2)$, and e_1 is independent of v_2 with a zero-mean normal distribution and variance, say, τ_1^2. Further, because (u_1, v_2) is independent of $\mathbf{z}$, e_1 is independent of $(\mathbf{z}, v_2)$. Now, plugging equation (16.28) into equation (16.26) gives

$$y_1 = \max(0, \mathbf{z}_1 \boldsymbol{\delta}_1 + \alpha_1 y_2 + \theta_1 v_2 + e_1) \tag{16.29}$$

where $e_1 \mid \mathbf{z}, v_2 \sim \mathrm{Normal}(0, \tau_1^2)$. It follows that, if we knew v_2, we would just estimate $\boldsymbol{\delta}_1$, α_1, θ_1, and τ_1^2 by standard censored Tobit. We do not observe v_2 because it depends on the unknown vector $\boldsymbol{\delta}_2$. However, we can easily estimate $\boldsymbol{\delta}_2$ by OLS in a first stage. The Smith-Blundell procedure is as follows:

Procedure 16.1: (a) Estimate the reduced form of y_2 by OLS; this step gives $\hat{\boldsymbol{\delta}}_2$. Define the reduced-form OLS residuals as $\hat{v}_2 = y_2 - \mathbf{z}\hat{\boldsymbol{\delta}}_2$.

(b) Estimate a standard Tobit of y_1 on $\mathbf{z}_1$, y_2, and $\hat{v}_2$. This step gives consistent estimators of $\boldsymbol{\delta}_1$, α_1, θ_1, and τ_1^2.

The usual t statistic on $\hat{v}_2$ reported by Tobit provides a simple test of the null H_0: $\theta_1 = 0$, which says that y_2 is exogenous. Further, under $\theta_1 = 0$, $e_1 = u_1$, and so normality of v_2 plays no role: as a *test* for endogeneity of y_2, the Smith-Blundell approach is valid without any distributional assumptions on the reduced form of y_2.

Example 16.4 (Testing Exogeneity of Education in the Hours Equation): As an illustration, we test for endogeneity of *educ* in the reduced-form hours equation in Example 16.3. We assume that *motheduc*, *fatheduc*, and *huseduc* are exogenous in the hours equation, and so these are valid instruments for *educ*. We first obtain $\hat{v}_2$ as the OLS residuals from estimating the reduced form for *educ*. When $\hat{v}_2$ is added to the Tobit model in Example 16.3 (without *unem* and *city*), its coefficient is 39.88 with t statistic $= .91$. Thus, there is little evidence that *educ* is endogenous in the equation. The test is valid under the null hypothesis that *educ* is exogenous even if *educ* does not have a conditional normal distribution.

When $\theta_1 \neq 0$, the second-stage Tobit standard errors and test statistics are not asymptotically valid because $\hat{\boldsymbol{\delta}}_2$ has been used in place of $\boldsymbol{\delta}_2$. Smith and Blundell (1986) contain formulas for correcting the asymptotic variances; these can be derived using the formulas for two-step M-estimators in Chapter 12. It is easily seen that joint normality of (u_1, v_2) is not absolutely needed for the procedure to work. It suffices that u_1 conditional on $\mathbf{z}$ and v_2 is distributed as Normal$(\theta_1 v_2, \tau_1^2)$. Still, this is a fairly restrictive assumption.

When $\theta_1 \neq 0$, the Smith-Blundell procedure does not allow us to estimate σ_1^2, which is needed to estimate average partial effects in corner solution outcomes. Nevertheless, we can obtain consistent estimates of the average partial effects by using methods similar to those in the probit case. Using the same reasoning in Section 15.7.2, the APEs are obtained by computing derivatives or differences of

$$\mathrm{E}_{v_2}[m(\mathbf{z}_1\boldsymbol{\delta}_1 + \alpha_1 y_2 + \theta_1 v_2, \tau_1^2)] \tag{16.30}$$

where $m(z, \sigma^2) \equiv \Phi(z/\sigma)z + \sigma\phi(z/\sigma)$ and $\mathrm{E}_{v_2}[\cdot]$ denotes expectation with respect to the distribution of v_2. Using the same argument as in Section 16.6.1, expression (16.30) can be written as $m(\mathbf{z}_1\boldsymbol{\delta}_1 + \alpha_1 y_2, \theta_1^2\tau_2^2 + \tau_1^2)$. Therefore, consistent estimators of the APEs are obtained by taking, with respect to elements of $(\mathbf{z}_1, y_2)$, derivatives or differences of

$$m(\mathbf{z}_1\hat{\boldsymbol{\delta}}_1 + \hat{\alpha}_1 y_2, \hat{\theta}_1^2\hat{\tau}_2^2 + \hat{\tau}_1^2) \tag{16.31}$$

where all estimates except $\hat{\tau}_2^2$ come from step b of the Smith-Blundell procedure; $\hat{\tau}_2^2$ is simply the usual estimate of the error variance from the first-stage OLS regression. As in the case of probit, obtaining standard errors for the APEs based on expression (16.31) and the delta method would be quite complicated. An alternative procedure, where $m(\mathbf{z}_1\hat{\boldsymbol{\delta}}_1 + \hat{\alpha}_1 y_2 + \hat{\theta}_1\hat{v}_{i2}, \hat{\tau}_1^2)$ is averaged across i, is also consistent, but it does not exploit the normality of v_2.

A full maximum likelihood approach avoids the two-step estimation problem. The joint distribution of (y_1, y_2) given $\mathbf{z}$ is most easily found by using

$$f(y_1, y_2 \mid \mathbf{z}) = f(y_1 \mid y_2, \mathbf{z})f(y_2 \mid \mathbf{z}) \tag{16.32}$$

just as for the probit case in Section 15.7.2. The density $f(y_2 \mid \mathbf{z})$ is Normal$(\mathbf{z}\boldsymbol{\delta}_2, \tau_2^2)$. Further, from equation (16.29), y_1 given $(y_2, \mathbf{z})$ follows a Tobit with latent mean

$$\mathbf{z}_1\boldsymbol{\delta}_1 + \alpha_1 y_2 + \theta_1 v_2 = \mathbf{z}_1\boldsymbol{\delta}_1 + \alpha_1 y_2 + (\eta_1/\tau_2^2)(y_2 - \mathbf{z}\boldsymbol{\delta}_2)$$

and variance $\tau_1^2 = \sigma_1^2 - (\eta_1^2/\tau_2^2)$, where $\sigma_1^2 = \text{Var}(u_1)$, $\tau_2^2 = \text{Var}(v_2)$, and $\eta_1 = \text{Cov}(u_1, v_2)$. Taking the log of equation (16.32), the log-likelihood function for each i is easily constructed as a function of the parameters $(\boldsymbol{\delta}_1, \alpha_1, \boldsymbol{\delta}_2, \sigma_1^2, \tau_2^2, \eta_1)$. The usual coditional maximum likelihood theory can be used for constructing standard errors and test statistics.

Once the MLE has been obtained, we can easily test the null hypothesis of exogeneity of y_2 by using the t statistic for $\hat{\theta}_1$. Because the MLE can be computationally more difficult than the Smith-Blundell procedure, it makes sense to use the Smith-Blundell procedure to test for endogeneity before obtaining the MLE.

If y_2 is a binary variable, then the Smith-Blundell assumptions cannot be expected to hold. Taking equation (16.26) as the structural equation, we could add

$$y_2 = 1[\mathbf{z}\boldsymbol{\pi}_2 + v_2 > 0] \tag{16.33}$$

and assume that (u_1, v_2) has a zero-mean normal distribution and is independent of $\mathbf{z}$; v_2 is standard normal, as always. Equation (16.32) can be used to obtain the log likelihood for each i. Since y_2 given $\mathbf{z}$ is probit, its density is easy to obtain: $f(y_2 \mid \mathbf{z}) = \Phi(\mathbf{z}\boldsymbol{\pi}_2)^{y_2}[1 - \Phi(\mathbf{z}\boldsymbol{\pi}_2)]^{1-y_2}$. The hard part is obtaining the conditional density $f(y_1 \mid y_2, \mathbf{z})$, which is done first for $y_2 = 0$ and then for $y_2 = 1$; see Problem 16.6. Similar comments hold if y_2 given $\mathbf{z}$ follows a standard Tobit model.

16.6.3 Heteroskedasticity and Nonnormality in the Latent Variable Model

As in the case of probit, both heteroskedasticity and nonnormality result in the Tobit estimator $\hat{\boldsymbol{\beta}}$ being inconsistent for $\boldsymbol{\beta}$. This inconsistency occurs because the derived density of y given $\mathbf{x}$ hinges crucially on $y^* \mid \mathbf{x} \sim \text{Normal}(\mathbf{x}\boldsymbol{\beta}, \sigma^2)$. This nonrobustness of the Tobit estimator shows that data censoring can be very costly: in the absence of censoring $(y = y^*)$, $\boldsymbol{\beta}$ could be consistently estimated under $\text{E}(u \mid \mathbf{x}) = 0$ [or even $\text{E}(\mathbf{x}'u) = 0$].

In corner solution applications, we must remember that the presence of heteroskedasticity or nonnormality in the latent variable model entirely changes the functional forms for $\text{E}(y \mid \mathbf{x}, y > 0)$ and $\text{E}(y \mid \mathbf{x})$. Therefore, it does not make sense to focus only on the inconsistency in estimating $\boldsymbol{\beta}$. We should study how departures from the homoskedastic normal assumption affect the estimated partial derivatives of the conditional mean functions. Allowing for heteroskedasticity or nonnormality in the latent variable model can be useful for generalizing functional form in corner solution applications, and it should be viewed in that light.

Specification tests can be based on the score approach, where the standard Tobit model is nested in a more general alternative. Tests for heteroskedasticity and nonnormality in the latent variable equation are easily constructed if the outer product of the form statistic (see Section 13.6) is used. A useful test for heteroskedasticity is obtained by assuming $\text{Var}(u \mid \mathbf{x}) = \sigma^2 \exp(\mathbf{z}\boldsymbol{\delta})$, where $\mathbf{z}$ is a $1 \times Q$ subvector of $\mathbf{x}$ ($\mathbf{z}$ does not include a constant). The Q restrictions H_0: $\boldsymbol{\delta} = \mathbf{0}$ can be tested using the LM statistic. The partial derivatives of the log likelihood $\ell_i(\boldsymbol{\beta}, \sigma^2, \boldsymbol{\delta})$ with respect to $\boldsymbol{\beta}$ and σ^2, evaluated at $\boldsymbol{\delta} = \mathbf{0}$, are given exactly as in equations (16.21) and (16.22). Further, we can show that $\partial\ell_i/\partial\boldsymbol{\delta} = \sigma^2 \mathbf{z}_i(\partial\ell_i/\partial\sigma^2)$. Thus the outer product of the score statistic is $N - \text{SSR}_0$ from the regression

$$1 \text{ on } \partial\hat{\ell}_i/\partial\boldsymbol{\beta}, \partial\hat{\ell}_i/\partial\sigma^2, \hat{\sigma}^2\mathbf{z}_i(\partial\hat{\ell}_i/\partial\sigma^2), \qquad i = 1, \dots, N$$

where the derivatives are evaluated at the Tobit estimates (the restricted estimates) and SSR_0 is the usual sum of squared residuals. Under H_0, $N - \text{SSR}_0 \overset{a}{\sim} \chi^2_Q$. Unfortunately, as we discussed in Section 13.6, the outer product form of the statistic can reject much too often when the null hypothesis is true. If maximum likelihood estimation of the alternative model is possible, the likelihood ratio statistic is a preferable alternative.

We can also construct tests of nonnormality that only require standard Tobit estimation. The most convenient of these are derived as conditional moment tests, which we discussed in Section 13.7. See Pagan and Vella (1989).

It is not too difficult to estimate Tobit models with u heteroskedastic if a test reveals such a problem. For data-censoring applications, it makes sense to directly compare the estimates of $\boldsymbol{\beta}$ from standard Tobit and Tobit with heteroskedasticity. But when $\text{E}(y \mid \mathbf{x}, y > 0)$ and $\text{E}(y \mid \mathbf{x})$ are of interest, we should look at estimates of these expectations with and without heteroskedasticity. The partial effects on $\text{E}(y \mid \mathbf{x}, y > 0)$ and $\text{E}(y \mid \mathbf{x})$ could be similar even though the estimates of $\boldsymbol{\beta}$ might be very different.

As a rough idea of the appropriateness of the Tobit model, we can compare the probit estimates, say $\hat{\gamma}$, to the Tobit estimate of $\gamma = \boldsymbol{\beta}/\sigma$, namely, $\hat{\boldsymbol{\beta}}/\hat{\sigma}$. These will never be identical, but they should not be statistically different. Statistically significant sign changes are indications of misspecification. For example, if $\hat{\gamma}_j$ is positive and significant but $\hat{\beta}_j$ is negative and perhaps significant, the Tobit model is probably misspecified.

As an illustration, in Example 15.2, we obtained the probit coefficient on *nwifeinc* as $-.012$, and the coefficient on *kidslt6* was $-.868$. When we divide the corresponding

Tobit coefficients by $\hat{\sigma} = 1{,}122.02$, we obtain about $-.0079$ and $-.797$, respectively. Though the estimates differ somewhat, the signs are the same and the magnitudes are similar.

It is possible to form a Hausman statistic as a quadratic form in $(\hat{\gamma} - \hat{\boldsymbol{\beta}}/\hat{\sigma})$, but obtaining the appropriate asymptotic variance is somewhat complicated. (See Ruud, 1984, for a formal discussion of this test.) Section 16.7 discusses more flexible models that may be needed for corner solution outcomes.

16.6.4 Estimation under Conditional Median Restrictions

It is possible to $\sqrt{N}$-consistently estimate $\boldsymbol{\beta}$ without assuming a particular distribution for u and without even assuming that u and $\mathbf{x}$ are independent. Consider again the latent variable model, but where the *median* of u given $\mathbf{x}$ is zero:

$$y^* = \mathbf{x}\boldsymbol{\beta} + u, \qquad \text{Med}(u \mid \mathbf{x}) = 0 \tag{16.34}$$

This equation implies that $\text{Med}(y^* \mid \mathbf{x}) = \mathbf{x}\boldsymbol{\beta}$, so that the median of y^* is linear in $\mathbf{x}$. If the distribution of u given $\mathbf{x}$ is symmetric about zero, then the conditional expectation and conditional median of y^* coincide, in which case there is no ambiguity about what we would like to estimate in the case of data censoring. If y^* given $\mathbf{x}$ is asymmetric, the median and mean can be very different.

A well-known result in probability says that, if $g(y)$ is a nondecreasing function, then $\text{Med}[g(y)] = g[\text{Med}(y)]$. (The same property does *not* hold for the expected value.) Then, because $y = \max(0, y^*)$ is a nondecreasing function,

$$\text{Med}(y \mid \mathbf{x}) = \max[0, \text{Med}(y^* \mid \mathbf{x})] = \max(0, \mathbf{x}\boldsymbol{\beta}) \tag{16.35}$$

Importantly, equation (16.35) holds under assumption (16.34) only; no further distributional assumptions are needed. In Chapter 12 we noted that the analogy principle leads to least absolute deviations as the appropriate method for estimating the parameters in a conditional median. Therefore, assumption (16.35) suggests estimating $\boldsymbol{\beta}$ by solving

$$\min_{\boldsymbol{\beta}} \sum_{i=1}^{N} |y_i - \max(0, \mathbf{x}_i\boldsymbol{\beta})| \tag{16.36}$$

This estimator was suggested by Powell (1984) for the censored Tobit model. Since $q(\mathbf{w}, \boldsymbol{\beta}) \equiv |y - \max(0, \mathbf{x}\boldsymbol{\beta})|$ is a continuous function of $\boldsymbol{\beta}$, consistency of Powell's estimator follows from Theorem 12.2 under an appropriate identification assumption. Establishing $\sqrt{N}$-asymptotic normality is much more difficult because the objective function is not twice continuously differentiable with nonsingular Hessian. Powell (1984, 1994) and Newey and McFadden (1994) contain applicable theorems.

Powell's method also applies to corner solution applications, but the difference between the conditional median of y and its conditional expectations becomes crucial. As shown in equation (16.35), $\mathrm{Med}(y \mid \mathbf{x})$ does not depend on the distribution of u given $\mathbf{x}$, whereas $\mathrm{E}(y \mid \mathbf{x})$ and $\mathrm{E}(y \mid \mathbf{x}, y > 0)$ do. Further, the median and mean functions have different shapes. The conditional median of y is zero for $\mathbf{x}\boldsymbol{\beta} \leq 0$, and it is linear in $\mathbf{x}$ for $\mathbf{x}\boldsymbol{\beta} > 0$. (One implication of this fact is that, when using the median for predicting y, the prediction is exact when $\mathbf{x}_i\hat{\boldsymbol{\beta}} \leq 0$ and $y_i = 0$.) By contrast, the conditional expectation $\mathrm{E}(y \mid \mathbf{x})$ is never zero and is everywhere a nonlinear function of $\mathbf{x}$. In the standard Tobit specification we can also estimate $\mathrm{E}(y \mid \mathbf{x}, y > 0)$ and various probabilities. By its nature, the LAD approach does not allow us to do so. We cannot resolve the issue about whether the median or mean is more relevant for determining the effects of the x_j on y. It depends on the context and is somewhat a matter of taste.

In some cases a quantile other than the median is of interest. Buchinsky and Hahn (1998) show how to estimate the parameters in a censored quantile regression model.

It is also possible to estimate $\mathrm{E}(y \mid \mathbf{x})$ and $\mathrm{E}(y \mid \mathbf{x}, y > 0)$ without specifying the distribution of u given $\mathbf{x}$ using semiparametric methods similar to those used to estimate index binary choice models without specifying the index function G. See Powell (1994) for a summary.

16.7 Some Alternatives to Censored Tobit for Corner Solution Outcomes

In corner solution applications, an important limitation of the standard Tobit model is that a single mechanism determines the choice between $y = 0$ versus $y > 0$ and the *amount* of y given $y > 0$. In particular, $\partial\mathrm{P}(y > 0 \mid \mathbf{x})/\partial x_j$ and $\partial\mathrm{E}(y \mid \mathbf{x}, y > 0)/\partial x_j$ have the same sign. In fact, in Section 16.2 we showed that the relative effects of continuous explanatory variables on $\mathrm{P}(y > 0 \mid \mathbf{x})$ and $\mathrm{E}(y \mid \mathbf{x}, y > 0)$ are identical. Alternatives to censored Tobit have been suggested to allow the initial decision of $y > 0$ versus $y = 0$ to be separate from the decision of *how much* y given that $y > 0$. These are often called **hurdle models** or **two-tiered models**. The hurdle or first tier is whether or not to choose positive y. For example, in the charitable contributions example, family characteristics may differently affect the decision to contribute at all and the decision on how much to contribute.

A simple two-tiered model for a corner solution variable is

$$\mathrm{P}(y = 0 \mid \mathbf{x}) = 1 - \Phi(\mathbf{x}\boldsymbol{\gamma}) \tag{16.37}$$

$$\log(y) \mid (\mathbf{x}, y > 0) \sim \mathrm{Normal}(\mathbf{x}\boldsymbol{\beta}, \sigma^2) \tag{16.38}$$

The first equation dictates the probability that y is zero or positive, and equation (16.38) says that, conditional on $y > 0$, $y \mid \mathbf{x}$ follows a *lognormal distribution*. If we define $w = 1[y > 0]$ and use

$$f(y \mid \mathbf{x}) = \mathrm{P}(w = 0 \mid \mathbf{x}) f(y \mid \mathbf{x}, w = 0) + \mathrm{P}(w = 1 \mid \mathbf{x}) f(y \mid \mathbf{x}, w = 1)$$

we obtain

$$f(y \mid \mathbf{x}) = 1[y = 0][1 - \Phi(\mathbf{x}\gamma)] + 1[y > 0]\Phi(\mathbf{x}\gamma)\phi[\{\log(y) - \mathbf{x}\boldsymbol{\beta}\}/\sigma]/(y\sigma)$$

since $\mathrm{P}[y > 0 \mid \mathbf{x}] = \Phi(\mathbf{x}\gamma)$ and $\phi[\{\log(y) - \mathbf{x}\boldsymbol{\beta}\}/\sigma]/(y\sigma)$ is the density of a lognormal random variable. For maximum likelihood analysis, a better way to write the density is

$$f(y \mid \mathbf{x}; \boldsymbol{\theta}) = [1 - \Phi(\mathbf{x}\gamma)]^{1[y=0]}\{\Phi(\mathbf{x}\gamma)\phi[\{\log(y) - \mathbf{x}\boldsymbol{\beta}\}/\sigma]/(y\sigma)\}^{1[y>0]}$$

for $y \geq 0$. If there are no restrictions on γ, $\boldsymbol{\beta}$, and σ^2, then the MLEs are easy to obtain: the log-likelihood function for observation i is

$$\ell_i(\boldsymbol{\theta}) = 1[y_i = 0] \log[1 - \Phi(\mathbf{x}\gamma)] + 1[y_i > 0]\{\log \Phi(\mathbf{x}_i\gamma) - \log(y_i)$$
$$- \tfrac{1}{2}\log(\sigma^2) - \tfrac{1}{2}\log(2\pi) - \tfrac{1}{2}[\log(y_i) - \mathbf{x}_i\boldsymbol{\beta}]^2/\sigma^2\}$$

The MLE of γ is simply the probit estimator using $w = 1[y > 0]$ as the binary response. The MLE of $\boldsymbol{\beta}$ is just the OLS estimator from the regression $\log(y)$ on $\mathbf{x}$ using those observations for which $y > 0$. A consistent estimator of $\hat{\sigma}$ is the usual standard error from this regression. Estimation is very simple because we *assume* that, conditional on $y > 0$, $\log(y)$ follows a classical linear model. The expectations $\mathrm{E}(y \mid \mathbf{x}, y > 0)$ and $\mathrm{E}(y \mid \mathbf{x})$ are easy to obtain using properties of the lognormal distribution:

$$\mathrm{E}(y \mid \mathbf{x}, y > 0) = \exp(\mathbf{x}\boldsymbol{\beta} + \sigma^2/2), \qquad \mathrm{E}(y \mid \mathbf{x}) = \Phi(\mathbf{x}\gamma)\exp(\mathbf{x}\boldsymbol{\beta} + \sigma^2/2)$$

and these are easily estimated given $\hat{\boldsymbol{\beta}}$, $\hat{\sigma}^2$, and $\hat{\gamma}$.

We cannot obtain the Tobit model as a special case of the model (16.37) and (16.38) by imposing parameter restrictions, and this inability makes it difficult to test the Tobit model against equations (16.37) and (16.38). Vuong (1989) suggests a general *model selection test* that can be applied to choose the best-fitting model when the models are nonnested. Essentially, Vuong shows how to test whether one log-likelihood value is significantly greater than another, where the null is that they have the same expected value.

Cragg (1971) suggests a different two-tiered model which, unlike equations (16.37) and (16.38), nests the usual Tobit model. Cragg uses the truncated normal distribution in place of the lognormal distribution:

$$f(y \mid \mathbf{x}, y > 0) = [\Phi(\mathbf{x}\boldsymbol{\beta}/\sigma)]^{-1}\{\phi[(y - \mathbf{x}\boldsymbol{\beta})/\sigma]/\sigma\}, \qquad y > 0$$

where the term $[\Phi(\mathbf{x}\boldsymbol{\beta}/\sigma)]^{-1}$ ensures that the density integrates to unity over $y > 0$. The density of y given $\mathbf{x}$ becomes

$$f(y \mid \mathbf{x}; \boldsymbol{\theta}) = [1 - \Phi(\mathbf{x}\boldsymbol{\gamma})]^{1[y=0]}\{\Phi(\mathbf{x}\boldsymbol{\gamma})[\Phi(\mathbf{x}\boldsymbol{\beta}/\sigma)]^{-1}[\phi(\{y - \mathbf{x}\boldsymbol{\beta}\}/\sigma)/\sigma]\}^{1[y>0]}$$

This equation is easily seen to yield the standard censored Tobit density when $\boldsymbol{\gamma} = \boldsymbol{\beta}/\sigma$. Fin and Schmidt (1984) derive the LM test of this restriction, which allows the Tobit model to be tested against Cragg's more general alternative. Problem 16.7 asks you to derive the conditional expectations associated with Cragg's model. It is legitimate to choose between Cragg's model and the lognormal model in equation (16.38) by using the value of the log-likelihood function. Vuong's (1989) approach can be used to determine whether the difference in log likelihoods is statistically significant.

If we are interested primarily in $\mathrm{E}(y \mid \mathbf{x})$, then we can model $\mathrm{E}(y \mid \mathbf{x})$ directly and use a least squares approach. We discussed the drawbacks of using linear regression methods in Section 16.1. Nevertheless, a linear model for $\mathrm{E}(y \mid \mathbf{x})$ might give good estimates on the partial effects for $\mathbf{x}$ near its mean value.

In Section 16.1 we also mentioned the possibility of modeling $\mathrm{E}(y \mid \mathbf{x})$ as an exponential function and using NLS or a quasi-MLE procedure (see Chapter 19) without any further assumptions about the distribution of y given $\mathbf{x}$. If a model for $\mathrm{P}(y = 0 \mid \mathbf{x})$ is added, then we can obtain $\mathrm{E}(y \mid \mathbf{x}, y > 0) = \exp(\mathbf{x}\boldsymbol{\beta})/[1 - \mathrm{P}(y = 0 \mid \mathbf{x})]$. Such methods are not common in applications, but this neglect could be partly due to confusion about which quantities are of interest for corner solution outcomes.

16.8 Applying Censored Regression to Panel Data and Cluster Samples

We now cover Tobit methods for panel data and cluster samples. The treatment is very similar to that for probit models in Section 15.8, and so we make it brief.

16.8.1 Pooled Tobit

As with binary response, it is easy to apply pooled Tobit methods to panel data or cluster samples. A panel data model is

$$y_{it} = \max(0, \mathbf{x}_{it}\boldsymbol{\beta} + u_{it}), \qquad t = 1, 2, \ldots, T \tag{16.39}$$

$$u_{it} \mid \mathbf{x}_{it} \sim \mathrm{Normal}(0, \sigma^2) \tag{16.40}$$

This model has several notable features. First, it does not maintain strict exogeneity of $\mathbf{x}_{it}$: u_{it} is independent of $\mathbf{x}_{it}$, but the relationship between u_{it} and $\mathbf{x}_{is}$, $t \neq s$, is unspecified. As a result, $\mathbf{x}_{it}$ could contain $y_{i,t-1}$ or variables that are affected by feedback. A second important point is that the $\{u_{it}: t = 1, \dots, T\}$ are allowed to be serially dependent, which means that the y_{it} can be dependent after conditioning on the explanatory variables. In short, equations (16.39) and (16.40) only specify a model for $\mathrm{D}(y_{it} \mid \mathbf{x}_{it})$, and $\mathbf{x}_{it}$ can contain any conditioning variables (time dummies, interactions of time dummies with time-constant or time-varying variables, lagged dependent variables, and so on).

The pooled estimator maximizes the partial log-likelihood function

$$\sum_{i=1}^{N} \sum_{t=1}^{T} \ell_{it}(\boldsymbol{\beta}, \sigma^2)$$

where $\ell_{it}(\boldsymbol{\beta}, \sigma^2)$ is the log-likelihood function given in equation (16.20). Computationally, we just apply Tobit to the data set *as if* it were one long cross section of size NT. However, without further assumptions, a robust variance matrix estimator is needed to account for serial correlation in the score across t; see Sections 13.8.2 and 15.8.1. Robust Wald and score statistics can be computed as in Section 12.6. The same methods work when each i represents a cluster and t is a unit within a cluster; see Section 15.8.6 for the probit case and Section 13.8.4 for the general case. With either panel data or cluster samples, the LR statistic based on the pooled Tobit estimation is not generally valid.

In the case that the panel data model is dynamically complete, that is,

$$\mathrm{D}(y_{it} \mid \mathbf{x}_{it}, y_{i,t-1}, \mathbf{x}_{i,t-1}, \dots) = \mathrm{D}(y_{it} \mid \mathbf{x}_{it}) \tag{16.41}$$

inference is considerably easier: all the usual statistics from pooled Tobit are valid, including likelihood ratio statistics. Remember, we are *not* assuming any kind of independence across t; in fact, $\mathbf{x}_{it}$ can contain lagged dependent variables. It just works out that dynamic completeness leads to the same inference procedures one would use on independent cross sections; see the general treatment in Section 13.8.

A general test for dynamic completeness can be based on the scores $\hat{\mathbf{s}}_{it}$, as mentioned in Section 13.8.3, but it is nice to have a simple test that can be computed from pooled Tobit estimation. Under assumption (16.41), variables dated at time $t-1$ and earlier should not affect the distribution of y_{it} once $\mathbf{x}_{it}$ is conditioned on. There are many possibilities, but we focus on just one here. Define $r_{i,t-1} = 1$ if $y_{i,t-1} = 0$ and $r_{i,t-1} = 0$ if $y_{i,t-1} > 0$. Further, define $\hat{u}_{i,t-1} \equiv y_{i,t-1} - \mathbf{x}_{i,t-1}\hat{\boldsymbol{\beta}}$ if $y_{i,t-1} > 0$. Then estimate the following (artificial) model by pooled Tobit:

$$y_{it} = \max[0, \mathbf{x}_{it}\boldsymbol{\beta} + \gamma_1 r_{i,t-1} + \gamma_2(1 - r_{i,t-1})\hat{u}_{i,t-1} + error_{it}]$$

using time periods $t = 2, \dots, T$, and test the joint hypothesis H_0: $\gamma_1 = 0$, $\gamma_2 = 0$. Under the null of dynamic completeness, $error_{it} = u_{it}$, and the estimation of $u_{i,t-1}$

does not affect the limiting distribution of the Wald, LR, or LM tests. In computing either the LR or LM test it is important to drop the first time period in estimating the restricted model with $\gamma_1 = \gamma_2 = 0$. Since pooled Tobit is used to estimate both the restricted and unrestricted models, the LR test is fairly easy to obtain.

In some applications it may be important to allow interactions between time dummies and explanatory variables. We might also want to allow the variance of u_{it} to change over time. In data-censoring cases, where $\mathrm{E}(y_{it}^* \mid \mathbf{x}_{it}) = \mathbf{x}_{it}\boldsymbol{\beta}$ is of direct interest, allowing changing variances over time could give us greater confidence in the estimate of $\boldsymbol{\beta}$. If $\sigma_t^2 = \mathrm{Var}(u_{it})$, a pooled approach still works, but $\ell_{it}(\boldsymbol{\beta}, \sigma^2)$ becomes $\ell_{it}(\boldsymbol{\beta}, \sigma_t^2)$, and special software may be needed for estimation.

With true data censoring, it is tricky to allow for lagged dependent variables in $\mathbf{x}_{it}$, because we probably want a linear, AR(1) model for the unobserved outcome, y_{it}^*. But including $y_{i,t-1}^*$ in $\mathbf{x}_{it}$ is very difficult, because $y_{i,t-1}^*$ is only partially observed. For corner solution applications, it makes sense to include functions of $y_{i,t-1}$ in $\mathbf{x}_{it}$, and this approach is straightforward.

16.8.2 Unobserved Effects Tobit Models under Strict Exogeneity

Another popular model for Tobit outcomes with panel data is the **unobserved effects Tobit model**. We can state this model as

$$y_{it} = \max(0, \mathbf{x}_{it}\boldsymbol{\beta} + c_i + u_{it}), \qquad t = 1, 2, \ldots, T \tag{16.42}$$

$$u_{it} \mid \mathbf{x}_i, c_i \sim \mathrm{Normal}(0, \sigma_u^2) \tag{16.43}$$

where c_i is the unobserved effect and $\mathbf{x}_i$ contains $\mathbf{x}_{it}$ for all t. Assumption (16.43) is a normality assumption, but it also imples that the $\mathbf{x}_{it}$ are strictly exogenous conditional on c_i. As we have seen in several contexts, this assumption rules out certain kinds of explanatory variables.

If these equations represent a data-censoring problem, then $\boldsymbol{\beta}$ is of primary interest. In corner solution applications we must be careful to specify what is of interest. Consistent estimation of $\boldsymbol{\beta}$ and σ_u^2 means we can estimate the partial effects of the elements of $\mathbf{x}_t$ on $\mathrm{E}(y_t \mid \mathbf{x}_t, c, y_t > 0)$ and $\mathrm{E}(y_t \mid \mathbf{x}_t, c)$ for given values of c, using equations (16.11) and (16.14). Under assumption (16.44), which follows, we can estimate $\mathrm{E}(c_i)$ and evaluate the partial effects at the estimated mean value. We will also see how to estimate the average partial effects.

Rather than cover a standard random effects version, we consider a more general Chamberlain-like model that allows c_i and $\mathbf{x}_i$ to be correlated. To this end, assume, just as in the probit case,

$$c_i \mid \mathbf{x}_i \sim \mathrm{Normal}(\psi + \overline{\mathbf{x}}_i\xi, \sigma_a^2) \tag{16.44}$$

where σ_a^2 is the variance of a_i in the equation $c_i = \psi + \bar{\mathbf{x}}_i\xi + a_i$. We could replace $\bar{\mathbf{x}}_i$ with $\mathbf{x}_i$ to be more general, but $\bar{\mathbf{x}}_i$ has at most dimension K. (As usual, $\mathbf{x}_{it}$ would not include a constant, and time dummies would be excluded from $\bar{\mathbf{x}}_i$ because they are already in $\mathbf{x}_{it}$.) Under assumptions (16.42)–(16.44), we can write

$$y_{it} = \max(0, \psi + \mathbf{x}_{it}\boldsymbol{\beta} + \bar{\mathbf{x}}_i\xi + a_i + u_{it}) \tag{16.45}$$

$$u_{it} \mid \mathbf{x}_i, a_i \sim \text{Normal}(0, \sigma_u^2), \qquad t = 1, 2, \ldots, T \tag{16.46}$$

$$a_i \mid \mathbf{x}_i \sim \text{Normal}(0, \sigma_a^2) \tag{16.47}$$

This formulation is very useful, especially if we assume that, conditional on $(\mathbf{x}_i, a_i)$ [equivalently, conditional on $(\mathbf{x}_i, c_i)$], the $\{u_{it}\}$ are serially independent:

$$(u_{i1}, \ldots, u_{iT}) \text{ are independent given } (\mathbf{x}_i, a_i) \tag{16.48}$$

Under assumptions (16.45)–(16.48), we have the **random effects Tobit model** but with $\bar{\mathbf{x}}_i$ as an additional set of time-constant explanatory variables appearing in each time period. Software that estimates a random effects Tobit model will provide $\sqrt{N}$-consistent estimates of ψ, $\boldsymbol{\beta}$, ξ, σ_u^2, and σ_a^2. We can easily test H_0: $\xi = \mathbf{0}$ as a test of the traditional Tobit random effects model.

In data-censoring applications, our interest lies in $\boldsymbol{\beta}$, and so—under the maintained assumptions—adding $\bar{\mathbf{x}}_i$ to the random effects Tobit model solves the unobserved heterogeneity problem.

If $\mathbf{x}_{it}$ contains a time-constant variable, say, w_i, we will not be able to estimate its effect unless we assume that its coefficient in ξ is zero. But we can still include w_i as an explanatory variable to reduce the error variance.

For corner solution applications, we can estimate either partial effects evaluated at $\text{E}(c)$ or average partial effects (APEs). As in Section 16.6.2, it is convenient to define $m(z, \sigma^2) \equiv \Phi(z/\sigma)z + \sigma\phi(z/\sigma)$, so that $\text{E}(y_t \mid \mathbf{x}, c) = m(\mathbf{x}_t\boldsymbol{\beta} + c, \sigma_u^2)$. A consistent estimator of $\text{E}(c_i)$ is $\hat{\psi} + \bar{\mathbf{x}}\hat{\xi}$, where $\bar{\mathbf{x}}$ is the sample average of the $\bar{\mathbf{x}}_i$, and so we can consistently estimate partial effects at the mean value by taking derivatives or differences of $m(\hat{\psi} + \mathbf{x}_t\hat{\boldsymbol{\beta}} + \bar{\mathbf{x}}\hat{\xi}, \hat{\sigma}_u^2)$ with respect to the elements of $\mathbf{x}_t$.

Estimating APEs is also relatively simple. APEs (at $\mathbf{x}_t = \mathbf{x}^o$) are obtained by finding $\text{E}[m(\mathbf{x}^o\boldsymbol{\beta} + c_i, \sigma_u^2)]$ and then computing partial derivatives or changes with respect to elements of $\mathbf{x}^o$. Since $c_i = \psi + \bar{\mathbf{x}}_i\xi + a_i$, we have, by iterated expectations,

$$\text{E}[m(\mathbf{x}^o\boldsymbol{\beta} + c_i, \sigma_u^2)] = \text{E}\{\text{E}[m(\psi + \mathbf{x}^o\boldsymbol{\beta} + \bar{\mathbf{x}}_i\xi + a_i, \sigma_u^2) \mid \mathbf{x}_i]\} \tag{16.49}$$

where the first expectation is with respect to the distribution of c_i. Since a_i and $\mathbf{x}_i$ are independent and $a_i \sim \text{Normal}(0, \sigma_a^2)$, the conditional expectation in equation (16.49) is obtained by integrating $m(\psi + \mathbf{x}^o\boldsymbol{\beta} + \bar{\mathbf{x}}_i\xi + a_i, \sigma_u^2)$ over a_i with respect to the

Normal$(0, \sigma_a^2)$ distribution. Since $m(\psi + \mathbf{x}^o\boldsymbol{\beta} + \overline{\mathbf{x}}_i\xi + a_i, \sigma_u^2)$ is obtained by integrating $\max(0, \psi + \mathbf{x}^o\boldsymbol{\beta} + \overline{\mathbf{x}}_i\xi + a_i + u_{it})$ with respect to u_{it} over the Normal$(0, \sigma_u^2)$ distribution, it follows that

$$\mathrm{E}[m(\psi + \mathbf{x}^o\boldsymbol{\beta} + \overline{\mathbf{x}}_i\xi + a_i, \sigma_u^2) \,|\, \mathbf{x}_i] = m(\psi + \mathbf{x}^o\boldsymbol{\beta} + \overline{\mathbf{x}}_i\xi, \sigma_a^2 + \sigma_u^2) \tag{16.50}$$

Therefore, the expected value of equation (16.50) (with respect to the distribution of $\overline{\mathbf{x}}_i$) is consistently estimated as

$$N^{-1}\sum_{i=1}^{N} m(\hat{\psi} + \mathbf{x}^o\hat{\boldsymbol{\beta}} + \overline{\mathbf{x}}_i\hat{\xi}, \hat{\sigma}_a^2 + \hat{\sigma}_u^2) \tag{16.51}$$

A similar argument works for $\mathrm{E}(y_t \,|\, \mathbf{x}, c, y_t > 0)$: sum $(\hat{\psi} + \mathbf{x}^o\hat{\boldsymbol{\beta}} + \overline{\mathbf{x}}_i\hat{\xi}) + \hat{\sigma}_v\lambda[(\hat{\psi} + \mathbf{x}^o\hat{\boldsymbol{\beta}} + \overline{\mathbf{x}}_i\hat{\xi})/\hat{\sigma}_v]$ in expression (16.51), where $\lambda(\cdot)$ is the inverse Mills ratio and $\hat{\sigma}_v^2 = \hat{\sigma}_a^2 + \hat{\sigma}_u^2$.

We can relax assumption (16.48) and still obtain consistent, $\sqrt{N}$-asymptotically normal estimates of the APEs. In fact, under assumptions (16.45)–(16.47), we can write

$$y_{it} = \max(0, \psi + \mathbf{x}_{it}\boldsymbol{\beta} + \overline{\mathbf{x}}_i\xi + v_{it}) \tag{16.52}$$

$$v_{it} \,|\, \mathbf{x}_i \sim \text{Normal}(0, \sigma_v^2), \qquad t = 1, 2, \ldots, T \tag{16.53}$$

where $v_{it} = a_i + u_{it}$. Without further assumptions, the v_{it} are *arbitrarily* serially correlated, and so maximum likelihood analysis using the density of $\mathbf{y}_i$ given $\mathbf{x}_i$ would be computationally demanding. However, we can obtain $\sqrt{N}$-asymptotically normal estimators by a simple pooled Tobit procedure of y_{it} on 1, $\mathbf{x}_{it}$, $\overline{\mathbf{x}}_i$, $t = 1, \ldots, T$, $i = 1, \ldots, N$. While we can only estimate σ_v^2 from this procedure, it is all we need—along with $\hat{\psi}$, $\hat{\boldsymbol{\beta}}$, and $\hat{\xi}$—to obtain the average partial effects based on expression (16.51). The robust variance matrix for partial MLE derived in Section 13.8.2 should be used for standard errors and inference. A minimum distance approach, analogous to the probit case discussed in Section 15.8.2, is also available.

When we are interested only in $\boldsymbol{\beta}$, such as in data-censoring cases or when we are interested in $\mathrm{Med}(y_t \,|\, \mathbf{x}, c) = \max(0, \mathbf{x}_t\boldsymbol{\beta} + c)$, it is useful to have an estimator of $\boldsymbol{\beta}$ that does not require distributional assumptions for u_{it} or c_i. Honoré (1992) uses a clever transformation that eliminates c_i and provides estimating equations for $\boldsymbol{\beta}$. See also Honoré and Kyriazidou (2000b) and Arellano and Honoré (in press).

16.8.3 Dynamic Unobserved Effects Tobit Models

We now turn to a specific dynamic model

$$y_{it} = \max(0, \mathbf{z}_{it}\boldsymbol{\delta} + \rho_1 y_{i,t-1} + c_i + u_{it}) \tag{16.54}$$

$$u_{it} \mid (\mathbf{z}_i, y_{i,t-1}, \ldots, y_{i0}, c_i) \sim \text{Normal}(0, \sigma_u^2), \qquad t = 1, \ldots, T \tag{16.55}$$

We can embellish this model in many ways. For example, the lagged effect of $y_{i,t-1}$ can depend on whether $y_{i,t-1}$ is zero or greater than zero. Thus, we might replace $\rho_1 y_{i,t-1}$ by $\eta_1 r_{i,t-1} + \rho_1(1 - r_{i,t-1})y_{i,t-1}$, where r_{it} is a binary variable equal to unity if $y_{it} = 0$. Or, we can let the variance of u_{it} change over time. The basic approach does not depend on the particular model.

The model in equation (16.54) is suitable only for corner solution applications. In data-censoring cases, it makes more sense to have a dynamic linear model $y_{it}^* = \mathbf{z}_{it}\boldsymbol{\delta} + \rho_1 y_{i,t-1}^* + c_i + u_{it}$ and then to introduce the data-censoring mechanism for each time period. This approach leads to $y_{i,t-1}^*$ in equation (16.54) and is considerably more difficult to handle.

The discussion in Section 15.8.4 about how to handle the initial value problem also holds here (see Section 13.9.2 for the general case). A fairly general and tractable approach is to specify a distribution for the unobserved effect, c_i, given the initial value, y_{i0}, and the exogenous variables in all time periods, $\mathbf{z}_i$. Let $h(c \mid y_0, \mathbf{z}; \gamma)$ denote such a density. Then the joint density of $(y_1, \ldots, y_T)$ given $(y_0, \mathbf{z})$ is

$$\int_{-\infty}^{\infty} \prod_{t=1}^{T} f(y_t \mid y_{t-1}, \ldots y_1, y_0, \mathbf{z}, c; \boldsymbol{\theta}) h(c \mid y_0, \mathbf{z}; \gamma)\, dc \tag{16.56}$$

where $f(y_t \mid y_{t-1}, \ldots y_1, y_0, \mathbf{z}, c; \boldsymbol{\theta})$ is the censored-at-zero normal distribution with mean $\mathbf{z}_t\boldsymbol{\delta} + \rho_1 y_{t-1} + c$ and variance σ_u^2. A natural specification for $h(c \mid y_0, \mathbf{z}; \gamma)$ is $\text{Normal}(\psi + \xi_0 y_0 + \mathbf{z}\xi, \sigma_a^2)$, where $\sigma_a^2 = \text{Var}(c \mid y_0, \mathbf{z})$. This leads to a fairly straightforward procedure. To see why, write $c_i = \psi + \xi_0 y_{i0} + \mathbf{z}_i\xi + a_i$, so that

$$y_{it} = \max(0, \psi + \mathbf{z}_{it}\boldsymbol{\delta} + \rho_1 y_{i,t-1} + \xi_0 y_{i0} + \mathbf{z}_i\xi + a_i + u_{it})$$

where the distribution of a_i given $(y_{i0}, \mathbf{z}_i)$ is $\text{Normal}(0, \sigma_a^2)$, and assumption (16.55) holds with a_i replacing c_i. The density in expression (16.56) then has the same form as the random effects Tobit model, where the explanatory variables at time t are $(\mathbf{z}_{it}, y_{i,t-1}, y_{i0}, \mathbf{z}_i)$. The inclusion of the initial condition in each time period, as well as the entire vector $\mathbf{z}_i$, allows for the unobserved heterogeneity to be correlated with the initial condition and the strictly exogenous variables. Standard software can be used to test for state dependence $(\rho_1 \neq 0)$.

Average partial effects can be estimated by modification of the probit results in Section 15.8.4 and the formulas in Section 16.8.2. See Wooldridge (2000e) for details.

Honoré (1993a) obtains orthogonality conditions that can be used in a method of moments framework to estimate $\boldsymbol{\delta}$ and ρ_1 in equation (16.54) without making distributional assumptions about c_i. The assumptions on u_{it} restrict the dependence across time but do not include distributional assumptions. Because no distributional assumptions are made, partial effects on the conditional mean cannot be estimated using Honoré's approach.

Problems

16.1. Let t_i^* denote the duration of some event, such as unemployment, measured in continuous time. Consider the following model for t_i^*:

$$t_i^* = \exp(\mathbf{x}_i\boldsymbol{\beta} + u_i), \qquad u_i \mid \mathbf{x}_i \sim \text{Normal}(0, \sigma^2)$$

$$t_i = \min(t_i^*, c)$$

where $c > 0$ is a known censoring constant.

a. Find $\text{P}(t_i = c \mid \mathbf{x}_i)$, that is, the probability that the duration is censored. What happens as $c \to \infty$?

b. What is the density of $\log(t_i)$ (given $\mathbf{x}_i$) when $t_i < c$? Now write down the full density of $\log(t_i)$ given $\mathbf{x}_i$.

c. Write down the log-likelihood function for observation i.

d. Partition $\boldsymbol{\beta}$ into the $K_1 \times 1$ and $K_2 \times 1$ vectors $\boldsymbol{\beta}_1$ and $\boldsymbol{\beta}_2$. How would you test H_0: $\boldsymbol{\beta}_2 = \mathbf{0}$? Be specific.

e. Obtain the log-likelihood function if the censoring time is potentially different for each person, so that $t_i = \min(t_i^*, c_i)$, where c_i is observed for all i. Assume that u_i is independent of $(\mathbf{x}_i, c_i)$.

16.2. In some occupations, such as major league baseball, salary floors exist. This situation can be described by the model

$$wage^* = \exp(\mathbf{x}\boldsymbol{\beta} + u), \qquad u \mid \mathbf{x} \sim \text{Normal}(0, \sigma^2)$$

$$wage = \max(c, wage^*)$$

where $c > 0$ is the known salary floor (the minimum wage), $wage^*$ is the person's true worth, and $\mathbf{x}$ contains productivity and demographic variables.

a. Show how to turn this into a standard censored Tobit model.

b. Why is $\text{E}(wage^* \mid \mathbf{x})$, rather than $\text{E}(wage^* \mid \mathbf{x}, wage^* > c)$ or $\text{E}(wage \mid \mathbf{x})$, of interest in this application?

16.3. Suppose that, for a random draw $(\mathbf{x}_i, y_i)$ from the population, y_i is a **doubly censored variable**:

$$y_i^* \mid \mathbf{x}_i \sim \text{Normal}(\mathbf{x}_i\boldsymbol{\beta}, \sigma^2)$$

$$y_i = a_1 \qquad \text{if } y_i^* \leq a_1$$

$$y_i = y_i^* \qquad \text{if } a_1 < y_i^* < a_2$$

$$y_i = a_2 \qquad \text{if } y_i^* \geq a_2$$

where $\mathbf{x}_i$ is $1 \times K$, $\boldsymbol{\beta}$ is $K \times 1$, and $a_1 < a_2$ are known censoring constants. This may be a data-censoring problem—for example, y^* may be both top coded and bottom coded in a survey—in which case we are interested in $\text{E}(y_i^* \mid \mathbf{x}_i) = \mathbf{x}_i\boldsymbol{\beta}$. Or, y_i may be the outcome of a constrained optimization problem with corners at a_1 and a_2, such as when y_i is the proportion of person i's pension assets invested in the stock market, so that $a_1 = 0$ and $a_2 = 1$.

a. Find $\text{P}(y = a_1 \mid \mathbf{x})$ and $\text{P}(y = a_2 \mid \mathbf{x})$ in terms of the standard normal cdf, $\mathbf{x}$, $\boldsymbol{\beta}$, and σ. For $a_1 < \mathscr{y} < a_2$, find $\text{P}(y \leq \mathscr{y} \mid \mathbf{x})$, and use this to find the density of y given $\mathbf{x}$ for $a_1 < \mathscr{y} < a_2$.

b. If $z \sim \text{Normal}(0, 1)$, it can be shown that $\text{E}(z \mid c_1 < z < c_2) = \{\phi(c_1) - \phi(c_2)\}/\{\Phi(c_2) - \Phi(c_1)\}$ for $c_1 < c_2$. Use this fact to find $\text{E}(y \mid \mathbf{x}, a_1 < y < a_2)$ and $\text{E}(y \mid \mathbf{x})$.

c. Consider the following method for estimating $\boldsymbol{\beta}$. Using only the uncensored observations, that is, observations for which $a_1 < y_i < a_2$, run the OLS regression of y_i on $\mathbf{x}_i$. Explain why this does not generally produce a consistent estimator of $\boldsymbol{\beta}$.

d. Write down the log-likelihood function for observation i; it should consist of three parts.

e. For a corner solution, how would you estimate $\text{E}(y \mid \mathbf{x}, a_1 < y < a_2)$ and $\text{E}(y \mid \mathbf{x})$?

f. Show that

$$\frac{\partial \text{E}(y \mid \mathbf{x})}{\partial x_j} = \{\Phi[(a_2 - \mathbf{x}\boldsymbol{\beta})/\sigma] - \Phi[(a_1 - \mathbf{x}\boldsymbol{\beta})/\sigma]\}\beta_j$$

Why is the scale factor multiplying β_j necessarily between zero and one?

g. For a corner solution outcome, suppose you obtain $\hat{\gamma}$ from a standard OLS regression of y_i on $\mathbf{x}_i$, using all observations. Would you compare $\hat{\gamma}_j$ to the Tobit estimate, $\hat{\beta}_j$? What would be a sensible comparison?

h. For data censoring, how would the analysis change if a_1 and a_2 were replaced with a_{i1} and a_{i2}, respectively, where u_i is independent of $(\mathbf{x}_i, a_{i1}, a_{i2})$?

16.4. Use the data in JTRAIN1.RAW for this question.

a. Using only the data for 1988, estimate a linear equation relating *hrsemp* to log(*employ*), *union*, and *grant*. Compute the usual and heteroskedasticity-robust standard errors. Interpret the results.

b. Out of the 127 firms with nonmissing data on all variables, how many have $hrsemp = 0$? Estimate the model from part a by Tobit. Find the estimated effect of *grant* on $\mathrm{E}(hrsemp \mid employ, union, grant, hrsemp > 0)$ at the average employment for the 127 firms and $union = 1$. What is the effect on $\mathrm{E}(hrsemp \mid employ, union, grant)$?

c. Are log(*employ*) and *union* jointly significant in the Tobit model?

d. In terms of goodness of fit for the conditional mean, do you prefer the linear model or Tobit model for estimating $\mathrm{E}(hrsemp \mid employ, union, grant)$?

16.5. Use the data set FRINGE.RAW for this question.

a. Estimate a linear model by OLS relating *hrbens* to *exper*, *age*, *educ*, *tenure*, *married*, *male*, *white*, *nrtheast*, *nrthcen*, *south*, and *union*.

b. Estimate a Tobit model relating the same variables from part a. Why do you suppose the OLS and Tobit estimates are so similar?

c. Add $exper^2$ and $tenure^2$ to the Tobit model from part b. Should these be included?

d. Are there significant differences in hourly benefits across industry, holding the other factors fixed?

16.6. Consider a Tobit model with an endogenous binary explanatory variable:

$$y_1 = \max(0, \mathbf{z}_1\boldsymbol{\delta}_1 + \alpha_1 y_2 + u_1)$$

$$y_2 = 1[\mathbf{z}\boldsymbol{\delta}_2 + v_2 > 0]$$

where (u_1, v_2) is independent of $\mathbf{z}$ with a bivariate normal distribution with mean zero and $\mathrm{Var}(v_2) = 1$. If u_1 and v_2 are correlated, y_2 is endogenous.

a. Find the density of the latent variable, y_1^*, given $(\mathbf{z}, y_2)$. [Hint: As shown in Section 16.6.2, the density of y_1 given $(\mathbf{z}, v_2)$ is normal with mean $\mathbf{z}_1\boldsymbol{\delta}_1 + \alpha_1 y_2 + \rho_1 v_2$ and variance $\sigma_1^2 - \rho_1^2$, where $\rho_1 = \mathrm{Cov}(u_1, v_2)$. Integrate against the density of v_2 given $(\mathbf{z}, y_2 = 1)$, as in equation (15.55), and similarly for $y_2 = 0$.]

b. Write down the log-likelihood function for the parameters $\boldsymbol{\delta}_1$, α_1, σ_1^2, $\boldsymbol{\delta}_2$, and ρ_1 for observation *i*.

16.7. Suppose that *y* given $\mathbf{x}$ follows Cragg's model from Section 16.7.

a. Show that $\mathrm{E}(y \mid \mathbf{x}, y > 0) = \mathbf{x}\boldsymbol{\beta} + \sigma\lambda(\mathbf{x}\boldsymbol{\beta}/\sigma)$, just as in the standard Tobit model.

b. Use part a and equation (16.8) to find $\mathrm{E}(y \mid \mathbf{x})$.

c. Show that the elasticity of $\mathrm{E}(y \mid \mathbf{x})$ with respect to, say, x_1, is the sum of the elasticities of $\mathrm{P}(y > 0 \mid \mathbf{x})$ and $\mathrm{E}(y \mid \mathbf{x}, y > 0)$.

16.8. Consider three different approaches for modeling $\mathrm{E}(y \mid \mathbf{x})$ when $y \geq 0$ is a corner solution outcome: (1) $\mathrm{E}(y \mid \mathbf{x}) = \mathbf{x}\boldsymbol{\beta}$; (2) $\mathrm{E}(y \mid \mathbf{x}) = \exp(\mathbf{x}\boldsymbol{\beta})$; and (3) y given $\mathbf{x}$ follows a Tobit model.

a. How would you estimate models 1 and 2?

b. Obtain three goodness-of-fit statistics that can be compared across models; each should measure how much sample variation in y_i is explained by $\hat{\mathrm{E}}(y_i \mid \mathbf{x}_i)$.

c. Suppose, in your sample, $y_i > 0$ for all i. Show that the OLS and Tobit estimates of $\boldsymbol{\beta}$ are identical. Does the fact that they are identical mean that the linear model for $\mathrm{E}(y \mid \mathbf{x})$ and the Tobit model produce the same estimates of $\mathrm{E}(y \mid \mathbf{x})$? Explain.

d. If $y > 0$ in the population, does a Tobit model make sense? What is a simple alternative to the three approaches listed at the beginning of this problem? What assumptions are sufficient for estimating $\mathrm{E}(y \mid \mathbf{x})$?

16.9. Let y be the percentage of annual income invested in a pension plan, and assume that a law caps this percentage at 10 percent. Thus, in a sample of data, we observe y_i between zero and 10, with pileups at the end points.

a. What model would you use for y?

b. Explain the conceptual difference between the outcomes $y = 0$ and $y = 10$. In particular, which limit can be viewed as a form of data censoring?

c. Suppose you want to ask, What is the effect on $\mathrm{E}(y \mid \mathbf{x})$ if the cap were increased from 10 to 11? How would you estimate this? (Hint: Call the upper bound a_2, and take a derivative.)

d. If there are no observations at $y = 10$, what does the estimated model reduce to?

16.10. Provide a careful derivation of equation (16.16). It will help to use the fact that $\mathrm{d}\phi(z)/\mathrm{d}z = -z\phi(z)$.

16.11. Let y be a corner solution response, and let $\mathrm{L}(y \mid 1, \mathbf{x}) = \gamma_0 + \mathbf{x}\boldsymbol{\gamma}$ be the linear projection of y onto an intercept and $\mathbf{x}$, where $\mathbf{x}$ is $1 \times K$. If we use a random sample on $(\mathbf{x}, y)$ to estimate γ_0 and $\boldsymbol{\gamma}$ by OLS, are the estimators inconsistent because of the corner solution nature of y? Explain.

16.12. Use the data in APPLE.RAW for this question. These are phone survey data, where each respondent was asked the amount of "ecolabeled" (or "ecologically friendly") apples he or she would purchase at given prices for both ecolabeled apples and regular apples. The prices are cents per pound, and *ecolbs* and *reglbs* are both in pounds.

a. For what fraction of the sample is $ecolbs_i = 0$? Discuss generally whether *ecolbs* is a good candidate for a Tobit model.

b. Estimate a linear regression model for *ecolbs*, with explanatory variables log(*ecoprc*), log(*regprc*), log(*faminc*), *educ*, *hhsize*, and *num5_17*. Are the signs of the coefficient for log(*ecoprc*) and log(*regprc*) the expected ones? Interpret the estimated coefficient on log(*ecoprc*).

c. Test the linear regression in part b for heteroskedasticity by running the regression $\hat{u}^2$ on 1, $\widehat{ecolbs}$, $\widehat{ecolbs}^2$ and carrying out an F test. What do you conclude?

d. Obtain the OLS fitted values. How many are negative?

e. Now estimate a Tobit model for *ecolbs*. Are the signs and statistical significance of the explanatory variables the same as for the linear regression model? What do you make of the fact that the Tobit estimate on log(*ecoprc*) is about twice the size of the OLS estimate in the linear model?

f. Obtain the estimated partial effect of log(*ecoprc*) for the Tobit model using equation (16.16), where the x_j are evaluated at the mean values. What is the estimated price elasticity (again, at the mean values of the x_j)?

g. Reestimate the Tobit model dropping the variable log(*regprc*). What happens to the coefficient on log(*ecoprc*)? What kind of correlation does this result suggest between log(*ecoprc*) and log(*regprc*)?

h. Reestimate the model from part e, but with *ecoprc* and *regprc* as the explanatory variables, rather than their natural logs. Which functional form do you prefer? (Hint: Compare log-likelihood functions.)

16.13. Suppose that, in the context of an unobserved effects Tobit (or probit) panel data model, the mean of the unobserved effect, c_i, is related to the time average of *detrended* $\mathbf{x}_{it}$. Specifically,

$$c_i = \left[(1/T)\sum_{t=1}^{T}(\mathbf{x}_{it} - \boldsymbol{\pi}_t)\right]\xi + a_i$$

where $\boldsymbol{\pi}_t = \mathrm{E}(\mathbf{x}_{it})$, $t = 1, \ldots, T$, and $a_i \mid \mathbf{x}_i \sim \mathrm{Normal}(0, \sigma_a^2)$. How does this extension of equation (16.44) affect estimation of the unobserved effects Tobit (or probit) model?

16.14. Consider the random effects Tobit model under assumptions (16.42), (16.43), and (16.48), but replace assumption (16.44) with

$c_i \mid \mathbf{x}_i \sim \text{Normal}[\psi + \bar{\mathbf{x}}_i\xi, \sigma_a^2 \exp(\bar{\mathbf{x}}_i\boldsymbol{\lambda})]$

See Problem 15.18 for the probit case.

a. What is the density of y_{it} given $(\mathbf{x}_i, a_i)$, where $a_i = c_i - \text{E}(c_i \mid \mathbf{x}_i)$?

b. Derive the log-likelihood function by first finding the density of $(y_{i1}, \ldots, y_{iT})$ given $\mathbf{x}_i$.

c. Assuming you have estimated $\boldsymbol{\beta}$, σ_u^2, ψ, ξ, σ_a^2, and $\boldsymbol{\lambda}$ by CMLE, how would you estimate the average partial effects?

16.15. Explain why the Smith and Blundell (1986) procedure (Procedure 16.1 in Section 16.6.2) extends immediately to the model

$$y_1 = \max[0, \mathbf{z}_1\boldsymbol{\delta}_1 + \mathbf{g}(y_2)\boldsymbol{\alpha}_1 + u_1]$$

where $\mathbf{g}(y_2)$ is a row vector of functions of y_2, under equation (16.27) and the assumption that (u_1, v_2) is bivariate normal and independent of $\mathbf{z}$. (See Problem 15.20 for the probit case.)

17 Sample Selection, Attrition, and Stratified Sampling

17.1 Introduction

Up to this point, with the exception of occasionally touching on cluster samples and independently pooled cross sections, we have assumed the availability of a random sample from the underlying population. This assumption is not always realistic: because of the way some economic data sets are collected, and often because of the behavior of the units being sampled, random samples are not always available.

A **selected sample** is a general term that describes a nonrandom sample. There are a variety of **selection mechanisms** that result in nonrandom samples. Some of these are due to sample design, while others are due to the behavior of the units being sampled, including nonresponse on survey questions and attrition from social programs. Before we launch into specifics, there is an important general point to remember: sample selection can only be an issue once the population of interest has been carefully specified. If we are interested in a subset of a larger population, then the proper approach is to specify a model for that part of the population, obtain a random sample from that part of the population, and proceed with standard econometric methods.

The following are some examples with nonrandomly selected samples.

Example 17.1 (Saving Function): Suppose we wish to estimate a saving function for all families in a given country, and the population saving function is

$$saving = \beta_0 + \beta_1 income + \beta_2 age + \beta_3 married + \beta_4 kids + u \tag{17.1}$$

where *age* is the age of the household head and the other variables are self-explanatory. However, we only have access to a survey that included families whose household head was 45 years of age or older. This limitation raises a sample selection issue because we are interested in the saving function for all families, but we can obtain a random sample only for a subset of the population.

Example 17.2 (Truncation Based on Wealth): We are interested in estimating the effect of worker eligibility in a particular pension plan [for example, a 401(k) plan] on family wealth. Let the population model be

$$wealth = \beta_0 + \beta_1 plan + \beta_2 educ + \beta_3 age + \beta_4 income + u \tag{17.2}$$

where *plan* is a binary indicator for eligibility in the pension plan. However, we can only sample people with a net wealth less than \$200,000, so the sample is selected on the basis of *wealth*. As we will see, sampling based on a response variable is much more serious than sampling based on an exogenous explanatory variable.

In these two examples data were missing on all variables for a subset of the population as a result of survey design. In other cases, units *are* randomly drawn from the population, but data are missing on one or more variables for some units in the sample. Using a subset of a random sample because of missing data can lead to a sample selection problem. As we will see, if the reason the observations are missing is appropriately exogenous, using the subsample has no serious consequences.

Our final example illustrates a more subtle form of a missing data problem.

Example 17.3 (Wage Offer Function): Consider estimating a wage offer equation for people of working age. By definition, this equation is supposed to represent *all* people of working age, whether or not a person is actually working at the time of the survey. Because we can only observe the wage offer for working people, we effectively select our sample on this basis.

This example is not as straightforward as the previous two. We treat it as a sample selection problem because data on a key variable—the wage offer, $wage^o$—are available only for a clearly defined subset of the population. This is sometimes called **incidental truncation** because $wage^o$ is missing as a result of the outcome of another variable, labor force participation.

The incidental truncation in this example has a strong self-selection component: people self-select into employment, so whether or not we observe $wage^o$ depends on an individual's labor supply decision. Whether we call examples like this sample selection or self-selection is largely irrelevant. The important point is that we must account for the nonrandom nature of the sample we have for estimating the wage offer equation.

In the next several sections we cover a variety of sample selection issues, including tests and corrections. Section 17.7 treats sample selection and the related problem of attrition in panel data. Stratified sampling, which arises out of sampling design, is covered in Section 17.8.

17.2 When Can Sample Selection Be Ignored?

In some cases, the fact that we have a nonrandom sample does not affect the way we estimate population parameters; it is important to understand when this is the case.

17.2.1 Linear Models: OLS and 2SLS

We begin by obtaining conditions under which estimation of the population model by 2SLS using the selected sample is consistent for the population parameters. These results are of interest in their own right, but we will also apply them to several specific models later in the chapter.

We assume that there is a population represented by the random vector $(\mathbf{x}, y, \mathbf{z})$, where $\mathbf{x}$ is a $1 \times K$ vector of explanatory variables, y is the scalar response variable, and $\mathbf{z}$ is a $1 \times L$ vector of instruments.

The population model is the standard single-equation linear model with possibly endogenous explanatory variables:

$$y = \beta_1 + \beta_2 x_2 + \cdots + \beta_K x_K + u \tag{17.3}$$

$$\mathrm{E}(u \mid \mathbf{z}) = 0 \tag{17.4}$$

where we take $x_1 \equiv 1$ for notational simplicity. The sense in which the instruments $\mathbf{z}$ are exogenous, given in assumption (17.4), is stronger than we need for 2SLS to be consistent when using a random sample from the population. With random sampling, the zero correlation condition $\mathrm{E}(\mathbf{z}'u) = \mathbf{0}$ is sufficient. *If* we could obtain a random sample from the population, equation (17.3) could be estimated by 2SLS under the condition $\mathrm{rank}[\mathrm{E}(\mathbf{z}'\mathbf{x})] = K$.

A leading special case is $\mathbf{z} = \mathbf{x}$, so that the explanatory variables are exogenous and equation (17.3) is a model of the conditional expectation $\mathrm{E}(y \mid \mathbf{x})$:

$$\mathrm{E}(y \mid \mathbf{x}) = \beta_1 + \beta_2 x_2 + \cdots + \beta_K x_K \tag{17.5}$$

But our general treatment allows elements of $\mathbf{x}$ to be correlated with u.

Rather than obtaining a random sample—that is, a sample representative of the population—we only use data points that satisfy certain conditions. Let s be a binary **selection indicator** representing a random draw from the population. By definition, $s = 1$ if we use the draw in the estimation, and $s = 0$ if we do not. Usually, we do not use observations when $s = 0$ because data on at least some elements of $(\mathbf{x}, y, \mathbf{z})$ are unobserved—because of survey design, nonresponse, or incidental truncation.

The key assumption underlying the validity of 2SLS on selected sample is

$$\mathrm{E}(u \mid \mathbf{z}, s) = 0 \tag{17.6}$$

There are some important cases where assumption (17.6) necessarily follows from assumption (17.4). If s is a deterministic function of $\mathbf{z}$, then $\mathrm{E}(u \mid \mathbf{z}, s) = \mathrm{E}(u \mid \mathbf{z})$. Such cases arise when selection is a fixed rule involving only the exogenous variables $\mathbf{z}$. Also, if selection is independent of $(\mathbf{z}, u)$—a sufficient condition is that selection is independent of $(\mathbf{x}, y, \mathbf{z})$—then $\mathrm{E}(u \mid \mathbf{z}, s) = \mathrm{E}(u \mid \mathbf{z})$.

In estimating equation (17.3), we apply 2SLS to the observations for which $s = 1$. To study the properties of the 2SLS estimator on the selected sample, let

$\{(\mathbf{x}_i, y_i, \mathbf{z}_i, s_i)\colon i = 1, 2, \ldots, N\}$ denote a random sample from the *population*. We use observation i if $s_i = 1$, but not if $s_i = 0$. Therefore, we do not actually have N observations to use in the estimation; in fact, we do not even need to know N.

The 2SLS estimator using the selected sample can be expressed as

$$\hat{\boldsymbol{\beta}} = \left[\left(N^{-1}\sum_{i=1}^{N} s_i\mathbf{z}_i'\mathbf{x}_i\right)'\left(N^{-1}\sum_{i=1}^{N} s_i\mathbf{z}_i'\mathbf{z}_i\right)^{-1}\left(N^{-1}\sum_{i=1}^{N} s_i\mathbf{z}_i'\mathbf{x}_i\right)\right]^{-1}$$

$$\times\left(N^{-1}\sum_{i=1}^{N} s_i\mathbf{z}_i'\mathbf{x}_i\right)'\left(N^{-1}\sum_{i=1}^{N} s_i\mathbf{z}_i'\mathbf{z}_i\right)^{-1}\left(N^{-1}\sum_{i=1}^{N} s_i\mathbf{z}_i' y_i\right)$$

Substituting $y_i = \mathbf{x}_i\boldsymbol{\beta} + u_i$ gives

$$\hat{\boldsymbol{\beta}} = \boldsymbol{\beta} + \left[\left(N^{-1}\sum_{i=1}^{N} s_i\mathbf{z}_i'\mathbf{x}_i\right)'\left(N^{-1}\sum_{i=1}^{N} s_i\mathbf{z}_i'\mathbf{z}_i\right)^{-1}\left(N^{-1}\sum_{i=1}^{N} s_i\mathbf{z}_i'\mathbf{x}_i\right)\right]^{-1}$$

$$\times\left(N^{-1}\sum_{i=1}^{N} s_i\mathbf{z}_i'\mathbf{x}_i\right)'\left(N^{-1}\sum_{i=1}^{N} s_i\mathbf{z}_i'\mathbf{z}_i\right)^{-1}\left(N^{-1}\sum_{i=1}^{N} s_i\mathbf{z}_i' u_i\right) \tag{17.7}$$

By assumption, $\mathrm{E}(u_i \mid \mathbf{z}_i, s_i) = 0$, and so $\mathrm{E}(s_i\mathbf{z}_i'u_i) = \mathbf{0}$ by iterated expectations. [In the case where s is a function of $\mathbf{z}$, this result shows why assumption (17.4) cannot be replaced with $\mathrm{E}(\mathbf{z}'u) = \mathbf{0}$.] Now the law of large numbers applies to show that plim $\hat{\boldsymbol{\beta}} = \boldsymbol{\beta}$, at least under a modification of the rank condition. We summarize with a theorem:

THEOREM 17.1 (Consistency of 2SLS under Sample Selection): In model (17.3), assume that $\mathrm{E}(u^2) < \infty$, $\mathrm{E}(x_j^2) < \infty$, $j = 1, \ldots, K$, and $\mathrm{E}(z_j^2) < \infty$, $j = 1, \ldots, L$. Maintain assumption (17.6) and, in addition, assume

$$\text{rank } \mathrm{E}(\mathbf{z}'\mathbf{z} \mid s = 1) = L \tag{17.8}$$

$$\text{rank } \mathrm{E}(\mathbf{z}'\mathbf{x} \mid s = 1) = K \tag{17.9}$$

Then the 2SLS estimator using the selected sample is consistent for $\boldsymbol{\beta}$ and $\sqrt{N}$-asymptotically normal. Further, if $\mathrm{E}(u^2 \mid \mathbf{z}, s) = \sigma^2$, then the usual asymptotic variance of the 2SLS estimator is valid.

Equation (17.7) essentially proves the consistency result. Showing that the usual 2SLS asymptotic variance matrix is valid requires two steps. First, under the homoskedasticity assumption in the population, the usual iterated expectations argument gives $\mathrm{E}(su^2\mathbf{z}'\mathbf{z}) = \sigma^2\mathrm{E}(s\mathbf{z}'\mathbf{z})$. This equation can be used to show that Avar $\sqrt{N}(\hat{\boldsymbol{\beta}} - \boldsymbol{\beta}) = \sigma^2\{\mathrm{E}(s\mathbf{x}'\mathbf{z})[\mathrm{E}(s\mathbf{z}'\mathbf{z})]^{-1}\mathrm{E}(s\mathbf{z}'\mathbf{x})\}^{-1}$. The second step is to show that the usual 2SLS estimator of σ^2 is consistent. This fact can be seen as follows. Under the homoskedasticity assumption, $\mathrm{E}(su^2) = \mathrm{E}(s)\sigma^2$, where $\mathrm{E}(s)$ is just the fraction of the subpopulation in the overall population. The estimator of σ^2 (without degrees-of-freedom adjustment) is

$$\left(\sum_{i=1}^{N} s_i\right)^{-1} \sum_{i=1}^{N} s_i \hat{u}_i^2 \tag{17.10}$$

since $\sum_{i=1}^{N} s_i$ is simply the number of observations in the selected sample. Removing the "^" from u_i^2 and applying the law of large numbers gives $N^{-1}\sum_{i=1}^{N} s_i \xrightarrow{p} \mathrm{E}(s)$ and $N^{-1}\sum_{i=1}^{N} s_i u_i^2 \xrightarrow{p} \mathrm{E}(su^2) = \mathrm{E}(s)\sigma^2$. Since the N^{-1} terms cancel, expression (17.10) converges in probability to σ^2.

If s is a function only of $\mathbf{z}$, or s is independent of $(\mathbf{z}, u)$, and $\mathrm{E}(u^2 \mid \mathbf{z}) = \sigma^2$—that is, if the homoskedasticity assumption holds in the original population—then $\mathrm{E}(u^2 \mid \mathbf{z}, s) = \sigma^2$. Without the homoskedasticity assumption we would just use the heteroskedasticity-robust standard errors, just as if a random sample were available with heteroskedasticity present in the population model.

When $\mathbf{x}$ is exogenous and we apply OLS on the selected sample, Theorem 17.1 implies that we can select the sample on the basis of the explanatory variables. Selection based on y or on endogenous elements of $\mathbf{x}$ is not allowed because then $\mathrm{E}(u \mid \mathbf{z}, s) \neq \mathrm{E}(u)$.

Example 17.4 (Nonrandomly Missing IQ Scores): As an example of how Theorem 17.1 can be applied, consider the analysis in Griliches, Hall, and Hausman (1978) (GHH). The structural equation of interest is

$$\log(wage) = \mathbf{z}_1\boldsymbol{\delta}_1 + abil + v, \qquad \mathrm{E}(v \mid \mathbf{z}_1, abil, IQ) = 0$$

and we assume that IQ is a valid proxy for $abil$ in the sense that $abil = \theta_1 IQ + e$ and $\mathrm{E}(e \mid \mathbf{z}_1, IQ) = 0$ (see Section 4.3.2). Write

$$\log(wage) = \mathbf{z}_1\boldsymbol{\delta}_1 + \theta_1 IQ + u \tag{17.11}$$

where $u = v + e$. Under the assumptions made, $\mathrm{E}(u \mid \mathbf{z}_1, IQ) = 0$. It follows immediately from Theorem 17.1 that, if we choose the sample excluding all people with IQs below a fixed value, then OLS estimation of equation (17.11) will be consistent. This problem is not quite the one faced by GHH. Instead, GHH noticed that the *probability* of IQ missing was higher at lower IQs (because people were reluctant to give permission to obtain IQ scores). A simple way to model this situation is $s = 1$ if $IQ + r \geq 0$, $s = 0$ if $IQ + r < 0$, where r is an unobserved random variable. If r is redundant in the structural equation *and* in the proxy variable equation for IQ, that is, if $\mathrm{E}(v \mid \mathbf{z}_1, abil, IQ, r) = 0$ and $\mathrm{E}(e \mid \mathbf{z}_1, IQ, r) = 0$, then $\mathrm{E}(u \mid \mathbf{z}_1, IQ, r) = 0$. Since s is a function of IQ and r, it follows immediately that $\mathrm{E}(u \mid \mathbf{z}_1, IQ, s) = 0$. Therefore, using OLS on the sample for which IQ is observed yields consistent estimators.

If r is correlated with either v or e, $\mathrm{E}(u \mid \mathbf{z}_1, IQ, s) \neq \mathrm{E}(u)$ in general, and OLS estimation of equation (17.11) using the selected sample would not consistently estimate $\boldsymbol{\delta}_1$ and θ_1. Therefore, even though IQ is exogenous in the population equation (17.11), the sample selection is not exogenous. In Section 17.4.2 we cover a method that can be used to correct for sample selection bias.

Theorem 17.1 has other useful applications. Suppose that $\mathbf{x}$ is exogenous in equation (17.3) and that s is a nonrandom function of $(\mathbf{x}, v)$, where v is a variable not appearing in equation (17.3). If (u, v) is independent of $\mathbf{x}$, then $\mathrm{E}(u \mid \mathbf{x}, v) = \mathrm{E}(u \mid v)$, and so

$$\mathrm{E}(y \mid \mathbf{x}) = \mathbf{x}\boldsymbol{\beta} + \mathrm{E}(u \mid \mathbf{x}, v) = \mathbf{x}\boldsymbol{\beta} + \mathrm{E}(u \mid v)$$

If we make an assumption about the functional form of $\mathrm{E}(u \mid v)$, for example, $\mathrm{E}(u \mid v) = \gamma v$, then we can write

$$y = \mathbf{x}\boldsymbol{\beta} + \gamma v + e, \qquad \mathrm{E}(e \mid \mathbf{x}, v) = 0 \tag{17.12}$$

where $e = u - \mathrm{E}(u \mid v)$. Because s is just a function of $(\mathbf{x}, v)$, $\mathrm{E}(e \mid \mathbf{x}, v, s) = 0$, and so $\boldsymbol{\beta}$ and γ can be estimated consistently by the OLS regression y on $\mathbf{x}$, v, using the selected sample. Effectively, including v in the regression on the selected subsample eliminates the sample selection problem and allows us to consistently estimate $\boldsymbol{\beta}$. [Incidentally, because v is independent of $\mathbf{x}$, we would not have to include it in equation (17.3) to consistently estimate $\boldsymbol{\beta}$ *if* we had a random sample from the population. However, including v would result in an asymptotically more efficient estimator of $\boldsymbol{\beta}$ when $\mathrm{Var}(y \mid \mathbf{x}, v)$ is homoskedastic. See Problem 4.5.] In Section 17.5 we will see how equation (17.12) can be implemented.

17.2.2 Nonlinear Models

Results similar to those in the previous section hold for nonlinear models as well. We will cover explicitly the case of nonlinear regression and maximum likelihood. See Problem 17.8 for the GMM case.

In the nonlinear regression case, if $\mathrm{E}(y \mid \mathbf{x}, s) = \mathrm{E}(y \mid \mathbf{x})$—so that selection is *ignorable* in the conditional mean sense—then NLS on the selected sample is consistent. Sufficient is that s is a deterministic function of $\mathbf{x}$. The consistency argument is simple: NLS on the selected sample solves

$$\min_{\boldsymbol{\beta}} N^{-1} \sum_{i=1}^{N} s_i [y_i - m(\mathbf{x}_i, \boldsymbol{\beta})]^2$$

so it suffices to show that $\boldsymbol{\beta}_o$ in $\mathrm{E}(y \mid \mathbf{x}) = m(\mathbf{x}, \boldsymbol{\beta}_o)$ minimizes $\mathrm{E}\{s[y - m(\mathbf{x}, \boldsymbol{\beta})]^2\}$ over $\boldsymbol{\beta}$. By iterated expectations,

$$\mathrm{E}\{s[y - m(\mathbf{x}, \boldsymbol{\beta})]^2\} = \mathrm{E}(s\mathrm{E}\{[y - m(\mathbf{x}, \boldsymbol{\beta})]^2 \mid \mathbf{x}, s\})$$

Next, write $[y - m(\mathbf{x}, \boldsymbol{\beta})]^2 = u^2 + 2[m(\mathbf{x}, \boldsymbol{\beta}_o) - m(\mathbf{x}, \boldsymbol{\beta})]u + [m(\mathbf{x}, \boldsymbol{\beta}_o) - m(\mathbf{x}, \boldsymbol{\beta})]^2$, where $u = y - m(\mathbf{x}, \boldsymbol{\beta}_o)$. By assumption, $\mathrm{E}(u \mid \mathbf{x}, s) = 0$. Therefore,

$$\mathrm{E}\{[y - m(\mathbf{x}, \boldsymbol{\beta})]^2 \mid \mathbf{x}, s\} = \mathrm{E}(u^2 \mid \mathbf{x}, s) + [m(\mathbf{x}, \boldsymbol{\beta}_o) - m(\mathbf{x}, \boldsymbol{\beta})]^2$$

and the second term is clearly minimized at $\boldsymbol{\beta} = \boldsymbol{\beta}_o$. We do have to assume that $\boldsymbol{\beta}_o$ is the *unique* value of $\boldsymbol{\beta}$ that makes $\mathrm{E}\{s[m(\mathbf{x}, \boldsymbol{\beta}) - m(\mathbf{x}, \boldsymbol{\beta}_o)]^2\}$ zero. This is the identification condition on the subpopulation.

It can also be shown that, if $\mathrm{Var}(y \mid \mathbf{x}, s) = \mathrm{Var}(y \mid \mathbf{x})$ and $\mathrm{Var}(y \mid \mathbf{x}) = \sigma_o^2$, then the usual, nonrobust NLS statistics are valid. If heteroskedasticity exists either in the population or the subpopulation, standard heteroskedasticity-robust inference can be used. The arguments are very similar to those for 2SLS in the previous subsection.

Another important case is the general conditional maximum likelihood setup. Assume that the distribution of $\mathbf{y}$ given $\mathbf{x}$ and s is the same as the distribution of $\mathbf{y}$ given $\mathbf{x}$: $\mathrm{D}(\mathbf{y} \mid \mathbf{x}, s) = \mathrm{D}(\mathbf{y} \mid \mathbf{x})$. This is a stronger form of ignorability of selection, but it always holds if s is a nonrandom function of $\mathbf{x}$, or if s is independent of $(\mathbf{x}, \mathbf{y})$. In any case, $\mathrm{D}(\mathbf{y} \mid \mathbf{x}, s) = \mathrm{D}(\mathbf{y} \mid \mathbf{x})$ ensures that the MLE on the selected sample is consistent and that the usual MLE statistics are valid. The analogy argument should be familiar by now. Conditional MLE on the selected sample solves

$$\max_{\boldsymbol{\theta}} N^{-1} \sum_{i=1}^{N} s_i \ell(\mathbf{y}_i, \mathbf{x}_i; \boldsymbol{\theta}) \tag{17.13}$$

where $\ell(\mathbf{y}_i, \mathbf{x}_i; \boldsymbol{\theta})$ is the log likelihood for observation i. Now for each $\mathbf{x}$, $\boldsymbol{\theta}_o$ maximizes $\mathrm{E}[\ell(\mathbf{y}, \mathbf{x}; \boldsymbol{\theta}) \mid \mathbf{x}]$ over $\boldsymbol{\theta}$. But $\mathrm{E}[s\ell(\mathbf{y}, \mathbf{x}; \boldsymbol{\theta})] = \mathrm{E}\{s\mathrm{E}[\ell(\mathbf{y}, \mathbf{x}; \boldsymbol{\theta}) \mid \mathbf{x}, s]\} = \mathrm{E}\{s\mathrm{E}[\ell(\mathbf{y}, \mathbf{x}; \boldsymbol{\theta}) \mid \mathbf{x}]\}$, since, by assumption, the conditional distribution of $\mathbf{y}$ given $(\mathbf{x}, s)$ does not depend on s. Since $\mathrm{E}[\ell(\mathbf{y}, \mathbf{x}; \boldsymbol{\theta}) \mid \mathbf{x}]$ is maximized at $\boldsymbol{\theta}_o$, so is $\mathrm{E}\{s\mathrm{E}[\ell(\mathbf{y}, \mathbf{x}; \boldsymbol{\theta}) \mid \mathbf{x}]\}$. We must make the stronger assumption that $\boldsymbol{\theta}_o$ is the unique maximum, just as in the previous cases: if the selected subset of the population is too small, we may not be able to identify $\boldsymbol{\theta}_o$. Inference can be carried out using the usual MLE statistics obtained from the selected subsample because the information equality now holds conditional on $\mathbf{x}$ and s under the assumption that $\mathrm{D}(\mathbf{y} \mid \mathbf{x}, s) = \mathrm{D}(\mathbf{y} \mid \mathbf{x})$. We omit the details.

Problem 17.8 asks you to work through the case of GMM estimation of general nonlinear models based on conditional moment restrictions.

17.3 Selection on the Basis of the Response Variable: Truncated Regression

Let $(\mathbf{x}_i, y_i)$ denote a random draw from a population. In this section we explicitly treat the case where the sample is selected on the basis of y_i.

In applying the following methods it is important to remember that there is an underlying population of interest, often described by a linear conditional expectation: $\mathrm{E}(y_i \mid \mathbf{x}_i) = \mathbf{x}_i\boldsymbol{\beta}$. If we could observe a random sample from the population, then we would just use standard regression analysis. The problem comes about because the sample we can observe is chosen at least partly based on the value of y_i. Unlike in the case where selection is based only on $\mathbf{x}_i$, selection based on y_i causes problems for standard OLS analysis on the selected sample.

A classic example of selection based on y_i is Hausman and Wise's (1977) study of the determinants of earnings. Hausman and Wise recognized that their sample from a negative income tax experiment was truncated because only families with income below 1.5 times the poverty level were allowed to participate in the program; no data were available on families with incomes above the threshold value. The truncation rule was known, and so the effects of truncation could be accounted for.

A similar example is Example 17.2. We do not observe data on families with wealth above \$200,000. This case is different from the top coding example we discussed in Chapter 16. Here, we observe *nothing* about families with high wealth: they are entirely excluded from the sample. In the top coding case, we have a random sample of families, and we always observe $\mathbf{x}_i$; the information on $\mathbf{x}_i$ is useful even if wealth is top coded.

We assume that y_i is a continuous random variable and that the selection rule takes the form

$$s_i = 1[a_1 < y_i < a_2]$$

where a_1 and a_2 are known constants such that $a_1 < a_2$. A good way to think of the sample selection is that we draw $(\mathbf{x}_i, y_i)$ randomly from the population. If y_i falls in the interval (a_1, a_2), then we observe both y_i and $\mathbf{x}_i$. If y_i is outside this interval, then we do not observe y_i or $\mathbf{x}_i$. Thus all we know is that there is some subset of the population that does not enter our data set because of the selection rule. We know how to characterize the part of the population not being sampled because we know the constants a_1 and a_2.

In most applications we are still interested in estimating $\mathrm{E}(y_i \mid \mathbf{x}_i) = \mathbf{x}_i\boldsymbol{\beta}$. However, because of sample selection based on y_i, we must—at least in a parametric context—specify a full conditional distribution of y_i given $\mathbf{x}_i$. Parameterize the conditional density of y_i given $\mathbf{x}_i$ by $f(\cdot \mid \mathbf{x}_i; \boldsymbol{\beta}, \boldsymbol{\gamma})$, where $\boldsymbol{\beta}$ are the conditional mean parameters and $\boldsymbol{\gamma}$ is a $G \times 1$ vector of additional parameters. The cdf of y_i given $\mathbf{x}_i$ is $F(\cdot \mid \mathbf{x}_i; \boldsymbol{\beta}, \boldsymbol{\gamma})$.

What we can use in estimation is the density of y_i conditional on $\mathbf{x}_i$ *and* the fact that we observe $(y_i, \mathbf{x}_i)$. In other words, we must condition on $a_1 < y_i < a_2$ or, equivalently, $s_i = 1$. The cdf of y_i conditional on $(\mathbf{x}_i, s_i = 1)$ is simply

$$\mathrm{P}(y_i \le y \mid \mathbf{x}_i, s_i = 1) = \frac{\mathrm{P}(y_i \le y, s_i = 1 \mid \mathbf{x}_i)}{\mathrm{P}(s_i = 1 \mid \mathbf{x}_i)}$$

Because y_i is continuously distributed, $\mathrm{P}(s_i = 1 \mid \mathbf{x}_i) = \mathrm{P}(a_1 < y_i < a_2 \mid \mathbf{x}_i) = F(a_2 \mid \mathbf{x}_i; \boldsymbol{\beta}, \boldsymbol{\gamma}) - F(a_1 \mid \mathbf{x}_i; \boldsymbol{\beta}, \boldsymbol{\gamma}) > 0$ for all possible values of $\mathbf{x}_i$. The case $a_2 = \infty$ corresponds to truncation only from below, in which case $F(a_2 \mid \mathbf{x}_i; \boldsymbol{\beta}, \boldsymbol{\gamma}) \equiv 1$. If $a_1 = -\infty$ (truncation only from above), then $F(a_1 \mid \mathbf{x}_i; \boldsymbol{\beta}, \boldsymbol{\gamma}) = 0$. To obtain the numerator when $a_1 < y < a_2$, we have

$$\mathrm{P}(y_i \le y, s_i = 1 \mid \mathbf{x}_i) = \mathrm{P}(a_1 < y_i \le y \mid \mathbf{x}_i) = F(y \mid \mathbf{x}_i; \boldsymbol{\beta}, \boldsymbol{\gamma}) - F(a_1 \mid \mathbf{x}_i; \boldsymbol{\beta}, \boldsymbol{\gamma})$$

When we put this equation over $\mathrm{P}(s_i = 1 \mid \mathbf{x}_i)$ and take the derivative with respect to the dummy argument y, we obtain the density of y_i given $(\mathbf{x}_i, s_i = 1)$:

$$p(y \mid \mathbf{x}_i, s_i = 1) = \frac{f(y \mid \mathbf{x}_i; \boldsymbol{\beta}, \boldsymbol{\gamma})}{F(a_2 \mid \mathbf{x}_i; \boldsymbol{\beta}, \boldsymbol{\gamma}) - F(a_1 \mid \mathbf{x}_i; \boldsymbol{\beta}, \boldsymbol{\gamma})} \tag{17.14}$$

for $a_1 < y < a_2$.

Given a model for $f(y \mid \mathbf{x}; \boldsymbol{\beta}, \boldsymbol{\gamma})$, the log-likelihood function for any $(\mathbf{x}_i, y_i)$ in the sample can be obtained by plugging y_i into equation (17.14) and taking the log. The CMLEs of $\boldsymbol{\beta}$ and $\boldsymbol{\gamma}$ using the selected sample are efficient in the class of estimators that do not use information about the distribution of $\mathbf{x}_i$. Standard errors and test statistics can be computed using the general theory of conditional MLE.

In most applications of truncated samples, the population conditional distribution is assumed to be $\mathrm{Normal}(\mathbf{x}\boldsymbol{\beta}, \sigma^2)$, in which case we have the **truncated Tobit model** or **truncated normal regression model**. The truncated Tobit model is related to the censored Tobit model for data-censoring applications (see Chapter 16), but there is a key difference: in censored regression, we observe the covariates $\mathbf{x}$ for *all* people, even those for whom the response is not known. If we drop observations entirely when the response is not observed, we obtain the truncated regression model. If in Example 16.1 we use the information in the top coded observations, we are in the censored regression case. If we drop all top coded observations, we are in the truncated regression case. (Given a choice, we should use a censored regression analysis, as it uses all of the information in the sample.)

From our analysis of the censored regression model in Chapter 16, it is not surprising that heteroskedasticity or nonnormality in truncated regression results in inconsistent estimators of $\boldsymbol{\beta}$. This outcome is unfortunate because, if not for the sample selection problem, we could consistently estimate $\boldsymbol{\beta}$ under $\mathrm{E}(y \mid \mathbf{x}) = \mathbf{x}\boldsymbol{\beta}$, without specifying $\mathrm{Var}(y \mid \mathbf{x})$ or the conditional distribution. Distribution-free methods for the truncated regression model have been suggested by Powell (1986) under the assumption of a symmetric error distribution; see Powell (1994) for a recent survey.

Truncating a sample on the basis of y is related to **choice-based sampling**. Traditional choice-based sampling applies when y is a discrete response taking on a finite number of values, where sampling frequencies differ depending on the outcome of y. [In the truncation case, the sampling frequency is one when y falls in the interval (a_1, a_2) and zero when y falls outside of the interval.] We do not cover choice-based sampling here; see Manksi and McFadden (1981), Imbens (1992), and Cosslett (1993). In Section 17.8 we cover some estimation methods for stratified sampling, which can be applied to some choice-based samples.

17.4 A Probit Selection Equation

We now turn to sample selection corrections when selection is determined by a probit model. This setup applies to problems different from those in Section 17.3, where the problem was that a survey or program was designed to intentionally exclude part of the population. We are now interested in selection problems that are due to incidental truncation, attrition in the context of program evalution, and general nonresponse that leads to missing data on the response variable or the explanatory variables.

17.4.1 Exogenous Explanatory Variables

The incidental truncation problem is motivated by Gronau's (1974) model of the wage offer and labor force participation.

Example 17.5 (Labor Force Participation and the Wage Offer): Interest lies in estimating $\mathrm{E}(w_i^{\mathrm{o}} \mid \mathbf{x}_i)$, where w_i^{o} is the hourly wage offer for a randomly drawn individual

i. If w_i^o were observed for everyone in the (working age) population, we would proceed in a standard regression framework. However, a potential sample selection problem arises because w_i^o is observed only for people who work.

We can cast this problem as a weekly labor supply model:

$$\max_h \ \text{util}_i(w_i^o h + a_i, h) \quad \text{subject to } 0 \le h \le 168 \tag{17.15}$$

where h is hours worked per week and a_i is nonwage income of person i. Let $s_i(h) \equiv \text{util}_i(w_i^o h + a_i, h)$, and assume that we can rule out the solution $h_i = 168$. Then the solution can be $h_i = 0$ or $0 < h_i < 168$. If $\mathrm{d}s_i/\mathrm{d}h \le 0$ at $h = 0$, then the optimum is $h_i = 0$. Using this condition, straightforward algebra shows that $h_i = 0$ if and only if

$$w_i^o \le -mu_i^h(a_i, 0)/mu_i^q(a_i, 0) \tag{17.16}$$

where $mu_i^h(\cdot,\cdot)$ is the marginal disutility of working and $mu_i^q(\cdot,\cdot)$ is the marginal utility of income. Gronau (1974) called the right-hand side of equation (17.16) the *reservation wage*, w_i^r, which is assumed to be strictly positive.

We now make the parametric assumptions

$$w_i^o = \exp(\mathbf{x}_{i1}\boldsymbol{\beta}_1 + u_{i1}), \qquad w_i^r = \exp(\mathbf{x}_{i2}\boldsymbol{\beta}_2 + \gamma_2 a_i + u_{i2}) \tag{17.17}$$

where (u_{i1}, u_{i2}) is independent of $(\mathbf{x}_{i1}, \mathbf{x}_{i2}, a_i)$. Here, $\mathbf{x}_{i1}$ contains productivity characteristics, and possibly demographic characteristics, of individual i, and $\mathbf{x}_{i2}$ contains variables that determine the marginal utility of leisure and income; these may overlap with $\mathbf{x}_{i1}$. From equation (17.17) we have the log wage equation

$$\log w_i^o = \mathbf{x}_{i1}\boldsymbol{\beta}_1 + u_{i1} \tag{17.18}$$

But the wage offer w_i^o is observed only if the person works, that is, only if $w_i^o \ge w_i^r$, or

$$\log w_i^o - \log w_i^r = \mathbf{x}_{i1}\boldsymbol{\beta}_1 - \mathbf{x}_{i2}\boldsymbol{\beta}_2 - \gamma_2 a_i + u_{i1} - u_{i2} \equiv \mathbf{x}_i\boldsymbol{\delta}_2 + v_{i2} > 0$$

This behavior introduces a potential sample selection problem if we use data only on working people to estimate equation (17.18).

This example differs in an important respect from top coding examples. With top coding, the censoring rule is known for each unit in the population. In Gronau's example, we do not know w_i^r, so we cannot use w_i^o in a censored regression analysis. If w_i^r were observed and exogenous and $\mathbf{x}_{i1}$ were always observed, then we would be in the censored regression framework (see Problem 16.3). If w_i^r were observed and exogenous but $\mathbf{x}_{i1}$ were observed only when w_i^o is, we would be in the truncated Tobit framework. But w_i^r is allowed to depend on unobservables, and so we need a new framework.

If we drop the i subscript, let $y_1 \equiv \log w^o$, and let y_2 be the binary labor force participation indicator, Gronau's model can be written for a random draw from the population as

$$y_1 = \mathbf{x}_1 \boldsymbol{\beta}_1 + u_1 \tag{17.19}$$

$$y_2 = 1[\mathbf{x}\boldsymbol{\delta}_2 + v_2 > 0] \tag{17.20}$$

We discuss estimation of this model under the following set of assumptions:

ASSUMPTION 17.1: (a) $(\mathbf{x}, y_2)$ are always observed, y_1 is observed only when $y_2 = 1$; (b) (u_1, v_2) is independent of $\mathbf{x}$ with zero mean; (c) $v_2 \sim \text{Normal}(0, 1)$; and (d) $\text{E}(u_1 \mid v_2) = \gamma_1 v_2$.

Assumption 17.1a emphasizes the sample selection nature of the problem. Part b is a strong, but standard, form of exogeneity of $\mathbf{x}$. We will see that Assumption 17.1c is needed to derive a conditional expectation given the selected sample. It is probably the most restrictive assumption because it is an explicit distributional assumption. Assuming $\text{Var}(v_2) = 1$ is without loss of generality because y_2 is a binary variable.

Assumption 17.1d requires linearity in the population regression of u_1 on v_2. It always holds if (u_1, v_2) is bivariate normal—a standard assumption in these contexts—but Assumption 17.1d holds under weaker assumptions. In particular, we do not need to assume that u_1 itself is normally distributed.

Amemiya (1985) calls equations (17.19) and (17.20) the **type II Tobit model**. This name is fine as a label, but we must understand that it is a model of sample selection, and it has nothing to do with y_1 being a corner solution outcome. Unfortunately, in almost all treatments of this model, y_1 is set to zero when $y_2 = 0$. Setting y_1 to zero (or any value) when $y_2 = 0$ is misleading and can lead to inappropriate use of the model. For example, it makes no sense to set the wage offer to zero just because we do not observe it. As another example, it makes no sense to set the price per dollar of life insurance (y_1) to zero for someone who did not buy life insurance (so $y_2 = 1$ if and only if a person owns a life insurance policy).

We also have some interest in the parameters of the selection equation (17.20); for example, in Gronau's model it is a reduced-form labor force participation equation. In program evaluation with attrition, the selection equation explains the probability of dropping out of the program.

We can allow a little more generality in the model by replacing $\mathbf{x}$ in equation (17.20) with $\mathbf{x}_2$; then, as will become clear, $\mathbf{x}_1$ would only need to be observed whenever y_1 is, whereas $\mathbf{x}_2$ must always be observed. This extension is not especially useful for something like Gronau's model because it implies that $\mathbf{x}_1$ contains elements that cannot also appear in $\mathbf{x}_2$. Because the selection equation is not typically a structural equation, it is undesirable to impose exclusion restrictions in equation (17.20). If a variable affecting y_1 is observed only along with y_1, the instrumental variables method that we cover in Section 17.4.2 is more attractive.

To derive an estimating equation, let $(y_1, y_2, \mathbf{x}, u_1, v_2)$ denote a random draw from the population. Since y_1 is observed only when $y_2 = 1$, what we can hope to estimate is $\mathrm{E}(y_1 \mid \mathbf{x}, y_2 = 1)$ [along with $\mathrm{P}(y_2 = 1 \mid \mathbf{x})$]. How does $\mathrm{E}(y_1 \mid \mathbf{x}, y_2 = 1)$ depend on the vector of interest, $\boldsymbol{\beta}_1$? First, under Assumption 17.1 and equation (17.19),

$$\mathrm{E}(y_1 \mid \mathbf{x}, v_2) = \mathbf{x}_1\boldsymbol{\beta}_1 + \mathrm{E}(u_1 \mid \mathbf{x}, v_2) = \mathbf{x}_1\boldsymbol{\beta}_1 + \mathrm{E}(u_1 \mid v_2) = \mathbf{x}_1\boldsymbol{\beta}_1 + \gamma_1 v_2 \tag{17.21}$$

where the second equality follows because (u_1, v_2) is independent of $\mathbf{x}$. Equation (17.21) is very useful. The first thing to note is that, if $\gamma_1 = 0$—which implies that u_1 and v_2 are uncorrelated—then $\mathrm{E}(y_1 \mid \mathbf{x}, v_2) = \mathrm{E}(y_1 \mid \mathbf{x}) = \mathrm{E}(y_1 \mid \mathbf{x}_1) = \mathbf{x}_1\boldsymbol{\beta}_1$. Because y_2 is a function of $(\mathbf{x}, v_2)$, it follows immediately that $\mathrm{E}(y_1 \mid \mathbf{x}, y_2) = \mathrm{E}(y_1 \mid \mathbf{x}_1)$. In other words, if $\gamma_1 = 0$, then there is no sample selection problem, and $\boldsymbol{\beta}_1$ can be consistently estimated by OLS using the selected sample.

What if $\gamma_1 \neq 0$? Using iterated expectations on equation (17.21),

$$\mathrm{E}(y_1 \mid \mathbf{x}, y_2) = \mathbf{x}_1\boldsymbol{\beta}_1 + \gamma_1 \mathrm{E}(v_2 \mid \mathbf{x}, y_2) = \mathbf{x}_1\boldsymbol{\beta}_1 + \gamma_1 h(\mathbf{x}, y_2)$$

where $h(\mathbf{x}, y_2) = \mathrm{E}(v_2 \mid \mathbf{x}, y_2)$. If we knew $h(\mathbf{x}, y_2)$, then, from Theorem 17.1, we could estimate $\boldsymbol{\beta}_1$ and γ_1 from the regression y_1 on $\mathbf{x}_1$ and $h(\mathbf{x}, y_2)$, using only the selected sample. Because the selected sample has $y_2 = 1$, we need only find $h(\mathbf{x}, 1)$. But $h(\mathbf{x}, 1) = \mathrm{E}(v_2 \mid v_2 > -\mathbf{x}\boldsymbol{\delta}_2) = \lambda(\mathbf{x}\boldsymbol{\delta}_2)$, where $\lambda(\cdot) \equiv \phi(\cdot)/\Phi(\cdot)$ is the inverse Mills ratio, and so we can write

$$\mathrm{E}(y_1 \mid \mathbf{x}, y_2 = 1) = \mathbf{x}_1\boldsymbol{\beta}_1 + \gamma_1 \lambda(\mathbf{x}\boldsymbol{\delta}_2) \tag{17.22}$$

Equation (17.22), which can be found in numerous places (see, for example, Heckman, 1979, and Amemiya, 1985) makes it clear that an OLS regression of y_1 on $\mathbf{x}_1$ using the selected sample omits the term $\lambda(\mathbf{x}\boldsymbol{\delta}_2)$ and generally leads to inconsistent estimation of $\boldsymbol{\beta}_1$. As pointed out by Heckman (1979), the presence of selection bias can be viewed as an omitted variable problem in the selected sample. An interesting point is that, even though only $\mathbf{x}_1$ appears in the population expectation, $\mathrm{E}(y_1 \mid \mathbf{x})$, other elements of $\mathbf{x}$ appear in the expectation on the subpopulation, $\mathrm{E}(y_1 \mid \mathbf{x}, y_2 = 1)$.

Equation (17.22) also suggests a way to consistently estimate $\boldsymbol{\beta}_1$. Following Heckman (1979), we can consistently estimate $\boldsymbol{\beta}_1$ and γ_1 using the selected sample by regressing y_{i1} on $\mathbf{x}_{i1}$, $\lambda(\mathbf{x}_i\boldsymbol{\delta}_2)$. The problem is that $\boldsymbol{\delta}_2$ is unknown, so we cannot compute the additional regressor $\lambda(\mathbf{x}_i\boldsymbol{\delta}_2)$. Nevertheless, a consistent estimator of $\boldsymbol{\delta}_2$ is available from the first-stage probit estimation of the selection equation.

Procedure 17.1: (a) Obtain the probit estimate $\hat{\boldsymbol{\delta}}_2$ from the model

$$\mathrm{P}(y_{i2} = 1 \mid \mathbf{x}_i) = \Phi(\mathbf{x}_i \boldsymbol{\delta}_2) \tag{17.23}$$

using all N observations. Then, obtain the estimated inverse Mills ratios $\hat{\lambda}_{i2} \equiv \lambda(\mathbf{x}_i \hat{\boldsymbol{\delta}}_2)$ (at least for $i = 1, \dots, N_1$).

(b) Obtain $\hat{\boldsymbol{\beta}}_1$ and $\hat{\gamma}_1$ from the OLS regression on the selected sample,

$$y_{i1} \text{ on } \mathbf{x}_{i1}, \hat{\lambda}_{i2}, \qquad i = 1, 2, \dots, N_1 \tag{17.24}$$

These estimators are consistent and $\sqrt{N}$-asymptotically normal.

The procedure is sometimes called **Heckit** after Heckman (1976) and the tradition of putting "it" on the end of procedures related to probit (such as Tobit).

A very simple test for selection bias is available from regression (17.24). Under the the null of no selection bias, H_0: $\gamma_1 = 0$, we have $\mathrm{Var}(y_1 \mid \mathbf{x}, y_2 = 1) = \mathrm{Var}(y_1 \mid \mathbf{x}) = \mathrm{Var}(u_1)$, and so homoskedasticity holds under H_0. Further, from the results on generated regressors in Chapter 6, the asymptotic variance of $\hat{\gamma}_1$ (and $\hat{\boldsymbol{\beta}}_1$) is not affected by $\hat{\boldsymbol{\delta}}_2$ when $\gamma_1 = 0$. Thus, a standard t test on $\hat{\gamma}_1$ is a valid test of the null hypothsesis of no selection bias.

When $\gamma_1 \neq 0$, obtaining a consistent estimate for the asymptotic variance of $\hat{\boldsymbol{\beta}}_1$ is complicated for two reasons. The first is that, if $\gamma_1 \neq 0$, then $\mathrm{Var}(y_1 \mid \mathbf{x}, y_2 = 1)$ is not constant. As we know, heteroskedasticity itself is easy to correct for using the robust standard errors. However, we should also account for the fact that $\hat{\boldsymbol{\delta}}_2$ is an estimator of $\boldsymbol{\delta}_2$. The adjustment to the variance of $(\hat{\boldsymbol{\beta}}_1, \hat{\gamma}_1)$ because of the two-step estimation is cumbersome—it is *not* enough to simply make the standard errors heteroskedasticity-robust. Some statistical packages now have this feature built in.

As a technical point, we do not need $\mathbf{x}_1$ to be a strict subset of $\mathbf{x}$ for $\boldsymbol{\beta}_1$ to be indentified, and Procedure 17.1 does carry through when $\mathbf{x}_1 = \mathbf{x}$. However, if $\mathbf{x}_i \hat{\boldsymbol{\delta}}_2$ does not have much variation in the sample, then $\hat{\lambda}_{i2}$ can be approximated well by a linear function of $\mathbf{x}$. If $\mathbf{x} = \mathbf{x}_1$, this correlation can introduce severe collinearity among the regressors in regression (17.24), which can lead to large standard errors of the elements of $\hat{\boldsymbol{\beta}}_1$. When $\mathbf{x}_1 = \mathbf{x}$, $\boldsymbol{\beta}_1$ is identified only due to the nonlinearity of the inverse Mills ratio.

The situation is not quite as bad as in Section 9.5.1. There, identification failed for certain values of the structural parameters. Here, we still have identification for any value of $\boldsymbol{\beta}_1$ in equation (17.19), but it is unlikely we can estimate $\boldsymbol{\beta}_1$ with much precision. Even if we can, we would have to wonder whether a statistically inverse Mills ratio term is due to sample selection or functional form misspecification in the population model (17.19).

Table 17.1
Wage Offer Equation for Married Women

Dependent Variable: log(*wage*)		
Independent Variable	OLS	Heckit
educ	.108	.109
	(.014)	(.016)
exper	.042	.044
	(.012)	(.016)
$exper^2$	−.00081	−.00086
	(.00039)	(.00044)
constant	−.522	−.578
	(.199)	(.307)
$\hat{\lambda}_2$	—	.032
		(.134)
Sample size	428	428
R-squared	.157	.157

Example 17.6 (Wage Offer Equation for Married Women): We use the data in MROZ.RAW to estimate a wage offer function for married women, accounting for potential selectivity bias into the workforce. Of the 753 women, we observe the wage offer for 428 working women. The labor force participation equation contains the variables in Table 15.1, including other income, age, number of young children, and number of older children—in addition to *educ*, *exper*, and $exper^2$. The results of OLS on the selected sample and the Heckit method are given in Table 17.1.

The differences between the OLS and Heckit estimates are practically small, and the inverse Mills ratio term is statistically insignificant. The fact that the intercept estimates differ somewhat is usually unimportant. [The standard errors reported for Heckit are the unadjusted ones from regression (17.24). If $\hat{\lambda}_2$ were statistically significant, we should obtain the corrected standard errors.]

The Heckit results in Table 17.1 use four exclusion restrictions in the structural equation, because *nwifeinc*, *age*, *kidslt6*, and *kidsge6* are all excluded from the wage offer equation. If we allow all variables in the selection equation to also appear in the wage offer equation, the Heckit estimates become very imprecise. The coefficient on *educ* becomes .119 (se = .034), compared with the OLS estimate .100 (se = .015). The coefficient on *kidslt6*—which now appears in the wage offer equation—is −.188 (se = .232) in the Heckit estimation, and −.056 (se = .009) in the OLS estimation. The imprecision of the Heckit estimates is due to the severe collinearity that comes from adding $\hat{\lambda}_2$ to the equation, because $\hat{\lambda}_2$ is now a function only of the explanatory variables in the wage offer equation. In fact, using the selected sample, regressing $\hat{\lambda}_2$ on the seven explanatory variables gives R-squared $= .962$. Unfortunately, comparing the OLS and Heckit results does not allow us to resolve some important issues. For example, the OLS results suggest that another young child reduces the wage offer by about 5.6 percent (t statistic ≈ -6.2), other things being equal. Is this effect real, or is it simply due to our inability to adequately correct for sample selection bias? Unless we have a variable that affects labor force participation without affecting the wage offer, we cannot answer this question.

If we replace parts c and d in Assumption 17.1 with the stronger assumption that (u_1, v_2) is bivariate normal with mean zero, $\text{Var}(u_1) = \sigma_1^2$, $\text{Cov}(u_1, v_2) = \sigma_{12}$, and $\text{Var}(v_2) = 1$, then partial maximum likelihood estimation can be used, as described generally in Problem 13.7. Partial MLE will be more efficient than the two-step procedure under joint normality of u_1 and v_2, and it will produce standard errors and likelihood ratio statistics that can be used directly (this conclusion follows from Problem 13.7). The drawbacks are that it is less robust than the two-step procedure and that it is sometimes difficult to get the problem to converge.

The reason we cannot perform full conditional MLE is that y_1 is only observed when $y_2 = 1$. Thus, while we can use the full density of y_2 given $\mathbf{x}$, which is $f(y_2 \mid \mathbf{x}) = [\Phi(\mathbf{x}\boldsymbol{\delta}_2)]^{y_2}[1 - \Phi(\mathbf{x}\boldsymbol{\delta}_2)]^{1-y_2}$, $y_2 = 0, 1$, we can only use the density $f(y_1 \mid y_2, \mathbf{x})$ when $y_2 = 1$. To find $f(y_1 \mid y_2, \mathbf{x})$ at $y_2 = 1$, we can use Bayes' rule to write $f(y_1 \mid y_2, \mathbf{x}) = f(y_2 \mid y_1, \mathbf{x}) f(y_1 \mid \mathbf{x}) / f(y_2 \mid \mathbf{x})$. Therefore, $f(y_1 \mid y_2 = 1, \mathbf{x}) = \text{P}(y_2 = 1 \mid y_1, \mathbf{x}) f(y_1 \mid \mathbf{x}) / \text{P}(y_2 = 1 \mid \mathbf{x})$. But $y_1 \mid \mathbf{x} \sim \text{Normal}(\mathbf{x}_1\boldsymbol{\beta}_1, \sigma_1^2)$. Further, $y_2 = 1[\mathbf{x}\boldsymbol{\delta}_2 + \sigma_{12}\sigma_1^{-2}(y_1 - \mathbf{x}_1\boldsymbol{\beta}_1) + e_2 > 0]$, where e_2 is independent of $(\mathbf{x}, y_1)$ and $e_2 \sim \text{Normal}(0, 1 - \sigma_{12}^2\sigma_1^{-2})$ (this conclusion follows from standard conditional distribution results for joint normal random variables). Therefore,

$$\text{P}(y_2 = 1 \mid y_1, \mathbf{x}) = \Phi\{[\mathbf{x}\boldsymbol{\delta}_2 + \sigma_{12}\sigma_1^{-2}(y_1 - \mathbf{x}_1\boldsymbol{\beta}_1)](1 - \sigma_{12}^2\sigma_1^{-2})^{-1/2}\}$$

Combining all of these pieces [and noting the cancellation of $\text{P}(y_2 = 1 \mid \mathbf{x})$] we get

$$\ell_i(\boldsymbol{\theta}) = (1 - y_{i2}) \log[1 - \Phi(\mathbf{x}_i\boldsymbol{\delta}_2)] + y_{i2}(\log \Phi\{[\mathbf{x}_i\boldsymbol{\delta}_2 + \sigma_{12}\sigma_1^{-2}(y_{i1} - \mathbf{x}_{i1}\boldsymbol{\beta}_1)]$$
$$\times (1 - \sigma_{12}^2\sigma_1^{-2})^{-1/2}\} + \log \phi[(y_{i1} - \mathbf{x}_{i1}\boldsymbol{\beta}_1)/\sigma_1] - \log(\sigma_1))$$

The partial log likelihood is obtained by summing $\ell_i(\boldsymbol{\theta})$ across *all* observations; $y_{i2} = 1$ picks out when y_{i1} is observed and therefore contains information for estimating $\boldsymbol{\beta}_1$.

Ahn and Powell (1993) show how to consistently estimate $\boldsymbol{\beta}_1$ without making any distributional assumptions; in particular, the selection equation need not have the probit form. Vella (1998) contains a recent survey.

17.4.2 Endogenous Explanatory Variables

We now study the sample selection model when one of the elements of $\mathbf{x}_1$ is thought to be correlated with u_1. Or, all the elements of $\mathbf{x}_1$ are exogenous in the population model but data are missing on an element of $\mathbf{x}_1$, and the reason data are missing might be systematically related to u_1. For simplicity, we focus on the case of a single endogenous explanatory variable.

The model in the population is

$$y_1 = \mathbf{z}_1\boldsymbol{\delta}_1 + \alpha_1 y_2 + u_1 \tag{17.25}$$

$$y_2 = \mathbf{z}\boldsymbol{\delta}_2 + v_2 \tag{17.26}$$

$$y_3 = 1(\mathbf{z}\boldsymbol{\delta}_3 + v_3 > 0) \tag{17.27}$$

The first equation is the structural equation of interest, the second equation is a linear projection for the potentially endogenous or missing variable y_2, and the third equation is the selection equation. We allow arbitrary correlation among u_1, v_2, and v_3.

The setup in equations (17.25)–(17.27) encompasses at least three cases of interest. The first occurs when y_2 is always observed but is endogenous in equation (17.25). An example is seen when y_1 is $\log(wage^{o})$ and y_2 is years of schooling: years of schooling is generally available whether or not someone is in the workforce. The model also applies when y_2 is observed only along with y_1, as would happen if $y_1 = \log(wage^{o})$ and y_2 is the ratio of the benefits offer to wage offer. As a second example, let y_1 be the percentage of voters supporting the incumbent in a congressional district, and let y_2 be intended campaign expenditures. Then $y_3 = 1$ if the incumbent runs for reelection, and we only observe (y_1, y_2) when $y_3 = 1$. A third application is to missing data only on y_2, as in Example 17.4 where y_2 is IQ score. In the last two cases, y_2 might in fact be exogenous in equation (17.25), but endogenous sample selection effectively makes y_2 endogenous in the selected sample.

If y_1 and y_2 were always observed along with $\mathbf{z}$, we would just estimate equation (17.25) by 2SLS if y_2 is endogenous. We can use the results from Section 17.2.1 to show that 2SLS with the inverse Mills ratio added to the regressors is consistent. Regardless of the data availability on y_1 and y_2, in the second step we use only observations for which both y_1 and y_2 are observed.

ASSUMPTION 17.2: (a) $(\mathbf{z}, y_3)$ is always observed, (y_1, y_2) is observed when $y_3 = 1$; (b) (u_1, v_3) is independent of $\mathbf{z}$; (c) $v_3 \sim \text{Normal}(0, 1)$; (d) $\mathrm{E}(u_1 \mid v_3) = \gamma_1 v_3$; and (e) $\mathrm{E}(\mathbf{z}'v_2) = \mathbf{0}$ and, writing $\mathbf{z}\boldsymbol{\delta}_2 = \mathbf{z}_1\boldsymbol{\delta}_{21} + \mathbf{z}_2\boldsymbol{\delta}_{22}$, $\boldsymbol{\delta}_{22} \neq \mathbf{0}$.

Parts b, c, and d are identical to the corresponding assumptions when all explanatory variables are observed and exogenous. Assumption e is new, resulting from the endogeneity of y_2 in equation (17.25). It is important to see that Assumption 17.2e is identical to the rank condition needed for identifying equation (17.25) in the absence of sample selection. As we will see, stating identification in the population is not always sufficient, but, from a practical point of view, the focus should be on Assumption 17.2e.

To derive an estimating equation, write (in the population)

$$y_1 = \mathbf{z}_1\boldsymbol{\delta}_1 + \alpha_1 y_2 + g(\mathbf{z}, y_3) + e_1 \tag{17.28}$$

where $g(\mathbf{z}, y_3) \equiv \mathrm{E}(u_1 \mid \mathbf{z}, y_3)$ and $e_1 \equiv u_1 - \mathrm{E}(u_1 \mid \mathbf{z}, y_3)$. By definition, $\mathrm{E}(e_1 \mid \mathbf{z}, y_3) = 0$. If we knew $g(\mathbf{z}, y_3)$ then, from Theorem 17.1, we could just estimate equation (17.28) by 2SLS on the selected sample ($y_3 = 1$) using instruments $[\mathbf{z}, g(\mathbf{z}, 1)]$. It turns out that we do know $g(\mathbf{z}, 1)$ up to some estimable parameters: $\mathrm{E}(u_1 \mid \mathbf{z}, y_3 = 1) = \gamma_1\lambda(\mathbf{z}\boldsymbol{\delta}_3)$. Since $\boldsymbol{\delta}_3$ can be consistently estimated by probit of y_3 on $\mathbf{z}$ (using the entire sample), we have the following:

Procedure 17.2: (a) Obtain $\hat{\boldsymbol{\delta}}_3$ from probit of y_3 on $\mathbf{z}$ using all observations. Obtain the estimated inverse Mills ratios, $\hat{\lambda}_{i3} = \lambda(\mathbf{z}_i\hat{\boldsymbol{\delta}}_3)$.

(b) Using the selected subsample (for which we observe both y_1 and y_2), estimate the equation

$$y_{i1} = \mathbf{z}_{i1}\boldsymbol{\delta}_1 + \alpha_1 y_{i2} + \gamma_1\hat{\lambda}_{i3} + error_i \tag{17.29}$$

by 2SLS, using instruments $(\mathbf{z}_i, \hat{\lambda}_{i3})$.

The steps in this procedure show that identification actually requires that $\mathbf{z}_2$ appear in the linear projection of y_2 onto $\mathbf{z}_1, \mathbf{z}_2$, *and* $\lambda(\mathbf{z}\boldsymbol{\delta}_3)$ in the selected subpopulation. It would be unusual if this statement were not true when the rank condition 17.2e holds in the population.

The hypothesis-of-no-selection problem (allowing y_2 to be endogenous or not), $\mathrm{H}_0\colon \gamma_1 = 0$, is tested using the usual 2SLS t statistic for $\hat{\gamma}_1$. When $\gamma_1 \neq 0$, standard errors and test statistics should be corrected for the generated regressors problem, as in Chapter 6.

Example 17.7 (Education Endogenous and Sample Selection): In Example 17.6 we now allow *educ* to be endogenous in the wage offer equation, and we test for sample selection bias. Just as if we did not have a sample selection problem, we need IVs for *educ* that do not appear in the wage offer equation. As in Example 5.3, we use parents' education (*motheduc*, *fatheduc*) and husband's education as IVs. In addition, we need some variables that affect labor force participation but not the wage offer; we use the same four variables as in Example 17.6. Therefore, all variables except *educ* (and, of course, the wage offer) are treated as exogenous.

Unless we have very reliable prior information, *all* exogenous variables should appear in the selection equation, and all should be listed as instruments in estimating equation (17.29) by 2SLS. Dropping some exogenous variables in either the selection equation or in estimating equation (17.29) imposes exclusion restrictions on a reduced-form equation, something that can be dangerous and is unnecessary. Therefore, in the labor force participation equation we include *exper*, *exper*^{2}, *nwifeinc*, *kidslt6*, *kidsge6*, *motheduc*, *fatheduc*, and *huseduc* (not *educ*). In estimating equation (17.29), the same set of variables, along with $\hat{\lambda}_3$, are used as IVs. The 2SLS coefficient on $\hat{\lambda}_3$ is .040 (se = .133), and so, again, there is little evidence of sample selection bias. The coefficient on *educ* is .088 (se = .021), which is similar to the 2SLS estimate obtained without the sample selection correction (see Example 5.3). Because there is little evidence of sample selection bias, the standard errors are not corrected for first-stage estimation of $\boldsymbol{\delta}_3$.

Importantly, Procedure 17.2 applies to any kind of endogenous variable y_2, including binary and other discrete variables, without any additional assumptions. This statement is true because the reduced form for y_2 is just a linear projection; we do not have to assume, for example, that v_2 is normally distributed or even independent of $\mathbf{z}$. As an example, we might wish to look at the effects of participation in a job training program on the subsequent wage offer, accounting for the fact that not all who participated in the program will be employed in the following period (y_2 is always observed in this case). If participation is voluntary, an instrument for it might be whether the person was randomly chosen as a potential participant.

Even if y_2 is exogenous in the population equation (17.25), when y_2 is sometimes missing we generally need an instrument for y_2 when selection is not ignorable [that is, $\mathrm{E}(u_1 \mid \mathbf{z}_1, y_2, y_3) \neq \mathrm{E}(u_1)$]. In Example 17.4 we could use family background variables and another test score, such as *KWW*, as IVs for *IQ*, assuming these are always observed. We would generally include all such variables in the reduced-form selection equation. Procedure 17.2 works whether we assume *IQ* is a proxy variable for ability or an indicator of ability (see Chapters 4 and 5).

As a practical matter, we should have at least *two* elements of $\mathbf{z}$ that are not also in $\mathbf{z}_1$; that is, we need at least two exclusion restrictions in the structural equation. Intuitively, for the procedure to be convincing, we should have at least one instrument for y_2 and another exogenous variable that determines selection. Suppose that the scalar z_2 is our only exogenous variable excluded from equation (17.25). Then, under random sampling, the equation would be just identified. When we account for sample selection bias, the Mills ratio term in equation (17.29) is a function of $\mathbf{z}_1$ and z_2. While the nonlinearity of the Mills ratio technically allows us to identify $\boldsymbol{\delta}_1$ and α_1, it is unlikely to work very well in practice because of severe multicollinearity among the IVs. This situation is analogous to using the standard Heckit method when there are no exclusion restrictions in the structural equation (see Section 17.4.1).

If we make stronger assumptions, it is possible to estimate model (17.25)–(17.27) by partial maximum likelihood of the kind discussed in Problem 13.7. One possibility is to assume that (u_1, v_2, v_3) is trivariate normal and independent of $\mathbf{z}$. In addition to ruling out discrete y_2, such a procedure would be computationally difficult. If y_2 is binary, we can model it as $y_2 = 1[\mathbf{z}\boldsymbol{\delta}_2 + v_2 > 0]$, where $v_2 \mid \mathbf{z} \sim \text{Normal}(0, 1)$. But maximum likelihood estimation that allows any correlation matrix for (u_1, v_2, v_3) is complicated and less robust than Procedure 17.2.

17.4.3 Binary Response Model with Sample Selection

We can estimate binary response models with sample selection if we assume that the latent errors are bivariate normal and independent of the explanatory variables. Write the model as

$$y_1 = 1[\mathbf{x}_1\boldsymbol{\beta}_1 + u_1 > 0] \tag{17.30}$$

$$y_2 = 1[\mathbf{x}\boldsymbol{\delta}_2 + v_2 > 0] \tag{17.31}$$

where the second equation is the sample selection equation and y_1 is observed only when $y_2 = 1$; we assume that $\mathbf{x}$ is always observed. For example, suppose y_1 is an employment indicator and $\mathbf{x}_1$ contains a job training binary indicator (which we assume is exogenous), as well as other human capital and family background variables. We might lose track of some people who are eligible to participate in the program; this is an example of sample attrition. If attrition is systematically related to u_1, estimating equation (17.30) on the sample at hand can result in an inconsistent estimator of $\boldsymbol{\beta}_1$.

If we assume that (u_1, v_2) is independent of $\mathbf{x}$ with a zero-mean normal distribution (and unit variances), we can apply partial maximum likelihood. What we need is the density of y_1 conditional on $\mathbf{x}$ and $y_2 = 1$. We have essentially found this density in Chapter 15: in equation (15.55) set $\alpha_1 = 0$, replace $\mathbf{z}$ with $\mathbf{x}$, and replace $\boldsymbol{\delta}_1$ with $\boldsymbol{\beta}_1$. The parameter ρ_1 is still the correlation between u_1 and v_2. A two-step procedure can be applied: first, estimate $\boldsymbol{\delta}_2$ by probit of y_2 on $\mathbf{x}$. Then, estimate $\boldsymbol{\beta}_1$ and ρ_1 in the second stage using equation (15.55) along with $\text{P}(y_1 = 0 \mid \mathbf{x}, y_2 = 1)$.

A convincing analysis requires at least one variable in $\mathbf{x}$—that is, something that determines selection—that is not also in $\mathbf{x}_1$. Otherwise, identification is off of the nonlinearities in the probit models.

Allowing for endogenous explanatory variables in equation (17.30) along with sample selection is difficult, and it could be the focus of future research.

17.5 A Tobit Selection Equation

We now study the case where more information is available on sample selection, primarily in the context of incidental truncation. In particular, we assume that selection is based on the outcome of a Tobit, rather than a probit, equation. The analysis of the models in this section comes from Wooldridge (1998). The model in Section 17.5.1 is a special case of the model studied by Vella (1992) in the context of testing for selectivity bias.

17.5.1 Exogenous Explanatory Variables

We now consider the case where the selection equation is of the censored Tobit form. The population model is

$$y_1 = \mathbf{x}_1\boldsymbol{\beta}_1 + u_1 \tag{17.32}$$

$$y_2 = \max(0, \mathbf{x}\boldsymbol{\delta}_2 + v_2) \tag{17.33}$$

where $(\mathbf{x}, y_2)$ is always observed in the population but y_1 is observed only when $y_2 > 0$. A standard example occurs when y_1 is the log of the hourly wage offer and y_2 is weekly or annual hours of labor supply.

ASSUMPTION 17.3: (a) $(\mathbf{x}, y_2)$ is always observed in the population, but y_1 is observed only when $y_2 > 0$; (b) (u_1, v_2) is independent of $\mathbf{x}$; (c) $v_2 \sim \text{Normal}(0, \tau_2^2)$; and (d) $\mathrm{E}(u_1 \mid v_2) = \gamma_1 v_2$.

These assumptions are very similar to the assumptions for a probit selection equation. The only difference is that v_2 now has an unknown variance, since y_2 is a censored as opposed to binary variable.

Amemiya (1985) calls equations (17.32) and (17.33) the **type III Tobit model**, but we emphasize that equation (17.32) is the structural population equation of interest and that equation (17.33) simply determines when y_1 is observed. In the labor economics example, we are interested in the wage offer equation, and equation (17.33) is a reduced-form hours equation. It makes no sense to define y_1 to be, say, zero, just because we do not observe y_1.

The starting point is equation (17.21), just as in the probit selection case. Now define the selection indicator as $s_2 = 1$ if $y_2 > 0$, and $s_2 = 0$ otherwise. Since s_2 is a function of $\mathbf{x}$ and v_2, it follows immediately that

$$E(y_1 \mid \mathbf{x}, v_2, s_2) = \mathbf{x}_1 \boldsymbol{\beta}_1 + \gamma_1 v_2 \tag{17.34}$$

This equation means that, if we could observe v_2, then an OLS regression of y_1 on $\mathbf{x}_1$, v_2 using the selected subsample would consistently estimate $(\boldsymbol{\beta}_1, \gamma_1)$, as we discussed in Section 17.2.1. While v_2 cannot be observed when $y_2 = 0$ (because when $y_2 = 0$, we only know that $v_2 \leq -\mathbf{x}\boldsymbol{\delta}_2$), for $y_2 > 0$, $v_2 = y_2 - \mathbf{x}\boldsymbol{\delta}_2$. Thus, if we knew $\boldsymbol{\delta}_2$, we would know v_2 whenever $y_2 > 0$. It seems reasonable that, because $\boldsymbol{\delta}_2$ can be consistently estimated by Tobit on the whole sample, we can replace v_2 with consistent estimates.

Procedure 17.3: (a) Estimate equation (17.33) by standard Tobit using all N observations. For $y_{i2} > 0$ (say $i = 1, 2, \ldots, N_1$), define

$$\hat{v}_{i2} = y_{i2} - \mathbf{x}_i \hat{\boldsymbol{\delta}}_2 \tag{17.35}$$

(b) Using observations for which $y_{i2} > 0$, estimate $\boldsymbol{\beta}_1$, γ_1 by the OLS regression

$$y_{i1} \text{ on } \mathbf{x}_{i1}, \hat{v}_{i2} \quad i = 1, 2, \ldots, N_1 \tag{17.36}$$

This regression produces consistent, $\sqrt{N}$-asymptotically normal estimators of $\boldsymbol{\beta}_1$ and γ_1 under Assumption 17.3.

The statistic to test for selectivity bias is just the usual t statistic on $\hat{v}_{i2}$ in regression (17.36). This was suggested by Vella (1992). Wooldridge (1998) showed that this procedure also solves the selection problem when $\gamma_1 \neq 0$.

It seems likely that there is an efficiency gain over Procedure 17.1. If v_2 were known and we could use regression (17.36) for the entire population, there would definitely be an efficiency gain: the error variance is reduced by conditioning on v_2 along with $\mathbf{x}$, and there would be no heteroskedasticity in the population. See Problem 4.5.

Unlike in the probit selection case, $\mathbf{x}_1 = \mathbf{x}$ causes no problems here: v_2 always has separate variation from $\mathbf{x}_1$ because of variation in y_2. We do not need to rely on the nonlinearity of the inverse Mills ratio.

Example 17.8 (Wage Offer Equation for Married Women): We now apply Procedure 17.3 to the wage offer equation for married women in Example 17.6. (We assume education is exogenous.) The only difference is that the first-step estimation is Tobit, rather than probit, and we include the Tobit residuals as the additional explanatory variables, not the inverse Mills ratio. In regression (17.36), the coefficient on $\hat{v}_2$ is $-.000053$ (se $= .000041$), which is somewhat more evidence of a sample selection problem, but we still do not reject the null hypothesis H_0: $\gamma_1 = 0$ at even the 15 percent level against a two-sided alternative. Further, the coefficient on *educ* is .103 (se $= .015$), which is not much different from the OLS and Heckit estimates. (Again, we use the usual OLS standard error.) When we include all exogenous variables in the wage offer equation, the estimates from Procedure 17.3 are much more stable than the Heckit estimates. For example, the coefficient on *educ* becomes .093 (se $= .016$), which is comparable to the OLS estimates discussed in Example 17.6.

For partial maximum likelihood estimation, we assume that (u_1, v_2) is jointly normal, and we use the density for $f(y_2 \mid \mathbf{x})$ for the entire sample and the conditional density $f(y_1 \mid \mathbf{x}, y_2, s_2 = 1) = f(y_1 \mid \mathbf{x}, y_2)$ for the selected sample. This approach is fairly straightforward because, when $y_2 > 0$, $y_1 \mid \mathbf{x}, y_2 \sim \mathrm{Normal}[\mathbf{x}_1\boldsymbol{\beta}_1 + \gamma_1(y_2 - \mathbf{x}\boldsymbol{\delta}_2), \eta_1^2]$, where $\eta_1^2 = \sigma_1^2 - \sigma_{12}^2/\tau_2^2$, $\sigma_1^2 = \mathrm{Var}(u_1)$, and $\sigma_{12} = \mathrm{Cov}(u_1, v_2)$. The log likelihood for observation i is

$$\ell_i(\boldsymbol{\theta}) = s_{i2} \log f(y_{i1} \mid \mathbf{x}_i, y_{i2}; \boldsymbol{\theta}) + \log f(y_{i2} \mid \mathbf{x}_i; \boldsymbol{\delta}_2, \tau_2^2) \tag{17.37}$$

where $f(y_{i1} \mid \mathbf{x}_i, y_{i2}; \boldsymbol{\theta})$ is the $\mathrm{Normal}[\mathbf{x}_{i1}\boldsymbol{\beta}_1 + \gamma_1(y_{i2} - \mathbf{x}_i\boldsymbol{\delta}_2), \eta_1^2]$ distribution, evaluated at y_{i1}, and $f(y_{i2} \mid \mathbf{x}_i; \boldsymbol{\delta}_2, \tau_2^2)$ is the standard censored Tobit density [see equation (16.19)]. As shown in Problem 13.7, the usual MLE theory can be used even though the log-likelihood function is not based on a true conditional density.

It is possible to obtain sample selection corrections and tests for various other nonlinear models when the selection rule is of the Tobit form. For example, suppose that the binary variable y_1 given $\mathbf{z}$ follows a probit model, but it is observed only when $y_2 > 0$. A valid test for selection bias is to include the Tobit residuals, $\hat{v}_2$, in a probit of y_1 on $\mathbf{z}$, $\hat{v}_2$ using the selected sample; see Vella (1992). This procedure also produces consistent estimates (up to scale), as can be seen by applying the maximum likelihood results in Section 17.2.2 along with two-step estimation results.

Honoré, Kyriazidou, and Udry (1997) show how to estimate the parameters of the type III Tobit model without making distributional assumptions.

17.5.2 Endogenous Explanatory Variables

We explicitly consider the case of a single endogenous explanatory variable, as in Section 17.4.2. We use equations (17.25) and (17.26), and, in place of equation (17.27), we have a Tobit selection equation:

$$y_3 = \max(0, \mathbf{z}\boldsymbol{\delta}_3 + v_3) \tag{17.38}$$

ASSUMPTION 17.4: (a) $(\mathbf{z}, y_3)$ is always observed, (y_1, y_2) is observed when $y_3 > 0$; (b) (u_1, v_3) is independent of $\mathbf{z}$; (c) $v_3 \sim \text{Normal}(0, \tau_3^2)$; (d) $\text{E}(u_1 \mid v_3) = \gamma_1 v_3$; and (e) $\text{E}(\mathbf{z}'v_2) = \mathbf{0}$ and, writing $\mathbf{z}\boldsymbol{\delta}_2 = \mathbf{z}_1\boldsymbol{\delta}_{21} + \mathbf{z}_2\boldsymbol{\delta}_{22}$, $\boldsymbol{\delta}_{22} \neq \mathbf{0}$.

Again, these assumptions are very similar to those used with a probit selection mechanism.

To derive an estimating equation, write

$$y_1 = \mathbf{z}_1\boldsymbol{\delta}_1 + \alpha_1 y_2 + \gamma_1 v_3 + e_1 \tag{17.39}$$

where $e_1 \equiv u_1 - \text{E}(u_1 \mid v_3)$. Since (e_1, v_3) is independent of $\mathbf{z}$ by Assumption 17.4b, $\text{E}(e_1 \mid \mathbf{z}, v_3) = 0$. From Theorem 17.1, if v_3 were observed, we could estimate equation (17.39) by 2SLS on the selected sample using instruments $(\mathbf{z}, v_3)$. As before, we can estimate v_3 when $y_3 > 0$, since $\boldsymbol{\delta}_3$ can be consistently estimated by Tobit of y_3 on $\mathbf{z}$ (using the entire sample).

Procedure 17.4: (a) Obtain $\hat{\boldsymbol{\delta}}_3$ from Tobit of y_3 on $\mathbf{z}$ using all observations. Obtain the Tobit residuals $\hat{v}_{i3} = y_{i3} - \mathbf{z}_i\hat{\boldsymbol{\delta}}_3$ for $y_{i3} > 0$.

(b) Using the selected subsample, estimate the equation

$$y_{i1} = \mathbf{z}_{i1}\boldsymbol{\delta}_1 + \alpha_1 y_{i2} + \gamma_1 \hat{v}_{i3} + error_i \tag{17.40}$$

by 2SLS, using instruments $(\mathbf{z}_i, \hat{v}_{i3})$. The estimators are $\sqrt{N}$-consistent and asymptotically normal under Assumption 17.4.

Comments similar to those after Procedure 17.2 hold here as well. Strictly speaking, identification really requires that $\mathbf{z}_2$ appear in the linear projection of y_2 onto $\mathbf{z}_1$, $\mathbf{z}_2$, and v_3 in the selected subpopulation. The null of no selection bias is tested using the 2SLS t statistic (or maybe its heteroskedasticity-robust version) on $\hat{v}_{i3}$. When $\gamma_1 \neq 0$, standard errors should be corrected using two-step methods.

As in the case with a probit selection equation, the endogenous variable y_2 can be continuous, discrete, censored, and so on. Extending the method to multiple endogenous explanatory variables is straightforward. The only restriction is the usual one for linear models: we need enough instruments to identify the structural equation. See Problem 17.6 for an application to the Mroz data.

An interesting special case of model (17.25), (17.26), and (17.38) is when $y_2 = y_3$. Actually, because we only use observations for which $y_3 > 0$, $y_2 = y_3^*$ is also allowed, where $y_3^* = \mathbf{z}\boldsymbol{\delta}_3 + v_3$. Either way, the variable that determines selection also appears in the structural equation. This special case could be useful when sample selection is caused by a corner solution outcome on y_3 (in which case $y_2 = y_3$ is natural) or because y_3^* is subject to data censoring (in which case $y_2 = y_3^*$ is more realistic). An example of the former occurs when y_3 is hours worked and we assume hours appears in the wage offer function. As a data-censoring example, suppose that y_1 is a measure of growth in an infant's weight starting from birth and that we observe y_1 only if the infant is brought into a clinic within three months. Naturally, birth weight depends on age, and so y_3^*—length of time between the first and second measurements, which has quantitiative meaning—appears as an explanatory variable in the equation for y_1. We have a data-censoring problem for y_3^*, which causes a sample selection problem for y_1. In this case, we would estimate a censored regression model for y_3 [or, possibly, $\log(y_3)$] to account for the data censoring. We would include the residuals $\hat{v}_{i3} = y_{i3} - \mathbf{z}_i\hat{\boldsymbol{\delta}}_3$ in equation (17.40) for the noncensored observations. As our extra instrument we might use distance from the child's home to the clinic.

17.6 Estimating Structural Tobit Equations with Sample Selection

We briefly show how a structural Tobit model can be estimated using the methods of the previous section. As an example, consider the structural labor supply model

$$\log(w^o) = \mathbf{z}_1\boldsymbol{\beta}_1 + u_1 \tag{17.41}$$

$$h = \max[0, \mathbf{z}_2\boldsymbol{\beta}_2 + \alpha_2 \log(w^o) + u_2] \tag{17.42}$$

This system involves simultaneity and sample selection because we observe w^o only if $h > 0$.

The general form of the model is

$$y_1 = \mathbf{z}_1\boldsymbol{\beta}_1 + u_1 \tag{17.43}$$

$$y_2 = \max(0, \mathbf{z}_2\boldsymbol{\beta}_2 + \alpha_2 y_1 + u_2) \tag{17.44}$$

ASSUMPTION 17.5: (a) $(\mathbf{z}, y_2)$ is always observed; y_1 is observed when $y_2 > 0$; (b) (u_1, u_2) is independent of $\mathbf{z}$ with a zero-mean bivariate normal distribution; and (c) $\mathbf{z}_1$ contains at least one element whose coefficient is different from zero that is not in $\mathbf{z}_2$.

As always, it is important to see that equations (17.43) and (17.44) constitute a model describing a population. If y_1 were always observed, then equation (17.43) could be estimated by OLS. If, in addition, u_1 and u_2 were uncorrelated, equation (17.44) could be estimated by censored Tobit. Correlation between u_1 and u_2 could be handled by the methods of Section 16.6.2. Now, we require new methods, whether or not u_1 and u_2 are uncorrelated, because y_1 is not observed when $y_2 = 0$.

The restriction in Assumption 17.5c is needed to identify the structural parameters $(\boldsymbol{\beta}_2, \alpha_2)$ ($\boldsymbol{\beta}_1$ is always identified). To see that this condition is needed, and for finding the reduced form for y_2, it is useful to introduce the latent variable

$$y_2^* \equiv \mathbf{z}_2\boldsymbol{\beta}_2 + \alpha_2 y_1 + u_2 \tag{17.45}$$

so that $y_2 = \max(0, y_2^*)$. If equations (17.43) and (17.45) make up the system of interest—that is, if y_1 and y_2^* are always observed—then $\boldsymbol{\beta}_1$ is identified without further restrictions, but identification of α_2 and $\boldsymbol{\beta}_2$ requires exactly Assumption 17.5c. This turns out to be sufficient even when y_2 follows a Tobit model and we have nonrandom sample selection.

The reduced form for y_2^* is $y_2^* = \mathbf{z}\boldsymbol{\delta}_2 + v_2$. Therefore, we can write the reduced form of equation (17.44) as

$$y_2 = \max(0, \mathbf{z}\boldsymbol{\delta}_2 + v_2). \tag{17.46}$$

But then equations (17.43) and (17.46) constitute the model we studied in Section 17.5.1. The vector $\boldsymbol{\delta}_2$ is consistently estimated by Tobit, and $\boldsymbol{\beta}_1$ is estimated as in Procedure 17.3. The only remaining issue is how to estimate the structural parameters of equation (17.44), α_2 and $\boldsymbol{\beta}_2$. In the labor supply case, these are the labor supply parameters.

Assuming identification, estimation of $(\alpha_2, \boldsymbol{\beta}_2)$ is fairly straightforward after having estimated $\boldsymbol{\beta}_1$. To see this point, write the reduced form of y_2 in terms of the structural parameters as

$$y_2 = \max[0, \mathbf{z}_2\boldsymbol{\beta}_2 + \alpha_2(\mathbf{z}_1\boldsymbol{\beta}_1) + v_2] \tag{17.47}$$

Under joint normality of u_1 and u_2, v_2 is normally distributed. Therefore, if $\boldsymbol{\beta}_1$ were *known*, $\boldsymbol{\beta}_2$ and α_2 could be estimated by standard Tobit using $\mathbf{z}_2$ and $\mathbf{z}_1\boldsymbol{\beta}_1$ as regressors. Operationalizing this procedure requires replacing $\boldsymbol{\beta}_1$ with its consistent estimator. Thus, using all observations, $\boldsymbol{\beta}_2$ and α_2 are estimated from the Tobit equation

$$y_{i2} = \max[0, \mathbf{z}_{i2}\boldsymbol{\beta}_2 + \alpha_2(\mathbf{z}_{i1}\hat{\boldsymbol{\beta}}_1) + error_i] \tag{17.48}$$

To summarize, we have the following:

Procedure 17.5: (a) Use Procedure 17.3 to obtain $\hat{\boldsymbol{\beta}}_1$.

(b) Obtain $\hat{\boldsymbol{\beta}}_2$ and $\hat{\alpha}_2$ from the Tobit in equation (17.48).

In applying this procedure, it is important to note that the explanatory variable in equation (17.48) is $\mathbf{z}_{i1}\hat{\boldsymbol{\beta}}_1$ for all i. These are *not* the fitted values from regression (17.36), which depend on $\hat{v}_{i2}$. Also, it may be tempting to use y_{i1} in place of $\mathbf{z}_{i1}\hat{\boldsymbol{\beta}}_1$ for that part of the sample for which y_{i1} is observed. This approach is not a good idea: the estimators are inconsistent in this case.

The estimation in equation (17.48) makes it clear that the procedure fails if $\mathbf{z}_1$ does not contain at least one variable not in $\mathbf{z}_2$. If $\mathbf{z}_1$ is a subset of $\mathbf{z}_2$, then $\mathbf{z}_{i1}\hat{\boldsymbol{\beta}}_1$ is a linear combination of $\mathbf{z}_{i2}$, and so perfect multicollinearity will exist in equation (17.48).

Estimating $\text{Avar}(\hat{\alpha}_2, \hat{\boldsymbol{\beta}}_2)$ is even messier than estimating $\text{Avar}(\hat{\boldsymbol{\beta}}_1)$, since $(\hat{\alpha}_2, \hat{\boldsymbol{\beta}}_2)$ comes from a three-step procedure. Often just the usual Tobit standard errors and test statistics reported from equation (17.48) are used, even though these are not strictly valid. By setting the problem up as a large GMM problem, as illustrated in Chapter 14, correct standard errors and test statistics can be obtained.

Under Assumption 17.5, a full maximum likelihood approach is possible. In fact, the log-likelihood function can be constructed from equations (17.43) and (17.47), and it has a form very similar to equation (17.37). The only difference is that nonlinear restrictions are imposed automatically on the structural parameters. In addition to making it easy to obtain valid standard errors, MLE is desirable because it allows us to estimate $\sigma_2^2 = \text{Var}(u_2)$, which is needed to estimate average partial effects in equation (17.44).

In examples such as labor supply, it is not clear where the elements of $\mathbf{z}_1$ that are not in $\mathbf{z}_2$ might come from. One possibility is a union binary variable, if we believe that union membership increases wages (other factors accounted for) but has no effect on labor supply once wage and other factors have been controlled for. This approach would require knowing union status for people whether or not they are working in the period covered by the survey. In some studies past experience is assumed to affect wage—which it certainly does—and is assumed not to appear in the labor supply function, a tenuous assumption.

17.7 Sample Selection and Attrition in Linear Panel Data Models

In our treatment of panel data models we have assumed that a balanced panel is available—each cross section unit has the same time periods available. Often, some time periods are missing for some units in the population of interest, and we are left with an **unbalanced panel**. Unbalanced panels can arise for several reasons. First, the survey design may simply rotate people or firms out of the sample based on prespecified rules. For example, if a survey of individuals begins at time $t = 1$, at time $t = 2$ some of the original people may be dropped and new people added. At $t = 3$ some additional people might be dropped and others added; and so on. This is an example of a **rotating panel**.

Provided the decision to rotate units out of a panel is made randomly, unbalanced panels are fairly easy to deal with, as we will see shortly. A more complicated problem arises when attrition from a panel is due to units electing to drop out. If this decision is based on factors that are systematically related to the response variable, even after we condition on explanatory variables, a sample selection problem can result—just as in the cross section case. Nevertheless, a panel data set provides us with the means to handle, in a simple fashion, attrition that is based on a time-constant, unobserved effect, provided we use first-differencing methods; we show this in Section 17.7.3.

A different kind of sample selection problem occurs when people do not disappear from the panel but certain variables are unobserved for at least some time periods. This is the incidental truncation problem discussed in Section 17.4. A leading case is estimating a wage offer equation using a panel of individuals. Even if the population of interest is people who are employed in the initial year, some people will become unemployed in subsequent years. For those people we cannot observe a wage offer, just as in the cross-sectional case. This situation is different from the attrition problem where people leave the sample entirely and, usually, do not reappear in later years. In the incidental truncation case we observe some variables on everyone in each time period.

17.7.1 Fixed Effects Estimation with Unbalanced Panels

We begin by studying assumptions under which the usual fixed effects estimator on the unbalanced panel is consistent. The model is the usual linear, unobserved effects model under random sampling in the cross section: for any i,

$$y_{it} = \mathbf{x}_{it}\boldsymbol{\beta} + c_i + u_{it}, \qquad t = 1, \ldots, T \tag{17.49}$$

where $\mathbf{x}_{it}$ is $1 \times K$ and $\boldsymbol{\beta}$ is the $K \times 1$ vector of interest. As before, we assume that N cross section observations are available and the asymptotic analysis is as $N \to \infty$. We explicitly cover the case where c_i is allowed to be correlated with $\mathbf{x}_{it}$, so that all elements of $\mathbf{x}_{it}$ are time varying. A random effects analysis is also possible under stronger assumptions; see, for example, Verbeek and Nijman (1992, 1996).

We covered the case where all T time periods are available in Chapters 10 and 11. Now we consider the case where some time periods might be missing for some of the cross section draws. Think of $t = 1$ as the first time period for which data on anyone in the population are available, and $t = T$ as the last possible time period. For a random draw i from the population, let $\mathbf{s}_i \equiv (s_{i1}, \ldots, s_{iT})'$ denote the $T \times 1$ vector of selection indicators: $s_{it} = 1$ if $(\mathbf{x}_{it}, y_{it})$ is observed, and zero otherwise. Generally, we have an unbalanced panel. We can treat $\{(\mathbf{x}_i, \mathbf{y}_i, \mathbf{s}_i): i = 1, 2, \ldots, N\}$ as a random sample from the population; the selection indicators tell us which time periods are missing for each i.

We can easily find assumptions under which the fixed effects estimator on the unbalanced panel is consistent by writing it as

$$\hat{\boldsymbol{\beta}} = \left(N^{-1}\sum_{i=1}^{N}\sum_{t=1}^{T} s_{it}\ddot{\mathbf{x}}_{it}'\ddot{\mathbf{x}}_{it}\right)^{-1}\left(N^{-1}\sum_{i=1}^{N}\sum_{t=1}^{T} s_{it}\ddot{\mathbf{x}}_{it}'\ddot{y}_{it}\right)$$

$$= \boldsymbol{\beta} + \left(N^{-1}\sum_{i=1}^{N}\sum_{t=1}^{T} s_{it}\ddot{\mathbf{x}}_{it}'\ddot{\mathbf{x}}_{it}\right)^{-1}\left(N^{-1}\sum_{i=1}^{N}\sum_{t=1}^{T} s_{it}\ddot{\mathbf{x}}_{it}'u_{it}\right) \tag{17.50}$$

where we define

$$\ddot{\mathbf{x}}_{it} \equiv \mathbf{x}_{it} - T_i^{-1}\sum_{r=1}^{T} s_{ir}\mathbf{x}_{ir}, \qquad \ddot{y}_{it} \equiv y_{it} - T_i^{-1}\sum_{r=1}^{T} s_{ir}y_{ir}, \qquad \text{and} \qquad T_i \equiv \sum_{t=1}^{T} s_{it}$$

That is, T_i is the number of time periods observed for cross section i, and we apply the within transformation on the available time periods.

If fixed effects on the unbalanced panel is to be consistent, we should have $\mathrm{E}(s_{it}\ddot{\mathbf{x}}_{it}'u_{it}) = 0$ for all t. Now, since $\ddot{\mathbf{x}}_{it}$ depends on all of $\mathbf{x}_i$ and $\mathbf{s}_i$, a form of strict exogeneity is needed.

ASSUMPTION 17.6: (a) $\mathrm{E}(u_{it} \mid \mathbf{x}_i, \mathbf{s}_i, c_i) = 0$, $t = 1, 2, \ldots, T$; (b) $\sum_{t=1}^{T} \mathrm{E}(s_{it}\ddot{\mathbf{x}}_{it}'\ddot{\mathbf{x}}_{it})$ is nonsingular; and (c) $\mathrm{E}(\mathbf{u}_i\mathbf{u}_i' \mid \mathbf{x}_i, \mathbf{s}_i, c_i) = \sigma_u^2\mathbf{I}_T$.

Under Assumption 17.6a, $\mathrm{E}(s_{it}\ddot{\mathbf{x}}_{it}'u_{it}) = \mathbf{0}$ from the law of iterated expectations [because $s_{it}\ddot{\mathbf{x}}_{it}$ is a function of $(\mathbf{x}_i, \mathbf{s}_i)$]. The second assumption is the rank condition on the expected outer product matrix, after accounting for sample selection; naturally, it rules out time-constant elements in $\mathbf{x}_{it}$. These first two assumptions ensure consistency of FE on the unbalanced panel.

In the case of a randomly rotating panel, and in other cases where selection is entirely random, $\mathbf{s}_i$ is independent of $(\mathbf{u}_i, \mathbf{x}_i, c_i)$, in which case Assumption 17.6a follows under the standard fixed effects assumption $\mathrm{E}(u_{it} \mid \mathbf{x}_i, c_i) = 0$ for all t. In this case, the natural assumptions on the population model imply consistency and asympotic normality on the unbalanced panel. Assumption 17.6a also holds under much weaker conditions. In particular, it does not assume anything about the relationship between $\mathbf{s}_i$ and $(\mathbf{x}_i, c_i)$. Therefore, if we think selection in all time periods is correlated with c_i or $\mathbf{x}_i$, but that u_{it} is mean independent of $\mathbf{s}_i$ given $(\mathbf{x}_i, c_i)$ for all t, then FE on the unbalanced panel is consistent and asymptotically normal. This conclusion may be a reasonable approximation, especially for short panels. What Assumption 17.6a rules out is selection that is partially correlated with the idiosyncratic errors, u_{it}.

A random effects analysis on the unbalanced panel requires much stronger assumptions: it effectively requires $\mathbf{s}_i$ and c_i to be independent. Random effects will be inconsistent if, say, in a wage offer equation, less able people are more likely to disappear from the sample. This conclusion is true even if $\mathrm{E}(c_i \mid \mathbf{x}_i) = 0$ (Assumption RE.1 from Chapter 10) holds in the underlying population; see Wooldridge (1995a) for further discussion.

When we add Assumption 17.6c, standard inference procedures based on FE are valid. In particular, under Assumptions 17.6a and 17.6c,

$$\mathrm{Var}\left(\sum_{t=1}^{T} s_{it}\ddot{\mathbf{x}}_{it}' u_{it}\right) = \sigma_u^2 \left[\sum_{t=1}^{T} \mathrm{E}(s_{it}\ddot{\mathbf{x}}_{it}'\ddot{\mathbf{x}}_{it})\right]$$

Therefore, the asymptotic variance of the fixed effects estimator is estimated as

$$\hat{\sigma}_u^2 \left(\sum_{i=1}^{N}\sum_{t=1}^{T} s_{it}\ddot{\mathbf{x}}_{it}'\ddot{\mathbf{x}}_{it}\right)^{-1} \tag{17.51}$$

The estimator $\hat{\sigma}_u^2$ can be derived from

$$\mathrm{E}\left(\sum_{t=1}^{T} s_{it}\ddot{u}_{it}^2\right) = \mathrm{E}\left[\sum_{t=1}^{T} s_{it}\mathrm{E}(\ddot{u}_{it}^2 \mid \mathbf{s}_i)\right] = \mathrm{E}\{T_i[\sigma_u^2(1 - 1/T_i)]\} = \sigma_u^2 \mathrm{E}[(T_i - 1)]$$

Now, define the FE residuals as $\hat{u}_{it} = \ddot{y}_{it} - \ddot{\mathbf{x}}_{it}\hat{\boldsymbol{\beta}}$ when $s_{it} = 1$. Then, because $N^{-1}\sum_{i=1}^{N}(T_i - 1) \xrightarrow{p} \mathrm{E}(T_i - 1)$,

$$\hat{\sigma}_u^2 = \left[N^{-1}\sum_{i=1}^{N}(T_i - 1)\right]^{-1} N^{-1}\sum_{i=1}^{N}\sum_{t=1}^{T} s_{it}\hat{u}_{it}^2 = \left[\sum_{i=1}^{N}(T_i - 1)\right]^{-1} \sum_{i=1}^{N}\sum_{t=1}^{T} s_{it}\hat{u}_{it}^2$$

is consistent for σ_u^2 as $N \to \infty$. Standard software packages also make a degrees-of-freedom adjustment by subtracting K from $\sum_{i=1}^{N}(T_i - 1)$. It follows that all of the usual test statistics based on an unbalanced fixed effects analysis are valid. In particular, the dummy variable regression discussed in Chapter 10 produces asymptotically valid statistics.

Because the FE estimator uses time demeaning, any unit i for which $T_i = 1$ drops out of the fixed effects estimator. To use these observations we would need to add more assumptions, such as the random effects assumption $\mathrm{E}(c_i \mid \mathbf{x}_i, \mathbf{s}_i) = 0$.

Relaxing Assumption 17.6c is easy: just apply the robust variance matrix estimator in equation (10.59) to the unbalanced panel. The only changes are that the rows of $\ddot{\mathbf{X}}_i$ are $s_{it}\ddot{\mathbf{x}}_{it}$ and the elements of $\hat{\mathbf{u}}_i$ are $s_{it}\hat{u}_{it}$, $t = 1, \ldots, T$.

Under Assumption 17.6, it is also valid to used a standard fixed effects analysis on any balanced subset of the unbalanced panel; in fact, we can condition on any outcomes of the s_{it}. For example, if we use unit i only when observations are available in all time periods, we are conditioning on $s_{it} = 1$ for all t.

Using similar arguments, it can be shown that any kind of differencing method on any subset of the observed panel is consistent. For example, with $T = 3$, we observe cross section units with data for one, two, or three time periods. Those units with $T_i = 1$ drop out, but any other combinations of differences can be used in a pooled OLS analysis. The analogues of Assumption 17.6 for first differencing—for example, Assumption 17.6c is replaced with $\mathrm{E}(\Delta\mathbf{u}_i\Delta\mathbf{u}_i' \mid \mathbf{x}_i, \mathbf{s}_i, c_i) = \sigma_e^2\mathbf{I}_{T-1}$—ensure that the usual statistics from pooled OLS on the unbalanced first differences are asymptotically valid.

17.7.2 Testing and Correcting for Sample Selection Bias

The results in the previous subsection imply that sample selection in a fixed effects context is only a problem when selection is related to the idiosyncratic errors, u_{it}. Therefore, any test for selection bias should test only this assumption. A simple test was suggested by Nijman and Verbeek (1992) in the context of random effects estimation, but it works for fixed effects as well: add, say, the lagged selection indicator, $s_{i,t-1}$, to the equation, estimate the model by fixed effects (on the unbalanced panel), and do a t test (perhaps making it fully robust) for the significance of $s_{i,t-1}$. (This method loses the first time period for *all* observations.) Under the null hypothesis, u_{it} is uncorrelated with s_{ir} for all r, and so selection in the previous time period should not be significant in the equation at time t. (Incidentally, it never makes sense to put s_{it} in the equation at time t because $s_{it} = 1$ for all i and t in the selected subsample.)

Putting $s_{i,t-1}$ does not work if $s_{i,t-1}$ is unity whenever s_{it} is unity because then there is no variation in $s_{i,t-1}$ in the selected sample. This is the case in attrition problems if (say) a person can only appear in period t if he or she appeared in $t-1$. An alternative is to include a lead of the selection indicator, $s_{i,t+1}$. For observations i that are in the sample every time period, $s_{i,t+1}$ is always zero. But for attriters, $s_{i,t+1}$ switches from zero to one in the period just before attrition. If we use fixed effects or first differencing, we need $T > 2$ time periods to carry out the test.

For incidental truncation problems it makes sense to extend Heckman's (1976) test to the unobserved effects panel data context. This is done in Wooldridge (1995a). Write the equation of interest as

$$y_{it1} = \mathbf{x}_{it1}\boldsymbol{\beta}_1 + c_{i1} + u_{it1}, \qquad t = 1, \ldots, T \tag{17.52}$$

Initially, suppose that y_{it1} is observed only if the binary selection indicator, s_{it2}, is unity. Let $\mathbf{x}_{it}$ denote the set of all exogenous variables at time t; we assume that these are observed in every time period, and $\mathbf{x}_{it1}$ is a subset of $\mathbf{x}_{it}$. Suppose that, for each t, s_{it2} is determined by the probit equation

$$s_{it2} = 1[\mathbf{x}_i\boldsymbol{\psi}_{t2} + v_{it2} > 0], \qquad v_{it2} \mid \mathbf{x}_i \sim \text{Normal}(0, 1) \tag{17.53}$$

where $\mathbf{x}_i$ contains unity. This is best viewed as a reduced-form selection equation: we let the explanatory variables in all time periods appear in the selection equation at time t to allow for general selection models, including those with unobserved effect and the Chamberlain (1980) device discussed in Section 15.8.2, as well as certain dynamic models of selection. A Mundlak (1978) approach would replace $\mathbf{x}_i$ with $(\mathbf{x}_{it}, \overline{\mathbf{x}}_i)$ at time t and assume that coefficients are constant across time. [See equation (15.68).] Then the parameters can be estimated by pooled probit, greatly conserving on degrees of freedom. Such conservation may be important for small N. For testing purposes, under the null hypothesis it does not matter whether equation (17.53) is the proper model of sample selection, but we will need to assume equation (17.53), or a Mundlak version of it, when correcting for sample selection.

Under the null hypothesis in Assumption 17.6a (with the obvious notational changes), the inverse Mills ratio obtained from the sample selection probit should not be significant in the equation estimated by fixed effects. Thus, let $\hat{\lambda}_{it2}$ be the estimated Mills ratios from estimating equation (17.53) by pooled probit across i and t. Then a valid test of the null hypothesis is a t statistic on $\hat{\lambda}_{it2}$ in the FE estimation on the unbalanced panel. Under Assumption 17.6c the usual t statistic is valid, but the approach works whether or not the u_{it1} are homoskedastic and serially uncorrelated: just compute the robust standard error. Wooldridge (1995a) shows formally that the first-stage estimation of $\boldsymbol{\psi}_2$ does not affect the limiting distribution of the t statistic under H_0. This conclusion also follows from the results in Chapter 12 on M-estimation.

Correcting for sample selection requires much more care. Unfortunately, under any assumptions that actually allow for an unobserved effect in the underlying selection equation, adding $\hat{\lambda}_{it2}$ to equation (17.52) and using FE does not produce consistent estimators. To see why, suppose

$$s_{it2} = 1[\mathbf{x}_{it}\boldsymbol{\delta}_2 + c_{i2} + a_{it2} > 0], \qquad a_{it2} \mid (\mathbf{x}_i, c_{i1}, c_{i2}) \sim \text{Normal}(0, 1) \tag{17.54}$$

Then, to get equation (17.53), v_{it2} depends on a_{it2} and, at least partially, on c_{i2}. Now, suppose we make the strong assumption $\text{E}(u_{it1} \mid \mathbf{x}_i, c_{i1}, c_{i2}, \mathbf{v}_{i2}) = g_{i1} + \rho_1 v_{it2}$, which would hold under the assumption that the (u_{it1}, a_{it2}) are independent across t conditional on $(\mathbf{x}_i, c_{i1}, c_{i2})$. Then we have

$$y_{it1} = \mathbf{x}_{it1}\boldsymbol{\beta}_1 + \rho_1 \mathrm{E}(v_{it2} \mid \mathbf{x}_i, \mathbf{s}_{i2}) + (c_{i1} + g_{i1}) + e_{it1} + \rho_1[v_{it2} - \mathrm{E}(v_{it2} \mid \mathbf{x}_i, \mathbf{s}_{i2})]$$

The composite error, $e_{it1} + \rho_1[v_{it2} - \mathrm{E}(v_{it2} \mid \mathbf{x}_i, \mathbf{s}_{i2})]$, is uncorrelated with any function of $(\mathbf{x}_i, \mathbf{s}_{i2})$. The problem is that $\mathrm{E}(v_{it2} \mid \mathbf{x}_i, \mathbf{s}_{i2})$ depends on all elements in $\mathbf{s}_{i2}$, and this expectation is complicated for even small T.

A method that does work is available using Chamberlain's approach to panel data models, but we need some linearity assumptions on the expected values of u_{it1} and c_{i1} given $\mathbf{x}_i$ and v_{it2}.

ASSUMPTION 17.7: (a) The selection equation is given by equation (17.53); (b) $\mathrm{E}(u_{it1} \mid \mathbf{x}_i, v_{it2}) = \mathrm{E}(u_{it1} \mid v_{it2}) = \rho_{t1} v_{it2}$, $t = 1, \ldots, T$; and (c) $\mathrm{E}(c_{i1} \mid \mathbf{x}_i, v_{it2}) = \mathrm{L}(c_{i1} \mid 1, \mathbf{x}_i, v_{it2})$

The second assumption is standard and follows under joint normality of (u_{it1}, v_{it2}) when this vector is independent of $\mathbf{x}_i$. Assumption 17.7c implies that

$$\mathrm{E}(c_{i1} \mid \mathbf{x}_i, v_{it2}) = \mathbf{x}_i \boldsymbol{\pi}_1 + \phi_{t1} v_{it2}$$

where, by equation (17.53) and iterated expectations, $\mathrm{E}(c_{i1} \mid \mathbf{x}_i) = \mathbf{x}_i \boldsymbol{\pi}_1 + \mathrm{E}(v_{it2} \mid \mathbf{x}_{it}) = \mathbf{x}_i \boldsymbol{\pi}_1$. These assumptions place no restrictions on the serial dependence in (u_{it1}, v_{it2}). They do imply that

$$\mathrm{E}(y_{it1} \mid \mathbf{x}_i, v_{it2}) = \mathbf{x}_{it1}\boldsymbol{\beta}_1 + \mathbf{x}_i \boldsymbol{\pi}_1 + \gamma_{t1} v_{it2} \tag{17.55}$$

where $\gamma_{t1} \equiv \rho_{t1} + \phi_{t1}$
Conditioning on $s_{it2} = 1$ gives

$$\mathrm{E}(y_{it1} \mid \mathbf{x}_i, s_{it2} = 1) = \mathbf{x}_{it1}\boldsymbol{\beta}_1 + \mathbf{x}_i \boldsymbol{\pi}_1 + \gamma_{t1} \lambda(\mathbf{x}_i \boldsymbol{\psi}_{t2})$$

Therefore, we can consistently estimate $\boldsymbol{\beta}_1$ by first estimating a probit of s_{it2} on $\mathbf{x}_i$ for each t and then saving the inverse Mills ratio, $\hat{\lambda}_{it2}$, all i and t. Next, run the pooled OLS regression using the selected sample:

$$y_{it1} \text{ on } \mathbf{x}_{it1}, \mathbf{x}_i, \hat{\lambda}_{it2}, d2_t \hat{\lambda}_{it2}, \ldots, dT_t \hat{\lambda}_{it2} \quad \text{for all } s_{it2} = 1 \tag{17.56}$$

where $d2_t$ through dT_t are time dummies. If γ_{t1} in equation (17.55) is constant across t, simply include $\hat{\lambda}_{it2}$ by itself in equation (17.56).

The asymptotic variance of $\hat{\boldsymbol{\beta}}_1$ needs to be corrected for general heteroskedasticity and serial correlation, as well as first-stage estimation of the $\boldsymbol{\psi}_{t2}$. These corrections can be made using the formulas for two-step M-estimation from Chapter 12; Wooldridge (1995a) contains the formulas.

If the selection equation is of the Tobit form, we have somewhat more flexibility. Write the selection equation now as

$$y_{it2} = \max(0, \mathbf{x}_i \boldsymbol{\psi}_{t2} + v_{it2}), \qquad v_{it2} \mid \mathbf{x}_i \sim \text{Normal}(0, \sigma_{t2}^2) \tag{17.57}$$

where y_{it1} is observed if $y_{it2} > 0$. Then, under Assumption 17.6, with the Tobit selection equation in place of equation (17.53), consistent estimation follows from the pooled regression (17.56) where $\hat{\lambda}_{it2}$ is replaced by the Tobit residuals, $\hat{v}_{it2}$ when $y_{it2} > 0$ $(s_{it2} = 1)$. The Tobit residuals are obtained from the T cross section Tobits in equation (17.57); alternatively, especially with small N, we can use a Mundlak-type approach and use pooled Tobit with $\mathbf{x}_i \boldsymbol{\psi}_{t2}$ replaced with $\mathbf{x}_{it} \boldsymbol{\delta}_2 + \bar{\mathbf{x}}_i \boldsymbol{\pi}_2$; see equation (16.52).

It is easy to see that we can add $\alpha_1 y_{it2}$ to the structural equation (17.52), provided we make an explicit exclusion restriction in Assumption 17.7. In particular, we must assume that $\mathrm{E}(c_{i1} \mid \mathbf{x}_i, v_{it2}) = \mathbf{x}_{i1} \boldsymbol{\pi}_1 + \phi_{t1} v_{it2}$, and that $\mathbf{x}_{it1}$ is a strict subset of $\mathbf{x}_{it}$. Then, because y_{it2} is a function of $(\mathbf{x}_i, v_{it2})$, we can write $\mathrm{E}(y_{it1} \mid \mathbf{x}_i, v_{it2}) = \mathbf{x}_{it1} \boldsymbol{\beta}_1 + \alpha_1 y_{it2} + \mathbf{x}_{i1} \boldsymbol{\pi}_1 + \gamma_{t1} v_{it2}$. We obtain the Tobit residuals, $\hat{v}_{it2}$ for each t, and then run the regression y_{it1} on $\mathbf{x}_{it1}, y_{it2}, \mathbf{x}_{i1}$, and $\hat{v}_{it2}$ (possibly interacted with time dummies) for the selected sample. If we do not have an exclusion restriction, this regression suffers from perfect multicollinearity. As an example, we can easily include hours worked in a wage offer function for panel data, provided we have a variable affecting labor supply (such as the number of young children) but not the wage offer.

A pure fixed effects approach is more fruitful when the selection equation is of the Tobit form. The following assumption comes from Wooldridge (1995a):

ASSUMPTION 17.8: (a) The selection equation is equation (17.57). (b) For some unobserved effect g_{i1}, $\mathrm{E}(u_{it1} \mid \mathbf{x}_i, c_{i1}, g_{i1}, \mathbf{v}_{i2}) = \mathrm{E}(u_{it1} \mid g_{i1}, v_{it2}) = g_{i1} + \rho_1 v_{it2}$.

Under part b of this assumption,

$$\mathrm{E}(y_{it1} \mid \mathbf{x}_i, \mathbf{v}_{i2}, c_{i1}, g_{i1}) = \mathbf{x}_{it1} \boldsymbol{\beta}_1 + \rho_1 v_{it2} + f_{i1} \tag{17.58}$$

where $f_{i1} = c_{i1} + g_{i1}$. The same expectation holds when we also condition on $\mathbf{s}_{i2}$ (since $\mathbf{s}_{i2}$ is a function of $\mathbf{x}_i$, $\mathbf{v}_{i2}$). Therefore, estimating equation (17.58) by fixed effects on the unbalanced panel would consistently estimate $\boldsymbol{\beta}_1$ and ρ_1. As usual, we replace v_{it2} with the Tobit residuals $\hat{v}_{it2}$ whenever $y_{it2} > 0$. A t test of H_0: $\rho_1 = 0$ is valid very generally as a test of the null hypothesis of no sample selection. If the $\{u_{it1}\}$ satisfy the standard homoskedasticity and serial uncorrelatedness assumptions, then the usual t statistic is valid. A fully robust test may be warranted. (Again, with an exclusion restriction, we can add y_{it2} as an additional explanatory variable.)

Wooldridge (1995a) discusses an important case where Assumption 17.8b holds: in the Tobit version of equation (17.54) with $(\mathbf{u}_{i1}, \mathbf{a}_{i2})$ independent of $(\mathbf{x}_i, c_{i1}, c_{i2})$ and $\mathrm{E}(u_{it1} \mid \mathbf{a}_{i2}) = \mathrm{E}(u_{it1} \mid a_{it2}) = \rho_1 a_{it2}$. The second-to-last equality holds under the common assumption that $\{(u_{it1}, a_{it2})\colon t = 1, \ldots, T\}$ is serially independent.

The preceding methods assume normality of the errors in the selection equation and, implicitly, the unobserved heterogeneity. Kyriazidou (1997) and Honoré and Kyriazidou (2000b) have proposed methods that do not require distributional assumptions. Dustmann and Rochina-Barrachina (2000) apply Wooldridge's (1995a) and Kyriazidou's (1997) methods to the problem of estimating a wage offer equation with selection into the work force.

17.7.3 Attrition

We now turn specifically to testing and correcting for attrition in a linear, unobserved effects panel data model. General attrition, where units may reenter the sample after leaving, is complicated. We analyze a common special case. At $t = 1$ a random sample is obtained from the relevant population—people, for concreteness. In $t = 2$ and beyond, some people drop out of the sample for reasons that may not be entirely random. We assume that, once a person drops out, he or she is out forever: attrition is an *absorbing* state. Any panel data set with attrition can be set up in this way by ignoring any subsequent observations on units after they initially leave the sample. In Section 17.7.2 we discussed one way to test for attrition bias when we assume that attrition is an absorbing state: include $s_{i,t+1}$ as an additional explanatory variable in a fixed effects analysis.

One method for correcting for attrition bias is closely related to the corrections for incidental truncation covered in the previous subsection. Write the model for a random draw from the population as in equation (17.49), where we assume that $(\mathbf{x}_{it}, y_{it})$ is observed for all i when $t = 1$. Let s_{it} denote the selection indicator for each time period, where $s_{it} = 1$ if $(\mathbf{x}_{it}, y_{it})$ are observed. Because we ignore units once they initially leave the sample, $s_{it} = 1$ implies $s_{ir} = 1$ for $r < t$.

The sequential nature of attrition makes first differencing a natural choice to remove the unobserved effect:

$$\Delta y_{it} = \Delta \mathbf{x}_{it}\boldsymbol{\beta} + \Delta u_{it}, \qquad t = 2, \dots, T$$

Conditional on $s_{i,t-1} = 1$, write a (reduced-form) selection equation for $t \geq 2$ as

$$s_{it} = 1[\mathbf{w}_{it}\boldsymbol{\delta}_t + v_{it} > 0], \qquad v_{it} \mid \{\Delta\mathbf{x}_{it}, \mathbf{w}_{it}, s_{i,t-1} = 1\} \sim \text{Normal}(0, 1) \tag{17.59}$$

where $\mathbf{w}_{it}$ must contain variables observed at time t for all units with $s_{i,t-1} = 1$. Good candidates for $\mathbf{w}_{it}$ include the variables in $\mathbf{x}_{i,t-1}$ and any variables in $\mathbf{x}_{it}$ that are observed at time t when $s_{i,t-1} = 1$ (for example, if $\mathbf{x}_{it}$ contains lags of variables or a variable such as age). In general, the dimension of $\mathbf{w}_{it}$ can grow with t. For example, if equation (17.49) is dynamically complete, then $y_{i,t-2}$ is orthogonal to Δu_{it}, and so it can be an element of $\mathbf{w}_{it}$. Since $y_{i,t-1}$ is correlated with $u_{i,t-1}$, it should not be included in $\mathbf{w}_{it}$.

If the $\mathbf{x}_{it}$ are strictly exogenous *and* selection does not depend on $\Delta\mathbf{x}_{it}$ once $\mathbf{w}_{it}$ has been controlled for, a reasonable assumption (say, under joint normality of Δu_{it} and v_{it}) is

$$\mathrm{E}(\Delta u_{it} \mid \Delta\mathbf{x}_{it}, \mathbf{w}_{it}, v_{it}, s_{i,t-1} = 1) = \mathrm{E}(\Delta u_{it} \mid v_{it}, s_{i,t-1} = 1) = \rho_t v_{it} \tag{17.60}$$

Then

$$\mathrm{E}(\Delta y_{it} \mid \Delta\mathbf{x}_{it}, \mathbf{w}_{it}, s_{it} = 1) = \Delta\mathbf{x}_{it}\boldsymbol{\beta} + \rho_t \lambda(\mathbf{w}_{it}\boldsymbol{\delta}_t), \qquad t = 2, \ldots, T \tag{17.61}$$

Notice how, because $s_{i,t-1} = 1$ when $s_{it} = 1$, we do not have to condition on $s_{i,t-1}$ in equation (17.61). It now follows from equation (17.61) that pooled OLS of Δy_{it} on $\Delta\mathbf{x}_{it}, d2_t\hat{\lambda}_{it}, \ldots, dT_t\hat{\lambda}_{it}$, $t = 2, \ldots, T$, where the $\hat{\lambda}_{it}$ are from the $T - 1$ cross section probits in equation (17.59), is consistent for $\boldsymbol{\beta}_1$ and the ρ_t. A joint test of H_0: $\rho_t = 0$, $t = 2, \ldots, T$, is a fairly simple test for attrition bias, although nothing guarantees serial independence of the errors.

There are two potential problems with this approach. For one, the first equality in equation (17.60) is restrictive because it means that $\mathbf{x}_{it}$ does not affect attrition once the elements in $\mathbf{w}_{it}$ have been controlled for. Second, we have assumed strict exogeneity of $\mathbf{x}_{it}$. Both these restrictions can be relaxed by using an IV procedure.

Let $\mathbf{z}_{it}$ be a vector of variables such that $\mathbf{z}_{it}$ is redundant in the selection equation (possibly because $\mathbf{w}_{it}$ contains $\mathbf{z}_{it}$) and that $\mathbf{z}_{it}$ is exogenous in the sense that equation (17.58) holds with $\mathbf{z}_{it}$ in place of $\Delta\mathbf{x}_{it}$; for example, $\mathbf{z}_{it}$ should contain $\mathbf{x}_{ir}$ for $r < t$. Now, using an argument similar to the cross section case in Section 17.4.2, we can estimate the equation

$$\Delta y_{it} = \Delta\mathbf{x}_{it}\boldsymbol{\beta} + \rho_2\, d2_t\hat{\lambda}_{it} + \cdots + \rho_T\, dT_t\hat{\lambda}_{it} + error_{it} \tag{17.62}$$

by instrumental variables with instruments $(\mathbf{z}_{it}, d2_t\hat{\lambda}_{it}, \ldots, dT_t\hat{\lambda}_{it})$, using the selected sample. For example, the pooled 2SLS estimator on the selected sample is consistent and asymptotically normal, and attrition bias can be tested by a joint test of H_0: $\rho_t = 0$, $t = 2, \ldots, T$. Under H_0, only serial correlation and heteroskedasticity adjustments are possibly needed. If H_0 fails we have the usual generated regressors problem for estimating the asymptotic variance. Other IV procedures, such as GMM, can also be used, but they too must account for the generated regressors problem.

Example 17.9 (Dynamic Model with Attrition): Consider the model

$$y_{it} = \mathbf{g}_{it}\boldsymbol{\gamma} + \eta_1 y_{i,t-1} + c_i + u_{it}, \qquad t = 1, \ldots, T \tag{17.63}$$

where we assume that $(y_{i0}, \mathbf{g}_{i1}, y_{i1})$ are all observed for a random sample from the population. Assume that $\mathrm{E}(u_{it} \mid \mathbf{g}_i, y_{i,t-1}, \ldots, y_{i0}, c_i) = 0$, so that $\mathbf{g}_{it}$ is strictly exogenous. Then the explanatory variables in the probit at time t, $\mathbf{w}_{it}$, can include $\mathbf{g}_{i,t-1}$, $y_{i,t-2}$, and further lags of these. After estimating the selection probit for each t, and differencing, we can estimate

$$\Delta y_{it} = \Delta \mathbf{g}_{it}\boldsymbol{\beta} + \eta_1 \Delta y_{i,t-1} + \rho_3\, d3_t \hat{\lambda}_{it} + \cdots + \rho_T\, dT_t \hat{\lambda}_{it} + error_{it}$$

by pooled 2SLS on the selected sample starting at $t = 3$, using instruments $(\mathbf{g}_{i,t-1}, \mathbf{g}_{i,t-2}, y_{i,t-2}, y_{i,t-3})$. As usual, there are other possibilities for the instruments.

Although the focus in this section has been on pure attrition, where units disappear entirely from the sample, the methods can also be used in the context of incidental truncation without strictly exogenous explanatory variables. For example, suppose we are interested in the population of men who are employed at $t = 0$ and $t = 1$, and we would like to estimate a dynamic wage equation with an unobserved effect. Problems arise if men become unemployed in future periods. Such events can be treated as an attrition problem if all subsequent time periods are dropped once a man first becomes unemployed. This approach loses information but makes the econometrics relatively straightforward, especially because, in the preceding general model, $\mathbf{x}_{it}$ will always be observed at time t and so can be included in the labor force participation probit (assuming that men do not leave the sample entirely). Things become much more complicated if we are interested in the wage offer for all working age men at $t = 1$ because we have to deal with the sample selection problem into employment at $t = 0$ and $t = 1$.

The methods for attrition and selection just described apply only to linear models, and it is difficult to extend them to general nonlinear models. An alternative approach is based on **inverse probability weighting (IPW)**, which can be applied to general M-estimation, at least under certain assumptions.

Moffitt, Fitzgerald, and Gottschalk (1999) (MFG) propose inverse probability weighting to estimate linear panel data models under possibly nonrandom attrition. [MFG propose a different set of weights, analogous to those studied by Horowitz and Manski (1998), to solve missing data problems. The weights we use require estimation of only one attrition model, rather than two as in MFG.] IPW must be used with care to solve the attrition problem. As before, we assume that we have a random sample from the population at $t = 1$. We are interested in some feature, such as the conditional mean, or maybe the entire conditional distribution, of y_{it} given $\mathbf{x}_{it}$. Ideally, at each t we would observe $(y_{it}, \mathbf{x}_{it})$ for any unit that was in the random sample at $t = 1$. Instead, we observe $(y_{it}, \mathbf{x}_{it})$ only if $s_{it} = 1$. We can easily solve the attrition problem if we assume that, conditional on observables in the first time period, say, $\mathbf{z}_{i1}$, $(y_{it}, \mathbf{x}_{it})$ is independent of s_{it}:

$$\mathrm{P}(s_{it} = 1 \mid y_{it}, \mathbf{x}_{it}, \mathbf{z}_{i1}) = \mathrm{P}(s_{it} = 1 \mid \mathbf{z}_{i1}), \qquad t = 2, \ldots, T \tag{17.64}$$

Assumption (17.64) has been called **selection on observables** because we assume that $\mathbf{z}_{i1}$ is a strong enough predictor of selection in each time period so that the distribution of s_{it} given $[\mathbf{z}_{i1}, (y_{it}, \mathbf{x}_{it})]$ does not depend on $(y_{it}, \mathbf{x}_{it})$. In the statistics literature, selection on observables is also called **ignorability of selection** conditional on $\mathbf{z}_{i1}$. [The more standard approach, where selection is given by equation (17.59) and Δu_{it} is correlated with v_{it}, is sometimes called **selection on unobservables**. These categorizations are not strictly correct, as selection in both cases depends on observables and unobservables, but they serve as useful shorthand.]

Inverse probability weighting involves two steps. First, for each t, we estimate a probit or logit of s_{it} on $\mathbf{z}_{i1}$. (A crucial point is that the same cross section units—namely, all units appearing in the first time period—are used in the probit or logit for each time period.) Let $\hat{p}_{it}$ be the fitted probabilities, $t = 2, \ldots, T$, $i = 1, \ldots, N$. In the second step, the objective function for (i, t) is weighted by $1/\hat{p}_{it}$. For general M-estimation, the objective function is

$$\sum_{i=1}^{N} \sum_{t=1}^{T} (s_{it}/\hat{p}_{it}) q_t(\mathbf{w}_{it}, \boldsymbol{\theta}) \tag{17.65}$$

where $\mathbf{w}_{it} \equiv (y_{it}, \mathbf{x}_{it})$ and $q_t(\mathbf{w}_{it}, \boldsymbol{\theta})$ is the objective function in each time period. As usual, the selection indicator s_{it} chooses the observations where we actually observe data. (For $t = 1$, $s_{it} = \hat{p}_{it} = 1$ for all i.) For least squares, $q_t(\mathbf{w}_{it}, \boldsymbol{\theta})$ is simply the squared residual function; for partial MLE, $q_t(\mathbf{w}_{it}, \boldsymbol{\theta})$ is the log-likelihood function.

The argument for why IPW works is rather simple. Let $\boldsymbol{\theta}_o$ denote the value of $\boldsymbol{\theta}$ that solves the population problem $\min_{\boldsymbol{\theta} \in \boldsymbol{\Theta}} \sum_{t=1}^{T} \mathrm{E}[q_t(\mathbf{w}_{it}, \boldsymbol{\theta})]$. Let $\boldsymbol{\delta}_t^o$ denote the true values of the selection response parameters in each time period, so that $\mathrm{P}(s_{it} = 1 \mid \mathbf{z}_{i1}) = p_t(\mathbf{z}_{i1}, \boldsymbol{\delta}_t^o) \equiv p_{it}^o$. Now, under standard regularity conditions, we can replace p_{it}^o with $\hat{p}_{it} \equiv p_t(\mathbf{z}_{i1}, \hat{\boldsymbol{\delta}}_t)$ without affecting the consistency argument. So, apart from regularity conditions, it is sufficient to show that $\boldsymbol{\theta}_o$ minimizes $\sum_{t=1}^{T} \mathrm{E}[(s_{it}/p_{it}^o) q_t(\mathbf{w}_{it}, \boldsymbol{\theta})]$ over $\boldsymbol{\Theta}$. But, from iterated expectations,

$$\begin{aligned} \mathrm{E}[(s_{it}/p_{it}^o) q_t(\mathbf{w}_{it}, \boldsymbol{\theta})] &= \mathrm{E}\{\mathrm{E}[(s_{it}/p_{it}^o) q_t(\mathbf{w}_{it}, \boldsymbol{\theta}) \mid \mathbf{w}_{it}, \mathbf{z}_{i1}]\} \\ &= \mathrm{E}\{[\mathrm{E}(s_{it} \mid \mathbf{w}_{it}, \mathbf{z}_{i1})/p_{it}^o] q_t(\mathbf{w}_{it}, \boldsymbol{\theta})\} = \mathrm{E}[q_t(\mathbf{w}_{it}, \boldsymbol{\theta})] \end{aligned}$$

because $\mathrm{E}(s_{it} \mid \mathbf{w}_{it}, \mathbf{z}_{i1}) = \mathrm{P}(s_{it} = 1 \mid \mathbf{z}_{i1})$ by assumption (17.64). Therefore, the probability limit of the weighted objective function is identical to that of the unweighted function *if* we had no attrition problem. Using this simple analogy argument, Wooldridge (2000d) shows that the inverse probability weighting produces a consistent,

$\sqrt{N}$-asymptotically normal estimator. The methods for adjusting the asymptotic variance matrix of two step M-estimators—described in Subsection 12.5.2—can be applied to the IPW M-estimator from (17.65). For reasons we will see, a sequential method of estimating attrition probabilities can be more attractive.

MFG propose an IPW scheme where the conditioning variables in the attrition probits change across time. In particular, at time t an attrition probit is estimated restricting attention to those units still in the sample at time $t-1$. (Out of this group, some are lost to attrition at time t, and some are not.) If we assume that attrition is an absorbing state, we can include in the conditioning variables, $\mathbf{z}_{it}$, all values of y and $\mathbf{x}$ dated at time $t-1$ and earlier (as well as other variables observed for all units in the sample at $t-1$). This approach is appealing because the ignorability assumption is much more plausible if we can condition on both recent responses and covariates. [That is, $\mathrm{P}(s_{it}=1 \mid \mathbf{w}_{it}, \mathbf{w}_{i,t-1}, \ldots, \mathbf{w}_{i1}, s_{i,t-1}=1) = \mathrm{P}(s_{it}=1 \mid \mathbf{w}_{i,t-1}, \ldots, \mathbf{w}_{i1}, s_{i,t-1}=1)$ is more likely than assumption (17.64).] Unfortunately, obtaining the fitted probabilities in this way and using them in an IPW procedure does not generally produce consistent estimators. The problem is that the selection models at each time period are not representative of the population that was originally sampled at $t=1$. Letting $p_{it}^{\mathrm{o}} = \mathrm{P}(s_{it}=1 \mid \mathbf{w}_{i,t-1}, \ldots, \mathbf{w}_{i1}, s_{i,t-1}=1)$, we can no longer use the iterated expectations argument to conclude that $\mathrm{E}[(s_{it}/p_{it}^{\mathrm{o}})q_t(\mathbf{w}_{it}, \boldsymbol{\theta})] = \mathrm{E}[q_t(\mathbf{w}_{it}, \boldsymbol{\theta})]$. Only if $\mathrm{E}[q_t(\mathbf{w}_{it}, \boldsymbol{\theta})] = \mathrm{E}[q_t(\mathbf{w}_{it}, \boldsymbol{\theta}) \mid s_{i,t-1}=1]$ for all $\boldsymbol{\theta}$ does the argument work, but this assumption essentially requires that $\mathbf{w}_{it}$ be independent of $s_{i,t-1}$.

It is possible to allow the covariates in the selection probabilities to increase in richness over time, but the MFG procedure must be modified. For the case where attrition is an absorbing state, Wooldridge (2000d), building on work for regression models by Robins, Rotnitzky, and Zhao (1995) (RRZ), shows that the following probabilities can be used in the IPW procedure:

$$p_{it}(\boldsymbol{\delta}_t^{\mathrm{o}}) \equiv \pi_{i2}(\gamma_2^{\mathrm{o}})\pi_{i3}(\gamma_3^{\mathrm{o}}) \cdots \pi_{it}(\gamma_t^{\mathrm{o}}), \qquad t = 2, \ldots, T \tag{17.66}$$

where

$$\pi_{it}(\gamma_t^{\mathrm{o}}) \equiv \mathrm{P}(s_{it}=1 \mid \mathbf{z}_{it}, s_{i,t-1}=1) \tag{17.67}$$

In other words, as in the MFG procedure, we estimate probit models at each time t, restricted to units that are in the sample at $t-1$. The covariates in the probit are essentially everything we can observe for units in the sample at time $t-1$ that might affect attrition. For $t = 2, \ldots, T$, let $\hat{\pi}_{it}$ denote the fitted selection probabilities. Then we construct the probability weights as the product $\hat{p}_{it} \equiv \hat{\pi}_{i2}\hat{\pi}_{i3} \cdots \hat{\pi}_{it}$ and use the objective function (17.65). Naturally, this method only works under certain assumptions. The key ignorability condition can be stated as

$$P(s_{it} = 1 \mid \mathbf{v}_{i1}, \ldots, \mathbf{v}_{iT}, s_{i,t-1} = 1) = P(s_{it} = 1 \mid \mathbf{z}_{it}, s_{i,t-1} = 1) \tag{17.68}$$

where $\mathbf{v}_{it} \equiv (\mathbf{w}_{it}, \mathbf{z}_{it})$. Now, we must include future values of $\mathbf{w}_{it}$ *and* $\mathbf{z}_{it}$ in the conditioning set on the left-hand side. Assumption (17.68) is fairly strong, but it does allow for attrition to be strongly related to past outcomes on y and $\mathbf{x}$ (which can be included in $\mathbf{z}_{it}$).

A convenient feature of the sequential method described above is that ignoring the first-stage estimation of the probabilities actually leads to *conservative* inference concerning $\boldsymbol{\theta}_0$: the (correct) asymptotic variance that adjusts for the first-stage estimation is actually smaller than the one that does not. See Wooldridge (2000d) for the general case and RRZ (1995) for the nonlinear regression case. See Wooldridge (2000d) for more on the pros and cons of using inverse probability weighting to reduce attrition bias.

17.8 Stratified Sampling

Nonrandom samples also come in the form of **stratified samples**, where different subsets of the population are sampled with different frequencies. For example, certain surveys are designed to learn primarily about a particular subset of the population, in which case that group is usually overrepresented in the sample. Stratification can be based on exogenous variables or endogenous variables (which are known once a model and assumptions have been specified), or some combination of these. As in the case of sample selection problems, it is important to know which is the case.

As mentioned in Section 17.3, choice-based sampling occurs when the stratification is based entirely on a discrete response variable. Various methods have been proposed for estimating discrete response models from choice-based samples under different assumptions; most of these are variations of maximum likelihood. Manski and McFadden (1981) and Cosslett (1993) contain general treatments, with the latter being a very useful survey. For a class of discrete response models, Cosslett (1981) proposed an efficient estimator, and Imbens (1992) obtained a computationally simple method of moments estimator that also achieves the efficiency bound. Imbens and Lancaster (1996) allow for general response variables in a maximum likelihood setting. Here, we focus on a simple, albeit often inefficient, method for estimating models in the context of two kinds of stratified sampling.

17.8.1 Standard Stratified Sampling and Variable Probability Sampling

The two most common kinds of stratification used in obtaining data sets in the social sciences are **standard stratified sampling (SS sampling)** and **variable probability sam-**

pling (VP sampling). In SS sampling, the population is first partitioned into J groups, $\mathcal{W}_1, \mathcal{W}_2, \ldots, \mathcal{W}_J$, which we assume are nonoverlapping and exhaustive. We let $\mathbf{w}$ denote the random variable representing the population of interest.

STANDARD STRATIFIED SAMPLING: For $j = 1, \ldots, J$, draw a random sample of size N_j from stratum j. For each j, denote this random sample by $\{\mathbf{w}_{ij}: i = 1, 2, \ldots, N_j\}$.

The strata sample sizes N_j are nonrandom. Therefore, the total sample size, $N = N_1 + \cdots + N_J$, is also nonrandom. A randomly drawn observation from stratum $j, \mathbf{w}_{ij}$, has distribution $\mathrm{D}(\mathbf{w} \mid \mathbf{w} \in \mathcal{W}_j)$. Therefore, while observations within a stratum are identically distributed, observations across strata are not. A scheme that is similar in nature to SS sampling is called **multinomial sampling**, where a stratum is first picked at random and then an observation is randomly drawn from the stratum. This *does* result in i.i.d. observations, but it does not correspond to how stratified samples are obtained in practice. It also leads to the same estimators as under SS sampling, so we do not discuss it further; see Cosslett (1993) or Wooldridge (1999b) for further discussion.

Variable probability samples are obtained using a different scheme. First, an observation is drawn at random from the population. If the observation falls into stratum j, it is kept with probability p_j. Thus, random draws from the population are discarded with varying frequencies depending on which stratum they fall into. This kind of sampling is appropriate when information on the variable or variables that determine the strata is relatively easy to obtain compared with the rest of the information. Survey data sets, including initial interviews to collect panel or longitudinal data, are good examples. Suppose we want to oversample individuals from, say, lower income classes. We can first ask an individual her or his income. If the response is in income class j, this person is kept in the sample with probability p_j, and then the remaining information, such as education, work history, family background, and so on can be collected; otherwise, the person is dropped without further interviewing.

A key feature of VP sampling is that observations within a stratum are discarded randomly. As discussed by Wooldridge (1999b), VP sampling is equivalent to the following:

VARIABLE PROBABILITY SAMPLING: Repeat the following steps N times:

1. Draw an observation $\mathbf{w}_i$ at random from the population.

2. If $\mathbf{w}_i$ is in stratum j, toss a (biased) coin with probability p_j of turning up heads. Let $h_{ij} = 1$ if the coin turns up heads and zero otherwise.

3. Keep observation i if $h_{ij} = 1$; otherwise, omit it from the sample.

The number of observations falling into stratum j is denoted N_j, and the number of data points we actually have for estimation is $N_0 = N_1 + N_2 + \cdots + N_J$. Notice that if N—the number of times the population is sampled—is fixed, then N_0 is a random variable: we do not know what each N_j will be prior to sampling. Also, we will not use information on the number of discarded observations in each stratum, so that N is not required to be known.

The assumption that the probability of the coin turning up heads in step 2 depends only on the stratum ensures that sampling is random within each stratum. This roughly reflects how samples are obtained for certain large cross-sectional and panel data sets used in economics, including the panel study of income dynamics and the national longitudinal survey.

To see that a VP sample can be analyzed as a random sample, we construct a population that incorporates the stratification. The VP sampling scheme is equivalent to first tossing all J coins before actually observing which stratum $\mathbf{w}_i$ falls into; this gives $(h_{i1}, \ldots, h_{iJ})$. Next, $\mathbf{w}_i$ is observed to fall into one of the strata. Finally, the outcome is kept or not depending on the coin flip for that stratum. The result is that the vector $(\mathbf{w}_i, \mathbf{h}_i)$, where $\mathbf{h}_i$ is the J-vector of binary indicators h_{ij}, is a random sample from a new population with sample space $\mathscr{W} \times \mathscr{H}$, where $\mathscr{W}$ is the original sample space and $\mathscr{H}$ denotes the sample space associated with outcomes from flipping J coins. Under this alternative way of viewing the sampling scheme, $\mathbf{h}_i$ is independent of $\mathbf{w}_i$. Treating $(\mathbf{w}_i, \mathbf{h}_i)$ as a random draw from the new population is not at odds with the fact that our estimators are based on a nonrandom sample from the original population: we simply use the vector $\mathbf{h}_i$ to determine which observations are kept in the estimation procedure.

17.8.2 Weighted Estimators to Account for Stratification

With variable probability sampling, it is easy to construct weighted objective functions that produce consistent and asymptotically normal estimators of the population parameters. It is useful to define a set of binary variables that indicate whether a random draw $\mathbf{w}_i$ is kept in the sample and, if so, which stratum it falls into:

$$r_{ij} = h_{ij} s_{ij} \tag{17.69}$$

By definition, $r_{ij} = 1$ for at most one j. If $h_{ij} = 1$ then $r_{ij} = s_{ij}$. If $r_{ij} = 0$ for all $j = 1, 2, \ldots, J$, then the random draw $\mathbf{w}_i$ does not appear in the sample (and we do not know which stratum it belonged to).

With these definitions, we can define the **weighted M-estimator**, $\hat{\theta}_w$, as the solution to

$$\min_{\theta \in \Theta} \sum_{i=1}^{N} \sum_{j=1}^{J} p_j^{-1} r_{ij} q(\mathbf{w}_i, \boldsymbol{\theta}) \tag{17.70}$$

where $q(\mathbf{w}, \boldsymbol{\theta})$ is the objective function that is chosen to identify the population parameters $\boldsymbol{\theta}_o$. Note how the outer summation is over all *potential* observations, that is, the observations that *would* appear in a random sample. The indicators r_{ij} simply pick out the observations that actually appear in the available sample, and these indicators also attach each observed data point to its stratum. The objective function (17.70) weights each observed data point in the sample by the inverse of the sampling probability. For implementation it is useful to write the objective function as

$$\min_{\boldsymbol{\theta} \in \boldsymbol{\Theta}} \sum_{i=1}^{N_0} p_{j_i}^{-1} q(\mathbf{w}_i, \boldsymbol{\theta}) \tag{17.71}$$

where, without loss of generality, the data points actually observed are ordered $i = 1, \ldots, N_0$. Since j_i is the stratum for observation i, $p_{j_i}^{-1}$ is the weight attached to observation i in the estimation. In practice, the $p_{j_i}^{-1}$ are the **sampling weights** reported with other variables in stratified samples.

The objective function $q(\mathbf{w}, \boldsymbol{\theta})$ contains all of the M-estimator examples we have covered so far in the book, including least squares (linear and nonlinear), conditional maximum likelihood, and partial maximum likelihood. In panel data applications, the probability weights are from sampling in an initial year. Weights for later years are intended to reflect both stratification (if any) and possible attrition, as discussed in Section 17.7.3 and in Wooldridge (2000d).

Wooldridge (1999b) shows that, under the same assumptions as Theorem 12.2 and the assumption that each sampling probability is strictly positive, the weighted M-estimator consistently estimates $\boldsymbol{\theta}_o$, which is assumed to uniquely minimize $\mathrm{E}[q(\mathbf{w}, \boldsymbol{\theta})]$. To see that the weighted objective function identifies $\boldsymbol{\theta}_o$, we use the fact that h_j is independent of $\mathbf{w}$ [and therefore of $(\mathbf{w}, s_j)$ for each j], and so

$$\begin{aligned} \mathrm{E}\left[\sum_{j=1}^{J} p_j^{-1} h_j s_j q(\mathbf{w}, \boldsymbol{\theta})\right] &= \sum_{j=1}^{J} p_j^{-1} \mathrm{E}(h_j) \mathrm{E}[s_j q(\mathbf{w}, \boldsymbol{\theta})] \\ &= \sum_{j=1}^{J} p_j^{-1} p_j \mathrm{E}[s_j q(\mathbf{w}, \boldsymbol{\theta})] = \mathrm{E}\left[\left(\sum_{j=1}^{J} s_j\right) q(\mathbf{w}, \boldsymbol{\theta})\right] = \mathrm{E}[q(\mathbf{w}, \boldsymbol{\theta})] \end{aligned} \tag{17.72}$$

where the final equality follows because the s_j sum to unity. Therefore, the expected value of the weighted objective function [over the distribution of $(\mathbf{w}, \mathbf{h})$] equals the expected value of $q(\mathbf{w}, \boldsymbol{\theta})$ (over the distribution of $\mathbf{w}$). Consistency of the weighted M-estimator follows under the regularity conditions in Theorem 12.2.

Asymptotic normality also follows under the same regularity conditions as in Chapter 12. Wooldridge (1999b) shows that a valid estimator of the asymptotic variance of $\hat{\boldsymbol{\theta}}_w$ is

$$\left[\sum_{i=1}^{N_0} p_{j_i}^{-1} \nabla_\theta^2 q_i(\hat{\boldsymbol{\theta}}_w)\right]^{-1} \left[\sum_{i=1}^{N_0} p_{j_i}^{-2} \nabla_\theta q_i(\hat{\boldsymbol{\theta}}_w)' \nabla_\theta q_i(\hat{\boldsymbol{\theta}}_w)\right] \left[\sum_{i=1}^{N_0} p_{j_i}^{-1} \nabla_\theta^2 q_i(\hat{\boldsymbol{\theta}}_w)\right]^{-1} \tag{17.73}$$

which looks like the standard formula for a robust variance matrix estimator except for the presence of the sampling probabilities p_{j_i}.

When $\mathbf{w}$ partitions as $(\mathbf{x}, \mathbf{y})$, an alternative estimator replaces the Hessian $\nabla_\theta^2 q_i(\hat{\boldsymbol{\theta}}_w)$ in expression (17.73) with $\mathbf{A}(\mathbf{x}_i, \hat{\boldsymbol{\theta}}_w)$, where $\mathbf{A}(\mathbf{x}_i, \boldsymbol{\theta}_o) \equiv \mathrm{E}[\nabla_\theta^2 q(\mathbf{w}_i, \boldsymbol{\theta}_o) \,|\, \mathbf{x}_i]$, as in Chapter 12. Asymptotic standard errors and Wald statistics can be obtained using either estimate of the asymptotic variance.

Example 17.10 (Linear Model under Stratified Sampling): In estimating the linear model

$$y = \mathbf{x}\boldsymbol{\beta}_o + u, \qquad \mathrm{E}(\mathbf{x}'u) = \mathbf{0} \tag{17.74}$$

by weighted least squares, the asymptotic variance matrix estimator is

$$\left(\sum_{i=1}^{N_0} p_{j_i}^{-1} \mathbf{x}_i'\mathbf{x}_i\right)^{-1} \left(\sum_{i=1}^{N_0} p_{j_i}^{-2} \hat{u}_i^2 \mathbf{x}_i'\mathbf{x}_i\right) \left(\sum_{i=1}^{N_0} p_{j_i}^{-1} \mathbf{x}_i'\mathbf{x}_i\right)^{-1} \tag{17.75}$$

where $\hat{u}_i = y_i - \mathbf{x}_i\hat{\boldsymbol{\beta}}_w$ is the residual after WLS estimation. Interestingly, this is simply the White (1980b) heteroskedasticity-consistent covariance matrix estimator applied to the stratified sample, where all variables for observation i are weighted by $p_{j_i}^{-1/2}$ before performing the regression. This estimator has been suggested by, among others, Hausman and Wise (1981). Hausman and Wise use maximum likelihood to obtain more efficient estimators in the context of the normal linear regression model, that is, $u \,|\, \mathbf{x} \sim \mathrm{Normal}(\mathbf{x}\boldsymbol{\beta}_o, \sigma_o^2)$. Because of stratification, MLE is not generally robust to failure of the homoskedastic normality assumption.

It is important to remember that the form of expression (17.75) in this example is not due to potential heteroskedasticity in the underlying population model. Even if $\mathrm{E}(u^2 \,|\, \mathbf{x}) = \sigma_o^2$, the estimator (17.75) is generally needed because of the stratified sampling. This estimator also works in the presence of heteroskedasticity of arbitrary and unknown form in the population, and it is routinely computed by many regression packages.

Example 17.11 (Conditional MLE under Stratified Sampling): When $f(\mathbf{y} \,|\, \mathbf{x}; \boldsymbol{\theta})$ is a correctly specified model for the density of $\mathbf{y}_i$ given $\mathbf{x}_i$ in the population, the inverse-probability-weighted MLE is obtained with $q_i(\boldsymbol{\theta}) \equiv -\log[f(\mathbf{y}_i \,|\, \mathbf{x}_i; \boldsymbol{\theta})]$. This estimator is consistent and asymptotically normal, with asymptotic variance estimator given by expression (17.73) [or, preferably, the form that uses $\mathbf{A}(\mathbf{x}_i, \hat{\boldsymbol{\theta}}_w)$].

A weighting scheme is also available in the standard stratified sampling case, but the weights are different from the VP sampling case. To derive them, let $Q_j = \mathrm{P}(\mathbf{w} \in \mathscr{W}_j)$ denote the population frequency for stratum j; we assume that the Q_j are *known*. By the law of iterated expectations,

$$\mathrm{E}[q(\mathbf{w}, \boldsymbol{\theta})] = Q_1 \mathrm{E}[q(\mathbf{w}, \boldsymbol{\theta}) \mid \mathbf{w} \in \mathscr{W}_1] + \cdots + Q_J \mathrm{E}[q(\mathbf{w}, \boldsymbol{\theta}) \mid \mathbf{w} \in \mathscr{W}_J] \tag{17.76}$$

for any $\boldsymbol{\theta}$. For each j, $\mathrm{E}[q(\mathbf{w}, \boldsymbol{\theta}) \mid \mathbf{w} \in \mathscr{W}_j]$ can be consistently estimated using a random sample obtained from stratum j. This scheme leads to the sample objective function

$$Q_1 \left[N_1^{-1} \sum_{i=1}^{N_1} q(\mathbf{w}_{i1}, \boldsymbol{\theta}) \right] + \cdots + Q_J \left[N_J^{-1} \sum_{i=1}^{N_J} q(\mathbf{w}_{iJ}, \boldsymbol{\theta}) \right]$$

where $\mathbf{w}_{ij}$ denotes a random draw i from stratum j and N_j is the nonrandom sample size for stratum j. We can apply the uniform law of large numbers to each term, so that the sum converges uniformly to equation (17.76) under the regularity conditions in Chapter 12. By multiplying and dividing each term by the total number of observations $N = N_1 + \cdots + N_J$, we can write the sample objective function more simply as

$$N^{-1} \sum_{i=1}^{N} (Q_{j_i}/H_{j_i}) q(\mathbf{w}_i, \boldsymbol{\theta}) \tag{17.77}$$

where j_i denotes the stratum for observation i and $H_j \equiv N_j/N$ denotes the fraction of observations in stratum j. Because we have the stratum indicator j_i, we can drop the j subscript on $\mathbf{w}_i$. When we omit the division by N, equation (17.77) has the same form as equation (17.71), but the weights are (Q_{j_i}/H_{j_i}) rather than $p_{j_i}^{-1}$ (and the arguments for why each weighting works are very different). Also, in general, the formula for the asymptotic variance is different in the SS sampling case. In addition to the minor notational change of replacing N_0 with N, the middle matrix in equation (17.73) becomes

$$\sum_{j=1}^{J} (Q_j^2/H_j^2) \left[\sum_{i=1}^{N_j} (\nabla_\theta \hat{q}_{ij} - \overline{\nabla_\theta q_j})' (\nabla_\theta \hat{q}_{ij} - \overline{\nabla_\theta q_j}) \right]$$

where $\nabla_\theta \hat{q}_{ij} \equiv \nabla_\theta q(\mathbf{w}_{ij}, \hat{\boldsymbol{\theta}}_w)$ and $\overline{\nabla_\theta q_j} \equiv N_j^{-1} \sum_{i=1}^{N_j} \nabla_\theta \hat{q}_{ij}$ (the within-stratum sample average). This approach requires us to explicitly partition observations into their respective strata. See Wooldridge (2001) for a detailed derivation. [If in the VP sampling case the population frequencies Q_j are known, it is better to use as weights $Q_j/(N_j/N_0)$ rather than p_j^{-1}, which makes the analysis look just like the SS sampling case. See Wooldridge (1999b) for details.]

If in Example 17.11 we have standard stratified sampling rather than VP sampling, the weighted MLE is typically called the **weighted exogenous sample MLE (WESMLE)**; this estimator was suggested by Manski and Lerman (1977) in the context of choice-based sampling in discrete response models. [Actually, Manski and Lerman (1977) use multinomial sampling where H_j is the probability of picking stratum j. But Cosslett (1981) showed that a more efficient estimator is obtained by using N_j/N, as one always does in the case of SS sampling; see Wooldridge (1999b) for an extension of Cosslett's result to the M-estimator case.]

Provided that the sampling weights Q_{j_i}/H_{j_i} or $p_{j_i}^{-1}$ are given (along with the stratum), analysis with the weighted M-estimator under SS or VP sampling is fairly straightforward, but it is not likely to be efficient. In the conditional maximum likelihood case it is certainly possible to do better. See Imbens and Lancaster (1996) for a careful treatment.

17.8.3 Stratification Based on Exogenous Variables

When $\mathbf{w}$ partitions as $(\mathbf{x}, \mathbf{y})$, where $\mathbf{x}$ is exogenous in a sense to be made precise, and stratification is based entirely on $\mathbf{x}$, the standard unweighted estimator on the stratified sample is consistent and asymptotically normal. The sense in which $\mathbf{x}$ must be exogenous is that $\boldsymbol{\theta}_{\text{o}}$ solves

$$\min_{\boldsymbol{\theta} \in \boldsymbol{\Theta}} \mathrm{E}[q(\mathbf{w}, \boldsymbol{\theta}) \mid \mathbf{x}] \tag{17.78}$$

for each possible outcome $\mathbf{x}$. This assumption holds in a variety of contexts with conditioning variables and correctly specified models. For example, as we discussed in Chapter 12, this holds for nonlinear regression when the conditional mean is correctly specified and $\boldsymbol{\theta}_{\text{o}}$ is the vector of conditional mean parameters; in Chapter 13 we showed that this holds for conditional maximum likelihood when the density of $\mathbf{y}$ given $\mathbf{x}$ is correct. It also holds in other cases, including quasi-maximum likelihood, which we cover in Chapter 19. One interesting observation is that, in the linear regression model (17.74), the exogeneity of $\mathbf{x}$ must be strengthened to $\mathrm{E}(u \mid \mathbf{x}) = 0$.

In the case of VP sampling, selection on the basis of $\mathbf{x}$ means that each selection indicator s_j is a deterministic function of $\mathbf{x}$. The unweighted M-estimator on the stratified sample, $\hat{\boldsymbol{\theta}}_u$, minimizes

$$\sum_{i=1}^{N} \sum_{j=1}^{J} h_{ij} s_{ij} q(\mathbf{w}_i, \boldsymbol{\theta}) = \sum_{i=1}^{N_0} q(\mathbf{w}_i, \boldsymbol{\theta})$$

Consistency follows from standard M-estimation results if we can show that $\boldsymbol{\theta}_{\mathrm{o}}$ uniquely solves

$$\min_{\boldsymbol{\theta} \in \Theta} \sum_{j=1}^{J} \mathrm{E}[h_j s_j q(\mathbf{w}, \boldsymbol{\theta})] \tag{17.79}$$

Since s_j is a function of $\mathbf{x}$ and h_j is independent of $\mathbf{w}$ (and therefore $\mathbf{x}$), $\mathrm{E}[h_j s_j q(\mathbf{w}, \boldsymbol{\theta}) \mid \mathbf{x}] = \mathrm{E}(h_j \mid \mathbf{x}) s_j \mathrm{E}[q(\mathbf{w}, \boldsymbol{\theta}) \mid \mathbf{x}] = p_j s_j \mathrm{E}[q(\mathbf{w}, \boldsymbol{\theta}) \mid \mathbf{x}]$ for each j. By assumption, $\mathrm{E}[q(\mathbf{w}, \boldsymbol{\theta}) \mid \mathbf{x}]$ is minimized at $\boldsymbol{\theta}_{\mathrm{o}}$ for all $\mathbf{x}$, and therefore so is $p_j s_j \mathrm{E}[q(\mathbf{w}, \boldsymbol{\theta}) \mid \mathbf{x}]$ (but probably not uniquely). By iterated expectations it follows that $\boldsymbol{\theta}_{\mathrm{o}}$ is a solution to equation (17.79). Unlike in the case of the weighted estimator, it no longer suffices to assume that $\boldsymbol{\theta}_{\mathrm{o}}$ uniquely minimizes $\mathrm{E}[q(\mathbf{w}, \boldsymbol{\theta})]$; we must directly assume $\boldsymbol{\theta}_{\mathrm{o}}$ is the unique solution to problem (17.79). This assumption could fail if, for example, $p_j = 0$ for some j—so that we do not observe part of the population at all. (Unlike in the case of the weighted estimator, $p_j = 0$ for at least some j is allowed for the unweighted estimator, subject to identification holding.) For example, in the context of linear wage regression, we could not identify the return to education if we only sample those with exactly a high school education.

Wooldridge (1999b) shows that the usual asymptotic variance estimators (see Section 12.5) are valid when stratification is based on $\mathbf{x}$ and we ignore the stratification problem. For example, the usual conditional maximum likelihood analysis holds. In the case of regression, we can use the usual heteroskedasticity-robust variance matrix estimator. Or, if we assume homoskedasticity in the population, the nonrobust form [see equation (12.58)] is valid with the usual estimator of the error variance.

When a generalized conditional information matrix equality holds, and stratification is based on $\mathbf{x}$, Wooldridge (1999b) shows that the unweighted estimator is more efficient than the weighted estimator. The key assumption is

$$\mathrm{E}[\nabla_{\theta} q(\mathbf{w}, \boldsymbol{\theta}_{\mathrm{o}})' \nabla_{\theta} q(\mathbf{w}, \boldsymbol{\theta}_{\mathrm{o}}) \mid \mathbf{x}] = \sigma_{\mathrm{o}}^2 \mathrm{E}[\nabla_{\theta}^2 q(\mathbf{w}, \boldsymbol{\theta}_{\mathrm{o}}) \mid \mathbf{x}] \tag{17.80}$$

for some $\sigma_{\mathrm{o}}^2 > 0$. When assumption (17.80) holds and $\boldsymbol{\theta}_{\mathrm{o}}$ solves equation (17.79), the asymptotic variance of the unweighted M-estimator is smaller than that for the weighted M-estimator. This generalization includes conditional maximum likelihood (with $\sigma_{\mathrm{o}}^2 = 1$) and nonlinear regression under homoskedasticity.

Very similar conclusions hold for standard stratified sampling. One useful fact is that, when stratification is based on $\mathbf{x}$, the estimator (17.73) is valid with $p_j = H_j/Q_j$ (and $N_0 = N$); therefore, we need not compute within-strata variation in the estimated score. The unweighted estimator is consistent when stratification is based on $\mathbf{x}$ and the usual asymptotic variance matrix estimators are valid. The unweighted estimator is also more efficient when assumption (17.80) holds. See Wooldridge (2001) for statements of assumptions and proofs of theorems.

Problems

17.1. a. Suppose you are hired to explain fire damage to buildings in terms of building and neighborhood characteristics. If you use cross section data on reported fires, is there a sample selection problem due to the fact that most buildings do not catch fire during the year?

b. If you want to estimate the relationship between contributions to a 401(k) plan and the match rate of the plan—the rate at which the employer matches employee contributions—is there a sample selection problem if you only use a sample of workers already enrolled in a 401(k) plan?

17.2. In Example 17.4, suppose that *IQ* is an indicator of *abil*, and *KWW* is another indicator (see Section 5.3.2). Find assumptions under which IV on the selected sample is valid.

17.3. Let $f(\cdot \mid \mathbf{x}_i; \boldsymbol{\theta})$ denote the density of y_i given $\mathbf{x}_i$ for a random draw from the population. Find the conditional density of y_i given $(\mathbf{x}_i, s_i = 1)$ when the selection rule is $s_i = 1[a_1(\mathbf{x}_i) < y_i < a_2(\mathbf{x}_i)]$, where $a_1(\mathbf{x})$ and $a_2(\mathbf{x})$ are known functions of $\mathbf{x}$. In the Hausman and Wise (1977) example, $a_2(\mathbf{x})$ was a function of family size because the poverty income level depends on family size.

17.4. Suppose in Section 17.4.1 we replace Assumption 17.1d with

$$\mathrm{E}(u_1 \mid v_2) = \gamma_1 v_2 + \gamma_2 (v_2^2 - 1)$$

(We subtract unity from v_2^2 to ensure that the second term has zero expectation.)

a. Using the fact that $\mathrm{Var}(v_2 \mid v_2 > -a) = 1 - \lambda(a)[\lambda(a) + a]$, show that

$$\mathrm{E}(y_1 \mid \mathbf{x}, y_2 = 1) = \mathbf{x}_1 \boldsymbol{\beta}_1 + \gamma_1 \lambda(\mathbf{x}\boldsymbol{\delta}_2) - \gamma_2 \lambda(\mathbf{x}\boldsymbol{\delta}_2)\mathbf{x}\boldsymbol{\delta}_2$$

[Hint: Take $a = \mathbf{x}\boldsymbol{\delta}_2$ and use the fact that $\mathrm{E}(v_2^2 \mid v_2 > -a) = \mathrm{Var}(v_2 \mid v_2 > -a) + [\mathrm{E}(v_2 \mid v_2 > -a)]^2$.]

b. Explain how to correct for sample selection in this case.

c. How would you test for the presence of sample selection bias?

17.5. Consider the following alternative to Procedure 17.2. First, run the OLS regression of y_2 on $\mathbf{z}$ and obtain the fitted values, $\hat{y}_2$. Next, get the inverse Mills ratio,

$\hat{\lambda}_3$, from the probit of y_3 on $\mathbf{z}$. Finally, run the OLS regression y_1 on $\mathbf{z}_1, \hat{y}_2, \hat{\lambda}_3$ using the selected sample.

a. Find a set of sufficient conditions that imply consistency of the proposed procedure. (Do not worry about regularity conditions.)

b. Show that the assumptions from part a are more restrictive than those in Procedure 17.2, and give some examples that are covered by Procedure 17.2 but not by the alternative procedure.

17.6. Apply Procedure 17.4 to the data in MROZ.RAW. Use a constant, *exper*, and $exper^2$ as elements of $\mathbf{z}_1$; take $y_2 = educ$. The other elements of $\mathbf{z}$ should include *age*, *kidslt6*, *kidsge6*, *nwifeinc*, *motheduc*, *fatheduc*, and *huseduc*.

17.7. Consider the model

$$y_1 = \mathbf{z}\boldsymbol{\delta}_1 + v_1$$

$$y_2 = \mathbf{z}\boldsymbol{\delta}_2 + v_2$$

$$y_3 = \max(0, \alpha_{31} y_1 + \alpha_{32} y_2 + \mathbf{z}_3\boldsymbol{\delta}_3 + u_3)$$

where $(\mathbf{z}, y_2, y_3)$ are always observed and y_1 is observed when $y_3 > 0$. The first two equations are reduced-form equations, and the third equation is of primary interest. For example, take $y_1 = \log(wage^o)$, $y_2 = educ$, and $y_3 = hours$, and then education and $\log(wage^o)$ are possibly endogenous in the labor supply function. Assume that (v_1, v_2, u_3) are jointly zero-mean normal and independent of $\mathbf{z}$.

a. Find a simple way to consistently estimate the parameters in the third equation allowing for arbitrary correlations among (v_1, v_2, u_3). Be sure to state any identification assumptions needed.

b. Now suppose that y_2 is observed only when $y_3 > 0$; for example, $y_1 = \log(wage^o)$, $y_2 = \log(benefits^o)$, $y_3 = hours$. Now derive a multistep procedure for estimating the third equation under the same assumptions as in part a.

c. How can we estimate the average partial effects?

17.8. Consider the following conditional moment restrictions problem with a selected sample. In the population, $\mathrm{E}[\mathbf{r}(\mathbf{w}, \boldsymbol{\theta}_o) \mid \mathbf{x}] = \mathbf{0}$. Let s be the selection indicator, and assume that

$$\mathrm{E}[\mathbf{r}(\mathbf{w}, \boldsymbol{\theta}_o) \mid \mathbf{x}, s] = \mathbf{0}$$

Sufficient is that $s = f(\mathbf{x})$ for a nonrandom function f.

a. Let $\mathbf{Z}_i$ be a $G \times L$ matrix of functions of $\mathbf{x}_i$. Show that $\boldsymbol{\theta}_o$ satisfies

$\mathrm{E}[s_i \mathbf{Z}_i' \mathbf{r}(\mathbf{w}_i, \boldsymbol{\theta}_o)] = \mathbf{0}$

b. Write down the objective function for the system nonlinear 2SLS estimator based on the selected sample. Argue that, under the appropriate rank condition, the estimator is consistent and $\sqrt{N}$-asymptotically normal.

c. Write down the objective function for a minimum chi-square estimator using the selected sample. Use the estimates from part b to estimate the weighting matrix. Argue that the estimator is consistent and $\sqrt{N}$-asymptotically normal.

17.9. Consider the problem of standard stratified sampling. Argue that when $\boldsymbol{\theta}_o$ solves equation (17.78) for each $\mathbf{x}$, $\boldsymbol{\theta}_o$ is identified in the population, stratification is based on $\mathbf{x}$, and $\overline{H}_j > 0$ for $j = 1, \ldots, J$, the unweighted estimator is consistent. {Hint: Write the objective function for the unweighted estimator as

$$\sum_{j=1}^{J} H_j \left[N_j^{-1} \sum_{i=1}^{N_j} q(\mathbf{w}_{ij}, \boldsymbol{\theta}) \right] \tag{17.81}$$

and assume that $H_j \to \overline{H}_j > 0$ as $N \to \infty$. If the strata are $\mathscr{X}_1, \mathscr{X}_2, \ldots, \mathscr{X}_J$, argue that equation (17.81) converges uniformly to

$$\overline{H}_1 \mathrm{E}[q(\mathbf{w}, \boldsymbol{\theta}) \mid \mathbf{x} \in \mathscr{X}_1] + \cdots + \overline{H}_J \mathrm{E}[q(\mathbf{w}, \boldsymbol{\theta}) \mid \mathbf{x} \in \mathscr{X}_J] \tag{17.82}$$

Why does $\boldsymbol{\theta}_o$ necessarily minimize expression (17.82)? Identification follows when you show that $\mathrm{E}[q(\mathbf{w}, \boldsymbol{\theta}) \mid \mathbf{x} \in \mathscr{X}_j]$ is uniquely minimized at $\boldsymbol{\theta}_o$ for at least one j.}

17.10. Consider model (17.25), where selection is ignorable in the sense that $\mathrm{E}(u_1 \mid \mathbf{z}, u_3) = 0$. However, data are missing on y_2 when $y_3 = 0$, and $\mathrm{E}(y_2 \mid \mathbf{z}, y_3) \neq \mathrm{E}(y_2 \mid \mathbf{z})$.

a. Find $\mathrm{E}(y_1 \mid \mathbf{z}, y_3)$.

b. If, in addition to Assumption 17.2, (v_2, v_3) is independent of $\mathbf{z}$ and $\mathrm{E}(v_2 \mid v_3) = \gamma_2 v_3$, find $\mathrm{E}(y_1 \mid \mathbf{z}, y_3 = 1)$.

c. Suggest a two-step method for consistently estimating $\boldsymbol{\delta}_1$ and α_1.

d. Does this method generally work if $\mathrm{E}(u_1 \mid \mathbf{z}, y_3) \neq 0$?

e. Would you bother with the method from part c if $\mathrm{E}(u_1 \mid \mathbf{z}, y_2, y_3) = 0$? Explain.

17.11. In Section 16.7 we discussed two-part models for a corner solution outcome, say, y. These models have sometimes been studied in the context of incidental truncation.

a. Suppose you have a parametric model for the distribution of y conditional on $\mathbf{x}$ and $y > 0$. (Cragg's model and the lognormal model from Section 16.7 are examples.) If you estimate the parameters of this model by conditional MLE, using only the observations for which $y_i > 0$, do the parameter estimates suffer from sample selection bias? Explain.

b. If instead you specify only $\mathrm{E}(y \mid \mathbf{x}, y > 0) = \exp(\mathbf{x}\boldsymbol{\beta})$ and estimate $\boldsymbol{\beta}$ by nonlinear least squares using observations for which $y_i > 0$, do the estimates suffer from sample selection bias?

c. In addition to the specification from part b, suppose that $\mathrm{P}(y = 0 \mid \mathbf{x}) = 1 - \Phi(\mathbf{x}\boldsymbol{\gamma})$. How would you estimate $\boldsymbol{\gamma}$?

d. Given the assumptions in parts b and c, how would you estimate $\mathrm{E}(y \mid \mathbf{x})$?

e. Given your answers to the first four parts, do you think viewing estimation of two-part models as an incidental truncation problem is appropriate?

17.12. Consider Theorem 17.1. Suppose that we relax assumption (17.6) to $\mathrm{E}(u \mid \mathbf{z}, s) = \mathrm{E}(u \mid s) = (1 - s)\alpha_0 + s\alpha_1$. The first equality is the assumption; the second is unrestrictive, as it simply allows the mean of u to differ in the selected and unselected subpopulations.

a. Show that 2SLS estimation using the selected subsample consistently estimates the slope parameters, $\beta_2, \ldots, \beta_K$. What is the plim of the intercept estimator? [Hint: Replace u with $(1 - s)\alpha_0 + s\alpha_1 + e$, where $\mathrm{E}(e \mid \mathbf{z}, s) = 0$.]

b. Show that $\mathrm{E}(u \mid \mathbf{z}, s) = \mathrm{E}(u \mid s)$ if (u, s) is independent of $\mathbf{z}$. Does independence of s and $\mathbf{z}$ seem reasonable?

17.13. Suppose that y given $\mathbf{x}$ follows a standard censored Tobit, where y is a corner solution response. However, there is at least one element of $\mathbf{x}$ that we can observe only when $y > 0$. (An example is seen when y is quantity demanded of a good or service, and one element of $\mathbf{x}$ is price, derived as total expenditure on the good divided by y whenever $y > 0$.)

a. Explain why we cannot use standard censored Tobit maximum likelihood estimation to estimate $\boldsymbol{\beta}$ and σ^2. What method can we use instead?

b. How is it that we can still estimate $\mathrm{E}(y \mid \mathbf{x})$, even though we do not observe some elements of $\mathbf{x}$ when $y = 0$?

18 Estimating Average Treatment Effects

18.1 Introduction

In this chapter we explicitly study the problem of estimating an **average treatment effect (ATE)**. An average treatment effect is a special case of an average partial effect: an ATE is an average partial effect for a binary explanatory variable.

Estimating ATEs has become important in the program evaluation literature, such as in the evaluation of job training programs. Originally, the binary indicators represented medical treatment or program participation, but the methods are applicable when the explanatory variable of interest is any binary variable.

We begin by introducing a counterfactual framework pioneered by Rubin (1974) and since adopted by many in both statistics and econometrics, including Rosenbaum and Rubin (1983), Heckman (1992, 1997), Imbens and Angrist (1994), Angrist, Imbens, and Rubin (1996), Manski (1996), Heckman, Ichimura, and Todd (1997), and Angrist (1998). The counterfactual framework allows us to define various treatment effects that may be of interest. Once we define the different treatment effects, we can study ways to consistently estimate these effects. We will not provide a comprehensive treatment of this rapidly growing literature, but we will show that, under certain assumptions, estimators that we are already familiar with consistently estimate average treatment effects. We will also study some extensions that consistently estimate ATEs under weaker assumptions.

Broadly, most estimators of ATEs fit into one of two categories. The first set exploits assumptions concerning *ignorability* of the treatment conditional on a set of covariates. As we will see in Section 18.3, this approach is analogous to the proxy variable solution to the omitted variables problem that we discussed in Chapter 4, and in some cases reduces exactly to an OLS regression with many controls. A second set of estimators relies on the availability of one or more instrumental variables that are redundant in the response equations but help determine participation. Different IV estimators are available depending on functional form assumptions concerning how unobserved heterogeneity affects the responses. We study IV estimators in Section 18.4.

In Section 18.5 we briefly discuss some further topics, including special considerations for binary and corner solution responses, using panel data to estimate treatment effects, and nonbinary treatments.

18.2 A Counterfactual Setting and the Self-Selection Problem

The modern literature on treatment effects begins with a counterfactual, where each individual (or other agent) has an outcome with and without treatment (where "treatment" is interpreted very broadly). This section draws heavily on Heckman (1992, 1997), Imbens and Angrist (1994), and Angrist, Imbens, and Rubin (1996) (hereafter AIR). Let y_1 denote the outcome with treatment and y_0 the outcome without treatment. Because an individual cannot be in both states, we cannot observe both y_0 and y_1; in effect, the problem we face is one of missing data.

It is important to see that we have made no assumptions about the distributions of y_0 and y_1. In many cases these may be roughly continuously distributed (such as salary), but often y_0 and y_1 are binary outcomes (such as a welfare participation indicator), or even corner solution outcomes (such as married women's labor supply). However, some of the assumptions we make will be less plausible for discontinuous random variables, something we discuss after introducing the assumptions.

The following discussion assumes that we have an independent, identically distributed sample from the population. This assumption rules out cases where the treatment of one unit affects another's outcome (possibly through general equilibrium effects, as in Heckman, Lochner, and Taber, 1998). The assumption that treatment of unit i affects only the outcome of unit i is called the **stable unit treatment value assumption (SUTVA)** in the treatment literature (see, for example, AIR). We are making a stronger assumption because random sampling implies SUTVA.

Let the variable w be a binary treatment indicator, where $w = 1$ denotes treatment and $w = 0$ otherwise. The triple (y_0, y_1, w) represents a random vector from the underlying population of interest. For a random draw i from the population, we write (y_{i0}, y_{i1}, w_i). However, as we have throughout, we state assumptions in terms of the population.

To measure the effect of treatment, we are interested in the difference in the outcomes with and without treatment, $y_1 - y_0$. Because this is a random variable (that is, it is individual specific), we must be clear about what feature of its distribution we want to estimate. Several possibilities have been suggested in the literature. In Rosenbaum and Rubin (1983), the quantity of interest is the **average treatment effect (ATE)**,

$$ATE \equiv \mathrm{E}(y_1 - y_0) \tag{18.1}$$

ATE is the expected effect of treatment on a randomly drawn person from the population. Some have criticized this measure as not being especially relevant for policy purposes: because it averages across the entire population, it includes in the average units who would never be eligible for treatment. Heckman (1997) gives the example of a job training program, where we would not want to include millionaires in computing the average effect of a job training program. This criticism is somewhat misleading, as we can—and would—exclude people from the population who would never be eligible. For example, in evaluating a job training program, we might restrict attention to people whose pretraining income is below a certain threshold; wealthy people would be excluded precisely because we have no interest in how job training affects the wealthy. In evaluating the benefits of a program such as Head Start, we could restrict the population to those who are actually eligible for the program or are likely to be eligible in the future. In evaluating the effectiveness of enterprise zones, we could restrict our analysis to block groups whose unemployment rates are above a certain threshold or whose per capita incomes are below a certain level.

A second quantity of interest, and one that has received much recent attention, is the **average treatment effect on the treated**, which we denote ATE_1:

$$ATE_1 \equiv \mathrm{E}(y_1 - y_0 \mid w = 1) \tag{18.2}$$

That is, ATE_1 is the mean effect for those who actually participated in the program. As we will see, in some special cases equations (18.1) and (18.2) are equivalent, but generally they differ.

Imbens and Angrist (1994) define another treatment effect, which they call a **local average treatment effect (LATE)**. LATE has the advantage of being estimable using instrumental variables under very weak conditions. It has two potential drawbacks: (1) it measures the effect of treatment on a generally unidentifiable subpopulation; and (2) the definition of LATE depends on the particular instrumental variable that we have available. We will discuss LATE in the simplest setting in Section 18.4.2.

We can expand the definition of both treatment effects by conditioning on covariates. If x is an observed covariate, the ATE conditional on x is simply $\mathrm{E}(y_1 - y_0 \mid x)$; similarly, equation (18.2) becomes $\mathrm{E}(y_1 - y_0 \mid x, w = 1)$. By choosing x appropriately, we can define ATEs for various subsets of the population. For example, x can be pretraining income or a binary variable indicating poverty status, race, or gender. For the most part, we will focus on ATE and ATE_1 without conditioning on covariates.

As noted previously, the difficulty in estimating equation (18.1) or (18.2) is that we observe only y_0 or y_1, not both, for each person. More precisely, along with w, the observed outcome is

$$y = (1 - w)y_0 + wy_1 = y_0 + w(y_1 - y_0) \tag{18.3}$$

Therefore, the question is, How can we estimate equation (18.1) or (18.2) with a random sample on y and w (and usually some observed covariates)?

First, suppose that the treatment indicator w is statistically independent of (y_0, y_1), as would occur when treatment is *randomized* across agents. One implication of independence between treatment status and the potential outcomes is that ATE and ATE_1 are identical: $\mathrm{E}(y_1 - y_0 \mid w = 1) = \mathrm{E}(y_1 - y_0)$. Furthermore, estimation of

ATE is simple. Using equation (18.3), we have

$$E(y \mid w = 1) = E(y_1 \mid w = 1) = E(y_1)$$

where the last equality follows because y_1 and w are independent. Similarly,

$$E(y \mid w = 0) = E(y_0 \mid w = 0) = E(y_0)$$

It follows that

$$ATE = ATE_1 = E(y \mid w = 1) - E(y \mid w = 0) \tag{18.4}$$

The right-hand side is easily estimated by a difference in sample means: the sample average of y for the treated units minus the sample average of y for the untreated units. Thus, randomized treatment guarantees that the difference-in-means estimator from basic statistics is unbiased, consistent, and asymptotically normal. In fact, these properties are preserved under the weaker assumption of **mean independence**: $E(y_0 \mid w) = E(y_0)$ and $E(y_1 \mid w) = E(y_1)$.

Randomization of treatment is often infeasible in program evaluation (although randomization of *eligibility* often is feasible; more on this topic later). In most cases, individuals at least partly determine whether they receive treatment, and their decisions may be related to the benefits of treatment, $y_1 - y_0$. In other words, there is **self-selection** into treatment.

It turns out that ATE_1 can be consistently estimated as a difference in means under the weaker assumption that w is independent of y_0, without placing any restriction on the relationship between w and y_1. To see this point, note that we can always write

$$\begin{aligned} E(y \mid w = 1) - E(y \mid w = 0) &= E(y_0 \mid w = 1) - E(y_0 \mid w = 0) + E(y_1 - y_0 \mid w = 1) \\ &= [E(y_0 \mid w = 1) - E(y_0 \mid w = 0)] + ATE_1 \end{aligned} \tag{18.5}$$

If y_0 is mean independent of w, that is,

$$E(y_0 \mid w) = E(y_0) \tag{18.6}$$

then the first term in equation (18.5) disappears, and so the difference in means estimator is an unbiased estimator of ATE_1. Unfortunately, condition (18.6) is a strong assumption. For example, suppose that people are randomly made eligible for a voluntary job training program. Condition (18.6) effectively implies that the participation decision is unrelated to what people would earn in the absence of the program.

A useful expression relating ATE_1 and ATE is obtained by writing $y_0 = \mu_0 + v_0$ and $y_1 = \mu_1 + v_1$, where $\mu_g = E(y_g)$, $g = 0, 1$. Then

$$y_1 - y_0 = (\mu_1 - \mu_0) + (v_1 - v_0) = ATE + (v_1 - v_0)$$

Taking the expectation of this equation conditional on $w = 1$ gives

$$ATE_1 = ATE + \mathrm{E}(v_1 - v_0 \mid w = 1)$$

We can think of $v_1 - v_0$ as the person-specific gain from participation, and so ATE_1 differs from ATE by the expected person-specific gain for those who participated. If $y_1 - y_0$ is not mean independent of w, ATE_1 and ATE generally differ.

Fortunately, we can estimate ATE and ATE_1 under assumptions less restrictive than independence of (y_0, y_1) and w. In most cases, we can collect data on individual characteristics and relevant pretreatment outcomes—sometimes a substantial amount of data. If, in an appropriate sense, treatment depends on the observables and not on the unobservables determining (y_0, y_1), then we can estimate average treatment effects quite generally, as we show in the next section.

18.3 Methods Assuming Ignorability of Treatment

We adopt the framework of the previous section, and, in addition, we let $\mathbf{x}$ denote a vector of observed covariates. Therefore, the population is described by $(y_0, y_1, w, \mathbf{x})$, and we observe y, w, and $\mathbf{x}$, where y is given by equation (18.3). When w and (y_0, y_1) are allowed to be correlated, we need an assumption in order to identify treatment effects. Rosenbaum and Rubin (1983) introduced the following assumption, which they called **ignorability of treatment** (given observed covariates $\mathbf{x}$):

ASSUMPTION ATE.1: Conditional on $\mathbf{x}$, w and (y_0, y_1) are independent.

For many purposes, it suffices to assume ignorability in a **conditional mean independence** sense:

ASSUMPTION ATE.1′: (a) $\mathrm{E}(y_0 \mid \mathbf{x}, w) = \mathrm{E}(y_0 \mid \mathbf{x})$; and (b) $\mathrm{E}(y_1 \mid \mathbf{x}, w) = \mathrm{E}(y_1 \mid \mathbf{x})$.

Naturally, Assumption ATE.1 implies Assumption ATE.1′. In practice, Assumption ATE.1′ might not afford much generality, although it does allow $\mathrm{Var}(y_0 \mid \mathbf{x}, w)$ and $\mathrm{Var}(y_1 \mid \mathbf{x}, w)$ to depend on w. The idea underlying Assumption ATE.1′ is this: if we can observe enough information (contained in $\mathbf{x}$) that determines treatment, then (y_0, y_1) might be mean independent of w, conditional on $\mathbf{x}$. Loosely, even though (y_0, y_1) and w might be correlated, they are uncorrelated once we partial out $\mathbf{x}$.

Assumption ATE.1 certainly holds if w is a deterministic function of $\mathbf{x}$, which has prompted some authors in econometrics to call assumptions like ATE.1 **selection on observables**; see, for example, Barnow, Cain, and Goldberger (1980, 1981), Heckman and Robb (1985), and Moffitt (1996). (We discussed a similar assumption in Section

17.7.3 in the context of attrition in panel data.) The name is fine as a label, but we must realize that Assumption ATE.1 does allow w to depend on unobservables, albeit in a restricted fashion. If $w = g(\mathbf{x}, a)$, where a is an unobservable random variable independent of $(\mathbf{x}, y_0, y_1)$, then Assumption ATE.1 holds. But a cannot be arbitrarily correlated with y_0 and y_1.

An important fact is that, under Assumption ATE.1′, the average treatment effect conditional on $\mathbf{x}$ and the average treatment effect of the treated, conditional on $\mathbf{x}$, are identical:

$$ATE_1(\mathbf{x}) \equiv \mathrm{E}(y_1 - y_0 \mid \mathbf{x}, w = 1) = \mathrm{E}(y_1 - y_0 \mid \mathbf{x}) = ATE(\mathbf{x})$$

because $\mathrm{E}(y_g \mid \mathbf{x}, w) = \mathrm{E}(y_g \mid \mathbf{x})$, $g = 0, 1$. However, the unconditional versions of the treatment effects are not generally equal. For clarity, define $r(\mathbf{x}) = \mathrm{E}(y_1 - y_0 \mid \mathbf{x}) = ATE(\mathbf{x})$. Then ATE is the expected value of $r(\mathbf{x})$ across the entire population, whereas ATE_1 is the expected value of $r(\mathbf{x})$ in the treated subpopulation. Mathematically,

$$ATE = \mathrm{E}[r(\mathbf{x})] \qquad \text{and} \qquad ATE_1 = \mathrm{E}[r(\mathbf{x}) \mid w = 1]$$

If we can estimate $r(\cdot)$, then ATE can be estimated by averaging across the entire random sample from the population, whereas ATE_1 would be estimated by averaging across the part of the sample with $w_i = 1$. We will discuss specific estimation strategies in the next subsection.

An interesting feature of Assumptions ATE.1 and ATE.1′—and one that is perhaps foreign to economists—is that they are stated without imposing any kind of model on joint or conditional distributions. It turns out that no more structure is needed in order to identify either of the treatment effects. We first show how the ignorability assumption relates to standard regression analysis.

18.3.1 Regression Methods

We can use equation (18.3), along with Assumption ATE.1′, to obtain estimators of $ATE(\mathbf{x})$, which can then be used to estimate ATE and ATE_1. First,

$$\begin{aligned}\mathrm{E}(y \mid \mathbf{x}, w) &= \mathrm{E}(y_0 \mid \mathbf{x}, w) + w[\mathrm{E}(y_1 \mid \mathbf{x}, w) - \mathrm{E}(y_0 \mid \mathbf{x}, w)] \\ &= \mathrm{E}(y_0 \mid \mathbf{x}) + w[\mathrm{E}(y_1 \mid \mathbf{x}) - \mathrm{E}(y_0 \mid \mathbf{x})]\end{aligned}$$

where the first equality follows from equation (18.3) and the second follows from Assumption ATE.1′. Therefore, under Assumption ATE.1′,

$$\mathrm{E}(y \mid \mathbf{x}, w = 1) - \mathrm{E}(y \mid \mathbf{x}, w = 0) = \mathrm{E}(y_1 \mid \mathbf{x}) - \mathrm{E}(y_0 \mid \mathbf{x}) = ATE(\mathbf{x}) \tag{18.7}$$

Because we have a random sample on $(y, w, \mathbf{x})$ from the relevant population, $r_1(\mathbf{x}) \equiv \mathrm{E}(y \mid \mathbf{x}, w = 1)$ and $r_0(\mathbf{x}) \equiv \mathrm{E}(y \mid \mathbf{x}, w = 0)$ are **nonparametrically identified**. That is, these are conditional expectations that depend entirely on observables, and so they can be consistently estimated quite generally. (See Härdle and Linton, 1994, for assumptions and methods.) For the purposes of identification, we can just assume $r_1(\mathbf{x})$ and $r_0(\mathbf{x})$ are known, and the fact that they are known means that $ATE(\mathbf{x})$ is identified. If $\hat{r}_1(\mathbf{x})$ and $\hat{r}_0(\mathbf{x})$ are consistent estimators (in an appropriate sense), using the random sample of size N, a consistent estimator of ATE under fairly weak assumptions is

$$A\hat{T}E = N^{-1} \sum_{i=1}^{N} [\hat{r}_1(\mathbf{x}_i) - \hat{r}_0(\mathbf{x}_i)]$$

while a consistent estimator of ATE_1 is

$$A\hat{T}E_1 = \left(\sum_{i=1}^{N} w_i\right)^{-1} \left\{\sum_{i=1}^{N} w_i [\hat{r}_1(\mathbf{x}_i) - \hat{r}_0(\mathbf{x}_i)]\right\}$$

The formula for $A\hat{T}E_1$ simply averages $[\hat{r}_1(\mathbf{x}_i) - \hat{r}_0(\mathbf{x}_i)]$ over the subsample with $w_i = 1$.

There are several implementation issues that arise in computing and using $A\hat{T}E$ and $A\hat{T}E_1$. The most obvious of these is obtaining $\hat{r}_1(\cdot)$ and $\hat{r}_0(\cdot)$. To be as flexible as possible, we could use nonparametric estimators, such as a **kernel estimator** (see Härdle and Linton, 1994). Obtaining reliable standard errors when we use nonparametric estimates can be difficult. An alternative is to use flexible parametric models, such as low-order polynomials that include interaction terms. [Presumably, we would also account for the nature of y in estimating $\mathrm{E}(y \mid \mathbf{x}, w = 1)$ and $\mathrm{E}(y \mid \mathbf{x}, w = 0)$. For example, if y is binary, we would use a flexible logit or probit; if y is a corner solution, we might use a flexible Tobit or a flexible exponential regression function.]

With plenty of data, a third possibility is to list all possible values that $\mathbf{x}$ can take, say, $\mathbf{c}_1, \mathbf{c}_2, \ldots, \mathbf{c}_M$, and to estimate $\mathrm{E}(y \mid \mathbf{x} = \mathbf{c}_m, w = 1)$ by averaging the y_i over all i with $\mathbf{x}_i = \mathbf{c}_m$ and $w_i = 1$; $\mathrm{E}(y \mid \mathbf{x} = \mathbf{c}_m, w = 0)$ is estimated similarly. For each m and $w = 0$ or 1, this method is just estimation of a mean using a sample average. Typically, M is large because $\mathbf{x}$ takes on many values, and many of the cells may have only a small number of observations.

Regardless of how $\hat{r}_1(\cdot)$ and $\hat{r}_0(\cdot)$ are obtained, to use the estimated treatment effects we need to obtain asymptotically valid standard errors. Generally, this task can be very difficult, especially if nonparametric methods are used in estimation.

Nevertheless, we will show how a linear regression model involving level effects and interactions can be used to obtain good estimates of the treatment effects as well as reliable standard errors.

Before we turn to standard regression models, we need to discuss a problem that can arise in the evaluation of programs, especially when flexible estimation of $\mathrm{E}(y \mid \mathbf{x}, w = 1)$ and $\mathrm{E}(y \mid \mathbf{x}, w = 0)$ is desirable. To illustrate the problem, suppose there is only one binary covariate, x, and Assumption ATE.1′ holds; for concreteness, x could be an indicator for whether pretraining earnings are below a certain threshold. Suppose that everyone in the relevant population with $x = 1$ participates in the program. Then, while we can estimate $\mathrm{E}(y \mid x = 1, w = 1)$ with a random sample from the population, we cannot estimate $\mathrm{E}(y \mid x = 1, w = 0)$ because we have no data on the subpopulation with $x = 1$ and $w = 0$. Intuitively, we only observe the counterfactual y_1 when $x = 1$; we never observe y_0 for any members of the population with $x = 1$. Therefore, $ATE(x)$ is not identified at $x = 1$.

If some people with $x = 0$ participate while others do not, we can estimate $\mathrm{E}(y \mid x = 0, w = 1) - \mathrm{E}(y \mid x = 0, w = 0)$ using a simple difference in averages over the group with $x = 0$, and so $ATE(x)$ is identified at $x = 0$. But if we cannot estimate $ATE(1)$, we cannot estimate the unconditional ATE because $ATE = \mathrm{P}(x = 0) \cdot ATE(0) + \mathrm{P}(x = 1) \cdot ATE(1)$. In effect, we can only estimate the ATE over the subpopulation with $x = 0$, which means that we must redefine the population of interest. This limitation is unfortunate: presumably we would be very interested in the program's effects on the group that always participates.

A similar conclusion holds if the group with $x = 0$ never participates in the program. Then $ATE(0)$ is not estimable because $\mathrm{E}(y \mid x = 0, w = 1)$ is not estimable. If some people with $x = 1$ participated while others did not, $ATE(1)$ would be identified, and then we would view the population of interest as the subgroup with $x = 1$. There is one important difference between this situation and the one where the $x = 1$ group always receives treatment: it seems perfectly natural to exclude from the population people who have no chance of treatment based on observed covariates. This observation is related to the issue we discussed in Section 18.2 concerning the relevant population for defining ATE. If, for example, people with very high preprogram earnings ($x = 0$) have no chance of participating in a job training program, then we would not want to average together $ATE(0)$ and $ATE(1)$; $ATE(1)$ by itself is much more interesting.

Although the previous example is extreme, its consequences can arise in more plausible settings. Suppose that $\mathbf{x}$ is a vector of binary indicators for pretraining income intervals. For most of the intervals, the probability of participating is strictly between zero and one. If the participation probability is zero at the highest income level, we simply exclude the high-income group from the relevant population. Unfortunately, if participation is certain at low income levels, we must exclude low-income groups as well.

As a practical matter, we often determine whether the probability of participation is one or zero by looking at the random sample. If we list the possible values of the explanatory variables, $\mathbf{c}_1, \ldots, \mathbf{c}_M$, as described earlier, the problem arises when there is a value, say $\mathbf{c}_m$, where all units with $\mathbf{x}_i = \mathbf{c}_m$ participate in the program. Because we cannot estimate $\mathrm{E}(y \mid \mathbf{x} = \mathbf{c}_m, w = 0)$, the subpopulation with $\mathbf{x} = \mathbf{c}_m$ must be excluded from the analysis.

We now turn to standard parametric regression methods for estimating ATE, and then briefly discuss estimating ATE_1. It is useful to decompose the counterfactual outcomes into their means and a stochastic part with zero mean, as we did at the end of Section 18.2:

$$y_0 = \mu_0 + v_0, \qquad \mathrm{E}(v_0) = 0 \tag{18.8}$$

$$y_1 = \mu_1 + v_1, \qquad \mathrm{E}(v_1) = 0 \tag{18.9}$$

Plugging these into equation (18.3) gives

$$y = \mu_0 + (\mu_1 - \mu_0)w + v_0 + w(v_1 - v_0) \tag{18.10}$$

This is a simple example of a **switching regression model**, where the outcome equations depend on the regime (treatment status in this case).

If we assume that $v_1 - v_0$ has zero mean conditional on $\mathbf{x}$, we obtain a standard regression model under Assumption ATE.1$'$.

PROPOSITION 18.1: Under Assumption ATE.1$'$, assume, in addition, that

$$\mathrm{E}(v_1 \mid \mathbf{x}) = \mathrm{E}(v_0 \mid \mathbf{x}) \tag{18.11}$$

Then $ATE_1 = ATE$, and

$$\mathrm{E}(y \mid w, \mathbf{x}) = \mu_0 + \alpha w + g_0(\mathbf{x}) \tag{18.12}$$

where $\alpha \equiv ATE$ and $g_0(\mathbf{x}) = \mathrm{E}(v_0 \mid \mathbf{x})$. If, in addition, $\mathrm{E}(v_0 \mid \mathbf{x}) = \eta_0 + \mathbf{h}_0(\mathbf{x})\boldsymbol{\beta}_0$ for some vector function $\mathbf{h}_0(\mathbf{x})$, then

$$\mathrm{E}(y \mid w, \mathbf{x}) = \gamma_0 + \alpha w + \mathbf{h}_0(\mathbf{x})\boldsymbol{\beta}_0 \tag{18.13}$$

where $\gamma_0 = \mu_0 + \eta_0$.

Proof: Under Assumption ATE.1$'$, $\mathrm{E}(y_1 \mid w, \mathbf{x}) = \mu_1 + \mathrm{E}(v_1 \mid \mathbf{x})$ and $\mathrm{E}(y_0 \mid w, \mathbf{x}) = \mu_0 + \mathrm{E}(v_0 \mid \mathbf{x})$. Under assumption (18.11), $\mathrm{E}(y_1 \mid w, \mathbf{x}) - \mathrm{E}(y_0 \mid w, \mathbf{x}) = \mu_1 - \mu_0$.

Therefore, by iterated expectations, $\mathrm{E}(y_1 \mid w) - \mathrm{E}(y_0 \mid w) = \mu_1 - \mu_0$, which implies that $ATE_1 = ATE$. The proof of equation (18.12) follows by taking the expectation of equation (18.10) given w, $\mathbf{x}$ and using Assumption ATE.1′ and assumption (18.11).

This proposition shows that when the predicted person-specific gain given $\mathbf{x}$ is zero—that is, when $\mathrm{E}(v_1 - v_0 \mid \mathbf{x}) = 0$—$\mathrm{E}(y \mid w, \mathbf{x})$ is additive in w and a function of $\mathbf{x}$, and the coefficient on w is the average treatment effect. It follows that standard regression methods can be used to estimate ATE. While nonlinear regression methods can be used if $\mathrm{E}(v_0 \mid \mathbf{x})$ is assumed to be nonlinear in parameters, typically we would use an assumption such as equation (18.13). Then, regressing y on an intercept, w, and $\mathbf{h}_0(\mathbf{x})$ consistently estimates the ATE. By putting enough controls in $\mathbf{x}$, we have arranged it so that w and unobservables affecting (y_0, y_1) are appropriately unrelated. In effect, $\mathbf{x}$ proxies for the unobservables. Using flexible functional forms for the elements of $\mathbf{h}_0(\mathbf{x})$ should provide a good approximation to $\mathrm{E}(v_0 \mid \mathbf{x})$.

The function $\mathbf{h}_0(\mathbf{x})\boldsymbol{\beta}_0$ in equation (18.13) is an example of a **control function**: when added to the regression of y on 1, w, it controls for possible self-selection bias. Of course, this statement is only true under the assumptions in Proposition 18.1.

Given Assumption ATE.1′, the additively separable form of equation (18.12) hinges crucially on assumption (18.11). Though assumption (18.11) might be reasonable in some cases, it need not generally hold. [A sufficient, but not necessary, condition for assumption (18.11) is $v_1 = v_0$ or $y_1 = \alpha + y_0$, which means the effect of treatment is the same for everyone in the population.] If we relax assumption (18.11), then we no longer have equality of ATE and ATE_1. Nevertheless, a regression formulation can be used to estimate ATE:

PROPOSITION 18.2: Under Assumption ATE.1′,

$$\mathrm{E}(y \mid w, \mathbf{x}) = \mu_0 + \alpha w + g_0(\mathbf{x}) + w[g_1(\mathbf{x}) - g_0(\mathbf{x})] \tag{18.14}$$

where $\alpha = ATE$, $g_0(\mathbf{x}) \equiv \mathrm{E}(v_0 \mid \mathbf{x})$, and $g_1(\mathbf{x}) \equiv \mathrm{E}(v_1 \mid \mathbf{x})$.

The proof of Proposition 18.2 is immediate by taking the expectation of equation (18.10) given $(w, \mathbf{x})$. Equation (18.14) is interesting because it shows that, under Assumption ATE.1′ only, $\mathrm{E}(y \mid w, \mathbf{x})$ is additive in w, a function of $\mathbf{x}$, and an interaction between w and another function of $\mathbf{x}$. The coefficient on w is the average treatment effect (but not generally ATE_1). To operationalize equation (18.14) in a parametric framework, we would replace $g_0(\cdot)$ and $g_1(\cdot)$ with parametric functions of $\mathbf{x}$; typically, these would be linear in parameters, say $\eta_0 + \mathbf{h}_0(\mathbf{x})\boldsymbol{\beta}_0$ and $\eta_1 + \mathbf{h}_1(\mathbf{x})\boldsymbol{\beta}_1$. For notational simplicity, assume that these are both linear in $\mathbf{x}$. Then we can write

$$\mathrm{E}(y \mid w, \mathbf{x}) = \gamma + \alpha w + \mathbf{x}\boldsymbol{\beta}_0 + w \cdot (\mathbf{x} - \boldsymbol{\psi})\boldsymbol{\delta} \tag{18.15}$$

where $\boldsymbol{\beta}_0$ and $\boldsymbol{\delta}$ are vectors of unknown parameters and $\boldsymbol{\psi} \equiv \mathrm{E}(\mathbf{x})$. Subtracting the mean from $\mathbf{x}$ ensures that ATE is the coefficient on w. In practice, either we would subtract off the known population mean from each element of $\mathbf{x}$, or, more likely, we would demean each element of $\mathbf{x}$ using the sample average. Therefore, under equation (18.15), we would estimate α as the coefficient on w in the regression

$$y_i \text{ on } 1, w_i, \mathbf{x}_i, w_i(\mathbf{x}_i - \bar{\mathbf{x}}), \qquad i = 1, 2, \ldots, N \tag{18.16}$$

where $\bar{\mathbf{x}}$ is the vector of sample averages. (Subtracting the sample averages rather than population averages introduces a generated regressor problem. However, as argued in Problem 6.10, the adjustments to the standard errors typically have minor effects.) The control functions in this case involve not just the $\mathbf{x}_i$, but also interactions of the covariates with the treatment variable. If desired, we can be selective about which elements of $(\mathbf{x}_i - \bar{\mathbf{x}})$ we interact with w_i.

Adding functions of $\mathbf{x}$, such as squares or logarithms, as both level terms and interactions, is simple, provided we demean any functions before constructing the interactions.

Because regression (18.16) consistently estimates $\boldsymbol{\delta}$, we can also study how the ATE given $\mathbf{x}$, that is, $ATE(\mathbf{x}) = \mathrm{E}(y_1 - y_0 \mid \mathbf{x})$, changes with elements of $\mathbf{x}$. In particular, for any $\mathbf{x}$ in the valid range,

$$A\hat{T}E(\mathbf{x}) = \hat{\alpha} + (\mathbf{x} - \bar{\mathbf{x}})\hat{\boldsymbol{\delta}}$$

We can then average this equation over interesting values of $\mathbf{x}$ to obtain the ATE for a subset of the population. For example, if $\mathbf{x}$ contains pretraining earnings or indicators for earnings groups, we can estimate how the ATE changes for various levels of pretraining earnings.

If the functions of $\mathbf{x}$ appearing in the regression are very flexible, problems with estimating $ATE(\mathbf{x})$ at certain values of $\mathbf{x}$ can arise. In the extreme case, we define dummy variables for each possible outcome on $\mathbf{x}$ and use these in place of $\mathbf{x}$. This approach results in what is known as a **saturated model**. We will not be able to include dummy variables for groups that are always treated or never treated, with the result that our estimator of ATE is for the population that excludes these groups.

To estimate ATE_1, write $ATE_1 = \alpha + [\mathrm{E}(\mathbf{x} \mid w = 1) - \boldsymbol{\psi}]\boldsymbol{\delta}$, and so a consistent estimator is

$$A\hat{T}E_1 = \hat{\alpha} + \left(\sum_{i=1}^{N} w_i\right)^{-1} \left[\sum_{i=1}^{N} w_i(\mathbf{x}_i - \bar{\mathbf{x}})\hat{\boldsymbol{\delta}}\right]$$

Obtaining a standard error for this estimator is somewhat complicated, but it can be done using the delta method or bootstrapping.

Example 18.1 (Effects of Enterprise Zones on Economic Development): Consider evaluating the effects of enterprise zone (EZ) designation on employment growth, for block groups in a particular state. Suppose that we have 1980 and 1990 census data, and that the EZ designation originated in the early 1980s. To account for the fact that zone designation is likely to depend on prior economic performance, and perhaps other block characteristics, we can estimate a model such as the following:

$$\begin{aligned} gemp = {} & \mu_0 + \alpha ez + \beta_1 \log(emp80) + \beta_2 \log(pop80) + \beta_3 percmanf80 \\ & + \beta_4 \log(housval80) + \beta_5 ez \cdot [\log(emp80) - m_1] + \beta_6 ez \cdot [\log(pop80) - m_2] \\ & + \beta_7 ez \cdot [percmanf80 - m_3] + \beta_8 ez \cdot [\log(housval80) - m_4] + error \end{aligned}$$

where the right-hand-side variables are a dummy variable for EZ designation, employment, population, percent of employment in manufacturing, and median housing value, all in 1980, and where the m_j are the sample averages.

The regression estimator (18.16), especially with flexible functions of the covariates, applies directly to what are called **regression discontinuity designs**. In this case, treatment is determined as a *nonstochastic* function of a covariate, say $w = f(s)$, where s is an element of $\mathbf{x}$ that has sufficient variation. The key is that f is a discontinuous function of s, typically a step function, $w = 1[s \leq s_0]$, where s_0 is a known threshold. The idea is that once s, which could be income level or class size, reaches a certain threshold, a policy automatically kicks in. (See, for example, Angrist and Lavy, 1999.) Because s is a nonrandom function of $\mathbf{x}$, the conditional independence assumption in Assumption ATE.1 must hold. The key is obtaining flexible functional forms for $g_0(\cdot)$ and $g_1(\cdot)$. Generally, we can identify α only if we are willing to assume that $g_0(\cdot)$ and $g_1(\cdot)$ are smooth functions of $\mathbf{x}$ (which is almost always the case when we estimate parametric or nonparametric regression functions). If we allow $g_0(\cdot)$ to be discontinuous in s—that is, with jumps—we could never distinguish between changes in y due to a change in s or a change in treatment status.

18.3.2 Methods Based on the Propensity Score

Rosenbaum and Rubin (1983) use the ignorability-of-treatment assumption differently in estimating ATE. Regression (18.16) makes functional form assumptions about $\mathrm{E}(v_0 \mid \mathbf{x})$ and $\mathrm{E}(v_1 \mid \mathbf{x})$, where v_0 and v_1 are unobserved. Alternatively, it turns out that ATE and ATE_1 can both be estimated by modeling

$$p(\mathbf{x}) \equiv \mathrm{P}(w = 1 \mid \mathbf{x}) \tag{18.17}$$

which is the probability of treatment given the covariates. The function $p(\mathbf{x})$, which is simply the response probability for treatment, is called the **propensity score** in the evaluation literature. Interestingly, ATE and ATE_1 can be written in terms of the propensity score.

PROPOSITION 18.3: Under Assumption ATE.1′, assume in addition that

$$0 < p(\mathbf{x}) < 1, \qquad \text{all } \mathbf{x} \tag{18.18}$$

Then

$$ATE = \mathrm{E}([w - p(\mathbf{x})]y/\{p(\mathbf{x})[1 - p(\mathbf{x})]\}) \tag{18.19}$$

and

$$ATE_1 = \mathrm{E}\{[w - p(\mathbf{x})]y/[1 - p(\mathbf{x})]\}/\mathrm{P}(w = 1) \tag{18.20}$$

Proof: Plugging equation (18.3) into the numerator inside the expectation in equation (18.19) gives

$$\begin{aligned}[w - p(\mathbf{x})]y &= [w - p(\mathbf{x})][(1 - w)y_0 + wy_1] \\ &= wy_1 - p(\mathbf{x})(1 - w)y_0 - p(\mathbf{x})wy_1\end{aligned}$$

Taking the expectation of this equation conditional on $(w, \mathbf{x})$ and using Assumption ATE.1′ gives

$$wm_1(\mathbf{x}) - p(\mathbf{x})(1 - w)m_0(\mathbf{x}) - p(\mathbf{x})wm_1(\mathbf{x})$$

where $m_j(\mathbf{x}) \equiv \mathrm{E}(y_j \mid \mathbf{x})$, $j = 0, 1$. Taking the expectation conditional on $\mathbf{x}$ gives

$$p(\mathbf{x})m_1(\mathbf{x}) - p(\mathbf{x})[1 - p(\mathbf{x})]m_0(\mathbf{x}) - [p(\mathbf{x})]^2 m_1(\mathbf{x}) = p(\mathbf{x})[1 - p(\mathbf{x})][m_1(\mathbf{x}) - m_0(\mathbf{x})]$$

because $p(\mathbf{x}) = \mathrm{E}(w \mid \mathbf{x})$. Therefore, the expected value of the term in equation (18.19) conditional on $\mathbf{x}$ is simply $[m_1(\mathbf{x}) - m_0(\mathbf{x})]$; iterated expectations implies that the right-hand side of equation (18.19) is $\mu_1 - \mu_0$.

Very similar reasoning shows that

$$\mathrm{E}\{[w - p(\mathbf{x})]y/[1 - p(\mathbf{x})] \mid \mathbf{x}\} = p(\mathbf{x})[m_1(\mathbf{x}) - m_0(\mathbf{x})]$$

Next, by iterated expectations,

$$\mathrm{E}\{p(\mathbf{x})[m_1(\mathbf{x}) - m_0(\mathbf{x})]\} = \mathrm{E}\{w[m_1(\mathbf{x}) - m_0(\mathbf{x})]\} = \mathrm{E}[w(y_1 - y_0)]$$

where the last equality follows from Assumption ATE.1′. But

$$\begin{aligned}\mathrm{E}[w(y_1 - y_0)] &= \mathrm{P}(w = 1)\mathrm{E}[w(y_1 - y_0) \mid w = 1] + \mathrm{P}(w = 0)\mathrm{E}[w(y_1 - y_0) \mid w = 0] \\ &= \mathrm{P}(w = 1)\mathrm{E}(y_1 - y_0 \mid w = 1)\end{aligned}$$

Therefore, the right-hand side of equation (18.20) is

$$\{\mathrm{P}(w = 1)\mathrm{E}(y_1 - y_0 \mid w = 1)\}/\mathrm{P}(w = 1) = ATE_1.$$

Rosenbaum and Rubin (1983) call Assumption ATE.1 *plus* condition (18.18) **strong ignorability of treatment** (given covariates $\mathbf{x}$). Proposition 18.3 shows, in a different way from Section 18.3.1, that ATE and ATE_1 are nonparametrically identified under strong ignorability of treatment: the response probability, $\mathrm{P}(y = 1 \mid \mathbf{x})$, can be assumed known for the purposes of identification analysis. Wooldridge (1999c) obtained equation (18.19) in the more general setting of a random coefficient model (see Section 18.5.3), while equation (18.20) is essentially due to Dehejia and Wahba (1999, Proposition 4), who make the stronger assumption ATE.1.

Condition (18.18) is precisely the restriction on the response probability that arose in Section 18.3.1 for identifying ATE. Equation (18.20) shows that ATE_1 is still identified if $p(\mathbf{x}) = 0$ for some $\mathbf{x}$, but this finding has little practical value because we probably want to exclude units that have no chance of being treated, anyway. Importantly, in estimating ATE or ATE_1, we rule out $p(\mathbf{x}) = 1$: we cannot estimate ATE or ATE_1 by including in the population units that are treated with certainty, conditional on $\mathbf{x}$.

Of course, to estimate ATE and ATE_1, we need an estimator of $p(\cdot)$. Rosenbaum and Rubin (1983) suggest using a flexible logit model, where $\mathbf{x}$ and various functions of $\mathbf{x}$—for example, quadratics and interactions—are included. [In this case there is no danger of $\hat{p}(\mathbf{x}) = 0$ or 1 because logit fitted values are strictly in the unit interval, but this functional form restriction might simply mask the problem in the population.] The propensity score can also be estimated using fully nonparametric methods—see, for example, Powell (1994) and Heckman, Ichimura, and Todd (1997). Here, we focus on flexible parametric methods. If $\hat{p}(\mathbf{x}) \equiv F(\mathbf{x}; \hat{\gamma})$ is such an estimator, where $\hat{\gamma}$ is obtained in a first-stage binary response estimation of w on $\mathbf{x}$, then a consistent estimator of ATE is

$$\hat{ATE} = N^{-1} \sum_{i=1}^{N} [w_i - \hat{p}(\mathbf{x}_i)] y_i / \{\hat{p}(\mathbf{x}_i)[1 - \hat{p}(\mathbf{x}_i)]\} \tag{18.21}$$

Interestingly, after simple algebra this estimator can be shown to be identical to an estimator due to Horvitz and Thompson (1952) for handling nonrandom sampling. Consistency under standard regularity conditions follows from Lemma 12.1. Similarly, a consistent estimator of ATE_1 is

$$\hat{ATE}_1 = \left(N^{-1}\sum_{i=1}^{N} w_i\right)^{-1}\left\{N^{-1}\sum_{i=1}^{N}[w_i - \hat{p}_i(\mathbf{x}_i)]y_i/[1-\hat{p}(\mathbf{x}_i)]\right\} \tag{18.22}$$

Notice that $N^{-1}\sum_{i=1}^{N} w_i$ is a consistent estimator of $\mathrm{P}(w=1)$. Obtaining valid asymptotic standard errors using the delta method is somewhat complicated, as we need a first-order representation for $\sqrt{N}(\hat{\gamma}-\gamma)$—see Section 12.5.2. Notice that only the predicted probabilities appear in equations (18.21) and (18.22). Therefore, different methods of estimating $p(\mathbf{x})$ that lead to similar predicted values $\hat{p}(\mathbf{x}_i)$ will tend to produce similar treatment effect estimates.

It turns out that the estimators in equations (18.21) and (18.22) not only are convenient, but also can be made to have the smallest asymptotic variances among estimators that are based only on Assumption ATE.1 and condition (18.18) (as well as several regularity conditions). Hirano, Imbens, and Ridder (2000) (HIR) have recently shown that (18.21) and (18.22) achieve the semiparametric efficiency bound obtained by Hahn (1998). In order to achieve the bound, HIR assume that $\hat{p}(\cdot)$ is a series estimator, so that the conditions in Newey (1994) can be verified. As a practical matter, series estimation is not ideal, because, for a binary response, it is identical to a linear probability model in functions of $\mathbf{x}$. Plus, it is difficult to estimate the asymptotic variance of the resulting estimators, $\hat{ATE}$ and $\hat{ATE}_1$. Probably little is lost by using a flexible logit or probit and then obtaining the standard errors by the usual delta method.

A simple, popular estimator in program evaluation is obtained from an OLS regression that simply includes the estimated propensity score, $\hat{p}(\mathbf{x})$, as an additional regressor:

$$y_i \text{ on } 1, w_i, \hat{p}(\mathbf{x}_i), \qquad i = 1, 2, \ldots, N \tag{18.23}$$

where the coefficient on w_i is the estimate of the treatment effect. In other words, the estimated propensity score plays the role of the control function. The idea is that the estimated propensity score should contain all the information in the covariates that is relevant for estimating the treatment effect. The question is, When does regression (18.23) consistently estimate the average treatment effect? The following is a special case of Wooldridge (1999c, Proposition 3.2):

PROPOSITION 18.4: In addition to Assumption ATE.1′, assume that $\mathrm{E}(y_1 - y_0 \mid \mathbf{x}) = m_1(\mathbf{x}) - m_0(\mathbf{x})$ is *uncorrelated* with $\mathrm{Var}(w \mid \mathbf{x}) = p(\mathbf{x})[1-p(\mathbf{x})]$. If the parametric estimator $\hat{p}(\cdot)$ is consistent and $\sqrt{N}$-asymptotically normal, then the OLS coefficient on

w from regression (18.23) is consistent and $\sqrt{N}$-asymptotically normal for the average treatment effect, ATE.

The assumption that $m_1(\mathbf{x}) - m_0(\mathbf{x})$ is uncorrelated with $\text{Var}(w \mid \mathbf{x})$ may appear unlikely, as both are functions of $\mathbf{x}$. However, remember that correlation is a linear measure of dependence. The conditional variance $\text{Var}(w \mid \mathbf{x})$ is a nonmonotonic quadratic in $p(\mathbf{x})$, while $m_1(\mathbf{x}) - m_0(\mathbf{x})$ is likely to be monotonic in many elements of $\mathbf{x}$; zero correlation might hold approximately. (This observation is analogous to the fact that if z is a standard normal random variable, then z and z^2 are uncorrelated.)

Using different auxiliary assumptions, Rosenbaum and Rubin (1983, Corollary 4.3) suggest a more general version of regression (18.23) for estimating ATE:

$$y_i \text{ on } 1, w_i, \hat{p}_i, w_i(\hat{p}_i - \hat{\mu}_p), \qquad i = 1, 2, \ldots, N \tag{18.24}$$

where $\hat{\mu}_p$ is the sample average of $\hat{p}_i$, $i = 1, 2, \ldots, N$.

PROPOSITION 18.5: Under Assumption ATE.1, assume in addition that $\text{E}[y_0 \mid p(\mathbf{x})]$ and $\text{E}[y_1 \mid p(\mathbf{x})]$ are linear in $p(\mathbf{x})$. Then the coefficient on w_i in regression (18.24) consistently estimates ATE.

Proof: Rosenbaum and Rubin (1983, Theorem 3) show that, under Assumption ATE.1, (y_0, y_1) and w are independent conditional on $p(\mathbf{x})$. For completeness, we present the argument. It suffices to show $\text{P}[w = 1 \mid y_0, y_1, p(\mathbf{x})] = \text{P}[w = 1 \mid p(\mathbf{x})]$ or $\text{E}[w \mid y_0, y_1, p(\mathbf{x})] = \text{E}[w \mid p(\mathbf{x})]$. But, under Assumption ATE.1, $\text{E}(w \mid y_0, y_1, \mathbf{x}) = \text{E}(w \mid \mathbf{x}) = p(\mathbf{x})$. By iterated expectations,

$$\text{E}[w \mid y_0, y_1, p(\mathbf{x})] = \text{E}[\text{E}(w \mid y_0, y_1, \mathbf{x}) \mid y_0, y_1, p(\mathbf{x})] = \text{E}[p(\mathbf{x}) \mid y_0, y_1, p(\mathbf{x})] = p(\mathbf{x})$$

We can now use this equation to obtain $\text{E}[y \mid w, p(\mathbf{x})]$. Write $y = y_0 + (\mu_1 - \mu_0)w + w(v_1 - v_0)$. We just showed that (y_0, y_1) and w are independent given $p(\mathbf{x})$, and so

$$\begin{aligned}\text{E}[y \mid w, p(\mathbf{x})] &= \text{E}[y_0 \mid p(\mathbf{x})] + (\mu_1 - \mu_0)w + w\{\text{E}[v_1 \mid p(\mathbf{x})] - \text{E}[v_0 \mid p(\mathbf{x})]\} \\ &= \delta_0 + \delta_1 p(\mathbf{x}) + (\mu_1 - \mu_0)w + \delta_2 w[p(\mathbf{x}) - \mu_p]\end{aligned}$$

under the linearity assumptions, where $\mu_p \equiv \text{E}[p(\mathbf{x})]$. {Remember, as v_1 and v_0 have zero means, the linear function of $p(\mathbf{x})$ must have a zero mean, too; we can always write it as $\delta_2[p(\mathbf{x}) - \mu_p]$.} This step completes the proof, as replacing μ_p with its sample average in the regression does not affect consistency (or asymptotic normality).

The linearity assumptions for $\text{E}[y_0 \mid p(\mathbf{x})]$ and $\text{E}[y_1 \mid p(\mathbf{x})]$ are probably too restrictive in many applications. As $p(\mathbf{x})$ is bounded between zero and one, $\text{E}[y_0 \mid p(\mathbf{x})]$ and $\text{E}[y_1 \mid p(\mathbf{x})]$ are necessarily bounded under linearity, which might be a poor assumption if the y_g have a wide support. If y is binary, linearity of these expected values is also questionable, but it could be a reasonable approximation. Of course, it is a simple matter to replace $\hat{p}_i$ with a low-order polynomial in $\hat{p}_i$, being sure to de-mean any term before constructing its interaction with w_i.

Example 18.2 (Effects of Job Training on Earnings): The data in JTRAIN2.RAW are from a job training experiment in the 1970s. The response variable is real earnings in 1978, measured in thousands of dollars. Real earnings are zero for men who did not work during the year. Training began up to two years prior to 1978. We use regressions (18.23) and (18.24) to estimate the average treatment effect. The elements of $\mathbf{x}$ are real earnings in 1974 and 1975, age (in quadratic form), a binary high school degree indicator (*nodegree*), marital status, and binary variables for black and Hispanic. In the first-stage probit of *train* on $\mathbf{x}$, only *nodegree* is statistically significant at the 5 percent level. Once we have the fitted propensity scores, we can run regression (18.23). This gives $\hat{\alpha} = 1.626$ (se $= .644$), where the standard error is not adjusted for the probit first-stage estimation. Job training is estimated to increase earnings by about \$1,626. Interestingly, this estimate is very close to the regression *re78* on 1, *train*, $\mathbf{x}$: $\hat{\alpha} = 1.625$ (se $= .640$); both are somewhat smaller than the simple comparison-of-means estimate, which is 1.794 (se $= .633$).

Adding the interaction term in regression (18.24), with $\hat{\mu}_p = .416$, lowers the estimate somewhat: $\hat{\alpha} = 1.560$ (se $= .642$). The interaction term (again, based on the usual OLS standard error) is marginally significant.

Regressions (18.23) and (18.24) are attractive because they account for possibly nonrandom assignment of treatment by including a single function of the covariates, the estimated propensity score. Compared with the regressions that include the full set of covariates, in flexible ways, possibly interacted with the treatment [as in equation (18.16)], the propensity score approach seems much more parsimonious. However, this parsimony is somewhat illusory. Remember, the propensity score is estimated by a first-stage probit or logit, where the treatment is the dependent variable and flexible functions of the elements of $\mathbf{x}$ are the explanatory variables. It is not obvious that estimating a flexible binary response model in the first stage is somehow better than the kitchen sink regression (18.16). In fact, if the propensity score were estimated using a linear probability model, regression (18.23) and regression (18.16) without the interaction terms would produce identical estimates of α. Also, using regression (18.23) or (18.24) makes it tempting to ignore the first-stage estimation of the propensity score in obtaining the standard error of the treatment effect (as we did in Example 18.2). At least in regression (18.16) we know that the standard error of $\hat{\alpha}$ is reliable; at worst, we must make the standard error robust to heteroskedasticity. In

Example 18.2, we have no way of knowing how much the sampling variation in the first-stage probit estimates would affect a properly computed standard error short of actually doing the calculations. Because the propensity score approach and the standard regression approach require different assumptions for consistency, neither generally dominates the other. [If anything, the linearity assumptions on $\mathrm{E}[y_0 \mid p(\mathbf{x})]$ and $\mathrm{E}[y_1 \mid p(\mathbf{x})]$ are less palatable than the linearity assumptions underlying equation (18.15).]

If we use the propensity score as in equation (18.21) then we need not make auxiliary assumptions as required by regressions (18.23) and (18.24). But we should still adjust the standard error of $\hat{ATE}$ to account for first-stage estimation of the propensity score. Apparently, not much work has been done comparing regression methods that use the propensity score with standard kitchen sink–type regressions, let alone comparing these procedures with the estimator from equation (18.21).

All the previous estimates of ATEs that use the estimated propensity score involve either regressions or formulas that appear similar to regressions in the sense that the propensity score is included in a sample average [see equations (18.21) and (18.22)]. Estimates of the propensity score are also used in a very different way in the treatment effect literature. Various **matching estimators** have been proposed, and asymptotic distributions are available in many cases. The matching approach suggested by Rosenbaum and Rubin (1983) is motivated by the following thought experiment. Suppose we choose a propensity score, $p(\mathbf{x})$, at random from the population. Then, we select two agents from the population sharing the chosen propensity score, where one agent receives treatment and the other does not. Under Assumption ATE.1, the expected difference in the observed outcomes for these agents is

$$\mathrm{E}[y \mid w = 1, p(\mathbf{x})] - \mathrm{E}[y \mid w = 0, p(\mathbf{x})] = \mathrm{E}[y_1 - y_0 \mid p(\mathbf{x})]$$

which is the ATE conditional on $p(\mathbf{x})$. By iterated expectations, averaging across the distribution of propensity scores gives $ATE = \mathrm{E}(y_1 - y_0)$.

An estimation strategy requires estimating the propensity scores, estimating the response differences for pairs matched on the basis of the estimated propensity scores, and then averaging over all such pairs. Because getting identical predicted probabilities is often unlikely, grouping into cells or local averaging is used instead. Effectively, agents with similar propensity scores are considered a match. Heckman, Ichimura, and Todd (1997) (HIT), Angrist (1998), and Dehejia and Wahba (1999) provide recent treatments of matching methods.

As with the regression methods discussed in Section 18.3.1, a practical problem with matching on the propensity score is that it can be hard to find treated and untreated agents with similar estimated propensity scores. HIT discuss trimming strategies in a nonparametric context and derive asymptotically valid standard errors. Similarly, the practice of grouping on the basis of the estimated propensity scores, and then ignoring the sampling variation in both the estimated propensity scores and the grouping when constructing standard errors and confidence intervals, may be misleading. HIT show how to obtain valid inference.

18.4 Instrumental Variables Methods

We now turn to instrumental variables estimation of average treatment effects when we suspect failure of the ignorability-of-treatment assumption (ATE.1 or ATE.1′). IV methods for estimating ATEs can be very effective if a good instrument for treatment is available. We need the instrument to predict treatment (after partialing out any controls). As we discussed in Section 5.3.1, the instrument should be redundant in a certain conditional expectation and unrelated to unobserved heterogeneity; we give precise assumptions in the following subsections.

Our primary focus in this section is on the average treatment effect defined in equation (18.1), although we touch on estimating ATE_1. In Section 18.4.2, we briefly discuss estimating the local average treatment effect.

18.4.1 Estimating the ATE Using IV

In studying IV procedures, it is useful to write the observed outcome y as in equation (18.10):

$$y = \mu_0 + (\mu_1 - \mu_0)w + v_0 + w(v_1 - v_0) \tag{18.25}$$

However, unlike in Section 18.3, we do not assume that v_0 and v_1 are mean independent of w, given $\mathbf{x}$. Instead, we assume the availability of instruments, which we collect in the vector $\mathbf{z}$. (Here we separate the extra instruments from the covariates, so that $\mathbf{x}$ and $\mathbf{z}$ do not overlap. In many cases $\mathbf{z}$ is a scalar, but the analysis is no easier in that case.)

If we assume that the stochastic parts of y_1 and y_0 are the same, that is, $v_1 = v_0$, then the interaction term disappears (and $ATE = ATE_1$). Without the interaction term we can use standard IV methods under weak assumptions.

Assumption ATE.2: (a) In equation (18.25), $v_1 = v_0$; (b) $\mathrm{L}(v_0 \mid \mathbf{x}, \mathbf{z}) = \mathrm{L}(v_0 \mid \mathbf{x})$; and (c) $\mathrm{L}(w \mid \mathbf{x}, \mathbf{z}) \neq \mathrm{L}(w \mid \mathbf{x})$.

All linear projections in this chapter contain unity, which we suppress for notational simplicity.

Under parts a and b of Assumption ATE.2, we can write

$$y = \delta_0 + \alpha w + \mathbf{x}\boldsymbol{\beta}_0 + u_0 \tag{18.26}$$

where $\alpha = ATE$ and $u_0 \equiv v_0 - \mathrm{L}(v_0 \mid \mathbf{x}, \mathbf{z})$. By definition, u_0 has zero mean and is uncorrelated with $(\mathbf{x}, \mathbf{z})$, but w and u_0 are generally correlated, which makes OLS estimation of equation (18.26) inconsistent. The redundancy of $\mathbf{z}$ in the linear projection $\mathrm{L}(v_0 \mid \mathbf{x}, \mathbf{z})$ means that $\mathbf{z}$ is appropriately excluded from equation (18.26); this is the part of identification that we cannot test (except indirectly using the overidentification test from Chapter 6). Part c means that $\mathbf{z}$ has predictive power in the linear projection of treatment on $(\mathbf{x}, \mathbf{z})$; this is the standard rank condition for identification from Chapter 5, and we can test it using a first-stage regression and heteroskedasticity-robust tests of exclusion restrictions. Under Assumption ATE.2, α [and the other parameters in equation (18.26)] are identified, and they can be consistently estimated by 2SLS. Because the only endogenous explanatory variable in equation (18.26) is binary, equation (18.25) is called a **dummy endogenous variable model** (Heckman, 1978). As we discussed in Chapter 5, there are no special considerations in estimating equation (18.26) by 2SLS when the endogenous explanatory variable is binary.

Assumption ATE.2b holds if the instruments $\mathbf{z}$ are independent of $(y_0, \mathbf{x})$. For example, suppose z is a scalar determining eligibility in a job training program or some other social program. Actual participation, w, might be correlated with v_0, which could contain unobserved ability. If eligibility is randomly assigned, it is often reasonable to assume that z is independent of $(y_0, \mathbf{x})$. Eligibility would positively influence participation, and so Assumption ATE.2c should hold.

Random assignment of eligibility is no guarantee that eligibility is a valid instrument for participation. The outcome of z could affect other behavior, which could feed back into u_0 in equation (18.26). For example, consider Angrist's (1990) draft lottery application, where draft lottery number is used as an instrument for enlisting. Lottery number clearly affected enlistment, so Assumption ATE.2c is satisfied. Assumption ATE.2b is also satisfied *if* men did not change behavior in unobserved ways that affect wage, based on their lottery number. One concern is that men with low lottery numbers may get more education as a way of avoiding service through a deferment. Including years of education in $\mathbf{x}$ effectively solves this problem. But what if men with high draft lottery numbers received more job training because employers did not fear losing them? If a measure of job training status cannot be included in $\mathbf{x}$, lottery number would generally be correlated with u_0. See AIR and Heckman (1997) for additional discussion.

As the previous discussion implies, the redundancy condition in Assumption ATE.2b allows the instruments $\mathbf{z}$ to be correlated with elements of $\mathbf{x}$. For example, in the population of high school graduates, if w is a college degree indicator and the instrument z is distance to the nearest college while attending high school, then z is allowed to be correlated with other controls in the wage equation, such as geographic indicators.

Under $v_1 = v_0$ and the key assumptions on the instruments, 2SLS on equation (18.26) is consistent and asymptotically normal. But if we make stronger assumptions, we can find a more efficient IV estimator.

ASSUMPTION ATE.2′: (a) In equation (18.25), $v_1 = v_0$; (b) $\mathrm{E}(v_0 \mid \mathbf{x}, \mathbf{z}) = \mathrm{L}(v_0 \mid \mathbf{x})$; (c) $\mathrm{P}(w = 1 \mid \mathbf{x}, \mathbf{z}) \neq \mathrm{P}(w = 1 \mid \mathbf{x})$ and $\mathrm{P}(w = 1 \mid \mathbf{x}, \mathbf{z}) = G(\mathbf{x}, \mathbf{z}; \gamma)$ is a known parametric form (usually probit or logit); and (d) $\mathrm{Var}(v_0 \mid \mathbf{x}, \mathbf{z}) = \sigma_0^2$.

Part b assumes that $\mathrm{E}(v_0 \mid \mathbf{x})$ is linear in $\mathbf{x}$, and so it is more restrictive than Assumption ATE.2b. It does not usually hold for discrete response variables y, although it may be a reasonable approximation in some cases. Under parts a and b, the error u_0 in equation (18.26) has a zero conditional mean:

$$\mathrm{E}(u_0 \mid \mathbf{x}, \mathbf{z}) = 0 \tag{18.27}$$

Part d implies that $\mathrm{Var}(u_0 \mid \mathbf{x}, \mathbf{z})$ is constant. From the results on efficient choice of instruments in Section 14.5.3, the optimal IV for w is $\mathrm{E}(w \mid \mathbf{x}, \mathbf{z}) = G(\mathbf{x}, \mathbf{z}; \gamma)$. Therefore, we can use a two-step IV method:

Procedure 18.1 (Under Assumption ATE.2′): (a) Estimate the binary response model $\mathrm{P}(w = 1 \mid \mathbf{x}, \mathbf{z}) = G(\mathbf{x}, \mathbf{z}; \gamma)$ by maximum likelihood. Obtain the fitted probabilities, $\hat{G}_i$. The leading case occurs when $\mathrm{P}(w = 1 \mid \mathbf{x}, \mathbf{z})$ follows a probit model.

(b) Estimate equation (18.26) by IV using instruments 1, $\hat{G}_i$, and $\mathbf{x}_i$.

There are several nice features of this IV estimator. First, it can be shown that the conditions sufficient to ignore the estimation of γ in the first stage hold; see Section 6.1.2. Therefore, the usual 2SLS standard errors and test statistics are asymptotically valid. Second, under Assumption ATE.2′, the IV estimator from step b is asymptotically efficient in the class of estimators where the IVs are functions of $(\mathbf{x}_i, \mathbf{z}_i)$; see Problem 8.11. If Assumption ATE.2d does not hold, all statistics should be made robust to heteroskedasticity, and we no longer have the efficient IV estimator.

Procedure 18.1 has an important robustness property. Because we are using $\hat{G}_i$ as an instrument for w_i, the model for $\mathrm{P}(w = 1 \mid \mathbf{x}, \mathbf{z})$ does *not* have to be correctly specified. For example, if we specify a probit model for $\mathrm{P}(w = 1 \mid \mathbf{x}, \mathbf{z})$, we do not need the probit model to be correct. Generally, what we need is that the linear projection of w onto $[\mathbf{x}, G(\mathbf{x}, \mathbf{z}; \gamma^*)]$ actually depends on $G(\mathbf{x}, \mathbf{z}; \gamma^*)$, where we use γ^* to denote the plim of the maximum likelihood estimator when the model is misspecified (see White, 1982a). These requirements are fairly weak when $\mathbf{z}$ is partially correlated with w.

Technically, α and $\boldsymbol{\beta}$ are identified even if we do not have extra exogenous variables excluded from $\mathbf{x}$. But we can rarely justify the estimator in this case. For concreteness, suppose that w given $\mathbf{x}$ follows a probit model [and we have no $\mathbf{z}$, or $\mathbf{z}$ does not appear in $\mathrm{P}(w = 1 \mid \mathbf{x}, \mathbf{z})$]. Because $G(\mathbf{x}, \gamma) \equiv \Phi(\gamma_0 + \mathbf{x}\gamma_1)$ is a nonlinear function of $\mathbf{x}$, it is not perfectly correlated with $\mathbf{x}$, so it can be used as an IV for w. This situation is very similar to the one discussed in Section 17.4.1: while identification holds for all values of α and $\boldsymbol{\beta}$ if $\gamma_1 \neq \mathbf{0}$, we are achieving identification off of the nonlinearity of $\mathrm{P}(w = 1 \mid \mathbf{x})$. Further, $\Phi(\gamma_0 + \mathbf{x}\gamma_1)$ and $\mathbf{x}$ are typically highly correlated. As we discussed in Section 5.2.6, severe multicollinearity among the IVs can result in very imprecise IV estimators. In fact, if $\mathrm{P}(w = 1 \mid \mathbf{x})$ followed a linear probability model, α would not be identified. See Problem 18.5 for an illustration.

Example 18.3 (Estimating the Effects of Education on Fertility): We use the data in FERTIL2.RAW to estimate the effect of attaining at least seven years of education on fertility. The data are for women of childbearing age in Botswana. Seven years of education is, by far, the modal amount of positive education. (About 21 percent of women report zero years of education. For the subsample with positive education, about 33 percent report seven years of education.) Let $y = children$, the number of living children, and let $w = educ7$ be a binary indicator for at least seven years of education. The elements of $\mathbf{x}$ are *age*, age^2, *evermarr* (ever married), *urban* (lives in an urban area), *electric* (has electricity), and *tv* (has a television).

The OLS estimate of ATE is $-.394$ (se = .050). We also use the variable *frsthalf*, a binary variable equal to one if the woman was born in the first half of the year, as an IV for *educ7*. It is easily shown that *educ7* and *frsthalf* are significantly negatively related. The usual IV estimate is much larger in magnitude than the OLS estimate, but only marginally significant: -1.131 (se = .619). The estimate from Procedure 18.1 is even bigger in magnitude, and very significant: -1.975 (se = .332). The standard error that is robust to arbitrary heteroskedasticity is even smaller. Therefore, using the probit fitted values as an IV, rather than the usual linear projection, produces a more precise estimate (and one notably larger in magnitude).

The IV estimate of education effect seems very large. One possible problem is that, because *children* is a nonnegative integer that piles up at zero, the assumptions underlying Procedure 18.1—namely, Assumptions ATE.2′a and ATE.2′b—might not be met. In Chapter 19 we will discuss other methods for handling integer responses.

In principle, it is important to recognize that Procedure 18.1 is *not* the same as using $\hat{G}$ as a *regressor* in place of w. That is, IV estimation of equation (18.26) is *not* the same as the OLS estimator from

$$y_i \text{ on } 1, \hat{G}_i, \mathbf{x}_i \tag{18.28}$$

Consistency of the OLS estimators from regression (18.28) relies on having the model for $\mathrm{P}(w = 1 \mid \mathbf{x}, \mathbf{z})$ correctly specified. If the first three parts of Assumption ATE.2′ hold, then

$$\mathrm{E}(y \mid \mathbf{x}, \mathbf{z}) = \delta_0 + \alpha G(\mathbf{x}, \mathbf{z}; \gamma) + \mathbf{x}\boldsymbol{\beta}$$

and, from the results on generated regressors in Chapter 6, the estimators from regression (18.28) are generally consistent. Procedure 18.1 is more robust because it does not require Assumption ATE.2′c for consistency.

Another problem with regression (18.28) is that the usual OLS standard errors and test statistics are not valid, for two reasons. First, if $\mathrm{Var}(u_0 \mid \mathbf{x}, \mathbf{z})$ is constant, $\mathrm{Var}(y \mid \mathbf{x}, \mathbf{z})$ cannot be constant because $\mathrm{Var}(w \mid \mathbf{x}, \mathbf{z})$ is not constant. By itself this is a minor nuisance because heteroskedasticity-robust standard errors and test statistics are easy to obtain. [However, it does call into question the efficiency of the estimator from regression (18.28).] A more serious problem is that the asymptotic variance of the estimator from regression (18.28) depends on the asymptotic variance of $\hat{\gamma}$ unless $\alpha = 0$, and the heteroskedasticity-robust standard errors do not correct for this.

In summary, using fitted probabilities from a first-stage binary response model, such as probit or logit, as an instrument for w is a nice way to exploit the binary nature of the endogenous explanatory variable. In addition, the asymptotic inference is always standard. Using $\hat{G}_i$ as an instrument does require the assumption that $\mathrm{E}(v_0 \mid \mathbf{x}, \mathbf{z})$ depends only on $\mathbf{x}$ and is linear in $\mathbf{x}$, which can be more restrictive than Assumption ATE.2b.

Allowing for the interaction $w(v_1 - v_0)$ in equation (18.25) is notably harder. In general, when $v_1 \neq v_0$, the IV estimator (using $\mathbf{z}$ or $\hat{G}$ as IVs for w) does not consistently estimate ATE (or ATE_1). Nevertheless, it is useful to find assumptions under which IV estimation does consistently estimate ATE. This problem has been studied by Angrist (1991), Heckman (1997), and Wooldridge (1997b), and we synthesize results from these papers.

Under the conditional mean redundancy assumptions

$$\mathrm{E}(v_0 \mid \mathbf{x}, \mathbf{z}) = \mathrm{E}(v_0 \mid \mathbf{x}) \qquad \text{and} \qquad \mathrm{E}(v_1 \mid \mathbf{x}, \mathbf{z}) = \mathrm{E}(v_1 \mid \mathbf{x}) \tag{18.29}$$

we can always write equation (18.25) as

$$y = \mu_0 + \alpha w + g_0(\mathbf{x}) + w[g_1(\mathbf{x}) - g_0(\mathbf{x})] + e_0 + w(e_1 - e_0) \tag{18.30}$$

where α is the ATE and

$$v_0 = g_0(\mathbf{x}) + e_0, \qquad \mathrm{E}(e_0 \mid \mathbf{x}, \mathbf{z}) = 0 \tag{18.31}$$

$$v_1 = g_1(\mathbf{x}) + e_1, \qquad \mathrm{E}(e_1 \mid \mathbf{x}, \mathbf{z}) = 0 \tag{18.32}$$

Given functional form assumptions for g_0 and g_1—which would typically be linear in parameters—we can estimate equation (18.30) by IV, where the error term is $e_0 + w(e_1 - e_0)$. For concreteness, suppose that

$$g_0(\mathbf{x}) = \eta_0 + \mathbf{x}\boldsymbol{\beta}_0, \qquad g_1(\mathbf{x}) - g_0(\mathbf{x}) = (\mathbf{x} - \boldsymbol{\psi})\boldsymbol{\delta} \tag{18.33}$$

where $\boldsymbol{\psi} = \mathrm{E}(\mathbf{x})$. If we plug these equations into equation (18.30), we need instruments for w *and* $w(\mathbf{x} - \boldsymbol{\psi})$ (note that $\mathbf{x}$ does not contain a constant here). If $q \equiv q(\mathbf{x}, \mathbf{z})$ is the instrument for w (such as the response probability in Procedure 18.1), the natural instrument for $w \cdot \mathbf{x}$ is $q \cdot \mathbf{x}$. (And, if q is the efficient IV for w, $q \cdot \mathbf{x}$ is the efficient instrument for $w \cdot \mathbf{x}$.) When will applying IV to

$$y = \gamma + \alpha w + \mathbf{x}\boldsymbol{\beta}_0 + w(\mathbf{x} - \boldsymbol{\psi})\boldsymbol{\delta} + e_0 + w(e_1 - e_0) \tag{18.34}$$

be consistent? If the last term disappears, and, in particular, if

$$e_1 = e_0 \tag{18.35}$$

then the error e_0 has zero mean given $(\mathbf{x}, \mathbf{z})$; this result means that IV estimation of equation (18.34) produces consistent, asymptotically normal estimators.

Assumption ATE.3: With y expressed as in equation (18.25), conditions (18.29), (18.33), and (18.35) hold. In addition, Assumption ATE.2′c holds.

We have the following extension of Procedure 18.1:

Procedure 18.2 (Under Assumption ATE.3): (a) Same as Procedure 18.1.
(b) Estimate the equation

$$y_i = \gamma + \alpha w_i + \mathbf{x}_i\boldsymbol{\beta}_0 + [w_i(\mathbf{x}_i - \bar{\mathbf{x}})]\boldsymbol{\delta} + error_i \tag{18.36}$$

by IV, using instruments 1, $\hat{G}_i$, $\mathbf{x}_i$, and $\hat{G}_i(\mathbf{x}_i - \bar{\mathbf{x}})$.

If we add Assumption ATE.2′d, Procedure 18.2 produces the efficient IV estimator [when we ignore estimation of $\mathrm{E}(\mathbf{x})$]. As with Procedure 18.1, we do not actually need the binary response model to be correctly specified for identification. As an alternative, we can use $\mathbf{z}_i$ and interactions between $\mathbf{z}_i$ and $\mathbf{x}_i$ as instruments, which generally results in testable overidentifying restrictions.

Technically, the fact that $\bar{\mathbf{x}}$ is an estimator of $\mathrm{E}(\mathbf{x})$ should be accounted for in computing the standard errors of the IV estimators. But, as shown in Problem 6.10, the adjustments for estimating $\mathrm{E}(\mathbf{x})$ can be expected to have a trivial effect on the standard errors; in practice, we can just use the usual or heteroskedasticity-robust standard errors.

Example 18.4 (An IV Approach to Evaluating Job Training): To evaluate the effects of a job training program on subsequent wages, suppose that $\mathbf{x}$ includes education, experience, and the square of experience. If z indicates eligibility in the program, we would estimate the equation

$$\begin{aligned}\log(wage) &= \mu_0 + \alpha\, jobtrain + \beta_{01} educ + \beta_{02} exper + \beta_{03} exper^2 \\ &\quad + \delta_1 jobtrain \cdot (educ - \overline{educ}) + \delta_2 jobtrain \cdot (exper - \overline{exper}) \\ &\quad + \delta_3 jobtrain \cdot (exper^2 - \overline{exper^2}) + error\end{aligned}$$

by IV, using instruments 1, z, *educ*, *exper*, $exper^2$, and interactions of z with all demeaned covariates. Notice that for the last interaction, we subtract off the average of $exper^2$. Alternatively, we could use in place of z the fitted values from a probit of *jobtrain* on $(\mathbf{x}, z)$.

Procedure 18.2 is easy to carry out, but its consistency generally hinges on condition (18.35), not to mention the functional form assumptions in equation (18.33). We can relax condition (18.35) to

$$\mathrm{E}[w(e_1 - e_0) \mid \mathbf{x}, \mathbf{z}] = \mathrm{E}[w(e_1 - e_0)] \tag{18.37}$$

We do *not* need $w(e_1 - e_0)$ to have zero mean, as a nonzero mean only affects the intercept. It is important to see that correlation between w and $(e_1 - e_0)$ does *not* invalidate the IV estimator of α from Procedure 18.2. However, we must assume that the covariance conditional on $(\mathbf{x}, \mathbf{z})$ is constant. Even if this assumption is not exactly true, it might be approximately true.

It is easy to see why, along with conditions (18.29) and (18.33), condition (18.37) implies consistency of the IV estimator. We can write equation (18.34) as

$$y = \xi + \alpha w + \mathbf{x}\boldsymbol{\beta}_0 + w(\mathbf{x} - \boldsymbol{\psi})\boldsymbol{\delta} + e_0 + r \tag{18.38}$$

where $r = w(e_1 - e_0) - \mathrm{E}[w(e_1 - e_0)]$ and $\xi = \gamma + \mathrm{E}[w(e_1 - e_0)]$. Under condition (18.37), $\mathrm{E}(r \mid \mathbf{x}, \mathbf{z}) = 0$, and so the composite error $e_0 + r$ has zero mean conditional on $(\mathbf{x}, \mathbf{z})$. Therefore, any function of $(\mathbf{x}, \mathbf{z})$ can be used as instruments in equation (18.38). Under the following modification of Assumption ATE.3, Procedure 18.2 is still consistent:

Assumption ATE.3′: With y expressed as in equation (18.25), conditions (18.29), (18.33), and (18.37) hold. In addition, Assumption ATE.2′c holds.

Even if Assumption ATE.2′d holds in addition to Assumption ATE.2′c, the IV estimator is generally not efficient because $\text{Var}(r \mid \mathbf{x}, \mathbf{z})$ would typically be heteroskedastic.

Angrist (1991) provided primitive conditions for assumption (18.37) in the case where $\mathbf{z}$ is independent of $(y_0, y_1, \mathbf{x})$. Then, the covariates can be dropped entirely from the analysis (leading to IV estimation of the simple regression equation $y = \xi + \alpha w + error$). We can extend those conditions here to allow $\mathbf{z}$ and $\mathbf{x}$ to be correlated. Assume that

$$\text{E}(w \mid \mathbf{x}, \mathbf{z}, e_1 - e_0) = h(\mathbf{x}, \mathbf{z}) + k(e_1 - e_0) \tag{18.39}$$

for some functions $h(\cdot)$ and $k(\cdot)$ and that

$$e_1 - e_0 \text{ is independent of } (\mathbf{x}, \mathbf{z}) \tag{18.40}$$

Under these two assumptions,

$$\begin{aligned} \text{E}[w(e_1 - e_0) \mid \mathbf{x}, \mathbf{z}] &= h(\mathbf{x}, \mathbf{z})\text{E}(e_1 - e_0 \mid \mathbf{x}, \mathbf{z}) + \text{E}[(e_1 - e_0)k(e_1 - e_0) \mid \mathbf{x}, \mathbf{z}] \\ &= h(\mathbf{x}, \mathbf{z}) \cdot 0 + \text{E}[(e_1 - e_0)k(e_1 - e_0)] \\ &= \text{E}[(e_1 - e_0)k(e_1 - e_0)] \end{aligned} \tag{18.41}$$

which is just an unconditional moment in the distribution of $e_1 - e_0$. We have used the fact that $\text{E}(e_1 - e_0 \mid \mathbf{x}, \mathbf{z}) = 0$ and that any function of $e_1 - e_0$ is independent of $(\mathbf{x}, \mathbf{z})$ under assumption (18.40). If we assume that $k(\cdot)$ is the identity function (as in Wooldridge, 1997b), then equation (18.41) is $\text{Var}(e_1 - e_0)$.

Assumption (18.40) is reasonable for continuously distributed responses, but it would not generally be reasonable when y is a discrete response or corner solution outcome. Further, even if assumption (18.40) holds, assumption (18.39) is violated when w given $\mathbf{x}$, $\mathbf{z}$, and $(e_1 - e_0)$ follows a standard binary response model. For example, a probit model would have

$$\text{P}(w = 1 \mid \mathbf{x}, \mathbf{z}, e_1 - e_0) = \Phi[\pi_0 + \mathbf{x}\boldsymbol{\pi}_1 + \mathbf{z}\boldsymbol{\pi}_2 + \rho(e_1 - e_0)] \tag{18.42}$$

which is not separable in $(\mathbf{x}, \mathbf{z})$ and $(e_1 - e_0)$. Nevertheless, assumption (18.39) might be a reasonable approximation in some cases. Without covariates, Angrist (1991) presents simulation evidence that suggests the simple IV estimator does quite well for estimating the ATE even when assumption (18.39) is violated.

Rather than assuming (18.39), different approaches are available, but they require different assumptions. We first consider a solution that involves adding a nonlinear function of $(\mathbf{x}, \mathbf{z})$ to equation (18.38) and estimating the resulting equation by 2SLS. We add to assumptions (18.40) and (18.42) a normality assumption,

$$e_1 - e_0 \sim \text{Normal}(0, \tau^2) \tag{18.43}$$

Under assumptions (18.40), (18.42), and (18.43) we can derive an estimating equation to show that ATE is usually identified.

To derive an estimating equation, note that conditions (18.40), (18.42), and (18.43) imply that

$$\text{P}(w = 1 \mid \mathbf{x}, \mathbf{z}) = \Phi(\theta_0 + \mathbf{x}\boldsymbol{\theta}_1 + \mathbf{z}\boldsymbol{\theta}_2) \tag{18.44}$$

where each theta is the corresponding pi multiplied by $[1 + \rho^2\tau^2]^{-1/2}$. If we let a denote the latent error underlying equation (18.44) (with a standard normal distribution), and define $c \equiv e_1 - e_0$, then conditions (18.40), (18.42), and (18.43) imply that (a, c) has a zero-mean bivariate normal distribution that is independent of $(\mathbf{x}, \mathbf{z})$. Therefore, $\text{E}(c \mid a, \mathbf{x}, \mathbf{z}) = \text{E}(c \mid a) = \xi a$ for some parameter ξ, and

$$\text{E}(wc \mid \mathbf{x}, \mathbf{z}) = \text{E}[w\text{E}(c \mid a, \mathbf{x}, \mathbf{z}) \mid \mathbf{x}, \mathbf{z}] = \xi\text{E}(wa \mid \mathbf{x}, \mathbf{z}).$$

Using the fact that $a \sim \text{Normal}(0, 1)$ and is independent of $(\mathbf{x}, \mathbf{z})$, we have

$$\begin{aligned}\text{E}(wa \mid \mathbf{x}, \mathbf{z}) &= \int_{-\infty}^{\infty} 1[\theta_0 + \mathbf{x}\boldsymbol{\theta}_1 + \mathbf{z}\boldsymbol{\theta}_2 + a \geq 0]a\phi(a)\,\text{d}a \\ &= \phi(-\{\theta_0 + \mathbf{x}\boldsymbol{\theta}_1 + \mathbf{z}\boldsymbol{\theta}_2\}) = \phi(\theta_0 + \mathbf{x}\boldsymbol{\theta}_1 + \mathbf{z}\boldsymbol{\theta}_2)\end{aligned} \tag{18.45}$$

where $\phi(\cdot)$ is the standard normal density. Therefore, we can now write

$$y = \gamma + \alpha w + \mathbf{x}\boldsymbol{\beta} + w(\mathbf{x} - \boldsymbol{\psi})\boldsymbol{\delta} + \xi\phi(\theta_0 + \mathbf{x}\boldsymbol{\theta}_1 + \mathbf{z}\boldsymbol{\theta}_2) + e_0 + r \tag{18.46}$$

where $r = wc - \text{E}(wc \mid \mathbf{x}, \mathbf{z})$. The composite error in (18.46) has zero mean conditional on $(\mathbf{x}, \mathbf{z})$, and so we can estimate the parameters using IV methods. One catch is the nonlinear function $\phi(\theta_0 + \mathbf{x}\boldsymbol{\theta}_1 + \mathbf{z}\boldsymbol{\theta}_2)$. We could use nonlinear two stage least squares, as described in Chapter 14. But a two-step approach is easier. First, we gather together the assumptions:

Assumption ATE.4: With y written as in equation (18.25), maintain assumptions (18.29), (18.33), (18.40), (18.42) (with $\boldsymbol{\pi}_2 \neq \mathbf{0}$), and (18.43).

Procedure 18.3 (Under Assumption ATE.4): (a) Estimate θ_0, $\boldsymbol{\theta}_1$, and $\boldsymbol{\theta}_2$ from a probit of w on $(1, \mathbf{x}, \mathbf{z})$. Form the predicted probabilities, $\hat{\Phi}_i$, along with $\hat{\phi}_i = \phi(\hat{\theta}_0 + \mathbf{x}_i\hat{\boldsymbol{\theta}}_1 + \mathbf{z}_i\hat{\boldsymbol{\theta}}_2)$, $i = 1, 2, \ldots, N$.

(b) Estimate the equation

$$y_i = \gamma + \alpha w_i + \mathbf{x}_i\boldsymbol{\beta}_0 + w_i(\mathbf{x}_i - \bar{\mathbf{x}})\boldsymbol{\delta} + \xi\hat{\phi}_i + error_i \tag{18.47}$$

by IV, using instruments $[1, \hat{\Phi}_i, \mathbf{x}_i, \hat{\Phi}_i(\mathbf{x}_i - \bar{\mathbf{x}}), \hat{\phi}_i]$.

The term $\hat{\phi}_i \equiv \phi(\hat{\theta}_0 + \mathbf{x}_i\hat{\boldsymbol{\theta}}_1 + \mathbf{z}_i\hat{\boldsymbol{\theta}}_2)$ in equation (18.47) is another example of a control function, although, unlike in Section 18.3, it is obtained from instrumental variables assumptions, rather than ignorability of treatment assumptions.

Even if $\xi \neq 0$, the effect of adding $\hat{\phi}_i$ to the estimate of α can be small. Consider the version of (18.46) without covariates $\mathbf{x}$ and with a scalar instrument, z:

$$y = \gamma + \alpha w + \xi\phi(\theta_0 + \theta_1 z) + u, \qquad \mathrm{E}(u \mid z) = 0 \tag{18.48}$$

This equation holds, for example, if the instrument z is independent of $(\mathbf{x}, v_0, v_1)$. The simple IV estimator of α is obtained by omitting $\phi(\theta_0 + \theta_1 z)$. If we use z as an IV for w, the simple IV estimator is consistent provided z and $\phi(\theta_0 + \theta_1 z)$ are uncorrelated. (Remember, having an omitted variable that is uncorrelated with the IV does not cause inconsistency of the IV estimator.) Even though $\phi(\theta_0 + \theta_1 z)$ is a function of z, these two variables might have small correlation because z is monotic while $\phi(\theta_0 + \theta_1 z)$ is symmetric about $-(\theta_0/\theta_1)$. This discussion shows that condition (18.37) is not necessary for IV to consistently estimate the ATE: It could be that while $\mathrm{E}[w(e_1 - e_0) \mid \mathbf{x}, \mathbf{z}]$ is not constant, it is roughly uncorrelated with $\mathbf{x}$ (or the functions of $\mathbf{x}$) that appear in (18.38), as well as with the functions of $\mathbf{z}$ used as instruments.

Equation (18.48) illustrates another important point: If $\xi \neq 0$ and the single instrument z is binary, α is not identified. Lack of identification occurs because $\phi(\theta_0 + \theta_1 z)$ takes on only two values, which means it is perfectly linearly related to z. So long as z takes on more than two values, α is generally identified, although the identification is due to the fact that $\phi(\cdot)$ is a different nonlinear function than $\Phi(\cdot)$. With $\mathbf{x}$ in the model $\hat{\phi}_i$ and $\hat{\Phi}_i$ might be collinear, resulting in imprecise IV estimates.

Because r in (18.46) is heteroskedastic, the instruments below (18.47) are not optimal, and so we might simply use $\mathbf{z}_i$ along with interactions of $\mathbf{z}_i$ with $(\mathbf{x}_i - \bar{\mathbf{x}})$ and $\hat{\phi}_i$ as IVs. If $\mathbf{z}_i$ has dimension greater than one, then we can test the overidentifying restrictions as a partial test of instrument selection and the normality assumptions. Of course, we could use the results of Chapter 14 to characterize and estimate the optimal instruments, but this is fairly involved [see, for example, Newey and McFadden (1994)].

A different approach to estimating the ATE when assumption (18.39) fails is to compute the expected value of y given the endogenous treatment and all exogenous variables: $\mathrm{E}(y \mid w, \mathbf{x}, \mathbf{z})$. Finding this expectation requires somewhat more by way of assumptions, but it also has some advantages, which we discuss later. For completeness, we list a set of assumptions:

ASSUMPTION ATE.4′: With y written as in equation (18.25), maintain assumptions (18.29) and (18.33). Furthermore, the treatment can be written as $w = 1[\theta_0 + \mathbf{x}\boldsymbol{\theta}_1 +$

$\mathbf{z}\boldsymbol{\theta}_2 + a \geq 0]$, where (a, e_0, e_1) is independent of $(\mathbf{x}, \mathbf{z})$ with a trivariate normal distribution; in particular, $a \sim \text{Normal}(0, 1)$.

Under Assumption ATE.4′, we can use calculations very similar to those used in Section 17.4.1 to obtain $\mathrm{E}(y \mid w, \mathbf{x}, \mathbf{z})$. In particular,

$$\mathrm{E}(y \mid w, \mathbf{x}, \mathbf{z}) = \gamma + \alpha w + \mathbf{x}\boldsymbol{\beta}_0 + w(\mathbf{x} - \boldsymbol{\psi})\boldsymbol{\delta} + \rho_1 w[\phi(\mathbf{q}\boldsymbol{\theta})/\Phi(\mathbf{q}\boldsymbol{\theta})] + \rho_2(1 - w)\{\phi(\mathbf{q}\boldsymbol{\theta})/[1 - \Phi(\mathbf{q}\boldsymbol{\theta})]\} \tag{18.49}$$

where $\mathbf{q}\boldsymbol{\theta} \equiv \theta_0 + \mathbf{x}\boldsymbol{\theta}_1 + \mathbf{z}\boldsymbol{\theta}_2$ and ρ_1 and ρ_2 are additional parameters. Heckman (1978) used this expectation to obtain two-step estimators of the switching regression model. [See Vella and Verbeek (1999) for a recent discussion of the switching regression model in the context of treatment effects.] Not surprisingly, (18.49) suggests a simple two-step procedure, where the first step is identical to that in Procedure 18.3:

Procedure 18.4 (Under Assumption ATE.4′): (a) Estimate θ_0, $\boldsymbol{\theta}_1$, and $\boldsymbol{\theta}_2$ from a probit of w on $(1, \mathbf{x}, \mathbf{z})$. Form the predicted probabilities, $\hat{\Phi}_i$, along with $\hat{\phi}_i = \phi(\hat{\theta}_0 + \mathbf{x}_i\hat{\boldsymbol{\theta}}_1 + \mathbf{z}_i\hat{\boldsymbol{\theta}}_2)$, $i = 1, 2, \ldots, N$.

(b) Run the OLS regression

$$y_i \text{ on } 1, w_i, \mathbf{x}_i, w_i(\mathbf{x}_i - \bar{\mathbf{x}}), w_i(\hat{\phi}_i/\hat{\Phi}_i), (1 - w_i)[\hat{\phi}_i/(1 - \hat{\Phi}_i)] \tag{18.50}$$

using all of the observations. The coefficient on w_i is a consistent estimator of α, the ATE.

When we restrict attention to the $w_i = 1$ subsample, thereby dropping w_i and $w_i(\mathbf{x}_i - \bar{\mathbf{x}})$, we obtain the sample selection correction from Section 17.4.1; see equation (17.24). (The treatment w_i becomes the sample selection indicator.) But the goal of sample selection corrections is very different from estimating an average treatment effect. For the sample selection problem, the goal is to estimate $\boldsymbol{\beta}_0$, which indexes $\mathrm{E}(y \mid \mathbf{x})$ in the population. By contrast, in estimating an ATE we are interested in the causal effect that w has on y.

It makes sense to check for joint significance of the last two regressors in regression (18.50) as a test of endogeneity of w. Because the coefficients ρ_1 and ρ_2 are zero under H_0, we can use the results from Chapter 6 to justify the usual Wald test (perhaps made robust to heteroskedasticity). If these terms are jointly insignificant at a sufficiently high level, we can justify the usual OLS regression without unobserved heterogeneity. If we reject H_0, we must deal with the generated regressors problem in obtaining a valid standard error for $\hat{\alpha}$.

Technically, Procedure 18.3 is more robust than Procedure 18.4 because the former does not require a trivariate normality assumption. Linear conditional expectations, along with the assumption that w given $(\mathbf{x}, \mathbf{z})$ follows a probit, suffice. In addition, Procedure 18.3 allows us to separate the issues of endogeneity of w and nonconstant treatment effect: if we ignore the estimation error involved with demeaning $\mathbf{x}_i$ in the interaction term—which generally seems reasonable—then a standard t-test (perhaps made robut to heteroskedasticity) for H_0: $\xi = 0$ is valid for testing the presence of $w(e_1 - e_0)$, even when w is endogenous.

Practically, the extra assumption in Procedure 18.4 is that e_0 is independent of $(\mathbf{x}, \mathbf{z})$ with a normal distribution. We may be willing to make this assumption, especially if the estimates from Procedure 18.3 are too imprecise to be useful. The efficiency issue is a difficult one because of the two-step estimation involved, but, intuitively, Procedure 18.4 is likely to be more efficient because it is based on $\mathrm{E}(y \mid w, \mathbf{x}, \mathbf{z})$. Procedure 18.3 involves replacing the unobserved composite error with its expectation conditional only on $(\mathbf{x}, \mathbf{z})$. In at least one case, Procedure 18.4 gives results when Procedure 18.3 cannot: when $\mathbf{x}$ is not in the equation and there is a single binary instrument.

Under a variant of Assumption ATE.3′, we can consistently estimate ATE_1 by IV. As before, we express y as in equation (18.25). First, we show how to consistently estimate $ATE_1(\mathbf{x})$, which can be written as

$$ATE_1(\mathbf{x}) = \mathrm{E}(y_1 - y_0 \mid \mathbf{x}, w = 1) = (\mu_1 - \mu_0) + \mathrm{E}(v_1 - v_0 \mid \mathbf{x}, w = 1)$$

The following assumption identifies $ATE_1(\mathbf{x})$:

Assumption ATE.3″: (a) With y expressed as in equation (18.25), the first part of assumption (18.29) holds, that is, $\mathrm{E}(v_0 \mid \mathbf{x}, \mathbf{z}) = \mathrm{E}(v_0 \mid \mathbf{x})$; (b) $\mathrm{E}(v_1 - v_0 \mid \mathbf{x}, \mathbf{z}, w = 1) = \mathrm{E}(v_1 - v_0 \mid \mathbf{x}, w = 1)$; and (c) Assumption ATE.2′c holds.

We discussed part a of this assumption earlier, as it also appears in Assumption ATE.3′. It can be violated if agents change their behavior based on $\mathbf{z}$. Part b deserves some discussion. Recall that $v_1 - v_0$ is the person-specific gain from participation or treatment. Assumption ATE.3″ requires that for those in the treatment group, the gain is not predictable given $\mathbf{z}$, once $\mathbf{x}$ is controlled for. Heckman (1997) discusses Angrist's (1990) draft lottery example, where z (a scalar) is draft lottery number. Men who had a large z were virtually certain to escape the draft. But some men with large draft numbers chose to serve anyway. Even with good controls in $\mathbf{x}$, it seems plausible that, for those who chose to serve, a higher z is associated with a higher gain to military service. In other words, for those who chose to serve, $v_1 - v_0$ and z are positively correlated, even after controlling for $\mathbf{x}$. This argument directly applies to estimation of ATE_1; the effect on estimation of ATE is less clear.

Assumption ATE.3″b is plausible when z is a binary indicator for eligibility in a program, which is randomly determined and does not induce changes in behavior other than whether or not to participate.

To see how Assumption ATE.3″ identifies $ATE_1(\mathbf{x})$, rewrite equation (18.25) as

$$\begin{aligned} y &= \mu_0 + g_0(\mathbf{x}) + w[(\mu_1 - \mu_0) + \mathrm{E}(v_1 - v_0 \mid \mathbf{x}, w = 1)] \\ &\quad + w[(v_1 - v_0) - \mathrm{E}(v_1 - v_0 \mid \mathbf{x}, w = 1)] + e_0 \\ &= \mu_0 + g_0(\mathbf{x}) + w \cdot ATE_1(\mathbf{x}) + a + e_0 \end{aligned} \tag{18.51}$$

where $a \equiv w[(v_1 - v_0) - \mathrm{E}(v_1 - v_0 \mid \mathbf{x}, w = 1)]$ and e_0 is defined in equation (18.31). Under Assumption ATE.3″a, $\mathrm{E}(e_0 \mid \mathbf{x}, \mathbf{z}) = 0$. The hard part is dealing with the term a. When $w = 0$, $a = 0$. Therefore, to show that $\mathrm{E}(a \mid \mathbf{x}, \mathbf{z}) = 0$, it suffices to show that $\mathrm{E}(a \mid \mathbf{x}, \mathbf{z}, w = 1) = 0$. [Remember, $\mathrm{E}(a \mid \mathbf{x}, \mathbf{z}) = \mathrm{P}(w = 0) \cdot \mathrm{E}(a \mid \mathbf{x}, \mathbf{z}, w = 0) + \mathrm{P}(w = 1) \cdot \mathrm{E}(a \mid \mathbf{x}, \mathbf{z}, w = 1)$.] But this result follows under Assumption ATE.3″b:

$$\mathrm{E}(a \mid \mathbf{x}, \mathbf{z}, w = 1) = \mathrm{E}(v_1 - v_0 \mid \mathbf{x}, \mathbf{z}, w = 1) - \mathrm{E}(v_1 - v_0 \mid \mathbf{x}, w = 1) = 0$$

Now, letting $r \equiv a + e_0$ and assuming that $g_0(\mathbf{x}) = \eta_0 + \mathbf{h}(\mathbf{x})\boldsymbol{\beta}_0$ and $ATE_1(\mathbf{x}) = \tau + \mathbf{f}(\mathbf{x})\boldsymbol{\delta}$ for some row vector of functions $\mathbf{h}(\mathbf{x})$ and $\mathbf{f}(\mathbf{x})$, we can write

$$y = \gamma_0 + \mathbf{h}_0(\mathbf{x})\boldsymbol{\beta}_0 + \tau w + [w \cdot \mathbf{f}(\mathbf{x})]\boldsymbol{\delta} + r, \qquad \mathrm{E}(r \mid \mathbf{x}, \mathbf{z}) = 0$$

All the parameters of this equation can be consistently estimated by IV, using any functions of $(\mathbf{x}, \mathbf{z})$ as IVs. [These would include include 1, $\mathbf{h}_0(\mathbf{x})$, $G(\mathbf{x}, \mathbf{z}; \hat{\gamma})$—the fitted treatment probabilities—and $G(\mathbf{x}, \mathbf{z}; \hat{\gamma}) \cdot \mathbf{f}(\mathbf{x})$.] The average treatment effect on the treated for any $\mathbf{x}$ is estimated as $\hat{\tau} + \mathbf{f}(\mathbf{x})\hat{\boldsymbol{\delta}}$. Averaging over the observations with $w_i = 1$ gives a consistent estimator of ATE_1.

18.4.2 Estimating the Local Average Treatment Effect by IV

We now discuss estimation of an evaluation parameter introduced by Imbens and Angrist (1994), the local average treatment effect (LATE), in the simplest possible setting. This requires a slightly more complicated notation. (More general cases require even more complicated notation, as in AIR.) As before, we let w be the observed treatment indicator (taking on zero or one), and let the counterfactual outcomes be y_1 with treatment and y_0 without treatment. The observed outcome y can be written as in equation (18.3).

To define $LATE$, we need to have an instrumental variable, z. In the simplest case z is a binary variable, and we focus attention on that case here. For each unit i in a random draw from the population, z_i is zero or one. Associated with the two possible outcomes on z are counterfactual treatments, w_0 and w_1. These are the treatment statuses we would observe if $z = 0$ and $z = 1$, respectively. For each unit, we observe only one of these. For example, z can denote whether a person is eligible for a particular program, while w denotes actual participation in the program.

Write the observed treatment status as

$$w = (1 - z)w_0 + zw_1 = w_0 + z(w_1 - w_0) \tag{18.52}$$

When we plug this equation into $y = y_0 + w(y_1 - y_0)$ we get

$$y = y_0 + w_0(y_1 - y_0) + z(w_1 - w_0)(y_1 - y_0)$$

A key assumption is

$$z \text{ is independent of } (y_0, y_1, w_0, w_1) \tag{18.53}$$

Under assumption (18.53), all expectations involving functions of (y_0, y_1, w_0, w_1), conditional on z, do not depend on z. Therefore,

$$\mathrm{E}(y \mid z = 1) = \mathrm{E}(y_0) + \mathrm{E}[w_0(y_1 - y_0)] + \mathrm{E}[(w_1 - w_0)(y_1 - y_0)]$$

and

$$\mathrm{E}(y \mid z = 0) = \mathrm{E}(y_0) + \mathrm{E}[w_0(y_1 - y_0)]$$

Subtracting the second equation from the first gives

$$\mathrm{E}(y \mid z = 1) - \mathrm{E}(y \mid z = 0) = \mathrm{E}[(w_1 - w_0)(y_1 - y_0)] \tag{18.54}$$

which can be written [see equation (2.49)] as

$$\begin{aligned} 1 \cdot \mathrm{E}&(y_1 - y_0 \mid w_1 - w_0 = 1)\mathrm{P}(w_1 - w_0 = 1) \\ &+ (-1)\mathrm{E}(y_1 - y_0 \mid w_1 - w_0 = -1)\mathrm{P}(w_1 - w_0 = -1) \\ &+ 0 \cdot \mathrm{E}(y_1 - y_0 \mid w_1 - w_0 = 0)\mathrm{P}(w_1 - w_0 = 0) \\ = {}& \mathrm{E}(y_1 - y_0 \mid w_1 - w_0 = 1)\mathrm{P}(w_1 - w_0 = 1) \\ &- \mathrm{E}(y_1 - y_0 \mid w_1 - w_0 = -1)\mathrm{P}(w_1 - w_0 = -1) \end{aligned}$$

To get further, we introduce another important assumption, called *monotonicity* by Imbens and Angrist:

$$w_1 \geq w_0 \tag{18.55}$$

In other words, we are ruling out $w_1 = 0$ and $w_0 = 1$. This assumption has a simple interpretation when z is a dummy variable representing assignment to the treatment group: anyone in the population who would be in the treatment group in the absence of assignment (or eligibility) would be in the treatment group if assigned to the treatment group. Units of the population who do not satisfy monotonicity are called *defiers*. In many applications, this assumption seems very reasonable. For example, if z denotes randomly assigned eligibility in a job training program, assumption (18.55) simply requires that people who would participate without being eligible would also participate if eligible.

Under assumption (18.55), $\mathrm{P}(w_1 - w_0 = -1) = 0$, so assumptions (18.53) and (18.55) imply

$$\mathrm{E}(y \mid z = 1) - \mathrm{E}(y \mid z = 0) = \mathrm{E}(y_1 - y_0 \mid w_1 - w_0 = 1)\mathrm{P}(w_1 - w_0 = 1) \tag{18.56}$$

In this setup, Imbens and Angrist (1994) define $LATE$ to be

$$LATE = \mathrm{E}(y_1 - y_0 \mid w_1 - w_0 = 1) \tag{18.57}$$

Because $w_1 - w_0 = 1$ is equivalent to $w_1 = 1$, $w_0 = 0$, $LATE$ has the following interpretation: it is the average treatment effect for those who would be induced to participate by changing z from zero to one. There are two things about $LATE$ that make it different from the other treatment parameters. First, it depends on the instrument, z. If we use a different instrument, then $LATE$ generally changes. The parameters ATE and ATE_1 are defined without reference to an IV, but only with reference to a population. Second, because we cannot observe both w_1 and w_0, we cannot identify the subpopulation with $w_1 - w_0 = 1$. By contrast, ATE averages over the entire population, while ATE_1 is the average for those who are actually treated.

Example 18.5 (LATE for Attending a Catholic High School): Suppose that y is a standardized test score, w is an indicator for attending a Catholic high school, and z is an indicator for whether the student is Catholic. Then, generally, $LATE$ is the mean effect on test scores for those individuals who choose a Catholic high school because they are Catholic. Evans and Schwab (1995) use a high school graduation indicator for y, and they estimate a probit model with an endogenous binary explanatory variable, as described in Section 15.7.3. Under the probit assumptions, it is possible to estimate ATE, whereas the simple IV estimator identifies $LATE$ under weaker assumptions.

Because $\mathrm{E}(y \mid z = 1)$ and $\mathrm{E}(y \mid z = 0)$ are easily estimated using a random sample, $LATE$ is identified if $\mathrm{P}(w_1 - w_0 = 1)$ is estimable *and* nonzero. Importantly, from the monotonicity assumption, $w_1 - w_0$ is a binary variable because $\mathrm{P}(w_1 - w_0 = -1) = 0$. Therefore,

$$\begin{aligned}\mathrm{P}(w_1 - w_0 = 1) &= \mathrm{E}(w_1 - w_0) = \mathrm{E}(w_1) - \mathrm{E}(w_0) = \mathrm{E}(w \mid z = 1) - \mathrm{E}(w \mid z = 0) \\ &= \mathrm{P}(w = 1 \mid z = 1) - \mathrm{P}(w = 1 \mid z = 0)\end{aligned}$$

where the second-to-last equality follows from equations (18.52) and (18.53). Each conditional probability can be consistently estimated given a random sample on (w, z). Therefore, the final assumption is

$$P(w = 1 \mid z = 1) \neq P(w = 1 \mid z = 0) \tag{18.58}$$

To summarize, under assumptions (18.53), (18.55), and (18.58),

$$LATE = [E(y \mid z = 1) - E(y \mid z = 0)]/[P(w = 1 \mid z = 1) - P(w = 1 \mid z = 0)] \tag{18.59}$$

Therefore, a consistent estimator is $\widehat{LATE} = (\bar{y}_1 - \bar{y}_0)/(\bar{w}_1 - \bar{w}_0)$, where $\bar{y}_1$ is the sample average of y_i over that part of the sample where $z_i = 1$ and $\bar{y}_0$ is the sample average over $z_i = 0$, and similarly for $\bar{w}_1$ and $\bar{w}_0$ (which are sample proportions). From Problem 5.13b, we know that $\widehat{LATE}$ is identical to the IV estimator of α in the simple equation $y = \delta_0 + \alpha w + error$, where z is the IV for w.

Our conclusion is that, in the simple case of a binary instrument for the binary treatment, the usual IV estimator consistently estimates $LATE$ under weak assumptions. See Angrist, Imbens, and Rubin (1996) and the discussants' comments for much more.

18.5 Further Issues

As we have seen in Sections 18.3 and 18.4, under certain assumptions, OLS or IV can be used to estimate average treatment effects. Therefore, at least in some cases, problems such as attrition or other forms of sample selection can be easily handled using the methods in Chapter 17. For example, in equation (18.34) under assumption (18.35), it is reasonable to assume that the assumptions of Procedure 17.2 hold, with the straightforward extension that the interaction between w_i (which plays the role of y_{i2}) and $(\mathbf{x}_i - \bar{\mathbf{x}})$ is added, along with the appropriate IVs. If the problem is attrition, we need some exogenous elements that affect attrition but do not appear in $\mathbf{x}$ or $\mathbf{z}$.

Other situations may require special attention, and we now briefly discuss some of these.

18.5.1 Special Considerations for Binary and Corner Solution Responses

The definitions of ATE and ATE_1, as well as $LATE$, are valid for any kind of response variable. ATE is simply $E(y_1) - E(y_0)$, and for this to be well defined we only need to assume that the expected values exist. If y_0 and y_1 are binary—such as employment indicators—the expected values are probabilities of success. If y_0 and y_1 are corner solution outcomes—such as labor supply—ATE and ATE_1 estimate the effect of treatment on the so-called unconditional expectation rather than, say,

$E(y_1 - y_0 \mid y_0 > 0)$. Still, ATE and ATE_1 are often of interest for corner solution outcomes.

If the average treatment effects as we defined them in Section 18.2 are still of interest, why do we need to consider alternative methods for estimating treatment effects? The answer is that some of the assumptions we have discussed are unrealistic for discrete or corner solution outcomes. For example, to arrive at equation (18.15), we assumed that $E(y_g \mid \mathbf{x})$ is linear in some functions of $\mathbf{x}$. Though these assumptions can be relaxed, the computation of valid standard errors is no longer straightforward because a linear regression no longer generally estimates ATE. [Expression (18.7) is general and does not impose any functional forms, and so it can be used as the basis for estimating ATE. We would simply estimate $E(y \mid \mathbf{x}, w = 1)$ and $E(y \mid \mathbf{x}, w = 0)$ in a way that is consistent with the features of y.]

Under ignorability of treatment, the propensity score approach is attractive because it requires no modeling of expectations involving y_0 or y_1. Only the propensity score needs to be modeled, and this is always a binary response probability.

When we cannot assume ignorability of treatment and must resort to IV methods, allowing for discrete and corner solution responses is theoretically harder. As we discussed in Section 18.4.1, conditions such as equation (18.33) cannot be literally true for binary and Tobit-like responses, and this condition appears in all of the assumptions for IV estimation. It is not easy to relax this assumption because if, say, y_g is a corner solution outcome, a reasonable model for $E(v_1 - v_0 \mid \mathbf{x})$ is not obvious.

Of course, it could be that, even if the assumptions in Section 18.4 cannot be exactly true, the IV methods may nevertheless produce reasonable estimates of ATE and ATE_1. Angrist's (1991) simulation evidence is compelling for binary responses, but he only studies the case without covariates.

As an alternative to the various treatment effect estimators covered in this chapter, we can use probit and Tobit models with a binary endogenous explanatory variable. The maximum likelihood estimator described in Section 15.7.3 requires a strong set of assumptions, but it delivers estimates of the exact average treatment effect, conditional on the exogenous variables, if the probit assumptions hold. Similarly, a Tobit model with a binary endogenous variable can be estimated by maximum likelihood (see Problem 16.6); again, estimates of ATE can be obtained directly.

18.5.2 Panel Data

The availability of panel data allows us to consistently estimate treatment effects without assuming ignorability of treatment and without an instrumental variable, provided the treatment varies over time and is uncorrelated with time-varying unobservables that affect the response.

If the treatment is assumed to have the same effect for each unit and if the effect is constant over time, fixed effects or first-differencing methods can be used, as described in Chapter 10. This approach works well when the treatment and control groups are designated based on time-constant variables and when treatment status is not constant across time. Of course, we must observe the responses and other controls for each cross section unit in at least two different time periods. A more complicated model allows the treatment effect to interact with observable variables and unobserved heterogeneity. For example, consider the model

$$y_{it} = \mathbf{x}_{it}\boldsymbol{\beta} + \alpha_1 w_{it} + c_i + w_{it}h_i + u_{it}$$

where w_{it} is a binary treatment indicator of some training program, y_{it} is the response variable, and c_i and h_i are unobserved heterogeneity. This is a special case of the model studied in Section 11.2.2. The average treatment effect is $\alpha_1 + \mathrm{E}(h_i)$, and we can use the methods of Section 11.2.2 to estimate α_1 and $\mathrm{E}(h_i)$.

The problem of attrition can be handled as in Section 17.7, provided the treatment effect has an additive form. If attrition is determined solely by whether the participant was not selected for the program, then no adjustments are needed if w_{it} is orthogonal to the idiosyncratic error, u_{it}: this is just attrition on the basis of exogenous explanatory variables.

18.5.3 Nonbinary Treatments

So far, we have restricted attention to the case where w is a binary variable. But we can also estimate average treatment effects when w takes on more than two values. The definitions of ATE, ATE_1, and $LATE$ are more complicated in this case because the counterfactual is more complicated; see Angrist and Imbens (1995) and Heckman (1997). Here, we focus on a **random coefficient model** for the observed outcome, as in Garen (1984), Heckman and Vytlacil (1998), and Wooldridge (1997b, 1999c). The average treatment effect is easy to define in this context, as it is just an average partial effect.

As in the case of binary treatment, two approaches can be used to identify ATE: we can assume ignorability of treatment, conditional on a set of covariates, or we can use an instrumental variables approach. In either case, the model is the same:

$$\mathrm{E}(y \mid w, \mathbf{c}) = a + bw \tag{18.60}$$

where $\mathbf{c} = (a, b)$ and a and b may both depend on observable covariates as well as unobserved heterogeneity. A more traditional approach would introduce observables and unobservables into the equation separately in a parametric fashion—usually, linear in a set of parameters—but this step is unnecessary when we are interested in estimating $\beta \equiv \mathrm{E}(b)$, which is the average partial effect of w on $\mathrm{E}(y \mid w, \mathbf{c})$.

It is important to see that, unlike in the binary treatment case, equation (18.60) imposes a functional form assumption. This is not as restrictive as it might seem, because a and b are allowed to depend on individual-specific observables and unobservables. Nevertheless, as we know, linear models can have drawbacks for binary and corner solution responses (unless w is binary).

When w is binary, equation (18.60) encompasses the counterfactual setup in Section 18.2, which we analyzed in Sections 18.3 and 18.4. Equation (18.3) shows this result immediately, where we take $a = y_0$ and $b = y_1 - y_0$.

We now establish identification of β under ignorability conditions. The assumptions are collected together as follows:

ASSUMPTION ATE.5: (a) Equation (18.60) holds. For a set of covariates $\mathbf{x}$, the following redundancy assumptions hold: (b) $\mathrm{E}(y \mid w, \mathbf{c}, \mathbf{x}) = \mathrm{E}(y \mid w, \mathbf{c})$; and (c) Conditional on $\mathbf{x}$, $\mathbf{c}$ is redundant in the first two conditional moments of w: $\mathrm{E}(w \mid \mathbf{x}, \mathbf{c}) = \mathrm{E}(w \mid \mathbf{x})$ and $\mathrm{Var}(w \mid \mathbf{x}, \mathbf{c}) = \mathrm{Var}(w \mid \mathbf{x})$.

Given the functional form assumption (18.60), Assumption ATE.5b is not very controversial because a and b can depend in an arbitrary way on $\mathbf{x}$. In effect, a and b already capture any dependence of $\mathrm{E}(y \mid w, \mathbf{c})$ on $\mathbf{x}$. Assumption ATE.5c is much more restrictive, but it is the analogue of the ignorability-of-treatment Assumption ATE.1′. In fact, when w is binary, Assumption ATE.1′ implies Assumption ATE.5c. For general w, Assumption ATE.5c is slightly less restrictive than assuming $(w, \mathbf{c})$ are independent given $\mathbf{x}$. The following is from Wooldridge (1999c, Proposition 3.1):

PROPOSITION 18.6: Under Assumption ATE.5, assume, in addition, that $\mathrm{Var}(w \mid \mathbf{x}) > 0$ for all $\mathbf{x}$ in the relevant population. Then

$$\beta = \mathrm{E}[\mathrm{Cov}(w, y \mid \mathbf{x}) / \mathrm{Var}(w \mid \mathbf{x})] \tag{18.61}$$

Because $\mathrm{Var}(w \mid \mathbf{x})$ and $\mathrm{Cov}(w, y \mid \mathbf{x})$ can be estimated generally, equation (18.61) shows that β is identified. If $\hat{m}(\cdot)$ and $\hat{h}(\cdot)$ are consistent estimators of $\mathrm{E}(w \mid \mathbf{x})$ and $\mathrm{Var}(w \mid \mathbf{x})$, respectively, a consistent estimator of β, under fairly weak assumptions, is $N^{-1} \sum_{i=1}^{N} [w_i - \hat{m}(\mathbf{x}_i)] y_i / \hat{h}(\mathbf{x}_i)$; this is the extension of equation (18.21) to the case of nonbinary treatments.

Estimating $m(\cdot)$ and $h(\cdot)$ is easily done using flexible parametric models that should reflect the nature of w. When w is binary, we simply estimate the propensity score. When w is a roughly continuous variable over a broad range, $\mathrm{E}(w \mid \mathbf{x})$ linear in functions of $\mathbf{x}$ and $\text{Var}(w \mid \mathbf{x})$ constant might be reasonable, in which case, as shown in Wooldridge (1999c), a "kitchen sink" regression of y on w and functions of $\mathbf{x}$ can consistently estimate β. Wooldridge (1999c) discusses additional examples, including when w is a count variable or a fractional variable (both of which we discuss in Chapter 19), and contains an example.

As a computational device, it is useful to see that consistent estimators of β can be computed using an instrumental variables approach. As shown in Wooldridge (1999c), under Assumption ATE.5 we can write

$$y = \beta w + \mathbf{g}(\mathbf{x})\boldsymbol{\theta} + v \tag{18.62}$$

where $\mathbf{g}(\cdot)$ is *any* vector function of $\mathbf{x}$ and $\text{E}[\mathbf{g}(\mathbf{x})'v] = \mathbf{0}$. Typically, we would include levels, squares, and cross products, or logarithms, as elements of $\mathbf{g}(\cdot)$. Adding $\mathbf{g}(\mathbf{x})$ is intended to effectively reduce the error variance. Further, if we define $r = [w - m(\mathbf{x})]/h(\mathbf{x})$, it can be shown that $\text{E}(rv) = 0$. Because r and w are highly correlated, we can use $[r, \mathbf{g}(\mathbf{x})]$ as IVs in equation (18.62). In practice, we replace each unknown r_i with $\hat{r}_i = [w_i - \hat{m}(\mathbf{x}_i)]/\hat{h}(\mathbf{x}_i)$, and use $(\hat{r}_i, \mathbf{g}_i)$ as the IVs for $(w_i, \mathbf{g}_i)$. This estimator is consistent and $\sqrt{N}$-asymptotically normal. Unfortunately, the sufficient conditions for ignoring estimation of the IVs in the first stage—see Section 6.1.2—are not always met in this application.

An alternative approach assumes that w is ignorable in $\text{E}(a \mid \mathbf{x}, w)$ and $\text{E}(b \mid \mathbf{x}, w)$. Under additional linearity assumptions, this leads directly to equation (18.15), regardless of the nature of w.

The previous methods assume some kind of ignorability of treatment. The IV approach also begins with equation (18.60). As in the binary treatment case, we separate the covariates ($\mathbf{x}$) and the IVs ($\mathbf{z}$). We assume both are redundant in equation (18.60):

$$\text{E}(y \mid w, \mathbf{c}, \mathbf{x}, \mathbf{z}) = \text{E}(y \mid w, \mathbf{c}) \tag{18.63}$$

Again, this assumption is noncontroversial once we specify the functional form in equation (18.60). Assumption (18.63) holds trivially in the counterfactual framework with binary treatment.

The difference between $\mathbf{x}$ and $\mathbf{z}$ is that a and b may have conditional means that depend on $\mathbf{x}$, but not on $\mathbf{z}$. For example, if w is a measure of class attendance, $\mathbf{x}$ might contain measures of student ability and motivation. By contrast, we assume $\mathbf{z}$ is redundant for explaining a and b, given $\mathbf{x}$. In the class attendance example, $\mathbf{z}$ might be indicators for different living situations or distances from residence to lecture halls. In effect, the distinction between $\mathbf{x}$ and $\mathbf{z}$ is the kind of distinction we make in structural models, where some "exogenous" variables ($\mathbf{x}$) are allowed to appear in the structural equation and others ($\mathbf{z}$) are not. Mathematically, we have

$$\mathrm{E}(a \mid \mathbf{x}, \mathbf{z}) = \mathrm{E}(a \mid \mathbf{x}), \qquad \mathrm{E}(b \mid \mathbf{x}, \mathbf{z}) = \mathrm{E}(b \mid \mathbf{x}). \tag{18.64}$$

Assumption (18.64) is completely analogous to assumption (18.29). For simplicity, we also assume the expectations are linear in $\mathbf{x}$:

$$\mathrm{E}(a \mid \mathbf{x}) = \gamma_0 + \mathbf{x}\boldsymbol{\gamma}, \qquad \mathrm{E}(b \mid \mathbf{x}) = \delta_0 + \mathbf{x}\boldsymbol{\delta} \tag{18.65}$$

Then we can write

$$y = \eta_0 + \mathbf{x}\boldsymbol{\gamma} + \beta w + w(\mathbf{x} - \boldsymbol{\psi})\boldsymbol{\delta} + u + w \cdot v + e \tag{18.66}$$

where $\boldsymbol{\psi} = \mathrm{E}(\mathbf{x})$, $u = a - \mathrm{E}(a \mid \mathbf{x}, \mathbf{z})$, $v = b - \mathrm{E}(b \mid \mathbf{x}, \mathbf{z})$, e is the error implied by equation (18.60), and so $\mathrm{E}(e \mid w, \mathbf{c}, \mathbf{x}, \mathbf{z}) = 0$. This equation is basically the same as equation (18.34), except that now w need not be binary. To apply IV to equation (18.66), it suffices that the composite error, $u + w \cdot v + e$, has a constant mean given $(\mathbf{x}, \mathbf{z})$. But $\mathrm{E}(u + e \mid \mathbf{x}, \mathbf{z}) = 0$, and so it suffices to assume

$$\mathrm{E}(w \cdot v \mid \mathbf{x}, \mathbf{z}) = \mathrm{E}(w \cdot v) \tag{18.67}$$

which is the same as $\mathrm{Cov}(w, v \mid \mathbf{x}, \mathbf{z}) = \mathrm{Cov}(w, v)$ because $\mathrm{E}(v \mid \mathbf{x}, \mathbf{z}) = 0$. When assumption (18.67) holds along with conditions (18.60), (18.63), (18.64), and (18.65) and an appropriate rank condition—essentially, w is partially correlated with $\mathbf{z}$—2SLS estimation of equation (18.66) consistently estimates all parameters except the intercept. The IVs would be $(1, \mathbf{x}, \mathbf{z}, z_1\mathbf{x}, \ldots, z_L\mathbf{x})$, or we could use $\hat{\mathrm{E}}(w \mid \mathbf{x}, \mathbf{z})$ and $\hat{\mathrm{E}}(w \mid \mathbf{x}, \mathbf{z}) \cdot \mathbf{x}$ as IVs for $[w, w(\mathbf{x} - \boldsymbol{\psi})]$, where $\hat{\mathrm{E}}(w \mid \mathbf{x}, \mathbf{z})$ is an estimate of $\mathrm{E}(w \mid \mathbf{x}, \mathbf{z})$. As before, in practice $\boldsymbol{\psi}$ would be replaced with $\bar{\mathbf{x}}$. The 2SLS estimator is $\sqrt{N}$-consistent and asymptotically normal. Generally, the error in equation (18.66) is heteroskedastic.

Condition (18.67) is the same one we used in the binary treatment case to justify the usual IV estimator. As we discussed in Section 18.4.1, condition (18.67) does not hold when $\mathrm{P}(w = 1 \mid \mathbf{x}, \mathbf{z})$ satisfies logit or probit binary response models. If w is a continuous treatment, condition (18.67) is more reasonable. For example, if $\mathrm{E}(w \mid \mathbf{x}, \mathbf{z}, v)$ is additive in v, then condition (18.67) holds when $\mathrm{Var}(v \mid \mathbf{x}, \mathbf{z})$ is constant, in which case $\mathrm{Cov}(w, v \mid \mathbf{x}, \mathbf{z}) = \sigma_v^2$. See Wooldridge (1997b, 2000f) for further discussion. Wooldridge (2000f) also covers more general cases when condition (18.67) is not true and the treatment is not binary.

Heckman and Vytlacil (1998) use similar assumptions in a general random coefficient model to arrive at a related estimation method. In their simplest approach,

Heckman and Vytlacil suggest a two-step estimator, where $\mathrm{E}(w \mid \mathbf{x}, \mathbf{z})$ is estimated using a linear model in the first stage and the fitted values are used in a second-stage regression. The preceding analysis shows that a linear functional form for $\mathrm{E}(w \mid \mathbf{x}, \mathbf{z})$ is not needed for the IV estimator to be consistent, although condition (18.67) generally is.

18.5.4 Multiple Treatments

Sometimes the treatment variable is not simply a scalar. For example, for the population of working high school graduates, w_1 could be credit hours at two-year colleges and w_2 credit hours at four-year colleges. If we make ignorability assumptions of the kind in Section 18.3.1, equation (18.15) extends in a natural way: each treatment variable appears by itself and interacted with the (demeaned) covariates. This approach does not put any restrictions on the nature of the treatments. Alternatively, as in Wooldridge (1999c), Assumption 18.5 extends to a vector $\mathbf{w}$, which leads to an extension of condition (18.60) for multiple treatments.

Wooldridge (2000f) shows how the IV methods in Section 18.4.1 extend easily to multiple treatments, binary or otherwise. For multiple binary treatments, a reduced-form probit is estimated for each treatment, and then terms $w_{ij}(\mathbf{x}_i - \bar{\mathbf{x}})$ and $\hat{\phi}_{ij}$ for each treatment j are added to equation (18.47). See Wooldridge (2000f) for further discussion. An approach based on finding $\mathrm{E}(y \mid w_1, \ldots, w_M, \mathbf{x}, \mathbf{z})$, for M treatments, is difficult but perhaps tractable in some cases.

Problems

18.1. Consider the difference-in-means estimator, $\bar{d} = \bar{y}_1 - \bar{y}_0$, where $\bar{y}_g$ is the sample average of the y_i with $w_i = g$, $g = 0, 1$.

a. Show that, as an estimator of ATE_1, the bias in $\bar{y}_1 - \bar{y}_0$ is $\mathrm{E}(y_0 \mid w = 1) - \mathrm{E}(y_0 \mid w = 0)$.

b. Let y_0 be the earnings someone would earn in the absence of job training, and let $w = 1$ denote the job training indicator. Explain the meaning of $\mathrm{E}(y_0 \mid w = 1) < \mathrm{E}(y_0 \mid w = 0)$. Intuitively, does it make sense that $\mathrm{E}(\bar{d}) < ATE_1$?

18.2. Show that $ATE_1(\mathbf{x})$ is identified under Assumption ATE.1′a; Assumption ATE.1′b is not needed.

18.3. Using the data in JTRAIN2.RAW, repeat the analysis in Example 18.2, using *unem78* as the response variable. For comparison, use the same $\mathbf{x}$ as in Example 18.2.

Compare the estimates from regressions (18.23) and (18.24), along with the estimate of ATE from linear regression *unem78* on 1, *train*, $\mathbf{x}$.

18.4. Carefully derive equation (18.45).

18.5. Use the data in JTRAIN2.RAW for this question.

a. As in Example 18.2, run a probit of *train* on 1, $\mathbf{x}$, where $\mathbf{x}$ contains the covariates from Example 18.2. Obtain the probit fitted values, say $\hat{\Phi}_i$.

b. Estimate the equation $re78_i = \gamma_0 + \alpha\, train_i + \mathbf{x}_i\gamma + u_i$ by IV, using instruments $(1, \hat{\Phi}_i, \mathbf{x}_i)$. Comment on the estimate of α and its standard error.

c. Regress $\hat{\Phi}_i$ on $\mathbf{x}_i$ to obtain the R-squared. What do you make of this result?

d. Does the nonlinearity of the probit model for *train* allow us to estimate α when we do not have an additional instrument? Explain.

18.6. In Procedure 18.2, explain why it is better to estimate equation (18.36) by IV rather than to run the OLS regression y_i on 1, $\hat{G}_i$, $\mathbf{x}_i$, $\hat{G}_i(\mathbf{x}_i - \bar{\mathbf{x}})$, $i = 1, \dots, N$.

18.7. Use the data in JTRAIN2.RAW for this question.

a. In the ignorability setup of Section 18.5.3, let $w = mostrn$, the number of months spent in job training. Assume that $\mathrm{E}(w \mid \mathbf{x}) = \exp(\gamma_0 + \mathbf{x}\gamma)$, where $\mathbf{x}$ contains the same covariates as in Example 18.2. Estimate the parameters by nonlinear least squares, and let $\hat{m}_i$ be the fitted values. Which elements of $\mathbf{x}$ are significant? (You may use the usual NLS standard errors.)

b. Suppose that $\mathrm{Var}(w \mid \mathbf{x}) = h(\mathbf{x}) = \delta_0 + \delta_1 \mathrm{E}(w \mid \mathbf{x}) + \delta_2 [\mathrm{E}(w \mid \mathbf{x})]^2$. Use the estimates from part a to estimate the δ_j. (Hint: Regress the squared NLS residuals on a quadratic in the NLS fitted values.) Are any of $\hat{h}_i$—the estimated variances—negative?

c. Form $\hat{r}_i = (w_i - \hat{m}_i)/\hat{h}_i$. Estimate equation (18.62) using $\hat{r}_i$ as an IV for w_i, where $\mathbf{g}(\mathbf{x}) = (1, \mathbf{x})$ and $y = re78$. Compare $\hat{\beta}$ with the OLS estimate of β.

18.8. In the IV setup of Section 18.5.3, suppose that $b = \beta$, and therefore we can write

$$y = a + \beta w + e, \qquad \mathrm{E}(e \mid a, \mathbf{x}, \mathbf{z}) = 0$$

Assume that conditions (18.64) and (18.65) hold for a.

a. Suppose w is a corner solution outcome, such as hours spent in a job training program. If $\mathbf{z}$ is used as IVs for w in $y = \gamma_0 + \beta w + \mathbf{x}\gamma + r$, what is the identification condition?

b. If w given $(\mathbf{x}, \mathbf{z})$ follows a standard Tobit model, propose an IV estimator that uses the Tobit fitted values for w.

c. If $\text{Var}(e \mid a, \mathbf{x}, \mathbf{z}) = \sigma_e^2$ and $\text{Var}(a \mid \mathbf{x}, \mathbf{z}) = \sigma_a^2$, argue that the IV estimator from part b is asymptotically efficient.

d. What is an alternative to IV estimation that would use the Tobit fitted values for w? Which method do you prefer?

e. If $b \neq \beta$, but assumptions (18.64) and (18.65) hold, how would you estimate β?

18.9. Consider the IV approach in Section 18.5.3, under assumptions (18.60), (18.63), (18.64), and (18.65). In place of assumption (18.67), assume that $\text{E}(w \mid \mathbf{x}, \mathbf{z}, v) = \exp(\pi_0 + \mathbf{x}\boldsymbol{\pi}_1 + \mathbf{z}\boldsymbol{\pi}_2 + \pi_3 v)$, where v is independent of $(\mathbf{x}, \mathbf{z})$ with $\text{E}[\exp(\pi_3 v)] = 1$. (Therefore, w is some nonnegative treatment.)

a. Show that we can write

$$y = \eta_0 + \mathbf{x}\gamma + \beta w + w \cdot (\mathbf{x} - \boldsymbol{\psi})\boldsymbol{\delta} + \xi \text{E}(w \mid \mathbf{x}, \mathbf{z}) + r$$

where $\text{E}(w \mid \mathbf{x}, \mathbf{z}) = \exp(\boldsymbol{\pi}_0 + \mathbf{x}\boldsymbol{\pi}_1 + \mathbf{z}\boldsymbol{\pi}_2)$, and $\text{E}(r \mid \mathbf{x}, \mathbf{z}) = 0$.

b. Use part a to show that β is not identified. {Hint: Let $q \equiv \text{E}(w \mid \mathbf{x}, \mathbf{z})$, and let h be any other function of $(\mathbf{x}, \mathbf{z})$. Does the linear projection of w on $[1, \mathbf{x}, h, h \cdot (\mathbf{x} - \boldsymbol{\psi}), q]$ depend on h?}

c. For $w > 0$ (strictly positive treatment), add the assumption that $E(u \mid v, x, z) = \rho v$. Find $E(y \mid w, x, z) = E(y \mid v, x, z)$ and propose a two-step estimator of β.

19 Count Data and Related Models

19.1 Why Count Data Models?

A **count variable** is a variable that takes on nonnegative integer values. Many variables that we would like to explain in terms of covariates come as counts. A few examples include the number of times someone is arrested during a given year, number of emergency room drug episodes during a given week, number of cigarettes smoked per day, and number of patents applied for by a firm during a year. These examples have two important characteristics in common: there is no natural a priori upper bound, and the outcome will be zero for at least some members of the population. Other count variables do have an upper bound. For example, for the number of children in a family who are high school graduates, the upper bound is number of children in the family.

If y is the count variable and $\mathbf{x}$ is a vector of explanatory variables, we are often interested in the population regression, $\mathrm{E}(y \mid \mathbf{x})$. Throughout this book we have discussed various models for conditional expectations, and we have discussed different methods of estimation. The most straightforward approach is a linear model, $\mathrm{E}(y \mid \mathbf{x}) = \mathbf{x}\boldsymbol{\beta}$, estimated by OLS. For count data, linear models have shortcomings very similar to those for binary responses or corner solution responses: because $y \geq 0$, we know that $\mathrm{E}(y \mid \mathbf{x})$ should be nonnegative for all $\mathbf{x}$. If $\hat{\boldsymbol{\beta}}$ is the OLS estimator, there usually will be values of $\mathbf{x}$ such that $\mathbf{x}\hat{\boldsymbol{\beta}} < 0$—so that the predicted value of y is negative.

For strictly positive variables, we often use the natural log transformation, $\log(y)$, and use a linear model. This approach is not possible in interesting count data applications, where y takes on the value zero for a nontrivial fraction of the population. Transformations could be applied that are defined for all $y \geq 0$—for example, $\log(1 + y)$—but $\log(1 + y)$ itself is nonnegative, and it is not obvious how to recover $\mathrm{E}(y \mid \mathbf{x})$ from a linear model for $\mathrm{E}[\log(1 + y) \mid \mathbf{x}]$. With count data, it is better to model $\mathrm{E}(y \mid \mathbf{x})$ directly and to choose functional forms that ensure positivity for any value of $\mathbf{x}$ and any parameter values. When y has no upper bound, the most popular of these is the exponential function, $\mathrm{E}(y \mid \mathbf{x}) = \exp(\mathbf{x}\boldsymbol{\beta})$.

In Chapter 12 we discussed nonlinear least squares (NLS) as a general method for estimating nonlinear models of conditional means. NLS can certainly be applied to count data models, but it is not ideal: NLS is relatively inefficient unless $\mathrm{Var}(y \mid \mathbf{x})$ is constant (see Chapter 12), and all of the standard distributions for count data imply heteroskedasticity.

In Section 19.2 we discuss the most popular model for count data, the Poisson regression model. As we will see, the Poisson regression model has some nice features. First, if y given $\mathbf{x}$ has a Poisson distribution—which used to be the maintained assumption in count data contexts—then the conditional maximum likelihood estimators are fully efficient. Second, the Poisson assumption turns out to be unnecessary for consistent estimation of the conditional mean parameters. As we will see in Section 19.2, the Poisson *quasi*–maximum likelihood estimator is fully robust to distributional misspecification. It also maintains certain efficiency properties even when the distribution is not Poisson.

In Section 19.3 we discuss other count data models, and in Section 19.4 we cover quasi-MLEs for other nonnegative response variables. In Section 19.5 we cover multiplicative panel data models, which are motivated by unobserved effects count data models but can also be used for other nonnegative responses.

19.2 Poisson Regression Models with Cross Section Data

In Chapter 13 we used the basic Poisson regression model to illustrate maximum likelihood estimation. Here, we study Poisson regression in much more detail, emphasizing the properties of the estimator when the Poisson distributional assumption is incorrect.

19.2.1 Assumptions Used for Poisson Regression

The basic Poisson regression model assumes that y given $\mathbf{x} \equiv (x_1, \ldots, x_K)$ has a Poisson distribution, as in El Sayyad (1973) and Maddala (1983, Section 2.15). The density of y given $\mathbf{x}$ under the Poisson assumption is completely determined by the conditional mean $\mu(\mathbf{x}) \equiv \mathrm{E}(y \mid \mathbf{x})$:

$$f(y \mid \mathbf{x}) = \exp[-\mu(\mathbf{x})][\mu(\mathbf{x})]^y / y!, \qquad y = 0, 1, \ldots \tag{19.1}$$

where $y!$ is y factorial. Given a parametric model for $\mu(\mathbf{x})$ [such as $\mu(\mathbf{x}) = \exp(\mathbf{x}\boldsymbol{\beta})$] and a random sample $\{(\mathbf{x}_i, y_i): i = 1, 2, \ldots, N\}$ on $(\mathbf{x}, y)$, it is fairly straightforward to obtain the conditional MLEs of the parameters. The statistical properties then follow from our treatment of CMLE in Chapter 13.

It has long been recognized that the Poisson distributional assumption imposes restrictions on the conditional moments of y that are often violated in applications. The most important of these is equality of the conditional variance and mean:

$$\mathrm{Var}(y \mid \mathbf{x}) = \mathrm{E}(y \mid \mathbf{x}) \tag{19.2}$$

The variance-mean equality has been rejected in numerous applications, and later we show that assumption (19.2) is violated for fairly simple departures from the Poisson model. Importantly, whether or not assumption (19.2) holds has implications for how we carry out statistical inference. In fact, as we will see, it is assumption (19.2), not the Poisson assumption per se, that is important for large-sample inference; this point will become clear in Section 19.2.2. In what follows we refer to assumption (19.2) as the **Poisson variance assumption**.

A weaker assumption allows the variance-mean ratio to be any positive constant:

$$\text{Var}(y \mid \mathbf{x}) = \sigma^2 \text{E}(y \mid \mathbf{x}) \tag{19.3}$$

where $\sigma^2 > 0$ is the variance-mean ratio. This assumption is used in the **generalized linear models (GLM)** literature, and so we will refer to assumption (19.3) as the **Poisson GLM variance assumption**. The GLM literature is concerned with quasi-maximum likelihood estimation of a class of nonlinear models that contains Poisson regression as a special case. We do not need to introduce the full GLM apparatus and terminology to analyze Poisson regression. See McCullagh and Nelder (1989).

The case $\sigma^2 > 1$ is empirically relevant because it implies that the variance is greater than the mean; this situation is called **overdispersion** (relative to the Poisson case). One distribution for y given $\mathbf{x}$ where assumption (19.3) holds with overdispersion is what Cameron and Trivedi (1986) call NegBin I—a particular parameterization of the negative binomial distribution. When $\sigma^2 < 1$ we say there is **underdispersion**. Underdispersion is less common than overdispersion, but underdispersion has been found in some applications.

There are plenty of count distributions for which assumption (19.3) does not hold—for example, the NegBin II model in Cameron and Trivedi (1986). Therefore, we are often interested in estimating the conditional mean parameters without specifying the conditional variance. As we will see, Poisson regression turns out to be well suited for this purpose.

Given a parametric model $m(\mathbf{x}, \boldsymbol{\beta})$ for $\mu(\mathbf{x})$, where $\boldsymbol{\beta}$ is a $P \times 1$ vector of parameters, the log likelihood for observation i is

$$\ell_i(\boldsymbol{\beta}) = y_i \log[m(\mathbf{x}_i, \boldsymbol{\beta})] - m(\mathbf{x}_i, \boldsymbol{\beta}) \tag{19.4}$$

where we drop the term $\log(y_i!)$ because it does not depend on the parameters $\boldsymbol{\beta}$ (for computational reasons dropping this term is a good idea in practice, too, as $y_i!$ gets very large for even moderate y_i). We let $\mathscr{B} \subset \mathbb{R}^P$ denote the parameter space, which is needed for the theoretical development but is practically unimportant in most cases.

The most common mean function in applications is the exponential:

$$m(\mathbf{x}, \boldsymbol{\beta}) = \exp(\mathbf{x}\boldsymbol{\beta}) \tag{19.5}$$

where $\mathbf{x}$ is $1 \times K$ and contains unity as its first element, and $\boldsymbol{\beta}$ is $K \times 1$. Under assumption (19.5) the log likelihood is $\ell_i(\boldsymbol{\beta}) = y_i\mathbf{x}_i\boldsymbol{\beta} - \exp(\mathbf{x}_i\boldsymbol{\beta})$. The parameters in model (19.5) are easy to interpret. If x_j is continuous, then

$$\frac{\partial \mathrm{E}(y \mid \mathbf{x})}{\partial x_j} = \exp(\mathbf{x}\boldsymbol{\beta})\beta_j$$

and so

$$\beta_j = \frac{\partial \mathrm{E}(y \mid \mathbf{x})}{\partial x_j} \cdot \frac{1}{\mathrm{E}(y \mid \mathbf{x})} = \frac{\partial \log[\mathrm{E}(y \mid \mathbf{x})]}{\partial x_j}$$

Therefore, $100\beta_j$ is the semielasticity of $\mathrm{E}(y \mid \mathbf{x})$ with respect to x_j: for small changes Δx_j, the percentage change in $\mathrm{E}(y \mid \mathbf{x})$ is roughly $(100\beta_j)\Delta x_j$. If we replace x_j with $\log(x_j)$, β_j is the elasticity of $\mathrm{E}(y \mid \mathbf{x})$ with respect to x_j. Using assumption (19.5) as the model for $\mathrm{E}(y \mid \mathbf{x})$ is analogous to using $\log(y)$ as the dependent variable in linear regression analysis.

Quadratic terms can be added with no additional effort, except in interpreting the parameters. In what follows, we will write the exponential function as in assumption (19.5), leaving transformations of $\mathbf{x}$—such as logs, quadratics, interaction terms, and so on—implicit. See Wooldridge (1997c) for a discussion of other functional forms.

19.2.2 Consistency of the Poisson QMLE

Once we have specified a conditional mean function, we are interested in cases where, other than the conditional mean, the Poisson distribution can be arbitrarily misspecified (subject to regularity conditions). When y_i given $\mathbf{x}_i$ does *not* have a Poisson distribution, we call the estimator $\hat{\boldsymbol{\beta}}$ that solves

$$\max_{\boldsymbol{\beta} \in \mathscr{B}} \sum_{i=1}^{N} \ell_i(\boldsymbol{\beta}) \tag{19.6}$$

the **Poisson quasi–maximum likelihood estimator (QMLE)**. A careful discussion of the consistency of the Poisson QMLE requires introduction of the true value of the parameter, as in Chapters 12 and 13. That is, we assume that for some value $\boldsymbol{\beta}_{\mathrm{o}}$ in the parameter space $\mathscr{B}$,

$$\mathrm{E}(y \mid \mathbf{x}) = m(\mathbf{x}, \boldsymbol{\beta}_{\mathrm{o}}) \tag{19.7}$$

To prove consistency of the Poisson QMLE under assumption (19.5), the key is to show that $\boldsymbol{\beta}_{\mathrm{o}}$ is the unique solution to

$$\max_{\boldsymbol{\beta} \in \mathscr{B}} \mathrm{E}[\ell_i(\boldsymbol{\beta})] \tag{19.8}$$

Then, under the regularity conditions listed in Theorem 12.2, it follows from this theorem that the solution to equation (19.6) is weakly consistent for $\boldsymbol{\beta}_{\mathrm{o}}$.

Wooldridge (1997c) provides a simple proof that $\boldsymbol{\beta}_{\mathrm{o}}$ is a solution to equation (19.8) when assumption (19.7) holds (see also Problem 19.1). It also follows from the general results on quasi-MLE in the **linear exponential family (LEF)** by Gourieroux, Monfort, and Trognon (1984a) (hereafter, GMT, 1984a). Uniqueness of $\boldsymbol{\beta}_{\mathrm{o}}$ must be assumed separately, as it depends on the distribution of $\mathbf{x}_i$. That is, in addition to assumption (19.7), identification of $\boldsymbol{\beta}_{\mathrm{o}}$ requires some restrictions on the distribution of explanatory variables, and these depend on the nature of the regression function m. In the linear regression case, we require full rank of $\mathrm{E}(\mathbf{x}_i'\mathbf{x}_i)$. For Poisson QMLE with an exponential regression function $\exp(\mathbf{x}\boldsymbol{\beta})$, it can be shown that multiple solutions to equation (19.8) exist whenever there is perfect multicollinearity in $\mathbf{x}_i$, just as in the linear regression case. If we rule out perfect multicollinearity, we can usually conclude that $\boldsymbol{\beta}_{\mathrm{o}}$ is identified under assumption (19.7).

It is important to remember that consistency of the Poisson QMLE does not require any additional assumptions concerning the distribution of y_i given $\mathbf{x}_i$. In particular, $\mathrm{Var}(y_i \mid \mathbf{x}_i)$ can be virtually anything (subject to regularity conditions needed to apply the results of Chapter 12).

19.2.3 Asymptotic Normality of the Poisson QMLE

If the Poission QMLE is consistent for $\boldsymbol{\beta}_{\mathrm{o}}$ without any assumptions beyond (19.7), why did we introduce assumptions (19.2) and (19.3)? It turns out that whether these assumptions hold determines which asymptotic variance matrix estimators and inference procedures are valid, as we now show.

The asymptotic normality of the Poisson QMLE follows from Theorem 12.3. The result is

$$\sqrt{N}(\hat{\boldsymbol{\beta}} - \boldsymbol{\beta}_{\mathrm{o}}) \xrightarrow{d} \mathrm{Normal}(0, \mathbf{A}_{\mathrm{o}}^{-1}\mathbf{B}_{\mathrm{o}}\mathbf{A}_{\mathrm{o}}^{-1}) \tag{19.9}$$

where

$$\mathbf{A}_{\mathrm{o}} \equiv \mathrm{E}[-\mathbf{H}_i(\boldsymbol{\beta}_{\mathrm{o}})] \tag{19.10}$$

and

$$\mathbf{B}_{\mathrm{o}} \equiv \mathrm{E}[\mathbf{s}_i(\boldsymbol{\beta}_{\mathrm{o}})\mathbf{s}_i(\boldsymbol{\beta}_{\mathrm{o}})'] = \mathrm{Var}[\mathbf{s}_i(\boldsymbol{\beta}_{\mathrm{o}})] \tag{19.11}$$

where we define $\mathbf{A}_{\mathrm{o}}$ in terms of minus the Hessian because the Poisson QMLE solves a maximization rather than a minimization problem. Taking the gradient of equation (19.4) and transposing gives the score for observation i as

$$\mathbf{s}_i(\boldsymbol{\beta}) = \nabla_{\beta} m(\mathbf{x}_i, \boldsymbol{\beta})'[y_i - m(\mathbf{x}_i, \boldsymbol{\beta})]/m(\mathbf{x}_i, \boldsymbol{\beta}) \tag{19.12}$$

It is easily seen that, under assumption (19.7), $\mathbf{s}_i(\boldsymbol{\beta}_o)$ has a zero mean conditional on $\mathbf{x}_i$. The Hessian is more complicated but, under assumption (19.7), it can be shown that

$$-\mathrm{E}[\mathbf{H}_i(\boldsymbol{\beta}_o) \mid \mathbf{x}_i] = \nabla_\beta m(\mathbf{x}_i, \boldsymbol{\beta}_o)' \nabla_\beta m(\mathbf{x}_i, \boldsymbol{\beta}_o) / m(\mathbf{x}_i, \boldsymbol{\beta}_o) \tag{19.13}$$

Then $\mathbf{A}_o$ is the expected value of this expression (over the distribution of $\mathbf{x}_i$). A fully robust asymptotic variance matrix estimator for $\hat{\boldsymbol{\beta}}$ follows from equation (12.49):

$$\left(\sum_{i=1}^N \hat{\mathbf{A}}_i\right)^{-1} \left(\sum_{i=1}^N \hat{\mathbf{s}}_i \hat{\mathbf{s}}_i'\right) \left(\sum_{i=1}^N \hat{\mathbf{A}}_i\right)^{-1} \tag{19.14}$$

where $\hat{\mathbf{s}}_i$ is obtained from equation (19.12) with $\hat{\boldsymbol{\beta}}$ in place of $\boldsymbol{\beta}$, and $\hat{\mathbf{A}}_i$ is the right-hand side of equation (19.13) with $\hat{\boldsymbol{\beta}}$ in place of $\boldsymbol{\beta}_o$. This is the fully robust variance matrix estimator in the sense that it requires only assumption (19.7) and the regularity conditions from Chapter 12.

The asymptotic variance of $\hat{\boldsymbol{\beta}}$ simplifies under the GLM assumption (19.3). Maintaining assumption (19.3) (where σ_o^2 now denotes the true value of σ^2) and defining $u_i \equiv y_i - m(\mathbf{x}_i, \boldsymbol{\beta}_o)$, the law of iterated expectations implies that

$$\begin{aligned}\mathbf{B}_o &= \mathrm{E}[u_i^2 \nabla_\beta m_i(\boldsymbol{\beta}_o)' \nabla_\beta m_i(\boldsymbol{\beta}_o) / \{m_i(\boldsymbol{\beta}_o)\}^2] \\ &= \mathrm{E}[\mathrm{E}(u_i^2 \mid \mathbf{x}_i) \nabla_\beta m_i(\boldsymbol{\beta}_o)' \nabla_\beta m_i(\boldsymbol{\beta}_o) / \{m_i(\boldsymbol{\beta}_o)\}^2] = \sigma_o^2 \mathbf{A}_o\end{aligned}$$

since $\mathrm{E}(u_i^2 \mid \mathbf{x}_i) = \sigma_o^2 m_i(\boldsymbol{\beta}_o)$ under assumptions (19.3) and (19.7). Therefore, $\mathbf{A}_o^{-1}\mathbf{B}_o\mathbf{A}_o^{-1} = \sigma_o^2 \mathbf{A}_o^{-1}$, so we only need to estimate σ_o^2 in addition to obtaining $\hat{\mathbf{A}}$. A consistent estimator of σ_o^2 is obtained from $\sigma_o^2 = \mathrm{E}[u_i^2 / m_i(\boldsymbol{\beta}_o)]$, which follows from assumption (19.3) and iterated expectations. The usual analogy principle argument gives the estimator

$$\hat{\sigma}^2 = N^{-1} \sum_{i=1}^N \hat{u}_i^2 / \hat{m}_i = N^{-1} \sum_{i=1}^N (\hat{u}_i / \sqrt{\hat{m}_i})^2 \tag{19.15}$$

The last representation shows that $\hat{\sigma}^2$ is simply the average sum of squared weighted residuals, where the weights are the inverse of the estimated nominal standard deviations. (In the GLM literature, the weighted residuals $\tilde{u}_i \equiv \hat{u}_i / \sqrt{\hat{m}_i}$ are sometimes called the **Pearson residuals**. In earlier chapters we also called them standardized residuals.) In the GLM literature, a degrees-of-freedom adjustment is usually made by replacing N^{-1} with $(N - P)^{-1}$ in equation (19.15).

Given $\hat{\sigma}^2$ and $\hat{\mathbf{A}}$, it is straightforward to obtain an estimate of $\mathrm{Avar}(\hat{\boldsymbol{\beta}})$ under assumption (19.3). In fact, we can write

$$\text{Av\hat{a}r}(\hat{\boldsymbol{\beta}}) = \hat{\sigma}^2\hat{\mathbf{A}}^{-1}/N = \hat{\sigma}^2\left(\sum_{i=1}^{N}\nabla_\beta\hat{m}_i'\nabla_\beta\hat{m}_i/\hat{m}_i\right)^{-1} \tag{19.16}$$

Note that the matrix is always positive definite when the inverse exists, so it produces well-defined standard errors (given, as usual, by the square roots of the diagonal elements). We call these the **GLM standard errors**.

If the Poisson variance assumption (19.2) holds, things are even easier because σ^2 is known to be unity; the estimated asymptotic variance of $\hat{\boldsymbol{\beta}}$ is given in equation (19.16) but with $\hat{\sigma}^2 \equiv 1$. The same estimator can be derived from the MLE theory in Chapter 13 as the inverse of the estimated information matrix (conditional on the $\mathbf{x}_i$); see Section 13.5.2.

Under assumption (19.3) in the case of overdispersion ($\sigma^2 > 1$), standard errors of the $\hat{\beta}_j$ obtained from equation (19.16) with $\hat{\sigma}^2 = 1$ will systematically underestimate the asymptotic standard deviations, sometimes by a large factor. For example, if $\sigma^2 = 2$, the correct GLM standard errors are, in the limit, 41 percent larger than the incorrect, nominal Poisson standard errors. It is common to see very significant coefficients reported for Poisson regressions—a recent example is Model (1993)—but we must interpret the standard errors with caution when they are obtained under assumption (19.2). The GLM standard errors are easily obtained by multiplying the Poisson standard errors by $\hat{\sigma} \equiv \sqrt{\hat{\sigma}^2}$. The most robust standard errors are obtained from expression (19.14), as these are valid under *any* conditional variance assumption. In practice, it is a good idea to report the fully robust standard errors along with the GLM standard errors and $\hat{\sigma}$.

If y given $\mathbf{x}$ has a Poisson distribution, it follows from the general efficiency of the conditional MLE—see Section 14.5.2—that the Poisson QMLE is fully efficient in the class of estimators that ignores information on the marginal distribution of $\mathbf{x}$.

A nice property of the Poisson QMLE is that it retains some efficiency for certain departures from the Poisson assumption. The efficiency results of GMT (1984a) can be applied here: if the GLM assumption (19.3) holds for some $\sigma^2 > 0$, the Poisson QMLE is efficient in the class of all QMLEs in the linear exponential family of distributions. In particular, the Poisson QMLE is more efficient than the nonlinear least squares estimator, as well as many other QMLEs in the LEF, some of which we cover in Sections 19.3 and 19.4.

Wooldridge (1997c) gives an example of Poisson regression to an economic model of crime, where the response variable is number of arrests of a young man living in California during 1986. Wooldridge finds overdispersion: $\hat{\sigma}$ is either 1.228 or 1.172, depending on the functional form for the conditional mean. The following example shows that underdispersion is possible.

Table 19.1
OLS and Poisson Estimates of a Fertility Equation

Dependent Variable: *children*		
Independent Variable	Linear (OLS)	Exponential (Poisson QMLE)
educ	−.0644 (.0063)	−.0217 (.0025)
age	.272 (.017)	.337 (.009)
age^2	−.0019 (.0003)	−.0041 (.0001)
evermarr	.682 (.052)	.315 (.021)
urban	−.228 (.046)	−.086 (.019)
electric	−.262 (.076)	−.121 (.034)
tv	−.250 (.090)	−.145 (.041)
constant	−3.394 (.245)	−5.375 (.141)
Log-likelihood value	—	−6,497.060
R-squared	.590	.598
$\hat{\sigma}$	1.424	.867

Example 19.1 (Effects of Education on Fertility): We use the data in FERTIL2. RAW to estimate the effects of education on women's fertility in Botswana. The response variable, *children*, is number of living children. We use a standard exponential regression function, and the explanatory variables are years of schooling (*educ*), a quadratic in age, and binary indicators for ever married, living in an urban area, having electricity, and owning a television. The results are given in Table 19.1. A linear regression model is also included, with the usual OLS standard errors. For Poisson regression, the standard errors are the GLM standard errors. A total of 4,358 observations are used.

As expected, the signs of the coefficients agree in the linear and exponential models, but their interpretations differ. For Poisson regression, the coefficient on *educ* implies that another year of education reduces expected number of children by about 2.2 percent, and the effect is very statistically significant. The linear model estimate implies that another year of education reduces expected number of children by about .064. (So, if 100 women get another year of education, we estimate they will have about six fewer children.)

The estimate of σ in the Poisson regression implies underdispersion: the variance is less than the mean. (Incidentally, the $\hat{\sigma}$'s for the linear and Poisson models are not comparable.) One implication is that the GLM standard errors are actually less than the corresponding Poisson MLE standard errors.

For the linear model, the R-squared is the usual one. For the exponential model, the R-squared is computed as the squared correlation coefficient between $children_i$ and $\widehat{children}_i = \exp(\mathbf{x}_i\hat{\boldsymbol{\beta}})$. The exponential regression function fits slightly better.

19.2.4 Hypothesis Testing

Classical hypothesis testing is fairly straightforward in a QMLE setting. Testing hypotheses about individual parameters is easily carried out using asymptotic t statistics after computing the appropriate standard error, as we discussed in Section 19.2.3. Multiple hypotheses tests can be carried out using the Wald, quasi–likelihood ratio, or score test. We covered these generally in Sections 12.6 and 13.6, and they apply immediately to the Poisson QMLE.

The Wald statistic for testing nonlinear hypotheses is computed as in equation (12.63), where $\hat{\mathbf{V}}$ is chosen appropriately depending on the degree of robustness desired, with expression (19.14) being the most robust. The Wald statistic is convenient for testing multiple exclusion restrictions in a robust fashion.

When the GLM assumption (19.3) holds, the quasi–likelihood ratio statistic can be used. Let $\breve{\boldsymbol{\beta}}$ be the restricted estimator, where Q restrictions of the form $\mathbf{c}(\breve{\boldsymbol{\beta}}) = \mathbf{0}$ have been imposed. Let $\hat{\boldsymbol{\beta}}$ be the unrestricted QMLE. Let $\mathscr{L}(\boldsymbol{\beta})$ be the quasi–log likelihood for the sample of size N, given in expression (19.6). Let $\hat{\sigma}^2$ be given in equation (19.15) (with or without the degrees-of-freedom adjustment), where the $\hat{u}_i$ are the residuals from the unconstrained maximization. The QLR statistic,

$$QLR \equiv 2[\mathscr{L}(\hat{\boldsymbol{\beta}}) - \mathscr{L}(\breve{\boldsymbol{\beta}})]/\hat{\sigma}^2 \tag{19.17}$$

converges in distribution to χ^2_Q under H_0, under the conditions laid out in Section 12.6.3. The division of the usual likelihood ratio statistic by $\hat{\sigma}^2$ provides for some degree of robustness. If we set $\hat{\sigma}^2 = 1$, we obtain the usual LR statistic, which is valid only under assumption (19.2). There is no usable quasi-LR statistic when the GLM assumption (19.3) does not hold.

The score test can also be used to test multiple hypotheses. In this case we estimate only the restricted model. Partition $\boldsymbol{\beta}$ as $(\boldsymbol{\alpha}', \boldsymbol{\gamma}')'$, where $\boldsymbol{\alpha}$ is $P_1 \times 1$ and $\boldsymbol{\gamma}$ is $P_2 \times 1$, and assume that the null hypothesis is

$$\mathrm{H}_0\colon \boldsymbol{\gamma}_\mathrm{o} = \bar{\boldsymbol{\gamma}} \tag{19.18}$$

where $\bar{\boldsymbol{\gamma}}$ is a $P_2 \times 1$ vector of specified constants (often, $\bar{\boldsymbol{\gamma}} = \mathbf{0}$). Let $\breve{\boldsymbol{\beta}}$ be the estimator of $\boldsymbol{\beta}$ obtained under the restriction $\boldsymbol{\gamma} = \bar{\boldsymbol{\gamma}}$ [so $\breve{\boldsymbol{\beta}} \equiv (\breve{\boldsymbol{\alpha}}', \bar{\boldsymbol{\gamma}}')'$], and define quantities under the restricted estimation as $\check{m}_i \equiv m(\mathbf{x}_i, \check{\boldsymbol{\beta}})$, $\check{u}_i \equiv y_i - \check{m}_i$, and $\nabla_\beta \check{m}_i \equiv (\nabla_\alpha \check{m}_i, \nabla_\gamma \check{m}_i) \equiv \nabla_\beta m(\mathbf{x}_i, \check{\boldsymbol{\beta}})$. Now weight the residuals and gradient by the inverse of nominal Poisson standard deviation, estimated under the null, $1/\sqrt{\check{m}_i}$:

$$\tilde{u}_i \equiv \check{u}_i/\sqrt{\check{m}_i}, \qquad \nabla_\beta \tilde{m}_i \equiv \nabla_\beta \check{m}_i/\sqrt{\check{m}_i} \tag{19.19}$$

so that the $\tilde{u}_i$ here are the Pearson residuals obtained under the null. A form of the score statistic that is valid under the GLM assumption (19.3) [and therefore under assumption (19.2)] is NR_u^2 from the regression

$$\tilde{u}_i \text{ on } \nabla_\beta \tilde{m}_i, \qquad i = 1, 2, \ldots, N \tag{19.20}$$

where R_u^2 denotes the uncentered R-squared. Under H_0 and assumption (19.3), $NR_u^2 \overset{a}{\sim} \chi^2_{P_2}$. This is identical to the score statistic in equation (12.68) but where we use $\tilde{\mathbf{B}} = \tilde{\sigma}^2 \tilde{\mathbf{A}}$, where the notation is self-explanatory. For more, see Wooldridge (1991a, 1997c).

Following our development for nonlinear regression in Section 12.6.2, it is easy to obtain a test that is completely robust to variance misspecification. Let $\tilde{\mathbf{r}}_i$ denote the $1 \times P_2$ residuals from the regression

$$\nabla_\gamma \tilde{m}_i \text{ on } \nabla_\alpha \tilde{m}_i \tag{19.21}$$

In other words, regress each element of the weighted gradient with respect to the restricted parameters on the weighted gradient with respect to the unrestricted parameters. The residuals are put into the $1 \times P_2$ vector $\tilde{\mathbf{r}}_i$. The robust score statistic is obtained as $N - \mathrm{SSR}$ from the regression

$$1 \text{ on } \tilde{u}_i \tilde{\mathbf{r}}_i, \qquad i = 1, 2, \ldots, N \tag{19.22}$$

where $\tilde{u}_i \tilde{\mathbf{r}}_i = (\tilde{u}_i \tilde{r}_{i1}, \tilde{u}_i \tilde{r}_{i2}, \ldots, \tilde{u}_i \tilde{r}_{iP_2})$ is a $1 \times P_2$ vector.

As an example, consider testing $\mathrm{H}_0\colon \boldsymbol{\gamma} = \mathbf{0}$ in the exponential model $\mathrm{E}(y \mid \mathbf{x}) = \exp(\mathbf{x}\boldsymbol{\beta}) = \exp(\mathbf{x}_1 \boldsymbol{\alpha} + \mathbf{x}_2 \boldsymbol{\gamma})$. Then $\nabla_\beta m(\mathbf{x}, \boldsymbol{\beta}) = \exp(\mathbf{x}\boldsymbol{\beta})\mathbf{x}$. Let $\check{\boldsymbol{\alpha}}$ be the Poisson QMLE obtained under $\boldsymbol{\gamma} = \mathbf{0}$, and define $\check{m}_i \equiv \exp(\mathbf{x}_{i1} \check{\boldsymbol{\alpha}})$, with $\check{u}_i$ the residuals. Now $\nabla_\alpha \check{m}_i = \exp(\mathbf{x}_{i1} \check{\boldsymbol{\alpha}})\mathbf{x}_{i1}$, $\nabla_\gamma \check{m}_i = \exp(\mathbf{x}_{i1} \check{\boldsymbol{\alpha}})\mathbf{x}_{i2}$, and $\nabla_\beta \tilde{m}_i = \check{m}_i \mathbf{x}_i / \sqrt{\check{m}_i} = \sqrt{\check{m}_i}\mathbf{x}_i$. Therefore, the test that is valid under the GLM variance assumption is NR_u^2 from the OLS regression $\tilde{u}_i$ on $\sqrt{\check{m}_i}\mathbf{x}_i$, where the $\tilde{u}_i$ are the weighted residuals. For the robust test, first obtain the $1 \times P_2$ residuals $\tilde{\mathbf{r}}_i$ from the regression $\sqrt{\check{m}_i}\mathbf{x}_{i2}$ on $\sqrt{\check{m}_i}\mathbf{x}_{i1}$; then obtain the statistic from regression (19.22).

19.2.5 Specification Testing

Various specification tests have been proposed in the context of Poisson regression. The two most important kinds are conditional mean specification tests and conditional variance specification tests. For conditional mean tests, we usually begin with a fairly simple model whose parameters are easy to interpret—such as $m(\mathbf{x}, \boldsymbol{\beta}) = \exp(\mathbf{x}\boldsymbol{\beta})$—and then test this against other alternatives. Once the set of conditioning variables $\mathbf{x}$ has been specified, all such tests are functional form tests.

A useful class of functional form tests can be obtained using the score principle, where the null model $m(\mathbf{x}, \boldsymbol{\beta})$ is nested in a more general model. Fully robust tests and less robust tests are obtained exactly as in the previous section. Wooldridge (1997c, Section 3.5) contains details and some examples, including an extension of RESET to exponential regression models.

Conditional variance tests are more difficult to compute, especially if we want to maintain only that the first two moments are correctly specified under H_0. For example, it is very natural to test the GLM assumption (19.3) as a way of determining whether the Poisson QMLE is efficient in the class of estimators using only assumption (19.7). Cameron and Trivedi (1986) propose tests of the stronger assumption (19.2) and, in fact, take the null to be that the Poisson distribution is correct in its entirety. These tests are useful if we are interested in whether y given $\mathbf{x}$ truly has a Poisson distribution. However, assumption (19.2) is not necessary for consistency or relative efficiency of the Poisson QMLE.

Wooldridge (1991b) proposes fully robust tests of conditional variances in the context of the linear exponential family, which contains Poisson regression as a special case. To test assumption (19.3), write $u_i = y_i - m(\mathbf{x}_i, \boldsymbol{\beta}_o)$ and note that, under assumptions (19.3) and (19.7), $u_i^2 - \sigma_o^2 m(\mathbf{x}_i, \boldsymbol{\beta}_o)$ is uncorrelated with any function of $\mathbf{x}_i$. Let $\mathbf{h}(\mathbf{x}_i, \boldsymbol{\beta})$ be a $1 \times Q$ vector of functions of $\mathbf{x}_i$ and $\boldsymbol{\beta}$, and consider the alternative model

$$\mathrm{E}(u_i^2 \mid \mathbf{x}_i) = \sigma_o^2 m(\mathbf{x}_i, \boldsymbol{\beta}_o) + \mathbf{h}(\mathbf{x}_i, \boldsymbol{\beta}_o)\boldsymbol{\delta}_o \tag{19.23}$$

For example, the elements of $\mathbf{h}(\mathbf{x}_i, \boldsymbol{\beta})$ can be powers of $m(\mathbf{x}_i, \boldsymbol{\beta})$. Popular choices are unity and $\{\mathrm{m}(\mathbf{x}_i, \boldsymbol{\beta})\}^2$. A test of H_0: $\boldsymbol{\delta}_o = \mathbf{0}$ is then a test of the GLM assumption. While there are several moment conditions that can be used, a fruitful one is to use the weighted residuals, as we did with the conditional mean tests. We base the test on

$$N^{-1} \sum_{i=1}^{N} (\hat{\mathbf{h}}_i / \hat{m}_i)' \{(\hat{u}_i^2 - \hat{\sigma}^2 \hat{m}_i)/\hat{m}_i\} = N^{-1} \sum_{i=1}^{N} \tilde{\mathbf{h}}_i' (\tilde{u}_i^2 - \hat{\sigma}^2) \tag{19.24}$$

where $\tilde{\mathbf{h}}_i = \hat{\mathbf{h}}_i / \hat{m}_i$ and $\tilde{u}_i = \hat{u}_i / \sqrt{\hat{m}_i}$. (Note that $\hat{\mathbf{h}}_i$ is weighted by $1/\hat{m}_i$, not $1/\sqrt{\hat{m}_i}$.) To turn this equation into a test statistic, we must confront the fact that its standardized limiting distribution depends on the limiting distributions of $\sqrt{N}(\hat{\boldsymbol{\beta}} - \boldsymbol{\beta}_o)$ and $\sqrt{N}(\hat{\sigma}^2 - \sigma_o^2)$. To handle this problem, we use a trick suggested by Wooldridge

(1991b) that removes the dependence of the limiting distribution of the test statistic on that of $\sqrt{N}(\hat{\sigma}^2 - \sigma_o^2)$: replace $\tilde{\mathbf{h}}_i$ in equation (19.24) with its demeaned counterpart, $\tilde{\mathbf{r}}_i \equiv \tilde{\mathbf{h}}_i - \bar{\mathbf{h}}$, where $\bar{\mathbf{h}}$ is just the $1 \times Q$ vector of sample averages of each element of $\tilde{\mathbf{h}}_i$. There is an additional purging that then leads to a simple regression-based statistic. Let $\nabla_\beta \hat{m}_i$ be the unweighted gradient of the conditional mean function, evaluated at the Poisson QMLE $\hat{\boldsymbol{\beta}}$, and define $\nabla_\beta \tilde{m}_i \equiv \nabla_\beta \hat{m}_i / \sqrt{\hat{m}_i}$, as before. The following steps come from Wooldridge (1991b, Procedure 4.1):

1. Obtain $\hat{\sigma}^2$ as in equation (19.15) and $\hat{\mathbf{A}}$ as in equation (19.16), and define the $P \times Q$ matrix $\hat{\mathbf{J}} = \hat{\sigma}^2 (N^{-1} \sum_{i=1}^N \nabla_\beta \hat{m}_i' \tilde{\mathbf{r}}_i / \hat{m}_i)$.
2. For each i, define the $1 \times Q$ vector

$$\hat{\mathbf{z}}_i \equiv (\tilde{u}_i^2 - \hat{\sigma}^2)\tilde{\mathbf{r}}_i - \hat{\mathbf{s}}_i' \hat{\mathbf{A}}^{-1} \hat{\mathbf{J}} \tag{19.25}$$

where $\hat{\mathbf{s}}_i \equiv \nabla_\beta \tilde{m}_i' \tilde{u}_i$ is the Poisson score for observation i.

3. Run the regression

$$1 \text{ on } \hat{\mathbf{z}}_i, \qquad i = 1, 2, \ldots, N \tag{19.26}$$

Under assumptions (19.3) and (19.7), $N - \text{SSR}$ from this regression is distributed asymptotically as χ_Q^2.

The leading case occurs when $\hat{m}_i = \exp(\mathbf{x}_i \hat{\boldsymbol{\beta}})$ and $\nabla_\beta \hat{m}_i = \exp(\mathbf{x}_i \hat{\boldsymbol{\beta}}) \mathbf{x}_i = \hat{m}_i \mathbf{x}_i$. The subtraction of $\hat{\mathbf{s}}_i' \hat{\mathbf{A}}^{-1} \hat{\mathbf{J}}$ in equation (19.25) is a simple way of handling the fact that the limiting distribution of $\sqrt{N}(\hat{\boldsymbol{\beta}} - \boldsymbol{\beta}_o)$ affects the limiting distribution of the unadjusted statistic in equation (19.24). This particular adjustment ensures that the tests are just as efficient as any maximum-likelihood-based statistic if $\sigma_o^2 = 1$ and the Poisson assumption is correct. But this procedure is fully robust in the sense that only assumptions (19.3) and (19.7) are maintained under H_0. For further discussion the reader is referred to Wooldridge (1991b).

In practice, it is probably sufficient to choose the number of elements in Q to be small. Setting $\hat{\mathbf{h}}_i = (1, \hat{m}_i^2)$, so that $\tilde{\mathbf{h}}_i = (1/\hat{m}_i, \hat{m}_i)$, is likely to produce a fairly powerful two-degrees-of-freedom test against a fairly broad class of alternatives.

The procedure is easily modified to test the more restrictive assumption (19.2). First, replace $\hat{\sigma}^2$ everywhere with unity. Second, there is no need to demean the auxiliary regressors $\tilde{\mathbf{h}}_i$ (so that now $\tilde{\mathbf{h}}_i$ can contain a constant); thus, wherever $\tilde{\mathbf{r}}_i$ appears, simply use $\tilde{\mathbf{h}}_i$. Everything else is the same. For the reasons discussed earlier, when the focus is on $\mathrm{E}(y \mid \mathbf{x})$, we are more interested in testing assumption (19.3) than assumption (19.2).

19.3 Other Count Data Regression Models

19.3.1 Negative Binomial Regression Models

The Poisson regression model nominally maintains assumption (19.2) but retains some asymptotic efficiency under assumption (19.3). A popular alternative to the Poisson QMLE is full maximum likelihood analysis of the NegBin I model of Cameron and Trivedi (1986). NegBin I is a particular parameterization of the negative binomial distribution. An important restriction in the NegBin I model is that it implies assumption (19.3) with $\sigma^2 > 1$, so that there cannot be underdispersion. (We drop the "o" subscript in this section for notational simplicity.) Typically, NegBin I is parameterized through the mean parameters $\boldsymbol{\beta}$ and an additional parameter, $\eta^2 > 0$, where $\sigma^2 = 1 + \eta^2$. On the one hand, when $\boldsymbol{\beta}$ and η^2 are estimated jointly, the maximum likelihood estimators are generally inconsistent if the NegBin I assumption fails. On the other hand, if the NegBin I distribution holds, then the NegBin I MLE is more efficient than the Poisson QMLE (this conclusion follows from Section 14.5.2). Still, under assumption (19.3), the Poisson QMLE is more efficient than an estimator that requires only the conditional mean to be correctly specified for consistency. On balance, because of its robustness, the Poisson QMLE has the edge over NegBin I for estimating the parameters of the conditional mean. If conditional probabilities need to be estimated, then a more flexible model is probably warranted.

Other count data distributions imply a conditional variance other than assumption (19.3). A leading example is the NegBin II model of Cameron and Trivedi (1986). The NegBin II model can be derived from a model of unobserved heterogeneity in a Poisson model. Specifically, let $c_i > 0$ be unobserved heterogeneity, and assume that

$$y_i \mid \mathbf{x}_i, c_i \sim \text{Poisson}[c_i m(\mathbf{x}_i, \boldsymbol{\beta})]$$

If we further assume that c_i is independent of $\mathbf{x}_i$ and has a gamma distribution with unit mean and $\text{Var}(c_i) = \eta^2$, then the distribution of y_i given $\mathbf{x}_i$ can be shown to be negative binomial, with conditional mean and variance

$$\text{E}(y_i \mid \mathbf{x}_i) = m(\mathbf{x}_i, \boldsymbol{\beta}), \tag{19.27}$$

$$\begin{aligned} \text{Var}(y_i \mid \mathbf{x}_i) &= \text{E}[\text{Var}(y_i \mid \mathbf{x}_i, c_i) \mid \mathbf{x}_i] + \text{Var}[\text{E}(y_i \mid \mathbf{x}_i, c_i) \mid \mathbf{x}_i] \\ &= m(\mathbf{x}_i, \boldsymbol{\beta}) + \eta^2 [m(\mathbf{x}_i, \boldsymbol{\beta})]^2 \end{aligned} \tag{19.28}$$

so that the conditional variance of y_i given $\mathbf{x}_i$ is a quadratic in the conditional mean. Because we can write equation (19.28) as $\text{E}(y_i \mid \mathbf{x}_i)[1 + \eta^2 \text{E}(y_i \mid \mathbf{x}_i)]$, NegBin II also implies overdispersion, but where the amount of overdispersion increases with $E(y_i \mid \mathbf{x}_i)$.

The log-likelihood function for observation i is

$$\ell_i(\boldsymbol{\beta}, \eta^2) = \eta^{-2} \log\left[\frac{\eta^{-2}}{\eta^{-2} + m(\mathbf{x}_i, \boldsymbol{\beta})}\right] + y_i \log\left[\frac{m(\mathbf{x}_i, \boldsymbol{\beta})}{\eta^{-2} + m(\mathbf{x}_i, \boldsymbol{\beta})}\right]$$

$$+ \log[\Gamma(y_i + \eta^{-2})/\Gamma(\eta^{-2})] \tag{19.29}$$

where $\Gamma(\cdot)$ is the gamma function defined for $r > 0$ by $\Gamma(r) = \int_0^\infty z^{r-1} \exp(-z)\,dz$.

You are referred to Cameron and Trivedi (1986) for details. The parameters $\boldsymbol{\beta}$ and η^2 can be jointly estimated using standard maximum likelihood methods.

It turns out that, for *fixed* η^2, the log likelihood in equation (19.29) is in the linear exponential family; see GMT (1984a). Therefore, if we fix η^2 at any positive value, say $\bar{\eta}^2$, and estimate $\boldsymbol{\beta}$ by maximizing $\sum_{i=1}^N \ell_i(\boldsymbol{\beta}, \bar{\eta}^2)$ with respect to $\boldsymbol{\beta}$, then the resulting QMLE is consistent under the conditional mean assumption (19.27) *only*: for fixed η^2, the negative binomial QMLE has the same robustness properties as the Poisson QMLE. (Notice that when η^2 is fixed, the term involving the gamma function in equation (19.29) does not affect the QMLE.)

The structure of the asymptotic variance estimators and test statistics is very similar to the Poisson regression case. Let

$$\hat{v}_i = \hat{m}_i + \bar{\eta}^2 \hat{m}_i^2 \tag{19.30}$$

be the estimated nominal variance for the given value $\bar{\eta}^2$. We simply weight the residuals $\hat{u}_i$ and gradient $\nabla_\beta \hat{m}_i$ by $1/\sqrt{\hat{v}_i}$:

$$\tilde{u}_i = \hat{u}_i / \sqrt{\hat{v}_i}, \qquad \nabla_\beta \tilde{m}_i = \nabla_\beta \hat{m}_i / \sqrt{\hat{v}_i} \tag{19.31}$$

For example, under conditions (19.27) and (19.28), a valid estimator of $\text{Avar}(\hat{\boldsymbol{\beta}})$ is

$$\left(\sum_{i=1}^N \nabla_\beta \hat{m}_i' \nabla_\beta \hat{m}_i / \hat{v}_i\right)^{-1}$$

If we drop condition (19.28), the estimator in expression (19.14) should be used but with the standardized residuals and gradients given by equation (19.31). Score statistics are modified in the same way.

When η^2 is set to unity, we obtain the **geometric QMLE**. A better approach is to replace η^2 by a first-stage estimate, say $\hat{\eta}^2$, and then estimate $\boldsymbol{\beta}$ by two-step QMLE. As we discussed in Chapters 12 and 13, sometimes the asymptotic distribution of the first-stage estimator needs to be taken into account. A nice feature of the two-step

QMLE in this context is that the key condition, assumption (12.37), can be shown to hold under assumption (19.27). Therefore, we can ignore the first-stage estimation of η^2.

Under assumption (19.28), a consistent estimator of η^2 is easy to obtain, given an initial estimator of $\boldsymbol{\beta}$ (such as the Poisson QMLE or the geometric QMLE). Given $\hat{\boldsymbol{\beta}}$, form $\hat{m}_i$ and $\hat{u}_i$ as the usual fitted values and residuals. One consistent estimator of η^2 is the coefficient on $\hat{m}_i^2$ in the regression (through the origin) of $\hat{u}_i^2 - \hat{m}_i$ on $\hat{m}_i^2$; this is the estimator suggested by Gourieroux, Monfort, and Trognon (1984b) and Cameron and Trivedi (1986). An alternative estimator of η^2, which is closely related to the GLM estimator of σ^2 suggested in equation (19.15), is a weighted least squares estimate, which can be obtained from the OLS regression $\tilde{\hat{u}}_i^2 - 1$ on $\hat{m}_i$, where the $\tilde{\hat{u}}_i$ are residuals $\hat{u}_i$ weighted by $\hat{m}_i^{-1/2}$. The resulting two-step estimator of $\boldsymbol{\beta}$ is consistent under assumption (19.7) only, so it is just as robust as the Poisson QMLE. It makes sense to use fully robust standard errors and test statistics. If assumption (19.3) holds, the Poisson QMLE is asymptotically more efficient; if assumption (19.28) holds, the two-step negative binomial estimator is more efficient. Notice that neither variance assumption contains the other as a special case for all parameter values; see Wooldridge (1997c) for additional discussion.

The variance specification tests discussed in Section 19.2.5 can be extended to the negative binomial QMLE; see Wooldridge (1991b).

19.3.2 Binomial Regression Models

Sometimes we wish to analyze count data conditional on a known upper bound. For example, Thomas, Strauss, and Henriques (1990) study child mortality within families conditional on number of children ever born. Another example takes the dependent variable, y_i, to be the number of adult children in family i who are high school graduates; the known upper bound, n_i, is the number of children in family i. By conditioning on n_i we are, presumably, treating it as exogenous.

Let $\mathbf{x}_i$ be a set of exogenous variables. A natural starting point is to assume that y_i given $(n_i, \mathbf{x}_i)$ has a binomial distribution, denoted Binomial $[n_i, p(\mathbf{x}_i, \boldsymbol{\beta})]$, where $p(\mathbf{x}_i, \boldsymbol{\beta})$ is a function bounded between zero and one. Usually, y_i is viewed as the sum of n_i independent Bernoulli (zero-one) random variables, and $p(\mathbf{x}_i, \boldsymbol{\beta})$ is the (conditional) probability of success on each trial.

The binomial assumption is too restrictive for all applications. The presence of an unobserved effect would invalidate the binomial assumption (after the effect is integrated out). For example, when y_i is the number of children in a family graduating from high school, unobserved family effects may play an important role.

As in the case of unbounded support, we assume that the conditional mean is correctly specified:

$$\mathrm{E}(y_i \mid \mathbf{x}_i, n_i) = n_i p(\mathbf{x}_i, \boldsymbol{\beta}) \equiv m_i(\boldsymbol{\beta}) \tag{19.32}$$

This formulation ensures that $\mathrm{E}(y_i \mid \mathbf{x}_i, n_i)$ is between zero and n_i. Typically, $p(\mathbf{x}_i, \boldsymbol{\beta}) = G(\mathbf{x}_i\boldsymbol{\beta})$, where $G(\cdot)$ is a cumulative distribution function, such as the standard normal or logistic function.

Given a parametric model $p(\mathbf{x}, \boldsymbol{\beta})$, the binomial quasi–log likelihood for observation i is

$$\ell_i(\boldsymbol{\beta}) = y_i \log[p(\mathbf{x}_i, \boldsymbol{\beta})] + (n_i - y_i) \log[1 - p(\mathbf{x}_i, \boldsymbol{\beta})] \tag{19.33}$$

and the binomial QMLE is obtained by maximizing the sum of $\ell_i(\boldsymbol{\beta})$ over all N observations. From the results of GMT (1984a), the conditional mean parameters are consistently estimated under assumption (19.32) only. This conclusion follows from the general M-estimation results after showing that the true value of $\boldsymbol{\beta}$ maximizes the expected value of equation (19.33) under assumption (19.32) only.

The **binomial GLM variance assumption** is

$$\mathrm{Var}(y_i \mid \mathbf{x}_i, n_i) = \sigma^2 n_i p(\mathbf{x}_i, \boldsymbol{\beta})[1 - p(\mathbf{x}_i, \boldsymbol{\beta})] = \sigma^2 v_i(\boldsymbol{\beta}) \tag{19.34}$$

which generalizes the nominal binomial assumption with $\sigma^2 = 1$. [McCullagh and Nelder (1989, Section 4.5) discuss a model that leads to assumption (19.34) with $\sigma^2 > 1$. But underdispersion is also possible.] Even the GLM assumption can fail if the binary outcomes comprising y_i are not independent conditional on $(\mathbf{x}_i, n_i)$. Therefore, it makes sense to use the fully robust asymptotic variance estimator for the binomial QMLE.

Owing to the structure of LEF densities, and given our earlier analysis of the Poisson and negative binomial cases, it is straightforward to describe the econometric analysis for the binomial QMLE: simply take $\hat{m}_i \equiv n_i p(\mathbf{x}_i, \hat{\boldsymbol{\beta}})$, $\hat{u}_i \equiv y_i - \hat{m}_i$, $\nabla_\beta \hat{m}_i \equiv n_i \nabla_\beta \hat{p}_i$, and $\hat{v}_i \equiv n_i \hat{p}_i(1 - \hat{p}_i)$ in equations (19.31). An estimator of σ^2 under assumption (19.34) is also easily obtained: replace $\hat{m}_i$ in equation (19.15) with $\hat{v}_i$. The structure of asymptotic variances and score tests is identical.

19.4 Other QMLES in the Linear Exponential Family

Sometimes we want to use a quasi-MLE analysis for other kinds of response variables. We will consider two here. The **exponential regression model** is well suited to strictly positive, roughly continuous responses. **Fractional logit regression** can be used when the response variable takes on values in the unit interval.

19.4.1 Exponential Regression Models

Just as in the Poisson regression model, in an exponential regression model we specify a conditional mean function, $m(\mathbf{x}, \boldsymbol{\beta})$. However, we now use the exponential quasi–log likelihood function, $\ell_i(\boldsymbol{\beta}) = -y_i/m(\mathbf{x}_i, \boldsymbol{\beta}) - \log[m(\mathbf{x}_i, \boldsymbol{\beta})]$. [The "exponential" in "exponential regression model" refers to the quasi-likelihood used, and not to the mean function $m(\mathbf{x}, \boldsymbol{\beta})$.] The most popular choice of $m(\mathbf{x}, \boldsymbol{\beta})$ happens to be $\exp(\mathbf{x}\boldsymbol{\beta})$.

The results of GMT (1984a) imply that, provided the conditional mean is correctly specified, the exponential QMLE consistently estimates the conditional mean parameters. Thus the exponential QMLE enjoys the same robustness properties as the Poisson QMLE.

The GLM variance assumption for exponential regression is

$$\mathrm{Var}(y \mid \mathbf{x}) = \sigma^2[\mathrm{E}(y \mid \mathbf{x})]^2 \tag{19.35}$$

When $\sigma^2 = 1$, assumption (19.35) gives the variance-mean relationship for the exponential distribution. Under assumption (19.35), σ is the **coefficient of variation**: it is the ratio of the conditional standard deviation of y to its conditional mean.

Whether or not assumption (19.35) holds, an asymptotic variance matrix can be estimated. The fully robust form is expression (19.14), but, in defining the score and expected Hessian, the residuals and gradients are weighted by $1/\hat{m}_i$ rather than $\hat{m}_i^{-1/2}$. Under assumption (19.35), a valid estimator is

$$\hat{\sigma}^2\left(\sum_{i=1}^{N} \nabla_\beta \hat{m}_i' \nabla_\beta \hat{m}_i / \hat{v}_i\right)^{-1}$$

where $\hat{\sigma}^2 = N^{-1}\sum_{i=1}^{N} \hat{u}_i^2/\hat{m}_i^2$ and $\hat{v}_i = \hat{m}_i^2$. Score tests and quasi–likelihood ratio tests can be computed just as in the Poisson case. Most statistical packages implement exponential regression with an exponential mean function; it is sometimes called the **gamma regression model** because the exponential distribution is a special case of the gamma distribution.

19.4.2 Fractional Logit Regression

Quasi-likelihood methods are also available when y is a variable restricted to the unit interval, $[0, 1]$. {By rescaling, we can cover the case where y is restricted to the interval $[a, b]$ for known constants $a < b$. The transformation is $(y - a)/(b - a)$.} Examples include fraction of income contributed to charity, fraction of weekly hours spent working, proportion of a firm's total capitalization accounted for by debt capital, and high school graduation rates. In some cases, each y_i might be obtained by dividing a count variable by an upper bound, n_i.

Given explanatory variables $\mathbf{x}$, a linear model for $\mathrm{E}(y \mid \mathbf{x})$ has the same strengths and weaknesses as the linear probability model for binary y. When y is *strictly* between zero and one, a popular alternative is to assume that the **log-odds transformation**, $\log[y/(1-y)]$, has a conditional expectation of the form $\mathbf{x}\boldsymbol{\beta}$. The motivation for using $\log[y/(1-y)]$ as a dependent variable in a linear model is that $\log[y/(1-y)]$ ranges over all real values as y ranges between zero and one. This approach leads to estimation of $\boldsymbol{\beta}$ by OLS. Unfortunately, using the log-odds transformation has two drawbacks. First, it cannot be used directly if y takes on the boundary values, zero and one. While we can always use adjustments for the boundary values, such adjustments are necessarily arbitrary. Second, even if y is strictly inside the unit interval, $\boldsymbol{\beta}$ is difficult to interpret: without further assumptions, it is not possible to recover an estimate of $\mathrm{E}(y \mid \mathbf{x})$, and with further assumptions, it is still nontrivial to estimate $\mathrm{E}(y \mid \mathbf{x})$. See Papke and Wooldridge (1996) and Problem 19.8 for further discussion.

An approach that avoids both these problems is to model $\mathrm{E}(y \mid \mathbf{x})$ as a logistic function:

$$\mathrm{E}(y \mid \mathbf{x}) = \exp(\mathbf{x}\boldsymbol{\beta})/[1 + \exp(\mathbf{x}\boldsymbol{\beta})] \tag{19.36}$$

This model ensures that predicted values for y are in $(0, 1)$ and that the effect of any x_j on $\mathrm{E}(y \mid \mathbf{x})$ diminishes as $\mathbf{x}\boldsymbol{\beta} \to \infty$. Just as in the binary logit model, $\partial \mathrm{E}(y \mid \mathbf{x})/\partial x_j = \beta_j g(\mathbf{x}\boldsymbol{\beta})$, where $g(z) = \exp(z)/[1 + \exp(z)]^2$. In applications, the partial effects should be evaluated at the $\hat{\beta}_j$ and interesting values of $\mathbf{x}$. Plugging in the sample averages, $\bar{\mathbf{x}}$, makes the partial effects from equation (19.36) roughly comparable to the coefficients from a linear regression for $\mathrm{E}(y \mid \mathbf{x})$: $\hat{\gamma}_j \approx \hat{\beta}_j g(\bar{\mathbf{x}}\hat{\boldsymbol{\beta}})$, where the $\hat{\gamma}_j$ are the OLS estimates from the linear regression of y on $\mathbf{x}$.

Given equation (19.36), one approach to estimating $\boldsymbol{\beta}$ is nonlinear least squares, as we discussed in Chapter 12. However, the assumption that implies relative efficiency of NLS—namely, $\mathrm{Var}(y \mid \mathbf{x}) = \sigma^2$—is unlikely to hold for fractional y. A method that is just as robust [in the sense that it consistently estimates $\boldsymbol{\beta}$ under assumption (19.36) only] is quasi-MLE, where the quasi-likelihood function is the binary choice log likelihood. Therefore, quasi–log likelihood for observation i is exactly as in equation (15.17) [with $G(\cdot)$ the logistic function], although y_i can be any value in $[0, 1]$. The mechanics of obtaining $\hat{\boldsymbol{\beta}}$ are identical to the binary response case.

Inference is complicated by the fact that the binary response density cannot be the actual density of y given $\mathbf{x}$. Generally, a fully robust variance matrix estimator and test statistics should be obtained. These are gotten by applying the formulas for the binomial case with $n_i \equiv 1$ and $p(\mathbf{x}, \boldsymbol{\beta}) \equiv \exp(\mathbf{x}\boldsymbol{\beta})/[1 + \exp(\mathbf{x}\boldsymbol{\beta})]$. The GLM assumption for fractional logit regression is given in assumption (19.34) with $n_i = 1$. See

Papke and Wooldridge (1996) for more details, as well as suggestions for specification tests and for an application to participation rates in 401(k) pension plans.

19.5 Endogeneity and Sample Selection with an Exponential Regression Function

With all of the previous models, standard econometric problems can arise. In this section, we will study two of the problems when the regression function for y has an exponential form: endogeneity of an explanatory variable and incidental truncation. We follow the methods in Wooldridge (1997c), which are closely related to those suggested by Terza (1998). Gurmu and Trivedi (1994) and the references therein discuss the problems of data censoring, truncation, and two-tier or hurdle models.

19.5.1 Endogeneity

We approach the problem of endogenous explanatory variables from an omitted variables perspective. Let y_1 be the nonnegative, in principle unbounded variable to be explained, and let $\mathbf{z}$ and $\mathbf{y}_2$ be observable explanatory variables (of dimension $1 \times L$ and $1 \times G_1$, respectively). Let c_1 be an unobserved latent variable (or unobserved heterogeneity). We assume that the (structural) model of interest is an omitted variables model of exponential form, written in the population as

$$\mathrm{E}(y_1 \mid \mathbf{z}, \mathbf{y}_2, c_1) = \exp(\mathbf{z}_1\boldsymbol{\delta}_1 + \mathbf{y}_2\boldsymbol{\gamma}_1 + c_1) \tag{19.37}$$

where $\mathbf{z}_1$ is a $1 \times L_1$ subset of $\mathbf{z}$ containing unity; thus, the model (19.37) incorporates some exclusion restrictions. On the one hand, the elements in $\mathbf{z}$ are assumed to be exogenous in the sense that they are independent of c_1. On the other hand, $\mathbf{y}_2$ and c_1 are allowed to be correlated, so that $\mathbf{y}_2$ is potentially endogenous.

To use a quasi-likelihood approach, we assume that $\mathbf{y}_2$ has a linear reduced form satisfying certain assumptions. Write

$$\mathbf{y}_2 = \mathbf{z}\boldsymbol{\Pi}_2 + \mathbf{v}_2 \tag{19.38}$$

where $\boldsymbol{\Pi}_2$ is an $L \times G_1$ matrix of reduced form parameters and $\mathbf{v}_2$ is a $1 \times G_1$ vector of reduced form errors. We assume that the rank condition for identification holds, which requires the order condition $L - L_1 \geq G_1$. In addition, we assume that $(c_1, \mathbf{v}_2)$ is independent of $\mathbf{z}$, and that

$$c_1 = \mathbf{v}_2\boldsymbol{\rho}_1 + e_1 \tag{19.39}$$

where e_1 is independent of $\mathbf{v}_2$ (and necessarily of $\mathbf{z}$). (We could relax the independence assumptions to some degree, but we cannot just assume that $\mathbf{v}_2$ is uncorrelated with $\mathbf{z}$

and that e_1 is uncorrelated with $\mathbf{v}_2$.) It is natural to assume that $\mathbf{v}_2$ has zero mean, but it is convenient to assume that $\mathrm{E}[\exp(e_1)] = 1$ rather than $\mathrm{E}(e_1) = 0$. This assumption is without loss of generality whenever a constant appears in $\mathbf{z}_1$, which should almost always be the case.

If $(c_1, \mathbf{v}_2)$ has a multivariate normal distribution, then the representation in equation (19.39) under the stated assumptions always holds. We could also extend equation (19.39) by putting other functions of $\mathbf{v}_2$ on the right-hand side, such as squares and cross products, but we do not show these explicitly. Note that $\mathbf{y}_2$ is exogenous if and only if $\boldsymbol{\rho}_1 = \mathbf{0}$.

Under the maintained assumptions, we have

$$\mathrm{E}(y_1 \mid \mathbf{z}, \mathbf{y}_2, \mathbf{v}_2) = \exp(\mathbf{z}_1 \boldsymbol{\delta}_1 + \mathbf{y}_2 \boldsymbol{\gamma}_1 + \mathbf{v}_2 \boldsymbol{\rho}_1) \tag{19.40}$$

and this equation suggests a strategy for consistently estimating $\boldsymbol{\delta}_1$, $\boldsymbol{\gamma}_1$, and $\boldsymbol{\rho}_1$. If $\mathbf{v}_2$ were observed, we could simply use this regression function in one of the QMLE earlier methods (for example, Poisson, two-step negative binomial, or exponential). Because these methods consistently estimate correctly specified conditional means, we can immediately conclude that the QMLEs would be consistent. [If y_1 conditional on $(\mathbf{z}, \mathbf{y}_2, c_1)$ has a Poisson distribution with mean in equation (19.37), then the distribution of y_1 given $(\mathbf{z}, \mathbf{y}_2, \mathbf{v}_2)$ has overdispersion of the type (19.28), so the two-step negative binomial estimator might be preferred in this context.]

To operationalize this procedure, the unknown quantities $\mathbf{v}_2$ must be replaced with estimates. Let $\hat{\boldsymbol{\Pi}}_2$ be the $L \times G_1$ matrix of OLS estimates from the first-stage estimation of equation (19.38); these are consistent estimates of $\boldsymbol{\Pi}_2$. Define $\hat{\mathbf{v}}_2 = \mathbf{y}_2 - \mathbf{z}\hat{\boldsymbol{\Pi}}_2$ (where the observation subscript is suppressed). Then estimate the exponential regression model using regressors $(\mathbf{z}_1, \mathbf{y}_2, \hat{\mathbf{v}}_2)$ by one of the QMLEs. The estimates $(\hat{\boldsymbol{\delta}}_1, \hat{\boldsymbol{\gamma}}_1, \hat{\boldsymbol{\rho}}_1)$ from this procedure are consistent using standard arguments from two-step estimation in Chapter 12.

This method is similar in spirit to the methods we saw for binary response (Chapter 15) and censored regression models (Chapter 16). There is one difference: here, we do not need to make distributional assumptions about y_1 or $\mathbf{y}_2$. However, we do assume that the reduced-form errors $\mathbf{v}_2$ are independent of $\mathbf{z}$. In addition, we assume that c_1 and $\mathbf{v}_2$ are linearly related with e_1 in equation (19.39) independent of $\mathbf{v}_2$. Later we will show how to relax these assumptions using a method of moments approach.

Because $\hat{\mathbf{v}}_2$ depends on $\hat{\boldsymbol{\Pi}}_2$, the variance matrix estimators for $\hat{\boldsymbol{\delta}}_1$, $\hat{\boldsymbol{\gamma}}_1$, and $\hat{\boldsymbol{\rho}}_1$ should generally be adjusted to account for this dependence, as described in Sections 12.5.2 and 14.1. Using the results from Section 12.5.2, it can be shown that estimation of $\boldsymbol{\Pi}_2$ does not affect the asymptotic variance of the QMLEs when $\boldsymbol{\rho}_1 = \mathbf{0}$, just as we saw when testing for endogeneity in probit and Tobit models. Therefore, *testing* for endogeneity of $\mathbf{y}_2$ is relatively straightforward: simply test H_0: $\boldsymbol{\rho}_1 = \mathbf{0}$ using a Wald or LM statistic. When $G_1 = 1$, the most convenient statistic is probably the t statistic on $\hat{v}_2$, with the fully robust form being the most preferred (but the GLM form is also useful). The LM test for omitted variables is convenient when $G_1 > 1$ because it can be computed after estimating the null model ($\boldsymbol{\rho}_1 = \mathbf{0}$) and then doing a variable addition test for $\hat{\mathbf{v}}_2$. The test has G_1 degrees of freedom in the chi-square distribution.

There is a final comment worth making about this test. The null hypothesis is the same as $\mathrm{E}(y_1 \mid \mathbf{z}, \mathbf{y}_2) = \exp(\mathbf{z}_1\boldsymbol{\delta}_1 + \mathbf{y}_2\boldsymbol{\gamma}_1)$. The test for endogeneity of $\mathbf{y}_2$ simply looks for whether a particular linear combination of $\mathbf{y}_2$ and $\mathbf{z}$ appears in this conditional expectation. For the purposes of getting a limiting chi-square distribution, it does not matter where the linear combination $\hat{\mathbf{v}}_2$ comes from. In other words, under the null hypothesis none of the assumptions we made about $(c_1, \mathbf{v}_2)$ need to hold: $\mathbf{v}_2$ need not be independent of $\mathbf{z}$, and e_1 in equation (19.39) need not be independent of $\mathbf{v}_2$. Therefore, as a test, this procedure is very robust, and it can be applied when $\mathbf{y}_2$ contains binary, count, or other discrete variables. Unfortunately, if $\mathbf{y}_2$ is endogenous, the correction does not work without something like the assumptions made previously.

Example 19.2 (Is Education Endogenous in the Fertility Equation?): We test for endogeneity of *educ* in Example 19.1. The IV for *educ* is a binary indicator for whether the woman was born in the first half of the year (*frsthalf*), which we assume is exogenous in the fertility equation. In the reduced-form equation for *educ*, the coefficient on *frsthalf* is $-.636$ (se $= .104$), and so there is a significant negative partial relationship between years of schooling and being born in the first half of the year.

When we add the first-stage residuals, $\hat{v}_2$, to the Poisson regression, its coefficient is .025, and its GLM standard error is .028. Therefore, there is little evidence against the null hypothesis that *educ* is exogenous. The coefficient on *educ* actually becomes larger in magnitude ($-.046$), but it is much less precisely estimated.

Mullahy (1997) has shown how to estimate exponential models when some explanatory variables are endogenous without making assumptions about the reduced form of $\mathbf{y}_2$. This approach is especially attractive for dummy endogenous and other discrete explanatory variables, where the linearity in equation (19.39) coupled with independence of $\mathbf{z}$ and $\mathbf{v}_2$ is unrealistic. To sketch Mullahy's approach, write $\mathbf{x}_1 = (\mathbf{z}_1, \mathbf{y}_2)$ and $\boldsymbol{\beta}_1 = (\boldsymbol{\delta}_1', \boldsymbol{\gamma}_1')'$. Then, under the model (19.37), we can write

$$y_1 \exp(-\mathbf{x}_1\boldsymbol{\beta}_1) = \exp(c_1)a_1, \qquad \mathrm{E}(a_1 \mid \mathbf{z}, \mathbf{y}_2, c_1) = 1 \tag{19.41}$$

If we assume that c_1 is independent of $\mathbf{z}$—a standard assumption concerning unobserved heterogeneity and exogenous variables—and use the normalization $\mathrm{E}[\exp(c_1)] = 1$, we have the conditional moment restriction

$$\mathrm{E}[y_1 \exp(-\mathbf{x}_1\boldsymbol{\beta}_1) \mid \mathbf{z}] = 1 \tag{19.42}$$

Because y_1, $\mathbf{x}_1$, and $\mathbf{z}$ are all observable, condition (19.42) can be used as the basis for generalized method of moments estimation. The function $g(y_1, \mathbf{y}_2, \mathbf{z}_1; \boldsymbol{\beta}_1) \equiv y_1 \exp(-\mathbf{x}_1\boldsymbol{\beta}_1) - 1$, which depends on observable data and the parameters, is uncorrelated with any function of $\mathbf{z}$ (at the true value of $\boldsymbol{\beta}_1$). GMM estimation can be used as in Section 14.2 once a vector of instrumental variables has been chosen.

An important feature of Mullahy's approach is that no assumptions, other than the standard rank condition for identification in nonlinear models, are made about the distribution of $\mathbf{y}_2$ given $\mathbf{z}$: we need not assume the existence of a linear reduced form for $\mathbf{y}_2$ with errors independent of $\mathbf{z}$. Mullahy's procedure is computationally more difficult, and testing for endogeneity in his framework is harder than in the QMLE approach. Therefore, we might first use the two-step quasi-likelihood method proposed earlier for testing, and if endogeneity seems to be important, Mullahy's GMM estimator can be implemented. See Mullahy (1997) for details and an empirical example.

19.5.2 Sample Selection

It is also possible to test and correct for sample selection in exponential regression models. The case where selection is determined by the dependent variable being above or below a known threshold requires full maximum likelihood methods using a truncated count distribution; you are referred to the book by Cameron and Trivedi (1998). Here, we assume that sample selection is related to an unobservable in the population model

$$\mathrm{E}(y_1 \mid \mathbf{x}, c_1) = \exp(\mathbf{x}_1\boldsymbol{\beta}_1 + c_1) \tag{19.43}$$

where $\mathbf{x}_1$ is a $1 \times K_1$ vector of exogenous variables containing a constant, and c_1 is an unobserved random variable. The full set of exogenous variables is $\mathbf{x}$, and c_1 is independent of $\mathbf{x}$. Therefore, *if* a random sample on $(\mathbf{x}_1, y_1)$ were available, $\boldsymbol{\beta}_1$ could be consistently estimated by a Poisson regression of y_1 on $\mathbf{x}_1$ (or by some other QMLE) under the normalization $\mathrm{E}[\exp(c_1)] = 1$.

A sample selection problem arises when a random sample on $(\mathbf{x}_1, y_1)$ from the relevant population is not available. Let y_2 denote a binary selection indicator, which is unity if $(\mathbf{x}_1, y_1)$ is observed and zero otherwise. We assume that y_2 is determined by $y_2 = 1[\mathbf{x}_2\boldsymbol{\delta}_2 + v_2 > 0]$, where $1[\cdot]$ is the indicator function, $\mathbf{x}_2$ is a subset of $\mathbf{x}$ (typically, $\mathbf{x}_2 = \mathbf{x}$), and v_2 is unobserved. This is a standard sample selection mechanism, where y_2 and $\mathbf{x}_2$ must be observable for all units in the population.

In this setting, sample selection bias arises when v_2 is correlated with c_1. In particular, if we write equation (19.43) with a multiplicative error, $y_1 = \exp(\mathbf{x}_1\boldsymbol{\beta}_1 + c_1)a_1$, with $\mathrm{E}(a_1 \mid \mathbf{x}, c_1) = 1$ by definition, we also assume that $\mathrm{E}(a_1 \mid \mathbf{x}, c_1, v_2) = \mathrm{E}(a_1) = 1$. In other words, selection may be correlated with c_1 but not a_1. This model is similar to the linear model with sample selection in Section 17.4.1 where the error in the regression equation can be decomposed into two parts, one that is correlated with v_2 (c_1) and one that is not (a_1).

To derive a simple correction, assume that (c_1, v_2) is independent of $\mathbf{x}$ and bivariate normal with zero mean; v_2 also has a unit variance, so that y_2 given $\mathbf{x}$ follows a probit model. These assumptions imply that $\mathrm{E}[\exp(c_1) \mid \mathbf{x}, v_2] = \mathrm{E}[\exp(c_1) \mid v_2] = \exp(\rho_0 + \rho_1 v_2)$ for parameters ρ_0 and ρ_1. Provided $\mathbf{x}_1$ contains a constant, we can use the normalization $\exp(\rho_0) = 1$, and we do so in what follows. Then $\mathrm{E}(y_1 \mid \mathbf{x}, v_2) = \exp(\mathbf{x}_1\boldsymbol{\beta}_1 + \rho_1 v_2)$, and so by iterated expectations,

$$\mathrm{E}(y_1 \mid \mathbf{x}, y_2 = 1) = \exp(\mathbf{x}_1\boldsymbol{\beta}_1)g(\mathbf{x}_2\boldsymbol{\delta}_2, \rho_1) \tag{19.44}$$

where $g(\mathbf{x}_2\boldsymbol{\delta}_2, \rho_1) \equiv \mathrm{E}[\exp(\rho_1 v_2) \mid v_2 > -\mathbf{x}_2\boldsymbol{\delta}_2]$. By integrating the function $\exp(\rho_1 v_2)$ against the truncated standard normal density conditional on $v_2 > -\mathbf{x}_2\boldsymbol{\delta}_2$, it can be shown that $g(\mathbf{x}_2\boldsymbol{\delta}_2, \rho_1) = \exp(\rho_1^2)\Phi(\rho_1 + \mathbf{x}_2\boldsymbol{\delta}_2)/\Phi(\mathbf{x}_2\boldsymbol{\delta}_2)$, where $\Phi(\cdot)$ is the standard normal cdf.

Given equation (19.44), we can apply a two-step method similar to Heckman's (1976) method for linear models that we covered in Chapter 17. First, run a probit of y_2 on $\mathbf{x}_2$ using the entire sample. Let $\hat{\boldsymbol{\delta}}_2$ be the probit estimator of $\boldsymbol{\delta}_2$. Next, on the selected subsample for which $(y_1, \mathbf{x}_1)$ is observed, use a QMLE analysis with conditional mean function $\exp(\mathbf{x}_1\boldsymbol{\beta}_1)g(\mathbf{x}_2\hat{\boldsymbol{\delta}}_2, \rho_1)$ to estimate $\boldsymbol{\beta}_1$ and ρ_1. If $\rho_1 \neq 0$, then, as usual, the asymptotic variance of $\hat{\boldsymbol{\beta}}_1$ and $\hat{\rho}_1$ should be adjusted for estimation of $\boldsymbol{\delta}_2$.

Testing $\rho_1 = 0$ is simple if we use the robust score test. This requires the derivative of the mean function with respect to ρ_1, evaluated at $\rho_1 = 0$. But $\partial g(\mathbf{x}_2\boldsymbol{\delta}_2, 0)/\partial\rho_1 = \lambda(\mathbf{x}_2\boldsymbol{\delta}_2)$, where $\lambda(\cdot)$ is the usual inverse Mills ratio that appears in linear sample selection contexts. Thus the derivative of the mean function with respect to ρ_1, evaluated at all estimates under the null, is simply $\exp(\mathbf{x}_1\hat{\boldsymbol{\beta}}_1)\lambda(\mathbf{x}_2\hat{\boldsymbol{\delta}}_2)$. This result gives the following procedure to test for sample selection: (1) let $\hat{\boldsymbol{\beta}}_1$ be a QMLE (for example, the Poisson) using the selected sample, and define $\hat{y}_{i1} \equiv \exp(\mathbf{x}_{i1}\hat{\boldsymbol{\beta}}_1)$, $\hat{u}_{i1} \equiv y_{i1} - \hat{y}_{i1}$, and $\tilde{u}_{i1} \equiv \hat{u}_{i1}/\sqrt{\hat{y}_{i1}}$ for all i in the selected sample; (2) obtain $\hat{\boldsymbol{\delta}}_2$ from the probit of y_2 onto $\mathbf{x}_2$, using the entire sample; denote the estimated inverse Mills ratio for each observation i by $\hat{\lambda}_{i2}$; and (3) regress $\tilde{u}_{i1}$ onto $\sqrt{\hat{y}_{i1}}\mathbf{x}_{i1}$, $\sqrt{\hat{y}_{i1}}\hat{\lambda}_{i2}$ using the selected sample, and use $N_1 R_u^2$ as asymptotically χ_1^2, where N_1 is the number of observations in the selected sample. This approach assumes that the GLM assumption holds under H_0. For the fully robust test, first regress $\sqrt{\hat{y}_{i1}}\hat{\lambda}_{i2}$ onto $\sqrt{\hat{y}_{i1}}\mathbf{x}_{i1}$ using the selected sample and save the residuals, $\tilde{r}_{i1}$; then regress 1 on $\tilde{u}_{i1}\tilde{r}_{i1}$, $i = 1, 2, \ldots, N_1$, and use $N_1 - \mathrm{SSR}$ as asymptotically χ_1^2.

19.6 Panel Data Methods

In this final section, we discuss estimation of panel data models, primarily focusing on count data. Our main interest is in models that contain unobserved effects, but we initially cover pooled estimation when the model does not explicitly contain an unobserved effect.

The pioneering work in unobserved effects count data models was done by Hausman, Hall, and Griliches (1984) (HHG), who were interested in explaining patent applications by firms in terms of spending on research and development. HHG developed random and fixed effects models under full distributional assumptions. Wooldridge (1999a) has shown that one of the approaches suggested by HHG, which is typically called the **fixed effects Poisson model**, has some nice robustness properties. We will study those here.

Other count panel data applications include (with response variable in parentheses) Rose (1990) (number of airline accidents), Papke (1991) (number of firm births in an industry), Downes and Greenstein (1996) (number of private schools in a public school district), and Page (1995) (number of housing units shown to individuals). The time series dimension in each of these studies allows us to control for unobserved heterogeneity in the cross section units, and to estimate certain dynamic relationships.

As with the rest of the book, we explicitly consider the case with N large relative to T, as the asymptotics hold with T fixed and $N \to \infty$.

19.6.1 Pooled QMLE

As with the linear case, we begin by discussing pooled estimation after specifying a model for a conditional mean. Let $\{(\mathbf{x}_t, y_t): t = 1, 2, \ldots, T\}$ denote the time series observations for a random draw from the cross section population. We assume that, for some $\boldsymbol{\beta}_o \in \mathscr{B}$,

$$\mathrm{E}(y_t \mid \mathbf{x}_t) = m(\mathbf{x}_t, \boldsymbol{\beta}_o), \qquad t = 1, 2, \ldots, T \tag{19.45}$$

This assumption simply means that we have a correctly specified parametric model for $\mathrm{E}(y_t \mid \mathbf{x}_t)$. For notational convenience only, we assume that the function m itself does not change over time. Relaxing this assumption just requires a notational change, or we can include time dummies in $\mathbf{x}_t$. For $y_t \geq 0$ and unbounded from above, the most common conditional mean is $\exp(\mathbf{x}_t\boldsymbol{\beta})$. There is no restriction on the time dependence of the observations under assumption (19.45), and $\mathbf{x}_t$ can contain any observed variables. For example, a static model has $\mathbf{x}_t = \mathbf{z}_t$, where $\mathbf{z}_t$ is dated contemporaneously with y_t. A finite distributed lag has $\mathbf{x}_t$ containing lags of $\mathbf{z}_t$. Strict exogeneity of $(\mathbf{x}_1, \ldots, \mathbf{x}_T)$, that is, $\mathrm{E}(y_t \mid \mathbf{x}_1, \ldots, \mathbf{x}_T) = \mathrm{E}(y_t \mid \mathbf{x}_t)$, is not assumed. In particular, $\mathbf{x}_t$ can contain lagged dependent variables, although how these might appear in nonlinear models is not obvious (see Wooldridge, 1997c, for some possibilities). A limitation of model (19.45) is that it does not explicitly incorporate an unobserved effect.

For each $i = 1, 2, \ldots, N$, $\{(\mathbf{x}_{it}, y_{it})\colon t = 1, 2, \ldots, T\}$ denotes the time series observations for cross section unit i. We assume random sampling from the cross section.

One approach to estimating $\boldsymbol{\beta}_o$ is pooled nonlinear least squares, which was introduced in Problem 12.6. When y is a count variable, a Poisson QMLE can be used. This approach is completely analogous to pooled probit and pooled Tobit estimation with panel data. Note, however, that we are not assuming that the Poisson distribution is true.

For each i the quasi–log likelihood for pooled Poisson estimation is (up to additive constants)

$$\ell_i(\boldsymbol{\beta}) = \sum_{t=1}^{T} \{y_{it} \log[m(\mathbf{x}_{it}, \boldsymbol{\beta})] - m(\mathbf{x}_{it}, \boldsymbol{\beta})\} \equiv \sum_{t=1}^{T} \ell_{it}(\boldsymbol{\beta}) \tag{19.46}$$

The **pooled Poisson QMLE** then maximizes the sum of $\ell_i(\boldsymbol{\beta})$ across $i = 1, \ldots, N$. Consistency and asymptotic normality of this estimator follows from the Chapter 12 results, once we use the fact that $\boldsymbol{\beta}_o$ maximizes $\mathrm{E}[\ell_i(\boldsymbol{\beta})]$; this follows from GMT (1984a). Thus pooled Poisson estimation is robust in the sense that it consistently estimates $\boldsymbol{\beta}_o$ under assumption (19.45) only.

Without further assumptions we must be careful in estimating the asymptotic variance of $\hat{\boldsymbol{\beta}}$. Let $\mathbf{s}_i(\boldsymbol{\beta})$ be the $P \times 1$ score of $\ell_i(\boldsymbol{\beta})$, which can be written as $\mathbf{s}_i(\boldsymbol{\beta}) = \sum_{t=1}^{T} \mathbf{s}_{it}(\boldsymbol{\beta})$, where $\mathbf{s}_{it}(\boldsymbol{\beta})$ is the score of $\ell_{it}(\boldsymbol{\beta})$; each $\mathbf{s}_{it}(\boldsymbol{\beta})$ has the form (19.12) but with $(\mathbf{x}_{it}, y_{it})$ in place of $(\mathbf{x}_i, y_i)$.

The asymptotic variance of $\sqrt{N}(\hat{\boldsymbol{\beta}} - \boldsymbol{\beta}_o)$ has the usual form $\mathbf{A}_o^{-1}\mathbf{B}_o\mathbf{A}_o^{-1}$, where $\mathbf{A}_o \equiv \sum_{t=1}^{T} \mathrm{E}[\nabla_\beta m_{it}(\boldsymbol{\beta}_o)' \nabla_\beta m_{it}(\boldsymbol{\beta}_o)/m_{it}(\boldsymbol{\beta}_o)]$ and $\mathbf{B}_o \equiv \mathrm{E}[\mathbf{s}_i(\boldsymbol{\beta}_o)\mathbf{s}_i(\boldsymbol{\beta}_o)']$. Consistent estimators are

$$\hat{\mathbf{A}} = N^{-1} \sum_{i=1}^{N} \sum_{t=1}^{T} \nabla_\beta \hat{m}_{it}' \nabla_\beta \hat{m}_{it} / \hat{m}_{it} \tag{19.47}$$

$$\hat{\mathbf{B}} = N^{-1} \sum_{i=1}^{N} \mathbf{s}_i(\hat{\boldsymbol{\beta}})\mathbf{s}_i(\hat{\boldsymbol{\beta}})' \tag{19.48}$$

and we can use $\hat{\mathbf{A}}^{-1}\hat{\mathbf{B}}\hat{\mathbf{A}}^{-1}/N$ for $\text{Av}\hat{\text{a}}\text{r}(\hat{\boldsymbol{\beta}})$. This procedure is fully robust to the presence of serial correlation in the score and arbitrary conditional variances. It should be used in the construction of standard errors and Wald statistics. The quasi-LR statistic is not usually valid in this setup because of neglected time dependence and possible violations of the Poisson variance assumption.

If the conditional mean is dynamically complete in the sense that

$$\mathrm{E}(y_t \mid \mathbf{x}_t, y_{t-1}, \mathbf{x}_{t-1}, \ldots, y_1, \mathbf{x}_1) = \mathrm{E}(y_t \mid \mathbf{x}_t) \tag{19.49}$$

then $\{\mathbf{s}_{it}(\boldsymbol{\beta}_o)\colon t = 1, 2, \ldots, T\}$ is serially uncorrelated. Consequently, under assumption (19.49), a consistent estimator of $\mathbf{B}$ is

$$\hat{\mathbf{B}} = N^{-1} \sum_{i=1}^{N} \sum_{t=1}^{T} \mathbf{s}_{it}(\hat{\boldsymbol{\beta}})\mathbf{s}_{it}(\hat{\boldsymbol{\beta}})' \tag{19.50}$$

Using this equation along with $\hat{\mathbf{A}}$ produces the asymptotic variance that results from treating the observations as one long cross section, but without the Poisson or GLM variance assumptions. Thus, equation (19.50) affords a certain amount of robustness, but it requires the dynamic completeness assumption (19.49).

There are many other possibilities. If we impose the GLM assumption

$$\mathrm{Var}(y_{it} \mid \mathbf{x}_{it}) = \sigma_o^2 m(\mathbf{x}_{it}, \boldsymbol{\beta}_o), \qquad t = 1, 2, \ldots, T \tag{19.51}$$

along with dynamic completeness, then $\mathrm{Avar}(\hat{\boldsymbol{\beta}})$ can be estimated by

$$\hat{\sigma}^2 \left(\sum_{i=1}^{N} \sum_{t=1}^{T} \nabla_\beta \hat{m}_{it}' \nabla_\beta \hat{m}_{it} / \hat{m}_{it} \right)^{-1} \tag{19.52}$$

where $\hat{\sigma}^2 = (NT - P)^{-1} \sum_{i=1}^{N} \sum_{t=1}^{T} \tilde{u}_{it}^2$, $\tilde{u}_{it} = \hat{u}_{it}/\sqrt{\hat{m}_{it}}$, and $\hat{u}_{it} = y_{it} - m_{it}(\hat{\boldsymbol{\beta}})$. This estimator results in a standard GLM analysis on the pooled data.

19.6.2 Specifying Models of Conditional Expectations with Unobserved Effects

We now turn to models that explicitly contain an unobserved effect. The issues that arise here are similar to those that arose in linear panel data models. First, we must know whether the explanatory variables are strictly exogenous conditional on an unobserved effect. Second, we must decide how the unobserved effect should appear in the conditional mean.

Given conditioning variables $\mathbf{x}_t$, strict exogeneity conditional on the unobserved effect c is defined just as in the linear case:

$$E(y_t \mid \mathbf{x}_1, \ldots, \mathbf{x}_T, c) = E(y_t \mid \mathbf{x}_t, c) \tag{19.53}$$

As always, this definition rules out lagged values of y in $\mathbf{x}_t$, and it can rule out feedback from y_t to future explanatory variables. In static models, where $\mathbf{x}_t = \mathbf{z}_t$ for variables $\mathbf{z}_t$ dated contemporaneously with y_t, assumption (19.53) implies that neither past nor future values of $\mathbf{z}$ affect the expected value of y_t, once $\mathbf{z}_t$ and c have been controlled for. This can be too restrictive, but it is often the starting point for analyzing static models.

A finite distributed lag relationship assumes that

$$E(y_t \mid \mathbf{z}_t, \mathbf{z}_{t-1}, \ldots, \mathbf{z}_1, c) = E(y_t \mid \mathbf{z}_t, \mathbf{z}_{t-1}, \ldots, \mathbf{z}_{t-Q}, c), \qquad t > Q \tag{19.54}$$

where Q is the length of the distributed lag. Under assumption (19.54), the strict exogeneity assumption conditional on c becomes

$$E(y_t \mid \mathbf{z}_1, \mathbf{z}_2, \ldots, \mathbf{z}_T, c) = E(y_t \mid \mathbf{z}_1, \ldots, \mathbf{z}_t, c) \tag{19.55}$$

which is less restrictive than in the purely static model because lags of $\mathbf{z}_t$ explicitly appear in the model; it still rules out general feedback from y_t to $(\mathbf{z}_{t+1}, \ldots, \mathbf{z}_T)$.

With count variables, a multiplicative unobserved effect is an attractive functional form:

$$E(y_t \mid \mathbf{x}_t, c) = c \cdot m(\mathbf{x}_t, \boldsymbol{\beta}_o) \tag{19.56}$$

where $m(\mathbf{x}_t, \boldsymbol{\beta})$ is a parametric function known up to the $P \times 1$ vector of parameters $\boldsymbol{\beta}_o$. Equation (19.56) implies that the partial effect of x_{tj} on $\log E(y_t \mid \mathbf{x}_t, c)$ does not depend on the unobserved effect c. Thus quantities such as elasticities and semi-elasticities depend only on $\mathbf{x}_t$ and $\boldsymbol{\beta}_o$. The most popular special case is the exponential model $E(y_t \mid \mathbf{x}_t, a) = \exp(a + \mathbf{x}_t\boldsymbol{\beta})$, which is obtained by taking $c = \exp(a)$.

19.6.3 Random Effects Methods

A **multiplicative random effects model** maintains, at a minimum, two assumptions for a random draw i from the population:

$$E(y_{it} \mid \mathbf{x}_{i1}, \ldots, \mathbf{x}_{iT}, c_i) = c_i m(\mathbf{x}_{it}, \boldsymbol{\beta}_o), \qquad t = 1, 2, \ldots, T \tag{19.57}$$

$$E(c_i \mid \mathbf{x}_{i1}, \ldots, \mathbf{x}_{iT}) = E(c_i) = 1 \tag{19.58}$$

where c_i is the unobserved, time-constant effect, and the observed explanatory variables, $\mathbf{x}_{it}$, may be time constant or time varying. Assumption (19.57) is the strict exogeneity assumption of the $\mathbf{x}_{it}$ conditional on c_i, combined with a regression function multiplicative in c_i. When $y_{it} \geq 0$, such as with a count variable, the most popular choice of the parametric regression function is $m(\mathbf{x}_t, \boldsymbol{\beta}) = \exp(\mathbf{x}_t \boldsymbol{\beta})$, in which case $\mathbf{x}_{it}$ would typically contain a full set of time dummies. Assumption (19.58) says that the unobserved effect, c_i, is mean independent of $\mathbf{x}_i$; we normalize the mean to be one, a step which is without loss of generality for common choices of m, including the exponential function with unity in $\mathbf{x}_t$. Under assumptions (19.57) and (19.58), we can "integrate out" c_i by using the law of iterated expectations:

$$\mathrm{E}(y_{it} \mid \mathbf{x}_i) = \mathrm{E}(y_{it} \mid \mathbf{x}_{it}) = m(\mathbf{x}_{it}, \boldsymbol{\beta}_o), \qquad t = 1, 2, \ldots, T \tag{19.59}$$

Equation (19.59) shows that $\boldsymbol{\beta}_o$ can be consistently estimated by the pooled Poisson method discussed in Section 19.6.1. The robust variance matrix estimator that allows for an arbitrary conditional variance and serial correlation produces valid inference. Just as in a linear random effects model, the presence of the unobserved heterogeneity causes the y_{it} to be correlated over time, conditional on $\mathbf{x}_i$.

When we introduce an unobserved effect explicitly, a random effects analysis typically accounts for the overdispersion and serial dependence implied by assumptions (19.57) and (19.58). For count data, the **Poisson random effects model** is given by

$$y_{it} \mid \mathbf{x}_i, c_i \sim \text{Poisson}[c_i m(\mathbf{x}_{it}, \boldsymbol{\beta}_o)] \tag{19.60}$$

$$y_{it}, y_{ir} \text{ are independent conditional on } \mathbf{x}_i, c_i, \qquad t \neq r \tag{19.61}$$

$$c_i \text{ is independent of } \mathbf{x}_i \text{ and distributed as Gamma}(\delta_o, \delta_o) \tag{19.62}$$

where we parameterize the gamma distribution so that $\mathrm{E}(c_i) = 1$ and $\mathrm{Var}(c_i) = 1/\delta_o \equiv \eta_o^2$. While $\mathrm{Var}(y_{it} \mid \mathbf{x}_i, c_i) = \mathrm{E}(y_{it} \mid \mathbf{x}_i, c_i)$ under assumption (19.60), by equation (19.28), $\mathrm{Var}(y_{it} \mid \mathbf{x}_i) = \mathrm{E}(y_{it} \mid \mathbf{x}_i)[1 + \eta_o^2 \mathrm{E}(y_{it} \mid \mathbf{x}_i)]$, and so assumptions (19.60) and (19.62) imply overdispersion in $\mathrm{Var}(y_{it} \mid \mathbf{x}_i)$. Although other distributional assumptions for c_i can be used, the gamma distribution leads to a tractable density for $(y_{i1}, \ldots, y_{iT})$ given $\mathbf{x}_i$, which is obtained after c_i has been integrated out. (See HHG, p. 917, and Problem 19.11.) Maximum likelihood analysis (conditional on $\mathbf{x}_i$) is relatively straightforward and is implemented by some econometrics packages.

If assumptions (19.60), (19.61), and (19.62) all hold, the conditional MLE is efficient among all estimators that do not use information on the distribution of $\mathbf{x}_i$; see Section 14.5.2. The main drawback with the random effects Poisson model is that it is sensitive to violations of the maintained assumptions, any of which could be false. (Problem 19.5 covers some ways to allow c_i and $\bar{\mathbf{x}}_i$ to be correlated, but they still rely on stronger assumptions than the fixed effects Poisson estimator that we cover in Section 19.6.4.)

A **quasi-MLE random effects analysis** keeps some of the key features of assumptions (19.60)–(19.62) but produces consistent estimators under just the conditional mean assumptions (19.57) and (19.58). Nominally, we maintain assumptions (19.60)–(19.62). Define $u_{it} \equiv y_{it} - \mathrm{E}(y_{it} \mid \mathbf{x}_{it}) = y_{it} - m(\mathbf{x}_{it}, \boldsymbol{\beta})$. Then we can write $u_{it} = c_i m_{it}(\boldsymbol{\beta}_o) + e_{it} - m_{it}(\boldsymbol{\beta}_o) = e_{it} + m_{it}(\boldsymbol{\beta}_o)(c_i - 1)$, where $e_{it} \equiv y_{it} - \mathrm{E}(y_{it} \mid \mathbf{x}_{it}, c_i)$. As we showed in Section 19.3.1,

$$\mathrm{E}(u_{it}^2 \mid \mathbf{x}_i) = m_{it}(\boldsymbol{\beta}_o) + \eta_o^2 m_{it}^2(\boldsymbol{\beta}_o) \tag{19.63}$$

Further, for $t \neq r$,

$$\mathrm{E}(u_{it} u_{ir} \mid \mathbf{x}_i) = \mathrm{E}[(c_i - 1)^2] m_{it}(\boldsymbol{\beta}_o) m_{ir}(\boldsymbol{\beta}_o) = \eta_o^2 m_{it}(\boldsymbol{\beta}_o) m_{ir}(\boldsymbol{\beta}_o) \tag{19.64}$$

where $\eta_o^2 = \mathrm{Var}(c_i)$. The serial correlation in equation (19.64) is reminiscent of the serial correlation that arises in linear random effects models under standard assumptions. This shows explicitly that we must correct for serial dependence in computing the asymptotic variance of the pooled Poisson QMLE in Section 19.6.1. The overdispersion in equation (19.63) is analogous to the variance of the composite error in a linear model. A QMLE random effects analysis exploits these nominal variance and covariance expressions but does not rely on either of them for consistency. If we use equation (19.63) while ignoring equation (19.64), we are led to a **pooled negative binomial analysis**, which is very similar to the pooled Poisson analysis except that the quasi–log likelihood for each time period is the negative binomial discussed in Section 19.3.1. See Wooldridge (1997c) for details.

If assumption (19.64) holds, it is more efficient—possibly much more efficient—to use this information. **Multivariate weighted nonlinear least squares (MWNLS)**—see Problem 12.10—can be used for these purposes. (See GMT, 1984b, for an application to a related model.) The MWNLS estimator in this context is essentially the same as the **generalized estimating equation (GEE)** approach of Zeger, Liang, and Albert (1988). In the GEE literature, the estimated model is called the **population-averaged model** (see Section 15.8.2 for the binary response case). For multiplicative models where c_i and $\mathbf{x}_i$ are independent, the distinction is unimportant.

The MWNLS estimator solves the problem

$$\min_{\boldsymbol{\beta}} \sum_{i=1}^{N} [\mathbf{y}_i - \mathbf{m}_i(\boldsymbol{\beta})]' \hat{\mathbf{W}}_i^{-1} [\mathbf{y}_i - \mathbf{m}_i(\boldsymbol{\beta})]$$

where $\hat{\mathbf{W}}_i$ is the $T \times T$ matrix with the elements from equation (19.63) down its diagonal and the elements from equation (19.64) as its off-diagonals; $\boldsymbol{\beta}_o$ is replaced with the pooled Poisson estimate, and η_o^2 is replaced by the estimate from the pooled regression $\tilde{u}_{it}^2 - 1$ on $\hat{m}_{it}$, $t = 1, \dots, T$, $i = 1, \dots, N$, where $\tilde{u}_{it} = (y_{it} - \hat{m}_{it})/\sqrt{\hat{m}_{it}}$ is the standardized residual. Under assumptions (19.63) and (19.64), the MWNLS estimator is relatively efficient among estimators that only require a correct conditional mean for consistency, and its asymptotic variance can be estimated as

$$\text{Av}\hat{\text{a}}\text{r}(\hat{\boldsymbol{\beta}}) = \left(\sum_{i=1}^{N} \nabla_\beta \hat{\mathbf{m}}_i' \hat{\mathbf{W}}_i^{-1} \nabla_\beta \hat{\mathbf{m}}_i\right)^{-1}$$

As with the other QMLEs, the WNLS estimator is consistent under assumptions (19.57) and (19.58) only, but if assumption (19.63) or (19.64) is violated, the variance matrix needs to be made robust. Letting $\hat{\mathbf{u}}_i \equiv \mathbf{y}_i - \mathbf{m}_i(\hat{\boldsymbol{\beta}})$ (a $T \times 1$ vector), the robust estimator is

$$\left(\sum_{i=1}^{N} \nabla_\beta \hat{\mathbf{m}}_i' \hat{\mathbf{W}}_i^{-1} \nabla_\beta \hat{\mathbf{m}}_i\right)^{-1} \left(\sum_{i=1}^{N} \nabla_\beta \hat{\mathbf{m}}_i' \hat{\mathbf{W}}_i^{-1} \hat{\mathbf{u}}_i \hat{\mathbf{u}}_i' \hat{\mathbf{W}}_i^{-1} \nabla_\beta \hat{\mathbf{m}}_i\right) \left(\sum_{i=1}^{N} \nabla_\beta \hat{\mathbf{m}}_i' \hat{\mathbf{W}}_i^{-1} \nabla_\beta \hat{\mathbf{m}}_i\right)^{-1}$$

This expression gives a way to obtain fully robust inference while having a relatively efficient estimator under the random effects assumptions (19.63) and (19.64).

GMT (1984b) cover a model that suggests an alternative form of $\hat{\mathbf{W}}_i$. The matrix $\hat{\mathbf{W}}_i$ can be modified for other nominal distributional assumptions, such as the exponential (which would be natural to apply to continuous, nonnegative y_{it}.) Any WNLS method is more robust than a fully parametric maximum likelihood analysis, such as that in assumptions (19.60)–(19.62). We must be aware that none of these methods produces consistent estimators if either the strict exogeneity assumption fails or $\mathrm{E}(c_i \mid \mathbf{x}_i)$ depends on $\mathbf{x}_i$.

19.6.4 Fixed Effects Poisson Estimation

HHG first showed how to do a fixed-effect-type analysis of count panel data models, which allows for arbitrary dependence between c_i and $\mathbf{x}_i$. Their fixed effects Poisson assumptions are (19.60) and (19.61), with the conditional mean given still by assumption (19.57). The key is that neither assumption (19.62) nor assumption (19.58) is maintained; in other words, arbitrary dependence between c_i and $\mathbf{x}_i$ is allowed. HHG take $m(\mathbf{x}_{it}, \boldsymbol{\beta}) = \exp(\mathbf{x}_{it}\boldsymbol{\beta})$, which is by far the leading case.

HHG use Andersen's (1970) conditional ML methodology to estimate $\boldsymbol{\beta}$. Let $n_i \equiv \sum_{t=1}^{T} y_{it}$ denote the sum across time of the counts across t. Using standard results on obtaining a joint distribution conditional on the sum of its components, HHG show that

$$\mathbf{y}_i \mid n_i, \mathbf{x}_i, c_i \sim \text{Multinomial}\{n_i, p_1(\mathbf{x}_i, \boldsymbol{\beta}_o), \ldots, p_T(\mathbf{x}_i, \boldsymbol{\beta}_o)\} \tag{19.65}$$

where

$$p_t(\mathbf{x}_i, \boldsymbol{\beta}) \equiv m(\mathbf{x}_{it}, \boldsymbol{\beta}) \Big/ \left[\sum_{r=1}^{T} m(\mathbf{x}_{ir}, \boldsymbol{\beta})\right] \tag{19.66}$$

Because this distribution does not depend on c_i, equation (19.65) is also the distribution of $\mathbf{y}_i$ conditional on n_i and $\mathbf{x}_i$. Therefore, $\boldsymbol{\beta}_o$ can be estimated by standard conditional MLE techniques using the multinomial log likelihood. The conditional log likelihood for observation i, apart from terms not depending on $\boldsymbol{\beta}$, is

$$\ell_i(\boldsymbol{\beta}) = \sum_{t=1}^{T} y_{it} \log[p_t(\mathbf{x}_i, \boldsymbol{\beta})] \tag{19.67}$$

The estimator $\hat{\boldsymbol{\beta}}$ that maximizes $\sum_{i=1}^{N} \ell_i(\boldsymbol{\beta})$ will be called the **fixed effects Poisson (FEP) estimator**. (Note that when $y_{it} = 0$ for all t, the cross section observation i does not contribute to the estimation.)

Obtaining the FEP estimator is computationally fairly easy, especially when $m(\mathbf{x}_{it}, \boldsymbol{\beta}) = \exp(\mathbf{x}_{it}\boldsymbol{\beta})$. But the assumptions used to derive the conditional log likelihood in equation (19.67) can be restrictive in practice. Fortunately, the FEP estimator has very strong robustness properties for estimating the parameters in the conditional mean. As shown in Wooldridge (1999a), the FEP estimator is consistent for $\boldsymbol{\beta}_o$ under the conditional mean assumption (19.57) only. Except for the conditional mean, the distribution of y_{it} given $(\mathbf{x}_i, c_i)$ is entirely unrestricted; in particular, there can be overdispersion or underdispersion in the latent variable model. Also, there is no restriction on the dependence between y_{it} and y_{ir}, $t \neq r$. This is another case where the QMLE derived under fairly strong nominal assumptions turns out to have very desirable robustness properties.

The argument that the FEP estimator is consistent under assumption (19.57) hinges on showing that $\boldsymbol{\beta}_o$ maximizes the expected value of equation (19.67) under assumption (19.57) only. This result is shown in Wooldridge (1999a). Uniqueness holds under general identification assumptions, but certain kinds of explanatory variables are ruled out. For example, when the conditional mean has an exponential form, it is easy to see that the coefficients on time-constant explanatory variables drop out of equation (19.66), just as in the linear case. Interactions between time-constant and time-varying explanatory variables are allowed.

Consistent estimation of the asymptotic variance of $\hat{\boldsymbol{\beta}}$ follows from the results on M-estimation in Chapter 12. The score for observation i can be written as

$$\mathbf{s}_i(\boldsymbol{\beta}) \equiv \nabla_\beta \ell_i(\boldsymbol{\beta}) = \sum_{t=1}^{T} y_{it}[\nabla_\beta p_t(\mathbf{x}_i, \boldsymbol{\beta})'/p_t(\mathbf{x}_i, \boldsymbol{\beta})]$$

$$\equiv \nabla_\beta \mathbf{p}(\mathbf{x}_i, \boldsymbol{\beta})'\mathbf{W}(\mathbf{x}_i, \boldsymbol{\beta})\{\mathbf{y}_i - \mathbf{p}(\mathbf{x}_i, \boldsymbol{\beta})n_i\} \tag{19.68}$$

where $\mathbf{W}(\mathbf{x}_i, \boldsymbol{\beta}) \equiv [\text{diag}\{p_1(\mathbf{x}_i, \boldsymbol{\beta}), \ldots, p_T(\mathbf{x}_i, \boldsymbol{\beta})\}]^{-1}$, $\mathbf{u}_i(\boldsymbol{\beta}) \equiv \mathbf{y}_i - \mathbf{p}(\mathbf{x}_i, \boldsymbol{\beta})n_i$, $\mathbf{p}(\mathbf{x}_i, \boldsymbol{\beta}) \equiv [p_1(\mathbf{x}_i, \boldsymbol{\beta}), \ldots, p_T(\mathbf{x}_i, \boldsymbol{\beta})]'$, and $p_t(\mathbf{x}_i, \boldsymbol{\beta})$ is given by equation (19.66).

The expected Hessian for observation i can be shown to be

$$\mathbf{A}_o \equiv \mathrm{E}[n_i \nabla_\beta \mathbf{p}(\mathbf{x}_i, \boldsymbol{\beta}_o)'\mathbf{W}(\mathbf{x}_i, \boldsymbol{\beta}_o)\nabla_\beta \mathbf{p}(\mathbf{x}_i, \boldsymbol{\beta}_o)]$$

The asymptotic variance of $\hat{\boldsymbol{\beta}}$ is $\mathbf{A}_o^{-1}\mathbf{B}_o\mathbf{A}_o^{-1}/N$, where $\mathbf{B}_o \equiv \mathrm{E}[\mathbf{s}_i(\boldsymbol{\beta}_o)\mathbf{s}_i(\boldsymbol{\beta}_o)']$. A consistent estimate of $\mathbf{A}$ is

$$\hat{\mathbf{A}} = N^{-1} \sum_{i=1}^{N} n_i \nabla_\beta \mathbf{p}(\mathbf{x}_i, \hat{\boldsymbol{\beta}})'\mathbf{W}(\mathbf{x}_i, \hat{\boldsymbol{\beta}})\nabla_\beta \mathbf{p}(\mathbf{x}_i, \hat{\boldsymbol{\beta}}) \tag{19.69}$$

and $\mathbf{B}$ is estimated as

$$\hat{\mathbf{B}} = N^{-1} \sum_{i=1}^{N} \mathbf{s}_i(\hat{\boldsymbol{\beta}})\mathbf{s}_i(\hat{\boldsymbol{\beta}})' \tag{19.70}$$

The robust variance matrix estimator, $\hat{\mathbf{A}}^{-1}\hat{\mathbf{B}}\hat{\mathbf{A}}^{-1}/N$, is valid under assumption (19.57); in particular, it allows for any deviations from the Poisson distribution and arbitrary time dependence. The usual maximum likelihood estimate, $\hat{\mathbf{A}}^{-1}/N$, is valid under assumptions (19.60) and (19.61). For more details, including methods for specification testing, see Wooldridge (1999a).

Applications of the fixed effects Poisson estimator, which compute the robust variance matrix and some specification test statistics, are given in Papke (1991), Page (1995), and Gordy (1999). We must emphasize that, while the leading application is to count data, the fixed effects Poisson estimator works whenever assumption (19.57) holds. Therefore, y_{it} could be a nonnegative continuous variable, or even a binary response if we believe the unobserved effect is multiplicative (in contrast to the models in Sections 15.8.2 and 15.8.3).

19.6.5 Relaxing the Strict Exogeneity Assumption

We end this chapter with a brief discussion about how to relax the strict exogeneity assumption in a multiplicative unobserved effects panel data model. In place of assumption (19.57) we assume

$$\mathrm{E}(y_{it} \mid \mathbf{x}_{i1}, \ldots, \mathbf{x}_{it}, c_i) = c_i m(\mathbf{x}_{it}, \boldsymbol{\beta}_o), \qquad t = 1, 2, \ldots, T \tag{19.71}$$

These are **sequential moment restrictions** of the kind we discussed in Chapter 11. The model (19.71) is applicable to static and distributed lag models with possible feedback, as well as to models with lagged dependent variables. Again, y_{it} need not be a count variable here.

Chamberlain (1992b) and Wooldridge (1997a) have suggested residual functions that lead to conditional moment restrictions. Assuming that $m(\mathbf{x}_{it}, \boldsymbol{\beta}) > 0$, define

$$r_{it}(\boldsymbol{\beta}) \equiv y_{it} - y_{i,t+1}[m(\mathbf{x}_{it}, \boldsymbol{\beta})/m(\mathbf{x}_{i,t+1}, \boldsymbol{\beta})], \qquad t = 1, \ldots, T-1 \tag{19.72}$$

Under assumption (19.72), we can use iterated expectations to show that $\mathrm{E}[r_{it}(\boldsymbol{\beta}_o) \mid \mathbf{x}_{i1}, \ldots, \mathbf{x}_{it}] = 0$. This expression means that any function of $\mathbf{x}_{i1}, \ldots, \mathbf{x}_{it}$ is uncorrelated with $r_{it}(\boldsymbol{\beta}_o)$ and is the basis for generalized method of moments estimation. One can easily test the strict exogeneity assumption in a GMM framework. For further discussion and details on implementation, as well as an alternative residual function, see Wooldridge (1997a).

Blundell, Griffith, and Windmeijer (1998) consider variants of moment conditions in a *linear feedback model*, where the mean function contains a lagged dependent variable, which enters additively, in addition to an exponential regression function in other conditioning variables with a multiplicated unobserved effect. They apply their model to the patents and R&D relationship.

A different approach is conditional maximum likelihood, as we discussed in Sections 15.8.4 and 16.8.3—see Section 13.9 for a general discussion. For example, if we want to estimate a model for y_{it} given $(\mathbf{z}_{it}, y_{i,t-1}, c_i)$, where $\mathbf{z}_{it}$ contains contemporaneous variables, we can model it as a Poisson variable with exponential mean $c_i \exp(\mathbf{z}_{it}\boldsymbol{\beta}_o + \rho_o y_{i,t-1})$. Then, assuming that $\mathrm{D}(y_{it} \mid \mathbf{z}_i, y_{i,t-1}, \ldots, y_{i0}, c_i) = \mathrm{D}(y_{it} \mid \mathbf{z}_{it}, y_{i,t-1}, c_i)$, we can obtain the density of $(y_{i1}, \ldots, y_{iT})$ given $(y_{i0}, \mathbf{z}_i, c_i)$ by multiplication; see equation (13.60). Given a density specification for $\mathrm{D}(c_i \mid y_{i0}, \mathbf{z}_i)$, we can obtain the conditional log likelihood for each i as in equation (13.62). A very convenient specification is $c_i = \exp(\alpha_o + \xi_o y_{i0} + \mathbf{z}_i \boldsymbol{\gamma}_o) a_i$, where a_i is independent of $(y_{i0}, \mathbf{z}_i)$ and distributed as Gamma(δ_o, δ_o). Then, for each t, y_{it} given $(y_{i,t-1}, \ldots, y_{i0}, \mathbf{z}_i, a_i)$ has a Poisson distribution with mean

$$a_i \exp(\alpha_o + \mathbf{z}_{it}\boldsymbol{\beta}_o + \rho_o y_{i,t-1} + \xi_o y_{i0} + \mathbf{z}_i \boldsymbol{\gamma}_o)$$

(As always, we would probably want aggregate time dummies included in this equation.) It is easy to see that the distribution of $(y_{i1}, \ldots, y_{iT})$ given $(y_{i0}, \mathbf{z}_i)$ has the random effects Poisson form with gamma heterogeneity; therefore, standard random effects Poisson software can be used to estimate $\alpha_o, \boldsymbol{\beta}_o, \rho_o, \xi_o, \gamma_o$, and δ_o. The usual conditional MLE standard errors, t statistics, Wald statistics, and likelihood ratio statistics are asymptotically valid for large N. See Wooldridge (2000e) for further details.

Problems

19.1. a. For estimating the mean of a nonnegative random variable y, the Poisson quasi–log likelihood for a random draw is

$$\ell_i(\mu) = y_i \log(\mu) - \mu, \qquad \mu > 0$$

(where terms not depending on μ have been dropped). Letting $\mu_o \equiv \mathrm{E}(y_i)$, we have $\mathrm{E}[\ell_i(\mu)] = \mu_o \log(\mu) - \mu$. Show that this function is uniquely maximized at $\mu = \mu_o$. This simple result is the basis for the consistency of the Poisson QMLE in the general case.

b. The exponential quasi–log likelihood is

$$\ell_i(\mu) = -y_i/\mu - \log(\mu), \qquad \mu > 0$$

Show that $\mathrm{E}[\ell_i(\mu)]$ is uniquely maximized at $\mu = \mu_o$.

19.2. Carefully write out the robust variance matrix estimator (19.14) when $m(\mathbf{x}, \boldsymbol{\beta}) = \exp(\mathbf{x}\boldsymbol{\beta})$.

19.3. Use the data in SMOKE.RAW to answer this question.

a. Use a linear regression model to explain *cigs*, the number of cigarettes smoked per day. Use as explanatory variables log(*cigpric*), log(*income*), *restaurn*, *white*, *educ*, *age*, and age^2. Are the price and income variables significant? Does using heteroskedasticity-robust standard errors change your conclusions?

b. Now estimate a Poisson regression model for *cigs*, with an exponential conditional mean and the same explanatory variables as in part a. Using the usual MLE standard errors, are the price and income variables each significant at the 5 percent level? Interpret their coefficients.

c. Find $\hat{\sigma}$. Is there evidence of overdispersion? Using the GLM standard errors, discuss the significance of log(*cigpric*) and log(*income*).

d. Compare the usual MLE likelihood ratio statistic for joint significance of log(*cigpric*) and log(*income*) with the QLR statistic in equation (19.17).

e. Compute the fully robust standard errors, and compare these with the GLM standard errors.

f. In the model estimated from part b, at what point does the effect of *age* on expected cigarette consumption become negative?

g. Do you think a two-part, or double-hurdle, model for count variables is a better way to model *cigs*?

19.4. Show that, under the conditional moment restriction $\mathrm{E}(y \mid \mathbf{x}) = m(\mathbf{x}, \boldsymbol{\beta}_o)$, the Poisson QMLE achieves the efficiency bound in equation (14.66) when the GLM variance assumption holds.

19.5. Consider an unobserved effects model for count data with exponential regression function

$$\mathrm{E}(y_{it} \mid \mathbf{x}_{i1}, \ldots, \mathbf{x}_{iT}, c_i) = c_i \exp(\mathbf{x}_{it}\boldsymbol{\beta})$$

a. If $\mathrm{E}(c_i \mid \mathbf{x}_{i1}, \ldots, \mathbf{x}_{iT}) = \exp(\alpha + \bar{\mathbf{x}}_i\boldsymbol{\gamma})$, find $\mathrm{E}(y_{it} \mid \mathbf{x}_{i1}, \ldots, \mathbf{x}_{iT})$.

b. Use part a to derive a test of mean independence between c_i and $\bar{\mathbf{x}}_i$. Assume under H_0 that $\mathrm{Var}(y_{it} \mid \mathbf{x}_i, c_i) = \mathrm{E}(y_{it} \mid \mathbf{x}_i, c_i)$, that y_{it} and y_{ir} are uncorrelated conditional on $(\mathbf{x}_i, c_i)$, and that c_i and $\mathbf{x}_i$ are independent. (Hint: You should devise a test in the context of multivariate weighted nonlinear least squares.)

c. Suppose now that assumptions (19.60) and (19.61) hold, with $m(\mathbf{x}_{it}, \boldsymbol{\beta}) = \exp(\mathbf{x}_{it}\boldsymbol{\beta})$, but assumption (19.62) is replaced by $c_i = a_i \exp(\alpha + \bar{\mathbf{x}}_i\boldsymbol{\gamma})$, where $a_i \mid \mathbf{x} \sim \mathrm{Gamma}(\delta, \delta)$. Now how would you estimate $\boldsymbol{\beta}$, α, and $\boldsymbol{\gamma}$, and how would you test $\mathrm{H}_0\colon \boldsymbol{\gamma} = 0$?

19.6. A model with an additive unobserved effect, strictly exogenous regressors, and a nonlinear regression function is

$$\mathrm{E}(y_{it} \mid \mathbf{x}_i, c_i) = c_i + m(\mathbf{x}_{it}, \boldsymbol{\beta}_o), \qquad t = 1, \ldots, T$$

a. For each i and t define the time-demeaned variables $\ddot{y}_{it} \equiv y_{it} - \bar{y}_i$ and, for each $\boldsymbol{\beta}$, $\ddot{m}_{it}(\boldsymbol{\beta}) = m(\mathbf{x}_{it}, \boldsymbol{\beta}) - (1/T)\sum_{r=1}^{T} m(\mathbf{x}_{ir}, \boldsymbol{\beta})$. Argue that, under standard regularity conditions, the pooled nonlinear least squares estimator of $\boldsymbol{\beta}_o$ that solves

$$\min_{\boldsymbol{\beta}} \sum_{i=1}^{N} \sum_{t=1}^{T} [\ddot{y}_{it} - \ddot{m}_{it}(\boldsymbol{\beta})]^2 \tag{19.73}$$

is generally consistent and $\sqrt{N}$-asymptotically normal (with T fixed). [Hint: Show that $\mathrm{E}(\ddot{y}_{it} \mid \mathbf{x}_i) = \ddot{m}_{it}(\boldsymbol{\beta}_o)$ for all t.]

b. If $\text{Var}(\mathbf{y}_i \mid \mathbf{x}_i, c_i) = \sigma_o^2 \mathbf{I}_T$, how would you estimate the asymptotic variance of the pooled NLS estimator?

c. If the variance assumption in part b does not hold, how would you estimate the asymptotic variance?

d. Show that the NLS estimator based on time demeaning from part a is in fact *identical* to the pooled NLS estimator that estimates $\{c_1, c_2, \ldots, c_N\}$ along with $\boldsymbol{\beta}_o$:

$$\min_{\{c_1, c_2, \ldots, c_N, \boldsymbol{\beta}\}} \sum_{i=1}^{N} \sum_{t=1}^{T} [y_{it} - c_i - m(\mathbf{x}_{it}, \boldsymbol{\beta})]^2 \tag{19.74}$$

Thus, this is another case where treating the unobserved effects as parameters to estimate does not result in an inconsistent estimator of $\boldsymbol{\beta}_o$. [Hint: It is easiest to concentrate out the c_i from the sum of square residuals; see Section 12.7.4. In the current context, for given $\boldsymbol{\beta}$, find $\hat{c}_i$ as functions of $\mathbf{y}_i, \mathbf{x}_i$, and $\boldsymbol{\beta}$. Then plug these back into equation (19.74) and show that the concentrated sum of squared residuals function is identical to equation (19.73).]

19.7. Assume that the standard Poisson fixed effects assumptions hold, so that, conditional on $(\mathbf{x}_i, c_i), y_{i1}, \ldots, y_{iT}$ are independent Poisson random variables with means $c_i m(\mathbf{x}_{it}, \boldsymbol{\beta}_o)$.

a. Show that, if we treat the c_i as parameters to estimate along with $\boldsymbol{\beta}_o$, then the conditional log likelihood for observation i (apart from terms not depending on c_i or $\boldsymbol{\beta}$) is

$$\begin{aligned} \ell_i(c_i, \boldsymbol{\beta}) &\equiv \log[f(y_{i1}, \ldots, y_{iT} \mid \mathbf{x}_i; c_i, \boldsymbol{\beta})] \\ &= \sum_{t=1}^{T} \{-c_i m(\mathbf{x}_{it}, \boldsymbol{\beta}) + y_{it}[\log(c_i)] + \log[m(\mathbf{x}_{it}, \boldsymbol{\beta})]\} \end{aligned}$$

where we now group c_i with $\boldsymbol{\beta}$ as a parameter to estimate. (Note that $c_i > 0$ is a needed restriction.)

b. Let $n_i = y_{i1} + \cdots + y_{iT}$, and assume that $n_i > 0$. For given $\boldsymbol{\beta}$, maximize $\ell_i(c_i, \boldsymbol{\beta})$ only with respect to c_i. Find the solution, $c_i(\boldsymbol{\beta}) > 0$.

c. Plug the solution from part b into $\ell_i[c_i(\boldsymbol{\beta}), \boldsymbol{\beta}]$, and show that

$$\ell_i[c_i(\boldsymbol{\beta}), \boldsymbol{\beta}] = \sum_{t=1}^{T} y_{it} \log[p_t(\mathbf{x}_i, \boldsymbol{\beta})] + (n_i - 1) \log(n_i)$$

d. Conclude from part c that the log-likelihood function for all N cross section observations, with $(c_1, \ldots, c_N)$ concentrated out, is

$$\sum_{i=1}^{N}\sum_{t=1}^{T} y_{it} \log[p_t(\mathbf{x}_i, \boldsymbol{\beta})] + \sum_{i=1}^{N}(n_i - 1)\log(n_i)$$

What does this mean about the conditional MLE from Section 19.6.4 and the estimator that treats the c_i as parameters to estimate along with $\boldsymbol{\beta}_o$?

19.8. Let y be a fractional response, so that $0 \leq y \leq 1$.

a. Suppose that $0 < y < 1$, so that $w \equiv \log[y/(1-y)]$ is well defined. If we assume the linear model $\mathrm{E}(w \mid \mathbf{x}) = \mathbf{x}\boldsymbol{\alpha}$, does $\mathrm{E}(y \mid \mathbf{x})$ have any simple relationship to $\mathbf{x}\boldsymbol{\alpha}$? What would we need to know to obtain $\mathrm{E}(y \mid \mathbf{x})$? Let $\hat{\boldsymbol{\alpha}}$ be the OLS estimator from the regression w_i on $\mathbf{x}_i$, $i = 1, \ldots, N$.

b. If we estimate the fractional logit model for $\mathrm{E}(y \mid \mathbf{x})$ from Section 19.4.2, should we expect the estimated parameters, $\hat{\boldsymbol{\beta}}$, to be close to $\hat{\boldsymbol{\alpha}}$ from part a? Explain.

c. Now suppose that y takes on the values zero and one with positive probability. To model this population feature we use a latent variable model:

$$y^* \mid \mathbf{x} \sim \mathrm{Normal}(\mathbf{x}\boldsymbol{\gamma}, \sigma^2)$$

$$\begin{aligned} y &= 0, \quad y^* \leq 0 \\ &= y^*, \quad 0 < y^* < 1 \\ &= 1, \quad y^* \geq 1 \end{aligned}$$

How should we estimate $\boldsymbol{\gamma}$ and σ^2? (Hint: See Problem 16.3.)

d. Given the estimate $\hat{\boldsymbol{\gamma}}$ from part c, does it make sense to compare the magnitude of $\hat{\gamma}_j$ to the corresponding $\hat{\alpha}_j$ from part a or the $\hat{\beta}_j$ from part b? Explain.

e. How might we choose between the models estimated in parts b and c? (Hint: Think about goodness of fit for the conditional mean.)

f. Now suppose that $0 \leq y < 1$. Suppose we apply fractional logit, as in part b, and fractional logit to the subsample with $0 < y_i < 1$. Should we necessarily get similar answers?

g. With $0 \leq y < 1$ suppose that $\mathrm{E}(y_i \mid \mathbf{x}_i, y_i > 0) = \exp(\mathbf{x}_i\boldsymbol{\delta})/[1 + \exp(\mathbf{x}_i\boldsymbol{\delta})]$. If we estimate $\boldsymbol{\delta}$ using the QMLE from Section 19.4.2, using only observations with $0 < y_i < 1$, is there a sample selection bias? Explain.

h. To the assumptions from part g add $\mathrm{P}(y_i = 0 \mid \mathbf{x}_i) = 1 - G(\mathbf{x}_i\boldsymbol{\eta})$, where $G(\cdot)$ is a differentiable, strictly increasing cumulative distribution function. How should we estimate $\mathrm{E}(y_i \mid \mathbf{x}_i)$?

19.9. Use the data in ATTEND.RAW to answer this question.

a. Estimate a linear regression relating *atndrte* to *ACT*, *priGPA*, *frosh*, and *soph*; compute the usual OLS standard errors. Interpret the coefficients on *ACT* and *priGPA*. Are any fitted values outside the unit interval?

b. Model $\mathrm{E}(atndrte \mid \mathbf{x})$ as a logistic function, as in Section 19.4.2. Use the QMLE for the Bernoulli log likelihood, and compute the GLM standard errors. What is $\hat{\sigma}$, and how does it affect the standard errors?

c. For $priGPA = 3.0$ and $frosh = soph = 0$, estimate the effect of increasing *ACT* from 25 to 30 using the estimated equation from part b. How does the estimate compare with that from the linear model?

d. Does a linear model or a logistic model provide a better fit to $\mathrm{E}(atndrte \mid \mathbf{x})$?

19.10. Use the data in PATENT.RAW for this exercise.

a. Estimate a pooled Poisson regression model relating *patents* to $lsales = \log(sales)$ and current and four lags of $lrnd = \log(1 + rnd)$, where we add one before taking the log to account for the fact that *rnd* is zero for some firms in some years. Use an exponential mean function and include a full set of year dummies. Which lags of *lrnd* are significant using the usual Poisson MLE standard errors?

b. Give two reasons why the usual Poisson MLE standard errors from part a might be invalid.

c. Obtain $\hat{\sigma}$ for the pooled Poisson estimation. Using the GLM standard errors (but without an adjustment for possible serial dependence), which lags of *lrnd* are significant?

d. Obtain the QLR statistic for joint significance of lags one through four of *lrnd*. (Be careful here; you must use the same set of years in estimating the restricted version of the model.) How does it compare to the usual LR statistic?

e. Compute the standard errors that are robust to an arbitrary conditional variance and serial dependence. How do they compare with the standard errors from parts a and c?

f. What is the estimated long-run elasticity of expected patents with respect to R&D spending? (Ignore the fact that one has been added to the R&D numbers before taking the log.) Obtain a fully robust standard error for the long-run elasticity.

g. Now use the fixed effects Poisson estimator, and compare the estimated lag coefficients to those from the pooled Poisson analysis. Estimate the long-run elasticity, and obtain its standard error. (Assume that the full set of FEP assumptions hold.)

19.11. a. For a random draw i from the cross section, assume that (1) for each time period t, $y_{it} \mid \mathbf{x}_i, c_i \sim \text{Poisson}(c_i m_{it})$, where $c_i > 0$ is unobserved heterogeneity and $m_{it} > 0$ is typically a function of only $\mathbf{x}_{it}$; and (2) $(y_{i1}, \dots, y_{iT})$ are independent conditional on $(\mathbf{x}_i, c_i)$. Derive the density of $(y_{i1}, \dots, y_{iT})$ conditional on $(\mathbf{x}_i, c_i)$.

b. To the assumptions from part a, add the assumption that $c_i \mid \mathbf{x}_i \sim \text{Gamma}(\delta, \delta)$, so that $\text{E}(c_i) = 1$ and $\text{Var}(c_i) = 1/\delta$. {The density of c_i is $h(c) = [\delta^\delta / \Gamma(\delta)] c^{\delta-1} \exp(-\delta c)$, where $\Gamma(\delta)$ is the gamma function.} Let $s = y_1 + \cdots + y_T$ and $M_i = m_{i1} + \cdots + m_{iT}$. Show that the density of $(y_{i1}, \dots, y_{iT})$ given $\mathbf{x}_i$ is

$$\left(\prod_{t=1}^{T} m_{it}^{y_t}/y_t!\right)[\delta^\delta/\Gamma(\delta)][\Gamma(M_i + s)/(M_i + \delta)^{(s+\delta)}]$$

[Hint: The easiest way to show this result is to turn the integral into one involving a $\text{Gamma}(s + \delta, M_i + \delta)$ density and a multiplicative term. Naturally, the density must integrate to unity, and so what is left over is the density we seek.]

19.12. For a random draw i from the cross section, assume that (1) for each t, $y_{it} \mid \mathbf{x}_i, c_i \sim \text{Gamma}(m_{it}, 1/c_i)$, where $c_i > 0$ is unobserved heterogeneity and $m_{it} > 0$; and (2) $(y_{i1}, \dots, y_{iT})$ are independent conditional on $(\mathbf{x}_i, c_i)$. The gamma distribution is parameterized so that $\text{E}(y_{it} \mid \mathbf{x}_i, c_i) = c_i m_{it}$ and $\text{Var}(y_{it} \mid \mathbf{x}_i, c_i) = c_i^2 m_{it}$.

a. Let $s_i = y_{i1} + \cdots + y_{iT}$. Show that the density of $(y_{i1}, y_{i2}, \dots, y_{iT})$ conditional on $(s_i, \mathbf{x}_i, c_i)$ is

$$f(y_1, \dots, y_T \mid s_i, \mathbf{x}_i, c_i) = \left[\Gamma(m_{i1} + \cdots + m_{iT}) / \prod_{t=1}^{T} \Gamma(m_{it})\right] \times \left[\left(\prod_{t=1}^{T} y_t^{m_{it}-1}\right) / s_i^{\{(m_{i1}+\cdots+m_{iT})-1\}}\right]$$

where $\Gamma(\cdot)$ is the gamma function. Note that the density does not depend on c_i. {Hint: If $Y_1, \dots, Y_T$ are independent random variables and $S = Y_1 + \cdots + Y_T$, the joint density of $Y_1, \dots, Y_T$ given $S = s$ is $f_1(y_1) \cdots f_{T-1}(y_{T-1}) f_T(s - y_1 - \cdots - y_{T-1}) / g(s)$, where $g(s)$ is the density of S. When Y_t has a $\text{Gamma}(\alpha_t, \lambda)$ distribution for each t, so that $f_t(y_t) = [\lambda^{\alpha_t}/\Gamma(\alpha_t)] y_t^{(\alpha_t - 1)} \exp(-\lambda y_t)$, $S \sim \text{Gamma}(\alpha_1 + \cdots + \alpha_T, \lambda)$.}

b. Let $m_t(\mathbf{x}_i, \boldsymbol{\beta})$ be a parametric function for m_{it}—for example, $\exp(\mathbf{x}_{it}\boldsymbol{\beta})$. Write down the log-likelihood function for observation i. The conditional MLE in this case is called the **fixed effects gamma estimator**.

20 Duration Analysis

20.1 Introduction

Some response variables in economics come in the form of a **duration**, which is the time elapsed until a certain event occurs. A few examples include weeks unemployed, months spent on welfare, days until arrest after incarceration, and quarters until an Internet firm files for bankruptcy.

The recent literature on duration analysis is quite rich. In this chapter we focus on the developments that have been used most often in applied work. In addition to providing a rigorous introduction to modern duration analysis, this chapter should prepare you for more advanced treatments, such as Lancaster's (1990) monograph.

Duration analysis has its origins in what is typically called **survival analysis**, where the duration of interest is survival time of a subject. In survival analysis we are interested in how various treatments or demographic characteristics affect survival times. In the social sciences, we are interested in any situation where an individual—or family, or firm, and so on—begins in an initial state and is either observed to exit the state or is censored. (We will discuss the exact nature of censoring in Sections 20.3 and 20.4.) The calendar dates on which units enter the initial state do not have to be the same. (When we introduce covariates in Section 20.2.2, we note how dummy variables for different calendar dates can be included in the covariates, if necessary, to allow for systematic differences in durations by starting date.)

Traditional duration analysis begins by specifying a population distribution for the duration, usually conditional on some explanatory variables (covariates) observed at the beginning of the duration. For example, for the population of people who became unemployed during a particular period, we might observe education levels, experience, marital status—all measured when the person becomes unemployed—wage on prior job, and a measure of unemployment benefits. Then we specify a distribution for the unemployment duration conditional on the covariates. Any reasonable distribution reflects the fact that an unemployment duration is nonnegative. Once a complete conditional distribution has been specified, the same maximum likelihood methods that we studied in Chapter 16 for censored regression models can be used. In this framework, we are typically interested in estimating the effects of the covariates on the expected duration.

Recent treatments of duration analysis tend to focus on the hazard function. The hazard function allows us to approximate the probability of exiting the initial state within a short interval, conditional on having survived up to the starting time of the interval. In econometric applications, hazard functions are usually conditional on some covariates. An important feature for policy analysis is allowing the hazard function to depend on covariates that change over time.

In Section 20.2 we define and discuss hazard functions, and we settle certain issues involved with introducing covariates into hazard functions. In Section 20.3 we show how censored regression models apply to standard duration models with single-cycle flow data, when all covariates are time constant. We also discuss the most common way of introducing unobserved heterogeneity into traditional duration analysis. Given parametric assumptions, we can test for duration dependence—which means that the probability of exiting the initial state depends on the length of time in the state—as well as for the presence of unobserved heterogeneity.

In Section 20.4 we study methods that allow flexible estimation of a hazard function, both with time-constant and time-varying covariates. We assume that we have grouped data; this term means that durations are observed to fall into fixed intervals (often weekly or monthly intervals) and that any time-varying covariates are assumed to be constant within an interval. We focus attention on the case with two states, with everyone in the population starting in the initial state, and single-cycle data, where each person either exits the initial state or is censored before exiting. We also show how heterogeneity can be included when the covariates are strictly exogenous.

We touch on some additional issues in Section 20.5.

20.2 Hazard Functions

The hazard function plays a central role in modern duration analysis. In this section, we discuss various features of the hazard function, both with and without covariates, and provide some examples.

20.2.1 Hazard Functions without Covariates

Often in this chapter it is convenient to distinguish random variables from particular outcomes of random variables. Let $T \geq 0$ denote the duration, which has some distribution in the population; t denotes a particular value of T. (As with any econometric analysis, it is important to be very clear about the relevant population, a topic we consider in Section 20.3.) In survival analysis, T is the length of time a subject lives. Much of the current terminology in duration analysis comes from survival applications. For us, T is the time at which a person (or family, firm, and so on) leaves the initial state. For example, if the initial state is unemployment, T would be the time, measured in, say, weeks, until a person becomes employed.

The cumulative distribution function (cdf) of T is defined as

$$F(t) = \mathrm{P}(T \leq t), \qquad t \geq 0 \tag{20.1}$$

The **survivor function** is defined as $S(t) \equiv 1 - F(t) = \mathrm{P}(T > t)$, and this is the probability of "surviving" past time t. We assume in the rest of this section that T is continuous—and, in fact, has a differentiable cdf—because this assumption simplifies statements of certain probabilities. Discreteness in observed durations can be viewed as a consequence of the sampling scheme, as we discuss in Section 20.4. Denote the density of T by $f(t) = \dfrac{dF}{dt}(t)$.

For $h > 0$,

$$\mathrm{P}(t \leq T < t + h \mid T \geq t) \tag{20.2}$$

is the probabilty of leaving the initial state in the interval $[t, t+h)$ given survival up until time t. The **hazard function** for T is defined as

$$\lambda(t) = \lim_{h \downarrow 0} \frac{\mathrm{P}(t \leq T < t + h \mid T \geq t)}{h} \tag{20.3}$$

For each t, $\lambda(t)$ is the instantaneous rate of leaving per unit of time. From equation (20.3) it follows that, for "small" h,

$$\mathrm{P}(t \leq T < t + h \mid T \geq t) \approx \lambda(t)h \tag{20.4}$$

Thus the hazard function can be used to approximate a conditional probability in much the same way that the height of the density of T can be used to approximate an unconditional probability.

Example 20.1 (Unemployment Duration): If T is length of time unemployed, measured in weeks, then $\lambda(20)$ is (approximately) the probability of becoming employed between weeks 20 and 21. The phrase "becoming employed" reflects the fact that the person was unemployed up through week 20. That is, $\lambda(20)$ is roughly the probability of becoming employed between weeks 20 and 21, conditional on having been unemployed through week 20.

Example 20.2 (Recidivism Duration): Suppose T is the number of months before a former prisoner is arrested for a crime. Then $\lambda(12)$ is roughly the probability of being arrested during the 13th month, conditional on not having been arrested during the first year.

We can express the hazard function in terms of the density and cdf very simply. First, write

$$\mathrm{P}(t \leq T < t + h \mid T \geq t) = \mathrm{P}(t \leq T < t + h)/\mathrm{P}(T \geq t) = \frac{F(t+h) - F(t)}{1 - F(t)}$$

When the cdf is differentiable, we can take the limit of the right-hand side, divided by h, as h approaches zero from above:

$$\lambda(t) = \lim_{h \downarrow 0} \frac{F(t+h) - F(t)}{h} \cdot \frac{1}{1 - F(t)} = \frac{f(t)}{1 - F(t)} = \frac{f(t)}{S(t)} \tag{20.5}$$

Because the derivative of $S(t)$ is $-f(t)$, we have

$$\lambda(t) = -\frac{d \log S(t)}{dt} \tag{20.6}$$

and, using $F(0) = 0$, we can integrate to get

$$F(t) = 1 - \exp\left[-\int_0^t \lambda(s)\, ds\right], \qquad t \geq 0 \tag{20.7}$$

Straightforward differentiation of equation (20.7) gives the density of T as

$$f(t) = \lambda(t) \exp\left[-\int_0^t \lambda(s)\, ds\right] \tag{20.8}$$

Therefore, all probabilities can be computed using the hazard function. For example, for points $a_1 < a_2$,

$$\mathrm{P}(T \geq a_2 \mid T \geq a_1) = \frac{1 - F(a_2)}{1 - F(a_1)} = \exp\left[-\int_{a_1}^{a_2} \lambda(s)\, ds\right]$$

and

$$\mathrm{P}(a_1 \leq T < a_2 \mid T \geq a_1) = 1 - \exp\left[-\int_{a_1}^{a_2} \lambda(s)\, ds\right] \tag{20.9}$$

This last expression is especially useful for constructing the log-likelihood functions needed in Section 20.4.

The shape of the hazard function is of primary interest in many empirical applications. In the simplest case, the hazard function is constant:

$$\lambda(t) = \lambda, \qquad \text{all } t \geq 0 \tag{20.10}$$

This function means that the process driving T is *memoryless*: the probability of exit in the next interval does not depend on how much time has been spent in the initial state. From equation (20.7), a constant hazard implies

$$F(t) = 1 - \exp(-\lambda t) \tag{20.11}$$

which is the cdf of the **exponential distribution**. Conversely, if T has an exponential distribution, it has a constant hazard.

When the hazard function is not constant, we say that the process exhibits **duration dependence**. Assuming that $\lambda(\cdot)$ is differentiable, there is **positive duration dependence** at time t if $\mathrm{d}\lambda(t)/\mathrm{d}t > 0$; if $\mathrm{d}\lambda(t)/\mathrm{d}t > 0$ for all $t > 0$, then the process exhibits positive duration dependence. With positive duration dependence, the probability of exiting the initial state increases the longer one is in the initial state. If the derivative is negative, then there is **negative duration dependence**.

Example 20.3 (Weibull Distribution): If T has a **Weibull distribution**, its cdf is given by $F(t) = 1 - \exp(-\gamma t^{\alpha})$, where γ and α are nonnegative parameters. The density is $f(t) = \gamma\alpha t^{\alpha-1}\exp(-\gamma t^{\alpha})$. By equation (20.5), the hazard function is

$$\lambda(t) = f(t)/S(t) = \gamma\alpha t^{\alpha-1} \tag{20.12}$$

When $\alpha = 1$, the Weibull distribution reduces to the exponential with $\lambda = \gamma$. If $\alpha > 1$, the hazard is monotonically increasing, so the hazard everywhere exhibits positive duration dependence; for $\alpha < 1$, the hazard is monotonically decreasing. Provided we think the hazard is monotonically increasing or decreasing, the Weibull distribution is a relatively simple way to capture duration dependence.

We often want to specify the hazard directly, in which case we can use equation (20.7) to determine the duration distribution.

Example 20.4 (Log-Logistic Hazard Function): The **log-logistic hazard** function is specified as

$$\lambda(t) = \frac{\gamma\alpha t^{\alpha-1}}{1 + \gamma t^{\alpha}} \tag{20.13}$$

where γ and α are positive parameters. When $\alpha = 1$, the hazard is monotonically decreasing from γ at $t = 0$ to zero as $t \to \infty$; when $\alpha < 1$, the hazard is also monotonically decreasing to zero as $t \to \infty$, but the hazard is unbounded as t approaches zero. When $\alpha > 1$, the hazard is increasing until $t = [(\alpha - 1)/\gamma]^{1-\alpha}$, and then it decreases to zero.

Straightforward integration gives

$$\int_0^t \lambda(s)\,ds = \log(1 + \gamma t^{\alpha}) = -\log[(1 + \gamma t^{\alpha})^{-1}]$$

so that, by equation (20.7),

$$F(t) = 1 - (1 + \gamma t^{\alpha})^{-1}, \qquad t \geq 0 \tag{20.14}$$

Differentiating with respect to t gives

$$f(t) = \gamma \alpha t^{\alpha-1}(1 + \gamma t^{\alpha})^{-2}$$

Using this density, it can be shown that $Y \equiv \log(T)$ has density $g(y) = \alpha \exp[\alpha(y - \mu)]/\{1 + \exp[\alpha(y - \mu)]\}^2$, where $\mu = -\alpha^{-1} \log(\gamma)$ is the mean of Y. In other words, $\log(T)$ has a **logistic distribution** with mean μ and variance $\pi^2/(3\alpha^2)$ (hence the name "log-logistic").

20.2.2 Hazard Functions Conditional on Time-Invariant Covariates

Usually in economics we are interested in hazard functions conditional on a set of covariates or regressors. When these do not change over time—as is often the case given the way many duration data sets are collected—then we simply define the hazard (and all other features of T) conditional on the covariates. Thus, the conditional hazard is

$$\lambda(t; \mathbf{x}) = \lim_{h \downarrow 0} \frac{\mathrm{P}(t \leq T < t + h \mid T \geq t, \mathbf{x})}{h}$$

where $\mathbf{x}$ is a vector of explanatory variables. All of the formulas from the previous subsection continue to hold provided the cdf and density are defined conditional on $\mathbf{x}$. For example, if the conditional cdf $F(\cdot \mid \mathbf{x})$ is differentiable, we have

$$\lambda(t; \mathbf{x}) = \frac{f(t \mid \mathbf{x})}{1 - F(t \mid \mathbf{x})} \tag{20.15}$$

where $f(\cdot \mid \mathbf{x})$ is the density of T given $\mathbf{x}$. Often we are interested in the partial effects of the x_j on $\lambda(t; \mathbf{x})$, which are defined as partial derivatives for continuous x_j and as differences for discrete x_j.

If the durations start at different calendar dates—which is usually the case—we can include indicators for different starting dates in the covariates. These allow us to control for seasonal differences in duration distributions.

An especially important class of models with time-invariant regressors consists of **proportional hazard models**. A proportional hazard can be written as

$$\lambda(t; \mathbf{x}) = \kappa(\mathbf{x})\lambda_0(t) \tag{20.16}$$

where $\kappa(\cdot) > 0$ is a nonnegative function of $\mathbf{x}$ and $\lambda_0(t) > 0$ is called the **baseline hazard**. The baseline hazard is common to all units in the population; individual hazard functions differ proportionately based on a function $\kappa(\mathbf{x})$ of observed covariates.

Typically, $\kappa(\cdot)$ is parameterized as $\kappa(\mathbf{x}) = \exp(\mathbf{x}\boldsymbol{\beta})$, where $\boldsymbol{\beta}$ is a vector of parameters. Then

$$\log \lambda(t; \mathbf{x}) = \mathbf{x}\boldsymbol{\beta} + \log \lambda_0(t) \tag{20.17}$$

and β_j measures the semielasticity of the hazard with respect to x_j. [If x_j is the log of an underlying variable, say $x_j = \log(z_j)$, β_j is the elasticity of the hazard with respect to z_j.]

Occasionally we are interested only in how the covariates shift the hazard function, in which case estimation of λ_0 is not necessary. Cox (1972) obtained a partial maximum likelihood estimator for $\boldsymbol{\beta}$ that does not require estimating $\lambda_0(\cdot)$. We discuss Cox's approach briefly in Section 20.5. In economics, much of the time we are interested in the shape of the baseline hazard. We discuss estimation of proportional hazard models with a flexible baseline hazard in Section 20.4.

If in the Weibull hazard function (20.12) we replace γ with $\exp(\mathbf{x}\boldsymbol{\beta})$, where the first element of $\mathbf{x}$ is unity, we obtain a proportional hazard model with $\lambda_0(t) \equiv \alpha t^{\alpha-1}$. However, if we replace γ in equation (20.13) with $\exp(\mathbf{x}\boldsymbol{\beta})$—which is the most common way of introducing covariates into the log-logistic model—we do not obtain a hazard with the proportional hazard form.

Example 20.1 (continued): If T is an unemployment duration, $\mathbf{x}$ might contain education, labor market experience, marital status, race, and number of children, all measured at the beginning of the unemployment spell. Policy variables in $\mathbf{x}$ might reflect the rules governing unemployment benefits, where these are known before each person's unemployment duration.

Example 20.2 (continued): To explain the length of time before arrest after release from prison, the covariates might include participation in a work program while in prison, years of education, marital status, race, time served, and past number of convictions.

20.2.3 Hazard Functions Conditional on Time-Varying Covariates

Studying hazard functions is more complicated when we wish to model the effects of time-varying covariates on the hazard function. For one thing, it makes no sense to specify the distribution of the duration T conditional on the covariates at only one time period. Nevertheless, we can still define the appropriate conditional probabilities that lead to a conditional hazard function.

Let $\mathbf{x}(t)$ denote the vector of regressors at time t; again, this is the random vector describing the population. For $t \geq 0$, let $\mathbf{X}(t)$, $t \geq 0$, denote the covariate path up through time t: $\mathbf{X}(t) \equiv \{\mathbf{x}(s): 0 \le s \le t\}$. Following Lancaster (1990, Chapter 2), we define the conditional hazard function at time t by

$$\lambda[t; \mathbf{X}(t)] = \lim_{h \downarrow 0} \frac{\mathrm{P}[t \le T < t+h \mid T \ge t, \mathbf{X}(t+h)]}{h} \tag{20.18}$$

assuming that this limit exists. A discussion of assumptions that ensure existence of equation (20.18) is well beyond the scope of this book; see Lancaster (1990, Chapter 2). One case where this limit exists very generally occurs when T is continuous and, for each t, $\mathbf{x}(t+h)$ is constant for all $h \in [0, \eta(t)]$ for some function $\eta(t) > 0$. Then we can replace $\mathbf{X}(t+h)$ with $\mathbf{X}(t)$ in equation (20.18) [because $\mathbf{X}(t+h) = \mathbf{X}(t)$ for h sufficiently small]. For reasons we will see in Section 20.4, we must assume that time-varying covariates are constant over the interval of observation (such as a week or a month), anyway, in which case there is no problem in defining equation (20.18).

For certain purposes, it is important to know whether time-varying covariates are **strictly exogenous**. With the hazard defined as in equation (20.18), Lancaster (1990, Definition 2.1) provides a definition that rules out feedback from the duration to future values of the covariates. Specifically, if $\mathbf{X}(t, t+h)$ denotes the covariate path from time t to $t+h$, then Lancaster's strict exogeneity condition is

$$\mathrm{P}[\mathbf{X}(t, t+h) \mid T \ge t+h, \mathbf{X}(t)] = \mathrm{P}[\mathbf{X}(t, t+h) \mid \mathbf{X}(t)] \tag{20.19}$$

for all $t \ge 0$, $h > 0$. Actually, when condition (20.19) holds, Lancaster says $\{\mathbf{x}(t): t > 0\}$ is "exogenous." We prefer the name "strictly exogenous" because condition (20.19) is closely related to the notions of strict exogeneity that we have encountered throughout this book. Plus, it is important to see that condition (20.19) has nothing to do with contemporaneous endogeneity: by definition, the covariates are **sequentially exogenous** (see Section 11.1.1) because, by specifying $\lambda[t; \mathbf{X}(t)]$, we are conditioning on current and past covariates.

Equation (20.19) applies to covariates whose entire path is well-defined whether or not the agent is in the initial state. One such class of covariates, called **external covariates** by Kalbfleisch and Prentice (1980), has the feature that the covariate path is independent of whether any particular agent has or has not left the initial state. In modeling time until arrest, these covariates might include law enforcement per capita in the person's city of residence or the city unemployment rate.

Other covariates are not external to each agent but have paths that are still defined after the agent leaves the initial state. For example, marital status is well-defined before and after someone is arrested, but it is possibly related to whether someone has been arrested. Whether marital status satisfies condition (20.19) is an empirical issue.

The definition of strict exogeneity in condition (20.19) cannot be applied to time-varying covariates whose path is not defined once the agent leaves the initial state. Kalbfleisch and Prentice (1980) call these **internal covariates**. Lancaster (1990, p. 28) gives the example of job tenure duration, where a time-varying covariate is wage paid on the job: if a person leaves the job, it makes no sense to define the future wage path in that job. As a second example, in modeling the time until a former prisoner is arrested, a time-varying covariate at time t might be wage income in the previous month, $t-1$. If someone is arrested and reincarcerated, it makes little sense to define future labor income.

It is pretty clear that internal covariates cannot satisfy any reasonable strict exogeneity assumption. This fact will be important in Section 20.4 when we discuss estimation of duration models with unobserved heterogeneity and grouped duration data. We will actually use a slightly different notion of strict exogeneity that is directly relevant for conditional maximum likelihood estimation. Nevertheless, it is in the same spirit as condition (20.19).

With time-varying covariates there is not, strictly speaking, such a thing as a proportional hazard model. Nevertheless, it has become common in econometrics to call a hazard of the form

$$\lambda[t; \mathbf{x}(t)] = \kappa[\mathbf{x}(t)]\lambda_0(t) \tag{20.20}$$

a **proportional hazard with time-varying covariates**. The function multiplying the baseline hazard is usually $\kappa[\mathbf{x}(t)] = \exp[\mathbf{x}(t)\boldsymbol{\beta}]$; for notational reasons, we show this depending only on $\mathbf{x}(t)$ and not on past covariates [which can always be included in $\mathbf{x}(t)$]. We will discuss estimation of these models, without the strict exogeneity assumption, in Section 20.4.2. In Section 20.4.3, when we multiply equation (20.20) by unobserved heterogeneity, strict exogeneity becomes very important.

The log-logistic hazard is also easily modified to have time-varying covariates. One way to include time-varying covariates parametrically is

$$\lambda[t; \mathbf{x}(t)] = \exp[\mathbf{x}(t)\boldsymbol{\beta}]\alpha t^{\alpha-1}/\{1 + \exp[\mathbf{x}(t)\boldsymbol{\beta}]t^{\alpha}\}$$

We will see how to estimate α and $\boldsymbol{\beta}$ in Section 20.4.2.

20.3 Analysis of Single-Spell Data with Time-Invariant Covariates

We assume that the population of interest is individuals entering the initial state during a given interval of time, say $[0, b]$, where $b > 0$ is a known constant. (Naturally, "individual" can be replaced with any population unit of interest, such as "family" or "firm.") As in all econometric contexts, it is very important to be explicit about the underlying population. By convention, we let zero denote the earliest calendar date that an individual can enter the initial state, and b is the last possible date. For example, if we are interested in the population of U.S. workers who became unemployed at any time during 1998, and unemployment duration is measured in years (with .5 meaning half a year), then $b = 1$. If duration is measured in weeks, then $b = 52$; if duration is measured in days, then $b = 365$; and so on.

In using the methods of this section, we typically ignore the fact that durations are often grouped into discrete intervals—for example, measured to the nearest week or month—and treat them as continuously distributed. If we want to explicitly recognize the discreteness of the measured durations, we should treat them as grouped data, as we do in Section 20.4.

We restrict attention to **single-spell data**. That is, we use, at most, one completed spell per individual. If, after leaving the initial state, an individual subsequently reenters the initial state in the interval $[0, b]$, we ignore this information. In addition, the covariates in the analysis are time invariant, which means we collect covariates on individuals at a given point in time—usually, at the beginning of the spell—and we do not re-collect data on the covariates during the course of the spell. Time-varying covariates are more naturally handled in the context of grouped duration data in Section 20.4.

We study two general types of sampling from the population that we have described. The most common, and the easiest to handle, is flow sampling. In Section 20.3.3 we briefly consider various kinds of stock sampling.

20.3.1 Flow Sampling

With **flow sampling**, we sample individuals who enter the state at some point during the interval $[0, b]$, and we record the length of time each individual is in the initial state. We collect data on covariates known at the time the individual entered the initial state. For example, suppose we are interested in the population of U.S. workers who became unemployed at any time during 1998, and we randomly sample from U.S. male workers who became unemployed during 1998. At the beginning of the unemployment spell we might obtain information on tenure in last job, wage on last job, gender, marital status, and information on unemployment benefits.

There are two common ways to collect flow data on unemployment spells. First, we may randomly sample individuals from a large population, say, all working-age individuals in the United States for a given year, say, 1998. Some fraction of these people will be in the labor force and will become unemployed during 1998—that is, enter the initial state of unemployment during the specified interval—and this group of people who become unemployed is our random sample of all workers who become unemployed during 1998. Another possibility is retrospective sampling. For example, suppose that, for a given state in the United States, we have access to unemployment records for 1998. We can then obtain a random sample of all workers who became unemployed during 1998.

Flow data are usually subject to **right censoring**. That is, after a certain amount of time, we stop following the individuals in the sample, which we must do in order to analyze the data. (Right censoring is the only kind that occurs with flow data, so we will often refer to right censoring as "censoring" in this and the next subsection.) For individuals who have completed their spells in the initial state, we observe the exact duration. But for those still in the initial state, we only know that the duration lasted as long as the tracking period. In the unemployment duration example, we might follow each individual for a fixed length of time, say, two years. If unemployment spells are measured in weeks, we would have right censoring at 104 weeks. Alternatively, we might stop tracking individuals at a fixed calendar date, say, the last week in 1999. Because individuals can become unemployed at any time during 1998, calendar-date censoring results in censoring times that differ across individuals.

20.3.2 Maximum Likelihood Estimation with Censored Flow Data

For a random draw i from the population, let $a_i \in [0, b]$ denote the time at which individual i enters the initial state (the "starting time"), let t_i^* denote the length of time in the initial state (the duration), and let $\mathbf{x}_i$ denote the vector of observed covariates. We assume that t_i^* has a continuous conditional density $f(t \mid \mathbf{x}_i; \boldsymbol{\theta})$, $t \geq 0$, where $\boldsymbol{\theta}$ is the vector of unknown parameters.

Without right censoring we would observe a random sample on $(a_i, t_i^*, \mathbf{x}_i)$, and estimation would be a standard exercise in conditional maximum likelihood. To account for right censoring, we assume that the observed duration, t_i, is obtained as

$$t_i = \min(t_i^*, c_i) \tag{20.21}$$

where c_i is the censoring time for individual i. In some cases, c_i is constant across i. For example, suppose t_i^* is unemployment duration for person i, measured in weeks. If the sample design specifies that we follow each person for at most two years, at which point all people remaining unemployed after two years are censored, then $c =$ 104. If we have a fixed calendar date at which we stop tracking individuals, the censoring time differs by individual because the workers typically would become unemployed on different calendar dates. If $b = 1$ year and we censor everyone at two years from the start of the study, the censoring times could range from 52 to 104 weeks.)

We assume that, conditional on the covariates, the true duration is independent of the starting point, a_i, and the censoring time, c_i:

$$D(t_i^* \mid \mathbf{x}_i, a_i, c_i) = D(t_i^* \mid \mathbf{x}_i) \tag{20.22}$$

where $D(\cdot \mid \cdot)$ denotes conditional distribution. Assumption (20.22) clearly holds when a_i and c_i are constant for all i, but it holds under much weaker assumptions. Sometimes c_i is constant for all i, in which case assumption (20.22) holds when the duration is independent of the starting time, conditional on $\mathbf{x}_i$. If there are seasonal effects on the duration—for example, unemployment durations that start in the summer have a different expected length than durations that start at other times of the year—then we may have to put dummy variables for different starting dates in $\mathbf{x}_i$ to ensure that assumption (20.22) holds. This approach would also ensure that assumption (20.22) holds when a fixed calendar date is used for censoring, implying that c_i is not constant across i. Assumption (20.22) holds for certain nonstandard censoring schemes, too. For example, if an element of $\mathbf{x}_i$ is education, assumption (20.22) holds if, say, individuals with more education are censored more quickly.

Under assumption (20.22), the distribution of t_i^* given $(\mathbf{x}_i, a_i, c_i)$ does not depend on (a_i, c_i). Therefore, if the duration is not censored, the density of $t_i = t_i^*$ given $(\mathbf{x}_i, a_i, c_i)$ is simply $f(t \mid \mathbf{x}_i; \boldsymbol{\theta})$. The probability that t_i is censored is

$$P(t_i^* \geq c_i \mid \mathbf{x}_i) = 1 - F(c_i \mid \mathbf{x}_i; \boldsymbol{\theta})$$

where $F(t \mid \mathbf{x}_i; \boldsymbol{\theta})$ is the conditional cdf of t_i^* given $\mathbf{x}_i$. Letting d_i be a censoring indicator ($d_i = 1$ if uncensored, $d_i = 0$ if censored), the conditional likelihood for observation i can be written as

$$f(t_i \mid \mathbf{x}_i; \boldsymbol{\theta})^{d_i}[1 - F(t_i \mid \mathbf{x}_i; \boldsymbol{\theta})]^{(1-d_i)} \tag{20.23}$$

Importantly, neither the starting times, a_i, nor the length of the interval, b, plays a role in the analysis. [In fact, in the vast majority of treatments of flow data, b and a_i are not even introduced. However, it is important to know that the reason a_i is not relevant for the analysis of flow data is the conditional independence assumption in equation (20.22).] By contrast, the censoring times c_i do appear in the likelihood for censored observations because then $t_i = c_i$. Given data on $(t_i, d_i, \mathbf{x}_i)$ for a random sample of size N, the maximum likelihood estimator of $\boldsymbol{\theta}$ is obtained by maximizing

$$\sum_{i=1}^{N} \{d_i \log[f(t_i \mid \mathbf{x}_i; \boldsymbol{\theta})] + (1 - d_i) \log[1 - F(t_i \mid \mathbf{x}_i; \boldsymbol{\theta})]\} \tag{20.24}$$

For the choices of $f(\cdot \mid \mathbf{x}; \boldsymbol{\theta})$ used in practice, the conditional MLE regularity conditions—see Chapter 13—hold, and the MLE is $\sqrt{N}$-consistent and asymptotically normal. [If there is no censoring, the second term in expression (20.24) is simply dropped.]

Because the hazard function can be expressed as in equation (20.15), once we specify f, the hazard function can be estimated once we have the MLE, $\hat{\boldsymbol{\theta}}$. For example, the Weibull distribution with covariates has conditional density

$$f(t \mid \mathbf{x}_i; \boldsymbol{\theta}) = \exp(\mathbf{x}_i\boldsymbol{\beta})\alpha t^{\alpha-1} \exp[-\exp(\mathbf{x}_i\boldsymbol{\beta})t^{\alpha}] \tag{20.25}$$

where $\mathbf{x}_i$ contains unity as its first element for all i. [We obtain this density from Example 20.3 with γ replaced by $\exp(\mathbf{x}_i\boldsymbol{\beta})$.] The hazard function in this case is simply $\lambda(t; \mathbf{x}) = \exp(\mathbf{x}\boldsymbol{\beta})\alpha t^{\alpha-1}$.

Example 20.5 (Weibull Model for Recidivism Duration): Let *durat* be the length of time, in months, until an inmate is arrested after being released from prison. Although the duration is rounded to the nearest month, we treat *durat* as a continuous variable with a Weibull distribution. We are interested in how certain covariates affect the hazard function for recidivism, and also whether there is positive or negative duration dependence, once we have conditioned on the covariates. The variable *workprg*—a binary indicator for participation in a prison work program—is of particular interest.

The data in RECID.RAW, which comes from Chung, Schmidt, and Witte (1991), are flow data because it is a random sample of convicts released from prison during the period July 1, 1977, through June 30, 1978. The data are retrospective in that they were obtained by looking at records in April 1984, which served as the common censoring date. Because of the different starting times, the censoring times, c_i, vary from 70 to 81 months. The results of the Weibull estimation are in Table 20.1.

In interpreting the estimates, we use equation (20.17). For small $\hat{\beta}_j$, we can multiply the coefficient by 100 to obtain the semielasticity of the hazard with respect to x_j. (No covariates appear in logarithmic form, so there are no elasticities among the $\hat{\beta}_j$.) For example, if *tserved* increases by one month, the hazard shifts up by about 1.4 percent, and the effect is statistically significant. Another year of education reduces the hazard by about 2.3 percent, but the effect is insignificant at even the 10 percent level against a two-sided alternative.

The sign of the *workprg* coefficient is unexpected, at least if we expect the work program to have positive benefits after the inmates are released from prison. (The result is not statistically different from zero.) The reason could be that the program is ineffective or that there is self-selection into the program.

For large $\hat{\beta}_j$, we should exponentiate and subtract unity to obtain the proportionate change. For example, at any point in time, the hazard is about $100[\exp(.477) - 1] = 61.1$ percent greater for someone with an alcohol problem than for someone without.

Table 20.1
Weibull Estimation of Criminal Recidivism

Explanatory Variable	Coefficient (Standard Error)
workprg	.091 (.091)
priors	.089 (.013)
tserved	.014 (.002)
felon	−.299 (.106)
alcohol	.447 (.106)
drugs	.281 (.098)
black	.454 (.088)
married	−.152 (.109)
educ	−.023 (.019)
age	−.0037 (.0005)
constant	−3.402 (0.301)
Observations	1,445
Log likelihood	−1,633.03
$\hat{\alpha}$	.806 (.031)

The estimate of α is .806, and the standard error of $\hat{\alpha}$ leads to a strong rejection of H_0: $\alpha = 1$ against H_0: $\alpha < 1$. Therefore, there is evidence of negative duration dependence, conditional on the covariates. This means that, for a particular ex-convict, the instantaneous rate of being arrested decreases with the length of time out of prison. When the Weibull model is estimated without the covariates, $\hat{\alpha} = .770$ (se $= .031$), which shows slightly more negative duration dependence. This is a typical finding in applications of Weibull duration models: estimated α without covariate tends to be less than the estimate with covariates. Lancaster (1990, Section 10.2) contains a theoretical discussion based on unobserved heterogeneity.

When we are primarily interested in the effects of covariates on the expected duration (rather than on the hazard), we can apply a censored Tobit analysis to the log of the duration. A Tobit analysis assumes that, for each random draw i, $\log(t_i^*)$ given $\mathbf{x}_i$ has a Normal$(\mathbf{x}_i\boldsymbol{\delta}, \sigma^2)$ distribution, which implies that t_i^* given $\mathbf{x}_i$ has a lognormal distribution. (The first element of $\mathbf{x}_i$ is unity.) The hazard function for a lognormal distribution, conditional on $\mathbf{x}$, is $\lambda(t; \mathbf{x}) = h[(\log t - \mathbf{x}\boldsymbol{\delta})/\sigma]/\sigma t$, where $h(z) \equiv \phi(z)/[1 - \Phi(z)]$, $\phi(\cdot)$ is the standard normal probability density function (pdf), and $\Phi(\cdot)$ is the standard normal cdf. The lognormal hazard function is not monotonic and does not have the proportional hazard form. Nevertheless, the estimates of the δ_j are easy to interpret because the model is equivalent to

$$\log(t_i^*) = \mathbf{x}_i\boldsymbol{\delta} + e_i \tag{20.26}$$

where e_i is independent of $\mathbf{x}_i$ and normally distributed. Therefore, the δ_j are semielasticities—or elasticities if the covariates are in logarithmic form—of the covariates on the *expected* duration.

The Weibull model can also be represented in regression form. When t_i^* given $\mathbf{x}_i$ has density (20.25), $\exp(\mathbf{x}_i\boldsymbol{\beta})(t_i^*)^\alpha$ is independent of $\mathbf{x}_i$ and has a unit exponential distribution. Therefore, its natural log has a **type I extreme value distribution**; therefore, we can write $\alpha \log(t_i^*) = -\mathbf{x}_i\boldsymbol{\beta} + u_i$, where u_i is independent of $\mathbf{x}_i$ and has density $g(u) = \exp(u)\exp\{\exp(-u)\}$. The mean of u_i is not zero, but, because u_i is independent of $\mathbf{x}_i$, we can write $\log(t_i^*)$ exactly as in equation (20.26), where the slope coefficents are given by $\delta_j = -\beta_j/\alpha$, and the intercept is more complicated. Now, e_i does not have a normal distribution, but it is independent of $\mathbf{x}_i$ with zero mean. Censoring can be handled by maximum likelihood estimation. The estimated coefficients can be compared with the censored Tobit estimates described previously to see if the estimates are sensitive to the distributional assumption.

In Example 20.5, we can obtain the Weibull estimates of the δ_j as $\hat{\delta}_j = -\hat{\beta}_j/\hat{\alpha}$. (Some econometrics packages, such as Stata, allow direct estimation of the δ_j and provide standard errors.) For example, $\hat{\delta}_{\text{drugs}} = -.281/.806 \approx -.349$. When the lognormal model is used, the coefficient on *drugs* is somewhat smaller in magnitude, about $-.298$. As another example, $\hat{\delta}_{\text{age}} = .0046$ in the Weibull estimation and $\hat{\delta}_{\text{age}} = .0039$ in the lognormal estimation. In both cases, the estimates have t statistics over six. For obtaining estimates on the expected duration, the Weibull and lognormal models give similar results. [Interestingly, the lognormal model fits the data notably better, with log likelihood $= -1{,}597.06$. This result is consistent with the findings of Chung, Schmidt, and Witte (1991).]

Sometimes we begin by specifying a parametric model for the hazard conditional on $\mathbf{x}$ and then use the formulas from Section 20.2 to obtain the cdf and density. This approach is easiest when the hazard leads to a tractable duration distribution, but there is no reason the hazard function must be of the proportional hazard form.

Example 20.6 (Log-Logistic Hazard with Covariates): A log-logistic hazard function with covariates is

$$\lambda(t; \mathbf{x}) = \exp(\mathbf{x}\boldsymbol{\beta})\alpha t^{\alpha-1}/[1 + \exp(\mathbf{x}\boldsymbol{\beta})t^{\alpha}] \tag{20.27}$$

where $x_1 \equiv 1$. From equation (20.14) with $\gamma = \exp(\mathbf{x}\boldsymbol{\beta})$, the cdf is

$$F(t \mid \mathbf{x}; \boldsymbol{\theta}) = 1 - [1 + \exp(\mathbf{x}\boldsymbol{\beta})t^{\alpha}]^{-1}, \qquad t \geq 0 \tag{20.28}$$

The distribution of $\log(t_i^*)$ given $\mathbf{x}_i$ is logistic with mean $-\alpha^{-1}\log\{\exp(\mathbf{x}\boldsymbol{\beta})\} = -\alpha^{-1}\mathbf{x}\boldsymbol{\beta}$ and variance $\pi^2/(3\alpha^2)$. Therefore, $\log(t_i^*)$ can be written as in equation (20.26) where e_i has a zero mean logistic distribution and is *independent* of $\mathbf{x}_i$ and $\boldsymbol{\delta} = -\alpha^{-1}\boldsymbol{\beta}$. This is another example where the effects of the covariates on the mean duration can be obtained by an OLS regression when there is no censoring. With censoring, the distribution of e_i must be accounted for using the log likelihood in expression (20.24).

20.3.3 Stock Sampling

Flow data with right censoring are common, but other sampling schemes are also used. With **stock sampling** we randomly sample from individuals that are in the initial state at a given point in time. The population is again individuals who enter the initial state during a specified interval, $[0, b]$. However, rather than observe a random sample of people flowing into the initial state, we can only obtain a random sample of individuals that are in the initial state at time b. In addition to the possibility of right censoring, we may also face the problem of **left censoring**, which occurs when some or all of the starting times, a_i, are not observed. For now, we assume that (1) we observe the starting times a_i for all individuals we sample at time b and (2) we can follow sampled individuals for a certain length of time after we observe them at time b. We also allow for right censoring.

In the unemployment duration example, where the population comprises workers who became unemployed at some point during 1998, stock sampling would occur if we randomly sampled from workers who were unemployed during the last week of 1998. This kind of sampling causes a clear sample selection problem: we necessarily exclude from our sample any individual whose unemployment spell ended before the last week of 1998. Because these spells were necessarily shorter than a year, we cannot just assume that the missing observations are randomly missing.

The sample selection problem caused by stock sampling is essentially the same situation we faced in Section 17.3, where we covered the truncated regression model. Therefore, we will call this the **left truncation** problem. Kiefer (1988) calls it **length-biased sampling**.

Under the assumptions that we observe the a_i and can observe some spells past the sampling date b, left truncation is fairly easy to deal with. With the exception of replacing flow sampling with stock sampling, we make the same assumptions as in Section 20.3.2.

To account for the truncated sampling, we must modify the density in equation (20.23) to reflect the fact that part of the population is systematically omitted from the sample. Let $(a_i, c_i, \mathbf{x}_i, t_i)$ denote a random draw from the population of all spells starting in $[0, b]$. We observe this vector if and only if the person is still in the initial state at time b, that is, if and only if $a_i + t_i^* \geq b$ or $t_i^* \geq b - a_i$, where t_i^* is the true duration. But, under the conditional independence assumption (20.22),

$$\mathrm{P}(t_i^* \geq b - a_i \mid a_i, c_i, \mathbf{x}_i) = 1 - F(b - a_i \mid \mathbf{x}_i; \boldsymbol{\theta}) \tag{20.29}$$

where $F(\cdot \mid \mathbf{x}_i; \boldsymbol{\theta})$ is the cdf of t_i^* given $\mathbf{x}_i$, as before. The correct conditional density function is obtained by dividing equation (20.23) by equation (20.29). In Problem 20.5 you are asked to adapt the arguments in Section 17.3 to also allow for right censoring. The log-likelihood function can be written as

$$\sum_{i=1}^{N} \{d_i \log[f(t_i \mid \mathbf{x}_i; \boldsymbol{\theta})] + (1 - d_i) \log[1 - F(t_i \mid \mathbf{x}_i; \boldsymbol{\theta})] - \log[1 - F(b - a_i \mid \mathbf{x}_i; \boldsymbol{\theta})]\} \tag{20.30}$$

where, again, $t_i = c_i$ when $d_i = 0$. Unlike in the case of flow sampling, with stock sampling both the starting dates, a_i, and the length of the sampling interval, b, appear in the conditional likelihood function. Their presence makes it clear that specifying the interval $[0, b]$ is important for analyzing stock data. [Lancaster (1990, p. 183) essentially derives equation (20.30) under a slightly different sampling scheme; see also Lancaster (1979).]

Equation (20.30) has an interesting implication. If observation i is right censored at calendar date b—that is, if we do not follow the spell after the initial data collection—then the censoring time is $c_i = b - a_i$. Because $d_i = 0$ for censored observations, the log likelihood for such an observation is $\log[1 - F(c_i \mid \mathbf{x}_i; \boldsymbol{\theta})] - \log[1 - F(b - a_i \mid \mathbf{x}_i; \boldsymbol{\theta})] = 0$. In other words, observations that are right censored at the data collection time provide no information for estimating $\boldsymbol{\theta}$, at least when we use equation (20.30). Consequently, the log likelihood in equation (20.30) does not identify $\boldsymbol{\theta}$ if *all* units are right censored at the interview date: equation (20.30) is identically zero. The intuition for why equation (20.30) fails in this case is fairly clear: our data consist only of $(a_i, \mathbf{x}_i)$, and equation (20.30) is a log likelihood that is conditional on $(a_i, \mathbf{x}_i)$. Effectively, there is no random response variable.

Even when we censor all observed durations at the interview date, we can still estimate $\boldsymbol{\theta}$, provided—at least in a parametric context—we specify a model for the conditional distribution of the starting times, $\mathrm{D}(a_i \mid \mathbf{x}_i)$. (This is essentially the problem analyzed by Nickell, 1979.) We are still assuming that we observe the a_i. So, for example, we randomly sample from the pool of people unemployed in the last week of 1998 and find out when their unemployment spells began (along with covariates). We do not follow any spells past the interview date. (As an aside, if we sample unemployed people during the last week of 1998, we are likely to obtain some observations where spells began before 1998. For the population we have specified, these people would simply be discarded. If we want to include people whose spells began prior to 1998, we need to redefine the interval. For example, if durations are measured in weeks and if we want to consider durations beginning in the five-year period prior to the end of 1998, then $b = 260$.)

For concreteness, we assume that $\mathrm{D}(a_i \mid \mathbf{x}_i)$ is continuous on $[0, b]$ with density $k(\cdot \mid \mathbf{x}_i; \boldsymbol{\eta})$. Let s_i denote a sample selection indicator, which is unity if we observe random draw i, that is, if $t_i^* \geq b - a_i$. Estimation of $\boldsymbol{\theta}$ (and $\boldsymbol{\eta}$) can proceed by applying CMLE to the density of a_i conditional on $\mathbf{x}_i$ *and* $s_i = 1$. [Note that this is the only density we can hope to estimate, as our sample only consists of observations $(a_i, \mathbf{x}_i)$ when $s_i = 1$.] This density is informative for $\boldsymbol{\theta}$ even if $\boldsymbol{\eta}$ is not functionally related to $\boldsymbol{\theta}$ (as would typically be assumed) because there are some durations that started and ended in $[0, b]$; we simply do not observe them. Knowing something about the starting time distribution gives us information about the duration distribution. (In the context of flow sampling, when $\boldsymbol{\eta}$ is not functionally related to $\boldsymbol{\theta}$, the density of a_i given $\mathbf{x}_i$ is uninformative for estimating $\boldsymbol{\theta}$; in other words, a_i is ancillary for $\boldsymbol{\theta}$.)

In Problem 20.6 you are asked to show that the density of a_i conditional on observing $(a_i, \mathbf{x}_i)$ is

$$p(a \mid \mathbf{x}_i, s_i = 1) = k(a \mid \mathbf{x}_i; \boldsymbol{\eta})[1 - F(b - a \mid \mathbf{x}_i; \boldsymbol{\theta})]/\mathrm{P}(s_i = 1 \mid \mathbf{x}_i; \boldsymbol{\theta}, \boldsymbol{\eta}) \tag{20.31}$$

$0 < a < b$, where

$$\mathrm{P}(s_i = 1 \mid \mathbf{x}_i; \boldsymbol{\theta}, \boldsymbol{\eta}) = \int_0^b [1 - F(b - u \mid \mathbf{x}_i; \boldsymbol{\theta})] k(u \mid \mathbf{x}_i; \boldsymbol{\eta})\, du \tag{20.32}$$

[Lancaster (1990, Section 8.3.3) essentially obtains the right-hand side of equation (20.31) but uses the notion of backward recurrence time. The argument in Problem 20.6 is more straightforward because it is based on a standard truncation argument.] Once we have specified the duration cdf, F, and the starting time density, k, we can use conditional MLE to estimate $\boldsymbol{\theta}$ and $\boldsymbol{\eta}$: the log likelihood for observation i is just the log of equation (20.31), evaluated at a_i. If we assume that a_i is independent of

$\mathbf{x}_i$ and has a uniform distribution on $[0, b]$, the estimation simplifies somewhat; see Problem 20.6. Allowing for a discontinuous starting time density $k(\cdot \mid \mathbf{x}_i; \boldsymbol{\eta})$ does not materially affect equation (20.31). For example, if the interval [0,1] represents one year, we might want to allow different entry rates over the different seasons. This would correspond to a uniform distribution over each subinterval that we choose.

We now turn to the problem of left censoring, which arises with stock sampling when we do not actually know when any spell began. In other words, the a_i are not observed, and therefore neither are the true durations, t_i^*. However, we assume that we can follow spells after the interview date. Without right censoring, this assumption means we can observe the time in the current spell since the interview date, say, r_i, which we can write as $r_i = t_i^* + a_i - b$. We still have a left truncation problem because we only observe r_i when $t_i^* > b - a_i$, that is, when $r_i > 0$. The general approach is the same as with the earlier problems: we obtain the density of the variable that we can at least partially observe, r_i in this case, conditional on observing r_i. Problem 20.8 asks you to fill in the details, accounting also for possible right censoring.

We can easily combine stock sampling and flow sampling. For example, in the case that we observe the starting times, a_i, suppose that, at time $m < b$, we sample a stock of individuals already in the initial state. In addition to following spells of individuals already in the initial state, suppose we can randomly sample individuals flowing into the initial state between times m and b. Then we follow all the individuals appearing in the sample, at least until right censoring. For starting dates after m ($a_i \geq m$), there is no truncation, and so the log likelihood for these observations is just as in equation (20.24). For $a_i < m$, the log likelihood is identical to equation (20.30) except that m replaces b. Other combinations are easy to infer from the preceding results.

20.3.4 Unobserved Heterogeneity

One way to obtain more general duration models is to introduce unobserved heterogeneity into fairly simple duration models. In addition, we sometimes want to test for duration dependence conditional on observed covariates *and* unobserved heterogeneity. The key assumptions used in most models that incorporate unobserved heterogeneity are that (1) the heterogeneity is *independent* of the observed covariates, as well as starting times and censoring times; (2) the heterogeneity has a distribution known up to a finite number of parameters; and (3) the heterogeneity enters the hazard function multiplicatively. We will make these assumptions. In the context of single-spell flow data, it is difficult to relax any of these assumptions. (In the special case of a lognormal duration distribution, we can relax assumption 1 by using Tobit methods with endogenous explanatory variables; see Section 16.6.2.)

Before we cover the general case, it is useful to cover an example due to Lancaster (1979). For a random draw i from the population, a Weibull hazard function conditional on observed covariates $\mathbf{x}_i$ and unobserved heterogeneity v_i is

$$\lambda(t; \mathbf{x}_i, v_i) = v_i \exp(\mathbf{x}_i \boldsymbol{\beta}) \alpha t^{\alpha-1} \tag{20.33}$$

where $x_{i1} \equiv 1$ and $v_i > 0$. [Lancaster (1990) calls equation (20.33) a *conditional hazard*, because it conditions on the unobserved heterogeneity v_i. Technically, almost all hazards in econometrics are conditional because we almost always condition on observed covariates.] Notice how v_i enters equation (20.33) multiplicatively. To identify the parameters α and $\boldsymbol{\beta}$ we need a normalization on the distribution of v_i; we use the most common, $\mathrm{E}(v_i) = 1$. This implies that, for a given vector $\mathbf{x}$, the average hazard is $\exp(\mathbf{x}\boldsymbol{\beta})\alpha t^{\alpha-1}$. An interesting hypothesis is H_0: $\alpha = 1$, which means that, conditional on $\mathbf{x}_i$ *and* v_i, there is no duration dependence.

In the general case where the cdf of t_i^* given $(\mathbf{x}_i, v_i)$ is $F(t \mid \mathbf{x}_i, v_i; \boldsymbol{\theta})$, we can obtain the distribution of t_i^* given $\mathbf{x}_i$ by integrating out the unobserved effect. Because v_i and $\mathbf{x}_i$ are independent, the cdf of t_i^* given $\mathbf{x}_i$ is

$$G(t \mid \mathbf{x}_i; \boldsymbol{\theta}, \boldsymbol{\rho}) = \int_0^\infty F(t \mid \mathbf{x}_i, v; \boldsymbol{\theta}) h(v; \boldsymbol{\rho})\, dv \tag{20.34}$$

where, for concreteness, the density of v_i, $h(\cdot; \boldsymbol{\rho})$, is assumed to be continuous and depends on the unknown parameters $\boldsymbol{\rho}$. From equation (20.34) the density of t_i^* given $\mathbf{x}_i$, $g(t \mid \mathbf{x}_i; \boldsymbol{\theta}, \boldsymbol{\rho})$, is easily obtained. We can now use the methods of Sections 20.3.2 and 20.3.3. For flow data, the log-likelihood function is as in equation (20.24), but with $G(t \mid \mathbf{x}_i; \boldsymbol{\theta}, \boldsymbol{\rho})$ replacing $F(t \mid \mathbf{x}_i; \boldsymbol{\theta})$ and $g(t \mid \mathbf{x}_i; \boldsymbol{\theta}, \boldsymbol{\rho})$ replacing $f(t \mid \mathbf{x}_i; \boldsymbol{\theta})$. We should assume that $\mathrm{D}(t_i^* \mid \mathbf{x}_i, v_i, a_i, c_i) = \mathrm{D}(t_i^* \mid \mathbf{x}_i, v_i)$ and $\mathrm{D}(v_i \mid \mathbf{x}_i, a_i, c_i) = \mathrm{D}(v_i)$; these assumptions ensure that the key condition (20.22) holds. The methods for stock sampling described in Section 20.3.3 also apply to the integrated cdf and density.

If we assume **gamma-distributed heterogeneity**—that is, $v_i \sim \mathrm{Gamma}(\delta, \delta)$, so that $\mathrm{E}(v_i) = 1$ and $\mathrm{Var}(v_i) = 1/\delta$—we can find the distribution of t_i^* given $\mathbf{x}_i$ for a broad class of hazard functions with multiplicative heterogeneity. Suppose that the hazard function is $\lambda(t; \mathbf{x}_i, v_i) = v_i \kappa(t; \mathbf{x}_i)$, where $\kappa(t; \mathbf{x}) > 0$ (and need not have the proportional hazard form). For simplicity, we suppress the dependence of $\kappa(\cdot\,;\cdot)$ on unknown parameters. From equation (20.7), the cdf of t_i^* given $(\mathbf{x}_i, v_i)$ is

$$F(t \mid \mathbf{x}_i, v_i) = 1 - \exp\left[-v_i \int_0^t \kappa(s; \mathbf{x}_i)\, ds\right] \equiv 1 - \exp[-v_i \xi(t; \mathbf{x}_i)] \tag{20.35}$$

where $\xi(t; \mathbf{x}_i) \equiv \int_0^t \kappa(s; \mathbf{x}_i)\, ds$. We can obtain the cdf of t_i^* given $\mathbf{x}_i$ by using equation (20.34). The density of v_i is $h(v) = \delta^\delta v^{\delta-1} \exp(-\delta v)/\Gamma(\delta)$, where $\mathrm{Var}(v_i) = 1/\delta$ and

$\Gamma(\cdot)$ is the gamma function. Let $\xi_i \equiv \xi(t; \mathbf{x}_i)$ for given t. Then

$$\int_0^{\infty} \exp(-\xi_i v)\delta^{\delta} v^{\delta-1} \exp(-\delta v)/\Gamma(\delta)\, dv$$

$$= [\delta/(\delta+\xi_i)]^{\delta} \int_0^{\infty} (\delta+\xi_i)^{\delta} v^{\delta-1} \exp[-(\delta+\xi_i)v]/\Gamma(\delta)\, dv$$

$$= [\delta/(\delta+\xi_i)]^{\delta} = (1+\xi_i/\delta)^{-\delta}$$

where the second-to-last equality follows because the integrand is the Gamma (δ, $\delta+\xi_i$) density and must integrate to unity. Now we use equation (20.34):

$$G(t \mid \mathbf{x}_i) = 1 - [1 + \xi(t; \mathbf{x}_i)/\delta]^{-\delta} \tag{20.36}$$

Taking the derivative of equation (20.36) with respect to t, using the fact that $\kappa(t; \mathbf{x}_i)$ is the derivative of $\xi(t; \mathbf{x}_i)$, yields the density of t_i^* given $\mathbf{x}_i$ as

$$g(t \mid \mathbf{x}_i) = \kappa(t; \mathbf{x}_i)[1 + \xi(t; \mathbf{x}_i)/\delta]^{-(\delta-1)} \tag{20.37}$$

The function $\kappa(t; \mathbf{x})$ depends on parameters $\boldsymbol{\theta}$, and so $g(t \mid \mathbf{x})$ should be $g(t \mid \mathbf{x}; \boldsymbol{\theta}, \delta)$. With censored data the vector $\boldsymbol{\theta}$ can be estimated along with δ by using the log-likelihood function in equation (20.24) (again, with G replacing F).

With the Weibull hazard in equation (20.33), $\xi(t; \mathbf{x}) = \exp(\mathbf{x}\boldsymbol{\beta})t^{\alpha}$, which leads to a very tractable analysis when plugged into equations (20.36) and (20.37); the resulting duration distribution is called the **Burr distribution**. In the log-logistic case with $\kappa(t; \mathbf{x}) = \exp(\mathbf{x}\boldsymbol{\beta})\alpha t^{\alpha-1}[1 + \exp(\mathbf{x}\boldsymbol{\beta})t^{\alpha}]^{-1}$, $\xi(t; \mathbf{x}) = \log[1 + \exp(\mathbf{x}\boldsymbol{\beta})t^{\alpha}]$. These equations can be plugged into the preceding formulas for a maximum likelihood analysis.

Before we end this section, we should recall why we might want to explicitly introduce unobserved heterogeneity when the heterogeneity is assumed to be independent of the observed covariates. The strongest case is seen when we are interested in testing for duration dependence conditional on observed covariates *and* unobserved heterogeneity, where the unobserved heterogeneity enters the hazard multiplicatively. As carefully exposited by Lancaster (1990, Section 10.2), ignoring multiplicative heterogeneity in the Weibull model results in asymptotically underestimating α. Therefore, we could very well conclude that there is negative duration dependence conditional on $\mathbf{x}$, whereas there is no duration dependence ($\alpha = 1$) conditional on $\mathbf{x}$ and v.

In a general sense, it is somewhat heroic to think we can distinguish between duration dependence and unobserved heterogeneity when we observe only a single cycle for each agent. The problem is simple to describe: because we can only estimate the distribution of T given $\mathbf{x}$, we cannot uncover the distribution of T given $(\mathbf{x}, v)$ unless we make extra assumptions, a point Lancaster (1990, Section 10.1) illustrates with an example. Therefore, we cannot tell whether the hazard describing T given $(\mathbf{x}, v)$ exhibits duration dependence. But, when the hazard has the proportional hazard form $\lambda(t; \mathbf{x}, v) = v\kappa(\mathbf{x})\lambda_0(t)$, it is possible to identify the function $\kappa(\cdot)$ and the baseline hazard $\lambda_0(\cdot)$ quite generally (along with the distribution of v). See Lancaster (1990, Section 7.3) for a presentation of the results of Elbers and Ridder (1982). Recently, Horowitz (1999) has demonstrated how to nonparametrically estimate the baseline hazard and the distribution of the unobserved heterogeneity under fairly weak assumptions.

When interest centers on how the observed covariates affect the mean duration, explicitly modeling unobserved heterogeneity is less compelling. Adding unobserved heterogeneity to equation (20.26) does not change the mean effects; it merely changes the error distribution. Without censoring, we would probably estimate $\boldsymbol{\beta}$ in equation (20.26) by OLS (rather than MLE) so that the estimators would be robust to distributional misspecification. With censoring, to perform maximum likelihood, we must know the distribution of t_i^* given $\mathbf{x}_i$, and this depends on the distribution of v_i when we explicitly introduce unobserved heterogeneity. But introducing unobserved heterogeneity is indistinguishable from simply allowing a more flexible duration distribution.

20.4 Analysis of Grouped Duration Data

Continuously distributed durations are, strictly speaking, rare in social science applications. Even if an underlying duration is properly viewed as being continuous, measurements are necessarily discrete. When the measurements are fairly precise, it is sensible to treat the durations as continuous random variables. But when the measurements are coarse—such as monthly, or perhaps even weekly—it can be important to account for the discreteness in the estimation.

Grouped duration data arise when each duration is only known to fall into a certain time interval, such as a week, a month, or even a year. For example, unemployment durations are often measured to the nearest week. In Example 20.2 the time until next arrest is measured to the nearest month. Even with grouped data we can generally estimate the parameters of the duration distribution.

The approach we take here to analyzing grouped data summarizes the information on staying in the initial state or exiting in each time interval in a sequence of binary outcomes. (Kiefer, 1988; Han and Hausman, 1990; Meyer, 1990; Lancaster, 1990; McCall, 1994; and Sueyoshi, 1995, all take this approach.) In effect, we have a panel data set where each cross section observation is a vector of binary responses, along with covariates. In addition to allowing us to treat grouped durations, the panel data approach has at least two additional advantages. First, in a proportional hazard specification, it leads to easy methods for estimating flexible hazard functions. Second, because of the sequential nature of the data, time-varying covariates are easily introduced.

We assume flow sampling so that we do not have to address the sample selection problem that arises with stock sampling. We divide the time line into $M+1$ intervals, $[0, a_1), [a_1, a_2), \ldots, [a_{M-1}, a_M), [a_M, \infty)$, where the a_m are known constants. For example, we might have $a_1 = 1, a_2 = 2, a_3 = 3$, and so on, but unequally spaced intervals are allowed. The last interval, $[a_M, \infty)$, is chosen so that any duration falling into it is censored at a_M: no observed durations are greater than a_M. For a random draw from the population, let c_m be a binary censoring indicator equal to unity if the duration is censored in interval m, and zero otherwise. Notice that $c_m = 1$ implies $c_{m+1} = 1$: if the duration was censored in interval m, it is still censored in interval $m+1$. Because durations lasting into the last interval are censored, $c_{M+1} \equiv 1$. Similarly, y_m is a binary indicator equal to unity if the duration ends in the mth interval and zero otherwise. Thus, $y_{m+1} = 1$ if $y_m = 1$. If the duration is censored in interval m ($c_m = 1$), we set $y_m \equiv 1$ by convention.

As in Section 20.3, we allow individuals to enter the initial state at different calendar times. In order to keep the notation simple, we do not explicitly show the conditioning on these starting times, as the starting times play no role under flow sampling when we assume that, conditional on the covariates, the starting times are independent of the duration and any unobserved heterogeneity. If necessary, starting-time dummies can be included in the covariates.

For each person i, we observe $(y_{i1}, c_{i1}), \ldots, (y_{iM}, c_{iM})$, which is a balanced panel data set. To avoid confusion with our notation for a duration (T for the random variable, t for a particular outcome on T), we use m to index the time intervals. The string of binary indicators for any individual is *not* unrestricted: we must observe a string of zeros followed by a string of ones. The important information is the interval in which y_{im} becomes unity for the first time, and whether that represents a true exit from the initial state or censoring.

20.4.1 Time-Invariant Covariates

With time-invariant covariates, each random draw from the population consists of information on $\{(y_1, c_1), \ldots, (y_M, c_M), \mathbf{x}\}$. We assume that a parametric hazard function is specified as $\lambda(t; \mathbf{x}, \boldsymbol{\theta})$, where $\boldsymbol{\theta}$ is the vector of unknown parameters. Let T denote the time until exit from the initial state. While we do not fully observe T, either we know which interval it falls into, or we know whether it was censored in a particular interval. This knowledge is enough to obtain the probability that y_m takes on the value unity given $(y_{m-1}, \dots, y_1)$, $(c_m, \dots, c_1)$, and $\mathbf{x}$. In fact, by definition this probability depends only on y_{m-1}, c_m, and $\mathbf{x}$, and only two combinations yield probabilities that are not identically zero or one. These probabilities are

$$\mathrm{P}(y_m = 0 \mid y_{m-1} = 0, \mathbf{x}, c_m = 0) \tag{20.38}$$

$$\mathrm{P}(y_m = 1 \mid y_{m-1} = 0, \mathbf{x}, c_m = 0), \qquad m = 1, \dots, M \tag{20.39}$$

(We define $y_0 \equiv 0$ so that these equations hold for all $m \geq 1$.) To compute these probabilities in terms of the hazard for T, we assume that the duration is conditionally independent of censoring:

$$T \text{ is independent of } c_1, \dots, c_M, \text{ given } \mathbf{x} \tag{20.40}$$

This assumption allows the censoring to depend on $\mathbf{x}$ but rules out censoring that depends on unobservables, after conditioning on $\mathbf{x}$. Condition (20.40) holds for fixed censoring or completely randomized censoring. (It may not hold if censoring is due to nonrandom attrition.) Under assumption (20.40) we have, from equation (20.9),

$$\begin{aligned} \mathrm{P}(y_m = 1 \mid y_{m-1} = 0, \mathbf{x}, c_m = 0) &= \mathrm{P}(a_{m-1} \leq T < a_m \mid T \geq a_{m-1}, \mathbf{x}) \\ &= 1 - \exp\left[-\int_{a_{m-1}}^{a_m} \lambda(s; \mathbf{x}, \boldsymbol{\theta})\, ds\right] \equiv 1 - \alpha_m(\mathbf{x}, \boldsymbol{\theta}) \end{aligned} \tag{20.41}$$

for $m = 1, 2, \dots, M$, where

$$\alpha_m(\mathbf{x}, \boldsymbol{\theta}) \equiv \exp\left[-\int_{a_{m-1}}^{a_m} \lambda(s; \mathbf{x}, \boldsymbol{\theta})\, ds\right] \tag{20.42}$$

Therefore,

$$\mathrm{P}(y_m = 0 \mid y_{m-1} = 0, \mathbf{x}, c_m = 0) = \alpha_m(\mathbf{x}, \boldsymbol{\theta}) \tag{20.43}$$

We can use these probabilities to construct the likelihood function. If, for observation i, uncensored exit occurs in interval m_i, the likelihood is

$$\left[\prod_{h=1}^{m_i - 1} \alpha_h(\mathbf{x}_i, \boldsymbol{\theta})\right][1 - \alpha_{m_i}(\mathbf{x}_i, \boldsymbol{\theta})] \tag{20.44}$$

The first term represents the probability of remaining in the initial state for the first $m_i - 1$ intervals, and the second term is the (conditional) probability that T falls into interval m_i. [Because an uncensored duration must have $m_i \leq M$, expression (20.44) at most depends on $\alpha_1(\mathbf{x}_i, \boldsymbol{\theta}), \ldots, \alpha_M(\mathbf{x}_i, \boldsymbol{\theta})$.] If the duration is censored in interval m_i, we know only that exit did not occur in the first $m_i - 1$ intervals, and the likelihood consists of only the first term in expression (20.44).

If d_i is a censoring indicator equal to one if duration i is uncensored, the log likelihood for observation i can be written as

$$\sum_{h=1}^{m_i-1} \log[\alpha_h(\mathbf{x}_i, \boldsymbol{\theta})] + d_i \log[1 - \alpha_{m_i}(\mathbf{x}_i, \boldsymbol{\theta})] \tag{20.45}$$

The log likelihood for the entire sample is obtained by summing expression (20.45) across all $i = 1, \ldots, N$. Under the assumptions made, this log likelihood represents the density of $(y_1, \ldots, y_M)$ given $(c_1, \ldots, c_M)$ and $\mathbf{x}$, and so the conditional maximum likelihood theory covered in Chapter 13 applies directly. The various ways of estimating asymptotic variances and computing test statistics are available.

To implement conditional MLE, we must specify a hazard function. One hazard function that has become popular because of its flexibility is a **piecewise-constant proportional hazard**: for $m = 1, \ldots, M$,

$$\lambda(t; \mathbf{x}, \boldsymbol{\theta}) = \kappa(\mathbf{x}, \boldsymbol{\beta})\lambda_m, \qquad a_{m-1} \le t < a_m \tag{20.46}$$

where $\kappa(\mathbf{x}, \boldsymbol{\beta}) > 0$ [and typically $\kappa(\mathbf{x}, \boldsymbol{\beta}) = \exp(\mathbf{x}\boldsymbol{\beta})$]. This specification allows the hazard to be different (albeit constant) over each time interval. The parameters to be estimated are $\boldsymbol{\beta}$ and $\boldsymbol{\lambda}$, where the latter is the vector of λ_m, $m = 1, \ldots, M$. {Because durations in $[a_M, \infty)$ are censored at a_M, we cannot estimate the hazard over the interval $[a_M, \infty)$.} As an example, if we have unemployment duration measured in weeks, the hazard can be different in each week. If the durations are sparse, we might assume a different hazard rate for every two or three weeks (this assumption places restrictions on the λ_m). With the piecewise-constant hazard and $\kappa(\mathbf{x}, \boldsymbol{\beta}) = \exp(\mathbf{x}\boldsymbol{\beta})$, for $m = 1, \ldots, M$, we have

$$\alpha_m(\mathbf{x}, \boldsymbol{\theta}) \equiv \exp[-\exp(\mathbf{x}\boldsymbol{\beta})\lambda_m(a_m - a_{m-1})] \tag{20.47}$$

Remember, the a_m are known constants (often $a_m = m$) and not parameters to be estimated. Usually the λ_m are unrestricted, in which case $\mathbf{x}$ does not contain an intercept.

The piecewise-constant hazard implies that the duration distribution is discontinuous at the endpoints, whereas in our discussion in Section 20.2, we assumed that the duration had a continuous distribution. A piecewise-continuous distribution causes no real problems, and the log likelihood is exactly as specified previously. Alternatively, as in Han and Hausman (1990) and Meyer (1990), we can assume that T

has a proportional hazard as in equation (20.16) with continuous baseline hazard, $\lambda_0(\cdot)$. Then, we can estimate $\boldsymbol{\beta}$ along with the parameters

$$\int_{a_{m-1}}^{a_m} \lambda_0(s)\, ds, \qquad m = 1, 2, \ldots, M$$

In practice, the approaches are the same, and it is easiest to just assume a piecewise-constant proportional hazard, as in equation (20.46).

Once the λ_m have been estimated along with $\boldsymbol{\beta}$, an estimated hazard function is easily plotted: graph $\hat{\lambda}_m$ at the midpoint of the interval $[a_{m-1}, a_m)$, and connect the points.

Without covariates, maximum likelihood estimation of the λ_m leads to a well-known estimator of the survivor function. Rather than derive the MLE of the survivor function, it is easier to motivate the estimator from the representation of the survivor function as a product of conditional probabilities. For $m = 1, \ldots, M$, the survivor function at time a_m can be written as

$$S(a_m) = \mathrm{P}(T > a_m) = \prod_{r=1}^{m} \mathrm{P}(T > a_r \mid T > a_{r-1}) \tag{20.48}$$

[Because $a_0 = 0$ and $\mathrm{P}(T > 0) = 1$, the $r = 1$ term on the right-hand side of equation (20.48) is simply $\mathrm{P}(T > a_1)$.] Now, for each $r = 1, 2, \ldots, M$, let N_r denote the number of people in the **risk set** for interval r: N_r is the number of people who have neither left the initial state nor been censored at time a_{r-1}, which is the beginning of interval r. Therefore, N_1 is the number of individuals in the initial random sample; N_2 is the number of individuals who did not exit the initial state in the first interval, less the number of individuals censored in the first interval; and so on. Let E_r be the number of people observed to leave in the rth interval—that is, in the interval $[a_{r-1}, a_r)$. A consistent estimator of $\mathrm{P}(T > a_r \mid T > a_{r-1})$ is $(N_r - E_r)/N_r$, $r = 1, 2, \ldots, M$. [We must use the fact that the censoring is ignorable in the sense of assumption (20.40), so that there is no sample selection bias in using only the uncensored observations.] It follows from equation (20.48) that a consistent estimator of the survivor function at time a_m is

$$\hat{S}(a_m) = \prod_{r=1}^{m} [(N_r - E_r)/N_r], \qquad m = 1, 2, \ldots, M \tag{20.49}$$

This is the **Kaplan-Meier estimator** of the survivor function (at the points $a_1, a_2, \ldots, a_M$). Lancaster (1990, Section 8.2) contains a proof that maximum likelihood estimation of the λ_m (without covariates) leads to the Kaplan-Meier estimator of the survivor function. If there are no censored durations before time a_m, $\hat{S}(a_m)$ is simply the fraction of people who have not left the initial state at time a_m, which is obviously consistent for $\mathrm{P}(T > a_m) = S(a_m)$.

In the general model, we do not need to assume a proportional hazard specification within each interval. For example, we could assume a log-logistic hazard within each interval, with different parameters for each m. Because the hazard in such cases does not depend on the covariates multiplicatively, we must plug in values of $\mathbf{x}$ in order to plot the hazard. Sueyoshi (1995) studies such models in detail.

If the intervals $[a_{m-1}, a_m)$ are coarser than the data—for example, unemployment is measured in weeks, but we choose $[a_{m-1}, a_m)$ to be four weeks for all m—then we can specify nonconstant hazards within each interval. The piecewise-constant hazard corresponds to an exponential distribution within each interval. But we could specify, say, a Weibull distribution within each interval. See Sueyoshi (1995) for details.

20.4.2 Time-Varying Covariates

Deriving the log likelihood is more complicated with time-varying covariates, especially when we do not assume that the covariates are strictly exogenous. Nevertheless, we will show that, if the covariates are constant within each time interval $[a_{m-1}, a_m)$, the form of the log likelihood is the same as expression (20.45), provided $\mathbf{x}_i$ is replaced with $\mathbf{x}_{im}$ in interval m.

For the population, let $\mathbf{x}_1, \mathbf{x}_2, \ldots, \mathbf{x}_M$ denote the outcomes of the covariates in each of the M time intervals, where we assume that the covariates are constant within an interval. This assumption is clearly an oversimplification, but we cannot get very far without it (and it reflects how data sets with time-varying covariates are usually constructed). When the covariates are internal and are not necessarily defined after exit from the initial state, the definition of the covariates in the time intervals is irrelevant; but it is useful to list covariates for all M time periods.

We assume that the hazard at time t conditional on the covariates up through time t depends only on the covariates at time t. If past values of the covariates matter, they can simply be included in the covariates at time t. The conditional independence assumption on the censoring indicators is now stated as

$$\mathrm{D}(T \mid T \geq a_{m-1}, \mathbf{x}_m, c_m) = \mathrm{D}(T \mid T \geq a_{m-1}, \mathbf{x}_m), \qquad m = 1, \ldots, M \tag{20.50}$$

This assumption allows the censoring decision to depend on the covariates during the time interval (as well as past covariates, provided they are either included in $\mathbf{x}_m$ or do not affect the distribution of T given $\mathbf{x}_m$). Under this assumption, the probability of exit (without censoring) is

$$\mathrm{P}(y_m = 1 \mid y_{m-1} = 0, \mathbf{x}_m, c_m = 0) = \mathrm{P}(a_{m-1} \le T < a_m \mid T \ge a_{m-1}, \mathbf{x}_m)$$
$$= 1 - \exp\left[-\int_{a_{m-1}}^{a_m} \lambda(s; \mathbf{x}_m, \boldsymbol{\theta})\, ds\right] \equiv 1 - \alpha_m(\mathbf{x}_m, \boldsymbol{\theta}) \tag{20.51}$$

We can use equation (20.51), along with $\mathrm{P}(y_m = 0 \mid y_{m-1} = 0, \mathbf{x}_m, c_m = 0) = \alpha_m(\mathbf{x}_m, \boldsymbol{\theta})$, to build up a partial log likelihood for person i. As we discussed in Section 13.8, this is only a partial likelihood because we are not necessarily modeling the joint distribution of $(y_1, \ldots, y_M)$ given $\{(\mathbf{x}_1, c_1), \ldots, (c_M, \mathbf{x}_M)\}$.

For someone censored in interval m, the information on the duration is contained in $y_{i1} = 0, \ldots, y_{i,m-1} = 0$. For someone who truly exits in interval m, there is additional information in $y_{im} = 1$. Therefore, the partial log likelihood is given by expression (20.45), but, to reflect the time-varying covariates, $\alpha_h(\mathbf{x}_i, \boldsymbol{\theta})$ is replaced by $\alpha_h(\mathbf{x}_{ih}, \boldsymbol{\theta})$ and $\alpha_{m_i}(\mathbf{x}_i, \boldsymbol{\theta})$ is replaced by $\alpha_{m_i}(\mathbf{x}_{i,m_i}, \boldsymbol{\theta})$.

Each term in the partial log likelihood represents the distribution of y_m given $(y_{m-1}, \ldots, y_1)$, $(\mathbf{x}_m, \ldots, \mathbf{x}_1)$, and $(c_m, \ldots, c_1)$. [Most of the probabilities in this conditional distribution are either zero or one; only the probabilities that depend on $\boldsymbol{\theta}$ are shown in expression (20.45).] Therefore, the density is *dynamically complete*, in the terminology of Section 13.8.3. As shown there, the usual maximum likelihood variance matrix estimators and statistics are asymptotically valid, even though we need not have the full conditional distribution of $\mathbf{y}$ given $(\mathbf{x}, \mathbf{c})$. This result would change if, for some reason, we chose not to include past covariates when in fact they affect the current probability of exit even after conditioning on the current covariates. Then the robust forms of the statistics covered in Section 13.8 should be used. In most duration applications we want dynamic completeness.

If the covariates are strictly exogenous and if the censoring is strictly exogenous, then the partial likelihood is the full conditional likelihood. The precise strict exogeneity assumption is

$$\mathrm{D}(T \mid T \ge a_{m-1}, \mathbf{x}, \mathbf{c}) = \mathrm{D}(T \mid T \ge a_{m-1}, \mathbf{x}_m), \qquad m = 1, \ldots, M \tag{20.52}$$

where $\mathbf{x}$ is the vector of covariates across all time periods and $\mathbf{c}$ is the vector of censoring indicators. There are two parts to this assumption. Ignoring the censoring, assumption (20.52) means that neither future nor past covariates appear in the hazard, once current covariates are controlled for. The second implication of assumption (20.52) is that the censoring is also strictly exogenous.

With time-varying covariates, the hazard specification

$$\lambda(t; \mathbf{x}_m, \boldsymbol{\theta}) = \kappa(\mathbf{x}_m, \boldsymbol{\beta})\lambda_m, \qquad a_{m-1} \le t < a_m \tag{20.53}$$

$m = 1, \ldots, M$, is still attractive. It implies that the covariates have a multiplicative effect in each time interval, and it allows the baseline hazard—the part common to all members of the population—to be flexible.

Meyer (1990) essentially uses the specification (20.53) to estimate the effect of unemployment insurance on unemployment spells. McCall (1994) shows how to allow for time-varying coefficients when $\kappa(\mathbf{x}_m, \boldsymbol{\beta}) = \exp(\mathbf{x}_m \boldsymbol{\beta})$. In other words, $\boldsymbol{\beta}$ is replaced with $\boldsymbol{\beta}_m$, $m = 1, \ldots, M$.

20.4.3 Unobserved Heterogeneity

We can also add unobserved heterogeneity to hazards specified for grouped data, even if we have time-varying covariates. With time-varying covariates and unobserved heterogeneity, it is difficult to relax the strict exogeneity assumption. Also, with single-spell data, we cannot allow general correlation between the unobserved heterogeneity and the covariates. Therefore, we assume that the covariates are strictly exogenous conditional on unobserved heterogeneity *and* that the unobserved heterogeneity is independent of the covariates.

The precise assumptions are given by equation (20.52) but where unobserved heterogeneity, v, appears in both conditioning sets. In addition, we assume that v is independent of $(\mathbf{x}, \mathbf{c})$ (which is a further sense in which the censoring is exogenous).

In the leading case of the piecewise-constant baseline hazard, equation (20.53) becomes

$$\lambda(t; v, \mathbf{x}_m, \boldsymbol{\theta}) = v\kappa(\mathbf{x}_m, \boldsymbol{\beta})\lambda_m, \qquad a_{m-1} \le t < a_m \tag{20.54}$$

where $v > 0$ is a continuously distributed heterogeneity term. Using the same reasoning as in Sections 20.4.1 and 20.4.2, the density of $(y_{i1}, \ldots, y_{iM})$ given $(v_i, \mathbf{x}_i, \mathbf{c}_i)$ is

$$\left[\prod_{h=1}^{m_i - 1} \alpha_h(v_i, \mathbf{x}_{ih}, \boldsymbol{\theta})\right][1 - \alpha_{m_i}(v_i, \mathbf{x}_{i,m_i}, \boldsymbol{\theta})]^{d_i} \tag{20.55}$$

where $d_i = 1$ if observation i is uncensored. Because expression (20.55) depends on the unobserved heterogeneity, v_i, we cannot use it directly to consistently estimate $\boldsymbol{\theta}$. However, because v_i is independent of $(\mathbf{x}_i, \mathbf{c}_i)$, with density $g(v; \boldsymbol{\delta})$, we can integrate expression (20.55) against $g(\cdot\,; \boldsymbol{\delta})$ to obtain the density of $(y_{i1}, \ldots, y_{iM})$ given $(\mathbf{x}_i, \mathbf{c}_i)$. This density depends on the observed data—$(m_i, d_i, \mathbf{x}_i)$—and the parameters $\boldsymbol{\theta}$ and $\boldsymbol{\delta}$. From this density, we construct the conditional log likelihood for observation i, and we can obtain the conditional MLE, just as in other nonlinear models with unobserved heterogeneity—see Chapters 15, 16, and 19. Meyer (1990) assumes that the distribution of v_i is gamma, with unit mean, and obtains the log-likelihood function in closed form. McCall (1994) analyzes a heterogeneity distribution that contains the gamma as a special case.

It is possible to consistently estimate $\boldsymbol{\beta}$ and λ without specifying a parametric form for the heterogeneity distribution; this approach results in a semiparametric maximum likelihood estimator. Heckman and Singer (1984) first showed how to perform this method with a Weibull baseline hazard, and Meyer (1990) proved consistency when the hazard has the form (20.54). The estimated heterogeneity distribution is discrete and, in practice, has relatively few mass points. The consistency argument works by allowing the number of mass points to increase with the sample size. Computation is a difficult issue, and the asymptotic distribution of the semiparametric maximum likelihood estimator has not been worked out.

20.5 Further Issues

The methods we have covered in this chapter have been applied in many contexts. Nevertheless, there are several important topics that we have neglected.

20.5.1 Cox's Partial Likelihood Method for the Proportional Hazard Model

Cox (1972) suggested a partial likelihood method for estimating the parameters $\boldsymbol{\beta}$ in a proportional hazard model without specifying the baseline hazard. The strength of Cox's approach is that the effects of the covariates can be estimated very generally, provided the hazard is of the form (20.16). However, Cox's method is intended to be applied to flow data as opposed to grouped data. If we apply Cox's methods to grouped data, we must confront the practically important issue of individuals with identical observed durations. In addition, with time-varying covariates, Cox's method evidently requires the covariates to be strictly exogenous. Estimation of the hazard function itself is more complicated than the methods for grouped data that we covered in Section 20.4. See Amemiya (1985, Chapter 11) and Lancaster (1990, Chapter 9) for treatments of Cox's partial likelihood estimator.

20.5.2 Multiple-Spell Data

All the methods we have covered assume a single spell for each sample unit. In other words, each individual begins in the initial state and then either is observed leaving the state or is censored. But at least some individuals might have multiple spells, especially if we follow them for long periods. For example, we may observe a person who is initially unemployed, becomes employed, and then after a time becomes unemployed again. If we assume constancy across time about the process driving unemployment duration, we can use multiple spells to aid in identification, particularly in models with heterogeneity that can be correlated with time-varying covariates. Chamberlain (1985) and Honoré (1993b) contain identification results when multiple spells are observed. Chamberlain allowed for correlation between the heterogeneity and the time-varying covariates.

Multiple-spell data are also useful for estimating models with unobserved heterogeneity when the regressors are not strictly exogenous. Ham and Lalonde (1996) give an example in which participation in a job training program can be related to past unemployment duration, even though eligibility is randomly assigned. See also Wooldridge (2000c) for a general framework that allows feedback to future explanatory variables in models with unobserved heterogeneity.

20.5.3 Competing Risks Models

Another important topic is allowing for more than two possible states. **Competing risks models** allow for the possibility that an individual may exit into different alternatives. For example, a person working full-time may choose to retire completely or work part-time. Han and Hausman (1990) and Sueyoshi (1992) contain discussions of the assumptions needed to estimate competing risks models, with and without unobserved heterogeneity.

Problems

20.1. Use the data in RECID.RAW for this problem.

a. Using the covariates in Table 20.1, estimate equation (20.26) by censored Tobit. Verify that the log-likelihood value is $-1{,}597.06$.

b. Plug in the mean values for *priors*, *tserved*, *educ*, and *age*, and the values $workprg = 0$, $felon = 1$, $alcohol = 1$, $drugs = 1$, $black = 0$, and $married = 0$, and plot the estimated hazard for the lognormal distribution. Describe what you find.

c. Using only the uncensored observations, perform an OLS regression of $\log(durat)$ on the covariates in Table 20.1. Compare the estimates on *tserved* and *alcohol* with those from part a. What do you conclude?

d. Now compute an OLS regression using all data—that is, treat the censored observations as if they are uncensored. Compare the estimates on *tserved* and *alcohol* from those in parts a and c.

20.2. Use the data in RECID.RAW to answer these questions:

a. To the Weibull model, add the variables *super* (=1 if release from prison was supervised) and *rules* (number of rules violations while in prison). Do the coefficient estimates on these new variables have the expected signs? Are they statistically significant?

b. Add *super* and *rules* to the lognormal model, and answer the same questions as in part a.

c. Compare the estimated effects of the *rules* variable on the expected duration for the Weibull and lognormal models. Are they practically different?

20.3. Consider the case of flow sampling, as in Section 20.3.2, but suppose that all durations are censored: $d_i = 1$, $i = 1, \ldots, N$.

a. Write down the log-likelihood function when all durations are censored.

b. Find the special case of the Weibull distribution in part a.

c. Consider the Weibull case where $\mathbf{x}_i$ only contains a constant, so that $F(t; \alpha, \beta) = 1 - \exp[-\exp(\beta)t^{\alpha}]$. Show that the Weibull log likelihood cannot be maximized for real numbers $\hat{\beta}$ and $\hat{\alpha}$.

d. From part c, what do you conclude about estimating duration models from flow data when all durations are right censored?

e. If the duration distribution is continuous, $c_i > b > 0$ for some constant b, and $\mathrm{P}(t_i^* < t) > 0$ for all $t > 0$, is it likely, in a large random sample, to find that all durations have been censored?

20.4. Suppose that, in the context of flow sampling, we observe covariates $\mathbf{x}_i$, the censoring time c_i, and the binary indicator d_i (=1 if the observation is uncensored). We never observe t_i^*.

a. Show that the conditional likelihood function has the binary response form. What is the binary "response"?

b. Use the Weibull model to demonstrate the following when we only observe whether durations are censored: if the censoring times c_i are constant, the parameters $\boldsymbol{\beta}$ and α are not identified. [Hint: Consider the same case as in Problem 20.3c, and show that the log likelihood depends only on the constant $\exp(\beta)c^{\alpha}$, where c is the common censoring time.]

c. Use the lognormal model to argue that, provided the c_i vary across i in the population, the parameters are generally identified. [Hint: In the binary response model, what is the coefficient on $\log(c_i)$?]

20.5. In this problem you are to derive the log likelihood in equation (20.30). Assume that $c_i > b - a_i$ for all i, so that we always observe part of each spell after the sampling date, b. In what follows, we supress the parameter vector, $\boldsymbol{\theta}$.

a. For $b - a_i < t < c_i$, show that $\mathrm{P}(t_i^* \leq t \mid \mathbf{x}_i, a_i, c_i, s_i = 1) = [F(t \mid \mathbf{x}_i) - F(b - a_i \mid \mathbf{x}_i)]/[1 - F(b - a_i \mid \mathbf{x}_i)]$.

b. Use part a to obtain the density of t_i^* conditional on $(\mathbf{x}_i, a_i, c_i, s_i = 1)$ for $b - a_i < t < c_i$.

c. Show that $\mathrm{P}(t_i = c_i \mid \mathbf{x}_i, a_i, c_i, s_i = 1) = [1 - F(c_i \mid \mathbf{x}_i)]/[1 - F(b - a_i \mid \mathbf{x}_i)]$.

d. Explain why parts b and c lead to equation (20.30).

20.6. Consider the problem of stock sampling where we do not follow spells after the sampling date, b, as described in Section 20.3.3. Let $F(\cdot \mid \mathbf{x}_i)$ denote the cdf of t_i^* given $\mathbf{x}_i$, and let $k(\cdot \mid \mathbf{x}_i)$ denote the continuous density of a_i given $\mathbf{x}_i$. We drop dependence on the parameters for most of the derivations. Assume that t_i^* and a_i are independent conditional on $\mathbf{x}_i$.

a. Let s_i denote a selection indicator, so that $s_i = 1(t_i^* \geq b - a_i)$. For any $0 < a < b$, show that

$$\mathrm{P}(a_i \leq a, s_i = 1 \mid \mathbf{x}_i) = \int_0^a k(u \mid \mathbf{x}_i)[1 - F(b - u \mid \mathbf{x}_i)]\, du$$

b. Derive equation (20.32). {Hint: $\mathrm{P}(s_i = 1 \mid \mathbf{x}_i) = \mathrm{E}(s_i \mid \mathbf{x}_i) = \mathrm{E}[\mathrm{E}(s_i \mid a_i, \mathbf{x}_i) \mid \mathbf{x}_i]$, and $\mathrm{E}(s_i \mid a_i, \mathbf{x}_i) = \mathrm{P}(t_i^* \geq b - a_i \mid \mathbf{x}_i)$.}

c. For $0 < a < b$, what is the cdf of a_i given $\mathbf{x}_i$ and $s_i = 1$? Now derive equation (20.31).

d. Take $b = 1$, and assume that the starting time distribution is uniform on $[0, 1]$ (independent of $\mathbf{x}_i$). Find the density (20.31) in this case.

e. For the setup in part d, assume that the duration cdf has the Weibull form, $1 - \exp[-\exp(\mathbf{x}_i\boldsymbol{\beta})t^{\alpha}]$. What is the log likelihood for observation i?

20.7. Consider the original stock sampling problem that we covered in Section 20.3.3. There, we derived the log likelihood (20.30) by conditioning on the starting times, a_i. This approach is convenient because we do not have to specify a distribution for the starting times. But suppose we have an acceptable model for $k(\cdot \mid \mathbf{x}_i; \boldsymbol{\eta})$, the (continuous) density of a_i given $\mathbf{x}_i$. Further, we maintain assumption (20.22) and assume $\mathrm{D}(a_i \mid c_i, \mathbf{x}_i) = \mathrm{D}(a_i \mid \mathbf{x}_i)$.

a. Show that the log-likelihood function conditional on $\mathbf{x}_i$, which accounts for truncation, is

$$\sum_{i=1}^{N}\{d_i \log[f(t_i \mid \mathbf{x}_i; \boldsymbol{\theta})] + (1 - d_i) \log[1 - F(t_i \mid \mathbf{x}_i; \boldsymbol{\theta})]$$

$$+ \log[k(a_i \mid \mathbf{x}_i; \boldsymbol{\eta})] - \log[\mathrm{P}(s_i = 1 \mid \mathbf{x}_i; \boldsymbol{\theta}, \boldsymbol{\eta})]\} \tag{20.56}$$

where $\mathrm{P}(s_i = 1 \mid \mathbf{x}_i; \boldsymbol{\theta}, \boldsymbol{\eta})$ is given in equation (20.32).

b. Discuss the trade-offs in using equation (20.30) or the log likelihood in (20.56).

20.8. In the context of stock sampling, where we are interested in the population of durations starting in $[0, b]$, suppose that we interview at date b, as usual, but we do not observe any starting times. {This assumption raises the issue of how we know individual i's starting time is in the specified interval, $[0, b]$. We assume that the interval is defined to make this condition true for all i.} Let $r_i^* = a_i + t_i^* - b$, which can be interpreted as the calendar date at which the spell ends minus the interview date. Even without right censoring, we observe r_i^* only if $r_i^* > 0$, in which case r_i^* is simply the time in the spell since the interview date, b. Assume that t_i^* and a_i are independent conditional on $\mathbf{x}_i$.

a. Show that for $r > 0$, the density of r_i^* given $\mathbf{x}_i$ is

$$h(r \mid \mathbf{x}_i; \boldsymbol{\theta}, \boldsymbol{\eta}) \equiv \int_0^b k(u \mid \mathbf{x}_i; \boldsymbol{\eta}) f(r + b - u \mid \mathbf{x}_i; \boldsymbol{\theta})\, du$$

where, as before, $k(a \mid \mathbf{x}_i; \boldsymbol{\eta})$ is the density of a_i given $\mathbf{x}_i$ and $f(t \mid \mathbf{x}_i; \boldsymbol{\theta})$ is the duration density.

b. Let $q > 0$ be a fixed censoring time after the interview date, and define $r_i = \min(r_i^*, q)$. Find $\mathrm{P}(r_i = q \mid \mathbf{x}_i)$ in terms of the *cdf* of r_i^*, say, $H(r \mid \mathbf{x}_i; \boldsymbol{\theta}, \boldsymbol{\eta})$.

c. Use parts a and b, along with equation (20.32), to show that the log likelihood conditional on observing $(r_i, \mathbf{x}_i)$ is

$$d_i \log[h(r_i \mid \mathbf{x}_i; \boldsymbol{\theta}, \boldsymbol{\eta})] + (1 - d_i) \log[1 - H(r_i \mid \mathbf{x}_i; \boldsymbol{\theta}, \boldsymbol{\eta})]$$

$$- \log\left\{\int_0^b [1 - F(b - u \mid \mathbf{x}_i; \boldsymbol{\theta})] k(u \mid \mathbf{x}_i; \boldsymbol{\eta})\, du\right\} \tag{20.57}$$

where $d_i = 1$ if observation i has not been right censored.

d. Simplify the log likelihood from part c when $b = 1$ and $k(a \mid \mathbf{x}_i; \boldsymbol{\eta})$ is the uniform density on $[0, 1]$.

20.9. Consider the Weibull model with multiplicative heterogeneity, as in equation (20.33), where v_i takes on only two values, $1/\rho$ and 0, with probabilities ρ and $1 - \rho$, respectively, where $0 < \rho < 1$. This parameterization imposes the normalization $\mathrm{E}(v_i) = 1$. You can think of a situation where there are only two types of people, type A ($v_i = 0$) and type B ($v_i = 1/\rho$).

a. Show that, as the difference between the two types grows, the probability of being type B must shrink to zero.

b. Find the cdf of t_i^* given $\mathbf{x}_i$.

c. Find the log-likelihood function for observation i in terms of α, $\boldsymbol{\beta}$, and ρ.

20.10. Let $0 < a_1 < a_2 < \cdots < a_{M-1} < a_M$ be a positive, increasing set of constants, and let T be a nonnegative random variable with $\mathrm{P}(T > 0) = 1$.

a. Show that, for any $m = 1, \ldots, M$, $\mathrm{P}(T > a_m) = \mathrm{P}(T > a_m \mid T > a_{m-1})\mathrm{P}(T > a_{m-1})$.

b. Use part a to prove equation (20.48).

References

Abrevaya, J. (1997), "The Equivalence of Two Estimators for the Fixed Effects Logit Model," *Economics Letters* 55, 41–43.

Ahn, H., and J. L. Powell (1993), "Semiparametric Estimation of Censored Selection Models with a Nonparametric Selection Mechanism," *Journal of Econometrics* 58, 3–29.

Ahn, S. C., and P. Schmidt (1995), "Efficient Estimation of Models for Dynamic Panel Data," *Journal of Econometrics* 68, 5–27.

Ai, C. (1997), "A Semiparametric Maximum Likelihood Estimator," *Econometrica* 65, 933–963.

Aitchison, J., and S. D. Silvey (1958), "Maximum-Likelihood Estimation of Parameters Subject to Constraints," *Annals of Mathematical Statistics* 29, 813–828.

Altonji, J. G., and L. M. Segal (1996), "Small-Sample Bias in GMM Estimation of Covariance Structures," *Journal of Business and Economic Statistics* 14, 353–366.

Amemiya, T. (1973), "Regression Analysis When the Dependent Variable Is Truncated Normal," *Econometrica* 41, 997–1016.

Amemiya, T. (1974), "The Nonlinear Two-Stage Least-Squares Estimator," *Journal of Econometrics* 2, 105–110.

Amemiya, T. (1985), *Advanced Econometrics*. Cambridge, MA: Harvard University Press.

Andersen, E. B. (1970), "Asymptotic Properties of Conditional Maximum Likelihood Estimators," *Journal of the Royal Statistical Society*, Series B, 32, 283–301.

Anderson, T. W., and C. Hsiao (1982), "Formulation and Estimation of Dynamic Models Using Panel Data," *Journal of Econometrics* 18, 67–82.

Andrews, D. W. K. (1989), "Power in Econometric Applications," *Econometrica* 57, 1059–1090.

Angrist, J. D. (1990), "Lifetime Earnings and the Vietnam Era Draft Lottery: Evidence from Social Security Administrative Records," *American Economic Review* 80, 313–336.

Angrist, J. D. (1991), "Instrumental Variables Estimation of Average Treatment Effects in Econometrics and Epidemiology," National Bureau of Economic Research Technical Working Paper Number 115.

Angrist, J. D. (1998), "Estimating the Labor Market Impact of Voluntary Military Service Using Social Security Data on Military Applicants," *Econometrica* 66, 249–288.

Angrist, J. D., and G. W. Imbens (1995), "Two-Stage Least Squares Estimation of Average Causal Effects in Models with Variable Treatment Intensity," *Journal of the American Statistical Association* 90, 431–442.

Angrist, J. D., G. W. Imbens, and D. B. Rubin (1996), "Identification and Causal Effects Using Instrumental Variables," *Journal of the American Statistical Association* 91, 444–455.

Angrist, J. D., and A. B. Krueger (1991), "Does Compulsory School Attendance Affect Schooling and Earnings?" *Quarterly Journal of Economics* 106, 979–1014.

Angrist, J. D., and V. Lavy (1999), "Using Maimonides' Rule to Estimate the Effect of Class Size on Scholastic Achievement," *Quarterly Journal of Economics* 114, 533–575.

Angrist, J. D., and W. K. Newey (1991), "Overidentification Tests in Earnings Functions with Fixed Effects," *Journal of Business and Economic Statistics* 9, 317–323.

Arellano, M. (1987), "Computing Robust Standard Errors for Within-Groups Estimators," *Oxford Bulletin of Economics and Statistics* 49, 431–434.

Arellano, M., and S. R. Bond (1991), "Some Specification Tests for Panel Data: Monte Carlo Evidence and an Application to Employment Equations," *Review of Economic Studies* 58, 277–298.

Arellano, M., and O. Bover (1995), "Another Look at the Instrumental Variables Estimation of Error-Component Models," *Journal of Econometrics* 68, 29–51.

Arellano, M., and B. E. Honoré (in press), "Panel Data: Some Recent Developments," *Handbook of Econometrics*, Volume 5, ed. E. Leamer and J. J. Heckman. Amsterdam: North Holland.

Ashenfelter, O., and A. B. Krueger (1994), "Estimates of the Economic Return to Schooling from a New Sample of Twins," *American Economic Review* 84, 1157–1173.

Ashenfelter, O., and C. E. Rouse (1998), "Income, Schooling, and Ability: Evidence from a New Sample of Identical Twins," *Quarterly Journal of Economics* 113, 253–284.

Ayers, I., and S. D. Levitt (1998), "Measuring Positive Externalities from Unobservable Victim Precaution: An Empirical Analysis of Lojack," *Quarterly Journal of Economics* 108, 43–77.

Baltagi, B. H. (1981), "Simultaneous Equations with Error Components," *Journal of Econometrics* 17, 189–200.

Baltagi, B. H. (1995), *Econometric Analysis of Panel Data*. New York: Wiley.

Baltagi, B. H., and Q. Li (1995), "Testing AR(1) Against MA(1) Disturbances in an Error Component Model," *Journal of Econometrics* 68, 133–151.

Barnow, B., G. Cain, and A. Goldberger (1980), "Issues in the Analysis of Selectivity Bias," *Evaluation Studies* 5, 42–59.

Bartik, T. J. (1987), "The Estimation of Demand Parameters in Hedonic Price Models," *Journal of Political Economy* 95, 81–88.

Bassett, G., and R. Koenker (1978), "Asymptotic Theory of Least Absolute Error Regression," *Journal of the American Statistical Association* 73, 618–622.

Bassi, L. J. (1984), "Estimating the Effect of Job Training Programs with Non-Random Selection," *Review of Economics and Statistics* 66, 36–43.

Bates, C. E., and H. White (1993), "Determination of Estimators with Minimum Asymptotic Covariances Matrices," *Econometric Theory* 9, 633–648.

Bera, A. K., and C. R. McKenzie (1986), "Alternative Forms and Properties of the Score Test," *Journal of Applied Statistics* 13, 13–25.

Berndt, E. R., B. H. Hall, R. E. Hall, and J. A. Hausman (1974), "Estimation and Inference in Nonlinear Structural Models," *Annals of Economic and Social Measurement* 3, 653–666.

Bhargava, A., L. Franzini, and W. Narendranathan (1982), "Serial Correlation and the Fixed Effects Model," *Review of Economic Studies* 49, 533–549.

Biddle, J. E., and D. S. Hamermesh (1990), "Sleep and the Allocation of Time," *Journal of Political Economy* 98, 922–943.

Billingsley, P. (1979), *Probability and Measure*. New York: John Wiley.

Blackburn, M., and D. Neumark (1992), "Unobserved Ability, Efficiency Wages, and Interindustry Wage Differentials," *Quarterly Journal of Economics* 107, 1421–1436.

Blundell, R., and S. Bond (1998), "Initial Conditions and Moment Restrictions in Dynamic Panel Data Models," *Journal of Econometrics* 87, 115–144.

Blundell, R., R. Griffith, and F. Windmeijer (1998), "Individual Effects and Dynamics in Count Data Models," mimeo, Institute of Fiscal Studies, London.

Bound, J., D. A. Jaeger, and R. M. Baker (1995), "Problems with Instrumental Variables Estimation When the Correlation between the Instruments and Endogenous Explanatory Variables Is Weak," *Journal of the American Statistical Association* 90, 443–450.

Breusch, T. S., G. E. Mizon, and P. Schmidt (1989), "Efficient Estimation Using Panel Data," *Econometrica* 57, 695–700.

Breusch, T. S., and A. R. Pagan (1979), "A Simple Test for Heteroskedasticity and Random Coefficient Variation," *Econometrica* 50, 987–1007.

Breusch, T. S., and A. R. Pagan (1980), "The LM Test and Its Applications to Model Specification in Econometrics," *Review of Economic Studies* 47, 239–254.

Breusch, T., H. Qian, P. Schmidt, and D. Wyhowski (1999), "Redundancy of Moment Conditions," *Journal of Econometrics* 91, 89–111.

Bronars, S. G., and J. Grogger (1994), "The Economic Consequences of Unwed Motherhood: Using Twin Births as a Natural Experiment," *American Economic Review* 84, 1141–1156.

Brown, B. W., and M. B. Walker (1995), "Stochastic Specification in Random Production Models of Cost-Minimizing Firms," *Journal of Econometrics* 66, 175–205.

Buchinsky, M. (1994), "Changes in the U.S. Wage Structure: Application of Quantile Regression," *Econometrica* 62, 405–458.

Buchinsky, M., and J. Hahn (1998), "An Alternative Estimator for the Censored Quantile Regression Model," *Econometrica* 66, 653–671.

Butler, J. S., and R. A. Moffitt (1982), "A Computationally Efficient Quadrature Procedure for the One-Factor Multinomial Probit Model," *Econometrica* 50, 761–764.

Cameron, A. C., and P. K. Trivedi (1986), "Econometric Models Based on Count Data: Comparisons and Applications of Some Estimators and Tests," *Journal of Applied Econometrics* 1, 29–53.

Cameron, A. C., and P. K. Trivedi (1998), *Regression Analysis of Count Data.* Cambridge: Cambridge University Press.

Card, D. (1995), "Using Geographic Variation in College Proximity to Estimate the Return to Schooling," in *Aspects of Labour Market Behavior: Essays in Honour of John Vanderkamp*, ed. L. N. Christophides, E. K. Grant, and R. Swidinsky. Toronto: University of Toronto Press, 201–222.

Case, A. C., and L. F. Katz (1991), "The Company You Keep: The Effects of Family and Neighborhood on Disadvantaged Youths," National Bureau of Economic Research Working Paper Number 3705.

Chamberlain, G. (1980), "Analysis of Covariance with Qualitative Data," *Review of Economic Studies* 47, 225–238.

Chamberlain, G. (1982), "Multivariate Regression Models for Panel Data," *Journal of Econometrics* 18, 5–46.

Chamberlain, G. (1984), "Panel Data," in *Handbook of Econometrics*, Volume 2, ed. Z. Griliches and M. D. Intriligator. Amsterdam: North Holland, 1247–1318.

Chamberlain, G. (1985), "Heterogeneity, Omitted Variable Bias, and Duration Dependence," in *Longitudinal Analysis of Labor Market Data*, ed. J. J. Heckman and B. Singer. Cambridge: Cambridge University Press, 3–38.

Chamberlain, G. (1987), "Asymptotic Efficiency in Estimation with Conditional Moment Restrictions," *Journal of Econometrics* 34, 305–334.

Chamberlain, G. (1992a), "Efficiency Bounds for Semiparametric Regression," *Econometrica* 60, 567–596.

Chamberlain, G. (1992b), "Comment: Sequential Moment Restrictions in Panel Data," *Journal of Business and Economic Statistics* 10, 20–26.

Chesher, A., and R. Spady (1991), "Asymptotic Expansions of the Information Matrix Test Statistic," *Econometrica* 59, 787–815.

Chung, C.-F., and A. Goldberger (1984), "Proportional Projections in Limited Dependent Variable Models," *Econometrica* 52, 531–534.

Chung, C.-F., P. Schmidt, and A. D. Witte (1991), "Survival Analysis: A Survey," *Journal of Quantitative Criminology* 7, 59–98.

Cornwell, C., P. Schmidt, and D. Wyhowski (1992), "Simultaneous Equations Models and Panel Data," *Journal of Econometrics* 51, 151–181.

Cornwell, C., and D. Trumball (1994), "Estimating the Economic Model of Crime with Panel Data," *Review of Economics and Statistics* 76, 360–366.

Cosslett, S. R. (1981), "Efficient Estimation of Discrete-Choice Models," in *Structural Analysis of Discrete Data with Econometric Applications*, ed. C. F. Manski and D. McFadden. Cambridge, MA: MIT Press, 51–111.

Cosslett, S. R. (1993), "Estimation from Endogenously Stratified Samples," in *Handbook of Statistics*, Volume 11, ed. G. S. Maddala, C. R. Rao, and H. D. Vinod. Amsterdam: North Holland, 1–43.

Costa, D. L. (1995), "Pensions and Retirements: Evidence from Union Army Veterans," *Quarterly Journal of Economics* 110, 297–319.

Cox, D. R. (1972), "Regression Models and Life Tables," *Journal of the Royal Statistical Society*, Series B, 34, 187–220.

Cragg, J. (1971), "Some Statistical Models for Limited Dependent Variables with Applications to the Demand for Durable Goods," *Econometrica* 39, 829–844.

Cragg, J. (1983), "More Efficient Estimation in the Presence of Heteroskedasticity of Unknown Form," *Econometrica* 51, 751–763.

Cragg, J. G., and S. G. Donald (1996), "Inferring the Rank of a Matrix," *Journal of Econometrics* 76, 223–250.

Currie, J., and N. Cole (1993), "Welfare and Child Health: The Link between AFDC Participation and Birth Weight," *American Economic Review* 83, 971–983.

Currie, J., and D. Thomas (1995), "Does Head Start Make a Difference?" *American Economic Review* 85, 341–364.

Cutler, D. M., and E. L. Glaeser (1997), "Are Ghettos Good or Bad?" *Quarterly Journal of Economics* 112, 827–872.

Davidson, J. (1994), *Stochastic Limit Theory*. Oxford: Oxford University Press.

Davidson, R., and J. G. MacKinnon (1984), "Convenient Specification Tests for Logit and Probit Models," *Journal of Econometrics* 24, 241–262.

Davidson, R., and J. G. MacKinnon (1985), "Heteroskedasticity-Robust Tests in Regression Directions," *Annale de l'INSÉÉ* 59/60, 183–218.

Davidson, R., and J. G. MacKinnon (1992), "A New Form of the Information Matrix Test," *Econometrica* 60, 145–147.

Davidson, R., and J. G. MacKinnon (1993), *Estimation and Inference in Econometrics*. New York: Oxford University Press.

Deaton, A. (1995), "Data and Econometric Tools for Development Analysis," in *Handbook of Development Economics*, Volume 3A, ed. J. Berhman and T. N. Srinivasan. Amsterdam: North Holland, 1785–1882.

Dehejia, R. H., and S. Wahba (1999), "Causal Effects in Non-Experimental Studies: Evaluating the Evaluation of Training Programs," *Journal of the American Statistical Association* 94, 1053–1062.

Donald, S. G., and H. J. Paarsch (1996), "Identification, Estimation, and Testing in Parametric Empirical Models of Auctions within the Independent Private Values Paradigm," *Econometric Theory* 12, 517–567.

Downes, T. M., and S. M. Greenstein (1996), "Understanding the Supply Decisions of Nonprofits: Modeling the Location of Private Schools," *Rand Journal of Economics* 27, 365–390.

Dustmann, C., and M. E. Rochina-Barrachina (2000), "Selection Correction in Panel Data Models: An Application to Labour Supply and Wages," mimeo, Department of Economics, University College London.

Eicker, F. (1967), "Limit Theorems for Regressions with Unequal and Dependent Errors," *Proceedings of the Fifth Berkeley Symposium on Mathematical Statistics and Probability* 1, 59–82. Berkeley: University of California Press.

Elbers, C., and G. Ridder (1982), "True and Spurious Duration Dependence: The Identifiability of the Proportional Hazard Model," *Review of Economic Studies* 49, 403–410.

El Sayyad, G. M. (1973), "Bayesian and Classical Analysis of Poisson Regression," *Journal of the Royal Statistical Society*, Series B, 35, 445–451.

Engle, R. F. (1982), "Autoregressive Conditional Heteroskedasticity with Estimates of the Variance of U.K. Inflation," *Econometrica* 50, 987–1008.

Engle, R. F. (1984), "Wald, Likelihood Ratio, and Lagrange Multiplier Statistics in Econometrics," in *Handbook of Econometrics*, Volume 2, ed. Z. Griliches and M. D. Intriligator. Amsterdam: North Holland, 776–828.

Epple, D. (1987), "Hedonic Prices and Implicit Markets: Estimated Demand and Supply Functions for Differentiated Products," *Journal of Political Economy* 95, 59–80.

Estrella, A. (1998), "A New Measure of Fit for Equations with Dichotomous Dependent Variables," *Journal of Business and Economic Statistics* 16, 198–205.

Evans, W. N., W. E. Oates, and R. M. Schwab (1992), "Measuring Peer Group Effects: A Study of Teenage Behavior," *Journal of Political Economy* 100, 966–991.

Evans, W. N., and R. M. Schwab (1995), "Finishing High School and Starting College: Do Catholic Schools Make a Difference?" *Quarterly Journal of Economics* 110, 941–974.

Fin, T., and P. Schmidt (1984), "A Test of the Tobit Specification Against an Alternative Suggested by Cragg," *Review of Economics and Statistics* 66, 174–177.

Fisher, F. M. (1965), "Identifiability Criteria in Nonlinear Systems: A Further Note," *Econometrica* 33, 197–205.

Foster, A. D., and M. R. Rosenzweig (1995), "Learning by Doing and Learning from Others: Human Capital and Technical Change in Agriculture," *Journal of Political Economy* 103, 1176–1209.

Friedberg, L. (1998), "Did Unilateral Divorce Raise Divorce Rates? Evidence from Panel Data," *American Economic Review* 88, 608–627.

Gallant, A. R. (1987), *Nonlinear Statistical Models.* New York: Wiley.

Gallant, A. R., and H. White (1988), *A Unified Theory of Estimation and Inference for Nonlinear Dynamic Models.* New York: Blackwell.

Garen, J. (1984), "The Returns to Schooling: A Selectivity Bias Approach with a Continuous Choice Variable," *Econometrica* 52, 1199–1218.

Geronimus, A. T., and S. Korenman (1992), "The Socioeconomic Consequences of Teen Childbearing Reconsidered," *Quarterly Journal of Economics* 107, 1187–1214.

Geweke, J., and M. P. Keane (in press), "Computationally Intensive Methods for Integration in Economics," *Handbook of Econometrics*, Volume 5, ed. E. Leamer and J. J. Heckman. Amsterdam: North Holland.

Goldberger, A. S. (1968), *Topics in Regression Analysis.* New York: Macmillan.

Goldberger, A. S. (1972), "Structural Equation Methods in the Social Sciences," *Econometrica* 40, 979–1001.

Goldberger, A. S. (1981), "Linear Regression after Selection," *Journal of Econometrics* 15, 357–366.

Goldberger, A. S. (1991), *A Course in Econometrics.* Cambridge, MA: Harvard University Press.

Gordy, M. B. (1999), "Hedging Winner's Curse with Multiple Bids: Evidence from the Portuguese Treasury Bill Auction," *Review of Economics and Statistics* 81, 448–465.

Gourieroux, C., A. Monfort, and C. Trognon (1984a), "Pseudo–Maximum Likelihood Methods: Theory," *Econometrica* 52, 681–700.

Gourieroux, C., A. Monfort, and C. Trognon (1984b), "Pseudo–Maximum Likelihood Methods: Applications to Poisson Models," *Econometrica* 52, 701–720.

Greene, W. (1997), *Econometric Analysis.* New York: Macmillan, 3rd edition.

Gregory, A. W., and M. R. Veall (1985), "On Formulating Wald Tests for Nonlinear Restrictions," *Econometrica* 53, 1465–1468.

Griliches, Z., B. H. Hall, and J. A. Hausman (1978), "Missing Data and Self-Selection in Large Panels," *Annale de l'INSÉÉ* 30/31, 137–176.

Griliches, Z., and J. A. Hausman (1986), "Errors in Variables in Panel Data," *Journal of Econometrics* 31, 93–118.

Griliches, Z., and W. M. Mason (1972), "Education, Income and Ability," *Journal of Political Economy*, Part II, 80, S74–S103.

Gronau, R. (1974), "Wage Comparisons—A Selectivity Bias," *Journal of Political Economy* 82, 1119–1143.

Gruber, J., and J. M. Poterba (1994), "Tax Incentives and the Decision to Purchase Health Insurance: Evidence from the Self-Employed," *Quarterly Journal of Economics* 109, 701–733.

Gurmu, S., and P. K. Trivedi (1994), "Recent Developments in Models of Event Counts: A Survey," University of Virginia Department of Economics Discussion Paper Number 261.

Haavelmo, T. (1943), "The Statistical Implications of a System of Simultaneous Equations," *Econometrica* 11, 1–12.

Hagy, A. P. (1998), "The Demand for Child Care Quality: An Hedonic Price Approach," *Journal of Human Resources* 33, 683–710.

Hahn, J. (1998), "On the Role of the Propensity Score in Efficient Semiparametric Estimation of Average Treatment Effects," *Econometrica* 66, 315–331.

Hahn, J. (1999), "How Informative is the Initial Condition in the Dynamic Panel Data Model with Fixed Effects?" *Journal of Econometrics* 93, 309–326.

Hajivassiliou, V. A. (1993), "Simulation Estimation Methods for Limited Dependent Variable Models," in *Handbook of Statistics*, Volume 11, ed. G. S. Maddala, C. R. Rao, and H. D. Vinod. Amsterdam: North Holland, 519–543.

Hajivassiliou, V. A., and P. A. Ruud (1994), "Classical Estimation Methods for LDV Models Using Simulation," in *Handbook of Econometrics*, Volume 4, ed. R. F. Engle and D. McFadden. Amsterdam: North Holland, 2383–2441.

Hall, A. (1987), "The Information Matrix Test for the Linear Model," *Review of Economic Studies* 54, 257–263.

Hall, P. (1994), "Methodology and Theory for the Bootstrap," in *Handbook of Econometrics*, Volume 4, ed. R. F. Engle and D. McFadden. Amsterdam: North Holland, 2341–2381.

Ham, J. C., and R. J. Lalonde (1996), "The Effect of Sample Selection and Initial Conditions in Duration Models: Evidence from Experimental Data on Training," *Econometrica* 64, 175–205.

Hamilton, J. D. (1994), *Time Series Analysis*. Princeton, NJ: Princeton University Press.

Han, A. K., and J. A. Hausman (1990), "Flexible Parametric Estimation of Duration and Competing Risk Models," *Journal of Applied Econometrics* 5, 1–28.

Hansen, L. P. (1982), "Large Sample Properties of Generalized Method of Moments Estimators," *Econometrica* 50, 1029–1054.

Härdle, W., and O. Linton (1994), "Applied Nonparametric Methods," in *Handbook of Econometrics*, Volume 4, ed. R. F. Engle and D. McFadden. Amsterdam: North Holland, 2295–2339.

Hausman, J. A. (1978), "Specification Tests in Econometrics," *Econometrica* 46, 1251–1271.

Hausman, J. (1983), "Specification and Estimation of Simultaneous Equations Models," in *Handbook of Econometrics*, Volume 1, ed. Z. Griliches and M. D. Intriligator. Amsterdam: North Holland, 391–448.

Hausman, J. A., B. H. Hall, and Z. Griliches (1984), "Econometric Models for Count Data with an Application to the Patents-R&D Relationship," *Econometrica* 52, 909–938.

Hausman, J. A., and D. L. McFadden (1984), "A Specification Test for the Multinomial Logit Model," *Econometrica* 52, 1219–1240.

Hausman, J. A., W. K. Newey, and W. E. Taylor (1987), "Efficient Estimation and Identification of Simultaneous Equation Models with Covariance Restrictions," *Econometrica* 55, 849–874.

Hausman, J. A., and W. E. Taylor (1981), "Panel Data and Unobservable Individual Effects," *Econometrica* 49, 1377–1398.

Hausman, J. A., and D. A. Wise (1977), "Social Experimentation, Truncated Distributions, and Efficient Estimation," *Econometrica* 45, 319–339.

Hausman, J. A., and D. A., Wise (1978), "A Conditional Probit Model for Qualitative Choice: Discrete Decisions Recognizing Interdependence and Heterogeneous Preferences," *Econometrica* 46, 403–426.

Hausman, J. A., and D. A. Wise (1981), "Stratification on an Endogenous Variable and Estimation: The Gary Income Maintenance Experiment," in *Structural Analysis of Discrete Data with Econometric Applications*, ed. C. F. Manski and D. McFadden. Cambridge, MA: MIT Press, 365–391.

Heckman, J. J. (1976), "The Common Structure of Statistical Models of Truncation, Sample Selection, and Limited Dependent Variables and a Simple Estimator for Such Models," *Annals of Economic and Social Measurement* 5, 475–492.

Heckman, J. J. (1978), "Dummy Endogenous Variables in a Simultaneous Equations System," *Econometrica* 46, 931–960.

Heckman, J. J. (1979), "Sample Selection Bias as a Specification Error," *Econometrica* 47, 153–161.

Heckman, J. J. (1981), "The Incidental Parameters Problem and the Problem of Initial Conditions in Estimating a Discrete Time–Discrete Data Stochastic Process," in *Structural Analysis of Discrete Data with Econometric Applications*, ed. C. F. Manski and D. McFadden. Cambridge, MA: MIT Press, 179–195.

Heckman, J. J. (1992), "Randomization and Social Program Evaluation," in *Evaluating Welfare and Training Programs*, ed. C. F. Manski and I. Garfinkel. Cambridge, MA: Harvard University Press, 201–230.

Heckman, J. J. (1997), "Instrumental Variables: A Study of Implicit Behavioral Assumptions Used in Making Program Evaluations," *Journal of Human Resources* 32, 441–462.

Heckman, J. J., and V. J. Hotz (1989), "Choosing among Alternative Nonexperimental Methods for Estimating the Impact of Social Programs: The Case of Manpower Training," *Journal of the American Statistical Association* 84, 862–875.

Heckman, J. J., H. Ichimura, and P. Todd (1997), "Matching as an Econometric Evaluation Estimator," *Review of Economic Studies* 65, 261–294.

Heckman, J. J., L. Lochner, and C. Taber (1998), "General-Equilibrium Treatment Effects," *American Economic Review* 88, 381–386.

Heckman, J. J., and R. Robb (1985), "Alternative Methods for Evaluating the Impact of Interventions," in *Longitudinal Analysis of Labor Market Data*, ed. J. J. Heckman and B. Singer. New York: Cambridge University Press, 156–245.

Heckman, J. J., and B. Singer (1984), "A Method for Minimizing the Impact of Distributional Assumptions in Econometric Models for Duration Data," *Econometrica* 52, 271–320.

Heckman, J. J., and E. Vytlacil (1998), "Instrumental Variables Methods for the Correlated Random Coefficient Model," *Journal of Human Resources* 33, 974–987.

Hendry, D. F. (1984), "Monte Carlo Experimentation in Econometrics," in *Handbook of Econometrics*, Volume 2, ed. Z. Griliches and M. D. Intriligator. Amsterdam: North Holland, 937–976.

Hirano, K., G. W. Imbens, and G. Ridder (2000), "Efficient Estimation of Average Treatment Effects Using the Estimated Propensity Score," mimeo, UCLA Department of Economics.

Holzer, H., R. Block, M. Cheatham, and J. Knott (1993), "Are Training Subsidies Effective? The Michigan Experience," *Industrial and Labor Relations Review* 46, 625–636.

Honoré, B. E. (1992), "Trimmed LAD and Least Squares Estimation of Truncated and Censored Regression Models with Fixed Effects," *Econometrica* 60, 533–565.

Honoré, B. E. (1993a), "Orthogonality Conditions for Tobit Models with Fixed Effects and Lagged Dependent Variables," *Journal of Econometrics* 59, 35–61.

Honoré, B. E. (1993b), "Identification Results for Duration Models with Multiple Spells," *Review of Economic Studies* 60, 241–246.

Honoré, B. E., and E. Kyriazidou (2000a), "Panel Data Discrete Choice Models with Lagged Dependent Variables," *Econometrica* 68, 839–874.

Honoré, B. E., and E. Kyriazidou (2000b), "Estimation of Tobit-Type Models with Individual Specific Effects," *Econometric Reviews* 19, 341–366.

Honoré, B. E., E. Kyriazidou, and C. Udry (1997), "Estimation of Type 3 Tobit Models Using Symmetric Trimming and Pairwise Comparisons," *Journal of Econometrics* 76, 107–128.

Horowitz, J. L. (1992), "A Smoothed Maximum Score Estimator for the Binary Response Model," *Econometrica* 60, 505–531.

Horowitz, J. L. (1993), "Semiparametric and Nonparametric Estimation of Quantal Response Models," in *Handbook of Statistics*, Volume 11, ed. G. S. Maddala, C. R. Rao, and H. D. Vinod. Amsterdam: North Holland, 45–72.

Horowitz, J. L. (1999), "Semiparametric Estimation of a Proportional Hazard Model with Unobserved Heterogeneity," *Econometrica* 67, 1001–1028.

Horowitz, J. L. (in press), "The Bootstrap," *Handbook of Econometrics*, Volume 5, ed. E. Leamer and J. J. Heckman. North Holland: Amsterdam.

Horowitz, J. L., and C. F. Manski (1998), "Censoring of Outcomes and Regressors Due to Survey Nonresponse: Identification and Estimation Using Weights and Imputations," *Journal of Econometrics* 84, 37–58.

Horvitz, D., and D. Thompson (1952), "A Generalization of Sampling without Replacement from a Finite Population," *Journal of the American Statistical Association* 47, 663–685.

Hoxby, C. M. (1994), "Does Competition among Public Schools Benefit Students and Taxpayers?" National Bureau of Economic Research Working Paper Number 4979.

Hoxby, C. M. (1996), "How Teachers' Unions Affect Education Production," *Quarterly Journal of Economics* 111, 671–718.

Hsiao, C. (1986), *Analysis of Panel Data*. Cambridge: Cambridge University Press.

Huber, P. J. (1967), "The Behavior of Maximum Likelihood Estimates under Nonstandard Conditions," in *Proceedings of the Fifth Berkeley Symposium in Mathematical Statistics*, Volume 1. Berkeley: University of California Press, 221–233.

Ichimura, H. (1993), "Semiparametric Least Squares (SLS) and Weighted SLS Estimation of Single-Index Models," *Journal of Econometrics* 58, 71–120.

Im, K. S., S. C. Ahn, P. Schmidt, and J. M. Wooldridge (1999), "Efficient Estimation of Panel Data Models with Strictly Exogenous Explanatory Variables," *Journal of Econometrics* 93, 177–201.

Imbens, G. W. (1992), "An Efficient Method of Moments Estimator for Discrete Choice Models with Choice-Based Sampling," *Econometrica* 60, 1187–1214.

Imbens, G. W., and J. D. Angrist (1994), "Identification and Estimation of Local Average Treatment Effects," *Econometrica* 62, 467–476.

Imbens, G. W., and T. Lancaster (1996), "Efficient Estimation and Stratified Sampling," *Journal of Econometrics* 74, 289–318.

Kahn, S., and K. Lang (1988), "Efficient Estimation of Structural Hedonic Systems," *International Economic Review* 29, 157–166.

Kakwani, N. (1967), "The Unbiasedness of Zellner's Seemingly Unrelated Regressions Equation Estimators," *Journal of the American Statistical Association* 62, 141–142.

Kalbfleisch, J. D., and R. L. Prentice (1980), *The Statistical Analysis of Failure Time Data*. New York: Wiley.

Kane, T. J., and C. E. Rouse (1995), "Labor-Market Returns to Two- and Four-Year Colleges," *American Economic Review* 85, 600–614.

Kao, C. (1999), "Spurious Regression and Residual-Based Tests for Cointegration in Panel Data," *Journal of Econometrics* 90, 1–44.

Keane, M. P. (1993), "Simulation Estimation for Panel Data Models with Limited Dependent Variables," in *Handbook of Statistics*, Volume 11, ed. G. S. Maddala, C. R. Rao, and H. D. Vinod. Amsterdam: North Holland, 545–571.

Keane, M. P., and R. A. Moffitt (1998), "A Structural Model of Multiple Welfare Participation and Labor Supply," *International Economic Review* 39, 553–589.

Keane, M. P., and D. E. Runkle (1992), "On the Estimation of Panel Data Models with Serial Correlation When Instruments Are Not Strictly Exogenous," *Journal of Business and Economic Statistics* 10, 1–9.

Keane, M. P., and K. I. Wolpin (1997), "The Career Decisions of Young Men," *Journal of Political Economy* 105, 473–522.

Kiefer, N. M. (1980), "Estimation of Fixed Effect Models for Time Series of Cross-Sections with Arbitrary Intertemporal Covariance," *Journal of Econometrics* 14, 195–202.

Kiefer, N. M. (1988), "Economic Duration Data and Hazard Functions," *Journal of Economic Literature* 26, 646–679.

Kiefer, N. M. (1989), "The ET Interview: Arthur S. Goldberger," *Econometric Theory* 5, 133–160.

Kiel, K. A., and K. T. McClain (1995), "House Prices during Siting Decision Stages: The Case of an Incinerator from Rumor through Operation," *Journal of Environmental Economics and Management* 28, 241–255.

Kinal, T. W. (1980), "The Existence of Moments of k-Class Estimators," *Econometrica* 48, 241–249.

Kinal, T., and K. Lahiri (1993), "On the Estimation of Simultaneous Error Components Models with an Application to a Model of Developing Country Foreign Trade," *Journal of Applied Econometrics* 8, 81–92.

Klein, R. W., and R. H. Spady (1993), "An Efficient Semiparametric Estimator for Discrete Choice Models," *Econometrica* 61, 387–421.

Koenker, R. (1981), "A Note on Studentizing a Test for Heteroskedasticity," *Journal of Econometrics* 17, 107–112.

Koenker, R., and G. Bassett (1978), "Regression Quantiles," *Econometrica* 46, 33–50.

Krueger, A. B. (1993), "How Computers Have Changed the Wage Structure: Evidence from Microdata, 1984–1989," *Quarterly Journal of Economics* 108, 33–60.

Kyriazidou, E. (1997), "Estimation of a Panel Data Sample Selection Model," *Econometrica* 65, 1335–1364.

Lahiri, K., and P. Schmidt (1978), "On the Estimation of Triangular Structural Systems," *Econometrica* 46, 1217–1221.

Lancaster, T. (1979), "Econometric Methods for the Duration of Unemployment," *Econometrica* 47, 939–956.

Lancaster, T. (1990), *The Econometric Analysis of Transition Data.* Cambridge: Cambridge University Press.

LeCam, L. (1953), "On Some Asymptotic Properties of Maximum Likelihood Estimates and Related Bayes Estimates," *University of California Publications in Statistics* 1, 277–328.

Lemieux, T. (1998), "Estimating the Effects of Unions on Wage Inequality in a Panel Data Model with Comparative Advantage and Nonrandom Selection," *Journal of Labor Economics* 16, 261–291.

Levine, P. B., T. A. Gustafson, and A. D. Velenchik (1997), "More Bad News for Smokers? The Effects of Cigarette Smoking on Wages," *Industrial and Labor Relations Review* 50, 493–509.

Levitt, S. D. (1996), "The Effect of Prison Population Size on Crime Rates: Evidence from Prison Overcrowding Legislation," *Quarterly Journal of Economics* 111, 319–351.

Levitt, S. D. (1997), "Using Electoral Cycles in Police Hiring to Estimate the Effect of Police on Crime," *American Economic Review* 87, 270–290.

Lewbel, A. (1998), "Semiparametric Latent Variable Model Estimation with Endogenous or Mismeasured Regressors," *Econometrica* 66, 105–121.

MacKinnon, J. G., and H. White (1985), "Some Heteroskedasticity Consistent Covariance Matrix Estimators with Improved Finite Sample Properties," *Journal of Econometrics* 29, 305–325.

MaCurdy, T. E. (1982), "The Use of Time Series Processes to Model the Error Structure of Earnings in a Longitudinal Data Analysis," *Journal of Econometrics* 18, 83–114.

Maddala, G. S. (1983), *Limited Dependent and Qualitative Variables in Econometrics.* Cambridge: Cambridge University Press.

Maloney, M. T., and R. E. McCormick (1993), "An Examination of the Role That Intercollegiate Athletic Participation Plays in Academic Achievement: Athlete's Feats in the Classroom," *Journal of Human Resources* 28, 555–570.

Manski, C. F. (1975), "Maximum Score Estimation of the Stochastic Utility Model of Choice," *Journal of Econometrics* 3, 205–228.

Manski, C. F. (1987), "Semiparametric Analysis of Random Effects Linear Models from Binary Panel Data," *Econometrica* 55, 357–362.

Manski, C. F. (1988), *Analog Estimation Methods in Econometrics*. New York: Chapman and Hall.

Manski, C. F. (1996), "Learning about Treatment Effects from Experiments with Random Assignment of Treatments," *Journal of Human Resources* 31, 709–733.

Manski, C. F., and S. Lerman (1977), "The Estimation of Choice Probabilities from Choice-Based Samples," *Econometrica* 45, 1977–1988.

Manski, C. F., and D. McFadden (1981), "Alternative Estimators and Sample Designs for Discrete Choice Analysis," in *Structural Analysis of Discrete Data with Econometric Applications*, ed. C. F. Manski and D. McFadden. Cambridge, MA: MIT Press, 2–50.

McCall, B. P. (1994), "Testing the Proportional Hazards Assumption in the Presence of Unmeasured Heterogeneity," *Journal of Applied Econometrics* 9, 321–334.

McCullagh, P., and J. A. Nelder (1989), *Generalized Linear Models*, second edition. New York: Chapman and Hall.

McDonald, J. B. (1996), "An Application and Comparison of Some Flexible Parametric and Semi-Parametric Qualitative Response Models," *Economics Letters* 53, 145–152.

McDonald, J. F., and R. A. Moffitt (1980), "The Uses of Tobit Analysis," *Review of Economics and Statistics* 62, 318–321.

McFadden, D. L. (1974), "Conditional Logit Analysis of Qualitative Choice Analysis," in *Frontiers in Econometrics*, ed. P. Zarembka. New York: Academic Press, 105–142.

McFadden, D. L. (1978), "Modeling the Choice of Residential Location," in *Spatial Interaction Theory and Residential Location*, ed. A. Karlqvist. Amsterdam: North Holland, 75–96.

McFadden, D. L. (1981), "Econometric Models of Probabilistic Choice," in *Structural Analysis of Discrete Data with Econometric Applications*, ed. C. F. Manski and D. McFadden. Cambridge, MA: MIT Press, 198–272.

McFadden, D. L. (1984), "Econometric Analysis of Qualitative Response Models," in *Handbook of Econometrics*, Volume 2, ed. Z. Griliches and M. D. Intriligator. Amsterdam: North Holland, 1395–1457.

McFadden, D. L. (1987), "Regression Based Specification Tests for the Multinomial Logit Model," *Journal of Econometrics* 34, 63–82.

Meyer, B. D. (1990), "Unemployment Insurance and Unemployment Spells," *Econometrica* 58, 757–782.

Meyer, B. D. (1995), "Natural and Quasi-Experiments in Economics," *Journal of Business and Economic Statistics* 13, 151–161.

Meyer, B. D., W. K. Viscusi, and D. L. Durbin (1995), "Workers' Compensation and Injury Duration: Evidence from a Natural Experiment," *American Economic Review* 85, 322–340.

Model, K. E. (1993), "The Effect of Marijuana Decriminalization on Hospital Emergency Drug Episodes: 1975–1978," *Journal of the American Statistical Association* 88, 737–747.

Moffitt, R. A. (1996), "Identification of Causal Effects Using Instrumental Variables: Comment," *Journal of the American Statistical Association* 91, 462–465.

Moffitt, R., J. Fitzgerald, and P. Gottschalk (1999), "Sample Attrition in Panel Data: The Role of Selection on Observables," *Annale d'Economie et de Statistique* 55/56, 129–152.

Montgomery, E., K. Shaw, and M. E. Benedict (1992), "Pensions and Wages: An Hedonic Price Theory Approach," *International Economic Review* 33, 111–128.

Moon, C.-G. (1988), "Simultaneous Specification Test in a Binary Logit Model: Skewness and Heteroskedasticity," *Communications in Statistics* 17, 3361–3387.

Moulton, B. (1990), "An Illustration of a Pitfall in Estimating the Effects of Aggregate Variables on Micro Units," *Review of Economics and Statistics* 72, 334–338.

Mroz, T. A. (1987), "The Sensitivity of an Empirical Model of Married Women's Hours of Work to Economic and Statistical Assumptions," *Econometrica* 55, 765–799.

Mullahy, J. (1997), "Instrumental-Variable Estimation of Count Data Models: Applications to Models of Cigarette Smoking Behavior," *Review of Economics and Statistics* 79, 586–593.

Mundlak, Y. (1978), "On the Pooling of Time Series and Cross Section Data," *Econometrica* 46, 69–85.

Newey, W. K. (1984), "A Method of Moments Interpretation of Sequential Estimators," *Economics Letters* 14, 201–206.

Newey, W. K. (1985), "Maximum Likelihood Specification Testing and Conditional Moment Tests," *Econometrica* 53, 1047–1070.

Newey, W. K. (1990), "Efficient Instrumental Variables Estimation of Nonlinear Models," *Econometrica* 58, 809–837.

Newey, W. K. (1993), "Efficient Estimation of Models with Conditional Moment Restrictions," in *Handbook of Statistics*, Volume 11, ed. G. S. Maddala, C. R. Rao, and H. D. Vinod. Amsterdam: North Holland, 419–454.

Newey, W. K. (1994), "The Asymptotic Variance of Semiparametric Estimators," *Econometrica* 62, 1349–1382.

Newey, W. K., and D. McFadden (1994), "Large Sample Estimation and Hypothesis Testing," in *Handbook of Econometrics*, Volume 4, ed. R. F. Engle and D. McFadden. Amsterdam: North Holland, 2111–2245.

Newey, W. K., and K. D. West (1987), "A Simple, Positive Semi-Definite Heteroskedasticity and Autocorrelation Consistent Covariance Matrix," *Econometrica* 55, 703–708.

Nickell, S. (1979), "Estimating the Probability of Leaving Unemployment," *Econometrica* 47, 1249–1266.

Nijman, T., and M. Verbeek (1992), "Nonresponse in Panel Data: The Impact on Estimates of a Life Cycle Consumption Function," *Journal of Applied Econometrics* 7, 243–257.

Orme, C. (1990), "The Small Sample Performance of the Information Matrix Test," *Journal of Econometrics* 46, 309–331.

Pagan, A. R. (1984), "Econometric Issues in the Analysis of Regressions with Generated Regressors," *International Economic Review* 25, 221–247.

Pagan, A. R., and F. Vella (1989), "Diagnostic Tests for Models Based on Individual Data: A Survey," *Journal of Applied Econometrics* 4, S29–59.

Page, M. (1995), "Racial and Ethnic Discrimination in Urban Housing Markets: Evidence from a Recent Audit Study," *Journal of Urban Economics* 38, 183–206.

Papke, L. E. (1991), "Interstate Business Tax Differentials and New Firm Location," *Journal of Public Economics* 45, 47–68.

Papke, L. E. (1994), "Tax Policy and Urban Development: Evidence From the Indiana Enterprise Zone Program," *Journal of Public Economics* 54, 37–49.

Papke, L. E. (1998), "How Are Participants Directing Their Participant-Directed Individual Account Pension Plans?" *American Economic Review* 88, 212–216.

Papke, L. E., and J. M. Wooldridge (1996), "Econometric Methods for Fractional Response Variables with an Application to 401(k) Plan Participation Rates," *Journal of Applied Econometrics* 11, 619–632.

Pesaran, M. H., and R. J. Smith (1995), "Estimating Long-Run Relationships from Dynamic Heterogeneous Panels," *Journal of Econometrics* 68, 79–113.

Phillips, P. C. B., and H. R. Moon (1999), "Linear Regression Limit Theory for Nonstationary Panel Data," *Econometrica* 67, 1057–1111.

Phillips, P. C. B., and J. Y. Park (1988), "On the Formulation of Wald Tests for Nonlinear Restrictions," *Econometrica* 56, 1065–1083.

Polachek, S., and M.-K. Kim (1994), "Panel Estimates of the Gender Earnings Gap: Individual-Specific Intercepts and Individual-Specific Slope Models," *Journal of Econometrics* 61, 23–42.

Porter, J. R. (1999), "Semiparametric Efficiency in Maximum Likelihood Variance Estimation," mimeo, Harvard University Department of Economics.

Powell, J. L. (1984), "Least Absolute Deviations Estimation for the Censored Regression Model," *Journal of Econometrics* 25, 303–325.

Powell, J. L. (1986), "Symmetrically Trimmed Least Squares Estimation for Tobit Models," *Econometrica* 54, 1435–1460.

Powell, J. L. (1994), "Estimation of Semiparametric Models," in *Handbook of Econometrics*, Volume 4, ed. R. F. Engle and D. McFadden. Amsterdam: North Holland, 2443–2521.

Powell, J. L., J. H. Stock, and T. M. Stoker (1989), "Semiparametric Estimation of Weighted Average Derivatives," *Econometrica* 57, 1403–1430.

Qian, H., and P. Schmidt (1999), "Improved Instrumental Variables and Generalized Method of Moments Estimators," *Journal of Econometrics* 91, 145–169.

Quah, D. (1994), "Exploiting Cross-Section Variations for Unit Root Inference in Dynamic Data," *Economics Letters* 44, 9–19.

Quandt, R. E. (1983), "Computational Problems and Methods," in *Handbook of Econometrics*, Volume 1, ed. Z. Griliches and M. D. Intriligator. Amsterdam: North Holland, 699–764.

Ramsey, J. B. (1969), "Tests for Specification Errors in Classical Linear Least Squares Regression Analysis," *Journal of the Royal Statistical Society*, Series B, 31, 350–371.

Rao, C. R. (1948), "Large Sample Tests of Hypotheses Involving Several Parameters with Applications to Problems of Estimation," *Proceedings of the Cambridge Philosophical Society* 44, 50–57.

Rivers, D., and Q. H. Vuong (1988), "Limited Information Estimators and Exogeneity Tests for Simultaneous Probit Models," *Journal of Econometrics* 39, 347–366.

Robins, J. A., A. Rotnitzky, and L. Zhao (1995), "Analysis of Semiparametric Regression Models for Repeated Outcomes in the Presence of Missing Data," *Journal of the American Statistical Association* 90, 106–121.

Romer, D. (1993), "Openness and Inflation: Theory and Evidence," *Quarterly Journal of Economics* 108, 869–903.

Rose, N. L. (1990), "Profitability and Product Quality: Economic Determinants of Airline Safety Performance," *Journal of Political Economy* 98, 944–961.

Rosenbaum, P. R., and D. B. Rubin (1983), "The Central Role of the Propensity Score in Observational Studies for Causal Effects," *Biometrika* 70, 41–55.

Rouse, C. E. (1995), "Democratization or Diversion? The Effect of Community Colleges on Educational Attainment," *Journal of Business and Economic Statistics* 13, 217–224.

Rubin, D. B. (1974), "Estimating Causal Effects of Treatments in Randomized and Nonrandomized Studies," *Journal of Education Psychology* 66, 688–701.

Rudin, W. (1976), *Principles of Mathematical Analysis*, 3rd edition. New York: McGraw-Hill.

Ruud, P. (1983), "Sufficient Conditions for Consistency of Maximum Likelihood Estimation Despite Misspecification of Distribution," *Econometrica* 51, 225–228.

Ruud, P. (1984), "Tests of Specification in Econometrics," *Econometric Reviews* 3, 211–242.

Ruud, P. (1986), "Consistent Estimation of Limited Dependent Variable Models Despite Misspecification of Distribution," *Journal of Econometrics* 32, 157–187.

Sander, W. (1992), "The Effect of Women's Schooling on Fertility," *Economics Letters* 40, 229–233.

Schmidt, P. (1976), *Econometrics*. New York: Marcel-Dekker.

Schmidt, P. (1990), "Three-Stage Least Squares with Different Instruments for Different Equations," *Journal of Econometrics* 43, 389–394.

Shapiro, M. D. (1984), "The Permanent Income Hypothesis and the Real Interest Rate: Some Evidence from Panel Data," *Economics Letters* 14, 93–100.

Shea, J. (1995), "Union Contracts and the Life-Cycle/Permanent Income Hypothesis," *American Economic Review* 85, 186–200.

Smith, R., and R. Blundell (1986), "An Exogeneity Test for a Simultaneous Equation Tobit Model with an Application to Labor Supply," *Econometrica* 54, 679–685.

Solon, G. (1985), "Comment on 'Benefits and Limitations of Panel Data' by C. Hsiao," *Econometric Reviews* 4, 183–186.

Staiger, D., and J. H. Stock (1997), "Instrumental Variables Regression with Weak Instruments," *Econometrica* 65, 557–586.

Stoker, T. M. (1986), "Consistent Estimation of Scaled Coefficients," *Econometrica* 54, 1461–1481.

Stoker, T. M. (1992), *Lectures on Semiparametric Econometrics*. Louvain-la-Neuve, Belgium: CORE Lecture Series.

Strauss, J., and D. Thomas (1995), "Human Resources: Empirical Modeling of Household and Family Decisions," in *Handbook of Development Economics*, Volume 3A, ed. J. Berhman and T. N. Srinivasan. Amsterdam: North Holland, 1883–2023.

Sueyoshi, G. T. (1992), "Semiparametric Proportional Hazards Estimation of Competing Risks Models with Time-Varying Covariates," *Journal of Econometrics* 51, 25–58.

Sueyoshi, G. T. (1995), "A Class of Binary Response Models for Grouped Duration Data," *Journal of Applied Econometrics* 10, 411–431.

Tauchen, G. (1985), "Diagnostic Testing and Evaluation of Maximum Likelihood Models," *Journal of Econometrics* 30, 415–443.

Tauchen, G. (1986), "Statistical Properties of Generalized Method-of-Moments Estimators of Structural Parameters Obtained from Financial Market Data," *Journal of Business and Economic Statistics* 4, 397–416.

Terza, J. V. (1998), "Estimating Count Models with Endogenous Switching: Sample Selection and Endogenous Treatment Effects," *Journal of Econometrics* 84, 129–154.

Theil, H. (1983), "Linear Algebra and Matrix Methods in Econometrics," in *Handbook of Econometrics*, Volume 1, ed. Z. Griliches and M. D. Intriligator. Amsterdam: North Holland, 5–65.

Thomas, D., J. Strauss, and M.-H. Henriques (1990), "Child Survival, Height for Age and Household Characteristics in Brazil," *Journal of Development Economics* 33, 197–234.

Tobin, J. (1956), "Estimation of Relationships for Limited Dependent Variables," *Econometrica* 26, 24–36.

Ullah, A., and H. D. Vinod (1993), "General Nonparametric Regression Estimation and Testing in Econometrics," in *Handbook of Statistics*, Volume 11, ed. G. S. Maddala, C. R. Rao, and H. D. Vinod. Amsterdam: North Holland, 85–116.

van der Klaauw, W. (1996), "Female Labour Supply and Marital Status Decisions: A Life-Cyle Model," *Review of Economic Studies* 63, 199–235.

Vella, F. (1992), "Simple Tests for Sample Selection Bias in Censored and Discrete Choice Models," *Journal of Applied Econometrics* 7, 413–421.

Vella, F. (1998), "Estimating Models with Sample Selection Bias: A Survey," *Journal of Human Resources* 33, 127–169.

Vella, F., and M. Verbeek (1998), "Whose Wages Do Unions Raise? A Dynamic Model of Unionism and Wage Rate Determination for Young Men," *Journal of Applied Econometrics* 13, 163–183.

Vella, F., and M. Verbeek (1999), "Estimating and Interpreting Models with Endogenous Treatment Effects," *Journal of Business and Economic Statistics* 17, 473–478.

Verbeek, M., and T. Nijman (1992), "Testing for Selectivity Bias in Panel Data Models," *International Economic Review* 33, 681–703.

Verbeek, M., and T. Nijman (1996), "Incomplete Panels and Selection Bias," in L. Matyas and P. Sevestre, eds., *The Econometrics of Panel Data*. Amsterdam: Kluwer Academic Publishers, 449–490.

Vuong, Q. (1989), "Likelihood Ratio Tests for Model Selection and Nonnested Hypotheses," *Econometrica* 57, 307–333.

Wald, A. (1940), "The Fitting of Straight Lines If Both Variables Are Subject to Error," *Annals of Mathematical Statistics* 11, 284–300.

White, H. (1980a), "Nonlinear Regression on Cross Section Data," *Econometrica* 48, 721–746.

White, H. (1980b), "A Heteroskedasticity-Consistent Covariance Matrix Estimator and a Direct Test for Heteroskedasticity," *Econometrica* 48, 817–838.

White, H. (1982a), "Maximum Likelihood Estimation of Misspecified Models," *Econometrica* 50, 1–26.

White, H. (1982b), "Instrumental Variables Regression with Independent Observations," *Econometrica* 50, 483–499.

White, H. (1984), *Asymptotic Theory for Econometricians*. Orlando, FL: Academic Press.

White, H. (1994), *Estimation, Inference and Specification Analysis*. Cambridge: Cambridge University Press.

Wolak, F. A. (1991), "The Local Nature of Hypothesis Tests Involving Inequality Constraints in Nonlinear Models," *Econometrica* 59, 981–995.

Wooldridge, J. M. (1990), "A Unified Approach to Robust, Regression-Based Specification Tests," *Econometric Theory* 6, 17–43.

Wooldridge, J. M. (1991a), "On the Application of Robust, Regression-Based Diagnostics to Models of Conditional Means and Conditional Variances," *Journal of Econometrics* 47, 5–46.

Wooldridge, J. M. (1991b), "Specification Testing and Quasi-Maximum Likelihood Estimation," *Journal of Econometrics* 48, 29–55.

Wooldridge, J. M. (1992), "Some Alternatives to the Box-Cox Regression Model," *International Economic Review* 33, 935–955.

Wooldridge, J. M. (1994), "Estimation and Inference for Dependent Processes," in *Handbook of Econometrics*, Volume 4, ed. R. F. Engle and D. L. McFadden. Amsterdam: North-Holland, 2639–2738.

Wooldridge, J. M. (1995a), "Selection Corrections for Panel Data Models under Conditional Mean Independence Assumptions," *Journal of Econometrics* 68, 115–132.

Wooldridge, J. M. (1995b), "Score Diagnostics for Linear Models Estimated by Two Stage Least Squares," in *Advances in Econometrics and Quantitative Economics*, ed. G. S. Maddala, P. C. B. Phillips, and T. N. Srinivasan. Oxford: Blackwell, 66–87.

Wooldridge, J. M. (1996), "Estimating Systems of Equations with Different Instruments for Different Equations," *Journal of Econometrics* 74, 387–405.

Wooldridge, J. M. (1997a), "Multiplicative Panel Data Models without the Strict Exogeneity Assumption," *Econometric Theory* 13, 667–678.

Wooldridge, J. M. (1997b), "On Two Stage Least Squares Estimation of the Average Treatment Effect in a Random Coefficient Model," *Economics Letters* 56, 129–133.

Wooldridge, J. M. (1997c), "Quasi-Likelihood Methods for Count Data," in *Handbook of Applied Econometrics*, Volume 2, ed. M. H. Pesaran and P. Schmidt. Oxford: Blackwell, 352–406.

Wooldridge, J. M. (1998), "Selection Corrections with a Censored Selection Variable," mimeo, Michigan State University Department of Economics.

Wooldridge, J. M. (1999a), "Distribution-Free Estimation of Some Nonlinear Panel Data Models," *Journal of Econometrics* 90, 77–97.

Wooldridge, J. M. (1999b), "Asymptotic Properties of Weighted M-Estimators for Variable Probability Samples," *Econometrica* 67, 1385–1406.

Wooldridge, J. M. (1999c), "Estimating Average Partial Effects under Conditional Moment Independence Assumptions," mimeo, Michigan State University Department of Economics.

Wooldridge, J. M. (2000a), *Introductory Econometrics: A Modern Approach.* Cincinnati, OH: South-Western.

Wooldridge, J. M. (2000c), "A Framework for Estimating Dynamic, Unobserved Effects Panel Data Models with Possible Feedback to Future Explanatory Variables," *Economics Letters* 68, 245–250.

Wooldridge, J. M. (2000d), "Inverse Probability Weighted M-Estimators for Sample Selection, Attrition, and Stratification," mimeo, Michigan State University Department of Economics.

Wooldridge, J. M. (2000e), "The Initial Conditions Problem for Dynamic, Nonlinear Panel Data Models with Unobserved Heterogeneity," mimeo, Michigan State University Department of Economics.

Wooldridge, J. M. (2000f), "Instrumental Variables Estimation of the Average Treatment Effect in the Correlated Random Coefficient Model," mimeo, Michigan State University Department of Economics.

Wooldridge, J. M. (2001), "Asymptotic Properties of Weighted M-Estimators for Standard Stratified Samples." *Econometric Theory* 17, 451–470.

Zeger, S. L., K.-Y. Liang, and P. S. Albert (1988), "Models for Longitudinal Data: A Generalized Estimating Equation Approach," *Biometrics* 44, 1049–1060.

Zeldes, S. P. (1989), "Consumption and Liquidity Constraints: An Empirical Investigation," *Journal of Political Economy* 97, 305–346.

Zellner, A. (1962), "An Efficient Method of Estimating Seemingly Unrelated Regressions and Tests of Aggregation Bias," *Journal of the American Statistical Association* 57, 500–509.

Ziliak, J. P. (1997), "Efficient Estimation with Panel Data When Instruments Are Predetermined: An Empirical Comparison of Moment-Condition Estimators," *Journal of Business and Economic Statistics* 15, 419–431.

Ziliak, J. P., and T. J. Kniesner (1998), "The Importance of Sample Attrition in Life Cycle Labor Supply Estimation," *Journal of Human Resources* 33, 507–530.

Ziliak, J. P., B. Wilson, and J. Stone (1999), "Spatial Dynamics and Heterogeneity in the Cyclicality of Real Wages," *Review of Economics and Statistics* 81, 227–236.

Index